FEMINIST FRONTIERS

SEVENTH EDITION

Verta Taylor

Nancy Whittier

Leila J. Rupp

Boston   Burr Ridge, IL   Dubuque, IA   Madison, WI   New York
San Francisco   St. Louis   Bangkok   Bogotá   Caracas   Kuala Lumpur
Lisbon   London   Madrid   Mexico City   Milan   Montreal   New Delhi
Santiago   Seoul   Singapore   Sydney   Taipei   Toronto

The **McGraw·Hill** Companies

Mc Graw Hill | Higher Education

FEMINIST FRONTIERS, SEVENTH EDITION

Published by McGraw-Hill, a business unit of The McGraw-Hill Companies, Inc., 1221 Avenue of the Americas, New York, NY, 10020. Copyright © 2007, 2004, 2001, 1997, 1993, 1989, 1983 by The McGraw-Hill Companies, Inc. All rights reserved. No part of this publication may be reproduced or distributed in any form or by any means, or stored in a database or retrieval system, without the prior written consent of The McGraw-Hill Companies, Inc., including, but not limited to, in any network or other electronic storage or transmission, or broadcast for distance learning.

Some ancillaries, including electronic and print components, may not be available to customers outside the United States.

This book is printed on acid-free paper.

2 3 4 5 6 7 8 9 0 FGR/FGR 0 9 8 7 6

ISBN-13: 978-0-07-319608-4
ISBN-10:   0-07-319608-8

Vice President and Editor-in-Chief: *Emily Barrosse*
Publisher: *Phillip A. Butcher*
Sponsoring Editor: *Sherith Pankratz*
Developmental Editor: *Kate Scheinman*
Senior Marketing Manager: *Daniel M. Loch*
Managing Editor: *Jean Dal Porto*
Senior Project Manager: *Becky Komro*
Art Director: *Jeanne Schreiber*

Interior Designer: *Marianna Kinigakis*
Cover Designer: *Mary Kazak*
Senior Supplement Producer: *Louis Swaim*
Media Project Manager: *Stacy Bentz*
Lead Production Supervisor: *Randy L. Hurst*
Composition: *9/11 Palatino Roman, by Interactive Composition Corporation*
Printing: *45# New Era Matte, Quebecor Fairfield*

About the Cover: Detail of painting by artist Russell D'Alessio, one of a series of works titled "Three Naked Ladies," is intended to encourage the feminine spirit into today's political and economic policies. The artist's studio is in Bar Harbor, Maine, where he lives and works with his wife, Linda, and their three children. Russell's paintings and graphics can be seen on his Web site (www.rdalessio.com).

Credits: The credits section for this book begins on page A-1 and is considered an extension of the copyright page.

Library of Congress Cataloging-in-Publication Data

Taylor, Verta A.
    Feminist frontiers/Verta Taylor, Nancy Whittier, Leila J. Rupp.—7th ed.
        p. cm.
    Includes bibliographical references.
    ISBN-13: 978-0-07-319608-4 (softcover : alk. paper)
    ISBN-10: 0-07-319608-8 (softcover : alk. paper)
    1. Feminism—United States. 2. Women—United States. 3. Sex role—United States. 4. Women—Cross-cultural studies.
    I. Whittier, Nancy, 1966- II. Rupp, Leila J., 1950- III. Title.
HQ1426.T397 2007
305.420973—dc22   2006041926

The Internet addresses listed in the text were accurate at the time of publication. The inclusion of a Web site does not indicate an endorsement by the authors or McGraw-Hill, and McGraw-Hill does not guarantee the accuracy of the information presented at these sites.

www.mhhe.com

For our students,
and for Jonah, Eva, and Isaac Weigand-Whittier

ABOUT THE EDITORS

VERTA TAYLOR is Professor and Chair of the Department of Sociology and an affiliated faculty member in Women's Studies at the University of California at Santa Barbara. She teaches courses on gender, feminism, women's studies, and social movements and has won numerous teaching awards, including an Ohio State University Distinguished Teaching Award, a Multicultural Teaching Award, an Outstanding Faculty Award from the Office of Gay, Lesbian, and Bisexual Student Services, and a University Distinguished Diversity Enhancement Award for her role as Chair of Undergraduate Studies in the Department of Sociology at Ohio State. She continues to be recognized for her teaching at the University of California. Professor Taylor also received the Sociologists for Women in Society's Mentoring Award and has served as Feminist Lecturer for Sociologists for Women in Society. She has served on more than a dozen editorial boards, as Chair of the Sex and Gender, Collective Behavior and Social Movement, and Sexuality Sections of the American Sociological Association, and as Chair of the Committee on the Status of Gay, Lesbian, Bisexual, and Transgender Sociologists of the American Sociological Association. She is the author of *Rock-a-by Baby: Feminism, Self-Help, and Postpartum Depression* and coauthor with Leila J. Rupp of *Survival in the Doldrums: The American Women's Rights Movement, 1945 to the 1960s* and *Drag Queens at the 801 Cabaret*, which won the 2005 book award from the Sex and Gender Section of the American Sociological Association. Her writings have appeared in numerous scholarly collections and journals, such as *Signs, Gender & Society, American Sociological Review, Social Problems, Mobilization, Qualitative Sociology, Journal of Women's History, Journal of Homosexuality*, and *Journal of Marriage and the Family*.

NANCY WHITTIER is Associate Professor and former chair of the Department of Sociology and a member of the Women's Studies Program Committee at Smith College. She teaches courses on gender, social movements, queer politics, and research methods. She is the author of *Feminist Generations: The Persistence of the Radical Women's Movement* and coeditor of *Social Movements: Identity, Culture, and the State*. Her work on the women's movement, social movement culture and collective identity, activist generations, and activism against child sexual abuse has appeared in numerous scholarly collections and journals.

LEILA J. RUPP is Professor and Chair of the Women's Studies Program at the University of California, Santa Barbara, where she holds affiliated appointments in the Departments of History and Sociology. A historian by training, she teaches introductory women's studies and courses on sexuality and women's movements. While teaching at Ohio State University, she received an Ohio State University Distinguished Teaching Award, a Multicultural Teaching Award, and an outstanding teaching award from the Ohio Academy of History. She also won awards at both Ohio State and the University of California for her contributions to gay, lesbian, bisexual, transgender, and queer students. She is the author of *Mobilizing Women for War: German and American Propaganda, 1939–1945, Worlds of Women: The Making of an International Women's Movement*, and *A Desired Past: A Short History of Same-Sex Love in America* and coauthor with Verta Taylor of *Survival in the Doldrums: The American Women's Rights Movement, 1945 to the 1960s* and *Drag Queens at the 801 Cabaret*, which won the 2005 book award from the Sex and Gender Section of the American Sociological Association. In addition, she has published numerous articles in journals and edited collections. She served as the editor of the *Journal of Women's History* from 1996 to 2004.

PREFACE

The first edition of *Feminist Frontiers* was conceived in the late 1970s at a time when many women inside and outside academia were beginning to recognize and challenge male domination. At the time of its publication, only a handful of books and anthologies written for classroom use presented a feminist perspective on the status of women.

The evolution of this book through seven editions reflects both the success of the women's movement and the incredible development of feminist scholarship over the past three decades. Women's studies courses have blossomed and spread to campuses in even the most conservative regions of the country. Feminist scholars have, in the meantime, refined and enlarged our understanding of how gender inequality operates and how it intersects with other systems of domination based on race, ethnicity, class, sexuality, nationality, and ability. There is no doubt that the situation of women has changed since the publication of the first edition of *Feminist Frontiers*. Gender inequality has not, however, disappeared.

We write this preface to the seventh edition of *Feminist Frontiers* with pride and excitement. We are proud to be part of the continuing women's movement; and we are excited about the burgeoning knowledge about how gender is connected to class, race, ethnicity, sexuality, and other differences and how forces of globalization in the contemporary world shape the experiences of women. We feel fortunate to be writing, teaching, and learning at a time when feminist thought and research are flourishing and deepening, despite the challenges we face in an increasingly conservative political climate. It is, simultaneously, a time to enjoy the bounty of feminist scholarship and to sow new feminist seeds. We are proud as well that this book represents a new collaboration, with historian and women's studies scholar Leila Rupp joining the tested team of Verta Taylor and Nancy Whittier.

We have enjoyed our collaboration across intellectual and generational perspectives, and we think that it has enriched the book.

We developed *Feminist Frontiers* for use as the major—or supplementary—text in courses on women's studies, gender studies, or the sociology of women or gender. Because this book offers a general framework for analyzing the status of women, it can also be used as a supplementary text in introductory sociology classes and in courses on social problems, comparative studies, and American studies.

Although we have retained some of the articles from previous editions of *Feminist Frontiers*—particularly writings that have become feminist classics—the book has been comprehensively updated to include more recent scholarship. Approximately half of the readings and boxes are new to this edition. We have selected readings that continue to emphasize the diversity of women's experiences and the intersections of gender with race, ethnicity, class, sexuality, nationality, and ability. We have strengthened the coverage of global issues, especially the impact of globalization on women. As in previous editions, the introductions to each section contain focused summaries of the readings, and their relationship to each other, as well as discussion questions for each reading.

ORGANIZATION

Feminist Frontiers is organized into four major parts, each introduced by a sociological and feminist analysis. **Part One: Introduction** begins with a section representing the diversity of women's experiences and gender systems. That is followed by a section on "Theoretical Perspectives," which presents social constructionist and intersectional theoretical approaches to gender. **Part Two: Gender, Culture, and Socialization** has two sections, "Representation, Language, and Culture" and

"Socialization." **Part Three: Social Organization of Gender** has five sections, providing readings on work, families, sexualities, bodies, and violence against women. **Part Four: Social Change** includes articles on global politics and the state and on social protest and women's movements.

CRITERIA FOR SELECTION

As we set about selecting articles for this edition, we found an abundance of excellent pieces. We used the following criteria for choosing what to include:

- We wanted each selection to be engagingly written and accessible in style and language to readers from different disciplinary backgrounds.
- As a testament to the tremendous growth in the depth and complexity of feminist scholarship, we sought selections exploring a wide range of theoretical and substantive issues.
- We wanted this anthology to reflect a diversity of racial, ethnic, class, sexual, and cultural experiences.
- Given the increasingly powerful forces of globalization in our contemporary world, we looked for articles on different countries and on the impact of globalization on women.
- We sought to capture the cross-disciplinary nature of gender research.

CHANGES IN THE SEVENTH EDITION

The seventh edition contains 25 new articles and 12 new boxed inserts, representing the most current scholarship and public debates and expanding our coverage of numerous issues important to feminist scholarship. We have deleted dated pieces while retaining readings that are classic in the field.

Central topics that continue to receive coverage in this edition include social constructionist theories of gender; feminist intersectionality theory; gendered and raced beauty standards; disability; gender socialization; gender segregation in the workplace; affirmative action; Latina domestic workers; Chicana and Mexicana motherhood and employment; Vietnamese transpacific marriages; gay and lesbian families; adolescent sexuality; menstruation and menopause; eating disorders among African-American, Latina, and white women; reproductive rights; rape on college campuses; men's organizing to end violence against women; sex education; violence against women of color; the global assembly line; women and welfare; women's movements; third-wave feminism; and queer politics.

Additions to the text focus especially on improving coverage of diverse ethnicities within the United States and of global issues, with new articles on such topics as identity issues for Latinas and Arab American women, the socialization of Filipina women in the United States, Black women raised in white communities, Korean immigrant manicurists, masculinities and globalization, Asian women fighting globalization, and women workers on the U.S.-Mexico border.

This edition offers many **new and central topics** including:

- Whiteness (Reading 2, Section 1 box)
- Gender and racial-ethnic identity for Latina and Arab American women (Reading 3)
- Transnational feminism (Reading 9)
- Masculinities and globalization (Reading 10)
- Women in rap music (Reading 14)
- Filipina women (Readings 17, 43)
- Black girls raised in predominantly white communities (Reading 18)
- Sexual harassment in schools (Section 4 box)
- Race and gender on the assembly line in World War II (Reading 20)
- Korean women manicurists in the United States (Reading 21)
- The bridal industry (Reading 23)
- Queer parenting (Reading 27)
- The marriage debates (Reading 27)
- Teen dating (Reading 29)
- Black sexual politics (Reading 30)
- A global history of same-sex sexuality (Reading 31)
- Being transgendered or transsexual (Section 7 box)
- Cosmetic genital surgery in the United States (Reading 35)
- The gender and cultural politics of cancer (Reading 37)
- Queerness and disability (Section 8 box)
- Sexuality and sexual assault in wartime (Reading 41)

- Asian women fighting globalization (Reading 43)
- Mexican-American women workers on the border (Reading 44)
- Femicide in Juárez (Section 10 box)
- Muslim women (Reading 45)
- Young feminists (Readings 48, 50, Section 11 box)

Although the core focus remains on women and gender, this edition continues to offer consistent coverage of men and masculinity.

NEW READINGS IN THE SEVENTH EDITION

Every section has been updated with new selections, and many have been comprehensively revised. Section One brings back from an earlier edition a classic piece by **Peggy McIntosh** on white privilege and male privilege, and improves the diversity of coverage by adding an article on Latina and Arab American women by **Laura Lopez and Frances Hasso** and a new boxed insert on being white in Hawai'i by **Judy Rohrer**. Section Two offers a classic article on theorizing difference by **Maxine Baca Zinn and Bonnie Thornton Dill**, and improves on global coverage by adding an excerpt from **Chandra Talpade Mohanty's** new book on transnational feminist theory and an article on masculinities and globalization by **R. W. Connell**.

The section on "Representation, Language, and Culture" adds better coverage of contemporary media through an article by **Cheryl Keyes** on women in rap music. A boxed insert on a feminist magazine launched in Baghdad provides a global perspective on feminist culture. Two new articles in the section on socialization provide a perspective on diverse ethnicities: **Yen Le Espiritu** on Filipina girls and **France Winddance Twine** on black girls raised in white communities. A boxed insert on sexual harassment in schools also appears in this section. **Eileen Boris** contributes an article on the complexities of gender and race in the World War II workforce in the section on "Work," as well as a boxed insert explaining why the issue of a living wage matters to women. **Miliann Kang** describes the gendered and embodied work of Korean nail technicians in the United States.

Section Six represents the diversity of families. A new article by **Melissa Morrison** covers the bridal craze,

another by **Kathleen Gerson** covers women's care work and work-family tensions, and **Nancy Naples** provides an update on queer parenting and debates over same-sex marriage. New pieces in "Sexualities" deal with changes and ethnic patterns in teen sexuality (by **Barbara Risman and Pepper Schwartz**), the politics of black sexuality (**Patricia Hill Collins**), the global history of same-sex sexuality (**Leila Rupp**), and being transgendered by **Susan Stryker**. Section Eight, "Bodies," is expanded with **Simone Weil Davis's** article that compares cosmetic genital surgery in the United States to African genital cutting, **Andrea Smith's** new piece on reproductive rights, **Barbara Ehrenreich** on the experience and cultural politics of breast cancer, and a personal narrative by **Eli Clare** on queerness and disability.

"Violence against Women" adds a new piece on war and sexuality and sexual assault from **Joane Nagel's** book on ethnosexual frontiers. Globalization is the focus of Section Ten, with new articles on the migration of Filipina women to Canada and the United States by **Grace Chang,** Mexican-American women workers in El Paso displaced by the North American Free Trade Agreement by **Sharon Ann Navarro,** the ongoing murder of women workers on the Mexican side of the border, and Muslim women in Afghanistan by **Lila Abu-Lughod**. Addressing one of the most important issues of state policies, **Gwendolyn Mink** covers women and welfare in the United States.

Young feminists are the focus of the new material in Section Eleven. **Pamela Aronson** covers "postfeminism" and **Susan Muaddi Darraj** describes being an Arab American feminist. We conclude with the Beijing Declaration on global women's rights and its reaffirmation in 2005.

CONNECTIONS AMONG SECTIONS

More than in previous editions, *Feminist Frontiers* makes connections among the topics appearing in different sections. For example, the concept of intersectionality, illustrated in the diverse and complex experiences covered in Section One and outlined in the theoretical articles in Section Two, can be traced through Kimberlé Crenshaw's classic article on violence against women of color in Section Nine and Andrea's Smith consideration of reproductive politics in the context of race, class, and ability. That we cannot talk of gender without acknowledging the ways that it is raced and classed is central to Yen Le Espiritu's article on Filipina girls, France Winddance Twine's piece on "brown-skinned white girls," Eileen Boris's article on workers during World War II, Miliann Kang's on Korean manicurists, Pierrette Hondagneu-Sotelo's on Latina domestics, Denise Segura's on Chicana and Mexicana mothers, Hung Cam Thai's on Vietnamese marriages, Patricia Hill Collins's on black sexual politics, Becky Wangsgaard Thompson's on eating disorders, Lila Abu-Lughod's on Muslim women, Gwendolyn Mink's on welfare, and Susan Muaddi Darraj's on Arab American feminism.

Likewise, global forces appear throughout the volume, not just in the section on global politics: in Chandra Talpade Mohanty's and R.W. Connell's theoretical articles in Section Two, "Ms. of Baghdad" in Section Three, Yen Le Espiritu's analysis of cross-national socialization practices in Section Four, the piece on Korean manicurists in Section Five, the articles on Mexican and Mexican-American women and Vietnamese marriages in Section Six, the consideration of same-sex sexuality around the globe in Section Seven, the consideration of African genital cutting in light of cosmetic labial surgery in the United States in Section Eight, Joane Nagel's piece on sexuality in wartime in Section Nine, and the overview of women's movements and the Beijing documents in Section Eleven.

Other issues, too, cross sections. Diverse sexualities, including transsexuality, transgenderism, and intersexuality, appear in Paula Gunn Allen's reflections on being Native American, Susan Stryker's transgender manifesto, Suzanne Kessler's consideration of surgery on intersexed infants, Eileen Boris's article on World War II, Nancy Naples's piece on queer parenting, the boxed insert "Stolen Bodies," the article on sexuality in wartime, and Cathy Cohen's article on queer politics. Other connections across sections focus on work, bodies, disability, beauty, youth, motherhood, and migration.

SUPPLEMENTS

Companion Web Site

The *Feminist Frontiers* Web site proves general information about the book and offers separate areas for students and instructors.

For the Student

The student side of the site is organized to correspond to the 11 sections in the text. There are practice test questions, an annotated list of Web links, links to Census 2000 updates, a glossary, and a comprehensive, annotated film/video guide.

For the Instructor

The instructor's side of the Web site, which is password-protected, includes the Instructor's Manual, an annotated list of Web links and links to Census 2000 updates, a glossary, and a comprehensive annotated film/video guide.

Visit the companion Web site at:

www.mhhe.com/taylorff7

Instructor's Resource CD (IRCD)

The following supplements are available to instructors on the Instructor's Resource CD:

Instructor's Manual

The Instructor's Manual is organized to correspond to the 11 sections in the text. It offers learning objectives, discussion questions, summaries of the key points of the section introductions and readings, suggestions for assignments and exercises, and an annotated list of Web links. The Instructor's Manual is also available (password-protected) on the companion Web site.

Test Bank

The Test Bank offers multiple-choice, short answer, and essay questions on the section introductions and the individual readings. It can be printed from the CD. It is also included as a **Computerized Test Bank.**

ACKNOWLEDGMENTS

We gratefully acknowledge the support, skill, and help of many people. We extend thanks to the authors of the articles, not only for writing the selected pieces but also for allowing us to reprint them here. At McGraw-Hill, we thank editors Sherith Pankratz, Kate Scheinman, and Becky Komro for their encouragement, astute advice, and attention to detail in the production of the book. We also thank Fred Courtright for his services as permissions editor. Amber Ault was instrumental in shaping some section introductions for the third edition of the book, and we continue to appreciate her contributions for this and for developing some of the content for both the Instructor's Manual and the companion Web site. Nicole Raeburn provided invaluable research assistance and revisions of the Test Bank for earlier editions of the book, and Lisa Leitz put her charisma as a teacher to use in developing the Web site and Instructor's Manual for this edition. We could not have completed this revision without the help of Kegan Allee, who brought her intellectual abilities, commitment to feminism, and incredible organizational skills to the project. From suggesting readings to assembling the manuscript, she was our mainstay. In addition, we are grateful to Eileen Boris for sharing with us her experience teaching the previous edition and suggesting potential articles. Finally, we express our appreciation to students in our classes on the sociology of women, sex and gender, and women's studies at Smith College and the University of California, Santa Barbara. They have contributed to the development of this anthology by their thoughtful responses to potential articles.

The following scholars served as reviewers in the development of the seventh edition of *Feminist Frontiers*:

Willow Aureala, University of Hawaii Center, West Hawaii; Dana Britton, Kansas State University; Karen C. Flynn, University of Illinois, Urbana–Champaign; Susan Freeman, Minnesota State University, Mankato; Kirsten Gardner, University of Texas San Antonio; Cris Mayo, University of Illinois, Urbana–Champaign; Amy Pardo, Mississippi University for Women; Lisa Van Zwoll, University of Georgia; and Ann Wetherilt, Emmanuel College.

This is the first edition of *Feminist Frontiers* to appear without the name of Laurel Richardson, who, together with Verta Taylor, initiated the project, so we express here our gratitude for her past contributions. Special thanks go to Kate Weigand, who provided feedback and insight into the collection's organization and offered consistent encouragement and companionship. Jonah, Eva, and Isaac Weigand-Whittier are a constant source of inspiration as we seek to reconstruct gender. To them and to the students and colleagues who have touched our lives positively, we express our gratitude.

Verta Taylor
Nancy Whittier
Leila J. Rupp

CONTENTS

PART ONE

INTRODUCTION

What is gender? Our gender, and what it means to us and to others, affects the ways we interact with each other, the kinds of relationships we form, and our positions in our communities. As an element of social relationships, gender operates at multiple levels to categorize and distinguish people. But gender is also about social institutions that distribute power, resources, and status among various groups of women and men. As we shall see, gender also interacts with race, class, ethnicity, and sexuality. In other words, gender means different things, and has different consequences for status and power, depending on race, class, ethnicity, and sexuality.

What does it mean to be a woman? Thinking about women's experiences is a complicated task because women have as many differences from each other as commonalities. On the one hand, women everywhere suffer restrictions, oppression, and discrimination because they are living in patriarchal societies. Yet gender is not the sole influence on any woman's life. Differences of race, ethnicity, class, sexuality, age, nation, region, and religion shape women's experiences. Moreover, these differences intersect with each other. For example, Asian-American women of various ages, sexual orientations, classes, and ethnic and national origins have different experiences.

The experience of being a woman may be quite different for distinct groups of women. For a white, upper-class, heterosexual American woman, for example, femininity might entail being economically dependent on her husband, perfecting a delicate and refined physical appearance, and achieving social influence through child-raising and volunteer work. Womanhood for a middle-class African-American woman might mean providing financial support for her children, holding influential and respected positions within her church and community, yet being stereotyped by the dominant white culture as sexually

promiscuous or unintelligent. For a Mexican immigrant to the United States, femininity might mean being a good mother—which, as Denise Segura suggests in Section Six, may mean working long hours in order to support her children.

The experiences of men are similarly varied. Although men benefit from power and privilege over women, some groups of men also exercise power over other men, while other groups of men are excluded from economic or political influence due to their race, class, nationality, or sexual identity. To understand the position of a particular man, in other words, we must consider his gender, race, class, sexuality, age, and so forth, in order to understand the particular advantages and disadvantages he faces.

In short, gender is defined in various ways for different groups. Gender definitions bring with them a distinct set of restrictions and disadvantages for members in each group, as well as privileges and sources of power or resistance. The task for you as students, and for scholars of gender, is to recognize the patterns and persistence of male dominance while simultaneously recognizing these variations.

As if matters were not complex enough, feminist scholars also recognize that individuals have unique constellations of experiences. Each of us has her or his own story to tell. Each of us has multiple alliances and identifications with groups that shift through time and social context. The religious identity of childhood may be shunted aside during young adulthood, for example, only to be reclaimed in later years. Self-definition as heterosexual may give way later in life to new identities as lesbian or bisexual. As biracial or bicultural or mixed-religion daughters, we might identify with the heritage of either parent or both. In addition, we have different degrees of allegiance to the gender standards of our particular groups. Some of us adopt prescriptions about masculinity or femininity wholeheartedly, others reject those prescriptions, and others adopt some aspects of socially approved gender standards and reject others. Some of us identify strongly with the category—woman or man—to which we are assigned, while some of us identify as transgendered and seek either to identify with the other gender category or to construct an alternate gender identity altogether. Although social forces such as sexism, racism, heterosexism, and class inequality shape our biographies, it is as individuals that we experience and make sense of our lives.

The task of feminist scholarship, and of this volume, is to illuminate the social and structural roots of our gendered experiences while recognizing the complicated and unique factors that shape our lives. Feminist research builds upon and links two levels of analysis: structure and biography. The structural level looks at social institutions and cultural practices that create and sustain gender inequalities and links those inequalities to other systems of oppression, such as racism, ageism, and homophobia. The biographical level honors each individual's expression of her own experience. It pays attention to how individuals represent themselves and recognizes personal voice. As a result, we can learn how difference and commonality are structurally rooted and personally experienced. We can see how larger social forces affect our own and others' lives.

Feminist research is not just about analyzing the ways that social structures shape and restrict the lives of women. Of course, it is important to document the inequalities faced by various groups of women and to examine the ways that women have been oppressed and victimized based on gender. Experiences such as discrimination in hiring and pay, sexual violence, and legal subordination, for example, are undeniably central to gender. Yet feminist scholarship also emphasizes the sources of power that women find: how they define themselves, influence their social contexts, and resist the restrictions that they face. The articles in this volume view women not as passive victims of patriarchal social structures, but as actors who exercise control over their own lives, find pleasure and fulfillment, and resist social constraints.

Further, feminist research is not just about documenting women's experiences. It is about recognizing the ways that gender shapes the lives of both women and men and analyzing a broad system of gender. The gender system affects not only the lives of individuals but also the organization of other institutions in the larger society. By documenting the influence of social structures on gender and highlighting individuals' complex mixture of domination, resistance, and complicity, feminist scholarship leads us to rethink the structural changes necessary to meet the needs of actual women and men.

Feminist theory and scholarship on gender, then, face a broad set of questions. Approaches to answering these questions vary enormously; we hope that you will recognize disagreement and debate, as well as cooperation, in the readings that follow. There are, however, some shared assumptions that run through the chapters in this book.

First, feminist scholars view gender as pervasive, as part of every feature of social life and individual identity. It is impossible, therefore, to analyze any part of social life as if it were gender neutral. As a result, feminist scholars challenge the male bias hidden under claims of scientific objectivity in academic research. As you read these articles and those in other classes, ask yourself how the social conditions and practices of doing research reinforce or challenge gender inequities.

Second, feminist researchers understand systems of oppression as interlocking. Race, class, ethnicity, sexuality, and other systems of domination affect how one experiences gender. Therefore, although gender is a basic fact of social life, women and men in different positions in society experience their gender and the power or oppression that results from it differently. Individuals also do not experience class, race, or gender as separate or separable entities. Just as feminist researchers challenge knowledge claims about "people" based on research on men, they question knowledge about "women" based on research on white, middle-class women.

Third, feminist scholars experiment with new ways of doing research, rethinking the relationship between the researcher and the researched. The scientific method of research assumes that there is a separation between the scholar and the subjects of research and that this separation is necessary to produce "objective" and "valid" research. Feminist researchers challenge this tenet. Treating women as "objects" of research contravenes feminist goals of equality by elevating the researcher's agenda and perspective above those of the researched. One of the major questions of feminist thought is how to do research that empowers both the researcher and the researched. How do we create social research practices in which researcher and researched collaborate in the process of interpreting the world?

For some, the solution has been to write about their own lives; some acknowledge directly how their own biases affect their work; some study groups of which they are a part; others do "participatory" or "action" research in which the researcher and the researched determine together the topics, methods, goals, and political action to follow from the project, so that the scholar is a participant in the project but not its leader.

These are not only theoretical concerns; they are important ethical questions. What right does a scholar have to write about another person's life? How should scholars write about the lives of those who are different from themselves? How can feminist scholars use the skills and privileges of academic practice to diminish social inequality?

We invite you to engage in reading, thinking about, and doing feminist research. We hope that you will consider some of the central questions that run through this book. What are the commonalities and differences among women or among men? What, if anything, do women of different classes, races, or sexualities share in common? We hope you will reflect on the complicated balance between oppression and resistance, or between the pervasive influence of society and the ways that individuals and groups find to define themselves and carve out meaningful lives. We encourage you to discuss your ideas, to debate the issues this volume raises with your friends and classmates, to agree or disagree with the authors here, and to come to your own conclusions. We hope that through this engagement, you will consider how gender has shaped your life and how gender intersects with the other systems of inequality that affect you. We hope that you will share your understandings with others, becoming a researcher yourself and a theorist of your own and others' lives so that you might help empower us all and transform society.

SECTION 1

Diversity and Difference

Conducting research about women has been the focus of feminist scholars from the 1960s to the present. In recent years, researchers have looked especially closely at the differences and commonalities among women, and have also examined how men's lives are shaped by cultural expectations of masculinity. Gender shapes women's and men's lives in complex ways, and scholars are interested in understanding these experiences in ways that can contribute to positive social change. Women everywhere face male dominance in various manifestations. Yet differences among women arise from factors like race, ethnicity, class, sexual orientation, age, geographic region, and religion. Further, not all men possess the same advantages or social power. Men of subordinate racial or ethnic groups, classes, or sexual orientations may have power relative to women in their own group but are subordinate in some ways to other men and to women in more powerful groups.

Recognizing that women are not a homogeneous group raises questions about the grounds for affiliation among women. Can we even speak of "women" as a meaningful category, or is the diversity among women too great for any generalization? The readings in this section discuss points of similarity and difference among women and among men. Although the readings in this section give only a sampling of the varied and rich experiences of women and men, they begin to illustrate the vast range of meanings that gender has for women and men in different groups. The readings in this section also provide some key analytical frameworks and concepts for understanding the tension between the significance of gender as a category by which people are grouped and the ways that gender is shaped by other forms of inequality and social distinctions.

One way of thinking about commonalities among women is the idea of oppression. As a concept, oppression has a long history in feminist scholarship. What does it mean? Why is it important to think about? The first selection, "Oppression," addresses these questions and raises some others. In the article, Marilyn Frye defines *oppression* as "living one's life confined and shaped by forces and barriers which are not accidental or occasional and hence avoidable, but are systematically related to each other in such a way as to catch one between and among them and restrict or penalize motion in any direction." The multiple sources of interrelated oppressions can make it difficult for people to recognize how the systems of oppression impinge on their lives or on the lives of others. Learning about and considering the effects of larger social forces can help one understand one's own life. Can you think of examples of how various barriers come together to restrict particular groups of women?

As you read the other articles in this section, can you use Frye's concept of oppression to think about the experiences they describe? What are the advantages and disadvantages of an emphasis on oppression?

The remaining readings in this section examine the distinctions among women's experiences by showing how race, ethnicity, and age shape the lives of specific groups of women. Whereas Frye emphasizes how structures of oppression constrict all women, Peggy McIntosh focuses on the often-unrecognized ways that white women benefit from their racial category. In "White Privilege and Male Privilege" McIntosh discusses the taken-for-granted systems and practices that privilege white women over women of color. She argues that much of what white women take for granted in daily life is in fact a result of their dominant social status. Documenting her own white privilege helps her understand how she benefits from this system and shows that racism cannot change through individual attitudes alone, but requires change in social institutions. How does her list of benefits from white privilege change your understanding of racism? How does it change your understanding of gender inequality or of the degree to which women of different races share oppression in common? Can you think of other advantages to add to her list? If you are a member of another privileged group, can you construct a list of the benefits you receive by virtue of your gender, class, sexual orientation, religion, or nationality? If you are a member of a subordinated group, can you list some of the ways you are disadvantaged? Most readers will have some statuses that grant them privilege (such as white skin, male gender, heterosexuality, U.S. nationality, youth, Christian religion) and some statuses that disadvantage them (such as nonwhite skin, female gender, lesbian, gay, or bisexual sexual orientation, non-U.S. nationality, age, non-Christian religion). In what ways do the forms of privilege and disadvantage that you possess interact? How does the boxed insert, "Haole [pronounced "how lee"] Girl," suggest that even white skin may carry different degrees of privilege and disadvantage in different settings?

In "Frontlines and Borders: Identity Thresholds for Latinas and Arab American Women," Laura Lopez and Frances Hasso discuss how women experience their racial-ethnic identities differently at white-dominant universities and in their own ethnic communities. Latina and Arab American students both experience the university as often hostile and culturally unfamiliar, but in different ways. Latinas faced stereotyping as unsuited for college education and found themselves left out of both Anglo and African-American social and political groups. Often coming from rich Latina cultural settings into a university with very few Latino/a students or faculty, they also felt culturally dislocated. Arab Americans, in contrast, were affected by tense political events in the

Middle East, and often "came out" as Arab American in response to comments that stereotyped all Arabs as terrorists. Both groups responded to these pressures by reaffirming their ethnic identities and often heightening them by relearning native languages, finding other students who shared their identities, and strengthening ties to family and community. As they strengthened community ties, they had to reckon with often-restrictive notions of gender and sexuality. In both home and university setting, the women negotiated borders between ethnic and Anglo culture and faced concerns with ethnic "authenticity." Both groups faced contradictory pressures about their physical appearance (to appear more or less "ethnic") and worried about how to manage their ethnic communities' expectations of women's sexuality. Gaining a college education had quite different effects on ethnic identity for the two groups: Latinas, who in this study were mostly first-generation college students, risked criticism from family and community for assimilating into Anglo culture; this was not an issue for the Arab American women in this study because their families were highly educated. It is, however, a common concern for a variety of different ethnic groups.

What ethnic, racial, and cultural groups are predominant on your campus? To what extent do other groups have access to their own cultural spaces and influence on the larger campus culture? How has your experience at college affected your own racial or ethnic identity, and how has this been shaped by your gender, whether you are a member of a minority or majority group?

Paula Gunn Allen, similarly, suggests that assumptions about what it means to be a woman in Anglo-European culture do not hold in American Indian cultures. In "Where I Come From Is Like This," she draws on her bicultural experiences to explore the contradictions between the images of women embedded in Anglo and American Indian culture. The images of American Indian women she grew up with are images of "practicality, strength, reasonableness, intelligence, wit, and competence," in contrast to Anglo-American ideas about women as "passive and weak." Again, we see the difficulty of generalizing about women's experiences. What are the assumptions about women that are part of your own culture?

The final selection emphasizes the difficulties of accurately analyzing how systems of oppression affect people's lives. In "The Master's Tools Will Never Dismantle the Master's House," Audre Lorde argues that feminists must critically examine their own use of dominant concepts in their analysis of women's lives. She suggests that academic knowledge is based in an institution that historically has excluded women and people of color, and asks whether that academic knowledge can undermine the inequalities on which it is based. Do you think that the "regular" methods of scholarship and science are adequate to the task of understanding the diversity among women and the complexity of the gender system? Will new tools be necessary? What might they be? Lorde argues that encouraging women to talk to each other across their differences promotes growth, creativity, and social change. Do these conversations across differences happen on your campus?

READING *1* *Marilyn Frye*

Oppression

It is a fundamental claim of feminism that women are oppressed. The word "oppression" is a strong word. It repels and attracts. It is dangerous and dangerously fashionable and endangered. It is much misused, and sometimes not innocently.

The statement that women are oppressed is frequently met with the claim that men are oppressed too. We hear that oppressing is oppressive to those who oppress as well as to those they oppress. Some men cite as evidence of their oppression their much-advertised inability to cry. It is tough, we are told, to be masculine. When the stresses and frustrations of being a man are cited as evidence that oppressors are oppressed by their oppressing, the word "oppression" is being stretched to meaninglessness; it is treated as though its scope includes any and all human experience of limitation or suffering, no matter the cause, degree, or consequence. Once such usage has been put over on us, then if ever we deny that any person or group is oppressed, we seem to imply that we think they never suffer and have no feelings. We are accused of insensitivity; even of bigotry. For women, such accusation is particularly intimidating, since sensitivity is one of the few virtues that have been assigned to us. If we are found insensitive, we may fear we have no redeeming traits at all and perhaps are not real women. Thus are we silenced before we begin: the name of our situation drained of meaning and our guilt mechanisms tripped.

But this is nonsense. Human beings can be miserable without being oppressed, and it is perfectly consistent to deny that a person or group is oppressed without denying that they have feelings or that they suffer. . . .

The root of the word "oppression" is the element "press." *The press of the crowd; pressed into military service; to press a pair of pants; printing press; press the button.* Presses are used to mold things or flatten them or reduce them in bulk, sometimes to reduce them by squeezing out the gases or liquids in them. Something pressed is something caught between or among forces and barriers which are so related to each other that jointly they restrain, restrict, or prevent the thing's motion or mobility. Mold. Immobilize. Reduce.

The mundane experience of the oppressed provides another clue. One of the most characteristic and ubiquitous features of the world as experienced by oppressed people is the double bind—situations in which options are reduced to a very few and all of them expose one to penalty, censure or deprivation. For example, it is often a requirement upon oppressed people that we smile and be cheerful. If we comply, we signal our docility and our acquiescence in our situation. We need not, then, be taken note of. We acquiesce in being made invisible, in our occupying no space. We participate in our own erasure. On the other hand, anything but the sunniest countenance exposes us to being perceived as mean, bitter, angry, or dangerous. This means, at the least, that we may be found "difficult" or unpleasant to work with, which is enough to cost one one's livelihood; at worst, being seen as mean, bitter, angry, or dangerous has been known to result in rape, arrest, beating, and murder. One can only choose to risk one's preferred form and rate of annihilation.

Another example: It is common in the United States that women, especially younger women, are in a bind where neither sexual activity nor sexual inactivity is all right. If she is heterosexually active, a woman is open to censure and punishment for being loose, unprincipled, or a whore. The "punishment" comes in the form of criticism, snide and embarrassing remarks, being treated as an easy lay by men, scorn from her more restrained female friends. She may have to lie and hide her behavior from her parents. She must juggle the risks of unwanted pregnancy and dangerous contraceptives. On the other hand, if she refrains from heterosexual activity, she is fairly constantly harassed by men who try to persuade her into it and pressure her to "relax" and "let her hair down"; she is threatened with labels like "frigid," "uptight," "man-hater," "bitch" and "cocktease." The same parents who would be disapproving of her sexual activity may be worried by her inactivity because it suggests she is not or will not be popular, or is not sexually normal. She may be charged with lesbianism. If a woman is raped, then if she has been heterosexually active she is subject to the presumption that she liked it (since her activity is presumed to show that she likes sex), and if she has not been heterosexually active, she is subject to the presumption that she liked it (since she is supposedly "repressed and frustrated"). Both heterosexual activity and heterosexual nonactivity are likely to be taken as proof that you wanted to be raped, and hence, of course, weren't *really* raped at all. You can't win. You are caught in a bind, caught between systematically related pressures.

Women are caught like this, too, by networks of forces and barriers that expose one to penalty, loss, or contempt whether one works outside the home or not, is on welfare or not, bears children or not, raises children or not, marries or not, stays married or not, is heterosexual, lesbian, both, or neither. Economic necessity; confinement to racial and/or sexual job ghettos; sexual harassment; sex discrimination; pressures of competing expectations and judgments about *women, wives,* and *mothers* (in the society at large, in racial and ethnic subcultures, and in one's own mind); dependence (full or partial) on husbands, parents, or the state; commitment to political ideas; loyalties to racial or ethnic or other "minority" groups; the demands of self-respect and responsibilities to others. Each of these factors exists in complex tension with every other, penalizing or prohibiting all of the apparently available options. And nipping at one's heels, always, is the endless pack of little things. If one dresses one way, one is subject to the assumption that one is advertising one's sexual availability; if one dresses another way, one appears to "not care about oneself" or to be "unfeminine." If one uses "strong language," one invites categorization as a whore or slut; if one does not, one invites categorization as a "lady"—one too delicately constituted to cope with robust speech or the realities to which it presumably refers.

The experience of oppressed people is that the living of one's life is confined and shaped by forces and barriers which are not accidental or occasional and hence avoidable, but are systematically related to each other in such a way as to catch one between and among them and restrict or penalize motion in any direction. It is the experience of being caged in: all avenues, in every direction, are blocked or booby-trapped.

Cages. Consider a birdcage. If you look very closely at just one wire in the cage, you cannot see the other wires. If your conception of what is before you is determined by this myopic focus, you could look at that one wire, up and down the length of it, and be unable to see why a bird would not just fly around the wire any time it wanted to go somewhere. Furthermore, even if, one day at a time, you myopically inspected each wire, you still could not see why a bird would have trouble going past the wires to get anywhere. There is no physical property of any one wire, *nothing* that the closest scrutiny could discover, that will reveal how a bird could be inhibited or harmed by it except in the most accidental way. It is only when you step back, stop looking at the wires one by one, microscopically, and take a macroscopic view of the whole cage, that you can see why the bird does not go anywhere; and then you will see it in a moment. It will require no great subtlety of mental powers. It is perfectly *obvious* that the bird is surrounded by a network of systematically related barriers, no one of which would be the least hindrance to its flight, but which, by their relations to each other, are as confining as the solid walls of a dungeon.

It is now possible to grasp one of the reasons why oppression can be hard to see and recognize: one can study the elements of an oppressive structure with great care and some good will without seeing the structure as a whole, and hence without seeing or being able to understand that one is looking at a cage and that there are people there who are caged, whose motion and mobility are restricted, whose lives are shaped and reduced.

The arresting of vision at a microscopic level yields such common confusion as that about the male door-opening ritual. This ritual, which is remarkably widespread across classes and races, puzzles many people, some of whom do and some of whom do not find it offensive. Look at the scene of the two people approaching a door. The male steps slightly ahead and opens the door. The male holds the door open while the female glides through. Then the male goes through. The door closes after them. "Now how," one innocently asks, "can those crazy women's libbers say that is oppressive? The guy *removed* a barrier to the lady's smooth and unruffled progress." But each repetition of this ritual has a place in a pattern, in fact in several patterns. One has to shift the level of one's perception in order to see the whole picture.

The door-opening pretends to be a helpful service, but the helpfulness is false. This can be seen by noting that it will be done whether or not it makes any practical sense. Infirm men and men burdened with packages will open doors for able-bodied women who are free of physical burdens. Men will impose themselves awkwardly and jostle everyone in order to get to the door first. The act is not determined by convenience or grace. Furthermore, these very numerous acts of unneeded or even noisome "help" occur in counterpoint to a pattern of men not being helpful in many practical ways in which women might welcome help. What *women* experience is a world in which gallant princes charming commonly make a fuss about being helpful and providing small services when help and services are of little or no use, but in which there are rarely ingenious and adroit princes at hand when substantial assistance is really wanted either in mundane affairs or in situations of threat, assault, or terror. There is no help with the (his) laundry; no help typing a report at 4:00 AM; no help in mediating disputes among relatives or children. There is nothing but advice that women should stay indoors after dark, be chaperoned by a man, or when it comes down to it, "lie back and enjoy it."

The gallant gestures have no practical meaning. Their meaning is symbolic. The door-opening and similar services provided are services which really are needed by people who are for one reason or another incapacitated—unwell, burdened with parcels, etc. So the message is that women are incapable. The detachment of the acts from the concrete realities of what women need and do not need is a vehicle for the message that women's actual needs and interests are unimportant or irrelevant.

Finally, these gestures imitate the behavior of servants toward masters and thus mock women, who are in most respects the servants and caretakers of men. The message of the false helpfulness of male gallantry is female dependence, the invisibility or insignificance of women, and contempt for women.

One cannot see the meanings of these rituals if one's focus is riveted upon the individual event in all its particularity, including the particularity of the individual man's present conscious intentions and motives and the individual woman's conscious perception of the event in the moment. It seems sometimes that people take a deliberately myopic view and fill their eyes with things seen microscopically in order not to see macroscopically. At any rate, whether it is deliberate or not, people can and do fail to see the oppression of women because they fail to see macroscopically and hence fail to see the various elements of the situation as systematically related in larger schemes.

As the cageness of the birdcage is a macroscopic phenomenon, the oppressiveness of the situations in which women live our various and different lives is a macroscopic phenomenon. Neither can be *seen* from a microscopic perspective. But when you look macroscopically you can see it—a network of forces and barriers which are systematically related and which conspire to the immobilization, reduction, and molding of women and the lives we live.

READING *2* **Peggy McIntosh**

White Privilege and Male Privilege

Through work to bring materials and perspectives from Women's Studies into the rest of the curriculum, I have often noticed men's unwillingness to grant that they are overprivileged in the curriculum, even though they may grant that women are disadvantaged. Denials that amount to taboos surround the subject of advantages that men gain from women's disadvantages. These denials protect male privilege from being fully recognized, acknowledged, lessened, or ended.

Thinking through unacknowledged male privilege as a phenomenon with a life of its own, I realized that since hierarchies in our society are interlocking, there was most likely a phenomenon of white privilege that was similarly denied and protected, but alive and real in its effects. As a white person, I realized I had been taught about racism as something that puts others at a disadvantage, but had been taught not to see one of its corollary aspects, White privilege, which puts me at an advantage.

I think whites are carefully taught not to recognize white privilege, as males are taught not to recognize male privilege. So I have begun in an untutored way to ask what it is like to have white privilege. This paper is a partial record of my personal observations and not a scholarly analysis. It is based on my daily experiences within my particular circumstances.

I have come to see white privilege as an invisible package of unearned assets that I can count on cashing in each day, but about which I was "meant" to remain oblivious. White privilege is like an invisible weightless knapsack of special provisions, assurances, tools, maps, guides, codebooks, passports, visas, clothes, compass, emergency gear, and blank checks.

Since I have had trouble facing white privilege, and describing its results in my life, I saw parallels here with men's reluctance to acknowledge male privilege. Only rarely will a man go beyond acknowledging that women are disadvantaged to acknowledging that men have unearned advantage, or that unearned privilege has not been good for men's development as human beings, or for society's development, or that privilege systems might ever be challenged and *changed*.

I will review here several types or layers of denial that I see at work protecting, and preventing awareness about, entrenched male privilege. Then I will draw parallels, from my own experience, with the denials that veil the facts of white privilege. Finally, I will list forty-six ordinary and daily ways in which I experience having white privilege, by contrast with my African-American colleagues in the same building. This list is not intended to be generalizable. Others can make their own lists from within their own life circumstances.

Writing this paper has been difficult, despite warm receptions for the talks on which it is based.[1] For describing white privilege makes one newly accountable. As we in Women's Studies work to reveal male privilege and ask men to give up some of their power so one who writes about having white privilege must ask, "Having described it, what will I do to lessen or end it."

The denial of men's overprivileged state takes many forms in discussions of curriculum change work. Some claim that men must be central in the curriculum because they have done most of what is important or distinctive in life or in civilization. Some recognize sexism in the curriculum but deny that it makes male students seem unduly important in life. Others agree that certain *individual* thinkers are male-oriented but deny that there is any *systemic* tendency in disciplinary frameworks or epistemology to overempower men as a group. Those men who do grant that male privilege takes institutionalized and embedded forms are still likely to deny that male hegemony has opened doors for them personally. Virtually all men deny that male overreward alone can explain men's centrality in all the inner sanctums of our most powerful institutions. Moreover, those few who will acknowledge that male privilege systems have overempowered them usually end up doubting that we could dismantle these privilege systems. They may say they will work to improve women's status, in the society or in the university, but they can't or won't support the idea of lessening men's. In curricular terms, this is the point at which they say that they regret they cannot use any of the interesting new scholarship on women because the syllabus is full. When the talk turns to giving men less cultural room, even the most thoughtful and fair-minded of the men I know will tend to reflect, or fall back on, conservative assumptions about the inevitability of present gender relations and distributions of power, calling on precedent or sociobiology and psychobiology to demonstrate that male domination is natural and follows inevitably from evolutionary pressures. Others resort to arguments from "experience" or religion or social responsibility or wishing and dreaming.

After I realized, through faculty development work in Women's Studies, the extent to which men work from a base of unacknowledged privilege, I understood that much of their oppressiveness was unconscious. Then I remembered the frequent charges from women of color that white women whom they encounter are oppressive. I began to understand why we are justly seen as oppressive, even when we don't see ourselves that way. At the very least, obliviousness of one's privileged state can make a person or group irritating to be with. I began to count the ways in which I enjoy unearned skin privilege and have been conditioned into oblivion about its existence, unable to see that it put me "ahead" in any way, or put my people ahead, overrewarding us and yet also paradoxically damaging us, or that it could or should be changed.

My schooling gave me no training in seeing myself as an oppressor, as an unfairly advantaged person, or as a participant in a damaged culture. I was taught to see myself as an individual whose moral state depended on her individual moral will. At school, we were not taught about slavery in any depth; we were not taught to see slaveholders as damaged people. Slaves were seen as the only group at risk of being dehumanized. My schooling followed the pattern which Elizabeth Minnich has pointed out: whites are taught to think of their lives as morally neutral, normative, and average, and also ideal, so that when we work to benefit others, this is seen as work that will allow "them" to be more like "us." I think many of us know how obnoxious this attitude can be in men.

After frustration with men who would not recognize male privilege, I decided to try to work on myself at least by identifying some of the daily effects of white privilege in my life. It is crude work, at this stage, but I will give here a list of special circumstances and conditions I experience that I did not earn but that I have been made to feel are mine by birth, by citizenship, and by virtue of being a conscientious law-abiding "normal" person of goodwill. I have chosen those conditions that I think in my case *attach somewhat more to skin-color privilege* than to class, religion, ethnic status, or geographical location, though these other privileging factors are intricately intertwined. As far as I can see, my African-American co-workers, friends, and acquaintances with whom I come into daily or frequent contact in this particular time, place, and line of work cannot count on most of these conditions.

1. I can, if I wish, arrange to be in the company of people of my race most of the time.
2. I can avoid spending time with people whom I was trained to mistrust and who have learned to mistrust my kind or me.
3. If I should need to move, I can be pretty sure of renting or purchasing housing in an area which I can afford and in which I would want to live.
4. I can be reasonably sure that my neighbors in such a location will be neutral or pleasant to me.
5. I can go shopping alone most of the time, fairly well assured that I will not be followed or harassed by store detectives.
6. I can turn on the television or open to the front page of the paper and see people of my race widely and positively represented.
7. When I am told about our national heritage or about "civilization," I am shown that people of my color made it what it is.
8. I can be sure that my children will be given curricular materials that testify to the existence of their race.
9. If I want to, I can be pretty sure of finding a publisher for this piece on white privilege.
10. I can be fairly sure of having my voice heard in a group in which I am the only member of my race.
11. I can be casual about whether or not to listen to another woman's voice in a group in which she is the only member of her race.
12. I can go into a bookshop and count on finding the writing of my race represented, into a supermarket and find the staple foods that fit with my cultural traditions, into a hairdresser's shop and find someone who can deal with my hair.
13. Whether I use checks, credit cards, or cash, I can count on my skin color not to work against the appearance that I am financially reliable.
14. I could arrange to protect our young children most of the time from people who might not like them.
15. I did not have to educate our children to be aware of systemic racism for their own daily physical protection.
16. I can be pretty sure that my children's teachers and employers will tolerate them if they fit school and workplace norms; my chief worries about them do not concern others' attitudes toward their race.
17. I can talk with my mouth full and not have people put this down to my color.
18. I can swear, or dress in secondhand clothes, or not answer letters, without having people attribute these choices to the bad morals, the poverty, or the illiteracy of my race.
19. I can speak in public to a powerful male group without putting my race on trial.
20. I can do well in a challenging situation without being called a credit to my race.
21. I am never asked to speak for all the people of my racial group.
22. I can remain oblivious to the language and customs of persons of color who constitute the world's majority without feeling in my culture any penalty for such oblivion.
23. I can criticize our government and talk about how much I fear its policies and behavior without being seen as a cultural outsider.
24. I can be reasonably sure that if I ask to talk to "the person in charge," I will be facing a person of my race.
25. If a traffic cop pulls me over or if the IRS audits my tax return, I can be sure I haven't been singled out because of my race.
26. I can easily buy posters, postcards, picture books, greeting cards, dolls, toys, and children's magazines featuring people of my race.
27. I can go home from most meetings of organizations I belong to feeling somewhat tied in, rather than isolated, out of place, outnumbered, unheard, held at a distance, or feared.
28. I can be pretty sure that an argument with a colleague of another race is more likely to jeopardize her chances for advancement than to jeopardize mine.
29. I can be fairly sure that if I argue for the promotion of a person of another race, or a program centering on race,

this is not likely to cost me heavily within my present setting, even if my colleagues disagree with me.

30. If I declare there is a racial issue at hand, or there isn't a racial issue at hand, my race will lend me more credibility for either position than a person of color will have.

31. I can choose to ignore developments in minority writing and minority activist programs, or disparage them, or learn from them, but in any case, I can find ways to be more or less protected from negative consequences of any of these choices.

32. My culture gives me little fear about ignoring the perspectives and powers of people of other races.

33. I am not made acutely aware that my shape, bearing, or body odor will be taken as a reflection on my race.

34. I can worry about racism without being seen as self-interested or self-seeking.

35. I can take a job with an affirmative action employer without having my co-workers on the job suspect that I got it because of my race.

36. If my day, week, or year is going badly, I need not ask of each negative episode or situation whether it has racial overtones.

37. I can be pretty sure of finding people who would be willing to talk with me and advise me about my next steps, professionally.

38. I can think over many options, social, political, imaginative, or professional, without asking whether a person of my race would be accepted or allowed to do what I want to do.

39. I can be late to a meeting without having the lateness reflect on my race.

40. I can choose public accommodation without fearing that people of my race cannot get in or will be mistreated in the places I have chosen.

41. I can be sure that if I need legal or medical help, my race will not work against me.

42. I can arrange my activities so that I will never have to experience feelings of rejection owing to my race.

43. If I have low credibility as a leader, I can be sure that my race is not the problem.

44. I can easily find academic courses and institutions that give attention only to people of my race.

45. I can expect figurative language and imagery in all of the arts to testify to experiences of my race.

46. I can choose blemish cover or bandages in "flesh" color and have them more or less match my skin.

I repeatedly forgot each of the realizations on this list until I wrote it down. For me, white privilege has turned out to be an elusive and fugitive subject. The pressure to avoid it is great, for in facing it I must give up the myth of meritocracy. If these things are true, this is not such a free country; one's life is not what one makes it; many doors open for certain people through no virtues of their own. These perceptions mean also that my moral condition is not what I had been led to believe. The appearance of being a good citizen rather than a troublemaker comes in large part from having all sorts of doors open automatically because of my color.

A further paralysis of nerve comes from literary silence protecting privilege. My clearest memories of finding such analysis are in Lillian Smith's unparalleled *Killers of the Dream,* and Margaret Andersen's review of Karen and Mamie Fields' *Lemon Swamp.* Smith, for example, wrote about walking toward black children on the street and knowing they would step into the gutter; Andersen contrasted the pleasure that she, as a white child, took on summer driving trips to the south with Karen Fields' memories of driving in a closed car stocked with all necessities lest, in stopping, her black family should suffer "insult, or worse." Adrienne Rich also recognizes and writes about daily experiences of privilege, but in my observation, white women's writing in this area is far more often on systemic racism than on our daily lives as light-skinned women.[2]

In unpacking this invisible knapsack of white privilege, I have listed conditions of daily experience that I once took for granted, as neutral, normal, and universally available to everybody, just as I once thought of a male-focused curriculum as the neutral or accurate account that can speak for all. Nor did I think of any of these perquisites as bad for the holder. I now think that we need a more finely differentiated taxonomy of privilege, for some of these varieties are only what one would want for everyone in a just society, and others give license to be ignorant, oblivious, arrogant, and destructive. Before proposing some more finely tuned categorization, I will make some observations about the general effects of these conditions on my life and expectations.

In this potpourri of examples, some privileges make me feel at home in the world. Others allow me to escape penalties or dangers that others suffer. Through some, I escape fear, anxiety, insult, injury, or a sense of not being welcome, not being real. Some keep me from having to hide, to be in disguise, to feel sick or crazy, to negotiate each transaction from the position of being an outsider or, within my group, a person who is suspected of having too close links with a dominant culture. Most keep me from having to be angry.

I see a pattern running through the matrix of white privilege, a pattern of assumptions that were passed on to me as a white person. There was one main piece of cultural turf; it was my own turf, and I was among those who could control the turf. I could measure up to the cultural standards and take advantage of the many options I saw around me to make what the culture would call a success of my life. *My skin color was an asset for any move I was educated to want to make.* I could think of myself as "belonging" in major ways and of making social systems work for me. I could freely disparage, fear, neglect, or be oblivious to anything outside of the dominant cultural forms. Being of the main culture, I could also criticize it fairly freely. My life was reflected back to me frequently enough so that I felt, with regard to my race, if not to my sex, like one of the real people.

Whether through the curriculum or in the newspaper, the television, the economic system, or the general look of people in the streets, I received daily signals and indications that my people counted and that others *either didn't exist or must be trying, not very successfully, to be like people of my race.* I was given cultural permission not to hear voices of people of other races or a tepid cultural tolerance for hearing or acting on such voices. I was also raised not to suffer seriously from anything that darker-skinned people might say about my group, "protected," though perhaps I should more accurately say *prohibited,* through the habits of my economic class and social group, from living in racially mixed groups or being reflective about interactions between people of differing races.

In proportion as my racial group was being made confident, comfortable, and oblivious, other groups were likely being made unconfident, uncomfortable, and alienated. Whiteness protected me from many kinds of hostility, distress, and violence, which I was being subtly trained to visit in turn upon people of color.

For this reason, the word "privilege" now seems to me misleading. Its connotations are too positive to fit the conditions and behaviors which "privilege systems" produce. We usually think of privilege as being a favored state, whether earned or conferred by birth or luck. School graduates are reminded they are privileged and urged to use their (enviable) assets well. The word "privilege" carries the connotation of being something everyone must want. Yet some of the conditions I have described here work to systemically overempower certain groups. Such privilege simply *confers dominance,* gives permission to control, because of one's race or sex. The kind of privilege that gives license to some people to be, at best, thoughtless and, at worst, murderous should not continue to be referred to as a desirable attribute. Such "privilege" may be widely desired without being in any way beneficial to the whole society.

Moreover, though "privilege" may confer power, it does not confer moral strength. Those who do not depend on conferred dominance have traits and qualities that may never develop in those who do. Just as Women's Studies courses indicate that women survive their political circumstances to lead lives that hold the human race together, so "underprivileged" people of color who are the world's majority have survived their oppression and lived survivors' lives from which the white global minority can and must learn. In some groups, those dominated have actually become strong through *not* having all of these unearned advantages, and this gives them a great deal to teach the others. Members of so-called privileged groups can seem foolish, ridiculous, infantile, or dangerous by contrast.

I want, then, to distinguish between earned strength and unearned power conferred systemically. Power from unearned privilege can look like strength when it is, in fact, permission to escape or to dominate. But not all of the privileges on my list are inevitably damaging. Some, like the expectation that neighbors will be decent to you, or that your race will not count against you in court, should be the norm in a just society and should be considered as the entitlement of everyone. Others, like the privilege not to listen to less powerful people, distort the humanity of the holders as well as the ignored groups. Still others, like finding one's staple foods everywhere, may be a function of being a member of a numerical majority in the population. Others have to do with not having to labor under pervasive negative stereotyping and mythology.

We might at least start by distinguishing between positive advantages that we can work to spread, to the point where they are not advantages at all but simply part of the normal civic and social fabric, and negative types of advantage that unless rejected will always reinforce our present hierarchies. For example, the positive "privilege" of belonging, the feeling that one belongs within the human circle, as Native Americans say, fosters development and should not be seen as privilege for a few. It is, let us say, an entitlement that none of us should have to earn; ideally it is an *unearned entitlement.* At present, since only a few have it, it is an *unearned advantage* for them. The negative "privilege" that gave me cultural permission not to take darker-skinned Others seriously can be seen as arbitrarily conferred dominance and should not be desirable for anyone. This paper results from a process of coming to see that some of the power that I originally saw as attendant on being a human being in the United States consisted in *unearned advantage* and *conferred dominance,* as well as other kinds of special circumstance not universally taken for granted.

In writing this paper I have also realized that white identity and status (as well as class identity and status) give me considerable power to choose whether to broach this subject and its trouble. I can pretty well decide whether to disappear and avoid and not listen and escape the dislike I may engender in other people through this essay, or interrupt, answer, interpret, preach, correct, criticize, and control to some extent what goes on in reaction to it. Being white, I am given considerable power to escape many kinds of danger or penalty as well as to choose which risks I want to take.

There is an analogy here, once again, with Women's Studies. Our male colleagues do not have a great deal to lose in supporting Women's Studies, but they do not have a great deal to lose if they oppose it either. They simply have the power to decide whether to commit themselves to more equitable distributions of power. They will probably feel few penalties whatever choice they make; they do not seem, in any obvious short-term sense, the ones at risk, though they and we are all at risk because of the behaviors that have been rewarded in them.

Through Women's Studies work I have met very few men who are truly distressed about systemic, unearned male advantage and conferred dominance. And so one question for me and others like me is whether we will be like them, or whether we will get truly distressed, even outraged, about unearned race advantage and conferred dominance and if so, what we will do to lessen them. In any case, we need to do more work in identifying how they actually affect our daily lives. We need more down-to-earth writing by people about these taboo subjects. We need more understanding of the ways in which white "privilege" damages white people, for these are not the same ways in which it damages the victimized. Skewed white psyches are an inseparable part of the picture, though I do not want to confuse the kinds of damage done to the holders of special assets and to those who suffer the deficits. Many, perhaps most, of our white students in the United States think that racism doesn't affect them because they are not people of color; they do not see "whiteness" as a racial identity. Many men likewise think that Women's Studies does not bear on their own existences because they are not female; they do not see themselves as having gendered identities. Insisting on the universal "effects" of "privilege" systems, then, becomes one of our chief tasks, and being more explicit about the *particular* effects in particular contexts is another. Men need to join us in this work.

In addition, since race and sex are not the only advantaging systems at work, we need to similarly examine the daily experience of having age advantage, or ethnic advantage, or physical ability, or advantage related to nationality, religion, or sexual orientation. Professor Marnie Evans suggested to me that in many ways the list I made also applies directly to heterosexual privilege. This is a still more taboo subject than race privilege: the daily ways in which heterosexual privilege makes some persons comfortable or powerful, providing supports, assets, approvals, and rewards to those who live or expect to live in heterosexual pairs. Unpacking that content is still more difficult, owing to the deeper embeddedness of heterosexual advantage and dominance and stricter taboos surrounding these.

But to start such an analysis I would put this observation from my own experience: The fact that I live under the same roof with a man triggers all kinds of societal assumptions about my worth, politics, life, and values and triggers a host of unearned advantages and powers. After recasting many elements from the original list I would add further observations like these:

1. My children do not have to answer questions about why I live with my partner (my husband).
2. I have no difficulty finding neighborhoods where people approve of our household.
3. Our children are given texts and classes that implicitly support our kind of family unit and do not turn them against my choice of domestic partnership.
4. I can travel alone or with my husband without expecting embarrassment or hostility in those who deal with us.
5. Most people I meet will see my marital arrangements as an asset to my life or as a favorable comment on my likability, my competence, or my mental health.
6. I can talk about the social events of a weekend without fearing most listeners' reactions.
7. I will feel welcomed and "normal" in the usual walks of public life, institutional and social.
8. In many contexts, I am seen as "all right" in daily work on women because I do not live chiefly with women.

Difficulties and dangers surrounding the task of finding parallels are many. Since racism, sexism, and heterosexism are not the same, the advantages associated with them should not be seen as the same. In addition, it is hard to isolate aspects of unearned advantage that derive chiefly from social class, economic class, race, religion, region, sex, or ethnic identity. The oppressions are both distinct and interlocking, as the Combahee River Collective statement of 1977 continues to remind us eloquently.[3]

One factor seems clear about all of the interlocking oppressions. They take both active forms that we can see and embedded forms that members of the dominant group are taught not to see. In my class and place, I did not see myself as racist because I was taught to recognize racism only in individual acts of meanness by members of my group, never in invisible systems conferring racial dominance on my group from birth. Likewise, we are taught to think that sexism or heterosexism is carried on only through intentional, individual acts of discrimination, meanness, or cruelty, rather than in invisible systems conferring unsought dominance on certain groups. Disapproving of the systems won't be enough to change them. I was taught to think that racism could end if white individuals changed their attitudes; many men think sexism can be ended by individual changes in daily behavior toward women. But a man's sex provides advantage for him whether or not he approves of the way in which dominance has been conferred on his group. A "white" skin in the United States opens many doors for whites whether or not we approve of the way dominance has been conferred on us. Individual acts can palliate, but cannot end, these problems. To redesign social systems, we need first to acknowledge their colossal unseen dimensions. The silences and denials surrounding privilege are the key political tool here. They keep the thinking about equality or equity incomplete, protecting unearned advantage and conferred dominance by making these taboo subjects. Most talk by whites about equal opportunity seems to me now to be about equal opportunity to try to get into a position of dominance while denying that *systems* of dominance exist.

Obliviousness about white advantage, like obliviousness about male advantage, is kept strongly inculturated in the United States so as to maintain the myth of meritocracy, the myth that democratic choice is equally available to all. Keeping most people unaware that freedom of confident action is there for just a small number of people props up those in power and serves to keep power in the hands of the same groups that have most of it already. Though systemic change takes many decades, there are pressing questions for me and I imagine for some others like me if we raise our daily consciousness on the perquisites of being light-skinned. What will we do with such knowledge? As we know from watching men, it is an open question whether we will choose to use unearned advantage to weaken invisible privilege systems and whether we will use any of our arbitrarily awarded power to try to reconstruct power systems on a broader base.

ACKNOWLEDGMENTS

I have appreciated commentary on this paper from the Working Papers Committee of the Wellesley College Center for Research on Women, from members of the Dodge seminar, and from many individuals, including Margaret Andersen, Sorel Berman, Joanne Braxton, Johnnella Butler, Sandra Dickerson, Marnie Evans, Beverly Guy-Sheftall, Sandra Harding, Eleanor Hinton Hoytt, Pauline Houston, Paul Lauter, Joyce Miller, Mary Norris, Gloria Oden, Beverly Smith, and John Walter.

NOTES

1. This paper was presented at the Virginia Women's Studies Association conference in Richmond in April 1986, and the American Educational Research Association conference in Boston in October 1986, and discussed with two groups of participants in the Dodge seminars for Secondary School Teachers in New York and Boston in the spring of 1987.

2. Andersen, Margaret, "Race and the Social Science Curriculum: A Teaching and Learning Discussion," *Radical Teacher*, November 1984, pp. 17–20. Smith, Lillian, *Killers of the Dream*, New York: W. W. Norton, 1949.

3. "A Black Feminist Statement," The Combahee River Collective, pp. 13–22 in G. Hull, P. Scott, B. Smith, Eds., *All the Women Are White, All the Blacks Are Men, but Some of Us Are Brave: Black Women's Studies*, Old Westbury, NY: The Feminist Press, 1982.

HAOLE GIRL: IDENTITY AND WHITE PRIVILEGE IN HAWAI'I

Judy Rohrer

This is a paper about what it means to be a white person in Hawai'i, what it means to be a haole. Hawaii's ethnically mixed population and history as an independent kingdom colonized by the United States makes being a white person here a completely different experience than anywhere else in the country. In Hawai'i, white does not blend in; it stands out. Having grown up in Hawai'i and now living here as an adult, I have struggled with my haole identity, mostly trying to figure out how to minimize, disguise, or get rid of it altogether. I have tried hard to be anything but da haole girl. Instead of continuing to try to escape, I decided to face it through research and writing. . . .

Who am I? It makes sense that I would have different answers at different times under different circumstances. Identity is relational, contested, contingent, negotiated, produced, manipulated, multiple, socially and historically constructed. In other words, it is never just one thing. "Our cultural identities are . . . always in a state of becoming, a journey in which we never arrive" (Hereniko 1994:407). Postmodern theorists encourage us to "play" with identities, putting them on and taking them off like hats or cloaks. Oppressed peoples are reclaiming and redefining their identities as sources of strength. Non-white feminist theorists have stressed the multiplicity, interconnectedness, and simultaneity of identities. I am not just a woman, but a white woman; not just a white woman, but a white lesbian; not just a white lesbian, but a white, educated, middle-class lesbian; not just a white, educated, middle-class lesbian, but a white, educated, middle-class, able-bodied lesbian. These identities are the ones about which I have spent the most time (re)constructing, thinking and educating myself. But what about haole? . . .

Use of the word haole can be found in pre-contact times in the *Kumulipo*, a creation chant and in written references to a type of pig, the pua'a haole. Most scholars agree that its earliest meanings were "foreigner, foreign, introduced, of foreign origin," as it is defined in the Pukui and Elbert *Hawaiian Dictionary*. Emily Hawkins, a Hawaiian language professor at the University of Hawai'i states, "it was a word used for outsiders, or things that were not from here."[1] One of the first references describing a white person, in this case an English captain, is found in a biography published in 1838.[2]

> I remember using knowledge of the epistemology of haole to try to counteract its sting.

> When local (non-Hawaiian) kids would call me haole, I would say, "Haole means foreigner. You're a foreigner here too."

> But it didn't matter.

> Haole had taken on new meanings through years of colonialism and neo-colonialism.

> The kids knew I was "da haole girl."

> Years later I'm coming to understand that too.

. . . We cannot escape being haole; we have been too well-trained and the term carries too much meaning and history. Haole is not a positive identity for most white people in Hawai'i, not something we claim with pride, but something ascribed to us by a history, a culture and a language we may know little about. Our feelings about the term range from ambivalence to anger. In fact, some of us spend a good deal of energy ignoring or denying our haoleness. It is difficult for us to know how to choose to be/become haole. At this time, what I am searching for are ways to be not *so* haole, ways to reconstruct my haole identity. If identities are really manipulated, negotiable, and produced, then I want to become a different haole without denying the historical and contemporary context that shapes the term. I remind myself that while Hawai'i *is* very multicultural, the history behind that ethnic mix has built today's structures of unequal power and domination. . . .

What has helped me in figuring out where to go from here is feminist writing which attempts to question, unveil and deconstruct whiteness. On a certain level, haole can be thought of as a name for white privilege situated in Hawai'i. . . .

I like the idea of being/becoming a "recovering haole." It is a subprocess of being a "recovering racist," a concept from anti-racism work. As a white person, I can never fully "recover" from being haole or racist, because these identities are so strongly constructed in our culture, in our beings. What I can do is work to acknowledge the privilege I have and act out of this self-awareness by becoming more accountable and responsible. This process of recovery is vital to my becoming a more whole person—vital, in fact, to my survival.

NOTES

1. As quoted in Vicki Viotti (1995:F8).
2. *Ibid.*

REFERENCES

Hereniko, Vilsoni. 1994. "Representations of Cultural Identities," pp. 406–434 in *Tides of History: The Pacific in the Twentieth Century,* edited by Kerry Howe, Robert Kiste and Brij Lal. Honolulu: University of Hawai'i Press.
Viotti, Vicki. 1995. "Haole: Is it a Dirty Word?" *Honolulu Advertiser* February 5:F8.

READING *3* **Laura M. Lopez**
Frances S. Hasso

Frontlines and Borders: Identity Thresholds for Latinas and Arab American Women[1]

INTRODUCTION

I would like to say that I longed not to be defined by the gaze of the other, but to look out upon the world through eyes rooted in the boundaries of my own identity. But it is true that for much of my life I thought if I looked long enough I would find someone to tell me who I am. Turning to the world for some reflection of myself, however, I found only distortion. (Majaj 1994: 67)

This essay compares the ways in which Latina and Arab American women students experienced their racial-ethnic and gender identities at "home" and in a university environment.[2] These women's experiences have for the most part been excluded by a black/white dichotomy that is especially dominant in the sociological literatures on race and gender. Comparing the experiences of these two pan-national, racially diverse groups enriches this literature by exploring how multiple sites of difference (race, class, national, cultural, and sexual) interact with systems of domination, and how these interactions, in turn, affect identity construction. Literally and figuratively, dominance and resistance are not black/white issues. Without undercutting the power of material and discursive anti-African American racism, this dichotomy limits analysis of racism against African Americans, excludes other racialized experiences, inhibits comparison across racialized groups, and, perhaps most importantly from our perspective, restricts the possibilities for alliances across racial-ethnic groups for the purpose of making social change.

While racial-ethnic identities in racist societies are defined and constructed by subordinate groups in a context of exclusion and misrepresentation, the process can also be empowering for minorities. In the educational system in particular, power relations are contradictory, producing

not only oppression but its opposition—and opposition, in turn, avails itself of power's blind spots and loopholes. The educational system's greater or lesser discriminatory and dehumanizing constructions of the "third world"-origin minority "identity" elicit the minority subject's destabilization of dominant ideology's logic, while oppression and discrimination in turn create the oppressed's desire for empowerment, equality, and justice. (Pérez 1993: 269)

In response to racism and the configuration of racial-ethnic identities, both the Arab American women and Latinas interviewed found the university to be an identity threshold—a place where racial-ethnic identity was reconfigured. Both groups of women were excluded and misrepresented in a variety of ways. As underrepresented minorities, the Latinas contended with a myriad of messages that they were unqualified to be university students *because* of their racial-ethnic backgrounds. This was compounded by a dichotomized racial-ethnic discourse that often excluded their experiences as Latinas. The Arab American women grew up in a popular culture that almost uniformly denigrated their Arab and/or Muslim backgrounds, and live in a social environment in which political discourse about the Middle East is generally both uninformed and highly charged. For the Arab Americans, political conflicts related to the Middle East played out on campus in ways that created identity "frontlines."

Whereas racial-ethnic identities were emphasized in the university, both groups of women focused on issues of authenticity when discussing their "homes"—family, community, or nation. Language-knowledge, class mobility, and obedience to racial-ethnic gender and sexual norms affected whether the women felt and/or were treated as "authentic" community members. In addition, both groups discussed physical appearance (skin color, hair texture, and body size) as a focus of discipline and control within and outside their communities. Rather than being mutually exclusive categories, "home" and university experiences interactively defined racial-ethnic and gender identities; at the same time, different identity issues were stressed in the two settings.

METHOD AND REPRESENTATION

The findings in this report stem from a joint fieldwork project undertaken in the 1993–4 academic year during a graduate qualitative research methods course at the University of Michigan, Ann Arbor. Using the same interview guide, Frances Hasso conducted one- to two-hour semi-structured interviews with eight Arab American women students, and Laura Lopez did the same with eight Latinas; the groups were evenly split between undergraduate and graduate students.[3] Together we conducted two group interviews that included both Arab Americans and Latinas, one of which was designed to share information and get feedback on preliminary analysis.

The eight Arab American women interviewed had parents originally from Egypt, Palestine, Lebanon, Morocco, and combinations of these countries; three of the women had Euro-American mothers, and one (Mona) had a Euro-American father. Seven of the Arab Americans were born in the US and one (Suha) was naturalized as an infant. Three of the women identified as Muslim and five as Christian (although only one in each category was practicing). None of the Arab American women's parents were divorced, although one (Hana) had parents who were separated.

The call for interviews with Latinas drew only Chicanas and Puerto Rican women. Of the four women who identified as being of Puerto Rican descent, three were born and raised in New York and one grew up in Puerto Rico. The birth mother of one Puerto Rican woman (Linda) was of Euro-American descent (her stepmother, however, was Puerto Rican), and the birth father of another Puerto Rican woman (Margaret) was Asian (although she was raised solely by her single mother). The remaining four Latinas were Chicanas/Mexican Americans from Texas and California, one of whom was born in Mexico and naturalized in the US soon thereafter. One Latina gave no religious identification, and the remainder identified as Catholics (five practicing and two non-practicing). Five of the eight Latinas grew up with both birth parents (although not all fathers were consistently present or financially supportive); two had spent their childhoods partly with divorced mothers and partly in blended families; and one was raised by a single mother.

Five of the eight Latinas were from poor or working-class backgrounds. Additionally, one Puerto Rican said she was "low to middle class" (Linda), a Chicana said she was "middle-class" (Emma), and the Puerto Rican from the island said she was "high middle-class" (Lisa). Both parents of two Puerto Rican women (Linda and Lisa) had bachelor degrees (one had an MA); the single mother of another Puerto Rican woman (Margaret) had earned a BA as an adult; and the father of one Chicana (Emma) had attended two years of college after earning a graduate equivalency diploma. The remaining four Latinas came from families in which neither parents nor siblings had ever attended college. Moreover, three of these women came from households in which neither parent had graduated from high school.

In contrast, all eight Arab American women had at least one college-educated parent (and usually both were college-educated). Seven out of the eight (Jamila is the exception) had at least one parent (and usually both) who had an advanced academic or professional degree. With the exception of one middle-class woman (Hana), all the remaining women came from upper middle-class backgrounds. While some of the women had spent parts of their childhoods living in the Arab world, when they lived in the US seven of the eight had grown up in mostly white, upper middle-class neighborhoods and went to schools (public and private) with similar characteristics. While they did not live in Arab neighborhoods, the parents of four women were involved in religious, professional, cultural, and/or political activities in Arab American communities.

It was not possible to compare the socio-economic indicators of the women interviewed with those of other Arab American and Latina/o students at the University of Michigan because of the absence of such data, including a complete lack of any information on Arab Americans as a group. According to university data, during the 1992–3 academic year, approximately 4.1 percent of the student body (undergraduate and graduate) were "Hispanic/Latino"; included in this category are persons of "Mexican, Puerto Rican, Cuban, Central or South American, or other Spanish culture or origin, regardless of race . . ." (University of Michigan, June 1993: 35).[4] During the 1992–3 academic year, approximately 76 percent of graduate and undergraduate students were categorized as "white," 8.4 percent as Asian American, 7.9 percent as African American, and 0.65 as Native American (University of Michigan, June 1993: 39, 41).

In this study, we are looking at "segments within segments" of communities intersected by a number of axes of difference, not least of which is that both "Arab American" and "Latina/o" are constructs that include different national, class, and religious backgrounds. In addition, while there are class differences among Arab Americans, US Census Bureau data indicate that they are significantly better off as a group than either Mexican Americans or Puerto Ricans, whose poor class standing has been connected to a long history of US colonization and exploitation of these two groups (Montejano 1987; Moore and Pachon 1993; Munóz, Jr 1989; Rodriguez 1989).[5] While there are many voices (e.g., men, working-class Arab American women, and upper middle-class Latinas) not represented in this study, those who are provide insights with respect to both racial-ethnic groups. Instead of emphasizing the representativeness of the women interviewed, we would prefer to stress the dynamic and context-specific nature of identity and identity formation, in keeping

with the goal of "partial, locatable, critical knowledges sustaining the possibility of webs of connections" (Behdad 1993: 45, citing D. Haraway).

Renalo Rosaldo (1989) and others have argued that knowledge and theorizing occurs relationally and is always a subjective process involving the researcher and the researched. Our own subjectivities and experiences as an Arab American woman and a Chicana provided critical insights throughout this research project. We undertook the project as two women of color for whom racism has been a tangible part of growing up in the United States and our university experiences. As members of these respective communities, we also had expectations about the types of issues that would resonate with the women we interviewed. At the same time, we approached the project from an inductive perspective, being careful to remain open to differences of subjectivity and experience. Indeed, while our social and class locations and experiences were sometimes similar to those of the women interviewed, they were also different in many respects. Like Laura, three of the Latinas interviewed had been primarily raised by a single or divorced mother and a number of them had struggled economically growing up. Unlike Frances, none of the Arab American women came from working-class backgrounds.

OPPOSITIONALITY AND IDENTITY

According to Chela Sandoval, "oppositional consciousness" is an ideological strategy for subordinated persons confronting domination. It refers to

> the capacity to re-center depending upon the kinds of oppression to be confronted . . . [and it also] depends upon the ability to read the current situation of power and self-consciously choosing and adopting the ideological form best suited to push against its configurations, a survival skill well-known to oppressed peoples. (Sandoval 1991: 14–15)

This type of consciousness allows "weav[ing] 'between and among' oppositional ideologies," much like the clutch of an automobile allows a driver to "select, engage, and disengage gears in a system for the transmission of power" (Sandoval 1991: 14).

For the Latinas and Arab Americans interviewed, identity was redefined in opposition to the racialized narratives operative on campus. That is, while race, class, and gender identities were bound together, because racial-ethnic identities were emphasized by the dominant culture, they were usually the most salient in the university; gender was not irrelevant, but *less* relevant than racial-ethnic identity. Exclusion and misrepresentation in this setting contributed to a more definitive sense of "Arabness" or "Latinaness," and the women often relayed identity "coming out" stories. It is not that racial-ethnic identity did not exist as an affirming process, but that oppositionality *on campus* redefined it.

Oppositionality operated in different ways for the Arab American women and Latinas. The Latinas redefined their identities in opposition to the university's predominantly white environment, white racism, and a Eurocentric curriculum; they were told that they were "unqualified" and did not "belong" in a myriad of ways in this setting. On another level, however, their experiences were also shaped by tension and exclusion by students of color who had limited definitions of race. For the Arab American women, oppositionality was very much related to the way international events played out on college campuses. The Middle East's political-economic importance, its real frontlines of war and political crises, its ubiquity in the news, and the treatment of such issues in classrooms created "frontlines" in the university that compelled women to make identity decisions.

THE "FORCED ALIENATION" OF LATINAS

[P]eople talk about assimilation in one voice and alienation in another voice and I don't think that they're that separate—not in my life—they're not. If you could take anything from, you know, what I just splurted out, it would be that, that my life has been one of confused assimilation and forced alienation. (Linda)

Upon their entrance to the university, most of the Latinas interviewed found themselves relocated from racially diverse or predominantly Latino/a neighborhoods to a largely white educational institution and city. Latino/a students' relatively low representation at the university defined and exacerbated their sense of oppositionality. One Chicana (Emma) characterized this low representation by saying, "it was a long time before I found another Mexican." A Puerto Rican woman (Janie), who had described the university and surrounding community as "too white-bread," said it took her a long time to find other people of color on campus.

Further, most of the Latinas interviewed left communities where their cultural events, music, and food were more readily accessible and came to study at a university that lacked many of the cultural comforts of "home." As Emma put it, "there's nothing here of what I am used to . . . like food, music, you know all these . . . I had to bring everything from back home to even have just a little bit."

Teresa, another Chicana observed:

It took me a while to figure out that they didn't have any Spanish radio stations . . . or TV stations [at that time] and it took me probably three months to figure out that the tortillas were in the frozen section . . . and the minute I opened the package I knew I wasn't going to like them. So that was really depressing.

Their sense of oppositionality to the dominant culture at the university was exacerbated by discriminatory encounters with white students and professors, and an academic discourse and environment that excluded their experiences. Margaret, a Puerto Rican/Chinese American student, related the following:

I've almost always had white professors—white male professors . . . here at the university . . . I don't know, I have always wondered about that because I go into the classroom and I never felt very comfortable talking to the professor . . . and I'm sure a lot of it is just me, but I wonder why it is that some of these other people feel so comfortable doing that, feel so comfortable being . . . loud or being whatever kind of way in class, which I wouldn't do because . . . maybe because it would attract too much attention, I don't know . . . [I] can't really be myself or feel comfortable enough to ask questions in the middle of class. I know that the one time when I did have a Black professor here in one of my hard sciences courses . . . I felt so comfortable—even though I rarely talked to the professor at all—but just walking in there, sitting down, I loved going to class because he was Black and I felt like "wow, somebody at least I feel like I can identify with," you know, who might at least be able to identify with me a little bit better.

Janie, also Puerto Rican, discussed feeling "out of place in school":

I was probably the only Latina . . . in all of my classes, which was really sad. And I think being from out-of-state, and being Puerto Rican, and being lower-class, I think everything was just very difficult. So when I got here I felt really alienated. I had a tough time with the politics of being in graduate school. I did not get along with my advisor . . . I just had a hard time.

A Chicana student encountered racist remarks on two different occasions at the beginning of her tenure in a PhD program. First, a white male literature professor criticized this US-born and educated woman (Anne) for her command of the English language, and she was within earshot on another occasion when another white male professor remarked that the students of color from her entering cohort "were just a joke." Linda, a Puerto Rican/Euro-American student, similarly noted:

I was insulted, I was stepped on, I was criticized, I was questioned [by white students and professors] . . . to the point that, even if I thought that they were nice people or they had some particular personality characteristic that I might have wanted to hang out with, it was impossible for me to do that and maintain a sense of self-worth . . . When people found out that I had minority fellowships, I was no longer a smart kid. You know, it wasn't the kind of research experience I had, it wasn't the college I went to, the classes I had, or the things that I said in class. It was that she's this minority, she has this fellowship. . . .

Feeling marginalized, the Latinas sought out other Latina/o students in social and political groups, and the few Latina/o professors on campus for mentorship. They attempted to build cultural spaces and small communities in opposition to an alienating academic community, which further contributed to a sense of "Latina-ness" or "woman of colorness," versus "them" or "whiteness." Some of the lighter-skinned Latinas even reacted negatively to being "mistaken for" or labeled as "white" by whites or other students of color in the university whose race thinking worked from only black/white scripts. Teresa, a light-skinned Chicana, relayed the following story about her first summer at the university:

I guess, again, coming from California it was OK to mix different groups and nobody ever had any problems with it, you know, and people knew who you were or at least they had been exposed to more groups than just blacks and whites. And when I got here this summer I went to a party and one of the black guys that was there said "Who brought that white bitch?" and who they were talking about was me and I overheard that so it was sort of like "well, do I cuss this motherfucker out . . . ?"

Significantly, her angry response was not because she had been called "bitch" by another man (i.e., he was offending her as a woman), but because she had been called a *white* bitch by an African American.

Thus, as a result of racialized-cultural opposition from whites (and sometimes, African Americans), and the lack of the cultural comforts of home, "Latina" became a critical part of these women's identities in the university. Emma summarized this feeling when she said "I've become more conscientious about it [being Latina] . . . because who thinks about it when you're all the same? . . . Being up here makes me more aware and more proud of who I am." In addition to increasingly associating predominantly or even exclusively with other Latinas/os, these Latinas also learned or brushed up on Spanish language skills as necessary, and all but one (a student in the physical sciences) focused on Latino/a issues in their studies.

ARAB AMERICAN "FRONTLINES"

[Misconceptions about the Middle East on campus] really stir feelings of rage and frustration [in me] and it's like an actual emotion rather than knowledge. And I think, how did it happen to me? What did my parents do to make me so wrapped up in it? . . . And my parents never—I almost wish they had—but they never sat me down and said: "This is the history of your [Palestinian] family. First they killed so and so." It just came out gradually, these things that happened, sad things and terrible things, but never explicitly. (Mona)

The racialized campus experiences of the Arab American women differed from those of the Latinas. They did not confront the dislocation experienced by the Latinas interviewed, largely because most of them came from upper middle-class backgrounds, lived in predominantly white neighborhoods, and attended schools with similar characteristics. Even as they remained "Arab" within their homes, as children, most of the Arab American women had assimilated in public contexts as much as they were allowed to until they became university students—avoiding "role conflict" by becoming "Americans by day and [Arabs] by night" (Swanson 1996: 244). When they reached the university, however, almost all were compelled to make identity decisions about their "Arab-ness"—whether or not to "come out," so to speak—largely in response to the way Middle East–related events played out on campuses.

These international events are highly politically charged and for the most part (mis)represented in both the media (Said 1981; Shaheen 1984; Shaheen 1993) and school and university classrooms. Recent examples include the 1990–1 Gulf War, the 1994 World Trade Center bombing, and the ongoing Arab-Israeli conflict. In university classroom situations, the Arab American women had to either disregard misrepresentations or racist characterizations of Arabs, Muslims, Islam, or Arab culture, or publicly confront their professors, teaching assistants, or fellow students. "Taking a stand" exposed their Arab American identities (if others did not already know), and often subjected them to being labelled a number of things that are assumed by the dominant culture to be inherently Arab or Muslim: "terroristic," anti-Semitic, violent, and unreasonably angry. As a result, confusion and silence were common responses to such misrepresentations.

(Mis)perceptions of the Arab-Israeli conflict in particular were often provocative for the Arab American women. One Palestinian/Euro-American graduate student remembered the following conversation with a white male housemate soon after arriving in Ann Arbor:

He was seeing a Jewish girlfriend and he just found out I was Palestinian and he said, "well, that puts me in an awkward position. . . . I'm going out with a Jewish girlfriend, and you being Palestinian." I said, "Yeah, but I mean we're adults here. Why does that make a difference?" [she laughs slightly] . . . And do you know what he said to me? He said, "If you ever did anything to hurt this girl, I will come after you and blow your head off." This is *a week* after I lived with this guy. And I was stuck with him for a whole four months. Can you believe that? (Katy)

This woman, whose hair is blondish and skin light-colored, told few others in her professional program that she is Palestinian American after this incident.

Another Palestinian/Euro-American graduate student discussed her ambivalent silence in classrooms at her "very Ivy League" undergraduate institution:

I mean, I didn't feel comfortable saying my opinions [about the Middle East] in class or in really any setting, except with close friends, and even then it would be a little hard. I have a lot of Jewish friends and stuff who have an amazing blind spot when it comes to certain things. But definitely not in classes; I would not give my opinion; I always was restraining myself and saying

I have to be diplomatic, I have to be understanding, I have to remember this, this, and the other thing, so I never actually brought it to a head by doing something. So, I just avoided it, but I knew I was consciously avoiding something, because I felt that it would cause trouble, but I can't prove that it would because I didn't. I had friends who told me about other incidents and it just scared me and I wasn't up to dealing with it. . . . (Mona)

Many women, including this Egyptian American undergraduate, remembered the 1990–1 Gulf War as making life particularly difficult for Arab Americans: "It was difficult because I have a lot of friends who are Jewish . . . And so, you know, it was—it was difficult . . . I was against the war and I didn't—I felt that most people were really just supporting the war out of blind patriotism and nothing else" (Amy). A Moroccan/Euro-American graduate student who had been politically active during the Gulf War described how she was accused at various points of being unpatriotic, un-American, and anti-Semitic: "I got obscene and pornographic hate mail, threatening me with rape . . . My classmates spread a rumor . . . that I had given up my American citizenship" (Hana). Anti-Muslim sentiment was at such heights during the Gulf War, that for the first time she began identifying herself as a *Muslim* Arab American: "I wanted to set myself as much apart [as possible] from this culture and in line with that culture . . . and I thought that was one way to do it" (Hana).

While these incidents were frightening and alienating for the Arab American women, they also galvanized most of them to study the political debates into which they were inextricably pulled, and to be prepared for intellectual confrontations. All except one (Katy) of the Arab American women interviewed became politically active, took courses on the Arab-Israeli and other regional conflicts, studied the Arab countries from which they originated, and/or focused their studies on the Arab world during college. A Lebanese American woman discussed the effects of a course she took on the Arab-Israeli conflict:

I became stronger with my identity as an Arab and a Lebanese . . . Why I did, I'm not sure . . . [When she was one of the few women and only Arab American to publicly disagree with the professor's and other students' analysis in a class of over 100 students] I don't know how to explain it, but I know I felt cornered [in class]. It's not because I'm anti-Jewish, but I am against what the Israeli government does. I'm against what the US does. Do you know what I'm saying? Um, so I identified more and more and that's where my Arab identity came into larger play. (Jamila)

Similar to the Latinas' responses to racism and exclusion on campus, all but one of the Arab American women learned or relearned Arabic, interrogated their families about their own histories, travelled to the Arab world, and/or socialized with other Arab Americans and Arabs. While many of the women became more comfortable with their "Arab-ness," most could not ignore the intertwining of oppositionality and identity. As one activist noted in relation to being attacked at the university for her political positions: "Isn't it funny how that [people attacking you] makes you feel more Arab, too? . . . it's sort of like opposition defines you" (Michelle). While oppositionality generally strengthened racial-ethnic identity, for three of the Arab American women (two of whom were bi-racial), "coming out" was a personal, not public, process. As indicated by their narratives, some of these women remained afraid of the reputational and professional consequences of confronting racism and stressing their racial-ethnic identities in the university. In addition, as they became more aware of their histories and backgrounds, the cultural dilemmas became more stark for most of the women, who found themselves in situations where they felt neither "Arab" nor "American," in practice redefining both identities.

"BORDERED" RACIAL/GENDER IDENTITIES

In the remainder of the paper, we address racial/gender identities by looking at physical appearance, language knowledge, class mobility, and sexuality. These issues were most (but not exclusively) relevant in "home" spaces, and were often tied to whether women were treated as "authentic" community members. Physical appearance, language knowledge, class mobility, and obedience to cultural rules of behavior about gender and sexuality were important both to how others identified the Latinas and Arab American women and how they self-identified. These were interdependent processes: identity was socially constructed in relation to how others defined them.

The concept of "home" has been discussed by a number of feminist scholars (Martin and Mohanty

1986; Pratt 1984). Martin and Mohanty argue that some feminist scholars' "pursuit of safe places and ever-narrower conceptions of community relies on unexamined notions of home, family, and nation, and severely limits the scope of the feminist inquiry and struggle" (1986: 191–2). Even though most needed "home" for comfort, security, and sustenance, the women interviewed problematized these locations as sites of restrictive sexual norms and essentialized definitions of the "authentic" Latina or Arab woman.

The "borders" metaphor captures the conflicts and contradictions that arose for the Latinas and Arab American women as they negotiated within limiting definitions of identity. Over the past decade, the metaphor has characterized the experiences and geopolitical spaces of Latinas/os as a colonized people: they are products of interaction and exchange between different cultures, races, and nations with often diametrically opposed ideologies and cultural practices (Anzaldua 1987; Saldivar-Hull 1991). Borders, therefore, divide two or more different states of existence that may contradict each other, making conflicts common for those whose identities straddle such borders. The concept is also a metaphor for the histories, experiences, and social spaces of other "hybrid" peoples who are compelled to live in borders because conventional spaces do not accept their multiple identities (Anzaldua 1987). Thus, borders are also margins of safety, spaces in which "hybridity" is allowed.

APPEARANCE BORDERS

The relationship between physical appearance and "bordered" racial/gender identities was stressed in the individual and group interviews by Latinas and Arab American women. The women varied in terms of their physical features: they were light to dark-skinned; had "kinky," "nappy," "big," or straight hair, ranging from black to blonde; and had differently shaped facial features and body sizes. However they identified themselves, the Arab American women were frequently thought to be Greek, Latina, African American, African/Euro-American, or white, and the Latinas were sometimes assumed to be African American or white.

Women in both groups felt that hair and body size have been significant foci of discipline and control in different contexts. They discussed unsuccessful attempts at feathering, perming, or straightening their hair in order to look like white teenagers, and the gendered implications of some of their mothers' pressures to contain their "big" hair into tight braids, knots, or with hair clips. One Latina believed this pressure was actually about containing girls' sexuality, and an Arab American woman explained such control with a different feminist argument:

> "[Y]our hair is too big, it's like uncontrollable." I think that's the thing about trying to keep women small, too, you know? . . . So why do we have to take up this much space [she curves both hands on the table facing each other about a foot apart], you know [everyone laughs]? (Michelle)

Both groups discussed body size standards within their communities as liberating in comparison to those dominant in US culture. Most US men, they believed, want "petite, they all want petite" (Amal). A Chicana joked about the US Southwest as a place "where men really appreciate women," and an Arab American woman joked about her father's Arab country of origin as "the only place in the world where I'm considered too thin." While variations in skin color occasionally came up as disciplinary issues *within* some homes and communities—with lighter skin considered more beautiful than darker skin for women—their discussions largely centered on how "external" groups perceived them based on their skin color.

The light-skinned Chicanas, as mentioned earlier, were often defined as white and ostracized by some students of color on campus. Carol said she "got literally ignored, brushed off by some people in the African American community because they thought I was white because I'm light skinned . . . Some of them didn't accept me as a person of color, they had to be told."

Conversely, Janie felt that it was difficult to be both black and Puerto Rican within the African American community:

> Last year I think I identified myself more with the racial aspect of it because I was getting so much— you know, it was like people were identifying me a lot by my race and it was frustrating for me. It was like "How can I explain to them? . . . I don't identify myself by my race, but then I don't want to be excluded and that was important for me . . . but last year I started . . . saying that I was black Puerto Rican.

Another black Puerto Rican woman who had attended a predominantly black university as an undergraduate found herself in a similar situation when she began applying for graduate schools:

> I put Puerto Rican on the box, or Hispanic, or whatever the box was at that time, my adviser told me "Why am I putting that?" and I said because that's what I am and he said "No, you're black" and I said, "You know, my grandfather is as African as your grandfather, but my experience isn't, my experience is a Puerto Rican experience." (Linda)

Thus, because discussions of race and ethnicity in the university were usually based on a black/white schema, the Latinas were often pigeon-holed into one or the other category, excluding their other identities and experiences.

All the darker-skinned Arab Americans said that as children they frequently wished they were lighter-skinned and lighter-haired, and less identifiably "Arab," especially during Middle East–related crises. Most had childhood memories of being called "niggers," "sand niggers," "Ayrabs," and "camel jockeys":

> [B]ecause my hair's really curly and very tight curls, I got all kinds of—you know, some people would think I was Black so they would call me "nigger." Some people knew that my parents were from Egypt, so they . . . would say "sand nigger," I got that a lot. (Amy)

In response to constant harassment for her brown skin and kinky hair, Amy admitted: "I felt bad. I mean, when I was eight, I wanted to have blonde, straight hair, this was my ideal. And now I realize how hideous I would look if I had blonde straight hair."

While the less phenotypically "Arab" women were much less likely to have their physical appearances be sources of difference during their childhoods, this physical blending was problematic later in life when they wanted to affirm their "Arabness." The dissonance between their identification as Arab Americans and their physical appearance contributed to feeling "phoney" when using a self-identifier such as "Arab American" or "woman of color." Indeed, three of the four bi-racial Arab American women wished they looked darker. For example, when asked if she considered herself a woman of color, Hana said:

> It's really interesting that you should ask me this question because this for me is one of the most difficult issues . . . because I look white. I mean, it's very difficult because it's an identification that I feel very strongly

about. And again, I think that very much came out of the Gulf War . . . But I sometimes feel ridiculous saying it ["I am a woman of color"] because for people looking at me it's like: "What's this person talking about?" Which has always been something that is extremely complicated for me because I always wanted to look like my—like I was an Arab.

Six of the eight Latinas strongly identified as women of color, whereas only two of the eight Arab American women did so. The two Latinas and two of the six Arab Americans who did not identify as women of color identified instead as a Chicana, Puerto Rican, Lebanese, and Egyptian, respectively. The generally weaker "women of color" identification among the Arab Americans may be related to the fact that their school and neighborhood interactions have largely been with white people. At the same time, six of the eight Arab Americans strongly believed that they were not white and all eight were ambivalent about being legally categorized as such.

LANGUAGE BORDERS

Language knowledge existed as a marker of authenticity in both communities. Four of the eight Latinas interviewed spoke Spanish fluently; two of the four who did not grow up speaking Spanish fluently sought to learn the language as adults. Among the Arab American women, with the exception of one who was fluent in Arabic, five were learning or relearning the language, and two said they wanted to learn it. Latinas and Arab American women who did not speak Spanish or Arabic fluently often felt inadequate as a result in their respective communities. Indeed, some of the Latinas interviewed whose first language was Spanish resented other Latinas/os who did not speak Spanish. As Emma put it: "[I]t really bugs me when some people are Mexican and they don't know Spanish."

Lack of language knowledge created a sense of distance from their racial-ethnic communities for both groups of women. As Margaret stated, "For me, not being fluent in Spanish has always been an insecurity . . . it has kind of been one of the things that has kept me apart from certain Latino communities . . . [because] there's some expectations on this campus that a Latino should speak Spanish." An Arab American similarly stated:

I've had long conversations about the significance of feeling at home nowhere. When I'm here [in the US],

I'm sure that I belong there [in the Arab world] and when I'm there, I'm sure I don't belong there . . . Language has been a big issue simply because a lot of them [my relatives abroad] I can't speak with. (Hana)

Some of the women who were not fluent in Arabic or Spanish attributed "loss" of language to social obstacles. One Chicana (Anne) said that her parents were physically and psychologically sanctioned for speaking Spanish in school and she believed this resulted in her being discouraged from speaking the language as a child. Margaret believed that English was her first language because her Puerto Rican mother was educated in a US convent, where she was punished for speaking Spanish. Linda similarly said, "I minored in Spanish in college . . . but it wasn't something that was reinforced in our lives."

Loss of language was relevant for three of the four Arab American women, both of whose parents were of Arab descent; the fourth woman was almost fluent as a result of consistently traveling between the Arab world and the US. Like the Latinas, these Arab American women discussed how US racism and ethno-centrism compelled them to forget their Arabic when they were young and/or resulted in teachers discouraging their parents from using the language with them. An Arab American who was frequently harassed by white children because of her physical appearance also discussed her own resistance to maintaining her Arabic language knowledge when she was younger:

I had a very bad attitude towards speaking Arabic. My mom would try to teach me periodically. You know, she'd get the books out and say, "Okay, this is *alef*, this is *bey*, this is *ley*" [the first three letters of the Arabic alphabet]. And I really—I mean, I very much did not want any part of Arabic. Like I remember being seven and eight and her trying to teach me, and I remember thinking, "This is America, we have to speak English.". . . To speak the [Arabic] language would only make me more a part of something I didn't want to be a part of. (Amy)

Amy, who was relearning the language, regretted this loss of Arabic as an adult and saw a powerful relationship between language knowledge and racial-ethnic identity:

I really regret their [her parents] not having spoken [Arabic] at home and my not having learned the language when I was much younger, when it would have been easier . . . And I really feel, too, since having been able to read and write a little bit, there is great power of the language to allow me to identify with that culture more. I just—it makes it so much easier when you get the window into that culture, do you know what I mean? (Amy)

CLASS BORDERS

Earlier, we discussed how many of the women interviewed were alienated in the academic setting and how in most cases this strengthened their racial-ethnic identities. A paradox arises for the Latinas, however, because many simultaneously feel alienated from their home communities as a result of their higher education and impending class mobility. Getting a university education created a distance—physically, economically and socially—between these Latinas and members of their families and communities, most of whom were poor to working-class and far less educated; they felt that their educations were privileging them in relation to their families and communities.

After being at the university for a year or so, a Chicana undergraduate from Texas (Emma) noted being disturbed and offended when she was told by a former teacher back home that she "sounded so different . . . so white." The interplay between class, race, and education was also apparent in her following statement:

> [W]hen I go back home with my family—because I am the first one to go to college and I was the second one to graduate from high school . . . now they see me as like "Oh, well Miss College here." I don't know. My whole family is proud of me, but it's like in a sense they're—some of them actually go "Oh, you think you're big shit because you're over there." (Emma)

Linda, a Puerto Rican graduate student, similarly stated:

> Earlier on it was hard to justify being here and wanting the education and . . . having my father telling me that I was distancing myself from the community . . . but society expects education to be that method by which you go about change, so when you go back there you're not part of that community anymore . . . [My family told me,] "College was OK, but what's this PhD

business?" . . . I want to go back, but there is still that issue of, first, where do you put a PhD in the middle of East Harlem?

Anne, a Chicana graduate student, was concerned about trying to balance efforts to help her community "without alienating or intimidating them." Another Chicana graduate student remarked that while her parents were proud of what she was accomplishing, they did not really understand what she was doing. When she does go home she is careful not to let her "academic hat" place her above others:

> I think my sister and my brother would be the first ones to slap me in the face—not literally, but you know—and say "You're at home now . . . don't impress us . . . we know you" . . . to them I'm still the same person [as when] I left . . . But I think to my parents it's much more of a big deal that I'm getting [a PhD] than probably to anybody else. Even though I don't think they understand it themselves . . . I guess in some sense I am my mother's dream come true, that she never went to school and at least I got that opportunity. (Teresa)

Education and upward mobility did not distance the Arab American women interviewed from their families and communities, for two related reasons: first, none of their families lived in Arab neighborhoods, where class differences are much more salient. And second, the women came from middle- to upper-middle-class backgrounds, in which at least one and usually both parents were highly educated. As one woman noted in response to this issue: "In fact, I feel like they've [her parents] obtained a certain level of education and there's actually great expectation on me to at least equal that or surpass it . . . So if anybody is feeling intellectual inferiority, it's me not them" (Amy).

SEXUALITY BORDERS[6]

The women interviewed discussed the often repressive aspects of "home" with respect to gender, sexuality, and sexual practices. Both groups believed that being a woman in Latino/a and Arab cultures had its own limitations, especially with respect to controlling their sexuality as unmarried women. In asking women to discuss their formal and informal sexual educations, the major themes that arose were silence, denial, and control. The two groups diverged in a number of ways, however, most importantly in that the Latinas were particularly concerned about not becoming pregnant, whereas the Arab American women were most concerned with the implications of losing their virginity.

Latina scholars have argued that the sexual repression of Latinas begins early, and girls are taught to be "submissive, virtuous, respectful of elders and helpful of our mothers, long suffering, deferring to men, industrious, and devoted" (Ramos 1987: xxvi); the most common strategy has been to deny "young women's imminent sexuality" (Castillo 1991: 32). As one Chicana said, her mother "didn't know" and "didn't want to know" about her sexual development and practices. If sex was discussed in the Latinas' homes, it was often bluntly discouraged. This angered the Latinas interviewed, and most were taught to be ashamed of sexuality. When asked about her informal sex education, one Puerto Rican woman responded: "I didn't get anything from my mother, absolutely nothing. I think she did such a poor job with that; I'm sorry, but she did [she laughs]. She really dodged it." This silence and denial with respect to sexuality affected her later when she "couldn't look her mother in the face" after her first experience of sexual intercourse. Almost all the Latinas received their sexual educations from peers, in school, and/or from television. According to another Chicana: "[My mom] just once told me 'if you have anything you want to talk to me about, just ask me.' And the first time we talked about menstruation was when I already had it . . . But as far as sex, never, never a conversation."

The sex education experiences of the Arab American women were more divided. Interestingly, all of the women whose parents are both Arab had very open discussions with one (not always the mother) or both parents about anatomy, sexuality, and even sexually transmitted diseases before the onset of their menstrual cycles. One woman said that she often tried on her older sister's and mother's sanitary napkins for fun before she got her first period, and another woman argued about female anatomy with her Arab father as an 11-year-old. Three of the four bi-racial Arab American women, in contrast, received little to no sexual education from their parents and were generally not encouraged to discuss sexuality issues. One of these women said that her first period was "traumatic—very traumatic . . . I didn't know how to deal with the irregularity and cramps . . . [I felt] isolated and abandoned [laughs], and I just survived." This woman, who was a virgin and engaged to be married, asked a number of questions about birth control during her individual interview.

While pre-marital sexual activity was discouraged by the Latinas' families, all the Arab American women received much stronger explicit and implicit messages that they should remain virgins until they married. "Nice Arab girls" were not supposed to lose their virginity before marriage. In order to control the sexuality of unmarried daughters, unchaperoned dating is generally strongly discouraged in Arab cultures, and Arab American girls are punished for violating these cultural norms (Aswad and Gray 1996). The virginity narrative was an especially strong source of internal conflict for the five Arab American women who had engaged in pre-marital sex. One respondent who eventually slept with a partner discussed this ambivalence:

I went through a phase for a while, because I think a lot of Arabs—in-between women go through—which is that "If I lose my virginity, I can't marry an Arab . . . It's awful, I mean it's awful. . . . I'm really glad that I didn't have sex earlier because my experiences with men have been on the whole extremely shitty and it seems to me like it would have just made everything worse.

A number of the Arab American women were sexually active with men but tried to abstain from intercourse. One of these women described her first experience of sexual intercourse with her Arab American boyfriend as a rape, which she believed he knew would force her to make a premature commitment to him: "Oh, yeah, I mean, I have slept with him, I wish we never did. I wish—because I know that I became more attached and closer to him. I think maybe, maybe . . . had I not slept with him, maybe I would not continue seeing him." Her primary concern after this was what would occur if she and her boyfriend did not marry: "What man is going to take me, a non-virgin, in our society?"

When asked if her parents had specifically warned her against having sex, an Arab American who had not engaged in sexual intercourse responded: "[T]hey never came out explicitly and said, you know, 'Don't sleep with anyone.' . . . [I]t was implicit in everything else that they said, do you know what I mean?" This Arab American demonstrated that ostracization from family and society was the most effective form of social control:

[I]t was always very clear in terms of sexual mores what was and wasn't permissible . . . [I]f I ever got pregnant and I wasn't married, that they would have nothing to do with me. That would be the end of it . . . And that, you know, instilled enough fear in me that I was never going to put myself in a situation, you know, where I would jeopardize my being related to them or them not having anything to do with me.[7]

The three Arab American women who had not engaged in pre-marital sex said that they were unwilling to do so until they married. One of these women stated that she remained a virgin

[n]ot because they'd [her parents] forbid me to, but just because I see—you know, sleeping with somebody is such an intimate thing and it binds you to them in ways that you're not bound to anybody else. And that's not something that . . . I just want to do with anyone.

Discussions about sex and the loss of virginity often brought up the fear of pregnancy or the consequences of unwanted early motherhood for the Latinas, a phenomenon highly informed by the fact that most of them came from poor to working-class backgrounds. These women had seen many friends and family members whose lives had been changed by early motherhood. One Puerto Rican woman said her "biggest fear was getting pregnant" at an early age as her mother had done when she was 19. She added, "[in] turning 19 and 20, for me to be able to make it that far and not to have a baby, that was like my goal in life." Fear of unplanned pregnancy also came up when women were asked their views of abortion, a right that all but one Latina strongly supported. The Arab American women, in contrast, were much more ambivalent about abortion. While five of the eight stated they were pro-choice, most believed abortion was morally wrong, and all expressed discomfort with the idea.

Despite the fact that many of the women grew up in households where sex was not discussed and/or sexual expression was discouraged, a number of the Latinas and Arab Americans spoke about transgressing some of these cultural norms. Two of the Latinas interviewed disclosed that they had engaged in sexual relationships with women as well as men, and another had experimented with a female friend as a pre-adolescent. One Chicana said that she had to "change her thinking" about expressing her sexuality because she grew up in a very "restricted" household. She didn't

want to be sexually repressed as she had seen her "father make [her] mother be." This theme is clearly articulated by a Puerto Rican, who said:

I've had to replace values. In the very beginning, that was part of my value system that "Oh, I can only be with one person" . . . but now that I've dated and that I've had—that I've been sexually intimate with people . . . it's not part of my value system anymore.

The Arab American women interviewed did not bring up sexual experiences with other women, possibly because they were uncomfortable discussing the issue. Five of the eight Arab American women interviewed had engaged in pre-marital sex despite strong messages to the contrary from their families and communities. Three of these women continued to feel ambivalent about their sexual activity, however, while two were more comfortable. According to one in the latter group:

[A]ll through high school, because my parents were so, like, "You can't date, you can't do this," that when I got to college, I was like, "Oh, let's check it out!" [We both laugh.]. . . I think that maybe when it all first started happening, I felt a little strange about it because I know that my parents were sort of like, "No pre-marital sex. No pre-marital sex.". . . But I don't feel like that about it anymore. . . I just do it because I think it's right and this is what I want to do and if you're not—. . . [I]f the person I want to marry does not accept that then that's not the kind of person I need to marry.

CONCLUSION

Whereas the Arab American women and Latinas interviewed differed along a variety of axes, all found the university to be a threshold for racial-ethnic identity. They discussed the university as a site where racial-ethnic identity was defined oppositionally, and "home" as culturally affirmative *and* a place with its own inflexible racial-ethnic/gender norms. Rather than being mutually exclusive categories, home and university sites emphasized different identity issues that were interactively defined. Although there is a common assumption, especially in non-academic circles, that racial-ethnic identities are natural and fixed, they are always being constructed and redefined in social interaction and through social practices. Anti-Arab and anti-Latina/o racisms were under-girded by different assumptions by the dominant culture, and, like identities, both were "performed" in daily interactions. While oppositional consciousness was governed by both "structural" location and context, subjective experiences ultimately meant that

these Latinas and Arab American women practiced a range of identity strategies over time and tailored them for different sites. They responded in a variety of ways to rigid identity categories, providing evidence that racial-ethnic identity is a process of both external social construction and political self-definition.

NOTES

1. The authors share equal responsibility for this article. We thank Judith A. Howard, the anonymous reviewers of *Qualitative Sociology*, Tomás Almagner, Natalie Bennett, Mark Chesler, Jeff Dillman, Janet Hart, Moon-Kie Jung, Maria Teresa Koreck, Michael Sulieman, Steve Sumida, and Patricia Zavella for reading and commenting on the paper, which we presented at the August 1995 meeting of the American Sociological Association in Washington, DC.

2. We use the term "racial-ethnic" to capture both the racialization of people of color by the dominant culture *and* the idea that people of color can affirmatively define their histories, languages, and customs. We assume that racial-ethnic identities are not stable or unitary, but socially constructed, contingent and historical (Hall 1992; McCarthy and Crichlow 1993; Omi and Winant 1994). Similarly, oppression based on gender, race, class, and sexuality is interlocking and the intersections of these identities are multiple and dynamic (Alarcon 1991; Collins 1990; Crenshaw 1991; Zinn and Dill 1994; Harris 1991; Martin and Mohanty 1986; Mohanty 1991). For women of color, then, multiple hierarchies condition and define their material positions and subjective experiences.

3. The Arab world encompasses 21 Arab countries in North Africa and Southwest Asia and the Occupied Palestinian Territories. The term "Middle East" refers to these Arabic-speaking countries, as well as Turkey, Iran, Israel, and sometimes Pakistan and Afghanistan. "Latina/o" is an umbrella term used to describe peoples of Latin American or Spanish origin, including Chicanos and Puerto Ricans. The students interviewed were recruited through solicitations on the Arab American Student Association and the Latino/a electronic mail networks, personal contact, and word of mouth. Those who agreed to participate in the

study were self-selected in that they identified as Arab Americans or Latinas and were willing to discuss identity issues. For convenience, we limited the sample to women who had US citizenship. We use pseudonyms to protect confidentiality.

4. The university does not track the specific racial-ethnic backgrounds of Latino/a students and does not keep records on their family income levels. In addition, it does not maintain separate records on Arab Americans, who are categorized as "white."

5. Based on 1990 census data, while the overall US official poverty rate was 13.1 percent, the rates were 26.3 percent for persons of Mexican origin, 31.7 percent for persons of Puerto Rican origin, and 14.5 percent for persons of Arab ancestry. Arab Americans 25 years or over were significantly more likely than the overall population to have received a high school diploma (82.4 compared to 75.2 percent), a bachelor's degree (36.3 to 20.3 percent), and a graduate degree 15.2 to 7.2 percent). Among Puerto Ricans, 53.4 percent received a high school diploma, 9.5 percent received a bachelor's degree, and 3.2 percent received a graduate degree. Among Mexican Americans the figures are 44.2 percent, 6.3 percent, and 2.0 percent, respectively (US Bureau of Census 1990).

6. The populations of Chicanas, Puerto Rican, and Arab American women students at the University of Michigan, Ann Arbor, are small. To safeguard confidentiality, which women were particularly concerned about when discussing sexuality, we do not attribute quotes in this section.

7. Aswad and Gray (1996) discuss the oppressive and affirmative tunetions of patrilineal family membership for Arabs and Arab Americans; Swanson (1996: 245) examines how these functions are used to "psychological[ly] coerce children [so as to] assure compliance with parental expectations."

REFERENCES

Alarcon, N. 1991. "The theoretical subject(s) of this bridge called my back and Anglo American feminism," in *Criticism in the Borderlands: Studies in Chicano Literature, Culture and Ideology,* H. Calderon and J. D. Saldivar (eds). Durham, NC: Duke University Press.

Anzaldua, G. 1987. *Borderlands/La Frontera: The New Mestiza.* San Francisco, CA: Aunt Lute Books.

Aswad, B. C., and N. A. Gray. 1996. "Challenges to the Arab-American family and ACCESS," in *Family and Gender among American Muslims: Issues Facing Middle Eastern Immigrants and Their Descendants,* B. C. Aswad and B. Bilgé (eds). Philadelphia, PA: Temple University Press.

Behdad, A. 1993. "Traveling to teach: Postcolonial critics in the American academy," in *Race, Identity, and Representation in*

Education, C. McCarthy and W. Crichlow (eds). New York, NY: Routledge.

Castillo, A. 1991. "La macha: Toward a beautiful whole self," in *Chicana Lesbians: The Girls Our Mothers Warned Us About,* C. Trujillo (ed.). Berkeley, CA: Third Woman Press.

Collins, P. H. 1990. *Black Feminist Thought: Knowledge, Consciousness, and the Politics of Empowerment.* Boston: Unwin Hyman.

Crenshaw, K. 1991. "Demarginalizing the intersection of race and sex: A Black feminist critique of anti-discrimination doctrine," in *Feminist Legal Theory: Readings in Law and Gender,* K. Bartlett and R. Kennedy (eds). Boulder, CO: Westview Press.

Hall, S. 1992. "The question of cultural identity," in *Modernity and Its Futures,* S. Hall, D. Held, and T. McGrew (eds). Cambridge: Polity Press.

Harris, A. 1991. "Race and essentialism in feminist legal theory," in *Feminist Legal Theory: Readings in Law and Gender,* K. Bartlett and R. Kennedy (eds). Boulder, CO: Westview Press.

Majaj, L. S. 1994. "Boundaries: Arab/American," in *Food for Our Grandmothers: Writings by Arab-American and Arab-Canadian Feminists,* J. Kadi (ed.). Boston, MA: South End Press.

Martin, Biddy and Chandra Talpade Mohanty, 1986. "Feminist Politics: What's home got to do with it?" in *Feminist Studies/Critical Studies,* Teresa de Lauretis (ed.). Bloomington, IN: Indiana University Press, 191–212.

Mohanty, C. 1991. "Under Western eyes: Feminist scholarship and colonial discourses," in *Third World Women and the Politics of Feminism,* C. Mohanty, A. Russo, and L. Torres (eds). Bloomington, IN: Indiana University Press.

Monlejano, D. 1987. *Anglos and Mexicans in the Making of Texas, 1836–1986.* Austin, TX: University of Texas Press.

Moore, J. and H. Pachon 1985. *Hispanics in the United States.* Englewood Cliffs, NJ: Prentice-Hall.

Munóz, C., Jr 1989. *Youth, Identity, Power: The Chicano Movement.* London: Verso.

Omi, M. and H. Winant, 1994. *Racial Formation in the United States: From the 1960s to the 1990s,* 2nd ed. New York, NY: Routledge.

Pérez, L. E. 1993. "Opposition and the education of Chicana/os," in *Race, Identity and Representation in Education,* C. McCarthy and W. Crichlow (eds). New York, NY: Routledge.

Pratt, Minnie, Bruce. 1984. "Identity: Skin blood heart," in *Yours in Struggle: Three Feminist Perspectives on Anti-Semitism and Racism,* Elly Bulkin, Minnie Bruce Pratt, and Barbara Smith. Brooklyn, NY: Long Haul Press.

Ramos, J. 1987. Introduction, in *Compañeras: Latina Lesbians (an Anthology),* J. Ramos (ed.). New York, NY: Latina Lesbian Project.

Rodriguez, C. E. 1989. *Puerto Ricans: Born in the U.S.A.* Boston, MA: Unwin Hyman.

Rosaldo, R. 1989. *Culture and Truth: The Remaking of Social Analysis.* Boston, MA: Beacon Press.

Said, E. W. 1981. *Covering Islam: How the Media and the Experts Determine How We See the Rest of the World.* New York, NY: Pantheon Books.

Saldivar-Hull, S. 1991. "Feminism on the border: From gender politics to geopolitics," in *Criticism in the Borderlands: Studies in Chicano Literature, Culture and Ideology,* H. Calderon and J. D. Saldivar (eds). Durham, NC: Duke University Press.

Sandoval, C. 1991. "U.S. third world feminism: The theory and method of oppositional consciousness in the postmodern world," *Genders* 10: 1–24.

Shaheen, J. G. 1993. "Aladdin: Animated racism." *Cineaste* 20(1): 49.

Shaheen, J. G. 1984. *The TV Arab.* Bowling Green, OH: Bowling Green State University Popular Press.

Swanson, J. C. 1996. "Ethnicity, marriage, and role conflict: The dilemma of a second-generation Arab-American," in *Family and Gender among American Muslims: Issues Facing Middle Eastern Immigrants and Their Descendants,* B. C. Aswad and B. Bilgé (eds). Philadelphia, PA: Temple University Press.

University of Michigan. 1993. *Faculty, Staff and Students of Color: A Statistical Profile for Academic Years 1982–83 through 1992–93.* Ann Arbor, MI: Office of Affirmative Action and Office of Minority Affairs (June).

US Bureau of the Census. 1990. "Persons of Hispanic origin in the U.S.," CP-3-3 (CPH-L-150), and "Ancestry of the population in the United States," CP-3-2 (CPH-L-149), in *1990 Census of Population and Housing.*

Zinn, M. B., and B. T. Dill (eds). 1994. *Women of Color in U.S. Society.* Philadelphia, PA: Temple University Press.

4 **Paula Gunn Allen**

Where I Come From Is Like This

I

Modern American Indian women, like their non-Indian sisters, are deeply engaged in the struggle to redefine themselves. In their struggle they must reconcile traditional tribal definitions of women with industrial and postindustrial non-Indian definitions. Yet while these definitions seem to be more or less mutually exclusive, Indian women must somehow harmonize and integrate both in their own lives.

An American Indian woman is primarily defined by her tribal identity. In her eyes, her destiny is necessarily that of her people, and her sense of herself as a woman is first and foremost prescribed by her tribe. The definitions of woman's roles are as diverse as tribal cultures in the Americas. In some she is devalued, in others she wields considerable power. In some she is a familial/clan adjunct, in some she is as close to autonomous as her economic circumstances and psychological traits permit. But in no tribal definitions is she perceived in the same way as are women in western industrial and postindustrial cultures.

In the West, few images of women form part of the cultural mythos, and these are largely sexually charged. Among Christians, the madonna is the female prototype, and she is portrayed as essentially passive: her contribution is simply that of birthing. Little else is attributed to her and she certainly possesses few of the characteristics that are attributed to mythic figures among Indian tribes. This image is countered (rather than balanced) by the witch/goddess/whore characteristics designed to reinforce cultural beliefs about women, as well as western adversarial and dualistic perceptions of reality.

The tribes see women variously, but they do not question the power of femininity. Sometimes they see women as fearful, sometimes peaceful, sometimes omnipotent and omniscient, but they never portray women as mindless, helpless, simple, or oppressed. And while the women in a given tribe, clan, or band may be all these things, the individual woman is provided with a variety of images of women from the interconnected supernatural, natural, and social worlds she lives in.

As a half-breed American Indian woman, I cast about in my mind for negative images of Indian women, and I find none that are directed to Indian women alone. The negative images I do have are of Indians in general and in fact are more often of males than of females. All these images come to me from non-Indian sources, and they are always balanced by a positive image. My ideas of womanhood, passed on largely by my mother and grandmothers, Laguna Pueblo women, are about practicality, strength, reasonableness, intelligence, wit, and competence. I also remember vividly the women who came to my father's store, the women who held me and sang to me, the women at Feast Day, at Grab Days, the women in the kitchen of my Cubero home, the women I grew up with; none of them appeared weak or helpless, none of them presented herself tentatively. I remember a certain reserve on those lovely brown faces; I remember the direct gaze of eyes framed by bright-colored shawls draped over their heads and cascading down their backs. I remember the clean cotton dresses and carefully pressed hand-embroidered aprons they always wore; I remember laughter and good food, especially the sweet bread and the oven bread they gave us. Nowhere in my mind is there a foolish woman, a dumb woman, a vain woman, or a plastic woman, though the Indian women I have known have shown a wide range of personal style and demeanor.

My memory includes the Navajo woman who was badly beaten by her Sioux husband; but I also remember that my grandmother abandoned her Sioux husband long ago. I recall the stories about the Laguna woman beaten regularly by her husband in the presence of her children so that the children would not believe in the strength and power of femininity. And I remember the women who drank, who got into fights with other women and with the men, and who often

31

won those battles. I have memories of tired women, partying women, stubborn women, sullen women, amicable women, selfish women, shy women, and aggressive women. Most of all I remember the women who laugh and scold and sit uncomplaining in the long sun on feast days and who cook wonderful food on wood stoves, in beehive mud ovens, and over open fires outdoors.

Among the images of women that come to me from various tribes as well as my own are White Buffalo Woman, who came to the Lakota long ago and brought them the religion of the Sacred Pipe, which they still practice; Tinotzin the goddess, who came to Juan Diego to remind him that she still walked the hills of her people and sent him with her message, her demand, and her proof to the Catholic bishop in the city nearby. And from Laguna I take the images of Yellow Woman, Coyote Woman, Grandmother Spider (Spider Old Woman), who brought the light, who gave us weaving and medicine, who gave us life. Among the Keres she is known as Thought Woman, who created us all and who keeps us in creation even now. I remember Iyatiku, Earth Woman, Corn Woman, who guides and counsels the people to peace and who welcomes us home when we cast off this coil of flesh as huskers cast off the leaves that wrap the corn. I remember Iyatiku's sister, Sun Woman, who held metals and cattle, pigs and sheep, highways and engines and so many things in her bundle, who went away to the east saying that one day she would return.

II

Since the coming of the Anglo-Europeans beginning in the fifteenth century, the fragile web of identity that long held tribal people secure has gradually been weakened and torn. But the oral tradition has prevented the complete destruction of the web, the ultimate disruption of tribal ways. The oral tradition is vital; it heals itself and the tribal web by adapting to the flow of the present while never relinquishing its connection to the past. Its adaptability has always been required, as many generations have experienced. Certainly the modern American Indian woman bears slight resemblance to her forebears—at least on superficial examination—but she is still a tribal woman in her deepest being. Her tribal sense of relationship to all that is continues to flourish. And though she is at times beset by her knowledge of the enormous gap between the life she lives and the life she was raised to live, and

while she adapts her mind and being to the circumstances of her present life, she does so in tribal ways, mending the tears in the web of being from which she takes her existence as she goes.

My mother told me stories all the time, though I often did not recognize them as that. My mother told me stories about cooking and childbearing; she told me stories about menstruation and pregnancy; she told me stories about gods and heroes, about fairies and elves, about goddesses and spirits; she told me stories about the land and the sky, about cats and dogs, about snakes and spiders; she told me stories about climbing trees and exploring the mesas; she told me stories about going to dances and getting married; she told me stories about dressing and undressing, about sleeping and waking; she told me stories about herself, about her mother, about her grandmother. She told me stories about grieving and laughing, about thinking and doing; she told me stories about school and about people; about darning and mending; she told me stories about turquoise and about gold; she told me European stories and Laguna stories; she told me Catholic stories and Presbyterian stories; she told me city stories and country stories; she told me political stories and religious stories. She told me stories about living and stories about dying. And in all of those stories she told me who I was, who I was supposed to be, whom I came from, and who would follow me. In this way she taught me the meaning of the words she said, that all life is a circle and everything has a place within it. That's what she said and what she showed me in the things she did and the way she lived.

Of course, through my formal, white, Christian education, I discovered that other people had stories of their own—about women, about Indians, about fact, about reality—and I was amazed by a number of startling suppositions that others made about tribal customs and beliefs. According to the un-Indian, non-Indian view, for instance, Indians barred menstruating women from ceremonies and indeed segregated them from the rest of the people, consigning them to some space specially designed for them. This showed that Indians considered menstruating women unclean and not fit to enjoy the company of decent (nonmenstruating) people, that is, men. I was surprised and confused to hear this because my mother had taught me that white people had strange attitudes toward menstruation: they thought something was bad about it, that it meant you were sick, cursed, sinful, and weak and that you had to be very careful during that time. She

AIN'T I A WOMAN?

Sojourner Truth

Well, children, where there is so much racket there must be something out of kilter. I think that twixt the negroes of the South and the women of the North, all talking about rights, the white men will be in a fix pretty soon. But what's all this here talking about?

That man over there says that women need to be helped into carriages, and lifted over ditches, and to have the best place everywhere. Nobody ever helps me into carriages, or over mud-puddles, or gives me any best place! And ain't I a woman? Look at me! Look at my arm! I have ploughed and planted, and gathered into barns, and no man could head me! And ain't I a woman? I could work as much and eat as much as a man—when I could get it—and bear the lash as well! And ain't I a woman? I have borne thirteen children, and seen them most all sold off to slavery, and when I cried out with my mother's grief, none but Jesus heard me! and ain't I a woman?

Then they talk about this thing in the head; what's this they call it? [Intellect, someone whispers.] That's it, honey. What's that got to do with women's rights or negro's rights? If my cup won't hold but a pint, and yours holds a quart, wouldn't you be mean not to let me have my little half-measure full?

Then that little man in black there, he says women can't have as much rights as men, 'cause Christ wasn't a woman! Where did your Christ come from? Where did your Christ come from? From God and a woman! Man had nothing to do with Him.

If the first woman God ever made was strong enough to turn the world upside down all alone, these women together ought to be able to turn it back, and get it right side up again! And now they is asking to do it, the men better let them.

Obliged to you for hearing me, and now old Sojourner ain't got nothing more to say.

---

taught me that menstruation was a normal occurrence, that I could go swimming or hiking or whatever else I wanted to do during my period. She actively scorned women who took to their beds, who were incapacitated by cramps, who "got the blues."

As I struggled to reconcile these very contradictory interpretations of American Indians' traditional beliefs concerning menstruation, I realized that the menstrual taboos were about power, not about sin or filth. My conclusion was later borne out by some tribes' own explanations, which, as you may well imagine, came as quite a relief to me.

The truth of the matter as many Indians see it is that women who are at the peak of their fecundity are believed to possess power that throws male power totally out of kilter. They emit such force that, in their presence, any male-owned or -dominated ritual or sacred object cannot do its usual task. For instance, the Lakota say that a menstruating woman anywhere near a yuwipi man, who is a special sort of psychic, spirit-empowered healer, for a day or so before he is to do his ceremony will effectively disempower him. Conversely, among many if not most tribes, important

ceremonies cannot be held without the presence of women. Sometimes the ritual woman who empowers the ceremony must be unmarried and virginal so that the power she channels is unalloyed, unweakened by sexual arousal and penetration by a male. Other ceremonies require tumescent women, others the presence of mature women who have borne children, and still others depend for empowerment on postmenopausal women. Women may be segregated from the company of the whole band or village on certain occasions, but on certain occasions men are also segregated. In short, each ritual depends on a certain balance of power, and the positions of women within the phases of womanhood are used by tribal people to empower certain rites. This does not derive from a male-dominant view; it is not a ritual observance imposed on women by men. It derives from a tribal view of reality that distinguishes tribal people from feudal and industrial people.

Among the tribes, the occult power of women, inextricably bound to our hormonal life, is thought to be very great; many hold that we possess innately the blood-given power to kill—with a glance, with a step, or with a judicious mixing of menstrual blood into somebody's soup. Medicine women among the Pomo of California cannot practice until they are sufficiently mature; when they are immature, their power is diffuse and is likely to interfere with their practice until time and experience have it under control. So women of the tribes are not especially inclined to see themselves as poor helpless victims of male domination. Even in those tribes where something akin to male domination was present, women are perceived as powerful, socially, physically, and metaphysically. In times past, as in times present, women carried enormous burdens with aplomb. We were far indeed from the "weaker sex," the designation that white aristocratic sisters unhappily earned for us all.

I remember my mother moving furniture all over the house when she wanted it changed. She didn't wait for my father to come home and help—she just went ahead and moved the piano, a huge upright from the old days, the couch, the refrigerator. Nobody had told her she was too weak to do such things. In imitation of her, I would delight in loading trucks at my father's store with cases of pop or fifty-pound sacks of flour. Even when I was quite small I could do it, and it gave me a belief in my own physical strength that advancing middle age can't quite erase. My mother used to tell me about the Acoma Pueblo women she had seen as a child carrying huge ollas (water pots) on their heads as they wound their way up the tortuous stairwell carved into the face of the "Sky City" mesa, a feat I tried to imitate with books and tin buckets. ("Sky City" is the term used by the Chamber of Commerce for the mother village of Acoma, which is situated atop a high sandstone table mountain.) I was never very successful, but even the attempt reminded me that I was supposed to be strong and balanced to be a proper girl.

Of course, my mother's Laguna people are Keres Indian, reputed to be the last extreme mother-right people on earth. So it is no wonder that I got notably nonwhite notions about the natural strength and prowess of women. Indeed, it is only when I am trying to get non-Indian approval, recognition, or acknowledgment that my "weak sister" emotional and intellectual ploys get the better of my tribal woman's good sense. At such times I forget that I just moved the piano or just wrote a competent paper or just completed a financial transaction satisfactorily or have supported myself and my children for most of my adult life.

Nor is my contradictory behavior atypical. Most Indian women I know are in the same bicultural bind: we vacillate between being dependent and strong, self-reliant and powerless, strongly motivated and hopelessly insecure. We resolve the dilemma in various ways: some of us party all the time; some of us drink to excess; some of us travel and move around a lot; some of us land good jobs and then quit them; some of us engage in violent exchanges; some of us blow our brains out. We act in these destructive ways because we suffer from the societal conflicts caused by having to identify with two hopelessly opposed cultural definitions of women. Through this destructive dissonance we are unhappy prey to the self-disparagement common to, indeed demanded of, Indians living in the United States today. Our situation is caused by the exigencies of a history of invasion, conquest, and colonization whose searing marks are probably ineradicable. A popular bumper sticker on many Indian cars proclaims: "If You're Indian You're In," to which I always find myself adding under my breath, "Trouble."

III

No Indian can grow to any age without being informed that her people were "savages" who interfered with the march of progress pursued by respectable, loving, civilized white people. We are the villains of the scenario when we are mentioned at all. We are absent from much of white history except when we are calmly, rationally, succinctly, and systematically dehumanized. On the few occasions we are noticed in any way other than as howling, blood-thirsty beings, we are acclaimed for our noble quaintness. In this definition, we are exotic curios. Our ancient arts and customs are used to draw tourist money to state coffers, into the pocketbooks and bank accounts of scholars, and into support of the American-in-Disneyland promoters' dream.

As a Roman Catholic child I was treated to bloody tales of how the savage Indians martyred the hapless priests and missionaries who went among them in an attempt to lead them to the one true path. By the time I was through high school I had the idea that Indians were people who had benefited mightily from the advanced knowledge and superior morality of the Anglo-Europeans. At least I had, perforce, that idea to lay beside the other one that derived from my daily experience of Indian life, an idea less dehumanizing and more accurate because it came from my mother and the other Indian people who raised me. That idea was that Indians are a people who don't tell lies, who care for their children and their old people. You never see an Indian orphan, they said. You always know when you're old that someone will take care of you—one of your children will. Then they'd list the old folks who were being taken care of by this child or that. No child is ever considered illegitimate among the Indians, they said. If a girl gets pregnant, the baby is still part of the family, and the mother is too. That's what they said, and they showed me real people who lived according to those principles.

Of course the ravages of colonization have taken their toll; there are orphans in Indian country now, and abandoned, brutalized old folks; there are even illegitimate children, though the very concept still strikes me as absurd. There are battered children and neglected children, and there are battered wives and women who have been raped by Indian men. Proximity to the "civilizing" effects of white Christians has not improved the moral quality of life in Indian country, though each group, Indian and white, explains the situation differently. Nor is there much yet in the oral tradition that can enable us to adapt to these inhuman changes. But a force is growing in that direction, and it is helping Indian women reclaim their lives. Their power, their sense of direction and of self will soon be visible. It is the force of the women who speak and work and write, and it is formidable.

Through all the centuries of war and death and cultural and psychic destruction have endured the women who raise the children and tend the fires, who pass along the tales and the traditions, who weep and bury the dead, who are the dead, and who never forget. There are always the women, who make pots and weave baskets, who fashion clothes and cheer their children on at powwow, who make fry bread and piki bread, and corn soup and chili stew, who dance and sing and remember and hold within their hearts the dream of their ancient peoples—that one day the woman who thinks will speak to us again, and everywhere there will be peace. Meanwhile we tell the stories and write the books and trade tales of anger and woe and stories of fun and scandal and laugh over all manner of things that happen every day. We watch and we wait.

My great-grandmother told my mother: Never forget you are Indian. And my mother told me the same thing. This, then, is how I have gone about remembering, so that my children will remember too.

R E A D I N G *5*   *Audre Lorde*

The Master's Tools Will Never Dismantle the Master's House

I agreed to take part in a New York University Institute for the Humanities conference a year ago, with the understanding that I would be commenting upon papers dealing with the role of difference within the lives of american [*sic*] women: difference of race, sexuality, class, and age. The absence of these considerations weakens any feminist discussion of the personal and the political.

It is a particular academic arrogance to assume any discussion of feminist theory without examining our many differences, and without a significant input from poor women, Black and Third World women, and lesbians. And yet, I stand here as a Black lesbian feminist, having been invited to comment within the only panel at this conference where the input of Black feminists and lesbians is represented. What this says about the vision of this conference is sad, in a country where racism, sexism, and homophobia are inseparable. To read this program is to assume that lesbian and Black women have nothing to say about existentialism, the erotic, women's culture and silence, developing feminist theory, or heterosexuality and power. And what does it mean in personal and political terms when even the two Black women who did present here were literally found at the last hour? What does it mean when the tools of a racist patriarchy are used to examine the fruits of that same patriarchy? It means that only the most narrow perimeters of change are possible and allowable.

The absence of any consideration of lesbian consciousness or the consciousness of Third World women leaves a serious gap within this conference and within the papers presented here. For example, in a paper on material relationships between women, I was conscious of an either/or model of nurturing which totally dismissed my knowledge as a Black lesbian. In this paper there was no examination of mutuality between women, no systems of shared support, no interdependence as exists between lesbians and women-identified women. Yet it is only in the patriarchal model of nurturance that women "who attempt to emancipate themselves pay perhaps too high a price for the results," as this paper states.

For women, the need and desire to nurture each other is not pathological but redemptive, and it is within that knowledge that our real power is rediscovered. It is this real connection which is so feared by a patriarchal world. Only within a patriarchal structure is maternity the only social power open to women.

Interdependency between women is the way to a freedom which allows the *I* to *be,* not in order to be used, but in order to be creative. This is a difference between the passive *be* and the active *being*.

Advocating the mere tolerance of difference between women is the grossest reformism. It is a total denial of the creative function of difference in our lives. Difference must be not merely tolerated, but seen as a fund of necessary polarities between which our creativity can spark like a dialectic. Only then does the necessity for interdependency become unthreatening. Only within that interdependency of different strengths, acknowledged and equal, can the power to seek new ways of being in the world generate, as well as the courage and sustenance to act where there are no charters.

Within the interdependence of mutual (nondominant) differences lies that security which enables us to descend into the chaos of knowledge and return with true visions of our future, along with the concomitant power to effect those changes which can bring that future into being. Difference is that raw and powerful connection from which our personal power is forged.

As women, we have been taught either to ignore our differences or to view them as causes for separation and suspicion rather than as forces for change. Without community there is no liberation, only the most vulnerable and temporary armistice between an individual and her oppression. But community must not mean a shedding of our differences, nor the pathetic pretense that these differences do not exist.

Those of us who stand outside the circle of this society's definition of acceptable women; those of us who have been forged in the crucibles of difference—those of us who are poor, who are lesbians, who are Black, who are older—know that *survival is not an academic skill.* It is learning how to stand alone, unpopular and sometimes reviled, and how to make common cause with those others identified as outside the structures in order to define and seek a world in which we can all flourish. It is learning how to take our differences and make them strengths. *For the master's tools will never dismantle the master's house.* They may allow us temporarily to beat him at his own game, but they will never enable us to bring about genuine change. And this fact is threatening only to those women who still define the master's house as their only source of support.

Poor women and women of Color know there is a difference between the daily manifestations of marital slavery and prostitution because it is our daughters who line 42nd Street. If white american [*sic*] feminist theory need not deal with the differences between us, and the resulting difference in our oppressions, then how do you deal with the fact that the women who clean your houses and tend your children while you attend conferences on feminist theory are, for the most part, poor women and women of Color? What is the theory behind racist feminism?

In a world of possibility for us all, our personal visions help lay the groundwork for political action. The failure of academic feminists to recognize difference as a crucial strength is a failure to reach beyond the first patriarchal lesson. In our world, divide and conquer must become define and empower.

Why weren't other women of Color found to participate in this conference? Why were two phone calls to me considered a consultation? Am I the only possible source of names of Black feminists? And although the Black panelist's paper ends on an important and powerful connection of love between women, what about interracial cooperation between feminists who don't love each other?

In academic feminist circles, the answer to these questions is often, "We did not know who to ask." But that is the same evasion of responsibility, the same copout, that keeps Black women's art out of women's exhibitions, Black women's work out of most feminist publications except for the occasional "Special Third World Women's Issue," and Black women's texts off your reading lists. But as Adrienne Rich pointed out in a recent talk, white feminists have educated themselves about such an enormous amount over the past ten years, how come you haven't also educated yourselves about Black women and the differences between us—white and Black—when it is key to our survival as a movement?

Women of today are still being called upon to stretch across the gap of male ignorance and to educate men as to our existence and our needs. This is an old and primary tool of all oppressors to keep the oppressed occupied with the master's concerns. Now we hear that it is the task of women of Color to educate white women—in the face of tremendous resistance—as to our existence, our differences, our relative roles in our joint survival. This is a diversion of energies and a tragic repetition of racist patriarchal thought.

Simone de Beauvoir once said: "It is in the knowledge of the genuine conditions of our lives that we must draw our strength to live and our reasons for acting."

Racism and homophobia are real conditions of all our lives in this place and time. *I urge each one of us here to reach down into that deep place of knowledge inside herself and touch that terror and loathing of any difference that lives there. See whose face it wears.* Then the personal as the political can begin to illuminate all our choices.

SECTION 2

Theoretical Perspectives

Theory is simply an effort to understand and explain the social world. Theories of gender are attempts to identify the major processes and social structures that give rise to the differences and inequalities between women and men and to analyze how these gender inequalities are connected to other major inequalities of race, class, sexuality, and nationality. You may notice as you read some of these selections that the language of theory is a bit different from some other forms of writing. Some of these readings may seem "harder" to you, and in fact, the language in some of them is more complex as the authors attempt to make sense of abstract and complicated social processes and as they summarize others' attempts to do so. We hope that you will not be intimidated by this. Every student is smart enough to understand "theory," and the effort you put into reading these works will be rewarded in two ways: You will grasp the fascinating and provocative ideas the authors put forward, and you will gain a sense of your own competence. We are all theorists of gender, after all, whether we construct our theories in formal academic language or in everyday discussions with friends.

One important distinction in feminist theory is between *sex*, or the biological characteristics of men and women, and *gender*, or the social statuses and meanings assigned to women and men. Gender is one of the most important social distinctions. Societies define men and women as separate and distinct categories, and stratification based on gender or sex is ubiquitous. Even our physical bodies (which might be considered an aspect of *sex*, or biology) are shaped and interpreted through societies' focus on differences

between women and men. For example, men are widely considered to be stronger than women, despite the fact that men's physical strength is also affected by social practices such as weight-training or manual labor. Women are considered to be biologically "softer" and more delicate than men, but these characteristics are produced in part by social practices such as hairstyle, clothing, and shaving body hair. Although there are undeniably physical or biological attributes that differ between women and men (including, but not limited to, reproductive organs), the distinction between biological sex and social gender is far from clear-cut.

Gender is also more than a feature of individuals. Behaviors are gendered (aggressive, nurturing), as are traits (strong, delicate) and even objects (pink or blue clothes, children's toys, power tools, and household gadgets). As we saw in the previous section, gender distinctions overlap with race, class, sexuality, nationality, and other statuses. Feminist scholars seek to understand how societies construct the meaning of being a woman or a man and how gender affects individual identities, the ways people interact with each other, how social institutions are organized, and inequality.

Explanations of gender inequality fall into two basic schools of thought: the essentialist and the social constructionist. The essentialist position holds that the behaviors of men and women are rooted in biological and genetic factors, including differences in hormonal patterns, physical size, aggressiveness, the propensity to "bond" with members of the same sex, and the capacity to bear children. For the essentialist, the sexual division of labor in human societies is rooted in the sexual determination that is found in all species, from ants to deer to primates. Viewing such differences as a natural outgrowth of human evolution, essentialists contend that sex-based differences in responsibilities and the natural superiority of the male are inevitable, functional, and necessary for the survival of the species.

The second school of thought, the social constructionist approach, bases its position on a growing body of historical and anthropological research that points to wide variations in gender behavior and in the sexual division of labor among human societies throughout time. Social constructionists contend that the diversity of cultural understandings of gender is too great to be explained by biological factors. Instead, they argue, male dominance only appears to be inevitable because cultural ideas and beliefs have arisen to justify and perpetuate sex-based stratification systems that entitle men to greater power, prestige, and wealth than women. While such ideologies do not cause gender inequality, they certainly justify it as natural.

Gender is simultaneously socially constructed—"made up," artificial, created by people out of quite flimsy bases—and very real in its ramifications for individuals and for the society as a whole. The task of theorists of gender is to explain this contradiction and the means by which gender becomes "real." The readings in this section present various approaches to understanding gender and its construction. In "'Night to His Day': The Social Construction of Gender," Judith Lorber outlines a social constructionist approach. She defines gender as a social institution that rests on the "socially constructed statuses" of "man" and "woman." Even the apparently dimorphic physical characteristics of the two sexes, Lorber argues, are socially interpreted and emphasized. How does the social institution of gender create *sameness* among members of each gender and *difference* between women and men? How are the genders ranked in a hierarchy that privileges men over women?

In "The Medical Construction of Gender," Suzanne Kessler illustrates the powerful role medicine plays in the social construction of the categories of male and female. Kessler challenges the notion that the biological distinctions between women and men are natural rather than subject to social construction. Drawing from interviews with medical experts who have had

extensive clinical experience managing babies born with genitals that are neither clearly male nor clearly female, Kessler discusses the standard practices used by the medical establishment to define the gender of intersexed infants. The primary consideration in physicians' gender assignments and corrective surgery is the ability to construct correctly formed genitals, not the other potential gender markers such as chromosomes, hormones, or psychological factors. Kessler argues that the view that gender consists of two mutually exclusive types—female and male—is created by these medical practices, despite biological evidence of greater natural variation in actual gender markers. Do you agree with the medical view that gender must be assigned immediately, decisively, and irreversibly when an intersexed child is born? What role, if any, do you think social factors should play in making decisions about gender identity? What does Kessler's article suggest about the relationship (if any) between biological differences and societal gender systems?

In "Theorizing Difference from Multiracial Feminism," Maxine Baca Zinn and Bonnie Thornton Dill develop a model of how race, class, and gender are related to each other. In this model, race and other "differences" among women are central to the task of understanding gender. Arguing that these different forms of inequality intersect with each other, Baca Zinn and Dill discuss how experiences of gender vary according to race and class. Their multiracial feminist perspective is relevant to the experiences of women and men of all races, because, they contend, categories of dominance and power are constructed in relationship to subordinate categories. As race, class, and gender intersect, they create both oppression and opportunity for various groups of people. Multiracial feminism is not simply a theory of inequality and oppression. Baca Zinn and Dill argue that individuals exercise their own agency, resisting the social structures that attempt to restrict them and finding ways to live satisfying lives.

Can you apply the multiracial feminist perspective to some of the readings from Section One, "Diversity and Difference"? Which of the readings take a multiracial feminist perspective, and what would that perspective add to the readings that do not? Can you analyze a currently relevant topic on your own campus or in your own community using a multiracial feminist perspective? How is this perspective different from other points of view on that topic? As you read the remaining selections in this volume, consider the ways in which they are informed by a multiracial feminist perspective.

Chandra Mohanty discusses the shifting categories of "Third World women," "feminism," and "Third World feminism," in "Feminism without Borders." She aims to define Third World women in a way that does not present them as a unified group, with any single culture or racial category. Instead, "Third World women" is an internally diverse group that is brought together by shared political allegiances and opposition to racism and imperialism. Similarly, the relationship between Third World women and feminism is varied. Mohanty argues that feminist politics have too often been linked to racism and imperialism, and yet Third World women's political actions address multiple oppressions simultaneously, including gender oppression. This is in part because the state has a strong effect on their lives (through its policies and through the ideologies about Third World women that it promotes). In this, Mohanty suggests that Third World women take what Baca Zinn and Dill would call a multiracial feminist perspective. But Mohanty, writing almost a decade after Baca Zinn and Dill wrote their essay, focuses more strongly on how Third World women's position is constructed within a *global* context. For Mohanty, analyzing Third World feminist politics is important for understanding industrial and postindustrial countries and politics as well, because of changing connections among countries, the rise of international corporations, and the migration of people from the Third World to industrialized countries. How would Mohanty understand recent developments in international trade agreements? Can you identify some current events that reflect the transnationalism that she discusses? What is the position of women in these events? As you read later selections in this volume, particularly those in Section Ten, try to apply Mohanty's perspective.

R. W. Connell follows Mohanty's concern with how transnationalism and gender affect each other.

Focusing specifically on the forms of masculinity that characterize global capitalism, Connell argues that masculinity is defined in different ways in different contexts and time periods. In contrast to theorists who see masculinity as having one single definition, Connell emphasizes how different versions of masculinity exist in relation to each other, with some kinds of masculinity, which he calls *hegemonic masculinity,* characterizing more powerful men, and other kinds of masculinity characterizing subordinated men. Although masculinities are constructed in specific contexts, Connell emphasizes that they are linked to a global gender order. The global gender order specifies divisions of labor among countries and individuals (through production, work, and trade), creates power relations between women and men and among different countries, structures emotions, and represents gender through culture. What examples does he give of the effects of the global gender order on local masculinities? Can you come up with some additional examples? How are the masculinities that prevail in your own community shaped by global forces?

Connell outlines the gender order and the prevailing masculinities during three major global time periods: conquest and settlement, empire, and postcolonial or neoliberal. What does he see as the major forms of masculinity during each period? In his final section, Connell discusses local variations on "transnational business masculinity." Look at articles or pictures in a newspaper for examples of transnational business masculinity, and consider the extent to which they represent a Western model. What possibilities for social change in the gender order does Connell identify, and what does he see as barriers to those changes?

As you consider the various ways of thinking about gender presented in these articles, with which do you agree? As you read the selections in the rest of the book, consider the questions raised here about what gender is; the extent to which women share commonalities of oppression or experience; how gender intersects with other forms of inequality such as race, class, or nationality; and how gender is part of our cultural systems of meaning and our institutions and social structures.

6 *Judith Lorber*

"Night to His Day": The Social Construction of Gender

Talking about gender for most people is the equivalent of fish talking about water. Gender is so much the routine ground of everyday activities that questioning its taken-for-granted assumptions and presuppositions is like thinking about whether the sun will come up.[1] Gender is so pervasive that in our society we assume it is bred into our genes. Most people find it hard to believe that gender is constantly created and recreated out of human interaction, out of social life, and is the texture and order of that social life. Yet gender, like culture, is a human production that depends on everyone constantly "doing gender" (West and Zimmerman 1987).

And everyone "does gender" without thinking about it. Today, on the subway, I saw a well-dressed man with a year-old child in a stroller. Yesterday, on a bus, I saw a man with a tiny baby in a carrier on his chest. Seeing men taking care of small children in public is increasingly common—at least in New York City. But both men were quite obviously stared at—and smiled at, approvingly. Everyone was doing gender—the men who were changing the role of fathers and the other passengers, who were applauding them silently. But there was more gendering going on that probably fewer people noticed. The baby was wearing a white crocheted cap and white clothes. You couldn't tell if it was a boy or a girl. The child in the stroller was wearing a dark blue T-shirt and dark print pants. As they started to leave the train, the father put a Yankee baseball cap on the child's head. Ah, a boy, I thought. Then I noticed the gleam of tiny earrings in the child's ears, and as they got off, I saw the little flowered sneakers and lace-trimmed socks. Not a boy after all. Gender done.

Gender is such a familiar part of daily life that it usually takes a deliberate disruption of our expectations of how women and men are supposed to act to pay attention to how it is produced. Gender signs and signals are so ubiquitous that we usually fail to note them—unless they are missing or ambiguous. Then we are uncomfortable until we have successfully placed the other person in a gender status; otherwise, we feel

socially dislocated. In our society, in addition to man and woman, the status can be *transvestite* (a person who dresses in opposite-gender clothes) and *transsexual* (a person who has had sex-change surgery). Transvestites and transsexuals carefully construct their gender status by dressing, speaking, walking, gesturing in the ways prescribed for women or men—whichever they want to be taken for—and so does any "normal" person.

For the individual, gender construction starts with assignment to a sex category on the basis of what the genitalia look like at birth.[2] Then babies are dressed or adorned in a way that displays the category because parents don't want to be constantly asked whether their baby is a girl or a boy. A sex category becomes a gender status through naming, dress, and the use of other gender markers. Once a child's gender is evident, others treat those in one gender differently from those in the other, and the children respond to the different treatment by feeling different and behaving differently. As soon as they can talk, they start to refer to themselves as members of their gender. Sex doesn't come into play again until puberty, but by that time, sexual feelings and desires and practices have been shaped by gendered norms and expectations. Adolescent boys and girls approach and avoid each other in an elaborately scripted and gendered mating dance. Parenting is gendered, with different expectations for mothers and for fathers, and people of different genders work at different kinds of jobs. The work adults do, as mothers and fathers and as low-level workers and high-level bosses, shapes women's and men's life experiences, and these experiences produce different feelings, consciousness, relationships, skills—ways of being that we call feminine or masculine.[3] All of these processes constitute the social construction of gender.

Gendered roles change—today fathers are taking care of little children, girls and boys are wearing unisex clothing and getting the same education, women and men are working at the same jobs. Although many traditional social groups are quite strict about maintaining gender differences, in other social groups they seem to be blurring. Then why the one-year-old's earrings? Why is it still so important to mark a child as a girl or a boy, to make sure she is not taken for a boy or he for a girl? What would happen if they were? They would, quite literally, have changed places in their social world.

To explain why gendering is done from birth, constantly and by everyone, we have to look not only at the way individuals experience gender but at gender as a social institution. As a social institution, gender is one of the major ways that human beings organize their lives. Human society depends on a predictable division of labor, a designated allocation of scarce goods, assigned responsibility for children and others who cannot care for themselves, common values and their systematic transmission to new members, legitimate leadership, music, art, stories, games, and other symbolic productions. One way of choosing people for the different tasks of society is on the basis of their talents, motivations, and competence—their demonstrated achievements. The other way is on the basis of gender, race, ethnicity—ascribed membership in a category of people. Although societies vary in the extent to which they use one or the other of these ways of allocating people to work and to carry out other responsibilities, every society uses gender and age grades. Every society classifies people as "girl and boy children," "girls and boys ready to be married," and "fully adult women and men," constructs similarities among them and differences between them, and assigns them to different roles and responsibilities. Personality characteristics, feelings, motivations, and ambitions flow from these different life experiences so that the members of these different groups become different kinds of people. The process of gendering and its outcome are legitimated by religion, law, science, and the society's entire set of values.

In order to understand gender as a social institution, it is important to distinguish human action from animal behavior. Animals feed themselves and their young until their young can feed themselves. Humans have to produce not only food but shelter and clothing. They also, if the group is going to continue as a social group, have to teach the children how their particular group does these tasks. In the process, humans reproduce gender, family, kinship, and a division of labor—social institutions that do not exist among animals. Primate social groups have been referred to as families, and their mating patterns as monogamy, adultery, and harems. Primate behavior has been used

to prove the universality of sex differences—as built into our evolutionary inheritance (Haraway 1978). But animals' sex differences are not at all the same as humans' gender differences; animals' bonding is not kinship; animals' mating is not ordered by marriage; and animals' dominance hierarchies are not the equivalent of human stratification systems. Animals group on sex and age, relational categories that are physiologically, not socially, different. Humans create gender and age-group categories that are socially, and not necessarily physiologically, different.[4]

For animals, physiological maturity means being able to impregnate or conceive; its markers are coming into heat (estrus) and sexual attraction. For humans, puberty means being available for marriage; it is marked by rites that demonstrate this marital eligibility. Although the onset of physiological puberty is signaled by secondary sex characteristics (menstruation, breast development, sperm ejaculation, pubic and underarm hair), the onset of social adulthood is ritualized by the coming-out party or desert walkabout or bar mitzvah or graduation from college or first successful hunt or dreaming or inheritance of property. Humans have rituals that mark the passage from childhood into puberty and puberty into full adult status, as well as for marriage, childbirth, and death; animals do not (van Gennep 1960). To the extent that infants and the dead are differentiated by whether they are male or female, there are different birth rituals for girls and boys and different funeral rituals for men and women (Biersack 1984, 132–33). Rituals of puberty, marriage, and becoming a parent are gendered, creating a "woman," a "man," a "bride," a "groom," a "mother," a "father." Animals have no equivalents for these statuses.

Among animals, siblings mate and so do parents and children; humans have incest taboos and rules that encourage or forbid mating between members of different kin groups (Lévi-Strauss 1956, [1949] 1969). Any animal of the same species may feed another's young (or may not, depending on the species). Humans designate responsibility for particular children by kinship; humans frequently limit responsibility for children to the members of their kinship group or make them into members of their kinship group with adoption rituals.

Animals have dominance hierarchies based on size or on successful threat gestures and signals. These hierarchies are usually sexed, and in some species, moving to the top of the hierarchy physically changes the sex (Austad 1986). Humans have stratification patterns based on control of surplus food, ownership of property, legitimate demands on others' work and sexual services, enforced determinations of who marries whom, and approved use of violence. If a woman replaces a man at the top of a stratification hierarchy, her social status may be that of a man, but her sex does not change.

Mating, feeding, and nurturant behavior in animals is determined by instinct and imitative learning and ordered by physiological sex and age (Lancaster 1974). In humans, these behaviors are taught and symbolically reinforced and ordered by socially constructed gender and age grades. Social gender and age statuses sometimes ignore or override physiological sex and age completely. Male and female animals (unless they physiologically change) are not interchangeable; infant animals cannot take the place of adult animals. Human females can become husbands and fathers, and human males can become wives and mothers, without sex-change surgery (Blackwood 1984). Human infants can reign as kings or queens.

Western society's values legitimate gendering by claiming that it all comes from physiology—female and male procreative differences. But gender and sex are not equivalent, and gender as a social construction does not flow automatically from genitalia and reproductive organs, the main physiological differences of females and males. In the construction of ascribed social statuses, physiological differences such as sex, stage of development, color of skin, and size are crude markers. They are not the source of the social statuses of gender, age grade, and race. *Social statuses* are carefully constructed through prescribed processes of teaching, learning, emulation, and enforcement. Whatever genes, hormones, and biological evolution contribute to human social institutions is materially as well as qualitatively transformed by social practices. Every social institution has a material base, but culture and social practices transform that base into something with qualitatively different patterns and constraints. The economy is much more than producing food and goods and distributing them to eaters and users; family and kinship are not the equivalent of having sex and procreating; morals and religions cannot be equated with the fears and ecstasies of the brain; language goes far beyond the sounds produced by tongue and larynx. No one eats "money" or "credit"; the concepts of "god" and "angels" are the subjects of theological disquisitions; not only words but objects, such as their flag, "speak" to the citizens of a country.

Similarly, gender cannot be equated with biological and physiological differences between human females and males. The building blocks of gender are *socially constructed statuses*. Western societies have only two genders, "man" and "woman." Some societies have three genders—men, women, and *berdaches* or *hijras* or *xaniths*. Berdaches, hijras, and xaniths are biological males who behave, dress, work, and are treated in most respects as social women; they are therefore not men, nor are they female women; they are, in our language, "male women."[5] There are African and American Indian societies that have a gender status called *manly hearted women*—biological females who work, marry, and parent as men; their social status is "female men" (Amadiume 1987; Blackwood 1984). They do not have to behave or dress as men to have the social responsibilities and prerogatives of husbands and fathers; what makes them men is enough wealth to buy a wife.

Modern Western societies' *transsexuals* and *transvestites* are the nearest equivalent of these crossover genders, but they are not institutionalized as third genders (Bolin 1987). Transsexuals are biological males and females who have sex-change operations to alter their genitalia. They do so in order to bring their physical anatomy into congruence with the way they want to live and with their own sense of gender identity. They do not become a third gender; they change genders. Transvestites are males who live as women and females who live as men but do not intend to have sex-change surgery. Their dress, appearance, and mannerisms fall within the range of what is expected from members of the opposite gender, so that they "pass." They also change genders, sometimes temporarily, some for most of their lives. Transvestite women have fought in wars as men soldiers as recently as the nineteenth century; some married women, and others went back to being women and married men once the war was over.[6] Some were discovered when their wounds were treated; others not until they died. In order to work as a jazz musician, a man's occupation, Billy Tipton, a woman, lived most of her life as a man. She died recently at seventy-four, leaving a wife and three adopted sons for whom she was husband and father, and musicians with whom she had played and traveled, for whom she was "one of the boys" (*New York Times* 1989).[7] There have been many other such occurrences of women passing as men to do more prestigious or lucrative men's work (Matthaei 1982, 192–93).[8]

Genders, therefore, are not attached to a biological substratum. Gender boundaries are breachable, and individual and socially organized shifts from one gender to another call attention to "cultural, social, or aesthetic dissonances" (Garber 1992, 16). These odd or deviant or third genders show us what we ordinarily take for granted—that people have to learn to be women and men. Men who cross-dress for performances or for pleasure often learn from women's magazines how to "do femininity" convincingly (Garber 1992, 41–51). Because transvestism is direct evidence of how gender is constructed, Marjorie Garber claims it has "extraordinary power . . . to disrupt, expose, and challenge, putting in question the very notion of the 'original' and of stable identity" (1992, 16).

GENDER BENDING

It is difficult to see how gender is constructed because we take it for granted that it's all biology, or hormones, or human nature. The differences between women and men seem to be self-evident, and we think they would occur no matter what society did. But in actuality, human females and males are physiologically more similar in appearance than are the two sexes of many species of animals and are more alike than different in traits and behavior (Epstein 1988). Without the deliberate use of gendered clothing, hairstyles, jewelry, and cosmetics, women and men would look far more alike.[9] Even societies that do not cover women's breasts have gender-identifying clothing, scarification, jewelry, and hairstyles.

The ease with which many transvestite women pass as men and transvestite men as women is corroborated by the common gender misidentification in Westernized societies of people in jeans, T-shirts, and sneakers. Men with long hair may be addressed as "miss," and women with short hair are often taken for men unless they offset the potential ambiguity with deliberate gender markers (Devor 1987, 1989). Jan Morris, in *Conundrum,* an autobiographical account of events just before and just after a sex-change operation, described how easy it was to shift back and forth from being a man to being a woman when testing how it would feel to change gender status. During this time, Morris still had a penis and wore more or less unisex clothing; the context alone made the man and the woman:

> Sometimes the arena of my ambivalence was uncomfortably small. At the Travellers' Club, for example, I was obviously known as a man of sorts—women were only allowed on the premises at all during a few hours of the day, and even then were hidden away as far as possible in lesser rooms or alcoves. But I had another club, only a few hundred yards away, where I

was known only as a woman, and often I went directly from one to the other, imperceptibly changing roles on the way—"Cheerio, sir," the porter would say at one club, and "Hello, madam," the porter would greet me at the other. (1975, 132)

Gender shifts are actually a common phenomenon in public roles as well. Queen Elizabeth II of England bore children, but when she went to Saudi Arabia on a state visit, she was considered an honorary man so that she could confer and dine with the men who were heads of a state that forbids unrelated men and women to have face-to-unveiled-face contact. In contemporary Egypt, lower-class women who run restaurants or shops dress in men's clothing and engage in unfeminine aggressive behavior, and middle-class educated women of professional or managerial status can take positions of authority (Rugh 1986, 131). In these situations, there is an important status change: These women are treated by the others in the situation as if they are men. From their own point of view, they are still women. From the social perspective, however, they are men.[10]

In many cultures, gender bending is prevalent in theater or dance—the Japanese kabuki are men actors who play both women and men; in Shakespeare's theater company, there were no actresses—Juliet and Lady Macbeth were played by boys. Shakespeare's comedies are full of witty comments on gender shifts. Women characters frequently masquerade as young men, and other women characters fall in love with them; the boys playing these masquerading women meanwhile, are acting out pining for the love of men characters.[11] In *As You Like It*, when Rosalind justifies her protective cross-dressing, Shakespeare also comments on manliness:

> *Were it not better,*
> *Because that I am more than common tall,*
> *That I did suit me all points like a man:*
> *A gallant curtle-axe upon my thigh,*
> *A boar-spear in my hand, and in my heart*
> *Lie there what hidden women's fear there will,*
> *We'll have a swashing and martial outside,*
> *As many other mannish cowards have*
> *That do outface it with their semblances.*
>
> (I, i, 115–22)

Shakespeare's audience could appreciate the double subtext: Rosalind, a woman character, was a boy dressed in girl's clothing who then dressed as a boy; like bravery, masculinity and femininity can be put on and taken off with changes of costume and role (Howard 1988, 435).[12]

M Butterfly is a modern play of gender ambiguities, which David Hwang (1989) based on a real person. Shi Peipu, a male Chinese opera singer who sang women's roles, was a spy as a man and the lover as a woman of a Frenchman, Gallimard, a diplomat (Bernstein 1986). The relationship lasted twenty years, and Shi Peipu even pretended to be the mother of a child by Gallimard. "She" also pretended to be too shy to undress completely. As "Butterfly," Shi Peipu portrayed a fantasy Oriental woman who made the lover a "real man" (Kondo 1990b). In Gallimard's words, the fantasy was "of slender women in chong sams and kimonos who die for the love of unworthy foreign devils. Who are born and raised to be perfect women. Who take whatever punishment we give them, and bounce back, strengthened by love, unconditionally" (Hwang 1989, 91). When the fantasy woman betrayed him by turning out to be the more powerful "real man," Gallimard assumed the role of Butterfly and, dressed in a geisha's robes, killed himself: "because 'man' and 'woman' are oppositionally defined terms, reversals . . . are possible" (Kondo 1990b, 18).[13]

But despite the ease with which gender boundaries can be traversed in work, in social relationships, and in cultural productions, gender statuses remain. Transvestites and transsexuals do not challenge the social construction of gender. Their goal is to be feminine women and masculine men (Kando 1973). Those who do not want to change their anatomy but do want to change their gender behavior fare less well in establishing their social identity. The women Holly Devor called "gender blenders" wore their hair short, dressed in unisex pants, shirts, and comfortable shoes, and did not wear jewelry or makeup. They described their everyday dress as women's clothing: One said, "I wore jeans all the time, but I didn't wear men's clothes" (Devor 1989, 100). Their gender identity was women, but because they refused to "do femininity," they were constantly taken for men (1987, 1989, 107–42). Devor said of them: "The most common area of complaint was with public washrooms. They repeatedly spoke of the humiliation of being challenged or ejected from women's washrooms. Similarly, they found public change rooms to be dangerous territory and the buying of undergarments to be a difficult feat to accomplish" (1987, 29). In an ultimate ironic twist, some of these women said "they would feel like transvestites if they were to wear dresses, and two women said that they had been called

transvestites when they had done so" (1987, 31). They resolved the ambiguity of their gender status by identifying as women in private and passing as men in public to avoid harassment on the street, to get men's jobs, and, if they were lesbians, to make it easier to display affection publicly with their lovers (Devor 1989, 107–42). Sometimes they even used men's bathrooms. When they had gender-neutral names, like Leslie, they could avoid the bureaucratic hassles that arose when they had to present their passports or other proof of identity, but because most had names associated with women, their appearance and their cards of identity were not conventionally congruent, and their gender status was in constant jeopardy.[14] When they could, they found it easier to pass as men than to try to change the stereotyped notions of what women should look like.

Paradoxically, then, bending gender rules and passing between genders do not erode but rather preserve gender boundaries. In societies with only two genders, the gender dichotomy is not disturbed by transvestites, because others feel that a transvestite is only transitorily ambiguous—is "really a man or woman underneath." After sex-change surgery, transsexuals end up in a conventional gender status—a "man" or a "woman" with the appropriate genitals (Eichler 1989). When women dress as men for business reasons, they are indicating that in that situation, they want to be treated the way men are treated; when they dress as women, they want to be treated as women:

> By their male dress, female entrepreneurs signal their desire to suspend the expectations of accepted feminine conduct without losing respect and reputation. By wearing what is "unattractive" they signify that they are not intending to display their physical charms while engaging in public activity. Their loud, aggressive banter contrasts with the modest demeanor that attracts men. . . . Overt signalling of a suspension of the rules preserves normal conduct from eroding expectations. (Rugh 1986, 131)

FOR INDIVIDUALS, GENDER MEANS SAMENESS

Although the possible combinations of genitalia, body shapes, clothing, mannerisms, sexuality, and roles could produce infinite varieties in human beings, the social institution of gender depends on the production and maintenance of a limited number of gender statuses and of making the members of these statuses similar to each other. Individuals are born sexed but not gendered, and they have to be taught to be masculine or feminine.[15] As Simone de Beauvoir said: "One is not born, but rather becomes, a woman . . . ; it is civilization as a whole that produces this creature . . . which is described as feminine" (1952, 267).

Children learn to walk, talk, and gesture the way their social group says girls and boys should. Ray Birdwhistell, in his analysis of body motion as human communication, calls these learned gender displays *tertiary sex characteristics* and argues that they are needed to distinguish genders because humans are a weakly dimorphic species—their only sex markers are genitalia (1970, 39–46). Clothing, paradoxically, often hides the sex but displays the gender.

In early childhood, humans develop gendered personality structures and sexual orientations through their interactions with parents of the same and opposite gender. As adolescents, they conduct their sexual behavior according to gendered scripts. Schools, parents, peers, and the mass media guide young people into gendered work and family roles. As adults, they take on a gendered social status in their society's stratification system. Gender is thus both ascribed and achieved (West and Zimmerman 1987). . . .

People go along with the imposition of gender norms because the weight of morality as well as immediate social pressure enforces them. Consider how many instructions for properly gendered behavior are packed into this mother's admonition to her daughter: "This is how to hem a dress when you see the hem coming down and so to prevent yourself from looking like the slut I know you are so bent on becoming" (Kincaid 1978).

Gender norms are inscribed in the way people move, gesture, and even eat. In one African society, men were supposed to eat with their "whole mouth, wholeheartedly, and not, like women, just with the lips, that is halfheartedly, with reservation and restraint" (Bourdieu [1980] 1990, 70). Men and women in this society learned to walk in ways that proclaimed their different positions in the society:

The manly man . . . stands up straight into the face of the person he approaches, or wishes to welcome. Ever on the alert, because ever threatened, he misses nothing of what happens around him. . . . Conversely, a well brought-up woman . . . is expected to walk with a slight stoop, avoiding every misplaced movement of her body, her head or her arms, looking down, keeping her eyes on the spot where she will next put her foot, especially if she happens to have to walk past the men's assembly. (70)

Many cultures go beyond clothing, gestures, and demeanor in gendering children. They inscribe gender directly into bodies. In traditional Chinese society, mothers bound their daughters' feet into three-inch stumps to enhance their sexual attractiveness. Jewish fathers circumcise their infant sons to show their covenant with God. Women in African societies remove the clitoris of prepubescent girls, scrape their labia, and make the lips grow together to preserve their chastity and ensure their marriageability. In Western societies, women augment their breast size with silicone and reconstruct their faces with cosmetic surgery to conform to cultural ideals of feminine beauty. Hanna Papanek (1979) notes that these practices reinforce the sense of superiority or inferiority in the adults who carry them out as well as in the children on whom they are done: The genitals of Jewish fathers and sons are physical and psychological evidence of their common dominant religious and familial status; the genitals of African mothers and daughters are physical and psychological evidence of their joint subordination.[16]

Sandra Bem (1981, 1983) argues that because gender is a powerful "schema" that orders the cognitive world, one must wage a constant, active battle for a child not to fall into typical gendered attitudes and behavior. In 1972, *Ms.* magazine published Lois Gould's fantasy of how to raise a child free of gender-typing. The experiment calls for hiding the child's anatomy from all eyes except the parents' and treating the child as neither a girl nor a boy. The child, called X, gets to do all the things boys *and* girls do. The experiment is so successful that all the children in X's class at school want to look and behave like X. At the end of the story, the creators of the experiment are asked what will happen when X grows up. The scientists' answer is that by then it will be quite clear what X is, implying that its hormones will kick in and it will be revealed as a female or male. That ambiguous, and somewhat contradictory, ending lets Gould off the hook; neither she nor we have any idea what someone brought up totally androgynously would be like sexually or socially as an adult. The hormonal input will not create gender or sexuality but will only establish secondary sex characteristics; breasts, beards, and menstruation alone do not produce social manhood or womanhood. Indeed, it is at puberty, when sex characteristics become evident, that most societies put pubescent children through their most important rites of passage, the rituals that officially mark them as fully gendered—that is, ready to marry and become adults.

Most parents create a gendered world for their newborn by naming, birth announcements, and dress. Children's relationships with same-gendered and different-gendered caretakers structure their self-identifications and personalities. Through cognitive development, children extract and apply to their own actions the appropriate behavior for those who belong in their own gender, as well as race, religion, ethnic group, and social class, rejecting what is not appropriate. If their social categories are highly valued, they value themselves highly; if their social categories are low status, they lose self-esteem (Chodorow 1974). Many feminist parents who want to raise androgynous children soon lose their children to the pull of gendered norms (Gordon 1990, 87–90). My son attended a carefully nonsexist elementary school, which didn't even have girls' and boys' bathrooms. When he was seven or eight years old, I attended a class play about "squares" and "circles" and their need for each other and noticed that all the girl squares and circles wore makeup, but none of the boy squares and circles did. I asked the teacher about it after the play, and she said, "Bobby said he was not going to wear makeup, and he is a powerful child, so none of the boys would either." In a long discussion about conformity, my son confronted me with the question of who the conformists were, the boys who followed their leader or the girls who listened to the woman teacher. In actuality, they both were, because they both followed same-gender leaders and acted in gender-appropriate ways. (Actors may wear makeup, but real boys don't.)

For human beings there is no essential femaleness or maleness, femininity or masculinity, womanhood or manhood, but once gender is ascribed, the social order constructs and holds individuals to strongly gendered norms and expectations. Individuals may vary on many of the components of gender and may shift genders temporarily or permanently, but they must fit into the limited number of gender statuses their society recognizes. In the process, they recreate their society's version of women and men: "If we do gender appropriately, we simultaneously sustain, reproduce, and render legitimate the institutional arrangements. . . . If we fail to do gender appropriately, we as individuals—not the institutional arrangements—may be called to

account (for our character, motives, and predispositions)" (West and Zimmerman 1987, 146).

The gendered practices of everyday life reproduce a society's view of how women and men should act (Bourdieu [1980] 1990). Gendered social arrangements are justified by religion and cultural productions and backed by law, but the most powerful means of sustaining the moral hegemony of the dominant gender ideology is that the process is made invisible; any possible alternatives are virtually unthinkable (Foucault 1972; Gramsci 1971).[17]

FOR SOCIETY, GENDER MEANS DIFFERENCE

The pervasiveness of gender as a way of structuring social life demands that gender statuses be clearly differentiated. Varied talents, sexual preferences, identities, personalities, interests, and ways of interacting fragment the individual's bodily and social experiences. Nonetheless, these are organized in Western cultures into two and only two socially and legally recognized gender statuses, "man" and "woman."[18] In the social construction of gender, it does not matter what men and women actually do; it does not even matter if they do exactly the same thing. The social institution of gender insists only that what they do is *perceived* as different.

If men and women are doing the same tasks, they are usually spatially segregated to maintain gender separation, and often the tasks are given different job titles as well, such as executive secretary and administrative assistant (Reskin 1988). If the differences between women and men begin to blur, society's "sameness taboo" goes into action (G. Rubin 1975, 178). At a rock-and-roll dance at West Point in 1976, the year women were admitted to the prestigious military academy for the first time, the school's administrators "were reportedly perturbed by the sight of mirror-image couples dancing in short hair and dress gray trousers," and a rule was established that women cadets could dance at these events only if they wore skirts (Barkalow and Raab 1990, 53).[19] Women recruits in the U.S. Marine Corps are required to wear makeup—at a minimum, lipstick and eye shadow—and they have to take classes in makeup, hair care, poise, and etiquette. This feminization is part of a deliberate policy of making them clearly distinguishable from men Marines. Christine Williams quotes a twenty-five-year-old woman drill instructor as saying: "A lot of the recruits who come here don't wear makeup; they're tomboyish or athletic. A lot of them have the preconceived idea that going into the military means they can still be a tomboy. They don't realize that you are a *Woman* Marine" (1989, 76–77).[20]

If gender differences were genetic, physiological, or hormonal, gender bending and gender ambiguity would occur only in hermaphrodites, who are born with chromosomes and genitalia that are not clearly female or male. Since gender differences are socially constructed, all men and all women can enact the behavior of the other, because they know the other's social script: "'Man' and 'woman' are at once empty and overflowing categories. Empty because they have no ultimate, transcendental meaning. Overflowing because even when they appear to be fixed, they still contain within them alternative, denied, or suppressed definitions" (Scott 1988, 49). Nonetheless, though individuals may be able to shift gender statuses, the gender boundaries have to hold, or the whole gendered social order will come crashing down.

Paradoxically, it is the social importance of gender statuses and their external markers—clothing, mannerisms, and spatial segregation—that makes gender bending or gender crossing possible—or even necessary. The social viability of differentiated gender statuses produces the need or desire to shift statuses. Without gender differentiation, transvestism and transsexuality would be meaningless. You couldn't dress in the opposite gender's clothing if all clothing were unisex. There would be no need to reconstruct genitalia to match identity if interests and lifestyles were not gendered. There would be no need for women to pass as men to do certain kinds of work if jobs were not typed as "women's work" and "men's work." Women would not have to dress as men in public life in order to give orders or aggressively bargain with customers.

Gender boundaries are preserved when transsexuals create congruous autobiographies of always having felt like what they are now. The transvestite's story also "recuperates social and sexual norms" (Garber 1992, 69). In the transvestite's normalized narrative, he or she "is 'compelled' by social and economic forces to disguise himself or herself in order to get a job, escape repression, or gain artistic or political 'freedom'" (Garber 1992, 70). The "true identity," when revealed, causes amazement over how easily and successfully the person passed as a member of the opposite gender, not a suspicion that gender itself is something of a put-on.

GENDER RANKING

Most societies rank genders according to prestige and power and construct them to be unequal, so that moving from one to another also means moving up or down the social scale. Among some North American Indian cultures, the hierarchy was male men, male women, female men, female women. Women produced significant durable goods (basketry, textiles, pottery, decorated leather goods), which could be traded. Women also controlled what they produced and any profit or wealth they earned. Since women's occupational realm could lead to prosperity and prestige, it was fair game for young men—but only if they became women in gender status. Similarly, women in other societies who amassed a great deal of wealth were allowed to become men—"manly hearts." According to Harriet Whitehead (1982):

> Both reactions reveal an unwillingness or inability to distinguish the sources of prestige—wealth, skill, personal efficacy (among other things)—from masculinity. Rather there is the innuendo that if a person performing female tasks can attain excellence, prosperity, or social power, it must be because that person is, at some level, a man. . . . A woman who could succeed at doing the things men did was honored as a man would be. . . . What seems to have been more disturbing to the culture—which means, for all intents and purposes, to the men—was the possibility that women, within their own department, might be onto a good thing. It was into this unsettling breach that the berdache institution was hurled. In their social aspect, women were complimented by the berdache's imitation. In their anatomic aspect, they were subtly insulted by his vaunted superiority. (108)

In American society, men-to-women transsexuals tend to earn less after surgery if they change occupations; women-to-men transsexuals tend to increase their income (Bolin 1988, 153–60; Brody 1979). Men who go into women's fields, like nursing, have less prestige than women who go into men's fields, like physics. Janice Raymond, a radical feminist, feels that transsexual men-to-women have advantages over female women because they were not socialized to be subordinate or oppressed throughout life. She says:

> We know that we are women who are born with female chromosomes and anatomy, and that whether or not we were socialized to be so-called normal women,

patriarchy has treated and will treat us like women. Transsexuals have not had this same history. No man can have the history of being born and located in this culture as a woman. He can have the history of *wishing* to be a woman and of *acting* like a woman, but this gender experience is that of a transsexual, not of a woman. Surgery may confer the artifacts of outward and inward female organs but it cannot confer the history of being born a woman in this society. (1979, 114)

Because women who become men rise in the world and men who become women fall, Elaine Showalter (1987) was very critical of the movie *Tootsie,* in which Dustin Hoffman plays an actor who passes as a woman in order to be able to get work. "Dorothy" becomes a feminist "woman of the year" for standing up for women's rights not to be demeaned or sexually harassed. Showalter feels that the message of the movie is double-edged: "Dorothy's 'feminist' speeches . . . are less a response to the oppression of women than an instinctive situational male reaction to being treated like a woman. The implication is that women must be taught by men how to win their rights. . . . It says that feminist ideas are much less threatening when they come from a man" (123). Like Raymond, Showalter feels that being or having been a man gives a transsexual man-to-woman or a man cross-dressed as a woman a social advantage over those whose gender status was always "woman."[21] The implication here is that there is an experiential superiority that doesn't disappear with the gender shift.

For one transsexual man-to-woman, however, the experience of living as a woman changed his/her whole personality. As James, Morris had been a soldier, foreign correspondent, and mountain climber; as Jan, Morris is a successful travel writer. But socially, James was far superior to Jan, and so Jan developed the "learned helplessness" that is supposed to characterize women in Western society:

We are told that the social gap between the sexes is narrowing, but I can only report that having, in the second half of the twentieth century, experienced life in both roles, there seems to me no aspect of existence, no moment of the day, no contact, no arrangement, no response, which is not different for men and for women. The very tone of voice in which I was now addressed, the very posture of the person next in the queue, the very feel in the air when I entered a room or sat at a restaurant table, constantly emphasized my change of status.

And if other's responses shifted, so did my own. The more I was treated as woman, the more woman I became. I adapted willy-nilly. If I was assumed to be incompetent at reversing cars, or opening bottles, oddly incompetent I found myself becoming. If a case was thought too heavy for me, inexplicably I found it so myself. . . . Women treated me with a frankness which, while it was one of the happiest discoveries of my metamorphosis, did imply membership of a camp, a faction, or at least a school of thought; so I found myself gravitating always towards the female, whether in sharing a railway compartment or supporting a political cause. Men treated me more and more as junior, . . . and so, addressed every day of my life as an inferior, involuntarily, month by month I accepted the condition. I discovered that even now men prefer women to be less informed, less able, less talkative, and certainly less self-centered than they are themselves; so I generally obliged them. (1975, 165–66)[22]

COMPONENTS OF GENDER

By now, it should be clear that gender is not a unitary essence but has many components as a social institution and as an individual status.[23]

As a social institution, gender is composed of:

Gender statuses, the socially recognized genders in a society and the norms and expectations for their enactment behaviorally, gesturally, linguistically, emotionally, and physically. How gender statuses are evaluated depends on historical development in any particular society.

Gendered division of labor, the assignment of productive and domestic work to members of different gender statuses. The work assigned to those of different gender statuses strengthens the society's evaluation of those statuses—the higher the status, the more prestigious and valued the work and the greater its rewards.

Gendered kinship, the family rights and responsibilities for each gender status. Kinship statuses reflect and reinforce the prestige and power differences of the different genders.

Gendered sexual scripts, the normative patterns of sexual desire and sexual behavior, as prescribed for the different gender statuses. Members of the dominant gender have more sexual prerogatives; members of a subordinate gender may be sexually exploited.

Gendered personalities, the combinations of traits patterned by gender norms of how members of different gender statuses are supposed to feel and behave. Social expectations of others in face-to-face interaction constantly bolster these norms.

Gendered social control, the formal and informal approval and reward of conforming behavior and the stigmatization, social isolation, punishment, and medical treatment of nonconforming behavior.

Gender ideology, the justification of gender statuses, particularly, their differential evaluation. The dominant ideology tends to suppress criticism by making these evaluations seem natural.

Gender imagery, the cultural representations of gender and embodiment of gender in symbolic language and artistic productions that reproduce and legitimate gender statuses. Culture is one of the main supports of the dominant gender ideology.

For an individual, gender is composed of:

Sex category, to which the infant is assigned at birth based on appearance of genitalia. With prenatal testing and sex-typing, categorization is prenatal. Sex category may be changed later through surgery or reinspection of ambiguous genitalia.

Gender identity, the individual's sense of gendered self as a worker and family member.

Gendered marital and procreative status, fulfillment or nonfulfillment of allowed or disallowed mating, impregnation, childbearing, kinship roles.

Gendered sexual orientation, socially and individually patterned sexual desires, feelings, practices, and identification.

Gendered personality, internalized patterns of socially normative emotions as organized by family structure and parenting.

Gendered processes, the social practices of learning, being taught, picking up cues, enacting behavior already learned to be gender appropriate (or inappropriate, if rebelling, testing), developing a gender identity, "doing gender" as a member of a gender status in relationships with gendered others, acting deferent or dominant.

Gender beliefs, incorporation of or resistance to gender ideology.

Gender display, presentation of self as a certain kind of gendered person through dress, cosmetics, adornments, and permanent and reversible body markers.

For an individual, all the social components are supposed to be consistent and congruent with perceived physiology. The actual combination of genes and genitalia, prenatal, adolescent, and adult hormonal input, and procreative capacity may or may not be congruous with each other and with sex-category assignment, gender identity, gendered sexual orientation and procreative status, gender display, personality, and work and family roles. At any one time, an individual's identity is a combination of the major ascribed statuses of gender, race, ethnicity, religion, and social class, and the individual's achieved statuses, such as education level, occupation or profession, marital status, parenthood, prestige, authority, and wealth. The ascribed statuses substantially limit or create opportunities for individual achievements and also diminish or enhance the luster of those achievements.

GENDER AS PROCESS, STRATIFICATION, AND STRUCTURE

As a social institution, gender is a process of creating distinguishable social statuses for the assignment of rights and responsibilities. As part of a stratification system that ranks these statuses unequally, gender is a major building block in the social structures built on these unequal statuses.

As a *process,* gender creates the social differences that define "woman" and "man." In social interaction throughout their lives, individuals learn what is expected, see what is expected, act and react in expected ways, and thus simultaneously construct and maintain the gender order: "The very injunction to be a given gender takes place through discursive routes: to be a good mother, to be a heterosexually desirable object, to be a fit worker, in sum, to signify a multiplicity of guarantees in response to a variety of different demands all at once" (Butler 1990, 145). Members of a social group neither make up gender as they go along nor exactly replicate in rote fashion what was done before. In almost every encounter, human beings produce gender, behaving in the ways they learned were appropriate for their gender status, or resisting or rebelling against these norms. Resistance and rebellion have altered gender norms, but so far they have rarely eroded the statuses.

Gendered patterns of interaction acquire additional layers of gendered sexuality, parenting, and work behaviors in childhood, adolescence, and adulthood. Gendered norms and expectations are enforced through informal sanctions of gender-inappropriate behavior by peers and by formal punishment or threat of punishment by those in authority should behavior deviate too far from socially imposed standards for women and men.

Everyday gendered interactions build gender into the family, the work process, and other organizations and institutions, which in turn reinforce gender expectations for individuals.[24] Because gender is a process, there is room not only for modification and variation by individuals and small groups but also for institutionalized change (Scott 1988, 7).

As part of a *stratification* system, gender ranks men above women of the same race and class. Women and men could be different but equal. In practice, the process of creating difference depends to a great extent on differential evaluation. As Nancy Jay (1981) says: "That which is defined, separated out, isolated from all else is A and pure. Not-A is necessarily impure, a random catchall, to which nothing is external except A and the principle of order that separates it from Not-A" (45). From the individual's point of view, whichever gender is A, the other is Not-A; gender boundaries tell the individual who is like him or her, and all the rest are unlike. From society's point of view, however, one gender is usually the touchstone, the normal, the dominant, and the other is different, deviant, and subordinate. In Western society, "man" is A, "wo-man" is Not-A. (Consider what a society would be like where woman was A and man Not-A.)

The further dichotomization by race and class constructs the gradations of a heterogeneous society's stratification scheme. Thus, in the United States, white is A, African American is Not-A; middle class is A, working class is Not-A, and "African-American women occupy a position whereby the inferior half of a series of these dichotomies converge" (Collins 1990, 70). The dominant categories are the hegemonic ideals, taken so for granted as the way things should be that white is not ordinarily thought of as a race, middle class as a class, or men as a gender. The characteristics of these categories define the Other as that which lacks the valuable qualities the dominants exhibit.

In a gender-stratified society, what men do is usually valued more highly than what women do because men do it, even when their activities are very similar or the same. In different regions of southern India, for example, harvesting rice is men's work, shared work, or women's work: "Wherever a task is done by women it is considered easy, and where it is done by [men] it is considered difficult" (Mencher 1988, 104). A gathering

and hunting society's survival usually depends on the nuts, grubs, and small animals brought in by the women's foraging trips, but when the men's hunt is successful, it is the occasion for a celebration. Conversely, because they are the superior group, white men do not have to do the "dirty work," such as housework; the most inferior group does it, usually poor women of color (Palmer 1989).

Freudian psychoanalytic theory claims that boys must reject their mothers and deny the feminine in themselves in order to become men: "For boys the major goal is the achievement of personal masculine identification with their father and sense of secure masculine self, achieved through superego formation and disparagement of women" (Chodorow 1978, 165). Masculinity may be the outcome of boys' intrapsychic struggles to separate their identity from that of their mothers, but the proofs of masculinity are culturally shaped and usually ritualistic and symbolic (Gilmore 1990).

The Marxist feminist explanation for gender inequality is that by demeaning women's abilities and keeping them from learning valuable technological skills, bosses preserve them as a cheap and exploitable reserve army of labor. Unionized men who could be easily replaced by women collude in this process because it allows them to monopolize the better paid, more interesting, and more autonomous jobs: "Two factors emerge as helping men maintain their separation from women and their control of technological occupations. One is the active gendering of jobs and people. The second is the continual creation of sub-divisions in the work processes, and levels in work hierarchies, into which men can move in order to keep their distance from women" (Cockburn 1985, 13).

Societies vary in the extent of the inequality in social status of their women and men members, but where there is inequality, the status "woman" (and its attendant behavior and role allocations) is usually held in lesser esteem than the status "man." Since gender is also intertwined with a society's other constructed statuses of differential evaluation—race, religion, occupation, class, country of origin, and so on—men and women members of the favored groups command more power, more prestige, and more property than the members of the disfavored groups. Within many social groups, however, men are advantaged over women. The more economic resources, such as education and job opportunities, are available to a group, the more they tend to be monopolized by men. In poorer groups that have few resources (such as working-class

African Americans in the United States), women and men are more nearly equal, and the women may even outstrip the men in education and occupational status (Almquist 1987).

As a *structure,* gender divides work in the home and in economic production, legitimates those in authority, and organizes sexuality and emotional life (Connell 1987, 91–142). As primary parents, women significantly influence children's psychological development and emotional attachments, in the process reproducing gender. Emergent sexuality is shaped by heterosexual, homosexual, bisexual, and sadomasochistic patterns that are gendered—different for girls and boys, and for women and men—so that sexual statuses reflect gender statuses.

When gender is a major component of structured inequality, the devalued genders have less power, prestige, and economic rewards than the valued genders. In countries that discourage gender discrimination, many major roles are still gendered; women still do most of the domestic labor and child-rearing, even while doing full-time paid work; women and men are segregated on the job and each does work considered "appropriate"; women's work is usually paid less than men's work. Men dominate the positions of authority and leadership in government, the military, and the law; cultural productions, religions, and sports reflect men's interests.

In societies that create the greatest gender difference, such as Saudi Arabia, women are kept out of sight behind walls or veils, have no civil rights, and often create a cultural and emotional world of their own (Bernard 1981). But even in societies with less rigid gender boundaries, women and men spend much of their time with people of their own gender because of the way work and family are organized. This spatial separation of women and men reinforces gendered differentness, identity, and ways of thinking and behaving (Coser 1986).

Gender inequality—the devaluation of "women" and the social domination of "men"—has social functions and a social history. It is not the result of sex, procreation, physiology, anatomy, hormones, or genetic predispositions. It is produced and maintained by identifiable social processes and built into the general social structure and individual identities deliberately and purposefully. The social order as we know it in Western societies is organized around racial, ethnic, class, and gender inequality. I contend, therefore, that the continuing purpose of gender as a modern social institution is to construct women as a group to be the subordinates of men as a group. The life of everyone placed in the status "woman" is "night to his day—that

has forever been the fantasy. Black to his white. Shut out of his system's space, she is the repressed that ensures the system's functioning" (Cixous and Clément [1975] 1986, 67).

THE PARADOX OF HUMAN NATURE

To say that sex, sexuality, and gender are all socially constructed is not to minimize their social power. These categorical imperatives govern our lives in the most profound and pervasive ways, through the social experiences and social practices of what Dorothy Smith calls the "everyday/everynight world" (1990, 31–57). The paradox of human nature is that it is *always* a manifestation of cultural meanings, social relationships, and power politics; "not biology, but culture, becomes destiny" (Butler 1990, 8). Gendered people emerge not from physiology or sexual orientation but from the exigencies of the social order, mostly from the need for a reliable division of the work of food production and the social (not physical) reproduction of new members. The moral imperatives of religion and cultural representations guard the boundary lines among genders and ensure that what is demanded, what is permitted, and what is tabooed for the people in each gender are well known and followed by most (Davies 1982). Political power, control of scarce resources, and, if necessary, violence uphold the gendered social order in the face of resistance and rebellion. Most people, however, voluntarily go along with their society's prescriptions for those of their gender status, because the norms and expectations get built into their sense of worth and identity as a certain kind of human being, and because they believe their society's way is the natural way. These beliefs emerge from the imagery that pervades the way we think, the way we see and hear and speak, the way we fantasize, and the way we feel.

There is no core or bedrock human nature below these endlessly looping processes of the social production of sex and gender, self and other, identity and psyche, each of which is a "complex cultural construction" (Butler 1990, 36). *For humans, the social is the natural.* Therefore, "in its feminist senses, gender cannot mean simply the cultural appropriation of biological sexual difference. Sexual difference is itself a fundamental—and scientifically contested—construction. Both 'sex' and 'gender' are woven of multiple, asymmetrical strands of difference, charged with multifaceted dramatic narratives of domination and struggle" (Haraway 1990, 140).

NOTES

1. Gender is, in Erving Goffman's words, an aspect of *Felicity's Condition*: "any arrangement which leads us to judge an individual's . . . acts not to be a manifestation of strangeness. Behind Felicity's Condition is our sense of what it is to be sane" (1983, 27). Also see Bem 1993; Frye 1983, 17–40; Goffman 1977.

2. In cases of ambiguity in countries with modern medicine, surgery is usually performed to make the genitalia more clearly male or female.

3. See J. Butler 1990 for an analysis of how doing gender *is* gender identity.

4. Douglas 1973; MacCormack 1980; Ortner 1974; Ortner and Whitehead 1981; Yanagisako and Collier 1987. On the social construction of childhood, see Ariès 1962; Zelizer 1985.

5. On the hijras of India, see Nanda 1990; on the xaniths of Oman, Wikan 1982, 168–86; on the American Indian berdaches, W. L. Williams 1986. Other societies that have similar institutionalized third-gender men are the Koniag of Alaska, the Tanala of Madagascar, the Mesakin of Nuba, and the Chukchee of Siberia (Wikan 1982, 170).

6. Durova 1989; Freeman and Bond 1992; Wheelwright 1989.

7. Gender segregation of work in popular music still has not changed very much, according to Groce and Cooper 1990, despite considerable androgyny in some very popular figures. See Garber 1992 on the androgyny. She discusses Tipton on pp. 67–70.

8. In the nineteenth century, not only did these women get men's wages, but they also "had male privileges and could do all manner of things other women could not: open a bank account, write checks, own property, go anywhere unaccompanied, vote in elections" (Faderman 1981, 44).

9. When unisex clothing and men wearing long hair came into vogue in the United States in the mid-1960s, beards and mustaches for men also came into style again as gender identifications.

10. For other accounts of women being treated as men in Islamic countries, as well as accounts of women and men cross-dressing in these countries, see Garber 1992, 304–52.

11. Dollimore 1986; Garber 1992, 32–40; Greenblatt 1987, 66–93; Howard 1988. For Renaissance accounts of sexual relations with women and men of ambiguous sex, see Laqueur 1990, 134–39. For modern accounts of women passing as men that other women find sexually attractive, see Devor 1989, 136–37; Wheelwright 1989, 53–59.

12. Females who passed as men soldiers had to "do masculinity," not just dress in a uniform (Wheelwright 1989, 50–78). On the triple entendres and gender resonances of Rosalind-type characters, see Garber 1992, 71–77.

13. Also see Garber 1992, 234–66.

14. Bolin describes how many documents have to be changed by transsexuals to provide a legitimizing "paper trail" (1988, 145–47). Note that only members of the same social group know which names are women's and which men's in their culture, but many documents list "sex."

15. For an account of how a potential man-to-woman transsexual learned to be feminine, see Garfinkel 1967, 116–85, 285–88. For a gloss on this account that points out how, throughout his encounters with Agnes, Garfinkel failed to see how he himself was constructing his own masculinity, see Rogers 1992.

16. Paige and Paige (1981, 147–49) argue that circumcision ceremonies indicate a father's loyalty to his lineage elders—"visible public evidence that the head of a family unit of their lineage is willing to trust others with his and his family's most valuable political asset, his son's penis" (147). On female circumcision, see El Dareer 1982; Lightfoot-Klein 1989; van der Kwaak 1992; Walker 1992. There is a form of female circumcision that removes only the prepuce of the clitoris and is similar to male circumcision, but most forms of female circumcision are far more extensive, mutilating, and spiritually and psychologically shocking than the usual form of male circumcision. However, among the Australian aborigines, boys' penises are slit and kept open, so that they urinate and bleed the way women do (Bettelheim 1962, 165–206).

17. The concepts of moral hegemony, the effects of everyday activities (praxis) on thought and personality, and the necessity of consciousness of these processes before political change can occur are all based on Marx's analysis of class relations.

18. Other societies recognize more than two categories, but usually no more than three or four (Jacobs and Roberts 1989).

19. Carol Barkalow's book has a photograph of eleven first-year West Pointers in a math class, who are dressed in regulation pants, shirts, and sweaters, with short haircuts. The caption challenges the reader to locate the only woman in the room.

20. The taboo on males and females looking alike reflects the U.S. military's homophobia (Berube and D'Emilio 1984). If you can't tell those with a penis from those with a vagina, how are you going to determine whether their sexual interest is heterosexual or homosexual unless you watch them having sexual relations?

21. Garber feels that *Tootsie* is not about feminism but about transvestism and its possibilities for disturbing the gender order (1992, 5–9).

22. See Bolin 1988, 149–50, for transsexual men-to-women's discovery of the dangers of rape and sexual harassment. Devor's "gender blenders" went in the opposite direction. Because they found that it was an advantage to be taken for men, they did not deliberately cross-dress, but they did not feminize themselves either (1989, 126–40).

23. See West and Zimmerman 1987 for a similar set of gender components.

24. On the "logic of practice," or how the experience of gender is embedded in the norms of everyday interaction and the structure of formal organizations, see Acker 1990; Bourdieu [1980] 1990; Connell 1987; Smith 1987.

REFERENCES

Acker, Joan. 1990. Hierarchies, jobs, and bodies: A theory of gendered organizations. *Gender & Society* 4: 139–58.

Almquist, Elizabeth M. 1987. Labor market gendered inequality in minority groups. *Gender & Society* 1: 400–14.

Amadiume, Ifi. 1987. *Male daughters, female husbands: Gender and sex in an African society.* London: Zed Books.

Ariés, Philippe. 1962. *Centuries of childhood: A social history of family life,* translated by Robert Baldick. New York: Vintage.

Austad, Steven N. 1986. Changing sex nature's way. *International Wildlife,* May–June, 29.

Barkalow, Carol, with Andrea Raab. 1990. *In the men's house.* New York: Poseidon Press.

Bem, Sandra Lipsitz. 1981. Gender schema theory: A cognitive account of sex typing. *Psychological Review* 88: 354–64.

———. 1983. Gender schema theory and its implications for child development: Raising gender-aschematic children in a gender-schematic society. *Signs* 8: 598–616.

———. 1993. *The lense of gender: Transforming the debate on sexual inequality.* New Haven: Yale University Press.

Bernard, Jessie. 1981. *The female world.* New York: Free Press.

Bernstein, Richard. 1986. France jails 2 in odd case of espionage. *New York Times,* 11 May.

Berube, Allan, and John D'Emilio. 1984. The military and lesbians during the McCarthy years. *Signs* 9: 759–75.

Bettelheim, Bruno. 1962. *Symbolic wounds: Puberty rites and the envious male.* London: Thames and Hudson.

Biersack, Aletta. 1984. Paiela "women-men": The reflexive foundations of gender ideology. *American Ethnologist* 11: 118–38.

Birdwhistell, Ray L. 1970. *Kinesics and context: Essays on body motion communications.* Philadelphia: University of Pennsylvania Press.

Blackwood, Evelyn. 1984. Sexuality and gender in certain Native American tribes: The case of cross-gender females. *Signs* 10: 27–42.

Bolin, Anne. 1987. Transsexualism and the limits of traditional analysis. *American Behavioral Scientist* 31: 41–65.

———. 1988. *In search of Eve: Transsexual rites of passage.* South Hadley, Mass.: Bergin & Garvey.

Bourdieu, Pierre. [1980] 1990. *The logic of practice.* Stanford, Calif.: Stanford University Press.

Brody, Jane E. 1979. Benefits of transsexual surgery disputed as leading hospital halts the procedure. *New York Times,* 2 October.

Butler, Judith. 1990. *Gender trouble: Feminism and the subversion of identity.* New York and London: Routledge.

Chodorow, Nancy. 1974. Family structure and feminine personality. In Rosaldo and Lamphere.

———. 1978. *The reproduction of mothering.* Berkeley: University of California Press.

Cixous, Hélène, and Catherine Clément. [1975] 1986. *The newly born woman,* translated by Betsy Wing. Minneapolis: University of Minnesota Press.

Cockburn, Cynthia. 1985. *Machinery of dominance: Women, men and technical know-how.* London: Pluto Press.

Collins, Patricia Hill. 1990. *Black feminist thought: Knowledge, consciousness, and the politics of empowerment.* Boston: Unwin Hyman.

Connell, R. [Robert] W. 1987. *Gender and power: Society, the person, and sexual politics.* Stanford, Calif.: Stanford University Press.

Coser, Rose Laub. 1986. Cognitive structure and the use of social space. *Sociological Forum* 1: 1–26.

Davies, Christie. 1982. Sexual taboos and social boundaries. *American Journal of Sociology* 87: 1032–63.

de Beauvoir, Simone. 1953. *The second sex,* translated by H. M. Parshley. New York: Knopf.

Devor, Holly. 1987. Gender blending females: Women and sometimes men. *American Behavioral Scientist* 31: 12–40.

———. 1989. *Gender blending: Confronting the limits of duality.* Bloomington: Indiana University Press.

Dollimore, Jonathan. 1986. Subjectivity, sexuality, and transgression: The Jacobean connection. *Renaissance Drama,* n.s. 17: 53–81.

Douglas, Mary. 1973. *Natural symbols.* New York: Vintage.

Durova, Nadezhda. 1989. *The calvary maiden: Journals of a Russian officer in the Napoleonic wars,* translated by Mary Fleming Zirin. Bloomington: Indiana University Press.

Eichler, Margrit. 1989. Sex change operations: The last bulwark of the double standard. In *Feminist frontiers,* edited by Laurel Richardson and Verta Taylor. New York: Random House.

El Dareer, Asma. 1982. *Woman, why do you weep? Circumcision and its consequences.* London: Zed Books.

Epstein, Cynthia Fuchs, 1988. *Deceptive distinctions: Sex, gender and the social order.* New Haven: Yale University Press.

Faderman, Lillian. 1981. *Surpassing the love of men: Romantic friendship and love between women from the Renaissance to the present.* New York: William Morrow.

Foucault, Michel. 1972. *The archeology of knowledge and the discourse on language,* translated by A. M. Sheridan Smith. New York: Pantheon.

Freeman, Lucy, and Alma Halbert Bond. 1992. *America's first woman warrior: The courage of Deborah Sampson.* New York: Paragon.

Frye, Marilyn. 1983. *The politics of reality: Essays in feminist theory.* Trumansburg, N.Y.: Crossing Press.

Garber, Marjorie. 1992. *Vested interests: Cross-dressing and cultural anxiety.* New York and London: Routledge.

Garfinkel, Harold. 1967. *Studies in ethnomethodology.* Englewood Cliffs, N.J.: Prentice-Hall.

Gilmore, David D. 1977. The arrangement between the sexes. *Theory and Society* 4: 301–33.

———. 1990. *Manhood in the making: Cultural concepts of masculinity.* New Haven: Yale University Press.

Goffman, Erving. 1977. The arrangement between the sexes. *Theory and Society* 4: 301–33.

———. Felicity's condition. *American Journal of Sociology* 89: 1–53.

Gordon, Tuula. 1990. *Feminist mothers.* New York: New York University Press.

Gramsci, Antonio. 1971. *Selections from the prison notebooks,* translated and edited by Quintin Hoare and Geoffrey Nowell Smith. New York: International Publishers.

Greenblatt, Stephen. 1987. *Shakespearean negotiations: The circulation of social energy in Renaissance England.* Berkeley: University of California Press.

Groce, Stephen B., and Margaret Cooper. 1990. Just me and the boys? Women in local-level rock and roll. *Gender & Society* 4: 220–29.

Haraway, Donna. 1978. Animal sociology and a natural economy of the body politic. Part I: A political physiology of dominance. *Signs* 4: 21–36.

———. 1990. Investment strategies for the evolving portfolio of primate females. In Jacobus, Keller, and Shuttleworth.

Howard, Jean E. 1988. Crossdressing, the theater, and gender struggle in early modern England. *Shakespeare Quarterly* 39: 418–41.

Hwang, David Henry. 1989. *M Butterfly.* New York: New American Library.

Jacobs, Sue-Ellen, and Christine Roberts. 1989. Sex, sexuality, gender, and gender variance. In *Gender and anthropology,* edited by Sandra Morgen. Washington, D.C.: American Anthropological Association.

Jay, Nancy. 1981. Gender and dichotomy. *Feminist Studies* 7: 38–56.

Kando, Thomas. 1973. *Sex change: The achievement of gender identity among feminized transsexuals.* Springfield, Ill.: Charles C. Thomas.

Kincaid, Jamaica. 1978. Girl. *The New Yorker,* 26 June.

Kondo, Dorinne K. 1990a. *Crafting selves: Power, gender, and discourses of identity in a Japanese workplace.* Chicago: University of Chicago Press.

———. 1990b. *M. Butterfly:* Orientalism, gender, and a critique of essentialist identity. Cultural Critique, no. 16 (Fall): 5–29.

Lancaster, Jane Beckman. 1974. *Primate behavior and the emergence of human culture.* New York: Holt, Rinehart and Winston.

Laqueur, Thomas. 1990. *Making sex: Body and gender from the Greeks to Freud.* Cambridge, Mass.: Harvard University Press.

Lévi-Strauss, Claude. 1956. The family. In *Man, culture, and society,* edited by Harry L. Shapiro, New York: Oxford.

———. [1949] 1969. *The elementary structures of kinship,* translated by J. H. Bell and J. R. von Sturmer. Boston: Beacon Press.

Lightfoot-Klein, Hanny. 1989. *Prisoners of ritual: An odyssey into female circumcision in Africa.* New York: Harrington Park Press.

MacCormack, Carol P. 1980. Nature, culture and gender: A critique. In *Nature, culture and gender,* edited by Carol P. MacCormack and Marilyn Strathern. Cambridge, England: Cambridge University Press.

Matthaei, Julie A. 1982. *An economic history of women's work in America.* New York: Schocken.

Mencher, Joan. 1988. Women's work and poverty: Women's contribution to household maintenance in South India. In Dwyer and Bruce.

Morris, Jan. 1975. *Conundrum.* New York: Signet.

Nanda, Serena. 1990. *Neither man nor woman: The hijiras of India.* Belmont, Calif.: Wadsworth.

New York Times. 1989. Musician's death at 74 reveals he was a woman. 2 February.

Ortner, Sherry B. 1974. Is female to male as nature is to culture? In Rosaldo and Lamphere.

Ortner, Sherry B., and Harriet Whitehead. 1981. Introduction: Accounting for sexual meanings. In Ortner and Whitehead (eds.).

Paige, Karen Ericksen, and Jeffrey M. Paige. 1981. *The politics of reproductive ritual.* Berkeley: University of California Press.

Palmer, Phyllis. 1989. *Domesticity and dirt: Housewives and domestic servants in the United States,* 1920–1945. Philadelphia: Temple University Press.

Papanek, Hanna. 1979. Family status production: The "work" and "non-work" of women. *Signs* 4: 775–81.

Raymond, Janice G. 1979. *The transsexual empire: The making of the she-male.* Boston: Beacon Press.

Reskin, Barbara F. 1988. Bringing the men back in: Sex differentiation and the devaluation of women's work. *Gender & Society* 2: 58–81.

Rogers, Mary F. 1992. They were all passing: Agnes, Garfinkel, and company. *Gender & Society* 6: 169–91.

Rosaldo, Michelle Zimbalist, and Louise Lamphere (eds.). 1974. *Woman, culture, and society.* Stanford, CA: Stanford University Press.

Rubin, Gayle. 1975. The traffic in women: Notes on the political economy of sex. In *Toward an anthropology of women,* ed. Rayna R[app] Reiter. New York: Monthly Review Press.

Rugh, Andrea B. 1986. *Reveal and conceal: Dress in contemporary Egypt.* Syracuse, N.Y.: Syracuse University Press.

Scott, Joan Wallach. 1988. *Gender and the politics of history.* New York: Columbia University Press.

Showalter, Elaine. 1987. Critical cross-dressing: Male feminists and the woman of the year. In *Men in feminism,* edited by Alice Jardine and Paul Smith. New York: Methuen.

Smith, Dorothy E. 1987. *The everyday world as problematic: A feminist sociology.* Toronto: University of Toronto Press.

———. 1990. *The conceptual practices of power: A feminist sociology of knowledge.* Toronto: University of Toronto Press.

van der Kwaak, Anke. 1992. Female circumcision and gender identity: A questionable alliance? *Social Science and Medicine* 35: 777–87.

van Gennep, Arnold. 1960. *The rites of passage,* trans. Monika B. Vizedom and Gabrielle L. Caffee. Chicago: University of Chicago Press.

Walker, Molly K. 1992. Maternal reactions to fetal sex. *Health Care for Women International* 13: 293–302.

West, Candace, and Don Zimmerman. 1987. Doing gender. *Gender & Society* 1: 125–51.

Wheelright, Julie. 1989. *Amazons and military maids: Women who cross-dressed in pursuit of life, liberty and happiness.* London: Pandora Press.

Whitehead, Harriet. 1982. The Bow and the Burden Strap: A New Look at Institutionalized Homosexuality in Native North America. In *Sexual meanings: The cultural construction of gender and sexuality,* edited by Sherry B. Ornter and Harriet Whitehead. New York: Cambridge University Press.

Wikan, Unni. 1982. *Behind the veil in Arabia: Women in Oman.* Baltimore, Md.: Johns Hopkins University Press.

Williams, Christine L. 1989. *Gender differences at work: Women and men in nontraditional occupations.* Berkeley: University of California Press.

Williams, Walter L. 1986. *The spirit and the flesh: Sexual diversity in American Indian culture.* Boston: Beacon Press.

Yanagisako, Sylvia Junko, and Jane Fishburne Collier. 1987. Toward a unified analysis of gender and kinship. In *Gender and kinship: Essays toward a unified analysis,* edited by Jane Fishburne Collier and Sylvia Junko Yanagisako. Berkeley: University of California Press.

Zelizer, Viviana A. 1985. *Pricing the priceless child: The changing social value of children.* New York: Basic Books.

R E A D I N G **Suzanne Kessler**

The Medical Construction of Gender

The birth of intersexed infants, babies born with genitals that are neither clearly male nor clearly female, has been documented throughout recorded time.[1] In the late twentieth century, medical technology has become sufficiently advanced to allow scientists to determine chromosomal and hormonal gender, which is typically taken to be the real, natural, biological gender, usually referred to as "sex."[2] Nevertheless, physicians who handle cases of intersexed infants consider several factors beside biological ones in determining, assigning, and announcing the gender of a particular infant. Indeed, biological factors are often preempted in physicians' deliberations by such cultural factors as the "correct" length of the penis and capacity of the vagina.

In the literature on intersexuality, issues such as announcing a baby's gender at the time of delivery, post-delivery discussions with the parents, and consultations with patients in adolescence are considered only peripherally to the central medical issues—etiology, diagnosis, and surgical procedures.[3] Yet members of medical teams have standard practices for managing intersexuality, which rely ultimately on cultural understandings of gender. The process and guidelines by which decisions about gender (re)construction are made reveal the model for the social construction of gender generally. Moreover, in the face of apparently incontrovertible evidence—infants born with some combination of "female" and "male" reproductive and sexual features—physicians hold an incorrigible belief that female and male are the only "natural" options. This paradox highlights and calls into question the idea that female and male are biological givens compelling a culture of two genders.

Ideally, to undertake an extensive study of intersexed infant case management, I would like to have had direct access to particular events, for example the deliveries of intersexed infants and the initial discussions among physicians, between physicians and parents, between parents, and among parents and family and friends of intersexed infants. The rarity with which intersexuality occurs, however, made this unfeasible.[4] Alternatively, physicians who have had considerable experience dealing with this condition were interviewed. I do not assume that their "talk" about how they manage such cases mirrors their "talk" in the situation, but their words do reveal that they have certain assumptions about gender and that they impose those assumptions via their medical decisions on the patients they treat.

Interviews were conducted with six medical experts (three women and three men) in the field of pediatric intersexuality: one clinical geneticist, three endocrinologists (two of them pediatric specialists), one psycho-endocrinologist, and one urologist. All of them have had extensive clinical experience with various inter-sexed syndromes, and some are internationally known researchers in the field of intersexuality. They were selected on the basis of their prominence in the field and their representing four different medical centers in New York City. Although they know one another, they do not collaborate on research and are not part of the same management team. All were interviewed in the spring of 1985 in their offices. The interviews lasted between forty-five minutes and one hour. Unless further referenced, all quotations in this chapter are from these interviews.[5]

THE THEORY OF INTERSEXUALITY MANAGEMENT

The sophistication of today's medical technology has led to an extensive compilation of various intersex categories based on the various causes of malformed genitals. The "true hermaphrodite" condition, where both ovarian and testicular tissue are present either in the same gonad or in opposite gonads, accounts for fewer than 5 percent of all cases of ambiguous genitals:[6] More commonly, the infant has either ovaries or testes, but the genitals are ambiguous. If the infant has two ovaries, the condition is referred to as female pseudohermaphroditism. If the infant has two testes, the condition is referred to as male pseudohermaphroditism. There are numerous causes of both forms of pseudohermaphroditism, and although there are life-threatening aspects to some of these conditions, having ambiguous genitals per se is not harmful to the infant's health.[7] Although most cases of ambiguous genitals do not represent true hermaphroditism, in keeping with the contemporary literature I will refer to all such cases as intersexed.

Current attitudes toward the intersex condition have been primarily influenced by three factors. First are the developments in surgery and endocrinology. Diagnoses of specific intersex conditions can be made with greater precision. Female genitals can be constructed that look much like "natural" ones, and some small penises can be enlarged with the exogenous application of hormones, although surgical skills are not sufficiently advanced to construct a "normal"-looking and -functioning penis out of other tissue.[8] Second, in the contemporary United States, the influence of the feminist movement has called into question the valuation of women according to strictly reproductive functions, and the presence or absence of functional gonads

is no longer the only or the definitive criterion for gender assignment. Third, psychological theorists focus on "gender identity" (one's sense of oneself as belonging to the female or male category) as distinct from "gender role" (cultural expectations of one's behavior as "appropriate" for a female or male).[9] The relevance of this new gender identity theory for rethinking cases of ambiguous genitals is that gender must be assigned as early as possible if gender identity is to develop successfully. As a result of these three factors, intersexuality is considered a treatable condition of the genitals, one that needs to be resolved expeditiously.

According to all of the specialists interviewed, management of intersexed cases is based upon the theory of gender proposed first by John Money, J. G. Hampson, and J. L. Hempson in 1955 and developed in 1972 by Money and Anke A. Ehrhardt. The theory argues that gender identity is changeable until approximately eighteen months of age.[10] "To use the Pygmalion allegory, one may begin with the same clay and fashion a god or a goddess."[11] The theory rests on satisfying several conditions: The experts must ensure that the parents have no doubt about whether their child is male or female; the genitals must be made to match the assigned gender as soon as possible; gender-appropriate hormones must be administered at puberty; and intersexed children must be kept informed about their situation with age-appropriate explanations. If these conditions are met, the theory proposes, the intersexed child will develop a gender identity in accordance with the gender assignment (regardless of the chromosomal gender) and will not question her or his assignment and request reassignment at a later age.

Supportive evidence for Money and Ehrhardt's theory is based on only a handful of repeatedly cited cases, but it has been accepted because of the prestige of the theoreticians and its resonance with contemporary ideas about gender, children, psychology, and medicine. Gender and children are malleable; psychology and medicine are the tools used to transform them. This theory is so strongly endorsed that it has taken on the character of gospel. "I think we [physicians] have been raised in the Money theory," one endocrinologist said. Another claimed, "We always approach the problem in a similar way and it's been dictated, to a large extent, by the work of John Money and Anke Ehrhardt because they are the only people who have published, at least in medical literature, any data, any guidelines." It is provocative that this physician immediately followed this assertion with: "And I don't know how effective it really is." Contradictory data are rarely cited in reviews of the literature, were not mentioned by any of the physicians interviewed, and have not reduced these physicians' belief in the theory's validity.[12]

The doctors interviewed concur with the argument that gender must be assigned immediately, decisively, and irreversibly, and that professional opinions be presented in a clear and unambiguous way. The psychoendocrinologist said that when doctors make a statement about the infant, they should "stick to it." The urologist said, "If you make a statement that later has to be disclaimed or discredited, you've weakened your credibility." A gender assignment made decisively, unambiguously, and irrevocably contributes, I believe, to the general impression that the infant's true, natural "sex" has been discovered, and that something that was there all along has been found. It also serves to maintain the credibility of the medical profession, reassure the parents, and reflexively substantiate Money and Ehrhardt's theory.

Also according to this theory, if corrective surgery is necessary, it should take place as soon as possible. If the infant is assigned the male gender, the initial stage of penis repair is usually undertaken in the first year, and further surgery is completed before the child enters school. If the infant is assigned the female gender, vulva repair (including clitoral reduction) is usually begun by three months of age. Money suggests that if reduction of phallic tissue were delayed beyond the neonatal period, the infant would have traumatic memories of having been castrated.[13] Vaginoplasty, in those females having an adequate internal structure (e.g., the vaginal canal is near its expected location), is done between the ages of one and four years. Girls who require more complicated surgical procedures might not be surgically corrected until preadolescence.[14] The complete vaginal canal is typically constructed only when the body is fully grown, following pubertal feminization with estrogen, although some specialists have claimed surgical success with vaginal construction in the early childhood years.[15] Although physicians speculate about the possible trauma of an early-childhood "castration" memory, there is no corresponding concern that vaginal reconstructive surgery delayed beyond the neonatal period is traumatic.

Even though gender identity theory places the critical age limit for gender reassignment between eighteen months and two years, the physicians acknowledge that diagnosis, gender assignment, and genital reconstruction cannot be delayed for as long as two years, since a clear gender assignment and correctly formed genitals will determine the kind of interactions parents will have with their child.[16] The geneticist argued that when parents "change a diaper and see genitalia that don't mean much in terms of gender assignment, I think it prolongs the negative response to the baby. . . . If you have clitoral enlargement that is so extraordinary that the parents can't distinguish between male and female, it is sometimes helpful to reduce that somewhat so that the parent views the child as female." Another physician concurred: Parents "need to go home and do their job as child rearers with it very clear whether it's a boy or a girl."

DIAGNOSIS

A premature gender announcement by an obstetrician, prior to a close examination of an infant's genitals, can be problematic. Money and his colleagues claim that the primary complications in case management of intersexed infants can be traced to mishandling by medical personnel untrained in sexology.[17] According to one of the pediatric endocrinologists interterviewed, obstetricians improperly educated about intersexed conditions "don't examine the babies closely enough at birth and say things just by looking, before separating legs and looking at everything, and jump to conclusions, because 99 percent of the time it's correct. . . . People get upset, physicians I mean. And they say things that are inappropriate." For example, he said that an inexperienced obstetrician might blurt out, "I think you have a boy, or no, maybe you have a girl." Other inappropriate remarks a doctor might make in postdelivery consultation with the parents include, "You have a little boy, but he'll never function as a little boy, so you better raise him as a little girl." As a result, said the pediatric endocrinologist, "the family comes away with the idea that they have a little boy, and that's what they wanted, and that's what they're going to get." In such cases, parents sometimes insist that the child be raised male despite the physicians' instructions to the contrary. "People have in mind certain things they've heard, that this is a boy, and they're not likely to forget that, or they're not likely to let it go easily." The urologist agreed that the first gender attribution is critical: "Once it's been announced, you've got a big problem on your hands." "One of the worst things is to allow them [the parents] to go ahead and give a name and tell everyone, and it turns out the child has to be raised in the opposite sex."[18]

Physicians feel that the mismanagement of such cases requires careful remedying. The psychoendocrinologist asserted, "When I'm involved, I spend hours with the parents to explain to them what has happened and how a mistake like that could be made, *or not really a mistake but a different decision*" [my emphasis]. One pediatric endocrinologist said, "I try to dissuade them from previous misconceptions and say, 'Well, I know what they meant, but the way they said it confused you. This is, I think, a better way to think about it.'" These statements reveal physicians' efforts not only to protect parents from concluding that their child is neither male nor female or both, but also to protect other physicians' decision-making processes. Case management involves perpetuating the notion that good medical decisions are based on interpretations of the infant's real "sex" rather than on cultural understandings of gender.

"Mismanagements" are less likely to occur in communities with major medical centers where specialists are prepared to deal with intersexuality and a medical team (perhaps drawing physicians from more than one teaching hospital) can be quickly assembled. The team typically consists of the original referring doctor (obstetrician or pediatrician), a pediatric endocrinologist, a pediatric surgeon (urologist or gynecologist), and a geneticist. In addition, a psychologist, psychiatrist, or psychoendocrinologist might play a role. If an infant is born with ambiguous genitals in a small community hospital without the relevant specialists on staff, the baby is likely to be transferred to a hospital where diagnosis and treatment are available. Intersexed infants born in poor rural areas where there is less medical intervention might never be referred for genital reconstruction. Many of these children, like those born in earlier historical periods, will grow up and live through adulthood with the genital ambiguity—somehow managing.

The diagnosis of intersexed conditions includes assessing the chromosomal sex and the syndrome that produced the genital ambiguity and may include medical procedures such as cytologic screening; chromosomal analysis; assessing serum electrolytes; hormone, gonadotropin, and steroids evaluation; digital examination; and radiographic genitography.[19] In any intersexed condition, if the infant is determined to be a genetic female (having an XX chromosome makeup), then the treatment—genital surgery to reduce the phallus size—can proceed relatively quickly, satisfying what the doctors believe are psychological and cultural

demands. For example, 21-hydroxylase deficiency, a form of female pseudohermaphroditism and one of the most common conditions, can be determined by a blood test within the first few days.

If, on the other hand, the infant is determined to have at least one Y chromosome, then surgery may be considerably delayed. A decision must be made whether to test the ability of the phallic tissue to respond to human chorionic gonadotropin (HCG), a treatment intended to enlarge the microphallus enough to be a penis. The endocrinologist explained, "You do HCG testing and you find out if the male can make testosterone. . . . You can get those results back probably within three weeks. . . . You're sure the male is making testosterone—but can he respond to it? It can take three months of waiting to see whether the phallus responds."

If the Y-chromosome infant cannot make testosterone or cannot respond to the testosterone it makes, the phallus will not develop, and the Y-chromosome infant will not be considered to be a male after all. Should the infant's phallus respond to the local application of testosterone or a brief course of intramuscular injections of low-potency androgen, the gender assignment problem is resolved, but possibly at some later cost, since the penis will not grow again at puberty when the rest of the body develops.[20] Money's case-management philosophy assumes that while it may be difficult for an adult male to have a much smaller than average penis, it is very detrimental to the morale of the young boy to have a micropenis.[21] In the former case, the male's manliness might be at stake, but in the latter case, his essential maleness might be. Although the psychological consequences of these experiences have not been empirically documented, Money and his colleagues suggest that it is wise to avoid the problems of both the micropenis in childhood and the still-undersized penis postpuberty by reassigning many of these infants to the female gender.[22] This approach suggests that for Money and his colleagues, chromosomes are less relevant in determining gender than penis size, and, by implication, that "male" is defined not by the genetic condition of having one Y and one X chromosome or by the production of sperm but by the aesthetic condition of having an "appropriately" sized penis.

The tests and procedures required for diagnosis (and consequently for gender assignment) can take several months.[23] Although physicians are anxious not to make premature gender assignments, their language suggests that it is difficult for them to take a completely neutral position and to think and speak only of *phallic tissue* that belongs to an infant whose gender has not yet been determined or decided. Comments such as "seeing whether the male can respond to testosterone" imply at least a tentative male gender assignment of an XY infant. The psychoendocrinologist's explanations to parents of their infant's treatment program also illustrate this implicit male gender assignment. "Clearly this baby has an underdeveloped phallus. But if the phallus responds to this treatment, we are fairly confident that surgical techniques and hormonal techniques will help this child to look like a boy. But we want to make absolutely sure and use some hormone treatments and see whether the tissue reacts." The mere fact that this doctor refers to the genitals as an "underdeveloped" phallus rather than an overdeveloped clitoris suggests that the infant has been judged to be, at least provisionally, a male. In the case of the undersized phallus, what is ambiguous is not whether this is a penis but whether it is "good enough" to remain one. If, at the end of the treatment period, the phallic tissue has not responded, what had been a potential penis (referred to in the medical literature as a "clitoropenis") is now considered an enlarged clitoris (or "penoclitoris"), and reconstructive surgery is planned as for the genetic female.

The time-consuming nature of intersex diagnosis and the assumption, based on the gender identity theory, that gender be assigned as soon as possible thus present physicians with difficult dilemmas. Medical personnel are committed to discovering the etiology of the condition in order to determine the best course of treatment, which takes time. Yet they feel an urgent need to provide an immediate assignment and genitals that look and function appropriately. An immediate assignment that will need to be retracted is more problematic than a delayed assignment, since reassignment carries with it an additional set of social complications. The endocrinologist interviewed commented: "We've come very far in that we can diagnose, eventually, many of the conditions. But we haven't come far enough. . . . We can't do it early enough. . . . Very frequently a decision is made before all this information is available, simply because it takes so long to make the correct diagnosis. And you cannot let a child go indefinitely, not in this society you can't. . . . There's pressure on parents [for a decision], and the parents transmit that pressure onto physicians."

A pediatric endocrinologist agreed: "At times you may need to operate before a diagnosis can be made. . . . In one case parents were told to wait on the announce-ment while the infant was treated to see if the phallus would grow when treated with androgens. After the first month passed and there was some growth, the parents said they had given the child a boy's name. They could only wait a month."

Deliberating out loud on the judiciousness of making parents wait for assignment decisions, the endocrinologist asked rhetorically, "Why do we do all these tests if in the end we're going to make the decision simply on the basis of the appearance of the genitalia?" This question suggests that the principles underlying physicians' decisions are cultural rather than biological, based on parental reaction and the medical team's perception of the infant's societal adjustment prospects given the way the child's genitals look or could be made to look. Moreover, as long as the decision rests largely on the criterion of genital appearance, and male is defined as having a "good-sized" penis, more infants will be assigned to the female gender than the male.

THE WAITING PERIOD: DEALING WITH AMBIGUITY

During the period of ambiguity between birth and assignment, physicians not only must evaluate the infant's prospects of becoming a good male but also must manage the parents' uncertainty about a genderless child. Physicians advise that parents postpone announcing the gender of the infant until a gender has been explicitly assigned. They believe that parents should not feel compelled to disclose the baby's "sex" to other people. The clinical geneticist interviewed said that physicians "basically encourage them [parents] to treat it [the infant] as neuter." One of the pediatric endocrinologists reported that in France parents confronted with this dilemma sometimes give the infant a neuter name such as Claude. The psychoendocrinologist concurred: "If you have a truly borderline situation, and you want to make it dependent on the hormone treatment . . . then the parents are . . . told, 'Try not to make a decision. Refer to the baby as "baby." Don't think in terms of boy or girl.'" Yet, when asked whether this is a reasonable request to make of parents in our society, the physician answered: "I don't think so. I think parents can't do it."[24]

New York State requires that a birth certificate be filled out within forty-eight hours of delivery, but the certificate need not be filed with the state for thirty days. The geneticist tells parents to insert "child of" instead of a name. In one case, parents filled out two birth registration forms, one for each gender, and they refused to sign either until a final gender assignment had been made.[25] One of the pediatric endocrinologists claimed, "I heard a story, I don't know if it's true or not. There were parents of a hermaphroditic infant who told everyone they had twins, one of each gender. When the gender was determined, they said the other had died."

The geneticist explained that when directly asked by parents what to tell others about the gender of the infant, she says, "Why don't you just tell them that the baby is having problems and as soon as the problems are resolved we'll get back to you." A pediatric endocrinologist echoes this suggestion in advising parents to say, "Until the problem is solved, [we] would really prefer not to discuss any of the details." According to the urologist, "If [the gender] isn't announced, people may mutter about it and may grumble about it, but they haven't got anything to get their teeth into and make trouble over for the child, or the parents, or whatever." In short, parents are asked to sidestep the infant's gender rather than admit that the gender is unknown, thereby collaborating in a web of white lies, ellipses, and mystifications.[26]

Even as physicians teach parents how to deal with those who may not find the infant's condition comprehensible or acceptable, they also must make the condition comprehensible and acceptable to the parents, normalizing the intersexed condition for them. In doing so, they help the parents consider the infant's condition in the most positive way. There are four key aspects to this "normalizing" process.

First, physicians teach parents usual fetal development and explain that all fetuses have the potential to be male or female. One of the endocrinologists explains, "In the absence of maleness, you have femaleness. . . . It's really the basic design. The other [intersex] is really a variation on a theme." This explanation presents the intersex condition as a natural phase of fetal development. Another endocrinologist "like[s] to show picture[s] to them and explain that at a certain point in development males and females look alike and then diverge for such and such reason." The professional literature suggests that doctors use diagrams that illustrate "nature's principle of using the same anlagen to produce the external genital parts of the male and female."[27]

Second, physicians stress the normalcy of other aspects of the infant. For example, the geneticist tells parents, "The baby is healthy, but there was a problem in the way the baby was developing." The endocrinologist says the infant has "a mild defect, [which] just like anything could be considered a birth defect, a mole, or a hemangioma." This language not only eases the blow

to the parents but also redirects their attention. Terms like "hermaphrodite" or "abnormal" are not used. The urologist said that he advised parents "about the generalization of sticking to the good things and not confusing people with something that is unnecessary."

Third, physicians (at least initially) imply that it is not the gender of the child that is ambiguous but the genitals. They talk about "undeveloped," "maldeveloped," or "unfinished" organs. From a number of the physicians interviewed came the following explanations:

> At a point in time the development proceeded in a different way, and sometimes the development isn't complete and we may have some trouble . . . in determining what the *actual* sex is. And so we have to do a blood test to help us. [my emphasis]
>
> The baby may be a female, which you would know after the buccal smear, but you can't prove it yet. If so, then it's a normal female with a different appearance. This can be surgically corrected.
>
> The gender of your child isn't apparent to us at the moment.
>
> While this looks like a small penis, it's actually a large clitoris. And what we're going to do is put it back in its proper position and reduce the size of the tip of it enough so it doesn't look funny, so it looks right.

Money and his colleagues report a case in which parents were advised to tell their friends that the reason their infant's gender was reannounced from male to female is that "the baby was . . . 'closed up down there.' [. . .] When the closed skin was divided, the female organs were revealed, and the baby discovered to be, *in fact,* a girl." [my emphasis] It was mistakenly assumed to be a male at first because "there was an excess of skin on the clitoris."[28]

The message in these examples is that the trouble lies in the doctor's ability to determine the gender, not in the baby's gender per se. The real gender will presumably be determined/proven by testing, and the "bad" genitals (which are confusing the situation for everyone) will be "repaired." The emphasis is not on the doctors' creating gender but in their completing the genitals. Physicians say that they "reconstruct" the genitals rather than "construct" them. The surgeons reconstitute from remaining parts what should have been there all along. The fact that gender in an infant is "reannounced" rather than "reassigned" suggests that the first announcement was a mistake because the announcer was confused by the genitals. The gender always was what it is now seen to be.[29]

Finally, physicians tell parents that social factors are more important in gender development than biological ones, even though they are searching for biological causes. In essence, the physicians teach the parents Money and Ehrhardt's theory of gender development.[30] In doing so, they shift the emphasis from the discovery of biological factors that are a sign of the "real" gender to providing the appropriate social conditions to produce the "real" gender. What remains unsaid is the apparent contradiction in the assumption that a "real" or "natural" gender can be or needs to be produced artificially. The physician/parent discussions make it clear to family members that gender is not a biological given [even though, of course, the physicians' own procedures for diagnosis assume that it is] and that gender is fluid: The psychoendocrinologist paraphrased an explanation to parents thus: "It will depend, ultimately, on how everybody treats your child and how your child is looking as a person. . . . I can with confidence tell them that generally gender [identity] clearly agrees with the assignment." A pediatric endocrinologist explained: "I try to impress upon them that there's an enormous amount of clinical data to support the fact that if you sex-reverse an infant . . . the majority of the time the alternative gender identity is commensurate with the socialization, the way that they're raised, and how people view them, and that seems to be the most critical."

The implication of these comments is that gender identity (of all children, not just those born with ambiguous genitals) is determined primarily by social factors, that the parents and community always construct the child's gender. In the case of intersexed infants, the physicians merely provide the right genitals to go along with the socialization. Of course at so-called normal births, when the infant's genitals are unambiguous, the parents are not told that the child's gender is ultimately up to socialization. In those cases, doctors do treat gender as a biological given.

SOCIAL FACTORS IN DECISION MAKING

Most of the physicians interviewed claimed that personal convictions of doctors ought to play no role in the decision-making process. The psychoendocrinologist explained:

I think the most critical factors [are] what is the possibility that this child will grow up with genitals which look like that of the assigned gender

and which will ultimately function according to gender. . . . That's why it's so important that it's a well-established team, because [personal convictions] can't really enter into it. It has to be what is surgically and endocrinologically possible for that baby to be able to make it. . . . It's really much more within medical criteria. I don't think many social factors enter into it.

While this doctor eschews the importance of social factors in gender assignment, she argues forcefully that social factors are extremely important in the development of gender identity. Indeed, she implies that social factors primarily enter the picture once the infant leaves the hospital.

In fact, doctors make decisions about gender on the basis of shared cultural values that are unstated, perhaps even unconscious, and therefore considered objective rather than subjective. Money states the fundamental rule for gender assignment: "Never assign a baby to be reared, and to surgical and hormonal therapy, as a boy, unless the phallic structure, hypospadiac or otherwise, is neonatally of at least the same caliber as that of same-aged males with small–average penises."[31] Elsewhere, he and his colleagues provide specific measurements for what qualifies as a micropenis: "A penis is, by convention, designated as a micropenis when at birth its dimensions are three or more standard deviations below the mean. . . . When it is correspondingly reduced in diameter with corpora that are vestigial, . . . it unquestionably qualifies as a micropenis."[32] A pediatric endocrinologist claimed that although "the [size of the] phallus is not the deciding factor, . . . if the phallus is less than two centimeters long at birth and won't respond to androgen treatments, then it's made into a female." There is no clearer statement of the formula for gender assignment than the one given by one well-published pediatric surgeon: "The decision to raise the child with male pseudohermaphroditism as a male or female is dictated entirely by the size of the phallus."[33]

These guidelines are clear, but they focus on only one physical feature, one that is distinctly imbued with cultural meaning. This becomes especially apparent in the case of an XX infant with normal female reproductive gonads and a "perfect" penis. Would the size and shape of the penis, in this case, be the deciding factor in assigning the infant as a "male," or would the "perfect" penis be surgically destroyed and female genitals created? Money notes that this dilemma would be complicated by the anticipated reaction of the parents to seeing "their apparent son lose his penis."[34] Other researchers concur that parents are likely to want to raise a child with a normal-shaped penis (regardless of size) as "male," particularly if the scrotal area looks normal and if the parents have had no experience with intersexuality.[35] Elsewhere, Money argues in favor of not neonatally amputating the penis of XX infants since fetal masculinization of brain structures would predispose them "almost invariably [to] develop behaviorally as tomboys, even when reared as girls."[36] This reasoning implies first that tomboyish behavior in girls is bad and should be avoided and second that it is preferable to remove the internal female organs, implant prosthetic testes, and regulate the "boy's hormones for his entire life than to overlook or disregard the perfection of the penis."[37]

The ultimate proof to the physicians that they intervened appropriately and gave the intersexed infant the correct gender assignment is that the reconstructed genitals look normal and function normally in adulthood. The vulva, labia, and clitoris should appear ordinary to the woman and her partner(s), and the vagina should be able to receive a normal-sized penis. Similarly, the man and his partner(s) should feel that his penis (even if somewhat smaller than the norm) looks and functions in an unremarkable way. Although there are no published data on how much emphasis the intersexed person, him- or herself, places upon genital appearance and functioning, physicians are absolutely clear about what they believe is important. The clinical geneticist said, "If you have . . . a seventeen-year-old young lady who has gotten hormone therapy and has breast development and pubic hair and no vaginal opening, I can't even entertain the notion that this young lady wouldn't want to have corrective surgery." The urologist summarized his criteria: "Happiness is the biggest factor. Anatomy is part of happiness." Money states, "The primary deficit [of not having sufficient penis]—and destroyer of morale—lies in being unable to satisfy the partner."[38] Another team of clinicians reveals its phallocentrism and argues that the most serious mistake in gender assignment is to create "an individual unable to engage in genital [heterosexual] sex."[39]

The equation of gender with genitals could have emerged only in an age when medical science can create genitals that appear to be normal and to function adequately, and an emphasis on the good phallus above all else could have emerged only in a culture that has rigid aesthetic and performance criteria for what constitutes maleness. The formulation "Good penis equals male; absence of good penis equals female" is treated in the literature and by the physicians interviewed as an objective criterion, operative in all cases. There is a striking lack of attention to the size and shape requirements of the female genitals, other than that the clitoris not be too big and that the vagina be able to receive a penis.[40]

In the late nineteenth century, when women's reproductive function was culturally designated as their essential characteristic, the presence or absence of ovaries (whether or not they were fertile) was held to be the ultimate criterion of gender assignment for hermaphrodites. As recently as 1955, there was some concern that if people with the same chromosomes or gonads paired off, even if they had different genitals, that "might bring the physician in conflict with the law for abetting the pursuit of (technically) illegal sex practices."[41] The urologist interviewed recalled a case from that period of a male child reassigned to "female" at the age of four or five because ovaries had been discovered. Nevertheless, doctors today, schooled in the etiology and treatment of the various intersex syndromes, view decisions based primarily on chromosomes or gonads as wrong, although, they complain, the conviction that the presence of chromosomes or gonads is the ultimate criterion "still dictates the decisions of the uneducated and uninformed."[42] Presumably the educated and informed now know that decisions based primarily on phallic size, shape, and sexual capacity are right.

While the prospect of constructing good genitals is the primary consideration in physicians' gender assignments, another extramedical factor was repeatedly cited by the six physicians interviewed—the specialty of the attending physician. Although intersexed infants are generally treated by teams of specialists, only the person who coordinates the team is actually responsible for the case. This person, acknowledged by the other physicians as having chief responsibility, acts as spokesperson to the parents. Although all of the physicians claimed that these medical teams work smoothly, with few differences of opinion, several of them mentioned decision-making orientations that are grounded in particular medical specializations. One endocrinologist stated, "The easiest route to take, where there is ever any question, . . . is to raise the child as female. . . . In this country, that is usual if the infant falls into the hands of a pediatric endocrinologist. . . . If the decision is made by the urologists, who are mostly males, . . . they're always opting, because they do the surgery, they're always feeling they can correct anything."

Another endocrinologist concurred: "[Most urologists] don't think in terms of dynamic processes. They're interested in fixing pipes and lengthening pipes, and not dealing with hormonal, and certainly not psychological issues. . . . 'What can I do with what I've got?'" Urologists were defended by the clinical geneticist: "Surgeons here, now I can't speak for elsewhere, they don't get into a situation where the child is a year old and they can't make anything."

Whether or not urologists "like to make boys," as one endocrinologist claimed, the following example from a urologist who was interviewed explicitly links a cultural interpretation of masculinity to the medical treatment plan. The case involved an adolescent who had been assigned the female gender at birth but was developing some male pubertal signs and wanted to be a boy. "He was ill-equipped," said the urologist, "yet we made a very respectable male out of him. He now owns a huge construction business—those big cranes that put stuff up on the building."

POSTINFANCY CASE MANAGEMENT

After the infant's gender has been assigned, parents generally latch onto the assignment as the solution to the problem—and it is. The physician as detective has collected the evidence, as lawyer has presented the case, and as judge has rendered a verdict. Although most of the interviewees claimed that parents are equal participants in the whole process, they gave no instances of parental participation prior to the gender assignment.[43] After the physicians assign the infant's gender, the parents are encouraged to establish the credibility of that gender publicly by, for example, giving a detailed medical explanation to a leader in their community, such as a physician or pastor, who will explain the situation to curious casual acquaintances. Money argues that "medical terminology has a special layman's magic in such a context, it is final and authoritative and closes the issue."[44] He also recommends that eventually the mother "settle [the] argument once and for all among her women friends by allowing some of them to see the baby's reconstructed genitalia." Apparently, the powerful influence of normal-looking genitals helps overcome a history of ambiguous gender.

Some of the same issues that arise in assigning gender recur some years later when, at adolescence, the child may be referred to a physician for counseling.[45] The physician then tells the adolescent many of the same things his or her parents had been told years before, with the same language. Terms like "abnormal," "disorder," "disease," and "hermaphroditism" are avoided; the condition is normalized and the child's gender is treated as unproblematic. One clinician explains to his patients that sex organs are different in appearance for each person, not just those who are intersexed. Furthermore, he tells the girls "that while most women menstruate, not all do . . . that conception is only a number of ways to become a parent; [and] that today some individuals are choosing not to become parents."[46] The clinical geneticist tells a typical female patient: "You are female. Female is not determined by your genes. Lots of other things determine being a woman. And you are a woman but you won't be able to have babies."

A case reported by one of the pediatric endocrinologists involving an adolescent female with androgen insensitivity provides an intriguing insight into the postinfancy gender-management process. She was told at the age of fourteen "that her ovaries weren't normal and had been removed. That's why she needed pills to look normal. . . . I wanted to convince her of her femininity. Then I told her she could marry and have normal sexual relations. . . . [Her] uterus won't develop but [she] could adopt children." The urologist interviewed was asked to comment on this handling of the counseling. "It sounds like a very good solution to it. He's stating the truth, and if you don't state the truth . . . then you're in trouble later." This is a strange version of "the truth," however, since the adolescent was chromosomally XY and was born with normal testes that produced normal quantities of androgen. There *were* no ovaries or uterus. Another pediatric endocrinologist, in commenting on the management of this case, hedged the issue by saying that he would have used a generic term like "the gonads." A third endocrinologist said she would say that the uterus had never formed.

Technically, these physicians are lying when, for example, they explain to an adolescent XY female with an intersexed history that her "ovaries . . . had to be removed because they were unhealthy or were producing 'the wrong balance of hormones.'"[47] We can presume that these lies are told in the service of what physicians consider a greater good—keeping individual/concrete genders as clear and uncontaminated as the notions of female and male are in the abstract. One clinician suggests that with some female patients it eventually may be possible to talk to them "about their gonads having some structures and features that are testicular-like."[48] This call for honesty may be based, at least partly, on the possibility of the child's discovering his or her chromosomal sex inadvertently from a buccal smear taken in a high school biology class. Today's litigious climate may be another encouragement.

In sum, the adolescent is typically told that certain internal organs did not form because of an endocrinological defect, not because those organs could never have developed in someone with her or his sex chromosomes. The topic of chromosomes is skirted.

There are no published studies on how these adolescents experience their condition and their treatment by doctors. An endocrinologist interviewed mentioned that her adolescent patients rarely ask specifically what is wrong with them, suggesting that they are accomplices in this evasion. In spite of the "truth" having been evaded, the clinician's impression is that "their gender identities and general senses of well-being and self-esteem appear not to have suffered."[49]

LESSONS FROM INTERSEX MANAGEMENT

Physicians conduct careful examinations of the intersexed infant's genitals and perform intricate laboratory procedures. They are interpreters of the body, trained and committed to uncovering the "actual" gender obscured by ambiguous genitals. Yet they also have considerable leeway in assigning gender, and their decisions are influenced by cultural as well as medical factors. What is the relationship between the physician as discoverer and the physician as determiner of gender? Where is the relative emphasis placed in discussions with parents and adolescents and in the consciousness of the physicians? It is misleading to characterize the doctors whose words are provided here as presenting themselves publicly to the parents as discoverers of the infant's real gender but privately acknowledging that the infant has no real gender other than the one being determined or constructed by the medical professionals. They are not hypocritical. It is also misleading to claim that the physicians' focus shifts from discovery to determination over the course of treatment: first the doctors regard the infant's gender as an unknown but discoverable reality; then the doctors relinquish their attempts to find the real gender and treat the infant's gender as something they must construct. They are not medically incompetent or deficient. Instead, I am arguing that the peculiar balance of discovery and determination throughout treatment permits physicians to handle very problematic cases of gender in the most unproblematic of ways.

This balance relies fundamentally on a particular conception of "natural."[50] Although the "deformity" of intersexed genitals would be immutable were it not for medical interference, physicians do not consider it natural. Instead, they think of, and speak of, the surgical/hormonal alteration of such "deformities" as natural because such intervention returns the body to what it ought to have been if events had taken their typical course. The nonnormative is converted into the normative, and the normative state is considered natural.[51] The genital ambiguity is remedied to conform to a "natural," that is, culturally indisputable gender dichotomy. Sherry Ortner's claim that the culture/nature distinction is itself a construction—a product of culture—is relevant here. Language and imagery help create and maintain a specific view of what is natural about the two genders and, I would argue, about the very idea of gender—that it consists of two exclusive types: female and male.[52] The belief that gender consists of two exclusive types is maintained and perpetuated by the medical community in the face of incontrovertible physical evidence that this is not mandated by biology.

The lay conception of human anatomy and physiology assumes a concordance among clearly dimorphic gender markers—chromosomes, genitals, gonads, hormones—but physicians understand that concordance and dimorphism do not always exist. Their understanding of biology's complexity, however, does not inform their understanding of gender's complexity. In order for intersexuality to be managed differently than it currently is, physicians would have to take seriously Money's assertion that it is a misrepresentation of epistemology to consider any cell in the body authentically male or female.[53] If authenticity for gender resides not in a discoverable nature but in someone's proclamation, then the power to proclaim something else is available. If physicians recognized that implicit in their management of gender is the notion that finally, and always, people construct gender, as well as the social systems that are grounded in gender-based concepts, the possibilities for real societal transformations would be unlimited. Unfortunately, neither in their representations to the families of the intersexed nor among themselves do the physicians interviewed for this study draw such far-reaching implications from their work. Their "understanding" that particular genders are medically (re)constructed in these cases does not lead them to see that gender *is always* constructed.

Accepting genital ambiguity as a natural option would require that physicians also acknowledge that genital ambiguity is "corrected" not because it is threatening to the infant's life but because it is threatening to the infant's culture.

Rather than admit to their role in perpetuating gender, physicians "psychologize" the issue by talking about the parents' anxiety and humiliation in being confronted with an anomalous infant. They talk as though they have no choice but to respond to the parents' pressure for a resolution of psychological discomfort and as though they have no choice but to use medical technology in the service of a two-gender culture. Neither the psychology nor the technology is doubted, since both shield physicians from responsibility. Indeed, for the most part, neither physicians nor parents emerge from the experience of intersex case management with a greater understanding of the social construction of gender. Society's accountability, like their own, is masked by the assumption that gender is a given. Thus, the medical management of intersexuality, instead of illustrating nature's failure to ordain gender in these isolated, "unfortunate" instances, illustrates physicians' and Western society's failure of imagination—the failure to imagine that each of their management decisions is a moment when a specific instance of biological "sex" is transformed into a culturally constructed gender.

NOTES

1. For historical reviews of the intersexed person in ancient Greece and Rome, see Leslie Fiedler, *Freaks: Myths and Images of the Second Self* and Vern Bullough, *Sexual Variance in Society and History.* For the Middle Ages and Renaissance, see Michel Foucault, *History of Sexuality.* For the eighteenth and nineteenth centuries, see Michel Foucault, *Herculine Barbin* and Alice Domurat Dreger, *Hermaphrodites and the Medical Invention of Sex.* For the early twentieth century, see Havelock Ellis, *Studies in the Psychology of Sex.*

2. Traditionally, the term "gender" has designated psychological, social, and cultural aspects of maleness and femaleness, and the term "sex" has specified the biological and presumably more objective components. Twenty years ago, Wendy McKenna and I introduced the argument that "gender" should be used exclusively to refer to anything related to the categories "female" and "male," replacing the term "sex," which would be restricted to reproductive and "lovemaking" activities (Kessler and McKenna). Our reasoning was (and still is) that this would emphasize the socially constructed, overlapping nature of all category distinctions, even the biological ones. We wrote about gender chromosomes and gender hormones even though, at the time, doing so seemed awkward. I continue this practice here, but I follow the convention of referring to people with mixed biological gender cues as "intersexed" or "intersexuals" rather than as "intergendered" or "intergenderals." The latter is more consistent with my position, but I want to reflect both medical and vernacular usage without using quotation marks each time.

3. See, for example: M. Bolkenius, R. Daum, and E. Heinrich, "Paediatric Surgical Principles in the Management of Children with Intersex"; Kenneth I. Glassberg, "Gender Assignment in Newborn Male Pseudohermaphrodites"; and Peter A. Lee et al., "Micropenis. I. Criteria, Etiologies and Classification."

4. It is difficult to get accurate statistics on the frequency of intersexuality. Chromosomal abnormalities (like XOXX or XXXY) are registered, but those conditions do not always imply ambiguous genitals, and most cases of ambiguous genitals do not involve chromosomal abnormalities. None of the physicians interviewed would venture a guess on frequency rates, but all claimed that intersexuality is rare. One physician suggested that the average obstetrician may see only two cases in twenty years. Another estimated that a specialist may see only one a year or possibly as many as five a year. A reporter who interviewed physicians at Johns Hopkins Medical Center wrote that they treat, at most, ten new patients a year (Melissa Hendricks, "Is It a Boy or a Girl?"). The numbers are considerably greater if one adopts a broader definition of intersexuality to include all "sex chromosome" deviations and any genitals that do not look, according to the culturally informed view of the moment, "normal" enough. A urologist at a Mt. Sinai School of Medicine symposium on Pediatric Plastic and Reconstructive Surgery (New York City, 16 May 1996) claimed that one of every three hundred male births involves some kind of genital abnormality. A meticulous analysis of the medical literature from 1955 to 1997 led Anne Fausto-Sterling and her students to conclude that the frequency of intersexuality may be as high as 2 percent of live births, and that between 0.1 and 0.2 percent of newborns undergo some sort of genital surgery (Melanie Blackless et al., "How Sexually Dimorphic Are We?"). The Intersex Society of North America (ISNA) estimates that about five intersex surgeries are performed in the United States each day.

5. Although the interviews in this chapter were conducted more than ten years ago, interviews with physicians conducted in the mid- to late 1990s and interviews conducted with parents of intersexed children during that same time

period . . . indicate that little has changed in the medical management of intersexuality. This lack of change is also evident in current medical management literature. See, for example, F. M. E. Slijper et al., "Neonates with Abnormal Genital Development Assigned the Female Sex: Parent Counseling," and M. Rohatgi, "Intersex Disorders: An Approach to Surgical Management."

6. Mariano Castro-Magana, Moris Angulo, and Platon J. Collipp, "Management of the Child with Ambiguous Genitalia."

7. For example, infants whose intersexuality is caused by congenital adrenal hyperplasia can develop severe electrolyte disturbances unless the condition is controlled by cortisone treatments. Intersexed infants whose condition is caused by androgen insensitivity are in danger of eventual malignant degeneration of the testes unless these are removed. For a complete catalog of clinical syndromes related to the intersexed condition, see Arye Lev-Ran, "Sex Reversal as Related to Clinical Syndromes in Human Beings."

8. Much of the surgical experimentation in this area has been accomplished by urologists who are trying to create penises for female-to-male transsexuals. Although there have been some advancements in recent years in the ability to create a "reasonable-looking" penis from tissue taken elsewhere on the body, the complicated requirements of the organ (requiring both urinary and sexual functioning) have posed surgical problems. It may be, however, that the concerns of the urologists are not identical to the concerns of the patients. While data are not yet available from the intersexed, we know that female-to-male transsexuals place greater emphasis on the "public" requirements of the penis (for example, being able to look normal while standing at the urinal or wearing a bathing suit) than on its functional requirements (for example, being able to achieve an erection) (Kessler and McKenna, 128–132). As surgical techniques improve, female-to-male transsexuals (and intersexed males) might increase their demands for organs that look and function better.

9. Historically, psychology has tended to blur the distinction between the two by equating a person's acceptance of her or his genitals with gender role and ignoring gender identity. For example, Freudian theory posited that if one had a penis and accepted its reality, then masculine gender role behavior would naturally follow (Sigmund Freud, "Some Psychical Consequences of the Anatomical Distinctions between the Sexes").

10. Almost all of the published literature on intersexed infant case management has been written or co-written by one researcher, John Money, professor of medical psychology and professor of pediatrics, emeritus, at Johns Hopkins University and Hospital, where he is director of the Psychohormonal Research Unit. Even the publications that are produced independently of Money reference him and reiterate his management philosophy. Although only one of the physicians interviewed has published with Money, they all essentially concur with his views and give the impression of a consensus that is rarely encountered in science. The one physician who raised some questions about Money's philosophy and the gender theory on which it is based has extensive experience with intersexuality in a nonindustrialized culture where the infant is matured differently with no apparent harm to gender development. Even though psychologists fiercely argue issues of gender identity and gender role development, doctors who treat intersexed infants seem untouched by these debates. There are still, in the late 1990s, few renegade voices from within the medical establishment. Why Money has been so single-handedly influential in promoting his ideas about gender is a question worthy of a separate substantial analysis. His management philosophy is conveyed in the following sources: John Money, J. G. Hampson, and J. L. Hampson, "Hermaphroditism: Recommendations Concerning Assignment of Sex, Change of Sex, and Psychologic Management"; John Money, *Sex Errors of the Body: Dilemmas, Education, Counseling;* John Money, Reynolds Potter, and Clarice S. Stoll, "Sex Reannouncement in Hereditary Sex Deformity: Psychology and Sociology of Habilitation"; Money and Ehrhardt; John Money, "Psychologic Consideration of Sex Assignment in Intersexuality"; John Money, "Psychological Counseling: Hermaphroditism"; John Money, Tom Mazur, Charles Abrams, and Bernard F. Norman, "Micropenis, Family Mental Health, and Neonatal Management: A Report on Fourteen Patients Reared as Girls"; and John Money, "Birth Defect of the Sex Organs: Telling the Parents and the Patient."

11. Money and Ehrhardt, 152.

12. One exception is the case followed by Milton Diamond in "Sexual Identity, Monozygotic Twins Reared in Discordant Sex Roles and a BBC Follow-up" and, with Keith Sigmundson, in "Sex Reassignment at Birth: Long-term Review and Clinical Applications."

13. Money, "Psychologic Consideration of Sex Assignment in Intersexuality."

14. Castro-Magana, Angulo, and Collipp.

15. Victor Braren et al., "True Hermaphroditism: A Rational Approach to Diagnosis and Treatment."

16. Studies of nonintersexed newborns have shown that, from the moment of birth, parents respond to their infant based on her or his gender. Jeffrey Rubin, F. J. Provenzano, and Z. Luria, "The Eye of the Beholder: Parents' Views on Sex of Newborns."

17. Money, Mazur, Abrams, and Norman.

18. There is evidence from other kinds of sources that once a gender attribution is made, all further information buttresses that attribution, and only the most contradictory new information will cause the original gender attribution to be questioned. Kessler and McKenna.

19. Castro-Magana, Angulo, and Collipp.

20. Money, "Psychologic Consideration of Sex Assignment in Intersexuality."

21. Technically, the term "micropenis" should be reserved for an exceptionally small but well-formed structure, a small, malformed "penis" should be referred to as a "microphallus" (Peter A. Lee et al.).

22. Money, Mazur, Abrams, and Norman, 26. A different view is argued by another leading gender-identity theorist: "When a little boy (with an imperfect penis) knows he is a male, he creates a penis that functions symbolically the same as those of boys with normal penises" (Robert J. Stoller, *Sex and Gender*).

23. W. Ch. Hecker, "Operative Correction of Intersexual Genitals in Children."

24. This way of presenting advice fails to understand that parents are part of a larger system. A pediatric endocrinologist told biologist Anne Fausto-Sterling that parents, especially young ones, are not independent actors. They rely on the advice of grandparents and older siblings, who, according to the physician, are more hysterical and push for an early gender assignment before all the medical data are analyzed (private communication, summer 1996).

25. Elizabeth Bing and Esselyn Rudikoff, "Divergent Ways of Parental Coping with Hermaphrodite Children."

26. These evasions must have many ramifications in everyday social interactions between parents, family, and friends. How people "fill in" the uncertainty such that interactions remain relatively normal is an interesting question that warrants further study. One of the pediatric endocrinologists interviewed acknowledged that the published literature discusses intersex management only from the physicians' point of view. He asks, "How [do parents] experience what they're told, and what [do] they remember . . . and carry with them?" One published exception to this neglect of the parents' perspective is a case study comparing two different coping strategies. The first couple, although initially distressed, handled the traumatic event by regarding the abnormality as an act of God. The second couple, more educated and less religious, put their faith in medical science and expressed a need to fully understand the biochemistry of the defect. Bing and Rudikoff.

27. Tom Mazur, "Ambiguous Genitalia: Detection and Counseling," and Money "Psychologic Consideration of Sex Assignment in Intersexuality," 218.

28. Money, Potter, and Stoll, 211.

29. The term "reassignment" is more commonly used to describe the gender changes of those who are cognizant of their earlier gender, e.g., transsexuals—people whose gender itself was a mistake.

30. Although Money and Ehrhardt's socialization theory is uncontested by the physicians who treat intersexuality and is presented to parents as a matter of fact, there is actually much debate among psychologists about the effect of prenatal hormones on brain structure and ultimately on gender-role behavior and even on gender identity. The physicians interviewed agreed that the animal evidence for prenatal brain organization is compelling but that

there is no evidence in humans that prenatal hormones have an inviolate or unilateral effect. If there is any effect of prenatal exposure to androgen, they believe it can easily be overcome and modified by psychosocial factors. It is this latter position, not the controversy in the field, that is communicated to the parents. For an argument favoring prenatally organized gender differences in the brain, see Milton Diamond, "Human Sexual Development: Biological Foundations for Social Development"; for a critique of that position, see Ruth Bleier, *Science and Gender. A Critique of Biology and Its Theories on Women*.

31. Money, "Psychological Counseling: Hermaphroditism," 610.

32. Money, Mazur, Abrams, and Norman, 18.

33. P. Donahoe, "Clinical Management of Intersex Abnormalities."

34. John Money, "Hermaphroditism and Pseudohermaphroditism."

35. Mojtaba Beheshti, Brian E. Hardy, Bernard M. Churchill, and Denis Daneman, "Gender Assignment in Male Pseudohermaphrodite Children." Of course, if the penis looked normal and the empty scrotum was overlooked, it might not be discovered until puberty that the male child was XX with a female internal structure.

36. Money, "Psychologic Consideration of Sex Assignment in Intersexuality," 216.

37. Weighing the probability of achieving a "perfect" penis against the probable trauma such procedures may entail is another social factor in decision making. According to an endocrinologist interviewed, if it seems that an XY infant with an inadequate penis would require as many as ten genital operations over a six-year period in order to have an adequate penis, the infant would be assigned the female gender. In this case, the endocrinologist's practical and compassionate concerns would override purely genital criteria.

38. Money, "Psychologic Consideration of Sex Assignment in Intersexuality," 217.

39. Castro-Magana, Angulo, and Collipp, 180.

40. It is unclear how much of this bias is the result of a general cultural devaluation of the female and how much is the result of physicians' belief in their ability to construct anatomically correct and functional female genitals.

41. John F. Oliven, *Sexual Hygiene and Pathology: A Manual for the Physician*.

42. Money, "Psychologic Consideration of Sex Assignment in Intersexuality," 215. Remnants of this anachronistic view can still be found, however, when doctors justify the removal of contradictory gonads on the grounds that they are typically sterile or at risk for malignancy (J. Dewhurst and D. B. Grant, "Intersex Problems"). Presumably, if the gonads were functional and healthy, their removal would provide an ethical dilemma for at least some medical professionals.

43. Although one set of authors argued that the views of the parents on the most appropriate gender for their child must be taken into account (Dewhurst and Grant, 1192),

the physicians interviewed here denied direct knowledge of this kind of participation. They claimed that they personally had encountered few, if any, cases of parents who insisted on their child being assigned a particular gender. Yet each had heard about cases where a family's ethnicity or religious background biased them toward males. None of the physicians recalled whether this preference for male offspring meant the parents wanted a male regardless of the "inadequacy" of the penis, or whether it meant that the parents would have greater difficulty with a less-than-perfect-male than with a "normal" female.

44. Money, "Psychological Counseling: Hermaphroditism," 613.

45. As with the literature on infancy, most of the published material on adolescents is on surgical and hormonal management rather than on social management. See, for example, Joel J. Roslyn, Eric W. Fonkalsrud, and Barbara Lippe, "Intersex Disorders in Adolescents and Adults."

46. Mazur, 421.

47. Dewhurst and Grant, 1193.

48. Mazur, 422.

49. Ibid.

50. For an extended discussion of different ways of conceptualizing what is natural, see Richard W. Smith, "What Kind of Sex Is Natural?"

51. This supports sociologist Harold Garfinkel's argument that we treat routine events as our *due* as social members and that we treat gender, like all normal forms, as a moral imperative. It is no wonder, then, that physicians conceptualize what they are doing as natural and unquestionably "right." Harold Garfinkel, *Studies in Ethnomethodology.*

52. Sherry B. Ortner, "Is Female to Male as Nature Is to Culture?"

53. Money, "Psychological Counseling: Hermaphroditism," 618.

REFERENCES

Beheshti, Mojtaba, Brian E. Hardy, Bernard M. Churchill, and Denis Daneman. "Gender Assignment in Male Pseudohermaphrodite Children." *Urology* 22, no. 6 (December 1983): 604–607.

Bing, Elizabeth and Esselyn Rudikoff. "Divergent Ways of Parental Coping with Hermaphrodite Children." *Medical Aspects of Human Sexuality* (December 1970): 73–88.

Blackless, Melanie, Anthony Charuvastra, Amanda Derryck, Anne Fausto-Sterling, Karl Lauzanne, and Ellen Lee. "How Sexually Dimorphic Are We?" Unpublished manuscript, 1997.

Bleier, Ruth. *Science and Gender: A Critique of Biology and Its Theories on Women.* New York: Pergamon Press, 1984.

Bolkenius, M., R. Daum, and E. Heinrich. "Paediatric Surgical Principles in the Management of Children with Intersex." *Progress in Pediatric Surgery* 17 (1984): 33–38.

Braren, Victor, John J. Warner, Ian M. Burr, Alfred Slonim, James A. O'Neill Jr., and Robert K. Rhamy. "True Hermaphroditism: A Rational Approach to Diagnosis and Treatment." *Urology* 15 (June 1980): 569–574.

Bullough, Vern. *Sexual Variance in Society and History.* New York: John Wiley and Sons, 1976.

Castro-Magana, Mariano, Moris Angulo, and Platon J. Collipp. "Management of the Child with Ambiguous Genitalia." *Medical Aspects of Human Sexuality* 18, no. 4 (April 1984): 172–188.

Dewhurst, J., and D. B. Grant. "Intersex Problems." *Archives of Disease in Childhood* 59 (July–December 1984): 1191–1194.

Diamond, Milton. "Human Sexual Development: Biological Foundations for Social Development." In *Human Sexuality in Four Perspectives,* ed. Frank A. Beach, 22–61. Baltimore: The Johns Hopkins University Press, 1976.

———. "Sexual Identity, Monozygotic Twins Reared in Discordant Sex Roles and a BBC Follow-Up." *Archives of Sexual Behavior* 11, no. 2 (1982): 181–186.

———, and Keith Sigmundson. "Sex Reassignment of Birth: Long-term Review and Clinical Applications." *Archives of Pediatric and Adolescent Medicine* 151 (May 1997): 298–304.

Donahoe, P. "Clinical Management of Intersex Abnormalities." *Current Problems in Surgery* 28 (1991): 519–579.

Dreger, Alice Domurat. *Hermaphrodites and the Medical Invention of Sex.* Cambridge: Harvard University Press, 1998.

Ellis, Havelock. *Studies in the Psychology of Sex.* New York: Random House, 1942.

Fiedler, Leslie. *Freaks: Myths and Images of the Second Self.* New York: Simon and Schuster, 1978.

Foucault, Michael. *Herculine Barbin.* New York: Pantheon Books, 1978.

———. *History of Sexuality.* New York: Pantheon Books, 1980.

Freud, Sigmund. "Some Psychical Consequences of the Anatomical Distinctions between the Sexes" (1925). In *The Complete Psychological Works,* trans. and ed. J. Strachy, vol. 18. New York: Norton, 1976.

Garfinkel, Harold. *Studies in Ethnomethodology.* Englewood Cliffs, N.J.: Prentice Hall, 1967.

Glassberg, Kenneth I. "Gender Assignment in Newborn Male Pseudohermaphrodites." *Urologic Clinics of North America* 7 (June 1980): 409–421.

Hecker, W. Ch. "Operative Correction of Intersexual Genitals in Children." *Progress in Pediatric Surgery* 17 (1984): 21–31.

Hendricks, Melissa. "Is It a Boy or a Girl?" *Johns Hopkins Magazine* 45, no. 5 (November 1993): 10–16.

Kessler, Suzanne J., and Wendy McKenna. *Gender: An Ethnomethodological Approach.* New York: Wiley-Interscience, 1978; Chicago: University of Chicago Press, 1985.

Lee, Peter A., Thomas Mazur, Robert Danish, James Amrhein, Robert M. Blizzard, John Money, and Claude J. Migeon. "Micropenis: I. Criteria, Etiologies and Classification." *The Johns Hopkins Medical Journal* 146 (1980): 156–163.

Lev-Ran, Arye. "Sex Reversal as Related to Clinical Syn-
dromes in Human Beings." In *Handbook of Sexology II:
Genetics, Hormones and Behavior,* ed. John Money and H.
Musaph, 157–173. New York: Elsevier, 1978.

Mazur, Tom. "Ambiguous Genitalia: Detection and Counseling."
Pediatric Nursing 9 (November/December 1983): 417–431.

Money, John. "Birth Defect of the Sex Organs: Telling the Parents and the Patient." *British Journal of Sexual Medicine* 10
(March 1983): 14.

———. "Hermaphroditism and Pseudohermaphroditism."
In *Gynecologic Endocrinology,* ed. Jay J. Gold, 449–464. New
York: Hoeber, 1968.

———. "Psychologic Consideration of Sex Assignment in
Intersexuality." *Clinics in Plastic Surgery* 1 (April 1974):
215–222.

———. "Psychological Counseling: Hermaphroditism." In *En-
docrine and Genetic Diseases of Childhood and Adolescence,* ed.
L. I. Gardner, 609–618. Philadelphia: W. B. Saunders, 1975.

———. Sex *Errors of the Body: Dilemmas, Education, Counseling.* Baltimore: The Johns Hopkins University Press, 1968.
Reprint, 1994.

———, and Anke A. Ehrhardt. *Man & Woman, Boy & Girl.*
Baltimore: The Johns Hopkins University Press, 1972.

———, J. G. Hampson, and J. L. Hampson. "Hermaphrodit-
ism: Recommendations Concerning Assignment of Sex,
Change of Sex, and Psychologic Management." *Bulletin of
The Johns Hopkins Hospital* 97 (1955): 284–300.

———, Tom Mazur, Charles Abrams, and Bernard F. Norman. "Micropenis, Family Mental Health, and Neonatal

Management: A Report on Fourteen Patients Reared as
Girls." *Journal of Preventive Psychiatry* 1, no. 1 (1981): 17–27.

———, Reynolds Potter, and Clarice S. Stoll. "Sex Reannouncement in Hereditary Sex Deformity: Psychology
and Sociology of Habilitation." *Social Science and Medicine*
3 (1969): 207–216.

Oliven, John F. *Sexual Hygiene and Pathology: A Manual for the
Physician.* Philadelphia: J. B. Lippincott Co., 1955.

Ortner, Sherry B. "Is Female to Male as Nature Is to Culture?"
In *Woman, Culture, and Society,* ed. Michelle Zimbalist
Rosaldo and Louise Lamphere, 67–87. Stanford, Calif.:
Stanford University Press, 1974.

Rohatgi, M. "Intersex Disorders: An Approach to Surgical
Management." *Indian Journal of Pediatrics* 59 (1992): 523–530.

Roslyn, Joel J., Eric W. Fonkalsrud, and Barbara Lippe. "Intersex Disorders in Adolescents and Adults." *The American
Journal of Surgery* 146 (July 1983): 138–144.

Rubin, Jeffrey, F. J. Provenzano, and Z. Luria. "The Eye of the
Beholder: Parents' Views on Sex of Newborns." *American
Journal of Orthopsychiatry* 44, no. 4 (1974): 512–519.

Slijper, F. M. E., S. L. S. Drop, J. C. Molenaar, and R. J.
Scholtmeijer. "Neonates with Abnormal Genital Devel-
opment Assigned the Female Sex: Parent Counseling."
Journal of Sex Education and Therapy 20, no. 1 (1994): 9–17.

Smith, Richard W. "What Kind of Sex Is Natural?" In *The Frontiers of Sex Research,* ed. Vern Bullough, 103–111. Buffalo:
Prometheus, 1979.

Stoller, Robert J. *Sex and Gender,* vol. 1. New York: J. Aronson,
1968.

R E A D I N G *8*   **Maxine Baca Zinn
Bonnie Thornton Dill**

Theorizing Difference from Multiracial Feminism

Women of color have long challenged the hegemony
of feminisms constructed primarily around the lives of
white middle-class women. Since the late 1960s, U.S.
women of color have taken issue with unitary theories
of gender. Our critiques grew out of the widespread
concern about the exclusion of women of color from
feminist scholarship and the misinterpretation of our
experiences,[1] and ultimately "out of the very discourses, denying, permitting, and producing difference."[2] Speaking simultaneously from "within and
against" *both* women's liberation *and* antiracist move-

ments, we have insisted on the need to challenge systems of domination,[3] not merely as gendered subjects
but as women whose lives are affected by our location
in multiple hierarchies.

Recently, and largely in response to these challenges,
work that links gender to other forms of domination is
increasing. In this article, we examine this connection
further as well as the ways in which difference and diversity infuse contemporary feminist studies. Our analysis draws on a conceptual framework that we refer to as
"multiracial feminism."[4] This perspective is an attempt

to go beyond a mere recognition of diversity and difference among women to examine structures of domination, specifically the importance of race in understanding the social construction of gender. Despite the varied concerns and multiple intellectual stances which characterize the feminisms of women of color, they share an emphasis on race as a primary force situating genders differently. It is the centrality of race, of institutionalized racism, and of struggles against racial oppression that link the various feminist perspectives within this framework. Together, they demonstrate that racial meanings offer new theoretical directions for feminist thought.

TENSIONS IN CONTEMPORARY DIFFERENCE FEMINISM

Objections to the false universalism embedded in the concept "woman" emerged within other discourses as well as those of women of color.[5] Lesbian feminists and postmodern feminists put forth their own versions of what Susan Bordo has called "gender skepticism."[6]

Many thinkers within mainstream feminism have responded to these critiques with efforts to contextualize gender. The search for women's "universal" or "essential" characteristics is being abandoned. By examining gender in the context of other social divisions and perspectives, difference has gradually become important—even problematizing the universal categories of "women" and "men." Sandra Harding expresses the shift best in her claim that "there are no gender relations *per se,* but only gender relations as constructed by and between classes, races, and cultures."[7]

Many feminists now contend that difference occupies center stage as *the* project of women studies today.[8] According to one scholar, "difference has replaced equality as the central concern of feminist theory."[9] Many have welcomed the change, hailing it as a major revitalizing force in U.S. feminist theory.[10] But if *some* priorities within mainstream feminist thought have been refocused by attention to difference, there remains an "uneasy alliance"[11] between women of color and other feminists.

If difference has helped revitalize academic feminisms, it has also "upset the apple cart" and introduced new conflicts into feminist studies.[12] For example, in a recent and widely discussed essay, Jane Rowland Martin argues that the current preoccupation with difference is leading feminism into dangerous traps. She fears that in giving privileged status to a predetermined set of analytic categories (race, ethnicity, and class), "we affirm the existence of nothing but difference." She asks, "How do we know that for us, difference does not turn on being fat, or religious, or in an abusive relationship?"[13]

We, too, see pitfalls in some strands of the difference project. However, our perspectives take their bearings from social relations. Race and class differences are crucial, we argue, not as individual characteristics (such as being fat) but insofar as they are primary organizing principles of a society which locates and positions groups within that society's opportunity structures.

Despite the much-heralded diversity trend within feminist studies, difference is often reduced to mere pluralism: a "live and let live" approach where principles of relativism generate a long list of diversities which begin with gender, class, and race and continue through a range of social structural as well as personal characteristics.[14] Another disturbing pattern, which bell hooks refers to as "the commodification of difference," is the representation of diversity as a form of exotica, "a spice, seasoning that livens up the dull dish that is mainstream white culture."[15] The major limitation of these approaches is the failure to attend to the power relations that accompany difference. Moreover, these approaches ignore the inequalities that cause some characteristics to be seen as "normal" while others are seen as "different" and thus, deviant.

Maria C. Lugones expresses irritation at those feminists who see only the *problem* of difference without recognizing *difference*.[16] Increasingly, we find that difference *is* recognized. But this in no way means that difference occupies a "privileged" theoretical status. Instead of using difference to rethink the category of women, difference is often a euphemism for women who differ from the traditional norm. Even in purporting to accept difference, feminist pluralism often creates a social reality that reverts to universalizing women:

> So much feminist scholarship assumes that when we cut through all of the diversity among women created by differences of racial classification, ethnicity, social class, and sexual orientation, a "universal truth" concerning women and gender lies buried underneath. But if we can face the scary possibility that no such certainty exists and that persisting in such a search will always distort or omit someone's experiences, with what do we replace this old way of thinking? Gender differences and gender politics begin to look very different if there is no essential woman at the core.[17]

WHAT IS MULTIRACIAL FEMINISM?

A new set of feminist theories have emerged from the challenges put forth by women of color. Multiracial feminism is an evolving body of theory and practice informed by wide-ranging intellectual traditions. This framework does not offer a singular or unified feminism but a body of knowledge situating women and men in multiple systems of domination. U.S. multiracial feminism encompasses several emergent perspectives developed primarily by women of color: African Americans, Latinas, Asian Americans, and Native Americans, women whose analyses are shaped by their unique perspectives as "outsiders within"—marginal intellectuals whose social locations provide them with a particular perspective on self and society.[18] Although U.S. women of color represent many races and ethnic backgrounds—with different histories and cultures—our feminisms cohere in their treatment of race as a basic social division, a structure of power, a focus of political struggle, and hence a fundamental force in shaping women's and men's lives.

This evolving intellectual and political perspective uses several controversial terms. While we adopt the label "multiracial," other terms have been used to describe this broad framework. For example, Chela Sandoval refers to "U.S. Third World feminisms,"[19] while other scholars refer to "indigenous feminisms." In their theory text-reader, Alison M. Jagger and Paula M. Rothenberg adopt the label "multicultural feminism."[20]

We use "multiracial" rather than "multicultural" as a way of underscoring race as a power system that interacts with other structured inequalities to shape genders. Within the U.S. context, race, and the system of meanings and ideologies which accompany it, is a fundamental organizing principle of social relationships.[21] Race affects all women and men, although in different ways. Even cultural and group differences among women are produced through interaction within a racially stratified social order. Therefore, although we do not discount the importance of culture, we caution that cultural analytic frameworks that ignore race tend to view women's differences as the product of group-specific values and practices that often result in the marginalization of cultural groups which are then perceived as exotic expressions of a normative center. Our focus on race stresses the social construction of differently situated social groups and their varying degrees of advantage and power. Additionally, this emphasis on race takes on increasing political importance in an era where discourse about race is governed by color-evasive language[22] and a preference for individual rather than group remedies for social inequalities. Our analyses insist upon the primary and pervasive nature of race in contemporary U.S. society while at the same time acknowledging how race both shapes and is shaped by a variety of other social relations.

In the social sciences, multiracial feminism grew out of socialist feminist thinking. Theories about how political economic forces shape women's lives were influential as we began to uncover the social causes of racial ethnic women's subordination. But socialist feminism's concept of capitalist patriarchy, with its focus on women's unpaid (reproductive) labor in the home failed to address racial differences in the organization of reproductive labor. As feminists of color have argued, "reproductive labor has divided along racial as well as gender lines, and the specific characteristics have varied regionally and changed over time as capitalism has reorganized."[23] Despite the limitations of socialist feminism, this body of literature has been especially useful in pursuing questions about the interconnections among systems of domination.[24]

Race and ethnic studies was the other major social scientific source of multiracial feminism. It provided a basis for comparative analyses of groups that are socially and legally subordinated and remain culturally distinct within U.S. society. This includes the systematic discrimination of socially constructed racial groups and their distinctive cultural arrangements. Historically, the categories of African American, Latino, Asian American, and Native American were constructed as both racially and culturally distinct. Each group has a distinctive culture, shares a common heritage, and has developed a common identity within a larger society that subordinates them.[25]

We recognize, of course, certain problems inherent in an uncritical use of the multiracial label. First, the perspective can be hampered by a biracial model in which only African Americans and whites are seen as racial categories and all other groups are viewed through the prism of cultural differences. Latinos and Asians have always occupied distinctive places within the racial hierarchy, and current shifts in the composition of the U.S. population are racializing these groups anew.[26]

A second problem lies in treating multiracial feminism as a single analytical framework, and its principle architects, women of color, as an undifferentiated category. The concepts "multiracial feminism," "racial ethnic women," and "women of color" "homogenize quite different experiences and can falsely universalize experiences across race, ethnicity, sexual orientation, and age."[27] The feminisms created by women of color exhibit a plurality of intellectual and political positions. We speak in many voices, with inconsistencies that are born of our different social locations. Multiracial feminism embodies this plurality and richness. Our intent is not to falsely universalize women of color. Nor do we wish to promote a new racial essentialism in place of the old gender essentialism. Instead, we use these concepts to examine the structures and experiences produced by intersecting forms of race and gender.

It is also essential to acknowledge that race is a shifting and contested category whose meanings construct definitions of all aspects of social life.[28] In the United States it helped define citizenship by excluding everyone who was not a white, male property owner. It defined labor as slave or free, coolie or contract, and family as available only to those men whose marriages were recognized or whose wives could immigrate with them. Additionally, racial meanings are contested both within groups and between them.[29]

Although definitions of race are at once historically and geographically specific, they are also transnational, encompassing diasporic groups and crossing traditional geographic boundaries. Thus, while U.S. multiracial feminism calls attention to the fundamental importance of race, it must also locate the meaning of race within specific national traditions.

THE DISTINGUISHING FEATURES OF MULTIRACIAL FEMINISM

By attending to these problems, multiracial feminism offers a set of analytic premises for thinking about and theorizing gender. The following themes distinguish this branch of feminist inquiry.

First, multiracial feminism asserts that gender is constructed by a range of interlocking inequalities, what Patricia Hill Collins calls a "matrix of domination."[30] The idea of a matrix is that several fundamental systems work with and through each other. People experience race, class, gender, and sexuality differently depending upon their social location in the structures of race, class, gender, and sexuality. For example, people of the same race will experience race differently depending upon their location in the class structure as working class, professional managerial class, or unemployed; in the gender structure as female or male; and in structures of sexuality as heterosexual, homosexual, or bisexual.

Multiracial feminism also examines the simultaneity of systems in shaping women's experience and identity. Race, class, gender, and sexuality are not reducible to individual attributes to be measured and assessed for their separate contribution in explaining given social outcomes, an approach that Elizabeth Spelman calls "popbead metaphysics," where a woman's identity consists of the sum of parts neatly divisible from one another.[31] The matrix of domination seeks to account for the multiple ways that women experience themselves as gendered, raced, classed, and sexualized.

Second, multiracial feminism emphasizes the intersectional nature of hierarchies at all levels of social life. Class, race, gender, and sexuality are components of both social structure and social interaction. Women and men are differently embedded in locations created by these cross-cutting hierarchies. As a result, women and men throughout the social order experience different forms of privilege and subordination, depending on their race, class, gender, and sexuality. In other words, intersecting forms of domination produce *both* oppression *and* opportunity. At the same time that structures of race, class, and gender create disadvantages for women of color, they provide unacknowledged benefits for those who are at the top of these hierarchies—whites, members of the upper classes, and males. Therefore, multiracial feminism applies not only to racial ethnic women but also to women and men of all races, classes, and genders.

Third, multiracial feminism highlights the relational nature of dominance and subordination. Power is the cornerstone of women's differences.[32] This means that women's differences are *connected* in systematic ways.[33] Race is a vital element in the pattern of relations among minority and white women. As Linda Gordon argues, the very meanings of being a white woman in the United States have been affected by the existence of subordinated women of color: "They intersect in conflict and in occasional cooperation, but always in mutual influence."[34]

Fourth, multiracial feminism explores the interplay of social structure and women's agency. Within the constraints of race, class, and gender oppression, women create viable lives for themselves, their families, and their communities. Women of color have resisted and often undermined the forces of power that control them. From acts of quiet dignity and steadfast determination to involvement in revolt and rebellion, women struggle to shape their own lives. Racial oppression has been a common focus of the "dynamic of oppositional agency" of women of color. As Chandra Talpade Mohanty points out, it is the nature and organization of women's opposition which mediates and differentiates the impact of structures of domination.[35]

Fifth, multiracial feminism encompasses wide-ranging methodological approaches, and like other branches of feminist thought, relies on varied theoretical tools as well. Ruth Frankenberg and Lata Mani identify three guiding principles of inclusive feminist inquiry: "building complex analyses, avoiding erasure, specifying location."[36] In the last decade, the opening up of academic feminism has focused attention on social location in the production of knowledge. Most basically, research by and about marginalized women has destabilized what used to be considered as universal categories of gender. Marginalized locations are well suited for grasping social relations that remained obscure from more privileged vantage points. Lived experience, in other words, creates alternative ways of understanding the social world and the experience of different groups of women within it. Racially informed standpoint epistemologies have provided new topics, fresh questions, and new understandings of women and men. Women of color have, as Norma Alarcón argues, asserted ourselves as subjects, using our voices to challenge dominant conceptions of truth.[37]

Sixth, multiracial feminism brings together understandings drawn from the lived experiences of diverse and continuously changing groups of women. Among Asian Americans, Native Americans, Latinas, and Blacks are many different national cultural and ethnic groups. Each one is engaged in the process of testing, refining, and reshaping these broader categories in its own image. Such internal differences heighten awareness of and sensitivity to both commonalities and differences, serving as a constant reminder of the importance of comparative study and maintaining a creative tension between diversity and universalization.

DIFFERENCE AND TRANSFORMATION

Efforts to make women's studies less partial and less distorted have produced important changes in academic feminism. Inclusive thinking has provided a way to build multiplicity and difference into our analyses. This has led to the discovery that race matters for everyone. White women, too, must be reconceptualized as a category that is multiply defined by race, class, and other differences. As Ruth Frankenberg demonstrates

in a study of whiteness among contemporary women, all kinds of social relations, even those that appear neutral, are, in fact, racialized. Frankenberg further complicates the very notion of a unified white identity by introducing issues of Jewish identity.[38] Therefore, the lives of women of color cannot be seen as a *variation* on a more general model of white American womanhood. The model of womanhood that feminist social science once held as "universal" is also a product of race and class.

When we analyze the power relations constituting all social arrangements and shaping women's lives in distinctive ways, we can begin to grapple with core feminist issues about how genders are socially constructed and constructed differently. Women's difference is built into our study of gender. Yet this perspective is quite far removed from the atheoretical pluralism implied in much contemporary thinking about gender.

Multiracial feminism, in our view, focuses not just on differences but also on the way in which differences and domination intersect and are historically and socially constituted. It challenges feminist scholars to go beyond the mere recognition and inclusion of difference to reshape the basic concepts and theories of our disciplines. By attending to women's social location based on race, class, and gender, multiracial feminism seeks to clarify the structural sources of diversity. Ultimately, multiracial feminism forces us to see privilege and subordination as interrelated and to pose such questions as: How do the existences and experiences of all people—women and men, different racial-ethnic groups, and different classes—shape the experiences of each other? How are those relationships defined and enforced through social institutions that are the primary sites for negotiating power within society? How do these differences contribute to the construction of both individual and group identity? Once we acknowledge that all women are affected by the racial order of society, then it becomes clear that the insights of multiracial feminism provide an analytical framework, not solely for understanding the experiences of women of color but for understanding *all* women, and men, as well.

NOTES

1. Maxine Baca Zinn, Lynn Weber Cannon, Elizabeth Higginbotham, and Bonnie Thornton Dill, "The Costs of Exclusionary Practices in Women's Studies," *Signs* 11 (winter 1986): 290–303.

2. Chela Sandoval, "U.S. Third World Feminism: The Theory and Method of Oppositional Consciousness in the Postmodern World," *Genders* (spring 1991): 1–24.

3. Ruth Frankenberg and Lata Mani, "Cross Currents, Crosstalk: Race, 'Postcoloniality,' and the Politics of Location," *Cultural Studies* 7 (May 1993): 292–310.

4. We use the term "multiracial feminism" to convey the multiplicity of racial groups and feminist perspectives.

5. A growing body of work on difference in feminist thought now exists. Although we cannot cite all the current work, the following are representative: Michèle Barrett, "The Concept of Difference," *Feminist Review* 26 (July 1987): 29–42; Christina Crosby, "Dealing with Difference," in *Feminists Theorize the Political,* ed. Judith Butler and Joan W. Scott (New York: Routledge, 1992), 130–43; Elizabeth Fox-Genovese, "Difference, Diversity, and Divisions in an Agenda for the Women's Movement," in *Color, Class, and Country: Experiences of Gender,* ed. Gay Young and Bette J. Dickerson (London: Zed Books, 1994), 232–48; Nancy A. Hewitt, "Compounding Differences," *Feminist Studies* 18 (summer 1992): 313–26; Maria C. Lugones, "On the Logic of Feminist Pluralism," in *Feminist Ethics,* ed. Claudia Card (Lawrence: University of Kansas Press, 1991), 35–44; Rita S. Gallin and Anne Ferguson, "The Plurality of Feminism: Rethinking 'Difference,'" in *The Woman and International Development Annual* (Boulder: Westview Press, 1993), 3: 1–16; and Linda Gordon, "On Difference," *Genders* 10 (spring 1991): 91–111.

6. Susan Bordo, "Feminism, Postmodernism, and Gender Skepticism," in *Feminism/Postmodernism,* ed. Linda J. Nicholson (London: Routledge, 1990), 133–56.

7. Sandra G. Harding, *Whose Science? Whose Knowledge? Thinking from Women's Lives* (Ithaca: Cornell University Press, 1991), 179.

8. Crosby, 131.

9. Fox-Genovese, 232.

10. Faye Ginsberg and Anna Lowenhaupt Tsing, Introduction to *Uncertain Terms, Negotiating Gender in American Culture,* ed. Faye Ginsberg and Anna Lowenhaupt Tsing (Boston: Beacon Press, 1990), 3.

11. Sandoval, 2.

12. Sandra Morgan, "Making Connections: Socialist-Feminist Challenges to Marxist Scholarship," in *Women and a New Academy: Gender and Cultural Contexts,* ed. Jean F. O'Barr (Madison: University of Wisconsin Press, 1989), 149.

13. Jane Rowland Martin, "Methodological Essentialism, False Difference, and Other Dangerous Traps," *Signs* 19 (spring 1994): 647.

14. Barrett, 32.

15. bell hooks, *Black Looks: Race and Representation* (Boston: South End Press, 1992), 21.

16. Lugones, 35–44.

17. Patricia Hill Collins, Foreword to *Women of Color in U.S. Society,* ed. Maxine Baca Zinn and Bonnie Thornton Dill (Philadelphia: Temple University Press, 1994), xv.

18. Patricia Hill Collins, "Learning from the Outsider Within: The Sociological Significance of Black Feminist Thought," *Social Problems* 33 (December 1986): 514–32.

19. Sandoval, 1.

20. Alison M. Jagger and Paula S. Rothenberg, *Feminist Frameworks: Alternative Theoretical Accounts of the Relations between Women and Men,* 3d ed. (New York: McGraw-Hill, 1993).

21. Michael Omi and Howard Winant, *Racial Formation in the United States: From the 1960s to the 1980s,* 2d ed. (New York: Routledge, 1994).

22. Ruth Frankenberg, *The Social Construction of Whiteness: White Women, Race Matters* (Minneapolis: University of Minnesota Press, 1993).

23. Evelyn Nakano Glenn, "From Servitude to Service Work: Historical Continuities in the Racial Division of Paid Reproductive Labor," *Signs* 18 (autumn 1992): 3. See also Bonnie Thornton Dill, "Our Mothers' Grief: Racial-Ethnic Women and the Maintenance of Families," *Journal of Family History* 13, no. 4 (1988): 415–31.

24. Morgan, 146.

25. Maxine Baca Zinn and Bonnie Thornton Dill, "Difference and Domination," in *Women of Color in U.S. Society,* 11–22.

26. See Omi and Winant, 53–76, for a discussion of racial formation.

27. Margaret L. Andersen and Patricia Hill Collins, *Race, Class, and Gender: An Anthology* (Belmont, Calif.: Wadsworth, 1992), xvi.

28. Omi and Winant.

29. Nazli Kibria, "Migration and Vietnamese American Women: Remaking Ethnicity," in *Women of Color in U.S. Society,* 247–61.

30. Patricia Hill Collins, *Black Feminist Thought: Knowledge, Consciousness, and the Politics of Empowerment* (Boston: Unwin Hyman, 1990).

31. Elizabeth Spelman, *Inessential Women: Problems of Exclusion in Feminist Thought* (Boston: Beacon Press, 1988), 136.

32. Several discussions of difference make this point. See Baca Zinn and Dill, 10; Gordon, 106; and Lynn Weber, in the "Symposium on West and Fenstermaker's 'Doing Difference,'" *Gender & Society* 9 (August 1995): 515–19.

33. Glenn, 10.

34. Gordon, 106.

35. Chandra Talpade Mohanty, "Cartographies of Struggle: Third World Women and the Politics of Feminism," in *Third World Women and the Politics of Feminism,* ed. Chandra Talpade Mohanty, Ann Russo, and Lourdes Torres (Bloomington: Indiana University Press, 1991), 13.

36. Frankenberg and Mani, 306.

37. Norma Alarcón, "The Theoretical Subject(s) of *This Bridge Called My Back* and Anglo-American Feminism," in *Making Face, Making Soul, Haciendo Caras: Creative and Critical Perspectives by Women of Color,* ed. Gloria Anzaldúa (San Francisco: Aunt Lute, 1990), 356.

38. Frankenberg. See also Evelyn Torton Beck, "The Politics of Jewish Invisibility.'" *NWSA Journal* (fall 1988): 93–102.

Feminism without Borders

. . . The world we occupy now [is] a world that is definable only in relational terms, a world traversed with intersecting lines of power and resistance, a world that can be understood only in terms of its destructive divisions of gender, color, class, sexuality, and nation, a world that must be transformed through a necessary process of "pivoting the center" (to use Bettina Aptheker's words), for the assumed center (Europe and the United States) will no longer hold. But it is also a world with powerful histories of resistance and revolution in daily life and as organized liberation movements. And it is these contours that define the complex ground for the emergence and consolidation of Third World women's feminist politics. (I use the term "Third World" to designate geographical location and sociohistorical conjunctures. It thus incorporates so-called minority peoples or people of color in the United States.)

In fact, one of the distinctive features of contemporary societies is the internationalization of economies and labor forces. In industrial societies, the international division of economic production consisted in the geographical separation of raw material extraction (in primarily the Third World) from factory production (in the colonial capitals). With the rise of transnational corporations that dominate and organize the contemporary economic system, however, factories have migrated in search of cheap labor, and the nation-state is no longer an appropriate socioeconomic unit for analysis. In addition, the massive migration of ex-colonial populations to the industrial metropolises of Europe to fill the need for cheap labor has created new kinds of multiethnic and multiracial social formations similar to those in the United States. Contemporary postindustrial societies, thus, invite cross-national and cross-cultural analyses for explanation of their own internal features and socioeconomic constitution. Moreover, contemporary definitions of the Third World can no longer have the same geographical contours and boundaries they had for industrial societies. In the postindustrial world, systemic socioeconomic and ideological processes position the peoples of Africa, Asia, Latin America, and the Middle East, as well as "minority" populations (people of color) in the United States and Europe, in similar relationships to the state.

Thus, charting the ground for an analysis of Third World women and the politics of feminism is no easy task. First, there are the questions of definition: Who/what is the Third World? Do Third World women make up any kind of a constituency? On what basis? Can we assume that Third World women's political struggles are necessarily "feminist"? How do we/they define feminism? And second, there are the questions about context: Which/whose history do we draw on to chart this map of Third World women's engagement with feminism? How do questions of gender, race, and nation intersect in determining feminisms in the Third World? Who produces knowledge about colonized peoples and from what space/location? What are the politics of the production of this particular knowledge? What are the disciplinary parameters of this knowledge? What are the methods used to locate and chart Third World women's self and agency? Clearly, questions of definition and context overlap; in fact, as we develop more complex, nuanced modes of asking questions and as scholarship in a number of relevant fields begins to address histories of colonialism, capitalism, race, and gender as inextricably interrelated, our very conceptual maps are redrawn and transformed. How we conceive of definitions and contexts, on what basis we foreground certain contexts over others, and how we understand the ongoing shifts in our conceptual cartographies—these are all questions of great importance in this particular cartography of Third World feminisms.

I write this cartography from my own particular political, historical, and intellectual location, as a Third World feminist trained in the United States, interested in questions of culture, knowledge production, and activism in an international context. The maps I draw are necessarily anchored in my own discontinuous locations. In this [reading], then, I attempt to formulate an initial and necessarily noncomprehensive response to the above questions. Thus this [reading] offers a very partial conceptual map: it touches upon certain contexts and foregrounds particular definitions and strategies. I see this as a map that will of necessity have to be redrawn as our analytic and conceptual skills and knowledge develop and transform the way we understand questions of history, consciousness, and agency. This [reading] will also suggest significant questions and directions for feminist analysis—an analysis that is made possible by the precise challenges posed by "race" and postcolonial studies to the second wave of white Western feminisms, and by feminist anticapitalist critique to economic globalization and neoliberalism. I believe that these challenges suggest new questions for feminist historiography and epistemology, as well as point toward necessary reconceptualizations of ideas of resistance, community, and agency in daily life.

DEFINITIONS: THIRD WORLD WOMEN AND FEMINISM

Unlike the history of Western (white, middle-class) feminisms, which has been explored in great detail over the last few decades, histories of Third World women's engagement with feminism are in short supply. There is a large body of work on "women in developing countries," but this does not necessarily engage feminist questions. A substantial amount of scholarship has accumulated on women in liberation movements, or on the role and status of women in individual cultures. However, this scholarship also does not necessarily engage questions of feminist historiography. Constructing such histories often requires reading against the grain of a number of intersecting progressive discourses (e.g., white feminist, Third World nationalist, and socialist), as well as the politically regressive racist, imperialist, sexist discourses of slavery, colonialism, and contemporary capitalism. The very notion of addressing what are often internally conflictual histories of Third World women's feminisms under a single rubric, in one chapter, may seem ludicrous—especially since the very meaning of the term "feminism" is continually contested. For, it can be argued, there are no simple ways of representing these diverse struggles and histories. Just as it is difficult to speak of a singular entity called "Western feminism," it is difficult to generalize about "Third World feminisms." But in much of my scholarship, I have chosen to foreground "Third World women" as an analytical and

political category; thus I want to recognize and analytically explore the links among the histories and struggles of Third World women against racism, sexism, colonialism, imperialism, and monopoly capital. I am suggesting, then, an "imagined community" of Third World oppositional struggles—"imagined" not because it is not "real" but because it suggests potential alliances and collaborations across divisive boundaries, and "community" because in spite of internal hierarchies within Third World contexts, it nevertheless suggests a significant, deep commitment to what Benedict Anderson, in referring to the idea of the nation, calls "horizontal comradeship."[1]

The idea of imagined community is useful because it leads us away from essentialist notions of Third World feminist struggles, suggesting political rather than biological or cultural bases for alliance. It is not color or sex that constructs the ground for these struggles. Rather, it is the way we think about race, class, and gender—the political links we choose to make among and between struggles. Thus, potentially, women of all colors (including white women) can align themselves with and participate in these imagined communities. However, clearly our relation to and centrality in particular struggles depend on our different, often conflictual, locations and histories. This, then, is what indelibly marks this discussion of Third World women and the politics of feminism together: imagined communities of women with divergent histories and social locations, woven together by the political threads of opposition to forms of domination that are not only pervasive but also systemic. An example of a similar construct is the notion of "communities of resistance," which refers to the broad-based opposition of refugee, migrant, and black groups in Britain to the idea of a common nation: Europe 1992 (now the European Union). "Communities of resistance," like "imagined communities," is a political definition, not an essentialist one. It is not based on any ahistorical notion of the inherent resistance and resilience of Third World peoples. It is, however, based on a historical, material analysis of the concrete disenfranchising effects of Europe 1992 on Third World communities in Britain and the necessity of forming "resistant/oppositional" communities that fight this. However, while such imagined communities are historically and geographically concrete, their boundaries are necessarily fluid. They have to be, since the operation of power is always fluid and changing. Thus I do not posit any homogeneous configuration of Third World women who form communities because they share a "gender" or a "race" or a "nation." As history (and recent feminist scholarship) teaches us, "races" and "nations" haven't been defined on the basis of inherent, natural characteristics; nor can we define "gender" in any transhistorical, unitary way.[2] So where does this leave us?

Geographically, the nation-states of Latin America, the Caribbean, sub-Saharan Africa, South and Southeast Asia, China, South Africa, and Oceania constitute the parameters of the non-European Third World. In addition, black, Latino, Asian, and indigenous peoples in the United States, Europe, and Australia, some of whom have historic links with the geographically defined Third World, also refer to themselves as Third World peoples. With such a broad canvas, racial, sexual, national, economic, and cultural borders are difficult to demarcate, shaped politically as they are in individual and collective practice.

THIRD WORLD WOMEN AS SOCIAL CATEGORY

. . . Scholars often locate "Third World women" in terms of the underdevelopment, oppressive traditions, high illiteracy, rural and urban poverty, religious fanaticism, and "overpopulation" of particular Asian, African, Middle Eastern, and Latin American countries. Corresponding analyses of "matriarchal" black women on welfare, "illiterate" Chicana farmworkers, and "docile" Asian domestic workers also abound in the context of the United States. Besides being normed on a white, Western (read: progressive/modern) or non-Western (read: backward/traditional) hierarchy, these analyses freeze Third World women in time, space, and history. For example, in analyzing indicators of Third World women's status and roles, Momsen and Townsend (1987) designate the following categories of analysis: life expectancy, sex ratio, nutrition, fertility, income-generating activities, education, and the new international division of labor. Of these, fertility issues and Third World women's incorporation into multinational factory employment are identified as two of the most significant aspects of "women's worlds" in Third World countries.

While such descriptive information is useful and necessary, these presumably "objective" indicators by no means exhaust the meaning of women's day-to-day lives. The everyday, fluid, fundamentally historical and dynamic nature of the lives of Third World women is here collapsed into a few frozen "indicators" of their well-being. Momsen and Townsend (1987) state that in fact fertility is the most studied aspect of women's lives

in the Third World (36). This particular fact speaks volumes about the predominant representations of Third World women in social-scientific knowledge production. And our representations of Third World women circumscribe our understanding and analysis of feminism as well as of the daily struggles women engage in these circumstances.

For instance, compare the analysis of fertility offered by Momsen and Townsend (as a social indicator of women's status) with the analysis of population policy and discussions on sexuality among poor Brazilian women offered by Barroso and Bruschini (1991). By analyzing the politics of family planning in the context of the Brazilian women's movement, and examining the way poor women build collective knowledge about sex education and sexuality, Barroso and Bruschini link state policy and social movements with the politics of everyday life, thus presenting us with a dynamic, historically specific view of the struggles of Brazilian women in the barrios. . . . Our definitions, descriptions, and interpretations of Third World women's engagement with feminism must necessarily be simultaneously historically specific and dynamic, not frozen in time in the form of a spectacle.

Thus if the above "social indicators" are inadequate descriptions/interpretations of women's lives, on what basis do Third World women form any constituency? First, just as Western women or white women cannot be defined as coherent interest groups, Third World women also do not constitute any automatic unitary group. Alliances and divisions of class, religion, sexuality, and history, for instance, are necessarily internal to each of the above groups. Second, ideological differences in understandings of the social mediate any assumption of a natural bond between women. After all, there is no logical and necessary connection between being female and becoming feminist. Finally, defining Third World women in terms of their "problems" or their "achievements" in relation to an imagined free white liberal democracy effectively removes them (and the liberal democracy) from history, freezing them in time and space.

A number of scholars in the United States have written about the inherently political definition of the term "women of color" (a term often used interchangeably with "Third World women," as I am doing here).[3] This term designates a political constituency, not a biological or even sociological one. It is a sociopolitical designation for people of African, Caribbean, Asian, and Latin American descent, and native peoples of the United States. It also refers to "new immigrants" to the United States in the last three decades: Arab,

Korean, Thai, Laotian, and so on. What seems to constitute "women of color" or "Third World women" as a viable oppositional alliance is a common context of struggle rather than color or racial identifications. Similarly, it is Third World women's oppositional political relation to sexist, racist, and imperialist structures that constitutes our potential commonality. Thus it is the common context of struggles against specific exploitative structures and systems that determines our potential political alliances. It is this common context of struggle, both historical and contemporary, that the next section charts and defines.

WHY FEMINISM?

Before proceeding to consider the structural, historical parameters that lead to Third World women's particular politics, we should understand how women in different sociocultural and historical locations formulate their relation to feminism. The term "feminism" is itself questioned by many Third World women. Feminist movements have been challenged on the grounds of cultural imperialism and of shortsightedness in defining the meaning of gender in terms of middle-class, white experiences, internal racism, classism, and homophobia. All of these factors, as well as the falsely homogeneous representation of the movement by the media, have led to a very real suspicion of "feminism" as a productive ground for struggle. Nevertheless, Third World women have always engaged with feminism, even if the label has been rejected in a number of instances. In the introduction to a collection of writings by black and Third World women in Britain (Grewal et al. 1988), the editors are careful to focus on the contradictions, conflicts, and differences among black women, while emphasizing that the starting point for all contributors has been "the historical link between us of colonialism and imperialism" (Grewal et al. 1988, 6). The editors maintain that this book, the first publication of its kind, is about the "idea of Blackness" in contemporary Britain:

> An idea as yet unmatured and inadequately defined, but proceeding along its path in both "real" social life and in the collective awareness of many of its subjects. Both as an idea and a process it is, inevitably, contradictory. Contradictory in its conceptualization because its linguistic expression is defined in terms of colour, yet it is an idea transcendent of colour. Contradictory in its material movements because the unity of action, conscious or otherwise, of Asians, Latin Americans and

Arabs, Caribbeans and Africans, gives political expression to a common "colour," even as the State-created fissures of ethnicity threaten to engulf and overwhelm us in islands of cultural exclusivity. (I)

This definition of the idea of "Blackness" in Britain, and of "the unity of action" as the basis for black and Third World women's engagement with feminist politics, echoes the idea of a common context of struggle. British colonialism and the migration of colonized populations to the "home country" form the common historical context for British Third World women, as do, for instance, contemporary struggles against racist immigration and naturalization laws.[4]

The text that corresponds to *Charting the Journey* in the U.S. context was published a few years earlier, in 1981: *This Bridge Called My Back: Writings by Radical Women of Color*.[5] In the introduction to this groundbreaking book, Cherríe Moraga and Gloria Anzaldúa delineate the major areas of concern for a broad-based political movement of U.S. Third World women:

- how visibility/invisibility as women of color forms our radicalism;
- the ways in which Third World women derive a feminist political theory specifically from our racial/cultural background and experience;
- the destructive and demoralizing effects of racism in the women's movement;
- the cultural, class, and sexuality differences that divide women of color;
- Third World women's writing as a tool for self-preservation and revolution; and
- the ways and means of a Third World feminist future. (Moraga and Anzaldúa 1981, xxiv)

A number of ideas central to Third World feminisms emerge from these two passages. Aida Hurtado (1989) adds a further layer: in discussing the significance of the idea "the personal is political" to communities of white women and women of color in the United States, she distinguishes between the relevance of the public/private distinction for American white middle- and upper-class women, and working-class women and women of color who have always been subject to state intervention in their domestic lives:

> Women of Color have not had the benefit of the economic conditions that underlie the public/private distinction. Instead the political consciousness of

women of Color stems from an awareness that the public is *personally* political. Welfare programs and policies have discouraged family life, sterilization programs have restricted reproduction rights, government has drafted and armed disproportionate numbers of people of Color to fight its wars overseas, and locally, police forces and the criminal justice system arrest and incarcerate disproportionate numbers of people of Color. There is no such thing as a private sphere for people of Color except that which they manage to create and protect in an otherwise hostile environment. (Hurtado 1989, 849)

Hurtado introduces the contemporary liberal, capitalist state as a major actor and focus of activity for women of color in the United States. Her discussion suggests that in fact, the politics of "personal life" may be differently defined for middle-class whites and for people of color.[6] Finally, Kumari Jayawardena, writing about feminist movements in Asia in the late nineteenth and early twentieth centuries, defines feminism as "embracing movements for equality within the current system and significant struggles that have attempted to change the system" (Jayawardena 1986, 2). She goes on to assert that these movements arose in the context of the formulation and consolidation of national identities that mobilized anti-imperialist movements during independence struggles and the remaking of precapitalist religious and feudal structures in attempts to "modernize" Third World societies. Here again, the common link between political struggles of women in India, Indonesia, and Korea, for instance, is the fight against racist, colonialist states and for national independence.

To sum up, Third World women's writings on feminism have consistently focused on the idea of the simultaneity of oppressions as fundamental to the experience of social and political marginality and the grounding of feminist politics in the histories of racism and imperialism; the crucial role of a hegemonic state in circumscribing their/our daily lives and survival struggles; the significance of memory and writing in the creation of oppositional agency; and the differences, conflicts, and contradictions internal to Third World women's organizations and communities. In addition, they have insisted on the complex interrelationships between feminist, antiracist, and nationalist struggles. In fact, the challenge of Third World feminisms to white, Western feminisms has been precisely this inescapable link between feminist and political

liberation movements. In fact, black, white, and other Third World women have very different histories with respect to the particular inheritance of post-fifteenth-century Euro-American hegemony: the inheritance of slavery, enforced migration, plantation and indentured labor, colonialism, imperial conquest, and genocide. Thus, Third World feminists have argued for the rewriting of history based on the specific locations and histories of struggle of people of color and postcolonial peoples, and on the day-to-day strategies of survival utilized by such peoples.

The urgency of rewriting and rethinking these histories and struggles is suggested by A. Sivanandan in his searing critique of the identity politics of the 1980s social movements in Britain, which, he argues, leads to a flight from class:

> For [the poor, the black, the unemployed] the distinction between the mailed fist and the velvet glove is a stylistic abstraction, the defining limit between consent and force a middle-class fabrication. Black youth in the inner cities know only the blunt force of the state, those on income support have it translated for them in a thousand not so subtle ways. If we are to extend the freedoms in civil society through a politics of hegemony, those who stand at the intersection of consent and coercion should surely be our first constituency and guide—a yardstick to measure our politics by. How do you extend a "politics of food" to the hungry, a "politics of the body" to the homeless, a "politics of the family" for those without an income? How do any of these politics connect up with the Third World? . . . Class cannot just be a matter of identity, it has to be the focus of commitment. (Sivanandan 1990, 18–19)

In foregrounding the need to build our politics around the struggles of the most exploited peoples of the world, and in drawing attention to the importance of a materialist definition of class in opposition to identity based social movements and discourses, Sivanandan underscores both the significance and the difficulty of rewriting counterhegemonic histories. His analysis questions the contemporary identity-based philosophy of social movements that define "discourse" as an adequate terrain of struggle. While discursive categories are clearly central sites of political contestation, they must be grounded in and informed by the material politics of everyday life, especially the daily life struggles for survival of poor people—those written out of history.

NOTES

1. Anderson 1983, esp. 11–16.
2. See Scott 1986 and essays in *Signs* 1989.
3. See, for instance, Chela Sandoval's work on the construction of the category "Women of Color" in the United States and her theorization of oppositional consciousness (Sandoval 1983, 1991, and 2000). Norma Alarcon 1990 offers an important conceptualization of Third World women as subjects in her essay "The Theoretical Subject(s) of *This Bridge Called My Back* and Anglo-American Feminism." See also Moraga and Anzaldúa 1981, hooks 1984, and Anzaldúa 1987 for similar conceptualizations.

4. Grewal, Kay, Landor, Lewis, and Parmar 1988, 1; see also Bryan et al. 1985, Bhabha et al. 1985, and *Feminist Review* 1984.
5. Moraga and Anzaldúa 1981.
6. My use of Hurtado's analysis is not meant to suggest that the state does not intervene in the "private" sphere of the white middle and upper classes; merely that historically, people of color and white people have a differential (and hierarchical) relation to state rule.

REFERENCES

Alarcon, Norma. 1989. "The Theoretical Subject(s) of *This Bridge Called My Back* and Anglo-American Feminism. In *Chicana Criticism in a Social Context,* edited by H. Calderon and J.D. Saldivar. Durham, NC: Duke University Press.

Anderson, Benedict. 1983. *Imagined Communities: Reflections on the Origin and Spread of Nationalism.* New York: Verso Books.

Anzaldúa, Gloria. 1987. *Borderlands/La Frontera: The New Mestiza.* San Francisco: Spinsters/Aunt Lute.

Barroso, Carmen, and Christina Bruschini. 1991. "Building Politics from Personal Lives: Discussions on Sexuality among Poor Women in Brazil." In *Third World Women and the Politics of Feminism,* edited by Chandra Talpade Mohanty, Ann Russo, and Lourdes Torres. Bloomington: Indiana University Press.

Bhaba, Jacqueline, et al. 1985. *Worlds Apart: Women under Immigration and Nationality Law.* London: Pluto Press.

Bryan, Beverly, et al. 1985. *The Heart of the Race: Black Women's Lives in Britain.* London: Virago.

Feminist Review. 1984. Special Issue: *Many Voices, One Chant: Black Feminist Perspectives.* Vol. 17 (Autumn).

Grewal, S., Jackie Kay, Liliane Landor, Gail Lewis, and Pratibha Parmar, eds. 1988. *Charting the Journey: Writings by Black and Third World Women.* London: Sheba Feminist Publishers.

hooks, bell. 1984. *Feminist Theory: From Margin to Center.* Boston: South End Press.

Hurtado, Aida. 1989. "Relating to Privilege: Seduction and Rejection in the Subordination of White Women and Women of Color." *Signs* 14, no. 4 (summer): 833–55.

Jayawardena, Kumari. 1986. *Feminism and Nationalism in the Third World.* London: Zed Press.

Momsen, Janet Henshall, and Janet G. Townsend. 1987. *Geography of Gender in the Third World.* Albany: State University of New York Press.

Moraga, Cherrie, and Gloria Anzaldúa. 1981. *This Bridge Called My Back: Writings by Radical Women of Color.* Albany: Kitchen Table Press.

Sandoval, Chela. 2000. *Methodology of the Oppressed.* Minneapolis: University of Minnesota Press.

———. 1991. "U.S. Third World: The Theory and Method of Oppositional Consciousness in the Postmodern World, *Genders* 10 (spring): 1–24.

———. 1983. "Women Respond to Racism: A Report on the National Women's Studies Association Conference, Storrs, Connecticut" Occasional Paper Series. Oakland, Calif.: Center for Third World Organizing, 1995.

Scott, Joan. 1986. "Gender: A Useful Category of Historical Analysis." *American Historical Review* 91, no. 5: 1053–75.

Signs. 1989. Special Issue: *Common Grounds and Crossroads: Race, Ethnicity and Class in Women's Lives.* Vol. 14, no. 4 (summer).

Sivandandan, A. 1990. "All That Melts into Air Is Solid: The Hokum of the New Times." *Race and Class* 31, no. 3: 1–30.

Masculinities and Globalization

The current wave of research and debate on masculinity stems from the impact of the women's liberation movement on men, but it has taken time for this impact to produce a new intellectual agenda. Most discussions of men's gender in the 1970s and early 1980s centered on an established concept, the male sex role, and an established problem: how men and boys were socialized into this role. There was not much new empirical research. What there was tended to use the more abstracted methods of social psychology (e.g., paper-and-pencil masculinity/femininity scales) to measure generalized attitudes and expectations in ill-defined populations. The largest body of empirical research was the continuing stream of quantitative studies of sex differences—which continued to be disappointingly slight (Carrigan, Connell, and Lee 1985).

The concept of a unitary male sex role, however, came under increasing criticism for its multiple over-simplifications and its incapacity to handle issues about power (Kimmel 1987; Connell 1987). New conceptual frameworks were proposed that linked feminist work on institutionalized patriarchy, gay theoretical work on homophobia, and psychoanalytic ideas about the person (Carrigan, Connell, and Lee 1985; Hearn 1987). Increasing attention was given to certain studies that located issues about masculinity in a fully described local context, whether a British printing shop (Cockburn 1983) or a Papuan mountain community (Herdt 1981). By the late 1980s, a genre of empirical research based on these ideas was developing, most clearly in sociology but also in anthropology, history, organization studies, and cultural studies. This has borne fruit in the 1990s in what is now widely recognized as a new generation of social research on masculinity and men in gender relations (Connell 1995; *Widersprueche* 1995; Segal 1997).

Although the recent research has been diverse in subject matter and social location, its characteristic focus is the construction of masculinity in a particular milieu or moment—a clergyman's family (Tosh 1991), a professional sports career (Messner 1992), a small group of gay men (Connell 1992), a bodybuilding gym (Klein 1993), a group of colonial schools (Morrell 1994), an urban police force (McElhinny 1994), drinking groups in bars (Tomsen 1997), a corporate office on the verge of a decision (Messerschmidt 1997). Accordingly, we might think of this as the "ethnographic moment" in masculinity research, in which the specific and the local are in focus. (This is not to deny that this work *deploys* broader structural concepts simply to note the characteristic focus of the empirical work and its analysis.)

The ethnographic moment brought a much-needed gust of realism to debates on men and masculinity, a corrective to the simplifications of role theory. It also provided a corrective to the trend in popular culture where vague discussions of men's sex roles were giving way to the mystical generalities of the mythopoetic movement and the extreme simplifications of religious revivalism.

Although the rich detail of the historical and field studies defies easy summary, certain conclusions emerge from this body of research as a whole. In short form, they are the following.

Plural Masculinities A theme of theoretical work in the 1980s, the multiplicity of masculinities has now been very fully documented by descriptive research. Different cultures and different periods of history construct gender differently. Striking differences exist, for instance, in the relationship of homosexual practice to dominant forms of masculinity (Herdt 1984). In multicultural societies, there are varying definitions and enactments of masculinity, for instance, between Anglo and Latino communities in the United States (Hondagneu-Sotelo and Messner 1994). Equally important, more than one kind of masculinity can be found within a given cultural setting or institution. This is particularly well documented in school studies (Foley 1990) but can also be observed in workplaces (Messerschmidt 1997) and the military (Barrett 1996).

Hierarchy and Hegemony These plural masculinities exist in definite social relations, often relations of hierarchy and exclusion. This was recognized early, in gay theorists' discussions of homophobia; it has become clear that the implications are far-reaching. There is generally a hegemonic form of masculinity, the most honored or desired in a particular context. For Western popular culture, this is extensively documented in research on media representations of masculinity (McKay and Huber 1992). The hegemonic form need not be the most common form of masculinity. Many men live in a state of some tension with, or distance from, hegemonic masculinity; others (such as sporting heroes) are taken as exemplars of hegemonic masculinity and are required to live up to it strenuously (Connell 1990a). The dominance of hegemonic masculinity over other forms may be quiet and implicit, but it may also be vehement and violent, as in the important case of homophobic violence.

Collective Masculinities Masculinities, as patterns of gender practice, are sustained and enacted not only by individuals but also by groups and institutions. This fact was visible in Cockburn's (1983) pioneering research on informal workplace culture, and it has been confirmed over and over: in workplaces (Donaldson 1991), in organized sport (Whitson 1990; Messner 1992), in schools (Connell 1996), and so on. This point must be taken with the previous two: institutions may construct multiple masculinities and define relationships between them. Barrett's (1996) illuminating study of hegemonic masculinity in the U.S. Navy shows how this takes different forms in the different subbranches of the one military organization.

Bodies as Arenas Men's bodies do not determine the patterns of masculinity, but they are still of great importance in masculinity. Men's bodies are addressed, defined and disciplined (as in sport; see Theberge 1991), and given outlets and pleasures by the gender order of society. But men's bodies are not blank slates. The enactment of masculinity reaches certain limits, for instance, in the destruction of the industrial worker's body (Donaldson 1991). Masculine conduct with a female body is felt to be anomalous or transgressive, like feminine conduct with a male body; research on gender crossing (Bolin 1988) shows the work that must be done to sustain an anomalous gender.

Active Construction Masculinities do not exist prior to social interaction, but come into existence as people act. They are actively produced, using the resources and strategies available in a given milieu. Thus the exemplary masculinities of sports professionals are not a product of passive disciplining, but as Messner (1992) shows, result from a sustained, active engagement with the demands of the institutional setting, even to the point of serious bodily damage from "playing hurt" and accumulated stress. With boys learning masculinities, much of what was previously taken as socialization appears, in close-focus studies of schools (Walker 1988; Thorne 1993), as the outcome of intricate and intense maneuvering in peer groups, classes, and adult-child relationships.

Contradiction Masculinities are not homogeneous, simple states of being. Close-focus research on masculinities commonly identifies contradictory desires and conduct; for instance, in Klein's (1993) study of bodybuilders, the contradiction between the heterosexual definition of hegemonic masculinity and the homosexual practice by which some of the bodybuilders finance the making of an exemplary body. Psychoanalysis provides the classic evidence of conflicts within personality, and recent psychoanalytic writing (Chodorow 1994; Lewes 1988) has laid some emphasis on the conflicts and emotional compromises within both hegemonic and subordinated forms of masculinity. Life-history research influenced by existential psychoanalysis (Connell 1995) has similarly traced contradictory projects and commitments within particular forms of masculinity.

Dynamics Masculinities created in specific historical circumstances are liable to reconstruction, and any pattern of hegemony is subject to contestation, in which a dominant masculinity may be displaced. Heward (1988) shows the changing gender regime of a boys' school responding to the changed strategies of the families in its clientele. Roper (1991) shows the displacement of a production-oriented masculinity among engineering managers by new financially oriented generic managers. Since the 1970s, the reconstruction of masculinities has been pursued as a conscious politics. Schwalbe's (1996) close examination of one mythopoetic group shows the complexity of the practice and the limits of the reconstruction.

If we compare this picture of masculinity with earlier understandings of the male sex role, it is clear that the ethnographic moment in research has already had important intellectual fruits.

Nevertheless, it has always been recognized that some issues go beyond the local. For instance, mythopoetic movements such as the highly visible Promise Keepers are part of a spectrum of masculinity politics; Messner (1997) shows for the United States that this spectrum involves at least eight conflicting agendas for the remaking of masculinity. Historical studies such as Phillips (1987) on New Zealand and Kimrnel (1996) on the United States have traced the changing public constructions of masculinity for whole countries over long periods; ultimately, such historical reconstructions are essential for understanding the meaning of ethnographic details.

I consider that this logic must now be taken a step further, and in taking this step, we will move toward a new agenda for the whole field. What happens in localities is affected by the history of whole countries, but what happens in countries is affected by the history of the world. Locally situated lives are now (indeed, have long been) powerfully influenced by geopolitical struggles, global markets, multinational corporations, labor migration, transnational media. It is time for this fundamental fact to be built into our analysis of men and masculinities.

To understand local masculinities, we must think in global terms. But how? That is the problem pursued in this article. I will offer a framework for thinking about masculinities as a feature of world society and for thinking about men's gender practices in terms of the global structure and dynamics of gender. This is by no means to reject the ethnographic moment in masculinity research. It is, rather, to think how we can use its findings more adequately.

THE WORLD GENDER ORDER

Masculinities do not first exist and then come into contact with femininities; they are produced together, in the process that constitutes a gender order. Accordingly, to understand the masculinities on a world scale, we must first have a concept of the globalization of gender.

This is one of the most difficult points in current gender analysis because the very conception is counterintuitive. We are so accustomed to thinking of gender as the attribute of an individual, even as an unusually intimate attribute, that it requires a considerable wrench to think of gender on the vast scale of global society. Most relevant discussions, such as the literature on women and development, fudge the issue.

They treat the entities that extend internationally (markets, corporations, intergovernmental programs, etc.) as ungendered in principle—but affecting unequally gendered recipients of aid in practice, because of bad policies. Such conceptions reproduce the familiar liberal-feminist view of the state as in principle gender-neutral, though empirically dominated by men.

But if we recognize that very large scale institutions such as the state are themselves gendered, in quite precise and specifiable ways (Comell 1990b), and if we recognize that international relations, international trade, and global markets are inherently an arena of gender formation and gender politics (Enloe 1990), then we can recognize the existence of a world gender order. The term can be defined as the structure of relationships that interconnect the gender regimes of institutions, and the gender orders of local society, on a world scale. That is, however, only a definition. The substantive questions remain: what is the shape of that structure, how tightly are its elements linked, how has it arisen historically, what is its trajectory into the future?

Current business and media talk about globalization pictures a homogenizing process sweeping across the world, driven by new technologies, producing vast unfettered global markets in which all participate on equal terms. This is a misleading image. As Hirst and Thompson (1996) show, the global economy is highly unequal and the current degree of homogenization is often overestimated. Multinational corporations based in the three major economic powers (the United States, European Union, and Japan) are the major economic actors worldwide.

The structure bears the marks of its history. Modern global society was historically produced as Wallerstein (1974) argued, by the economic and political expansion of European states from the fifteenth century on and by the creation of colonial empires. It is in this process that we find the roots of the modern world gender order. Imperialism was, from the start, a gendered process. Its first phase, colonial conquest and settlement, was carried out by gender-segregated forces, and it resulted in massive disruption of indigenous gender orders. In its second phase, the stabilization of colonial societies, new gender divisions of labor were produced in plantation economies and colonial cities, while gender ideologies were linked with racial hierarchies and the cultural defense of empire. The third phase, marked by political decolonization, economic neocolonialism, and the current growth of world markets and structures of financial control, has seen gender divisions of labor remade on a massive scale in the "global factory" (Fuentes and Ehrenreich 1983), as well as the spread of gendered violence alongside Western military technology.

The result of this history is a partially integrated, highly unequal and turbulent world society, in which gender relations are partly but unevenly linked on a global scale. The unevenness becomes clear when different substructures of gender (Connell 1987; Walby 1990) are examined separately.

The Division of Labor   A characteristic feature of colonial and neocolonial economies was the restructuring of local production systems to produce a male wage worker–female domestic worker couple (Mies 1986). This need not produce a "housewife" in the Western suburban sense, for instance, where the wage work involved migration to plantations or mines (Moodie 1994). But it has generally produced the identification of masculinity with the public realm and the money economy and of femininity with domesticity, which is a core feature of the modern European gender system (Holter 1997).

Power Relations   The colonial and postcolonial world has tended to break down purdah systems of patriarchy in the name of modernization, if not of women's emancipation (Kandiyoti 1994). At the same time, the creation of a westernized public realm has seen the growth of large-scale organizations in the form of the state and corporations, which in the great majority of cases are culturally masculinized and controlled by men. In *comprador* capitalism, however, the power of local elites depends on their relations with the metropolitan powers, so the hegemonic masculinities of neocolonial societies are uneasily poised between local and global cultures.

Emotional Relations   Both religious and cultural missionary activity has corroded indigenous homosexual and cross-gender practice, such as the native American *berdache* and the Chinese "passion of the cut sleeve" (Hinsch 1990). Recently developed Western models of romantic heterosexual love as the basis for marriage and of gay identity as the main alternative have now circulated globally—though as Altman (1996) observes, they do not simply displace indigenous models, but interact with them in extremely complex ways.

Symbolization   Mass media, especially electronic media, in most parts of the world follow North American and European models and relay a great deal of metropolitan content; gender imagery is an important part of what is circulated. A striking example is the reproduction of a North American imagery of femininity by Xuxa, the blonde television superstar in Brazil (Simpson 1993). In counterpoint, exotic gender imagery has been used in the marketing strategies of newly industrializing countries (e.g., airline advertising from Southeast Asia)—a tactic based on the longstanding combination of the exotic and the erotic in the colonial imagination (Jolly 1997).

Clearly, the world gender order is not simply an extension of a traditional European-American gender order. That gender order was changed by colonialism, and elements from other cultures now circulate globally. Yet in no sense do they mix on equal terms, to produce a United Colours of Benetton gender order. The culture and institutions of the North Atlantic countries are hegemonic within the emergent world system. This is crucial for understanding the kinds of masculinities produced within it.

THE REPOSITIONING OF MEN AND THE RECONSTITUTION OF MASCULINITIES

The positioning of men and the constitution of masculinities may be analyzed at any of the levels at which gender practice is configured: in relation to the body, in personal life, and in collective social practice. At each level, we need to consider how the processes of globalization influence configurations of gender.

Men's bodies are positioned in the gender order, and enter the gender process, through body-reflexive practices in which bodies are both objects and agents (Connell 1995)—including sexuality, violence, and labor. The conditions of such practice include where one is and who is available for interaction. So it is a fact of considerable importance for gender relations that the global social order distributes and redistributes bodies, through migration, and through political controls over movement and interaction.

The creation of empire was the original "elite migration," though in certain cases mass migration followed. Through settler colonialism, something close to the gender order of Western Europe was reassembled in North America and in Australia. Labor migration within the colonial systems was a means by which gender practices were spread, but also a means by which they were reconstructed, since labor migration was itself a gendered process—as we have seen in relation to the gender division of labor. Migration from the colonized world to the metropole became (except for Japan) a mass process in the decades after World War II. There is also migration within the periphery, such as the creation of a very large immigrant labor force, mostly from other Muslim countries, in the oil-producing Gulf states.

These relocations of bodies create the possibility of hybridization in gender imagery, sexuality, and other forms of practice. The movement is not always toward synthesis, however, as the race/ethnic hierarchies of colonialism have been recreated in new contexts, including the politics of the metropole. Ethnic and racial conflict has been growing in importance in recent years, and as Klein (1997) and Tillner (1997) argue, this is a fruitful context for the production of masculinities oriented toward domination and violence. Even without the context of violence, there can be an intimate interweaving of the formation of masculinity with the formation of ethnic identity, as seen in the study by Poynting, Noble, and Tabar (1997) of Lebanese youths in the Anglo-dominant culture of Australia.

At the level of personal life as well as in relation to bodies, the making of masculinities is shaped by global forces. In some cases, the link is indirect, such as the working-class Australian men caught in a situation of structural unemployment (Connell 1995), which arises from Australia's changing position in the global economy. In other cases, the link is obvious, such as the executives of multinational corporations and the financial sector servicing international trade. The requirements of a career in international business set up strong pressures on domestic life: almost all multinational executives are men, and the assumption in business magazines and advertising directed toward them is that they will have dependent wives running their homes and bringing up their children.

At the level of collective practice, masculinities are reconstituted by the remaking of gender meanings and the reshaping of the institutional contexts of practice. Let us consider each in turn.

The growth of global mass media, especially electronic media, is an obvious "vector" for the globalization of gender. Popular entertainment circulates stereotyped gender images, deliberately made attractive for marketing purposes. The example of Xuxa in Brazil has already been mentioned. International news media are also controlled or strongly influenced from the metropole and circulate Western definitions of authoritative masculinity, criminality, desirable femininity, and so on. But there are limits to the power of global mass communications. Some local centers of mass entertainment differ from the Hollywood model, such as the Indian popular film industry centered in Bombay. Further, media research emphasizes that audiences are highly selective in their reception of media messages, and we must allow for popular recognition of the fantasy in mass entertainment. Just as economic globalization can be exaggerated, the creation of a global culture is a more turbulent and uneven process than is often assumed (Featherstone 1995).

More important, I would argue, is a process that began long before electronic media existed, the export of institutions. Gendered institutions not only circulate definitions of masculinity (and femininity), as sex role theory notes. The functioning of gendered institutions, creating specific conditions for social practice, calls into existence specific patterns of practice. Thus, certain patterns of collective violence are embedded in the organization and culture of a Western-style army, which are different from the patterns of precolonial violence. Certain patterns of calculative egocentrism are embedded in the working of a stock market; certain patterns of rule following and domination are embedded in a bureaucracy.

Now, the colonial and postcolonial world saw the installation in the periphery, on a very large scale, of a range of institutions on the North Atlantic model: armies, states, bureaucracies, corporations, capital markets, labor markets, schools, law courts, transport systems. These are gendered institutions and their functioning has directly reconstituted masculinities in the periphery. This has not necessarily meant photocopies of European masculinities. Rather, pressures for change are set up that are inherent in the institutional form.

To the extent that particular institutions become dominant in world society, the patterns of masculinity embedded in them may become global standards. Masculine dress is an interesting indicator: almost every political leader in the world now wears the uniform of the Western business executive. The more common pattern, however, is not the complete displacement of local patterns but the articulation of the local gender order with the gender regime of globalmodel institutions. Case studies such as Hollway's (1994) account of bureaucracy in Tanzania illustrate the point; there, domestic patriarchy articulated with masculine authority in the state in ways that subverted the government's formal commitment to equal opportunity for women.

We should not expect the overall structure of gender relations on a world scale simply to mirror patterns known on the smaller scale. In the most vital of respects, there is continuity. The world gender order is unquestionably patriarchal, in the sense that it privileges men over women. There is a patriarchal dividend for men arising from unequal wages, unequal labor force participation, and a highly unequal structure of ownership, as well as cultural and sexual privileging. This has been extensively documented by feminist work on women's situation globally (e.g., Taylor 1985), though its implications for masculinity have mostly been ignored. The conditions thus exist for the production of a hegemonic masculinity on a world scale, that is to say, a dominant form of masculinity that embodies, organizes, and legitimates men's domination in the gender order as a whole.

The conditions of globalization, which involve the interaction of many local gender orders, certainly multiply the forms of masculinity in the global gender order. At the same time, the specific shape of globalization, concentrating economic and cultural power on an unprecedented scale, provides new resources for dominance by particular groups of men. This dominance may become institutionalized in a pattern of masculinity that becomes, to some degree, standardized across localities. I will call such patterns *globalizing masculinities,* and it is among them, rather than narrowly within the metropole, that we are likely to find candidates for hegemony in the world gender order.

GLOBALIZING MASCULINITIES

In this section, I will offer a sketch of major forms of globalizing masculinity in the three historical phases identified above in the discussion of globalization.

Masculinities of Conquest and Settlement

The creation of the imperial social order involved peculiar conditions for the gender practices of men. Colonial conquest itself was mainly carried out by segregated groups of men—soldiers, sailors, traders, administrators, and a good many who were all these by turn (such as the Rum Corps in early New South Wales, Australia). They were drawn from the more segregated occupations and milieu in the metropole, and it is likely that the men drawn into colonization tended to be the more rootless. Certainly the process

of conquest could produce frontier masculinities that combined the occupational culture of these groups with an unusual level of violence and egocentric individualism. The vehement contemporary debate about the genocidal violence of the Spanish conquistadors—who in fifty years completely exterminated the population of Hispaniola—points to this pattern (Bitterli 1989).

The political history of empire is full of evidence of the tenuous control over the frontier exercised by the state—the Spanish monarchs unable to rein in the conquistadors, the governors in Sydney unable to hold back the squatters and in Capetown unable to hold back the Boers, gold rushes breaking boundaries everywhere, even an independent republic set up by escaped slaves in Brazil. The point probably applies to other forms of social control too, such as customary controls on men's sexuality. Extensive sexual exploitation of indigenous women was a common feature of conquest. In certain circumstances, frontier masculinities might be reproduced as a local cultural tradition long after the frontier had passed, such as the gauchos of southern South America and the cowboys of the western United States.

In other circumstances, however, the frontier of conquest and exploitation was replaced by a frontier of settlement. Sex ratios in the colonizing population changed, as women arrived and locally born generations succeeded. A shift back toward the family patterns of the metropole was likely. As Cain and Hopkins (1993) have shown for the British empire, the ruling group in the colonial world as a whole was an extension of the dominant class in the metropole, the landed gentry, and tended to reproduce its social customs and ideology. The creation of a settler masculinity might be the goal of state policy, as it seems to have been in late-nineteenth-century New Zealand, as part of a general process of pacification and the creation of an agricultural social order (Phillips 1987). Or it might be undertaken through institutions created by settler groups, such as the elite schools in Natal studied by Morrell (1994).

The impact of colonialism on the construction of masculinity among the colonized is much less documented, but there is every reason to think it was severe. Conquest and settlement disrupted all the structures of indigenous society, whether or not this was intended by the colonizing powers (Bitierli 1989). Indigenous gender orders were no exception. Their disruption could result from the pulverization of indigenous communities (as in the seizure of land in eastern North America and southeastern Australia), through gendered labor migration (as in gold mining with Black labor in South Africa; see Moodie 1994), to ideological attacks on local gender arrangements (as in the missionary assault on the *berdache* tradition in North America; see Williams 1986). The varied course of resistance to colonization is also likely to have affected the making of masculinities. This is clear in the region of Natal in South Africa, where sustained resistance to colonization by the Zulu kingdom was a key to the mobilization of ethnic-national masculine identities in the twentieth century (Morrell 1996).

Masculinities of Empire

The imperial social order created a hierarchy of masculinities, as it created a hierarchy of communities and races. The colonizers distinguished "more manly" from "less manly" groups among their subjects. In British India, for instance, Bengali men were supposed effeminate while Pathans and Sikhs were regarded as strong and warlike. Similar distinctions were made in South Africa between Hottentots and Zulus, in North America between Iroquois, Sioux, and Cheyenne on one side, and southern and southwestern tribes on the other.

At the same time, the emerging imagery of gender difference in European culture provided general symbols of superiority and inferiority. Within the imperial "poetics of war" (MacDonald 1994), the conqueror was virile, while the colonized were dirty, sexualized, and effeminate or childlike. In many colonial situations, indigenous men were called "boys" by the colonizers (e.g., in Zimbabwe; see Shire 1994). Sinha's (1995) interesting study of the language of political controversy in India in the 1880s and 1890s shows how the images of "manly Englishman" and "effeminate Bengali" were deployed to uphold colonial privilege and contain movements for change. In the late nineteenth century, racial barriers in colonial societies were hardening rather than weakening, and gender ideology tended to fuse with racism in forms that the twentieth century has never untangled.

The power relations of empire meant that indigenous gender orders were generally under pressure from the colonizers, rather than the other way around. But the colonizers too might change. The barriers of late colonial racism were not only to prevent pollution from below but also to forestall "going native," a well-recognized possibility—the starting point, for instance, of Kipling's famous novel *Kim* ([1901] 1987). The pressures, opportunities, and profits of empire might also work changes in gender arrangements among the colonizers, for instance, the division of labor in households with a large supply of indigenous workers as domestic servants (Bulbeck 1992). Empire might also affect the gender order of the metropole itself by changing gender ideologies, divisions of labor, and the nature of the metropolitan state. For instance, empire figured prominently as a source of masculine imagery in Britain, in the Boy Scouts, and in the cult of Lawrence of Arabia (Dawson 1991). Here we see examples of an important principle: the interplay of gender dynamics between different parts of the world order.

The world of empire created two very different settings for the modernization of masculinities. In the periphery, the forcible restructuring of economics and workforces tended to individualize, on one hand, and rationalize, on the other. A widespread result was masculinities in which the rational calculation of self-interest was the key to action, emphasizing the European gender contrast of rational man/irrational woman. The specific form might be local—for instance, the Japanese "salaryman," a type first recognized in the 1910s, was specific to the Japanese context of large, stable industrial conglomerates (Kinmonth 1981). But the result generally was masculinities defined around economic action, with both workers and entrepreneurs increasingly adapted to emerging market economies.

In the metropole, the accumulation of wealth made possible a specialization of leadership in the dominant classes, and struggles for hegemony in which masculinities organized around domination or violence were split from masculinities organized around expertise. The class compromises that allowed the development of the welfare state in Europe and North America were paralleled by gender compromises—gender reform movements (most notably the women's suffrage movement) contesting the legal privileges of men and forcing concessions from the state. In this context, agendas of reform in masculinity emerged: the temperance movement, compassionate marriage, homosexual rights movements, leading eventually to the pursuit of androgyny in "men's liberation" in the 1970s (Kimmel and Mosmiller 1992). Not all reconstructions of masculinity, however, emphasized tolerance or moved toward androgyny. The vehement masculinity politics of fascism, for instance, emphasized dominance and difference and glorified violence, a pattern still found in contemporary racist movements (Tillner 1997).

Masculinities of Postcolonialism and Neoliberalism

The process of decolonization disrupted the gender hierarchies of the colonial order and, where armed struggle was involved, might have involved a deliberate cultivation of masculine hardness and violence (as in South Africa; see Xaba 1997). Some activists and theorists of liberation struggles celebrated this, as a necessary response to colonial violence and emasculation; women in liberation struggles were perhaps less impressed. However one evaluates the process, one of the consequences of decolonization was another round of disruptions of community-based gender orders and another step in the reorientation of masculinities toward national and international contexts.

Nearly half a century after the main wave of decolonization, the old hierarchies persist in new shapes. With the collapse of Soviet communism, the decline of postcolonial socialism, and the ascendancy of the new right in Europe and North America, world politics is more and more organized around the needs of transnational capital and the creation of global markets.

The neoliberal agenda has little to say, explicitly, about gender: it speaks a gender-neutral language of "markets," "individuals," and "choice." But the world in which neoliberalism is ascendant is still a gendered world, and neoliberalism has an implicit gender politics. The "individual" of neoliberal theory has in general the attributes and interests of a male entrepreneur, the attack on the welfare state generally weakens the position of women, while the increasingly unregulated power of transnational corporations places strategic power in the hands of particular groups of men. It is not surprising, then, that the installation of capitalism in Eastern Europe and the former Soviet Union has been accompanied by a reassertion of dominating masculinities and, in some situations, a sharp worsening in the social position of women.

We might propose, then, that the hegemonic form of masculinity in the current world gender order is the masculinity associated with those who control its dominant institutions: the business executives who operate in global markets, and the political executives who interact (and in many contexts, merge) with them. I will call this *transnational business masculinity*. This is not readily available for ethnographic study, but we can get some clues to its character from its reflections in management literature, business journalism, and corporate self-promotion, and from studies of local business elites (e.g., Donaldson 1997).

As a first approximation, I would suggest this is a masculinity marked by increasing egocentrism, very conditional loyalties (even to the corporation), and a declining sense of responsibility for others (except for purposes of image making). Gee, Hull and Lankshear (1996), studying recent management textbooks, note the peculiar construction of the executive in "fast capitalism" as a person with no permanent commitments, except (in effect) to the idea of accumulation itself. Transnational business masculinity is characterized by a limited technical rationality (management theory), which is increasingly separate from science.

Transnational business masculinity differs from traditional bourgeois masculinity by its increasingly libertarian sexuality, with a growing tendency to commodify relations with women. Hotels catering to businessmen in most parts of the world now routinely offer pornographic videos, and in some parts of the world, there is a well-developed prostitution industry catering for international businessmen. Transnational business masculinity does not require bodily force, since the patriarchal dividend on which it rests is accumulated by impersonal, institutional means. But corporations increasingly use the exemplary bodies of elite sportsmen as a marketing tool (note the phenomenal growth of corporate "sponsorship" of sport in the last generation) and indirectly as a means of legitimation for the whole gender order.

MASCULINITY POLITICS ON A WORLD SCALE

Recognizing global society as an arena of masculinity formation allows us to pose new questions about masculinity politics. What social dynamics in the global arena give rise to masculinity politics, and what shape does global masculinity politics take?

The gradual creation of a world gender order has meant many local instabilities of gender. Gender instability is a familiar theme of poststructuralist theory, but this school of thought takes as a universal condition a situation that is historically specific. Instabilities range from the disruption of men's local cultural dominance as women move into the public realm and higher education, through the disruption of sexual identities that produced "queer" politics in the metropole, to the shifts in the urban intelligentsia that produced "the new sensitive man" and other images of gender change.

One response to such instabilities, on the part of groups whose power is challenged but still dominant, is to reaffirm *local* gender orthodoxies and hierarchies. A masculine fundamentalism is, accordingly, a common response in gender politics at present. A soft version, searching for an essential masculinity among myths and symbols, is offered by the mythopoetic men's movement in the United States and by the religious revivalists of the Promise Keepers (Messner 1997). A much harder version is found, in that country, in the right-wing militia movement brought to world attention by the Oklahoma City bombing (Gibson 1994), and in contemporary Afghanistan, if we can trust Western media reports, in the militant misogyny of the Taliban. It is no coincidence that in the two latter cases, hardline masculine fundamentalism goes together with a marked anti-internationalism. The world system—rightly enough—is seen as the source of pollution and disruption.

Not that the emerging global order is a hotbed of gender progressivism. Indeed, the neoliberal agenda for the reform of national and international economics involves closing down historic possibilities for gender reform. I have noted how it subverts the gender compromise represented by the metropolitan welfare state. It has also undermined the progressive-liberal agendas of sex role reform represented by affirmative action programs, anti-discrimination provisions, child care services, and the like. Right-wing parties and governments have been persistently cutting such programs, in the name of either individual liberties or global competitiveness. Through these means, the patriarchal dividend to men is defended or restored, without an *explicit* masculinity politics in the form of a mobilization of men.

Within the arenas of international relations, the international state, multinational corporations, and global markets, there is nevertheless a deployment of masculinities and a reasonably clear hegemony. The transnational business masculinity described above has had only one major competitor for hegemony in recent decades, the rigid, control-oriented masculinity of the military, and the military-style bureaucratic dictatorships of Stalinism. With the collapse of Stalinism and the end of the cold war, Big Brother (Orwell's famous parody of this form of masculinity) is a fading threat, and the more flexible, calculative, egocentric masculinity of the fast capitalist entrepreneur holds the world stage.

We must, however, recall two important conclusions of the ethnographic moment in masculinity research: that different forms of masculinity exist together and that hegemony is constantly subject to challenge. These are possibilities in the global arena too. Transnational business masculinity is not completely homogeneous; variations of it are embedded in different parts of the world system, which may not be completely compatible. We may distinguish a Confucian variant, based in East Asia, with a stronger commitment to hierarchy and social consensus, from a secularized Christian variant, based in North America, with more hedonism and individualism and greater tolerance for social conflict. In certain arenas, there is already conflict between the business and political leaderships embodying these forms of masculinity: initially over human rights versus Asian values, and more recently over the extent of trade and investment liberalization.

If these are contenders for hegemony, there is also the possibility of opposition to hegemony. The global circulation of "gay" identity (Altman 1996) is an important indication that nonhegemonic masculinities may operate in global arenas, and may even find a certain political articulation, in this case around human rights and AIDS prevention.

REFERENCES

Altman, Dennis. 1996. Rupture or continuity? The internationalisation of gay identities. *Social Text* 48 (3): 77–94.

Barrett, Frank J. 1996. The organizational construction of hegemonic masculinity: The case of the U.S. Navy. *Gender Work and Organization* 3 (3): 129–42.

BauSteineMaenner, ed. 1996. *Kritische Maennerforschung* [Critical research on men]. Berlin: Argument.

Bitterli, Urs. 1989. *Cultures in conflict: Encounters between European and non-European cultures, 1492–1800,* Stanford, CA: Stanford University Press.

Bolin, Anne. 1988. *In search of Eve: Transsexual rites of passage.* Westport, CT: Bergin & Garvey.

Bulbeck, Chilla. 1992. *Australian women in Papua New Guinea: Colonial passages 1920–1960.* Cambridge, U.K.: Cambridge University Press.

Cain, P. J., and A. G. Hopkins. 1993. *British Imperialism: Innovation and expansion, 1688–1914.* New York: Longman.

Carrigan, Tim, Bob Connell, and John Lee. 1985. Toward a new sociology of masculinity. *Theory and Society* 14 (5): 551–604.

Chodorow, Nancy. 1994. *Femininities, masculinities, sexualities: Freud and beyond.* Lexington: University Press of Kentucky.

Cockburn, Cynthia. 1983. *Brothers: Male dominance and technological change.* London: Pluto.

Cohen, Jon. 1991. NOMAS: Challenging male supremacy. *Changing Men* (Winter/Spring): 45–46.

Connell, R. W. 1987. *Gender and power.* Cambridge, MA: Polity.

———. 1990a. An iron man: The body and some contradictions of hegemonic masculinity. In *Sport, men and the gender order: Critical feminist perspectives,* edited by Michael A. Messner and Donald F. Sabo, 83–95. Champaign, IL: Human Kinetics Books.

———. 1990b. The state, gender and sexual politics: Theory and appraisal. *Theory and Society* 19:507–44.

———. 1992. A very straight gay: Masculinity, homosexual experience and the dynamics of gender. *American Sociological Review* 57 (6): 735–5l.

———. 1995. *Masculinities.* Cambridge, MA: Polity.

———. 1996. Teaching the boys: New research on masculinity, and gender strategies for schools. *Teachers College Record* 98 (2): 206–35.

Cornwall, Andrea, and Nancy Lindisfarne, eds. 1994. *Dislocating masculinity: Comparative ethnographies.* London: Routledge.

Dawson, Graham. 1991. The blond Bedouin: Lawrence of Arabia, imperial adventure and the imagining of English-British masculinity. In *Manful assertions: Masculinities in Britain since 1800,* edited by Michael Roper and John Tosh, 113–44. London: Routledge.

Donaldson, Mike. 1991. *Time of our lives: Labour and love in the working class.* Sydney: Allen & Unwin.

———. 1997. Growing up very rich: The masculinity of the hegemonic. Paper presented at the conference Masculinities: Renegotiating Genders, June, University of Wollongong, Australia.

Enloe, Cynthia. 1990. *Bananas, beaches and bases: Making feminist sense of international politics.* Berkeley: University of California Press.

Featherstone, Mike. 1995. *Undoing culture: Globalization, postmodernism and identity.* London: Sage.

Foley, Douglas E. 1990. *Learning capitalist culture: Deep in the heart of Tejas.* Philadelphia: University of Pennsylvania Press.

Fuentes, Annette, and Barbara Ehrenreich. 1983. *Women in the global factory.* Boston: South End.

Gee, James Paul, Glynda Hall, and Colin Lankshear. 1996. *The new work order: Behind the language of the new capitalism.* Sydney: Allen & Unwin.

Gender Equality Ombudsman. 1997. *The father's quota.* Information sheet on parental leave entitlements, Oslo.

Gibson, J. William. 1994. *Warrior dreams: Paramilitary culture in post-Vietnam America.* New York: Hill and Wang.

Hagemann-White, Carol, and Maria S. Rerrich, eds. 1988. *FrauenMaennerBilder* (Women, imaging, men). Bielefeld: AJZ-Verlag.

Hearn, Jeff. 1987. *The gender of oppression: Men, masculinity and the critique of Marxism.* Brighton, U.K.: Wheatsheaf.

Herdt, Gilbert H. 1981. *Guardians of the flutes: Idioms of masculinity.* New York: McGraw-Hill.

———. ed. 1984. *Ritualized homosexuality in Melanesia.* Berkeley: University of California Press.

Heward, Christine. 1988. *Making a man of him: Parents and their sons' education at an English public school 1929–1950.* London: Routledge.

Hinsch, Bret. 1990. *Passions of the cut sleeve: The male homosexual tradition in China.* Berkeley: University of California Press.

Hirst, Paul, and Grahame Thompson. 1996. *Globalization in question: The international economy and the possibilities of governance.* Cambridge, MA: Polity.

Hollstein, Walter. 1992. *Machen Sie Platz, mein Herr! Teilen statt Herrschen* [Sharing instead of dominating]. Hamburg: Rowohlt.

Hollway, Wendy. 1994. Separation, integration and difference: Contradictions in a gender regime. In *Power/gender: Social relations in theory and practice,* edited by H. Lorraine Radtke and Henderikus Stam, 247–69. London: Sage.

Holter, Oystein Gullvag. 1997. Gender, patriarchy and capitalism: A social forms analysis. Ph.D. diss., University of Oslo, Faculty of Social Science.

Hondagneu-Sotelo, Pierrette, and Michael A. Messner. 1994. Gender displays and men's power: The "new man" and the Mexican immigrant man. In *Theorizing masculinities,* edited by Harry Brod and Michael Kaufman, 200–218. Twin Oaks, CA: Sage.

Ito Kimio. 1993. *Otokorashisa-no-yukue* [Directions for masculinities]. Tokyo: Shinyo-sha.

Jolly, Margaret. 1997. From point Venus to Bali Ha'i: Eroticism and exoticism in representations of the Pacific. In *Sites of desire, economies of pleasure: Sexualities in Asia and the Pacific,* edited by Lenore Manderson and Margaret Jolly, 99–122. Chicago: University of Chicago Press.

Kandiyoti, Deniz. 1994. The paradoxes of masculinity: Some thoughts on segregated societies. In *Dislocating masculinity: Comparative ethnographies,* edited by Andrea Cornwall and Nancy Lindisfame, 197–213. London: Routledge.

Kaufman, Michael. 1997. Working with men and boys to challenge sexism and end men's violence. Paper presented at UNESCO expert group meeting on Male Roles and Masculinities in the Perspective of a Culture of Peace, September, Oslo.

Kimmel, Michael S. 1987. Rethinking "masculinity": New directions in research. In *Changing men: New directions in research on men and masculinity,* edited by Michael S. Kimmel, 9–24. Newbury Park, CA: Sage.

———. 1996. *Manhood in America: A cultural history.* New York: Free Press.

Kimmel, Michael S., and Thomas P. Mosmiller, eds. 1992. *Against the tide: Pro-feminist men in the United States, 1776–1990, a documentary history.* Boston: Beacon.

Kindler, Heinz. 1993. *Maske(r)ade: Jungen- und Maenner-arbeit fuer die Pratis* [Work with youth and men]. Neuling: Schwaebisch Gmuend und Tuebingen.

Kinmonth, Earl H. 1981. *The self-made man in Meiji Japanese thought: From Samurai to salary man.* Berkeley: University of California Press.

Kipling, Rudyard. [1901] 1987. *Kim*. London: Penguin.

Klein, Alan M. 1993. *Little big men: Bodybuilding subculture and gender construction.* Albany: State University of New York Press.

Klein, Uta. 1997. Our best boys: The making of masculinity in Israeli society. Paper presented at UNESCO expert group meeting on Male Roles and Masculinities in the Perspectives of a Culture of Peace, September, Oslo.

Lewes, Kenneth. 1988. *The psychoanalytic theory of male homosexuality.* New York: Simon & Schuster.

MacDonald, Robert H. 1994. *The language of empire: Myths and metaphors of popular imperialism, 1880–1918.* Manchester, U.K.: Manchester University Press.

McElhinny, Bonnie. 1994. An economy of affect: Objectivity, masculinity and the gendering of police work. In *Dislocating masculinity: Comparative ethnographies,* edited by Andrea Cornwall and Nancy Lindisfarne, 159–71. London: Routledge.

McKay, Jim, and Debbie Huber. 1992. Anchoring media images of technology and sport. *Women's Studies International Forum* 15 (2): 205–18.

Messerschmidt, James W. 1997. *Crime as structured action: Gender, race, class, and crime in the making.* Thousand Oaks, CA: Sage.

Messner, Michael A. 1992. *Power at play: Sports and the problem of masculinity.* Boston: Beacon.

———. 1997. *The politics of masculinities: Men in movements.* Thousand Oaks, CA: Sage.

Metz-Goeckel, Sigrid, and Ursula Mueller. 1986. *Der Mann: Die Brigitte-Studie* [The male]. Beltz: Weinheim & Basel.

Mies, Maria. 1986. *Patriarchy and accumulation on a world scale: Women in the international division of labour.* London: Zed.

Moodie, T. Dunbar. 1994. *Going for gold: Men, mines, and migration.* Johannesburg: Witwatersand University Press.

Morrell, Robert. 1994. Boys, gangs, and the making of masculinity in the White secondary schools of Natal, 1880–1930. *Masculinities* 2 (2): 56–82.

———. ed. 1996. *Political economy and identities in KwaZulu-Natal: Historical and social perspectives.* Durban, Natal: Indicator Press.

Nakamura, Akira. 1994. *Watashi-no Danseigaku* [My men's studies]. Tokyo: Kindaibugei-sha.

Oftung, Knut, ed. 1994. *Menns bilder og bilder av menn* [Images of men]. Oslo: Likestillingsradet.

Phillips, Jock. 1987. *A man's country? The image of the Pakeha male—a history.* Auckland: Penguin.

Poynting, S., G. Noble, and P. Tabar. 1997. "Intersections" of masculinity and ethnicity: A study of male Lebanese immigrant youth in Western Sydney. Paper presented at the conference Masculinities: Renegotiating Genders, June, University of Wollongong, Australia.

Roper, Michael. 1991. Yesterday's model: Product fetishism and the British company man, 1945–85. In *Manful assertions: Masculinities in Britain since 1800,* edited by Michael Roper and John Tosh, 190–211. London: Routledge.

Schwalbe, Michael. 1996. *Unlocking the iron cage: The men's movement, gender, politics, and the American culture.* New York: Oxford University Press.

Segal, Lynne. 1997. *Slow motion: Changing masculinities, changing men.* 2d ed. London: Virago.

Seidler, Victor J. 1991. *Achilles heel reader: Men, sexual politics and socialism.* London: Routledge.

Shire, Chenjerai. 1994. Men don't go to the moon: Language, space and masculinities in Zimbabwe. In *Dislocating masculinity: Comparative ethnographies,* edited by Andrea Cornwall and Nancy Lindisfarne, 147–58. London: Routledge.

Simpson, Amelia. 1993. *Xuxa: The mega-marketing of a gender, race and modernity.* Philadelphia: Temple University Press.

Sinha, Mrinalini. 1995. *Colonial masculinity: The manly Englishman and the effeminate Bengali in the late nineteenth century.* Manchester, U.K.: Manchester University Press.

Taylor, Debbie. 1985. Women: An analysis. In *Women: A world report,* 1–98. London: Methuen.

Theberge, Nancy. 1991. Reflections on the body in the sociology of sport. *Quest* 43:123–34.

Thorne, Barrie. 1993. *Gender play: Girls and boys in school.* New Brunswick. NJ: Rutgers University Press.

Tillner, Georg. 1997. Masculinity and xenophobia. Paper presented at UNESCO meeting on Male Roles and Masculinities in the Perspective of a Culture of Peace, September, Oslo.

Tomsen, Stephen. 1997. A top night: Social protest, masculinity and the culture of drinking violence. *British Journal of Criminology* 37 (1): 90–103.

Tosh, John. 1991. Domesticity and manliness in the Victorian middle class: The family of Edward White Benson. In *Manful assertions: Masculinities in Britain since 1800,* edited by Michael Roper and John Tosh, 44–73. London: Routledge.

United Nations Educational, Scientific and Cultural Organization (UNESCO). 1997. *Male roles and masculinities in the perspective of a culture of peace: Report of expert group meeting, Oslo, 24–28 September 1997.* Paris: Women and a Culture of Peace Programme, Culture of Peace Unit, UNESCO.

Walby, Sylvia. 1990. *Theorizing patriarchy.* Oxford, U.K.: Blackwell.

Walker, James C. 1988. *Louts and legends: Male youth culture in an inner-city school.* Sydney: Allen & Unwin.

Wallerstein, Immanuel. 1974. *The modern world-system: Capitalist agriculture and the origins of the European world-economy in the sixteenth century.* New York: Academic Press.

Whitson, David. 1990. Sport in the social construction of masculinity. In *Sport, men, and the gender order: Critical feminist perspectives,* edited by Michael A. Messner and Donald F. Sabo, 19–29. Champaign, IL: Human Kinetics Books.

Widersprueche. 1995. Special Issue: Maennlichkeiten. Vol. 56/57.

Williams, Walter L. 1986. *The spirit and the flesh: Sexual diversity in American Indian culture.* Boston: Beacon.

Xaba, Thokozani. 1997. Masculinity in a transitional society: The rise and fall of the "young lions." Paper presented at the conference Masculinities in Southern Africa, June, University of Natal-Durban, Durban.

WOMANIST

Alice Walker

Womanist

1. From *Womanish*. (Opp. of "girlish," i.e., frivolous, irresponsible, not serious.) A black feminist or feminist or feminist or color. From the black folk expression of mothers to female children, "You acting womanish," i.e., like a woman. Usually referring to outrageous audacious, courageous or *willful* behavior. Wanting to know more and in greater depth than is considered "good" for one. Interested in grown-up doings. Acting grown up. Being grown up. Interchangeable with another black folk expression: "You trying to be grown," Responsible. In charge. *Serious.*

　　. . .

2. *Also:* A woman who loves other women, sexually and/or nonsexually. Appreciates and prefers women's culture, women's emotional flexibility (values tears as natural counterbalance of laughter), and women's strength. Sometimes loves individual men, sexually and/or nonsexually. Committed to survival and wholeness of entire people, male *and* female. Not a separatist, except periodically, for health. Traditionally universalist, as in: "Mama, why are we brown, pink, and yellow, and our cousins are white, beige, and black?" Ans.: "Well, you know the colored race is just like a flower garden, with every color flower represented." Traditionally capable, as in: "Mama, I'm walking to Canada and I'm taking you and a bunch of other slaves with me." Reply: "It wouldn't be the first time."

　　. . .

3. Loves music. Loves dance. Loves the moon. *Loves* the Spirit. Loves love and food and roundness. Loves struggle. *Loves* the Folk. Loves herself. *Regardless.*

　　. . .

4. Womanist is to feminist as purple to lavender.

PART TWO

GENDER, CULTURE, AND SOCIALIZATION

Everyone is born into a culture—a set of shared ideas about the nature of reality, standards of right and wrong, and concepts for making sense of social interactions. These ideas are put into practice through behaviors, language, images, and material objects. As totally dependent infants we are socialized—taught the rules, roles, and relationships of the social world we will inherit. In the process of growing up, we learn to think, act, and feel as we are "supposed to." As adults, we are embedded in our culture's assumptions and images of gender.

One of the earliest and most deeply seated ideas to which we are socialized is that of gender identity: the idea that "I am a boy" or "I am a girl." Because the culture promotes strong ideas about what boys and girls are like, most children learn to think of themselves in terms of their gender identity (their "boyness" or "girlness") and adopt behaviors that are sex-assigned in our culture. Thus, for example, a girl who plays quietly with dolls is viewed as behaving in a feminine or "ladylike" manner, and a boy who plays with trucks is seen as appropriately masculine, "all boy." Children who do not display these gender-stereotypical behaviors may face disapproval or punishment from adults and teasing or shunning by other children. Consciously or unconsciously, adults and peers categorize children as boys or girls, respond to and regard them differently, and encourage them to adopt behaviors and attitudes on the basis of their sex. We raise, in effect, two different kinds of children: girls and boys.

Parents are strong socializing influences, and they provide the first and most deeply experienced socialization. Despite claims to the contrary, American parents treat girls and boys differently. Boys and girls have different toys, names, and room decor and adults play with them in different ways. The stores in which parents shop for children's toys or clothing have separate aisles for boys' and girls' items, which can easily be identified by the dominant color. (Waves of pink packaging are a clue that the aisle contains girls' items.) Even if parents monitor their actions in the hope of preventing sexism from affecting their child, other socializing influences—schools, mass media, and other children—bear down on children.

One of the primary socializing influences is language. All languages teach their culture's ideas about men and women. They do it "naturally": when we learn to talk, we also learn the thought patterns and communication styles of our culture. Those patterns and styles reinforce differentiation by sex and perpetuate sex stereotyping, although the kind of stereotyping may vary from language to language. In the English language, for example, the generic man is supposed to include males and females, as well as people of all races and ethnicities; but in linguistic practice it does not, as Richardson shows in Selection 11. People other than white and male are linguistically tagged in writing and in speech. For example, occupational categories are sex- or race-tagged if the person's sex or race does not fit cultural stereotypes about who will be in those occupations. Consider: doctor/woman doctor/black woman doctor; nurse/male nurse/Asian male nurse. Linguistic tags convey normative expectations about who should occupy particular positions in society and about the normality or legitimacy of white men's claim to powerful positions. When a child asks, "Were there any cave women?" for example, we realize the picture conveyed by the term "cavemen."

As societies become more complex, increasingly the mass media have become centralized agents that transmit dominant cultural beliefs. Movements toward cultural heterogeneity are thwarted through the homogenizing effects of television, in particular. Television presents gender stereotypes in their purest and simplest forms. Whether the program is about African-American families, lawyers at work, white teenagers, talking animals, or a bachelor's search for the perfect wife, the stereotyping messages about gender and race are endlessly repetitive. Children in the United States spend more time watching television than they spend in school or interacting with parents or peers. Moreover, they believe that what they see on television is an accurate representation of how the world is and should be organized. White middle-class male dominance and sexualized, passive femininity are the repetitive themes.

The socialization effected by the family, language, and the mass media is continued in the educational system. Schools are formally charged with teaching the young. While teaching reading, writing, and arithmetic, however, schools also teach conventional views of gender. They do so through patterns of staffing (male principals and custodians, female teachers and food servers), curriculum, the sex segregation of sports and activities (whether formal or informal), and different expectations for boys and girls. Children themselves reinforce these messages through sex-segregated play and teasing children who do not conform.

Socialization—whether through the home, the school, language, or the mass media—creates and sustains gender differences. Boys are taught that they will inherit the privileges and prestige of manhood and that they must be tough, aggressive, and interested in trucks, airplanes, and sports. Girls, in contrast, learn that they are less socially valuable than boys and that they should be quiet, pretty, and interested in dolls, fashion, and boys. Subcultures that promote values and beliefs different from the mainstream do exist, and individuals do not necessarily internalize every message from the dominant culture. In fact, many children and adults challenge the culture of gender difference directly, and many others live their lives in ways that do not conform to the stereotypes and expectations for their gender. Nevertheless, traditional cultural views of gender are ubiquitous and powerful.

Through powerful social institutions, then, children learn and consume a culture. Our culture is one that views men and masculinity as superior to women and femininity. It is a system that assigns different behaviors and attitudes to males and females and that further distinguishes between people of different racial and ethnic groups. As adults we continue to be shaped by the books and magazines we read, the movies we see, the music we enjoy, and the people with whom we spend time. The ways that gender is portrayed or represented in the culture—in mass media, schools, public discussions—provide us with our conceptual tools for thinking about men and women. It becomes nearly impossible to think about gender without being shaped by the images that surround us.

The readings in this part of Feminist Frontiers illustrate and explain different aspects of cultural constructions of gender and the socialization process. These systems of meaning shape how we understand ourselves and the social institutions that form our society. The readings document both the prevalence of conventional understandings in the culture and the presence of alternative messages. As you read, consider what kinds of influences conventional representations of gender have and what sources exist for challenging these images.

SECTION *3*

Representation, Language, and Culture

Images of gender are pervasive in our lives. In our language, mass media, and daily lives, we encounter particular images of what it means to be a woman or a man. Often we take these images for granted, and the ways that women and men are represented seem natural or inevitable. Language and media representations of gender shape the way we view ourselves and our relationships to each other and to the world around us. This section explores the images of women and men expressed in language and mass media.

Laurel Richardson's "Gender Stereotyping in the English Language" demonstrates the major ways in which sexism pervades the structure and standard usage of modern American English. Her analysis reveals different expectations of women and men embedded in the language and shows how we internalize and reinforce gender differences, as we read, write, and speak English or hear it spoken. The reading raises questions about the relationships between language and social life, including connections between linguistic change and other forms of social change. What are some examples of sexist or nonsexist language? If you speak or have studied another language, compare its gender structure to that of English. Do you think using nonsexist language affects people's attitudes about women? How? An interesting question for classroom debate is whether the word "guy" or the phrase "you guys" is gender neutral.

Debra Gimlin describes one of the consequences of cultural messages of beauty on women: the high rates of cosmetic surgery. In "Cosmetic Surgery: Paying for Your Beauty," she discusses the phenomenal rise in the United States of elective cosmetic surgeries such as liposuction, breast augmentation (and reduction), blepharoplasty (eyelid surgery), face-lift, and chemical peel. Ninety percent of patients undergoing such procedures are women. Criticism of such surgeries focus not only on the risks and costs but also on the increasing pressure for women to take advantage of medical advances to fight aging, imperfection, and ethnic deviations from an Anglo-Saxon ideal of beauty.

Yet Gimlin, in interviewing women who had undergone plastic surgery at a Long Island clinic, challenges the notion that women are simply dupes of the culture. She finds that women set realistic and limited goals—not the attainment of perfect beauty—when they seek plastic surgery, and that the surgery is often successful in making them feel better about their bodies and themselves. At the same time, they feel the need to construct elaborate defenses for having made this choice. Gimlin offers a complex view of cosmetic surgery. Do you think cosmetic surgery is a reasonable choice for women? How important are cultural ideals in making women dislike parts of their bodies? Can you imagine seeking cosmetic surgery for yourself?

Some of the women Gimlin interviewed disliked their Jewish or Italian noses or Asian eyes. Race, ethnicity, and class have a great deal to do with American ideas of beauty. Ingrid Banks, author of a book called *Hair Matters*, argues in "Hair Still Matters" that hair continues to carry complex meanings for African-American women. From Venus Williams's controversial beaded braids to the butch haircut of Rebecca (on the television show *The Practice*), African-American women's hair makes statements about race, gender, sexuality, and culture. Banks listens to the voices of African-American women talking about how hair is perceived by others and how they feel about their own hair. And she connects the issue of hair to global issues of beauty and women's bodies. Given cultural images of white women with long flowing hair, is it surprising that long hair signals femininity for many African-American women? What do different hairstyles signal about the people who choose to wear them? Do you judge people's femininity and sexuality based on hairstyle?

In "Empowering Self, Making Choices, Creating Spaces: Black Female Identity via Rap Music Performance," Cheryl Keyes discusses how rap provides "spaces from which to deliver powerful messages from Black female and Black feminist perspectives." She identifies four main categories of women rappers: Queen Mother, Fly Girl, Sista with Attitude, and Lesbian. What are the main characteristics of each category? Can you think of additional examples of each category? Are there other categories that you might add?

The Fly Girl emphasizes her appearance and independent sexuality. Keyes suggests that Fly Girls do not simply reflect mainstream white standards of beauty, but draw on more flexible African-American beauty cultures to emphasize larger bodies. To what extent do Fly Girls challenge the emphasis on beauty as a defining feature of women, and to what extent do they reflect that emphasis? "Sistas with Attitude," Keyes suggests, are a topic of debate among other female rappers. In their image as assertive bad girls, Sistas with Attitude reclaim the term "bitch" to describe themselves. What are the arguments in favor of the use of this word, and what are the arguments against it? With which perspective do you agree? Keyes argues that, in each category, artists are presenting images of strong Black women and advocating political stances that often include Black feminism. In what ways does Keyes see rappers in each category as reflecting Black feminism? Do you agree with her interpretation?

We cannot emphasize too strongly the importance of language and media images in the construction of our understanding of women's and men's positions in society. We are exposed to these images continually. Because the language we have acquired and the images we use are so deeply rooted and inseparable, it is very difficult for us to break free of them, to see and describe the world and our experiences in non-sexist ways. Yet women and other subordinate groups do attempt to construct alternative systems of meaning and draw strength from cultures of resistance. The power to define has a major influence on our conceptions of others and ourselves.

Gender Stereotyping in the English Language

Everyone in our society, regardless of class, ethnicity, sex, age, or race, is exposed to the same language, the language of the dominant culture. Analysis of verbal language can tell us a great deal about a people's fears, prejudices, anxieties, and interests. A rich vocabulary on a particular subject indicates societal interests or obsessions (e.g., the extensive vocabulary about cars in America). And different words for the same subject (such as *freedom fighter* and *terrorist, passed away* and *croaked, make love* and *ball*) show that there is a range of attitudes and feelings in the society toward that subject.

It should not be surprising, then, to find differential attitudes and feelings about men and women rooted in the English language. Although English has not been completely analyzed, six general propositions concerning these attitudes and feelings about males and females can be made.

First, in terms of grammatical and semantic structure, women do not have a fully autonomous, independent existence; they are part of man. The language is not divided into male and female with distinct conjugations and declensions, as many other languages are. Rather, *women* are included under the generic *man*. Grammar books specify that the pronoun *he* can be used generically to mean *he or she*. Further, *man*, when used as an indefinite pronoun, grammatically refers to both men and women. So, for example, when we read *man* in the following phrases we are to interpret it as applying to both men and women: "man the oars," "one small step for man, one giant step for mankind," "man, that's tough," "man overboard," "man the toolmaker," "alienated man," "garbageman." Our rules of etiquette complete the grammatical presumption of inclusivity. When two persons are pronounced "man and wife," Miss Susan Jones changes her entire name to Mrs. Robert Gordon (Vanderbilt, 1972). In each of these correct usages, women are a part of man; they do not exist autonomously. The exclusion of women is

well expressed in Mary Daly's ear-jarring slogan "the sisterhood of man" (1973:7–21).

However, there is some question as to whether the theory that *man* means everybody is carried out in practice (see Bendix, 1979; Martyna, 1980). For example, an eight-year-old interrupts her reading of "The Story of the Cavemen" to ask how we got here without cavewomen. A ten-year-old thinks it is dumb to have a woman post*man*. A beginning anthropology student believes (incorrectly) that all shamans ("witch doctors") are males because her textbook and professor use the referential pronoun *he*.

But beginning language learners are not the only ones who visualize males when they see the word *man*. Research has consistently demonstrated that when the generic *man* is used, people visualize men, not women (Schneider & Hacker, 1973; DeStefano, 1976; Martyna, 1978; Hamilton & Henley, 1982). DeStefano, for example, reports that college students choose silhouettes of males for sentences with the word *man* or *men* in them. Similarly, the presumably generic *he* elicits images of men rather than women. The finding is so persistent that linguists doubt whether there actually is a semantic generic in English (MacKay, 1983).

Man, then, suggests not humanity but rather male images. Moreover, over one's lifetime, an educated American will be exposed to the prescriptive *he* more than a million times (MacKay, 1983). One consequence is the exclusion of women in the visualization, imagination, and thought of males and females. Most likely this linguistic practice perpetuates in men their feelings of dominance over and responsibility for women, feelings that interfere with the development of equality in relationships.

Second, in actual practice, our pronoun usage perpetuates different personality attributes and career aspirations for men and women. Nurses, secretaries, and elementary school teachers are almost invariably referred to as *she;* doctors, engineers, electricians, and presidents as *he.* In one classroom, students referred to an unidentified child as *he* but shifted to *she* when discussing the child's parent. In a faculty discussion of the problems of acquiring new staff, all architects, engineers, security officers, faculty, and computer programmers were referred to as *he;* secretaries and file clerks were referred to as *she.* Martyna (1978) has noted that speakers consistently use *he* when the referent has a high-status occupation (e.g., doctor, lawyer, judge) but shift to *she* when the occupations have lower status (e.g., nurse, secretary).

Even our choice of sex ascription to nonhuman objects subtly reinforces different personalities for males and females. It seems as though the small (e.g., kittens), the graceful (e.g., poetry), the unpredictable (e.g., the fates), the nurturant (e.g., the church, the school), and that which is owned and/or controlled by men (e.g., boats, cars, governments, nations) represent the feminine, whereas that which is a controlling forceful power in and of itself (e.g., God, Satan, tiger) primarily represents the masculine. Even athletic teams are not immune. In one college, the men's teams are called the Bearcats and the women's teams the Bearkittens.

Some of you may wonder whether it matters that the female is linguistically included in the male. The inclusion of women under the pseudogeneric *man* and the prescriptive *he,* however, is not a trivial issue. Language has tremendous power to shape attitudes and influence behavior. Indeed, MacKay (1983) argues that the prescriptive *he* "has all the characteristics of a highly effective propaganda technique": frequent repetition, early age of acquisition (before age six), covertness (*he* is not thought of as propaganda), use by high-prestige sources (including university texts and professors), and indirectness (presented as though it were a matter of common knowledge). As a result, the prescriptive affects females' sense of life options and feelings of well-being. For example, Adamsky (1981) found that women's sense of power and importance was enhanced when the prescriptive *he* was replaced by *she.*

Awareness of the impact of the generic *man* and prescriptive *he* has generated considerable activity to change the language. One change, approved by the Modern Language Association, is to replace the prescriptive *he* with the plural *they*—as was accepted practice before the eighteenth century. Another is the use of *he or she.* Although it sounds awkward at first, the *he or she* designation is increasingly being used in the media and among people who have recognized

the power of the pronoun to perpetuate sex stereotyping. When a professor, for example, talks about "the lawyer" as "he or she," a speech pattern that counteracts sex stereotyping is modeled. This drive to neutralize the impact of pronouns is evidenced further in the renaming of occupations: a policeman is now a police officer, a postman is a mail carrier, a stewardess is a flight attendant.

Third, linguistic practice defines females as immature, incompetent, and incapable and males as mature, complete, and competent. Because the words *man* and *woman* tend to connote sexual and human maturity, common speech, organizational titles, public addresses, and bathroom doors frequently designate the women in question as *ladies.* Simply contrast the different connotations of *lady* and *woman* in the following common phrases:

> *Luck, be a lady (woman) tonight.*
> *Barbara's a little lady (woman).*
> *Ladies' (Women's) Air Corps.*

In the first two examples, the use of *lady* desexualizes the contextual meaning of *woman.* So trivializing is the use of *lady* in the last phrase that the second is wholly anomalous. The male equivalent, *lord,* is never used, and its synonym, *gentleman,* is used infrequently. When *gentleman* is used, the assumption seems to be that certain culturally condoned aspects of masculinity (e.g., aggressivity, activity, and strength) should be set aside in the interests of maturity and order, as in the following phrases:

> *A gentlemen's (men's) agreement.*
> *A duel between gentlemen (men).*
> *He's a real gentleman (man).*

Rather than feeling constrained to set aside the stereotypes associated with *man,* males frequently find the opposite process occurring. The contextual connotation of *man* places a strain on males to be continuously sexually and socially potent, as the following examples reveal:

> *I was not a man (gentleman) with her tonight.*
> *This is a man's (gentleman's) job.*
> *Be a man (gentleman).*

Whether males, therefore, feel competent or anxious, valuable or worthless in particular contexts is influenced by the demands placed on them by the expectations of the language.

Not only are men infrequently labeled *gentlemen,* but they are infrequently labeled *boys.* The term *boy* is reserved for young males, bellhops, and car attendants, and as a putdown to those males judged inferior. *Boy* connotes immaturity and powerlessness. Only occasionally do males "have a night out with the boys." They do not talk "boy talk" at the office. Rarely does our language legitimize carefreeness in males. Rather, they are expected, linguistically, to adopt the responsibilities of manhood.

On the other hand, women of all ages may be called *girls.* Grown females "play bridge with the girls" and indulge in "girl talk." They are encouraged to remain childlike, and the implication is that they are basically immature and without power. Men can become men, linguistically, putting aside the immaturity of childhood; indeed, for them to retain the openness and playfulness of boyhood is linguistically difficult.

Further, the presumed incompetence and immaturity of women are evidenced by the linguistic company they keep. Women are categorized with children ("women and children first"), the infirm ("the blind, the lame, the women"), and the incompetent ("women, convicts, and idiots"). The use of these categorical designations is not accidental happenstance; "rather these selectional groupings are powerful forces behind the actual expressions of language and are based on distinctions which are not regarded as trivial by the speakers of the language" (Key, 1975:82). A total language analysis of categorical groupings is not available, yet it seems likely that women tend to be included in groupings that designate incompleteness, ineptitude, and immaturity. On the other hand, it is difficult for us to conceive of the word *man* in any categorical grouping other than one that extends beyond humanity, such as "Man, apes, and angels" or "Man and Superman." That is, men do exist as an independent category capable of autonomy; women are grouped with the stigmatized, the immature, and the foolish. Moreover, when men are in human groupings, they are invariably first on the list ("men and women," "he and she," "man and wife"). This order is not accidental but was prescribed in the sixteenth century to honor the worthier party.

Fourth, in practice women are defined in terms of their sexual desirability (to men); men are defined in terms of their sexual prowess (over women). Most slang words in reference to women refer to their sexual desirability to men (e.g., *dog, fox, broad, ass, chick*). Slang about men refers to their sexual prowess over women (e.g., *dude, stud, hunk*). The fewer examples given for men is not an oversight. An analysis of sexual slang, for example, listed more than a thousand words and phrases that derogate women sexually but found "nowhere near this multitude for describing men" (Kramarae, 1975:72). Farmer and Henley (cited in Schulz, 1975) list five hundred synonyms for *prostitute,* for example, and only sixty-five for *whoremonger.* Stanley (1977) reports two hundred twenty terms for a sexually promiscuous woman and only twenty-two for a sexually promiscuous man. Shuster (1973) reports that the passive verb form is used in reference to women's sexual experiences (e.g., *to be laid, to be had, to be taken*), whereas the active tense is used in reference to the male's sexual experience (e.g., *lay, take, have*). Being sexually attractive to males is culturally condoned for women and being sexually powerful is approved for males. In this regard, the slang of the street is certainly not countercultural; rather, it perpetuates and reinforces different expectations in females and males as sexual objects and performers.

Further, we find sexual connotations associated with neutral words applied to women. A few examples should suffice. A male academician questioned the title of a new course, asserting it was "too suggestive." The title? "The Position of Women in the Social Order." A male tramp is simply a hobo, but a female tramp is a slut. And consider the difference in connotation of the following expressions:

> *It's easy.*
> *He's easy.*
> *She's easy.*

In the first, we assume something is "easy to do"; in the second, we might assume a professor is an "easy grader" or a man is "easygoing." But when we read "she's easy," the connotation is "she's an easy lay."

In the world of slang, men are defined by their sexual prowess. In the world of slang and proper speech, women are defined as sexual objects. The rule in practice seems to be: If in doubt, assume that *any* reference to a women has a sexual connotation. For both genders, the constant bombardment of prescribed sexuality is bound to have real consequences.

Fifth, women are defined in terms of their relations to men; men are defined in terms of their relations to the world at large. A good example is seen in the words *master* and *mistress*. Originally these words had the same meaning—"a person who holds power over servants." With the demise of the feudal system, however, these words took on different meanings. The masculine variant metaphorically refers to power over something; as in "He is the master of his trade"; the feminine variant metaphorically (although probably not in actuality) refers to power over a man sexually, as in "She is Tom's mistress." Men are defined in terms of their power in the occupational world, women in terms of their sexual power over men.

The existence of two contractions for Mistress (*Miss* and *Mrs.*) and but one for Mister (*Mr.*) underscores the cultural concern and linguistic practice: women are defined in relation to men. Even a divorced woman is defined in terms of her no-longer-existing relation to a man (she is still *Mrs. Man's Name*). But apparently the divorced state is not relevant enough to the man or to the society to require a label. A divorced woman is a *divorcée*, but what do you call a divorced man? The recent preference of many women to be called *Ms.* is an attempt to provide for women an equivalency title that is not dependent on marital status.

Sixth, a historical pattern can be seen in the meanings that come to be attached to words that originally were neutral: those that apply to women acquire obscene and/or debased connotations, but no such pattern of derogation holds for neutral words referring to men. The processes of *pejoration* (the acquiring of an obscene or debased connotation) and *amelioration* (the reacquiring of a neutral or positive connotation) in the English language in regard to terms for males and females have been studied extensively by Muriel Schulz (1975).

Leveling is the least derogative form of pejoration. Through leveling, titles that originally referred to an elite class of persons come to include a wider class of persons. Such democratic leveling is more common for female designates than for males. For example, contrast the following: *lord–lady; baronet–dame; governor–governess*.

Most frequently what happens to words designating women as they become pejorated, however, is that they come to denote or connote sexual wantonness. *Sir* and *mister*, for example, remain titles of courtesy, but at some time *madam, miss*, and *mistress* have come to designate, respectively, a brothelkeeper, a prostitute, and an unmarried sexual partner of a male (Schulz, 1975:66).

Names for domestic helpers, if they are females, are frequently derogated. *Hussy,* for example, originally meant "housewife." *Laundress, needlewoman, spinster* ("tender of the spinning wheel"), and *nurse* all referred to domestic occupations within the home, and all at some point became slang expressions for prostitute or mistress.

Even kinship terms referring to women become denigrated. During the seventeenth century, *mother* was used to mean "a bawd"; more recently *mother* (*mothuh f—*) has become a common derogatory epithet (Cameron, 1974). Probably at some point in history every kinship term for females has been derogated (Schulz, 1975:66).

Terms of endearment for women also seem to follow a downward path. Such pet names as Tart, Dolly, Kitty, Polly, Mopsy, Biddy, and Jill all eventually became sexually derogatory (Schulz, 1975:67). *Whore* comes from the same Latin root as *care* and once meant "a lover of either sex."

Indeed, even the most neutral categorical designations—*girl, female, woman, lady*—at some point in their history have been used to connote sexual immorality. *Girl* originally meant "a child of either sex"; through the process of semantic degeneration it eventually meant "a prostitute." Although *girl* has lost this meaning, *girlie* still retains sexual connotations. *Woman* connoted "a mistress" in the early nineteenth century; *female* was a degrading epithet in the latter part of the nineteenth century; and when *lady* was introduced as a euphemism, it too became deprecatory. "Even so neutral a term as *person*, when it was used as substitute for *woman*, suffered [vulgarization]" (Mencken, 1963:350, quoted in Schulz, 1975:71).

Whether one looks at elite titles, occupational roles, kinship relationships, endearments, or age-sex categorical designations, the pattern is clear. Terms referring to females are pejorated—"become negative in the middle instances and abusive in the extremes" (Schulz, 1975:69). Such semantic derogation, however, is not evidenced for male referents. *Lord, baronet, father, brother, nephew, footman, bowman, boy, lad, fellow, gentleman, man, male*, and so on "have failed to undergo the derogation found in the history of their corresponding feminine designations" (Schulz, 1975:67). Interestingly, the male word, rather than undergoing derogation, frequently is replaced by a female referent when the speaker wants to debase a male. A weak man, for example, is referred to as a *sissy* (diminutive of *sister*), and an army recruit during basic training is called a *pussy*. And when one is swearing at a male, he is referred to as a *bastard* or a *son of a bitch*—both appellations that impugn the dignity of a man's mother.

In summary, these verbal practices are consistent with the gender stereotypes that we encounter in everyday life. Women are thought to be a part of man, nonautonomous, dependent, relegated to roles that require few skills, characteristically incompetent and immature, sexual objects, best defined in terms of their relations to men. Males are visible, autonomous and independent, responsible for the protection and containment of women, expected to occupy positions on the basis of their high achievement or physical power, assumed to be sexually potent, and defined primarily by their relations to the world of work. The use of the language perpetuates the stereotypes for both genders and limits the options available for self-definition.

REFERENCES

Adamsky, C. 1981. "Changes in pronominal usage in a classroom situation." *Psychology of Women Quarterly* 5:773–79.

Bendix, J. 1979. "Linguistic models as political symbols: Gender and the generic 'he' in English." In J. Orasanu, M. Slater, and L. L. Adler, eds., *Language, Sex and Gender: Does la différence Make a Difference?* pp. 23–42. New York: New Academy of Science Annuals.

Cameron, P. 1974. "Frequency and kinds of words in various social settings, or What the hell's going on?" In M. Truzzi, ed., *Sociology for Pleasure,* pp. 31–37. Englewood Cliffs, N.J.: Prentice Hall.

Daly, M. 1973. *Beyond God the Father.* Boston: Beacon Press.

DeStefano, J. S. 1976. Personal communication. Columbus: Ohio State University.

Hamilton, N., & Henley, N. 1982. "Detrimental consequences of the generic masculine usage." Paper presented to the Western Psychological Association meetings, Sacramento.

Key, M. R. 1975. *Male/Female Language.* Metuchen, N.J.: Scarecrow Press.

Kramarae, Cheris. 1975. "Woman's speech: Separate but unequal?" In Barrie Thorne and Nancy Henley, eds., *Language and Sex: Difference and Dominance,* pp. 43–56. Rowley, Mass.: Newbury House.

MacKay, D. G. 1983. "Prescriptive grammar and the pronoun problem." In B. Thorne, C. Kramarae, and N. Henley, eds., *Language, Gender, and Society,* pp. 38–53. Rowley, Mass.: Newbury House.

Martyna, W. 1978. "What does 'he' mean? Use of the generic masculine." *Journal of Communication* 28:131–38.

Martyna, W. 1980. "Beyond the 'he/man' approach: The case for nonsexist language." *Signs* 5:482–93.

Mencken, H. L. 1963. *The American Language.* 4th ed. with supplements. Abr. and ed. R. I. McDavis. New York: Knopf.

Schneider, J., & Hacker, S. 1973. "Sex role imagery in the use of the generic 'man' in introductory texts: A case in the sociology of sociology." *American Sociologist* 8:12–18.

Schulz, M. R. 1975. "The semantic derogation of women." In B. Thorne and N. Henley, eds., *Language and Sex: Difference and Dominance,* pp. 64–75. Rowley, Mass.: Newbury House.

Shuster, Janet. 1973. "Grammatical forms marked for male and female in English." Unpublished paper. Chicago: University of Chicago.

Stanley, J. P. 1977. "Paradigmatic woman: The prostitute." In D. L. Shores, ed., *Papers in Language Variation.* Birmingham: University of Alabama Press.

Vanderbilt, A. 1972. *Amy Vanderbilt's Etiquette.* Garden City, N.Y.: Doubleday.

THE *Ms.* OF BAGHDAD

Lauren Sandler

In the lobby of the Palestine hotel, everyone knows Estabarak Al Shamre. "She's the one who is different," says the receptionist, pointing across a room bustling with foreign journalists, Iraqi businessmen and veiled women. There, standing confidently on platform mules, is a 25-year-old in a bell-bottomed suit, and heavily lined eyes and lips. In the States, Al Shamre would hardly be the picture of a feminist editor exposing, at grave risk, abuses against women. But in Iraq, where her magazine stands alongside newly available copies of *Vogue* and *Marie Claire,* that's exactly what she has begun to do.

"In Iraq, some women are not brave enough to speak out about what has happened here. But we are, and our magazine will help Iraqi women to speak out as well," says Al Shamre. "Now we are willing to say anything, because finally we don't fear anything."

Nisf Al Dunia, Arabic for "half the world," is the first women's magazine to debut post-Saddam. Its decided difference from the women's magazines it replaces provides an allegory for the potential for free expression—especially for women—since the war. *Nisf Al Dunia* is filled with stories about women's oppression in Iraq. One exposes sexual abuse at a Baghdad mental institution. Another narrates a woman's years on the run from Saddam.

That woman is Al Shamre herself, writing under a pen name for fear of exposure in her own country. She married a man whose tribe was involved in an assassination attempt on Saddam Hussein that claimed instead the life of one of Saddam's stand-ins, and she lived on the lam in Europe for years until leaving her husband out of exhaustion and fear.

The publication of the former dictator's image, not to mention most of the stories that make up the magazine's content, was unimaginable in the world of Iraqi publishing under the regime. *Nisf Al Dunia* reads like a manifesto compared to its predecessors. For years, Al Shamre was writing privately about wrongs against women, even doing her own clandestine reporting, although magazines such as the regime-supported *Ishtar* would never have published her. She'd lock her writing away in a secret drawer. Just a year ago she destroyed her work in fear that Saddam's secret police would discover it.

Al Shamre has resurrected her writings to give them a public life in her magazine—like the stories she collected of five women who were raped and impregnated that became a centerpiece of the second issue.

Nisf Al Dunia will also take on all religious parties in Iraq with a highly controversial look at temporary marriages. In Islam, no woman is allowed to engage in sexual intercourse outside of marriage. But Shia Islam permits "temporary marriage," when a woman can be married under Allah, though not under the state, for an established period of time—say, three months—to experience the benefits of marriage, usually financial ones. Sunni Islam is opposed to this practice, as are Christians in Iraq, and so most temporary marriages exist only in secret in this society that fears scandal almost as much as the former regime. For the upcoming issue of the magazine, Al Shamre has interviewed clerics from the two sects, as well as psychiatrists and women veiled to protect their identity. She takes on extremists of all stripes in a story so controversial, she can discuss it only in whispers over 7-Up in the quiet hotel bar.

Also in the next issue, her narrative of her years fleeing Saddam will continue. And in some ways, to Al Shamre, that's the true marker of liberation in Iraq.

"So many women I know, like myself, we have lived through hell; we've had the most horrendous experiences here. But now we get to tell those stories, to expose the truth. The horrors haven't stopped, with the lack of security for women here... all the kidnapping and raping that gets worse all the time... but at least we can talk about it openly for the first time," she says, stubbing out a cigarette with a manicured hand and swiftly lighting another. "And that's revolutionary here."

Cosmetic Surgery: Paying for Your Beauty

After several unsuccessful attempts to schedule an appointment, I finally managed to meet with Jennifer, a twenty-nine-year-old grade school teacher who volunteered to talk with me about her cosmetic surgery. On a typically cold November afternoon, I spoke with Jennifer in her apartment on the south shore of Long Island. Jennifer is 5 feet 6 inches tall and has long, straight blonde hair and expressive light blue eyes. That day she was dressed in an oversized gray pullover and black sweatpants. While we talked, she peeled and sliced the crudites that would be her contribution to the potluck engagement party that she was attending later that evening.

During our conversation, I noticed that by far the most prominent feature in her small studio apartment was the enormous black and chrome stair-climbing machine set slightly off from the center of the living room/bedroom. I learned that Jennifer spends forty minutes each day on this machine and works out with weights at a nearby gym three to four times a week. She eats no meat, very little oil or fat, and no sweets, and she drinks very little alcohol. Despite her rigorous body work routine, Jennifer's legs have remained a disappointment to her. Rather than lean and muscular, they look, by her account, thick and shapeless—particularly around her lower thighs and knees. Jennifer says that her decision to have liposuction was motivated primarily by her inability to reshape her legs through diet and exercise. During the procedure, the fatty deposits were removed from the insides of Jennifer's knees, making her legs appear slimmer and more toned.

Jennifer acknowledged her own significant ambivalence about taking surgical steps to alter her body. If possible, she would have preferred to shape her legs through aerobics, weight training, and dieting, rather than through liposuction, which Jennifer described as a final and desperate option. By her account, plastic surgery was the only way to alter physical attributes that she referred to as "genetic flaws," features that she could change through no other available means. Expressing some shame, as she says, "for taking the easy way out," Jennifer's guilt is not so great that she regrets having surgery. Indeed, she plans to have a second liposuction in the near future, this time to remove the fatty tissue from her upper and inner thighs.

Cosmetic surgery stands, for many theorists and social critics, as the ultimate invasion of the human body for the sake of physical beauty. It epitomizes the astounding lengths to which contemporary women will go to obtain bodies that meet current ideals of attractiveness. As such, plastic surgery is perceived by many to be qualitatively different from aerobics, hair styling, or even dieting. In this view, cosmetic surgery is not about controlling one's own body but is instead an activity so extreme, so invasive that it can only be interpreted as subjugation. Even more than women who may participate in other types of body-shaping activities, those who undergo cosmetic surgery appear to many observers—both casual and academic—to be so obsessed with physical appearance that they are willing to risk their very existence to become more attractive.

Not surprisingly, cosmetic surgery has been attacked by the scores of feminist writers who criticize body work generally.[1] While these attacks may be well deserved, the cosmetic surgery industry is expanding rapidly nevertheless. Board-certified plastic surgeons performed more than 2.2 million procedures in 1999, a 44 percent increase since 1996 and striking 153 percent increase since 1992. Liposuction, the most common cosmetic procedure in the United States, was performed 230,865 times (up 57 percent since 1996 and 264 percent since 1992), at a cost of approximately $2,000 per patient. Breast augmentation, with its price tag of nearly $3,000, was the second most common procedure, at 167,318 (a 51 percent increase since 1996). Blepharoplasty (eyelid surgery), the third most common, was performed on 142,033 patients at a cost of just under $3,000, followed by face-lift (72,793) at over $5,000, and chemical peel (51,519), at nearly $1,300.[2] Ninety percent of these operations are performed on women, as are virtually all breast augmentations and reductions, 87 percent of liposuctions, 91 percent of face-lifts, and 85 percent of blepharoplastics. In 1999, American women had 167,318 breast augmentations, 120,160 blepharoplasties, 201,083 liposuction procedures, and 66,096 face-lifts.[3]

Although strategies for surgically altering the body's appearance have been available for centuries, the practice has only recently become a mass phenomenon. Until recently, patients were most often men disabled by war or industrial accidents. Now the recipients are overwhelmingly women who are dissatisfied with their looks.[4] Today, aesthetic operations make up 45 percent of all plastic surgery.[5]

Cosmetic surgery is one of the fastest-growing specialities in American medicine.[6] Although the total number of physicians in the United States has little more than doubled in the last quarter of a century, the number of plastic surgeons has increased fourfold. At the end of World War II, there were only about 100 plastic surgeons in the country; in 1965, there were 1,133. By 1990, that number had tripled to 3,850. Moreover, these figures may underrepresent the total number of individuals performing aesthetic procedures today. Because it is not necessary to be a licensed plastic surgeon to perform cosmetic surgery, procedures such as face-lifts, eyelid corrections, and chemical peels may be performed by other specialists, such as dermatologists.[7]

Criticisms of surgical alternation of the female body multiply nearly as rapidly as the procedures themselves. One of the main critiques of cosmetic surgery derives from the dangers involved. Cosmetic surgery is undeniably painful and risky, and each operation involves specific potential complications. For instance, pain, numbness, bruising, discoloration, and depigmentation frequently follow a liposuction, often lingering up to six months after the operation. Face-lifts can damage nerves, leaving the patient's face permanently numb. More serious complications include fat embolisms, blood clots, fluid depletion, and even death. Health experts estimate that the chance of serious side effects from breast augmentation are between 30 percent and 50 percent. The least dramatic and most common of these include decreased sensitivity in the nipples, painful swelling or congestion of the breasts, and hardening of the breasts that makes it difficult to lie down comfortably or to raise the arms without shifting the implants.[8] More serious is the problem of encapsulation, in which the body reacts to foreign materials by forming a capsule of fibrous tissue around the implants. This covering can sometimes be broken down manually by the surgeon, but, even when successful, the procedure is extremely painful. When it is unsuccessful, the implants must be removed; in some cases, the surgeon must chisel the hardened substance from the patient's chest wall.

Clearly, the recipient of cosmetic surgery may emerge from the operation in worse shape than when she went in. Unsuccessful breast augmentations are often disfiguring, leaving the patient with unsightly scars and deformation. An overly tight face-lift produces a "zombie" look, in which the countenance seems devoid of expression. Following liposuction, the skin can develop a corrugated, uneven texture.

Finally, some criticisms of plastic surgery focus on the implications of such procedures for contemporary conceptualizations of the body and identity. Cosmetic surgery has expanded alongside specific technological developments, including advances in medical equipment like magnifying lenses, air drills for severing bone and leveling skin, and improved suturing materials, all of which enable surgical interventions to be performed with better results and less trauma for the patient.[9] According to some critics, these developments, and the increasing flexibility in body altering that they permit, are linked to cultural discourses likening the body to what Susan Bordo has called "cultural plastic." The body is now understood as having a potential for limitless change, "undetermined by history, social location or even individual biography."[10] Not only has the body come to stand as a primary symbol of identity, but it is a symbol with an unlimited capacity for alteration and modification. The body is not a dysfunctional object requiring medical intervention but a commodity, not unlike "a car, a refrigerator, a house, which can be continuously upgraded and modified in accordance with new interests and greater resources."[11] The body is a symbol of selfhood, but its relation to its inhabitant is shaped primarily by the individual's capacity for material consumption.

Of the various forms of body work, plastic surgery is surely the hardest to justify. The physical dangers are real. The symbolic damage done to all women by the apparent surrender of some to unattainable ideals of beauty is significant. Yet the criticisms also leave out a good deal. Most important, the criticisms operate either at the grand level of cultural discourse or the highly grounded level of physiological effect. As a result, they overlook the experience of the women who have plastic surgery. In this [reading], after first discussing the role of the doctor as a gatekeeper to plastic surgery, I focus on that experience.

First—and most important to those who undergo it—plastic surgery often works. This fact stands in contrast to a rhetoric that concentrates on the unattainable character of contemporary beauty ideals, portraying plastic surgery as a Sisyphean task. Critics of plastic surgery imply that those who undergo it will complete one operation only to discover some new flaw. Yet this is not the case. Somewhat to my surprise, many of the women I interviewed expressed enormous satisfaction with their procedures. While some did, indeed, intend to return for additional operations, others seemed content to have fixed a particular "flaw." I do not mean to argue that all contemporary ideals of beauty are, in fact, attainable. They are not. Neither do I mean to argue that women in contemporary America can escape the nagging self-doubts caused by those unattainable ideals. They cannot. But the ambitions of those women who undergo plastic surgery often stop far short of attaining ideal beauty. And given these limited ambitions—and within the cultural space marked out for the expression of female beauty—plastic surgery frequently achieves the exact goals intended by those who undergo it.

Second, criticisms of plastic surgery directed at gender issues often understate the extent to which this activity involves gender at an intersection with age, race, ethnicity, and even class. Many women surely undertake plastic surgery, most notably in the case of breast enlargement, to enhance distinctively female attributes. Others, however—Jewish and Italian women who have rhinoplasty, Chinese and Japanese women who have their eyes reshaped—do so in a distinctively ethnic context. And many others have plastic surgery in an attempt to reproduce the bodies of their youth. If plastic surgery speaks to the depredations of gender domination, we should recognize that it also speaks to the depredations of Anglo-Saxon ideals of beauty and the idealization of youth.

Third, the criticisms of plastic surgery ignore the complicated process by which the women who undergo surgical procedures integrate them into their identities. If not in feminist theory, then in popular culture, there lies an implicit notion that the benefits of plastic surgery are somehow inauthentic and, therefore, undeserved. Although the critics of plastic surgery insist that appearance should not be the measure of a woman's worth, the women who have plastic surgery are nonetheless participants in a culture in which appearance is taken as an expression of an inner state. To be able to purchase a new nose or wider eyes or thinner thighs seems, then, to sever the relationship between inner states and their outer expression. Where the women in aerobics classes are working hard to detach their identities from their bodies, the women who undergo plastic surgery must work even harder to reattach their identities to their new appearances. On the one hand, they are using plastic surgery to tell a story about themselves: I am the woman with svelte thighs or a button nose. On the other hand, they must also tell a story about plastic surgery in order to counter the charges of its inauthenticity. They must somehow show, to themselves even more than to others, that the new appearance is both deserved and a better indicator of the self than the old appearance—an appearance necessarily repositioned as "accidental." The result, then, is that the woman who has plastic surgery finds herself in a double bind. She is unhappy with her appearance, and so she takes the only steps she can to improve it. No matter how successful her efforts are—or how pleased she is with their outcome—the woman must ultimately defend her decision to purchase appearance and identity.

RESEARCH AND METHODS

The research for this [reading] involved fieldwork in a Long Island plastic surgery clinic and interviews with the surgeon and twenty of his female patients. Finding a location to study cosmetic surgery proved difficult because many women hesitate to admit that they have undergone such procedures and physicians are bound by doctor-patient confidentiality. Having organized my research around interviews and fieldwork in identifiable physical locations, I knew that I wanted to talk with a single surgeon's female patients, rather than a "snowball" sample of surgery clients, whom I could have located easily through advertisements in local newspapers, gyms, universities, or hairstyling salons. As a result, I needed to find a cosmetic surgeon who would permit me access to patients. My search for this doctor took nearly six months, during which time I contacted over twenty clinics and interviewed seven physicians.

I eventually chose to focus on the clinic of Dr. John Norris, a local surgeon specializing in aesthetic procedures. My discussions with the six other physicians proved to be a rich source of data about the cosmetic surgery industry and cosmetic surgeons themselves. I learned, for example, that cosmetic surgeons are frequently critical of their female clientele, seeing them as obsessed and impossible to please. Moreover, often believing that the physical imperfections that their clients observe are insignificant, surgeons sometimes suspect their patients of trying to solve emotional problems by altering their bodies.

I met John Norris at the gym where I studied aerobics. As a member of the gym, I spent a considerable amount of time there each week, both in research and on my own body work. John and his wife, Monica, were gym regulars who, like me, tended to exercise in the mornings, and I saw them several times each week. Even though I had met him previously, I contacted John formally, as I did the other cosmetic surgeons in the area. I explained my project to his receptionist and made an appointment to speak with him. After our second meeting, I asked John to allow me to interview twenty of his female clients. He agreed and asked his receptionist to contact women who might be willing to talk with me. After obtaining his patients' approval, John provided me with their names and telephone numbers. This procedure surely biased my sample in favor of successful cases. In addition to interviewing patients (one of whom I was able to interview both before and after she had surgery), I conducted several interviews with John. I also attended informational sessions at another local clinic to learn more about many of these procedures.

John conducts his enormously successful practice in two offices, one on Long Island and the other in Manhattan. I spoke with him at some length about his interest in aesthetic plastic surgery. He explained that although he had originally aspired to be a sculptor, he soon decided that a career in art would not provide an adequate income. As his interest in science developed, John opted instead for a medical career and for what he now refers to as the "excitement of sculpting human appearance." Believing that his work helps his patients to feel more satisfied with the way they look, more desirable, and more confident in their professional and private lives, John says that he derives enormous satisfaction from his career.

John is interested not only in "sculpting" the appearances of others; he is himself heavily involved in the culture of body work. In particular, John has participated in bodybuilding since he was fifteen years old and, at age fifty-one, still participates regularly in bodybuilding competitions. Moreover, John has personally undergone plastic surgery to remove the "love handles" that he says will develop at his waistline unless he maintains a body composition of no more than 3 percent body fat. As his medical career has progressed, John's training and competition have both fueled and been fueled by his interest in using surgery to rework the aesthetics of the body. While he began his career doing reconstructive and burn-correcting surgery in addition to cosmetic procedures, he now focuses almost exclusively on aesthetic plastic surgery, which he finds equally rewarding and more enjoyable.

Similar to the staff of Pamela's Hair Salon [discussed in another part of *Body Work: Beauty and Self-image in American Culture* (Berkeley: University of California Press, 2002), from which this reading is taken], John is a "true believer" in beauty ideology. Like the stylists, John not only dispenses the means of altering appearance but also is deeply involved in reworking his own appearance. Nevertheless, he is differentiated from them by his higher social status. Like Pamela's staff, John is able both to assess his clients' appearance "flaws" and to suggest particular techniques for correcting them. But, unlike Pamela's staff—and primarily because of his status as a medical professional—John's patients nearly always accept his advice. Simply put, John is different from Pamela's stylists because he not only dispenses "beauty" to his patients but also shapes the choices they make about their appearances.

Moreover, John regularly denies surgical candidates access to the body work he provides. He is selective in choosing his clientele, screening patients to ensure that they are suitable for the operations they request. Listening to the client's description of her physical imperfections, John determines whether or not her complaint is reasonable—whether or not her nose is really inappropriate for her face, her breasts are really too small, her ankles are really too thick, and so on. In making such judgments, John (like the beauticians at Pamela's) blurs the line between technique and aesthetics, effectively broadening his area of expertise.

While understanding his activity as a process of determining the "appropriateness" of surgical candidates, he actually selects patients based in large part on his personal taste and sense of aesthetics. As a purveyor of body work, John positions himself not only as a surgeon but also as an expert in contemporary standards for female beauty.

In deciding whether patients are suitable candidates for the procedures they request, John judges not only the aesthetics of their appearance but also their psychological health. By his own account, John attempts to determine whether patients are trying to deal with personal crises (such as divorce) through plastic surgery. John says that when he talks with potential patients about their motivations for having cosmetic surgery, many express sadness or fear regarding a significant personal relationship, even to the point of breaking down in tears in his office. This reaction, he claims, suggests that patients should seek the services of "some other type" of professional presumably, a psychologist or marital counselor—rather than those of a cosmetic surgeon.

John has come to categorize patients in four conceptual types, distinguished primarily by their motivations for having surgery. The first of the groups includes individuals who are "self-motivated and realistic." These patients pursue surgery as a means of bringing their appearances in line with their inner self. Claiming that their bodies fail to represent them as the people they truly are, individuals in this group explain their desire for cosmetic surgery with statements such as "I don't feel like an old person. I don't want to look like one," or "I exercise and diet. I want to look like I do." These candidates, according to John, are adequately prepared for cosmetic surgery, with expectations that will likely be met by the procedures they undergo.

The second type of patient seeks out plastic surgery to please someone else. In John's description, this patient—usually a woman—is going through a painful breakup and, hoping that changing her appearance will reignite her partner's interest, turns to plastic surgery as a "last-ditch effort" to save her relationship. Breast augmentation—which, John notes with some amusement, is the surgical procedure most likely to precede divorce—is a common request among members of this category. John typically refuses to perform such procedures on patients who hope to use plastic surgery to solve some personal problem.

The third group in John's typology involves children, usually brought to the office by their parents. According to John, these patients' parents frequently say things such as "She has her father's nose," which the parents, rather than the children themselves, judge as unattractive and requiring change. John makes it a practice to ask the adolescents what they think about the particular body part. According to him, they tend to be relatively satisfied with the "nose" or other problematic feature, finding it far less objectionable than the parents do. John advises parents not to "fix what isn't broken," to give the child a few years to "grow into" the feature and then broach the topic of surgery again if they feel it necessary.

The last group includes individuals John refers to as "flighty," who want surgery for any number of "bizarre" reasons. As an example, John described one woman who wanted to have rhinoplasty because a favorite movie star had undergone the procedure. In another case, a potential patient requested breast augmentation in order to look more like a celebrity her boyfriend admired. In such cases, John refuses to operate because he considers these individuals to be psychologically unstable and impossible to satisfy.

All told, John claims that he rejects two or three requests per week. His ability and willingness to deny service suggest another comparison between the plastic surgeon and the hairstylist: John is less dependent on his clientele than are the beauticians at Pamela's, who have little choice concerning whose hair they style or how they style it. At the same time, John's decisions to reject patients are linked to his medical and legal responsibility for the surgeries that he performs. Indeed, his motivations for denying surgical procedures suggest a wariness about trying to satisfy the desires of individuals whose expectations are unreasonable and who might hold him legally responsible for their inevitable dissatisfaction. In this sense, John is even more vulnerable to his clients than are the stylists at Pamela's. While a beautician might lose a client who dislikes her haircut, John could potentially lose much more to a patient who claims that he is responsible for some physical deformity, particularly if that patient decides to sue.

The patients I interviewed ranged in age from twenty-four to fifty. The procedures they underwent included breast augmentations, nose jobs, face-lifts, eye-reshaping procedures, tummy tucks, and liposuctions. All of the women were Asian-American or European American; three were of Semitic ancestry;

and all but one (a full-time mother) held salaried jobs or were students at the time of the interviews. They were employed as opticians, medical technicians, receptionists, insurance agents, teachers, office administrators, hairstylists, and secretaries.

THE STORY OF A FACE-LIFT: ANN MARIE

Ann Marie, a slender, soft-spoken fifty-year-old medical technician with upswept blonde hair, was one of the first patients I interviewed. Married to her current and only husband for nearly thirty years, Ann Marie carries herself with a careful gentility. Dressed in snug-fitting woolen pants, low-heeled brown pumps and a fuzzy light mauve sweater, Ann Marie invites me into her small, tidy home and asks if I would like coffee. Anxious to begin my first interview, I refuse. Ann Marie brings her own drink back from the kitchen in a tiny, flower-painted china cup and saucer and begins telling me about her experiences with plastic surgery.

Ann Marie is not at all shy about discussing her face-lift. She actually seems eager to tell me the reasons for her decision. Her appearance began to change in her late thirties and forties when she developed "puffiness underneath the eyes" and "drooping upper eyelids." Most unattractive, by Ann Marie's account, "the skin of my throat started getting creepy." In her words, "You get to an age" when "you look in the mirror and see lines that were not there before." Because her physical appearance had begun to reflect the aging process, she explains, "All of a sudden, the need [for cosmetic surgery] was there."

While Ann Marie describes her need for a face-lift as "sudden," she had planned to have the procedure long before. She recalls that "about ten years ago," she spoke with several close friends about having a face-lift at some point in the future. She explains, "We talked about it a long time ago. I guess I have never accepted the axiom of growing old gracefully. I have always sworn I would never picture myself as a chubby old lady." Ann Marie and her friends "talked and decided that when the time was just right, we would definitely do it." Ann Marie is the only member of the group who actually went through with surgery.

Despite her resolve, Ann Marie did not enter into cosmetic surgery lightly. Instead, for several years she "thought about it from time to time. There was a lot to be considered." Among the issues she contemplated

were the physical dangers involved in the operation, the risk of looking worse after the surgery than before, and the importance of choosing a well-qualified doctor with an excellent reputation. She explains, "You are putting your face in the hands of a surgeon; there is the possibility of absolute disaster, very possibly permanently. You have to choose the surgeon very carefully."

Ann Marie chose John Norris to perform the face-lift. Largely because he had performed an emergency procedure for her just over one year earlier, Ann Marie claims that she felt completely comfortable with him. "John was recommended to me by my dermatologist. I had an infection on my face; it was quite serious. The dermatologist told me I had to go to a plastic surgeon, and John was the only one he would recommend." Because of the dermatologist's recommendation and her satisfaction with John's earlier work, Ann Marie returned to him for the face-lift. She visited his office in Long Island for a consultation and, not long after her appointment, decided to go ahead with the procedure.

During their first meeting, Ann Marie had what she refers to as two "surprises": one was the price of the operation and the other the news that she would have to stop smoking. According to Ann Marie, John explained that "you will not heal as well if you continue to smoke. Because it impedes circulation, smoking decreases your ability to heal properly." She says, "The most difficult part was to stop smoking. I was puffing away a pack and a half a day for over twenty years." John told Ann Marie that she would not be able to smoke for three months before the surgery. She says, "I thought, What? I will never be able to do this. But I did, I stopped cold. That was the real sacrifice for me."

While giving up cigarettes may have been the greatest sacrifice for Ann Marie, there were clearly many others. For a full year, Ann Marie had to work "one day job, one night job, occasionally a third job" to afford the surgery. She had to "bank" four weeks of overtime at her primary job so she could take time off to recover from the procedure. She also postponed repairs on her home. She explains, "There were things my house needed, but my feeling was, I needed a face-lift more than my house did."

By providing me with a long and detailed account of her need for a face-lift and the sacrifices she was willing to make to have the procedure, Ann Marie hints at an awareness that her behavior is somehow subject to criticism, that it might be construed by others as superficial or shallow. With a hint of defensiveness, Ann Marie explains that she "needed" the face-lift—despite its financial costs and physical risks—not merely because she is concerned with her appearance, but because of pressures in "the work-field." She says, "Despite the fact that we have laws against age discrimination, employers do find ways of getting around it. I know women my age who do not get jobs or are relieved of jobs because of age. . . . [The face-lift] will ensure my work ability." Ann Marie, by her account, decided to have cosmetic surgery not due to narcissism but to concern for her professional well-being. Justifying her behavior as a career decision, she implies that she is sensitive to the social disapproval of plastic surgery, that she knows that the behavior requires some justification.

Even though Ann Marie believes that looking younger will help her professionally, she also admits that she has "not seen anything that has really changed in that area." Instead, the procedure has affected her primarily "on a personal basis, a social basis." Explaining these effects in more detail, she says, "I meet people I haven't seen for two or three years who will say, 'There is something different about you, but I don't know what it is.' I met a sister of a very good friend of mine in June, which is five months after my surgery. She looked at me and said, 'I don't know you.' I said, 'Of course you do. I've known you nearly all of my life.' She realized who I was and was astounded at my appearance."

This incident, along with several similar ones, has, by Ann Marie's account, improved her self-image. By attributing these experiences—and the resulting improvement in her self-perception—to her face-lift, Ann Marie justifies her decision to have cosmetic surgery. In contemporary Western culture, "feeling good" about oneself is understood to be worth considerable effort because it makes us better workers, spouses, and citizens. Among children, self-esteem is credited with the ability to improve grades and to discourage sex and illegal drug use. Ann Marie explains her choice to have plastic surgery as "a matter of personal esteem. If you feel you look better, you feel better about yourself." By granting cosmetic surgery the power to provide self-esteem, Ann Marie—like many of the other women I spoke with—effectively legitimizes an otherwise illegitimate activity.

At the same time, Ann Marie's defensiveness suggests that she is somewhat self-conscious about her choice. She describes her decision to have a face-lift as "not purely vanity," and then adds, "If it is vanity, so what? That does not make me a bad person. I don't want to look bad. I don't want to look my age. I want to look younger. I want smoother skin." By her account, Ann Marie is not "bad" or vain; in fact, she is actually a good person, as evidenced by the other forms of body work in which she participates. She explains, "My weight is only a variance of six pounds heavier from what it was thirty years ago. I keep in shape in addition to the surgery. I jog, I exercise, I diet." Ann Marie has maintained her physical appearance of youth in every way possible—failing only to control the appearance of her facial skin, which she could not keep from "getting creepy." In her account, Ann Marie deserved the surgery—an act tinged with deception—because she has proved her moral character through other (physically demanding and highly symbolic) forms of work on her body. Ann Marie is entitled to an appearance that reflects those efforts, even if that appearance is obtainable only through cosmetic surgery.

"A DEEP, DARK SECRET": HAVING LIPOSUCTION

John arranged for me to speak with a twenty-seven-year-old woman named Bonnie who was planning to have cosmetic surgery. In sharp contrast to the other women I interviewed, Bonnie was hesitant to speak with me about the procedure, because, as she later said, she considered it to be "a deep, dark secret" that she had discussed with no one but her husband of five months. Bonnie worked out at the same gym that both John and I attended. Because she and I were previously acquainted, John suggested that Bonnie speak with me about the procedure she was considering, and she agreed. Over the next six months, Bonnie and I met several times to discuss cosmetic surgery; during that period, she decided to have liposuction, underwent the procedure, and recovered from it.

Having recently completed a master's degree at a New England university, Bonnie moved to the east end of Long Island to take a position as a chemist in a pharmaceutical firm. She explained to me that over the years she had spoken casually to various women about cosmetic surgery and had "fantasized about" having liposuction herself, though she had never considered it seriously. Prior to having the operation, Bonnie told me why she was reluctant to have cosmetic surgery:

> It's always seemed to me to be one step too far. I have dieted and exercised my whole life, and sometimes I've gone over the edge and done some things that probably weren't very healthy, but I could always stop myself before I became totally obsessed. I guess I have always thought that I would never get so obsessed that I would allow my body to be cut into just so I could look better. At least that's what I had always hoped. I couldn't imagine myself as one of "them," as one of those weak women who would go that far.

Despite her stated objections to cosmetic surgery and her characterization of its patients as "weak," Bonnie underwent liposuction on the outside of her upper thighs. Bonnie described this area of her body as "flabby, no matter what I do. I exercise five or six times a week; I cycle with my husband. I do all the weight lifting that is supposed to tone up the muscles in those areas. Nothing works!" Nevertheless, Bonnie never seriously investigated the procedure until she finished graduate school and began full-time employment. She explained, "This is the first time I've ever made enough money to think about doing something like this. The liposuction will cost $2,000, which is less than it usually costs because I won't have to have general anesthesia, but it's still a lot of money."

Referring to her new job and home, Bonnie noted that she would never have considered having cosmetic surgery while she was living near her family and friends. "I wouldn't want any of my friends or my family to know about it, only my husband. My family would all be like, 'You don't need to have that done. You're crazy. You are thin enough already.' That doesn't keep me from thinking these lumps on my thighs are really ugly. They are the only thing I see when I look in the mirror."

Bonnie's hesitance to discuss liposuction with her friends stems from her perception of cosmetic surgery as part of a process of "giving in to pressure, giving in to these ideals about how women should look, when none of us real women are ever going to look like that." Bonnie believes that her friends would react to her interest in plastic surgery by making her "feel so ashamed, like I am not strong enough to accept myself like I am."

Unlike most of John's patients, Bonnie articulates her ambivalence about plastic surgery primarily in political rather than personal terms. Her description of her friends' imagined objections is one of many examples of her concern with the political meaning of her actions. In another, Bonnie explains that her own political view of cosmetic surgery is the main source of her conflict over having the procedure. She says, "I am not worried about problems with the operation itself. I know that Dr. Norris has a great reputation. I've talked to other people at the gym who have used him, and they were all really happy. He does so much of this stuff, I'm sure he's really good at it." Bonnie's concerns focus instead on the social and cultural significance of her action. "If I am proud to be a woman, then I should be proud to look like a woman, with a woman's butt and a woman's thighs." Reacting to her own accusations, she notes, "I am proud to be a woman, but I really hate it when I get a glimpse of my backside and I just look big. I feel terrible knowing that it is those areas of my body which are understood to be most 'female' that I dislike the most." Expressing her interest in cosmetic surgery as her only viable option for reducing her dissatisfaction with her appearance, she adds,

> I don't really know how to get around it, though, because I really do not like those parts of my figure. Plastic surgery seems like a pretty good way, and really, a pretty easy way, to deal with that dissatisfaction, to put those negative feelings behind me . . . to move on with the rest of my life. . . . I'd love to get dressed for work in the morning and have only the work in front of me, rather than, you know, what's literally behind me, be the thing that concerns me the most.

Bonnie is explicitly aware that the body and the self are linked. When she says that she dislikes the "female" parts of her figure, one can easily imagine replacing the term "figure" with the term "self." Indeed, it is Bonnie's ambivalence about her female identity that is most troubling to her; eradicating the physical signs of femininity—and the flaws inherent in those attributes—may enable her to construct a self that she believes to be less imperfect, more culturally acceptable, and that will allow her to focus more attention on other activities and concerns, including her career, the sports she enjoys, and her new marriage. At the same time, her decision to undergo liposuction comes at a considerable cost; Bonnie says explicitly that, if possible, she would prefer to change her perceptions rather than her body. The "pressure" she feels, however, limits her ability to rework her self-image, leaving her to choose between plastic surgery and a negative self-concept, two options that are unsatisfying. Bonnie's decision to undergo liposuction suggests that, in the end, the costs associated with plastic surgery are somehow less significant than those attached to her appearance flaws.

Obviously, Ann Marie and Bonnie present two quite disparate facets of the concerns women face as they consider having cosmetic surgery. While Ann Marie struggled to meet the financial and physical requirements of her face-lift, Bonnie agonized over the political dimension of her decision to have liposuction. So distinct are these preoccupations, in fact, that they can be conceptualized as opposite ends of a continuum, along which the perspectives of the other eighteen women I interviewed can be placed. For most of these women, the political implications of cosmetic surgery, though not entirely insignificant, were far less important than they were for Bonnie. The other women I interviewed were more often concerned with the health risks and financial costs of cosmetic surgery and with how they would look after their procedures.

While Ann Marie's and Bonnie's preoperative anxieties took different forms, both constructed elaborate justifications for plastic surgery. Like the other women I interviewed, Bonnie responds to the negative identity implications of plastic surgery by explaining that she has done all that is humanly possible to alter an imperfect body but that no act short of plastic surgery will allow her to live peacefully with herself. Invariably, the women's accounts involve bodies that were flawed in some way for which the individual claimed not to be responsible. Each woman's body was imperfect not because she had erred in her body work but because of aging, genetics, or some other physical condition that she could not control. Their flawed bodies are inaccurate indicators of character, and so they effectively lie about who the women really are. Accounts like these permit women to engage in cosmetic procedures with less guilt. Plastic surgery becomes for them not an act of deception but an attempt to align body with self.

"THE BODY I WAS MEANT TO HAVE": WHY WOMEN HAVE COSMETIC SURGERY

Whereas some writers have dealt with cosmetic surgery as if it were an attempt to attain idealized female beauty in order to gain the approval of men,[12]

the women I interviewed claim that their goal in undergoing plastic surgery is neither to become beautiful nor to be beautiful specifically for husbands, boyfriends, or other significant individuals. Rather, they alter their bodies for their own satisfaction, in effect utilizing such procedures to create what they consider a normal appearance, one that reflects a normal self. While I do not accept their accounts without some skepticism, I believe that women who have plastic surgery are not necessarily doing so in order to become beautiful or to please particular individuals. Instead they are responding to highly restrictive notions of normality and the "normal" self, notions that neither apply to the population at large (in fact, quite the reverse) nor leave space for ethnic variation. Plastic surgery "works" for women who have these procedures, but it works only within the context of a culture of appearance that is less about beauty than it is about control based on the physical representations of gender, age, and ethnicity.

My respondents claim that prior to having surgery, some particular physical feature stood in the way of their looking "normal." This feature distinguished them from others and prohibited them from experiencing "a happy, regular life," as Marcy, a twenty-five-year-old student, put it. Marcy decided at twenty-one to have the bony arch in the middle of her nose removed and its tip shortened. Before the procedure, Marcy had never been involved in a romantic relationship, a fact that she attributed to her "hook" nose and unattractive appearance. Marcy says, "I have always felt terrible about how pronounced it was. No matter how I wore my hair, it was in the middle of my face, and everybody noticed it. It's not like I could just wear my bangs long."

Marcy decided to have rhinoplasty near a date that was particularly symbolic for her. "I was having my nose done just before Valentine's Day. I thought to myself, maybe if I have my nose done for Valentine's Day, by next Valentine's Day, I'll have a Valentine!" Although she did not find a Valentine for the following year—she explained that dating "didn't happen until a few years later"—Marcy claimed that over time, the surgery allowed her to experience pleasure that she would otherwise have missed.

Because Marcy uses cosmetic surgery to make herself more appealing to others, her experience seemingly supports the criticisms of authors like Naomi Wolf. However, Marcy stresses that she does not expect plastic surgery to make her beautiful. Neither does she believe that winning male affection requires her to be beautiful. Quite the contrary, Marcy clearly imagines that a merely normal appearance is sufficient to garner the male attention she desires.

The women describe several ways in which their physical features have kept them from living ordinary lives. For example, Barbara, a twenty-nine-year-old bookkeeper, says that her breasts—which were, by her account, too small to fill out attractive clothing—made her appear "dumpy" and ill-proportioned. Her "flaw" contributed to a negative self-image, which in turn served to limit the education and career goals Barbara set for herself, the friendships she fostered, and the romantic and sexual relationships she pursued. Barbara decided to have her breasts augmented (from a 36A to a 36D) to become, in her words, "more attractive to myself and others." While her larger breasts have in fact made Barbara feel more attractive, she, like other patients I interviewed, nevertheless laments women's inability to be self-confident despite their physical shortcomings. She says, "For women, the appearance is the important thing. That's too bad that we can't worry about not being judged. [Small breasts] made a big difference in how I felt myself being perceived and how I felt about myself as a person."

Because physical attractiveness shapes the way women are "judged," appearance must be protected as women age. Like Ann Marie, several of the patients I interviewed underwent cosmetic procedures aimed at reducing the natural signs of aging. These women claim that aging had changed an acceptable appearance into an unacceptable one that reflected negatively on their identity. For instance, Sue, a forty-four-year-old optician, decided to have the loose skin around her eyes tightened. She discusses her motivations for having the operation: "My eyes had always been all right, nice eyes. I guess I had always liked my face pretty well, but with age, the skin around them started getting puffy. They just didn't look nice anymore. I looked tired, tired and old. That's why I had them fixed." While Sue had, according to her own account, once been satisfied with her appearance, she grew to dislike her face as the signs of aging became apparent. She used cosmetic surgery to regain the face she liked "pretty well."

Several women told me that they chose to have cosmetic surgery not to make themselves beautiful or outstanding in any particular way but simply to regain normal physical characteristics they had lost through aging.[13] Like Sue and Ann Marie, Tina, a forty-eight-year-old receptionist, used cosmetic surgery to combat the physical changes associated with growing older. Tina underwent liposuction to reduce what she referred to as "secretarial spread," the widening of her hips and buttocks that she believed had come with her twenty-five-year career in office management. She explains, "When I was younger, I had nice hips, curvy but narrow enough, and my rear was well-shaped. After a lifetime of sitting, growing older and flabbier, it had gotten really huge." Tina hoped to restore her appearance to its more youthful form. Believing that her only means of doing so was cosmetic surgery, Tina opted to have liposuction rather than surrender to the aging process that had so drastically altered her body.

Youth—or at least a youthful appearance—is not the only characteristic women attempt to construct or regain through aesthetic procedures. Indeed, three of the patients I interviewed—all under the age of thirty—had cosmetic surgery to reduce the physical markers of ethnicity. These women underwent procedures intended to make their physical features more Anglo-Saxon. Marcy, a Jewish woman, notes that her rhinoplasty removed physical features "more frequently associated with Jewish people." Jodie, a twenty-eight-year-old student who also had her nose reshaped, says, "I had this Italian bump on my nose. It required a little shaving. Now, it looks better." By a "better" nose, Jodie implies a more Anglo-Saxon, less Italian, and therefore less ethnic nose. And Kim, a twenty-two-year-old Taiwanese American student, underwent a procedure to make her eyes appear more oval in shape. She said, "[Taiwanese people] regard girls with wide, bright eyes as beautiful. My eyes used to look a little bit as if I was staring at somebody. The look is not soft; it is a very stiff look." While none of these women consciously attempted to detach themselves from ethnicity, they nevertheless chose to ignore the fact that their efforts to appear "normal" explicitly diminished the physical markers of that ethnicity. Seemingly indifferent to this loss, they accept the notion that normalized (i.e., Anglo-Saxon) features are more attractive than ethnic ones.

All the women claimed that plastic surgery was, for them, a logical, carefully thought-out response to distressing circumstances that could not be otherwise remedied. They now perceive themselves to be more socially acceptable, more normal, and, in several cases, more outgoing. As Bonnie explains, "I got exactly what I wanted from this. My body isn't extraordinarily different, but now, I feel like, well, I have a cute bottom. I have a cuter figure. I don't feel like the one with the big butt anymore. And for me, that lets me put my body issues away pretty much."

At the same time, displaying some remnants of her original ambivalence about cosmetic surgery, Bonnie notes, "I wish that I could have said, 'To hell with it, I am going to love my body the way it is' . . . but I had tried to do that for fifteen years, and it didn't work." She adds, "Now, I know I'll never look like Cindy Crawford, but I can walk around and feel like everything is good enough."

Women who undergo plastic surgery report various other benefits. For instance, some say that they can now wear clothes that they could not have worn prior to their operations; others attest to having greater self-confidence or to being more extroverted. Jennifer explains, "When I walk out that door in the morning, my head might be a little bit higher when I'm wearing a certain outfit. Like, before I had [liposuction] done, it used to be, I feel good, but I hope no one will notice that my legs aren't too nice."

These women now wear bathing suits, dresses with low-cut necklines, and feminine and revealing lingerie. Wearing these clothes, and believing themselves to be attractive in them, shapes the women's perceptions of themselves and increases their self-confidence. Tara, a twenty-seven-year-old student, told me that before she had breast augmentation surgery, she avoided wearing bathing suits in public and rarely shopped for bras. She says, "[Breast augmentation] has given me more self-confidence than I ever had. I fit in when I'm with my girlfriends now. Before, I never went to the beach with anybody around. After I had [plastic surgery], I couldn't wait to buy a bra. I could never buy one before because I was so pathetically small." Having plastic surgery made Tara appear more "normal." She is now able to participate in activities from which she previously felt excluded.

Barbara, who also had breast augmentation surgery, recounted a similar experience. She says, "I used to wear super-padded bras when I dressed up, but they just never did it for me. I didn't look like the other women. But now, like tonight, I am going to a party, and I know I'll be able to fill out the dress." She added,

"[Breast augmentation] has made me feel very confident. I think that's the difference."

Sandra, a forty-three-year-old office manager who had liposuction to reduce her "thick thighs" and "saddlebag" hips, explains that she underwent the procedure not only to appear youthful and wear feminine clothing, but also to approximate a cultural ideal involving social class. "I used to put on nice clothes and still look like a bag lady, you know, unsophisticated. Now I feel like I can wear good clothes and look like they are appropriate for me. Now, my body fits the clothes." Sandra likens appearance to a tableau of social class, both in the context of the clothing one chooses and the extent to which one's body appears to be "appropriate" for that clothing (and the social standing that it implies). Simply put, before Sandra's surgery, her "flabby" body had less class than her clothing. Her body undermined her efforts to use appearance to stake out a particular social location. In effect, it not only made her clothing an ineffective class identifier but also invalidated her claims to a particular status. Plastic surgery, however, has allowed Sandra to display social class through clothing. Cosmetic surgery legitimizes Sandra's claims to social status.

Other women I interviewed also claimed that cosmetic surgery helped them feel more self-confident. For example, Kim says, "I guess I feel better when I am out with friends, like maybe people will think I am attractive. I feel attractive and I guess, I act more attractive." Thus, the women imagine that they are now perceived more favorably and so behave in a manner that they believe is appropriate for "attractive" women. At the same time, the women recognize that they may simply be imagining others' perceptions of them and that their behaviors may have changed independently of any alteration in the way they are viewed. Kim says, "Maybe nobody even notices, but I feel like I look better. I guess just thinking I look better changes the way I act a little."

Nearly all of the women told me that their romantic partners believed the cosmetic procedures were unnecessary. Before her breast augmentation procedure, Tara's boyfriend voiced significant apprehension. "He was very, very frightened about it. He kept on telling me, 'I love you just the way you are,' that type of thing." And Barbara's fiance blamed himself for her dissatisfaction with her breasts. She recalls, "My fiance thought he was doing something wrong

that would make me feel like this about myself."
In many cases, the women's partners attempted to
convince them not to undergo the surgery. Jennifer
says her boyfriend "tried to talk me out of it, but finally he decided, 'If it's going to make you happy, go
ahead and do it.'" Some of John's patients report that
their partners have had mixed reactions to the results
of the procedures. Barbara says that even though she
has always considered her husband a "breast man, because his eyes would pop out if he saw a big-breasted
woman," he nevertheless told her that she was "perfect" with small breasts. She adds, laughing, "He still
says he liked me better before, but I'll tell you, I can't
keep him off of me. I keep saying I'm taking them
back for a refund."

The frequency with which I heard such assertions
points to the considerable importance women attach
to having "freely" chosen to have cosmetic surgery,
independent of coercion by their lovers or the desire
to please someone other than themselves. These assertions make sense in light of the women's accounts of
their surgery. Plastic surgery cannot be both something
women "deserve" and something that they are forced
or manipulated into doing. In their accounts, plastic
surgery is positioned as a final option for correcting
a tormenting problem. This conception of plastic surgery is clearly inconsistent with an image of acts forced
on them by others—particularly others who might actually benefit more from the procedures than do the
women themselves.

PLASTIC SURGERY AND
INAUTHENTICITY: THE HIGH PRICE
OF BODY WORK

In turning "abnormal" bodies into "normal" ones,
plastic surgery succeeds: the woman who participates
in plastic surgery comes to possess the foundation (i.e.,
a normal body) of a normative self. However, plastic
surgery fails as a method for constructing a positive
self-concept because of the negative social and political meanings attached to it. Women participate in cosmetic surgery in a world that limits their choices and
in which the flawed body is taken as a sign of a flawed
character. Despite the negative connotations of plastic
surgery, women opt to engage in such procedures because the alternative is more detrimental to self-image.
However, most of the women I interviewed carry with
them the burden of their decisions; the process of deal-

ing with that burden exacts from them a considerable
price.

Some of the costs of cosmetic surgery—including
the danger of physical damage and the high financial
price—are obvious to those who have undergone these
procedures and perhaps even to those who have not.
Most of these women had plastic surgery only after
serious consideration (often accompanied by research
into the medical technology involved in the operations).
Likewise, few could easily afford the surgery they underwent; nearly all of them had to sacrifice some other
large purchase or to weather financial hardship. Some
have accrued considerable debt, while others had
to request financial help from relatives. Only a very
few of the women had health insurance that covered
part of the cost.

Other costs associated with cosmetic surgery,
while less concrete, are no less substantial. Specifically, after surgery, women must attempt to deal with
the taint of inauthenticity these procedures imply.
Although the body appears more normal, the character becomes suspect, with the self, by implication,
becoming deviant. The unacceptable act of cosmetic
surgery displaces the normative body as an indicator
of character. Although the women I interviewed do
not formulate the complexities and contradictions involved in their activities in the way I have here, their
accounts show that they struggle with a self-concept
that continues to be deviant despite their now-normal
appearance. Indeed, the accounts themselves—which
attempt to deny inauthenticity by positioning cosmetic surgery as somehow owed to the women who
partake of it—show that plastic surgery fails to align
body and self.

These accounts suggest a singular conclusion
with regard to the success of plastic surgery for
establishing the normative identity. Women like
Ann Marie and Bonnie—like participants in the
aerobics classes [discussed in another part of *Body
Work*]—invoke their rigorous body work regimens
as evidence of moral rectitude and as the basis for
their entitlement to cosmetic surgery. But although
cosmetic surgery patients and aerobics participants
seem to rely on the same symbols of identity, for
women who undergo cosmetic surgery, those symbols fail to mitigate the body's negative implications
for self. Had these women accepted their body work
as an adequate indicator of identity, they would
not have needed to turn to plastic surgery to correct their bodies' failings. Moreover, still needing

to establish the "deceptive" act of plastic surgery as irrelevant to self (and to position the surgically altered, normative body as the true indicator of selfhood), these women revert to accounts that have already proved unsuccessful. Indeed, the negative implications for self inherent in cosmetic surgery require women to resort to accounts that they know—consciously or not—fail to support the normative identity. In so doing, these women attest to the failure of cosmetic surgery to position the transformed body as symbolic of self. Simply put, if plastic surgery were a successful method for constructing identity, these women would argue that the surgically altered body—rather than body work that has proved unsuccessful at shaping the body or establishing the self—serves to symbolize identity.

CONCLUSION

My research points to three general conclusions. The first bears on the reasons women have plastic surgery and suggests a modification of the criticisms of such procedures. The second bears on the ways in which women create accounts of plastic surgery, which are ignored by the criticisms of plastic surgery to date. The third returns more sympathetically to those criticisms.

None of the women I spoke to embarked casually on plastic surgery. The costs associated with these procedures—measured in dollars and the risk of physical damage—are well known. Although physicians may serve as gatekeepers by preventing some women from undergoing surgery, they rarely recruit patients directly. When surgeons actively market their practices—as did John Norris—they tend to do so indirectly, through advertisements in local magazines and shopping malls. And the women I interviewed did not report that they underwent surgery at the urging of a husband, parent, lover, or friend. Rather, the decision to seek surgery seems to have been theirs alone, at least in the immediate circumstances. To be sure, these decisions were shaped by broader cultural considerations—by notions of what constitutes beauty, by distinctively ethnic notions of beauty, and, most important, by the assumption that a woman's worth is measured by her appearance. Yet to portray the women I talked to as cultural dupes, as passively submitting to the demands of beauty, is to misrepresent them badly. A more appropriate image, I would suggest, is to present them as savvy cultural negotia-

tors, attempting to make out as best they can within a culture that limits their options. Those who undergo plastic surgery may (ultimately) be misguided, but they are not foolish. They know what they are doing. Their goals are realistic, and they in fact achieve most of what they set out to accomplish with plastic surgery. Although their actions surely do, in the long run, contribute to the reproduction of a beauty culture that carries heavy costs for them and for all women, in the short run they have succeeded in their own limited purposes.

Second, plastic surgery requires a defense. Much like the women I studied in the aerobics classes, those who underwent plastic surgery are working hard to justify themselves. But the accounts of the women who have plastic surgery are very different from those of the women who attend the aerobics classes. The aerobics women use hard physical work as an indicator of character that allows them to sever their conception of the self from the body. In contrast, the women who have had plastic surgery work hard to reattach the self to the body. First, they must convince themselves that they deserve the surgery, whether by the hard work they put in at the gym or the effort they invest in saving the money for the procedure. In so doing, they make the surgery psychologically and ideologically their own. Second, they must convince themselves that their revised appearance is authentically connected to the self.[14] To do this, they invoke essentialist notions of the self and corresponding notions of the body as accidental, somehow inessential or a degeneration from a younger body that better represented who they truly are.

I do not mean these observations as a defense of plastic surgery so much as an effort to understand that surgery and its implications. Indeed, if we are to distinguish plastic surgery from other forms of body work, we can do so on precisely the grounds I have just suggested. I am not convinced that reducing facial wrinkles is somehow less "real" than dyeing hair from gray to brown or even that eye surgery or rhinoplasty is somehow less authentic than a decision to have straight rather than curly hair. However, what characterizes the efforts of women in aerobics, hair salons, and, . . . in NAAFA [National Association to Advance Fat Acceptance], is that they attempt, in somewhat different ways and with varying degrees of success, to neutralize appearance as a measure of character. Far more than the other women I studied, the women who undergo plastic surgery help to reproduce some of the worst aspects of the beauty culture, not so much through the act of the surgery itself as through their ideological efforts to restore appearance as an indicator of character.

My own criticisms of plastic surgery are tempered by observations of [other] women described in [my book], *Body Work*. Although I have characterized plastic surgery as a research "site," parallel to an aerobics class or a group of women in a hair salon or the members of NAAFA, this parallel is in certain respects misleading. In the hair salon, in the aerobics class, and especially in NAAFA, I found women working together to find common solutions to a shared problem. But women who underwent plastic surgery were not a group in the same sense. For the most part, they did not know each other. They did not speak to each other. And although they may have had common problems with a common solution, they did not develop this solution cooperatively. In the other settings I studied, the local production of an alternative culture was very much in evidence. In the plastic surgery group, however, there were the aesthetic judgments of the plastic surgeon, the ignored opposition of friends and family, but no culture of its own. The women in the aerobics class, in the hair salon, and especially in NAAFA, all challenged a beauty culture, however haltingly, however partially. In contrast, the women who undergo plastic surgery are simply making do within a culture that they believe judges and rewards them for their looks.

NOTES

1. Ann Dally. *Women under the Knife: A History of Surgery* (London: Hutchinson Radius, 1991); Eugenia Kaw, "Opening Faces: The Politics of Cosmetic Surgery and Asian-American Women," in *Many Mirrors: Body Image and Social Relations,* ed. N. Sank (New Brunswick, N.J.: Rutgers University Press, 1994), 241–65.

2. American Society of Plastic and Reconstructive Surgeons, *1999 Plastic Surgery Procedural Statistics* (Arlington Heights, Ill.: American Society of Plastic and Reconstructive Surgeons, www.plasticsurgery.org, March 2000); American Society of Plastic and Reconstructive Surgeons, *1999 Average Surgeon's Fees* (Arlington Heights, Ill.: American Society of Plastic and Reconstructive Surgeons, www.plasticsurgery .org., March 2000). Generally, surgeons' fees do not include anesthesia, operating-room facilities, or other related expenses.

3. American Society of Plastic and Reconstructive Surgeons, *1999 Gender Distribution. Cosmetic Procedures* (Arlington Heights, Ill.: American Society of Plastic and Reconstructive Surgeons, www.plasticsurgery. org., March 2000).

4. American Society of Plastic and Reconstructive Surgeons, *1999 Plastic Surgery Procedural Statistics* (Arlington Heights, Ill.: www.plasticsurgery.org, March 2000).

5. Joachim Gabka and Ekkehard Vaubel, *Plastic Surgery Past and Present: Origin and History of Modern Lines of Incision* (Basle: Karger, 1983), 29.

6. Susan Faludi, *Backlash: The Undeclared War on Women* (New York: Crown, 1991), 217.

7. Kathy Davis, *Reshaping the Female Body: The Dilemma of Cosmetic Surgery* (New York: Routledge, 1995), 21.

8. Robert M. Goldwyn, ed., *Long-Term Results in Plastic and Reconstructive Surgery*, 2d ed. (Boston: Little, Brown, 1980).

9. Barbara Meredith, *A Change for the Better* (London: Grafton Books, 1988).

10. Susan Bordo, "'Material Girl': The Effacements of Postmodern Culture," *Michigan Quarterly Review* 29 (1990): 657.

11. Joan Finkelstein, *The Fashioned Self* (Philadelphia: Temple University Press, 1991), 87.

12. Naomi Wolf; *The Beauty Myth: How Images of Beauty Are Used against Women* (New York: William Morrow, 1991).

13. See Davis, *Reshaping the Female Body,* for similar findings.

14. Concern about authenticity may well be class-specific; however, because my sample is based on references from a plastic surgeon, it is likely to include those patients who are least troubled by what they have done.

THE MYTH OF THE PERFECT BODY

Roberta Galler

A woman was experiencing severe abdominal pain. She was rushed to the emergency room and examined, then taken to the operating room, where an appendectomy was performed. After surgery, doctors concluded that her appendix was fine but that she had VD. It never occurred to them that this woman had a sexual life at all, because she was in a wheelchair.

I saw a woman who had cerebral palsy at a neuro-muscular clinic. She was covered with bruises. After talking with her, it became clear that she was a battered wife. I brought her case to the attention of the medical director and social worker, both progressive practitioners who are knowledgeable about resources for battered women. They said, "But he supports her. Who else will take care of her? And besides, if she complains, the court might take custody of her children."

As a feminist and psychotherapist I am politically and professionally interested in the impact of body image on a woman's self-esteem and sense of sexuality. However, it is as a woman with a disability that I am personally involved with these issues. I had polio when I was ten years old, and now with arthritis and some new aches and pains I feel in a rather exaggerated fashion other effects of aging, a progressive disability we all share to some degree.

Although I've been disabled since childhood, until the past few years I didn't know anyone else with a disability and in fact *avoided* knowing anyone with a disability. I had many of the same fears and anxieties which many of you who are currently able-bodied might feel about close association with anyone with a disability. I had not opted for, but in fact rebelled against, the prescribed role of dependence expected of women growing up when I did and which is still expected of disabled women. I became the "exceptional" woman, the "super-crip," noted for her independence. I refused to let my identity be shaped by my disability. I wanted to be known for *who* I am and not just by what I physically cannot do.

Although I was not particularly conscious of it at the time, I was additionally burdened with extensive conflicts about dependency and feelings of shame over my own imperfections and realistic limitations. So much of my image and definition of myself had been rooted in a denial of the impact of my disability. Unfortunately, my values and emphasis on independence involved an assumption that any form of help implied dependence and was therefore humiliating.

As the aging process accelerated the impact of my disability, it became more difficult to be stoic or heroic or ignore my increased need for help at times. This personal crisis coincided in time with the growing national political organization of disabled persons who were asserting their rights, demanding changes in public consciousness and social policy, and working to remove environmental and attitudinal barriers to the potential viability of their lives.

Disabled women also began a dialogue within the feminist community. On a personal level it has been through a slow process of disability consciousness-raising aided by newly found "sisters in disability," as well as through profoundly moving discussions with close, non-disabled friends that we, through mutual support and self-disclosure, began to explore our feelings and to shed the shame and humiliation associated with needing help. We began to understand that to need help did not imply helplessness nor was it the opposite of independence. This increased appreciation of mutual interdependence as part of the human condition caused us to reexamine the feminist idea of autonomy versus dependence.

Feminists have long attacked the media image of "the Body Beautiful" as oppressive, exploitative,

(continued)

and objectifying. Even in our attempts to create alternatives, however, we develop standards which oppress some of us. The feminist ideal of autonomy does not take into account the realistic needs for help that disabled, aging—and, in fact, most—women have. The image of the physically strong "superwoman" is also out of reach for most of us.

As we began to develop disability consciousness, we recognized significant parallels to feminist consciousness. For example, it is clear that just as society creates an ideal of beauty which is oppressive for us all, it creates an ideal model of the physically perfect person, who is not beset with weakness, loss, or pain. It is toward these distorted ideals of perfection in form and function that we all strive and with which we identify.

The disabled (and aging) woman poses a symbolic threat by reminding us how tenuous that model, "the myth of the perfect body," really is, and we might want to run from this thought. The disabled woman's body may not meet the standard of "perfection" in either image, form, or function. On the one hand, disabled women share the social stereotype of women in general as being weak and passive, and in fact are depicted as the epitome of the incompetent female. On the other hand, disabled women are not viewed as women at all, but portrayed as helpless, dependent children in need of protection. She is not seen as the sexy, but the sexless, object, asexual, neutered, unbeautiful and unable to find a lover. This stigmatized view of the disabled woman reflects a perception of assumed inadequacy on the part of the nondisabled.

For instance, disabled women are often advised by professionals not to bear children, and are (within race and class groupings) more likely to be threatened by or be victims of involuntary sterilization. Concerns for reproductive freedom and child custody, as well as rape and domestic violence, often exclude the disabled woman by assuming her to be an asexual creature. The perception that a disabled woman couldn't possibly get a man to care for or take care of her underlies the instances where professionals have urged disabled women who have been victims of brutal battery to stay with abusive males. Members of the helping professions often assume that no other men would want them.

Disability is often associated with sin, stigma, and a kind of "untouchability." Anxiety, as well as a sense of vulnerability and dread, may cause others to respond to the "imperfections" of a disabled woman's body with terror, avoidance, pity and or guilt. In a special *Off Our Backs* issue on disabled women, Jill Lessing postulated that it is "through fear and denial that attitudes of repulsion and oppression are acted out on disabled people in ways ranging from our solicitous good intentions to total invisibility and isolation."*

Even when the disabled woman is idealized for surmounting all obstacles, she is the recipient of a distancing admiration, which assumes her achievement to be necessary compensation for a lack of sexuality, intimacy, and love. The stereotype of the independent "super-crip," although embodying images of strength and courage, involves avoidance and denial of the realities of disability for both the observer and the disabled woman herself.

These discomforts may evoke a wish that disabled women remain invisible and that their sexuality be a hidden secret. However, disabled (and aging) women are coming out; we are beginning to examine our issues publicly, forcing other women to not only address the issues of disability but reexamine their attitudes toward their own limitations and lack of perfection, toward oppressive myths, standards, and social conditions which affect us all. . . .

*Jill Lessing. "Denial and Disability," *Off Our Backs*, vol. xi, no. 5. May 1981, p. 21.

Hair Still Matters

Williams' beaded braids, though popular with her fans and part of her identity the past few years, have long been a matter of annoyance to some opponents even when they don't come undone. . . . To bead or not to bead, that is the question now facing Williams. For the moment, she plans only to braid them a little tighter. "I shouldn't have to change," she said. "I like my hair."

—*Associated Press, 1999*

INTRODUCTION

I've always liked tennis, as both a player and fan. But who knew back in 1999 when Venus Williams was beginning to light a fire to the women's professional circuit that my interest in tennis and my scholarly research on black women and hair would collide? Though troubled by the racial, gendered, and cultural meanings of Williams being penalized for wearing beads in her hair during the Australian Open, I knew that once again I had some phat fodder for continuing to argue that hair STILL matters for black women.[1] The expectation to conform to white standards is nothing new in a society that privileges whiteness, and the expectation is becoming magnified for blacks in predominantly white spaces like professional tennis. In fact, in the late 1990s, descriptions of Venus Williams and basketball sensation Allen Iverson often included allusions to their hairstyles, braided and in rows, respectively. The coded racial language of sportscasters' coverage of Williams's tennis matches or Iverson's basketball games is indicative of the fascination and discomfort that white mainstream U.S. society continues to feel regarding African Americans in general, and particular black hairstyles and what they signify, whether real or imagined. Like the Afro, Williams's beaded braids and Iverson's cornrows are exotic to some and

threatening to others because they display a black aesthetic that is linked to an authentic or radical blackness in the imagination of many whites. Still, the gendered component of Williams's sanctioning during her 1999 match is equally as important as the racial one. For example, Williams choice of hairstyle was rooted outside of mainstream constructions of femininity. By wearing beaded braids, Williams's expression of racialized gender sent the message to a predominantly white professional women's tennis circuit that mainstream constructions of womanhood are insufficient in understanding black women's relationship to beauty culture. In fact, Williams's hairstyle sent a bold statement that the very notion of what constitutes femininity must not only be contested, but our understanding of womanhood must be expanded. Feminist scholars have done well in unmasking the gender politics of femininity and sexuality that are embedded in how the female body has been, for example, treated in popular media and science (Jaggar and Bord 1989; Bordo 1993). The female body in general, as a site where both empowerment and repression are played out, must be central to feminist projects in the 21st century. From a woman's right to choose what happens to her body with regard to abortion to female circumcision to the covering of women's bodies among Muslims, feminists, locally and globally, must continue to illuminate the contexts under which women's bodies are politicized, as well as depoliticized.

SITUATING HAIR IN ACADEMIA AND POPULAR CULTURE

To be sure, this is not fetish or trendy scholarship. Hair has been of interest to social theorists spanning the 20th century from Freud to Robin D. G. Kelley. Psychoanalysts were waxing theoretical poetic about the sexual symbolism of hair during the earlier period (Freud 1922). In reaction to psychoanalytic readings of hair symbolism, social meanings of hair emerged. More specifically in the latter part of the century, scholars focusing on blacks and hair emphasize the importance of hair among blacks in relationship to Africa (Morrow 1973), enslavement (Patterson 1982), constructions of race (Mercer 1990), skin color, self-esteem, ritual, aesthetics, and adornment (Mercer 1990), appropriate grooming practices (Tyler 1990), images of beauty, politics, and identity (Grier and Cobbs 1968; Mercer 1990), and the intersection of race and gender (Craig 1997; Kelley 1997).

The scholarship on blacks and hair highlighting the difference that gender makes in understanding hairstyling practices among African Americans provides a similar gender intervention to that within general hair theorizing scholarship (Eilberg-Schwartz and Doniger 1995).

Several works have been written that engage beauty culture and black women (Giddings 1984; Hill Collins 1990; Caraway 1991; Rooks 1996; Craig 2002). In particular, discussions by black women moved the debate about hair among people of African descent to one that also focuses on experience (Okazawa-Rey et al. 1986; Benton Rushing 1988; hooks 1988; Walker 1988; Hill Collins 1990; Caldwell 1991; Norsworthy 1991; Cleage 1993; Wade Gayles 1993; Davis 1994; Jones 1994; Gibson 1995; DuCille 1996; Rooks 1996). In these works the authors discuss personal experiences involving hair that intersect with race, gender, motherhood, freedom, law, appropriation, and identity. In one of the most important texts focusing on black women and hair, *Hair Raising: Beauty, Culture, and African American Women,* Noliwe Rooks (1996) examines black hair care advertisements at the turn of the century in her investigation of how dominant or mainstream ideologies of race and beauty forced African American women to produce and sell beauty products for an African American female market. Rooks makes a strong case for understanding why gendered investigations of hair meanings in black communities are central for understanding how black women negotiate mainstream beauty culture. More recently, provocative texts that examine the history of black hair in the U.S. (Byrd and Tharps, 2001) and personal reflections on hair (Harris and Johnson, 2001) have contributed greatly to scholarship on black women and hair.

Similar to early anthropological writings that do not take into consideration the difference culture and gender make in understandings about hair, early feminist discussions about the relationship between femininity and hair focus on hair as an indelible marker of femininity. For example, Susan Brownmiller (1984) conflates

the meanings of hair by reducing the interpretation of "good" hair and "bad" hair to mean the same thing for black women as it does for white women. Brownmiller collapses these terms despite racial and cultural difference. Her analysis demonstrates why these types of comparisons are problematic and how they disclaim the cultural significance of hair for black women by treating the issue as if it were *merely* a women's issue, and not an issue that traverses lines of race and culture.

Black hair is certainly not simply an academic matter. In fact, the debates that scholars engage are clearly indicative of real-world tensions, as the literature on blacks and hair demonstrates. Within the context of black popular culture, hair has always been "pop." Spike Lee films such as *School Daze* and *Jungle Fever*, as well as the prime-time TV shows *Any Day Now, Girlfriends, Moesha, The Parkers,* and *The Practice,* have engaged the politically charged issue of black women's hair. For example, in Spike Lee's *School Daze,* a scene unfolds in the film that illustrates the intraracial tensions embedded in constructions of "good" hair and "bad" hair. In one episode of Lifetime Television Network's drama *Any Day Now,* a story line involving the different cultural meanings that black and white women ascribe to hair grooming practices illustrates difference race makes in understanding how women relate to beauty culture.

Rap artists such as Lauryn Hill and her former Fugees crew, The Lost Boyz, and The Roots have laced particular songs with explicit references to nappy hair.[2] Preceding the attention given to black hair on prime time and in popular music in the late 20th century and early 21st century was the emergence of the Afro almost three decades ago. Though today the Afro has less political meaning, in the late 1960s it was associated with a movement and a black woman. The movement was black power and the black woman was (and still is, even without her late 1960s, early 1970s Afro) Angela Davis. During an interview for *Hair Matters,* Taylor, a forty-eight-year-old accountant, reminisced about her desire to wear an "Angela Davis Afro" during the early 1970s. Similar yet different from Davis's recognition that law enforcement officers used her image (i.e., Afro) as a reason to detain and harass black women, Taylor explained that it was her Afro and *assumed* gender that led to her being detained during the early 1970s:

When Afros came out, I wanted to wear an Afro. So I did everything and I finally got me a great big huge Angela Davis Afro. Whenever I would wear my Afro

I'd get pulled over by the police because I drove a very sleek car and they always thought from the back of the head that I had to be male a lot of times because we [Black women and Black men] all wore the same hairstyle.

Taylor's understanding of why she was detained by police officers was based on both her Afro and mistaken gender-identity. Whereas Taylor presented an image of the Afro-wearing militant as male, which was supported by the general perception of the black militant at the time, Davis describes how race and gender merged to stigmatize and repress black women, a point that would surface almost twenty years later when black women's hair was at the center of legal battles.

In the late 1980s black female employees went to court to challenge a policy by Hyatt Hotels and American Airlines against the wearing of braids.[3] These companies couched their policy in terms that related to "appropriate" grooming practices, which they argued braids violated. In November 1996, another hair controversy hit a sururban middle school in Chicago. *The Atlanta Journal/Atlanta Constitution* ran a story that highlighted a ban on hairstyles, along with certain clothes and jewelry that school officials defined as "gang related paraphernalia." Hairstyles such as cornrows, dreadlocks, braids, and ponytails for boys would lead to suspension; hairstyles with zigzag parts for girls were disallowed. With a similar argument as the one used against Hyatt Hotels and American Airlines, critics argued that the school's policy appeared to restrict African Americans. To add, the weekly ABC news show *20/20* aired a segment that examined the tensions that many black professional women face when hair is at issue. Oprah Winfrey dedicated an entire show to the "black hair question." As the *Los Angeles Times* reported in an article that examined the rise in natural hairstyles among black women (and men), the *20/20* episode illustrated how "one woman was terminated because management saw her hairstyle as 'extreme,' and another woman was written up because her braids were deemed 'too ethnic'" (George 1998, E4).

MY RESEARCH ON BLACK WOMEN AND HAIR

My research is a departure from previous research and discussions as it serves as the first empirical study that examines why hair matters to black women and girls. Prior to my research, an empirically based book

that centers on black women's views was absent in the literature and to this end, the study fills a void in the literature. Given that I identified a gap in research on this topic, how did I go about collecting data? By the fall of 1998, I completed forty-three individual interviews and five focus group interviews with African-American women and girls. The interviewees consisted of girls and women ranging from ages 12 to 76, from various walks of life. Individuals were recruited and interviewed in the San Francisco Bay area, Los Angeles, Santa Barbara, and Atlanta. During a focus group interviewee, Wixie, a 45-year-old physician explained to me, "There's always a question of race, money, and sex. But I think for black women, it's race, money, sex, and hair. It transcends a cosmetic [or esthetic] issue because it is at the base historically, culturally, and socially." Indeed, the argument here presents hair as a cultural tool that shapes black women's ideas about race, gender, class, sexuality and images of beauty and power. In addition, my research illustrates that hair matters for black women are never merely arrested within esthetics. Indeed, it serves cultural theorists well in paying close to attention to why hair matters to black women. In stating that hair matters, I argue that identity matters.

HAIR AND FEMININITY

On January 3, 1999, hair, in relationship to black women, made prime time again on the ABC weekly one-hour drama *The Practice*. The show focuses on a group of attorneys in a Boston law firm. In this particular episode, Lucy, the white female receptionist in her early twenties, asks the black female attorney, Rebecca, if she's a lesbian. Rebecca, somewhat puzzled, replies no, but wonders why anyone would assume she is a lesbian. Lucy replies, "With that rump and no guy in your life, and that crop-cut butchy-do hair [I just assumed you were a lesbian]." Rebecca commences to wonder if the reason she doesn't get asked out is because she "looks butch." Though Rebecca's femininity is marked through her shapely posterior, which is loaded with racialized images of Black women's bodies, her hair becomes the ultimate marker of both her womanhood and sexuality. Ideas about the relationship between hair, femininity, and sexuality, as well as images of beauty and male perceptions of femininity, surfaced as the women and girls addressed the question of whether hair is associated with femininity in any way.

Several of the women explained how long hair is associated with femininity and how their beliefs have been nurtured through the mainstream media or other external forces. For example Pearl, a 45-year-old college counselor, explained that she felt most sexy with long hair:

PEARL: Oh I have [associated hair with femininity]. I think the sexiest hairstyle was for me, and this could come from advertisements, television, anywhere, was when my hair was longer and it was piled on top of my head and I would always have little ringlets on the side. And that could also be from my southern background and that's how southern women wore their hair a long time ago. It could stem from my mom. I'm not exactly sure where those images come from but I would look in the mirror and I would see how I look and say, "God, that is sexy, that looks gorgeous."

Pearl also associated her perception of long hair with her southern roots and mother, but still questioned how she learned what is feminine or sexy. Aria, a 30-year-old undergraduate student, also explained the relationship between long hair, femininity, and constructions of beauty but unlike Pearl, Aria perceived this relationship through gender and racial readings of hair:

ARIA: Oh please, yes. If I said no I'd be lying because for years we have been inundated with magazine pictures of white women and their beautiful bodies and their long flowing locks. We have seen commercials, they're [white women] in the magazine ads. You see them in school flippin' their hair all through the classroom. I mean I sit in class and I see these women changing their hairstyles in a fifty-minute class at least four different times, you know. It's like come on. We have romance novels that accentuate the long, silken tresses so there's so many different mediums that portray [long] hair as beautiful, as feminine, as silky. And then if you have a lack of hair, then your femininity sometimes is questioned.

Aria pointed to the white women on TV, in magazines, and in romance novels with long, flowing hair as representative of femininity in U.S. society. Therefore, femininity is not merely associated with long hair as described by Pearl but with white women. Aria made a connection to the historical construction of womanhood, also known as the "cult of the lady" or the "cult of true womanhood" that represented 19th century U.S. Victorian society (Giddings 1984). Similar to Aria's construction of femininity that does not include black women, this was also the case with the cult of true womanhood. Given that the cult was based on a socioeconomic class hierarchy,[4] as well as racist and sexist ideologies, there was no place for black women regardless of class status in the definition of "true" womanhood.

Aria ends by stating that if a woman lacks hair, her femininity is questioned. This idea was common among the women. They associated their understanding of what short hair means in relationship to sexuality and masculinity. Dianne, a 50-year-old retired material handler, explained that an understanding of what it means to be male and female is embedded in readings of hair length. She also presented a different way of approaching the image of long flowing hair among black women:

DIANNE: Oh yeah. Right or wrong, you'll say stuff like that's a feminine cut, that's not a feminine cut, or whatever. I think to the extent that you have this long flowing hair that's perceived as very feminine. And the shorter you go, the less feminine it seems to be. So I definitely think that there's some association with that. And the whole interesting thing with the long hair [is] that [it] has some tie back to mainstream culture because not a lot of people in our community have this flowing long hair, but that's defined as being feminine. So when [women] go really short, [people say] that looks too mannish or something. My sister got her hair cut really short one time and she was like, "oh now people are going to think that I look like a boy or something."

In Dianne's explanation of the relationship between femininity and hair, she presented a scale in which long hair (feminine) and short hair (masculine) exists at the extremes. "Mannish" is associated with "looking like a boy" and long, flowing hair becomes a powerful feminine trait. However, Dianne questioned placing the image of long flowing hair among black people outside of black communities when she stated that based on her observations, there is not a critical mass of black folk who have long flowing hair. The more telling issue is how black people in general, and black women in particular, understand these meanings and how ideas that link long hair to femininity are actually acted out. In fact Indigo, a 28-year-old independent filmmaker and teacher, explained how her decision to grow dreadlocks has allowed her to fulfill the dream of having long hair.

INDIGO: I think certainly. I've just begun to take a look at the issue of dreadlocks because I look at myself and all my life I wanted to have long hair and now I get to have it with dreadlocks. The longer I let it grow I can have this long, flowing hair. Of course it won't look like Cheryl Tiegs's hair or, you know, Farah Fawcett's, but it will be my own hair.

Although similar to Aria's observation that white women's hair is the standard of long, flowing hair, Indigo sees length as outweighing texture. She demonstrated her perception of femininity through hair, and although she recognizes the problem in reinforcing the belief that long hair characterizes femininity, she challenged mainstream standards of beauty through the length of her dreadlocks. Although she doesn't have the stuff, in terms of texture and color, as do Tiegs and Fawcett, she does possess the feminine trait, long hair. Thus, Indigo's reading of hair permits black women to sit at the table of femininity, despite historical constructions of what constitutes womanhood and, therefore, beauty. But the desire to have long hair relates to perceptions of what is considered feminine and it is associated with white women. That is, even with long dreadlocks, the model of long hair, and therefore femininity, is white women like Cheryl Tiegs and Farah Fawcett.

Indigo also explained how shaving her head and having short hair shaped her understanding about hair and femininity. Like other women, she discussed the relationship between sexuality or perceived sexuality with hair, particularly in relationship to lesbianism.

INDIGO: For women, you know, it is a very important part of your appearance. Your face, your hair. I mean you can still be feminine and have no hair on your head. But you know, we have these judgments that only certain women can pull that off. I mean actually be bald, and still be considered feminine. I know when I shaved off [my hair or the] many times I've had my hair short, I was trying to compensate with earrings and all this kind of stuff. Trying not to wear as many pants because I felt like I was going to be, you know, categorized as a dyke, or you know, just deemed unattractive.

Cheryl, Jean, Kaliph, and Barbara[5] made similar comments in linking hair to sexuality, as well as being masculine:

CHERYL: Yeah, I think it is, unfortunately. I cut my hair [short] [and] the day I did it I went out to a club with my girl [in the nonromantic sense]. It wasn't that crowded, so we were kinda hangin' out together and I think we went on the dance floor. We weren't even really dancing together but we were, you know, dancing without partners and somebody came up to me and asked me if like we were together as like a lesbian couple. And she [my friend] wears dreads. And I was like, it's the hair, isn't it?

JEAN: Oh yeah, definitely. So you know, especially in this town [San Francisco Bay Area, California] people see a haircut and they say, oh, dyke.

KALIPH: Yes, definitely yes because, and now I'm thinking in terms of length and lack of length. I hear one of the concerns among my friends who wear their hair short and natural, that there is sometimes a misperception around sexuality like, oh you must be a lesbian if you wear your hair like that. And by definition if you're a lesbian that somehow there's a lack of femininity, you know, you're trying to be a man. You're trying to be male, masculine. So I think there is something about hair, particularly length of hair, that speaks to being feminine and being a woman.

BARBARA: In my view, no. But some men will see a woman with short hair, real short hair, and will think negatively. [Like] a butch cut. I've heard that.

Words such as "butch" and "dyke" describe how ideas about sexuality can be read through hair. Sexual identities are often placed on individuals based on hair, which is why Cheryl concluded that it was her short haircut and her friend's dreadlocks that made others think they were a lesbian couple on the dance floor. Kaliph even shared that she has black female friends with close-cropped and natural hair that are concerned with being perceived as lesbian. Kaliph explained that hair length is related not only to sexuality but also to female attractiveness. For example, when Indigo compensated for the lack of hair on her head, she did so by accentuating what she understood as feminine. It was Indigo's concern with being labeled a lesbian and therefore unfeminine that guided her practice of wearing big earrings and more skirts and dresses. In fact, as if in a dialogue with Indigo, Mrs. Franklin, a 70-year-old retired instructor's assistant, supported this reading of hair and femininity:

MRS. FRANKLIN: Yes, I do [think hair is associated with femininity]. Because I like to see women with hair. Most women when they have their hair short, [they] got to get up in the morning [and start] puttin' on make-up, puttin' on earrings and all this kind of stuff so people won't take a second look and say, "Is that a man or a lady?"

Even though Mrs. Franklin appeared to be making a presumption that women with short hair have to highlight their femininity, her thoughts resonate in Indigo's personal account of her insecurities about how her womanhood, in relationship to sexuality, would be read. What Mrs. Franklin and Indigo demonstrate is that black women understand that femininity cannot be reduced to one thing. Although hair is important in black women's understanding of what constitutes femininity, it is not the only marker. However, their comments also contradict their understanding of a more complicated reading of femininity because if a black woman has long hair, it is not necessary for her to "play up" her femininity by adorning her body in ways that are defined as "feminine." Even if hair is only one of many markers of femininity, or lack thereof, it is definitely one of the most powerful.

Habiba is a 50-year-old writer and teacher. In her reading of the relationship between hair and femininity, she also discussed long hair but used the example of (black) men wearing dreads as indicative of femininity. Femininity is still read through long hair, but Habiba challenged the belief that only women possess feminine characteristics when they have long hair. She also *explicitly* stated that hair is associated with femininity *and* sexuality:

HABIBA: [Hair is associated with femininity] and sexuality. People often times have their hands in each others hair, pubic [for example]. So [hair] is very, very sensual. Very, very feminine. And I think men growing the long hair, men with dreads, are also activating that. What is it? They're activating the feminine side. Yes, yes, yes. For men to have the long hair and the dreads. Oh, that's incredible.

Habiba also provided a different view of the sexual nature of hair. Her reading of the relationship between hair and sexuality involves sensuality. Although her discussion supports how long hair is associated with femininity, Habiba's perception of what it means to be masculine is not questioned when she sees black men with long hair. Unlike the explanations of what it means for a woman to wear particular short hairdos[6] that are perceived as male "do's'" Habiba questioned static notions of gender identities for women and men even as she supported the idea that long hair is associated with femininity. However it is Semple's critique of gender readings of hair (she is a 22-year-old undergraduate student), like that posed by Habiba's, that view long hair as feminine, that present a challenge to how gender is socially constructed. Unlike other women, Semple discussed this matter within the context of black males and how their hairstyling practices relate to how they are perceived:

SEMPLE: Is hair associated with femininity? I mean, I can see where we've maybe been socialized to think certain hairstyles [are feminine]. [The artist formally known as] Prince is always thought of as being out the box because he wants to wear a perm and a short cut. Michael Jackson got a little bob cut and people wanted to feminize that whole image. But at the same time, a brother can grow locks down his back and still be seen as extremely masculine. I mean brothers are wearing braids now and people are still [associating certain hairstyles with femininity]. I mean there's an element of "gang society" who walks around with permed hair and curls in their hair.

Unlike Habiba, Semple sees long dreadlocks worn by black men as indicative of masculinity, not femininity. Styles or lengths that are perceived as feminine do not necessarily question the masculinity or sexuality of black men. Semple's discussion of femininity as being read through the hairstyling practices of black men provided a different lens from which to view how black women understand gender through their ideas about hair. Although Semple discussed the hairstyling practices of Michael Jackson and The Artist as influencing their feminization, it is in her discussion of gang culture and the hairstyling practices among younger black males, particularly those in urban areas, that undoubtedly influence and have been influenced by hip-hop culture and rap music, that she contested feminine constructions of hair. Although I am in no way suggesting that rap artist Snoop Dog is a gangster, his hairstyling practices sheds light on Semple's critique. When Snoop appeared on the MTV Music Awards show in New York City a few years ago his hair was freshly straightened with lots of "Shirley Temple" curls. A year or two later, he was on the same awards show with straightened hair that touched his shoulders. Despite Snoop's hairstyling practices that imitate popular hairstyling practices by (Black) women, his "manhood" is not called into question. Like other younger black males who are straightening their hair, wearing braids and cornrows, as well as barrettes and rubber bands, their hair, Snoop is still seen as masculine. In a recent DJ Quik music video "Youz a Gangsta," Snoop appears with individual braids with beads dangling elegantly at the end of each braid. DJ Quik's hairstyle changes from cornrows to a straightened style by the end of the video. In another recent video, "Thug Mentality," rap artist Krayzie Bone appears with beautiful cornrows, and one of his possee members stands by his side with the same type of braided and beaded style as Snoop in DJ Quik's video. The video represents the life of a thug, with car chases and gambling rounding out the message of the video. Despite their hairdos, in both of these videos, the masculinity and sexuality of the main characters are never questioned because they are gangstas and thugs. This was true in the 1970s as well within the urban pimp culture scene. No one challenged Ron O'Neal's masculinity in the blaxploitation film *Super Fly*. If anything, he was hyper-masculinized and seen as the perfect example of a "brother's brother." That is, a man's man. He had women, money, sharp clothes, a nice apartment, and a fancy car. And he had straightened ("fly") hair.

What Semple's observation suggests is that gender identity is not static, but given the comments by other women who addressed the relationship between hair and femininity, a nonstatic or even a cross-reading of gender does not occur when women's hair styling practices resemble those that are considered masculine. Whereas all black men are not labeled as feminine or gay when they sport hairdos that are perceived as feminine, when black women wear their hair close-cropped, for example, they are constructed as being unfeminine, unattractive, masculine, and lesbian. As Indigo and Mrs. Franklin's comments demonstrate above, women have to play up their femininity in other ways.

CONCLUSION: FEMININITY, HAIR, AND GLOBALIZATION

Hair still matters, and though differences arise in different cultural and political contexts, for women, hair is never *simply* arrested within the aesthetic. Though global-studies scholars are raising important questions concerning globalization and its relationship to not merely Western societies, but the entire planet, hair went global a while back. "Through the seventies, stock imported from Europe was the only hair product sold to what the industry calls the 'Caucasian Trade.' Now that the European market is drying up, Asian hair goes to all races, in most cases, unless specially ordered. When you buy human hair in lengths for weaving and braiding, in wigs, and as male-replacement product, what you buy nine times out often is Asian hair (Jones, 1994, p. 282). The average woman from Asia growing her hair for profit lives in poverty. It is an eerie feeling to realize that though these women will most likely remain living in a cycle of poverty, their hair exists within a global context.

Hair has gone global culturally as well. During the post-September 11 era, hair matters continue to make news, though within a different global and cultural context than what went down with Venus Williams in Australia in 1999. Consider the eyes of the Western/Christian world not merely on the Taliban restrictions placed on Afghani women, but also on the wider Islamic faith's teachings concerning the presentation of the female body. The hijab (veil) that covers the hair continues to be a source of great debate within and outside feminist circles. With the downfall of the Taliban government, some Afghani women proudly shed the all-encompassing burka (full body veil). However, many women continue to follow Afghan culture by continuing to wear the burka. As feminists, we would be remiss if we discounted the views of Islamic women outside and inside of Afghanistan who continue to don the hijab. Certainly, the issue of covering women's bodies among Muslims cannot be disengaged from patriarchy and the state, but as my research on U.S. black women conveys, women must be given a platform to speak, to theorize, about *their* existence from *their* various standpoints. As 22-year-old Mahbobo Sidiqi stated as she and the other women shed their burkas after entering a classroom at the University of Kabul to sit for college entrance exams along with men in February 2000 "My head is free. . . . No more headaches" (*Miami Herald,* February 7: 2002). Indeed, hair still matters, and it matters for women of color in profound ways as exemplified by what we can learn by recent events in the global culture.

ACKNOWLEDGMENT

I am indebted to Hung Cam Thai for his insightful comments and unwavering support. He is one of the finest *feminists* that I know.

NOTES

1. Ingrid Banks, *Hair Matters: Beauty, Power, and Black Women's Consciousness* (New York: New York University Press, 2000).
2. See Lauryn Hill's "Doo Wop (That Thing)," the Fugees' "Nappy Hair," and The Lost Boyz album "Love, Peace, and Nappiness."
3. See Paulette Caldwell's (1991) discussion of these cases.
4. For example, poor and working-class women, regardless of race, were not viewed as "true women." Those women who had to work outside of the home for economic necessity were excluded from the definition of a lady.
5. Cheryl is a 22-year-old graduate student, Jean is a 37-year-old architect, Kaliph is a 28-year-old graduate student, and Barbara is a 49-year-old Administrative Assistant II.
6. Not all short hairdos worn by women are viewed as unfeminine; what is meant here is particularly those hairdos that resemble traditional men's hairdos (e.g., short, cropped, buzz cuts).

REFERENCES

Banks, Ingrid. 2000. *Hair Matters: Beauty, Power and Black Women's Consciousness.* New York: University Press.

Benton Rushing, Andrea. 1988. "Hair-Raising." *Feminist Studies* 14(2) (Summer): 325–335.

Bordo, Susan. 1993. *Unbearable Weight: Feminism, Western Culture, and the Body.* Berkeley: University of California Press.

Brownmiller, Susan. 1984. *Femininity.* New York: London Press/Simon & Schuster.

Byrd, Ayana D., and Lori L. Tharps. 2001. *Hair Story: Untangling the Roots of Black Hair in America.* New York: St. Martin's Press.

Caldwell, Paulette M. 1991. "A Hair Piece: Perspectives on the Intersection of Race and Gender." *Duke Law Review*: 365–397.

Caraway, Nancie. 1991. *Segregated Sisterhood: Racism and the Politics of American Feminism.* Knoxville: University of Tennessee Press.

Cleage, Pearl. 1993. "Hairpeace: Requirement for Afro-American Women Writers to Discuss Hair." *African-American Review* 27(1) (Spring): 37.

Craig, Maxine. 2002. *Ain't I a Beauty Queen? Black Women, Beauty, and the Politics of Race.* New York: Oxford University Press.

———. 1997. "The Decline and the Fall of the Conk; or, How to Read a Process." *Fashion Theory: The Journal of Dress, Body and Culture* 1(4) (December): 399–419.

Davis, Angela Y. 1994. "Afro Images: Politics, Fashion, and Nostalgia." *Critical Inquiry* 21(1) (Autumn): 37.

DuCille, Ann. 1996 *Skin Trade.* Cambridge: Harvard University Press.

Eilberg-Schwartz, Howard, and Wendy Doniger, eds. 1995. *Off With Her Head! The Denial of Woman's Identity in Myth, Religion, and Culture.* Berkeley: University of California Press.

Freud, Sigmund. 1922. "Medusa's Hair." In *Collected Papers,* 105–106. London: Hogarth Press and the Institute of Psychoanalysis.

George, Lynell. 1998. "The Natural Look." *The Los Angeles Times,* August 6, E1.

Gibson, Aliona. 1995. *Nappy: Growing Up Black and Female in America.* New York: Harlem River Press.

Giddings, Paula. 1984. *When and Where I Enter: The Impact of Black Women on Race and Sex in America.* New York: Bantam Books.

Grier, William H. & Price M. Cobbs. 1968. *Black Rage.* New York: Basic Books.

Harris, Juliette, and Pamela Johnson. 2001. *Tenderheaded: A Comb-Bending Collection of Hair Stories.* New York: Pocket Books.

Hill Collins, Patricia. 1990. *Black Feminist Thought: Knowledge, Consciousness, and the Politics of Empowerment.* London: Harper Collins.

hooks, bell. 1988. "Straightening Our Hair." *Z Magazine* (Summer): 14–18.

Jagger, Alison, and Bordo, Susan. 1989. *Gender/Body/Knowledge: Feminist Reconstructions of Knowing.* Newark, NJ: Rutgers University Press.

Jones, Lisa. 1994. *Bulletproof Diva: Tales of Race, Sex, and Hair.* New York: Doubleday.

Kelley, Robin D.G. 1997. "Nap Time: Historicizing the Afro." *Fashion Theory: The Journal of Dress, Body and Culture* 1(4) (December): 339–351.

Mercer, Kobena. 1990. "Black Hair/Style Politics." In *Out There: Marginalization and Contemporary Cultures,* Russell Ferguson et al., eds., 247–264. New York & The New Museum of Contemporary Art & MIT Press.

Morrow, Willie. 1973. *400 Years Without a Comb.* San Diego: Black Publishers of San Diego.

Norsworthy, Kym. 1991. "Hair Discovery." *Real News,* 2(1): 3, 8.

Okazawa-Rey, Margo, et al. 1986. "Black Women and the Politics of Skin Color and Hair." *Women's Studies Quarterly* 14 (1 and 2) (Spring/Summer): 13–14

Patterson, Orlando. 1982. *Slavery and Social Death: A Comparative Study.* Cambridge: Harvard University Press.

Rooks, Noliwe. 1996. *Hair Raising: Beauty, Culture, and African American Women.* New Brunswick, NJ: Rutgers University Press.

Shipp, E. R. 1988. "Are Cornrows Right for Work?" *Essence,* February, 109–110.

Tyler, Bruce M. 1990. "Black Hairstyles: Cultural and Sociopolitical Implications." *The Western Journal of Black Studies* 14(4) 235–250.

Wade-Gayles, Gloria. 1993. "The Making of a Permanent Afro." In *Pushed Back to Strength: A Black Woman's Journey Home,* 133–158. Boston: Beacon Press.

Walker, Alice. 1988. "Oppressed Hair Puts a Ceiling on the Brain." In *Living by the Word,* 69–74. Orlando: Harcourt Brace Jovanovich.

READING *14*   **Cheryl L. Keyes**

Empowering Self, Making Choices, Creating Spaces: Black Female Identity via Rap Music Performance

Critics and scholars have often associated rap music with urban male culture. However, females have been involved in the history of this music since its early years. This article explores Black women's contribution to and role in shaping rap music. In examining female rappers, this study engages an interdisciplinary model that employs cultural studies, feminist theory, and mass mediation theory of popular culture, and it employs an ethnographic concept, the "interpretive community," in its analysis.

Observers of rap music began to notice the proliferation of successful female rap acts during the 1990s. Though rap has often been presented as a male-dominated form by the media, women have been a part of the rap scene since its early commercial years. In general, "females were always into rap, had their little crews and were known for rocking parties, schoolyards, whatever it was; and females rocked just as hard as males [but] the male was just first to be put on wax [record]" (Pearlman 1988:26). Rap music journalist Havelock Nelson notes, "While women have always been involved artistically with rap throughout the '80s, artists like [MC] Lyte, [Queen] Latifah, Roxanne Shanté,

and [Monie] Love have had to struggle to reach a level of success close to that of male rappers" (1993:77). Challenging male rappers' predominance, female rap artists have not only proven that they have lyrical skills; in their struggle to survive and thrive within this tradition, they have created spaces from which to deliver powerful messages from Black female and Black feminist perspectives.

Data utilized in this study derive from interviews (1993–1996) with "cultural readers" (Bobo 1995)—African American female performers, audience members, and music critics—referred to in this essay as an "interpretive community." In *Black Women as Cultural Readers,* film critic–scholar Jacqueline Bobo explores the concept of "interpretive community" as a movement comprising Black female cultural producers, critics and scholars, and cultural consumers (1995:22). She writes,

> As a group, the women make up what I have termed an interpretive community, which is strategically placed in relation to cultural works that either are created by black women or feature them in significant ways.

Working together the women utilize representations of black women that they deem valuable in productive and politically useful ways. (1995:22)

Because much of the criticism of Black female independent film makers' works stems from male or white perspectives, Bobo finds it necessary to distinguish the interpretive community—Black women involved in making or consuming these films—in order to accurately determine the actual intent and effect of these films. Bobo's thesis of the interpretive community is appropriate to this examination of women in rap because rap music is a form transmitted by recorded and video performances. More importantly, the classifications of women rappers are based on the constructions of an interpretive community, as observed via recorded performance and personal interviews. When rapper MC Lyte was asked, for example, if she felt that there is a distinct female rap category, she separated women rappers into three groups, referred to as "crews," reigning in three periods—the early 1980s, the mid-1980s through the early 1990s, and the late 1990s: "Sha-Rock, Sequence, to me, that's the first crew. Then you got a second crew, which is Salt-N-Pepa, Roxanne Shanté, The Real Roxanne, me, Latifah, Monie [Love], and Yo-Yo…. Then after that you got Da Brat, Foxy Brown, Lil' Kim, Heather B" (1996).[1]

Queried about specific categories, both rap music performers and female audience members frequently used the buzzwords *fly* and *attitude* (as in "girlfriend got attitude"), leading me to more clearly discern the parameters of categories. My initial category of "Black Diva" in early interviews for the grand posture of these women was later revised to "Queen Mother" after one female observer convincingly said *diva* denotes a posture of arrogance and pretentiousness as opposed to that of a regal and self-assured woman, qualities that she identified with the Queen Latifah types (see Penrice 1995).

In the female rap tradition, four distinct categories of women rappers emerge in rap music performance: "Queen Mother," "Fly Girl," "Sista with Attitude," and "Lesbian." Black female rappers can, however, shift between these categories or belong to more than one simultaneously. More importantly, each category mirrors certain images, voices, and lifestyles of African American women in contemporary urban society. Let us now examine the four categories or images of Black women introduced to rap by specific female rappers or emcees (MCs) and considered by the interpretive

community in general as representative of and specific to African American female identity in contemporary urban culture.

QUEEN MOTHER

The "Queen Mother" category comprises female rappers who view themselves as African-centered icons, an image often suggested by their dress. In their lyrics, they refer to themselves as "Asiatic Black women," "Nubian queens," "intelligent Black women," or "sistas droppin' science to the people," suggestive of their self-constructed identity and intellectual prowess. The "queen mother" is, however, associated with African traditional court culture. For instance, in the 16th-century Benin Kingdom of southeastern Nigeria, she was the mother of a reigning king. Because of her maternal connection to the king, she garnered certain rights and privileges, including control over districts and a voice in the national affairs of the state. During his reign, a commemorative head made of brass was sculpted in her honor adorned with a beaded choker, headdress, and crown, along with a facial expression capturing her reposed manner.[2]

It is certainly possible that female rap artists may know of the historical significance of African queens; women in this category adorn their bodies with royal or Kente cloth strips, African headdresses, goddess braid styles, and ankh-stylized jewelry. Their rhymes embrace Black female empowerment and spirituality, making clear their self-identification as African, woman, warrior, priestess, and queen. Queen mothers demand respect not only for their people but for Black women, who are "to be accorded respect by . . . men," observes Angela Y. Davis (1998:122). Among those women distinguished by the interpretive community as Queen Mother types are Queen Kenya, Queen Latifah, Sister Souljah, Nefertiti, Queen Mother, Rage, Isis, and Yo-Yo.

Queen Kenya, a member of hip-hop's Zulu Nation, was the first female MC to use *Queen* as a stage name.[3] But the woman of rap who became the first solo female MC to commercially record under the name "Queen" is Dana "Queen Latifah" Owens. Queen Latifah's initial singles "Princess of the Posse" and "Wrath of My Madness" (1988), followed by her debut album *All Hail the Queen* (1989), established her regal identity. They include such lyrics as, "You try to be down, you can't take my crown from me," and "I'm on the scene, I'm the Queen of Royal Badness." Latifah' whose Arabic name means "feminine, delicate, and kind," explains the origin of her stage name:

My cousin, who's Muslim, gave me that name [Latifah] when I was eight. Well [in rap], I didn't want to be MC Latifah. It didn't sound right. I didn't want to come out like old models. So *queen* just popped into my head one day, and I was like, "Me, Queen Latifah." It felt good saying it, and I felt like a queen. And you know, I am a queen. And every Black woman is a queen. (1993)

Latifah's maternal demeanor, posture, and full figure contribute to the perception of her as a queen mother. Although Queen Latifah acknowledges that others perceived her as motherly even at age 21, she tries to distance herself from the label: "I wish I wasn't seen as a mother, though. I don't really care for that. Just because I take a mature stance on certain things, it gives me a motherly feel . . . maybe because I am full-figured. I am mature, but I'm twenty-one" (quoted in Green 1991:33). The ambiguity of Latifah's motherly image follows what feminist scholars Joan Radner and Susan Lanser identify as a form of coding in women's folk culture called *distraction*: a device used to "drown out or draw attention away from the subversive power of a feminist message" (1993:15). Queen Latifah finds that her stature and grounded perspective cause fans to view her as a maternal figure or as a person to revere or, at times, fear. However, Latifah attempts to mute her motherly image offstage, as evidenced in the above interview, indicating to fans that she remains, nonetheless, a modest, down-to-earth, and ordinary person in spite of her onstage "Queen of Royal Badness" persona.

Despite the ambiguity, Queen Latifah represents a particular type of mother figure to her audience. In *Black Feminist Thought,* sociologist Patricia Hill Collins recognizes that, in the African American community, some women are viewed as "othermothers." Collins explains.

Black women's involvement in fostering African-American community development forms the basis for community-based power. This is the type of "strong Black woman" they see around them in traditional African-American communities. Community othermothers work on behalf of the Black community by expressing ethics of caring and personal accountability which embrace conceptions of transformative and mutuality . . . community othermothers become identified

as power figures through furthering the community's well-being. (1990:132)

Queen Latifah's othermother posture is no doubt reflected most vividly through her lyrics, which, at times, address political-economic issues facing Black women and the Black community as a whole. In Latifah's song "The Evil that Men Do" (1989) from *All Hail the Queen,* "she isolates several of the difficulties commonly experienced by young black women [on welfare]" (Forman 1994:44) and shows how the powers that be are apathetic to Black women who are trying to beat the odds. . . .

Another example of Queen Latifah's role as queen mother of rap resonates in her platinum single "Ladies First" (1989), ranked in the annals of rap music history as the first political commentary rap song by a female artist. The lyrics of "Ladies First" respond primarily to males who believe that females cannot create rhymes. . . .

The video version is far more political, containing live footage of South Africa's apartheid riots overlaid with photographic stills of Black heroines—Winnie Mandela, Rosa Parks, Angela Davis, Harriet Tubman, and Madame C.J. Walker.[4] Pan-Africanism is tacitly evoked with these images—South Africa's political struggle against segregation and a salute to Winnie Mandela, the mother of this struggle, who is presented among U.S. Black women—reminders of Black liberation. Additionally, the bond between Black women in the United States and the United Kingdom is alluded to through the appearance of Monie Love of England, whom Queen Latifah refers to as "my European partner." These images locate Latifah as a queen mother and equal partner among those Black queens who struggled for the freedom of Black people.

Perceived by the interpretive community as a queen mother of rap, Queen Latifah opened the doors for other Afrocentric female MCs, such as Sister Souljah. Souljah, a former associate of the Black nationalist rap group Public Enemy, launched her first LP in 1992. The LP, *360 Degrees of Power,* features the rap single "The Final Solution: Slavery's Back in Effect," in which "Souljah imagines a police state where blacks fight the reinstitution of slavery" (Leland 1992:48). With her candid and somewhat quasipreachy style of delivery, she earned the title "raptivist" from her followers. Souljah's fame grew after her speech at the Reverend Jesse Jackson's Rainbow Coalition Leadership Summit in 1992, where she chided African Americans who murder one another for no apparent reason by figuratively suggesting, "Why not take a week and kill white people[?]" (Leland 1992:48). As a consequence, Souljah was ridiculed as a propagator of hate by presidential candidate Bill Clinton. In the wake of the controversy, her record sales plummeted dramatically while her "raptivist" messages skyrocketed with television appearances on talk shows like *The Phil Donahue Show* and speeches on the university lecture circuit. While Sister Souljah advocates racial, social, and economic parity in her rap messages, she also looks within the community to relationship issues between Black men and women in her lyrics and her semiautobiographical book *No Disrespect* (1994:xiv).

Although Nefertiti, Isis, and Queen Mother Rage are categorized as queen mothers via their names, lyrics, or attire, female rapper Yo-Yo is also regarded by the interpretive community as a queen mother.[5] Her lyrics illustrate her political ideology of Black feminism and female respectability, as advanced by her organization, the Intelligent Black Women Coalition (I.B.W.C.), which she discusses on her debut LP *Make Way for the Motherlode* (1991). But Yo-Yo's image—long auburn braids and very short tight-fitting *pum-pum* shorts (worn by Jamaican dance hall women performers)—and her gyrating hip dancing also position her in the next category, "Fly Girl."

FLY GIRL

Fly describes someone in chic clothing and fashionable hairstyles, jewelry, and cosmetics, a style that grew out of the blaxploitation films of the late 1960s through the mid-1970s. These films include *Shaft* (1971), *Superfly* (1972), *The Mack* (1973), and *Foxy Brown* (1974), a film that inspired one MC to adopt the movie's title as her moniker. The fly persona in these films influenced a wave of Black contemporary youth who, in turn, resurrected flyness and its continuum in hip-hop culture. During the early 1980s, women rappers, including Sha Rock of funky Four Plus One, the trio Sequence, and soloist Lady B, dressed in what was then considered by their audiences as fly.

They wore short skirts, sequined fabric, high-heeled shoes, and prominent makeup. By 1985, the hip-hop community further embraced the fly image via the commercial recording of "A Fly Girl," by the male rap group Boogie Boys, and an answer rap during the same year, "A Fly Guy," by female rapper Pebblee-Poo. The Boogie Boys describe a fly girl as a woman "who wants

you to see her name, her game and her ability"; to do so, "she sports a lot of gold, wears tight jeans, leather mini skirts, a made-up face, has voluptuous curves, but speaks her mind" (1987).

By the mid-1980s, many female MCs began contesting the "fly girl" image because they wanted their audiences to focus more on their rapping skills than on their dress styles. Despite this changing trend, the female rap trio Salt-N-Pepa—Salt, Pepa, and Spinderella—nevertheless canonized the ultimate fly girl posture of rap by donning short, tight-fitting outfits, leather clothing, ripped jeans or punk clothing, glittering gold jewelry (i.e., earrings and necklaces), long sculpted nails, prominent makeup, and hairstyles ranging from braids and wraps to waves, in ever-changing hair coloring.

Rap's fly girl image is, however, far more than a whim, for it highlights aspects of Black women's bodies considered undesirable by American mainstream standards of beauty (Roberts 1998). Through performance, Salt-N-Pepa are "flippin da script" (deconstructing dominant ideology) by wearing clothes that accent their full breasts and rounded buttocks and thighs, considered beauty markers of Black women by Black culture (Roberts 1998). Moreover, they portray via performance the fly girl as a party-goer, an independent woman, but, additionally, an erotic subject rather than an objectified one.

Female rappers' reclamation of the *fly* resonates with the late Audre Lorde's theory of the erotic as power (Davis 1998:172). In Lorde's influential essay, "Uses of the Erotic," she reveals the transformative power of the erotic in Black women's culture: "Our erotic knowledge empowers us, becomes a lens through which we scrutinize all aspects of our existence, forcing us to evaluate those aspects honestly in terms of their meaning within our lives" (1984:57). Cultural critic and scholar bell hooks further articulates that Black women's erotic consciousness is textualized around issues of body esteem: "Erotic pleasure requires of us engagement with the realm of the senses . . . the capacity to be in touch with sensual reality; to accept and love our bodies; [to work] toward self-recovery issues around body esteem; [and] to be empowered by a healing eroticism" (1993:116, 121–122, 124).

Black fly girls express a growing awareness of their erotic selves by sculpting their own personas and, as folklorist Elaine Lawless (1998) puts it, "writing their own bodies." For example, Salt-N-Pepa describe themselves as "women [who have] worked hard to keep our bodies in shape; we're proud to show them off": moreover, "we're not ashamed of our sexuality; for we're Salt-N-Pepa—sexier and more in control" (quoted in Rogers 1994:31).

Another aspect of the fly girl persona is independence. Salt notes that "the image we project reflects the real independent woman of the '90s" (quoted in Chyll 1994:20). But for many women of rap, achieving a sense of independence from an entrepreneurial perspective has not been easy. For instance, it is common knowledge in the rap community that during Salt-N-Pepa's early years, their lyrics and hit songs ("I'll Take Your Man," "Push It," "Tramp," and "Shake Your Thang") were mainly written by their manager/producer Hurby "Luvbug" Azor, until the *Black's Magic* (1990) LP, on which Salt (Cheryl James) ventured into writing and producing the single "Expression," which went platinum. *Black's Magic* also contains Salt-N-Pepa's "Let's Talk about Sex" (written by Azor), which Salt later rewrote for a public service announcement song and video "Let's Talk about AIDS" in 1992.

On Salt-N-Pepa's fourth LP, *Very Necessary* (1993), the group wrote and produced most of the selections. The songs "Shoop" and "Whatta Man" from that album stand out as celebratory songs that deserve note.[6] In the video versions of both songs, the three women scrutinize desirable men, ranging from business types to "ruffnecks" (a fly guy associated with urban street culture). The "Shoop" video turns the tables on the male rappers; in it "ladies see a bunch of bare-chested, tight-bunned brothers acting like sex *objects,* servicing it up to us in our videos," said Salt (quoted in Rogers 1994:31, emphasis added). In "Whatta Man," on the other hand, Salt-N-Pepa praise their significant others in the areas of friendship, romance, and parenting as the female rhythm and blues group En Vogue joins them in singing the chorus, "Whatta man, whatta man, whatta man, whatta mighty good man."

Other women whom the interpretive community categorizes as *fly* are Left-Eye and Yo-Yo. Left Eye is the rapper of the hip-hop/rhythm and blues hybrid group TLC (*T-Boz, Left* Eye, and Chili). When TLC first appeared on the music scene with the debut LP *Oooooooohhh . . . On the TLC Tip* (1992), their baggy style of dress ran counter to the revealing apparel of hip-hop's typical fly girl and invited their full-figured audience to do the same. TLC's T-Boz said, "We like to wear a lot of baggy stuff because for one, it's comfortable, and two, many of our fans don't have the so-called perfect figure; we don't want them to feel like they

can't wear what we're wearing" (quoted in Horner 1993:16). Throughout the 1990s, TLC remained steadfast with the message to women of all sizes regarding mental and physical wellness and body esteem, as underscored in both music and video performances of the single "Unpretty" (1999).

Like Salt-N-Pepa, TLC has made delivering "safe sex" messages *a priority.* While both groups do so through lyrics, TLC underscores the messages visually through wearing certain accoutrements. Left Eye of the trio wears a condom in place of an eyeglass lens, while other members of the group attach colored condom packages to their clothes. TLC's warning about unprotected sex, emphasized by the condoms they wear, is conveyed powerfully in their award-winning "Waterfalls" from their second LP, *CrazySexyCool* (1994). The message is amplified in the video: A man decides to follow his partner's wish not to use a condom. Following this encounter, he notices a lesion on his face, which suggests that he has contracted the virus that causes AIDS. TLC's espousal of being fly and sexually independent undoubtedly comes hand in hand with sexual responsibility via their lyrics and image.

Like TLC, Yo-Yo also delivers a serious message, which earns her a place among the queen mothers. But her gyrating hips, stylish auburn braids, short, tight-fitting outfits, and pronounced facial makeup also categorize her as fly. Yo-Yo writes about independent, empowered Black women, championing African American sisterhood in "The I.B.W.C. National Anthem" and "Sisterland" from *Make Way for the Motherlode* (1991). She takes on sexuality in "You Can't Play with My Yo-Yo" and "Put a Lid on It," which, as their titles suggest, explore being sexually in control and being sexually irresponsible.

In 1996, Yo-Yo moved beyond the shadow of her mentor Ice Cube with her fourth LP, *Total Control,* for which she served as executive producer. Following this success, Yo-Yo began a column entitled "Yo, Yo-Yo" in the hip-hop magazine *Vibe,* in which she addresses questions about male-female relationships and interpersonal growth in the name of I.B.W.C.

Since the late 1990s, female MC, songwriter, and producer Missy "Misdemeanor" Elliott has joined the fly girl ranks. Mesmerized by her debut LP *Supa Dupa Fly* (1997) and her single "The Rain," female fans also admire her finger-wave hairstyle, known to some as "Missy [finger] waves," and her ability to carry off the latest hip-hop fashions on her full-figured frame. Elliott has occasionally appeared in television advertisements for the youth fashion store Gap. She no doubt succeeds as a full-figured *fly* woman, breaking new ground in an area too often seen as off-limits to all but the most slender and "correctly" proportioned. In staking her claim to rap music's fly girl category, Elliott further reclaims sexuality and eros as healing power for all Black women, regardless of size. However, with her single "She's a Bitch" from her sophomore LP *Da Real World* (1999), Missy "Misdemeanor" Elliott appends another image to her fly girl posture. Her usage of *bitch* makes a self-statement about being a mover and shaker, on- and offstage, in rap's male-dominated arena, and thus she shares much in common with the next category, "Sista with Attitude."

SISTA WITH ATTITUDE

According to Black English scholar Geneva Smitherman, "'tude, a diminutive form of attitude, can be defined as an aggressive, arrogant, defiant, I-know-I'm-BAD pose or air about oneself; or an oppositional or negative outlook or disposition" (1994:228). Prototypes of this category are grouped according to "'tude": Roxanne Shanté, Bytches with Problems (BWP), and Da Brat are known for their frankness; MC Lyte exudes a hardcore/no-nonsense approach; Boss is recognized for her gangsta bitch posture; and Mia X advances a militaristic stance, all in the name of her predominantly male posse No Limit Soldiers.[7]

In general, "Sista with Attitude" comprises female MCs who value attitude as a means of empowerment and present themselves accordingly. Many of these "sistas" (sisters) have reclaimed the word *bitch,* viewing it as positive rather than negative and using the term to entertain or provide cathartic release. Other sistas in the interpretive community are troubled by that view. These women, such as Lauryn Hill, have "refused to be labeled a 'bitch' because such appellations merely mar the images of young African American females" (1994; see also Harmony, quoted in Donahue 1991). The reclaimers counter this argument with the opinion that "it's not what you're called but what you answer to" (MC Lyte 1993). Some women of rap take a middle road, concurring that *bitch* can be problematic depending on who uses the term, how it is employed, and to whom one refers. As Queen Latifah explains.

I don't really mind the term…. I play around with it I use it with my home girls like, "Bitch are you crazy?" Bitch is a fierce girl. [Or.] "That bitch is so crazy, girl."

You know, that's not harmful [But.] "This stupid bitch just came down here talking … ," now that's meant in a harmful way. So it's the meaning behind the word that to me decides whether I should turn it off or listen to it. (1993)

Female MCs revise the standard definition of *bitch,* from an "aggressive woman who challenges male authority" (Penrice 1995) to an aggressive or assertive female who subverts patriarchal rule. Lyndah of the duo BWP explained, "We use 'Bytches' [to mean] a strong, positive, aggressive woman who goes after what she wants. We take that on today … and use it in a positive sense" (quoted in Donahue 1991).[8]

By the mid- to late 1990s, the "Sista with Attitude" category was augmented with rappers Lil' Kim and Foxy Brown, who conflate fly and hardcore attitudes in erotic lyrics and video performances, bordering both "Fly Girl" and "Sista with Attitude" categories. In doing so, they are designated by some as the "mack divas," "Thelma and Louise of rap" (Gonzales 1997:62), or "bad girls of hip-hop" (Morgan 1997). Foxy Brown, whose name is derived from Pam Grier's 1974 screen character, emulates the powerful, desirable, yet dangerous woman: "I think it's every girl's dream to be fly" (Gonzales 1997:63). Although Lil' Kim's debut album *Hard Core* (1996) and Foxy Brown's *Ill Na Na* (1997) have garnered platinum status, some members of the interpretive community criticize them for being "highly materialistic, violent, lewd" (Morgan 1997:77), an impression exacerbated by their affiliation with male gangsta rap–style crews: Lil' Kim is associated with Junior M.A.F.I.A., and Foxy Brown is connected with The Firm.

The bad girl image also parallels the "badman" character (such as John Hardy, Dolemite, and Stackolee) peculiar to the African American oral narrative. African American oral narratives commonly exploit the "badman" or "bad nigguh" types in the toast, a long poetic narrative form that predates rap.[9] In these narratives, Black badmen boast about their sexual exploits with women, wild drinking binges, and narrow brushes with the law, symbolic of "white power" (Roberts 1989:196). The feminist rendering of "the badman" includes those sistas who brag about partying and smoking "blunts" (marijuana) with their men; seducing, repressing, and sexually emasculating male characters;[10] or "dissin'" (verbally downplaying) their would-be female or male competitors—all through figurative speech.[11]

Some female observers I queried felt that sistas with attitude merely exist on the periphery of rap and are seen as just "shootin' off at the mouth." These artists are not highly respected for their creative skills; rather, they are viewed as misusing sex and feminism and devaluing Black men. In an *Essence* magazine article, hip-hop feminist Joan Morgan states that the new "bad girls of hip-hop" may not have career longevity because "feminism is not simply about being able to do what the boys do—get high, talk endlessly about their wee-wees and what have you. At the end of the day, it's the power women attain by making choices that increase their range of possibilities" (1997:132). Morgan further argues that Black women's power—on- and offstage—is sustained by "those sisters who selectively ration their erotic power" (1997:133).

Despite the controversies, sistas with attitude have acquired respect from their peers for their mastery of figurative language and rhyme. They simply refuse to be second best.

LESBIAN

While representatives of the "Queen Mother," "Fly Girl," and "Sista with Attitude" categories came into prominence during the mid- to late 1980s, the "Lesbian" category emerged from the closet during the late 1990s. Not only does the female audience term this category "Lesbian," but the artist who has given recognition to this division is among the first to rap about and address the lesbian lifestyle from a Black woman's perspective. Though other Black rap artists rumored to be gay/lesbian have chosen to remain closeted in a scene described as "notoriously homophobic" (Dyson, quoted in Jamison 1998:AR34), Queen Pen's "Girlfriend," from her debut LP *My Melody* (1997), represents a "breakthrough for queer culture" (Walters 1998:60).[12] "Girlfriend" signifies on or indirectly plays on Black lesbian love interest with a parody of the refrain section of Me'Shell Ndegeocello's "If That's Your Boyfriend (He Wasn't Last Night)." Ndegeocello, who is openly lesbian, appears on "Girlfriend," performing vocals and bass guitar. In "Girlfriend," Queen Pen positions herself as the suitor in a lesbian relationship. While this song may be a "breakthrough for queer culture," other issues still complicate Black female artists' willingness to openly address gay and lesbian culture in their performances.

Black lesbian culture and identity have been concerned with issues of race and role-play, note Lisa M. Walker (1993) and Ekua Omosupe (1991). Drawing on the critical works of Audre Lorde (1982, 1984), Omosupe notes that lesbian identity, similar to feminism, represents white lesbian culture or white women to the exclusion of women of color. In this regard, Black lesbians are at times forced to live and struggle against white male patriarchal culture on the one side and white lesbian culture, racism, and general homophobia on the other (Omosupe 1991:105). Corroborating issues of race privilege raised by the Black lesbian community, Queen Pen contends that certain licenses are afforded to white openly lesbian performers like Ellen DeGeneres and k.d. lang, who do not have to pay as high a price for their candidness as lesbians of color: "But you know, Ellen [DeGeneres] can talk about any ol' thing and it's all right. With everybody, it's all right. With 'Girlfriend,' I'm getting all kinds of questions" (quoted in Duvernay 1998:88).[13] She continues, "This song is buggin' everyone out right now. [If] you got Ellen; you got k.d., why shouldn't urban lesbians go to a girl club and hear their own thing?" (quoted in Jamison 1998:AR34).

Queen Pen further stresses in performance her play on image, which suggests "role-play," another crucial issue to Black lesbian culture. Walker asserts, "Role-play among black lesbians involves a resistance to the homophobic stereotype . . . lesbian as 'bulldagger,' a pejorative term within (and outside) the black community used to signal the lesbian as a woman who wants to be a man" (1993:886). On her album cover, Queen Pen exudes a "femme" image through wearing lipstick, a chic hairstyle, and stylish dress. However, in performance, as observed in Blackstreet's "No Dignity" (1996), one notices how Queen Pen "drowns out" her femme album cover image by appropriating "B-Boy" gestures (cool pose and bopped gait) commonly associated with male hip-hop culture. Regardless of issues concerning race privilege and role-play, Queen Pen concludes that in "two or three years from now, people will say I was the first female to bring the lesbian life to light [in an open way] on wax. It's reality. What's the problem?" (quoted in Jamison 1998:AR34).

CONCLUSION

Women are achieving major strides in rap music by continuing to chisel away at stereotypes about females as artists in a male-dominated tradition and by (re)defining women's culture and identity from a Black feminist perspective. Although rap continues to be predominantly male, female MCs move beyond the shadows of male rappers in diverse ways. Some have become exclusively known for their lyrical "skillz," while others have used a unique blend of musical styles or a combination of singer-rapper acts, as is apparent with Grammy awardees Left Eye of TLC and Lauryn Hill.

Women of rap still face, nevertheless, overt sexism regarding their creative capabilities. Female rapper Princesa recalls, "Only when I led them [male producers] to believe that a man had written or produced my stuff did they show interest" (quoted in Cooper 1989:80). Mass-mediation scholar Lisa Lewis notes that, in the popular music arena, "the ideological division between composition and performance serves to devalue women's role in music making and cast doubt on female creativity in general" (1990:57). However, female MCs of the 1990s have defied the sexist repression by writing their own songs, producing records, and even starting their own record companies, as with Salt-N-Pepa's *Very Necessary* (1993), Lauryn Hill's 1999 Grammy Award–winning LP *The Miseducation of Lauryn Hill* (1998), and Queen Latifah's record company, Flavor Unit. Additionally, Queen Latifah's Grammy Award–winning single "U.N.I.T.Y." (1993) challenges those males who use *bitch/ho* appellations in their lyrics.

While the majority of scholarly studies on female rappers locate Black women's voices in rap, they present only a partial rendering of female representation.[14]

These works tend to focus on females' attitudes and responses to sexual objectification, ignoring the many roles and issues of women and female rappers. Rap music scholar Tricia Rose says female MCs should be evaluated not only with regard to male rappers and misogynist lyrics "but also in response to a variety of related issues, including dominant notions of femininity, feminism, and black female sexuality. At the very least, black women rappers are in dialogue with one another, black men, black women, and dominant American culture as they struggle to define themselves" (1994:147–148). In rap music performance, a "black female-self emerges as a variation [on] several unique themes" (Etter-Lewis 1991:43).

More importantly, female rappers, most of whom are Black, convey their views on a variety of issues concerning identity, sociohistory, and esoteric beliefs shared by young African American women. Female rappers have attained a sense of distinction through revising and reclaiming Black women's history and perceived destiny. They use their performances as platforms to refute, deconstruct, and reconstruct alternative visions of their identity. With this platform, rap music becomes a vehicle by which Black female rappers seek empowerment, make choices, and create spaces for themselves and other sistas.

NOTES

Earlier drafts of this article were presented on the panel "Women Performers as Traditionalists and Innovators." at Resounding Women in World Music: A Symposium sponsored by the World Music Institute and Hunter College/City University of New York Graduate Program in Ethnomusicology, New York, 10–12 November 1995; and as a paper. "'Ain't Nuthin' but a She-Thing' Women. Race and Representation in Rap," at the 42nd Annual Meetings of the Society for Ethnomusicology with the International Association for the Study of Popular Music (USA Chapter), Pittsburgh, 22–26 October 1997. I wish to thank Lou-Ann Crouther, Phyllis May-Machunda, the late Gerald L. Davis, and the anonymous reviewers of the *Journal of American Folklore* for their suggestions on earlier drafts, as well as Corinne Lightweaver, whose invaluable comments contributed to the article's refinement.

1. The following is a list of other artists who make up a roster of female MCs: Antoinette (Next Plateau), Bahamadia (EMI), Conscious Daughters (Priority), Eve (Ruff Ryders), Finesse and Synquis (MCA), Gangsta Boo (Relativity), Heather B (MCA), Lady of Rage (Death Row), Ladybug

(Pendulum), MC Smooth (Crush Music), MC Trouble (Motown), Mercedes (No Limit), Nikki D (Def Jam), Nonchalant (MCA), Oaktown's 3–5–7 (Capital), Rah Digga (Flipmode), Solé (Dream Works), and 350 (Rap-a-Lot).

2. Accordingly, sculpting the queen mother's head was established in Benin by King Oba Esigies during the 16th century. Sieber and Walker (1987:93) note that, during Esigies's reign, he commissioned a sculpted head made of bronze of his mother, Idia, and placed it in his palace to commemorate her role in the Benn-Idah war, thereby including, for the first time, queen mothers in the cult of royal ancestors. In addition to Sieber and Walker's work, refer to Ben-Amos 1995 and Ben-Amos and Rubin 1983 for photographs and a brief discussion of queen mother heads of Benin.

3. The Zulu Nation is an organization that was founded in the Bronx during the mid-1970s by DJ Afrika Bambaataa. He contends that the Zulu Nation is a youth organization that incorporates a philosophy of nonviolence and in which inner-city youths compete artistically as break-dancers, rhyming emcees (rappers), disc jockeys, and graffiti artists rather than physically with knives and guns. Bambaataa's

Zulu Nation laid the foundation for hip-hop, a youth arts movement comprising the above arts, and an "attitude" rendered in the form of a distinct dress, language, and gesture—all of which is articulated via performance by rap music artists (see Keyes 1996).

4. For a more detailed analysis of this video, see Roberts 1994.

5. Isis once performed with the Black nationalist group X-Clan. After leaving this group, she also adopted a new stage name, Lin Que.

6. "Whatta Man" is adapted from Linda Lyndell's 1968 hit "What a Man."

7. For a more in-depth discussion of this category, refer to the section on female rappers in my book, *Rap Music and Street Consciousness* (Champaign: University of Illinois Press, 2002).

8. Another aspect of speech play is the manner in which sistas with attitude refer to men in their rap songs affectionately or insultingly as "motherfuckas" or "my niggas."

9. For further information about the toast, see Roger Abrahams (1970) and Darryl Dance (1978).

10. This emasculation can occur when sistas with attitude refer to their male competitors or suitors as "motherfuckas" or "niggas." Because the element of signifying is aesthetically appealing in this style of rap, these terms may have both negative and positive meanings depending on context.

11. Examples of selected rap songs that portray the distinct characteristics of sistas with attitude include the following:

Boss, "I Don't Give a Fuck" and "Mai Sista Izza Bitch," *Bom Gangstaz* (1993), Bytches with Problems, "Two Minute Brother" and "Shit Popper," *The Bytches* (1991); Da Brat, "Da Shit Ya Can't Fuc Wit" and "Fire It Up," *Funkdafied* (1994); Foxy Brown. "Ill Na Na" and "Letter to the Firm," *Ill Na Na* (1997); Lil' Kim, "Big Momma Thang" and "Spend a Little Doe," *Hard Core* (1996); MC Lyte, "Paper Thin," *Lyte as a Rock* (1988), and "Steady F . . . king," *Ain't No Other* (1993); Roxanne Shanté, "Big Mama," *The Bitch Is Back* (1992).

12. While "Queen Pen" is a play on "King Pin," Queen Pen uses this moniker to indicate that she "pens" (or writes) her own lyrics. A skill that some believe female MCs lack in comparison with male rappers. Although "Girlfriend" and other selections on Queen Pen's LP were cowritten and produced by Teddy Riley, inventor of new jack swing style (a rap rhythm and blues hybrid). Queen Pen's real name (Lynise Walters) appears on all songs. In the music industry, it is not unusual for producers to take cowriting credit on their mentees' debut works. The discussion of Riley's input on "Girlfriend" is discussed by Laura Jamison (1998).

13. When asked about "Girlfriend" in her interview in *Rap Pages* with Duvernay (1998), Queen Pen asserts that there are other nonlesbian songs on her debut album *My Melody*, including "Get Away," which discusses domestic violence.

14. For more on this topic, see Berry 1994, Forman 1994, Goodall 1994, Guevara 1987, and Rose 1994.

REFERENCES

Abrahams, Roger. 1970. *Deep Down in the Jungle. Negro Narrative Folklore from the Streets of Philadelphia.* Chicago: Aldine Publishing.

Ben-Amos, Paula Girshick. 1995. *The Art of Benin.* Rev. edition. Washington, D.C.: Smithsonian Institution Press.

Ben-Amos, Paula Girshick, and Arnold Rubin, eds. 1983. *The Art of Power, the Power of Art: Studies in Benin Iconography.* Los Angeles: Museum of Cultural History.

Berry, Venise T. 1994. Feminine or Masculine: The Conflicting Nature of Female Images in Rap Music. In *Cecilia Reclaimed: Feminist Perspectives on Gender and Music,* ed. Susan C. Cook and Judy S. Tsou, pp. 183–201. Urbana: University of Illinois Press.

Bobo, Jacqueline. 1995. *Black Women as Cultural Readers.* New York: Columbia University Press.

Chyll, Chuck. 1994. Musical Reactions: Sexy Rap or Credibility Gap? *Rap Masters* 7(7): 9–20.

Collins, Patricia Hill. 1990. *Black Feminist Thought: Knowledge, Consciousness, and the Politics of Empowerment.* London: Harper Collins Academic.

Cooper, Carol. 1989. Girls Ain't Nothin' but Trouble. *Essence* (April):80, 119.

Dance, Daryl. 1978. *Shuckin' and Jivin': Folklore from Contemporary Black Americans.* Bloomington: Indiana University Press.

Davis, Angela Y. 1998. *Blues Legacies and Black Feminism: Gertrude "Ma" Rainey, Bessie Smith, and Billie Holiday.* New York: Pantheon Books.

Donahue, Phil. 1991. Female Rappers Invade the Male Rap Industry. The Phil Donahue Show Transcript #3216, 29 May.

Duvernay, Ava. 1998. Queen Pen: Keep "EM Guessin" *Rap Pages* (May):86–88.

Etter-Lewis, Gwendolyn. 1991. Black Women's Life Stories: Reclaiming Self in Narrative Texts. In *Women's Words: The Feminist Practice of Oral History,* ed. Sherna Berger Gluck and Daphne Patai, pp. 43–59. New York: Routledge.

Forman, Murray. 1994. Movin' Closer to an Independent Funk: Black Feminist Theory, Standpoint, and Women in Rap. *Women's Studies* 23:35–55.

Gonzales, A. Michael. 1997. Mack Divas. *The Source* (February):62–64.

Goodall, Nataki. 1994. Depend on Myself: T.L.C. and the Evolution of Black Female Rap. *Journal of Negro History* 79(1):85–93.

Green, Kim. 1991. The Naked Truth. *The Source* (November):32–34, 36.

Guevara, Nancy. 1987. Women Writin' Rappin' Breakin'. In *The Year Left,* 2nd ed. Mike Davis, Manning Marable, Fred Pfeil, and Michael Sprinker, pp. 160–175. New York: Verso Press.

Hill, Lauryn. 1994. Panelist. Hip-Hop Summit for New Music, Seminar 15, New York, 20 July.

hooks, bell. 1993. *Sisters of the Yam: Black Women and Self-Recovery.* Boston: South End Press.

Horner, Cynthia. 1993. TLC: The Homegirls with Style! *Right On!* (February): 16–17.

Jamison, Laura. 1998. A Feisty Female Rapper Breaks a Hip-Hop Taboo. *Sunday New York Times,* 18 January: AR34.

Keyes, Cheryl L. 1996. At the Crossroads: Rap Music and Its African Nexus. *Ethnomusicology* 40(2): 223–248. In *Rap Music and Street Consciousness.* 2002. Champaign: University of Illinois Press.

Lawless, Elaine J. 1998. Claiming Inversion: Lesbian Constructions of Female Identity as Claims for Authority. *Journal of American Folklore* 11 (439):3–22.

Leland, John. 1992. Souljah on Ice. *Newsweek,* 29 June: 46–52.

Lewis, Lisa. 1990. *Gender Politics and MTV: Voicing the Difference.* Philadelphia: Temple University Press.

Lorde, Audre. 1982. *Zimi: A New Spelling of My Name.* Trumansburg. N.Y.: Crossing Press.

———. 1984. *Sister Outsider.* Freedom, Calif.: Crossing Press.

MC Lyte. 1993. Musical guest. Arsenio Hall Show, 8 October.

———. 1996. Interview by the author. Irvine, Calif., 11 August.

Morgan, Joan. 1997. The Bad Girls of Hip-Hop. *Essence* (March): 76–77, 132–134.

Nelson, Havelock. 1993. New Female Rappers Play for Keeps. *Billboard,* 10 July 1, 77.

Omosupe, Ekua. 1991. Black/Lesbian/Bulldagger. *differences* 3(2):101–111.

Pearlman, Jill. 1988. Girls Rappin' Round Table. *The Paper* (summer):25–27.

Penrice, Ronda. 1995. Interview by the author. *Manhattan,* 11 November.

Queen Latifah. 1993. Interview by the author. Jersey City. 8 July.

Radner, Joan Newlon, and Susan S. Lanser. 1993. Strategies of Coding in Women's Culture. In *Feminist Messages: Coding in Women's Folk Culture,* ed. Joan Newlon Radner, pp. 1–29. Urbana: University of Illinois Press.

Roberts, Deborah. 1998. Beautiful Women. 20/20, ABC Transcript #1796, 30 March.

Roberts, John W. 1989. *From Trickster to Badman: The Black Folk Hero in Slavery and Freedom.* Philadelphia: University of Pennsylvania.

Roberts, Robin. 1994. "Ladies First": Queen Latifah's Afrocentric Feminist Music Video. *African American Review* 28(2):245–257.

Rogers, E. Charles. 1994. The Salt-N-Pepa Interview. *Rap Masters* 7(7) July:30–31.

Rose, Tricia. 1994. *Black Noise: Rap Music and Black Culture in Contemporary America.* Hanover, N.H.: Wesleyan University Press.

Sieber, Roy, and Roslyn Adele Walker. 1987. *African Art in the Cycle of Life.* Washington, D.C.: Smithsonian Institution Press.

Sister Souljah. 1994. *No Disrespect.* New York: Random House.

Smitherman, Geneva. 1994. *Black Talk: Words and Phrases from the Hood to the Amen Corner.* New York: Houghton Mifflin Co.

Walker, Lisa M. 1993. How to Recognize a Lesbian: The Cultural Politics of Looking Like What You Are. *Signs: Journal of Women in Culture and Society* 18(4):866–889.

Walters, Barry. 1998. My Melody (sound recording review). *Advocate* 755 (17 March):59–60.

DISCOGRAPHY

Boogie Boys. 1987[1985]. A Fly Girl. *Rap vs. Rap: The Answer Album.* Priority 4XL-9506.

Boss. 1993. *Born Gangstaz:* Def Jam/Columbia OT 52903.

Bytches with Problems. 1991. *The Bytches.* No Face/RAL CT 47068.

Da Brat. 1994. *Funkdafied.* Chaos/Columbia OT 66164.

Foxy Brown. 1997. *Ill Na Na.* Def Jam 547028.

Funky Four Plus One. Rapping and Rocking the House. *Great Rap Hits.* Sugar Hill SH 246.

Lauryn Hill. 1998. *The Miseducation of Lauryn Hill.* Ruffhouse/Columbia CT69035.

Lil' Kim. 1996. *Hard Core.* Big Beat Records/Atlantic 92733–2.

MC Lyte. 1988. *Lyte as a Rock.* First Priority Music/Atlantic 7 90905–1.

———. 1993. *Ain't No Other.* First Priority Music/Atlantic 7 92230–4.

Missy "Misdemeanor" Elliott. 1997. *Supa Dupa Fly.* The Gold Mind, Inc./EastWest 62062–2.

———. 1999. *Da Real World.* The Gold Mine, Inc./East West 62244–4.

Queen Latifah. 1989. *All Hail the Queen.* Tommy Boy TBC 1022.

———. 1991. *Nature of a Sista'.* Tommy Boy TBC 9007.

———. 1993. U.N.I.T.Y. *Black Reign.* Motown 37463–6370–4.

Queen Pen. 1997. *My Melody.* Lil' Man/Interscope INTC-90151.

Roxanne Shanté. 1992. *The Bitch Is Back.* Livin' Large 3001.

———. 1995. Roxanne's Revenge. *Roxanne Shanté's Greatest Hits.* Cold Chillin'/Warner Brothers 5007.

Salt-N-Pepa. 1986. *Hot, Cool and Vicious.* Next Plateau/London 422–828362–2.

———. 1990. *Black's Magic.* Next Plateau/London 422–828362–2.

———. 1993. *Very Necessary.* Next Plateau/London P2–28392.

Sister Souljah. 1992. *360 Degrees of Power.* Epic EK-48713.

TLC. 1992. *Oooooooohhh . . . On the TLC Tip.* LaFace/Arista 26003–2.

———. 1994. *CrazySexyCool.* LaFace/Arista AC 26009–2.

———. 1999. Unpretty. *FanMail.* LaFace/Arista 26055–4.

Yo-Yo. 1991. *Make Way for the Motherlode.* EastWest/Atlantic 791605–2.

———. 1996. *Total Control.* EastWest/Atlantic 61898.

SECTION *4*

Socialization

We are born into cultures that have definite ideas about men and women and their appropriate attitudes, values, and behaviors, although those ideas may differ dramatically across time and place. The dominant U.S. culture defines certain traits as masculine or feminine and values behaviors, occupations, and attitudes deemed the characteristics of men more highly than those associated with women. It assumes that what men do is right and normal. Women are judged in accordance with how well they conform to the male standard. This way of thinking is known as *androcentrism*. As children, we learn to see ourselves and others as girls or boys and to judge our own and others' behaviors according to standards of gender-appropriate behavior. If we don't know a person's gender, we barely know how to interact, which is why people whose gender cannot be easily discerned or is easily mistaken have such a hard time.

The articles in this section analyze the complex process of gender socialization from various perspectives. Learning about our culture begins in the family. We learn about gender not only from what our parents say but from what they do. When mothers have primary responsibility for raising children, both girls and boys learn that nurturing is more a responsibility of women than of men. Gender socialization continues in schools, peer groups, and religious institutions, and can be ongoing throughout life, as we learn the expectations of our college contexts, our workplaces, and the families we form as adults.

As we have all experienced, schools play an important role in gender socialization. By the time children are in school, they not only have been socialized into their

gender but also are able to negotiate how and in which situations gender will be socially salient. Barrie Thorne, in "Girls and Boys Together . . . But Mostly Apart: Gender Arrangements in Elementary Schools," argues for a more complex idea of gender as socially constructed and context specific. In her observations of social relations among children in elementary school, she finds that boys and girls are segregated and seen as different in the classroom and on the playground both because of teachers' actions and because children socialize each other. Did your own experiences in elementary school conform to the patterns Thorne describes?

A new concern with boys has emerged in the past few years. In "What Are Little Boys Made Of?" Michael Kimmel discusses the different ways that popular discourse defines the problems that confront boys, from violence to attention deficit disorder to the pressure to appear emotionally invulnerable. Kimmel argues that there are clear problems facing boys, but that these problems stem from cultural expectations and peer pressure to conform to a narrow definition of masculinity. He critiques authors who argue that testosterone or other biological features make boys more violent, or more active, or less adapted to educational settings than girls. Instead, he suggests, boys' lives can be improved by not only addressing the emotional straitjacket forced upon them by gender norms but also taking a feminist approach to eliminating gender inequality. Do you agree with Kimmel's argument? How are his observations about boys' experiences similar to those that Thorne describes? Can you think of examples from your own experiences of the pressures placed on boys to conform to masculinity?

Because the culture differentiates not only along gender lines but according to race, ethnicity, and class as well, our socialization experiences also differ along these lines. What a woman of color, for example, needs to teach her sons and daughters to enable them to survive in a white-male-dominated society is different from what a white mother needs to teach her children. These kinds of racial differences, in turn, are compounded by differences in class status, as the last article illustrates. Yen Le Espiritu, in "We Don't Sleep Around Like White Girls Do," explores the ways that gendered sexual norms in Filipina American families serve as a strategy of resistance to oppression for the community as a whole and at the same time limit the autonomy of Filipina women. By emphasizing the sexual looseness of white girls, Filipina girls and their parents assert their moral superiority and counter the stereotypes of Filipinas as either prostitutes or submissive mail-order brides. Rather than consider dominant white conceptions of racial and ethnic "others,"

Espiritu looks at Filipina constructions of whiteness. What generational differences are there between the Filipina girls Espiritu studies and their parents? What is the Filipina American notion of white society? Do you think it is accurate?

France Winddance Twine, in "Brown-Skinned White Girls," also considers whiteness in her study of black girls raised in predominantly white middle-class communities. She finds that these young women grow up with a white identity and only in college develop a black or biracial identity. Once again, we see the ways that class, race, ethnicity, and gender intersect in shaping people's experiences and identities. What forces are at work in shifting the students' identities from white to black or biracial? How do the experiences of black students compare to those of the Latinas and Arab Americans explored in Section One?

Socialization, as we can see, is not a simple process. Are there any common factors, do you think, in the socialization of girls across class and ethnic differences?

Girls and Boys Together . . . But Mostly Apart: Gender Arrangements in Elementary Schools

Throughout the years of elementary school, children's friendships and casual encounters are strongly separated by sex. Sex segregation among children, which starts in preschool and is well established by middle childhood, has been amply documented in studies of children's groups and friendships (e.g., Eder & Hallinan, 1978; Schofield, 1981) and is immediately visible in elementary school settings. When children choose seats in classrooms or the cafeteria, or get into line, they frequently arrange themselves in same-sex clusters. At lunchtime, they talk matter-of-factly about "girls' tables" and "boys' tables." Playgrounds have gendered turfs, with some areas and activities, such as large playing fields and basketball courts, controlled mainly by boys, and others—smaller enclaves like jungle-gym areas and concrete spaces for hopscotch or jump rope—more often controlled by girls. Sex segregation is so common in elementary schools that it is meaningful to speak of separate girls' and boys' worlds.

Studies of gender and children's social relations have mostly followed this "two worlds" model, separately describing and comparing the subcultures of girls and boys (e.g., Lever, 1976; Maltz & Borker, 1983). In brief summary: Boys tend to interact in larger, more age-heterogeneous groups (Lever, 1976; Waldrop & Halverson, 1975; Eder & Hallinan, 1978). They engage in more rough and tumble play and physical fighting (Maccoby & Jacklin, 1974). Organized sports are both a central activity and a major metaphor in boys' subcultures; they use the language of "teams" even when not engaged in sports, and they often construct interaction in the form of contests. The shifting hierarchies of boys' groups (Savin-Williams, 1976) are evident in their more frequent use of direct commands, insults, and challenges (Goodwin, 1980).

Fewer studies have been done of girls' groups (Foot, Chapman, & Smith, 1980; McRobbie & Garber, 1975), and—perhaps because categories for description and analysis have come more from male than female experience—researchers have had difficulty seeing and analyzing girls' social relations. Recent work has begun to correct this skew. In middle childhood, girls' worlds are less public than those of boys; girls more often interact in private places and in smaller groups or friendship pairs (Eder & Hallinan, 1978; Waldrop & Halverson, 1975). Their play is more cooperative and turn-taking (Lever, 1976). Girls have more intense and exclusive friendships, which take shape around keeping and telling secrets, shifting alliances, and indirect ways of expressing disagreement (Goodwin, 1980; Lever, 1976; Maltz & Borker, 1983). Instead of direct commands, girls more often use directives which merge speaker and hearer, e.g., "let's" or "we gotta" (Goodwin, 1980).

Although much can be learned by comparing the social organization and subcultures of boys' and of girls' groups, the separate-worlds approach has eclipsed full, contextual understanding of gender and social relations among children. The separate-worlds model essentially involves a search for group sex differences and shares the limitations of individual sex difference research. Differences tend to be exaggerated and similarities ignored, with little theoretical attention to the integration of similarity and difference (Unger, 1979). Statistical findings of difference are often portrayed as dichotomous, neglecting the considerable individual variation that exists; for example, not all boys fight, and some have intense and exclusive friendships. The sex difference approach tends to abstract gender from its social context, to assume that males and females are qualitatively and permanently different (with differences perhaps unfolding through separate developmental lines). These assumptions mask the possibility that gender arrangements and patterns of similarity and difference may vary by situation, race, social class, region, or subculture.

Sex segregation is far from total, and is a more complex and dynamic process than the portrayal of separate worlds reveals. Erving Goffman (1977) has observed that sex segregation has a "with–then apart" structure; the sexes segregate periodically, with separate spaces, rituals, groups, but they also come together and are, in crucial ways, part of the same world. This is certainly true in the social environment of elementary schools. Although girls and boys do interact as boundaried collectivities—an image suggested by the separate-worlds approach—there are other occasions when they work or play in relaxed and integrated ways. Gender is less central to the organization and meaning of some situations than others. In short, sex segregation is not static, but is a variable and complicated process.

To gain an understanding of gender which can encompass both the "with" and the "apart" of sex segregation, analysis should start not with the individual, nor with a search for sex differences, but with social relationships. Gender should be conceptualized as a system of relationships rather than as an immutable and dichotomous given. Taking this approach, I have organized my research on gender and children's social relations around questions like the following: How and when does gender enter into group formation? In a given situation, how is gender made more or less salient or infused with particular meanings? By what rituals, processes, and forms of social organization and conflict do "with–then apart" rhythms get enacted? How are these processes affected by the organization of institutions (e.g., different types of schools, neighborhoods, or summer camps), varied settings (e.g., the constraints and possibilities governing interaction on playgrounds vs. classrooms), and particular encounters?

METHODS AND SOURCES OF DATA

This study is based on two periods of participant observation. In 1976–1977 I observed for eight months in a largely working-class elementary school in California, a school with 8 percent Black and 12 percent Chicana/o students. In 1980 I did fieldwork for three months in a Michigan elementary school of similar size (around 400 students), social class, and racial composition. I observed in several classrooms—a kindergarten, a second grade, and a combined fourth–fifth grade—and in

school hallways, cafeterias, and playgrounds. I set out to follow the round of the school day as children experience it, recording their interactions with one another, and with adults, in varied settings.

Participant observation involves gaining access to everyday, "naturalistic" settings and taking systematic notes over an extended period of time. Rather than starting with preset categories for recording, or with fixed hypotheses for testing, participant observers record detail in ways which maximize opportunities for discovery. Through continuous interaction between observation and analysis, "grounded theory" is developed (Glaser & Strauss, 1967).

The distinctive logic and discipline of this mode of inquiry emerges from: (1) theoretical sampling—being relatively systematic in the choice of where and whom to observe in order to maximize knowledge relevant to categories and analysis which are being developed; and (2) comparing all relevant data on a given point in order to modify emerging propositions to take account of discrepant cases (Katz, 1983). Participant observation is a flexible, open-ended and inductive method, designed to understand behavior within, rather than stripped from, social context. It provides richly detailed information anchored in everyday meanings and experience.

DAILY PROCESSES OF SEX SEGREGATION

Sex segregation should be understood not as a given, but as the result of deliberate activity. The outcome is dramatically visible when there are separate girls' and boys' tables in school lunchrooms or sex-separated groups on playgrounds. But in the same lunchroom one can also find tables where girls and boys eat and talk together, and in some playground activities the sexes mix. By what processes do girls and boys separate into gender-defined and relatively boundaried collectivities? And in what contexts, and through what processes, do boys and girls interact in less gender-divided ways?

In the school settings I observed, much segregation happened with no mention of gender. Gender was implicit in the contours of friendship, shared interest, and perceived risk which came into play when children chose companions—in their prior planning, invitations, seeking of access, saving of places, denials of entry, and allowing or protesting of "cuts" by those who violated the rules for lining up. Sometimes children formed mixed-sex groups for play, eating, talking, working on a classroom project, or moving through space. When adults or children explicitly invoked gender—and this was nearly always in ways which separated girls and boys—boundaries were heightened and mixed-sex interaction became an explicit arena of risk.

In the schools I studied, the physical space and curricula were not formally divided by sex, as they have been in the history of elementary schooling (a history evident in separate entrances to old school buildings, where the words "Boys" and "Girls" are permanently etched in concrete). Nevertheless, gender was a visible marker in the adult-organized school day. In both schools, when the public address system sounded, the principal inevitably opened with: "Boys and girls. . . . ," and in addressing clusters of children, teachers and aides regularly used gender terms ("Heads down, girls"; "The girls are ready and the boys aren't"). These forms of address made gender visible and salient, conveying an assumption that the sexes are separate social groups.

Teachers and aides sometimes drew upon gender as a basis for sorting children and organizing activities. Gender is an embodied and visual social category which roughly divides the population in half, and the separation of girls and boys permeates the history and lore of schools and playgrounds. In both schools—although through awareness of Title IX, many teachers had changed this practice—one could see separate girls' and boys' lines moving, like caterpillars, through the school halls. In the fourth–fifth-grade classroom the teacher frequently pitted girls against boys for spelling and math contests. On the playground in the Michigan school, aides regarded the space close to the building as girls' territory, and the playing fields "out there" as boys' territory. They sometimes shooed children of the other sex away from those spaces, especially boys who ventured near the girls' area and seemed to have teasing in mind.

In organizing their activities, both within and apart from the surveillance of adults, children also explicitly invoked gender. During my fieldwork in the Michigan school, I kept daily records of who sat where in the lunchroom. The amount of sex segregation varied: it was least at the first-grade tables and almost total among sixth-graders. There was also variation from classroom to classroom within a given age and from day to day. Actions like the following heightened the gender divide: In the lunchroom, when the two second-grade tables were filling, a high-status boy walked by the inside table, which had a scattering of both boys and girls, and said loudly, "Oooo, too many girls," as he headed for a seat at the far table. The boys at the inside table picked up their trays and moved, and no other boys sat at the inside table, which the pronouncement had effectively made taboo. In the end, that day (which was not the case every day), girls and boys ate at separate tables.

Eating and walking are not sex-typed activities, yet in forming groups in lunchrooms and hallways children often separated by sex. Sex segregation assumed added dimensions on the playground, where spaces, equipment, and activities were infused with gender meanings. My inventories of activities and groupings on the playground showed similar patterns in both schools: boys controlled the large fixed spaces designated for team sports (baseball diamonds, grassy fields used for football or soccer); girls more often played closer to the building, doing tricks on the monkey bars (which, for sixth-graders, became an area for sitting and talking) and using cement areas for jump rope, hopscotch, and group games like four-square. (Lever, 1976, provides a good analysis of sex-divided play.) Girls and boys most often played together in kickball, and in group (rather than team) games like four-square, dodgeball, and handball. When children used gender to exclude others from play, they often drew upon beliefs connecting boys to some activities and girls to others: A first-grade boy avidly watched an all-female game of jump rope. When the girls began to shift positions, he recognized a means of access to the play and he offered, "I'll swing it." A girl responded, "No way, you don't know how to do it, to swing it. You gotta be a girl." He left without protest. Although children sometimes ignored pronouncements about what each sex could or could not do, I never heard them directly challenge such claims.

When children had explicitly defined an activity or a group as gendered, those who crossed the boundary—especially boys who moved into female-marked space—risked being teased. ("Look! Mike's in the girls' line!"; "That's a girl over there," a girl said loudly, pointing to a boy sitting at an otherwise all-female table in the lunchroom.) Children, and occasionally adults, used teasing—especially the tease of "liking" someone of the other sex, or of "being" that sex by virtue of being in their midst—to police gender boundaries. Much of the teasing drew upon heterosexual romantic definitions, making cross-sex interaction risky and increasing social distance between boys and girls.

RELATIONSHIPS BETWEEN THE SEXES

Because I have emphasized the "apart" and ignored the occasions of "with," this analysis of sex segregation falsely implies that there is little contact between girls and boys in daily school life. In fact, relationships between girls and boys—which should be studied as fully as, and in connection with, same-sex relationships—are of several kinds:

1. "Borderwork," or forms of cross-sex interaction which are based upon and reaffirm boundaries and asymmetries between girls' and boys' groups.
2. Interactions which are infused with heterosexual meanings.
3. Occasions where individuals cross gender boundaries to participate in the world of the other sex.
4. Situations where gender is muted in salience, with girls and boys interacting in more relaxed ways.

Borderwork

In elementary school settings, boys' and girls' groups are sometimes spatially set apart. Same-sex groups sometimes claim fixed territories such as the basketball court, the bars, or specific lunchroom tables. However, in the crowded, multifocused, and adult-controlled environment of the school, groups form and disperse at a rapid rate and can never stay totally apart. Contact between girls and boys sometimes lessens sex segregation, but gender-defined groups also come together in ways which emphasize their boundaries.

"Borderwork" refers to interaction across, yet based upon and even strengthening, gender boundaries. I have drawn this notion from Fredrik Barth's (1969) analysis of social relations which are maintained across ethnic boundaries without diminishing dichotomized ethnic status.[1] His focus is on more macro, ecological arrangements; mine is on face-to-face behavior. But the insight is similar: groups may interact in ways which strengthen their borders, and the maintenance of ethnic (or gender) groups can best be understood by examining the boundary that defines the groups, "not the cultural stuff that it encloses" (Barth, 1969:15). In elementary schools there are several types of borderwork: contests or games where gender-defined teams compete; cross-sex rituals of chasing and pollution; and group invasions. These interactions are asymmetrical, challenging the separate-but-parallel model of "two worlds."

Contests   Boys and girls are sometimes pitted against each other in classroom competitions and playground games. The fourth–fifth-grade classroom had a boys' side and a girls' side, an arrangement that reemerged each time the teacher asked children to choose their own desks. Although there was some within-sex shuffling, the result was always a spatial moiety system—boys on the left, girls on the right—with the exception of one girl (the "tomboy" whom I'll describe later), who twice chose a desk with the boys and once with the girls. Drawing upon and reinforcing the children's self-segregation, the teacher often pitted the boys against the girls in spelling and math competitions, events marked by cross-sex antagonism and within-sex solidarity. The teacher introduced a math game; she would write addition and subtraction problems on the board, and a member of each team would race to be the first to write the correct answer. She wrote two scorekeeping columns on the board: "Beastly Boys". . . . "Gossipy Girls." The boys yelled out, as several girls laughed, "Noisy girls! Gruesome girls!" The girls sat in a row on top of their desks; sometimes they moved collectively, pushing their hips or whispering "Pass it on." The boys stood along the wall, some reclining against desks. When members of either group came back victorious from the front of the room, they would do the "giving five" hand-slapping ritual with their team members.

On the playground a team of girls occasionally played a team of boys, usually in kickball or team two-square. Sometimes these games proceeded matter-of-factly, but if gender became the explicit basis of team solidarity, the interaction changed, becoming more antagonistic and unstable. Two fifth-grade girls played against two fifth-grade boys in a team game of two-square. The game proceeded at an even pace until an argument ensued about whether the ball was out or on the line. Karen, who had hit the ball, became annoyed, flashed her middle finger at the other team, and called to a passing girl to join their side. The boys then called out to other boys, and cheered as several arrived to play. "We got five and you got three!" Jack yelled. The game continued, with the girls yelling, "Bratty boys! Sissy boys!" and the boys making noises—"Weee haw," "Ha-ha-ha"—as they played.

Chasing   Cross-sex chasing dramatically affirms boundaries between girls and boys. The basic elements of chase and elude, capture and rescue (Sutton-Smith, 1971) are found in various kinds of tag with formal rules and in informal episodes of chasing which punctuate life on playgrounds. These episodes begin with a provocation (taunts like "You can't get me!" or "Slobber monster!"; bodily pokes or the grabbing of possessions). A provocation may be ignored or responded to by chasing. Chaser and chased may then alternate roles. In an ethnographic study of chase sequences on a school playground, Christine Finnan (1982) observes that chases vary in number of chasers to chased (e.g., one chasing one or five chasing two); form of provocation (a taunt or a poke); outcome (an episode may end when the chased outdistances the chaser, or with a brief touch, being wrestled to the ground, or the recapturing of a hat or a ball); and use of space (there may or may not be safety zones).

Like Finnan (1982) and Sluckin (1981), who studied a playground in England, I found that chasing has a gendered structure. Boys frequently chase one another, an activity which often ends in wrestling and mock fights. When girls chase girls, they are usually less physically aggressive; they less often, for example, wrestle one another to the ground.

Cross-sex chasing is set apart by special names— "girls chase the boys"; "boys chase the girls"; "the chase"; "chasers"; "chase and kiss"; "kiss chase"; "kissers and chasers"; "kiss or kill"—and by children's animated talk about the activity. The names vary by region and school, but contain both gender and sexual meanings (this form of play is mentioned, but only briefly analyzed, in Finnan, 1982; Sluckin, 1981; Parrott, 1972; and Borman, 1979).

In "boys chase the girls" and "girls chase the boys" (the names most frequently used in both the California and Michigan schools) boys and girls become, by definition, separate teams. Gender terms override individual identities, especially for the other team ("Help, a girl's chasin' me!"; "C'mon, Sarah, let's get that boy"; "Tony, help save me from the girls"). Individuals may also grab someone of their sex and turn them over to the opposing team: Ryan grabbed Billy from behind, wrestling him to the ground. "Hey, girls, get 'im," Ryan called.

Boys more often mix episodes of cross-sex with same-sex chasing. Girls more often have safety zones, places like the girls' restroom or an area by the school wall, where they retreat to rest and talk (sometimes in animated postmortems) before new episodes of cross-sex chasing begin.

Early in the fall in the Michigan school, where chasing was especially prevalent, I watched a second-grade boy teach a kindergarten girl how to chase. He slowly ran backwards, beckoning her to pursue him, as he called, "Help, a girl's after me." In the early grades chasing mixes with fantasy play, e.g., a first-grade boy who played "sea monster," his arms out-flung and his voice growling, as he chased a group of girls. By third grade, stylized gestures—exaggerated stalking motions, screams (which only girls do), and karate kicks—accompany scenes of chasing.

Names like "chase and kiss" mark the sexual meanings of cross-sex chasing, a theme I return to later. The threat of kissing—most often girls threatening to kiss boys—is a ritualized form of provocation. Cross-sex chasing among sixth-graders involves elaborate patterns of touch and touch avoidance, which adults see as sexual. The principal told the sixth-graders in the Michigan school that they were not to play "pom-pom," a complicated chasing game, because it entailed "inappropriate touch."

Rituals of Pollution   Cross-sex chasing is sometimes entwined with rituals of pollution, as in "cooties," where specific individuals or groups are treated as contaminating or carrying "germs." Children have rituals for transferring cooties (usually touching someone else and shouting, "You've got cooties!"), for immunization (e.g., writing "CV" for "cootie vaccination" on their arms), and for eliminating cooties (e.g., saying "no gives" or using "cootie catchers" made of folded paper) (described in Knapp & Knapp, 1976). While girls may give cooties to girls, boys do not generally give cooties to one another (Samuelson, 1980).

In cross-sex play, either girls or boys may be defined as having cooties, which they transfer through chasing and touching. Girls give cooties to boys more often than vice versa. In Michigan, one version of cooties is called "girl stain"; the fourth-graders whom Karkau (1973) describes used the phrase "girl touch." "Cootie queens" or "cootie girls" (there are no "kings" or "boys") are female pariahs, the ultimate school untouchables, seen as contaminating not only by virtue of gender, but also through some added stigma such as being overweight or poor.[2] That girls are seen as more polluting than boys is a significant asymmetry, which echoes cross-cultural patterns, although in other cultures female pollution is generally connected to menstruation and not applied to prepubertal girls.

Invasions   Playground invasions are another asymmetric form of borderwork. On a few occasions I saw girls invade and disrupt an all-male game, most memorably a group of tall sixth-grade girls who ran onto the playing field and grabbed a football which was in play. The boys were surprised and frustrated, and, unusual for boys this old, finally tattled to the aide. But in the majority of cases, boys disrupt girls' activities rather than vice versa. Boys grab the ball from girls playing four-square, stick feet into a jump-rope and stop an ongoing game, and dash through the area of the bars where girls are taking turns performing, sending the rings flying. Sometimes boys ask to join a girls' game and then, after a short period of seemingly earnest play, disrupt the game. Two second-grade boys begged to "twirl" the jump rope for a group of second-grade girls who had been jumping for some time. The girls agreed, and the boys began to twirl. Soon, without announcement, the boys changed from "seashells, cockle bells" to "hot peppers" (spinning the rope very fast), and tangled the jumper in the rope. The boys ran away laughing.

Boys disrupt girls' play so often that girls have developed almost ritualized responses: they guard their ongoing play, chase boys away, and tattle to the aides. In a playground cycle which enhances sex segregation, aides who try to spot potential trouble before it occurs sometimes shoo boys away from areas where girls are playing. Aides do not anticipate trouble from girls who seek to join groups of boys, with the exception of girls intent on provoking a chase sequence. And indeed, if they seek access to a boys' game, girls usually play with boys in earnest rather than breaking up the game.

A close look at the organization of borderwork—or boundaried interactions between the sexes—shows that the worlds of boys and girls may be separate, but they are not parallel, nor are they equal. The worlds of girls and boys articulate in several asymmetric ways:

1. On the playground, boys control as much as ten times more space than girls, when one adds up the area of large playing fields and compares it with the much smaller areas where girls predominate. Girls, who play closer to the building, are more often watched over and protected by the adult aides.
2. Boys invade all-female games and scenes of play much more than girls invade boys'. This, and boys' greater control of space, correspond with other findings about the organization of gender, and inequality, in our society: compared with men and boys, women and girls take up less space, and their space and talk are more often violated and interrupted (Greif, 1982; Henley, 1977; West & Zimmerman, 1983).
3. Although individual boys are occasionally treated as contaminating (e.g., a third-grade boy who both boys and girls said was "stinky" and "smelled like pee"), girls are more often defined as polluting. This pattern ties to themes that I discuss later: it is more taboo for a boy to play with (as opposed to invade) girls, and girls are more sexually defined than boys.

A look at the boundaries between the separated worlds of girls and boys illuminates within-sex hierarchies of status and control. For example, in the sex-divided seating in the fourth–fifth-grade classroom, several boys recurringly sat near "female space": their desks were at the gender divide in the classroom, and they were more likely than other boys to sit at a predominantly female table in the lunchroom. These boys—two nonbilingual Chicanos and an overweight "loner" boy who was afraid of sports—were at the bottom of the male hierarchy. Gender is sometimes used as a metaphor for male hierarchies; the inferior status of boys at the bottom is conveyed by calling them "girls." Seven boys and one girl were playing basketball. Two younger boys came over and asked to play. While the girl silently stood, fully accepted in the company of players, one of the older boys disparagingly said to the younger boys, "You girls can't play."[3]

In contrast, the girls who more often travel in the boys' world, sitting with groups of boys in the lunchroom or playing basketball, soccer, and baseball with them, are not stigmatized. Some have fairly high status with other girls. The worlds of girls and boys are asymmetrically arranged, and spatial patterns map out interacting forms of inequality.

Heterosexual Meanings

The organization and meanings of gender (the social categories "woman/man," "girl/boy") and of sexuality vary cross-culturally (Ortner & Whitehead, 1981)—and, in our society, across the life course. Harriet Whitehead (1981) observed that in our (Western) gender system, and that of many traditional North American Indian cultures, one's choice of a sexual object, occupation, and dress and demeanor are closely associated with gender. However, the "center of gravity" differs in the two gender systems. For Indians, occupational pursuits provide the primary imagery of gender; dress and demeanor are secondary, and sexuality is least important. In our system, at least for adults, the order is reversed: heterosexuality is central to our definitions of "man" and "woman" ("masculinity/femininity") and the relationships that obtain between them, whereas occupation and dress/demeanor are secondary.

Whereas erotic orientation and gender are closely linked in our definitions of adults, we define children as relatively asexual. Activities and dress/demeanor are more important than sexuality in the cultural meanings of "girl" and "boy." Children are less heterosexually defined than adults, and we have nonsexual imagery for relations between girls and boys. However, both children and adults sometimes use heterosexual language—"crushes," "like," "goin' with," "girlfriends," and "boyfriends"—to define cross-sex relationships. This language increases through the years of elementary school; the shift to adolescence consolidates a gender system organized around the institution of heterosexuality.

In everyday life in the schools, heterosexual and romantic meanings infuse some ritualized forms of interaction between groups of boys and girls (e.g., "chase and kiss") and help maintain sex segregation. "Jimmy likes Beth" or "Beth likes Jimmy" is a major form of teasing, which a child risks in choosing to sit by or walk with someone of the other sex. The structure of teasing and children's sparse vocabulary for relationships between girls and boys are evident in the following conversation, which I had with a group of third-grade girls in the lunchroom. Susan asked me what I was doing, and I said I was observing the things children do and play. Nicole volunteered, "I like running, boys chase all the girls. See Tim over there? Judy chases him all around the school. She likes him." Judy, sitting across the table, quickly responded, "I hate him. I like him for a friend." "Tim loves Judy," Nicole said in a loud, singsong voice.

In the younger grades, the culture and lore of girls contain more heterosexual romantic themes than those of boys. In Michigan, the first-grade girls often jumped rope to a rhyme which began: "Down in the valley where the green grass grows, there sat Cindy [name of jumper], as sweet as a rose. She sat, she sat, she sat so sweet. Along came Jason and kissed her on the cheek. First comes love, then comes marriage, then along comes Cindy with a baby carriage." Before a girl took her turn at jumping, the chanters asked her, "Who do you want to be your boyfriend?" The jumper always proffered a name, which was accepted matter-of-factly. In chasing, a girl's kiss carried greater threat than a boy's kiss; "girl touch," when defined

as contaminating, had sexual connotations. In short, starting at an early age, girls are more sexually defined than boys.

Through the years of elementary school, and increasing with age, the idiom of heterosexuality helps maintain the gender divide. Cross-sex interactions, especially when children initiate them, are fraught with the risk of being teased about "liking" someone of the other sex. I learned of several close cross-sex friendships, formed and maintained in neighborhoods and church, which went underground during the school day.

By the fifth grade a few children began to affirm, rather than avoid, the charge of having a girlfriend or a boyfriend; they introduced the heterosexual courtship rituals of adolescence. In the lunchroom in the Michigan school, as the tables were forming, a high-status fifth-grade boy called out from his seat at the table: "I want Trish to sit by me." Trish came over, and almost like a king and queen, they sat at the gender divide—a row of girls down the table on her side, a row of boys on his. In this situation, which inverted earlier forms, it was not a loss but a gain in status to publicly choose a companion of the other sex. By affirming his choice, the boy became unteasable (note the familiar asymmetry of heterosexual courtship rituals: the male initiates). This incident signals a temporal shift in arrangements of sex and gender.

Traveling in the World of the Other Sex

Contests, invasions, chasing, and heterosexually defined encounters are based upon and reaffirm boundaries between girls and boys. In another type of cross-sex interaction, individuals (or sometimes pairs) cross gender boundaries, seeking acceptance in a group of the other sex. Nearly all the cases I saw of this were tomboys—girls who played organized sports and frequently sat with boys in the cafeteria or classroom. If these girls were skilled at activities central in the boys' world, especially games like soccer, baseball, and basketball, they were pretty much accepted as participants.

Being a tomboy is a matter of degree. Some girls seek access to boys' groups but are excluded; other girls limit their "crossing" to specific sports. Only a few—such as the tomboy I mentioned earlier, who chose a seat with the boys in the sex-divided fourth–fifth grade—participate fully in the boys' world. That particular girl was skilled at the various organized sports which boys played in different seasons of the year. She was also adept at physical fighting and at using the forms of arguing, insult, teasing, naming, and sports-talk of the boys' sub-culture. She was the only Black child in her classroom, in a school with only 8 percent Black students; overall that token status, along with unusual athletic and verbal skills, may have contributed to her ability to move back and forth across the gender divide. Her unique position in the children's world was widely recognized in the school. Several times, the teacher said to me, "She thinks she's a boy."

I observed only one boy in the upper grades (a fourth-grader) who regularly played with all-female groups, as opposed to "playing at" girls' games and seeking to disrupt them. He frequently played jump rope and took turns with girls doing tricks on the bars, using the small gestures—for example, a helpful push on the heel of a girl who needed momentum to turn her body around the bar—which mark skillful and earnest participation. Although I never saw him play in other than an earnest spirit, the girls often chased him away from their games, and both girls and boys teased him. The fact that girls seek and have more access to boys' worlds than vice versa, and the fact that girls who travel with the other sex are less stigmatized for it, are obvious asymmetries, tied to the asymmetries previously discussed.

Relaxed Cross-Sex Interactions

Relationships between boys and girls are not always marked by strong boundaries, heterosexual definitions, or interacting on the terms and turfs of the other sex. On some occasions girls and boys interact in relatively comfortable ways. Gender is not strongly salient nor explicitly invoked, and girls and boys are not organized into boundaried collectivities. These "with" occasions have been neglected by those studying gender and children's relationships, who have emphasized either the model of separate worlds (with little attention to their articulation) or heterosexual forms of contact.

Occasions when boys and girls interact without strain, when gender wanes rather than waxes in importance, frequently have one or more of the following characteristics:

1. The situations are organized around an absorbing task, such as a group art project or creating a radio show, which encourages cooperation and lessens attention to gender. This pattern accords with other studies finding that cooperative activities reduce

group antagonism (e.g., Sherif & Sherif, 1953, who studied divisions between boys in a summer camp; and Aronson et al., 1978, who used cooperative activities to lessen racial divisions in a classroom).

2. Gender is less prominent when children are not responsible for the formation of the group. Mixed-sex play is less frequent in games like football, which require the choosing of teams, and more frequent in games like handball or dodgeball, which individuals can join simply by getting into a line or a circle. When adults organize mixed-sex encounters—which they frequently do in the classroom and in physical education periods on the playground—they legitimize cross-sex contact. This removes the risk of being teased for choosing to be with the other sex.

3. There is more extensive and relaxed cross-sex interaction when principles of grouping other than gender are explicitly invoked—for example, counting off to form teams for spelling or kickball, dividing lines by hot lunch or cold lunch, or organizing a work group on the basis of interests or reading ability.

4. Girls and boys may interact more readily in less public and crowded settings. Neighborhood play, depending on demography, is more often sex- and age-integrated than play at school, partly because with fewer numbers, one may have to resort to an array of social categories to find play partners or to constitute a game. And in less crowded environments there are fewer potential witnesses to "make something of it" if girls and boys play together.

Relaxed interactions between girls and boys often depend on adults to set up and legitimize the contact.[4] Perhaps because of this contingency—and the other, distancing patterns which permeate relations between girls and boys—the easeful moments of interaction rarely build to close friendship. Schofield (1981) makes a similar observation about gender and racial barriers to friendship in a junior high school.

IMPLICATIONS FOR DEVELOPMENT

I have located social relations within an essentially spatial framework, emphasizing the organization of children's play, work, and other activities within specific settings and in one type of institution, the school. In contrast, frameworks of child development rely upon temporal metaphors, using images of growth and transformation over time. Taken alone, both spatial and temporal frameworks have shortcomings; fitted together, they may be mutually correcting.

Those interested in gender and development have relied upon conceptualizations of "sex-role socialization" and "sex differences." Sexuality and gender, I have argued, are more situated and fluid than these individualist and intrinsic models imply. Sex and gender are differently organized and defined across situations, even within the same institution. This situational variation (e.g., in the extent to which an encounter heightens or lessens gender boundaries, or is infused with sexual meanings) shapes and constrains individual behavior. Features which a developmental perspective might attribute to individuals and understand as relatively internal attributes unfolding over time may, in fact, be highly dependent on context. For example, children's avoidance of cross-sex friendship may be attributed to individual gender development in middle childhood. But attention to varied situations may show that this avoidance is contingent on group size, activity, adult behavior, collective meanings, and the risk of being teased.

A focus on social organization and situation draws attention to children's experiences in the present. This helps correct a model like "sex-role socialization," which casts the present under the shadow of the future, or presumed "endpoints" (Speier, 1976). A situated analysis of arrangements of sex and gender among those of different ages may point to crucial disjunctions in the life course. In the fourth and fifth grades, culturally defined heterosexual rituals ("goin' with") begin to suppress the presence and visibility of other types of interaction between girls and boys, such as nonsexualized and comfortable interaction and traveling in the world of the other sex. As "boyfriend/girlfriend" definitions spread, the fifth-grade tomboy I described had to work to sustain "buddy" relationships with boys. Adult women who were tomboys often speak of early adolescence as a painful time when they were pushed away from participation in boys' activities. Other adult women speak of the loss of intense, even erotic ties with other girls when they entered puberty and the rituals of dating, that is, when they became absorbed into the situation of heterosexuality (Rich, 1980). When Lever (1976) describes best-friend relationships among fifth-grade girls as preparation for dating, she imposes heterosexual ideologies onto a present which should be understood on its own terms.

As heterosexual encounters assume more importance, they may alter relations in same-sex groups. For example, Schofield (1981) reports that for sixth- and seventh-grade children in a middle school, the popularity of girls with other girls was affected by their popularity with boys, while boys' status with other boys did not depend on their relations with girls. This is an asymmetry familiar from the adult world; men's relationships with one another are defined through varied activities (occupations, sports), while relationships among women—and their public status—are more influenced by their connections to individual men.

A full understanding of gender and social relations should encompass cross-sex as well as within-sex interactions. "Borderwork" helps maintain separate, gender-linked subcultures, which, as those interested in development have begun to suggest, may result in different milieux for learning. Daniel Maltz and Ruth Borker (1983), for example, argue that because of different interactions within girls' and boys' groups, the sexes learn different rules for creating and interpreting friendly conversation, rules which carry into adulthood and help account for miscommunication between men and women. Carol Gilligan (1982) fits research on the different worlds of girls and boys into a theory of sex differences in moral development. Girls develop a style of reasoning, she argues, which is more personal and relational; boys develop a style which is more positional, based on separateness. Eleanor Maccoby (1982), also following the insight that because of sex segregation, girls and boys grow up in different environments, suggests implications for gender-differentiated prosocial and antisocial behavior.

This separate-worlds approach, as I have illustrated, also has limitations. The occasions when the sexes are together should also be studied, and understood as contexts for experience and learning. For example, asymmetries in cross-sex relationships convey a series of messages: that boys are more entitled to space and to the nonreciprocal right of interrupting or invading the activities of the other sex; that girls are more in need of adult protection, lower in status, more defined by sexuality, and may even be polluting. Different types of cross-sex interaction—relaxed, boundaried, sexualized, or taking place on the terms of the other sex—provide different contexts for development.

By mapping the array of relationships between and within the sexes, one adds complexity to the overly static and dichotomous imagery of separate worlds. Individual experiences vary, with implications for development. Some children prefer same-sex groupings; some are more likely to cross the gender boundary and participate in the world of the other sex; some children (e.g., girls and boys who frequently play "chase and kiss") invoke heterosexual meanings, while others avoid them.

Finally, after charting the terrain of relationships, one can trace their development over time. For example, age variation in the content and form of border-work, or of cross- and same-sex touch, may be related to differing cognitive, social, emotional, or physical capacities, as well as to age-associated cultural forms. I earlier mentioned temporal shifts in the organization of cross-sex chasing, from mixing with fantasy play in the early grades to more elaborately ritualized and sexualized forms by the sixth grade. There also appear to be temporal changes in same- and cross-sex touch. In kindergarten, girls and boys touch one another more freely than in fourth grade, when children avoid relaxed cross-sex touch and instead use pokes,

pushes, and other forms of mock violence, even when the touch clearly expresses affection. This touch taboo is obviously related to the risk of seeming to *like* someone of the other sex. In fourth grade, same-sex touch begins to signal sexual meanings among boys as well as between boys and girls. Younger boys touch one another freely in cuddling (arm around shoulder) as well as mock-violence ways. By fourth grade, when homophobic taunts like "fag" become more common among boys, cuddling touch begins to disappear for boys, but less for girls.

Overall, I am calling for more complexity in our conceptualizations of gender and of children's social relationships. Our challenge is to retain the temporal sweep, looking at individual and group lives as they unfold over time, while also attending to social structure and context and to the full variety of experiences in the present.

ACKNOWLEDGMENTS

I would like to thank Jane Atkinson, Nancy Chodorow, Arlene Daniels, Peter Lyman, Zick Rubin, Malcolm Spector, Avril Thorne, and Margery Wolf for comments on an earlier version of this paper. Conversations with Zella Luria enriched this work.

NOTES

1. I am grateful to Frederick Erickson for suggesting the relevance of Barth's analysis.
2. Sue Samuelson (1980) reports that in a racially mixed playground in Fresno, California, Mexican-American but not Anglo children gave cooties. Racial as well as sexual inequality may be expressed through these forms.
3. This incident was recorded by Margaret Blume, who, for an undergraduate research project in 1982, observed in the California school where I earlier did fieldwork. Her observations and insights enhanced my own, and I would like to thank her for letting me cite this excerpt.
4. Note that in daily school life depending on the individual and the situation, teachers and aides sometimes lessened and at other times heightened sex segregation.

REFERENCES

Aronson, E., et al. 1978. *The Jigsaw Classroom.* Beverly Hills, Calif.: Sage.

Barth, F., ed. 1969. *Ethnic Groups and Boundaries.* Boston: Little, Brown.

Borman, K. M. 1979. "Children's interactions in playgrounds," *Theory into Practice* 18: 251–57.

Eder, D., & Hallinan, M. T. 1978. "Sex differences in children's friendships." *American Sociological Review* 43: 237–50.

Finnan, C. R. 1982. "The ethnography of children's spontaneous play." In G. Spindler, ed., *Doing the Ethnography of Schooling,* pp. 358–80. New York: Holt, Rinehart & Winston.

Foot, H. C., Chapman, A. J., & Smith, J. R. 1980. "Introduction." *Friendship and Social Relations in Children,* pp. 1–14. New York: Wiley.

Gilligan, C. 1982. *In a Different Voice: Psychological Theory and Women's Development.* Cambridge: Harvard University Press.

Glaser, B. G., & Strauss, A. L. 1967. *The Discovery of Grounded Theory.* Chicago: Aldine.

Goffman, E. 1977. "The arrangement between the sexes." *Theory and Society* 4: 301–36.

Goodwin, M. H. 1980. "Directive-response speech sequences in girls' and boys' task activities." In S. McConnell-Ginet, R. Borker, & N. Furman, eds., *Women and Language in Literature and Society,* pp. 157–73. New York: Praeger.

Greif, E. B. 1982. "Sex differences in parent–child conversations." *Women's Studies International Quarterly* 3: 253–8.

Henley, N. 1977. *Body Politics: Power, Sex, and Nonverbal Communication.* Englewood Cliffs, N.J.: Prentice-Hall.

Karkau, K. 1973. *Sexism in the Fourth Grade.* Pittsburgh: KNOW, Inc. (pamphlet).

Katz, J. 1983. "A theory of qualitative methodology: The social system of analytic fieldwork." In R. M. Emerson, ed., *Contemporary Field Research,* pp. 127–48. Boston: Little, Brown.

Knapp, M., & Knapp, H. 1976. *One Potato, Two Potato: The Secret Education of American Children.* New York: W. W. Norton.

Lever, J. 1976. "Sex differences in the games children play." *Social Problems* 23: 478–87.

Maccoby, E. 1982. "Social groupings in childhood: Their relationship to prosocial and antisocial behavior in boys and girls." Paper presented at conference on The Development of Prosocial and Antisocial Behavior, Voss, Norway.

Maccoby, E., & Jacklin, C. 1974. *The Psychology of Sex Differences.* Stanford, Calif.: Stanford University Press.

Maltz, D. N., & Borker, R. A. 1983. "A cultural approach to male–female miscommunication." In J. J. Gumperz, ed., *Language and Social Identity,* pp. 195–216. New York: Cambridge University Press.

McRobbie, A., & Garber, J. 1975. "Girls and subcultures." In S. Hall & T. Jefferson, eds., *Resistance through Rituals,* pp. 209–23. London: Hutchinson.

Ortner, S. B., & Whitehead, H. 1981. *Sexual Meanings.* New York: Cambridge University Press.

Parrott, S. 1972. "Games children play: Ethnography of a second-grade recess." In J. P. Spradley & D. W. McCurdy, eds., *The Cultural Experience,* pp. 206–19. Chicago: Science Research Associates.

Rich, A. 1980. "Compulsory heterosexuality and lesbian existence." *Signs* 5: 631–60.

Samuelson, S. 1980. "The cooties complex." *Western Folklore* 39: 198–210.

Savin-Williams, R. C. 1976. "An ethological study of dominance formation and maintenance in a group of human adolescents." *Child Development* 47: 972–79.

Schofield, J. W. 1981. "Complementary and conflicting identities: Images and interaction in an interracial school." In S. R. Asher & J. M. Gottman, eds., *The Development of Children's Friendships,* pp. 53–90. New York: Cambridge University Press.

Sherif, M., & Sherif, C. 1953. *Groups in Harmony and Tension.* New York: Harper.

Sluckin, A. 1981. *Growing Up in the Playground.* London: Routledge & Kegan Paul.

Speier, M. 1976. "The adult ideological viewpoint in studies of childhood." In A. Skolnick, ed., *Rethinking Childhood,* pp. 168–86. Boston: Little, Brown.

Sutton-Smith, B. 1971. "A syntax for play and games." In R. E. Herron and B. Sutton-Smith, eds., *Child's Play,* pp. 298–307. New York: Wiley.

Unger, R. K. 1979. "Toward a redefinition of sex and gender." *American Psychologist* 34: 1085–94.

Waldrop, M. F., & Halverson, C. F. 1975. "Intensive and extensive peer behavior: Longitudinal and cross-sectional analysis." *Child Development* 46: 19–26.

West, C., & Zimmerman, D. H. 1983. "Small insults: A study of interruptions in cross-sex conversations between unacquainted persons." In B. Thorne, C. Kramarae, & N. Henley, eds., *Language, gender, and society.* Rowley, Mass.: Newbury House.

Whitehead, H. 1981. "The bow and the burden strap: A new look at institutionalized homosexuality in Native America." In S. B. Ortner & H. Whitehead, eds., *Sexual Meanings,* pp. 80–115. New York: Cambridge University Press.

HOSTILE HALLWAYS

American Association of University Women

Sexual harassment is a major problem for many students. Not unlike their adult counterparts in the workplace, children in school are experiencing unwanted advances. Students, however, are required by law to remain in school and thus have the right to be safe there. . . .

The AAUW Educational Foundation [underwrote] this in-depth survey of girls, boys, and sexual harassment in public schools.

The Survey

The survey was conducted in February and March 1993. A total of 1,632 field surveys was completed by public school students in grades 8 through 11, from 79 schools across the continental United States. . . . This study contains representative samples for Hispanic, white, and African American students. . . .

Students were provided with the following definition: **Sexual harassment is *unwanted* and *unwelcome* sexual behavior which interferes with your life. Sexual harassment is not behaviors that you *like* or *want* (for example: wanted kissing, touching, or flirting). . . .**

Sexual harassment in school is an experience common to the vast majority of 8th-to-11th-grade students in America's public schools. Clearly the most alarming finding of this survey is that fully 4 out of 5 students (81%) report that they have been the target of some form of sexual harassment during their school lives.

Who Is Being Harassed?

Among the 81% who report being harassed, the gender gap is surprisingly narrow: 85% of girls and 76% of boys surveyed say they have experienced unwanted and unwelcome sexual behavior that interferes with their lives. The gap widens, however, when we look at frequency. If we consider the statistics for the 58% of students who report experiencing at least one form of harassment "often" or "occasionally," we see a 17-point gender gap: 66% of girls and 49% of boys. Of those experiencing harassment, 1 in 4 report being

targeted "often." The percentage of girls reporting this is 31, compared with 18% of the boys.

In the racial breakdowns of sexual harassment in school there are greater gaps among boys than there are among girls. For all the boys surveyed: African Americans (81%) are more likely to have experienced sexual harassment than whites (75%) and Hispanics (69%). For all the girls surveyed: 87% of whites report having experienced sexual harassment, compared with 84% of African Americans and 82% of Hispanics.

When Does Sexual Harassment Start?

A student's first experience of sexual harassment is most likely to occur in the middle school/junior high years of 6th to 9th grade: 47% of the students who have been harassed fall into this group—40% of boys and 54% of girls. One-third of those students (32%) who have been harassed first experience such unwelcome behavior before 7th grade. . . . Four in 10 African American girls (42%) and Hispanic girls (40%) have been targeted this early, compared with 31% of white girls. Some students (6%) first experienced unwanted advances before the 3rd grade—notably 10% of Hispanic girls. . . .

What Forms of Sexual Harassment Are Students Experiencing?

Although the lines often blur, it is generally understood that there are different types and varying degrees of sexual harassment. This survey categorized 14 forms of harassment, half physical (grabbing, pinching, forced kissing, for example) and half involving no physical contact (including making sexual comments, spreading sexual rumors, and flashing).

At one end of the spectrum, two-thirds of all students surveyed say they have been the targets of **sexual comments, jokes, gestures, or looks**—76% of girls and 56% of boys report having experienced this most common form of harassment. At the other extreme, 11% report being **forced to do something sexual other than kissing**—13% of girls and 9% of boys say they have experienced this form of unwelcome sexual behavior. In between is a variety of sexual harassment experiences, both physical and nonphysical.

The second most common form of sexual harassment involves **touching, grabbing and/or pinching in a sexual way** (53%), as reported by 65% of girls and 42% of boys—a 23-point gender gap.

Among the 46% of students who say they have been **intentionally brushed up against in a sexual way,** the gender gap is a significant 21 points: 57% of girls and 36% of boys. African American girls (64%) are more likely to have experienced this physical form of harassment than white girls (58%) and Hispanic girls (49%). Among boys, nearly half of all African Americans (49%), compared with 34% of whites and 29% of Hispanics, have been targets of this behavior.

The gender gap narrows in the case of **mooning and flashing,** with 49% of girls and 41% of boys reporting this experience. There are significant disparities along racial/ethnic lines, for both girls and boys. White girls (54%) are much more likely to have experienced this harassment than Hispanic (38%) and African American (35%) girls. Roughly equal percentages of white boys (43%) and African American boys (41%) have been flashed or mooned when they did not want to be, compared with only 29% of Hispanic boys.

More than one-third of students (37%) have been the **target of sexual rumors**—the fifth most common form of sexual harassment in school. Among girls: 42% have been victimized this way—African Americans (49%), whites (42%), and Hispanics (33%). Among boys: 34% have had this experience—African Americans (36%), whites (34%), and Hispanics (29%).

The sixth most common form of sexual harassment in school is **having one's clothes pulled at in a sexual way.** One-third of students have experienced this, with girls (38%) more likely than boys (28%) to have been targeted. Again, African American girls (47%) have been subject to this behavior much more often than white (37%) and Hispanic (32%) girls. A similar pattern holds true for boys: African Americans (38%), Hispanics and whites (26% each)—a gap of 12 points.

Slightly less than one-third of students (32%) have been **shown, given, or left unwanted sexual pictures or notes.** Interestingly, boys (34%) are

more likely than girls (31%) to have been targeted in this way. Hispanic boys (27%) have been subject to this less often than white (33%) and African American (34%) boys.

More than 1 in 4 students (27%) say they have been **blocked or cornered in a sexual way,** with more than twice as many girls (38%) as boys (17%) reporting this. Among girls, 48% of African Americans have experienced this, compared with 36% of both whites and Hispanics. Roughly the same relative racial/ethnic breakdowns exist for boys.

Almost 1 in 5 students (19%) say they have been the **target of written sexual messages/graffiti** on bathroom walls, lockers, etc., with boys and girls reporting virtually equal experiences.

Among the 18% of students who say they have been **forced to kiss someone** when they did not want to, there is a gender gap of 9 points: 23% of girls and 14% of boys have been subjected to this behavior. Among girls: African Americans (30%), Hispanics (27%), and whites (22%). Among boys: African Americans (22%), Hispanics (16%), and whites (12%).

Among the 17% of students who have been **called gay or lesbian** when they did not want to be, there is a pattern-breaking gender gap of 13 points: boys (23%) are more than twice as likely as girls (10%) to have been targeted. While there are no significant racial/ethnic differences among boys, Hispanic girls (5%) were only half as likely to have experienced this behavior as African American (11%) and white (10%) girls.

Of the 16% of students who say they have **had their clothing pulled off or down,** the gender breakdown is nearly equal. Of all the subgroups, African American boys (23%—nearly 1 in 4) were most likely to have been targeted.

A troubling 1 in 10 students (11%) say they have been **forced to do something sexual at school other than kissing**—13% of girls and 9% of boys. Among boys, 1 in 5 African Americans (19%) report having been targeted, compared with 13% of Hispanic boys and 6% of white boys.

Lastly, 7% of students say they have **been spied on while they dressed or showered at school,** with equal percentages of girls and boys having been targeted, though 11% say they could not be sure if they had been victimized in this way.

(continued)

Who Are the Harassers ... and Why Do They Do It?

Of the 81%* who have been targets of sexual harassment in school, 18% say they have been harassed by a school employee (such as a teacher, coach, bus driver, teacher's aide, security guard, principal, or counselor)—1 in 4 girls (25%) and 1 in 10 boys (10%). African American girls (33%) are more likely to have been targeted by a school employee, compared with white (25%) and Hispanic (17%) girls.

But as disturbing as these numbers are, they are dwarfed by student reports of peer-to-peer harassment. Of those who say they have been harassed, nearly 4 in 5 (79%) have been targeted by a current or former student at school—86% of girls and 71% of boys. Among girls who have been harassed: 81% report having been harassed by a male acting alone, 57% by a group of males, 11% by a mixed group of males and females, 10% by a female acting alone, and 3% by a group of females. Among boys who have been harassed: 57% report having been harassed by a female acting alone, 35% by a group of females, 25% by a male acting alone, 14% by a group of males, and 13% by a mixed group of females and males. . . .

Whom Do Students Tell?

The answer, in broad terms, is that students do not routinely report sexual harassment incidents to adults. In addition, boys who have been harassed are more likely than girls to have told no one (27% and 19%, respectively).

A scant 7% of sexually harassed students say they have told a teacher about the experience, with girls twice as likely as boys to have done this. Just under 1 in 4 (23%) have reported the incidents to parents or other family members—approximately 1 in 3 girls (34%) and 1 in 10 boys (11%), with Hispanic boys (20%) almost twice as likely to respond this way as white and African American boys (11% and 10%, respectively).

By far, most reporting takes place on a peer-to-peer basis: 63% of sexually harassed students have told a friend (49% of boys and 77% of girls).

*The statistics in this survey—except where noted—refer to the 81% of students who report some experience of sexual harassment in school.

Those students who have remained silent and told no one number 23%.

The Impact

. . . The findings clearly indicate that although a hostile learning environment has serious implications for both girls and boys, girls report greater problems as a result of sexual harassment, with higher percentages of African American girls reporting this, compared with white and Hispanic girls.

What Is the Educational Impact of Sexual Harassment?

Nearly 1 in 4 students (23%) who have been sexually harassed say that one outcome of the experience is **not wanting to attend school:** 33% of girls report this—39% of African Americans, compared with 33% of white and 29% of Hispanic girls. In comparison, 12% of boys respond this way: 14% of whites, 9% of African Americans, and 8% of Hispanics. Nearly 1 in 4 girls (24%) say that harassment caused them to **stay home from school or cut a class.**

Nearly 1 in 4 students (23%) report **not wanting to talk as much in class** after experiencing harassment. Once again, the gender gap is considerable, with 32% of girls and 13% of boys thus affected. Almost half the African American girls who have been harassed (42%) respond this way, compared with Hispanic girls (35%) and white girls (30%).

Slightly more than 1 in 5 (21%) students who have been sexually harassed say the experience has made it **harder to pay attention in school,** 28% of girls and 13% of boys claim this. Similarly, 16% of students say they have **made a lower grade on a test or paper** as a result of harassment, with 23% of girls and 9% of boys responding in this fashion. Once more, those girls most affected are African American (28%); the numbers are 23% and 22%, respectively, for Hispanics and whites. Of the 13% who say sexual harassment resulted in **making a lower grade in class,** 1 in 5 girls (20%) and 6% of boys report this. African American girls (24%—nearly 1 in 4), again, are most affected, compared with white girls (19%) and Hispanic girls (15%).

One in 6 (16%) report that they have **found it hard to study;** 22% of girls answered this way—27% of African Americans, 26% of Hispanics, and 21% of whites.

Thoughts about changing schools are reported by 12% of students who have been harassed—18% of girls respond this way. Conforming to an unfortunate pattern, African American girls (26%) are more likely to have considered this than white and Hispanic girls (17% each). A small number of students (3%) state that they actually have **changed schools** as a result of sexual harassment.

Finally, 4% say that the experience of sexual harassment has made them **doubt whether they have what it takes to graduate from high school;** 5% of girls say this—almost 1 in 10 (9%) African Americans, 5% of Hispanics, and 4% of whites.

What Is the Emotional Impact of Sexual Harassment?

While half of all students (50%) who have been harassed state that they have suffered **embarrassment,** nearly 2 in 3 girls (64%) report feeling this way, compared with 36% of boys. White girls and boys feel this in greater numbers than their African American and Hispanic counterparts. Racial/ethnic breakdown for girls: whites (66%), Hispanics (58%), African Americans (55%). For boys: whites (40%), African Americans (25%), Hispanics (30%).

Similarly, 37% percent of students say that sexual harassment has caused them to **feel self-conscious**—more than 1 in 2 girls (52%) report this, compared with 1 in 5 boys (21%). Racial/ethnic breakdown for girls: whites (54%), African Americans (47%), Hispanics (44%); for boys: whites (24%), African Americans (14%), Hispanics (22%).

Slightly less than one-third of students (29%) say sexual harassment makes them **feel less sure or less confident about themselves**—43% of girls and 14% of boys say this, a very wide gender gap. Racial/ethnic breakdown for girls: whites (44%), African Americans and Hispanics (38% each); for boys: whites (16%), Hispanics (9%), and African Americans (8%).

When asked if sexual harassment has caused them to **feel afraid or scared,** nearly 1 in 4 (24%)

say yes—39% of girls and 8% of boys respond this way, with no marked racial/ethnic gaps. And while slightly more than 1 in 5 sexually harassed students (21%) say that sexual harassment has caused them to **doubt whether they can have a happy romantic relationship,** nearly 1 in 3 girls (30%) report this, compared with 12% of boys. Again, higher percentages of African American girls (38%) respond this way, compared with Hispanic girls (33%) and white girls (27%). For boys, this feeling is more common among Hispanics (16%) and whites (14%). The percentage for African American boys, 8%, is notably smaller compared with the 38% of African American girls who feel this way.

Adolescence is a critical time in the evolution of self-image. In fact, 17% say that sexual harassment has caused them to **feel confused about who they are.** One in 4 girls (25%) react this way; nearly 1 in 3 (31%) Hispanics, 25% of whites, and 21% of African Americans—compared with 1 in 10 boys (9%); 13% of Hispanics, 9% of whites, and 7% of African Americans. . . .

Students were asked which of the following phrases—very upset, somewhat upset, not very upset, not at all upset—best describes how they felt right after being harassed. While 1 in 4 students (25%) report that they were "very upset," 39% of girls—more than 1 in 3—report this, compared with 10% of boys. And **while nearly half the students (48%) say they were "very upset" or "somewhat upset," an alarming 70% of girls respond this way, compared with only 24% of boys.**

Also important to note is that twice as many boys (25%) as girls (13%) say they were not sure how they felt.

What Are the Behavioral Consequences?

Nearly 1 in 2 students (49%) who have been harassed say they **avoid the person(s) who harassed them;** a whopping 69% of girls, compared with 27% of boys, report responding this way. Slightly less than 1 in 4 students (23%) say they **stay away from particular places in the school or on the school grounds;** 34% of girls report this—41% of African Americans, 37% of Hispanics, and 32% of whites—compared with 12% of boys.

(continued)

Further, nearly 1 in 4 students (22%) say that sexual harassment has at least on one occasion caused them to **change their seats in class;** 31% of girls respond this way—42% of African American girls, 30% of white girls, and 28% of Hispanic girls—compared with 12% of boys. More than 1 in 10 (12%) have **stopped attending a particular activity or sport;** 17% of girls (nearly 1 out of 5) react this way—27% of Hispanics, 22% of African Americans, and 16% of whites—compared with 6% of boys.

One in 10 students (10%) report **changing their group of friends**—14% of girls and 6% of boys respond in this fashion. The numbers are the same for the incidence of those who **changed the way they come to or go home from school** (10% of students; 14% of girls and 6% of boys), although in this category there is a notable racial/ethnic gap: 25%) of African American girls react this way, compared with 20% of Hispanic girls and 12% of white girls.

The Worst Harassment—Being Called Gay

Sexual identity is a sensitive issue for adolescents. During this time, being called gay or lesbian is disturbing to a majority of students. Indeed, when students were asked to what degree they would be upset if they were the targets of the 14 different types of sexual harassment outlined in the survey, 86% of all students surveyed said they would be "very upset" if they were called gay or lesbian: 85% of boys and 87% of girls. No other type of harassment—including actual physical abuse—provoked a reaction this strong among boys.

In terms of actual experience, 17% of students say they have been called gay or lesbian. Boys (23%) are more than twice as likely as girls (10%) to have been targeted this way, with no significant racial/ethnic variations. Among the boys, 4% say this has occurred often; 5%, occasionally; 14%, rarely. Twice as many Hispanic boys (8%) say they are often called gay, compared with 4% each for African American and white boys.

Of those boys who have been called gay, nearly 3 in 5 (58%) say they have called someone else gay: 61% of whites, 51% of African Americans, and 45% of Hispanics.

The Challenge

This survey, comprised of voices as well as numbers, shapes a picture that demands attention: sexual harassment in school—in hallways, classrooms, and beyond—is wide-spread, with both girls and boys being targeted by their peers as well as adults. Clearly, the process of getting an education is a large enough challenge for most students without the added challenge of contending with sexual harassment in school.

At the most basic, schools must have sexual harassment policies that are clearly communicated and routinely enforced. The mere fact that more than half the students surveyed (57%) do not know if their school has a policy on sexual harassment is disturbing. . . .

This survey . . . also raises some important questions. Does adult sexual harassment have roots in school-based behavior? When behavior is shrugged off as permissible because it is widespread and "boys will be boys," are we unwittingly setting the stage for abusive behavior later on? Do students harass because they themselves are harassed?

The statements and statistics presented here add up to an undeniable mandate: parents, teachers, and administrators must acknowledge that sexual harassment in school is creating a hostile environment that compromises the education of America's children. Sexual harassment is clearly and measurably taking a toll on a significant percentage of students' educational, emotional, and behavioral lives. And although girls are experiencing more harassment—and suffering graver consequences—in the end, sexual harassment is everyone's problem. For when children's self-esteem and development are hampered, the repercussions echo throughout our society.

What Are Little Boys Made Of?

To hear some tell it, there's a virtual war against boys in America. Best-sellers' subtitles counsel us to "protect" boys, to "rescue" them. Inside, we hear how boys are failing at school, where their behavior is increasingly seen as a problem. Therapists advise anguished parents about boys' fragility, their hidden despair and despondence. Boys, we read, are depressed, suicidal, emotionally shut down.

And why? It depends on whom you ask. The backlash chorus—the cultural rights as well as the authors of some of these books—chant "feminism." Because of feminism, they say, America has been so focused on girls that we've forgotten about the boys. Other writers blame patterns of male development, while still others find in feminism not the problem but its solution.

There's no question that there's a boy crisis. Virtually all the books cite the same statistics: boys are four to five times more likely to kill themselves than girls, four times more likely to be diagnosed as emotionally disturbed, three times more likely to be diagnosed with attention deficit disorder, and 15 times more likely to be victims of violent crime. The debate concerns the nature of the crisis, its causes, and, of course, its remedies. The startling number of advice manuals that have appeared in the past couple of years—almost all by male therapists—alternate between psychological diagnoses and practical advice about how to raise boys.

One group, epitomized by therapist Michael Gurian (*A Fine Young Man, The Wonder of Boys*), suggests that boys are both doing worse than ever and doing worse than girls thanks to feminists' efforts. Gurian argues that as feminists have changed the rules, they've made boys the problem. By minimizing the importance of basic biological differences, and establishing girls' standards as the ones all children must follow, feminists have wrecked boyhood. Along with Australian men's movement guru Steve Biddulph (*Raising Boys*), Gurian argues that our educational system forces naturally rambunctious boys to conform to a regime of obedience. With testosterone surging through their little limbs, boys are commanded to sit still, raise their hands, and take naps.

To hear these critics tell it, we're no longer allowing boys to be boys. We've misunderstood boy biology, and cultural meddling—especially by misinformed women—won't change a thing. It's nature, not nurture, that propels boys towards obnoxious behavior, violence, and sadistic experiments on insects. What makes boys boys is, in a word, testosterone, that magical, catch-all hormone that drives them toward aggression and risk-taking, and challenging this fact gives them the message, Gurian says, that "boyhood is defective."

This facile biological determinism mars otherwise insightful observations. Gurian adroitly points out the nearly unbearable pressure on young boys to conform, to resort to violence to solve problems, to disrupt classroom decorum. But he thinks it's entirely due to biology—not peer culture, media violence, or parental influence. And Biddulph agrees: "Testosterone equals vitality," he writes. All we have to do is "honor it and steer it into healthy directions." This over-reliance on biology leads both writers to overstate the differences between the sexes and ignore the differences among boys and among girls. To argue that boys have a harder time in school ignores all reliable evidence from sources such as Myra and David Sadker's *Failing at Fairness: How America's Schools Cheat Girls.*

These misdiagnoses lead to some rather bizarre excuses for boys' behavior, and to the celebration of all things masculine as the simple product of that pubertal chemical elixir. In *The Wonder of Boys*, Gurian cites bewilderingly incongruous rites of passage, such as "military boot camp, fraternity hazings, graduation day, and bar mitzvah," as essential parts of every boy's life. Hazing and bar mitzvahs? Have you read any reports of boys dying at the hands of other boys at bar mitzvahs? Biddulph explains boys' refusal to listen to adult authority by reference to the "fact" that their ear canals develop in irregular spurts, "leading to a period of hearing loss." And did you know that baritone singers in Welsh choruses have more testosterone than tenors—and have more sex! Where do they get this stuff?

More chilling, though, are their strategies for intervention. Gurian suggests reviving corporal punishment both at home and at school—but only when administered privately with cool indifference and never in the heat of adult anger. (He calls it "spanking responsibly.") Biddulph, somewhat more moderately, proposes that boys start school a year later than girls, so they'll be on a par intellectually.

The problem is, there's plenty of evidence that boys are not "just boys" everywhere and in the same ways. If it's all biological, why is the slightest deviation from expected manly behavior so cruelly punished? Why aren't Norwegian or French or Swiss boys as violent, homophobic, and misogynist as many are in the U.S.? Boys are not doomed to be victims of what Alan Alda once facetiously called "testosterone poisoning." On the contrary, they can become men who express their emotions and treat their partners respectfully, who listen as well as act, and who love and nurture their children.

But how do we get there? Another group of therapists, including Dan Kindlon and Michael Thompson, and William Pollack, eschew testosterone-tinged testimonials and treat masculinity as an ideology to be challenged. For them, we need to understand the patterns of boys' development to more effectively intervene and set boys on the path to a manhood of integrity.

To do that, Kindlon and Thompson write in *Raising Cain,* we must contend with the "culture of cruelty" that forces a boy to deny emotional neediness, "routinely disguise his feelings," and end up emotionally isolated. In *Real Boys*, Pollack calls it the "Boy Code" and the "mask of masculinity"—a kind of swaggering attitude that boys embrace to hide their fears, suppress dependency and vulnerability, and present a stoic front.

These two books are the biggest sellers and their authors the most visible experts on boyhood. Pollack's book is far better. The most influenced by feminism, his observations provide an important parallel to psychologist Carol Gilligan's work on how assertive, confident, and proud girls "lose their voices" when they hit adolescence. At the same moment, Pollack says, boys find the inauthentic voice of bravado, of constant posturing, of foolish risk-taking and gratuitous violence. The

Boy Code teaches them that they are supposed to be in power and thus to act like it. They "ruffle in a manly pose," as Yeats once put it, "for all their timid heart."

Unfortunately, these therapists' explanations don't always track. For one thing they all use examples drawn from their clinical practices but then generalize casually from their clients to all boys. And, alas, "all" is limited almost entirely to middle-class, suburban white boys. Cute blond boys stare at us from the books' covers, while inside the authors ignore large numbers of boys whose pain and low self-esteem may have to do with insecurities and anxieties that are more economically and politically rooted. Gurian's books disingenuously show one boy of color on each cover, but there's nary a mention of them inside. Kindlon and Thompson generalize from their work at an elite prep school.

If all the boys are white and middle class, at least they're not all straight. Most therapists treat homosexuality casually, dropping in a brief reference, "explaining" it as biological, and urging compassion and understanding before returning to the more "important" stuff. Only Pollack devotes a sensitive and carefully thought-out chapter to homosexuality and he actually uses the term "homophobia."

The cause of all this posturing and posing is not testosterone, of course, but privilege. In adolescence, both boys and girls get their first real dose of gender inequality, and that is what explains their different paths. The interventions recommended by Kindlon and Thompson—allowing boys to have their emotions; accepting a high level of activity; speaking their language; treating them with respect; using discipline to guide and build; modeling manhood as emotionally attached (all of which are good suggestions and applicable to girls, also)—don't address male entitlement. Indeed, of the male therapists, only Pollack and James Gilligan (*Violence*) even seem to notice it. For the others, boys' troubles are all about fears suppressed, pain swallowed. Kindlon and Thompson write that the "culture of cruelty imposes a code of silence on boys, requiring them to suffer without speaking of it and to be silent witnesses to acts of cruelty to others."

The books that are written with an understanding of male privilege—and the need to challenge it—are the ones that offer the most useful tools to improve boys' lives. Books by Myriam Miedzian and by Olga Silverstein and Beth Rashbaum, published several years ago, offer critiques of traditional boyhood and well-conceived plans for support and change. Eschewing biological determinism, these books see in feminism a blueprint for transforming both boyhood and manhood. Feminism encourages men—and their sons—to be more emotionally open and expressive, to develop empathic skills, and to channel emotional outbursts away from violence. And feminism demands the kinds of societal changes that make this growth possible.

That's all the more necessary, because there really is a boy crisis in America—not the crisis of inverted proportions that claims boys are the new victims of a feminist-inspired agenda run amok. The real boy crisis usually goes by another name. We call it "teen violence," "youth violence," "gang violence," "violence in the schools." Let's face facts: men and boys are responsible for 85 percent of all violent crimes in this country, and their victims are overwhelmingly male as well. From an early age, boys learn that violence is not only an acceptable form of conflict resolution, but one that is admired. Four times more teenage boys than teenage girls think fighting is appropriate when someone cuts into the front of a line. Half of all teenage boys get into a physical fight each year.

"Rescuing" or "protecting" isn't the answer, say British high school teachers Jonathan Salisbury and David Jackson. As their title, *Challenging Macho Values*, shouts, they want to take issue with traditional masculinity, to disrupt the facile "boys will be boys" model, and to erode boys' sense of entitlement. And for Paul Kivel (*Boys Will Be Men*), raising boys to manhood means confronting racism, sexism, and homophobia—both in our communities and in ourselves. These books are loaded with hands-on practical advice to help adolescents raise issues, confront fears, and overcome anxieties, and to help teachers dispel myths, encourage cooperation, and discourage violent solutions to perceived problems. Salisbury and Jackson's book will be most valuable to teachers seeking to transform disruptive behavior; Kivel's is geared more to parents, to initiate and continue those sensitive and difficult conversations. The most valuable material helps parents and teachers deconstruct sexuality myths and challenge sexual harassment and violence. "We believe that masculine violence is intentional, deliberate, and purposeful," write Salisbury and Jackson. "It comes from an attempt by men and boys to create and sustain a system of masculine power and control that benefits them every minute of the day." Forget testosterone; it's sexism! Even if these two books are less gracefully written and more relentlessly critical of traditional boyhood, they are the only ones to recognize that not all boys are the same, and that one key to enabling boys to express a wider range of emotions is to challenge the power and privilege that is part of their cultural heritage.

Gilligan and Miedzian, along with James Garbarino (*Lost Boys*), understand that the real boy crisis is a crisis of violence—specifically the cultural prescriptions that equate masculinity with the capacity for violence. Garbarino's fortuitously timed study of youthful offenders locates the origins of men's violence in the way boys swallow anger and hurt. Among the boys he studied, "deadly petulance usually hides some deep emotional wounds, a way of compensating through an exaggerated sense of grandeur for an inner sense of violation, victimization, and injustice." In other words, as one prison inmate put it, "I'd rather be wanted for murder than not wanted at all."

Gilligan is even more specific. In his insightful study of violence, he places its origins in "the fear of shame and ridicule, and the overbearing need to prevent others from laughing at oneself by making them weep instead." The belief that violence is manly is not carried on any chromosome, not soldered into the wiring of the right or left hemisphere, not juiced by testosterone. (Half of all boys don't fight, most don't carry weapons, and almost all don't kill: are they not boys?) Boys learn it. Violence, Gilligan writes, "has far more to do with the cultural construction of manhood than it does with the hormonal substrates of biology."

That's where feminism comes in. Who, after all, has offered the most trenchant critique of that cultural construction but feminists? That's why the books written by women and men that use a feminist perspective (Gilligan, Kivel, Miedzian, Pollack, Salisbury and Jackson, and Silverstein and Rashbaum) are far more convincing than those that either repudiate it (Gurian, Biddulph) or ignore it (Kindlon and Thompson).

Frankly, I think the antifeminists such as Gurian and Biddulph (and the right wing in general) are the real male bashers. When they say boys will be boys, they mean boys will be uncivilized animals. In their view, males are biologically propelled to be savage, predatory, sexually omnivorous creatures, hard-wired for violence. As a man, I find this view insulting.

Feminists imagine, and demand, that men (and boys) can do better. Feminism offers the possibility of a new boyhood and a new masculinity based on a passion for justice, a love of equality, and the expression of a full range of feelings.

"We Don't Sleep Around Like White Girls Do": Family, Culture, and Gender in Filipina American Lives

I want my daughters to be Filipino especially on sex. I always emphasize to them that they should not participate in sex if they are not married. We are also Catholic. We are raised so that we don't engage in going out with men while we are not married. And I don't like it to happen to my daughters as if they have no values. I don't like them to grow up that way, like the American girls.

          —*Filipina immigrant mother*

I found that a lot of the Asian American friends of mine, we don't date like white girls date. We don't sleep around like white girls do. Everyone is really mellow at dating because your parents were constraining and restrictive.

          —*Second-generation Filipina daughter*

Focusing on the relationship between Filipino immigrant parents and their daughters, this article argues that gender is a key to immigrant identity and a vehicle for racialized immigrants to assert cultural superiority over the dominant group. In immigrant communities, culture takes on a special significance: not only does it form a lifeline to the home country and a basis for group identity in a new country, it is also a base from which immigrants stake their political and sociocultural claims on their new country (Eastmond 1993, 40). For Filipino immigrants, who come from a homeland that was once a U.S. colony, cultural reconstruction has been especially critical in the assertion of their presence in the United States—a way to counter the cultural

I gratefully acknowledge the many useful suggestions and comments of George Lipsitz, Vince Rafael, Lisa Lowe, Joane Nagel, Diane Wolf, Karen Pyke, and two anonymous reviewers for *Signs.* I also would like to thank all those Filipinos/as who participated in this study for their time, help, and insights into immigrant lives.

Americanization of the Philippines, to resist the assimilative and alienating demands of U.S. society, and to reaffirm to themselves their self-worth in the face of colonial, racial, class, and gendered subordination. Before World War II, Filipinos were barred from becoming U.S. citizens, owning property, and marrying whites. They also encountered discriminatory housing policies, unfair labor practices, violent physical encounters, and racist as well as anti-immigrant discourse.[1] While blatant legal discrimination against Filipino Americans is largely a matter of the past, Filipinos continue to encounter many barriers that prevent full participation in the economic, social, and political institutions of the United States (Azores-Gunter 1986–87; Cabezas, Shinagawa, and Kawaguchi 1986–87; Okamura and Agbayani 1997). Moreover, the economic mobility and cultural assimilation that enables white ethnics to become "unhyphenated whites" is seldom extended to Filipino Americans (Espiritu 1994). Like other Asians, the Filipino is "always seen as an immigrant, as the 'foreigner-within,' even when born in the United States" (Lowe 1996, 5). Finally, although Filipinos have been in the United States since the middle of the 1700s and Americans have been in the Philippines since at least the late 1800s, U.S. Filipinos—as racialized nationals, immigrants, and citizens—are "still practically an invisible and silent minority" (San Juan 1991, 117). Drawing from my research on Filipino American families in San Diego, California, I explore in this article the ways racialized immigrants claim through gender the power denied them by racism.

My epigraphs, quotations of a Filipina immigrant mother and a second-generation Filipina daughter, suggest that the virtuous Filipina daughter is partially constructed on the conceptualization of white women as sexually immoral. This juxtaposition underscores the fact that femininity is a relational category, one that is co-constructed with other racial and cultural categories.

These narratives also reveal that women's sexuality and their enforced "morality" are fundamental to the structuring of social inequalities. Historically, the sexuality of racialized women has been systematically demonized and disparaged by dominant or oppressor groups to justify and bolster nationalist movements, colonialism, and/or racism. But as these narratives indicate, racialized groups also criticize the morality of white women as a strategy of resistance—a means of asserting a morally superior public face to the dominant society.

By exploring how Filipino immigrants characterize white families and white women, I hope to contribute to a neglected area of research: how the "margins" imagine and construct the "mainstream" in order to assert superiority over it. But this strategy is not without costs. The elevation of Filipina chastity (particularly that of young women) has the effect of reinforcing masculinist and patriarchal power in the name of a greater ideal of national/ethnic self-respect. Because the control of women is one of the principal means of asserting moral superiority, young women in immigrant families face numerous restrictions on their autonomy, mobility, and personal decision making. Although this article addresses the experiences and attitudes of both parents and children, here I am more concerned with understanding the actions of immigrant parents than with the reactions of their second-generation daughters.

STUDYING FILIPINOS IN SAN DIEGO

San Diego, California has long been a favored area of settlement for Filipinos and is today the third-largest U.S. destination for Filipino immigrants (Rumbaut 1991, 220).[2] As the site of the largest U.S. naval base and the Navy's primary West Coast training facility, San Diego has been a primary area of settlement for Filipino navy personnel and their families since the early 1900s. As in other Filipino communities along the Pacific Coast, the San Diego community grew dramatically in the twenty-five years following passage of the 1965 Immigration Act. New immigration contributed greatly to the tripling of San Diego county's Filipino American population from 1970 to 1980 and its doubling from 1980 to 1990. In 1990, nearly 96,000 Filipinos resided in the county. Although they made up only 4 percent of the county's general population, they constituted close to 50 percent of the Asian American population (Espiritu 1995). Many post-1965 Filipino immigrants have come to San Diego as professionals—most conspicuously as health care

workers. A 1992 analysis of the socioeconomic characteristics of recent Filipino immigrants in San Diego indicated that they were predominantly middle-class, college-educated, and English-speaking professionals who were more likely to own than rent their homes (Rumbaut 1994). At the same time, about two-thirds of the Filipinos surveyed indicated that they had experienced racial and ethnic discrimination (Espiritu and Wolf, forthcoming).

The information on which this article is based comes mostly from in-depth interviews that I conducted with almost one hundred Filipinos in San Diego.[3] Using the "snowball" sampling technique, I started by interviewing Filipino Americans whom I knew and then asking them to refer me to others who might be willing to be interviewed. In other words, I chose participants not randomly but rather through a network of Filipino American contacts whom the first group of respondents trusted. To capture the diversity within the Filipino American community, I sought and selected respondents of different backgrounds and with diverse viewpoints. The sample is about equally divided between first-generation immigrants (those who came to the United States as adults) and Filipinas/os who were born and/or raised in the United States. It is more difficult to pinpoint the class status of the people I interviewed. To be sure, they included poor working-class immigrants who barely eked out a living, as well as educated professionals who thrived in middle- and upper-class suburban neighborhoods. However, the class status of most was much more ambiguous. I met Filipinos/as who toiled as assembly workers but who, through the pooling of income and finances, owned homes in middle-class communities. I also discovered that class status was transnational, determined as much by one's economic position in the Philippines as by that in the United States. For example, I encountered individuals who struggled economically in the United States but owned sizable properties in the Philippines. And I interviewed immigrants who continued to view themselves as "upper class" even while living in dire conditions in the United States. These examples suggest that the upper/middle/working-class typology, while useful, does not capture the complexity of immigrant lives. Reflecting the prominence of the U.S. Navy in San Diego, more than half of my respondents were affiliated with or had relatives affiliated with the U.S. Navy.

My tape-recorded interviews, conducted in English, ranged from three to ten hours each and took place in offices, coffee shops, and homes. My questions were open-ended and covered three general areas: family and immigration history, ethnic identity and practices, and community development among San Diego's Filipinos. The interviewing process varied widely: some respondents needed to be prompted with specific questions, while others spoke at great length on their own. Some chose to cover the span of their lives; others focused on specific events that were particularly important to them. The initial impetus for this article on the relationship between immigrant parents and their daughters came from my observation that the dynamics of gender emerged more clearly in the interviews with women than in those with men. Because gender has been a marked category for women, the mothers and daughters I interviewed rarely told their life stories without reference to the dynamics of gender (see Personal Narratives Group 1989, 4–5). Even without prompting, young Filipinas almost always recounted stories of restrictive gender roles and gender expectations, particularly of parental control over their whereabouts and sexuality.

I believe that my own personal and social characteristics influenced the actual process of data collection, the quality of the materials that I gathered, and my analysis of them. As a Vietnam-born woman who immigrated to the United States at the age of twelve, I came to the research project not as an "objective" outsider but as a fellow Asian immigrant who shared some of the life experiences of my respondents. During the fieldwork process, I did not remain detached but actively shared with my informants my own experiences of being an Asian immigrant woman: of being perceived as an outsider in U.S. society, of speaking English as a second language, of being a woman of color in a racialized patriarchal society, and of negotiating intergenerational tensions within my own family. I do not claim that these shared struggles grant me "insider status" into the Filipino American community; the differences in our histories, cultures, languages, and, at times, class backgrounds, remain important. But I do claim that these shared experiences enable me to bring to the work a comparative perspective that is implicit, intuitive, and informed by my own identities and positionalities—and with it a commitment to approach these subjects with both sensitivity and rigor. In a cogent call for scholars of color to expand on the premise of studying "our own" by studying other "others," Ruby Tapia argues that such implicitly comparative projects arc important because they permit us to "highlight the different and *differentiating* functional forces of racialization" (1997, 2). It is

with this deep interest in discovering—and forging—commonalities out of our specific and disparate experiences that I began this study on Filipino Americans in San Diego.

"AMERICAN" AND WHITENESS: "TO ME, AMERICAN MEANS WHITE"

In U.S. racial discourse and practices, unless otherwise specified, "Americans" means "whites" (Lipsitz 1998, 1). In the case of Asian Americans, U.S. exclusion acts, naturalization laws, and national culture have simultaneously marked Asians as the inassimilable aliens and whites as the quintessential Americans (Lowe 1996). Excluded from the collective memory of who constitutes a "real" American, Asians in the United States, even as citizens, remain "foreigners-within"—"non-Americans." In a study of third- and later-generation Chinese and Japanese Americans, Mia Tuan (1998) concludes that, despite being longtime Americans, Asians—as racialized ethnics—are often assumed to be foreign unless proven otherwise. In the case of Filipinos who emigrated from a former U.S. colony, their formation as racialized minorities does not begin in the United States but rather in a "homeland" already affected by U.S. economic, social, and cultural influences (Lowe 1996, 8).

Cognizant of this racialized history, my Filipino respondents seldom identify themselves as American. As will be evident in the discussion below, they equate "American" with "white" and often use these two terms interchangeably. For example, a Filipina who is married to a white American refers to her husband as "American" but to her African American and Filipino American brothers-in-law as "black" and "Filipino," respectively. Others speak about "American ways," "American culture," or "American lifestyle" when they really mean *white* American ways, culture, and lifestyle. A Filipino man who has lived in the United States for thirty years explains why he still does not identify himself as American: "I don't see myself just as an American because I cannot hide the fact that my skin is brown. To me, American means white." A second-generation Filipina recounted the following story when asked whether she defined herself as American:

> I went to an all-white school. I knew I was different. I wasn't American. See, you are not taught that you're American because you are not white. When I was in the tenth grade, our English teacher asked us what our nationality was, and she goes how many of you

are Mexican, how many of you are Filipino, and how many of you are Samoan and things like that. And when she asked how many of you are American, just the white people raised their hands.

Other Asian Americans also conflate *American* and *white.* In an ethnographic study of Asian American high school students, Stacey Lee reports that Korean immigrant parents often instructed their children to socialize only with Koreans and "Americans." When asked to define the term *American,* the Korean students responded in unison with "White! Korean parents like white" (Lee 1996, 24). Tuan (1998) found the same practice among later-generation Chinese and Japanese Americans: the majority use the term *American* to refer to whites.

CONSTRUCTING THE DOMINANT GROUP: THE MORAL FLAWS OF WHITE AMERICANS

Given the centrality of moral themes in popular discussions on racial differences, Michele Lamont (1997) has suggested that morality is a crucial site to study the cultural mechanisms of reproduction of racial inequality. While much has been written on how whites have represented the (im)-morality of people of color (Collins 1991; Marchetti 1993; Hamamoto 1994), there has been less critical attention to how people of color have represented whites.[4] Shifting attention from the otherness of the subordinate group (as dictated by the "mainstream") to the otherness of the dominant group (as constructed by the "margins"), this section focuses on the alternative frames of meaning that racially subordinate groups mobilize to (re)define their status in relation to the dominant group. I argue that female morality—defined as women's dedication to their families and sexual restraint—is one of the few sites where economically and politically dominated groups can construct the dominant group as other and themselves as superior. Because womanhood is idealized as the repository of tradition, the norms that regulate women's behaviors become a means of determining and defining group status and boundaries. As a consequence, the burdens and complexities of cultural representation fall most heavily on immigrant women and their daughters. Below, I show that Filipino immigrants claim moral distinctiveness for their community by re-presenting "Americans" as morally flawed, themselves as family-oriented model minorities, and their wives and daughters as paragons of morality.

FAMILY-ORIENTED MODEL MINORITIES: "WHITE WOMEN WILL LEAVE YOU"

In his work on Italian immigrant parents and children in the 1930s, Robert Anthony Orsi (1985) reports that the parents invented a virtuous Italy (based on memories of their childhood) that they then used to castigate the morality of the United States and their U.S.-born or -raised children. In a similar way, many of my respondents constructed their "ethnic" culture as principled and "American" culture as deviant. Most often, this morality narrative revolves around family life and family relations. When asked what set Filipinos apart from other Americans, my respondents—of all ages and class backgrounds—repeatedly contrasted close-knit Filipino families to what they perceived to be the more impersonal quality of U.S. family relations.[5] In the following narratives, "Americans" are characterized as lacking in strong family ties and collective identity, less willing to do the work of family and cultural maintenance, and less willing to abide by patriarchal norms in husband/wife relations:

> American society lacks caring. The American way of life is more individual rather than collective. The American way is to say I want to have my own way. (Filipina immigrant, fifty-four years old)
>
> Our [Filipino] culture is different. We are more close-knit. We tend to help one another. Americans, ya know, they are all right, but they don't help each other that much. As a matter of fact, if the parents are old, they take them to a convalescent home and let them rot there. We would never do that in our culture. We would nurse them; we would help them until the very end. (Filipino immigrant, sixty years old)
>
> Our [Filipino] culture is very communal. You know that your family will always be there, that you don't have to work when you turn eighteen, you don't have to pay rent when you are eighteen, which is the American way of thinking. You also know that if things don't work out in the outside world, you can always come home and mommy and daddy will always take you and your children in. (Second-generation Filipina, thirty-three years old)
>
> Asian parents take care of their children. Americans have a different attitude. They leave their children to their own resources. They get baby sitters to take care of their children or leave them in day care. That's why when they get old, their children don't even care about them. (Filipina immigrant, forty-six years old)

Implicit in negative depictions of U.S. families as uncaring, selfish, and distant is the allegation that white women are not as dedicated to their families as Filipina women are to theirs. Several Filipino men who married white women recalled being warned by their parents and relatives that "white women will leave you." As one man related, "My mother said to me, 'Well, you know, don't marry a white person because they would take everything that you own and leave you.'" For some Filipino men, perceived differences in attitudes about women's roles between Filipina and non-Filipina women influenced their marital choice. A Filipino American navy man explained why he went back to the Philippines to look for a wife:

My goal was to marry a Filipina. I requested to be stationed in the Philippines to get married to a Filipina. I'd seen the women here and basically they are spoiled. They have a tendency of not going along together with their husband. They behave differently. They chase the male, instead of the male, the normal way of the traditional way is for the male to go after the female. They have sex without marrying. They want to do their own things. So my idea was to go back home and marry somebody who has never been here. I tell my son the same thing: if he does what I did and finds himself a good lady there, he will be in good hands.

Another man who had dated mostly white women in high school recounted that when it came time for him to marry, he "looked for the kind of women" he met while stationed in the Philippines: "I hate to sound chauvinistic about marriages, but Filipinas have a way of making you feel like you are a king. They also have that tenderness, that elegance. And we share the same values about family, education, religion, and raising children."

The claims of family closeness are not unique to Filipino immigrants. For example, when asked what makes their group distinctive, Italian Americans (di Leonardo 1984), Vietnamese Americans (Kibria 1993), South Asian Americans (Hickey 1996), and African Americans (Lamont 1997) all point proudly to the close-knit character of their family life. Although it is difficult to know whether these claims are actual perceptions or favored self-legitimating answers, it is nevertheless important to note the gender implications of these claims. That is, while both men and women identify the family system as a tremendous source of cultural pride, it is women—through their unpaid housework and kin work—who shoulder the primary responsibility for maintaining family closeness. As the organizers of family rituals, transmitters of homeland folklores, and socializers of young children, women have been crucial for the maintenance of family ties and cultural traditions. In a study of kinship, class, and gender among California Italian Americans, di Leonardo argues that women's kin work, "the work of knitting households together into 'close, extended families,'" maintains the family networks that give ethnicity meaning (1984, 229).

Because the moral status of the community rests on women's labor, women, as wives and daughters, are expected to dedicate themselves to the family. Writing on the constructed image of ethnic family and gender, di Leonardo argues that "a large part of stressing ethnic identity amounts to burdening women with increased responsibilities for preparing special foods, planning rituals, and enforcing 'ethnic' socialization of children" (1984, 222). A twenty-three-year-old Filipina spoke about the reproductive work that her mother performed and expected her to learn:

In my family, I was the only girl, so my mom expected a lot from me. She wanted me to help her to take care of the household. I felt like there was a lot of pressure on me. It's very important to my mom to have the house in order: to wash the dishes, to keep the kitchen in order, vacuuming, and dusting and things like that. She wants me to be a perfect housewife. It's difficult. I have been married now for about four months and my mother asks me every now and then what have I cooked for my husband. My mom is also very strict about families getting together on holidays, and I would always help her to organize that. Each holiday, I would try to decorate the house for her, to make it more special.

The burden of unpaid reproductive and kin work is particularly stressful for women who work outside the home. In the following narrative, a Filipina wife and mother described the pulls of family and work that she experienced when she went back to school to pursue a doctoral degree in nursing:

The Filipinos, we are very collective, very connected. Going through the doctoral program, sometimes I think it is better just to forget about my relatives and just concentrate on school. All that connectedness, it steals parts of myself because all of my energies are devoted to my family. And that is the reason why I think Americans are successful. The majority of the American people they can do what they want. They don't feel guilty because they only have a few people to relate to. For us Filipinos, it's like roots under the tree, you have all these connections. The Americans are more like the trunk. I am still trying to go up to the trunk of the tree but it is too hard. I want to be more independent, more like the Americans. I want to be good to my family but what about me? And all the things that I am doing. It's hard. It's always a struggle.

It is important to note that this Filipina interprets her exclusion and added responsibilities as only racial when they are also gendered. For example, when she says, "the American people they can do what they want," she ignores the differences in the lives of white men and white women—the fact that most white women experience similar competing pulls of family, education, and work.

RACIALIZED SEXUALITY AND (IM)MORALITY: "IN AMERICA, . . . SEX IS NOTHING"

Sexuality, as a core aspect of social identity, is fundamental to the structuring of gender inequality (Millett 1970). Sexuality is also a salient marker of otherness and has figured prominently in racist and imperialist ideologies (Gilman 1985; Stoler 1991). Historically, the sexuality of subordinate groups—particularly that of racialized women—has been systematically stereotyped by the dominant groups.[6] At stake in these stereotypes is the construction of women of color as morally lacking in the areas of sexual restraint and traditional morality. Asian women—both in Asia and in the United States—have been racialized as sexually immoral, and the "Orient"—and its women—has long served as a site of European male-power fantasies, replete with lurid images of sexual license, gynecological aberrations, and general perversion (Gilman 1985, 89). In colonial Asia in the nineteenth and early twentieth centuries, for example, female sexuality was a site for colonial rulers to assert their moral superiority and thus their supposed natural and legitimate right to rule. The colonial rhetoric of moral superiority was based on the construction of colonized Asian women as subjects of sexual desire and fulfillment and European colonial women as the paragons of virtue and the bearers of a redefined colonial morality

(Stoler 1991). The discourse of morality has also been used to mark the "unassimilability" of Asians in the United States. At the turn of the twentieth century, the public perception of Chinese women as disease-ridden, drug-addicted prostitutes served to underline the depravity of "Orientals" and played a decisive role in the eventual passage of exclusion laws against all Asians (Mazumdar 1989, 3–4). The stereotypical view that all Asian women were prostitutes, first formed in the 1850s, persisted. Contemporary American popular culture continues to endow Asian women with an excess of "womanhood," sexualizing them but also impugning their sexuality (Espiritu 1997, 93).

Filipinas—both in the Philippines and in the United States—have been marked as desirable but dangerous "prostitutes" and/or submissive "mail-order brides" (Halualani 1995; Egan 1996). These stereotypes emerged out of the colonial process, especially the extensive U.S. military presence in the Philippines. Until the early 1990s, the Philippines, at times unwillingly, housed some of the United States's largest overseas airforce and naval bases (Espiritu 1995, 14). Many Filipino nationalists have charged that "the prostitution problem" in the Philippines stemmed from U.S. and Philippine government policies that promoted a sex industry—brothels, bars, and massage parlors—for servicemen stationed or on leave in the Philippines. During the Vietnam War, the Philippines was known as the "rest and recreation" center of Asia, hosting approximately ten thousand U.S. servicemen daily (Coronel and Rosca 1993; Warren 1993). In this context, *all* Filipinas were racialized as sexual commodities, usable and expendable. A U.S.-born Filipina recounted the sexual harassment she faced while visiting Subic Bay Naval Station in Olongapo City:

> One day, I went to the base dispensary. . . . I was dressed nicely, and as I walked by the fire station, I heard catcalls and snide remarks being made by some of the firemen. . . . I was fuming inside. The next thing I heard was, "How much do you charge?" I kept on walking. "Hey, are you deaf or something? How much do you charge? You have a good body." That was an incident that I will never forget. (Quoted in Espiritu 1995, 77)

The sexualized racialization of Filipina women is also captured in Marianne Vilanueva's short story "Opportunity" (1991). As the protagonist, a "mail-order bride" from the Philippines, enters a hotel lobby to meet her American fiancé, the bellboys snicker and whisper *puta* (whore): a reminder that U.S. economic and cultural colonization in the Philippines always forms a backdrop to any relations between Filipinos and Americans (Wong 1993, 53).

Cognizant of the pervasive hypersexualization of Filipina women, my respondents, especially women who grew up near military bases, were quick to denounce prostitution, to condemn sex laborers, and to declare (unasked) that they themselves did not frequent "that part of town." As one Filipina immigrant said,

> Growing up [in the Philippines], I could never date an American because my dad's concept of a friendship with an American is with a G.I. The only reason why my dad wouldn't let us date an American is that people will think that the only way you met was because of the base. I have never seen the inside of any of the bases because we were just forbidden to go there.

Many of my respondents also distanced themselves culturally from the Filipinas who serviced U.S. soldiers by branding them "more Americanized" and "more Westernized." In other words, these women were sexually promiscuous because they had assumed the sexual mores of white women. This characterization allows my respondents to symbolically disown the Filipina "bad girl" and, in so doing, to uphold the narrative of Filipina sexual virtuosity and white female sexual promiscuity. In the following narrative, a mother who came to the United States in her thirties contrasted the controlled sexuality of women in the Philippines with the perceived promiscuity of white women in the United States:

> In the Philippines, we always have chaperons when we go out. When we go to dances, we have our uncle, our grandfather, and auntie all behind us to make sure that we behave in the dance hall. Nobody goes necking outside. You don't even let a man put his hand on your shoulders. When you were brought up in a conservative country, it is hard to come here and see that it is all freedom of speech and freedom of action. Sex was never mentioned in our generation. I was thirty already when I learned about sex. But to the young generation in America, sex is nothing.

Similarly, another immigrant woman criticized the way young American women are raised: "Americans are so liberated. They allow their children, their girls, to go out even when they are still so young." In contrast, she stated that, in "the Filipino way, it is very important, the value of the woman, that she is a virgin when she gets married."

The ideal "Filipina," then, is partially constructed on the community's conceptualization of white women. She is everything that they are not: she is sexually modest and dedicated to her family; they are sexually promiscuous and uncaring. Within the context of the dominant culture's pervasive hypersexualization of Filipinas, the construction of the "ideal" Filipina—as family-oriented and chaste—can be read as an effort to reclaim the morality of the community. This effort erases the Filipina "bad girl," ignores competing sexual practices in the Filipino communities, and uncritically embraces the myth of "Oriental femininity." Cast as the embodiment of perfect womanhood and exotic femininity, Filipinas (and other Asian women) in recent years have been idealized in U.S. popular culture as more truly "feminine" (i.e., devoted, dependent, domestic) and therefore more desirable than their more modern, emancipated sisters (Espiritu 1997, 113). Capitalizing on this image of the "superfemme," mail-order bride agencies market Filipina women as "'exotic, subservient wife imports' for sale and as alternatives for men sick of independent 'liberal' Western women" (Halualani 1995, 49; see also Ordonez 1997, 122).

Embodying the moral integrity of the idealized ethnic community, immigrant women, particularly young daughters, are expected to comply with male-defined criteria of what constitute "ideal" feminine virtues. While the sexual behavior of adult women is confined to a monogamous, heterosexual context, that of young women is denied completely (see Dasgupta and DasGupta 1996, 229–31). In the next section, I detail the ways Filipino immigrant parents, under the rubric of "cultural preservation," police their daughters' behaviors in order to safeguard their sexual innocence and virginity. These attempts at policing generate hierarchies and tensions within immigrant families—between parents and children and between brothers and sisters.

THE CONSTRUCTION(S) OF THE "IDEAL" FILIPINA: "BOYS ARE BOYS AND GIRLS ARE DIFFERENT"

As the designated "keepers of the culture" (Billson 1995), immigrant women and their behavior come under intensive scrutiny both from men and women of their own groups and from U.S.-born Americans (Gabbacia 1994, xi). In a study of the Italian Harlem community from 1880 to 1950, Orsi reports that "all the community's fears for the reputation and integrity of the domus came to focus on the behavior of young women" (1985, 135). Because women's moral and sexual loyalties were deemed central to the maintenance of group status, changes in female behavior, especially that of growing daughters, were interpreted as signs of moral decay and ethnic suicide and were carefully monitored and sanctioned (Gabbacia 1994, 113).

Although details vary, young women of various groups and across space and time—for example, second-generation Chinese women in San Francisco in the 1920s (Yung 1995), U.S.-born Italian women in East Harlem in the 1930s (Orsi 1985), young Mexican women in the Southwest during the interwar years (Ruiz 1992), and daughters of Caribbean and Asian Indian immigrants on the East Coast in the 1990s (Dasgupta and DasGupta 1996; Waters 1996)—have identified strict parental control on their activities and movements as the primary source of intergenerational conflict. Recent studies of immigrant families also identify gender as a significant determinant of parent-child conflict, with daughters more likely than sons to be involved in such conflicts and instances of parental derogation (Rumbaut and Ima 1988; Woldemikael 1989; Matute-Bianchi 1991; Gibson 1995).

Although immigrant families have always been preoccupied with passing on their native culture, language, and traditions to both male and female children, it is daughters who have the primary burden of protecting and preserving the family. Because sons do not have to conform to the image of an "ideal" ethnic subject as daughters do, they often receive special day-to-day privileges denied to daughters (Haddad and Smith 1996, 22–24; Waters 1996, 75–76). This is not to say that immigrant parents do not place undue expectations on their sons; rather, these expectations do not pivot around the sons' sexuality or dating choices.[7] In contrast, parental control over the movement and action of daughters begins the moment they are perceived as young adults and sexually vulnerable. It regularly consists of monitoring their whereabouts and forbidding dating (Wolf 1997). For example, the immigrant parents I interviewed seldom allowed their daughters to date, to stay out late, to spend the night at a friend's house, or to take an out-of-town trip.

Many of the second-generation women I spoke to complained bitterly about these parental restrictions. They particularly resented what they saw as gender inequity in their families: the fact that their parents placed far more restrictions on their activities and movements than on their brothers'. Some decried the fact that even their younger brothers had more freedom than they did. "It was really hard growing up because my parents would let my younger brothers do what they wanted but I didn't get to do what I wanted even though I was the oldest. I had a curfew and my brothers didn't. I had to ask if I could go places and they didn't. My parents never even asked my brothers when they were coming home." As indicated in the following excerpt, many Filipino males are cognizant of this double standard in their families:

My sister would always say to me, "It's not fair, just because you are a guy, you can go wherever you want." I think my parents do treat me and my sister differently. Like in high school, maybe 10:30 at night, which is pretty late on a school night, and I say I have to go pick up some notes at my friend's house, my parents wouldn't say anything. But if my sister were to do that, there would be no way. Even now when my sister is in college already, if she wants to leave at midnight to go to a friend's house, they would tell her that she shouldn't do it.

When questioned about this double standard, parents generally responded by explaining that "girls are different":

I have that Filipino mentality that boys are boys and girls are different. Girls are supposed to be protected, to be clean. In the early years, my daughters have to have chaperons and curfews. And they know that they have to be virgins until they get married. The girls always say that is not fair. What is the difference between their brothers and them? And my answer always is, "In the Philippines, you know, we don't do that. The girls stay home. The boys go out." It was the way that I was raised. I still want to have part of that culture instilled in my children. And I want them to have that to pass on to their children.

Even among self-described Western-educated and "tolerant" parents, many continue to ascribe to "the Filipino way" when it comes to raising daughters. As one college-educated father explains,

Because of my Western education, I don't raise my children the way my parents raised me. I tended to be a little more tolerant. But at times, especially in certain issues like dating, I find myself more towards the Filipino way in the sense that I have only one daughter so I tended to be a little bit stricter. So the double standard kind of operates: it's alright for the boys to explore the field but I tended to be overly protective of my daughter. My wife feels the same way because the boys will not lose anything, but the daughter will lose something, her virginity, and it can be also a question of losing face, that kind of thing.

Although many parents discourage or forbid dating for daughters, they still fully expect these young women to fulfill their traditional roles as women: to marry and have children. A young Filipina recounted the mixed messages she received from her parents:

This is the way it is supposed to work: Okay, you go to school. You go to college. You graduate. You find a job. *Then* you find your husband, and you have children. That's the whole time line. *But* my question is, if you are not allowed to date, how are you supposed to find your husband? They say "no" to the whole dating scene because that is secondary to your education, secondary to your family. They do push marriage, but at a later date. So basically my parents are telling me that I should get married and I should have children but that I should not date.

In a study of second-generation Filipino Americans in northern California, Diane Wolf (1997) reports the same pattern of parental pressures: Parents expect daughters to remain virgins until marriage, to have a career, *and* to combine their work lives with marriage and children.

The restrictions on girls' movement sometimes spill over to the realm of academics. Dasgupta and DasGupta (1996, 230) recount that in the Indian American community, while young men were expected to attend faraway competitive colleges, many of their female peers were encouraged by their parents to go to the local colleges so that they could live at or close to home. Similarly, Wolf (1997, 467) reports that some Filipino parents pursued contradictory tactics with their children, particularly their daughters, by pushing them to achieve academic excellence in high school but then "pulling the emergency brake" when they contemplated college by expecting them to stay at home, even if it meant going

to a less competitive college, or not going at all. In the following account, a young Filipina relates that her parents' desire to "protect" her surpassed their concerns for her academic preparation:

My brother [was] given a lot more opportunity educationally. He was given the opportunity to go to Miller High School that has a renowned college preparatory program but [for] which you have to be bussed out of our area.[8] I've come from a college prep program in junior high and I was asked to apply for the program at Miller. But my parents said "No, absolutely not." This was even during the time, too, when Southside [the neighborhood high school] had one of the lowest test scores in the state of California. So it was like, "You know, mom, I'll get a better chance at Miller." "No, no, you're going to Southside. There is no ifs, ands, or buts. Miller is too far. What if something happens to you?" But two years later, when my brother got ready to go on to high school, he was allowed to go to Miller. My sister and I were like, "Obviously, whose education do you value more? If you're telling us that education is important, why do we see a double standard?"

The above narratives suggest that the process of parenting is gendered in that immigrant parents tend to restrict the autonomy, mobility, and personal decision making of their daughters more than that of their sons. I argue that these parental restrictions are attempts to construct a model of Filipina womanhood that is chaste, modest, nurturing, and family-oriented. Women are seen as responsible for holding the cultural line, maintaining racial boundaries, and marking cultural difference. This is not to say that parent-daughter conflicts exist in all Filipino immigrant families. Certainly, Filipino parents do not respond in a uniform way to the challenges of being racial-ethnic minorities, and I met parents who have had to change some of their ideas and practices in response to their inability to control their children's movements and choices:

I have three girls and one boy. I used to think that I wouldn't allow my daughters to go dating and things like that, but there is no way I could do that. I can't stop it. It's the way of life here in America. Sometimes you kind of question yourself, if you are doing what is right. It is hard to accept but you got to accept it. That's the way they are here. (Professional Filipino immigrant father)

My children are born and raised here, so they do pretty much what they want. They think they know everything. I can only do so much as a parent. . . . When I try to teach my kids things, they tell me that I sound like an old record. They even talk back to me sometimes. . . . The first time my daughter brought her boyfriend to the house, she was eighteen years old. I almost passed away, knocked out. Lord, tell me what to do? (Working-class Filipino immigrant mother)

These narratives call attention to the shifts in the generational power caused by the migration process and to the possible gap between what parents say they want for their children and their ability to control the young. However, the interview data do suggest that intergenerational conflicts are socially recognized occurrences in Filipino communities. Even when respondents themselves had not experienced intergenerational tensions, they could always recall a cousin, a girlfriend, or a friend's daughter who had.

SANCTIONS AND REACTIONS: "THAT IS NOT WHAT A DECENT FILIPINO GIRL SHOULD DO"

I do not wish to suggest that immigrant communities are the only ones in which parents regulate their daughters' mobility and sexuality. Feminist scholars have long documented the construction, containment, and exploitation of women's sexuality in various societies (Maglin and Perry 1996). We also know that the cultural anxiety over unbounded female sexuality is most apparent with regard to adolescent girls (Tolman and Higgins 1996, 206). The difference is in the ways immigrant and nonimmigrant families sanction girls' sexuality. To control sexually assertive girls nonimmigrant parents rely on the gender-based good girl/bad girl dichotomy in which "good girls" are passive, threatened sexual objects while "bad girls" are active, desiring sexual agents (Tolman and Higgins 1996). As Dasgupta and DasGupta write, "the two most pervasive images of women across cultures are the goddess and whore, the good and bad women" (1996, 236). This good girl/bad girl cultural story conflates femininity with sexuality, increases women's vulnerability to sexual coercion, and justifies women's containment in the domestic sphere.

Immigrant families, though, have an additional strategy: they can discipline their daughters as racial/national subjects as well as gendered ones. That is, as self-appointed guardians of "authentic" cultural memory, immigrant parents can attempt to regulate

their daughters' independent choices by linking them to cultural ignorance or betrayal. As both parents and children recounted, young women who disobeyed parental strictures were often branded "non-ethnic," "untraditional," "radical," "selfish," and "not caring about the family." Female sexual choices were also linked to moral degeneracy, defined in relation to a narrative of a hegemonic white norm. Parents were quick to warn their daughters about "bad" Filipinas who had become pregnant outside marriage.[9] As in the case of "bar girls" in the Philippines, Filipina Americans who veered from acceptable behaviors were deemed "Americanized"—as women who have adopted the sexual mores and practices of white women. As one Filipino immigrant father described "Americanized" Filipinas: "They are spoiled because they have seen the American way. They go out at night. Late at night. They go out on dates. Smoking. They have sex without marrying."

From the perspective of the second-generation daughters, these charges are stinging. The young women I interviewed were visibly pained—with many breaking down and crying—when they recounted their parents' charges. This deep pain, stemming in part from their desire to be validated as Filipina, existed even among the more "rebellious" daughters. One twenty-four-year-old daughter explained:

My mom is very traditional. She wants to follow the Filipino customs, just really adhere to them, like what is proper for a girl, what she can and can't do, and what other people are going to think of her if she doesn't follow that way. When I pushed these restrictions, when I rebelled and stayed out later than allowed, my mom would always say, "That is not what a decent Filipino girl should do. You should come home at a decent hour. What are people going to think of you?" And that would get me really upset, you know, because I think that my character is very much the way it should be for a Filipina. I wear my hair long, I wear decent makeup. I dress properly, conservative. I am family oriented. It hurts me that she doesn't see that I am decent, that I am proper and that I am not going to bring shame to the family or anything like that.

This narrative suggests that even when parents are unable to control the behaviors of their children, their (dis)approval remains powerful in shaping the emotional lives of their daughters (see Wolf 1997). Although better-off parents can and do exert greater controls over their children's behaviors than do poorer parents (Wolf 1992; Kibria 1993), I would argue that all immigrant parents—regardless of class background—possess this emotional hold on their children. Therein lies the source of their power: As immigrant parents, they have the authority to determine if their daughters are "authentic" members of their racial-ethnic community. Largely unacquainted with the "home" country, U.S.-born children depend on their parents' tutelage to craft and affirm their ethnic self and thus are particularly vulnerable to charges of cultural ignorance and/or betrayal (Espiritu 1994).

Despite these emotional pains, many young Filipinas I interviewed contest and negotiate parental restrictions in their daily lives. Faced with parental restrictions on their mobility, young Filipinas struggle to gain some control over their own social lives, particularly over dating. In many cases, daughters simply misinform their parents of their whereabouts or date without their parents' knowledge. They also rebel by vowing to create more egalitarian relationships with their own husbands and children. A thirty-year-old Filipina who is married to a white American explained why she chose to marry outside her culture:

> In high school, I dated mostly Mexican and Filipino. It never occurred to me to date a white or black guy. I was not attracted to them. But as I kept growing up and my father and I were having all these conflicts, I knew that if I married a Mexican or a Filipino, [he] would be exactly like my father. And so I tried to date anyone that would not remind me of my dad. A lot of my Filipina friends that I grew up with had similar experiences. So I knew that it wasn't only me. I was determined to marry a white person because he would treat me as an individual.[10]

Another Filipina who was labeled "radical" by her parents indicated that she would be more open-minded in raising her own children: "I see myself as very traditional in upbringing but I don't see myself as constricting on my children one day and I wouldn't put the gender roles on them. I wouldn't lock them into any particular way of behaving." It is important to note that even as these Filipinas desired new gender norms and practices for their own families, the majority hoped that their children would remain connected to Filipino culture.

My respondents also reported more serious reactions to parental restrictions, recalling incidents of

someone they knew who had run away, joined a gang, or attempted suicide. A Filipina high-school counselor relates that most of the Filipinas she worked with "are really scared because a lot of them know friends that are pregnant and they all pretty much know girls who have attempted suicide." A 1995 random survey of San Diego public high schools conducted by the Federal Centers for Disease Control and Prevention (CDC) found that, in comparison with other ethnic groups, female Filipino students had the highest rates of seriously considering suicide (45.6 percent) as well as the highest rates of actually attempting suicide (23 percent) in the year preceding the survey. In comparison, 33.4 percent of Latinas, 26.2 percent of white women, and 25.3 percent of black women surveyed said they had suicidal thoughts (Lau 1995).

CONCLUSION

Mainstream American society defines white middle-class culture as the norm and whiteness as the unmarked marker of others' difference (Frankenberg 1993). In this article, I have shown that many Filipino immigrants use the largely gendered discourse of morality as one strategy to decenter whiteness and to locate themselves above the dominant group, demonizing it in the process. Like other immigrant groups, Filipinos praise the United States as a land of significant economic opportunity but simultaneously denounce it as a country inhabited by corrupted and individualistic people of questionable morals. In particular, they criticize American family life, American individualism, and American women (see Gabbacia 1994, 113). Enforced by distorting powers of memory and nostalgia, this rhetoric of moral superiority often leads to patriarchal calls for a cultural "authenticity" that locates family honor and national integrity in the group's female members. Because the policing of women's bodies is one of the main means of asserting moral superiority, young women face numerous restrictions on their autonomy, mobility, and personal decision making. This practice of cultural (re)construction reveals how deeply the conduct of private life can be tied to larger social structures.

The construction of white Americans as the "other" and American culture as deviant serves a dual purpose: It allows immigrant communities both to reinforce patriarchy through the sanctioning of women's (mis)behavior and to present an unblemished, if not morally superior, public face to the dominant society.

Strong in family values, heterosexual morality, and a hierarchical family structure, this public face erases the Filipina "bad girl" and ignores competing (im)moral practices in the Filipino communities. Through the oppression of Filipina women and the denunciation of white women's morality, the immigrant community attempts to exert its moral superiority over the dominant Western culture and to reaffirm to itself its self-worth

in the face of economic, social, political, and legal subordination. In other words, the immigrant community uses restrictions on women's lives as one form of resistance to racism. This form of cultural resistance, however, severely restricts the lives of women, particularly those of the second generation, and it casts the family as a potential site of intense conflict and oppressive demands in immigrant lives.

NOTES

1. Cordova 1983; Sharma 1984; Scharlin and Villanueva 1992; Jung 1999.
2. Filipino settlement in San Diego dates back to 1903, when a group of young Filipino *pensionados* enrolled at the State Normal School (now San Diego State University).
3. My understanding of Filipino American lives is also based on the many conversations I have had with my Filipino American students at the University of California, San Diego, and with Filipino American friends in the San Diego area and elsewhere.
4. A few studies have documented the ways racialized communities have represented white Americans. For example, in his anthropological work on Chicano joking, José Limón (1982) reports that young Mexican Americans elevate themselves over whites through the telling of "Stupid-American" jokes in which an Anglo American is consistently duped by a Mexican character. In her interviews with African American working-class men, Michele Lamont (1997) finds that these men tend to perceive Euro Americans as immoral, sneaky, and not to be trusted. Although these studies provide an interesting and compelling window into racialized communities' views of white Americans, they do not analyze how the rhetoric of moral superiority often depends on gender categories.
5. Indeed people around the world often believe that Americans have no real family ties. For example, on a visit to my family in Vietnam, my cousin asked me earnestly if it was true that American children put their elderly parents in nursing homes instead of caring for them at home. She was horrified at this practice and proclaimed that, because they care for their elders, Vietnamese families are morally superior to American families.

6. Writing on the objectification of black women, Patricia Hill Collins (1991) argues that popular representations of black females—mammy, welfare queen, and Jezebel—all pivot around their sexuality, either desexualizing or hypersexualizing them. Along the same line, Native American women have been portrayed as sexually excessive (Green 1975), Chicana women as "exotic and erotic" (Mirande 1980), and Puerto Rican and Cuban women as "tropical bombshells, . . . sexy, sexed and interested" (Tafolla 1985, 39).
7. The relationship between immigrant parents and their sons deserves an article of its own. According to Gabbacia, "Immigrant parents fought with sons, too, but over different issues: parents' complaints about rebellious sons focused more on criminal activity than on male sexuality or independent courtship" (1994, 70). Moreover, because of their mobility, young men have more means to escape—at least temporarily—the pressures of the family than young women. In his study of Italian American families, Orsi reports that young men rebelled by sleeping in cars or joining the army, but young women did not have such opportunities (1985, 143).
8. The names of the two high schools in this excerpt are fictitious.
9. According to a 1992 health assessment report of Filipinos in San Francisco, Filipino teens have the highest pregnancy rates among all Asian groups and, in 1991, the highest rate of increase in the number of births as compared with all other racial or ethnic groups (Tiongson 1997, 257).
10. The few available studies on Filipino American intermarriage indicate a high rate relative to other Asian groups. In 1980, Filipino men in California recorded the highest intermarriage rate among all Asian groups, and Filipina women had the second-highest rate, after Japanese American women (Agbayani-Siewert and Revilla 1995, 156).

REFERENCES

Agbayani-Siewert, Pauline, and Linda Revilla. 1995. "Filipino Americans." In *Asian Americans: Contemporary Trends and Issues,* ed. Pyong Gap Min, 134–68. Thousand Oaks, Calif.: Sage.

Azores-Gunter, Tania Fortunata M. 1986–87. "Educational Attainment and Upward Mobility: Prospects for Filipino Americans." *Amerasia Journal* 13(1):39–52.

Billson, Janet Mancini. 1995. *Keepers of the Culture: The Power of Tradition in Women's Lives.* New York: Lexington.

Cabezas, Amado, Larry H. Shinagawa, and Gary Kawaguchi. 1986–87. "New Inquiries into the Socioeconomic Status of Pilipino Americans in California." *Amerasia Journal* 13(1):1–21.

Collins, Patricia Hill. 1991. *Black Feminist Thought: Knowledge, Consciousness, and the Politics of Empowerment.* New York: Routledge.

Cordova, Fred. 1983. *Filipinos: Forgotten Asian Americans, a Pictorial Essay, 1763–1963.* Dubuque, Iowa: Kendall/Hunt.

Coronel, Sheila, and Ninotchka Rosca. 1993. "For the Boys: Filipinas Expose Years of Sexual Slavery by the U.S. and Japan." *Ms.,* November/December, 10–15.

Dasgupta, Shamita Das, and Sayantani DasGupta. 1996. "Public Face, Private Space: Asian Indian Women and Sexuality." In *"Bad Girls/Good Girls": Women, Sex, and Power in the Nineties,* ed. Nan Bauer Maglin and Donna Perry, 226–43. New Brunswick, N.J.: Rutgers University Press.

di Leonardo, Micaela. 1984. *The Varieties of Ethnic Experience: Kinship, Class, and Gender among California Italian-Americans.* Ithaca, N.Y.: Cornell University Press.

Eastmond, Marita. 1993. "Reconstructing Life: Chilean Refugee Women and the Dilemmas of Exile." In *Migrant Women: Crossing Boundaries and Changing Identities,* ed. Gina Buijs, 35–53. Oxford: Berg.

Egan, Timothy. 1996. "Mail-Order Marriage, Immigrant Dreams and Death." *New York Times,* May 26, 12.

Espiritu, Yen Le. 1994. "The Intersection of Race, Ethnicity, and Class: The Multiple Identities of Second Generation Filipinos." *Identities* 1(2–3):249–73.

———. 1995. *Filipino American Lives.* Philadelphia: Temple University Press.

———. 1997. *Asian American Women and Men: Labor, Laws, and Love.* Thousand Oaks, Calif.: Sage.

Espiritu, Yen Le, and Diane L. Wolf. Forthcoming. "The Paradox of Assimilation: Children of Filipino Immigrants in San Diego." In *Ethnicities: Children of Immigrants in America,* ed. Ruben Rumbaut and Alejandro Portes. Berkeley: University of California Press; New York: Russell Sage Foundation.

Frankenberg, Ruth. 1993. *White Women, Race Matters: The Social Construction of Whiteness.* Minneapolis: University of Minnesota Press.

Gabbacia, Donna. 1994. *From the Other Side: Women, Gender, and Immigrant Life in the U.S., 1820–1990.* Bloomington: Indiana University Press.

Gibson, Margaret A. 1995. "Additive Acculturation as a Strategy for School Improvement." In *California's Immigrant Children: Theory, Research, and Implications for Educational Policy,* ed. Ruben Rumbaut and Wayne A. Cornelius, 77–105. La Jolla: Center for U.S.-Mexican Studies, University of California, San Diego.

Gilman, Sander L. 1985. *Difference and Pathology: Stereotypes of Sexuality, Race, and Madness.* Ithaca, N.Y.: Cornell University Press.

Green, Rayna. 1975. "The Pocahontas Perplex: The Image of Indian Women in American Culture." *Massachusetts Review* 16(4):698–714.

Haddad, Yvonne Y., and Jane I. Smith. 1996. "Islamic Values among American Muslims." In *Family and Gender among American Muslims: Issues Facing Middle Eastern Immigrants and Their Descendants,* ed. Barbara C. Aswad and Barbara Bilge, 19–40. Philadelphia: Temple University Press.

Halualani, Rona Tamiko. 1995. "The Intersecting Hegemonic Discourses of an Asian Mail-Order Bride Catalog: Pilipina 'Oriental Butterfly' Dolls for Sale." *Women's Studies in Communication* 18(1):45–64.

Hamamoto, Darrell Y. 1994. *Monitored Peril: Asian Americans and the Politics of Representation.* Minneapolis: University of Minnesota Press.

Hickey, M. Gail. 1996. "'Go to College, Get a Job, and Don't Leave the House without Your Brother': Oral Histories with Immigrant Women and Their Daughters." *Oral History Review* 23(2):63–92.

Jung, Moon-Kie. 1999. "No Whites: No Asians: Race, Marxism and Hawaii's Pre-emergent Working Class." *Social Science History* 23(3):357–93.

Kibria, Nazli. 1993. *Family Tightrope: The Changing Lives of Vietnamese Immigrant Community.* Princeton, N.J.: Princeton University Press.

Lamont, Michele. 1997. "Colliding Moralities between Black and White Workers." In *From Sociology to Cultural Studies: New Perspectives,* ed. Elisabeth Long, 263–85. New York: Blackwell.

Lau, Angela. 1995. "Filipino Girls Think Suicide at Number One Rate." *San Diego Union-Tribune,* February 11, A-1.

Lee, Stacey J. 1996. *Unraveling the "Model Minority" Stereotype: Listening to Asian American Youth.* New York: Teachers College Press.

Limón, José E. 1982. "History, Chicano Joking, and the Varieties of Higher Education: Tradition and Performance as Critical Symbolic Action." *Journal of the Folklore Institute* 19(2/3):141–66.

Lipsitz, George. 1998. *The Possessive Investment in Whiteness: How White People Profit from Identity Politics.* Philadelphia: Temple University Press.

Lowe, Lisa. 1996. *Immigrant Acts: On Asian American Cultural Politics.* Durham, N.C.: Duke University Press.

Maglin, Nan Bauer, and Donna Perry. 1996. "Introduction." In *"Bad Girls/Good Girls": Women, Sex, and Power in the Nineties,* ed. Nan Bauer Maglin and Donna Perry, xiii–xxvi. New Brunswick, N.J.: Rutgers University Press.

Marchetti, Gina. 1993. *Romance and the "Yellow Peril": Race, Sex, and Discursive Strategies in Hollywood Fiction.* Berkeley: University of California Press.

Matute-Bianchi, Maria Eugenia. 1991. "Situational Ethnicity and Patterns of School Performance among Immigrant and Nonimmigrant Mexican-Descent Students." In *Minority Status and Schooling: A Comparative Study of Immigrant and Involuntary Minorities,* ed. Margaret A. Gibson and John U. Ogbu, 205–47. New York: Garland.

Mazumdar, Suchetta. 1989. "General Introduction: A Woman-Centered Perspective on Asian American History." In *Making Waves: An Anthology by and about Asian American Women,* ed. Asian Women United of California, 1–22. Boston: Beacon.

Millett, Kate. 1970. *Sexual Politics.* Garden City, N.Y.: Doubleday.

Mirande, Alfredo. 1980. "The Chinano Family: A Reanalysis of Conflicting Views." In *Rethinking Marriage, Child Rearing, and Family Organization,* ed. Arlene S. Skohick and Jerome H. Skolnick, 479–93. Berkeley: University of California Press.

Okamura, Jonathan, and Amefil Agbayani. 1997. "*Pamantasan:* Filipino American Higher Education." In *Filipino Americans: Transformation and Identity,* ed. Maria P. Root, 183–97. Thousand Oaks, Calif.: Sage.

Ordonez, Raquel Z. 1997. "Mail-Order Brides: An Emerging Community." In *Filipino Americans: Transformation and Identity,* ed. Maria P. Root, 121–42. Thousand Oaks, Calif.: Sage.

Orsi, Robert Anthony. 1985. *The Madonna of 115th Street: Faith and Community in Italian Harlem, 1880–1950.* New Haven, Conn.: Yale University Press.

Personal Narratives Group. 1989. "Origins." In *Interpreting Women's Lives: Feminist Theory and Personal Narratives,* ed. Personal Narratives Group, 3–15. Bloomington: Indiana University Press.

Ruiz, Vicki L. 1992. "The Flapper and the Chaperone: Historical Memory among Mexican-American Women." In *Seeking Common Ground: Multidisciplinary Studies,* ed. Donna Gabbacia. Westport, Conn.: Greenwood.

Rumbaut, Ruben. 1991. "Passages to America: Perspectives on the New Immigration." *In America at Century's End,* ed. Alan Wolfe, 208–44. Berkeley: University of California Press.

———. 1994. "The Crucible Within: Ethnic Identity, Self-Esteem, and Segmented Assimilation among Children of Immigrants." *International Migration Review* 28(4):748–94.

Rumbaut, Ruben, and Kenji Ima. 1988. *The Adaptation of Southeast Asian Refugee Youth: A Comparative Study.* Washington, D.C.: U.S. Office of Refugee Resettlement.

San Juan, E., Jr. 1991. "Mapping the Boundaries: The Filipino Writer in the U.S." *Journal of Ethnic Studies* 19(1):117–31.

Scharlin, Craig, and Lilia V. Villanueva. 1992. *Philip Vera Cruz: A Personal History of Filipino Immigrants and the Farmworkers Movement.* Los Angeles: University of California, Los Angeles Labor Center, Institute of Labor Relations, and Asian American Studies Center.

Sharma, Miriam. 1984. "Labor Migration and Class Formation among the Filipinos in Hawaii, 1906–46." In *Labor Immigration under Capitalism: Asian Workers in the United States before World War II;* ed. Lucie Cheng and Edna Bonacich, 579–611. Berkeley: University of California Press.

Stoler, Ann Laura. 1991. "Carnal Knowledge and Imperial Power: Gender, Race, and Morality in Colonial Asia." In *Gender at the Crossroads of Knowledge: Feminist Anthropology in the Postmodern Era,* ed. Micaela di Leonardo, 51–104. Berkeley: University of California Press.

Tafolla, Carmen. 1985. *To Split a Human: Mitos, Machos y la Mujer Chicana.* San Antonio, Tex.: Mexican American Cultural Center.

Tapia, Ruby. 1997. "Studying Other 'Others.'" Paper presented at the Association of Pacific Americans in Higher Education, San Diego, Calif., May 24.

Tiongson, Antonio T., Jr. 1997. "Throwing the Baby out with the Bath Water." In *Filipino Americans: Transformation and Identity,* ed. Maria P. Root, 257–71. Thousand Oaks, Calif.: Sage.

Tolman, Deborah L., and Tracy E. Higgins. 1996. "How Being a Good Girl Can Be Bad for Girls." In *"Bad Girls/Good Girls": Women, Sex, and Power in the Nineties,* ed. Nan Bauer Maglin and Donna Perry, 205–25. New Brunswick, N.J.: Rutgers University Press.

Tuan, Mia. 1998. *Forever Foreigners or Honorary Whites? The Asian Ethnic Experience Today.* New Brunswick, N.J.: Rutgers University Press.

Villanueva, M. 1991. *Ginseng and Other Tales from Manila.* Corvallis, Oreg.: Calyx.

Warren, Jenifer. 1993. "Suit Asks Navy to Aid Children Left in Philippines." *Los Angeles Times,* March 5, A3.

Waters, Mary C. 1996. "The Intersection of Gender, Race, and Ethnicity in Identity Development of Caribbean American Teens." In *Urban Girls: Resisting Stereotypes, Creating Identities,* ed. Bonnie J. Ross Leadbeater and Niobe Way, 65–81. New York: New York University Press.

Woldemikael, T. M. 1989. *Becoming. Black American: Haitians and American Institutions in Evanston, Illinois.* New York: AMS Press.

Wolf, Diane L. 1992. *Factory Daughters: Gender; Household Dynamics, and Rural Industrialization in Java.* Berkeley: University of California Press.

———. 1997. "Family Secrets: Transnational Struggles among Children of Filipino Immigrants." *Sociological Perspectives* 40(3):457–82.

Wong, Sau-ling. 1993. *Reading Asian American Literature: From Necessity to Extravagance.* Princeton, N.J.: Princeton University Press.

Yung, Judy. 1995. *Unbound Feet: A Social History of Chinese Women in San Francisco.* Berkeley: University of California Press.

Brown-Skinned White Girls: Class, Culture, and the Construction of White Identity in Suburban Communities

Both what constitutes a race and how one recognizes a racial difference are culturally determined. Whether two individuals regard themselves as of the same or of different races depends not on the degree or similarity of their genetic material but on whether history, tradition and personal training and experiences *have brought them to regard themselves as belonging to the same group or different groups.*

—*J. C. King*, The Biology of Race

The empirical research generated by feminist scholars has provided little ethnographic data about the role of suburban residence in the acquisition of a racialized gender identity, particularly among U.S.-born women of African descent.[1] In this essay I will draw on material taken from ethnographic research to examine the importance of residence in middle-class suburban communities in the acquisition of a racially neutral identity among African-descent women. I first provide a specific case study of how *some* African-descent girls, in the absence of a politicized African American residential community, acquired a white cultural identity and not a black consciousness before leaving home to attend college. I then show how this identity shifted when it was challenged by a different residential and discursive milieu—that of the University of California at Berkeley.

I will analyze the social construction of identity among African-descent women who, as children, acquired white identities in their middle-class suburban communities. Feminist theorists have begun to address the social construction of whiteness and identity among women in the United States, but they have not yet addressed women who are not of exclusive or predominant European ancestry.[2] Biologically essentialist precepts that suggest one must be of exclusive European ancestry to have access to a white cultural identity can also be found in the works of cultural anthropologists interested in the social construction and enactment of whiteness.[3] Yet cultural anthropologists have been unable to explain the white identity claims and the "shifts" in racial consciousness that occur among African-descent women who have been "raised white."[4] Cultural anthropologists have assumed that a white identity that does not involve "passing" is not available to African-descent women who possess biological markers that place them in a nonwhite category. This essay departs from the previous scholarship on the construction of racialized gender identities by addressing the experiences of a neglected group of white women: women of mixed-race African descent. The experiences of African-descent women will highlight both the limits of "social constructionism" and the role that socioeconomic status plays in the construction of white identity in middle- and upper-class milieus.

In her book *Belonging in America: Reading between the Lines,* the cultural anthropologist Constance Perrin examines the meanings of kinship, friendship, privacy, and cultural belonging by examining how residents of middle-class suburban communities negotiate their relationships and maintain boundaries between themselves and their neighbors.[5] Although this book provides an excellent analysis and examination of the meaning of belonging to a suburban residential community, by choosing to interview only whites, whom she refers to as "Americans," Perrin reproduces the notion that middle-class suburban communities do not have any African-descent residents. She thus effectively erases all Americans of African, Asian, or multiracial descent in her discussion. Perrin defines her sample of suburban Americans as follows:

> I began by listening to suburbanites all around the country talk about their neighboring experiences. Wanting to hear "American ideas," I listened to men and women living in what is generally regarded as the "mainstream," those who have at least reached the suburban, single-family detached episode of the American Dream. The "American middle-class"; not knowing what it is any more precisely than anyone else, I've relied on this indigenous ideal of suburban residence and home ownership, which immediately implies another defining characteristic, namely white race. . . . I found that Americans see renters, blacks, children, the elderly, people with low incomes, together with signs of them in housing and geographical location, as being culturally unsettling.[6]

Any discussion of Americans of African and/or Asian descent living in suburban communities should include an analysis of the *historically specific* moment. Since 1960 the registered births to black-white couples in the United States have more than quintupled, from 9,600 in 1960 to 51,000 in 1988.[7] Although there are no accurate figures on the exact number of African-descent adolescents and young adults living in suburban communities, the significant increase in interracial marriages, particularly those involving a middle-class black spouse, means that an increasing number of African-descent children are growing up immersed in predominantly white, middle-class, suburban communities.

AFRICAN-DESCENT WOMEN AND THE SOCIAL CONSTRUCTION OF WHITENESS

A significant body of literature that interrogates the construction and enactment of whiteness and white identities has emerged since 1980.[8] However, this literature does not address the experiences of African-descent whites, assuming instead that Americans who claim and assert a white identity are exclusively of European descent. I am employing the term *white* to refer to a historically constituted identity that during other historical moments has excluded European Americans and non-Europeans who are *today* recognized by both Anglo-Americans and the U.S. government as unhyphenated whites.[9] I discuss the historical coconstruction of black and nonblack identities in the United States elsewhere.[10]

As I will discuss later in this essay, the women I interviewed described their white identity as class-linked and restricted to *middle-* and *upper-middle-class* segments of the U.S. European American community.

This essay expands the analysis of racialized gender identities in middle-class suburban communities by examining how white identities are constructed and enacted by African-descent women. The central question I asked is, How do brown-skinned women of mixed African descent become socially constructed as white girls in the local context of a *middle-class* suburban community? In other words, what social conditions are necessary for the acquisition of a white identity by African-descent girls? My research is a response to the feminist scholarship on racialized gender identities and expands the discussion of racial identity and racial consciousness within the feminist literature on white women by addressing the experiences of a group of women who *shifted* their racial self-identifications from a white to a black or biracial identity during early adulthood.

Studies of suburban communities have not explicitly examined how adolescents and young adults of African descent negotiate their *cultural and racial identities*. The women interviewed in this study were the natural daughters of U.S.-born African American fathers and European American, European Jewish American, or Asian (born and raised outside the United States and later naturalized U.S. citizens as adults) mothers. By examining the construction and meaning of whiteness in the lives of African-descent women who became socially constructed as white prior to puberty and were subsequently reconstructed as black or biracial in a different geographical and cultural setting—the Berkeley campus of the University of California—this essay both expands on and departs from the previous literature on white identity and whiteness.

RESEARCH METHODOLOGY

My research is based on the transcripts of interviews I conducted with a nonrandom and nonclinical population of sixteen multiracial women of *known* African ancestry who self-identified as being of multiracial heritage, and were attending the Berkeley campus of the University of California during the 1990–91 academic year. I initially gained access to informants as a graduate student instructor of African and American Indian ancestry involved with a group of undergraduate students raised in multiracial families who established a campus student organization at the University of California at Berkeley in 1989. I recruited additional volunteers from introductory classes in the Departments of Anthropology and Sociology. Additional informants volunteered through a process of snowball sampling in which interviewees were asked to identify students from multiracial families who they believed might be interested in participating.[11]

I conducted audiotaped and videotaped interviews between October 1990 and November 1991 on the Berkeley campus. The interviews ranged from two to three hours per session and were structured by a series of preselected topics that included racial self-identification, childhood experiences, counteridentification in public settings, dating, ethnic affiliations, and shifts in ethnic and cultural identities.[12]

I interviewed a total of twenty-five female and male undergraduate students, but this essay draws on data only from my interviews with women of known African ancestry. These students had been raised by at least one white or Asian parent and had grown up in predominantly white middle-class suburban communities. My sample included individuals who were raised by both biological parents, one biological parent and a stepparent, or two adoptive parents. With one exception, all of the women I interviewed had U.S.-born black fathers. Three participants had Asian mothers who, at the time of their marriage to U.S. black men, were citizens of Korea, Japan, or Jamaica. The participants included ten women of European descent, three of Asian descent (Chinese, Korean, Japanese), and three of European Jewish descent. None of the women interviewed from this sample had an African American mother. The women had origins in fifteen different suburban communities in five states: California, Colorado, Hawaii, New York, and Texas.

"RAISED WHITE": THE MIDDLE-CLASS SUBURBAN EXPERIENCE

One social condition that *all* the women I interviewed identified as central to their experience of being "raised white" was their immersion in a family and social network that did not identify itself in *racial* terms. As children these women had been the culturally "unmarked" intimates of European American middle-class children; they had not been conscious of being perceived as culturally distinct from their peers. Not being distinguished from European American peers in everyday

interactions was critical to the maintenance of a white cultural identity. I am *not* referring to physical distinctions in color, hair texture, or body type here. What I mean is that as children they experienced themselves as culturally neutral, as not deviating from their peer group. In other words, these African-descent women who acquired a white cultural identity did not position themselves, and were not positioned by those around them, as culturally distinct from their peers of no known African descent in terms of behavior, dress codes, speech patterns, leisure interests, or food preferences.

Whitney,[13] a female student who was adopted at birth, is the biological offspring of a U.S. black father and a European American white mother. She was raised in a racially exclusive middle-class suburban community in northern California in an all-white family, geographically and socially isolated from blacks and other nonwhites. Whitney was culturally indistinguishable from her monoracial adoptive sister, who shared the same communication style, clothing style, interests, friendship networks, and experience growing up in a European American family that embraced color-blindness as an ideal. When asked to describe her childhood and her family, Whitney described her family as white, her friends as white, and herself as culturally white.

FWT: How would you describe the ethnic and racial background of your adoptive parents?

WHITNEY: White. They are definitely white and had white culture . . . just the mainstream everyday. Now I am finding out this difference [between white and black culture] because of my boyfriend, who is black and has a black family. I get to see the difference between white—when people say white and black culture.[14]

Women of African descent who are socialized into a middle-class family network and a predominantly middle- or upper-middle-class suburban community may acquire a white identity as children despite possessing biological markers of African ancestry such as brown skin and dry, curly hair. Natasha, a young woman of African descent who was raised by her biological mother, a second-generation Russian Jewish woman, and her Anglo-American stepfather, described how she self-identified as an adolescent. Her parents separated when she was an infant, and Natasha had maintained no cultural ties and had no social contact with her biological father, whom she described as a "black American professional." Growing up, she had had no contact with any of her paternal relatives.

NATASHA: Until I got to high school I wouldn't tell people that I was black. I just told them that I was Caucasian. I mean I don't know if they believed me. I am Caucasian. . . . I didn't identify with [my black American father] at all. . . . My best friend would always have to tell people "she's Caucasian." She didn't know [about my African ancestry]. . . . I was assimilated not by choice but just by the way I was raised. I didn't try to fit into white culture. I *was* white culture. Both my parents were white.[15]

Note that Natasha is speaking from her present position as a self-identified "black Jew." She is interpreting her past experiences as a person who has recently acquired a black consciousness and identity. In this discussion of her childhood, she says that she previously self-identified as "Caucasian," but her white friend had to "verify" her white identity for others when questions were raised by her olive-colored skin. What did it mean for Natasha to self-identify as Caucasian? She explained during the interview that she had identified as Caucasian on the basis of both her *cultural training* and *biological* factors. As the *daughter* of a white Jewish American mother and an Anglo-American father, she claimed a white identity. In other words, she relied on both her social location in a family of European descent and her biological relationship to a birth mother of second-generation Russian ancestry to name and claim a white cultural identity before puberty.

The acquisition of a white cultural identity begins in childhood and requires a confluence of factors. Being raised by a white parent is often a necessary but not a sufficient condition for the establishment of a white identity. Individuals with Asian parents (Chinese, Korean, and Japanese) were also able to acquire a white cultural identity in their predominantly white suburban milieu and white schools.

Structural and Social Isolation from Nonwhites

The important role that middle-class entitlement played in the shift of Jews from nonwhite to white, as a group, has been explored by the anthropologist Karen Brodkin Sacks. However, this inclusion of Jewish Americans into middle-class suburbia was not extended to African Americans before the Civil Rights movement. In their analysis and critique of perceptions of the suburbs, William Sharpe and Leonard Wallock argue that recent scholars of suburbia have emphasized the independence of the suburbs from the cities and claim that it represents a new "urban" environment.[16] The authors argue against recent characterizations of the suburbs and discuss the social exclusivity of the suburban environment, contending that despite the increasing diversity of suburban communities, "suburbia has remained an essentially exclusive domain. For example, in 1980, blacks constituted just 6.1% of suburbanites, as compared to 23.4% of city dwellers. That same year, only 8.2% of suburbanites reported incomes below the federal poverty line as compared to 17.2% of city residents. Minorities and the poor are still excluded from the suburbs."[17]

A cultural and social milieu dominated by consumerism continues to characterize many, though not all middle-class suburban communities. My participants described growing up in and feeling a sense of cultural belonging to an economically and racially exclusive environment where identity was based on middle-classdom and purchasing power. How do socioeconomic segregation and status generate a social context in which African-descent adolescents who are *not* physically qualified for whiteness by virtue of their skin color, hair type, and other markers gain access to a white *cultural* experience as suburban residents?

Research suggests that gender division of reproductive labor in suburban communities has not changed radically, so, particularly in the event of divorce or separation, their African American fathers typically did assume the pivotal role in the socialization for the women I interviewed.[18] Furthermore like their middle-class peers of no known or visible African ancestry, these women grew up structurally and socially isolated from minority groups and working-class whites. Rebecca, a woman of European Jewish and African ancestry raised in a white suburban community in New York, described her social isolation from black students before her family moved from a white suburban community to an urban area of New York City and she began attending a racially mixed junior high school.

REBECCA: . . . so I was always isolated pretty much.
FWT: Isolated from whom?
REBECCA: From black kids. There were, like, two other black kids in my class.

The social segregation revealed in the above quote parallels the research findings of Ruth Frankenberg, who has provided scholars with a map of the "social geography" of white women's childhood. With few exceptions, the middle-class women I interviewed had had very limited, if any, daily social contact with blacks or other nonwhites before attending college.

WHITE MOTHERS AND THEIR DAUGHTERS: COLOR-BLINDNESS AND THE CULTURE OF RACIAL NEUTRALITY

What do African-descent women learn from their mothers as children growing up in middle-class homes and communities? Recent and past feminist research on motherhood provides very little empirical data on how European American mothers transfer a white racial identity to their children.[19] Black feminist scholars have theorized more about the intersection of race and class on the transfer of identity between mothers and daughters, but this does not add to our understanding of transracial motherhood.[20] There is some ethnographic data on the attitudes of white adoptive mothers of African-descent women, and Ruth Frankenberg provides a model for understanding the ideological milieu inherited by African-descent women raised by middle-class mothers of European or Asian descent. The study described here did not involve interviews with any mothers, so I can discuss only daughters' discussion of their relationships with their mothers *after* they had constructed a "black" identity.

Whiteness as a Position of Racial Neutrality

In addition to being immersed in European American families living in residentially segregated communities of middle- and upper-middle-class whites, some informants identified racial "neutrality" as an ideological condition necessary to acquiring a white identity. They defined racial "neutrality" as the childhood experience of seeing themselves as racially *invisible*, or racially neutral. Their Asian American and European American mothers played a critical role in providing an experience of racial neutrality in the home, and this enabled them to experience their class (and gender) identity as more primary than their African heritage. Racial visibility seemed linked to whether or not my participants felt stigmatized on the basis of being nonwhite in appearance. Angela, an eighteen-year-old woman who was raised by her biological mother and

her stepfather, described how race or racial difference was never mentioned in her family.

ANGELA: I look back at my family pictures and there's this white family and there's me in it. Like, wow, I never actually felt that I was [racially] different from my family. None of [my white relatives] actually said, "Why is your skin darker?" Never. I totally never thought about [skin color]. You know on my black side there's my brother who's mixed but looks white.[21]

Like her peers, Angela was not trained by her mother to a racially marked identity. She was not culturally trained to self-identify as racially visible, as children who grow up in poorer or more diverse communities are.[22]

Jessica, a twenty-one-year-old woman who was raised by her single Anglo-American mother and never lived with her African American father, described how she acquired a racially neutral identity in her suburban community. Her mother had never *racialized* her, had never told her that she belonged to the black racial category or any other racial group. Like many of her peers of no known African ancestry, she was *not* conscious of having a *racial* identity as a child, meaning that she did not acquire a black identity as a child.

JESSICA: Well, my mother is very idealistic. She was just. She would never use the word "race." She would never say I was black or white. She would just say "you're special." . . . She gave me a real sense of self but not a sense of a racial self.[23]

The African-descent women who claimed a white identity saw themselves as culturally and politically neutral and not targeted as members of a racial group until they were placed in an environment with a significant number of politicized people of color (African Americans/blacks, Mexican Americans/Chicanos). Mimi, the daughter of a Chinese American father and a mother of Chinese and African descent from the West Indies, described the "color-blind" and racially neutral analysis she was trained to embrace by her family.

MIMI: [My family] is not racist. But they're very assimilated, They're not prejudiced, but in terms of their ideals, their standards, I think they've adopted white ideals and white standards. You know those sort of people who are "race neutral." . . . They don't see [racial identity] as defining them at all. . . . They try to ignore differences, and when I say to people "I'm black," I'm saying, "I am different and I want you to notice and not act like it's not an issue." And not to discriminate against me for it but to recognize and appreciate it.[24]

Although Mimi's mother is of African descent and chemically straightens her hair to emphasize her Asian heritage, she was forbidden by Mimi's father to discuss her African ancestry, and *never* discussed it with her children. Although Mimi identified herself as black and Asian at the time she was interviewed, she reported that prior to *leaving* suburban community and prior to being integrated into the black campus community, she self-identified as culturally white.

In the context of a middle-class suburbia, being raised white involved having everyday social interactions and intimate contact with individuals who embraced a racially neutral identity. Having contact in which they were not differentiated or treated as culturally different from their peers or their family members enabled these African-descent children to experience the world as color-blind. They inhabited the same world as their middle-class peers. They were not excluded from any activities and were not aware of being perceived as different before puberty. Several women could not recall any situation in which they felt stigmatized or marked as different from their peers before adolescence (around twelve years of age).

The childhood experiences of my middle-class participants revealed that becoming culturally white required growing up immersed in a racially exclusive residential, academic, and social community and not being singled out as culturally distinct by white peers. Their mothers and peers had not called attention to markers of difference, thus they had not learned to experience themselves as racially *visible*. All described a childhood in which they had experienced a feeling of cultural belonging and acceptance. Individuals who had acquired their parents by birth or adoption were raised, as are many white children, to see themselves as "normal" or racially neutral. They were culturally trained not to see their skin color and physiognomy as relevant markers of cultural difference in the company of their siblings or peers.

Unconsciousness of racial position, a critical characteristic of the women who self-identified as white, was greatest among women who had been raised by white or Asian mothers. They saw themselves as racially neutral with regard to their membership in a middle-class suburban cultural community. However, this racial neutrality ceased being the primary interpretative framework through which these women described themselves prior to their attendance at the University of California at Berkeley, which appeared to provide an ideological milieu for these women as children.

Whiteness as a Position of Middle-Class Privilege

The women I interviewed identified their socioeconomic-economic status as one basis for their claim to a white cultural identity. In other words, they argued that they had been white because they had the same *material* privileges and socioeconomic-economic advantages as their suburban peers. Hence, white identity was inextricably linked to a middle-class economic position. For example, poor people of European descent did not represent whiteness to the middle-class women I interviewed. When they talked about whites, they referred *exclusively* to economically privileged European Americans. It was their access to material privileges as members of middle-class families that gave them access to a white cultural identity. Her status as the daughter of a professional psychologist enabled Angela to claim and name herself white. Angela's description of why she did not feel excluded from white social networks identifies her excellent grades, her interests, her friendships with whites, and her material privileges.

ANGELA: I just remember filling out college applications. I'd [ask] my mother, "Mom what should I put? Should I put black or white?" "Put 'other.' Put 'biracial.'" My [white] counselor at school actually told me, "You have to put black because you're over whatever percentage." If it was 30 percent or 20 percent you're considered black. So I thought, "Okay," so I ended up listing myself as black.

FWT: How did you feel about that?

ANGELA: It was weird. I got lots of scholarships for being black, for being a minority. For my grades and stuff. I remember my best friend, Laurie, telling me, "Wow, you're really lucky that you're black and getting all of these privileges. I wish I was black." . . . I act white and everything. I kinda didn't really deserve them. People don't really consider me—black, like [economically] underprivileged, people who deserve this kind of scholarship because they are a minority. . . . I totally don't feel like one.[25]

In the above statement Angela's European American counselor imposes on her an *exclusive* definition of whiteness and an *inclusive* definition of blackness. Numerous scholars have argued that in the contemporary United States, as in the past, whiteness is constructed as a category that is restricted to non-African-descent people, while blackness continues to be culturally constructed as a category that can include people of a range of racial and ethnic backgrounds. In other words, while the white category in the United States has expanded to include previously excluded groups such as southern and eastern Europeans, it continues to exclude mixed-race African-descent people born in the United States.[26]

The importance of material consumption in conferring an identity that makes residents of any racial background culturally invisible and acceptable members of the community cannot be overstated. Sharpe and Wallock argue that the "culture of consumption merely reinforces the homogeneity it supposedly erodes. Consumer culture is built to conformist standards because it must appeal to many people to achieve commercial success. At the same time that it solidifies group identity, however, status-conscious consumerism also magnifies the social distinctions that mark off one group from another."[27] The women I interviewed had learned to link their ability to consume with a racially neutral identity. They had access to a racially neutral (read "culturally white") identity because of their purchasing power, their ability to consume the same products as their middle-class suburban peers of no known African ancestry. An example of this logic can be found in the following comments by a woman of Chinese and African ancestry:

MIMI: My parents raised us in a very sheltered way. Both of them came from underprivileged backgrounds. My father is a doctor, though, and he was able to make it up the ladder. He is a big-time capitalist. He makes a lot of money and wants to keep it, so we had a lot of opportunities when we were younger. We didn't lack anything materially. . . . I think a lot of people of color in this country don't have the opportunities that money affords them. We did. None of us ever lacked anything [materially] that we saw white people [buying]. . . . That's why [racial privilege] is not an issue for them. And simply because it is not in the realm of their experience, they tend to discount [racial inequality]. It doesn't seem real

to them. They're like "we have this and this and this, so what is this issue about color!"[28]

The above quote reveals the relationship between the ability to purchase material goods and the development of a class versus a racial allegiance. Mimi described being raised to see her *class* position, her position as a consumer, as more important than her color or racial heritage. In other words, she had been culturally trained by her parents to privilege her identity as a consumer, not as a member of a racial group. She described her sense of cultural belonging as a product of her material experiences as a resident of a suburban community. She said that she did not experience herself as "different" from her white peers because of her ability to purchase the same things.

Angela, the biological daughter of a European American mother and an African American father who self-identified as white, described feeling uncomfortable self-identifying as "black" on her college applications. She defined being black as an economic category, a category to which she did not belong by virtue of her *economic status* and cultural training. Moreover, she resisted self-identifying as black, although her school counselor identified her as black on the basis of her father's African ancestry. Like Mimi, Angela equated being middle class with having a white identity: "I associate myself with being white." Since she identified herself as a member of a privileged economic class, self-identifying as white meant not being "underprivileged" and not being poor. In Angela's interpretive framework, claiming a white identity meant claiming her class identity as a middle-class person. Neither Mimi nor Angela had experienced material deprivation or social stigma as academic achievers in their peer groups. Neither reported any encounters with antiblack racism or any form of racialized discrimination. Their definition of whiteness excludes poor whites and links a culturally white identity to a middle-class position. Academic success and not being excluded from the middle class thus were the signifiers of white cultural identity.

The experience of becoming culturally white was class-linked and regionally specific to the suburbs for these women. The process of acquiring a white cultural identity may not occur in the same manner or at all among individuals who grow up in predominantly middle-class communities of color, multiracial suburban communities, working-class suburban communities, or lower-income white urban communities.

White Identity as an Expression and Embodiment of Individualism

Interviews with the daughters of European American and Asian American (born and raised in Asia) women revealed a constellation of ideological conditions under which African-descent girls acquired a white identity. In addition to experiencing racial neutrality, they had been encouraged to define themselves primarily as individuals. In their attempts to establish a link with their daughters, the mothers minimized phenotypic differences and instead emphasized their daughters' class identity and their identity as individuals. Frankenberg describes this perspective as "power-evasive" or "color-blind." Being raised white and middle class emerged as being linked to learning to privilege specific ideological positions, namely the tendency to self-identify first as an individual with no links to a specific racialized or ethnic community.

Angela reported that she had not been conscious of being treated as a member of a racially visible or stigmatized group before attending the University of California. This brown-skinned woman of visible African ancestry, who *continued to self-identify as white* despite being counteridentified by other students (including her friends of European descent who self-identify as white), described being unconscious of any antiblack racial discrimination before attending Barkeley. She had not experienced herself as racially visible at all. She described the differences between her experiences and those of brown-skinned students who self-identified as black in her high school.

ANGELA: I went to a black student union meeting once. The black students talked about all the times they felt biased against or discriminated against. I sat there and listened. I had never [experienced racial discrimination]. Like they talked about not getting into classes because they were black. Nobody would talk to them because they were black. I've never, ever felt that.[29]

Like the white feminist Minnie Bruce Pratt, who stated that until she lost her racialized gender privileges as a white, married, heterosexual woman she had never experienced herself as a member of a stigmatized or oppressed group, my informants argued that they were not conscious of belonging to a stigmatized group and that they had never experienced discrimination. All had been taught (like their white peers) to

be *indifferent* to racial issues. Thus, in addition to being a racially neutral site, white identity involves indifference to race(ism) or racialized issues. Blackness is conflated with being oppressed, and whiteness is conflated with the privilege of "normalcy." The families of the women I interviewed, like their neighbors, took the position that racial identity was not important in their lives.

Ayesha, a woman who was raised by a white mother and a black American father, delineated individualism as both a white cultural practice and as an ideological position. While she described her father in terms of his relationship to a larger black political community, she described her mother as an individual unconnected to a larger community. Her mother's individualism was presented as a salient aspect of her white identity; her lack of commitment and responsibility to a specific community were presented by Ayesha as a signifier of her whiteness. Ayesha cited her obligations to a racialized community as defining her in opposition to her white mother, who interpreted her problems as individual issues, not as collective ones.

AYESHA: My mother. Just certain things that she did were in a lot of ways distinctively white. . . . Also I think, her being a white woman, she doesn't really have any connection [to a racial community], whereas my father definitely has a community . . . with a historical situation. He has a definite connection [to a racial group]. Whereas my mother seems to be very individualistic. . . . She can turn her back on everything and say I'm going to be my own person, the hell with this whole thing [social problems].[30]

Her mother's identity as a white woman enabled her to respond to her environment in a certain way—to isolate herself and make decisions as an individual. In other words, she did not have to claim a racial identity, the identity of a member of a racial group.

White Identity as a Comfort Zone

Feeling comfortable—unself-conscious and not engaging in self-censorship—in the presence of people who self-identify as white emerged as yet another necessary social condition for the enactment and acquisition of a white cultural identity. Being culturally white requires being familiar with and comfortable functioning in milieus culturally controlled and dominated by whites. My informants defined the white experience as growing up and feeling comfortable with middle-class people who did not self-identify as members of a *racialized* group, being familiar with their cultural norms, and, most important, feeling comfortable interacting with middle-class whites. Individuals who self-identify as black generally learn within the family at a very early age to maintain a certain suspicion and social distance with nonblacks. In order to survive in a white-dominated society, blacks have learned to censor themselves, not to be completely open in their interactions with whites.[31] In contrast, not feeling the need to restrict the topics discussed to limit the interaction is a sign of white identity.

This "comfort zone" emerged as one of the primary distinctions between African-descent women who self-identified as black or biracial and those who self-identified as white. Whitney, an eighteen-year-old olive-skinned woman with naturally blonde and curly hair who had been adopted and raised by a white family, summed up her relationship to whites in this way.

WHITNEY: To tell you the truth I feel comfortable around white people because I've lived with them my whole life. I'm not really [self-conscious], whereas my [black boyfriend] doesn't trust white people. . . . He's not, like, paranoid, but he's more cautious around white people than he is around black people. Whereas I'm not that way.[32]

African-descent women like Whitney who have previously self-identified as white are distinguished by their high level of comfort in social interactions with European Americans who do not claim a racially marked identity. They have learned to feel comfortable in racially exclusive milieus that exclude most people of African descent. It is the shift to seeing whites as *racially* other that signals the beginning of the loss of white identity.

CHALLENGES TO WHITE IDENTITY: PUBERTY, DATING, AND THE LOSS OF RACIAL NEUTRALITY

Disjunctions between my informants' experiences as racially neutral and their counteridentification by their peers as nonwhite began around puberty. Several women described first becoming conscious of the limits that their physical appearance (brown skin, curly hair, and other biological markers of African ancestry) placed on their ability to experience the world as white

at puberty. In retrospect, speaking as blacks, these women interpreted these experiences as disruptions, but they did not relinquish their white cultural identity in response to these incidents of rejection, which I shall refer to as "boundary events" (after Barth).[33] Not being desired by their male peers as dating partners and being excluded by their male and female friends from full participation in the dating game did, however, force them to acknowledge that they were perceived as "different" by their peers.

Formal dating rituals (for heterosexuals) in suburbia generally begin in junior high or high school. The public selection of an individual as a desirable partner is a critical way of both expressing allegiance to a social group and affirming one's membership in a social network. It was at this moment that many of my female informants first became conscious of being marked as racially nonwhite by their peers and began the process of "losing" their position of racial neutrality. Whitney described how her sister and white friends pressured her to date the one black male in her high school.

WHITNEY: High school is such a time when you're just really exposed to the dating atmosphere, and it's exciting and everybody thinks it's cool if you're [dating]. . . . I didn't date the first two years. . . [in high school]. Not that I wasn't interested in guys. Not that I didn't [stutters], I think [long pause], I don't know. A lot of [my experiences] were racial [pauses]. I think I had some problems because I was black. And . . . practically all of my [adoptive European American] sister's friends and all of my friends were trying to get me and this black man set up. They were pushing for us to go out together so it was like automatically assumed that because we were both black that we should [date]. . . . Why was it that I could only date a black man?[34]

Whitney never dated the black man, and two years later she began dating one of her peers who was not of any known or visible African descent. She did not date any self-identified black men until she began attending the University of California at Berkeley.

Jessica, a twenty-one-year-old woman who was raised in a suburban community by her Anglo-American mother, a single parent, described how she began to lose her position of racial neutrality when she entered junior high school. When asked to describe how this transformation in her consciousness and identity occurred, she immediately described her relationships with her white male peers.

JESSICA: Growing older and being in a community that was predominantly white and not having the same interactions with white boys that my friends were having . . . not being ostracized [by peers] because I was [socially] accepted to a large extent. But in terms of [dating] relationships with boys and men . . . I wasn't accepted as having those intimate relationships with [white] boys that my [female] friends were having at those ages.[35]

The experiences of Rebecca, an eighteen-year-old Jewish woman of African descent, echo those of Jessica with regard to being excluded from the potential pool of dating partners by white male peers:

REBECCA: In junior high . . . other people [my female peers] were going out with [white] boyfriends and I always recognized the fact that I was not— I was not chosen by the [white] guys at school.

An analysis of their dating relationships reveals that patterns of exclusion and antiblack racism began to operate in my informants during puberty. For women of color, being selected by a male as a "public" romantic partner is an important aspect of the white socioeconomic-cultural experience. During puberty, they became aware that they were not desired by their male peers or pursued by them as potential romantic partners. In fact, dating emerged as the critical arena for initial confrontations with racism. A twenty-one-year-old woman who grew up in an all-white town in northern California described a change in her consciousness about her white identity when she entered junior high school.

JESSICA: It wasn't that people often referred to me in racial terms. It's just that I became more aware of myself as being different [from peers]. I came to the realization that I wasn't white, but I still lacked a racial consciousness. I wasn't aware of my racial identity. I was just aware that I wasn't white.

How did Jessica become aware of this difference? Dating and marriage are two critical arenas where the marking and enforcement of "difference" occurs. Ruth Frankenberg's research on interracial relationships revealed that white women are socialized across class and region in the United States to see blacks as, at best, inappropriate dating and marital partners, and, at worst, dangerous and deviant.[36]

During puberty, dating becomes an arena where the boundaries of whiteness are drawn by the exclusion of individuals of known African descent from the pool of dating partners. A woman must be desired and publicly recognized as the legitimate romantic partner of a white male in order to maintain a white cultural identity. Her peer groups must affirm and support the selection of the partner for her to be seen as white. Silence about their African ancestry also plays a role for such women. The peer group must either be unaware of the African ancestry or choose to ignore it and not emphasize it as significant marker of difference in order for a white cultural identity within one's peer group to be maintained.

However, being rejected by their male peers did *not immediately* result in either the relinquishment of a white identity or of the acquisition of a black or biracial identity. That occurred only *after* these young women arrived at Berkeley. These women were able to fully reinterpret their experiences in junior high school and high school only after they had relinquished their white cultural identity.

BECOMING BLACK AT BERKELEY: LEAVING A WHITE CULTURAL IDENTITY AT HOME

Identity is not static. It's constantly changing. It's constantly evolving. So while perhaps during their first two years at Berkeley [multiracial] students decide to identify as black or Chicano, or Asian, that identity could change in two years. . . . Racial identity is constantly going to change.[37]

Tamala, a woman of African and European descent who was adopted at birth, had had very limited contact with blacks. As she described it, before attending the University of California she had been a white person. When I interviewed her she was in the process of acquiring a black cultural identity. She was being culturally retrained by her African American boyfriend and peers in the black campus community at Berkeley.

TAMALA: Before I came to Cal I was white. I was all white culturally. . . . [Here] I am perceived as black. I'm treated as black so I don't have a problem with being black. . . . But it's a difficult situation. It's really hard.[38]

With one exception, all of the women described a shift in their identity and their consciousness during their first two years in college. Attendance at Berkeley was the common shared cultural experience and the most recent significant event in their lives. At the time of the interviews, they were between the ages of eighteen and twenty-five years and were adjusting to the climate of heightened racial consciousness and ethnic politics on the Berkeley campus.

The Berkeley experience challenged their ideology of individualism. They were no longer able to be "just individuals." Their prior identity as racially neutral (read "white") middle-class girls was abruptly challenged. The politicized communities of color would not allow them to avoid claiming a nonwhite racial identity. At the moment that they became conscious of their cultural whiteness (like their mono-racial peers of no known African ancestry) they were encouraged to embrace and assert a post-civil rights "black identity by their incorporation and recruitment into the black campus community. According to the *Diversity Project Report*, a report produced by the Institute for the Study of Social Change, "a process of racial and ethnic crystallization takes place at Berkeley. This process may be described in terms of the current literature on race as one of racialization, a development where social relations that were formerly defined in terms or factors other than race come to be defined in racial terms."[39]

The heightened sense of racial and ethnic consciousness that exists at Berkeley pressures students of any African ancestry to recognize and claim a black racial identity as part of their campus socialization process. In addition, allegiance to one's racial group must be demonstrated in terms of dating preferences and participation in racially based social clubs and professional, political, and academic organizations.[40] Social spaces are visibly racialized spaces on the Berkeley campus by the institution of "ethnic" parties that exclude whites. These racialized events and spaces generate ethnic group solidarity while also marking individuals who participate as racially marked members of a group.

Angela, an eighteen-year-old raised by her exclusively European-descent biological mother and an adoptive stepfather, felt uncomfortable in all-black environments but not in exclusively white environments. Her best friends were white. She dated white men exclusively and self-identified as white despite her obvious African American features.

ANGELA: At the beginning of the year I was invited to all of the African American activities that they have here [at Berkeley]. I went to some of these events and I [when] I was walking down Sproul Plaza, some black guy called out at me "Sistah, Sistah," . . . they would just call me. I kinda felt uncomfortable because I feel that I'm just [an individual] and I don't need to stick together with any [group]. I just need to be myself.

FWT: In what way do you feel that you can't be yourself at those black campus events?

ANGELA: Well . . . I'm there because I'm black so I'm black when I'm there. So I'm supposed to act black.[41]

Note that it was her presence at a specific social event that defined Angela as black ("I'm black when I'm there"). Angela did not feel comfortable in social spaces racially marked as nonwhite—spaces that excluded white people. Exclusively black locations imposed a black cultural identity on Angela that contradicted the white social identity she acquired as a child and adolescent. She was not comfortable in black spaces because, as a person who self-identified as black on her college admissions application and was identified by others as black based on her skin color and physical appearance, she was unable to assert a white cultural identity in this setting. Being in a social space that excluded white people, and racialized whites by this exclusion process, forced Angela to align herself racially with blacks. Angela described feeling uncomfortable being pressured to ally herself with a racial group (although she was allied with whites). She described wanting to just be "me"—an individual—and emphasized how her status as an individual was denied in this setting.

Angela did not wish to be racially "marked" or visible as black because it contradicted her core identity as a racially neutral *middle-class* person. She experienced herself as neutral, just like her middle-class white peers who were not under pressure to embrace a black identity. At one point during the interview Angela described black students as "extreme" and implied that blacks are deviant, in opposition to *her* identity as a "normal" person.

ANGELA: They're more aggressive. They've always been more aggressive [in social interactions] . . . . They've always been like, well, fighting for their equality and stuff. They've been really violent [unlike whites].

For Angela, blackness emerged only in relation to a "normal" identity—normal being those individuals who are not visible because of their cultural conformity. A white identity emerges as an unmarked cultural identity that is predicated on not being excluded from white social circles and not being included in all-black cultural settings that intentionally exclude nonblacks. Social spaces that are racially marked as "not white" by the presence of blacks and the exclusion of whites prevent multiracial women from asserting their white cultural identity.

ACQUIRING A PARADIGM: LEARNING TO SEE THROUGH A RACIAL LENS

A change in perception emerged as one of the most important indicators of the shift from a white identity to a black or biracial one. My research revealed a link between interpretive framework and the experience of being white culturally. My informants described being white as a way of perceiving and responding in social interactions. Whiteness emerged as an interpretive frame—a way of explaining and understanding social relations. In other words, it is an analytical posture used to decode social interactions. Whitney, a woman who self-identified as white before arriving at Berkeley, described the shift in her interpretive frame generated by her romantic relationship with her boyfriend, who embraced an African American identity. Her immersion in African American studies courses and the African American community provided her with an alternative paradigm, a way of interpreting her social world that was not "color- or power-evasive."[42] Her ability to decode racist assumptions and ideas became nuanced.

WHITNEY: Raishan was talking to this [black] woman at the bank. And she goes, "Yea, when you make your millions." And this white woman, who also worked at the bank, overheard them. And she goes, "How is he going to make millions, he's not a rapper or an athlete." See, that's a racial statement because she doesn't think that blacks could—are capable of doing anything except for being a rapper or an athlete. But I wouldn't have caught on to that if I hadn't been more aware like I am now . . . in high school I would have caught on to that. I'm more cued to that type of thing. I'm a different person now.[43]

Whitney had been culturally retrained through her relationship with her boyfriend and had begun to learn how to recognize everyday racism—something that children who grow up in households with parents who self-identify as black are often taught at an early age, although learning to recognize everyday racism can be taught by a parent who does not have a black identity and may not be taught to children by their African-descent parents.

A critical shift from a white identity to a biracial or black identity occurred for several women when they began exclusively dating men who embraced an African American identity. Establishing romantic relationships with black men also signaled to their parents and peers that they were embracing and privileging their African American ancestry over their cultural training as racially neutral. Dating relationships were no longer framed as just a matter of "individual choice" but instead became political decisions. Several women described feeling deprived of their ability to choose when they found themselves being encouraged to date men who were of African heritage and being rejected by some European American male peers. Rebecca described how her Russian Jewish American mother responded to her shift to dating men who identified as black.

REBECCA: And my mom is wondering, "[When] are you going to date a white person?" . . . She feels hurt because she sees me identifying with my African American cultural [heritage], and my [black father] didn't raise me. He didn't do anything for me . . . especially when we have a conversation about who I'm dating and almost everybody that I bring home is black. Almost everybody. And all the pictures on my wall. Almost everybody is black. . . . And I don't think she realizes that it's not a choice that I have. I mean it kinda was because I kind of made the switch [from a white to a black identity] on my own, but it wasn't really like if I wanted to make a conscious choice to be white, I have the option.[44]

Rebecca also described a pattern of subtle rejection and an increased awareness that she was not perceived as physically attractive by her male peers. She was not "chosen" and did not actively pursue white men in dating relationships, so she found herself being selected by men of African American descent. Aesthetics seemed to play a key role in the politics of exclusion as my informants got older. Judged (by European American men) on the basis of their physical attributes, they found themselves unable to compete with their female peers whose features more closely approximated the popular ideals of European American beauty.

Rebecca, like other women, also began to shift her identity away from a racially neutral one that emphasized individualism, and toward a racialized collective identity that emphasized her political and cultural connection to an African-descent community by dating men who embraced an African American identity.

Self-Censorship: Increased Social Distance and the Loss of the Comfort Zone

The comfort zone, characterized by an absence of self-censorship, did not survive in the politicized Berkeley campus, where an ethic of color-blindness was not embraced or defined as desirable by a vocal segment of the student body. As a result, my informants reported an increase in self-censorship and increased social distance between themselves and their parents. They began to censor themselves in front of people who did not self-identify as black or biracial. They learned that there are topics that are taboo in the presence of people who claim a racially neutral identity. This knowledge was accompanied by the loss of their parents' racial neutrality. Relatives who had been perceived as racially neutral became racialized. As Whitney learned to experience the world as a self-identified black, she began to experience increased cultural distance between herself and her adoptive mother. She gradually relinquished her previous ideological framework. This is illustrated by her recollection of a home visit with her mother.

WHITNEY: We were talking to Vincent's roommate. Vincent's roommate is black but he always [dates] white women. And I felt myself—when we were telling my mom about this one white girl that he brought over and . . . we didn't tell her what race she was. But we were just talking about him bringing home the ugliest women. "They're so ugly." And I go, "Yeah, Mom, and they're—" I stopped myself. "Yeah, Mom, and they're all white women." I can't tell my mom that. You know I never would have said that in high school. . . . But I find myself [thinking] in this kind of mentality. Like thinking, Whitney, think of your biological parents. That was them. Black and white . . . it's little things like that are so hard and I feel that I can't [talk about this]. I haven't shared this with my mom yet. . . .

Maybe I'm afraid that she won't understand. That she can't understand because I'm [learning from the black community] that white people don't understand [racism] or can't identify with [racial] problems, so that's where I'm in a conflict.[45]

Several women brought up the issue of their mothers not being able to understand them as black or biracial women. Once they had acquired an interpretive framework that was different from their mothers', they no longer saw themselves as occupying the same position as their mothers and did not evaluate their relationships in the same way. Whitney's relinquishment of a white identity and her acquisition of a black identity involved learning to make the distinction between whites and blacks in terms of what topics should be censored in the presence of nonblacks. She began to see her mother as not able to engage in a culturally competent fashion in discussions that addressed racial identity and racism.

CONCLUSIONS

The experiences of African-descent girls who shifted from a white to a black or biracial identity reveal that the one significant aspect of the construction of "white" identity is an interpretive framework that privileges individualism and racial neutrality. This essay both supports and expands the research of previous feminist scholars of whiteness by providing specific case studies of African-descent girls raised in suburban communities and their acquisition of a color- and power-evasive paradigm that enabled them to construct a racially neutral (white) identity. This essay also shows that a white identity is available (prior to attending a university) to a segment of the economically privileged and residentially segregated African-descent female community.

The African-descent women I interviewed had a white identity available to them as children growing up in middle- and upper-middle-class suburban communities. This identity was contingent on their being raised in residentially, socially, and socioeconomically segregated milieus. Such segregation has specific ideological consequences for the construction of white identity among African-descent women of multiracial heritage. African-descent women who have biological markers of "difference" but are not culturally or economically distinct from their peers may acquire a white identity as children. However, my research also reveals the limits of white identity claims after puberty and after women of visible African ancestry relocate to a politicized campus community.

In this essay I provide compelling evidence that a white, and later a black, identity is socially constructed and can be enacted under specific economic, demographic, and social conditions. All the women I interviewed stated that they had learned a great deal about their heritage and their identity by enrolling in African American and ethnic studies courses. These courses compensated for the lack of information they had received at home from their parents and served to reposition them both culturally and racially. Courses in African American/black studies and ethnic studies provided an anchor for the identity transition of students who had previously self-identified as white. This has implications for the cultural training of European American students of no known African heritage. It suggests that students of exclusively European descent could not only unlearn to see themselves as racially neutral but could also be taught to privilege a cultural connection to their African American cultural heritage as Americans, even if their cultural training and experiences prior to college did not give them access to a black cultural identity.

The Black Power movement and the Civil Rights movement played critical roles in the institutionalization of a reconstructed black identity accessible to African-descent students from a range of sociocultural backgrounds. During the 1960s and 1970s U.S. blacks fought for the establishment of academic departments and programs centered on the experiences and contributions of black Americans. Through course curricula and campus events, black/African American studies and ethnic studies departments have provided African-descent and other students with access to alternative paradigms that challenge the discourses of individualism and power evasion. At the University of California women of African-descent are socialized into a post-civil rights black identity that privileges and centers their African American heritage as *more politically* and socially relevant than their non-African (Asian and European) heritage.

Further research, particularly longitudinal studies involving a larger and more diverse sample of women and men from a range of socioeconomic-economic and regional backgrounds, is needed to evaluate the impact of class on the construction of racialized gender identities. Studies that examine differences *within* families between siblings who may acquire different racial identities are also needed. Since I did not have access to the siblings of my participants, I am unable to theorize about the impact of these identity shifts on siblings and other members of the family system.

I cannot say anything about the experiences of African-descent women in *working-class* suburban communities. Ethnographic studies that do not neglect the experiences of working-class, middle-class, and upper-middle-class African-descent suburban residents are needed to expand our understanding of the *meaning* of a white (and hence black) identity in various socioeconomic-economic and regional communities. This study challenges the notion that racial identities are fixed, natural, and unmalleable even in the face of phenotypical constraints. It also suggests that despite the persistence of overt antiblack racism in the contemporary United States, Asian American and European American mothers may play a pivotal role in transferring a racially neutral identity to their daughters. Moreover, the cultural practices and ideologies of mothers generate a racially neutral milieu in which their mixed-race daughters experience themselves as unmarked. My research demonstrates that a *racially neutral* experience and cultural identity are available (at least prior to puberty and attendance at a university) to an economically privileged segment of the African-descent female community raised by Asian or European American mothers.

NOTES

I thank Ara Wilson, Gloria Cuadraz, Jennifer Pierce, Naheed Islam, Sarah Murray, John Wolfe, and Jonathan W. Warren for their insightful comments and suggestions on the first draft of this essay. This essay also benefited from the critical reading and comments of my colleagues at the University of Washington, Caroline Chang Simpson and Judith Howard. Finally, I thank Kristin Luker at the University of California at Berkeley, who inspired me to write this paper, which is based on a study I began while enrolled in her graduate seminar on qualitative research methods.

1. Suzanne Caruthers, "Catching Sense: Learning From Our Mothers to Be Black and Female," in *Uncertain Terms: Negotiating Gender in American Culture,* ed. Faye Ginsburg and Anna Lowenhauptising (Boston: Beacon Press, 1990); Patricia Hill Collins, *Black Feminist Thought: Knowledge, Consciousness, and the Politics of Empowerment* (London: HarperCollins Academe, 1989).

2. Kathleen Blee, *Women of the Klan: Racism and Gender in the 1920s* (Berkeley: University of California Press, 1991); Ruth Frankenberg, *White Women, Race Matters: The Social*

Construction of Whiteness (Minneapolis: University of Minnesota Press. 1993); Minnie Bruce Pratt, "Identity: Skin Blood Heart," in *Yours in Struggle: Three Feminist Perspectives on Anti-Semitism and Racism*, ed. Elly Bulkin, Minnie Bruce Pratt, and Barbara Smith (Brooklyn: Long Haul Press, 1984); Karen Sacks, "How Did Jews Become White Folks?" in *Race*, ed. Steven Gregory and Roger Sanjek (New Brunswick: Rutgers University Press, 1994), 78–102.

3. Virginia Dominguez, *White by Definition: Social Classification in Creole Louisiana* (New Brunswick: Rutgers University Press, 1986); Ruth Frankenberg, "Whiteness and Americanness: Examining Constructions of Race, Culture, and Nation in White Women's Life Narratives," in *Race*, ed. Steven Gregory and Roger Sanjek (New Brunswick: Rutgers University Press, 1994), 62–77; Sacks, "How Did Jews Become White Folks?"

4. Signithia Fordham and John Ogbu, "Black Students' Success: Coping with the 'Burden of Acting White,'" *Urban Review* 18 (1986). This essay departs from Fordham and Ogbu's ideas of "acting white" by examining the experiences of African-descent women who had not acquired a black identity before attending college.

5. Constance Perrin, *Belonging in America: Reading between the Lines* (Madison: University of Wisconsin Press, 1988).

6. Ibid., 5–7.

7. Elizabeth Atkins, "For Many Mixed-Race Americans Life Isn't Simply Black or White," *New York Times*, June 5, 1991.

8. Reginald Horsman, *Race and Manifest Destiny: The Origins of American Racial Anglo-Saxonism* (Cambridge: Harvard University Press, 1981); Alexander Saxton, *The Rise and Fall of the White Republic: Class, Politics, and Mass Culture in Nineteenth Century America* (New York: Verso, 1990); David Roediger, *The Wages of Whiteness: Race and the Making of the American Working Class* (New York: Verso, 1991); bell hooks, "Representations of Whiteness in the Black Imagination," in *Black Looks: Race and Representation* (Boston: South End Press, 1991); Toni Morrison, *Playing in the Dark: Whiteness and the Literary Imagination* (Cambridge: Harvard University Press, 1992); Vron Ware, *Beyond the Pale: White Women, Racism, and History* (London: Verso, 1992); Ruth Frankenberg, *White Women, Race Matters*; Charles Gallagher, "White Reconstruction in the University," *Socialist Review* 94, nos. 1–2 (1995): 165–87; Tomas Almaguer, *Racial Fault Lines: The Historical Origins of White Supremacy in California* (Berkeley: University of California Press, 1994), 17–74.

9. For a discussion of the transformations and expansion of the "white" category see Sacks, "How Did Jews Become White Folks?"; Noel Ignatiev, *How the Irish Became White* (London: Routledge, 1996); Jonathan Warren and France Winddance Twine, "White Americans, the New Minority? Non-Blacks and the Ever-Expanding Boundaries of Whiteness," *Journal of Black Studies*, in press.

10. Warren and Twine, "White Americans, the New Minority."

11. During the first phase of this research project, I recruited volunteers who had been raised in multiracial families or *any* ethnic or racial background. After conducting interviews with two students of Asian and European American heritage, I decided to restrict my focus to students of known African descent. The history of slavery and the concentration of African Americans primarily in the rural South and the urban North has generated a unique experience that distinguishes African Americans, as a group, from American Indians, Asian Americans, and European Americans. I further decided to restrict this study to individuals who had one parent who self-identified as black or African American. This provided not only a "control" but also a common denominator that facilitated a more nuanced analysis of racial consciousness and racial labeling within multiracial families.

12. Francine Winddance Twine, Jonathan W. Warren, and Francisco Ferrandiz, *Just Black: Multiracial Identity* (New York: Filmmakers Library, 1991).

13. All names of participants used in this paper are pseudonyms. No names of specific suburban communities are used, although the names of larger geographical regions and the names of states have been retained.

14. Transcript of interview conducted on March 30, 1991.

15. Transcript of interview conducted on October 5, 1990.

16. William Sharpe and Leonard Wallock, "Bold New City or Built-up Burb? Redefining Contemporary Suburbia," *American Quarterly* 46, no. 1 (1994): 1–30.

17. Ibid., 7.

18. Arlie Hochschild, *The Second Shift: Working Parents and the Revolution at Home* (New York: Viking Press, 1989).

19. Nancy Chodorow, *The Reproduction of Mothering: Psychoanalysis and the Sociology of Gender* (Berkeley: University or California Press, 1978); Evelyn Nakano Glenn, Grace Chang, and Linda Rennie Forcey, *Mothering: Ideology, Experience and Agency* (New York: Routledge, 1994).

20. Suzanne Caruthers, "Catching Sense."

21. Transcript of interview conducted on November 25, 1991.

22. John Langston Gwaltney, *Drylongso: A Self-Portrait of Black America* (New York: Random House, 1980).

23. Transcript of interview conducted on October 15, 1990.

24. Transcript of interview conducted on April 8, 1991.

25. Transcript of interview conducted on November 25, 1991.

26. For a discussion of how mixed-race African-descent people continue to be constructed as unqualified for the white category, see Virginia Dominguez, *White by Definition: Social Classification in Creole Louisiana;* and F. Floyd David, *Who Is Black? One Nation's Definition* (University Park: Pennsylvania State University Press, 1991). For a discussion of the classification of African-descent people from North Africa, see Soheir Morsy, "Beyond the Honorary White Classification of Egyptians: Societal Identity in Historical Context," in *Race, ed.* Steven Gregory and Roger Sanjek (New Brunswick: Rutgers University Press, 1994).

27. Sharpe and Wallock, "Bold New City," 11.

28. Transcript of interview conducted on May 10, 1991.

29. Transcript of interview conducted on November 25, 1991.

30. Transcript of interview conducted on October 24, 1990.

31. Philomena Essed, *Everyday Racism: Reports from Women of Two Cultures* (Claremont, Calif.: Hunter House, 1990). This book compares the experiences of African-descent women (Surinamese) living in the Netherlands with those of African American women living in the San Francisco Bay area. Essed found differences in the cultural training of U.S. black American women and African-descent women in Holland. African-descent U.S. women had been trained as children to see and respond to everyday occurrences of racism in a sophisticated manner while Surinamese women generally lacked this training. In addition, Essed found that the socialization process for African American children (in monoracial black families) included learning how to deal with racism. In other words, African-descent children raised by two self-identified black parents in U.S. homes are taught to distinguish between covert and overt racism and to censor in the presence of nonblacks and whites. Hence, their early cultural training cues them to detect subtle forms of racism, which distinguishes them, in most cases, from children raised by European Americans in the United States.

32. Transcript of interview conducted on March 30, 1991.

33. Fredric Barth, ed., *Ethnic Groups and Boundaries* (Boston: Little, Brown, 1969), 294.

34. Transcription of interview conducted on March 30, 1991.

35. Transcript of interview conducted on March 20, 1991.

36. Frankenberg, *White Women, Race Matters,* 71–101.

37. Transcript of interview conducted on October 15, 1990.

38. Transcript of interview conducted on February 15, 1991.

39. Institute for the Study or Social Change, *Diversity Project: The Final Report* (Berkeley: Institute for the Study of Social Change, 1991), 44. This report, which examines the impact of the dramatic demographic shifts in the student population at Berkeley on campus life, is based on interviews conducted between February 1989 and April 1991 with 291 students and sixty-nine focus groups divided along lines of race. In addition to surveying student attitudes on affirmative action and other issues, the report illuminates the socioeconomic-political terrain that students from diverse racial and socioeconomic-economic backgrounds must negotiate on entering Berkeley.

40. For a more detailed discussion of the role that dating partners play in the identity shifts of multiracial college students, see "Heterosexual Alliances: The Romantic Management of Racial Identity," in *The Multiracial Experience: Racial Borders as the New Frontier,* ed. Maria P. P. Root (New York: Sage, 1996).

41. Transcript of interview conducted on November 25, 1991.

42. Frankenberg, *White Women, Race Matters.*

43. Transcript of interview conducted on March 20, 1991.

44. Transcript of interview conducted on May 13, 1991.

45. Transcript of interview conducted on March 30, 1991.

PART THREE

SOCIAL ORGANIZATION
OF GENDER

The processes of gender socialization that begin in early childhood prepare us for participation in society as adult women and men. Socialization alone, however, cannot account for the differences in power and prestige between men and women in almost all societies. Gender encompasses more than the socialized differences between individual women and men. As Judith Lorber pointed out in Section Two, gender also affects the way that social institutions—from family to medicine to politics—are structured. Key to feminist analyses is an understanding of the role of a society's institutions in perpetuating gender inequality.

Like other forms of social inequality, gender inequality includes the unequal distribution of three different kinds of valued commodities. First, inequality entails differential access to power, defined as the ability to carry out one's will despite opposition. Second, inequality includes differential access to the sources of prestige, defined as the ability to command respect, honor, and deference. Third, differential access to wealth, or economic and material resources, is important to inequality. Those who have access to anyone of these resources—power, prestige, or wealth—occupy a position from which they are likely to achieve access to the others and thereby reinforce their status over those who have less. In the case of gender-stratified social systems, men's greater access to power, prestige, and wealth enhances their opportunities to exploit women and decreases women's ability to resist.

Of course, not all men have equal access to prestige, power, or wealth. Men of subordinated racial or ethnic groups, working-class and poor men, disabled men, and many gay or old men are also excluded from socially sanctioned sources of power, prestige, and wealth. Women,

too, vary in their degree of access to power, prestige, and wealth; white or upper-class women receive benefits from their class and race even while they are penalized for their gender. As we have seen, gender is one system of domination that interacts with other systems based on race, class, ethnicity, sexuality, nation, and ability. The task of feminist scholars is to trace the intersections of gender and other systems of domination, examining the varied ways that gender inequality is expressed and reinforced in social institutions.

Institutions construct systems of inequality in a variety of ways. Economic and legal systems; political, educational, medical, religious, and familial institutions; mass media; and the institutions of science and technology reinforce the ideology of women's inferiority and preserve men's greater access to power, wealth, and prestige. How? The structures of institutions are gendered in that they privilege men and those traits labeled masculine and they penalize women and the traits labeled feminine. Such institutions engage in practices that discriminate against women, exclude or devalue women's perspectives, and perpetuate the idea that differences between women and men and the dominance of men are natural. In addition, the control of these institutions usually rests in the hands of men, and social scientists understand that dominant groups tend to behave in ways that enhance their own power.

Institutions establish various kinds of rewards and punishments that encourage women to behave in submissive ways, and such submissive behavior in turn perpetuates the idea that women are naturally submissive. For example, a complex social system in the United States exerts strong pressures on women to enter into heterosexual marriages. Families train daughters to be wives and mothers; high school events require opposite-sex dates; college fraternities and sororities promote heterosexual coupling; widespread violence against women encourages them, ironically, to seek male protection; and men's higher incomes mean that heterosexual marriage tends to improve a woman's standard of living.

A woman's failure to marry constitutes a violation of social prescriptions and often leaves her economically disadvantaged and socially suspect. On the other hand, despite women's increasing participation in the paid labor force, in heterosexual marriage the burden of care work—raising children and attending to the home—still usually falls disproportionately on women, a dynamic that helps maintain the inequality between men and women in the work world.

It is important to reiterate that gender stratification is not the only form of inequality affecting women's and men's lives and the structure of social institutions. Institutions that disadvantage racial or ethnic groups, older people, the disabled, the poor, or particular religious or class-based groups also discriminate against both women and men who belong to those groups. Understanding women's oppression as a function of the social organization of gender necessitates understanding the intersectionality of systems of domination.

The following articles examine how particular institutions express, construct, and maintain gender inequality. They analyze the ways that women's subordination is maintained in work, families, sexuality, treatment of and attitudes about bodies, and violence against women. The articles do not simply document women's submission, however. They also describe the ways that women and men in various groups resist oppression and attempt to exercise control over their choices and their lives. To what extent are women or men able to resist the structures of gender, and to what extent are they controlled by gendered institutions?

SECTION 5

Work

Work for pay influences many aspects of our lives: our economic prosperity, our social status, where we live, our relationships with family members and friends, our health, and our access to health care. Our work experiences influence how we come to view others, ourselves, and the social world around us. Reciprocally, how we are situated in society often influences the kind of work we do and our compensation for that work.

In traditional societies, division of labor based on sex and age did not necessarily correspond to differences in the importance assigned to different tasks: "women's work" might be considered just as socially valuable as "men's work." In societies like the United States, however, social divisions of labor based on gender, race/ethnicity, age, and other factors reflect and perpetuate power differences among groups. As we have already seen in Section One, "Diversity and Difference" and Section Two, "Theoretical Perspectives," gender is profoundly shaped by class and race/ethnicity in ways that are especially critical in the realm of work.

This section begins with Christine Bose and Rachel Whaley's exploration of the continued concentration of women in predominantly female and men in predominantly male occupations. The most common occupations for women include secretary, cashier, and nurse, while truck drivers and carpenters are almost always men. Bose and Whaley discuss the different ways of measuring sex segregation, the nature of sex segregation in white-collar, pink-collar, clerical, and blue-collar jobs, and the various explanations for the persistence of sex segregation into the twenty-first

century. They also argue that sex segregation matters: it is a cause of inequities in earnings (see the table on wages) and leads to tokenism and lack of occupational mobility. Thinking about the people you know, how many are in non–sex-segregated jobs? What factors hinder people from finding work outside the traditional gender-appropriate occupations? How important is outright discrimination compared to people's socialization? Has affirmative action made a difference (see the boxed insert on the realities of affirmative action)? What do you think can be done to end sex segregation in the labor force?

"You Wouldn't Want One of 'Em Dancing with Your Wife" looks back in time to explore the gender and racial dynamics involved in the labor force during World War II. Eileen Boris shows how wartime demands for labor opened up jobs for black men and women, raising fears among some white workers of bodily contact and "social equality" with African Americans. Taking off from a novel and analyzing complaints of discrimination to a wartime agency responsible for fair employment practices, Boris provides a concrete example of the ways that race, class, gender, and sexuality together shape the story of interactions on shopfloors, streetcars, and other public spaces. Fears of intimacy, especially between black men and white women, played just as important a role in the organization of work and the responses of workers as the more obvious economic factors. How would you describe the different interests of white men, black men, white women, and black women in the context of the wartime labor force? What does the story of the World War II workforce tell us about racialized

193

gender and gendered race? What has changed in American society since the end of the war in 1945?

The next article in this section looks at another form of gendered and embodied labor—work in nail salons. Just as Latin American immigrant women are funneled into domestic work in Los Angeles, in New York, Korean women predominate as manicurists. Here again, class and race/ethnicity are central, not just in terms of the characteristics of the labor force, but also with regard to the style of what Miliann Kang calls "body labor" expected by clients. In her rich ethnographic study, Kang differentiates between white upper- and middle-class women's interest in pampering, black working-class women's preference for technical skill, and the expectation of efficiency at a reasonable price on the part of the clients of a mixed-race mid-level salon. Like Hondagneu-Sotelo's domestic workers, Kang's manicurists are part of a global economy that is shaped by gender, class, and race/ethnicity. In what ways are the manicurists similar to domestics in Los Angeles? In what ways are they different? What do the different interests of their clients tell us about racialized gender? What other jobs involve "body labor"? What does Kang see as positive about the interactions among women that she documents?

Sex segregation and racial/ethnic patterns of employment are also at the heart of Pierrette Hondagneu-Sotelo's study of Latina domestic workers in Los Angeles. Talking with immigrant women, mostly from Latin America, who work as live-in and live-out nannies and housekeepers and as housecleaners, Hondagneu-Sotelo learns why they choose particular kinds of jobs at different times. New immigrants without the support of family and friends must often take jobs as live-ins, the least desirable position because of the lack of privacy, social isolation, long hours, incessant demands, and low pay. We hear how these Latina women feel about the houses they must clean, the children they care for, the food (or lack thereof) their employers provide. We understand why, as soon as they can, women choose to work on a live-out basis, in their own homes and communities, and why some choose housecleaning as the most autonomous job.

Hondagneu-Sotelo puts these women's experiences into the context of immigration, transnational motherhood, and racial stereotyping. What do the experiences of Latina domestic workers tell us about gender, ethnicity, and employment? What determines whether they see their jobs as good jobs? What can be done to improve their lives? Think about the relationship between their lives and the lives of the women who employ them. What do the experiences of Latina domestics tell us about why a living wage is a women's issue (see boxed insert)?

As these articles demonstrate, women's race, ethnicity, nationality, age, and class backgrounds affect both the structural opportunities available to them in the labor force and their interpretations of these experiences. What experiences, if any, do you think women in the labor force share by virtue of their gender?

READING *19*

Christine E. Bose
Rachel Bridges Whaley

Sex Segregation in the U.S. Labor Force

Sex segregation in the workplace is manifested in many ways—in the extent to which women and men are concentrated in different industries, establishments, occupations, and jobs, and in the extent to which any particular job is dominated by workers of one sex. An occupation is usually considered female or male dominated if it is at least 75 percent female or male. For example, 7 of the 10 most common occupations for women are dominated by female workers including secretary (98 percent), cashier (78 percent), and registered nurse (93 percent) (Women's Bureau 1999) (see Table 1). Similarly, the majority of the most common occupations for men are male dominated, such as truck driver (94 percent) and carpenter (98 percent) (U.S. Census Bureau 1998a) (see Table 2). The only occupation among the top 10 (largest numbers) for both men and women is miscellaneous salaried manager, which is 70 percent male (Women's Bureau 1999). Such occupational "integration" is rare and its positive effects are frequently diluted because the particular jobs offered by employers or firms are sex segregated.

Occupational segregation may entail the physical separation of workers of different social groups (sex and racial or ethnic groups). For example, between 1920 and 1940 in North Carolina's tobacco industry, workers were physically separated and segregated into sex-typed and race-typed tasks. Black women tobacco workers were located in one building or on one floor, designed for "dirty" prefabrication work such as

TABLE 1 TEN MOST COMMON OCCUPATIONS FOR WOMEN, 1998

Women's Common Occupations[1]	Percent Women
Secretaries	98
Cashiers	78
Managers and administrators, n.e.c.[1]	30
Sales supervisors and proprietors	40
Registered nurses	93
Nursing aides, orderlies, and attendants	89
Elementary school teachers	84
Bookkeepers, accounting clerks	93
Waiters and waitresses	78
Sales workers, other commodities[2]	68
Average labor-force occupation	46

[1]Not elsewhere classified or miscellaneous.
[2]Includes foods, drugs, health, and other commodities.

TABLE 2 TEN MOST COMMON OCCUPATIONS FOR MEN, 1998

Men's Common Occupations	Percent Women
Managers and administrators, n.e.c.	30
Truck drivers	5
Sales supervisors and proprietors	40
Construction laborers	16
Freight, stock, and material handlers	24
Janitors and cleaners	35
Fabricators and assemblers	33
Carpenters	1
Cooks	41
Sales representatives, commodities, wholesale	26

Source: U.S. Census, Statistical Abstract accessed on 4/10/00 at http://www.census.gov/prod/99pubs/99statab/sec13.pdf
Note: Occupational categories drawn from this source are slightly less detailed than those for women's occupations.

stripping the leaves, and white women were in another building or on another floor, inspecting and packing the product. Meanwhile black men hauled materials between locales and white men acted as supervisors and inspectors (Jones 1984). A more recent example can be found in the baking industry. Female bakers are located in retail establishments (e.g., supermarkets) while men make up the majority of wholesale bakers (Steiger and Reskin 1990).

The sex segregation of any occupation can change over time, even while the segregation of the entire labor force remains fairly stable. Occupations are more likely to shift from male to female domination than the reverse. Public-school teaching made this transition in the late nineteenth century; clerical workers, telephone operators, waiters and waitresses, and bank tellers were resegregated by the middle of the twentieth century from male to female jobs. More recently, residential real estate sales and pharmacy work have become female dominated. Women have made significant inroads into other male-dominated jobs such as bartending and insurance adjustment, which now appear to be sex integrated but may be merely in transit to becoming female dominated. According to Barbara Reskin and Patricia Roos (1990), the fundamental reason that a job is resegregated from male to female domination is a shortage of male workers. That shortage occasionally happens when an occupation is rapidly expanding, using up the supply of suitable men. In most cases, however, men are leaving a job that has become less attractive because the work process has been downgraded in terms of skills or the job rewards are less. Consequently, the decrease in prestige and pay of an occupation occurs before women enter it. As a result, women's integration into apparently prestigious male-dominated jobs can be a hollow victory.

MEASURING SEX SEGREGATION

One way to understand the extent to which men and women do different work is to examine the proportion of workers of the same sex in each occupation, as was done above. To this end, it is seen that most men and women work in occupations where workers of the same sex predominate. Indeed, only a fraction of women work in occupations that are dominated by men (Kraut and Luna 1992).

Another method is to examine the extent to which male and female workers are clustered in a small number of occupations. Reskin and Irene Padavic (1994) report that 33 percent of women workers are employed in the top 10 occupations sex-typed female compared to about 25 percent of men being clustered in the top 10 occupations sex-typed male.

The most common way to measure sex segregation is to calculate an index of sex segregation, also called an *index of dissimilarity*, which ranges from 0 to 100. Its value is interpreted as the percentage of workers of one sex that would have to change occupations so that men and women have the same distribution in each occupation. An index of 0 implies perfect integration while an index of 100 suggests that the sexes are completely segregated from each other. In 1990 the index was 53, which means 53 percent of women workers (or approximately 28 million individuals) would need to be redistributed into other occupations if all occupations were to have the same percentage of women and men that are in the entire labor force (Reskin and Padavic 1994).

Researchers have calculated the occupational sex segregation index, using the preferred detailed Census job categories, for different historical periods. It is generally agreed that the index stayed fairly high and steady, between 65 and 69, from 1900 through 1960 (Gross 1968) and perhaps as late as 1970 (Jacobs 1989). If one focuses on nonagricultural jobs, there was only a six-point decline in sex segregation in the 60 years between 1910 and 1970, dropping from 74 to 68. Through the 1970s, however, it dropped another 8 points to 60 in 1980 (Jacobs 1989b). In the 1980s, the segregation index continued to drop but at a much slower rate (Reskin and Roos 1990).

In 1940 a comparable index of occupational *race* segregation, calculated separately for blacks and whites of each sex, was rather high at 65 among women and 44 among men. These rates actually increased through 1960 but declined thereafter with the advent of affirmative-action legislation. By 1980, the greater racial segregation among working women had declined to match that of men, reaching 26 to men's 30 by 1990 (King 1992; Reskin 1994). During this same 50-year time span, occupational sex segregation rates among both blacks and whites remained almost twice as high as race segregation among men (Reskin and Padavic 1994). Indeed, Joyce Jacobsen (1994) has concluded that the slowed decline in occupational sex segregation, combined with high rates of firm-level segregation, make it unlikely that sex segregation rates will become as low as race segregation rates by the 2000 census.

SEX SEGREGATION IN SPECIFIC CATEGORIES OF OCCUPATIONS

White-Collar Occupations

As a group, white-collar occupations typically command high salaries, prestige, and autonomy. Yet further inspection reveals considerable variation in their earnings as well as considerable sex segregation. There is a hierarchy of occupations within the classification white-collar. Imagine a pyramid. Executives, physicians, lawyers, and college professors are at the top of the pyramid, while nurses, librarians, and elementary school and secondary-school teachers form part of the middle third. The bottom third includes clerical workers, sales workers, and some service workers. More women are in white-collar occupations today than ever before but where?

In 1900 only 9 percent of women workers were employed in professional occupations and only 1 percent in managerial occupations. Ninety years later 17 percent of working women are in a professional specialty and 11 percent are in executive, administrative, and managerial occupations (U.S. Census Bureau 1990). In fact, women are 49 percent of all workers in executive, administrative, and managerial occupations and 53 percent in professfonal specialties, respectively (U.S. Census Bureau 1998a). Does this mean occupational sex segregation is no longer a problem? Unfortunately the answer is no.

Industry, firm, and job segregation channels women into the lower-paid, less autonomous, and less prestigious positions that often lack opportunities for upward advancement. For example, although women are about 50 percent of financial managers, they tend to be segregated in small bank branches rather than in loan and investment departments at headquarters (Silver 1981, cited in Reskin and Phipps 1988). Women are 63 percent of personnel and labor relations managers, a service-focused occupation with median annual earnings of $50,080, but only 35 percent of managers in marketing, advertising, and public relations who earn an average $57,100 a year (U.S. Census Bureau 1998a; U.S. Bureau of Labor Statistics 1997).

Women are currently about 27 percent of all lawyers, a remarkable increase from the 1900 figure of .8 percent. Yet, in a recent study of 200 male and female lawyers, Patricia MacCorquodale and Gary Jensen found that "Not a single respondent, male or female, would choose an equally qualified female attorney over a male attorney when considering who would command more respect in court" (1993, 590). Stereotypes and prejudices influence which firms hire women lawyers, the cases they are given, and whether they make partner. Research suggests that the path to partnership is considerably more demanding for women, who must present themselves as "super lawyers" to dissuade the sexist doubts of current partners (Kay and Hagan 1998, 741).

The barriers that women face when they attempt to move into higher-status positions, with greater responsibility, decision-making power, and authority, are widespread in male-dominated occupations. The phenomenon is so common that it has been termed the *glass-ceiling effect*, a phrase that helps people visualize the very real barrier to upward mobility on the job for women workers. The glass ceiling is created by a variety of organizational barriers and discrimination. . . .

Although the gender balance in the broad categories of executive, administrative, and managerial occupations and professional specialties appears to be about 50–50 and thousands of women are managers, doctors, and college professors, occupational segregation continues to limit women's options. In fact, 70 percent of women professionals, but only 27 percent of men professionals, are employed as teachers, librarians, and counselors or in health assessment and treating occupations such as nurse or dietitian (U.S. Census Bureau 1990).

Pink-Collar Occupations

There is a cluster of white-collar occupations that are more commonly labeled pink-collar occupations because they are female dominated. For example, women are approximately 93 percent of registered nurses, 98 percent of preschool and kindergarten teachers, 84 percent of elementary-school teachers, and 81 percent of librarians (U.S. Census Bureau 1998a; Women's Bureau 1999). These professional jobs are occasionally labeled semiprofessions because they lack some of the characteristics that identify an occupation as professional. Semiprofessions tend to be less prestigious, have less autonomy, and command lower salaries than full professions. Nursing and teaching at the elementary-school level are among the top 10 occupations for women, but women earn an average of only $38,168 as registered nurses and $35,204 as elementary-school teachers. Semiprofessionals are usually located in a bureaucratic setting where persons other than fellow professional workers set most administrative rules and professional norms.

In contrast to the relatively large proportion of women who have attempted to enter traditionally male-dominated occupations (e.g., manager, doctor, or lawyer), men are much less likely to enter the traditionally female-dominated domain of pink-collar occupations. Currently, 8 percent of registered nurses, 16 percent of elementary-school teachers, and 20 percent of librarians are men (U.S. Census Bureau 1998a; Women's Bureau 1999). Contrary to the lower wages that women command when they enter male-dominated occupations, men who enter female-dominated occupations often receive higher wages than women in similar positions. Yet the wage gap is almost negligible in nursing and elementary-school teaching, where women earn 95 percent and 90 percent of what men earn. It is important that both women and men who work in female-dominated occupations earn relatively less than women and men who work in male-dominated occupations; "women's work" is generally devalued and underpaid (England and Herbert 1993). Men in female-dominated occupations often find themselves on the fast track or on a "glass escalator"; upward mobility is encouraged and supported for them, for example, in occupations such as bank teller or airline flight attendant.

Clerical Occupations

The history of clerical work represents an example of the feminization of an occupation. At the beginning of the twentieth century, women were only 4 percent of clerical workers. Clerical work was a small, male-dominated occupation with relatively high prestige; it incorporated a diversity of tasks ranging from correspondence to bookkeeping. As the economy grew to be dominated by business and as paperwork proliferated, the need for clerical workers increased drastically. Employers drew on the ready supply of educated, working-class women who were eager to leave domestic service and factory work and enter these "cleaner" jobs. Companies intentionally divided up and restructured clerical work, creating female-dominated typists, whose jobs were mechanized by the previously invented typewriter, and filers, both having less autonomy than the accounting, bookkeeping, and cashier work initially reserved for men (Davies 1982).

Today women are 99 percent of secretaries, 94 percent of typists, and 97 percent of receptionists (U.S. Census Bureau 1998a), while being only 31 percent of shipping clerks, 41 percent of purchasing managers, and 57 percent of accountants and auditors. Secretarial work now employs more women than any other occupation. Compared to other prevalent women's occupations, the median weekly salary for secretaries ($430) is ranked fifth, well behind the higher earnings of the top-ranked registered nurses ($734) (Women's Bureau 1999). Secretarial work and other clerical positions tend to have short promotion ladders and typically do not lead to professional or managerial positions (Nakano Glenn and Feldberg 1989). Over the last century, clerical work has become tedious, requires power skills, and is highly supervised. Clerical workers are often overeducated and find the work does not allow them to utilize all their skills (Nakano Glenn and Feldberg 1989).

Blue-Collar Occupations

Approximately 39 percent of men and 11 percent of women work in blue-collar occupations, which are counted by the Census under the headings of precision production, craft, and repair occupations and as machine operators, fabricators, and laborers (U.S. Census Bureau 1990). Like most occupational categories, blue-collar work includes a diverse array of occupations ranging from skilled through semiskilled to unskilled. Four blue-collar jobs—truck driver, carpenter, construction laborer, and automobile mechanic—were among the 10 leading occupations for men in 1990. All four are almost completely male dominated ranging from 99 percent (automobile mechanic) to 89 percent male (truck driver). Except for skilled occupations (e.g., electrician, carpenter, and plumber) and supervisory positions, blue-collar work offers little room for autonomy or creativity, requires hard physical labor, and is often dangerous.

Blue-collar work appeals to women although they find it hard to gain access to such positions. Historically, work in the manufacturing sector, particularly in unionized mills and plants, offered several advantages over the service jobs traditionally open to women. A study of women in the steel industry in the 1970s found that they preferred the higher wages, job security, health-care benefits, opportunity for shift work, and slower pace of blue-collar work over the harsh reality of working in sales or waitressing (Fonow 1993). In fact these tangible benefits outweighed the negative experiences in blue-collar work.

EXPLANATIONS OF SEX SEGREGATION

The history of work in the United States and elsewhere reveals a pattern of sex typing, defining some jobs as appropriate for men and others as women's work. But the origins of sex segregation in work are usually attributed to emerging industrialization. Sex segregation was created, in part, by gendered social expectations for women and men. For example, the ideas surrounding men as breadwinners and the "family wage" functioned to keep married women out of the labor force; and when single, divorced, or widowed women worked, these notions kept their wages lower than men's. The assumption was that all women had fathers and then husbands to care for them. Since men were considered the typical employees, part-time work, which women needed to be compatible with children's school hours, was virtually nonexistent except in the form of factory outwork or taking in laundry. Legal barriers constrained women's opportunities as well. Protective legislation limited women's options by defining how many hours, when (day versus night), and in which occupations they could work. In a reciprocal fashion, such segregation reinforced gendered power relations by limiting women's access to good jobs and by increasing their dependency on men. Through these processes, jobs became gendered. In other words, certain job titles as well as work tasks and skills became defined as male as distinct from female. This process is almost unnoticeable except when a job is newly created (and fought over by men and women) or its stereotype changes. A clear example of the latter case is the redefinition of clerical work as women's work by 1940 when, previously, it had been dominated by men.

Present-day researchers explain sex segregation in a variety of ways ranging from theories about individuals' behaviors to those emphasizing labor-market processes and social structure. The earliest sociological explanation focused on individual socialization, suggesting that the gender-stereotypical lessons people learn in childhood about masculine men and feminine women determine the academic fields they study and the occupations they choose. This view, however, is only partially supported. The jobs available to members of different social groups, such as women, blacks, or Hispanics, play a much greater role in determining our occupational status than any gender (or race) lessons we were taught as children. Workers are constrained by the opportunities available to them, by structural forces external to individuals.

One of the most important economic perspectives that, like socialization theory, focuses on individuals is human capital theory. Human capital is considered to be those characteristics or skills that make a worker more productive and attractive to an employer. To explain why women are predominantly employed in female-dominated occupations, human-capital theorists make many assumptions. First, they assume that all workers choose educational fields and occupations primarily with an eye toward maximizing lifetime earnings. They further assume that women consider work to be secondary to family and are only employed for short periods of time. Following from these assumptions, human-capital theorists expect women to select educational fields that require little investment in training and occupations that require skills that will not depreciate during occasional absences from the labor force. The assumption is that the resulting female-dominated occupations will be low skilled, have short career ladders, be amenable to intermittent employment, and pay more at entry than male-dominated jobs, where pay increases depend on on-the-job training. These assumptions are based on a 1950s understanding of women's roles.

Thus it is not surprising that researchers have shown that the human-capital perspective does not explain occupational sex segregation. It cannot explain why women enter low-skilled, female-dominated jobs when there are low-skilled, male-dominated jobs available. Worse still, most female-dominated occupations do not make it any easier to combine work and family than male-dominated occupations.

Counter to human-capital or socialization theorists, structural theorists argue that features of work can create behaviors, rather than individual behavior shaping occupational characteristics. For example, working in female-dominated occupations that are monotonous, have poor benefits and low wages, and lack autonomy can lead to high turnover rates. Researchers found that the same negative occupational characteristics lead to turnover among male workers, too (Reskin and Hartmann 1986). In other words, jobs can influence the attitudes, ambitions, and job preferences of workers, who are malleable and responsive to changing job situations.

The notion that institutional forces largely determine people's life chances is central to the various social-structural perspectives on occupational sex segregation. Social-control theory points to the social pressures that women and men encounter before and during employment. Both men and women are often discouraged from seeking employment in sex-atypical positions. Steel mill jobs were offered to women only after a federal court ordered steel companies to end discrimination against them. Even then the mills and male workers did not embrace the idea of women workers with open arms. In fact, women applicants reported feeling strongly discouraged by management, who questioned their interest and ability to deal with the negative aspects of the work (Fonow 1993). Men who attempt to enter traditionally female occupations are similarly discouraged by questions concerning their sexual orientation, manhood, and reasons for wanting to work with children or patients (Williams 1992).

In spite of such stereotyping, working people are not merely at the mercy of social institutions. They are also active participants in shaping sex segregation. Both sex typing and race typing of jobs can develop out of workers' struggles over new or existing occupations (Baron 1991; Milkman 1987). When the occupations of typist (originally called typewriter) or computer programmer were created, workers contended over which sex should fill them. When the existing occupation of typesetter changed from using hot-metal type to electronic composition in the 1970s, women actively entered jobs that men chose to leave (Roos 1990). Such resegregation in jobs from male to female is partially, but not entirely, responsible for the gradual decline in sex segregation during the 1980s (Jacobs 1989b).

Other processes, such as hiring procedures, help explain why women find employment in female-dominated occupations. When employers depend upon referrals from current employees for new employees, they tend to receive applications from workers of the same sex and race as those currently employed. The reason is that workers' informal networks of friends and family tend to include people of their own sex or racial group. Thus if an employer asks white men for referrals, names of other white men are proposed. Informal networks have been found to be very helpful for applicants; the sharing of information about job openings and promotion opportunities is critical to gaining access to higher-status and better-paying positions. This benefit, however, appears to be an advantage only for men. When women rely upon informal networks to learn about job openings, more often than not they end up in female-dominated occupations (Drentea 1998). When employers use open-recruitment methods, which they have to do if they are subject to affirmative-action laws, they are more likely to receive applications from workers who differ in sex, race, and ethnicity.

Open recruitment does not guarantee women access to sex-atypical jobs, however. Other organizational barriers make it difficult for women to break away from female-dominated occupations. For example, apprenticeship programs for various blue-collar jobs may have age limits, so that women who try to enter programs after having children are deemed too old, or they may require unnecessary previous experience including high school shop class. Seniority systems that are not plantwide and thus not transferable across departments may discourage women in clerical positions from taking more traditionally male jobs. The use of secretarial and typing pools in large offices hurts women's opportunities to be noticed and considered for promotion. Recent evidence suggests that sex segregation has a feedback effect. That is, employers tend to promote or hire women into management-level positions only if other women currently hold positions at the same level (Cohen, Broschak, and Haveman 1998). In other words, promotion or advancement in management for women occurs more often in female-dominated ladders. Until employers take the "risk" and hire women for positions not currently held by women, current practices will perpetuate sex segregation.

While many organizational or geographic barriers to sex-atypical occupations are grounded in administrative policies that have little to do with an employer's prejudices, discriminatory actions by employers and other male workers play an important role in the perpetuation of segregation. Recall the situation of women lawyers discussed above. Current law firm partners, who make decisions about granting new partnerships, have prejudices that can make it difficult for women to obtain partner status (Kay and Hagan 1998). Although discrimination against workers on the basis of sex and race is illegal, it persists nonetheless, as evidenced by the number of legitimate complaints of discrimination heard by the Equal Employment Opportunity Commission and other institutions.

CONSEQUENCES OF SEX SEGREGATION

Why does it matter that men and women are physically separated at work? What are the implications of sex-typed occupations? Sex segregation in the workplace matters for the same reason that the U.S.

Supreme Court outlawed school segregation in 1964; among socially unequal groups, separate is not equal. The separation of men and women, as well as members of different racial or ethnic groups, into different jobs makes it easier to treat them differently and helps maintain stereotypes about men's and women's work-related characteristics (skills, aspirations, experience). It makes possible the devaluation of women's skills and abilities.

The remainder of this [reading] briefly highlights some of the major consequences of occupational sex segregation, including the wage gap, tokenism, and hindered mobility. Other consequences include women's lower Social Security and retirement benefits as a result of earning less during employment and having worked in less profitable industries that may not provide pensions (Hogan, Perrucci, and Wilmoth 2000). Sexual harassment appears to be a major consequence of sex segregation. When women are a numerical minority in an office or section of a plant, they are very likely to experience various forms of sexual harassment ranging from hostile environment to sexual coercion. . . .

The wage gap is a major consequence of occupational sex segregation. Among full-time, year-round workers age 25 years and over, women earn an average of 74 cents for every men's dollar (U.S. Bureau of Labor Statistics, 1999). The current wage gap represents a historical narrowing of earnings inequality; between 1930 and 1980 it fluctuated between 55 and 64 percent (Reskin and Padavic 1994, 103). However, only two-fifths of women's wage improvement in the last 20 years is due to an increase in their real wages; the remaining three-fifths is due to the fall in men's real wages.

Occupational sex segregation helps explain the wage gap in several ways. First, women and men work in different occupations. The occupations in which men predominate pay higher wages. Second, even when one compares women and men in the same occupational grouping, one finds that sex segregation in industries, establishments, departments, and jobs results in lower wages for women workers. Women engineers earn $800 less per week than men engineers (Andersen 1997, 105). The median weekly income for female machine operators is $228, yet for male machine operators it is $415 (Andersen 1997, 105). Although the occupations of engineer and machine operator are male dominated, sales occupations appear well integrated; 50 percent of sales workers are women (U.S.

Census Bureau 1998a); however, retail or wholesale, men and women sell different items. In large department stores, for example, men sell large appliances on commission, while women work in noncommission departments such as sportswear. Consequently, the median weekly earning for men in this "integrated" occupational category is $603 while women earn $352 (U.S. Census Bureau 1998b). The broad categorization of sales occupations only appears integrated. Upon closer examination, the segregation of women into the retail industry and into positions such as cashier reveal the extent to which sales occupations are really not integrated. Third, female-dominated jobs often have a shorter career ladder and fewer possibilities for upward job mobility. As a result, women's jobs not only have a glass ceiling but also a "sticky floor" (Berheide 1992).

Researchers have debated the extent to which sex segregation actually explains the wage gap. Other explanations point to human-capital characteristics, job characteristics, and organizational and regional differences. Donald Tomaskovic-Devey (1995) compared the ability of sex composition to explain the wage gap in both jobs and occupations. He found that the number of women employees in jobs explains 46 percent of the earnings differential for women and men while sex composition in occupations explains 33 percent. Similarly, the segregation of men and women into different occupations and industries when they begin their careers explains 42 percent of the earnings gap while gender differences in human capital and occupational aspirations account for only 14 and 10 percent of the gap, respectively (Marini and Fan 1997). . . .

Women and men who enter nontraditional occupations may encounter varieties of "boundary heightening" by majority-group members; this situation also occurs when people of color enter predominantly white organizations (Kanter 1977). When one class of worker makes up only 15 percent of a work group or organization, majority-group members are likely to act in ways that strengthen or make more visible the differences between their own group and the minority group. Much of this activity involves discriminatory treatment that may have direct impact on a token person's work environment, physical and mental well-being, and opportunity for advancement. In the case of female tokens, employee events may take on a decidedly masculine theme involving football or cars to which female coworkers may not even be invited. Thus women may be effectively excluded from the informal networks that prove so important in obtaining better jobs. Dress codes also set women apart in a very visible manner. In addition to boundary-heightening actions, majority-group workers may attempt to discourage women workers altogether. When women first entered steel work, male workers attempted to sabotage their work. Women fire fighters report concerns as to whether co-workers will back them up in dangerous situations. Finally, when women are members of a token group in the workplace they are often "oversupervised" and scrutinized.

The discriminatory treatment of women in male-dominated occupations does not mirror the experience of men in female-dominated occupations. Although female nurses and librarians often interact with male nurses and librarians in stereotypical ways (e.g., asking a male nurse to help change a tire), male tokens receive more rewards as a result of their numerical minority than disadvantages (Williams 1992). For example, rather than being labeled a "bitch" or an "Iron Maiden" for working hard and overachieving, a man in a sex-atypical position will be encouraged to move ahead and will often be placed on the fast track. The glass escalator experienced by many token male employees reveals the extent to which the token's experience is dependent upon gender. Female and male tokens are not treated similarly by co-workers, potential mentors, and bosses.

In sum, the consequences of occupational segregation are substantial. Occupations can provide income, autonomy, security, social status, and upward mobility. Occupational segregation, however, serves as a major institutional factor shaping and limiting women's (and men's) employment options, ultimately, reinforcing a gendered distribution of power and social status.

CONCLUSION

Throughout much of the twentieth century, rates of occupational sex segregation were consistent and high, only declining since 1970 from 68 to 53. In white-collar, pink-collar, clerical, and blue-collar occupations, the jobs at the top of the hierarchy tend to be male dominated; when women are allowed into those specialties, it is usually because the jobs have changed in some way to be less attractive to men. Although occupational segregation per se is not illegal, discriminatory hiring and promotion practices are prohibited in firms covered by affirmative-action legislation. Unfortunately, many states are overturning affirmative-action laws and policies. This trend is likely to slow any progress made toward the inclusion of more women and minorities in highly skewed male occupations. The best-supported explanations for the persistence of occupational sex segregation are those that focus on institutional and socially constructed antecedents rather than individual characteristics or gender differences. Perhaps surprisingly, the rapid, large increase in women's recorded employment over the last few decades has done proportionately little to reduce occupational sex stereotyping and the overall sex segregation of workers. Attitudes about the desirability of women's work may have changed, but the social organization of the specific jobs women hold has not always done so. Some occupations have become more sex integrated or have switched from male to female dominated. Yet other factors have counterbalanced this trend, including the decline of sex-integrated occupations in agriculture or the growth of new and existing sex-segregated occupations in the service sector. The consequence is continuing high rates of sex segregation that foster gender inequities.

REFERENCES

Andersen, Margaret L. (1997). *Thinking About Women: Sociological Perspectives on Sex and Gender.* Boston: Allyn and Bacon.

Baron, Ava. (1991). *Work Engendered: Toward a New History of American Labor.* Ithaca, NY: Cornell University Press.

Berheide, Catherine White. (1992). "Women still 'stuck' in low level jobs." *Women in Public Services: A Bulletin for the Center for Women in Government* 3 (Fall). Albany: Center for Women in Government, State University of New York.

Cohen, Lisa E., Joseph P. Broschak, and Heather A. Haveman. (1998). "And then there were more? The effect of organizational sex composition on the hiring and promotion of managers." *American Sociological Review,* 63:711–727.

Davies, Margery W. (1982). *Women's Place Is at the Typewriter: Office Work and Office Workers 1870–1930.* Philadelphia: Temple University Press.

Drentea, Patricia. (1998). "Consequences of women's formal and informal job search methods for employment in female-dominated jobs." *Gender & Society,* 12:321–338.

England, Paula and Melissa S. Herbert. (1993). "The pay of men in 'female' occupations: Is comparable worth only for women?" Pp. 28–48 in *Doing "Women's Work": Men in Nontraditional Occupations.* Christine L. Williams (ed.). Newbury Park, CA: Sage.

Fonow, Mary Margaret. (1993). "Occupation/ steelworker: Sex/ female." Pp. 217–222 in *Feminist Frontiers III.* Laurel Richardson and Verta Taylor (eds.). New York: McGraw-Hill.

Gross, Edward. (1968). "*Plus ça change:* The sexual segregation of occupations over time." *Social Problems,* 16:198–208.

Hogan, Richard, Carolyn C. Perrucci, and Janet M. Wilmoth. (2000). "Gender inequality in employment and retirement income effects of marriage, industrial sector, and self-employment." Pp. 27–54 in *Advances in Gender Research, Vol. 4, Social Change for Women and Children.* Vasilikie Demos and Marcia Texler Segal (eds.). Stamford, CT: JAI.

Jacobs, Jerry. (1989). "Long-term trends in occupational segregation by sex." *American Journal of Sociology,* 95: 160–173.

Jacobsen, Joyce P. (1994). "Trends in work force sex segregation. 1960–1990." *Social Science Quarterly,* 75(1): 204–211.

Jones, Beverly W. (1984). "Race, sex, and class; black female tobacco workers in Durham, North Carolina, 1920–1940, and the development of female consciousness." Pp. 228–233 in *Feminist Frontiers IV.* Laurel Richardson, Verta Taylor, and Nancy Whittier (eds.). New York: McGraw-Hill.

Kanter, Rosabeth Moss. (1977). *Men and Women of the Corporation.* New York: Basic.

Kay, Fiona M. and John Hagan. (1998). "Raising the bar: The gender stratification of law-firm capital." *American Sociological Review,* 63:728–743.

King, Mary C. (1992). "Occupational segregation by race and sex, 1940–88." *Monthly Labor Review,* 115:30–36.

Kraut, Karen and Molly Luna. (1992). *Work and Wages: Facts on Women and People of Color in the Workforce.* Washington, DC: National Committee on Pay Equity.

MacCorquodale, Patricia and Gary Jensen. (1993). "Women in the law: Partners or tokens?" *Gender & Society,* 7:582–593.

Marini, Margaret Mooney and Pi-Ling Fan. (1997). "The gender gap in earnings at career entry." *American Sociological Review,* 62:588–604.

Milkman, Ruth. (1987). *Gender at Work: The Dynamics of Job Segregation by Sex During World War II.* Urbana: University of Illinois Press.

Nakano Glenn, Evelyn and Roslyn L. Feldberg. (1989). "Clerical work: The female occupation." Pp. 287–311 in *Women: A Feminist Perspective.* Jo Freeman (ed.). Mountain View, CA: Mayfield.

Reskin, Barbara F. (1994). "Segregating workers: Occupational differences by sex, race, and ethnicity." Paper presented at the annual meeting of the Population Association of America in San Francisco.

Reskin, Barbara F. and Heidi I. Hartmann. (1986). *Women's Work, Men's Work: Sex Segregation on the Job.* Washington, DC: National Academy Press.

Reskin, Barbara F. and Irene Padavic. (1994). *Women and Men at Work.* Thousand Oaks, CA: Pine Forge.

Reskin, Barbara F. and Polly A. Phipps. (1988). "Women in male-dominated professional and managerial occupations." Pp. 190–205 in *Women Working: Theories and Facts in Perspective,* Second Edition. Ann Helton Stromberg and Shirley Harkess (eds.). Mountain View, CA: Mayfield.

Reskin, Barbara F. and Patricia A. Roos (eds.). (1990). *Job Queues, Gender Queues: Explaining Women's Inroads into Male Occupations.* Philadelphia: Temple University Press.

Roos, Patricia A. (1990). "Hot-metal to electronic composition: Gender, technology, and social change." Pp. 275–298 in *Job Queues, Gender Queues: Explaining Women's Inroads into Male Occupations.* Barbara F. Reskin and Patricia A. Roos (eds.). Philadelphia: Temple University Press.

Silver, Catherine Bodare. (1981). "Public bureaucracy and private enterprise in the U.S.A. and France: Contexts for the attainment of executive positions by women." In *Access to Power: Cross-National Studies of Women and Elites.* Cynthia Fuchs Epstein and Rose Laub Coser (eds.). London: George Allen and Unwin.

Steiger, Thomas and Barbara F. Reskin. (1990). "Baking and baking off: Deskilling and the changing sex makeup of bakers." Pp. 257–274 in *Job Queues, Gender Queues: Explaining Women's Inroads into Male Occupations.* Barbara F. Reskin and Patricia A. Roos (eds.). Philadelphia: Temple University Press.

Tomaskovic-Devey, Donald. (1995). "Sex composition and gendered earnings inequality: A comparison of job and occupational models." Pp. 23–56 in *Gender Inequality at Work.* Jerry A. Jacobs (ed.). Thousand Oaks, CA: Sage.

U.S. Bureau of Labor Statistics. (1997). "Table 1. Table A-1. National employment and wage data from the occupational employment statistics survey by occupation, 1997."

[Web Page]. Accessed 3 August 1999. Available at http://stats.bls.gov;80/news.release/ocwage.t01.htm.

———. (1999). "D-20 median weekly earnings of full-time wage and salary workers by selected characteristics." [Web Page]. Accessed 13 August 1999. Available at http://www.bls.gov/cpseeq.htm.

U.S. Census Bureau. (1990). "Table 20. Occupation of employed persons: 1990." P. 20 in *Census of the Population. Social and Economic Characteristics. United States.* Washington, DC: Bureau of the Census.

———. (1998a). *The Official Statistics™.* "No. 672. Employed civilians, by occupations, sex, race, and Hispanic origin: 1983 and 1997." *Statistical Abstract of the United States.* [Web Page]. Accessed 7 August 1999. Available at http://www.census.gov/prod/3/98pubs/98statab/cc98stab.htm.

———. (1998b). *The Official Statistics™.* "No. 696. Full-time wage and salary workers—number and earnings: 1985 to 1997." *Statistical Abstract of the United States.* [Web Page]. Accessed 7 August 1999. Available at http://www.census.gov/prod/3/98pubs/98statab/cc98stab.htm.

Williams, Christine L. (1992). "The glass escalator: Hidden advantages for men in the 'female' professions." Pp. 193–207 in *Men's Lives,* Third Edition. Michael S. Kimmel and Michael A. Messner (eds.). Boston: Allyn and Bacon.

Women's Bureau, Department of Labor. (1999) "20 leading occupations of employed women: 1998 annual averages." [Web Page]. Accessed 7 August 1999. Available at http://www.dol.gov/dol/wb/public/wb_pubs/201ead98.htm.

The co-authors have equally contributed to this chapter and their order is alphabetical.

MEDIAN ANNUAL EARNINGS OF FULL-TIME, YEAR-ROUND WORKERS BY EDUCATION, RACE, AND HISPANIC ORIGIN, 1999

Irene Padavic and Barbara Reskin

Education	WOMEN			
	All Races	White	Black	Hispanic
Overall	$27,137	$27,600	$25,082	$20,242
Less than high school	$15,704	$15,661	$13,544	$13,879
High school graduate	$21,970	$22,247	$20,609	$19,923
Some college	$26,456	$26,850	$25,209	$24,236
Associate's degree	$30,129	$30,302	$27,198	$24,744
Bachelor's degree	$36,340	$36,672	$34,692	$31,996
Master's degree	$45,345	$45,772	$41,780	$43,718
Professional degree	$56,726	$59,223	*	*
Doctoral degree	$56,345	$58,577	*	*

Education	MEN			
	All Races	White	Black	Hispanic
Overall	$38,427	$40,138	$30,926	$25,242
Less than high school	$22,576	$22,981	$21,619	$18,960
High school graduate	$32,098	$33,147	$27,408	$25,291
Some college	$37,245	$38,463	$31,961	$31,446
Associate's degree	$40,474	$40,928	$31,206	$36,212
Bachelor's degree	$51,005	$51,606	$40,805	$41,467
Master's degree	$61,776	$61,691	$52,308	$50,410
Professional degree	$96,275	$96,863	*	*
Doctoral degree	$76,858	$80,359	*	*

Source: U.S. Census Bureau 2000. Current Population Reports, P60–209. "Money Income in the United States 1999." Table 10. Washington, D.C.: U.S. Government Printing Office. www.census.gov/prod/2000pubs/p60-209.pdf
Note: The categories of white and black include both Hispanics and non-Hispanics; the category Hispanic includes Hispanics of any race.
*No data were available for these categories due to small sample sizes.

"You Wouldn't Want One of 'Em Dancing with Your Wife": Racialized Bodies on the Job in World War II

There were a lot of women workers on board, mostly white. Whenever I passed the white women looked at me, some curiously, some coyly, some with open hostility. Some just stared with blank hard eyes. Few ever moved aside to let me pass. . . . Now and then some of the young white women gave me an opening to make a pass, but I'd never made one: at first because the coloured workers seemed as intent on protecting the white women from the coloured men as the white men were, probably because they wanted to prove to the white folks they could work with white women without trying to make them. . . .

—*"Bob Jones" in Chester Himes,*
If He Hollers Let Him Go, 1945

Racialized bodies dominate Chester Himes's home-front novel of social rage just as they provided a terrain of struggle in the wartime industry that forms its setting.[1] Obsessed with manhood and color, protagonist Bob Jones chafes under cultural notions of gender and race. This angry young African American migrant from Cleveland is a leaderman at a Los Angeles shipyard. Yet whites constantly undermine his authority as a supervisor. A white woman secretary keeps his blueprints locked away. A white Georgian foreman refuses to release a white woman tacker to Jones's all-black crew. Madge, "a peroxide blonde with a large-featured, overly made-up face" from Texas, taunts him through her whiteness, sure that white men "had to protect her from black rapists."[2] Her insulting refusal to work for Jones (she calls him "nigger") provokes him to curse her ("screw you then, you cracker bitch!"), leading to his demotion.[3]

At the novel's climax, Madge locks Jones into a cabin berth, crying "rape" when inspectors discover them. Though rejecting the sexual overtures of this

southern temptress, he becomes ensnarled anyway in the rape-lynching complex that has colonized his mind as well as the imagination of white co-workers.[4] The novel ends when Madge withdraws her charge of rape—"a patriotic gesture comparable only to the heroism of men in battle," the shipyard President explains, that would avoid the racial conflict ever threatening to disrupt industrial output.[5] Jones is forced to enter the army, a no-choice plea bargain for possessing a concealed gun. . . .

If He Hollers Let Him Go echoes the shopfloor and sidewalk conflict experienced by working people in the crowded production centers of the second World War. It dramatizes the pyschological hurt among African American men that fatter wartime paychecks failed to assure. "Fair" employment—that is, without discrimination—did not necessarily bring dignity. It was not the same as "equal" employment—similar job placements—in a society still burdened by legalized segregation and cultural constructions that differentiated people by their race *and* gender. Racialized understandings of manhood and womanhood—of the black male rapist, the pure white female, and the uncleanly black woman—provided an arena for the wartime debate over fair employment, one connected to larger structures of power and authority. . . .

The field investigations and complaints of discrimination to the President's Committee on Fair Employment Practices (FEPC) during the war, like . . . Himes's imaginative novel, serve as lenses into the complex dynamics of race and gender within class society. Though scholars often attempt to disaggregate the working of "race" from "gender," these constructions have existed in conjunction with one another to transform profoundly the ways that each works alone. Insight into "the inseparable unity of race and gender" derives from black women's studies which long has recognized the racial construction of gender, class, and sexuality.[6] But this paradigmatic definition of one category of anaysis in terms of the others is even more interactive than usually noted. Race itself is gendered, as historian Tessie Liu contends; it "functions through controlling sexuality and sexual behavior."[7] Constructed through gendered representations, race in turn reconstructs gender identities and class hierarchies. The concept of racialized gender reflects this interaction. It not only assumes differences based on race among women and men and differences based on gender among groups defined by race, ethnicity, or nationhood. It further stands as "a primary field within which or by means of which power is articulated," to extend the insight that historian Joan Scott brought to discussions of gender, deriving its meaning from political struggle and in turn offering a language through which politics operates and people comprehend their lives.[8] . . .

During World War II, African Americans sought equality of treatment, the end of legal segregation and unequal facilities, an integrated army, and better paying defense jobs. But they struggled to be heard against a discourse that displaced demands for economic equity into openings for sexual intimacy. This article deviates from the dominant economistic reading of industrial conflict during the Second World War by focusing on what cultural theorist Robyn Wiegman has called "the transformation of the economic into the sexual"[9] through analysis of confrontations sparked by bodily closeness on shopfloors, streetcars, and other public spaces. Some of these involved white women who refused to share toilet and dressing facilities with black ones; some were rank and file workers defying their unions; employer strategies to divide the laboring force encouraged others. In doing so, it begins to study white resistance to the African American quest for equality by moving from the workplace through the neighborhood to confront "fears of sexual mixing and its consequences."[10]

Though bound by the rules of segregation, blacks and whites in the South had lived in closer proximity than elsewhere in the nation. Many white Northerners and Westerners had little contact with African Americans. Wartime population shifts and labor needs pierced such boundaries and generated interaction, especially in such expanded production centers as Los Angeles, California's East Bay, and Detroit, precisely at a time when accelerated entrance of white women into factories also challenged women's and men's proper places.[11] Still, as subordinate workers, wives,

canteen hostesses, and other objects of the male gaze, white and black women often stood as bodies through which black as well as white men constructed their own masculinity.

In emphasizing the connections among sexuality, race, and gender, this portrait leaves to others the task of disaggregating worker and management responses by region, union, and industry. Instead, it relies on critical race and gender theory, cultural analysis, and social history to move beyond the terms of the existing scholarly debate over the relationship between race and class. That debate often treats gender as separate, sometimes parallel, but rarely central to understanding the nexus between race and class, themselves both engendered indentities and categories of analysis.[12]

THE PRESIDENT'S COMMITTEE ON FAIR EMPLOYMENT PRACTICE

Through Executive Order 8802, President Franklin D. Roosevelt created the FEPC in June 1941 to end discrimination in employment related to the war effort. FEPC targeted African Americans and other racial minorities, Jews and other religious minorities, and noncitizens or those not of United States nationality. However, African Americans filed more than 90 percent of the complaints. FEPC did not include women as a separate category, only as members of other, covered groups. A subsequent Executive Order, 9346, reconstituted the Committee as an independent agency in May 1943 under the Office of Emergency Management; this occurred after an earlier transfer of FEPC to the War Manpower Commission (WMC) in 1942.[13]

FEPC was a weak agency; it worked by complaint only and could not impose sanctions or file its own court cases. It held public and private hearings, attempting to jawbone adherence to the Presidential order. It often failed to upgrade the jobs of black workers or even get them hired. But its dedicated biracial staff of administrators and field officers tirelessly investigated business, unions, the military, and government, including the Federal Employment Service, creatively bringing recalcitrants to the attention of agencies that had enforcement teeth. . . .

Throughout its lifetime (1941–1946), the FEPC faced challenges from opponents. Southern Democrats filibustered its appropriations and blocked legislation to create a permanent agency; conservative northern Republicans agreed that it undermined "freedom of contract," linking government regulation of industry with government interference with personal association. A Mississippi congressman expressed this connection when he declared: "the relation between the employer and the employee is intimate"; one from Louisiana spoke of forcing "employers of the Nation, particularly in the South, to intermix the Negro along with his white employees."[14]

These congressmen fought against the agency as an attempt to "saddle social equality upon Dixie," as the African American *Pittsburgh Courier* described Southern white opinion.[15] Senator Richard Russell (D-Georgia) in 1946 attacked FEPC as a "measure . . . which would have a tendency to bring about social equality and intermingling and amalgamation of the races."[16] A Texas Democratic candidate for Congress condemned the agency for having 60 percent of its personnel as "negroes. Some of the black executives have white women for secretaries," he charged. Others lambasted FEPC for making white and black women use the same bathrooms. Georgia Governor Eugene Talmadge charged "Negroes of the North, finding a lot of craven politicians amenable to their desires, have succeeded in creating a condition under which white and colored persons are mixed indiscriminately in various departments at Washington." FEPC was unsettling the natural order of things, further abetting a social liberalism symbolized by First Lady Eleanor Roosevelt's support for civil rights.[17]

This defensiveness against "social equality" suggests how wartime conditions threatened the racialized gendered regime, in part by undermining the southern system of cheap labor. Black migration to war production centers cut the supply of field workers, but so too did money sent home from defense work and the military. Black women became less dependent on field work just as the greater options of black men led them to demand more control over tenancy. Labor shortages meant that white farm wives took to the fields during harvest time. Black women also left domestic service, which led to rumors of "Eleanor Clubs" or "Disappointment Clubs" with the "motto 'A white woman in every kitchen by Christmas.'" Such clubs would allow members "to 'get even' with their former white employers for past grievances."[18]

During a time when the behavior of African American soldiers—their courage in combat and their dating of British, Australian, and other "white" women—further upset inherited expectations, the homefront also offered possibilities for disruption and protest, spaces to contest sexualized representations of African Americans and challenge the use of social equality as a barrier to economic equality.[19] The "Double Victory" campaign, after all, connected battlefront and homefront, defeat of the Nazis with victory against Jim Crow.[20]

THE HOMEFRONT AS A SITE OF INTIMACY

Men as well as women had their bodies racialized in the contest over fair employment during World War II. Congressional investigation of the "checkerboarding" of the merchant marine, or sending to sea racially mixed crews, illuminates how the discourse of social equality justified job discrimination. In some workplaces, like mines, black and white men labored beside each other, but ships were particular places of intimacy, with homosocial—if not homoerotic—undertones.[21] Secretary of the Navy Frank Knox, who refused to use black men for anything other than mess crews, rejected the idea that "Negro and white sailors should be compelled to live together."[22] The Seafarers' International Union admitted black members, but complained to a special investigative committee under the conservative Virginia Democrat Howard W. Smith that the War Shipping Administration (WSA) deliberately sent out black and white men for the same ships. This bypassed the union's "rotary hiring hall system," which union spokesmen called, "fair and equitable in every way, which enables whites to share ships' quarters with whites and Negroes with Negroes." The union claimed equal wages, working conditions, and membership rights for African Americans, but black workers suffered from occupational segregation by race and held lesser paying jobs in the Steward's Department. Because their task was to cook and serve food, they did not eat with the rest of the crew.[23]

Yet the union charged the WSA with

> misrepresenting or concealing the facts when it recruits boys from American homes and then tries to compel them to depart abruptly from old-time family traditions to share eating and sleeping quarters on American ships with members of another race, particularly when such a condition is not at all necessary and is disruptive of rather than helpful to the war effort.[24]

Or as one congressional opponent of the FEPC put it, "human nature" meant that white men "have set ideas as to how they want to sleep or how they want to live. They haven't any prejudice against the colored men."[25]

In this tale, not only did racial separation (in the form of separate but equal) aid the war by maintaining full efficiency, but "family," "tradition," and "American" stood apart from men of African descent. Economic power, as well as social authority, was at stake.

All parties to the seafarers' dispute felt, as another congressman explained, "the colored men ought to have the right to work just like the white man."[26] Defenders of the union claimed equality of opportunity, while asserting that the circumstances of shiplife determined which men went to which ship. Administration officials clashed with congressmen over this interpretation of "equality." One Assistant Deputy Administrator of the WSA dodged inquiries over whether the FEPC executive orders "require[d] in any way the social intermingling of different races" by arguing that FEPC sought "full manpower utilization," but felt unable to answer if there was "any emphasis at all . . . on social equality." However, the Atlantic Coast Regional Representative admitted that "the order does not require" social intermingling, though "full utilization of manpower" included "employment" which took place "aboard ship" as well as "ashore" and "in the Government." Men who work on ships lived on them at the same time. Congressional inquisitors pushed him to admit that such employment would lead to social equality. In this case, equal opportunity and "social intermingling" merged into each other. But Representative Claire Hoffman (R-Mich.) was unsatisfied that social equality was anything but another name for intermarriage. A hearing about men on ship degenerated into questions about whether men and women of different races could choose to marry each other. The (il)logic became: men on ships lead to miscegenation.[27]

Rumors of social equality countered African American assertiveness. During the Spring of 1944 in Dallas, "a large group of Negroes," whose votes had ushered in the Congress of Industrial Organization (CIO) at their plant, became dissatisfied with both the union contract and the pace of War Labor Board (WLB) deliberations over an equal pay complaint. They went to the WLB offices, "acting in their own behalf"—"an extraordinary occurrence" in Texas, according to the FEPC regional director. They protested in a context in which "rumors, the dissemination of leaflets, news articles tending to rile up the people" poisoned relations between white and black workers. Employees heard "that a Negro worker passed a note to a white woman worker in which he asked her to meet him after work." White workers could read the leaflet, "Do You Want

Your Daughter to Marry a Negro?" which had "been spot dropped all over Texas." The FEPC sought to defuse tensions prior to the July Democratic National Convention, but the presence of black men and white women at the same workplaces offered kindling to those who desired to enflame white racial interests in the face of black economic demands.[28] . . .

Fear of bodily closeness was real: It sparked workplace confrontations that interrupted war production and brought charges of discrimination before the FEPC. Shortages of housing and transportation intensified gender mixing among the races in public spaces as well as workplaces. As one white bus rider in Alabama complained,

> "You have paid your fare to be transported to work, only to have some negro hanging over you "with" his body touching you from time to time—or worse, "hanging over the white women and girls."[29]

Rumors of black "'bumpers' and 'pushers' clubs" circulated among whites in Detroit and other cities, some spread by "an upper-middle class white group."[30] A Los Angeles shipfitter recorded a conversation with his AFL representative who justified a "Negro Auxiliary" by reminding him, "Our unions give social affairs. You wouldn't want one of 'em dancing with your wife, would you."[31]

A schism actually developed "over the question of interracial social functions" at the P. R. Mallory Plant in Indianapolis in late 1944 when Local 1005 of the United Electrical Workers (UE-CIO) planned a union dance. The company personnel director feared that "such functions" would "crystallize the sentiments of a good many white workers, not only against mixed social gatherings, but also against the Negro workers as a whole" and thus "jeopardise the continued success of the Mallory upgrading program for Negro workers." As with Communist unionists at other UE plants, here militant support of integration challenged the practices of the white workforce, in this case one more politically and socially conservative than the International.[32] But not all black workers lobbied for integration; most had "refrained from attending, by tacit agreement," previous dances. The FEPC investigator noted:

> Although its members have voiced very little opposition to the employment and upgrading of Negroes, and there has been surprisingly little racial friction in work situations, they have not yet reached the stage

where they can face the social equality bugaboo with equanimity. They tend to feel that only people with communistic leanings openly favor such equality.[33]

White local union officers sought to "maneuver" both the company personnel manager and black members of the union bargaining committee to sabotage interracial dances; they connected "social equality" to communists and both to the loss of control over their local to a more radical, distant International. This association they shared with southern opponents of FEPC, who later would condemn the ClO's "Operation Dixie" by linking social equality, trade unionism, and communism.[34] In contrast, the FEPC and the International representative agreed that "no CIO local can put itself in the position of favoring segregation in any form," and thus rejected either racially separate meetings to determine the make-up of social functions or segregated functions themselves. Despite a postponed union dance and separate company Christmas parties, P. R. Mallory continued to employ black workers, hiring about 500 black women (out of 800 women) in early January for a new battery division.[35]

From management's perspective, forced integration might disrupt shopfloor routines. From that of labor militants, lack of integration reinforced divisions within the union that would curtail a solidarity which might be needed against the company. By separating themselves socially, workers undermined the equality promised by the CIO and the quest for a more democratic America. Though the CIO tried to promote a "culture of unity" through dances and other social events, as historian Lisabeth Cohen has argued, rank and file unionists did not necessarily include African Americans in that culture. Black social scientists St. Clair Drake and Horace R. Cayton discovered resistance even in the late 1930s to "social extensions of economic contact." As "an Italian president of a steel workers' women's auxiliary" informed "another white woman":

> My husband and I have said to each other, you give them a foot and they'll take a yard. If you ask them to your dances they'll come and they don't just dance with each other but some of them will try to dance with white people. If they do, the white women will just stop going to the dances.

Though recognizing African Americans as fellow "workers" and "that, really, they *are* human," she felt

guilty—"not liberal enough"—for thinking "there's something about colored men that just makes you *afraid*. I don't know what it is, but you have a certain *fear* . . . there's something about them—that black skin." Black women, however, evoked in her no comparable fears.[36] Whites focused on the black body, describing black coworkers in terms of neatness, cleaniness, voice pitch, overall deportment, and physical proximity to their own bodies.[37] . . .

These fears and apprehensions occurred against a backdrop of sexual harassment and brutality toward African American women that fully matched the vile rhetoric of Southern Democratic Congressmen. The *Pittsburgh Courier* noted the hypocrisy of [the] call for racial purity when respectable black women in Washington, D.C., "schoolteachers, professionals, war-widows, co-eds . . . are so molested by white men (to whom all colored women are simply objects of prey) that they cannot walk a single block . . . without being invited to 'come go for a nice ride.' "[38] A serviceman's wife had to leave a better paying job at the Pennsylvania Railway after refusing the advances of the white foreman.[39] White men raped black schoolgirls and soldiers' wives; they beat and sometimes killed black women. But they never received punishment equal to the long prison sentences and occasional lynching that black men still faced for even calling a white woman on a phone. These white assailants included policemen and landlords intent on enforcing southern racial and social hierarchies.[40] A partial exception to the degrading treatment of black women came with the response to the Abbeville, Alabama kidnap and rape of Recy Taylor, "22-year-old mother and wife of a U.S. soldier." After northern radicals and southern liberals created a *cause celebre*, the governor promised "to press charges."[41] The rhetorical protection of white women continued to mask attacks on black women into the 1940s. But such incidents also suggest that wartime rhetoric and economic change encouraged black women to challenge the place set aside for them in the white South.

SHOPFLOOR CONFRONTATIONS

Southern white males certainly defined physical proximity between white women and black men as objectionable. At a Birmingham, Alabama sheet metal mill, white union members struck for a day because "the clocking lines for Negroes and whites had been placed too close together." As the committeeman for the steelworkers union noted, black men "had no business in the line with the white ladies and wished they would segregate them." Although black workers had other things on their minds—"to get out and take a bath and go home"—than sharing a line with "ladies" (the customary appellation for white women), "Negro Sam" reportedly told him, "if one stubbed his toe and happened to brush against a white woman they could not make her or any one believe it was not done on purpose." White men defended white womanhood, their control of the shopfloor, and their hold on skilled jobs. The company responded by segregating facilities.[42]

White women themselves objected to working with both black men and women. According to the vice-president of the Mobile-based Alabama Dry Dock and Shipbuilding Company, white "young bucks and girls" attacked black men upgraded to welding jobs on 24 May 1943. The company had hired white women over black men and women after they had "scraped the bottom of the barrel as far as [white] men are concerned." Such women would come to constitute 11.6 percent of the workforce, numbering over 3,000. They became socialized into aspects of the work culture of the shipyards. So perhaps it was not surprising that "Women Joined Men in Clubbing and Stoning Negro Ship Workers," reported the liberal New York daily *PM*. They used "bricks and iron bars." "A white lady," one black man noted, "hit me over the head with a broom handle." In surveying the incident, a national official of the Marine and Shipbuilding Workers of America suggested that white women had started the violence by "belabor[ing] colored women with sticks and stones and *then* white men began to beat colored male workers." Among the precipitating rumors was one that "a Negro welder had killed a white woman the night before." The *Mobile Register* blamed "indiscreet mingling of white and negro workers."[43] What appeared as economic conflict expressed fears of proximity and took violent physical form.

A more peaceful incident occurred in St. Louis at the U.S. Cartridge Company that same month. Management and trade union officers often predicted that white women would stop work with the introduction of black workers; here they did. White women walked off the job when the company transferred some fifty to seventy black floormen and material handlers from the segregated black building to their unit.[44] Local black activist David Grant blamed management for segregating the plant in the first place. Before a congressional committee, he explained that

management . . . could not get any white men. They were not available. In other words, they had created this situation. These women, who had been working in this plant, had their minds set on the condition as it existed, and they would not work with these Negroes in there. So they quit work.[45]

Black male workers, in turn, refused to labor under a white foreman.[46]

There were economic consequences to separating black and white bodies. Segregation undermined seniority and had a negative effect on the employment and retention of black women, who had been the last hired. Mrs. Beatrice Marshall complained to the FEPC that a newspaper advertised in September 1943 for "2,000 women wanted to make bullets. No experience. No training period. Good pay." But women meant white women for personnel told her that they were not hiring anymore for building 202; they were not recruiting women for the "colored" building. Bertha Brown likewise suffered from the company's policy of segregation when she was laid off, although she had more seniority than some whites. Truly plant-wide seniority (seniority was plant-wide except for building 202) would have placed black and white women in much closer proximity and might have forced white women to work next to black men, what had led to the May walkout by the white women. Significantly, the company differentiated the kind of ammunition it had white and black workers make, so that their expertise was not exactly interchangeable.[47] This segregation of black workers on their own product in their own division/building resembled the strategy deployed by other companies that separated women workers and relegated their seniority to divisions established only for the duration of the war. Employers and unions could thus by-pass the issue of "equal pay for equal work" by claiming different work.[48] In late December 1944, FEPC ordered U.S. Cartridge to hire and promote black workers, but by then, the war and heightened production were nearly over.[49] These examples illustrate how management reinforced white shopfloor resistance; its decisions maintained racial separation.

THE TOILET AS A SITE OF STRUGGLE

The toilet and bathroom, places for the most private bodily functions, became sites of conflict; their integration starkly symbolized social equality. Atlanta segregationists attempted to block the opening of a regional office of the FEPC in November 1943 by refusing office space to the FEPC's biracial staff, who would not only interview black plaintiffs there but also share the building's toilets with other federal agencies. After pressure from regional congressmen failed and the office opened, newspaper and political harassment persisted. Cries of " 'brazen negress' and 'carpetbaggers'" greeted the hiring of an African American woman secretary. Talmadge fanned white opinion when he spoke of the introduction of "a flat-nosed mulatto" and reported, "the white girls were stunned at first." After appealing to his successor, Governor Ellis Arnall, to stop a travesty, Talmadge claimed that "the white women painted a large sign on the rest room door that said 'White Only,' but this 'BRAZEN LITTLE NEGRO' ignored it." A new toilet built for FEPC black employees ended the commotion. A former FEPC official told historian Merl Reed that the Regional Director "became so exasperated that he sent to Eleanor Roosevelt memoranda drafted on toilet paper."[50]

Concepts of purity that distinguished white women from African Americans lay behind discriminatory acts.[51] White workers based moral judgments on physical appearance; as one woman admitted, "I always thought colored people were not clean and smelled bad and weren't as good as white people." Manuals for managers attempted to counter notions fanned by racist southern politicians "that Negroes have a peculiar body odor; that it is unpleasant to remain in close proximity to them" and "that there is an extraordinarily high incidence of social disease among Negroes." Syphilis rates were high among whites as well as blacks in areas of "low economic status." Still some employers acted as if high black rates of syphilis were "a well-known scientific fact." A hospital in Oakland, California, for example, refused to hire "experienced Negro girls" as dieticians because "Negroes couldn't pass Wassermann tests." A New York State handbook reminded managers that "the possibility of acquiring a venereal disease by contact with a toilet is exceeding remote." Such manuals also pointed out that black women and men not only cleaned public and private toilets but care for children, prepare food, and "handle much of the linen and make up the beds of many white Americans." A domestic's touch could be ignored in ways that bodily closeness at the job apparently could not; private service work reinforced racialized gender hierarchies in ways that public intimacy undermined them.[52]

Despite the attempt by some managers to alleviate fears, "the cleanliness taboo" generated resistance to using the same toilet, shower, and locker room facilities, especially on the part of white women.[53] Sometimes these resisters merely threatened to leave work to see if they could push management to remove black women, but "had no intention of really going through with their threat because they knew it might jeopardize their own jobs," as happened at a Buffalo, New York aircraft factory.[54] Other times they shut down production. Fifteen hundred United Automobile Union members walked out in the spring of 1944 when Chevrolet Motors refused "to rehire seven woman workers who had balked at working alongside four Negro women," who presumably would use the same toilets. When more than half the labor force of the U.S. Rubber Company in Detroit struck a few months before, they demanded that black women machinists "be transferred" or the company provide separate toilets for them. In contrast, lack of racial friction at Pullman's railroad operations may have derived from company adherence to segregated toilets and related facilities.[55] . . .

The experience of discrimination was gendered. Previously crowded into service and agricultural labor and thus thought of as a non-industrial workforce, African American women labored against stereotypical images of their bodies, against representations as Mammy or Sapphire.[56] Not only did they receive "the left-over and undesirable jobs in war industries," but they confronted barriers of "physical types . . . and intangibles not imposed on white female workers." Personnel managers drew upon the picture of the fat black woman to reject applicants. As one such woman recalled, "one time they say we was to old and the next time we were too fat. I only weight 165—5 feet 3 inch—46 years and still these [white] women weight 200 pound and some much older then 50 years."[57] African American women had to engage in additional maintenance or survival labor, a form of self and community care work, to reproduce themselves as neater, pleasanter, more cooperative than their white counterparts, to make whites feel more comfortable around them. They had to dress well and act respectable in public, whether engaging in the activities of everyday life or protesting discrimination.[58]

Regarded as different, black and white women saw each other as racialized bodies, not merely gendered ones, and so would develop insults that impugned the womanhood of the other. One group of black women at General Electric refused to work after a white woman inspector allegedly "called a colored woman worker either 'Black Son of a Bitch' or 'Black Heifer.'" The army feared "possible violence."[59] At the Fisk Tire and Rubber Company, Chicopee Falls, Massachusetts, a white woman "alleged that the colored girl was in a state of pregnancy. The girl happens to be unmarried," the FEPC regional director reported, "and the rumor spread like wildfire through the shop. It affected the girl so badly that she went to her doctor and procured a certificate stating that she was not in a state of pregnancy."[60] Given feelings of racial superiority, that white women rejected black women having any authority over them hardly surprises. At a California draft board, a white man was promoted supervisor rather than a black woman because white women rejected the notion of "a Negro [telling] white people what to do."[61] The belief that women could not get along with each other—that "we needed a man to keep peace and harmony between the girls"[62]— reflected the reality of some workplaces and offered an excuse for discrimination in others. Men continued to predominate as supervisors, with gender-mixed black crews coming under male leadership.

THE SPECTER OF SOCIAL EQUALITY

Worker responses to wartime integration occured in a political context in which demagogic politicians vilified the FEPC. Working people worried about social equality. "As the friendships became more intimate the white employee speculated as to how friendly he might become with a Negro employee without admitting him to 'social equality,'" participant observer Bernice Reed noted of a West coast aircraft factory. "A white female employee" wondered, "'If I go to X's house to visit his wife and babies will that be socializing? I wouldn't call that socializing, would you, just to go by to see his babies?" Most interracial friendships stopped at the plant gate, but Reed concluded that "management accommodated to integration of Negro employees less readily than non-supervisory employees."[63]

The promise of social equality—confused by its opponents with non-discrimination in the workplace— challenged the larger social and political hierarchies

that gripped the nation. Shopfloor integration—where black and white, male and female bodies labored in close proximity—stood as the material and symbolic embodiment of social equality. In seeking to exclude African Americans from war jobs, white workers reacted to what they perceived to be more than an economic threat. Women as well as men recoiled from "black skin." Fear of the other, of different bodies, encapsulated wartime tensions, disruptions, and insecurities. This is not to argue that all or most white workers responded to racial pornography; racial demagogues had no monopoly on image painting. Alternative signifiers certainly existed and trade union leadership, from the CIO and especially from its left-led unions, at times provided a counterpoint to both local union racism and the fear of social equality.[64]

Throughout the Jim Crow era, white supremacists had embodied opposition to social, political, and economic equality in the menacing figure of the black male rapist and the demeaning image of the uncleanly black woman. What was new during WWII was an official ideology of pluralist inclusion that facilitated the transformation of the foreign born into the American but also delegitimated racism in the face of Nazism. The federal government, however tentative, became involved in combating workplace discrimination among employers as well as unions. State action further encouraged the aspirations of African Americans who demanded fair treatment from a country for which their men were dying. Black workers claimed the rights of citizenship on the job as well as in the community. They believed in fairness, and asked to be "treated as an American and not as a Negro," to be just a man, as Bob Jones dreamed.[65] Such a vision remained tied to the equation of masculinity with freedom that had distinguished the black liberation movement even before the abolition of slavery.[66] It neglected black women's distinct experiences, just as FEPC failed to include sex. Nonetheless, the wartime struggle for fair employment illuminates the simultaneity of race and gender in the self-construction, social perception, and, not the least, scholarly re-construction of identity that mark the quest for equity and justice at century's end no less than during World War II.

NOTES

I would like to thank Cindy Aron, Ava Baron, Patricia Cooper, Robin D. G. Kelley, Andrew Kersten, Dan Letwin, Nelson Lichtenstein, Bruce Nelson, Laura Tabili, Deborah Gray White and the editors, reviewers, and board of *American Quarterly* for comments on previous versions of this article. The Faculty Research Program in the Social Sciences, Humanities, and Education, Howard University, funded this project.

1. Epigraph from Chester Himes, *If He Hollers Let Him Go* (1947; New York, 1986), 18. Doubleday originally published this novel in 1945. Robert E. Skinner, "The Black Man in the Literature of Labor: The Early Novels of Chester Himes," *Labor's Heritage* 1 (July 1989): 50–65; Stephen F. Milliken, *Chester Himes: A Critical Appraisal* (Columbia, Mo., 1976), 70–96; James Lundquist, *Chester Himes* (New York, 1976), 26–47; Gilbert H. Muller, *Chester Himes* (Boston, 1989), 20–29; for his works, Michel Fabre, et al., *Chester Himes: An Annotated Primary and Secondary Bibliography* (New York, 1992).

2. Himes, *If He Hollers*, 19, 125. For Madge in context, Phyllis R. Klotman, "The White Bitch Archetype in Contemporary Black Fiction," *Bulletin of the Midwest Modern Language Association* 6 (spring 1973): 96–110. Following the novel itself, I refer to Madge by her first name.

3. Himes, *If He Hollers*, 27.

4. See the now classic statement by Jacqueline Dowd Hall, "'The Mind That Burns in Each Body': Women, Rape, and Racial Violence," in *Powers of Desire: The Politics of Sexuality*, ed. Ann Snitow, Christine Stansell, and Sharon Thompson (New York, 1983), 328–49; and Hall's *Revolt against Chivalry: Jessie Daniel Ames and the Women's Campaign against Lynching*, rev. ed. (New York, 1993).

5. Himes, *If He Hollers*, 201.

6. Evelyn Brooks Higginbotham, "African-American Women's History and the Metalanguage of Race," *Signs: Journal of Women in Culture and Society* 17 (winter 1992): 273.

7. Tessie Liu, "Teaching the Differences Among Women from a Historical Perspective: Rethinking Race and Gender as Social Categories," in *Unequal Sisters: A Multicultural Reader in U.S. Women's History*, ed. Vicki L. Ruiz and Ellen Carol DuBois, 2d ed. (New York, 1994), 571, 577.

8. Joan Scott, "Gender: A Useful Category of Historical Analysis," in her *Gender and the Politics of History* (New York, 1988), 45–46. In formulating the concept "racialized gender," I have relied on Evelyn Nakano Glenn, "From Servitude to Service Work: Historical Continuities in the Racial Division of Paid Reproductive Labor," *Signs: Journal of Women in Culture and Society* 18 (fall 1992): 1–43; Fiona Williams, *Social Policy: A Critical Introduction to Issues of Race, Gender and Class* (Cambridge, 1989); Gwendolyn Mink, *The Wages of Motherhood: Inequality in the Welfare State, 1917–1942* (Ithaca, N.Y., 1995).

9. Robyn Wiegman, *American Anatomies: Theorizing Race and Gender* (Durham, N.C., 1995), 100.

10. Gary Gerstle, "Working-Class Racism: Broaden the Focus," *International Labor and Working-Class History* 44 (fall 1993): 33–40.

11. On wartime boom towns and their tensions, see, for example, Marilynn S. Johnson, *The Second Gold Rush: Oakland and the East Bay in World War II* (Berkeley, Calif., 1993). Historians disagree on whether the war years challenged women's place. For different interpretations, see D'Ann Campbell, *Women at War with America: Private Lives in a Patriotic Era* (Cambridge, Mass., 1984), 74–76, 107; Susan Hartmann, *The Home Front and Beyond: American Women in the 1940s* (Boston, 1982), 77–82.

12. In "What If Labor Were Not White and Male? Recentering Working-Class History and Reconstructing Debate on Unions and Race," *International Labor and Working-Class History* 51 (spring 1997), 72–95, David Roediger recognizes the necessity of the approach called for here. Bruce Nelson's otherwise fine essay "Class, Race and Democracy in the CIO: The 'New' Labor History Meets the 'Wages of Whiteness,'" *International Review of Social History* 41 (Dec. 1996): 351–74, neglects gender. In contrast, he skillfully weaves gendered concerns into the overall analysis in "Organized Labor and the Struggle for Black Equality in Mobile during World War II," *Journal of American History* 80 (Dec. 1993): 952–88. See also, Kevin Boyle. "The Kiss: Racial and Gender Conflict in a 1950s Automobile Factory," *Journal of American History* 84 (Sept. 1997): 496–523; Herbert Hill, "The Problem of Race in American Labor History," *Reviews in American History* 24 (June 1996): 189–208 discusses race and class separate from gender. Outside of historians of women, Robin D. G. Kelley most skillfully engenders analysis of the black working-class in *Race Rebels: Culture, Politics, and the Black Working Class* (New York, 1994). See also, Tera W. Hunter, *To 'Joy My Freedom: Southern Black Women's Lives and Labors After the Civil War* (Cambridge, Mass., 1997).

13. Roosevelt was responding to pressure from A. Philip Randolph and his March on Washington Movement. Merl E. Reed, *Seedtime for the Modern Civil Rights Movement: The President's Committee on Fair Employment Practice 1941–1946* (Baton Rouge, La., 1991); also see, Herbert Hill, *Black Labor and the American Legal System: Race, Work, and the Law* (Madison, Wisc., 1985), 173–381; Donna Cooper Hamilton and Charles V. Hamilton, *The Dual Agenda: The African-American Struggle for Civil and Economic Equality* (New York, 1997), 43–66; Paul D. Moreno, *From Direct Action to Affirmative Action: Fair Employment Law and Policy in America, 1933–1972* (Baton Rouge, La., 1997), 66–83.

14. For example, Representative Whittington (D-Miss.), 12 July 1945, *Congressional Record–House*, 7490; Representative Charles E. McKenzie (D-La.), 26 June 1945, *Appendix to the Congressional Record*, A 3083; for a Northern Republican opponent, Claire Hoffman (R-Mich.), 2 Feb. 1949, *Congressional Record–House*, 771.

15. "What About the FEPC?" *Pittsburgh Courier*, 17 Apr. 1943. For the black press, Lee Finkle, *Forum for Protest: The Black Press During World War II* (Madison, N.J., 1975).

16. Said during FEPC filibuster, as quoted by Smith, *Killers of the Dream*, 78.

17. On race and FEPC personnel, Hon. O. C. Fisher of Texas in the House of Representatives, 20 June 1944, *Proposed Permanent F.E.P.C. Would Outlaw Segregation Laws and Change Economic System* (Washington, D.C., 1944), 4, 7 [not printed at government expense], box 4, file: "July–Dec. 1944";

"Governor Talmadge Right About Social Equality Move," from Gladsden, Ala., *Times*, 21 June 1942, in FEPC "Press Clippings Digest," no.4, 6 July 1942, 17, box 3, file: "Aug.–Dec. 42," both in FEPC-FDR Library. On Eleanor Roosevelt, Joanna Schneider Zangrando and Robert L. Zangrando, "ER and Black Civil Rights," in *Without Precedent: The Life and Career of Eleanor Roosevelt*, ed. Joan Hoff-Wilson and Marjorie Lightman (Bloomington, Ind., 1984), 88–107.

18. See, for example, confidential report, "Race Tension and Farm Wages in the Rural South," 22 Sept. 1943, esp. 2–5, attached to letter to Jonathan Daniels from Arthur Raper, 25 Sept. 1945, in box 4, file: "Aug.–Sept. 43," FEPC-FDR Library; S.I. Hayakawa, "Second Thoughts: The Mythical 'Eleanor Clubs,'" *Chicago Defender*, 5 Feb. 1944; "New 'Disappointment Club' Rumors Have Dixie Worried," *Chicago Defender*, 22 Jan. 1944; Howard W. Odum, *Race and Rumors of Race: The American South in the Early Forties* (Chapel Hill, N.C., 1943), 73–80.

19. George Padmore, "Mixed Offspring Creates New Social Problem in England," *Pittsburgh Courier*, 18 Nov. 1944, 4; "Bias Prevents GI from Bringing French Bride to Home in States," *Pittsburgh Courier*, 22 Sept. 1945, 11; War Department, Washington, D.C., Ag. 291.1 (11 Sept. 43), Subject: Overseas Marriages of Military Personnel. To: The Commander-in-Chief, Southwest Pacific Area, attached to Stanley J. Grogan to Jonathan Daniels, 22 May 1944, box 4, folder: A-J 44, FEPC-FDR Library.

20. On the double V campaign, see Pfeffer, *A. Philip Randolph*, 45–88; for the homefront during the war, Earl Lewis, *In Their Own Interests: Race, Class, and Power in Twentieth-Century Norfolk, Virginia* (Berkeley, Calif., 1991), pp. 167–98; Joe William Trotter, Jr., *Black Milwaukee: The Making of an Industrial Proletariat, 1915–45* (Urbana, Ill., 1985), pp. 147–95; August Meier and Elliott Rudwick, *Black Detroit and the Rise of the UAW* (New York: Oxford Univ. Press, 1979); Sally M. Miller and Daniel A. Cornford, eds., *American Labor in the Era of World War II* (Westport, Conn., 1995), esp. those in pt. III, "Race, Gender, and Community"; Gretchen Lemke-Santangelo, *Abiding Courage: African American Migrant Women and the East Bay Community* (Chapel Hill, N.C., 1996).

21. For a discussion of sailors and homosexuality, see George Chauncy, *Gay New York: Gender, Urban Culture and the Making of the Gay Male World, 1890–1940* (New York, 1994), 76–86. For another case of male "physical proximity" involving long-haul trucking, see *Final Report: Fair Employment Practice Committee, June 28, 1946* (Washington, D.C., 1947), 22–23.

22. Press Release, "President Roosevelt Opposes Negro March on Washington," 4, report of conference of 18 June 1941, in C. R. Dellums Papers, carton 23, folder: "March on Washington," Bancroft Library, Univ. of California, Berkeley.

23. Indeed, FEPC found that the union excluded blacks from some of their traditional jobs, such as firemen, much as the railroad brotherhoods were doing. Testimony of John Hawk, Sec.-Tres. in House of Representatives, U.S., *Report of Proceedings, Hearing Held before Special Committee to Investigate Executive Agencies*, 25 Feb. 1944 (Washington, D.C., 1944), 2313, 2315–19. For FEPC findings, "Seafarers International Union (SIU) of North America," summary, reel 2H Office Files: Ross, folder: "Final Report—Difficult Cases"; press release, draft for Sept. 1945, "President's Committee on Fair Employment Practice," [on SIU], reel 3H, Office Files–Ross, folder: "Misc.," both in FEPC Papers.

24. Hawk in *Report of Proceedings*, 25 Feb. 1944, 2327.

25. Comment by Representative Jennings, House of Representatives, U.S., *Report of Proceedings, Hearing Held before Special Committee of the House of Representatives to Investigate Acts of Executive Agencies beyond the Scope of Their Authority*, 1 Mar. 1944 (Washington, D.C., 1944), 2392. For another account of such attitudes, see Malcolm Ross, *All Manner of Men* (New York, 1948), 114, 134.

26. Ibid., 2393.

27. Ibid., testimony of Marshall Dimock, 2406, and Craig S. Vincent, 2424–40, esp. 2425.

28. "Office Memorandum from Leonard M. Brin, Director, Region 10 to Will Maslow, Director of Field Operations, 19 May 1944, subject: Race Tension," in reel 63H, folder: "Tension Area Reports," FEPC papers.

29. Quoted in Nelson, "Organized Labor and the Struggle for Black Equality," 966, 979–81, for significance of the "sexual factor" in workplace confrontations between blacks and whites.

30. Swan to McKnight, from report for 15 July [1944?], in reel 75H, folder: "Tension File, July 1943–Oct. 1945: Michigan (Entry 37)," FEPC Papers.

31. Letter to U.S. FEPC from Gordon L'Allemsea [sic.], Los Angeles, 19 Nov. 1943, reel 112F, folder: "Boilermakers' Auxiliary Union Issue, 20 Aug. 1943, Exhibit C," FEPC Papers. Unions who refused to admit African Americans as equal members established "auxiliaries" during the war as a response to employer hirings and government pressure. Black workers filed complaints with the FEPC and in the courts against such separate but unequal representation.

32. Gerald Zahavi, "Passionate Commitments: Race, Sex, and Communism at Schenectady General Electric, 1932–1954," *Journal of American History* 83 (Sept. 1996): 514–48.

33. Memorandum, to Elmer W. Henderson from Joy Schultz, "Subject: Racial Problems Which Have Developed Recently at the P.R. Mallory Plant in Indianapolis," 25 Jan. 1945, "Tension File, July 1943–Oct. 1945: Illinois, Chicago," reel 75H, FEPC Papers.

34. Barbara S. Griffith, *The Crisis of American Labor: Operation Dixie and the Defeat of the CIO* (Philadelphia, 1988).

35. Memorandum, to Elmer W. Henderson from Joy Schultz, "Subject: Racial Problems Which Have Developed Recently at the P. R. Mallory Plant."

36. Lizabeth Cohen, *Making a New Deal: Industrial Workers in Chicago, 1919–1939* (Cambridge, 1991), 333–49; St. Clair Drake and Horace R. Cayton *Black Metropolis: A Study of*

Negro Life in a Northern City, 2 vols. (1945; rev. ed., 1962; New York, 1970), 1:330, 1:332.

37. Bernice Anita Reed, "Accommodation between Negro and White Employees in a West Coast Aircraft Industry 1942–1944," *Social Forces* 26 (1947): 77–82. I would like to thank David Roediger for bringing this article to my attention.

38. Ric Roberts, "While 'The Man' Bilbo Raves: Colored Women Subject to Insults from Thrill-Seeking Whites in D.C.," *Pittsburgh Courier*, 22 Sept. 1945, 17.

39. "Spurns Attention of Boss; Faces Charges, Loses Time," *Pittsburgh Courier*, 23 June 1945, 3.

40. The black press is full of examples: "Youth Phones White Woman, Killed; Whites Rape Negro Girl, Freed," *Pittsburgh Courier*, 2 June 1945, 3; "Florida Prisoner Lynched, "*Pittsburgh Courier*, 20 Oct. 1945, 1, 5; "Walks into Station, Gets Life for 'Rape'," *Pittsburgh Courier*, 8 Dec. 1945; "White Miamian Confesses Brutal Slaying of Negro Sweetheart," *Pittsburgh Courier*, 25 Nov. 1944, 15; "Shreveport Cops Face Charges for Beating Woman," *Chicago Defender*, 1 Apr. 1944, 3; "Mississippi Cops Slug GI's Wife Unconscious," *Pittsburgh Courier*, 3 Feb. 1945, 5; "White Georgians Beat Second Negro Woman," *Pittsburgh Courier*, 3 Nov. 1945, 14; "White Rapist Not Arrested," *Pittsburgh Courier*, 29 Sept. 1945; "Three Whites Allowed Bonds after Raping Negro Girl," *Pittsburgh Courier*, 10 Feb. 1945, 2.

41. "Kidnapping, Rape Spur Move for Equal Justice," *Pittsburgh Courier*, 9 Dec. 1944, 3; "Governor Sparks to Press Charges Against Rapists Following Protests," *Pittsburgh Courier*, 23 Dec. 1944, 1, 4; "Negro GI Needs Assurance Against Recy Taylor Repeat," *Pittsburgh Courier*, 19 May 1945, 3; "Sheriff Manhandles White Woman on Recy Taylor Case," *Pittsburgh Courier*, 19 Aug. 1945, 3; see also, Robin D. G. Kelley, *Hammer and Hoe: Alabama Communists During the Great Depression* (Chapel Hill, N.C., 1990), 223.

42. Archibald describes similar jostling and uneasy proximity of black and white workers at the exits of Moore Dry Dock in Oakland, California. See *Shipyard Worker*, 76. Division of Research, Bureau of Special Services, "Newspaper Clippings, May 10–June 16, 1944, No. 10," 12 July 1944: "Birmingham (Fairfield), Alabama, box 12, file: "OWI," FEPC-FDR Library; "Minutes of Meeting with Grievance Committee of the United Steelworkers of America Affiliated with the USA Local 1131," box SG12417, folder: 9, Governor Sparks Papers, Alabama Department of Archives and History. Document provided by Bruce Nelson, who uses it to make a related point in "Organized Labor and the Struggle for Black Equality," 980–81.

43. Bureau of Special Services, Office of War Information, "Mobile: Race Friction Disrupts War Production," Division of Research, Report No. 01, 9, 14, box 7, file: "OWI 1943," FEPC-FDR Library; Victor H. Bernstein, "The Story of a Race Riot: Women Joined Men in Clubbing and Stoning Negro Ship Workers," *PM*, 31 May 1943, 4. I follow the account in Nelson, "Organized Labor and Black Equality in Mobile," esp. 953, 960–62, 978–80.

44. For example, a Los Angeles transit company official "warned" at a FEPC hearing "that 90 percent of the 214 women operators and conductorettes would quit work if any Negro were upgraded." The Amalgamated agreed, but there was only one quit from the upgrading of about fifty black workers, still a low and perhaps not threatening number. "Opening Statement by Malcolm Ross, Chairman, President's Committee on Fair Employment Practice. Capital Transit Company Hearing, 15 Jan. 1945, U.S. Court of Appeals Courtroom, Washington, D.C.," 4–5, box 7, file: "Capital Transit," FEPC-FDR Library.

45. Howard Woods, "Strike Called in Protest of Negro Labor," *Chicago Defender*, 22 May 1943; Transcript of Hearing, "Fair Employment Practices," 6 June 1944, House of Representatives, Committee on Labor, 82, in St. Louis Scrapbook, 100, Collection of the Brotherhood of Sleeping Car Porters, Chicago Historical Society (referred afterwards as Testimony of David Grant).

46. Howard Woods, "Dusk Till Dawn," *Chicago Defender*, 19 June 1943; Testimony of David Grant, 6 June 1944, 100.

47. "In The Matter of the President's Committee on Fair Employment Practice ex rel Irene Johnson, Beatrice Marshall, Bertha Brown, Margie Foster, John W. Joiner, Jr., Ollie M. Haynes and Emilie T. Lee v. U.S. Cartridge Co. Respondent," Case No. 63, 2 Aug. 1944, 4–5, 19, roll 20H, file: "U.S. Cartridge Co," FEPC Papers.

48. Ruth Milkman, *Gender at Work: The Dynamics of Job Segregation by Sex during World War II* (Urbana, Ill., 1987), esp. 49–64, 104–27.

49. FEPC could not enforce its decision, though. "Decision Case No. 65: Cease and Desist Order," 23 Dec. 1944, 12, roll 20E, file, "U.S. Cartridge Co.," FEPC Papers. The company opened an integrated unit by Apr. 1945, see letter to Malcolm Ross from B. E. Bassett, 18 Apr. 1945, roll 20E, file, "U.S. Cartridge Co.," FEPC Papers roll 20H, file, "U.S. Cartridge Co.," FEPC Papers.

50. I am indebted to Merl Reed for this incident. See, Reed, *Seedtime for the Modern Civil Rights Movement*, 223–25.

51. The classic statement is Mary Douglas, *Purity and Danger An Analysis of Concepts of Pollution and Taboo* (London, 1966). She links ideas of dirt with symbolic systems. For a recent application, Ann McClintock, *Imperial Leather: Race, Gender and Sexuality in the Colonial Contest* (New York, 1995), esp. 207–31; for a brilliant analysis of the significance of bathrooms, see Patricia A. Cooper and Ruth Oldenziel, "Cherished Classifications: Construction of Gender/Race on the Pennsylvania Railroad during World War II," *Feminist Studies* (forthcoming).

52. Reed, "Accommodation between Negro and White Employees," 81; Council for Democracy, "Experience in Negro Employment," typescript, 8; Council for Democracy, "Skilled Negro Labor: A Suggested Guide for The Employer In Introducing Negroes As New Workers," July 1943, typescript, attached to letter to Jonathan Daniels from Ernest Angell, 10 Sept. 1943, 1–2, both in box 7,

file: "Miscellaneous," FEPC-FDR Library; "Final Report," typescript, roll 2H, office files: Ross, folder: "Final Report, West Coast," FEPC Papers; John A. Davis, *How Management Can Integrate Negroes in War Industries* (New York State War Council, Committee on Discrimination in Employment, 1942), 26–28. For racist comments on black cleanliness and health, see for example, letter of Eugene Bull Connor, 7 Aug. 1942, attached to Memorandum for Dr. MacLean, 18 Aug. 1942, box 3, file, "Aug.–Dec. 42," in FEPC-FDR Library; "Will Your Daughter Marry a Negro? When You Vote—Vote White," leaflet attached to letter to Franklin D. Roosevelt from [undecipherable signature], Dept. of Justice, Texarkana, Texas, 26 June 1944; Hon. O. C. Fisher, *Proposed Permanent F.E.P.C. Would Outlaw Segregation*, 4, 7. For analysis of domestic service, dirt, race, and racism, Phyllis Palmer, *Domesticity and Dirt: Housewives and Domestic Servants in the United States, 1920–1945* (Philadelphia, 1989), 137–51.

53. Numbers here are impressionistic. The New York State study, *How Management Can Integrate Negroes in War Industries* canvassed 32 personnel managers and drew upon investigations into about 175 companies by the state Committee on Discrimination in Employment (p. 3); The Council for Democracy studied 150 industries, see title page, "Skilled Negro Labor."

54. Davis, *How Management Can Integrate Negroes in War Industries*, 5.

55. Research Division, Bureau of Special Services, "Newspaper Clippings, Apr. 15 to May 4, 1944. No. 8," 11 May 1944, 2, box 4, file: "OWI," FEPC-FDR Library; Lipsitz, *Rainbow at Midnight*, 77; Susan E. Hirsh, "No Victory at the Workplace: Women and Minorities at Pullman During World War II," *The War in American Culture*, 249; see also, Nancy F. Gabin, *Feminism in the Labor Movement: Women and the United Automobile Workers, 1935–1975* (Ithaca, N.Y., 1990), 79, 88–89.

56. Deborah Gray White, *Ar'n't I a Woman? Female Slaves in the Plantation South* (New York, 1985), 27–61.

57. Lorenzo F. Davis, "Negro War Worker—Asset or Liability? America Must Decide Now," *Semi-Annual Report* (Brooklyn Urban League Industrial Department), 6–7, attached to letter to Jonathan Daniels from Francis J. Haas, 2 Sept. 1943, box 4, file: "Aug.–Sept. 43," FEPC-FDR Library; Letter from Alice Jones, Oakland, Ca., 15 Nov. 1942, in file, "Moore Drydock," FEPC Papers, San Bruno Branch, National Archives. I have kept original spelling and grammer. For black women during the war, see Karen Anderson, "Last Hired, First Fired: Black Women Workers during World War II," *Journal of American History* 69 (June 1982): 82–97; Jacqueline Jones, *Labor of Love, Labor of Sorrow: Black Women, Work, and the Family* (New York, l985), 211–22.

58. This labor comes through in Reed, "Accommodation between Negro and White Employees," 81–82. For a fine discussion of the uses of respectability in wartime protest, see Melinda Chateauvert, *"Marching Together": Women of the*

Brotherhood of Sleeping Car Porters (Urbana, Ill., 1997), 155, 178–79.

59. Point Breeze Salaried Employees' Association, Michael L. Enright, President to Brigadier General Garmer, 12 Jan. 1944, in entry 188, box 29, folder: "Individual Grievances and Complaints"; J. T. R. Memorandum to Colonel Thurman and Major Cross, 28 Jan. 1944, entry 188, box 28, folder: "Memorandum for the Files"; Balfour S. Jeffrey, Captain, Memorandum for the Files, "Subject: Incidental Strike in Cable Terminating Department," 31 Dec. 1943, entry 188, box 28, folder: "Memorandum for the Files"; Report by Agent Hays, Western Electric Company, 30 Dec. 1943, entry 188, box 28, folder: "Memorandum for the Files," all in RG153, Judge Advocate General Papers, National Archives. I would like to thank Kenneth Durr for these documents.

60. From Edward Lawson to Will Maslow, "Re: Situation at Fisk Tire and Rubber Company, Chicopee Falls, Mass.," 27 Jan. 1945, in "Tension File, July 1943–Oct. 1945," reel 75H, FEPC papers.

61. Letter to Regional Manager, Twelfth U.S. Civil Service District, San Francisco, California from Mrs. Thelma Johnson, 9 Nov. 1942; C. L. Dellums, "Facts Existing on Draft Board #73"; letter to Your Excellency Culbert L. Olson, Governor of California from Dellums, 15 Oct. 1942; letter to Colonel K. H. Leitch from Dellums, subject, "Chief Clerk of Local Board No. 73," 31 Oct. 1942; letter to Governor Olson from Dellums, 4 Nov. 1942; letter to Leitch from Dellums, 9 Dec. 1942, all in Dellums Papers, file: "Local Draft Board #73."

62. Letter to Colonel K. H. Leitch from C. L. Dellums, Subject: "Chief Clerk of Local Board #73," 31 Oct. 1942, Dellums Papers, file: "Local Draft Board #73." Dellums, a Vice-President of the Brotherhood of Sleeping Car Porters, was a major leader in Bay Area civil rights activity; he served as a member of this Oakland, Cal. draft board. See also, Letter to Assistant Attorney General Tom C. Clark from J. Edgar Hoover, [6] Oct. 1943 on "Racial Unrest, Boeing Aircraft Corporation," box 6, file: "Labor Department," FEPC-FDR Library.

63. Reed, "Accommodation between Negro and White Employees," 83–84.

64. Michael Goldfield, "Race and the CIO: The Possibilities for Racial Egalitarianism during the 1930s and 1940s," *International Labor and Working Class History* 44 (fall 1993): 1–32, argues for potential interracial unity; see also, Robert Korstad and Nelson Lichtenstein, "Opportunities Found and Lost: Labor, Radicals, and the Early Civil Rights Movement," *Journal of American History* 75 (Dec. 1988): 786–811. Marshall F. Stevenson Jr., however, suggests whatever progress existed came from the demands of black trade unionists; see his "Beyond Theoretical Models: The Limited, Possibilities of Racial Egalitarianism," *International Labor and Working-Class History* 44 (fall 1993): 45–52.

      While I am more convinced by arguments stressing investment in whiteness, counterexamples show white workers defending and working together with black ones. For example, Shelton Stromquist, *Solidarity* and *Survival: An Oral History of Iowa Labor in the Twentieth Century* (Iowa City, Ia., 1993), 136–39; Michael K. Honey, *Southern Labor and Black Civil Rights; Organizing Memphis Workers* (Urbana, Ill., 1993), 177–213; Meier and Rudwick, *Black Detroit*, 138–53. For alternative discourse at the time, William Fisher, "And Here is Democracy in Action in a War Plant . . . Negroes and Whites Work in Harmony," *PM's Daily Picture Magazine*, 25 June 1945, 12–13.

65. "Quotations from interviews," ii, attached to Office of War Information, Bureau of Intelligence, "Negroes and the War: A Study in Baltimore and Cincinnati," Special Report Number 16, Division of Surveys, 21 July 1942, file: "OWI," FEPC-FDR Library.

66. James Horton, "Freedom's Yoke: Gender Conventions Among AnteBellum Free Blacks," *Feminist Studies* 12 (spring 1986): 51–76.

R E A D I N G *21*   *Miliann Kang*

The Managed Hand: The Commercialization of Bodies and Emotions in Korean Immigrant–Owned Nail Salons

The title of Hochschild's (1983) groundbreaking study of emotional labor, *The Managed Heart*, provides a rich metaphor for the control and commercialization of human feeling in service interactions. The title of this article, "The Managed Hand," plays on Hochschild's to capture the commercialization of both human feelings and bodies and to introduce the concept of body labor, the provision of body-related services and the management of feelings that accompanies it. By focusing on the case study of Korean immigrant manicurists and their relations with racially and socioeconomically diverse female customers in New York City nail salons, I broaden the study of emotional labor to illuminate its neglected

Author's note: I would like to thank Catherine Berheide, C. N. Le, Jennifer Lee, Sara Lee, Susan Walzer and Chris Bose, Minjeong Kim, and the *Gender & Society* anonymous reviewers for valuable comments and suggestions. My dissertation committee at New York University, Craig Calhoun, Jeff Goodwin, and Ruth Horowitz, and readers, Troy Duster and Kathleen Gerson, guided the theory and research design. Thanks to Liann Kang, Wi Jo Kang, Nora Choi-Lee, Jung-hwa Hwang, Eunja Lee, Eunji Lee, and especially Jiwon Lee for research assistance. Research was supported in part by New York University, the Social Science Research Council's Committee on International Migration, Skidmore College, and Grinnell College. By recognizing this study with the Cheryl Allyn Miller award, Sociologists for Women in Society provided encouragement and intellectual community. I am grateful to Myra Marx Ferree, Mitchell Duneier, and members of the Feminist Seminar and Race and Ethnicity Seminar for inviting me to present and for responding to an earlier version of this article at the University of Wisconsin–Madison, 2001.

embodied dimensions and to examine the intersections of gender, race, and class in its performance.

The past decade has witnessed a turn toward "Bringing Bodies Back In" (Frank 1990) to theory and research in sociology and feminist scholarship. What can be gained by "bringing the body back in" to the study of emotional labor and, more broadly, of gendered work? What are the dimensions of body labor, and what factors explain the variation in the quality and quantity of its performance? An embodied perspective on gendered work highlights the feminization of the body-related service sector and the proliferation of intricate practices of enhancing the appearance of the female body. A race, gender, and class perspective highlights the increasing role of working-class immigrant women in filling body-related service jobs and the racialized meanings that shape the processes of emotional management among service workers.

This study compares nail salons in three racially and socioeconomically diverse settings, employing participant observation and in-depth interviews ($N = 62$) in the tradition of feminist ethnography and the extended case method. After providing a brief overview of the case study of Korean-owned nail salons in New York City, the data presentation maps out the physical and emotional dimensions of body labor in three different nail salons and explains patterns of variation according to the race and class of the clientele and neighborhood.

In addition to contributing original empirical research on Korean immigrant women's work in the new and expanding niches of body service work, this article broadens the scholarship on emotional labor by addressing its performance by racial-ethnic and immigrant women in the global service economy. It demonstrates how the gendered processes of physical and emotional labor in nail salon work are seeped with race and class meanings that reinforce broader structures of inequality and ideologies of difference between women.

THEORETICAL FRAMEWORK

Emotional Labor in Body Service Work: Race, Gender, and Class Intersections

Work on the body requires not only physical labor but extensive emotional management, or what Hochschild's (1983) seminal work describes as emotional labor. The concept of body labor makes two important contributions to the study of emotional labor: (1) It explores the embodied dimensions of emotional labor and (2) it investigates the intersections of race, gender, and class in shaping its performance. By bringing together an embodied analysis of emotional labor with an integrative race, gender, and class perspective, I show how this case study of nail salon work retheorizes emotional labor to have greater applicability to gendered occupations dominated by racialized immigrant women.

Building on Hochschild's (1983) work, studies of emotional labor have illuminated the increasing prevalence of emotional management in specific occupations and industries, the gendered composition of the emotional labor force, wage discrimination, burnout, and other occupational health issues (Hall 1993; Leidner 1999; Lively 2000; Wharton 1999). Steinberg and Figart (1999) provide a comprehensive overview of the field that examines both qualitative case studies of the contours of emotional labor in specific work sites and quantitative investigations of its prevalence and its impact on job satisfaction and compensation. Despite the many dimensions of emotional labor that have been addressed by feminist scholars, the body-related contours of emotional labor as it is manifested in low-wage service work dominated by racial-ethnic women, particularly in the beauty industry, have yet to be examined in depth.

While the study of beauty and the beauty industry presents a rich opportunity to explore the emotional work involved in servicing female bodies, this literature has focused attention almost exclusively on the experiences of middle-class white women consumers and their physical and psychological exploitation by the male-dominated beauty industry (Banner 1983; Bordo 1993; Chapkis 1986; Wolf 1991), neglecting the substandard working conditions, unequal power relations, and complex emotional lives of the women who provide these services. Several excellent ethnographies of beauty salons (Gimlan 1996; Kerner Furman 1997) have explored the dimensions of class and age in beauty shop culture, but they have not addressed the experiences of women of color as either customers or body service workers. Studies of the bodies of women of color, while illuminating cultural representations of racialized bodies as inferior and exotic (hooks 1990) and studying the politics of body alteration, particularly regarding hair (Banks 2000; Rooks 1996), have also neglected the actual interactions between consumers and providers of body-related services and the hierarchies that govern these exchanges.

In addition to neglecting emotional work in body service jobs, the literature on emotional labor has framed the processes of interactive service work primarily through a gender lens and paid less attention to the crosscutting influences of gender, race and class. Russsell Hochschild's original case study of flight attendants and subsequent applications to other female-dominated occupations have emphasized the gendered employment experiences of native-born white women as paralegals (Pierce 1995), nannies and au pairs (Macdonald 1996), fast food and insurance sales workers (Leidner 1993), and police officers (Schmitt and Yancey Martin 1999). My research expands this work not only in its empirical focus on immigrant women of color doing gendered, emotional labor but through the theoretical framework of race, gender, and class as "interactive systems" and "interlocking categories of experience" (Anderson and Hill Collins 2001, xii). This framework critiques additive models that append race and class to the experiences of white middle-class women and instead highlights the simultaneity and reciprocity of race, gender, and class in patterns of social relations and in the lives of individuals (Baca Zinn 1989; Hill Collins 1991; hooks 1981; Hurtado 1989; Nakano Glenn 1992; Ngan-Ling Chow 1994). Thus, I demonstrate that different expectations or "feeling rules" (Hochschild 1983, x) shape the performance of emotional labor by women according to the racial and class context.

Drawing from Hochschild's (1983) definition of emotional labor, I incorporate this intersectional analysis to define important parallels and distinctions between the concepts of body labor and emotional labor. First, Hochschild's definition of emotional labor focuses on a particular form that "requires one to induce or suppress feeling in order to sustain the outward countenance that produces the proper state of mind in others—in this case, the sense of being cared for in a convivial and safe place" (1983, 7). While Hochschild develops this definition in reference to the specific case of flight attendants and the feeling rules that govern their work, this kind of caring, attentive service has become a widely generalized definition, rather than being regarded as one particular form of emotional labor performed by mostly white, middle-class women largely for the benefit of white, middle- and upper-class men. Korean-owned nail salons thus serve as a contrasting site to explore other forms of emotional labor that emerge in work sites that are differently gendered, differently racialized, and differently classed. The patterns of emotional labor described in this study can illuminate similar sites in which emotional labor involves women serving women (as opposed to mainly women serving men), and is not necessarily governed by the social feeling rules of white, middle-class America.

Furthermore, while Hochschild and other scholars of emotional labor have examined certain embodied aspects of emotional labor concerned with gendered bodily display, ranging from control of weight to smiles, this study highlights emotional management regarding bodily contact in service interactions. The dynamics of extended physical contact between women of different racial and class positions complicate and intensify the gendered performance of emotional labor. Body labor not only demands that the service worker present and comport her body in an appropriate fashion but also that she induces customers' positive feelings about their own bodies. This is a highly complicated enterprise in a culture that sets unattainable standards for female beauty and pathologizes intimate, nurturing physical contact between women, while it normalizes unequal relations in the exchange of body services.

By investigating the understudied area of body-related service occupations through an intersectional race, gender, and class analysis, this study of body labor reformulates the concept of emotional labor to dramatize how the feeling rules governing its exchange are shaped by interlocking oppressions that operate at the macro level (Hill Collins 1991) and then emerge as different styles of emotional service at the micro level.

BACKGROUND FOR THE STUDY

In this section, I provide context for my study by describing nail salons as a niche for Korean immigrant women's work and discussing the dynamics of race and ethnicity in its development. As one of the few arenas in which immigrant and native-born women encounter each other in regular, sustained, physical contact, Korean immigrant women–owned nail salons in New York City illuminate the complex performance and production of race, gender, and class as they are constructed in feminized work sites in the global service economy. Since the early 1980s, Korean women in New York City have pioneered this new ethnic niche with more than 2,000 Korean-owned nail salons throughout the metropolitan area, or approximately 70 percent of the total, as estimated by the Korean American Nail Association of New York. Each salon employs an average of five workers, suggesting an occupational niche of roughly 10,000 women. While the New York State licensing bureau does not keep track of nail salon licenses by ethnic group, their figures reveal an overall 41-percent growth in the nail industry (from 7,562 licensed nail technicians in 1996 to 10,684 in 2000) in New York City, Westchester County, and Nassau County. These numbers undercount a sizable number of women who do not possess licenses or legal working status.

While concentrating on Korean immigrant women, this study examines both race and ethnicity as salient categories of analysis. I designate the salon owners and workers according to ethnicity, but I recognize shared racial positions that push not only Korean but also other Asian immigrant women into this niche. For example, in New York, there is a significant presence of Chinese- and Vietnamese- as well as Korean-owned nail salons, and on the West Coast, the niche is almost solely dominated by Vietnamese women (www.nailsmag.com). Common factors such as limited English-language ability, unrecognized professional credentials from their countries of origin, undocumented immigration status, and coethnic resources in the form of labor, start-up capital, and social networks explain why Asian immigrant women of various ethnic groups cluster in the nail salon industry. Similarities across Asian ethnic groups include not only the human capital of the women themselves but also the conditions of the labor market and the U.S. racial hierarchy that they encounter. Through their shared race, gender, and class locations, Asian women have been coveted as productive and docile workers, whose "nimble fingers" (Ong 1987) make them desirable and exploitable in an increasingly feminized, impoverished, and un-protected labor force (Cheng and Bonacich 1984; Hu-DeHart 1999). Racialized perceptions of Asian women as skilled in detailed handiwork and massage further contribute to customers' preference for their manicur-ing services, as evidenced by the fact that many cus-tomers racially identify the salons as owned by Asians or "Orientals," as opposed to by specific ethnic group.

In sum, because it would be methodologically un-sound to generalize findings based on a limited sam-ple of Korean women to include all Asian immigrant women in the nail industry, this study maintains ethnic-ity as the significant category for describing the workers and owners but frames differences between the custom-ers and variation in service interactions according to race. Thus, I discuss the different dimensions of Korean-immigrant women's performance of body labor through the integrative lens of race, gender, and class rather than a more specific focus on Korean ethnicity.

RESEARCH DESIGN AND METHOD

This study situates itself within feminist methodology and epistemology by beginning from the standpoint of women to investigate the "relations of ruling" in con-temporary capitalist society (Smith 1987). At the same time, it does not privilege gender as the only or the most important framework for defining and investigating dif-ferences and aims instead for an understanding of race, gender, and class as crosscutting forces. By examining contrasting patterns of body labor between women of different racial and class backgrounds, this study recon-structs theories of emotional labor by addressing its em-bodied dimensions and the simultaneous influence of gender, race, and class on its performance. In doing so, it follows the extended case method of making critical in-terventions in existing theory by explaining anomalies between similar phenomena, rather than seeking gener-alizations toward the discovery of new theory, as in the contrasting approach of grounded theory. According to Burawoy (1991, 281), the primary architect of the ex-tended case method, "The importance of the single case lies in what it tells us about society as a whole rather than about the population of similar cases." Thus, my study examines cases of specific nail salons, not to for-mulate generalizations about all similar nail salons but instead to explain how social forces influence variation in the service interactions at these sites.

The data collection for this project involved 14 months of fieldwork in New York City nail salons. The research

design included in-depth interviews ($N = 62$) and par-ticipant observation at three sites: (1) "Uptown Nails," located in a predominantly white, middle- and upper-class commercial area; (2) "Downtown Nails," located in a predominantly Black (African American and Ca-ribbean) working- and lower-middle-class commercial neighborhood; and (3) "Crosstown Nails," located in a racially mixed lower-middle and middle-class residen-tial and commercial area. I spent at least 50 hours at each salon over the course of several months. In the case of Crosstown Nails, which was located near my home, vis-its were shorter (2 to 3 hours) and more frequent (several times a week). The other two salons required long com-mutes, so I usually visited once a week for 6 to 7 hours.

In addition to hundreds of unstructured conversa-tional interviews conducted as a participant-observer, the research included in-depth structured interviews with 10 Korean nail salon owners, 10 Korean nail salon workers, 15 Black customers, and 15 white customers. The customers interviewed at each salon are as follows. Uptown Nails included a lawyer, professor, pharmacist, flight attendant, secretary, personal trainer, accessories importer, homemaker (formerly a computer program-mer), fashion designer, and real estate broker. Custom-ers interviewed at Downtown Nails included a pack-age clerk, student/waitress, student/mother, grocery cashier, ambulatory service driver, county government administrative assistant, laboratory technician, nanny, therapist, and elementary school principal. At Cross-town Nails, I interviewed 10 customers (five white, five Black). The white customers included a bartender, high school teacher, hairdresser, homemaker, and retired in-surance bookkeeper. The Black customers included a clinical researcher, theater technician/musician, man-agement consultant, homemaker, and student.

In-depth interviews averaged 45 minutes for custom-ers and two hours for owners and workers. Customers were interviewed in English at the salon while they were having their manicures, and when necessary, a follow-up meeting or telephone interview was arranged. Own-ers and workers were interviewed in both Korean and English, depending on their preference and level of flu-ency. Bilingual research assistants helped with transla-tion, transcription, and follow-up interviews. I tape-recorded interviews in which consent was given, but in cases in which respondents refused, I took extensive handwritten notes that I typed immediately afterward. Both customers and service providers are referred to by pseudonyms that approximate the names they use in the salons. This convention captures the naturalistic setting where even coworkers commonly refer to each other by the "American name" that they employ at work. I have added a surname to citations and descriptions of owners and workers to differentiate customers from service providers.

Finally, I conducted key respondent interviews with two officials of the Korean Nail Salon Association of New York, two Korean ethnic press journalists, one New York State licensing official, and a representative of a Korean-operated nail school. I interviewed two Vietnamese nail salon owners and one Chinese and one Russian manicurist to provide preliminary comparisons to other ethnically owned nail salons. To provide comparisons to other Korean-owned small businesses, I engaged in limited participant observation in a Korean-owned grocery store and interviewed the owner and manager.

FINDINGS

The Contours of Body Labor

Body labor involves the exchange of body-related services for a wage and the performance of physical and emotional labor in this exchange. My study's findings illustrate three dimensions of body labor: (1) the physical labor of attending to the bodily appearance and pleasure of customers, (2) the emotional labor of managing feelings to display certain feeling states and to create and respond to customers' feelings regarding the servicing of their bodies, and (3) variation in the performance of body labor as explained through the intersection of gender with race and class. These dimensions vary across the different research sites and emerge as three distinct patterns of body labor provision: (1) high-service body labor involving physical pampering and emotional attentiveness serving mostly middle- and upper-class white female customers, (2) expressive body labor involving artistry in technical skills and communication of respect and fairness when serving mostly working- and lower-middle-class African American and Caribbean female customers, and (3) routinized body labor involving efficient, competent physical labor and courteous but minimal emotional labor when serving mostly lower-middle and middle-class racially mixed female customers. The data presentation admittedly flattens some of the variation within each site to clarify distinctions between them, but this typology highlights the dominant physical and emotional style of service at each salon.

Uptown Nails: High-Service Body Labor

A seasoned Korean manicurist who has worked at Uptown Nails for nearly 10 years, Esther Lee is in high demand for her relaxing and invigorating hand massages. She energetically kneads, strokes, and pushes pressure points, finishing off the massage by holding each of the customer's hands between her own and alternately rubbing, slapping, and gently pounding them with the flare that has wooed many a customer into a regular nail salon habit. Margie, a white single woman in her mid-30s who works for an accounting firm, smiles appreciatively and squeezes Esther's hand: "I swear, I couldn't stay in my job without this!" Esther reciprocates a warm, somewhat shy smile.

Uptown Nails boasts leafy green plants, glossy framed pictures of white fashion models showing off well-manicured hands, recent fashion magazine subscriptions stacked neatly on a coffee table, and classical CDs on the stereo system. The salon has been in operation for 13 years, and three of the six employees have worked there for more than 10 years. The customers sit quietly sipping their cappuccinos, updating their appointment books, or at times politely conversing with each other about the weather or the color of the nail polish they are wearing. Located in a prosperous business district of Manhattan, an Uptown Nails manicuring experience involves not only the filing and polishing of nails but attention to the customer's physical and emotional comfort. From the gentle removal of undernail dirt, to the careful trimming of cuticles and buffing of calluses, to the massaging of hands and feet, Korean manicurists literally rub up against their customers, who are mostly white middle- and upper-class women. The owner, one of the earliest pioneers in the nail salon industry, currently operates six very profitable salons in prime Manhattan locations and visits this salon only once a week to take care of paperwork. The owner, manager, and employees are all middle-aged Korean women with fluent English-language ability, reflecting the greater expectations for communications with customers. The physical dimensions of body labor in Uptown Nails, including hot cotton towels, bowls of warm soaking solution, sanitized utensils, and calming background music, all indicate considerable attention to creating a pleasurable sensory experience for the customer. Particular attention is given to avoiding nicks and cuts and sterilizing and apologizing profusely when they occur.

In addition to this extensive physical pampering, Uptown Nails prioritizes the emotional needs of customers regarding the servicing of their bodies. The mostly white middle-class customers at this salon place great importance on emotional attentiveness as a crucial component of the service interaction. Kathy, a personal trainer, elaborated,

> Having them done is a pleasure, a luxury. Doing them myself is tedious, having them done is a treat. It's the whole idea of going and having something nice done for myself. If I do them myself, it's just routine upkeep of my body—like washing your hair or keeping your clothes clean. . . . Of course it makes it more enjoyable if they are friendly and can talk to you. If they can't remember my name that's okay, but I think they should recognize me.

The proper performance of body labor thus transforms a hygienic process, otherwise equated with washing hair or clothes, into a richly rewarding physical and emotional experience. The satisfaction Kathy experiences from the manicure derives not only from the appearance of the nails but the feeling of being special that accompanies attentive body servicing. To generate this feeling, customers expect the manicurist to display a caring demeanor and engage in pleasant one-on-one conversation with them.

Service providers recognize customers' high expectations with regard to both the physical and emotional dimensions of body labor, and they respond accordingly. Judy Cha, a 34-year-old who immigrated in 1993, describes the emotional and physical stressors that accompany high-service body labor, particularly giving massages to earn tips and engaging in conversation.

> Three years ago we didn't give a lot of massages but now customers ask more and more. It makes me weak and really tired. . . . I guess because I don't have the right training to do it in a way that doesn't tire my body. Some manicurists give massage all the time to get tips, but sometimes I don't even ask them if I'm tired. Owners keep asking you to ask them, but on days I'm not feeling well, I don't ask. . . . One of my biggest fears working in the salon is, what if I don't understand what the customer is saying? They don't really talk in detail, just say, "how is the weather." But in order to have a deeper relationship, I need to get past that and to improve my English. It makes it very stressful.

Thus, manicurists work hard to conform to the high service expectations of middle-class white women, but while the performance of caring, attentive emotional labor is noticeably higher than that afforded in the other research sites, it often does not meet customers' expectations. In particular, many Uptown Nails customers disapprove of the use of Korean language by the manicurists as a violation of proper attentiveness in beauty service transactions and suspect that they are being talked about (Kang 1997).

Cathy Hong, a 32-year-old manicurist who immigrated in 1999, sums up the assumptions many of the Uptown Nails customers have regarding access to a regular manicure delivered with high-service body labor: "These women get their nails done regularly because it has become a habit to them, they take if for granted. Just as we wash our face daily, American women get their nails done."

Downtown Nails: Expressive Body Labor

Entering another borough, the scene inside Downtown Nails differs as radically as the neighborhoods in which these two salons are located. Squeezed between a Caribbean bakery and a discount clothing store, a worn-out signboard displays the single word "NAILS" and a painting of a graceful, well-manicured hand holding a long-stemmed rose and pointing to a staircase leading to the second-story entrance. Upon being buzzed in through the locked door, the customer is greeted with a display of hundreds of brightly colored airbrushed nail tips lining an entire wall. The noise level in the salon is high, as various electronic nail-sculpting tools create a constant buzz to match the flow of the lively conversations among the mostly Black customers. On a weekend afternoon, Downtown Nails is filled to capacity, and the wait for a preferred "nail artist" can be more than an hour. Mostly Caribbean and African American women, the customers engage in animated conversations while sharing coco buns and currant rolls from the downstairs bakery. The banter ranges from vivid accounts of a recent mugging near the salon to news about the pay freeze in the nearby hospital where many of the women work as nurses or technicians.

A far cry from the spa-like pampering experience of Uptown Nails, a nail job at Downtown Nails is closer to a stint on a factory assembly line: highly mechanized and potentially toxic. Absent are the elaborate sanitizing machines and solutions, let alone the soft pampering touches. Despite these appearances, body labor at Downtown Nails involves a complex mix of physical and emotional labor that accommodates customers' desires to express a unique sense of self through their nail designs and their expectations that service providers demonstrate both individual respect and appreciation to the community.

The manicurists, or nail artists, provide less of the traditional, attentive style of emotional labor but focus their emotional management on communicating a sense of respect and fairness. These women tend to be more recent immigrants from more working-class backgrounds with less English-language fluency and are more likely to be working without legal immigration status or licenses. The owners, Mr. and Mrs. Lee, are a married couple, both formerly school teachers, who immigrated in 1981 to pursue better educational opportunities for their children. Two years after their arrival, they opened a salon in this location because the rent was affordable, the customer base was strong, and they reside in a nearby neighborhood. The customers at Downtown Nails span a broad range in socioeconomic status but most are working to lower-middle class.

The importance of the physical appearance of the nails themselves as opposed to the pampering experience of receiving these services is dramatized by customers' concern with the design of the nails versus the massage and other services that customers at Uptown Nails regard as integral and Downtown Nails customers view as extraneous. Jamilla, a 26-year-old African American part-time student and waitress, proudly displays her inch-and-a-half-long nails, each one adorned with the skyline of New York City in bold black, framed by an orange and yellow sunset. A regular patron of Downtown Nails for six years, she explains why she is willing to spend "$50–$60 every two weeks" for elaborate hand-painted designs:

> Because I don't like looking like anyone else. My nails say "me." They're the first thing people notice about me. I have big hands for a female. I never had those long, thin ladylike fingers. My father used to say my hands were bigger than his. I want long nails because they make my hands look more feminine.

Indicating a preference for nails that reflect very different norms of femininity than the demure, pastel tones prevalent at Uptown Nails, Jamilla elaborates further on her nail aesthetics. "It all depends on my mood. Like this design makes me feel like I'm on top of the city, like it can't bring me down [laughing]. . . . No one's gonna mess with you when you got nails like these." Jamilla's pride in having originally designed nails that no one else can reproduce suggests the importance of her nails as an expression of her individuality that

also communicate a sense of self-efficacy and protection, as indicated in her comments that no one would "mess" with a woman with nails like hers. To meet the expectations of customers such as Jamilla, body labor at Downtown Nails calls for development of expertise in sculpting and painting original nail designs rather than in the soothing, pampering services offered at Uptown Nails. Thus, the physical demands of body labor are not less but simply of a different type.

Similarly, the emotional dimensions of body labor at Downtown Nails are not different in degree so much as kind. The customer's race and class location intersect to produce much lower expectations among working-class Black customers for emotional attentiveness than the white middle-class women at Uptown Nails. While it is clearly less attentive, Serena, an African American grocery store cashier, assesses the emotional labor at Downtown Nails positively.

> It's very good, I'm satisfied with it. They really just do the nails, no massages. That's fine with me. I just go in with my Walkman and listen to some good music and maybe just have a little basic conversation.

Customers at Downtown Nails rarely are on a first-name basis with the service providers, and their preference for a particular manicurist is based much more on her technical skills than her emotional attentiveness. Serena elaborated,

> There are a few people I like and I go to whoever's open, but I'll stay away from certain people. I know they're not good cause I hear other people complain—I see someone come back and say that their nail cracked the next day, or I see someone get nicked with a filer. . . . No, it's not because they're rude or anything, it's because I know they don't do a good job. . . . Just like some people just can't do hair, some people just can't do nails.
>
> [Regarding relations with her current manicurist] I feel comfortable with her, but it's more that she does an excellent job. If a wrap cracks or looks funny or I lose a nail, I'm not going back to her no matter how nice she is.

While many working-class Black customers like Serena give little importance to a caring, attentive emotional display, they demand another style of emotional labor.

Emotional labor at Downtown Nails calls less for sensitivity to pampering of individual customers and more for demonstration of values of respect and fairness that recognize the complex dynamics of Korean businesses operating in Black neighborhoods. This includes efforts such as sponsoring a Christmas party to thank customers for their patronage, participating in community events, displaying Afro-centric designs, and playing R&B and rap music. Mrs. Lee, the co-owner of the salon, allows regulars to run an informal tab when they are short of money and keeps a change jar that customers dip into for bus fare, telephone calls, or other incidentals. It is not uncommon for customers to drop by even when they are not getting their nails done to use the bathroom or leave shopping bags behind the front desk while they complete errands. These efforts at "giving back to the community" entail a distinct form of emotional labor that conforms not to white middle-class women's feeling rules of privilege and pampering but to Black working-class women's concerns about being treated with respect and fairness.

Jamilla described the importance of a sense of fairness and respect to Black customers and how this demands a particular form of emotional labor from Korean manicurists.

> It's kind of a Catch-22. Some customers feel like they're getting disrespected if you don't refer back to them or if you're having a side conversation. Then the Koreans get upset and think African Americans have an attitude, which then makes them talk more about us. You see, in the African American community, you can't outright say anything you want to say because we always have our guard up. We get it all the time, from the cops or whoever. I've seen it in the Hispanic community too—this thing about honor and respect. "Don't disrespect me just because I'm Black or Hispanic. What I say does count."

Thus, while the caring, pampering style of service is virtually absent at Downtown Nails, another form of emotional labor is necessary to negotiate and avoid conflicts with customers that can quickly become racialized into heated confrontations (Lee 2002). Serena described a scene at another salon that illustrates how the failure to perform appropriately respectful emotional labor can quickly erupt into shouting matches that take on racialized and anti-immigrant overtones: "I've seen some customers really go off on them, 'You're not in your country, speak English.'" Her comments underscore how the race and class of the neighborhood complicate the processes of emotional management inside the salons.

Although disagreements between Downtown Nails' customers and workers do arise, at times resulting in heated exchanges, the relations in the salon are congenial overall, as the expressive style of emotional labor enables customers and service providers to voice and, for the most part, "work out" their differences. Mrs. Lee explained that she prefers serving Black customers for this reason and actually moved back to working in a low-income Black neighborhood after working for a period in Long Island.

> Working in the white neighborhood didn't match my personality. I don't deal well with picky customers. . . . In the Black neighborhood, it's more relaxed. They don't leave tips but they don't expect so much service either. . . . [In Long Island] they want you to go slow and spend time with them. Here I just concentrate on doing a good job and working quickly.

Service providers invest less energy in displaying and creating convivial feeling states, which in some cases allows for a genuine affinity with Black customers and less of a sense of burnout from the effort involved in the manufacture of falsely convivial feelings.

Expressive body labor thus prioritizes both the meanings of the nails as a form of self-expression to working-class Black customers and the expression of symbolic but tangible efforts to respond to the feeling rules of respect and fairness governing Korean immigrant service providers in predominantly Black working-class neighborhoods.

Crosstown Nails: Routinized Body Labor

Located on the second floor above a fashionable boutique, Crosstown Nails is clean but sparse and utilitarian. In many ways, this salon is representative of the most prevalent style of service offered in Korean-owned nail salons: fast, cheap, basic manicures and pedicures with no frills. The McDonald's of the nail salon industry, Crosstown Nails offers a manicure that is standardized and predictable in both its physical and emotional aspects.

This salon often has customers waiting, but even when it is busy, the line moves quickly as each customer is whisked in and out of the manicuring seat with crisp efficiency. The customer chooses her nail color, presents it to the manicurist who asks her to specify the desired shape of the nail, and then soaks her nails briefly in a softening solution. Depending on her preference, her nails are either trimmed or pushed back. The manicurist offers to give a massage, but it is perfunctory and lasts usually not more than a minute. After carefully layering on two coats of polish and a quick-drying topcoat, the customer moves to a heated hand dryer where she converses with other customers or more often "zones out."

Many customers come from the neighboring hospital during lunch hour or after work. Situated on the edge of a fashionable, high-rent, racially diverse residential district and a lower-income but also racially mixed neighborhood, Crosstown Nails captures the broad range of customer interactions that many Korean service providers negotiate in a given day. In large, high-immigrant-receiving cities such as New York, service interactions often involve multiracial rather than binary interactions between Korean and Blacks or Koreans and whites.

Susan Lee, age 39, founded Crosstown Nails in 1989 and is the sole owner. Divorced with one son, age 10, she emigrated in 1982 from Seoul with her husband, a graduate student. She graduated college with a degree in tourism and worked as a travel agent in Korea. In New York City, she first worked in a retail store in Manhattan, then began to work in a nail salon in Brooklyn to support her husband while he studied. After their marriage ended, she brought her mother from Korea in 1988 and with her help opened a convenience store, which failed shortly thereafter. She then opened Crosstown Nails a year later, and the business has thrived.

The secret of Crosstown Nail's success is its ability to appeal to customers who lack excess disposable income and normally would not indulge in a professional manicure but are attracted by the convenience and price. Julia, a white bartender, commented,

> I'm kind of a ragamuffin, so it kind of surprises me that I get them done as often as I do, which is still much less than most people in the city. It's just so easy to do here, and cheap.

Julia's description of herself as a "ragamuffin" suggests that she does not adhere to strict codes of femininity in her dress or other beauty routines, as indicated by her casual peasant skirt and no makeup. Nonetheless, easy and cheap access draws her into purchasing regular manicures.

Many customers at Crosstown Nails seek manicures not as a pampering experience or as creative expression but as a utilitarian measure to enhance their self-presentation at work. Merna, an Afro-Caribbean clinical researcher, explained,

> I only get them done about every two months. I don't want to get attached to it. For some women it's such a

ritual, it becomes a job—maintaining the tips and stuff. I'm presenting my hands all day long so it's worth it to me to spend some time and money to make sure they look good.

Merna regards manicured nails as a professional asset more than a core aspect of a gendered self. Thus, the style of her nails and the meaning she gives to them is more similar to the white middle-class customers at Crosstown Nails than to the Black working-class customers at Downtown Nails.

In general, middle-class Black customers like Merna mostly exhibited similar nail aesthetics to those of middle-class white women, suggesting the greater importance of class over race in influencing nail styles and expectations of body labor, particularly in routinized settings such as Crosstown Nails.

DISCUSSION

The concept of emotional labor addresses how service providers present and manipulate their feelings to communicate a sense of caring and attentiveness to customers, or in Hochschild's (1983, 6) words, where "the emotional style of offering service is part of the service itself." This study of interactions in Korean-owned nail salons enriches the literature on emotional labor by expanding it to include embodied dimensions, or body labor. The embodied aspects of emotional labor not only heighten the intensity of commercialized feeling exchanges but they also point out variation in these exchanges beyond the white middle-class settings explored by most researchers. Nail salon services, and body labor more generally, are gendered work processes, but they are enacted in different forms according to the influences of race and class.

In what ways is nail salon work gendered? In what ways are these gendered work processes remolded by race and class? Understanding the influence of race and class on the gendered performance of body labor in Korean-owned nail salons illuminates how gendered work processes reflect and reproduce racial and class inequalities at the level of social structures. Nail salon work is gendered in four major dimensions: (1) It involves mostly female actors, as both service providers and customers; (2) it focuses on the construction of beauty according to feminine norms; (3) it is situated in feminized, semiprivate spaces; and (4) it involves the gendered performance of emotional labor.

In describing each of these dimensions, I do not emphasize how socialized gender roles are acted out in these establishments, but rather how gender operates as a social institution that lays the groundwork for the very existence of these businesses and frames the interactions that occur within them. Thus, I conceptualize these small businesses according to the model of gendered institutions (Marx Ferree and Hall 1996) and examine how they are constructed from the ground up through gendered ideologies, relations, and practices that sustain systematic gender inequality at the micro level of sex differences, at the meso level of group conflict, and the macro levels of power, social control, and the division of labor. At the same time, I argue that as gendered institutions, they cannot be separated from forces of racial and class inequality.

If, as Paul Gilroy (1993, 85) asserted, "gender is the modality in which race is lived," then race, and I argue class as well, are lived in these nail salons and other body-service sites as differences in gendered styles of body labor. Interactions in Korean female immigrant–owned nail salons illustrate how the gendered practices of body labor become the locus of expressing and negotiating race and class hierarchies between white, Black, and Asian women. High-service body labor, as performed at Uptown Nails, is similar to the style of caring, attentive emotional labor practiced by Hochschild's flight attendants and conforms to the feeling rules of white middle-class women. Expressive body labor focuses on the physical appearance and artistry of the nails and the communication of respect and fairness in serving mostly working- and lower-middle-class African American and Caribbean women customers at Downtown Nails. Routinized body labor stresses efficiency, predictability, affordability, and competency in physical labor and a courteous but no-frills style of emotional labor geared toward mostly lower-middle- and middle-class racially mixed female customers at Crosstown Nails.

These patterns of body labor conform to the racial and class positions of the customers and the associated feeling rules that define their service expectations. At Uptown Nails, race, gender, and class intersect to produce an emotionally and physically pampering form of body labor that conforms to the expectations of white, professional women for caring and attentive service. These women have high expectations regarding massages, cleanliness, sensitive touch, and friendly conversation while Black, working-class women at Downtown Nails expect minimal pampering and focus on the appearance, originality, and durability of the nails themselves. At Crosstown Nails, class prevails over race as both Black

and white women of middling socioeconomic status view the nails instrumentally as a no-nonsense professional asset rather than conforming to traditional notions of pampered femininity. Thus, they trade off the physical pleasure and emotional attentiveness of high-service treatment for the convenience and price of routinized body labor.

Black middle-class women at Crosstown Nails share this instrumental view of nails and a preference for a routinized, hassle-free manicure. The style of nails and the meaning given to them by Black middle-class women radically differ from the working-class Black women at Downtown Nails, who value nail art as a form of self-expression and demand emotional labor that communicates respect and fairness. This contrast between the Black middle-class and working-class women customers at Crosstown and Downtown Nails again suggests the greater salience of class over race in determining the type of body labor.

What structural factors explain the differences in the provision of body labor in these three sites? These body labor types, while enacted at the micro level, reflect the social conditions of the neighborhoods in which the salons are located and the clientele they serve. Because of the reliance on tips in white middle-class neighborhoods, service providers have greater incentive to cater to the emotional needs of customers such as those at Uptown Nails to increase their earnings. In the Black working-class neighborhoods where tipping is not a widespread practice, nail salon workers guarantee their economic livelihood by establishing a base of regular customers who seek them out for their technical and artistic abilities more than their emotional or physical attentiveness. In routinized body labor settings serving lower-middle-class women of mixed races, service providers maximize their earnings by generating a high turnover of customers who receive satisfactory but not special emotional and physical treatment.

These patterns of body labor service reflect and reproduce racial and class inequalities between women. Korean service providers learn to respond to white middle- and upper-class customers' emotional pampering and physical pleasure, thereby reinforcing the invisible sense of privilege claimed by these customers. The expressive practices of creating artful nails and troubleshooting potential problems with Black working-class customers, while helping to smooth relations, can also serve to emphasize racial meanings in these interactions and enforce a sense of difference. The routinized style of body labor reflects the generic social position of women whose bodies are neither privileged nor pathologized but simply treated with routine efficiency.

CONCLUSIONS

Exchanges of manicuring services set up complex emotional and embodied interactions between diverse women. In introducing and exploring the dimensions of body labor, this article challenges the scholarship on emotional labor to take more seriously the growth in body-related service jobs and to address the differences in these service interactions not simply in terms of gendered processes but through the lens of race, gender, and class intersections. Thus, not only does the concept of body labor add embodied dimensions to emotional labor, but it also makes it more applicable to low-wage service work performed by immigrant women of color.

This study situates the practice of body labor in Korean-owned nail salons within the restructuring of the global economy and the transplantation of the practices of enhancing bodily appearance from private households into new forms of public urban space. A manicure is no longer something a woman gives herself, her daughter, or a girlfriend in the quiet of her own bathroom, but it is something that she increasingly purchases in a nail salon. In purchasing these services, she not only expands the boundaries of the service economy to include formerly private regimens of personal hygiene, but she also encounters the "other," often an immigrant woman of different racial and class background through physical contact that can generate highly charged feelings on both sides. These feelings manifest and are worked out differently in distinct styles of body labor that emerge through the intersection of gendered work processes with customers' racial and class positions and their associated service expectations.

Although so far I have drawn parallels between this process of exchanging body services for a wage with the commercialization of feelings in emotional labor, another parallel can be drawn to the encroachment of the capitalist system into the area of social reproduction. Nakano Glenn (1992) and others have illuminated how the performance of household work such as cleaning, cooking, and caring for children and the elderly has become increasingly part of the capitalist market, and these low-paying, unprotected jobs (nanny, elderly caregiver, nurses, aide) are most often filled by immigrant women of color. This study has illustrated how similar to these dynamics of commodifying reproductive labor and farming it out at low wages to less privileged women, body services and the emotional labor accompanying it (what I have conceptualized as body labor) have become increasingly commercialized and designated as racialized immigrant women's work.

Additional dimensions of body labor that I will explore in further studies include (1) the impact of this work on the women who perform it and the ways they conform to or resist its pressures, (2) the role of managers in supervising body labor, (3) the variation between body labor in nonessential beauty services such as nail salon work versus the work of social reproduction, and, as previously mentioned, (4) the ethnic-specific dimensions of Korean-Black and Korean-white relations. While this article has concentrated on my case study of nail salons, the concept of body labor can be applied to many other occupations, especially female-dominated service professions in which service providers and customers are of different race and class origins, including hairdressers, masseuses, nannies, nurses, doctors, personal trainers, and prostitutes.

Finally, in mapping out the racial, gendered, and classed complexity of body labor, this article highlights a kernel of social change that lies in negotiating service interactions between women of different classes, racial and ethnic backgrounds, and immigrant statuses. While these interactions often mimic structures of power and privilege, they also create opportunities to contest these structures. The Korean salon owner of Downtown Nails learns to respect and show appreciation for Black working-class patrons. Korean manicurists at Uptown Nails assert their knowledge and expertise over their white middle-class customers. Routinized service at Crosstown Nails equalizes treatment of women across race and class.

From the customer's side, a weekly trip to the local nail salon can become a lesson in relating to a woman of a radically different social position, whom she would rarely encounter in her own milieu. As these emotional and embodied interactions reflect larger systems of status and power, by rewriting the unspoken feeling rules of these interactions, women can take small but important steps in the creation of more equal relations with other women. Nakano Glenn (2002, 16–17) wrote that "contesting race and gender hierarchies may involve challenging everyday assumptions and practices, take forms that do not involve direct confrontation, and occur in locations not considered political." Exchanges involving body labor in Korean-owned nail salons are one such location where these everyday assumptions and practices can be recognized and possibly renegotiated.

REFERENCES

Anderson, Margaret, and Patricia Hill Collins. 2001. *Race, class, and gender: An anthology.* Belmont, CA: Wadsworth.

Baca Zinn, Maxine. 1989. Family, race, and poverty in the eighties. *Signs: Journal of Women in Culture and Society* 14:856–74.

Banks, Ingrid. 2000. *Hair matters: Beauty, power, and Black women's consciousness.* New York: New York University Press.

Banner, Lois. 1983. *American beauty.* New York: Alfred A. Knopf.

Bordo, Susan. 1993. *Unbearable weight: Feminism, Western culture and the body.* Berkeley: University of California Press.

Burawoy, Michael. 1991. *Ethnography unbound.* Berkeley: University of California Press.

Chapkis, Wendy. 1986. *Beauty secrets.* Boston: South End.

Cheng, Lucie, and Edna Bonacich. 1984. *Labor immigration under capitalism: Asian workers in the United States before World War 2.* Berkeley: University of California Press.

Frank, Arthur W. 1990. Bringing bodies back in: A decade review. *Theory, Culture, and Society* 7:131–62.

Gilroy, Paul. 1993. *The Black Atlantic: Modernity and double consciousness.* Cambridge, MA: Harvard University Press.

Gimlan, Debra. 1996. Pamela's place: Power and negotiation in the hair salon. *Gender & Society* 10:505–26.

Hall, Elaine J. 1993. Waitering/waitressing: Engendering the work of table servers. *Gender & Society* 7:329–46.

Hill Collins, Patricia. 1991. *Black feminist thought: Knowledge, consciousness, and the politics of empowerment.* New York: Routledge.

Hochschild, Arlie. 1983. *The managed heart: The commercialization of human feeling.* Berkeley: University of California Press.

hooks, bell. 1981. *Ain't I a woman: Black women and feminism.* Boston: South End.

———. 1990. *Black looks: Race and representation.* Boston: South End.

Hu-DeHart, Evelyn. 1999. *Across the Pacific: Asian Americans and globalization.* Philadelphia: Temple University Press.

Hurtado, Aida. 1989. Relating to privilege: Seduction and rejection in the subordination of white women and women of color. *Signs: Journal of Women in Culture and Society* 14:833–55.

Kang, Miliann. 1997. Manicuring race, gender, and class: Service interactions in New York City Korean nail salons. *Race, Gender, and Class* 4:143–64.

Kerner Furman, Frida. 1997. *Facing the mirror: Older women and the beauty shop culture.* New York: Routledge.

Lee, Jee-Young Jennifer. 2002. *Civility in the city: Blacks, Jews, and Koreans in urban America.* Cambridge, MA: Harvard University Press.

Leidner, Robin. 1993. *Fast food, fast talk: Service work and the routinization of everyday life.* Berkeley: University of California Press.

———. 1999. Emotional labor in service work. *Annals of the American Academy of Political and Social Science* 561:81–95.

Lively, Kathryn. 2000. Reciprocal emotion management: Working together to maintain stratification in private law firms. *Work and Occupations* 27:32–63.

Macdonald, Cameron. 1996. Shadow mothers: Nannies, au pairs, and invisible work. In *Working in the service society,* edited by Cameron Lynne Macdonald and Carmen Sirianni. Philadelphia: Temple University Press.

Marx Ferree, Myra, and Elaine J. Hall. 1996. Rethinking stratification from a feminist perspective: Gender, race, and class in mainstream textbooks. *American Sociological Review* 61:929–50.

Nakano Glenn, Evelyn. 1992. From servitude to service work: Historical continuities in the racial division of paid reproductive labor. *Signs: Journal of Women in Culture and Society* 18:1–43.

———. 2002. *Unequal freedom: How race and gender shaped American citizenship and labor.* Cambridge, MA: Harvard University Press.

Ngan-Ling Chow, Esther. 1994. Asian American women at work. In *Women of color in U.S. society,* edited by Maxine Baca Zinn and Bonnie Dill Thornton. Philadelphia: Temple University Press.

Ong, Aihwa. 1987. *Spirits of resistance and capitalist discipline: Factory women in Malaysia.* Albany: State University of New York Press.

Pierce, Jennifer L. 1995. *Gender trials: Emotional lives in contemporary law firms.* Berkeley: University of California Press.

Rooks, Noliwe. 1996. *Hair rising: Beauty, culture, and African American women.* New Brunswick. NJ: Rutgers University Press.

Schmitt, Frederika E., and Patricia Yancey Martin. 1999. Unobtrusive mobilization by an institutionalized rape crisis center: "All we do comes from victims." *Gender & Society* 13:364–84.

Smith, Dorothy. 1987. *The everyday world as problematic: A feminist sociology.* Boston: Northeastern University Press.

Steinberg, Ronnie, and Deborah Figart. 1999. Emotional labor since *The Managed Heart. Annals of the American Academy of Political and Social Science* 561:8–26.

Wharton, Amy. 1999. The psychological consequences of emotional labor. *Annals of the American Academy of Political and Social Science* 561:158–77.

Wolf, Naomi. 1991. *The beauty myth: How images of beauty are used against women.* New York: William Morrow.

THE REALITIES OF AFFIRMATIVE ACTION IN EMPLOYMENT

Barbara Reskin

Affirmative action policies and practices reduce job discrimination against minorities and white women, although their effects have not been large. Some critics charge that affirmative action's positive effects have been offset by its negative effects on white men, on productivity, and on the merit system.

For many people, the most troubling aspect of affirmative action is that it may discriminate against majority-group members (Lynch 1997). According to 1994 surveys, 70 to 80 percent of whites believed that affirmative action sometimes discriminates against whites (Steeh and Krysan 1996, p. 139). Men are more likely to believe that a woman will get a job or promotion over an equally or more qualified man than they are to believe that a man will get a promotion over an equally or more qualified woman (Davis and Smith 1996).

Several kinds of evidence indicate that whites' fears of reverse discrimination are exaggerated. Reverse discrimination is rare both in absolute terms and relative to conventional discrimination.[1] On every measured outcome, African-American men were much more likely than white men to experience discrimination, and Latinos were more likely than non-Hispanic men to experience discrimination (Heckman and Siegelman 1993, p. 218). Statistics on the numbers and outcomes of complaints of employment discrimination also suggest that reverse discrimination is rare.

According to national surveys, relatively few whites have experienced reverse discrimination. Only 5 to 12 percent of whites believe that their race has cost them a job or a promotion, compared to 36 percent of African Americans (Steeh and Krysan 1996, pp. 139–40). Of 4,025 Los Angeles workers, 45 percent of African Americans and 16 percent of Latinos said that they had been refused a job because of their race, and 16 percent of African Americans and 8 percent of Latinos reported that they had been discriminated against in terms of pay or a promotion (Bobo and Suh 1996, Table 1). In contrast, of the 863 whites surveyed, less than 3 percent had ever experienced discrimination in pay or promotion,

and only one mentioned reverse discrimination. Nonetheless, two-thirds to four-fifths of whites (but just one-quarter of African Americans) surveyed in the 1990s thought it likely that less qualified African Americans won jobs or promotions over more qualified whites (Taylor 1994a; Davis and Smith 1994; Steeh and Krysan 1996, p. 139).[2]

Alfred Blumrosen's (1996, pp. 5–6) exhaustive review of discrimination complaints filed with the Equal Employment Opportunity Commission offers additional evidence that reverse discrimination is rare. Of the 451,442 discrimination complaints filed with the EEOC between 1987 and 1994, only 4 percent charged reverse discrimination (see also Norton 1996, pp. 44–5).[3] Of the 2,189 discrimination cases that federal appellate courts decided between 1965 and 1985, *less* than 5 percent charged employers with reverse discrimination (Burstein 1991, p. 518).

Allegations of reverse discrimination are less likely than conventional discrimination cases to be supported by evidence. Of the approximately 7,000 reverse-discrimination complaints filed with the EEOC in 1994, the EEOC found only 28 credible (Crosby and Herzberger 1996, p. 55). Indeed, U.S. district and appellate courts dismissed almost all the reverse-discrimination cases they heard between 1990 and 1994 as lacking merit.

How can we reconcile the enormous gulf between whites' perceptions that they are likely to lose jobs or promotions because of affirmative action and the small risk of this happening? The white men who brought reverse-discrimination suits presumably concluded that their employers' choices of women or minorities could not have been based on merit, because men are accustomed to being selected for customarily male jobs (*New York Times*, March 31, 1995).[4] Most majority-group members who have not had a first-hand experience of competing unsuccessfully with a minority man or woman or a white woman cite media reports as the source of their impression that affirmative action prompts employers to favor minorities and women (Hochschild 1995, pp. 144, 308).[5] It seems

(continued)

likely that politicians' and the media's emphasis on "quotas" has distorted the public's understanding of what is required and permitted in the name of affirmative action (Entman 1997).

There is no evidence that affirmative action reduces productivity or that workers hired under affirmative action are less qualified than other workers. In the first place, affirmative action plans that compromise valid educational and job requirements are illegal. Hiring unqualified workers or choosing a less qualified person over a more qualified one because of their race or sex is illegal and is not condoned in the name of affirmative action (U.S. Department of Labor, Employment Standards Administration n.d. (b), p. 2). Second, to the extent that affirmative action gives women and minority men access to jobs that more fully exploit their productive capacity, their productivity and that of their employers should increase.

Although many Americans believe that affirmative action means that less qualified persons are hired and promoted (Verhovek 1997, p. 32), the evidence does not bear this out. According to a study of more than 3,000 workers hired in entry-level jobs in a cross-section of firms in Atlanta, Boston, Detroit, and Los Angeles, the performance evaluations of women and minorities hired under affirmative action did not differ from those of white men or female or minority workers for whom affirmative action played no role in hiring (Holzer and Neumark 1998). In addition, Columbus, Ohio, female and minority police officers hired under an affirmative action consent decree performed as well as white men (Kern 1996). Of nearly 300 corporate executives surveyed in 1979, 72 percent believed that minority hiring did not impair productivity (*Wall Street Journal* 1979); 41 percent of CEOs surveyed in 1995 said affirmative action improved corporate productivity (Crosby and Herzberger 1996, p. 86).[6]

The consequences of affirmative action reach beyond workers and employers by increasing the pools of skilled minority and female workers. When affirmative action prompts employers to hire minorities or women for positions that serve the public, it can bring services to communities that would otherwise be underserved. For example, African-American and Hispanic physicians are more likely than whites and Anglos to practice in minority communities (Komaromy et al. 1996). Graduates of the Medical School at the University of California at San Diego who were admitted under a special admissions program were more likely to serve inner-city and rural communities and saw more poor patients than those admitted under the regular procedures (Perm, Russell, and Simon 1986).

Women's and minorities' employment in nontraditional jobs also raises the aspirations of other members of excluded groups by providing role models and by signaling that jobs are open to them. Some minorities and women do not pursue jobs or promotions because they expect to encounter discrimination (Mayhew 1968, p. 313). By reducing the perception that discriminatory barriers block access to certain lines of work, affirmative action curtails this self-selection (Reskin and Roos 1990, p. 305). In addition, the economic gains provided by better jobs permit beneficiaries to invest in the education of the next generation.

The tension between affirmative action and merit is the inevitable result of the conflict between our national values and what actually occurs in the nation's workplaces. As long as discrimination is more pervasive than affirmative action, it is the real threat to meritocracy. But because no one will join the debate on behalf of discrimination, we end up with the illusion of a struggle between affirmative action and merit.

NOTES

1. Lynch's (1989, p. 53) search for white male Southern Californians who saw themselves as victims of reverse discrimination turned up only 32 men.
2. Younger whites, those from more privileged backgrounds, and those from areas with larger black populations—especially black populations who were relatively well off—were the most likely to believe that blacks benefited from preferential treatment (Taylor 1994b).

3. Two percent were by white men charging sex, race, or national-origin discrimination (three-quarters of these charged sex discrimination), and 1.8 percent were by white women charging race discrimination (Blumrosen 1996, p. 5).
4. Occupational segregation by sex, race, and ethnicity no doubt contributes to this perception by reinforcing the notion that one's sex, color, or ethnicity is naturally related to the ability to perform a particular job.

5. The disproportionate number of court-ordered interventions to curtail race and sex discrimination in cities' police and fire departments (Martin 1991) and the large number of court challenges by white men (Bureau of National Affairs 1995, pp. 5–12) probably contributed to the public's impression that hiring quotas are common.

6. No data were provided on the proportion who believed that affirmative action hampered productivity.

REFERENCES

Blumrosen, Alfred W. 1996. *Declaration*. Statement Submitted to the Supreme Court of California in Response to Proposition 209, September 26.

Bobo, Larry, and Susan A. Suh. 1996. "Surveying Racial Discrimination: Analyses from a Multi-Ethnic Labor Market." Working Paper No. 75, Russell Sage Foundation, New York.

Bureau of National Affairs. 1995. *Affirmative Action after Adarand: A Legal, Regulatory, Legislative Outlook*. Washington, DC: The Bureau of National Affairs.

Burstein, Paul. 1991. "'Reverse Discrimination' Cases in the Federal Courts: Mobilization by a Countermovement." *Sociological Quarterly* 32:511–28.

Crosby, Faye J., and Sharon D. Herzberger. 1996. "For Affirmative Action." Pp. 3–109 in *Affirmative Action: Pros and Cons of Policy and Practice*, ed. R. J. Simon. Washington, DC: American University Press.

Davis, James A., and Tom W. Smith. 1994. *General Social Survey* [MRDF]. Chicago, IL: National Opinion Research Center [producer, distributor].

———. 1996. *General Social Survey* [MRDF]. Chicago, IL: National Opinion Research Center [producer, distributor].

Entman, Robert M. 1997. "Manufacturing Discord: Media in the Affirmative Action Debate." *Press/Politics* 2:32–51.

Heckman, James J., and Peter Siegelman. 1993. "The Urban Institute Audit Studies: Their Methods and Findings." Pp. 187–229 in *Clear and Convincing Evidence. Measurement of Discrimination in America*, ed. M. Fix and R. J. Struyk. Washington, DC: The Urban Institute.

Hochschild, Jennifer. 1995. *Facing Up to the American Dream*. Princeton, NJ: Princeton University Press.

Holzer, Harry J., and David Neumark. Forthcoming 1998. "Are Affirmative Action Hires Less Qualified? Evidence from Employer–Employee Data on New Hires." *Journal of Labor Economics*.

Kern, Leesa. 1996. "Hiring and Seniority: Issues in Policing in the Post-Judicial Intervention Period." Department of Sociology, Ohio State University, Columbus, OH: Unpublished manuscript.

Komaromy, Miriam, Kevin Grumbach, Michael Drake, Karen Vranizan, Nicole Lurie, Dennis Keane, and Andrew Bindman. 1996. "The Role of Black and Hispanic Physicians in Providing Health Care for Underserved Populations." *New England Journal of Medicine* 334:1305–10.

Lynch, Frederick R. 1989. *Invisible victims: White Males and the Crisis of Affirmative Action*. New York: Greenwood.

———. 1997. The *Diversity Machine: The Drive to Change the White Male Workplace*. New York: Free Press.

Martin, Susan E. 1991. "The Effectiveness of Affirmative Action: The Case of Women in Policing." *Justice Quarterly* 8:489–504.

Mayhew, Leon. 1968. *Law and Equal Opportunity: A Study of Massachusetts Commission against Discrimination*. Cambridge, MA: Harvard University Press.

New York Times. 1995. "Reverse Discrimination Complaints Rare. Labor Study Reports." *New York Times*, March 31, p. A23.

Norton, Eleanor Holmes. 1996. "Affirmative Action in the Workplace." Pp. 39–48 in *The Affirmative Action Debate*, ed. G. Curry. Reading, MA: Addison-Wesley.

Penn, Nolan E., Percy J. Russell, and Harold J. Simon. 1986. "Affirmative Action at Work: A Survey of Graduates of the University of California at San Diego Medical School." *American Journal of Public Health* 76: 1144–46.

Reskin, Barbara F., and Patricia Roos. 1990. *Job Queues, Gender Queues*. Philadelphia, PA: Temple University Press.

Steeh, Charlotte, and Maria Krysan. 1996. "The Polls—Trends. Affirmative Action and the Public, 1970–1995." *Public Opinion Quarterly* 60:128–58.

Taylor, Marylee C. 1994a. "Beliefs about the Preferential Hiring of Black Applicants: Sure It Happens, But I've Never Seen It." Pennsylvania State University, University Park, PA. Unpublished manuscript.

———. 1994b. "Impact of Affirmative Action on Beneficiary Groups: Evidence from the 1990 General Social Survey." *Basic and Applied Social Psychology* 15: 143–78.

U.S. Department of Labor, Employment Standards Administration, Office of Federal Contract Compliance Programs [cited as OFCCP]. The Rhetoric and the Reality about Federal Affirmative Action at the OFCCP." Washington, DC: U.S. Department of Labor.

Verhovek, Sam Howe. 1997. "In Poll, Americans Reject Means but Not Ends of Racial Diversity." *New York Times*, December 14, 1, 32.

Wall Street Journal. 1979. "Labor Letter: A Special News Report on People and Their Jobs in Offices, Fields and Factories: Affirmative Action Is Accepted by Most Corporate Chiefs." *Wall Street Journal*, April 3, p. 1.

Maid in L.A.

The title of this [reading] was inspired by Mary Romero's 1992 book, *Maid in the U.S.A.*, but I am also taking the pun to heart: most Latina immigrant women who do paid domestic work in Los Angeles had no prior experience working as domestics in their countries of origin. Of the 153 Latina domestic workers that I surveyed at bus stops, in ESL classes, and in parks, fewer than 10 percent reported having worked in other people's homes, or taking in laundry for pay, in their countries of origin. This finding is perhaps not surprising, as we know from immigration research that the poorest of the poor rarely migrate to the United States; they simply cannot afford to do so.

Some of the Latina immigrant women who come to Los Angeles grew up in impoverished squatter settlements, others in comfortable homes with servants. In their countries of origin, these women were housewives raising their own children, or college students, factory workers, store clerks, and secretaries; still others came from rural families of very modest means. Regardless of their diverse backgrounds, their transformation into housecleaners and nanny/housekeepers occurs in Los Angeles. I emphasize this point because images in popular culture and the media more or less identify Latinas with domestic workers—or, more precisely, as "cleaning gals" and "baby-sitters," euphemisms that mask American discomfort with these arrangements. Yet they take on these roles only in the United States, at various points in their own migration and settlement trajectories, in the context of private households, informal social networks, and the larger culture's racialized nativism.

Who are these women who come to the United States in search of jobs, and what are those jobs like? Domestic work is organized in different ways, and in this [reading] I describe live-in, live-out, and house-cleaning jobs and profile some of the Latina immigrants who do them and how they feel about their work. The [reading] concludes with a discussion of why it is that Latina immigrants are the primary recruits to domestic work, and I examine what they and their employers have to say about race relations and domestic work.

LIVE-IN NANNY/HOUSEKEEPER JOBS

For Maribel Centeno, newly arrived from Guatemala City in 1989 at age twenty-two and without supportive family and friends with whom to stay, taking a live-in job made a lot of sense. She knew that she wouldn't have to spend money on room and board, and that she could soon begin saving to pay off her debts. Getting a live-in job through an agency was easy. The *señora*, in her rudimentary Spanish, only asked where she was from, and if she had a husband and children. Chuckling, Maribel recalled her initial misunderstanding when the *señora*, using her index finger, had drawn an imaginary "2" and "3" in the palm of her hand. "I thought to myself, well, she must have two or three bedrooms, so I said, fine. 'No,' she said. 'Really, really big.' She started counting, 'One, two, three, four . . . two-three rooms.' It was twenty-three rooms! I thought, huy! On a piece of paper, she wrote '$80 a week,' and she said, 'You, child, and entire house.' So I thought, well, I have to do what I have to do, and I happily said, 'Yes.'"

"I arrived on Monday at dawn," she recalled, "and I went to the job on Wednesday evening." When the *señora* and the child spoke to her, Maribel remembered "just laughing and feeling useless. I couldn't understand anything." On that first evening, the *señora* put on classical music, which Maribel quickly identified. "I said, 'Beethoven.' She said, 'Yeah,' and began asking me in English, 'You like it?' I said 'Yes,' or perhaps I said, 'Si,' and she began playing other cassettes, CDs. They had Richard Clayderman and I recognized it, and when I said that, she stopped in her tracks, her jaw fell open, and she just stared at me. She must have been thinking, 'No schooling, no preparation, no English, how does she know this music?'" But the *señora*, perhaps because of the language difficulty, or perhaps because she felt upstaged by her live-in's knowledge of classical music, never did ask. Maribel desperately wanted the *señora* to respect her, to recognize that she was smart, educated, and cultivated in the arts. In spite of her best status-signaling efforts, "They treated me," she said, "the same as any other girl from the countryside." She never got the verbal recognition that she desired from the *señora*.

Maribel summed up her experiences with her first live-in job this way: "The pay was bad. The treatment was, how shall I say? It was cordial, a little, uh, not racist, but with very little consideration, very little respect." She liked caring for the little seven-year-old boy, but keeping after the cleaning of the twenty-three-room house, filled with marble floors and glass tables, proved physically impossible. She eventually quit not because of the polishing and scrubbing, but because being ignored devastated her socially.

Compared to many other Latina immigrants' first live-in jobs, Maribel Centeno's was relatively good. She was not on call during all her waking hours and throughout the night, the parents were engaged with the child, and she was not required to sleep in a child's bedroom or on a cot tucked away in the laundry room. But having a private room filled with amenities did not mean she had privacy or the ability to do simple things one might take for granted. "I had my own room, with my own television, VCR, my private bath, and closet, and a kind of sitting room—but everything in miniature, Thumbelina style," she said. "I had privacy in that respect. But I couldn't do many things. If I wanted to walk around in a T-shirt, or just feel like I was home, I couldn't do that. If I was hungry in the evening, I wouldn't come out to grab a banana because I'd have to walk through the family room, and then everybody's watching and having to smell the banana. I could never feel at home, never. Never, never, never! There's always something invisible that tells you this is not your house, you just work here."

It is the rare California home that offers separate maid's quarters, but that doesn't stop families from hiring live-ins; nor does it stop newly arrived Latina migrant workers from taking jobs they urgently need. When live-ins cannot even retreat to their own rooms, work seeps into their sleep and their dreams. There is no time off from the job, and they say they feel confined, trapped, imprisoned.

"I lose a lot of sleep," said Margarita Gutiérrez, a twenty-four-year-old Mexicana who worked as a live-in nanny/housekeeper. At her job in a modest-sized

condominium in Pasadena, she slept in a corner of a three-year-old child's bedroom. Consequently, she found herself on call day and night with the child, who sometimes went several days without seeing her mother because of the latter's schedule at an insurance company. Margarita was obliged to be on her job twenty-four hours a day; and like other live-in nanny/housekeepers I interviewed, she claimed that she could scarcely find time to shower or brush her teeth. "I go to bed fine," she reported, "and then I wake up at two or three in the morning with the girl asking for water, or food." After the child went back to sleep, Margarita would lie awake, thinking about how to leave her job but finding it hard to even walk out into the kitchen. Live-in employees like Margarita literally have no space and no time they can claim as their own.

Working in a larger home or staying in plush, private quarters is no guarantee of privacy or refuge from the job. Forty-four-year-old Elvia Lucero worked as a live-in at a sprawling, canyon-side residence, where she was in charge of looking after twins, two five-year-old girls. On numerous occasions when I visited her there, I saw that she occupied her own bedroom, a beautifully decorated one outfitted with delicate antiques, plush white carpet, and a stenciled border of pink roses painstakingly painted on the wall by the employer. It looked serene and inviting, but it was only three steps away from the twins' room. Every night one of the twins crawled into bed with Elvia. Elvia disliked this, but said she couldn't break the girl of the habit. And the parents' room lay tucked away at the opposite end of the large (more than 3,000 square feet), L-shaped house.

Regardless of the size of the home and the splendor of the accommodations, the boundaries that we might normally take for granted disappear in live-in jobs. They have, as Evelyn Nakano Glenn has noted, "no clear line between work and non-work time," and the line between job space and private space is similarly blurred.[1] Live-in nanny/housekeepers are at once socially isolated and surrounded by other people's territory; during the hours they remain on the employers' premises, their space, like their time, belongs to another. The sensation of being among others while remaining invisible, unknown and apart, of never being able to leave the margins, makes many live-in employees sad, lonely, and depressed. Melancholy sets in and doesn't necessarily lift on the weekends.

Rules and regulations may extend around the clock. Some employers restrict the ability of their live-in employees to receive telephone calls, entertain friends, attend evening ESL classes, or see boyfriends during the workweek. Other employers do not impose these sorts of restrictions, but because their homes are located on remote hillsides, in suburban enclaves, or in gated communities, their live-in nanny/housekeepers are effectively kept away from anything resembling social life or public culture. A Spanish-language radio station, or maybe a *telenovela*, may serve as their only link to the outside world.

Food—the way some employers hoard it, waste it, deny it, or just simply do not even have any of it in their kitchens—is a frequent topic of discussion among Latina live-in nanny/housekeepers. These women are talking not about counting calories but about the social meaning of food on the job. Almost no one works with a written contract, but anyone taking a live-in job that includes "room and board" would assume that adequate meals will be included. But what constitutes an adequate meal? Everyone has a different idea, and using the subject like a secret handshake, Latina domestic workers often greet one another by talking about the problems of managing food and meals on the job. Inevitably, food enters their conversations.

No one feels the indignities of food more deeply than do live-in employees, who may not leave the job for up to six days at a time. For them, the workplace necessarily becomes the place of daily sustenance. In some of the homes where they work, the employers are out all day. When these adults return home, they may only snack, keeping on hand little besides hot dogs, packets of macaroni and cheese, cereal, and peanut butter for the children. Such foods are considered neither nutritious nor appetizing by Latina immigrants, many of whom are accustomed to sitting down to meals prepared with fresh vegetables, rice, beans, and meat. In some employers' homes, the cupboards are literally bare. Gladys Villedas recalled that at one of her live-in jobs, the *señora* had graciously said, "'Go ahead, help yourself to anything in the kitchen.' But at times," she recalled, "there was nothing, nothing in the refrigerator! There was nothing to eat!" Even in lavish kitchens outfitted with Subzero refrigerators and imported cabinetry, food may be scarce. A celebrity photographer of luxury homes that appear in posh magazines described to a reporter what he sees when he opens the doors of some of Beverly Hills' refrigerators: "Rows of cans of Diet Coke, and maybe a few remains of pizza."[2]

Further down the class ladder, some employers go to great lengths to economize on food bills. Margarita Gutiérrez claimed that at her live-in job, the husband did the weekly grocery shopping, but he bought things in small quantities—say, two potatoes that would be served in half portions, or a quarter of a watermelon to last a household of five all week. He rationed out the bottled water and warned her that milk would make her fat. Lately, she said, he was taking both her and the children to an upscale grocery market where they gave free samples of gourmet cheeses, breads, and dips, urging them all to fill up on the freebies. "I never thought," exclaimed Margarita, formerly a secretary in Mexico City, "that I would come to this country to experience hunger!"

Many women who work as live-ins are keenly aware of how food and meals underline the boundaries between them and the families for whom they work. "I never ate with them," recalled Maribel Centeno of her first live-in job. "First of all, she never said, 'Come and join us,' and secondly, I just avoided being around when they were about to eat." Why did she avoid mealtime? "I didn't feel I was part of that family. I knew they liked me, but only because of the good work I did, and because of the affection I showered on the boy; but apart from that, I was just like the gardener, like the pool man, just one more of their staff." Sitting down to share a meal symbolizes membership in a family, and Latina employees, for the most part, know they are not just like one of the family.

Food scarcity is not endemic to all of the households where these women work. In some homes, ample quantities of fresh fruits, cheeses, and chicken stock the kitchens. Some employer families readily share all of their food, but in other households, certain higher-quality, expensive food items may remain off-limits to the live-in employees, who are instructed to eat hot dogs with the children. One Latina live-in nanny/housekeeper told me that in her employers' substantial pantry, little "DO NOT TOUCH" signs signaled which food items were not available to her; and another said that her employer was always defrosting freezer-burned leftovers for her to eat, some of it dating back nearly a decade.

Other women felt subtle pressure to remain unobtrusive, humble, and self-effacing, so they held back from eating even when they were hungry. They talked a lot about how these unspoken rules apply to fruit. "Look, if they [the employers] buy fruit, they buy three bananas, two apples, two pears. So if I eat one, who took it? It's me," one woman said, "they'll know it's me." Another nanny/housekeeper recalled: "They would bring home fruit, but without them having to say it, you just knew these were not intended for you. You understand this right away, you get it." Or as another put it, "*Las Americanos* have their apples counted out, one for each day of the week." Even fruits growing in the garden are sometimes contested. In Southern California's agriculture-friendly climate, many a residential home boasts fruit trees that hang heavy with oranges, plums, and peaches, and when the Latina women who work in these homes pick the fruit, they sometimes get in trouble.[3] Eventually, many of the women solve the food problem by buying and bringing in their own food; early on Monday mornings, you see them walking with their plastic grocery bags, carting, say, a sack of apples, some chicken, and maybe some prepared food in plastic containers.

The issue of food captures the essence of how Latina live-in domestic workers feel about their jobs. It symbolizes the extent to which the families they work for draw the boundaries of exclusion or inclusion, and it marks the degree to which those families recognize the live-in nanny/housekeepers as human beings who have basic human needs. When they first take their jobs, most live-in nanny/housekeepers do not anticipate spending any of their meager wages on food to eat while on the job, but in the end, most do—and sometimes the food they buy is eaten by members of the family for whom they work.

Although there is a wide range of pay, many Latina domestic workers in live-in jobs earn less than minimum wage for marathon hours: 93 percent of the live-in workers I surveyed in the mid-1990s were earning less than $5 an hour (79 percent of them below minimum wage, which was then $4.25), and they reported working an average of sixty-four hours a week.[4] Some of the most astoundingly low rates were paid for live-in jobs in the households of other working-class Latino immigrants, which provide some women their first job when they arrive in Los Angeles. Carmen Vasquez, for example, had spent several years working as a live-in for two Mexican families, earning only $50 a week. By comparison, her current salary of $170 a week, which she was earning as a live-in nanny/housekeeper in the hillside home of an attorney and a teacher, seemed a princely sum.

Many people assume that the rich pay more than do families of modest means, but working as a live-in in an exclusive, wealthy neighborhood, or in a twenty-three-room house, provides no guarantee of a high salary. Early one Monday morning in the fall of 1995, I was

standing with a group of live-in nanny/housekeepers on a corner across the street from the Beverly Hills Hotel. As they were waiting to be picked up by their employers, a large Mercedes sedan with two women (a daughter and mother or mother-in-law?) approached, rolled down the windows, and asked if anyone was interested in a $150-a-week live-in job. A few women jotted down the phone number, and no one was shocked by the offer. Gore Vidal once commented that no one is allowed to fail within a two-mile radius of the Beverly Hills Hotel, but it turns out that plenty of women in that vicinity are failing in the salary department. In some of the most affluent Westside areas of Los Angeles—in Malibu, Pacific Palisades, and Bel Air—there are live-in nanny/housekeepers earning $150 a week. And in 1999, the *Los Angeles Times* Sunday classified ads still listed live-in nanny/housekeeper jobs with pay as low as $100 and $125.[5] Salaries for live-in jobs, however, do go considerably higher. The best-paid live-in employee whom I interviewed was Patricia Paredes, a Mexicana who spoke impeccable English and who had legal status, substantial experience, and references. She told me that she currently earned $450 a week at her live-in job. She had been promised a raise to $550, after a room remodel was finished, when she would assume weekend housecleaning in that same home. With such a relatively high weekly salary she felt compelled to stay in a live-in job during the week, away from her husband and three young daughters who remained on the east side of Los Angeles. The salary level required that sacrifice.

But once they experience it, most women are repelled by live-in jobs. The lack of privacy, the mandated separation from family and friends, the round-the-clock hours, the food issues, the low pay, and especially the constant loneliness prompt most Latina immigrants to seek other job arrangements. Some young, single women who learn to speak English fluently try to move up the ranks into higher-paying live-in jobs. As soon as they can, however, the majority attempt to leave live-in work altogether. Most live-in nanny/housekeepers have been in the United States for five years or less; among the live-in nanny/housekeepers I interviewed, only two (Carmen Vasquez and the relatively high-earning Patricia Paredes) had been in the United States for longer than that. Like African American women earlier in the century, who tired of what the historian Elizabeth Clark-Lewis has called "the soul-destroying hollowness of live-in domestic work,"[6] most Latina immigrants try to find other options.

Until the early 1900s, live-in jobs were the most common form of paid domestic work in the United States, but through the first half of the twentieth century they were gradually supplanted by domestic "day work."[7] Live-in work never completely disappeared, however, and in the last decades of the twentieth century, it revived with vigor, given new life by the needs of American families with working parents and young children—and, as we have seen, by the needs of newly arrived Latina immigrants, many of them unmarried and unattached to families. When these women try to move up from live-in domestic work, they see few job alternatives. Often, the best they can do is switch to another form of paid domestic work, either as a live-out nanny/housekeeper or as a weekly housecleaner. When they do such day work, they are better able to circumscribe their work hours, and they earn more money in less time.[8]

LIVE-OUT NANNY/HOUSEKEEPERS

When I first met twenty-four-year-old Ronalda Saavedra, she was peeling a hard-boiled egg for a dog in the kitchen of a very large home where I was interviewing the employer. At this particular domestic job, the fifth she had held since migrating from El Salvador in 1991, she arrived daily around one in the afternoon and left after the children went to bed. On a typical day, she assisted the housekeeper, a middle-aged woman, with cleaning, laundry, and errands, and at three o'clock she drove off in her own car to pick up the children—a nine-year-old boy, whom she claimed was always angry, and his hyperactive six-year-old brother.

Once the children were put to bed, Ronalda Saavedra drove home to a cozy apartment that she shared with her brother in the San Fernando Valley. When I visited her, I saw that it was a tiny place, about half the size of the kitchen where we had first met; but it was pleasantly outfitted with new bleached oak furniture, and the morning sunshine that streamed in through a large window gave it a cheerful, almost spacious feel. Ronalda kept a well-stocked refrigerator, and during our interview she served me *pan dulce*, coffee, and honeydew melon.

Like many other women, Ronalda had begun her work stint in the United States with a live-in job, but she vastly preferred living out. She slept through the night in peace, attended ESL classes in the morning, ate what she wanted when she wanted it, and talked daily on the phone with her fiancé. All this was possible because live-out jobs are firmly circumscribed. Even when women find it difficult to say no to their employers when they are asked, at the last minute, to stay and work another hour or two, they know they will eventually retreat to their own places. So while the workday tasks and rhythms are similar to those of live-ins, the job demands on live-outs stop when they exit the houses where they work and return to their own homes, usually small and sometimes crowded apartments located in one of Los Angeles' many Latino neighborhoods. For such women with husbands or with children of their own, live-out jobs allow them to actually live with their family members and see them daily.

Live-out nanny/housekeepers also earn more money than live-ins. Most of them work eight or nine hours a day, and of those I surveyed, 60 percent worked five days a week or fewer. Their mean hourly wages were $5.90—not an exorbitant wage by any means, but above the legal minimum, unlike the wages of their peers in live-in jobs. Ronalda earned $350 for her forty-hour workweek, making her hourly wage $8.75. On top of this, her employer gave her an additional $50 to cover gasoline expenses, as Ronalda spent a portion of each afternoon driving on errands, such as going to the dry cleaners, and ferrying the children home from school and then to and from soccer practices, music lessons, and so on. In the suburban landscape of Los Angeles, employers pay an extra premium for nanny/housekeepers who can provide this shuttling service. Only Latina nanny/housekeepers with experience, strong references, English skills, and an impressive array of certificates and licenses enjoy earnings that reach Ronalda's level.

Today, most Americans who hire a domestic worker to come into their homes on a daily basis do so in order to meet their needs for *both* housecleaning and child care. Most Latina nanny/housekeepers work in households where they are solely responsible for these tasks, and they work hard to fit in the cleaning and laundry (most of them don't cook) while the children are napping or at school. Some of them feel, as one woman said, that they need to be "octopuses," with busy arms extended simultaneously in all directions. A big part of their job requires taking care of the children; and various issues with the children present nanny/housekeepers with their greatest frustrations. Paradoxically, they also experience some of their deepest job satisfaction with these children with whom they spend so much time.

After what may be years of watching, feeding, playing with, and reprimanding the same child from birth to elementary school, day in and day out, some nanny/housekeepers grow very fond of their charges and look back nostalgically, remembering, say, when a child took her first steps or first learned nursery rhymes in Spanish. Ronalda, an articulate, highly animated woman who told stories using a lot of gestures and facial expressions, talked a great deal about the children she had cared for in her various jobs. She imitated the voices of children she had taken care of, describing longingly little girls who were, she said, "*muy* nice" or "*tan* sweet," and recalled the imaginary games they would play. Like many other nanny/housekeepers, she wept freely when she remembered some of the intimate and amusing moments she had spent with children she no longer saw. She also described other children who, she said, were dour, disrespectful, and disobedient.

Many live-out nanny/housekeepers made care work—the work of keeping the children clean, happy, well nourished, and above all safe—a priority over housecleaning duties. This sometimes created conflicts with their employers, who despite saying that their children should come first still expected a spotless house. "The truth is," explained Teresa Portillo, who looked after a child only on the weekends, "when you are taking care of children, you can't neglect anything, absolutely nothing! Because the moment you do, they do whatever little *travesura*, and they scrape their knees, cut themselves or whatever." Nanny/housekeepers fear they will be sent to jail if anything happens to the children.

Feeding the children is a big part of the job. Unlike their live-in peers, when live-out nanny/ housekeepers talk about food, they're usually concerned with what the children eat or don't eat. Some of them derive tremendous pleasure and satisfaction from bringing the children special treats prepared at their own homes— maybe homemade flan or *pan con crema*, or simply a mango. Some nanny/housekeepers are also in charge, to their dismay, of feeding and cleaning the children's menagerie of pets. Many feel disgusted when they have to bathe and give eyedrops to old, sick dogs, or clean the cages of iguanas, snakes, lizards, and various rodents. But these tasks are trivial in comparison to the difficulties they encounter with hard-to-manage children. Mostly, though, they complain about permissive, neglectful parents.

Not all nanny/housekeepers bond tightly with their employers' children, but most are critical of what they perceive as their employers' careless parenting—or, more accurately, mothering, for their female employers typically receive the blame. They see mothers who may spend, they say, only a few minutes a day with their babies and toddlers, or who return home from work after the children are asleep. Soraya Sanchez said she could understand mothers who work "out of necessity," but all other mothers, she believed, hired nanny/housekeepers because they just didn't like being with their own kids. "*La Americana* is very selfish, she only thinks about herself," she said. "They prefer not to be with their children, as they find it's much easier to pay someone to do that." Her critique was shared by many nanny/housekeepers; and those with children of their own, even if they didn't live with them, saw their own mothering as far superior. "I love my kids, they don't. It's just like, excuse the word, 'shitting kids'" said Patricia Paredes. "What they prefer is to go to the salon, get their nails done, you know, go shopping, things like that. Even if they're home all day, they don't want to spend time with the kids because they're paying somebody to do that for them." For many Latina nanny/housekeepers, seething class resentments find expression in the rhetoric of comparative mothering.

When Latina immigrant women enter the homes of middle-class and upper-middle-class Americans, they encounter ways of raising children very different from those with which they are familiar. As Julia Wrigley's research has shown, the child-rearing values of many Latina and Caribbean nannies differ from those of their employers, but most are eager to do what middle-class parents want—to adopt "time out" discipline measures instead of swatting, or to impose limits on television viewing and Nintendo.[9] Some of them not only adapt but come to genuinely admire and appreciate such methods of child rearing. Yet they, too, criticize the parenting styles they witness close up in the homes where they work.

Some nanny/housekeepers encounter belligerent young children, who yell at them, call them names, and throw violent temper tantrums; and when they do, they blame the parents. They are aghast when parents, after witnessing a child scratch or bite or spit at them, simply shrug their shoulders and ignore such behavior. Parents' reactions to these incidents were a litmus test of sorts. Gladys Villedas, for example, told me that at her job, a five-year-old "grabbed my hair and pulled it really hard. Ay! It hurt so much I started crying! It really hurt my feelings because never in my own country, when I was raising my children, had this happened to me. Why should this happen to me here?" When she complained to her employer, she said the employer had simply consulted a child-rearing manual and explained that it was "a stage." Not all nanny/housekeepers encounter physically abusive children, but when they do, they prefer parents who allow them the authority to impose discipline, or who back them up by firmly instructing their children that it is not okay to kick or slap the nanny. Nanny/housekeepers spoke glowingly about these sorts of employers.

When nanny/housekeepers see parent-child interactions in the homes where they work, they are often put off and puzzled by what they observe. In these moments, the huge cultural gulf between Latina nanny/housekeepers and their employers seems even wider than they had initially imagined. In the home where Maribel Centeno was working as a live-out nanny/housekeeper, she spent the first few hours of her shift doing laundry and housecleaning, but when a thirteen-year-old boy, of whom she was actually very fond, arrived home from school, her real work began. It was his pranks, which were neither malicious nor directed at her, and parental tolerance of these, that drove her crazy. These adolescent pranks usually involved items like water balloons, firecrackers, and baking soda made to look like cocaine. Recently the boy had tacked up on his parents' bedroom door a condom filled with a small amount of milk and a little sign that read, "Mom and Dad, this could have been my life." Maribel thought this was inappropriate behavior; but more bewildering and disturbing than the boy's prank was his mother's reaction—laughter. Another nanny/housekeeper had reacted with similar astonishment when, after a toddler tore apart a loaf of French bread and threw the pieces, balled like cotton, onto the floor, the father came forward not to reprimand but to record the incident with a camcorder. The regularity with which their employers waste food astounds them, and drug use also raises their eyebrows. Some nanny/housekeepers are instructed to give Ritalin and Prozac to children as young as five or six, and others tell of parents and teens locked in their separate bedrooms, each smoking marijuana.

Nanny/housekeepers blame permissive and neglectful parents, who they feel don't spend enough time with their own children, for the children's unruly behavior and for teen drug use. "The parents, they say 'yes' to everything the child asks," complained one woman. "Naturally," she added, "the children are going to act spoiled." Another nanny/housekeeper analyzed the situation this way: "They [the parents] feel guilty because they don't spend that much time with the kids, and they want to replace that missed time, that love, with toys."

Other nanny/housekeepers prided themselves on taming and teaching the children to act properly. "I really had to battle with these children just to get them to pay attention to me! When I started with them, they had no limits, they didn't pick up their toys, and they couldn't control their tempers. The eldest—oof! He used to kick and hit me, and in public! I was mortified," recalled Ronalda Saavedra. Another woman remarked of children she had looked after, "These kids listened to me. After all, they spent most of the time with me, and not with them [the parents]. They would arrive at night, maybe spend a few moments with the kids, or maybe the kids were already asleep." Elvia Areola highlighted the injustice of rearing children whom one will never see again. Discussing her previous job, she said, "I was the one who taught that boy to talk, to walk, to read, to sit! Everything! She [the child's mother] almost never picked him up! She only picked him up when he was happy." Another nanny/housekeeper concluded, "These parents don't really know their own children. Just playing with them, or taking them to the park, well, that's not raising children. I'm the one who is with them every day."

Nanny/housekeepers must also maneuver around jealous parents, who may come to feel that their children's affections have been displaced. "The kids fall in love with you and they [the parents] wonder why. Some parents are jealous of what the kids feel toward you," said Ronalda Saavedra, "I'm not going to be lying, 'I'm your mommy,' but in a way, children go to the person who takes care of them, you know? That's just the way it is." For many nanny/housekeepers, it is these ties of affection that make it possible for them to do their job by making it rewarding. Some of them say they can't properly care for the children without feeling a special fondness for them; others say it just happens naturally. "I fall in love with all of these children. How can I not? That's just the way I am," one nanny/housekeeper told me. "I'm with them all day, and when I go home, my husband complains that that's all I talk about, what they did, the funny things they said." The nanny/housekeepers, as much as they felt burdened by disobedient children, sometimes felt that these children were also a gift of sorts, one that parents—again, the mothers—did not fully appreciate. "The babies are so beautiful!" gushed Soraya Sanchez. "How is it that a mother can lose those best years, when their kids are babies. I mean, I remember going down for a nap with these little babies, how we'd cuddle. How is it that a person who has the option of enjoying that would prefer to give that experience to a stranger?" Precisely because of such feelings, many Latina immigrants who have children try to find a job that is compatible with their own family lives. Housecleaning is one of those jobs.

HOUSECLEANERS

Like many working mothers, every weekday morning Marisela Ramírez awoke to dress and feed her preschooler, Tomás, and drive him to school (actually, a Head Start program) before she herself ventured out to work, navigating the dizzying array of Los Angeles freeways. Each day she set off in a different direction headed for a different workplace. On Mondays she maneuvered her way to Pasadena, where she cleaned the stately home of an elderly couple; on Tuesdays she alternated between cleaning a home in the Hollywood Hills and a more modest-sized duplex in Glendale; and Wednesdays took her to a split-level condominium in Burbank. You had to keep alert, she said, to remember where to go on which days and how to get there!

By nine o'clock she was usually on the job, and because she zoomed through her work she was able to finish, unless the house was extremely dirty, by one or two in the afternoon. After work, there were still plenty of daylight hours left for Marisela to take Tomás to the park, or at least to take him outside and let him ride down the sidewalk on his kid-sized motorized vehicle before she started dinner. Working as a housecleaner allowed Marisela to be the kind of wife and mother she wanted to be. Her job was something she did, she said, "because I have to"; but unlike her peers who work in live-in jobs, she enjoyed a fairly regular family life of her own, one that included cooking and eating family meals, playing with her son, bathing him, putting him to bed, and then watching *telenovelas* in the evenings with her husband and her sister. On the weekends, family socializing took center stage, with *carne asadas* in the park; informal gatherings with her large Mexican family, which extended throughout Los Angeles; and music from her husband, who worked as a gardener but played guitar in a weekend *ranchera* band.

Some might see Marisela Ramírez as just another low-wage worker doing dirty work, but by her own account—and gauging by her progress from her starting point—she had made remarkable occupational strides. Marisela had begun working as a live-in

nanny/housekeeper in Los Angeles when she was only fifteen years old. Ten years later, the move from live-in work to housecleaning had brought her higher hourly wages, a shorter workweek, control over the pace of work, and flexibility in arranging when she worked. Cleaning different houses was also, she said, less boring than working as a nanny/housekeeper, which entailed passing every single day "in just one house, all week long with the same routine, over and over."

For a while she had tried factory work, packaging costume jewelry in a factory warehouse located in the San Fernando Valley, but Marisela saw housecleaning as preferable on just about every count. "In the factory, one has to work very, very fast!" she exclaimed. "And you can't talk to anybody, you can't stop, and you can't rest until it's break time. When you're working in a house, you can take a break at the moment you wish, finish the house when you want, and leave at the hour you decide. And it's better pay. It's harder work, yes," she conceded, "but it's better pay."

"How much were you earning at the factory?" I asked.

"Five dollars an hour; and working in houses now, I make about $11, or even more. Look, in a typical house, I enter at about 9 A.M., and I leave at 1 P.M., and they pay me $60. It's much better [than factory work]." Her income varied, but she could usually count on weekly earnings of about $300. By pooling these together with her husband's and sister's earnings, she was able to rent a one-bedroom bungalow roofed in red tile, with a lawn and a backyard for Tomás's sandbox and plastic swimming pool. In Mexico, Marisela had only studied as far as fifth grade, but she wanted the best for Tomás. Everyone doted on him, and by age four he was already reading simple words.

Of the housecleaners I surveyed, the majority earned, like Marisela, between $50 and $60 per housecleaning, which usually took about six hours. This suggests an average hourly wage of about $9.50, but I suspect the actual figure is higher.[10] Women like Marisela, who drive their own cars and speak some English, are likely to earn more than the women I surveyed, many of whom ride the buses to work. Marisela was typical of the housecleaners whom I surveyed in having been in the United States for a number of years. Unlike nanny/housekeepers, most of the housecleaners who were mothers themselves had all their children with them in the United States. Housecleaning, as Mary Romero has noted, is a job that is quite compatible with having a family life of one's own.

Breaking into housecleaning is tough, often requiring informal tutelage from friends and relatives. Contrary to the image that all women "naturally" know how to do domestic work, many Latina domestic workers discover that their own housekeeping experiences do not automatically transfer to the homes where they work. As she looked back on her early days in the job, Marisela said, "I didn't know how to clean or anything. My sister taught me." Erlinda Castro, a middle-aged women who had already run her own household and raised five children in Guatemala, had also initially worked in live-in jobs when she first came to Los Angeles. Yet despite this substantial domestic experience, she recalled how mystified she was when she began housecleaning. "Learning how to use the chemicals and the liquids" in the different households was confusing, and, as friends and employers instructed her on what to do, she began writing down in a little notebook the names of the products and what they cleaned. Some women learn the job by informally apprenticing with one another, accompanying a friend or perhaps an aunt on her housecleaning jobs.

Establishing a thriving route of *casas* requires more than learning which cleaning products to use or how to clean quickly and efficiently. It also involves acquiring multiple jobs, which housecleaners typically gain by asking their employers if they have friends, neighbors, or acquaintances who need someone to clean their houses; and because some attrition is inevitable, they must constantly be on the lookout for more *casas*. Not everyone who wants to can fill up her entire week.

To make ends meet when they don't have enough houses to clean, Latina housecleaners in Los Angeles find other ways to earn income. They might prepare food—say, tamales and *crema*—which they sell door-to-door or on the street; or they might sell small amounts of clothing that they buy wholesale in the garment district, or products from Avon, Mary Kay cosmetics, and Princess House kitchenware. They take odd jobs, such as handing out flyers advertising dental clinics or working at a swap meet; or perhaps they find something more stable, such as evening janitorial work in office buildings. Some housecleaners work swing shift in garment factories, while others work three days a week as a nanny/housekeeper and try to fill the remaining days with housecleaning jobs. Some women supplement their husband's income by cleaning only one or two houses a week, but more often they patch together a number of jobs in addition to housecleaning.

Housecleaning represents, as Romero has written, the "modernization" of paid domestic work. Women who clean different houses on different days sell their labor services, she argues, in much the same way that a vendor sells a product to various customers.[11] The housecleaners themselves see their job as far preferable to that of a live-in or live-out nanny/housekeeper. They typically work alone, during times when their employers are out of the home; and because they are paid "by the job" instead of by the hour, they don't have to remain on the job until 6 or 7 P.M., an advantage much appreciated by women who have families of their own. Moreover, because they work for different employers on different days, they are not solely dependent for their livelihood on one boss whom they see every single day. Consequently, their relationships with their employers are less likely to become highly charged and conflictual; and if problems do arise, they can leave one job without jeopardizing their entire weekly earnings. Since child care is not one of their tasks, their responsibilities are more straightforward and there are fewer points of contention with employers. Housecleaning is altogether less risky.

Housecleaners also see working independently and informally as more desirable than working for a commercial cleaning company. "The companies pay $5 an hour," said Erlinda Castro, whose neighbor worked for one, "and the women have to work their eight hours, doing up to ten, twenty houses a day! One does the vacuuming, the other does the bathroom and the kitchen, and like that. It's tremendously hard work, and at $5 an hour? Thank God, I don't have to do that." Two of the women I interviewed, one now a live-out nanny/housekeeper and the other a private housecleaner, had previously worked for cleaning services, and both of them complained bitterly about their speeded-up work pace, low pay, and tyrannical bosses.

Private housecleaners take enormous pride in their work. When they finish their job, they can see the shiny results, and they are proud of their job autonomy, their hours, their pay, and, most important, what they are able to do with their pay for themselves and for their families. Yet housecleaning brings its own special problems. Intensive cleaning eventually brings physical pain, and sometimes injury. "Even my bones are tired," said fifty-three-year-old Lupe Vélez; and even a relatively young woman like Celestina Vigil at age thirty-three was already reporting back problems that she attributed to her work. While most of them have only fleeting contact with their employers, and many said they work for "good people," just about everyone has suffered, they said, "inconsiderate persons" who exhort them to work faster, humiliate them, fail to give raises, add extra cleaning tasks without paying extra, or unjustly accuse them of stealing or of ruining a rug or upholstery. And the plain old hard work and stigma of cleaning always remain, as suggested by the answer I got when I asked a housecleaner what she liked least about her job. "The least?" she said, with a wry smile. "Well, that you have to clean."

DOMESTIC JOB TRAJECTORIES AND TRANSNATIONAL MOTHERHOOD

As we have seen, private paid domestic work is organized into suboccupations, each with different pay scales, tasks, and hours.[12] Although they share many similarities, each job arrangement has its own different problems and rewards. In this section I discuss the movement between the three suboccupations and some of the family characteristics of the women who fill these jobs.

Some researchers have called live-in domestic work "the bridging occupation," because in various periods and places, it allowed rural migrant women to acculturate to the city and learn new ways of living.[13] Unlike Irish immigrant women or the black women who went from the South to the North to work as domestics in the early twentieth century, and unlike many private domestics in Europe and Latin America in the past, most Latina immigrants doing paid domestic work in the United States are *not* new to the city. Yet for many of them in Los Angeles today, especially those who are single and have very limited options for places to work and live, live-in jobs do serve as an initial occupational step. As Table 1 shows, new arrivals and women who have lived in the United States five years or less concentrate in live-in jobs (60 percent). In contrast, the majority of housecleaners (83 percent) and live-out nanny/ housekeepers (69 percent) have lived in the United States for more than five years. Some begin their live-in jobs literally within forty-eight hours after arriving in Los Angeles, while some housecleaners have lived in the United States for twenty years or more. For newly arrived immigrant women without papers, a live-in job in a private home may feel safer, as private homes in middle- and upper-middle-class neighborhoods are rarely, if ever, threatened by Immigration and Naturalization Service raids.[14]

TABLE I   TYPE OF DOMESTIC WORK, LENGTH OF RESIDENCE IN THE UNITED STATES, AND MEAN HOURLY WAGES

	Live-ins (percent) (n = 30)	Live-outs (percent) (n = 64)	Housecleaners (percent) (n = 59)
Five years or less in United States	60	31	17
More than five years in United States	40	69	83
Mean hourly wage	$3.80	$5.90	$9.50

As the years pass, the women who took live-in jobs learn some English, gain knowledge of other job possibilities, and learn to use their social networks to their occupational advantage. Most of them eventually move out of live-in work. Some return to their countries of origin, and others look to sales, factory work, or janitorial work. But given the low pay of those jobs—in 1999, garment workers in Los Angeles were earning $5.00 an hour, and nonunion janitors with six years of experience were earning $6.30 an hour—many of them transition into some form of domestic day work.[15] As they abandon their live-in positions for live-out nanny/housekeeper and housecleaner jobs, their wages increase. For these women, the initial misery suffered in their live-in jobs makes other domestic work look if not good then at least tolerable—and certainly better than where they started.

For Latina immigrants in Los Angeles today, live-in domestic work does serve as an occupational bridge of sorts, but it often leads only to other types of domestic jobs. These individual trajectories match historical transformations in the occupation. Much as live-in jobs were once the dominant form of paid domestic work, and then gave way to arrangements in which domestics continued to work daily for one employer but lived with their own families, and finally to modernized "job work" or periodic housecleaning, so many Latina immigrants today traverse these three different types of jobs. Some roughly follow the historical order, moving from live-in to live-out nanny/ housekeeper jobs, and then to housecleaning, but their modest occupational mobility does not always follow such a linear course.

As Mexican and Central American immigrant women move into live-out and housecleaning jobs, their family lives change. With better pay and fewer hours of work, they become able to live with their own family members. Among those I surveyed, about 45 percent of the women doing day work were married, but only 13 percent of the live-ins were married. Most women who have husbands and children with them in Los Angeles do not wish to take live-in jobs; moreover, their application for a live-in job is likely to be rejected if they reveal that they have a husband, a boyfriend, or children living in Los Angeles. As one job seeker in an employment agency waiting room put it, "You can't have a family, you can't have anyone [if you want a live-in job]." Live-out nanny/housekeepers often face this family restriction too, as employers are wary of hiring someone who may not report for work when her own children come down with the flu.

Their subminimum wages and long hours make it impossible for many live-in workers to bring their children to Los Angeles; other live-ins are young women who do not have children of their own. Once they do have children who are either born in or have immigrated to Los Angeles, most women try to leave live-in work to be with them. Not all the women can do so, and sometimes their finances or jobs force them to send the children "back home" to be reared by grandmothers. Clearly, performing domestic work for pay, especially in a live-in job, is often incompatible with caring for one's own family and home.[16]

The substantial proportion of Latina domestic workers in Los Angeles whose children stay in their countries of origin are in the same position as many Caribbean women working in domestic jobs on the East Coast, and as the Filipinas who predominate in domestic jobs in many cities around the globe. This is what I label "transnational motherhood" . . . ; in a 1997 article Ernestine Avila and I coined this term as we examined how Latina immigrant domestic workers are transforming their own meanings of motherhood to accommodate these spatial and temporal separations.[17] As Table 2 suggests, these arrangements are most common among women with live-in jobs, but live-in domestic workers and single mothers are not the only ones who rely on them.[18]

These transnational arrangements are not altogether new. The United States has a long history of incorporating people of color through coercive systems of labor that do not recognize family rights, including the right to care for one's own family members. As others have pointed out, slavery and contract labor systems were organized to maximize economic productivity, and

TABLE 2   TYPE OF DOMESTIC WORK, MARITAL STATUS, AND LOCATION OF CHILDREN

	Live-ins (percent) (n = 30)	Live-outs (percent) (n = 64)	Housecleaners (percent) (n = 59)
Single (included the widowed, divorced, or separated)	87	55	54
Married	13	45	46
	Domestic Workers with Children		
	(n = 16)	(n = 53)	(n = 45)
All children in United States	18	58	76
At least one child "back home"	82	42	24

offered few supports to sustain family life.[19] Today, international labor migration and the job characteristics of paid domestic work, especially live-in work, virtually impose transnational motherhood on many Mexican and Central American women who have children of their own.

At the other end of the spectrum are the housecleaners, who earn higher wages than live-ins (averaging $9.50 an hour vs. $3.80) and who work fewer hours per week than live-ins (twenty-three vs. sixty-four). The majority of them (76 percent) have all their children in the United States, and they are the least likely to experience transnational spatial and temporal separations from their children. Greater financial resources and more favorable job terms enhance housecleaners' abilities to bring their children to the United States. As we have seen, weekly housecleaning is dominated by relatively well-established women with more years of experience in the United States, who speak some English, who have a car, and who have job references. Because their own position is more secure, they are also more likely to have their children here. And because they tend to work fewer hours per week, have greater flexibility in scheduling, and earn higher wages than the live-ins, they can live with and care for their children.

With respect to their ability to care for their own children, live-out nanny/housekeepers fall between live-ins and weekly cleaners—predictably, since they are also in an intermediate position in their earnings, rigidity of schedule, and working hours. Live-out domestic workers, according to the survey, earn $5.90 an hour and work an average workweek of thirty-five hours, and 42 percent of those who are mothers reported having at least one of their children in their country of origin.

THE DOMINANCE OF CENTRAL AMERICAN AND MEXICAN IMMIGRANT WOMEN

Paid domestic work has long been a racialized and gendered occupation, but why today are Central American women hugely over-represented in these jobs in Los Angeles in comparison with Mexicans (whose immigrant population is of course many times larger)? In the survey I conducted of 153 Westside Latina domestic workers, 75 percent of the respondents were from Central America; of those, most were from El Salvador and Guatemala. And in census counts, Salvadoran and Guatemalan women are, respectively, twelve times and thirteen times more likely than the general population to be engaged in private domestic work in Los Angeles.[20] Numerous studies paint a similar picture in other major U.S. cities, such as Washington, D.C., Houston, and San Francisco; one naturally wonders why this should be so.[21]

In Los Angeles, the heavy concentration of Central American women in paid domestic work is partially explained by the location of L.A.'s primary Central American immigrant neighborhood, the Pico-Union/Westlake area, just west of the small, high-rise downtown. As UCLA sociologist David Lopez and his colleagues explain, "A large proportion of Central Americans tend to reside closer to the middle-class neighborhoods of the Westside and the San Fernando Valley . . . while Mexicans are concentrated in the more isolated areas east and south of Downtown Los Angeles.[22] It is certainly quicker to drive or take a bus to the Westside from the Pico Union area than it is from East L.A. But there is more to this story than spatial location and L.A. transportation systems: distinct migration patterns have also influenced these occupational concentrations.

Mexican migration to the United States goes back over a hundred years, initially driven by labor recruitment programs designed to bring in men to work in agriculture. Since the late 1960s, it has shifted from a primarily male population of temporary or sojourner workers to one that includes women and entire families; these newcomers have settled in rural areas, cities,

and suburbs throughout the United States, but disproportionately in California. Many Mexican women who migrated in the 1970s and 1980s were accompanied by their families and were aided by rich social networks; the latter helped prevent the urgency that leads new immigrants to take live-in jobs. Even those unmarried Mexican women who did migrate on their own, despite being opposed and sometimes stigmatized by their family and community, were often assisted by friends and more sympathetic family members. By the 1990s, more unmarried Mexican women were going north, encouraged in part by help from female friends and kin. When Mexican women arrive in the United States, many of them enjoy access to well-developed, established communities whose members have long been employed in various industries, particularly agriculture, construction, hotels, food-processing plants, and garment factories. Compared to their Central American peers, Mexican women are more likely to have financial support from a husband; because fewer Mexican immigrant women must work outside their home, they have lower rates of overall participation in the labor force than do Central American women.[23] Their social networks also give Mexican women greater variety in their employment options; paid domestic work is only one of their alternatives.

Salvadoran and Guatemalan women migrating to the United States have done so under different circumstances than Mexican women. For Central Americans coming to *el norte*, there was no long-standing labor program recruiting men who could then bring, or encourage the migration of, their wives and daughters. In fact, as Terry Repak's study shows, some of the early pioneers of Salvadoran migration to Washington, D.C., were women, themselves informally recruited by individual members of the diplomatic corps precisely because they were desired as private domestics.[24] More significantly, Salvadoran and Guatemalan women and men left their countries in haste, often leaving their children behind, as they fled the civil wars, political violence, and economic upheaval of the 1980s. Theirs are immigrant communities that subsisted without legal status for nearly two decades, grew rapidly, and remain very poor. Even Guatemalan and Salvadoran women who arrived in the United States in the late 1980s and early 1990s could not count on finding communities of well-established compatriots who could quickly and efficiently situate them in jobs in restaurants, hotels, factories, or other industries. In fact, as some of the most compelling ethnographies of

Salvadorans in San Francisco and on Long Island have shown, Central Americans' relatively shallow U.S. roots have left their social networks extremely impoverished and sometimes fractured.[25] For Central American women arriving on their own, without husbands and children in tow, desperate and lacking information about jobs—and at a crucial historical moment when American families were seeking to resolve their own child care and housekeeping problems—live-in jobs were both attractive and available.

Family structures and marriage patterns may have also contributed to the preponderance of Central American women in paid domestic work. El Salvador has traditionally had one of the lowest marriage rates in the hemisphere, especially among the urban poor, where common-law marriages and legacies of internal and intra–Central America labor migration—mostly for work on coffee plantations—have encouraged the formation of female-headed households.[26] Thus Salvadoran women have been more likely to migrate on their own and accept live-in jobs.[27] Their large numbers in this lowest rung of domestic work would then explain their eventual disproportionate concentration in all types of private paid domestic work, following the pattern discussed above.

The experience of Central American women might also be compared to that of Asian immigrant women, who have been entering the United States at increasing rates. The latter are an extremely heterogeneous group, but on average—and this is particularly true of Chinese, Indian, and Filipina women—they arrive with much higher levels of education, better English language skills, and more professional credentials than do their Latina peers. They are also more likely to have legal status; and members of some groups, especially Korean immigrant women, enjoy access to jobs in family businesses and ethnic enclaves.[28] At the same time, the generally poorer and less-educated women from Vietnam, Laos, and Cambodia have been able to withstand periods of underemployment and unemployment because they are officially sanctioned political refugees and therefore enjoy access to welfare and resettlement assistance from the federal government. While some individual Asian immigrant women are working in paid domestic work, they have not developed social networks that channel them into this niche.

It is particularly striking that Filipina immigrants predominate in this occupation elsewhere around the globe, but not in the United States. Worldwide, about two-thirds of Filipina migrants in countries as different as Italy, Canada, Hong Kong, Taiwan, Singapore, Saudi Arabia, and Jordan, do paid domestic work; but in the United States, their high levels of education and fluent English enable most of them to enter higher status occupations that require more skills than does domestic work. In 1990, 71 percent of the Filipinas in the United States were working in managerial, professional, technical/sales, and administrative support jobs, and only 17 percent were employed in service jobs.[29] They are disproportionately concentrated in the health professions, the result of formal recruitment programs designed to fill U.S. nursing shortages.[30] Experience in the health professions leads many Filipinas to take jobs in elder care; and though some work as nanny/housekeepers in Los Angeles, many of them as live-ins, in my numerous discussions with employers, Latina employees, attorneys, and owners and employees of domestic employment agencies, no one ever mentioned Filipina housecleaners.

Nevertheless, Filipina immigrants are doing paid domestic work in the United States. Interviews conducted by Rhacel Parreñas with twenty-six Filipina domestic workers in Los Angeles reveal that many of these women have college diplomas and are working in homes because they are older and face age discrimination; they tend to earn more as care providers for the elderly ($425 per week) and more as nanny/housekeepers ($350 per week) than do Latina immigrants in these same jobs.[31] When it comes to caring for their children, some employers prefer Filipina nanny/housekeepers because they speak English well (English is the official language of schools and universities in the Philippines), and because they tend to be highly educated. Paradoxically, these qualities may predispose some employers to *not* choose Filipinas as domestic employees. At three domestic employment agencies, the owners told me that they rarely placed Filipina job applicants, because they were deemed "uppity," demanding, and likely to lie about their references. Racial preferences, as the next section suggests, shape the formation of Latina domestic workers and their employment in Los Angeles.

NARRATIVES OF RACIAL PREFERENCES

In a race-conscious society, everyone has racial preferences and prejudices, and Latina domestic workers and the women who employ them are no exception. When choosing someone to work in their homes, many employers prefer Latinas, because as "others" in language, race-ethnicity, and social class, they are outside white, English-speaking, middle-class social circles and are thus seen as unlikely to reveal family secrets and intimacies. If they do tell someone about the family fight they witnessed, that someone is likely to be another Latina nanny or a member of their own family—in either case, no one who matters to the employers. This fear of exposure sometimes prevents employers from choosing white, English-speaking job candidates. "She was non-Hispanic, and I wasn't sure if I could trust her," said one woman of a prospective employee. Another employer had been advised not to hire a white woman as a nanny/housekeeper because an immigrant would be less likely to recognize her philanthropic family's name and to engage in bribery or kidnapping. Other women told me that they did not want a European au pair or midwestern (white) teenager taking care of their children because they would probably be young, irresponsible teens, more interested in cavorting with boyfriends, cruising the beach, and stargazing in Hollywood than in doing their job. Employers may also prefer to hire Latina nannies, as research conducted by Julia Wrigley suggests, because they view them as more submissive than whites.[32]

While some of the older employers I interviewed had hired African American housecleaners and domestics in the past, none were now doing so. Of the relatively few black women working in paid domestic work in contemporary Los Angeles, most are immigrants from Belize and Brazil, and some employers remain adamantly opposed to hiring black women to work in their homes. One domestic employment agency owner told me that some clients had requested that he never send black women to interview for a job. And at an informal luncheon, arranged by one of the employer interviewees, one of them cleared her throat and then offered, with some awkward hesitation, "Uhm, ah, I would never hire a black woman. I'd be too scared to, and I'd be especially scared if her boyfriend came around." The women, all of them relatively upper-class white matrons, had nodded in silent agreement. The old stereotype of the bossy black maid is apparently alive and well, now joined by newer terrifying images associated with young black men; but since African-American women are not pursuing domestic work jobs in Los Angeles, most employers need never confront their own racial fears directly. It is, after all, Latina immigrant women who are queuing up for domestic jobs in private homes.

When I talked with them, most employers expressed genuine appreciation for the effort, dedication, and work that these women put into their homes and children. They viewed Latina domestic workers as responsible, trustworthy, and reliable employees who have "a really strong work ethic." And while plenty of employers spoke at length about Latina women as ideally suited to caring for children, relying on images of Latinas as exceptionally warm, patient, and loving mothers, there was no similar racialized image of cleanliness. No one said, for instance, "She cleans like a Mexican." Such a phrase may sound offensive, but the absence of any such generalization is striking when nearly everyone hired to do cleaning in Los Angeles is Mexican or Central American.

Indeed, some of the employers I interviewed did make this kind of statement—to associate their own northern European heritage with superior cleaning and hygiene. A few of them offered remarks such as "People associate very clean homes with Dutch people," or "My mother's German and she cleans, you know, like Germans clean." These women did not necessarily claim that they were excellent cleaners, only that they belonged to racial-ethnic groups associated with cleanliness. None of them described their domestic employees as "dirty," but the adjective has been commonly featured in racial epithets directed at Mexicans in the Southwest and at domestic workers just about everywhere. The historian Phyllis Palmer, who has written compellingly about dirt, domesticity, and racialized divisions among women, notes that while dirt and housework connote inferior morality, white middle-class women transcend these connotations by employing women different from themselves to do the work. "Dirtiness," Palmer notes, "appears always in a constellation of the suspect qualities that, along with sexuality, immorality, laziness, and ignorance, justify social rankings of race, class and gender. The 'slut,' initially a shorthand for 'slattern' or kitchen maid, captures all of these personifications in a way unimaginable in a male persona."[33]

Employers are not the only ones who hold strong racial-ethnic preferences and prejudices. Latina domestic workers at the bus stops, at the agencies, and in the public parks readily agreed on who were their worst employers: Armenians, Iranians, Asians, Latinos, blacks, and Jews, especially Israeli Jews. "I'll never work again for *un chino!*" or "*Los armenios* [Armenians] are the worst," they tell each other. These statements were echoed in the individual interviews, as well as by the preferences job candidates register at employment agencies, and they seem to mirror what Latino men who work as day laborers think about their similarly racialized employers in Los Angeles.[34] Anyone marked as "nonwhite," it seems, is at risk of being denounced as a cheap, abusive, and oppressive employer, one to be avoided at all costs.

There are a number of factors at work here. Many of the employers in these racial-ethnic groups are immigrants themselves, albeit entrepreneurial and professional immigrants with substantially more resources than the Latinas they hire to care for their homes and children. Many had belonged to elites in their countries of origin, accustomed to having servants in their homes who would be expected to perform all sorts of jobs on demand. Some of them bring these expectations with them when they come to the United States. When Latina domestic workers are expected to massage the señora's feet with oil, or scrub the kitchen floor on their hands and knees, they take offence. Others are wholly unprepared to iron Hindu saris, or to follow kosher food preparation and serving practices in the homes of Orthodox Jews. At the same time, the immigrant and ethnic employers may have been accustomed in their countries of origin to paying slave wages, and the tenuous financial situations of some makes them unable to pay minimum wage. Some newly arrived women who find their first job working as a live-in for other working-class Latino immigrant families may receive as little as $25 or $50 a week in exchange for their round-the-clock services.

Latina immigrants also operate under racist assumptions, many of which they learn in the United States. They quickly pick up the country's racial hierarchies and racist stereotypes. "Jews are cheap," "Mexican Americans and blacks are lazy," or *"Los chinos* are too bossy," they say. The regional racial hierarchy also fixes Jews, Armenians, and Iranians in low positions. *"Los Americanos,"* the term they typically use to refer to employers marked only "white," are almost never singled out by ethnicity and are rarely criticized or negatively labeled as a group.

Conversely, Latina domestic workers single out the race of particular employers who happen to be both "bad employers" and "racialized" as nonwhite. One Mexican housecleaner who maintained that Latino employers were among the most exploitative was Lupe Vélez. When I probed why she felt this way, she cited as evidence her experiences with one employer, a man from Monterrey, Mexico. A large, verbally abusive

man, he had called her a pig, he went out of his way to deny her food when he sat down to eat with his family, and he had unfairly accused her of scratching and ruining a stove top. These deeply felt, painful experiences were recounted tearfully.

Yet as we talked longer, I discovered that in Los Angeles, Lupe had worked in three different Latino homes; she spoke of a Mexican American teacher who had treated her well and paid her fairly. Mutual fondness, respect, and closeness had grown between the two, who had unsuccessfully conspired at matchmaking between their young adult children. How could she maintain that Latinos were the "worst" employers when in fact a Mexican American had been among her best employers? In recalling her bad experience with the Mexican man, Lupe Vélez singled out his racial-ethnic identity. As she recalled that painful experience, his being Mexican and consistently acting abusively toward her became the most salient features about him. She applied "Latino," a racial marker, to this man, labeled an abusive, bad employer, but not to the teacher whom she had favored.

I suspect that when Latina domestic workers denounce Jewish employers, a similar process is at work. In those cases, they may only identify as Jewish those employers who are abusive and who are, as Orthodox Jews or recently emigrated Israeli Jews, unambiguously marked as Jewish. They might not recognize the other Jews for whom they work. Or perhaps Latina domestic workers' disdain for Jewish employers is testimony to the force of contemporary anti-Semitism. It is no small irony that a major provider of legal services for Latina domestic workers in Los Angeles is a Jewish nonprofit organization.[35]

Some Latina domestic workers related counter-narratives, criticizing their peers for relying on racial stereotypes and hasty racial judgments. One Salvadoran housecleaner cited her Moroccan employer as one of the most gracious because she always served her a hot lunch, sitting down to chat with her; another related her appreciation of an African American bachelor, an ex-basketball player, who kept a messy house but paid her very generously; still another felt warmly toward her Korean employer who did not pay well, but who passed many choice housecleaning jobs on to her. Yet the voices of these women were drowned out by the louder, frequently blanket condemnations that other Latina domestic workers offered about their racially marked minority and immigrant employers. Amid the public clamor of racialized nativism that propelled California ballot initiatives against health and education services for undocumented immigrants and their children, against affirmative action, and against bilingual education (Propositions 187, 209, and 227 respectively), Latina immigrant domestic workers learn their own version of regional racism.

In this [reading], I conveyed briefly some of the life textures and the daily trials and triumphs experienced by Latina immigrants who work as housecleaners, live-out nanny/housekeepers, and live-in nanny/housekeepers. The Mexican, Salvadoran, and Guatemalan women who occupy these jobs come from diverse class, regional, and cultural locations, and they bring different expectations to their jobs. Once in the United States, however, they share a set of similar experiences part because of the way that their domestic work is structured.

NOTES

1. Glenn 1986: 141.
2. Lacher 1997: 1.
3. One nanny/housekeeper told me that a señora had admonished her for picking a bag of fruit, and wanted to charge her for it; another claimed that her employer had said she would rather watch the fruit fall off the branches and rot than see her eat it.
4. Many Latina domestic workers do not know the amount of their hourly wages; and because the lines between their work and nonwork tend to blur, live-in nanny/housekeepers have particular difficulty calculating them. In the survey questionnaire I asked live-in nanny/housekeepers how many days a week they worked, what time they began their job, and what time they ended, and I asked them to estimate how many hours off they had during an average workday (39 percent said they had no time off, but 32 percent said they had a break of between one and three hours). Forty-seven percent of the women said they began their workday at 7 A.M. or earlier, with 62 percent ending their workday at 7 P.M. or later. With the majority of them (71 percent) working five days a week, their average workweek was sixty-four hours. This estimate may at first glance appear inflated; but consider a prototypical live-in nanny/housekeeper who works, say, five days a week, from 7 A.M. until 9 P.M., with one and a half hours off during the children's nap time (when she might take a break to lie down or watch television). Her on-duty work hours would total sixty-four and a half hours per week. The weekly pay of live-in nanny/housekeepers surveyed ranged from $130 to $400, averaging $242. Dividing this figure by sixty-four yields an hourly wage of $3.80. None of the live-in nanny/housekeepers were charged for room and board—and . . . this practice is regulated by law—but 86 percent said they brought food with them to their jobs. The majority reported being paid in cash.
5. See, e.g., Employment Classified Section 2, *Los Angeles Times*, June 6, 1999, G9.
6. Clark-Lewis 1994: 123. "After an average of seven years," she notes in her analysis of African American women who had migrated from the South to Washington, D.C., in the early twentieth century, "all of the migrant women grew to dread their live-in situation. They saw their occupation as harming all aspects of their life" (124). Nearly all of these women transitioned into day work in private homes. This pattern is being repeated by Latina immigrants in Los Angeles today, and it reflects local labor market opportunities and constraints. In Houston, Texas, where many Mayan Guatemalan immigrant women today work as live-ins, research by Jacqueline Maria Hagan (1998) points to the tremendous obstacles they face in leaving live-in work. In Houston, housecleaning is dominated by better-established immigrant women, by Chicanas and, more recently, by the commercial cleaning companies—so it is hard for the Maya to secure those jobs. Moreover, Hagan finds that over time, the Mayan women who take live-in jobs see their own social networks contract, further reducing their internal job mobility.
7. Several factors explain the shift to day work, including urbanization, interurban transportation systems, and smaller private residences. Historians have also credited the job preferences of African American domestic workers, who rejected the constraints of live-in work and chose to live with their own families and communities, with helping to promote this shift in the urban North after 1900 (Katzman 1981; Clark-Lewis 1994: 129–35). In many urban regions of the United States, the shift to day work accelerated during World War I, so that live-out arrangements eventually became more prevalent (Katzman 1981; Palmer 1989). Elsewhere, and for different groups of domestic workers, these transitions happened later in the twentieth century. Evelyn Nakano Glenn (1986: 143) notes that Japanese immigrant and Japanese American women employed in domestic work in the San Francisco Bay Area moved out of live-in jobs and into modernized day work in the years after World War II.
8. Katzman 1981; Glenn 1986.
9. Wrigley 1995.
10. Keep in mind that the survey questionnaire was administered at three different types of sites: bus stops, ESL evening classes, and parks where nannies congregate with the children in their charge. Housecleaners who drive and have their own cars, and who speak some English, typically earn more money and are able to clean more houses per week. Because my survey is biased toward Latina

domestic workers who ride the buses and attend ESL classes, those housecleaners earning higher wages are not taken into account.

11. Romero 1992.

12. In addition to the jobs of live-in nanny/housekeepers, live-out nanny/housekeepers, and weekly or biweekly housecleaners, an increasingly important and growing segment of the domestic workforce is engaged in elder care. That, too, is organized in different ways; and though the occupation lies beyond the parameters of this study (much of it is formally organized and contracted for by the state or medical organizations), some Latina immigrants are privately contracted for jobs as elders' companions and caretakers, as *damas de compañía.*

13. Smith 1973; McBride 1976.

14. The only news report of INS raids involving nannies working in private homes in Los Angeles that came to my attention as I did this research involved a nanny working for a top-ranking Latino INS agent, Jorge Guzman. In 1996 armed plainclothes INS agents illegally raided Guzman's home, and allegedly fondled and made sexual advances toward the domestic worker. Guzman claimed that the raid was part of a ten-year program of internal anti-Latino harassment directed at him. After he filed suit, the U.S. Justice Department agreed to pay him $400,000 to settle (McDonnell 1999).

15. Personal communication, Cynthia Cranford, March 1999; Cleeland 1999.

16. Rollins 1985; Glenn 1986; Romero 1992. See Romero 1997 for a study focusing on the perspective of domestic workers' children. Although the majority of respondents in that study were children of day workers, and none appear to have been children of transnational mothers, they still recall that their mothers' occupation had significant costs for them.

17. Hondagneu-Sotelo and Avila 1997.

18. Central American women seem more likely than Mexican women to leave their children in their country of origin, even if their husbands are living with them in the United States, perhaps because of the multiple dangers and costs associated with undocumented travel from Central America to the United States. The civil wars of the 1980s, continuing violence and economic uncertainty, greater difficulties and costs associated with crossing multiple national borders, and stronger cultural legacies of socially sanctioned consensual unions may also contribute to this pattern for Central Americans.

19. Glenn 1986; Dill 1988.

20. The figures on Salvadoran and Guatemalan women are taken from an analysis of the 1990 census data by the sociologists David E. Lopez, Eric Popkin, and Edward Telles (1996); they also found that Mexican immigrants were only 2.3 times as likely as those in the general population to be engaged in paid domestic work.

21. See Salzinger 1991; Hagan 1994, 1998; Repak 1995.

22. Lopez, Popkin, and Telles 1996: 298.

23. According to 1990 PUMS Census data, about 70 percent of Central American women between the ages of 24 and 60 in Los Angeles County are in the labor force, while only 56 percent of their Mexican peers are. Among this same group, 71 percent of Mexican immigrant women but only 56 percent of their Central American peers are married and living with a spouse. To put it even more starkly, 28 percent of Mexican immigrant women and 43 percent of Central American women report living with family members or adults other than their spouses.

24. Repak 1995.

25. Mahler 1995; Menjívar 2000.

26. Some studies estimate that as many as 50 percent of poor households in San Salvador were formed by "free unions" rather than marriage by law. This pattern is related not just to internal and intra-Central American labor migration but also to urban poverty, as there is no need to secure inheritance rights when there is no property to share (Nieves 1979; Repak 1995).

27. Countries with traditions of consensual marriages afford women more migration opportunities (Donato 1992).

28. A survey conducted in Los Angeles and Orange County in 1986 revealed that 45 percent of Korean immigrants were self-employed; many were business owners in the Korean ethnic economy (Min 1996: 48).

29. Mar and Kim 1994.

30. Between 1966 and 1985 nearly 25,000 Filipina nurses came to work in the United States, and another 10,000 came between 1989 and 1991. Filipinas who were formally recruited through government programs then informally recruited their friends and former nursing school classmates (Ong and Azores 1994).

31. Parreñas 2001

32. Wrigley 1995.

33. Palmer 1989: 140.

34. Personal communication with UCLA professor Abel Valenzuela, fall 1998.

35. Bet Tzedek Legal Services.

REFERENCES

Clark-Lewis, Elizabeth. 1994. *Living In, Living Out: African American Domestics in Washington, D.C. 1910–1940.* Washington, D.C.: Smithsonian Institution Press.

Cleeland, Nancy. 1999. "Garment Jobs: Hard, Bleak, and Vanishing." *Los Angeles Times*, March 11, A1, A14–16.

Dill, Bonnie Thornton. 1988. "'Making Your Job Good Yourself': Domestic Service and the Construction of Personal Dignity." In *Women and the Politics of Empowerment*, edited by Ann Bookman and Sandra Morgen, 33–52. Philadelphia: Temple University Press.

Donato, Katharine. 1992. "Understanding U.S. Immigration: Why Some Countries Send Women and Others Send Men." In *Seeking Common Ground: Multidisciplinary Studies of Immigrant Women in the United States,* edited by Donna Gabaccia, 159–84. Westport, Conn.: Praeger.

Glenn, Evelyn Nakano. 1986. *Issei, Nisei, Warbride.* Philadelphia: Temple University Press.

Hagan, Jacqueline Maria. 1994. *Deciding to Be Legal: A Maya Community in Houston.* Philadelphia: Temple University Press.

———. 1998. "Social Networks, Gender, and Immigrant Incorporation." *American Sociological Review* 63: 55–67.

Hondagneu-Sotelo, Pierrette, and Ernestine Avila. 1997. "'I'm Here, But I'm There': The Meanings of Latina Transnational Motherhood." *Gender and Society* 11: 548–71.

Katzman, David M. 1981. *Seven Days a Week: Women and Domestic Service in Industrializing America.* Urbana: University of Illinois Press.

Lacher, Irene. 1997. "An Interior Mind." *Los Angeles Times,* March 16, E1, E3.

Lopez, David E., Eric Popkin, and Edward Telles. 1996. "Central Americans: At the Bottom, Struggling to Get Ahead." In *Ethnic Los Angeles,* edited by Roger Waldinger and Mehdi Bozorgmehr, 279–304. New York: Russell Sage Foundation.

Mahler, Sarah J. 1995. *American Dreaming: Immigrant Life on the Margins.* Princeton: Princeton University Press.

Mar, D., and M. Kim. 1994. "Historical Trends." In *The State of Asian Pacific America: Economic Diversity, Issues, and Policies,* edited by Paul Ong, 13–30. Los Angeles: LEAP Asian Pacific American Public Policy Institute and UCLA Asian American Studies Center.

McBride, Theresa. 1976. *The Domestic Revolution: The Modernization of Household Service in England and France, 1820–1920.* New York: Holmes and Meier.

McDonnell, Patrick J. 1999. "U.S. to Pay $400,000 to INS Agent in Bias Suit." *Los Angeles Times,* January 21, B1, B5.

Menjívar, Cecilia. 2000. *Fragmented Ties: Salvadoran Immigrant Networks in America.* Berkeley: University of California Press.

Min, Pyong Gap. 1996. *Caught in the Middle: Korean Communities in New York and Los Angeles.* Berkeley: University of California Press.

Nieves, Isabel, 1979. "Household Arrangements and Multiple Jobs in San Salvador." *Signs* 5:139–50.

Ong, Paul, and Tania Azores. 1994. "Health Professionals on the Front Line." In *The State of Asian Pacific America: Economic Diversity, Issues, and Policies,* edited by Paul Ong, 139–63. Los Angeles: LEAP Asian Pacific American Public Policy Institute and UCLA Asian American Studies Center.

Palmer, Phyllis. 1989. *Domesticity and Dirt: Housewives and Domestic Servants in the United States, 1920–1945.* Philadelphia: Temple University Press.

Parrenas, Rhacel Salazar. 2001. *Servants of Globalization: Women, Migration, and Domestic Work.* Stanford University Press.

Repak, Terry A. 1995. *Waiting on Washington: Central American Workers in the Nation's Capital.* Philadelphia: Temple University Press.

Rollins, Judith. 1985. *Between Women: Domestics and Their Employers.* Philadelphia: Temple University Press.

Romero, Mary. 1992. *Maid in the U.S.A.* New York: Routledge.

Romero, Mary. 1997. "Who Takes Care of the Maid's Children? Exploring the Costs of Domestic Service." In *Feminism and Families,* edited by Hilde L. Nelson, 63–91. New York: Routledge.

Salzinger, Leslie. 1991. "A Maid by Any Other Name: The Transformation of 'Dirty Work' by Central American Immigrants." In *Ethnography Unbound: Power and Resistance in the Modern Metropolis,* by Michael Burawoy et al., 139–60. Berkeley: University of California Press.

Smith, Margo L. 1973. "Domestic Service as a Channel of Upward Mobility for the Lower-Class Woman: The Lima Case." In *Female and Male in Latin America: Essays,* edited by Ann Pescatello, 192–207. Pittsburgh: University of Pittsburgh Press.

Wrigley, Julia. 1995. *Other People's Children.* New York: Basic Books.

THE LIVING WAGE AS A WOMEN'S ISSUE

Eileen Boris

Why is the living wage a women's issue? First, women will benefit the most from the introduction of living wages. Women are the largest group of low-income workers; among women, single mothers and women of color are the lowest paid. Women compose 60% of minimum wage workers when, even with California's recent increase to nearly $7 an hour, the minimum wage is dollars below a living wage. In an era when over half of women are in the labor force and the majority of mothers with small children are employed, women need a salary that allows them to make ends meet as much as men do. We can't count on men to support us, even if we wanted to. Those with partners understand that during periods of recession and spiraling costs of living, even two jobs may not be enough if none pay a living wage.

Second, living wages can counter welfare reform's race to the bottom. Marriage often isn't forever and sometimes parents never marry. For women who become household heads, welfare reform has shredded the safety net of public assistance. "Work-first" requirements flood the service sector with former recipients whose abundance serves to maintain low wages and counter the organizing efforts of immigrant, especially Latino, workers in hotels and nursing homes. Living wages help to stabilize all wages.

Third, a living wages ordinance might just keep the city from contracting out work, bypassing unionization. Women in public employee unions not only receive higher wages and greater benefits but also are more likely to have social supports to aid the juggling of family and wage labor.

Finally, the living wage promises to re-value the work of care. In a locale like Santa Barbara, those making less than a living wage cluster in service occupations funded by the state and often administrated and performed by non-profits: such as elder care, child care, and home health care. These are the jobs dismissed as unskilled because the work consists of tasks performed often by women for family members. Rather than again basing pay on the identity of the worker, we need to reward the identity of the work. A decent standard of living for all within our community benefits us all.

SECTION 6

Families

Families are a fundamental social unit. In families we develop a sense of ourselves as individuals and as members of a primary group. We internalize messages about our position in our communities, our nations, and the world. We are taught systems of belief, usually consistent with the society in which we live, about appropriate roles for particular kinds of people. For example, we learn to think differently about men and women, elders and children, and people of various races, classes, and social statuses. We also learn how we are expected to treat the people we encounter in the world around us.

It is within families that members of a society first develop ideas and feelings about themselves as gendered individuals. When we are children, the socialization we receive contains strong messages about the appropriate attitudes and behaviors for males and females. When we are adults, families are where we spend much of our time, divide up the work of meeting our physical and emotional needs, and care for others, such as children or aging family members. Families usually divide up these interpersonal roles according to what they consider appropriate for men or women. Yet families come in many forms, even within one society. The normative family structure of a married mother and father, in which the man is employed outside the home while the woman cares for their children no longer represents the majority of families. Instead, a family may be a single parent with children, a couple with no children, lesbian or gay parents and their children, or a group of people who share a household. As a result, individuals' experiences with families vary widely.

Feminist scholars examine the family as a major source of the reproduction of sexism in a society. Researchers ask questions about how the organization of family life supports women's oppression in society through its ideologies, economics, distribution of domestic tasks, and intimate relations. Reciprocally, researchers examine the impact of demographic, technological, economic, and political structures on women's and men's power and positions in their families.

At the same time, feminist researchers examine families as a source of women's strength and resistance. Alternative family forms are one way to restructure family lives; in addition, families may provide a source of resistance to other forms of oppression, such as racism or poverty. Feminist family studies emphasize the ways that race, ethnicity, sexuality, and class influence our family experiences.

In the first selection, "Bridal Wave," Melissa Morrison discusses American cultural obsession with weddings. From rampant weddings on television to a plethora of wedding books and magazines, to a whole industry dedicated to planning and producing the "perfect wedding," weddings occupy a central position in American life. Mass media representations of weddings, Morrison contends, promote a very expensive model of the perfect wedding and encourage consumers to desire weddings that imitate those of celebrities and the wealthy. Morrison argues that the event of the wedding, in fact, is emphasized in popular culture far more than the actual marriage relationship that it formalizes. Reality TV shows are only one reflection of this pattern. Despite the media wedding frenzy, actual couples often choose to live together rather than marrying, and marry, on average, at later ages. And while the presidential administration of George W. Bush has invested in attempts to promote marriage for low-income people, opposition to same-sex marriage remains entrenched. Yet ironically, legalization of same-sex marriage would produce large increases in earnings for the wedding industry.

What are the components of the "perfect wedding," as depicted in mainstream culture? How does this compare to weddings that you have attended? How do mass media depictions of weddings influence what people expect of their own weddings? Do you agree with Morrison that weddings are emphasized to the detriment of actual marriages?

In the next selection, "Moral Dilemmas, Moral Strategies, and the Transformation of Gender: Lessons from Two Generations of Work and Family Change," Kathleen Gerson addresses some of the issues that arise after the fairy-tale wedding. For young heterosexual women and men, dividing up the responsibilities of earning income and caring for children and home is a major challenge. Gerson argues that the idea that women and men have different moral responsibilities— with women responsible for caring for others and men for supporting others through their work—is at the core of this dilemma. While women are seen as achieving fulfillment through connections to others, men's fulfillment is seen as coming from their independent efforts in the work world. Although this ideology remains powerful, Gerson shows that contemporary reality is far different. Large numbers of women work for pay, and men's incomes have declined so that many of them could no longer play the breadwinner role in any case. Yet change in the work of caring for others has been slower, with women still expected to do the bulk of child care while employers are reluctant to accommodate the caring work of either women or men employees.

When Gerson interviewed women and men coming of age around the turn of the millennium, she found that they sought to achieve relationships in which they could be both autonomous and connected, and in which they would share work and child care. Reflecting on their own parents, who were the first generation to raise children after the changes wrought

by feminism, they viewed mothers' employment and fathers' involvement with children very positively. And overall, neither young men nor young women expected to find fulfillment solely through either work or family. Young women, however, were less likely than young men to prefer traditional gender relationships, and both women and men had fallback positions in case their ideals did not occur: women felt strongly that they wanted to be economically self-supporting, and men expected to be the primary breadwinners despite desiring connections with wives and children.

The conflicts are large between economic needs to work and the desire for personal autonomy, on the one hand, and caring demands and the desire for intimacy and connection, on the other. Yet Gerson suggests that these dilemmas also create the possibility for change, as women and men wrestle with their own hopes and confront the social institutions that make those hopes difficult to realize. What are your own expectations about work and family? What kinds of jobs and family support systems would you need in order to fulfill these expectations? To what extent have you been able to fulfill these expectations, if you have already formed your own independent household? As you reflect on the choices and situations faced by your own parents, how do your experiences compare to theirs, and to those of the people Gerson interviewed? What changes have occurred in family and paid labor over the past generation, and what has remained unchanged? What do you see as the main obstacles to further change in work and family lives?

The ways that heterosexual women balance work and family vary according to class, ethnicity, culture, and nationality. Denise Segura analyzes how Chicana and Mexicana immigrant mothers view their lives as employed mothers in "Working at Motherhood: Chicana and Mexicana Immigrant Mothers and Employment." She finds that many Mexicana immigrants in the study viewed working for pay as an important part of motherhood because the income helped support their families. Many Chicana mothers, in contrast, who had grown up in the United States, had been socialized with the American notion of a separation between spheres of work and family and therefore expressed more ambivalence about combining employment and mothering. The article illustrates how the meaning and practice of motherhood are socially constructed and thus vary among different groups of women. How is the relationship between working outside the home and raising children defined in the culture in which you grew up?

In "For Better or Worse: Gender Allures in the Vietnamese Global Marriage Market," Hung Cam Thai shows how ideas of gender shape marriage strategies in quite different ways for Vietnamese male migrants to the United States and for women living in Vietnam. Women in Vietnam, he argues, are expected to "marry up" to men who are more highly educated, better employed, and older. But women who pursue higher education may lose their opportunity to marry up—in effect, "pricing themselves out" of the marriage market because by the time they finish their education, they are not only too highly educated but too old to marry up. Reluctant to marry down in Vietnam and sacrifice their status and independence, they look for spouses who have immigrated to the United States, hoping to find a more egalitarian gender system there. Men in the United States, in contrast, often find themselves in low-status and low-paying jobs, despite education or higher class status in Vietnam. For them, a wife from Vietnam provides the hope of a traditional marriage in which they can gain the respect that they have lost in the workplace. As Thai shows, these women and men bring very different hopes to their marriages, both shaped by complicated intersections of gender, nationality, class, and culture. What do you think will happen to couples like these? How do their expectations compare to those of other cultures and communities with which you are familiar?

Nancy Naples, in "Queer Parenting in the New Millennium," argues that lesbian and gay parents produce social change simply by living their daily lives openly. The *heteronormative* family that she discusses is one in which a man and woman, married to each other,

bear and raise children and gain social approval and legal benefits. Both queer parenthood and queer marriage, Naples suggest, have the potential to challenge the dominance of this heteronormative model of family. Yet that model remains very influential, as Naples shows. She juxtaposes her own legally and socially marginal experience as an expectant nonbiological mother, in which she must come out as a lesbian in order to claim her status as parent with her partner's experience of being welcomed into the sisterhood of women by sharing pregnancy stories with heterosexual women. The widespread political opposition to the legalization of same-sex marriage is another indication of the marginalization of queer families. As Naples discusses, there has been considerable debate within gay and lesbian activist organizations about whether same-sex marriage is an important political goal, or whether it would simply promote assimilation by queer people into a heterosexual model. What is Naples' conclusion about this debate? What is your opinion? To what extent do you think that visible lesbian and gay parents contribute to social change? What media representations of lesbian or gay parenting or marriage can you think of, and how do these compare to the hostile political climate that Naples describes?

For most women, these articles suggest, family relationships are a complicated mixture of accommodation and resistance to gender oppression. Nevertheless, expectations and experiences within families differ for women and men of different races, ethnicities, classes, and sexual identities. In what ways do women, in these readings and in your own observation, accept or challenge traditional definitions of their family roles? How do they make choices about the relationship of paid employment to mothering? How do they gain power and fulfillment through family relationships, and how do these relationships constrict them? How are the answers to these questions different for men?

Bridal Wave

It's wedding season. Actually, it's wedding year. You might even say it's wedding millennium.

Seems like every time I turn on the TV these days, I'm blinded by the white of yet another Vera Wang gown: *For Better or for Worse, A Wedding Story, 'Til Death Do Us Part: Carmen & Dave, In Style's* annual celebrity wedding TV special, the dowry exchange known as *Trista & Ryan's Wedding*—it's all nuptials, all the time. When the one-off Fox special *Who Wants to Marry a Multi-Millionaire?* first aired a mere four years ago, viewers were shocked—shocked!—that something as superficial as a TV game show could unite a man and woman in the eyes of god and country. Today, the culminating prize of second-generation reality shows like *The Bachelor* and *The Bachelorette* is a ring, and no one even shrugs. Not since Charles and Diana's televised 1981 nuptials has marriage been such a ratings-grabber. The difference is that while the Prince and Princess of Wales had a TV marriage because they were well known, these days people are well known because they get married on TV.

It's the same story at the magazine rack: There are no fewer than 10 wedding-themed titles at my nearest Borders, each as thick as an encyclopedia and as chock-full of information. They inform brides-to-be (and bride wannabes) about everything they could possibly need to know for the ceremony: the best lipstick for wedding photos, how to style an updo, which bouquet suits an allergy-prone bride, where to buy a gold-leaf fondant cake, where to seat divorced parents.

The ostentatious, overly labored displays of emotion; the formulaic plots; the urgency to skip over relationship-building and get directly to the act—it all looks a lot like porn. The same way porn shows the act of lovemaking without reference to love, wedding porn fetishistically focuses on the ceremony without reference to the profound sentiments—and contemporary problems—that it represents. And so, from *The Bachelorette* to *Modern Bride,* the wedding itself has become the point of marriage. Any reference to what comes afterwards, i.e., the stuff women's magazines refer to as the "work" of marriage, well . . . hey, did we mention that Trista's shoes are the most expensive ever made for a wedding?

Offscreen, marriage is actually in something of a slump. Fewer Americans are marrying and more are choosing to live together instead (11 million in 2000, compared to 6.4 million a decade earlier). If they do marry, they're waiting longer to do it (the average age is 25 for women, up from 20 in 1960). With the average wedding costing more than $22,000 (up 50 percent from 1990), the "wedding-industrial complex," as sociologist Chrys Ingraham identified it in her 1999 book *White Weddings: Romancing Heterosexuality in Popular Culture,* has a huge stake in making the wedding, if not marriage itself, look like the latest must-have.

The bridal industry and ratings-hungry TV networks aren't the only ones waving the wedding flag these days. In fact, wedding porn has found some strange bedfellows, as a pop culture that was already wedding-saturated has been enlisted in a PR offensive by the Bush administration to bring heteros back onto the matrimonial ark. Bush's $1.5 billion effort aims to encourage low-income couples to tie the knot, yet the fact that marriage is no longer a social and financial necessity for a woman's survival and a man's reputation means the campaign must avoid pointing out that, like sex, the part that follows the big climax is far messier and more complicated than the ecstatic moment would lead us to believe.

However, President Bush was quick to clarify that he was talking about brides and grooms, not brides and brides. Though the Bush administration would presumably gnaw off its collective legs before declaring itself in step with Hollywood, on the subject of queer nuptials, the two entities seem to be in tacit agreement. Because on television, the story's much the same: The far right can say what they will about Hollywood's liberal agenda, but while a flurry of real-life same-sex weddings have occurred in San Francisco and

Massachusetts, on TV the only gay people featured in weddings are wedding planners and stylists. The *Queer Eye* guys may be busy readying some slob for his up-coming nuptials, but the Fab Five won't be putting on Armani tuxes for their own walks down the aisle any-time soon. *Will & Grace*, groundbreaking for its portrayal of gays, only allows its straight female stars—first Grace, now Karen—to marry in its season-finale weddings.

Even celebrities who used to scandalize with their bed-hopping are now troth-pledging. Death-obsessed Jane's Addiction guitarist Dave Navarro and profes-sional babe Carmen Electra may have gone about it unconventionally—their wedding invitation, pho-tographed by David LaChappelle, showed them as corpses on his-and-hers morgue slabs—but their MTV reality series, *'Til Death Do Us Part,* revealed a couple consumed by the minutiae of event planning, and fol-lowed them through cake tastings, dress fittings, first-dance-song-choosing (they selected Sade's "By Your Side"), and prewedding yoga and colonics sessions. The Bush administration, despite seeming unaware of any pop culture since Steve & Eydie, was surely rubbing its beringed hands together in glee through-out: If these two heathens can find it in their hearts to merge their tax status, surely they'll set an example for America's pierced and tattooed youth.

Back in the day, Dan Quayle knew just how power-ful a televised example could be when he condemned the fictional Murphy Brown for bearing a child out of wedlock. These days Marriage Savers, a promarriage advocacy group founded by former newsman Mike McManus, attributes the fact that a majority of Ameri-cans believe it's a good idea for couples to live together before marriage to the influence of movies and TV shows that depict wanton cohabitation. More to the point, Celia Duncan, the editor of British *CosmoGIRL!*, credited a recent 1.6 percent bump in British marriages to celebrity nuptials like those of the former Posh Spice to soccer star David Beckham. "The fact that so many celebrities are getting married does make a difference," she's quoted as saying in the U.K. business journal *Total Business Online* in November 2002. "They have a huge sway on society."

Stateside, nothing says traditional American val-ues like weddings—they're big, they're expensive, and they involve a lot of shopping. In *White Weddings*, Ingraham points out that TV, movie, and celebrity weddings reaffirm outdated stereotypes: that women are concerned primarily with romantic love and shop-ping; that they're willing to give up their own careers or ideals for the status and perceived security of being a wife; and that a relationship is "true" only if it's codi-fied by marriage—which, by default, restricts it to het-erosexuals. And the events are invariably celebrations of well-off white people with the occasional brides-maid of color thrown in as a nod to multiculturalism.

What's onscreen clearly reflects the wedding indus-try's targeted consumer: upper-income whites. Ingraham quotes the statistic that today's newlyweds earn twice the country's average household income and that whites (the race featured almost exclusively in bridal-magazine photos) marry at a higher rate than blacks or Hispanics. More tellingly, she points out the ways in which media consolidation has made the wedding-as-spectacle culturally ubiquitous. Media monolith Disney, for example, is the parent company of a dozen film production and distribution companies, including Touchstone Pictures, which made the *Father of the Bride* movies. It also owns ABC, home of *The Bachelor* and *The Bachelorette.* And among its 25-plus cable networks is Lifetime, which broadcasts wedding specials like *The "I Do" Diaries* and *Royal Weddings.* Of course, Disney's classic animated fairy tales like *Cinderella, Snow White and the Seven Dwarfs, Beauty and the Beast,* and *The Lit-tle Mermaid* typically end in weddings, and that's no doubt the inspiration for Disney's wedding business at its theme parks. (The "Ultimate Fairy Tale Wedding," available for a hundred grand, features a glass carriage that parades the bride down Main Street to meet her prince, who rides a white stallion.)

Women's magazines and the likes of *People* have al-ways chronicled the weddings of Hollywood's bright-est stars, but celebrity weddings have more recently be-come a genre of their own. *In Style* has taken the nuptial stargazing to new levels of obsession. It's not enough to feature "57 Pages of Dream Weddings," as prom-ised in the February 2004 issue; now *In Style* publishes a separate celebrity wedding issue as thick as *Modern Bride* and its doorstop ilk, and broadcasts ABC specials on some of the weddings featured in the magazine.

In Style Weddings functions under the assumption that if you're going to get married, you might as well get married like a celebrity—and, in its parlance, that includes everyone from *Sabrina, the Teenage Witch* star Melissa Joan Hart to former Jerry Seinfeld squeeze Shoshanna Lonstein. The spring 2004 issue featured nearly 500 pages of information and instruction: Readers learned that Debbie Matenopoulos's five-tier cake was made by the Cake Divas, that Lonstein served sea bass at her reception, and that Geraldo

Rivera bought his rings at Harry Winston. (No mention was made of the fact that it was Rivera's fifth time down the aisle.)

Journalists have written of the *In Style* "curse"—weddings or engagements that are no sooner celebrated in the magazine than they disappear faster than the latest Bennifer flick; victims have included J. Lo and Ojani Noa, J. Lo and Puff Daddy (as he was known at the time), Tara Reid and Carson Daly, and Drew Barrymore and Tom Green. The banner example is *In Style*'s March 2001 issue, which featured actor Courtney Thorne-Smith in her wedding dress on its cover, with a lengthy account of her Hawaii wedding within. By the time the issue came out, Thorne-Smith was already in the process of divorcing.

But as long as the caterers got paid, who cares? The stars of hit Fox series and actor-singer hyphenates can write off such expensive debacles as lessons in personal growth (and subjects for discussion in future magazine interviews). It's not so easy for the 401(k) class and those below. In that light, it's worth wondering how President Bush figures that marriage is the solution to poverty: If the couples have the kind of wedding pop culture encourages them to have, they'll be even poorer than when they started out. *In Style*'s spring wedding issue was chockablock with reasons why weddings are so pricey—some obvious (Reem Acra veil, $3,000; rose and snowberry bouquet, $350; vineyard rental for ceremony, $5,000) and some not so obvious (bride's handbag, $690; yo-yo favors for the kids, $2.50 a pop; wine carrier gift for out-of-town guests, $78 each).

It's wedding as shopping spree, and the implication seems to be, the more expensive the wedding, the more successful the marriage. Trista and Ryan's December 2003 nuptials, detailed exhaustively in a three-episode ABC reality miniseries, took the wedding-as-shopping metaphor to its most ostentatious level. Apart from the bride's aforementioned diamond-studded shoes, which the show's publicity repeatedly mentioned, the broadcast ran a tally of the items that added up to a $3.77 million ceremony: $750,000 location; $500,000 in pink roses; $155,000 for reception food and drink; $75,000 wedding dress; $15,000 wedding cake. Given that money is always cited as one of the most contentious issues for married couples, it would seem that the industry is sabotaging its own aim. Then again, maybe that's the point: Multiple marriages mean multiple expenditures.

Along those lines, it also seems that the wedding industry couldn't disagree more with the Bush administration's stringent anti–gay marriage stance. How could they, when snatching a piece of the gay wedding cake translates into such huge revenues? Forbes.com recently calculated a $16.8 billion annual "gay-marriage windfall" if laws were changed to legalize same-sex marriages. Specifically, the April 4, 2004, article noted, companies like Tiffany, Williams-Sonoma, and Marriott International would nicely benefit (it went on to helpfully provide their New York Stock Exchange abbreviations for any early investors). Forbes.com based its calculations on the assumption that gay couples would marry at the same rates as heterosexual couples, and spend the same amount of money, figuring, for example, $1.66 billion on collective engagement rings and $1.7 billion on honeymoons.

I'm not pretending to be such a savvy feminist that I'm impervious to wedding porn's siren song; I've fallen victim myself. Spending time with *In Style Weddings* had the same effect on me as an afternoon with *Vogue:* I was overtaken by the Fever. By the time I had reached the account of *Dawson's Creek* star Kerr Smith's Palm Springs nuptials, I had my own wedding planned: the Monique Lhuillier gown, the Audrey Hepburn upsweep, my mother's wedding ring. I wanted the party. I wanted all my family and friends to fly in and look at me at my most princesslike. (I'd gift them each with a wine basket for their effort.) Despite my own carefully deliberated belief that marriage is not for me, I still wanted a fondant cake decorated with my and my partner's initials.

I don't blame every entry in the current glut of wedding-themed shows for craven commercialism and fairy-tale portrayals. A recent episode of TLC's *A Wedding Story* (oddly enough, the least commercial of the current wedding media) revealed what it is, beyond the consumer booty and vicarious celebrity, that attracts us to wedding coverage. The episode was about a Liberian couple who had been separated by civil war, lost touch, then found each other again after each had escaped to the United States. At their best, partnerships can be seen as the symbolic opposite of war. They're about building lives, not destroying them. And weddings—when separated from the rampant heterosexual consumerism that too often attends them—are the threshold of creation: of a new family, new alliances, and new generations.

But this episode was exceptional, like a porno with a plot. And most of the audience was likely sitting there with the remote, poised for the butter-cream-frosted money shot.

ABSTINENCE-ONLY: BREEDING IGNORANCE

Mary-Jane Wagle

Imagine a driver's education course in which teachers show students grisly photos of traffic accidents but never tell them to stop at red lights or buckle their seat belts, and you've a pretty good idea of what abstinence-only sex education is like. Abstinence-only programs try to scare and shame teens, teaching only the negative consequences of sexuality without telling young people what they can do to stay safe and healthy.

Now a congressional staff analysis on the content of the federally funded sex education programs used in 25 states reveals they're just plain wrong. The report found that more than 80 percent of abstinence-only curricula contain false, misleading or distorted information about reproductive health.

The analysis, released by Rep. Henry Waxman, D-Calif., found that many of these curricula contain false information about the effectiveness of contraceptives and the risks of abortion. Several of the curricula contain basic scientific errors and present religious views as proven fact. Some curricula also treat gender stereotypes as scientific truth.

Here are some examples: In several abstinence-only programs, students are erroneously told that condoms fail to protect against HIV and that pregnancy occurs one out of every seven times that couples use a condom. One textbook states that touching another person's genitals "can result in pregnancy." Another suggests that 5 percent to 10 percent of women who have legal abortions will become sterile as a result.

One curriculum refers to a 43-day-old fetus as "a thinking person." Another incorrectly lists exposure to sweat and tears as risk factors for HIV transmission. And one textbook sanctimoniously instructs teenagers: "Women gauge their happiness and judge their success on their relationships. Men's happiness and success hinge on their accomplishments."

California has been wise enough to see through the hype of abstinence-only sex education, and it continues to be one of the few states that refuse to accept the federal funding for abstinence-only curricula.

Californians mandate HIV/AIDS education in our schools and require that all sexuality education is comprehensive and medically accurate. And our attention to the needs of our state's youth has paid off. Our teen pregnancy rate has fallen by 40 percent over the last 10 years—the largest decrease of any state except Alaska.

Abstinence-only curricula, such as those being pushed and funded by the Bush administration, aren't just riddled with errors—they clearly have no positive effect on the behavior of teens. Researchers at Columbia University found that while virginity "pledge" programs did help some of the participants delay sex, 88 percent still had premarital sex.

Additionally, the rates of sexually transmitted infections among pledgers showed no statistically significant difference from non-pledgers.

Despite these problems, the federal government will squander an astonishing $168 million for these programs in fiscal 2005. Although this falls short of the $270 million President Bush initially proposed, it more than doubles the amount in 2001. Meanwhile, programs that work go unfunded.

Proponents of abstinence-only sex education believe that knowledge can be dangerous. Ignorance, however, can be fatal. Last week, we marked World AIDS Day. When our young people are at risk of HIV infection as well as other sexually transmitted infections, it is unconscionable to deprive them of information that can save their lives.

Moral Dilemmas, Moral Strategies, and the Transformation of Gender: Lessons from Two Generations of Work and Family Change[1]

Choosing between self-interest and caring for others is one of the most fundamental dilemmas facing all of us. To reconcile this dilemma, modern societies in general—and American society in particular—have tried to divide women and men into different moral categories. Since the rise of industrialism, the social organization of moral responsibility has expected women to seek personal development by caring for others and men to care for others by sharing the rewards of independent achievement.

Although labeled "traditional," this gendered division of moral labor represents a social form and cultural mandate that rose to prominence in the mid-twentieth century but reached an impasse as the postindustrial era opened new avenues for work and family life. (Among the voluminous works on this subject, see Kimmel 1996; Ryan 1981; Welter 1966.) At the outset of the twenty-first century, women and men face rising conflicts over how to resolve the basic tensions between family and work, public and private, autonomy and commitment. They are searching for new strategies for reconciling an "independent self" with commitment to others.

While the long-term trajectory of change remains unclear, new social conditions have severely undermined the link between gender and moral obligation. The young women and men who have come of age amid this changing social landscape face risks and dangers, but they also inherit an unprecedented opportunity to forge new, more egalitarian ways to balance self-development with commitment to others. To enable them to do so, however, we must reshape work and family institutions in ways that overcome beliefs and practices that presume gender differences in moral responsibility.

Drawing on insights from my research on how contemporary young women and men negotiate the conflicts between family and work, I explore how new social conditions are compelling them to reconsider traditional strategies for reconciling self-development with caring for others. Social change has undermined earlier resolutions to these dilemmas but does not offer clear avenues for creating new ones. My research on the "children of the gender revolution" suggests that young women and men cannot rely on inflexible gender categories to resolve the conflict between autonomy and care, but they are encountering social and cultural obstacles to creating gender-neutral strategies for apportioning moral labor.

GENDER, SOCIAL THEORY, AND THE DIVISION OF MORAL LABOR

Across a wide range of traditions, social theorists remain concerned with the tension between autonomy and commitment. From de Tocqueville to Bellah, cultural theorists have spoken of a conflict between individualism and commitment in American life (Bellah et al. 1985; de Tocqueville [1832] 1969). From Parsons on, functionalist sociologists have distinguished between instrumental and expressive functions.[2] And economists, especially those who advocate human capital and rational choice approaches, separate the public domain of the market from the private sphere of the home (Becker 1981).

Despite their differences, all of these theoretical approaches rely on gender difference, either implicitly or explicitly, to reconcile the theoretical and practical conflicts between self-interest and social obligation. Psychological approaches, for example, emphasize that early childhood socialization leads girls and boys to develop contrasting orientations toward morality and care, self and others. Even rational choice approaches, which argue that self-interested calculation underlies all human action, assume that women and men possess different tastes and abilities, making it more efficient for women to specialize in domestic care and men to specialize in the world of paid work (for another critique, see England 1993).

Despite a vast amount of research demonstrating that the temperamental differences among women and among men are far greater than the differences between them, the appeal of a theoretical lens assuming a gender dichotomy in moral orientation remains strong.[3] It provides a way to resolve the universal human tension between self-interest and self-sacrifice as well as the social tensions between the marketplace and domestic work. Yet, it does so at a great cost. In its starkest terms, this framework justifies gender inequality by cloaking socially constructed gender categories with moral authority. It draws a sharp gender divide, suggesting that women can be for themselves by being for others, while men can be for others by being for themselves. Transgressing these boundaries continues to risk social disapproval or worse.[4]

Feminists have been understandably ambivalent about the moral dichotomization of gender. Some have implicitly adopted the classical framework while criticizing its underpinnings and consequences. Those emphasizing psychological processes have most clearly restated the idea that women and men diverge in their orientations toward self and others, although they see women's caring capacities as a special strength and mark of virtue. Gilligan argues, for example, that women's "ethic of care" should be as valued and esteemed as men's "ethic of rights" (Gilligan 1982; Gilligan, Ward, and Taylor 1989). And Chodorow's theory of mothering contends that the unequal, asymmetrical social organization of parenting causes women to seek connection and men to seek separation.[5] Most of those who emphasize women's distinct "moral voice" acknowledge that it is socially constructed and that it deserves to be accorded equal (or greater) value. Yet, they stop short of asking whether women and men—as social groups—actually possess different moral capacities and outlooks.

While it is important to assert that it is just as valuable to pursue emotional connection and provide care as it is to create an independent self or provide economically for a family, it is also critical to question the premise that women and men can be separated into distinct, opposed, or unchanging moral categories. As Epstein argues, any vision of dichotomous gender distinctions is not only inaccurate; it is also an ideological construct that justifies and reinforces inequality. Connell points out that "masculinities" and "femininities" vary across historical time and space. Lorber and Risman, among others, question the concept of gender itself, pointing to the social paradoxes and cultural contradictions to which all human actors must respond in constructing their public and private selves. These theorists recognize that gender is a social institution, not an inherent trait, and that it shapes organizations and opportunity structures as well as personal experiences (Connell 1987, 1995; Epstein 1988; Lorber 1994; Risman 1998).

There are good analytic and empirical reasons to reject the use of gender to resolve the knotty moral conflicts between public and private, work and family, self and other. It is difficult to avoid the conclusion that using gender in this way is more prescriptive than descriptive. Such approaches may depict how women and men *should* behave, but they do not provide an accurate description or explanation of how women and men actually *do* behave or how they *would* behave if alternative options were available. Certainly, the proportion who have conformed to gendered injunctions about appropriate moral choices has varied substantially across societies, subcultures, and historical periods. Countless women and men have been labeled "deviant" for their reluctance or inability to uphold idealized conceptions of gender. A framework of gendered moralities helps justify inequalities and stigmatize those who do not conform.

THE INSTITUTIONAL ROOTS OF THE CURRENT IMPASSE

Assigning women and men to distinct, homogeneous moral groups may have seemed natural, desirable, and inevitable when social majorities lived in, or aspired to live in, male breadwinner/female caretaker households, but the demographic and ideological underpinnings of this framework are eroding. At the outset of a new century, new generations of young adults cannot rely on notions of gendered differences in moral capacities to make viable or satisfying work and family choices. Yet, they face a set of contradictory institutional changes that makes it difficult to devise new ways of responding to moral conflicts.

Changes in women's economic and social fortunes have both allowed them to work and required them to seek self-sufficiency. More diverse and fluid sexual partnerships have given women more choice about when or whether to marry and have children, but they have also left women less able to count on a male partner for economic support. The expansion of women's employment has offered them new opportunities to seek personal and social commitments outside the home, but it has also intensified the devaluation of full-time domesticity.[6] And the decline of the male "family wage" has left even stably married women in need of independent earnings. In short, a deeply rooted set of institutional transformations has given women new options to pursue an independent life while eroding the option to confine their commitments to domestic care (Gerson 1985).

The fading of the male breadwinner household has altered men's options as well, albeit in different ways.[7] Men, like women, have more freedom to enter or leave a relationship, making it easier to avoid long-term commitment. Yet, they are also less able to compel a female partner to stay in a relationship or to confine herself to the home. Men who find it difficult to support a household on their own are less empowered to claim the privileges accorded a "household head" or to set the terms under which wives and children will live. As a group, men thus now have more opportunity to flee moral obligations to support women and children, but they also face new pressures to become more involved in caring for others (Gerson 1993).

Women now claim the right and the need to seek autonomy and personal gratification beyond caring commitments, and men are no longer routinely able or willing to provide care by supporting others economically. While these changes have undermined established systems of gender difference, they have not provided a clear avenue for creating a new balance between autonomy and connection. To the contrary, a lack of change in other gendered arrangements has created new structural and cultural contradictions. At the workplace, employers no longer routinely pay enough to support a partner at home, but they are, if anything, more demanding of a worker's time, asking parents to risk short- and long-run penalties for the time they take to care for their families (Fuchs Epstein et al. 1999; Gerson and Jacobs 2001; Jacobs and Gerson 2001; Raymon 2001). And although divorce and out-of-wedlock childbearing have left more children dependent on their mothers' earnings, women continue to face constricted work and career opportunities (Jacobs 1989, forthcoming; Reskin and Roos 1990; Williams 1995). These persistent inequalities, which give priority to paid work and to men's earnings, clash with women's and men's changing options and constraints.

FROM MORAL DIFFERENCE TO MORAL DILEMMAS

The erosion of social supports for traditional conceptions of moral obligation has prompted the search for new ways to balance family and work, but the contradictory nature of this change has also produced enduring political debates and rising social dilemmas. Cultural conservatives decry the rise of nontraditional families and the expansion of public opportunities for women, claiming that these changes represent a decline of morality in America. Social progressives, in contrast, applaud the expansion of opportunity, personal choice, and tolerance for diversity but are concerned that the spheres of family and work are colliding. Workplaces seem more demanding, local communities seem to be losing civic engagement, and families seem starved for time and resources (Hochschild 1997; Jacobs and Gerson forthcoming; Putnam 2000; Schor 1992). As it has become increasingly difficult to carve out equal space for the unpaid caring work that women have historically performed, women and men alike are facing apparently irreconcilable choices between caring and self-sufficiency. The classic tension between individualism and commitment now assumes new forms and is being experienced in intensified ways.

In a context where broad, multilayered social changes clash with continuing inequalities, it is more fruitful to focus on moral dilemmas than on moral differences. A dilemma is a difficult, perplexing, or ambiguous choice between equally undesirable (or desirable) alternatives, while *moral* involves a concern with the rules of right conduct (*Webster's dictionary* 1992). Of course, we experience many moral dilemmas in deeply personal ways. They become social, however, when institutional and cultural contexts make it difficult or impossible for individuals to make a socially sanctioned choice—when, for example, all options invite disapproval but action is nevertheless required.[8]

The current period poses many such situations. In forming adult relationships, how do women and men weigh the need and desire for achieving autonomy with the hope of establishing an enduring commitment?

In caring for a new generation, how do parents balance the need to spend time with their children and the need to earn enough to support them? In crafting a personal identity, how do individuals choose between attaining independence and building connections to others? These situations are *dilemmas* because they pose choices that have no institutionalized or unambiguously "correct" resolutions. They are *social* because they arise from the way that social change structures available options and creates conflicts, ambiguities, and inconsistencies. They are *moral* because others judge these choices, forcing new generations either to change or to reproduce prevailing moral codes. Socially structured moral dilemmas force us to move beyond habits and routines to develop and justify new actions and beliefs.[9]

Studying the creation of, and strategic responses to, socially structured moral dilemmas helps to illuminate the processes of gender change. It allows us to see how the definitions and practices of gender unfold as individuals develop responses to contradictory social options. Focusing on dilemmas allows us to view gender as an "incomplete" institution. Gendered responses do not reflect inherent gender differences but are instead strategies developed by differently situated social actors coping with ambiguous circumstances. Change is possible in this framework but never guaranteed. It becomes more likely when social arrangements create conflicts that require innovative responses. To expand on West and Zimmerman's (1987) notion of "doing gender," such circumstances create conditions in which it becomes possible to "redo" gender and, potentially, to "undo" gender, that is, to either recreate or change the daily experiences and practices of gender. Contemporary young women and men confront just such circumstances. Analyzing their coping strategies provides a lens through which to view the future contours of gender, work, and family.

STUDYING GENDER CHANGE: FINDINGS FROM A NEW GENERATION

During the last several decades, I have studied two pivotal generations. My earlier research examined how the women and men who came of age in the 1970s and 1980s helped forge changes in gender, work, and family life as they reacted to new structural and cultural conditions (Gerson 1985, 1993). My current research focuses on how the generation who grew up in these changing households and are now entering adulthood are responding to a world where nontraditional

family forms predominate and gender inequality has been seriously questioned. In significant ways, the older group can be viewed as the "parents of the gender revolution" and the generation now coming of age as the "children of the revolution" (Gerson 2001). They have watched their parents cope with the erosion of the breadwinner-homemaker ethos, and they must now devise their own strategies in the face of continuing work and family change.

To discover how new generations are experiencing and responding to these vast social changes, I conducted in-depth, life history interviews with 120 young women and men between the ages of 18 and 32. They were randomly selected from a range of economic and social contexts, including inner-city, outer-city, and suburban neighborhoods throughout the New York metropolitan area. They are evenly divided between women and men, with an average age of 24, and are economically and racially diverse, with 54 percent non-Hispanic whites, 21 percent African Americans, 18 percent Hispanics, and 8 percent Asians.

Most lived in families that underwent changes that cannot be captured in the static categories of household types. That said, a large majority lived in some form of nontraditional arrangement before reaching 18. About 40 percent lived in a single-parent home at some point in their childhood, and 7 percent saw their parents break up after they left home.[10] About one-third grew up in homes where both parents held full-time jobs of relatively equal importance, at least at some point during their childhood.[11] The remaining 27 percent described growing up in homes that were generally traditional in the sense that mothers worked intermittently, secondarily, or not at all, although most of these households underwent some form of change as mothers went to work or marriages faced crises. As a whole, the group experienced the full range of changes now emerging in family, work, and gender arrangements.

The interviews reveal how growing up amid a shifting gender and family order has prompted a new generation to rethink the age-old conflict between self-interest and responsibility to others. Taking lessons from their parents and their parents' generation, but facing new quandaries of their own, these young women and men are crafting moral strategies that challenge traditional views of gender. Their emerging views on how to balance autonomy and commitment, to define care, and to develop a personal identity amid ambiguous social shifts are presented below. While these views suggest a blurring of gender boundaries, they also underscore how persisting obstacles are creating a gap between young women's and men's emerging egalitarian aspirations and their far more limited opportunities for achieving them. The next section thus considers how pervasive barriers to both gender equality and work-family integration are creating a new gender divide between women who seek personal independence and men who worry about losing traditional privileges.

NEW DILEMMAS, AMBIGUOUS STRATEGIES

How does this generation view its moral choices? As adult partnerships have become more fluid and voluntary, they are grappling with how to form relationships that balance commitment with autonomy and self-sufficiency. As their mothers have become essential and often sole breadwinners for their households, they are searching for new ways to define care that do not force them to choose between spending time with their children and earning an income. And in the face of rising work-family conflicts, they are looking for definitions of personal identity that do not pit their own development against creating committed ties to others. As young women and men wrestle with these dilemmas, they are questioning a division of moral responsibility that poses a conflict between personal development and caring for others.

Seeking Autonomy, Establishing Commitment

The decline of permanent marriage has raised new and perplexing questions about how to weigh the need and desire for self-sufficiency against the hope of creating an enduring partnership. In wrestling with this quandary, young women and men draw on lessons learned in their families and personal relationships. Yet, they also recognize that past experiences and encounters can provide, at best, a partial and uncertain blueprint for the future.

Few of the women and men who were interviewed reacted in a rigidly moralistic way to their parents' choices. Among those whose parents chose to divorce (or never marry), about 45 percent viewed the breakup as a prelude to growing difficulty, but the other 55 percent supported the separation and felt relief in its aftermath. Danisha, a 21-year-old African American, concluded that conflict would have emerged had her parents stayed together:

> I have personally met a lot of miserable children whose parents stayed together. For me, it would have been worse—because eventually, a lot of the civility they had toward each other would have broken down into hostility. They got out while it was good.

And at 26, Erica, who grew up in a white middle-class suburb, supported her parents' decision to separate and received more support from each of them in its aftermath:

> I knew my parents were going to get divorced, because I could tell they weren't getting along. They were acting out roles rather than being involved. They were really drifting apart, so it was something perfectly natural to me. In the new situation, I spent more valuable time with my parents as individuals. So time with my father and mother was more meaningful to me and more productive.

Among those whose parents stayed together, almost 60 percent were pleased with and, indeed, inspired by, their parents' lifelong commitment, but about 40 percent concluded that a breakup would have been better than the persistently unhappy, conflict-ridden relationship they watched unfold. Amy, a 24-year-old Asian American, explains:

> I always felt my parents would have divorced if they didn't have kids and didn't feel it was so morally wrong. They didn't really stick together because they were in love. I know all couples go through fights and stuff, but growing up, it seemed like they fought a lot, and each of them has made passing comments—like "Oh, I would have divorced your mom by now" or "I would have left your dad a thousand times." [So] I wouldn't have broken down or been emotionally stressed if my parents divorced. I didn't want to hear the shouting, and I didn't want to see my mom cry anymore. And I was also afraid of my dad, because he would never lay a hand on my mom, but he's scary. He could be violent.

Whether their parents stayed together or parted, most concluded that neither steadfast commitment nor choosing to leave has moral meaning in the abstract. The value of enduring commitment depends on the quality of the relationship it embodies.

When considering their own aspirations, almost everyone hopes to establish a committed, lasting relationship with one partner. Yet, they also hold high standards for what a relationship should provide and anticipate risks in sustaining such a commitment. Across the divides of gender, race, and class, most agree that a satisfying and worthwhile relationship should offer a balance between autonomy and sharing, sacrifice and support. At 26, Michael, an African American who was raised by his mother in a working-class suburb, is convinced that only economic independence can provide a proper base for commitment with his girlfriend:

I don't want the fifties type of marriage, where I come home with a briefcase and she's cooking. She doesn't have to cook. I just want her to have a career of her own. I want things to be comfortable. And somewhere down the line, if I lose my job or things start going crazy in the marriage, I want to be able to set my goals, and she can do what she wants, because we both have this economic base and the attitude to do it. That's what marriage is about.

Amy imagines a partnership that is equal and fluid, capable of adapting to circumstances without relinquishing equity:

I want a fifty-fifty relationship, where we both have the potential of doing everything. Both of us working, and in dealing with kids, it would be a matter of who has more flexibility with regard to their career. And if neither does, then one of us will have to sacrifice for one period, and the other for another.

Most acknowledge, however, that finding a lasting and satisfying relationship represents an ideal that is hard to reach. If it proves unattainable, they agree that being alone is better than remaining in an unhappy or destructive union. Building a full life thus means developing the self in multiple ways. At 29, Maria, who grew up in a close-knit Hispanic household where both parents worked, is careful to build her life in many directions:

I want to be with somebody, to have this person to share your life with—that you're there for as much as they're there for you. But I can't settle. If I don't find it, then I cannot live in sorrow. It's not the only thing that's ultimately important. If I didn't have my family, if I didn't have a career, if I didn't have friends, or if I didn't have the things that I enjoy doing, I would be equally unhappy. This is just one thing. Maybe it takes a little bit more of the pie than some other things—but it's still just a slice of the pie.

Across the range of personal family experiences, most also agree that children suffer more from an unhappy home than from separated parents.[12] Miranda, whose parents parted when her father returned to Mexico in her teens, looks back from the vantage point of 27 and concludes,

For people to stay together in spite of themselves, just for the child, they're damaging the child. It's almost like a false assumption that you can do something for the sake of the child while you're being drained. Because the life is getting sucked out of you. How can you give life when it's sucked out of you?

Women and men both wonder if it is possible to establish relationships that strike a good balance between self-affirmation and commitment, providing and receiving support. Having observed their parents and others struggle with varying degrees of success against the strictures of traditional gender categories, they are hopeful but guarded about the possibilities for resolving the tension between autonomy and commitment in their own lives.[13] At 20, Chris, a Native American whose parents shared work and caretaking, is thus beginning to wonder:

I thought you could just have a relationship, that love and being happy was always needed in life, and I've learned that you've got to be able to draw that line. It's a difficult thing, and you've got to know how to do it. And that would be my fear. Where am I cutting into my job too much? Where am I cutting into the relationship too much? And how do I divide it, and can it actually be done at all? Can you blend these two parts of your world?

Care as Time, Care as Money

If the rise of fluid adult partnerships has heightened the strains between commitment and autonomy, then the rise of employed mothers and the decline of sole male breadwinners have made the meaning of care ambiguous. Now that most children—whether living in single-parent or two-parent households—depend on the earnings of their mothers, parents face conflicts in balancing the need to provide economic support with the need to devote time and attention.

Rigid notions of gendered caring do not fit well with most family experiences, and the majority express support for parents who transgressed traditional gender categories. Among those who grew up in two-earner households, four out of five support such an arrangement, most with enthusiasm. Across race, class, and gender groups, they believe that two incomes provided the family with increased economic resources, more flexibility against the buffeting of economic winds, and greater financial security. For Serena, a 26-year-old African American, her parents' two jobs allowed her to avoid the privations of her friends and peers:

> Both my parents worked and a lot of parents in this neighborhood, one stayed home or some were on welfare. So a lot of my peers thought we were, like, upper class because both parents had cars and we went to private schools. When I was in my late teens and actually realized where I fit into the picture, it made me really appreciate my parents.

And Jason, also 26 and white, finds inspiration in his upwardly mobile parents' example as hard workers who made things better for their children in the process:

> I would say [both parents' working] made things better for the family because their being so dedicated to providing, to working, they helped that ethic of having to work and not wasting time. So it's instilled in me and my sister the ethic to work.

Of course, this means they see a mother's employment as largely beneficial. Whether in a two-parent or single-parent home, women and men agree that an independent base enhanced a mother's sense of self, contributed to greater parental equality, and provided an uplifting model. Rachel, 24 and from a white, working-class background, explains,

> I don't think that I missed out on anything. I think it served as a more realistic model. I've heard all that stuff about how children need a parent at home, but I don't think that having her stay home with me, particularly considering her temper, would have been anything other than counterproductive. The reality is that I'm going to have to work, and a lot of women in her generation chose not to work and did or didn't have the option. She had a choice, and she did what she wanted, and I think that's really great.

Kevin, 25 and from a middle-class, white family, agrees:

> For quite a while, my mom was the main breadwinner. She was the one who was the driving force in earning money. My mother's persona was really hard working, and that's something I've strived to be with and to emulate. I didn't think it was wrong in any way. I actually feel it's a very positive thing. Whatever my relationships, I always want and appreciate people who work, and I'm talking about female involvement. It's part of who I am, and it makes me very optimistic knowing that hard work can get you somewhere.

They also deemed highly involved fathers, whether in two-earner or single-parent households, as worthy examples. Daniel, now 23, describes his Irish father's atypical working hours and parental involvement:

> My father was always around. He's a fire fighter, so he had a lot of free time. When he was home, he was usually coaching me and my brother or cooking dinner or taking us wherever we wanted to go. He was the only cook up until me and my brother started doing it. So I want to make sure that, if I get married and have kids, I'm there for my kids.

In contrast, those who grew up in a largely traditional household expressed more ambivalence. Although half felt fortunate to have had a mother devoted primarily to their care, the other half would have preferred for their mothers to pursue a more independent life. At 21, Justin, who grew up in a white, largely middle-class suburb, looks back on his mother's domestic focus with a strong conviction that it took its toll on the whole household:

> She was very involved [and] always around. And I appreciated it, but I felt guilty that maybe I was taking too much. It's just that she wasn't happy. And she didn't give us any responsibilities at all. I guess that made her feel good to have someone rely on her. She felt needed more. And in the long run, obviously that's not something good.

And at 30, Sarah, also white and middle-class, agreed, pointing out that a mother's "sacrifice" may evoke mixed feelings:

> I wish my mom had worked so that she would have been happier. Her identity was very much as

a mother, and that was a sort of a void and pain. Because that's all she was, and that was not enough. She would say that it was, but that's not what I saw. She just seemed really unhappy a lot of time. She was just overinvolved with us, and if we did something separate from her, that was a major problem. I wouldn't mind her being supermom if that was really okay with her. But I got the message that she was giving up all of this other stuff to do it, and we should feel bad about it.

Breadwinning fathers may also elicit mixed reactions. Their economic contributions are appreciated but not necessarily deemed sufficient. A good father, most concluded, takes time and offers emotional support as well. At 29, Nick, who grew up in a white working-class neighborhood and remembers feeling frustrated by his own father's distance, is seeking joint custody of his own young daughter:

I have seen a lot of guys who have kids and have never changed a diaper, have never done anything for this child. Don't call yourself daddy. Even when she was saying, "Oh, she might not be yours," it didn't matter to me. This child is counting on me.

In this context, care becomes a slippery concept. Across family circumstances, these young adults judge an ideal parent—whether mother or father—to be one who supports her or his children both economically and emotionally. At 21, Antonio, who grew up in a three-generational Hispanic household and whose father died of alcoholism, has concluded that fathers should give their children the time and emotional support typically expected of a mother:

[An ideal father] is a strong, balanced man. He's a daddy but he has the understanding of a mommy. He can care for you and protect you and guide you. . . . That's what I want to do with my kids. I want to make sure that I have time. I don't want to leave them in front of a TV set all day, because what they're learning is not coming from me. So I want to be there or, if not, I want to be in a position where I can take you with me.

If fathers should resemble traditional conceptions of mothers, then mothers should resemble fathers when it comes to work outside the home. Gabriel, a white 25-year-old who was raised by his father after his parents divorced when he was in grade school, explains,

In terms of splitting parental stuff, it should be even. Kids need a mother and a father. And I'm really not high on the woman giving up her job. I have never wanted to have a wife who didn't make a salary. But not for the sake of leeching off of her, but so that she was independent.

And Miranda agrees that mothering means providing money as well as care:

My mother has completely and entirely dedicated herself to me in the true sense; she has always been very selfless and very involved and fully responsible for me financially. I wouldn't feel comfortable if I didn't think I could make that kind of commitment.

If such an ideal proves beyond reach, as many expect it will be, women and men agree that families should apportion moral labor however best fits their circumstances—whether or not this means conforming to classic notions of gender difference. Mothers can and often do demonstrate care through paid work and fathers through involvement. Now 26 and raising a child on her own, Crystal, an African American, rejects a natural basis for mothering:

I don't really believe in the mother instinct. I don't believe that's natural. Some people really connect with their children, and some people just don't. I think it should be whoever is really going to be able to be there for that child.

In the end, the material and emotional support a child receives matters more than the type of household arrangement in which it is provided. Michelle, a 24-year-old of Asian descent who watched her parents struggle in an unhappy marriage and then separate after she and her brother left home, focuses on emotional support rather than family composition:

As long as the child feels supported and loved, that's the most important thing. Whether it's a two-parent home, a single-parent home, the mother is working, or anything, it's just really important for the child to have a good, strong foundation.

Identity through Love, Identity through Work

In a world where partnerships are fragile and domesticity is devalued, young women and men are confronting basic questions about identity and self-interest. Do they base their personal well-being and sense of self on public pursuits or private attachments? What balance can or should be struck between them?

In pondering their parents' lives, most could find no simple way to define or measure self-interest. While a minority uphold traditional gendered identities, most do not find such resolutions viable. Women are especially likely to conclude that it is perilous to look to the home as the sole source of satisfaction or survival. Reflecting on the many examples of mothers and other women who languished at home, who were bereft when marriages broke up, or who found esteem in the world of paid work, 9 out of 10 express the hope that their lives will include strong ties to the workplace and public pursuits. Sarah, now a psychologist with a long-term lesbian partner who works "constantly," has high hopes but also nagging worries:

> I have a lot of conflicts now—work versus home and all of that stuff. But I would feel successful if I had a life with a lot of balance and that I'd made time for people who were important to me and made a real commitment to the people that I care about. And also, to work—I would be dedicated to work. And work and home would be connected. It would all be integrated, and it would be an outgrowth of my general way of being.

On the other side of the gender divide, many men have also become skeptical of work-centered definitions of masculine identity. As traditional jobs have given way to unpredictable shifts in work prospects, they are generally guarded about the prospect of achieving stable work careers. Having observed fathers and friends who found work either dissatisfying or too demanding, two-thirds of the men concluded that, while important, work alone could not provide their lives with meaning. These young men hope to balance paid work and personal attachments without having to sacrifice the self for a job or paycheck. Traditional views persist, but they increasingly compete with perspectives that define identity in more fluid ways. Widely shared by those who grew up in different types of families, these outlooks also transcend class and race differences. They cast doubt on some postfeminist assertions that a "new traditionalism" predominates among young women and men (Crittenden 1999). When asked how he would like to divide caretaking and breadwinning, Kevin considers the possibilities:

> Whoever can do it and whoever's capable of doing it, but it should be divided evenly. If there's something

I can't do, just that I don't have the talent to do it, I would hope the other person would be able to. And the same goes the other way. My parents were like that. It was a matter of who was able to do what. There were hundreds of times when my dad made our lunches. And my sister claims that his were better than my mom's.

Yet, beyond the apparent similarities, a gender divide emerges. With one-third of men—but far fewer women—preferring traditional arrangements over all others, women are more likely to uphold flexible views of gender for themselves and their partners. More important, women and men both distinguish between their ideals and their chances of achieving them. If most hope to integrate family and work—and to find partners with whom to share the rewards and burdens of both—far fewer believe they can achieve this lofty aspiration. It is difficult to imagine integrating private with public obligations when most workplaces continue to make it difficult to balance family and job. And it is risky to build a life dependent on another adult when relationships are unpredictable. In this context, both women and men acknowledge that their actual options may fall substantially short of their ideals. For women, finding the right job and the right partner may seem too much to expect. Maria laments,

> Sometimes I ask myself if it's unrealistic to want everything. I think a lot of people would settle for something that is not what they wished, and, to me, that feels worse. It's a Catch 22, because you could wait so long, you never get anything, or you could settle for something and then be cut off from something else.

And men agree, although they are more likely to focus on the constraints of the workplace, as Peter, 27 and white, implies: "I want as even a split as possible. But with my hours, I don't think it could be very even."

AN EMERGING GENDER DIVIDE: AUTONOMY AND NEOTRADITIONALISM AS FALLBACK POSITIONS

The ideal of a balanced self continues to collide with an intransigent social world. New generations must thus develop contingent strategies for less than ideal circumstances. If egalitarian aspirations cannot be reached, what options remain? Here, women and men tend to diverge. Indeed, even as they are developing similar ideals, they are preparing for different outcomes. If an egalitarian commitment proves unworkable, most men would prefer a form of "modified traditionalism" in which they remain the primary if not sole family bread-winner and look to a partner to provide the lion's share of domestic care. Women, in contrast, tend to look toward autonomy as preferable to any form of tradition-alism that would leave them and their children econom-ically dependent on someone else.

As young women and men consider the difficulties of building balanced, integrated lives, they move from ideals to consider the fallback positions that would help them avert worst-case scenarios. Here, as we see below, the gender gap widens. Women, in hoping to avoid economic and social dependence, look toward autonomy, while men, in hoping to retain some tradi-tional privileges, look toward modified forms of tradi-tional arrangements. Yet, both groups hope to resolve these conflicts as they construct their lives over time.

Women and Autonomy

Among the women, 9 out of 10 hope to share family and work in a committed, mutually supportive, and egalitarian way. Yet, most are skeptical that they can find a partner or a work situation that will allow them to achieve this ideal. Integrating caretaking with com-mitted work remains an uphill struggle, and it seems risky to count on a partner to sustain a shared vision in the long run. Even a modified version of tradition-alism appears fraught with danger, for it creates eco-nomic vulnerability and constricted options in the event that a relationship sours or a partner decides to leave. Four out of five women thus prefer autonomy to a traditional marriage, concluding that going it alone is better than being trapped in an unhappy relationship or being abandoned by an unreliable partner. Danisha explains,

> Let's say that my marriage doesn't work. I won't ever go into marriage believing that, but just in case, I want to establish myself, because I don't ever want to end up, like, "What am I gonna do?" I want to be able to do what I have to do and still be okay. You can't take a cavalier attitude that things will just work out. Things will work out if you put some effort into making it work out.

Autonomy for women means, at its core, economic self-sufficiency. A life that is firmly rooted in the world of paid work provides the best safeguard against being

stuck in a destructive relationship or being left without the means to support a family. Healthy relationships, they reason, are based on a form of economic individu-alism in which they do not place their economic fate in the hands of another. Rachel declares,

> I'm not afraid of being alone, but I am afraid of being with somebody who's a jerk. I can spend the rest of my life alone, and as long as I have my sisters and my friends, I'm okay. I want to get married and have chil-dren, but I'm not willing to just do it. It has to be under the right circumstances with the right person.

Men and Neotraditionalism

Young men express more ambivalence about the choice between autonomy and traditionalism. If a committed, egalitarian ideal proves out of reach, about 40 percent would opt for independence, preferring to stress the autonomous self so long associated with manhood and now increasingly affirmed by women as well. But six out of 10 men would prefer a modified traditionalism in which two earners need not mean complete equal-ity. This split among men reflects the mix of options they confront. Work remains central to constructing a masculine identity, but it is difficult to find work that offers either economic security or good opportunities for family involvement. Without these supports, men are torn between avoiding family commitments and trying to retain some core advantages provided by tra-ditional arrangements.

From men's perspective, opting for the autonomy conferred by remaining unmarried, unattached, or childless relieves them of the economic burden of earn-ing a family wage in an uncertain economy, but it also risks cutting them off from close, committed, and lasting intimate connections. A neotraditional arrangement, in contrast, offers the chance to create a family built around shared breadwinning but less than equal caretaking. In this scenario, men may envision a dual-earner arrange-ment but still expect their partner to place family first and weave work around it. Josh, a white 27-year-old who was raised by his father after his mother was diag-nosed with severe mental illness, asserts,

> All things being equal, it should be shared. It may sound sexist, but if somebody's gonna be the bread-winner, it's going to be me. First of all, I make a better salary. If she made a much better salary, then I would stay home, but I always feel the need to work, even if

it's in the evenings or something. And I just think the child really needs the mother more than the father at a young age.

Modified traditionalism provides a way for men to cope with economic uncertainties and women's shifting status without surrendering some valued privileges. It collides, however, with women's growing desire for equality and rising need for economic self-sufficiency.

Resolving Moral Dilemmas over Time

In the absence of institutional supports, postponing ultimate decisions becomes a key strategy for resolving the conflicts between commitment and self-development. For women as much as men, the general refrain is, "You can't take care of others if you don't take care of yourself." Michael wants to be certain his girlfriend has created a base for herself at the workplace before they marry, hoping to increase the chances the marriage will succeed and to create a safety net if it fails:

There are a lot of problems when two people are not compatible socially, economically. When Kim gets these goals under her belt, and I have my goals established, it'll be a great marriage. You have to nurture the kind of marriage you want. You have to draw it out before you can go into it.

For Jennifer, 19 and white, autonomy also comes first. Commitment may follow, but only when she knows there is an escape route if the relationship deteriorates:

I will have to have a job and some kind of stability before considering marriage. Too many of my mother's friends went for that—let him provide everything—and they're stuck in a relationship they're not happy with because they can't provide for themselves or the children they now have. The man is not providing for them the way they need, or he's just not a good person. Most of them have husbands who make a lot more money, or they don't even work at all, and they're very unhappy, but they can't leave. So it's either welfare or putting up with somebody else's crap.

Establishing an independent base becomes an essential step on the road to other goals, and autonomy becomes a prerequisite for commitment. This devel-

opmental view rejects the idea that individualism and commitment are in conflict by defining the search for independence as a necessary part of the process of becoming able to care for others. To do that, women as well as men tend to look to work, and its promise of autonomy, to complete the self. For those with children as well as those who are childless, lifelong commitments can be established when "you feel good enough about yourself to create a good relationship." Shauna, a 30-year-old African American who was raised by her mother and stepfather, explains,

If you're not happy with yourself, then you can't be happy with someone else. I'm not looking for someone to fill a void. I think that's what a lot of people do when they look for relationships, and that's not what it's about. It's about sharing yourself with the other person, and when you're content and happy with who you are, then you can give more of yourself to someone else, and that's the type of person that I want to be with.

These strategies are deeply felt and intensely private responses to social and personal conflicts that seem intractable. More fundamental solutions await the creation of systematic supports for balancing work and family and for providing women and men with equal opportunities at the workplace and in the home. Without these supports, new generations must cope as best they can, remaining both flexible and guarded. Andrew, a white 27-year-old, has concluded that rigid positions are not helpful in an unpredictable world:

I would like to have an equal relationship, but I don't have a set definition for what that would be like. I would be fine if both of us were working and we were doing the same thing, but it would depend on what she wants, too. If she thought, "Well, at this point in my life, I don't want to work," or if I felt that way, then it would be fine for one person to do more work in some respects. But I would like it to be equal—just from what I was exposed to and what attracts me.

Anita, a 26-year-old Hispanic, agrees:

I don't want to be on my own for the rest of my life, but right now it's fine, so I can figure out who I am. I don't want to look back later and say I totally ignored my needs. I'm realizing that things are so impermanent, and my expectations can only get me so far.

CONCLUSION: TOWARD A NEW MORAL ORDER?

Deeply rooted social and cultural changes have created new moral dilemmas while undermining a traditional gendered division of moral labor. The widespread and interconnected nature of these changes suggests that a fundamental, irreversible realignment is under way. Less clear is whether it will produce a more gender-equal moral order or will, instead, create new forms of inequality. The long-term implications are necessarily cloudy, but this ambiguity has created some new opportunities along with new risks.

While large-scale social forces are propelling change in a general direction, the specific forms it takes will depend on how women and men respond, individually and collectively, to the dilemmas they face. Those who have come of age during this period are adopting a growing diversity of moral orientations that defies dichotomous gender categories. Their experiences point to a growing desire for a social order in which women and men alike are afforded the opportunity to integrate the essential life tasks of achieving autonomy and caring for others.

Yet, persistent inequalities continue to pose dilemmas, especially for those who aspire to integrate home and work in a balanced, egalitarian way. To understand these processes, we need to focus on the social conditions that create such dilemmas and can transform, and potentially dissolve, the link between gender and moral responsibility. Of course, eradicating this link might only mean that women are allowed to adopt the moral strategies once reserved for men. We also need to discover how to enable everyone, regardless of gender, class, or family situation, to balance care of others with care of self.

The possibilities have never been greater for creating humanistic, rather than gendered, conceptions of moral obligation. New moral dilemmas have prompted women and men to develop innovative strategies, but the long-term resolution of these dilemmas depends on reorganizing our social institutions to foster gender equality and a better balance between family and work. Freud once commented that a healthy person is able "to love and to work." Achieving this vision depends on creating a healthy society, where all citizens are able to combine love and work in the ways they deem best.

NOTES

1. My deep thanks go to Sociologists for Women in Society for honoring me with the 1998 Feminist Lectureship and to the sociology departments and Women's Studies Programs at the University of Georgia and the University of North Texas for their generous support and warm hospitality.

2. See, especially, Parsons and Bales (1955). In important ways, Parsons's focus on instrumental and expressive functions parallels the psychoanalytic focus on the developmental processes of attachment and separation, such as those presented by Bowlby (1969, 1973).

3. Kimmel (2000) presents an excellent summary of the evidence on the temperamental variability within gender groups and the smaller and shrinking differences between them.

4. The concept of *vicarious identity,* for example, was once used to argue that women can meet their identity needs by taking pride in the achievements of their husbands and children. While many contemporary critiques of rising individualism ignore the issue of gender, they have emerged just as women are seeking the right to the kind of autonomy men have historically enjoyed.

5. Chodorow (1978, 1990) distinguished between women's "permeable" and men's "impermeable" ego boundaries, a distinction that parallels the analysis of Parsons and Bales (1955), which relies on notions of "expressive" and

"instrumental" functions and predispositions to explain why women are more involved in, and responsible for, family caretaking.

6. The transformation from welfare to workfare as a framework for providing support for poor single mothers provides an example of this process. Another is the rise of "mommy wars," in which both full-time and employed mothers feel compelled to defend their respective choices by contesting the appropriateness of each other's parenting strategies.

7. Even at its height, male breadwinning was largely confined to white, middle-class households. Today, however, women, men, and children across all races and classes now live in circumstances that depart significantly from this once predominant model. Current trends show that two-thirds of mothers with preschool children are employed outside the home, 60 percent of married couples have two earners (while 77 percent of cohabiting couples have two earners), and 47 percent of the labor force is female. Among children under 18 in 2000, 27 percent live with a single parent (22 percent live with a single mother, and 5 percent with a single father), and one in three births is to an unmarried mother (Lewin 2001).

8. A vivid example of a "damned if you do and damned if you don't" situation can be found in Hays's (1996) analysis

of the "cultural contradictions of motherhood," in which women are expected to practice intensive mothering even as they seek a life outside the home.

9. In Giddens's (1979) language, they cause people to move from "practical consciousness" to "discursive consciousness." Behavior becomes action because it is has new social meaning.

10. Of this group, more than 27 percent lived largely with a single parent, including 7 percent whose parents shared joint custody and 5 percent who lived with single, custodial fathers. The rest saw one or both of their parents remarry and form a new, two-parent household.

11. A larger proportion of households were dual-earning, but they varied in the degree of equality between parents' jobs and did not necessarily include both biological parents.

12. Amato and Booth (1997) confirmed this viewpoint. Respondents also argue that both parents should sustain strong ties to their children whether or not they remain together.

13. Cancian (1987) provided an in-depth analysis of innovative attempts among couples to create interdependent relationships, in which both women and men are responsible for love.

REFERENCES

Amato, Paul, and Alan Booth. 1997. *A generation at risk: Growing up in an era of family upheaval.* Cambridge, MA: Harvard University Press.

Becker, Gary. 1981. *A treatise on the family.* Cambridge, MA: Harvard University Press.

Bellah, Robert N., Richard Madsen, William M. Sullivan, Ann Swidler, and Steven M. Tipton. 1985. *Habits of the heart: Individualism and commitment in American life.* Berkeley and Los Angeles: University of California Press.

Bowlby, John. 1969. *Attachment.* Vol. 1 of *Attachment and loss.* New York: Basic Books.

———. 1973. *Separation: Anxiety and anger.* Vol. 2 of *Attachment and loss.* New York: Basic Books.

Cancian, Francesca M. 1987. *Love in America: Gender and self-development.* Cambridge, UK, and New York: Cambridge University Press.

Chodorow, Nancy. 1978. *The reproduction of mothering: Psychoanalysis and the sociology of gender.* Berkeley and Los Angeles: University of California Press.

———. 1990. *Feminism and psychoanalytic theory.* New Haven, CT: Yale University Press.

Connell, R. W. 1987. *Gender and power.* Stanford, CA: Stanford University Press.

———. 1995. *Masculinities.* Berkeley and Los Angeles: University of California Press.

Crittenden, Danielle. 1999. *What our mothers didn't tell us: Why happiness eludes the modern woman.* New York: Simon & Schuster.

de Tocqueville, Alexis. [1832] 1969. *Democracy in America.* Reprint, New York: Anchor Books.

England, Paula. 1993. The separative self: Androcentric bias in neoclassical assumptions. In *Beyond economic man: Feminist theory and economics,* edited by Marianne A. Ferber and Julie A. Nelson. Chicago: University of Chicago Press.

Epstein, Cynthia F. 1988. *Deceptive distinctions: Sex, gender and the social order.* New Haven, CT: Yale University Press.

Fuchs Epstein, Cynthia, Carol Seron, Bonnie Oglensky, and Robert Saute. 1999. *The part-time paradox: Time norms and professional lives.* New York: Routledge.

Gerson, Kathleen. 1985. *Hard choices: How women decide about work, career, and motherhood.* Berkeley and Los Angeles: University of California Press.

———. 1993. *No man's land: Men's changing commitments to family and work.* New York: Basic Books.

———. 2001. Children of the gender revolution: Some theoretical questions and findings from the field. In *Restructuring work and the life course,* edited by Victor W. Marshall, Walter R. Heinz, Helga Krueger, and Anil Verma. Toronto, Canada: University of Toronto Press.

Gerson, Kathleen, and Jerry A. Jacobs. 2001. Changing the structure and culture of work: Work-family conflict, work flexibility, and gender equity in the modern workplace. In *Working families: The transformation of the American home,* edited by Rosanna Hertz and Nancy Marshall. Berkeley and Los Angeles: University of California Press.

Giddens, Anthony. 1979. *Central problems in social theory: Action, structure, and contradiction in social analysis.* Berkeley and Los Angeles: University of California Press.

Gilligan, Carol. 1982. *In a different voice: Psychological theory and women's development.* Cambridge, MA: Harvard University Press.

Gilligan, Carol, Janie V. Ward, and Jill M. Taylor. 1989. *Mapping the moral terrain: A contribution of women's thinking to psychological theory and education.* Cambridge, MA: Harvard University Press.

Hays, Sharon. 1996. *The cultural contradictions of motherhood.* New Haven, CT: Yale University Press.

Hochschild, Arlie R. 1997. *The time bind: When work becomes home and home becomes work.* New York: Metropolitan Books.

Jacobs, Jerry A. 1989. *Revolving doors: Sex segregation and women's careers.* Palo Alto, CA: Stanford University Press.

———. Forthcoming. The future of occupational sex segregation. *Contexts* 1 (1).

Jacobs, Jerry A., and Kathleen Gerson. 2001. Overworked individuals or overworked families? Explaining trends in work, leisure, and family time. *Work and Occupations* 28 (1): 40–63.

———. Forthcoming. *The time divide: Work, family, and social policy in a hurried era.* Cambridge, MA: Harvard University Press.

Kimmel, Michael. 1996. *Manhood in America: A cultural history.* New York: Free Press.

———. 2000. *The gendered society.* New York: Oxford University Press.

Lewin, Tamar. 2001. Children's well-being improves, report says. *New York Times,* July 19.

Lorber, Judith. 1994. *Paradoxes of gender.* New Haven, CT: Yale University Press.

Parsons, Talcott, and Robert F. Bales. 1955. *Family, socialization, and interaction process.* Glencoe, IL: Free Press.

Putnam, Robert. 2000. *Bowling alone: The collapse and revival of American community.* New York: Simon & Schuster.

Raymon, Paula M. 2001. *Beyond the bottom line: The search for dignity at work.* New York: St. Martin's.

Reskin, Barbara F., and Patricia A. Roos. 1990. *Job queues, gender queues: Explaining women's inroads into male occupations.* Philadelphia: Temple University Press.

Risman, Barbara J. 1998. *Gender vertigo: American families in transition.* New Haven, CT: Yale University Press.

Ryan, Mary. 1981. *Cradle of the middle class.* New York and Cambridge, UK: Cambridge University Press.

Schor, Juliet. 1992. *The overworked American: The unexpected decline of leisure.* New York: Basic Books.

Webster's dictionary of the English language. 1992. Chicago: J. G. Ferguson.

Welter, Barbara. 1966. The cult of true womanhood: 1820–1860. *American Quarterly* 18 (summer): 151–74.

West, Candace, and Don H. Zimmerman. 1987. Doing gender. *Gender & Society* 1:125–51.

Williams, Christine L. 1995. *It's still a man's world: Men who do women's work.* Berkeley and Los Angeles: University of California Press.

R E A D I N G *25*   *Denise A. Segura*

Working at Motherhood: Chicana and Mexicana Immigrant Mothers and Employment[1]

In North American society, women are expected to bear and assume primary responsibility for raising their children. This socially constructed form of motherhood encourages women to stay at home during their children's early or formative years, and asserts activities that take married mothers out of the home (for instance, paid employment) are less important or "secondary" to their domestic duties.[2] Motherhood as a social construction rests on the ideological position that women's biological abilities to bear and suckle children are "natural," and therefore fundamental to women's "fulfillment." This position, however, fails to appreciate that motherhood is a culturally formed structure whose meanings can vary and are subject to change.

Despite the ideological impetus to mother at home, over half of all women with children work for wages.[3]

The growing incongruence between social ideology and individual behaviors has prompted some researchers to suggest that traditional gender role expectations are changing (for example, greater acceptance of women working outside the home).[4] The profuse literature on the "ambivalence" and "guilt" employed mothers often feel when they work outside the home, however, reminds us that changes in expectations are neither absolute nor uncontested.

Some analysts argue that the ambivalence felt by many employed mothers stems from their discomfort in deviating from a socially constructed "idealized mother," who stays home to care for her family.[5] This image of motherhood, popularized in the media, schoolbooks, and public policy, implies that the family and the economy constitute two separate spheres, private and public. Hood argues, however, that the notion of a private–public dichotomy largely rests on the experiences of white, leisured women and lacks immediate relevance to less privileged women (for instance, immigrant women, women of color), who have historically been important economic actors both inside and outside the home.[6] The view that the relationship between motherhood and employment varies by class, race, and/or culture raises several important questions. Do the ideology of motherhood and the "ambivalence" of employed mothers depicted within American sociology and feminist scholarship pertain to women of Mexican descent in the United States? Among these women, what is the relation between the ideological constructions of motherhood and employment? Is motherhood mutually exclusive from employment among Mexican-heritage women from different social locations?

In this [reading] I explore these questions using qualitative data gathered from thirty women of Mexican descent in the United States—both native-born Chicanas (including two Mexico-born women raised since preschool years in the US) and resident immigrant Mexicanas.[7] I illustrate that notions of motherhood for Chicanas and Mexicanas are embedded in different ideological constructs operating within two systems of patriarchy. Contrary to the expectations of acculturation models, I find that Mexicanas frame motherhood in ways that foster a more consistent labor market presence than do Chicanas. I argue that this distinction—typically bypassed in the sociological literature on motherhood, women and work, or Chicano Studies—is rooted in their dissimilar social locations—that is, the "social spaces" they engage within the social structure created by the intersection of class, race, gender, and culture.[8]

I propose that Mexicanas, raised in a world where economic and household work often merged, do not dichotomize social life into public and private spheres, but appear to view employment as one workable domain of motherhood. Hence, the more recent the time of emigration, the less ambivalence Mexicanas express regarding employment. Chicanas, on the other hand, raised in a society that celebrates the expressive functions of the family and obscures its productive economic functions, express higher adherence to the ideology of stay-at-home motherhood and correspondingly more ambivalence toward full-time employment—even when they work.

These differences between Mexicanas and Chicanas challenge current research on Mexican-origin women that treats them as a single analytic category (for instance, "Hispanic") as well as research on contemporary views of motherhood that fails to appreciate diversity among women. My examination of the intersection of motherhood and employment among Mexican immigrant women also reinforces emerging research focusing on women's own economic and social motivations to emigrate to the United States (rather than the behest of husbands and/or fathers).[9]

My analysis begins with a brief review of relevant research on the relationship between motherhood and employment. Then I explore this relationship in greater detail, using in-depth interview data. I conclude by discussing the need to recast current conceptualizations of the dilemma between motherhood and employment to reflect women's different social locations.

THEORETICAL CONCERNS

The theoretical concerns that inform this research on Chicana/Mexicana employment integrate feminist analyses of the hegemonic power of patriarchy over work and motherhood with a critique of rational choice models and other models that overemphasize modernity and acculturation. In much of the literature on women and work, familial roles tend to be portrayed as important constraints on both women's labor market entry and mobility. Differences among women related to immigrant status, however, challenge this view.

Within rational choice models, motherhood represents a prominent social force behind women's job decisions. Becker and Polachek, for example, argue that women's "preference" to mother is maximized in jobs that exact fewer penalties for interrupted employment, such as part-time, seasonal, or clerical work.[10] According to this view, women's pursuit of their rational self-interest reinforces their occupational segregation within low-paying jobs (for example, clerical work) and underrepresentation in higher-paying, male-dominated jobs that typically require significant employer investments (for example, specialized training). Employers may be reluctant to "invest" in or train women workers who, they perceive, may leave a job at any time for familial reasons.[11] This perspective views motherhood as a major impediment to employment and mobility. But it fails to consider that the organization of production has developed in ways that make motherhood an impediment. Many feminist scholars view this particular development as consistent with the hegemonic power of patriarchy.

Distinct from rational choice models, feminist scholarship directs attention away from individual preferences to consider how patriarchy (male domination/female subordination) shapes the organization of production, resulting in the economic, political, and social subordination of women to men.[12] While many economists fail to consider the power of ideological constructs such as "family" and "motherhood" in shaping behavior among women, employers, and the organization of production itself, many feminist scholars focus on these power dynamics.

Within feminist analyses, motherhood as an ideology obscures and legitimizes women's social subordination because it conceals particular interests within the rubric of a universal prerogative (reproduction). The social construction of motherhood serves the interest of capital by providing essential childbearing, child care, and housework at a minimal cost to the state, and sustains women as a potential reservoir of labor power, or a "reserve army of labor."[13] The strength of the ideology of motherhood is such that women continue to try to reconcile the "competing urgencies"[14] of motherhood and employment despite the lack of supportive structures at work or within the family.

Because employers view women as mothers (or future mothers), they encounter discrimination in job entry and advancement.[15] Because women are viewed as mothers, they also work a "second shift" at home.[16] The conflict between market work and family work has caused considerable ambivalence within women. Berg, for example, notes that one of the dominant themes in analyzing women and work is the "guilt" of employed mothers based on "espousing something different" from their own mothers.[17]

The notion Berg describes of "conflict" or "guilt" rests on several suppositions. The first assumption is that motherhood is a unilaterally oppressive state; the second, that employed mothers feel guilt; and the third, that today's employed mothers do not have working mothers (which partially explains their "guilt feelings"). Inasmuch as large numbers of working-class, immigrant, and racial ethnic women have long traditions of working in the formal and informal economic sectors, such assumptions are suspect.

Research on women of Mexican descent and employment indicates their labor force participation is lower than that of other women when they have young children.[18] Moreover, Chicanas and Mexicanas are occupationally segregated in the lowest-paying of female-dominated jobs.[19] Explanations for their unique employment situation range from analyses of labor market structures and employer discrimination[20] to deficient individual characteristics (for instance, education, job skills)[21] and cultural differences.[22]

Analyses of Chicana/Mexicana employment that utilize a cultural framework typically explain the women's lower labor force participation, higher fertility, lower levels of education, and higher levels of unemployment as part of an ethnic or cultural tradition.[23] That is, as this line of argument goes, Chicano/Mexican culture emphasizes a strong allegiance to an idealized form of motherhood and a patriarchal ideology that frowns upon working wives and mothers and does not encourage girls to pursue higher education or employment options. These attitudes are supposed to vary by generation, with immigrant women (from Mexico) holding the most conservative attitudes.[24]

There are two major flaws in the research on Chicana/Mexicana employment, however. First, inconsistency in distinguishing between native-born and resident immigrant women characterizes much of this literature. Second, overreliance on linear acculturation persists. Both procedures imply either that Chicanas and Mexicanas are very similar, or that they lie on a sort of "cultural continuum," with Mexican immigrants at one end holding more conservative behaviors and attitudes grounded in traditional (often rural) Mexican culture, and U.S.-born Chicanos holding an amalgamation of cultural traditions from Mexico and the United States.[25] In terms of motherhood and employment, therefore, Mexicanas should have more "traditional" ideas about motherhood than U.S.-born Chicanas. Since the traditional ideology of motherhood typically refers to women staying home to "mother" children rather than going outside the home to work, Mexicanas theoretically should not be as willing to work as Chicanas or North American women in general—unless there is severe economic need. This formulation, while logical, reflects an underlying emphasis on modernity—or the view that "traditional" Mexican culture lags behind North American culture in developing behaviors and attitudes conducive to participating fully in modern society.[26] Inasmuch as conventional North American views of motherhood typically idealize labor market exit to care for children, embracing this prototype may be more conducive to maintaining patriarchal privilege (female economic subordination to men) than facilitating economic progress generally. In this sense, conceptualizations of motherhood that affirm its economic character may be better accommodating to women's market participation in the United States.

The following section discusses the distinct views of motherhood articulated by Chicanas and Mexicanas and their impact on employment attitudes and behaviors. In contrast to the notion that exposure to North American values enhances women's incentives to work, proportionately more Chicanas than Mexicanas express ambivalence toward paid employment when they have children at home. I analyze these differences among a selected sample of clerical, service, and operative workers.

METHOD AND SAMPLE

This paper is based on in-depth interviews with thirty Mexican-origin women—thirteen Chicanas and seventeen Mexicanas—who had participated in the 1978 to 79 or 1980 to 81 cohorts of an adult education and employment training program in the greater San Francisco Bay Area.[27] All thirty respondents had been involved in a conjugal relationship (either legal marriage or informal cohabitation with a male partner) at some point in their lives before I interviewed them in 1985, and had at least one child under eighteen years of age. At the time of their interviews, six Chicanas and fourteen Mexicanas were married; seven Chicanas and three Mexicanas were single parents.

On the average, the married Chicanas have 1.2 children at home; the Mexicanas report 3.5 children. Both Chicana and Mexicana single mothers average 1.6 children. The children of the Chicanas tend to be preschool age or in elementary school. The children of the Mexicanas exhibit a greater age range (from infant to late adolescence), reflecting their earlier marriages and slightly older average age.

With respect to other relevant characteristics, all but two Mexicanas and five Chicanas had either a high school diploma or its equivalent (GED). The average age was 27.4 years for the Chicanas and thirty-three years for the Mexicanas.[28] Upon leaving the employment training program, all the women secured employment. At the time of their interviews, about half of the Chicanas ($n = 7$); and three-fourths of the Mexicanas ($n = 12$) were employed. Only two out of the seven (28 percent) employed Chicanas worked full-time (thirty-five or more hours per week) whereas nine out of the twelve (75 percent) employed Mexicanas worked full-time. Most of the Chicanas found clerical or service jobs (for example, teacher assistants); most

of the Mexicanas labored in operative jobs or in the service sector (for example, hotel maids), with a small minority employed as clerical workers.

I gathered in-depth life and work histories from the women to ascertain:

1. What factors motivated them to enter, exit, and stay employed in their specific occupations;
2. whether familial roles or ideology influenced their employment consistency; and
3. whether other barriers limited their job attachment and mobility.

My examination of the relationship between motherhood and employment forms part of a larger study of labor market stratification and occupational mobility among Chicana and Mexican immigrant women.[29]

MOTHERHOOD AND EMPLOYMENT

Nearly all of the respondents, both Chicana and Mexicana, employed and nonemployed, speak of motherhood as their most important social role. They differ sharply in their employment behaviors and views regarding the relationship between motherhood and market work. Women fall into four major groups. The first group consists of five *Involuntary Nonemployed Mothers,* who are not employed but care full-time for their children. All of these women want to be employed at least part-time. They either cannot secure the job they want and/or feel pressured to be at home mothering full-time.

The second group consists of six *Voluntary Nonemployed Mothers* who are not employed but remain out of the labor force by *choice.* They feel committed to staying at home to care for preschool and/or elementary school age children.

The third category, *Ambivalent Employed Mothers,* includes eleven employed women. They have either preschool or elementary school age children. Women in this group believe that employment interferes with motherhood and feel "guilty" when they work outside the home. Despite these feelings, they are employed at least part-time.

The fourth group, *Nonambivalent Employed Mothers,* includes eight employed women. What distinguishes these women from the previous group is their view that employment and motherhood seem compatible social dynamics irrespective of the age of their children. All eight women are Mexicanas. Some of these women believe employment could be problematic, however, *if* a family member could not care for their children or be at home for the children when they arrived from school.

Chicanas tend to fall in the second and third categories, whereas Mexicanas predominate in the first and fourth groups. Three reasons emerged as critical in explaining this difference:

1. the economic situations of their families;
2. labor market structure (four-fifths of the nonemployed Mexicanas were involuntarily unemployed); and
3. women's conceptualizations of motherhood, in particular, their expressed *need* to mother.

Age of the women and number of children did not fall into any discernible pattern; therefore, I did not engage them in depth within my analysis.

First, I consider the situation of the Voluntary Nonemployed Mothers, including three married Chicanas, one single-parent Mexicana, and one single-parent Chicana. All but one woman exited the labor market involuntarily (for reasons such as layoffs or disability). All five women remain out of the labor force by choice. Among them, the expressed need to mother appears strong—overriding all other concerns. They view motherhood as mutually exclusive from employment. Lydia, a married Chicana with a small toddler, articulates this perspective:

Right now, since we've had the baby, I feel, well he [her husband] feels the same way, that I want to spend this time with her and watch her grow up. See, because when I was small my grandmother raised me so I felt this *loss* [her emphasis] when my grandmother died. And I've never gotten that *real love,* that mother love from my mother. We have a friendship, but we don't have that "motherly love." I want my daughter to know that I'm here, especially at her age, it's very important for them to know that when they cry that mama's there. Even if it's not a painful cry, it's still important for them to know that mommy's there. She's my number one—she's all my attention. . . . so working-wise, it's up to [her husband] right now.

Susana, a Chicana single parent with a five-year-old child, said:

I'm the type of person that has always wanted to have a family. I think it was more like I didn't have

a family-type home when I was growing up. I didn't have a mother and a father and the kids all together in the same household all happy. I didn't have that. And that's what I want more than anything! I want to be different from my mother, who has worked hard and is successful in her job. I don't want to be successful in the same way.

Lydia, Susana, and the other voluntarily unemployed Chicanas adamantly assert that motherhood requires staying home with their children. Susana said: "A good mother is there for her children all the time when they are little and when they come home from school." All the Chicanas in this category believe that motherhood means staying home with children—even if it means going on welfare (AFDC). This finding is similar to other accounts of working-class women.[30]

The sense shared among this group of women that motherhood and employment are irreconcilable, especially when children are of preschool age, is related to their social locations. A small minority of the Chicanas had been raised by nonemployed mothers ($n = 3$). They feel they should stay at home with their children as long as it's economically feasible. Most of the Chicanas, however, resemble Lydia and Susana, who had been raised by employed mothers. Although these women recognize that their mothers had worked out of economic need, they believe they did not receive sufficient love and care from their mothers. Throughout their interviews, this group of Chicanas expressed hostility and resentment against their employed mothers for leaving them with other caretakers. These feelings contribute to their decisions to stay at home with their children, and/or their sense of "guilt" when they are employed. Their hostility and guilt defy psychoanalytic theories that speculate that the cycle of gender construction locking women into "exclusive mothering" roles can be broken if the primary caretaker (the mother) undertakes more diverse roles.[31] Rather, Chicanas appear to value current conceptualizations of motherhood that prioritize the expressive work of the mother, as distinct from her economic activities.

This group of Chicanas seems to be pursuing the social construction of motherhood that is idealized within their ethnic community, their churches, and society at large.[32] Among Chicanos and Mexicanos the image of *la madre* as self-sacrificing and holy is a powerful standard against which women often compare themselves.[33] The Chicana informants also seem to accept the notion that women's primary duty is to provide for the emotional welfare of the children, and that economic activities which take them outside the home are secondary. Women's desire to enact the socially constructed motherhood ideal was further strengthened by their conviction that many of their current problems (for instance, low levels of education, feelings of inadequacy, single parenthood) are related to growing up in families that did not conform to the stay-at-home mother/father-as-provider configuration. Their evaluation of the close relationship between motherhood and economic or emotional well-being of offspring parallels popular emphasis on the primacy of individual efforts and the family environment to emotional vigor and achievement.[34]

Informants in this group speak to a complex dimension of mothering and gender construction in the Chicano/Mexicano communities. These women reject their employed mothers' organization of family life. As children, most had been cared for by other family members, and now feel closer to their grandmothers or other female relatives than to their own biological mothers. This causes them considerable pain—pain they want to spare their own children. Many, like Susana, do not want to be "successful" in the tradition of their own employed mothers. Insofar as "success" means leaving their children with other caretakers, it contradicts their conceptualization of motherhood. Rather, they frame "success" in more affective terms: having children who are happy and doing well in school. This does not suggest that Chicanas disagree with the notion that having a good job or a lucrative career denotes "success." They simply feel that successful careers could and should be deferred until their children are older (for instance, in the upper grades of elementary school) and doing well academically and emotionally.

Only one married Mexicana, Belen, articulated views similar to those of the Chicanas. Belen left the labor market in 1979 to give birth and care for her newborn child. It is important to note that she has a gainfully employed husband who does not believe mothers should work outside the home. Belen, who has two children and was expecting a third when I interviewed her, said:

> I wanted to work or go back to school after having my first son, but my husband didn't want me to. He said, "No one can take care of your child the way you can." He did not want me to work. And I did not feel right having someone else care for my son. So I decided to wait until my children were older.

Belen's words underscore an important dynamic that impacted on both Mexicana and Chicana conceptualizations of motherhood: spousal employment and private patriarchy. Specifically, husbands working in full-time, year-round jobs with earnings greater than those of their wives tended to pressure women to mother full-time. Women who succumb to this pressure become economically dependent on their husbands and reaffirm male authority in the organization of the family. These particular women tend to consider motherhood and employment in similar ways. This suggests that the form the social construction of motherhood takes involves women's economic relationship to men as well as length of time in the United States.

Four Mexicanas and one Chicana were involuntarily nonemployed. They had been laid off from their jobs or were on temporary disability leave. Three women (two Mexicanas/one Chicana) were seeking employment; the other two were in the last stages of pregnancy but intended to look for a job as soon as possible after their child's birth. All five women reported feeling "good" about being home with their children but wanted to rejoin the labor force as soon as possible. Ideologically these women view motherhood and employment as reconcilable social dynamics. As Isabel, an unemployed production worker, married with eight children, said:

> I believe that women always work more. We who are mothers work to maintain the family by working outside, but also inside the house caring for the children.

Isabel voiced a sentiment held by all of the informants—that women work hard at motherhood. Since emigrating to the U.S. about a decade ago, Isabel had been employed nearly continuously, with only short leaves for childbearing. Isabel and nearly all of the Mexicanas described growing up in environments where women, men, and children were important economic actors. In this regard they are similar to the Nonambivalent Employed Mothers—all of whom are also Mexicanas. They tended not to dichotomize social life in the same way as the Voluntary Nonemployed Chicanas and Ambivalent Employed informants.

Although all of the Chicanas believe that staying home best fulfills their mother roles, slightly fewer than half actually stay out of the labor market to care for their young children. The rest of the Chicanas are employed and struggling to reconcile motherhood with employment. I refer to these women as Ambivalent Employed

Mothers. They express guilt about working and assert they *would not work* if they did not have to for economic reasons. Seven of these women are Chicanas; four are Mexicanas.

To try and alleviate their guilt and help meet their families' economic goals, most of the Chicanas work in part-time jobs. This option permits them to be home when their children arrive from school. Despite this, they feel guilty and unhappy about working. As Jenny, a married Chicana with two children, ages two and four, who is employed part-time, said:

> Sure, I feel guilty. I *should* [her emphasis] be with them [her children] while they're little. He [her husband] really feels that I should be with my kids all the time. And it's true.

Despite their guilt, most of the women in this group remain employed because their jobs offer them the means to provide for family economic betterment—a goal that transcends staying home with their children. However, women's utilization of economic rationales for working sometimes served as a smokescreen for individualistic desires to "do something outside the home" and to establish a degree of autonomy. Several women, for example, stated that they enjoyed having their "own money." When I asked these women to elaborate, they typically retreated to a familistic stance. That is, much of *her* money is used *for the family* (for example, child care, family presents, clothing). When money is used *for the woman* (makeup, going out with the girls) it is often justified as necessary for her emotional well-being, which in turn helps her to be a good wife and mother.

The Mexicana mothers who are employed express their ambivalence somewhat differently from the Chicanas. One Mexicana works full-time; the other three are employed part-time. Angela, a Mexicana married with one child and employed full-time as a seamstress, told me with glistening eyes:

> Always I have had to work. I had to leave my son with the baby-sitter since he was six months old. It was difficult. Each baby-sitter has their own way of caring for children, which isn't like yours. I know the baby-sitter wouldn't give him the food I left. He always had on dirty diapers and was starving when I would pick him up. But there wasn't any other recourse. I had to work. I would just clean him and feed him when I got home.

Angela's "guilt" stemmed from her inability to find good, affordable child care. Unlike most of the Mexicanas, who had extensive family networks, Angela and her husband had few relatives to rely on in the U.S. Unlike the Chicana informants, Angela did not want to exit the labor market to care for her child. Her desire is reinforced by economic need; her husband is irregularly employed.[35] For the other three Mexicanas in this group, guilt as an employed mother appears to have developed with stable spousal employment. That is, the idea of feeling guilty about full-time employment emerged *after* husbands became employed in secure, well-paying jobs and "reminded" them of the importance of stay-at-home, full-time motherhood. Lourdes, who was married with eight children and working as a part-time hotel maid said:

> I was offered a job at a—factory, working from eleven at night to seven in the morning. But I had a baby and so I wasn't able to work. I would have liked to take the job because it paid $8.25 an hour. I couldn't though, because of my baby. And my husband didn't want me to work at night. He said, "If we both work at night, who will take care of the children?" So I didn't take the job.

To thwart potential guilt over full-time employment and to ease marital tension (if she had taken this job she would have earned more money than her husband), Lourdes declined this high-paying job. When her child turned two, she opted to work part-time as a hotel maid. Lourdes, and the other Mexicanas employed part-time, told me that they *would* work full-time *if* their husbands supported their preferences. Mexicanas' ambivalence, then, is related to unease about their children's child care situations, as well as to anger at being held accountable to a narrow construction of motherhood enforced by their husbands.

All Ambivalent Employed Mothers report worrying about their children while at work. While this does not necessarily impair their job performance, it adds another psychological or emotional burden on their shoulders. This burden affects their ability to work full-time (overtime is especially problematic) or seek the means (especially schooling) to advance in their jobs.

Women seem particularly troubled when they have to work on weekends. This robs them of precious family time. As Elena, a Chicana single parent with two children, ages nine and three, who works part-time as a hotel maid, said:

> Yes, I work on weekends. And my kids, you know how kids are—they don't like it. And it's hard. But I hope to find a job soon where the schedule is fixed and I won't have to work on weekends—because that time should be for my kids.

There is a clear sense among the women I interviewed that a boundary between *time for the family* and *market time* should exist. During times when this boundary folds, women experience both internal conflict (within the woman herself) and external conflict (among family members). They regard jobs that overlap on family time with disfavor and unhappiness. When economic reasons compel women to work during what they view as family time, they usually try to find as quickly as possible a different job that allows them to better meet their mother roles.

Interestingly, the Chicanas appear less flexible in reconciling the boundaries of family time and market time than the Mexicanas. That is, Chicanas overwhelmingly "choose" part-time employment to limit the amount of spillover time from employment on motherhood and family activities. Mexicanas, on the other hand, overwhelmingly work full-time ($n = 9$) and attempt to do both familial caretaking and market work as completely as possible.

This leads us to consider the fourth category I call Nonambivalent Employed Mothers. This category consists of Mexicana immigrants, both married and single-parent (six and two women, respectively). Mexicanas in this group do not describe motherhood as a *need* requiring a separate sphere for optimal realization. Rather, they refer to motherhood as one function of womanhood compatible with employment insofar as employment allows them to provide for their family's economic subsistence or betterment. As Pilar, a married Mexicana with four children, employed full-time as a line supervisor in a factory, said: "I work to help my children. That's what a mother should do." This group of Mexicanas does not express *guilt* over leaving their children in the care of others so much as *regret* over the limited amount of time they could spend with them. As Norma, a Mexicana full-time clerical worker who is married with two children ages three and five, said:

> I don't feel guilty for leaving my children because if I didn't work they might not have the things they have now.... Perhaps if I had to stay at home I would feel guilty and

frustrated. I'm not the type that can stay home twenty-four hours a day. I don't think that would help my children any because I would feel pressured at being cooped up [*encerrada*] at home. And that way I wouldn't have the same desire to play with my daughters. But now, with the time we have together, we do things that we want to, like run in the park, because there's so little time.

All of the Mexicanas in this group articulate views similar to Norma's. Their greater comfort with the demands of market and family work emanates from their social locations. All of the Mexicanas come from poor or working-class families, where motherhood embraced both economic and affective features. Their activities were not viewed as equal to those of men, however, and ideologically women saw themselves as *helping* the family rather than *providing* for it.

Few Mexicanas reported that their mothers were wage-laborers ($n = 3$); rather, they described a range of economic activities they remembered women doing "for the family."[36] Mexicanas from rural villages ($n = 7$) recounted how their mothers had worked on the land and made assorted products or food to sell in local marketplaces. Mexicanas from urban areas ($n = 5$) also discussed how their mothers had been economically active. Whether rural or urban, Mexicanas averred that their mothers had taught them to "help" the family as soon as possible. As Norma said:

> My mother said: "It's one thing for a woman to lie around the house but it's a different thing for the work that needs to be done. As the saying goes, Work is never done; the work does you in [*El trabajo acaba con uno; uno nunca acaba con el trabajo*]."

Lourdes and two other Mexicanas cleaned houses with their mothers after school. Other mothers sold clothes to neighbors, cooked and sold food, or did assorted services for pay (for example, giving penicillin shots to neighbors). The Mexicanas do not view these activities as "separate" or less important than the emotional nurturing of children and family. Rather, they appreciate both the economic and the expressive as important facets of motherhood.

Although the Mexicanas had been raised in worlds where women were important economic actors, this did not signify gender equality. On the contrary, male privilege, or patriarchy, characterizes the organization of the family, the economy, and the polity in both rural and urban Mexican society.[37] In the present study, Mexicanas indicated that men wielded greater authority in the family, the community, and the state than women. Mexicanas also tended to uphold male privilege in the family by viewing both domestic work and women's employment as "less important" than the work done by men. As Adela, a married Mexicana with four children, said: "Men are much stronger and do much more difficult work than women." Mexicanas also tended to defer to husbands as the "head" of the family—a position they told me was both "natural" and "holy."[38]

WORKING AT MOTHERHOOD

The differences presented here between the Chicanas and Mexicanas regarding motherhood and employment stem from their distinct social locations. Raised in rural or working-class families in Mexico, the Mexicanas described childhoods where they and their mothers actively contributed to the economic subsistence of their families by planting crops, harvesting, selling homemade goods, and cleaning houses. Their situations resonate with what some researchers term a family economy, where all family members work at productive tasks differentiated mainly by age and sex.[39] In this type of structure, there is less distinction between economic life and domestic life. Motherhood in this context is both economic and expressive, embracing employment as well as child-rearing.

The family economy the Mexicanas experienced differs from the family organization that characterizes most of the Chicanas' childhoods. The Chicanas come from a world that idealizes a male wage earner as the main economic "provider," with women primarily as consumers and only secondarily as economic actors.[40] Women in this context are mothers first, wage earners second. Families that challenge this structure are often discredited, or perceived as dysfunctional and the source of many social problems.[41] The ambivalence Chicanas recurrently voice stems from their belief in what Kanter calls "the myth of separate worlds."[42] They seek to realize the popular notion or stereotype that family is a separate structure—a haven in a heartless world. Their attachment to this ideal is underscored by a harsh critique of their own employed mothers and themselves *when* they work full-time. Motherhood framed within this context appears irreconcilable with employment.

There are other facets to the differences between Chicanas and Mexicanas. The Mexicanas, as immigrant women, came to the United States with a vision of improving the life chances of their families and themselves. This finding intersects with research on "selective immigration." That is, Mexican immigrants tend to possess higher levels of education than the national average in Mexico, and a wide range of behavioral characteristics (for instance, high achievement orientation) conducive to success in the United States.[43]

The Mexicanas emigrated hoping to work—hence their high attachment to employment, even in physically demanding, often demeaning jobs. Mexican and Chicano husbands support their wives' desires to work *so long as* this employment does not challenge the patriarchal structure of the family. In other words, so long as the Mexicanas: (1) articulate high attachment to motherhood *and* family caretaker roles, (2) frame their employment in terms of family economic goals, and (3) do not ask men to do equal amounts of housework or child care, they encounter little resistance from husbands or other male family members.

When Mexican and Chicano husbands secure good jobs, however, they begin pressuring wives to quit working or to work only part-time. In this way, Mexican and Chicano men actively pursue continuity of their superordinate position within the family. This suggests that the way motherhood is conceptualized in both the Mexican and Chicano communities, particularly with respect to employment, is wedded to male privilege, or patriarchy. Ironically, then, Mexicanas' sense of employment's continuity with motherhood enhances their job attachment but does not challenge a patriarchal family structure or ethos.

Similarly, Chicanas' preference for an idealized form of motherhood does not challenge male privilege in their community. Their desire to stay at home to mother exercised a particularly strong influence on the employment behavior of single-parent Chicanas and women with husbands employed in relatively good jobs. This preference reflects an adherence to an idealized, middle-class lifestyle that glorifies women's domestic roles, as well as to maintenance of a patriarchal family order. Chicanas feel they should stay at home to try and provide their children with the mothering they believe children should have—mothering that many of them had not experienced. Chicanas also feel compelled by husbands and the larger community to maintain the status of men as "good providers." Men earning wages adequate to provide for their families' needs usually urged their wives to leave the labor market. While the concept of the good provider continues to be highly valued in our society, it also serves as a rationale that upholds male privilege ideologically and materially, and reinforces the myth of separate spheres that emanates from the organization of the family and the economy.

CONCLUSION

By illustrating how Chicanas and Mexicanas differ in their conceptualizations and organization of the motherhood and employment nexus, this study demonstrates how motherhood is a culturally formed structure with various meanings and subtexts. The vitality of these differences among a group whose members share a common historical origin and many cultural attributes underscores the need for frameworks that analyze diversity among all groups of women. Most essential to such an undertaking is a critique of the privileging of the "separate spheres" concept in analyses of women and work.

The present study provides additional coherence to recent contentions that the private–public dichotomy lacks immediate relevance to less privileged women (for instance, Chicana and Mexican immigrant women). In the process of illustrating how Chicanas and Mexicanas organized the interplay between motherhood and employment, it became clear that a more useful way of understanding this intersection might be to problematize motherhood itself. Considering motherhood from the vantage point of women's diverse social locations revealed considerable heterogeneity in how one might speak of it. For example, motherhood has an economic component for both groups of women, but it is most strongly expressed by Mexicana immigrants. The flavor of the expressive, however, flows easily across both groups of women, and for the Mexicanas embraces the economic. What this suggests is that the dichotomy of the separate spheres lacks relevance to Chicanas and Mexicanas and other women whose social origins make economic work necessary for survival.

This leads us to consider the relative place and function of the ideology of motherhood prevalent in our society. Motherhood constructed to privilege the woman who stays at home serves a myriad of functions. It pushes women to dichotomize their lives rather than develop a sense of fluidity across roles, responsibilities, and preferences. Idealized, stay-at-home motherhood eludes most American women with children. As an ideology, however, it tells them what "should be," rendering them failures *as women* when they enter the labor market. Hence the feelings of ambivalence that characterized employed mothers' lives for the most part—except those who had not yet internalized these standards. The present research provided examples of such women, along with the understanding that other women from different social locations may demonstrate distinct ways of organizing the motherhood–employment nexus as well.

Feminist analyses of women and work emphasize the role of patriarchy to maintain male privilege and domination economically and ideologically. It is important to recognize that male privilege is not experienced equally by all men, and that patriarchy itself can be expressed in different ways. The present study found that notions of motherhood among Mexicanas and Chicanas are embedded in different ideological constructs operating within two systems of patriarchy. For Mexicanas, patriarchy takes the form of a corporate family model, with all members contributing to the common good. For Chicanas, the patriarchal structure centers more closely around a public–private dichotomy that idealizes men as economic providers and women primarily as caretakers-consumers.

The finding that women from more "traditional" backgrounds (such as rural Mexico) are likely to approach full-time employment with less ambivalence than more "American" women (such as the Chicanas) rebuts linear acculturation models that assume a negative relationship between ideologies (such as motherhood) constructed within "traditional" Mexican society and employment. It also complements findings on the negative relationship between greater length of time in the United States and high aspirations among Mexicans.[44] This suggests that employment problems (for example, underemployment, unemployment) are related less to "traditional" cultural configurations than to labor market structure and employment policies. Understanding the intersections between employment policy, social ideology, and private need is a necessary step toward expanding possibilities for women in our society.

NOTES

1. This article is a revised version of "Ambivalence or Continuity? Motherhood and Employment among Chicanas and Mexican Immigrant Women," *AZTLAN, International Journal of Chicano Studies Research* (1992). I would like to thank Maxine Baca Zinn, Evelyn Nakano Glenn, Arlie Hochschild, Beatriz Pesquera, and Vicki Ruiz for their constructive feedback and criticism of earlier drafts of this paper. A special thanks goes to Jon Cruz for his assistance in titling this paper. Any remaining errors or inconsistencies are my own responsibility. This research was supported in part by a 1986–87 University of California President's Postdoctoral Fellowship.

2. Betsy Wearing, *The Ideology of Motherhood, A Study of Sydney Suburban Mothers* (Sydney: George Allen and Unwin, 1984); Barbara J. Berg, *The Crisis of the Working Mother, Resolving the Conflict between Family and Work* (New York: Summit Books, 1986); Nancy Folbre "The Pauperization of Motherhood: Patriarchy and Public Policy in the United States," *Review of Radical Political Economics* 16 (1984). The view that mothers should not work outside the home typically pertains to married women. Current state welfare policies (e.g., Aid to Families with Dependent Children [AFDC], workfare) indicate that single, unmarried mothers belong in the labor force, not at home caring for their children full-time. See Naomi Gerstel and Harriet Engel Gross, "Introduction," in N. Gerstel and H. E. Gross, eds., *Families and Work* (Philadelphia: Temple University Press, 1987), pp. 1–12; Deborah K. Zinn and Rosemary C. Sarri, "Turning Back the Clock on Public Welfare," in *Signs: Journal of Women in Culture and Society* 10 (1984), pp. 355–370; Nancy Folbre "The Pauperization of Motherhood"; Nancy A. Naples, "A Socialist Feminist Analysis of the Family Support Act of 1988," AFFILIA 6 (1991), pp. 23–38.

3. Allyson Sherman Grossman, "More than Half of All Children Have Working Mothers," Special Labor Force Reports—Summaries, *Monthly Labor Review* (February 1982), pp. 41–43; Howard Hayghe, "Working Mothers Reach Record Number in 1984," *Monthly Labor Review* 107 (December 1984), pp. 31–34; U.S. Bureau of The Census "Fertility of American Women: June 1990," *Current Population Report,* Series P-20, No. 454 (Washington D.C.: United States Government Printing Office, 1991). In June 1990, over half (53.1 percent) of women between the ages of 18 and 44 who had had a child in the last year were in the labor force. This proportion varied by race: 54.9 percent of white women, 46.9 percent of Black women, and 44.4 percent of Latinas were in the labor force. See U.S. Bureau of the Census (1991), p. 5.

4. Simon and Landis report that a 1986 Gallup Poll indicates that support for married women to work outside the home is considerably greater than 1938 levels: 76 percent of women and 78 percent of men approve (1989: 270). Comparable 1938 levels are 25 percent and 19 percent, respectively, of women and men. The 1985 Roper Poll finds the American public adhering to the view that a husband's career supersedes that of his wife: 72 percent of women and 62 percent of men agree that a wife should quit her job and relocate if her husband is offered a good job in another city (1989: 272). In the reverse situation, 20 percent of women and 22 percent of men believe a husband should quit his job and relocate with his wife (1989: 272). Simon and Landis conclude: "The Women's Movement has not radicalized the American woman: she is still prepared to put marriage and children ahead of her career and to allow her husband's status to determine the family's position in society" (1989: 269). Rita J. Simon and Jean M. Landis, "Women's and Men's Attitudes about a Woman's Place and Role," *Public Opinion Quarterly* 53 (1989), pp. 265–276.

5. Arlie Hochschild with Anne Machung, *The Second Shift, Working Parents and the Revolution at Home* (New York: Viking Penguin Books, 1989); Kathleen Gerson, *Hard Choices* (Berkeley: University of California Press, 1985); Barbara J. Berg, *The Crisis of the Working Mother, Resolving the Conflict between Family and Work* (New York: Summit Books, 1986). The concept of "separate spheres" is approached in a variety of ways and often critiqued. See Michele Barrett, *Women's Oppression Today, Problems in Marxist Feminist Analysis* (London: Verso Press, 1980); Nona Glazer "Servants to Capital: Unpaid Domestic Labor and Paid Work," *Review of Radical Economics* 16 (1984), pp. 61–87. Zaretsky contends that distinct family and market spheres arose with the development of industrial capitalism: "Men and women came to see the family as separate from the economy, and personal life as a separate sphere of life divorced from the larger economy." See Eli Zaretsky, *Capitalism, The Family and Personal Life* (New York: Harper Colophon Books, 1976), p. 78. This stance is substantially different from that of early radical feminist approaches, including Firestone, who argued that the separation antedates history. See Shulamith Firestone, *The Dialectic of Sex* (New York: Bantam Books, 1970). Other scholars assert that the relations of production and reproduction are intertwined and virtually inseparable. See Heidi Hartmann, "Capitalism, Patriarchy and Job Segregation by Sex," in Martha Blaxall and Barbara Reagan, eds., *Women and the Work Place* (Chicago: University of Chicago Press, 1976), pp. 137–169.

6. Hood argues that the "ideal" of stay-at-home motherhood and male provider has historically been an unrealistic standard for families outside the middle and upper classes. She points out that early surveys of urban workers indicate between 40 and 50 percent of all families supplemented their income with the earnings of wives and children. See Jane C. Hood, "The Provider Role: Its Meaning and Measurement," *Journal of Marriage and the Family* 48 (May 1986), pp. 349–359.

7. It should be noted that native-born status is not an essential requirement for the ethnic label "Chicana/o." There are numerous identifiers used by people of Mexican descent, including: Chicana/o, Mexican, Mexican-American, Mexicana/o, Latina/o, and Hispanic. Often people of Mexican descent use two or three of the above labels, depending on the social situation (e.g., "Mexican-American" in the family or "Chicana/o" at school). See John A. Garcia, "Yo Soy Mexicano . . . : Self-identity and Sociodemographic Correlates," *Social Science Quarterly* 62 (March, 1981), pp. 88–98; Susan E. Keefe and Amado M. Padilla, *Chicano Ethnicity* (Albuquerque, NM: University of New Mexico Press, 1987). My designation of study informants as either "Chicana" or "Mexicana" represents an analytic separation that facilitates demonstrating the heterogeneity among this group.

8. Patricia Zavella, "Reflections on Diversity among Chicanos," *Frontiers* 2 (1991), p. 75.

9. See Rosalia Solorzano-Torres, "Female Mexican Immigrants in San Diego County," in V. L. Ruiz and S. Tiano, eds., *Women on the U.S.-Mexico Border: Responses to Change* (Boston: Allen and Unwin, 1987), pp. 41–59; Reynaldo Baca and Bryan Dexter, "Mexican Women, Migration and Sex Roles," *Migration Today* 13 (1985), pp. 14–18; Sylvia Guendelman and Auristela Perez-Itriago, "Double Lives: The Changing Role of Women in Seasonal Migration," *Women's Studies* 13 (1987), pp. 249–271.

10. Gary S. Becker, "Human Capital, Effort, and the Sexual Division of Labor," *Journal of Labor Economics* 3 (1985 Supplement), pp. S33–S58; Gary S. Becker, *A Treatise on the Family* (Cambridge, MA: Harvard University Press, 1981); Solomon W. Polachek, "Occupational Self-Selection: A Human Capital Approach to Sex Differences in Occupational Structure," *Review of Economics and Statistics* 63 (1981), pp. 60–69; S. Polachek, "Occupational Segregation among Women: Theory, Evidence, and a Prognosis" in C. B. Lloyd, E. S. Andrews and C. L. Gilroy, eds., *Women in the Labor Market* (New York: Columbia University Press, 1981), pp. 137–157; S. Polachek, "Discontinuous Labor Force Participation and Its Effect on Women's Market Earnings," in C. Lloyd, ed., *Sex Discrimination and the Division of Labor* (New York: Columbia University Press, 1975), pp. 90–122. Becker's classic treatise, *Human Capital*, uses the following example borrowed from G. Stigler, "The Economics of Information," *Journal of Political Economy* (June 1961): "Women spend less time in the labor force than men and, therefore, have less incentive than residents of the area to invest in knowledge of specific consumption activities." See Gary S. Becker, *Human Capital* (Chicago: University of Chicago Press, 1975), p. 74.

11. Some institutional economists argue that "statistical discrimination" is one critical labor market dynamic that often impedes women and minorities. See Kenneth Arrow, "Economic Dimensions of Occupational Segregation: Comment I," *Signs: Journal of Women in Culture and Society* 1 (1987), pp. 233–237; Edmund Phelps, "The Statistical Theory of Racism and Sexism," in A. H. Amsden, ed., *The Economics of Women and Work* (New York: St. Martin's Press, 1980), pp. 206–210. This perspective suggests that prospective employers often lack detailed information about individual applicants and therefore utilize statistical averages and normative views of the relevant group(s) to which the applicant belongs in their hiring decisions (e.g., college-educated men tend to be successful and committed employees; all women are potential mothers; or women tend to exit the labor force for childbearing).

Bielby and Baron pose an important critique to the underlying rationale of statistical discrimination. They argue that utilizing perceptions of group differences between the sexes is "neither as rational nor as efficient as the economists believe." That is, utilizing stereotypical notions of "men's work" and "women's work" is often costly to employers and therefore irrational. This suggests that sex segregation is embedded in organizational policies which reflect and reinforce "belief systems that are also rather inert." See William T. Bielby and James N. Baron, "Undoing Discrimination: Job Integration and Comparable Worth," in C. Bose and G. Spitze, eds., *Ingredients for Women's Employment Policy* (New York: State University of New York Press, 1987), p. 216, pp. 221–222.

12. Annette Kuhn, "Structure of Patriarchy and Capital in the Family," in A. Kuhn and Annemarie Wolfe, eds., *Feminism and Materialism: Women and Modes of Production* (London: Routledge and Kegan Paul, 1978); Heidi Hartmann, "Capitalism, Patriarchy, and Job Segregation by Sex," in Martha Blaxall and Barbara Reagan, eds., *Women and the Work Place* (Chicago: University of Chicago Press, 1976), pp. 137–169; H. Hartmann, "The Family as the Locus of Gender, Class, and Political Struggle: The Example of Housework," *Signs: Journal of Women in Culture and Society* 6 (1981), pp. 366–394; Michele Barrett, *Women's Oppression Today, Problems in Marxist Feminist Analysis* (London: Verso Press, 1980).

13. Lourdes Beneria and Martha Roldan, *The Crossroads of Class and Gender, Industrial Homework, Subcontracting, and Household Dynamics in Mexico City* (Chicago: The University of Chicago Press, 1987); L. Beneria and Gita Sen, "Accumulation, Reproduction, and Women's Role in Economic Development: Boserup Revisited," in E. Leacock and H. I. Safa, eds., *Women's Work: Development and Division of Labor by Gender* (Massachusetts: Bergin and Garvey Publishers, 1986), pp. 141–157; Dorothy Smith, "Women's Inequality and the Family," in N. Gerstel and H. E. Gross, eds., *Families and Work* (Philadelphia: Temple University Press, 1987), pp. 23–54.

14. This phrase was coined by Arlie R. Hochschild and quoted in Lillian B. Rubin, *Intimate Strangers, Men and Women Together* (New York: Harper and Row, 1983).

15. Rosabeth Moss Kanter, *Men and Women in the Corporation* (New York: Basic Books, 1977). Bielby and Baron note: "Employers expect certain behaviors from women (e.g., high turnover) and therefore assign them to routine tasks and dead-end jobs. Women respond by exhibiting the very behavior employers expect, thereby reinforcing the stereotype." Bielby and Baron, "Undoing Discrimination: Job Integration and Comparable Worth," p. 221.

16. Arlie Hochschild with Anne Machung, *The Second Shift, Working Parents and the Revolution of Home* (New York: Viking Penguin Books, 1989).

17. Barbara J. Berg, *The Crisis of the Working Mother, Resolving the Conflict between Family and Work* (New York: Summit Books, 1986), p. 42.

18. Howard Hayghe, "Working Mothers Reach Record Number in 1984," *Monthly Labor Review* 107 (December 1984), pp. 31–34; U.S. Bureau of the Census, "Fertility of American Women: June 1990" in Current Population Report, Series P-20, No. 454 (Washington D.C.: United States Government Printing Office, 1991); U.S. Bureau of Census Report, "Fertility of American Women: June 1986" in

Current Population Report, Series P-20. No. 421 (Washington, D.C.: United States Government Printing Press). In June 1986 (the year closest to the year I interviewed the respondents where I found relevant data), 49.8 percent of all women with newborn children were in the labor force. Women demonstrated differences in this behavior: 49.7 percent of white women, 51.1 percent of Black women, and 40.6 percent of Latinas with newborn children were in the labor force. See U.S. Bureau of the Census "Fertility of American Women: June 1986" (1987), p. 5.

19. Bonnie Thornton Dill, Lynn Weber Cannon, and Reeve Vanneman, "Pay Equity: An Issue of Race, Ethnicity, and Sex" (Washington D.C.: National Commission on Pay Equity, February, 1987); Julianne Malveaux and Phyllis Wallace, "Minority Women in the Workplace," in K. S. Koziara, M. Moskow, and L. Dewey Tanner, eds., *Women and Work: Industrial Relations Research Association Research Volume* (Washington D.C.: Bureau of National Affairs, 1987), pp. 265–298; Vicki L. Ruiz, "'And Miles to go. . . .': Mexican Women and Work, 1930–1985" in L. Schlissel, V. L. Ruiz, and J. Monk, eds., *Western Women, Their Land, Their Lives* (Albuquerque: University of New Mexico Press, 1988), pp. 117–136.

20. Mario Barrera, *Race and Class in the Southwest: A Theory of Racial Inequality* (Notre Dame, IN: University of Notre Dame Press, 1979); Tomas Almaguer, "Class, Race, and Chicano Oppression," in *Socialist Revolution* 5 (1975), pp. 71–99; Denise Segura, "Labor Market Stratification: The Chicana Experience," *Berkeley Journal of Sociology* 29 (1984), pp. 57–91.

21. Marta Tienda and P. Guhleman, "The Occupational Position of Employed Hispanic Women," in G. J. Borjas and M. Tienda, eds., *Hispanics in the U.S. Economy* (New York: Academic Press, 1985), pp. 243–273.

22. Edgar J. Kranau, Vicki Green, and Gloria Valencia-Weber, "Acculturation and the Hispanic Woman: Attitudes towards Women, Sex-Role Attribution, Sex-Role Behavior, and Demographics," *Hispanic Journal of Behavioral Sciences* 4 (1982), pp. 21–40; Alfredo Mirande and Evangelina Enriquez, *La Chicana, The Mexican American Woman* (Chicago: The University of Chicago Press, 1979).

23. Kranau, Green, and Valencia-Weber, "Acculturation and the Hispanic Woman," pp. 21–40; Alfredo Mirande, *The Chicano Experience: An Alternative Perspective* (Notre Dame: University of Notre Dame Press, 1985).

24. Vilma Ortiz and Rosemary Santana Cooney, "Sex-Role Attitudes and Labor Force Participation among Young Hispanic Females and Non-Hispanic White Females," *Social Science Quarterly* 65 (June 1984), pp. 392–400.

25. Susan E. Keefe and Amado M. Padilla, *Chicano Ethnicity* (Albuquerque, NM: University of New Mexico Press, 1987); Richard H. Mendoza, "Acculturation and Sociocultural Variability," in J. L. Martinez Jr. and R. H. Mendoza, eds., *Chicano Psychology,* 2nd ed. (New York: Academic Press, 1984), pp. 61–75.

26. Maxine Baca Zinn, "Mexican-American Women in the Social Sciences," *Signs: Journal of Women in Culture and Society* 8 (1982), pp. 259–272. M. Baca Zinn, "Employment and Education of Mexican-American Women: The Interplay of Modernity and Ethnicity in Eight Families," *Harvard Educational Review* 50 (February 1980), pp. 47–62. M. Baca Zinn, "Chicano Family Research: Conceptual Distortions and Alternative Directions," *Journal of Ethnic Studies* 7 (1979), pp. 59–71.

27. For additional information on the methods and sample selection, I refer the reader to Denise A. Segura, "Chicanas and Mexican Immigrant Women in the Labor Market: A Study of Occupational Mobility and Stratification," unpublished Ph.D. dissertation, Department of Sociology, University of California, Berkeley (1986).

28. The ages of the Chicanas range from 23 to 42 years. The Mexicanas reported ages from 24 to 45. The age profile indicates that most of the women were in peak childbearing years.

29. Denise A. Segura, "Chicanas and Mexican Immigrant Women in the Labor Market."

30. For an example, see Betsy Wearing, *The Ideology of Motherhood, A Study of Sydney Suburban Mothers* (Sydney: George Allen and Unwin, 1984).

31. For an example, see Nancy Chodorow, *The Reproduction of Mothering* (Berkeley: University of California Press, 1979).

32. Manuel Ramirez III and Alfredo Castaneda, *Cultural Democracy, Bicognitive Development, and Education* (New York: Academic Press, 1974); Robert F. Peck and Rogelio Diaz-Guerrero, "Two Core-Culture Patterns and the Diffusion of Values Across Their Borders," *International Journal of Psychology* 2 (1967), pp. 272–282; Javier I. Escobat and E. T. Randolph, "The Hispanic and Social Networks," in R. M. Becerra, M. Karno, and J. I. Escobar, eds., *Mental Health and Hispanic Americans: Clinical Perspectives* (New York: Grune and Stratton, 1982).

33. Alfredo Mirande and Evangelina Enriquez, *La Chicana, The Mexican American Woman* (Chicago: The University of Chicago Press, 1979); Margarita Melville, "Introduction" and "Matrascence" in M. B. Melville, ed., *Twice a Minority: Mexican American Women* (St. Louis: The C. V. Mosby Co., 1980), pp. 1–16; Gloria Anzaldúa, *Borderlands, La Frontera: The New Mestiza* (San Francisco: Spinsters/Aunt Lute Book Co., 1987); Linda C. Fox, "Obedience and Rebellion: Re-Vision of Chicana Myths of Motherhood," *Women's Studies Quarterly* (Winter, 1983), pp. 20–22.

34. Talcott Parsons and Robert Bales, *Family, Socialization, and Interaction Processes* (New York: Free Press, 1955); Robert H. Bradley and Bettye M. Caldwell, "The Relation of Infants' Home Environments to Achievement Test Performance in First Grade: A Follow-up Study," *Child Development* 55 (1984), pp. 803–809; Toby L. Parcel and Elizabeth G. Menaghan, "Maternal Working Conditions and Child Verbal Facility: Studying the Intergenerational Transmission of Inequality from Mothers to Young Children," *Social Psychology*

Quarterly 53 (1990), pp. 132–147; Avshalom Caspi and Glen H. Elder, "Emergent Family Patterns: The Intergenerational Construction of Problem Behavior and Relationships," in R. Hinde and J. Stevenson Hinde, eds., *Understanding Family Dynamics* (New York: Oxford University Press, 1988).

35. For a full discussion of the interplay between economic goals and economic status of the respondents and their employment decisions, I refer the reader to Denise Segura, "The Interplay of Familism and Patriarchy on Employment among Chicana and Mexican Immigrant Women," in the *Renato Rosaldo Lecture Series Monograph* 5 (Tucson, AZ: The University of Arizona, Center for Mexican American Studies, 1989), pp. 35–53.

36. Two of the Mexicanas reported that their mothers had died while they were toddlers and therefore they were unable to discuss their economic roles.

37. Patricia M. Fernandez-Kelly, "Mexican Border Industrialization, Female Labor-Force Participation and Migration," in J. Nash and M. P. Fernandez-Kelly, eds., *Women, Men, and the International Division of Labor* (Albany: State University of New York Press, 1983), pp. 205–223; Sylvia Guendelman and Auristela Perez-Itriago, "Double Lives: The Changing Role of Women in Seasonal Migration," *Women's Studies* 13 (1987), pp. 249–271; Reynaldo Baca and Dexter Bryan, "Mexican Women, Migration and Sex Roles," *Migration Today* 13 (1985), pp. 14–18.

38. Research indicates religious involvement plays an important role in gender beliefs. See Ross K. Baker, Laurily K. Epstein, and Rodney O. Forth, "Matters of Life and Death: Social, Political, Religious Correlates of Attitudes on Abortion," *American Politics Quarterly* 9 (1981), pp. 89–102; Charles E. Peek and Sharon Brown, "Sex Prejudice among White Protestants: Like or Unlike Ethnic Prejudice?" *Social Forces* 59 (1980), pp. 169–185. Of particular interest for the present study is that involvement in fundamentalist Christian churches is positively related to adherence to traditional gender role ideology. See Clyde Wilcox and Elizabeth Adell Cook, "Evangelical Women and Feminism: Some Additional Evidence," *Women and Politics* 9 (1989), pp. 27–49; Clyde Wilcox, "Religious Attitudes and Anti-Feminism: An Analysis of the Ohio Moral Majority," *Women and Politics* 48 (1987), pp. 1041–1051. Half of the Mexicanas (and all but two Chicanas) adhered to the Roman Catholic religion; half belonged to various fundamentalist Christian churches (e.g., Assembly of God). Two Chicanas belonged to other Protestant denominations. I noticed that the women who belonged to the Assembly of God tended to both work full-time in the labor market and voice the strongest convictions of male authority in the family. During their interviews many of the women brought out the Bible and showed me the biblical passages that authorized husbands to "rule" the family. Catholic women also voiced traditional beliefs regarding family structure but did not invoke God.

39. Frances Rothstein, "Women and Men in the Family Economy: An Analysis of the Relations Between the Sexes in Three Peasant Communities," *Anthropological Quarterly* 56 (1983), pp. 10–23; Ruth Schwartz Cowan, "Women's Work, Housework, and History: The Historical Roots of Inequality in Work-Force Participation," in N. Gerstel and H. E. Gross, eds., *Families and Work* (Philadelphia: Temple University, 1987), pp. 164–177; Louise A. Tilly and Joan W. Scott, *Women, Work, and Family* (New York: Holt, Rinehart, and Winston, 1978).

40. Jessie Bernard, "The Rise and Fall of the Good Provider Role," *American Psychologist* 36 (1981), pp. 1–12; J. Bernard, *The Future of Motherhood* (New York: Penguin Books, 1974); Jane C. Hood, "The Provider Role: Its Meaning and Measurement," *Journal of Marriage and the Family* 48 (May, 1986), pp. 349–359.

41. Lorraine O. Walker and Mary Ann Best, "Well-Being of Mothers with Infant Children: A Preliminary Comparison of Employed Women and Homemakers," *Women and Health* 17 (1991), pp. 71–88; William J. Doherty and Richard H. Needle, "Psychological Adjustment and Substance Use among Adolescents Before and After a Parental Divorce," *Child Development* 62 (1991), pp. 328–337; Eugene E. Clark and William Ramsey, "The Importance of Family and Network of Other Relationships in Children's Success in School," *International Journal of Sociology of the Family* 20 (1990), pp. 237–254.

42. Rosabeth Moss Kanter, *Men and Women of the Corporation* (New York: Basic Books, 1977).

43. John M. Chavez and Raymond Buriel, "Reinforcing Children's Effort: A Comparison of Immigrant, Native-Born Mexican American and Euro-American Mothers," *Hispanic Journal of Behavioral Sciences* 8 (1986), pp. 127–142; Raymond Buriel, "Integration with Traditional Mexican-American Culture and Sociocultural Adjustment" in J. L. Martinez, Jr. and R. H. Mendoza, eds., *Chicano Psychology,* 2nd ed. (New York: Academic Press, 1984), pp. 95–130; Leo R. Chavez, "Households, Migration and Labor Market Participation: The Adaptation of Mexicans to Life in the United States," *Urban Anthropology* 14 (1985), pp. 301–346.

44. Raymond Buriel, "Integration with Traditional Mexican-American Culture and Sociocultural Adjustment," in J. L. Martinez, Jr. and R. H. Mendoza, eds., *Chicano Psychology,* 2nd ed. (New York: Academic Press, 1984), pp. 95–130. In their analysis of differences in educational goals among Mexican-Americans, Buriel and his associates found that: "third-generation Mexican Americans felt less capable of fulfilling their educational objectives." See Raymond Buriel, Silverio Caldaza, and Richard Vasquez, "The Relationship of Traditional Mexican American Culture to Adjustment and Delinquency among Three Generations of Mexican American Adolescents," *Hispanic Journal of Behavioral Sciences* 4 (1982), p. 50. Similar findings were reported by Nielsen and Fernandez: "We find that students whose families have been in the U.S. longer have *lower*

[their emphasis] aspirations than recent immigrants." See Francois Nielsen and Roberto M. Fernandez, *Hispanic Students in American High Schools: Background Characteristics and Achievement* (Washington D.C.: United States Government Printing Office, 1981), p. 76.

In their analysis of Hispanic employment, Bean and his associates reported an unexpected finding—that English-proficient Mexican women exhibit a greater "constraining influence of fertility" on their employment vis-à-vis Spanish-speaking women. They speculate that more acculturated Mexican women may have "a greater desire for children of higher quality," and therefore "be more likely to devote time to the informal socialization and education of young children." They wonder "why this should hold true for English-speaking but not Spanish-speaking women." See Frank D. Bean, C. Gray Swicegood, and Allan G. King, "Role Incompatibility and the Relationship between Fertility and Labor Supply among Hispanic Women" in G. J. Borjas and M. Tienda, eds., *Hispanics in the U.S. Economy* (New York: Academic Press, 1985), p. 241.

READING *26*   *Hung Cam Thai*

For Better or Worse: Gender Allures in the Vietnamese Global Marriage Market

Men and women like Minh and Thanh have dreams, but their dreams clash. He wants the best of tradition and she wants the best of modernity. He believes the respect he has been searching for did not arrive with him when he migrated to the United States almost 20 years ago, but instead was left back safely in Vietnam. She feels that the marital respect she needs is waiting for her in the United States and that she will get it when she joins him through marriage migration. Minh, 37, represents one of the more than two million *Viet Kieus*, or Vietnamese people living overseas, who make up an aging diaspora that largely began in the mid-1970s,

This is a revised version of another paper previously published under the title "Clashing Dreams: Highly–Educated Vietnamese Brides and Their Low-Wage Overseas Husbands," in *Global Woman* (New York: Metropolitan Books, 2003), edited by Arlie Russell Hochschild and Barbara Ehrenreich. Versions of this paper were also presented at the 2002 annual meetings of American Sociological Association in Chicago, and at the 2003 annual meetings of the West and the Pacific Regional Association for Asian American Studies in Pomona, California. I would like to very much thank Arlie Russell Hochschild, Barbara Ehrenreich, Verta Taylor, and Leila Rupp for comments on previous drafts. Thanks to Ingrid Banks for conversations and feedback. And to Barrie Thorne for guidance at every step of the way.

after the postwar years. He is also one of over a million *Viet Kieus* who returned to visit family and friends during the year 2000, a dramatic increase from the 160,000 who did so in 1993 (Nhat 1999). Thanh, 32, will soon join Minh as one of over 200,000 women *and* men worldwide who come to the United States each year through marriage migration, the number one mechanism for contemporary *legal* migration to the United States. In general, females have dominated in U.S.-bound migration since the 1930s (Houstoun, Kramer, and Barrett 1984) and, historically, women more often than men have migrated as spouses (Thornton 1992). Women currently make up more than 65 percent of all marriage migrants. While male marriage migrants make up about a quarter of all men who enter the United States each year, female marriage migrants make up over 40 percent of all women who enter (USINS 1999a; USINS 1999b).

During 14 months of fieldwork done in phases in Vietnam and in the United States from 1997 to 2001, I got to know couples like Minh and Thanh. In addition to understanding their distinct national and local cultures, I paid particular attention to some of their most private matrimonial thoughts—thoughts that they have not yet disclosed to each other. For they are in a migration waiting period, a period in which the women are waiting to be united with their husbands through migration. In this distinct and emergent global marriage market, the immigrant Vietnamese men typically go to Vietnam to marry through arrangement and subsequently return to their places of residence in the Vietnamese diaspora (most are from the United States, Canada, France, and Australia) to initiate paperwork to sponsor their wives. During this waiting period, I came to know them by first entering the lives of the brides in Vietnam and later the U.S.-based grooms.

The marriage of Minh and Thanh characterizes a distinct and growing global stream over the past 40 years of immigrant or immigrant-origin men returning to their home countries for marriage partners through processes of family-forming migration (Lievans 1999), thus significantly transforming gender and race relations in the communities of both origin and destination. Same-ethnic individuals constitute an estimated two-thirds of all marriage migration couples, and among international marriage migrants of U.S. non-citizen permanent residents, who are presumably immigrants, almost 90 percent of them are women (Thornton 1992; USINS 1999a; USINS 1999b). Like many international marriages between same-ethnic individuals, especially in Asia, the marriage of Minh and Thanh was arranged. While there are varying flexible meanings of marriage arrangements and class compositions, I focus on marriages of the two "unmarriageables"—highly educated women in Vietnam and overseas Vietnamese men who do low-wage work. These couples make up roughly 55 percent ($n = 38$) of the 69 marriages I studied.

GLOBALIZATION AND MARRIAGE SQUEEZES ACROSS THE VIETNAMESE DIASPORA

Before I began this study, I was fully aware that Vietnamese people worldwide are pressed unusually, if not uniquely, by what demographer Daniel Goodkind (1997) calls the "double marriage squeeze," which has resulted from a high male mortality rate during the Vietnam War and the larger number of men than women who emigrated during the last quarter of the 20th century. A shortage of one sex or the other in the age group in which marriage generally occurs is often termed a marriage squeeze (Guttentag and Secord 1983). The Vietnamese double marriage squeeze specifically refers to the low ratio of males to females in Vietnam and the unusually high ratio of males to females in the Vietnamese diaspora, especially in Australia and in the United States. For example, by

1999, among people between the ages of 30 to 34 years in Vietnam, statistically speaking, there were approximately 92 men for every 100 women. At the other end of the diaspora in 2000, among Vietnamese Americans between 25 to 29 years, there were 129 men for every 100 women; for the age group of 30 to 34, there were about 135 men for every 100 women. While these numbers are important, they tell only part of the story about the recent dramatic rise in Vietnamese transpacific marriages. The link between demographic numbers, intensified transnational and global processes in Vietnam and worldwide, new contours of kinship, and the intersection of gender and class in marriage markets throughout the Vietnamese diaspora provides a much more in-depth look at social processes involved in the emergence of a Vietnamese transpacific marriage market.

The most striking aspect about marriages of the two unmarriageables like Minh and Thanh is that they have globalized and reversed the marriage gradient, an old and almost universal pattern that women "marry up" and men "marry down," which is to say women marry older men who earn more money and have more education and, conversely, men marry younger women who earn less money and have less education (Fitzgerald 1999). But depending on the measure one uses in the marriages I studied, it is difficult to tell who is "from below." In demographic marriage market language (Guttentag and Secord 1983), women worldwide often find that the pool of marriageable men declines as they move up the educational ladder. Thanh is part of this emerging group of highly educated women in Vietnam who have delayed or avoided marriage with local men. These women have found the pool of marriageable men in Vietnam, who are employed and successful relative to them, to be too small. More importantly, Thanh's status as a highly educated woman made her unmarriageable to many men still influenced by the Asian and Confucian ideologies of hierarchical relations in terms of gender, age, and class. Like highly educated African-American women, women like Thanh in Vietnam are a "surplus" relative to their educated male counterparts. Minh, on the other hand, belongs to a group of surplus men, accumulated in part by the scattering of post-war Vietnamese migration, who are unable to find marriage partners partly because of their current low-wage work status. Some of these men, though certainly not all, experienced tremendous downward mobility as they migrated overseas.

Men like Minh who work in the low-wage labor market made up 80 percent of the men in my study.

These men generally work for hourly wages, though some work in ethnic enterprises where salaries are negotiated "under the table." For the most part, they work long hours for low pay. In contrast, women like Thanh represent almost 70 percent of the brides. These women come from college-educated backgrounds, with about 40 percent having advanced degrees and working as doctors, lawyers, computer programmers, and the like. The remaining 60 percent are teachers, service sector workers in foreign companies, etc. To be sure, not all college-educated women in my study married low-wage working men, and not all low-wage working men married college-educated women. Men like Minh and women like Thanh are unmarriageable along both gender and class lines. Statistically, because of the double marriage squeeze, there is simply a surplus of women relative to men in Vietnam and a surplus of *Viet Kieu* men relative to *Viet Kieu* women overseas. But their unmarriageability does not end there. If the demography of the double marriage squeeze is a structural condition propelling these transpacific marriages, the cultural belief in the marriage gradient is perhaps a more powerful force driving these marriages. Vietnamese women and men worldwide have not dared to break the marriage-gradient norm in their local marriage market. They believe, as other unmarriageables do, that by globalizing the gradient, they have somehow solved the potential problem of breaking the marriage-gradient norm. That is, if a man is from a first-world country, he has the "up," while a woman from third-world Vietnam has the "down." And though it is no surprise that the economic divide between the "first-world" and "third-world" would inherently penetrate deeply into the private lives of Vietnamese transpacific couples, it is not always clear *who* has the third-world life in marriages of the two unmarriageables.

Globalization seems like a perfect solution to the dual problem facing the Vietnamese diaspora of "too few women here" and "too few men there," yet there is an untold story about the unanticipated collision of gender ideologies and strategies many of these couples will face.

Couples like Minh and Thanh—the unmarriageables—will bump into a clash of dreams as the women join their husbands overseas. Looking far across the Pacific, both were enamored, not necessarily by the economic, but powerfully by the gender allures of the other side: on one end of the Vietnamese diaspora, for educated women like Thanh, a man living overseas in a modern country will respect women more than men still held back by ancient traditions in Vietnam; on the other end of the diaspora, for low-wage working men like Minh, it is precisely these ancient traditions that he desired and perceived are still maintained by women in Vietnam, the sort of traditions that he believes have been eroded by America's modernity.

Both have turned to the old and new, relying foremost on the tradition of marriage arrangements vis-à-vis family members to introduce them to each other. Yet, it is the new globalizing culture of Vietnam that offered them that opportunity. In 1986, after having no contact with the outside world for over a decade, the Vietnamese government adopted a new economic policy known as *doi moi*. It did not end state ownership, but encouraged private enterprise, free markets, and global engagement. Particularly in the 1990s, Saigon was reemerging as a major international city, first within the Asian landscape and soon to the rest of the world. At the time, Vietnam was in the news and was projected to be one of Asia's next "tigers" (Pierre 2000). Recognizing an enticing labor and consumer market of 80 million people, foreign companies were eager to move their factories there and make their products known. Globalization rapidly opened impersonal markets of capital, goods, and labor, and in conjunction with these markets, it also opened a rather personal market of emotions and marriages. Like global corporations and factories that recently moved to Vietnam because of its large supply of labor, one of the reasons *Viet Kieu* men go there for brides is because they have a much larger selection of marriage partners. However, unlike locals who eagerly work at foreign factories mainly for the monetary rewards, Vietnamese transpacific brides don't always share the same reasons for choosing to marry *Viet Kieu* men.

THE HIGHLY EDUCATED BRIDE'S STORY

Twenty years ago, Thanh's father was a math teacher at Le Buon Phong, a prestigious high school in Saigon. After the war, Thanh's uncle, her mother's younger brother, and his family were among the few thousands of Vietnamese who were airlifted out of Vietnam on April 30, 1975, when Saigon surrendered to North Vietnamese military troops. They eventually settled in Houston, one of the larger Vietnamese enclaves in the United States, and started a successful restaurant business specializing in *pho*, the popular Vietnamese beef noodle soup. Remittances—money sent back—from

Thanh's uncle helped her parents open a small candy factory in the late 1980s which now has over 40 employees. Like the "new class of everywhere" in the global economy, her parents are now members of a class that represents a small but very visible percentage of families in Vietnam who enjoy access to overseas resources, such as Thanh's uncle and the remittances he sends home. They are part of a *Viet Kieu economy*, of which remittance plays an important role, that has grown from roughly $35 million in 1993 to an estimated $2 billion in 2000 (Pierre 2000). The remittance upward mobility is of course associated with Thanh's educational and social mobility. It has helped Thanh, her parents' only child, earn not only a good high school education, but also continue to study law and take lessons at international English schools in Saigon.

After graduating from Le Buon Phong High School, Thanh and a small group of her female friends did not choose early marriage, a path that most of their peers took soon after high school. Although Thanh and her friends did want to marry one day, they all wanted to further their schooling. Of her seven close female friends from high school, only one did not go to college. That friend opted for early marriage. The rest, including Thanh, quietly took various professional routes. Most went into fields traditionally reserved for women, including education and nursing. Two went on for higher education. Thanh obtained a law degree, and the other friend went on to become a prestigious physician at Vinh Bien, a private hospital catering to Saigon's middle class. Four of the seven, now in their early 30s, remain single. The pathways of Thanh and her four friends who chose singlehood illustrate a quiet gender revolution among highly educated women in Vietnam. These women have opted for singlehood in a culture where marriage is not only presumed, but often coerced. And if marriage is not achieved by a certain age, women and men are often dismissively referred to as simply "*e*," a derogatory term referring to commodities that are unmarketable. In contrast, women (often young and beautiful) and men (often educated and financially secure) who fare well on the marriage market are considered "*dat*," or scarce goods. As Thanh explained to me:

I am already "e" in Vietnam. You know, at thirty-two here, it's hard to find a decent husband. I knew that when I decided to get a good education here that many men would be intimidated by me. But it was important to me to get an education, and I know that

for women, marriage is more important. In Asian cultures, but maybe in Vietnam especially, the men do not want their wives to be better than them. I think for me it's harder, too, because my parents are successful here so on the outside [to the outsider] we are very successful.

In truth, Thanh is not completely "e" for there have been several men who, sometimes with their families, have come to propose marriage to her. In contemporary Vietnam, arranging marriage remains common practice, though more so in villages than in urban areas. For women in Vietnam, especially those who have passed the social marriageability age, individual and family success often come with being unmarriageable. Thanh had several proposals for marriage arrangements when she was in her mid-20s before she got her law degree, all from men who wanted to marry down socially and economically. Now, at age thirty-two and highly educated, she believes that marrying up is no longer an option as there are few available men in that category. Marrying down is not an appealing choice either, although she has many suitors in that category. Speaking in the marriage gradient mode, Thanh explains:

When I look up, there are few men "up there" who I could see as suitable husbands. But those men, the few men I know who have more education and who are more successful than I am, usually want to marry young, beautiful women. To them, I am now too old. The backward thing about life is that the men below are very unappealing. And of course there are many of them! There are many, many non-quality men I could choose from, but that's what they are—non-quality.

Thanh's marriage procrastination was partially anchored in her confused class and gender status, for her educational and remittance upward mobility puts her one up locally, but one down globally. On the one hand, if by tradition, a man is to be above her, he must be the one to provide economically, but given that she married a low-wage worker, she may end up being the one to seek economic security through her own means. On the other hand, by traditional Vietnamese culture, Thanh knows her high educational status would not necessarily help her escape the gender subordination in marital life in Vietnam for few men she knows respect women in the everyday contours of marriage. On our third and final interview, Thanh and I walked along the Saigon River early one evening. As the city's buildings rose arrogantly in the background through the din of countless motorcycles, cycles, and taxis, she explained to me, with a sense of disconsolation:

> In Vietnam, it is hard being single, female, and old. People will criticize and laugh at you. People always ask me, "Where are your husband and children? And when I think about that, I realize that I have two choices. I can marry a man in Vietnam who is much less educated and less successful than me who I will have to support and who will likely abuse me emotionally or physically or dominate me in every possible way. Or I can marry a *Viet Kieu* man. *At least Viet Kieu men live in modern countries where they respect women.*

Ultimately, Thanh's priority, as an educated woman, in the selection of a marriage partner is for someone to respect her and for a marriage in which a man does not control her like most men in Vietnam she observes do. As Thanh explained to me:

> When I find a nice man "below" me who I could marry, he wouldn't want to marry me because he's afraid that I'll take control of the house or that if anything goes wrong in the marriage, I could turn to my family for help. Most men in Vietnam want to control their wives, they want their wives to be subordinate even when she is more successful and educated. That leaves me with very few choices in Vietnam, you see, because I for sure don't want a man to take control of me.

THE LOW-WAGE WORKING GROOM'S STORY

Through complicated logics of transnationality, Thanh found a suitable spouse across the Pacific. But if Thanh's desire for respect was prompted by her educational and remittance upward mobility, her husband's need for respect was prompted by his migratory downward mobility. Minh, whose hands, facial expressions, and graying hair make him seem older than his 37 years, was the only member of his family to leave Vietnam during "wave II" of the boat refugee exodus that took place after the war (Zhou and Bankston 1998). As the eldest son, he holds a position of distinction and responsibility of six siblings in a family of educators. Both of his parents were teachers of philosophy at Le Buon Phong, where they have known Thanh's parents

for many years. Today, three of Minh's sisters are teachers and his two brothers are successful merchants in Saigon.

In 1985, at the age of 21, Minh, then a man of intellectual ambition and curiosity, had just completed his third year of engineering school when his parents asked him if he wanted to go to America. They didn't know anyone overseas at the time, but they knew of several people, among the many hundreds of thousands of refugees, who had fled and safely reached a Western country. Of those who successfully made the trip, over 90 percent eventually settled in France, Australia, Canada, or the United States (Merli 1997). Minh's parents also knew that as many as half of the refugees on any particular boat trip did not succeed. They died along the way due to starvation, pirate attacks, and often, in the case of women and children, rape and murder en route to a refugee camp. Many were also caught by the Vietnamese government and severely punished with long prison sentences. Nevertheless, his parents were confident that he would make it and have a better life abroad. After all, they spent their entire life savings to put him on one of the safest and most reputable boats run by private individuals, to leave the Mekong Delta for Western lands of opportunity via refugee camps in Southeast Asia. Like the Underground Railroad established for slave escapes during the American civil war, details about these refugee boats were kept secret. But unlike the railroads, the boats were made accessible only to wealthy or well-connected families. Many who were not wealthy, such as Minh's family, managed to pool their resources so that one person could go, usually a son. They saw this as an investment made with a hope of high returns, as in the case of Minh's family.

Today, Minh considers himself one of the lucky ones. After surviving two years—a lifetime to Minh—in a refugee camp in Malaysia, he was selected in 1987 for entry to the United States. Many people he met at the camp ended up in less desirable places, like Finland, Belgium, or Hungary. As with current migration from Vietnam, the United States was then considered the top destination choice, followed by Canada, France, and Australia. Minh arrived in rural Wyoming under the sponsorship of a local Catholic church. Like many of the churches scattered across the United States who sponsored Indochinese refugees from the late 1970s to the mid-1990s (Zhou and Bankston 1998), his church sponsored only one individual. He spent the first five years of his life in America as the only person of color in a rural town in Wyoming, the name of which he doesn't even want to remember. Like many Vietnamese refugees of the past three decades, Minh decided to migrate a second time. He wanted to go to Little Saigon, the most highly concentrated Vietnamese enclave outside of Vietnam, located in a seemingly quiet Los Angeles suburb, though today plagued by urban problems reported regularly by the media (Leonard and Tran 2000a; 2000b; *Los Angeles Times* 1995; Marosi and Tran 2000; Paddock and Dizon 1991; Terry 1999). But he had little money and no connections in or around Los Angeles. Then one day, in one of the Vietnamese-produced newspapers in the United States that flourished following the influx of refugees, Minh read about a Chinese restaurant called the Panda Garden that needed dishwashers. Unfortunately, it was not in Los Angeles but in a small town called Quincy, ninety miles from Seattle. Minh heard that Seattle also had many Vietnamese people and he thought a move there would bring him closer to other refugees.

Eleven years later, at age 37, Minh still lives in Quincy and works at the Panda Garden. He is now a deep fryer and an assistant cook, which is several steps up from the dishwashing position he was first given. Although to him, an assistant cook carries less stigma than a dishwasher, it is far from the engineering career he envisaged in his pre-migration years. Though known as one of the best and most authentic ethnic restaurants in town, the Panda mainly serves a "white American" clientele who, according to the owners, probably wouldn't know the differences between authentic Chinese food and Sara Lee frozen dinners. Quincy is similar to many suburban towns in Middle America—not quite rural, but far from urban. People who live here drive to Seattle to shop and eat if they have money, but stay in town if they want to see a movie. Minh knows five other Vietnamese people in the town, all men, and three of them work with him at the restaurant. He shares a modest three-bedroom apartment with the barest of furnishings with these co-workers.

Similar to many *Viet Kieu* people, Minh is a good example of a giver caught in the irony of a remittance-ship. Receivers of remittances enjoy first-world consumption, while their givers often only enjoy it when they go to Vietnam: on returning to a first-world setting, some givers like Minh, regress to a third-world consumption pattern. Like Thanh's family, Minh's family enjoys remittances, albeit much smaller ones than Thanh's family enjoys from her uncle. He earns approximately $1,400 a month in Quincy and sends $500 of that back to his family. That amount is much higher

than the average of $160 the grooms in my study send to their wives and/or families on a monthly basis. At $900, his remaining budget would be considered way below the poverty level anywhere in the United States. But his family has more than enough constant capital from his remittances to keep connected in the small, though conspicuous, circles of families who have overseas kin networks.

And while Minh's family enjoy their new consumption patterns, Minh finds himself lacking the luxury they afford—most importantly the luxury of having the kind of respect he was used to before migration, particularly the kind of respect he once had in intimate markets. Minh remembered vividly that in his early 20s, he had been considered a good catch among his peers. He was heading for an engineering career and was from a well-respected family. Recounting stories of masculinity from his early adulthood, Minh told me that young men he knew had not one, but several, girlfriends at a time, and that it was accepted and celebrated. After all, life after the war was particularly difficult for many families he knew. But he was relatively fortunate, for his parents were well-respected teachers with a small, but steady, income and, therefore, could afford to spend small amounts of money on leisure activities and materials that bought them some status in their pre-remittance circles. As he told me in one conversation when we were talking, with beers and cigarettes in our hands, rather loudly in the hot and sizzling kitchen where he worked:

> Life here now is not like life in Vietnam back then. My younger brothers and sisters used to respect me a lot because I was going to college and I was about to get my degree. Many young women I met at the time liked me, too, because I came from a good family and I had status [dia di]. But now, because I don't have a good job here, people don't pay attention to me. That's the way my life has been since I came to the United States. And I don't know if I'm lucky or unlucky, but I think it's hard for a [Vietnamese] man to find a wife here if he doesn't make good money. If you have money, everyone will pay attention [to you], but if you don't, you have to live by yourself.

For the most part, that's what Minh has done in the 16 years since he arrived in the United States. In his social world, Minh believes money can, and often does, buy love, and that if you don't have much of it, you live "by yourself." His yearly income puts him just above the poverty level for a single man, but when I did a budget analysis of his expenditures, I discovered that after remittances, his available funds place him well below the poverty level. The long hours that often accompany low-wage work have also made it particularly difficult for him to meet and court marriage partners. If Minh worked long hours for a law firm or a large business corporation, he would not only get financial rewards, but also the status and prestige which men often use as a trade-off in marriage markets. If he were a blue collar white man in Quincy, he could go to church functions, bowling alleys, or bars to meet and court women in the local marriage market. For Minh—a single immigrant man—who does low-wage work in a low-status job with long hours in Middle America, the prospect of marriage has been, and remains, low. Like highly educated women such as Thanh, men like Minh are on the market for more than just intimacy. They are on it for respect, a sense of respect for marital life which they perceive they cannot find in their local marriage market. For men in general, but especially for working-class men, as sociologist Lillian Rubin (1994) argues in a compelling study, a sense of self is deeply connected to the ability to provide economically for the family. For low-wage workers like Minh, the ability to provide, or lack thereof, is sharply linked to earning respect in marital life. As Minh movingly explained to me:

> I don't know if other men told you this, but I think the main reason why a lot of *Viet Kieu* men go back to Vietnam for a wife is because the women here [*Viet Kieu*] do not respect their husbands if the husbands can not make a lot of money. I think that's why there are a lot of *Viet Kieu* women who marry white men, because the white men have better jobs than us. Many *Viet Kieu* women, even though they are not attractive and would not be worth much if there were a lot of them, would not even look at men like me because we can't buy them the fancy house or the nice cars. *I need my wife to respect me as her husband. If your wife doesn't respect you, who will?*

AND SO THEY MEET

Although Minh was headed for upward mobility in 1985 before he migrated to the United States, and would have become an engineer one day if he had remained in Vietnam, he is now an assistant cook and has spent the bulk of his adult working life in the confines of a small Chinese restaurant in Middle America. He hasn't read a book in recent memory. In fact, he didn't have much to share about what he does, except work, or what he owns, except a used Toyota Tercel he recently bought. Meanwhile, Thanh is a relatively successful lawyer in urban Saigon, where Chanel perfume from Paris and American designer Ann Taylor's shirts are essential components of her daily life. Thanh speaks very good English, the language we used when she and I met in Vietnam; Minh and I spoke Vietnamese when I interviewed him in Quincy, Washington. Thanh is currently attending an international adult English school to obtain her English proficiency degree and her current reading list includes Fitzgerald's *The Great Gatsby*. She often prides herself on the fact that she is not as thin as the average woman in Vietnam, nor does she conform to the stereotypical image of Vietnamese women with long, straight black hair. Instead, Thanh has a perm with red highlights and she spends a large part of her leisure time taking aerobics classes at the Saigonese Women's Union, an emerging activity among Saigon's middle class. Pointing to her access to and practice of modernity, she often joked, "Some people in Vietnam think that I'm a *Viet Kieu* woman."

Minh and Thanh, thus, live in noticeably different social worlds. They were united by a network of kin and acquaintanceship that was spatially separated, yet held together by the histories, memories, and connections of the prewar years. This network of kin helped arrange the marriage of the two and started when Minh's siblings expressed concerns that their eldest brother appeared lonely and "needed" a wife, though they never asked him. After all, he was the eldest brother and the only sibling not yet married and still childless. The average age of marriage for his three younger sisters was 21 and for his two brothers, 24. His next brother's eldest child is now attending her first year at Le Buon Phong High School, a sign to Minh that he's getting old. Minh was often embarrassed when asked, "Why didn't you bring your lady friend back to visit us, too?" What his family did not understand on his first few visits back was that long hours of work, as well as the scarcity of Vietnamese women (relative to men) in the United States in general and Quincy in particular, were reasons why the "lady friend generally was too busy to make the trip home *this time*."

If Minh's choice to return to Vietnam to find a wife was propelled by siblings and then followed by his individual discretion, Thanh's entrance into the transpacific marriage market was the complete opposite. Both faced structural and demographic limitations in their local marriage markets, but in different and reversed ways. On the one hand, Minh knew very *few* Vietnamese-American women, and those he knew usually earned the same amount of, or more, money than he did, which made him a *less* attractive marriage candidate in the United States. Research has shown that in the low-wage labor market among Asian Americans, especially in California, women tend to get jobs more easily, work longer hours, and earn more money than men (Espiritu 1999). In contrast, Thanh knew *many* single men in Saigon, but those she knew were far below her in educational status and made much *less* money than she did working as a part-time lawyer and for her father's factory, all of which made her a *less* attractive marriage candidate in Vietnam. By Vietnamese standards—and for some, by any global standard—women like Thanh come from solidly middle-class backgrounds, through acquired or inherited wealth, educational mobility, or remittances. Thanh's education, combined with the income she and her family generate, have been real trade-offs on the transpacific marriage market. As Thanh explained to me:

Any *Viet Kieu* man can come here to find a wife. And he can surely find a beautiful woman if he wants because there are many beautiful young women willing to marry anyone to go overseas. I think there is something different when you talk about *Viet Kieu* men coming back here to marry. They look for a real marriage. And a marriage that will last forever. And so it's important to them to check everything about the woman they will marry and her background. These men [*Viet Kieu* men] want a woman who is educated and who comes from an educated family, because that means she comes from a good family. And if her family has money, he knows she just doesn't want to marry him to go overseas because she already has a comfortable life in Vietnam.

Fearful that they may be seen as sex-workers, local women in Vietnam who want a transpacific spouse rarely allow themselves to be courted by foreign men in public spaces as is the case for women in Taiwan, Thailand, Singapore, Malaysia, Hong Kong, and other Asian countries I've visited and learned about. According to most women and men I talked to in Vietnam, *Viet Kieu* men often come back and visit

local bars and dance clubs in search of "one-night stands" either with prostitutes or non-prostitutes, but they would never marry women they meet in those public spaces. If women are fearful of the possibility of being sexually exploited, *Viet Kieu* men are wary of being used as a "bridge" to cross the Pacific (Ong 1999). These reasons, as well as the availability of transnational networks, have propelled women in Vietnam and Vietnamese men who live overseas to rely on the old practice of marriage arrangements by family and kin members, rather than engaging in individual courtship, what we call "free love" practices of choosing a marriage partner. As in the case of arranged marriages among other ethnic groups, marriage candidates in the Vietnamese diaspora believe that family members make the best judgements in their interests when looking for a spouse. Here, Thanh explained the logics of marriage arrangements that may seem illogical to a foreigner:

It's very easy to trick people now. Both men and women can trick each other. Women will pretend to love so they can go abroad and men will pretend to love so they can get a one-night relationship. And so that is why people will choose a family member who could investigate both sides for them. Most of the cases I know are similar to mine. Usually a *Viet Kieu* man says he wants a wife, and then he will call a family here who will search for him. His family member will try to contact friends, neighbors, whoever he can in search of a suitable wife who happens to also be waiting for an overseas man to court her. There's always a lot of women willing to marry a *Viet Kieu* man, even though she may never have thought about it until someone asks them. If you have a family member to choose for you, as my uncle helped me get to know my husband, you will end up with a real marriage. Otherwise, it can be risky for both people if they meet each other on their own.

The marriage arrangement between Minh and Thanh was initiated by Minh's parents, who have known Thanh's family for over two decades. Even though Thanh's father taught at Le Buon Phong two decades ago, and was a friend and colleague of Minh's parents, the current consumption gap between the two families has created a social distance over the years. When Minh's siblings convinced him to search for a wife in Vietnam, he was hesitant at first, but later followed their advice when his parents promised that they would invest time and care in finding the most suitable spouse. According to Minh, however, they were surprised to discover that arranging a marriage for a *Viet Kieu* was more complicated than they had anticipated:

> I thought that it would be easy for them to find some-one. I thought all they had to do was mention a few things to their friends, and within days, they could describe a few possible people to me. But my parents told me that they were afraid that women just wanted to use our family to go abroad. We had many people get involved, many people wanted to be matchmak-ers for the family and added so much anxiety and fear about people's intentions. But the first choice for them was to find a woman from a wealthy family so that they were sure she wasn't just interested in money because if she has money, she would already be comfortable in Vietnam. And it would have been best if she had family in the United States already, because we would know that they already have overseas people who help them out so they would not expect to become dependent on us. In Vietnamese, you know, there is this saying, "When you choose a spouse, you are choosing his/her whole family."

Thanh's family was finally contacted by Minh's par-ents, a traditional way of arranging marriages in which a groom's parents represent him to propose, often with rituals and a ceremonial language that date back for centuries. Like most brides in my study, Thanh relied on an overseas relative—in this case, Thanh's uncle, Tuan—for advice on Minh's economic and social situ-ation in the United States. The family discovered that Minh was a low-wage worker, but a full-time worker nonetheless. Virtually all of the locals I met in Vietnam viewed overseas men as a two-tiered group: the "suc-cessful" who succeeded in owning ethnic enterprises or through obtaining an education, and the "indolent" without full-time jobs who were perceived as being welfare-dependent or as participants in underground economies, such as gambling. Some saw the latter group as men who took up valuable "spots" that oth-ers from Vietnam could have filled. "If I had gotten a chance to go," I heard many men say, "I would be so rich by now." Most people, however, did not have an explanation for a man like Minh, who is neither lazy nor extremely successful. Thanh's uncle, Tuan, seemed to know more men in Houston who were not only unemployed, but also alcoholics and gamblers. Her

parents were worried that their daughter was unmar-riageable as there was certainly no shortage of young and younger women in Vietnam for local men *her* age to marry. In addition, Thanh was already convinced that she was "*e.*" All three were concerned that Thanh was facing a life of permanent singlehood for she was getting old by Vietnamese standards. In the back and front of these pre-arrangement thoughts, all three parties—Thanh's uncle, her parents, and herself—saw the option of marrying Minh, a *Viet kieu* man, more desirable than marrying a local man in Vietnam. For Thanh's parents, Minh's status as a full-time worker *and* someone who sent remittances back home to his family translated into a potentially suitable husband. For her uncle, most *Viet Kieu* single men he knew were part of an underclass of which Minh was not a part. For Thanh, Minh's geographical advantage translated into something socially priceless: a man living in a modern country will respect women.

CLASH OF DREAMS

Women like Thanh want a respectful marriage based on principles of gender equality. By these principles, women expect to work for a wage, share in making social and economic decisions for their future house-holds, and have their husbands share in the house-hold division of labor. Above all, they did *not* want to live in multi-generational households serving as the dutiful daughter-in-law and housewife, the two often inseparable and presumed roles historically delegated to women in Vietnam. Many express that reluctance, for they know numerous *Viet Kieu* men who live with their parents or plan to do so in the future when their parents are old. The women's concern about having to live in multi-generational households is anchored in the fact that in Vietnamese culture, and more gener-ally in Asia, elderly parents prefer to, and often do, live with their sons, usually the eldest one. Much less is known about the fact that it is their daughters-in-law, the wives of their sons, who do the fundamental daily caring work.

For Thanh, living with one's in-laws is the most symbolic act of feminine submission. For Minh, a wife's insistence on a nuclear household represents a desire for an equal marriage—and is one of the gen-dered anxieties of modernity:

> Vietnamese women, they care for their husbands and they are more traditional. I think non-VN women and

Viet Kieu women, are too modern. They just want to be equal with their husbands and I don't think that it is the way husband and wife should be. [What do you mean?] I mean that husband and wife should not be equal. The wife should listen to husband most of the time. That is how they will have a happy life together. If the woman try to be equal they will have problems. . . . I know many Vietnamese men here who abandon their parents because their wives refuse to live with their parents. If my parents were in America, I would definitely plan for them to live with me when they are old. But because they are in Vietnam, they are living with one of my brothers.

Instead of seeking peasant village women or uneducated ones like white Europeans and Americans who search for wives through commercialized systems of mail-order brides, men like Minh seek marriage arrangement with educated women as part of a careful gender strategy for a perceived future marital stability. Minh outlines his strategy:

For me, I want to marry an educated woman because she comes from a good, educated family. It's very hard to find a poor woman or an uneducated woman who comes from an uneducated family, because if they are uneducated [the family] they don't know how to teach their daughters about morals and values. I know many men, *Viet Kieu* and foreign men, who go to Vietnam to marry beautiful young women, but they don't ask why do those women marry them? Those women only want to use their beauty to go overseas and they will leave their husbands when they get the chance. They can use their beauty to find other men. I would never marry a beautiful girl from a poor, uneducated family. You see, the educated women, they know it's important marry and stay married forever. As they say in Vietnam, "tram nam han phuc," [a hundred years of happiness]. Educated women must protect their family's reputation in Vietnam by having a happy marriage, not end in divorce.

UNIMAGINABLE FUTURES

At first glance, Minh and Thanh seem as if they are from different social worlds, two worlds accidentally assembled by a complex Vietnamese history. But once closely acquainted with them, we learn that they are very much alike. First is the class of their past—both sets of their parents were educated and middle class. Second, they are both lonely human faces of globalization who lack the emotional and intimate details that adults of their social worlds enjoy. Most importantly, it seems, because of the gendered meanings embedded in their opposite trails of class mobility, they both long for marital respect, the kind of respect they perceive is scarce in their local marriage market. From Minh's side of the gender scene, he experienced downward mobility quickly and immensely as a result of migration and is eager to get back the respect he has lost. Thanh, a woman who has, in part, priced herself out of the local marriage market by acquiring a higher education, paid for by a remittance upward mobility, wants a man who respects her as an equal and as a woman who embraces modernity. He wants to regain what he sees as something men like him have lost, while she has, in part, challenged the local marriage norm and, in effect, the "control-norm" in the gender world of Vietnam.

The global forces and global histories that have mobilized their marriage—and their clashed dreams—will assuredly usher in marital conflicts. These conflicts will lead to several possibilities as women quietly migrate to join their husbands overseas. In a happy global story, Minh will join in the feminist revolution and leave behind the tradition he never had as he moves forward with his new marriage. I believe some, but few, men will join women in this revolution. In a tragic global story, these couples may end in divorce or worse, women like Thanh will be abused by their husbands. Many women like Thanh have thought about this possibility and have told me that their connection to transnational networks will ensure that they avoid abusive marriages. The most likely possibility for married couples like Minh and Thanh is that men will get what they want in the market of respect and women will consent to subordination in the name of family and kinship. Thanh will enjoy some aspects of modernity she cannot acquire in Vietnam, but she will be burdened by tradition she doesn't expect to see in the United States. For she will be going from a patriarchal frying pan to a patriarchal fire, but with one big difference. In the United States she has more support for her desire for gender equity where more women dare to quit a marriage if they don't get it. But she has the powerful burden of tradition in Vietnam to hold her back from choosing this option.

In Vietnam, marriage is an important matter not only because it unites two people, but also because it has significant implications for extended networks of kin (Tran 1991). In a culture where divorce is stigmatized and where saving face is a sacred activity especially among the educated and middle class, if Thanh daringly divorces her husband, she will cause her family and kin a loss of reputation in Vietnam and overseas, a risk she told me she is unlikely to take. If she stays in the marriage, she will give up her need for the respect and equality she thinks are waiting for her in the United States. And she will likely serve as the traditional wife Minh needs in order for him to gain back the respect he left back in Vietnam almost 20 years ago. Simply put, Vietnamese politics of kinship promise that couples like Minh and Thanh will remain married—for better or worse.

REFERENCES

Espiritu, Yen Le. 1999. "Gender and Labor in Asian Immigrant Families." *American Behavioral Scientist* 42: 628–647.

Fitzgerald, Tina Katherine. 1999. *Who Marries Whom? Attitudes in Marital Partner Selection.* Ph.D. Dissertation: University of Colorado.

Goodkind, Daniel. 1997. "The Vietnamese Double Marriage Squeeze." *The Center for Migration Studies of New York* 31: 108–128.

Guttentag, Marcia, and Paul F. Secord. 1983. *Too Many Women? The Sex Ratio Question.* Beverly Hills: Sage Publications.

Houstoun, Marion F., Roger G. Kramer, and Joan Mackin Barrett. 1984. "Female Predominance in Immigration to the United States since 1930s: A First Look." *International Migration Review* 18: 908–963.

Leonard, Jack, and Mai Tran. 2000a. "Agents Target Little Saigon Crime Groups." *Los Angeles Times*, October 7, p. A1.

Leonard, Jack, and Mai Tran. 2000b. "Probes Take Aim at Organized Crime in Little Saigon; Crackdown: Numerous Agencies Target Gambling, Drug Sales, Counterfeit Labels and Credit Card Scams." *Los Angeles Times*, October 7, p. B7.

Lievans, John. 1999. "Family Forming Migration from Turkey and Morocco to Belgium." *International Migration Review* 33: 717–744.

Los Angeles Times. 1995. "Cooler Days in Little Saigon." *Los Angeles Times*, August 8, p. B8.

Marosi, Richard, and Mai Tran. 2000. "Little Saigon Raids Dismantle Crime Ring, Authorities Say; Probe: Asian Syndicate Supplied Most Illegal Gambling Machines in Orange County, Police Say. Fifteen Are Arrested." *Los Angeles Times*, September 29, p. B3

Merli, Giovanna M. 1997. "Estimation of International Migration for Vietnam, 1979–1989." Unpublished Paper, Department of Sociology and Center for Studies in Demography and Ecology. Seattle: University of Washington.

Nhat, Hong. 1999. "Hankering for '*Viet Kieu*' Money." P. 12 in *Vietnam Economic News* 9, no. 50 (December).

Ong, Aihwa. 1999. *Flexible Citizenship: The Cultural Logics of Transnationality.* Durham, N.C.: Duke University Press.

Paddock, Richard C., and Lily Dizon. 1991. "3 Vietnamese brothers in shoot-out led troubled lives." P. A3 in *Los Angeles Times*.

Pierre, Andrew J. 2000. "Vietnam's Contradictions." *Foreign Affairs* 79.

Rubin, Lillian. 1994. *Families on the Fault Line: America's Working Class Speaks About the Family, the Economy, Race and Ethnicity.* New York: Harper Collins Press.

Terry, Don. 1999. "Passions of Vietnam War are Revived in Little Saigon; Shop's Ho Chi Minh Poster Sets off Violence." *New York Times*, February 11, p. A20.

Thornton, Michael C. 1992. "The Quiet Immigration: Foreign Spouses of U.S. Citizens, 1945–1985." Pp. 64–76 in *Racially Mixed People in America*, edited by Maria P. Root. Newbury Park, CA: Sage Publications.

Tran, Dinh Huou. 1991. "Traditional Families in Vietnam and the Influence of Confucianism." Pp. 27–53 in *Sociological Studies on the Vietnamese Family*, edited by Rita Lijestrom and Tuong Lai. Hanoi: Social Sciences Publishing House.

USINS. 1999a. "International Matchmaking Organizations: A Report to Congress by the Immigration & Naturalization Service." *A Report to Congress*.

USINS. 1999b. *Statistical Yearbook of the Immigration and Naturalization Service, 1997.* Washington, D.C.: U.S. Government Printing Office.

Zhou, Min, and Carl L. Bankston. 1998. *Growing Up American: How Vietnamese Children Adapt to Life in the United States.* New York: Russell Sage Foundation.

Queer Parenting in the New Millennium

Earlier this year, the SWS Executive Council passed a resolution opposing a U.S. constitutional amendment prohibiting same-sex marriage. On 13 July, the Federal Marriage Amendment, which is designed as a constitutional amendment that would define marriage as the union of a man and a woman, reached the Senate floor.[1] Many senators expressed dismay that the legislation was brought to the floor for debate given the obvious lack of votes needed for passage (a constitutional amendment must be approved by two-thirds majority of both the Senate and the House of Representatives). However, sponsors of the legislation argued that their haste in bringing the vote to the Senate floor was prompted by the judicial decision in Massachusetts to permit same-sex marriage, which "could spread throughout the nation and undermine traditional marriage" (Hulse 2004).

Many conservative politicians believe that the Defense of Marriage Act, which was signed into law by President Bill Clinton in 1996,[2] does not go far enough in protecting "traditional marriage." President George W. Bush, who called for the constitutional amendment early in 2004, argues that same-sex marriage would undermine "the welfare of children and the stability of society."[3] Of course, feminist sociologists have long pointed out that it is poverty, not failure to marry, that contributes most to the instability of families and undermines children's welfare. Yet the Bush administration has earmarked approximately one million dollars to promote traditional marriage for women receiving public assistance in the legislation to reauthorize the welfare program Temporary Assistance to Needy Families. The contradictory expressions of support for marriage as a cure for many of the ills in society for different-sex couples and the opposition to marriage for same-sex couples has led even those of us who

were critics of gay and lesbian movement organizations' focus on obtaining marriage rights to rethink our positions (Walters 2004).

I recall a campus visit to the University of California–Irvine, by Torie Osborn, former executive director of the National Gay and Lesbian Task Force organization, who was invited by the gay and lesbian faculty and staff group to discuss her book *Coming Home to America* (1996). When she began to talk about the campaign for same-sex marriage, several faculty members and graduate students in the audience became quite impatient, stressing that this normalizing goal would lead inevitably to assimilation into a heterosexist regime, undermine radical queer organizing, and further marginalize those who did not fit into a monogamous dyad. Furthermore, they passionately argued, same-sex marriage serves to co-opt efforts to decouple legal rights from the institution of marriage (Fineman 1995; O'Brien 2004). As more people lay claim to the institution, political struggles for universal health care, tax benefits, and other benefits that now accrue primarily through marriage will lose constituents. Osborn forcefully explained that she had just concluded a multicity tour to promote her book and, much to her surprise, was greeted with a tremendous level of passion and mobilizing efforts around same-sex marriage, civil unions, and partnership legislation. She believed that this energy could be tapped for other progressive issues. Accordingly, she argued, organizers need to meet people where they are and help facilitate their political goals, not criticize them for a lack of consciousness around the constraints of marriage as a patriarchal and heterosexist institution.

Some members of the gay, lesbian, bisexual, and transgendered community who argue against organizing on behalf of same-sex marriage assert that this issue is of little interest to communities of color and that it is primarily white, middle-class lesbians and gay men who will reap the benefits of marriage. In contrast, in a survey of attendees at Black Gay Pride events in

Author's note: My thanks to Mary Bernstein for sharing her research and insights and for reviewing earlier drafts of this article and to Valerie Jenness and Jodi O'Brien for their helpful comments.

2000, 30 percent ranked marriage/domestic partnership as one of "the three most important issues facing the Black GLBT [gay, lesbian, bisexual, transgendered] community" (Battle et al. 2002, 26–27). In addition, the researchers found that women surveyed were "more likely than men and transgender people to view marriage and domestic partnership as a key issue for Black GLBT people" (Battle et al. 2002, 27). Since more than one thousand benefits accrue to couples through marriage, the economic benefits are sizable. Same-sex marriage would diminish the cost of legal paperwork that lesbians and gay men must complete to protect themselves and their children (Chambers 2001).

Protection of children is often used as the primary justification for the defense of traditional marriage legislation.[4] But of course, gays and lesbians already have children and will continue to do so despite the challenges they often face in the process (Dalton 2001). In fact, in the United States, in states such as Connecticut (where I live), gays and lesbians can apply to be coparents to the children they have with their partners despite the fact that they cannot marry.[5] Queer parenting can destabilize gender essentialism and other taken-for-granted assumptions about gender, sexuality, and family as well as pose challenges to regimes of normalization that shape contemporary institutions (Sullivan 2001). Of course, gay and lesbian parents are not a new phenomenon. In fact, it has been 15 years since the publication of *Heather Has Two Mommies* (Newman and Souza 1989), a children's book that has been banned from public school libraries in a number of U.S. cities. With the establishment of sperm banks and advances in reproductive technologies, gays and lesbians as well as infertile heterosexual couples, single women, and professional women who desire more control over the timing of births have been able to expand their reproductive options, at least if they have the funds to pay for these services. However, in some states, lesbians and single women can be denied infertility treatment (Murphy 2001).

In the context of the heated debate over same-sex marriage, my partner and I are expecting twin girls. As lesbians, our decision to have children poses a direct challenge to the heteronormativity that pervades everyday life. After a series of interviews with obstetricians in the area and a few hospital tours of labor and delivery facilities, my partner and I decided to work with a lesbian nurse midwife who is located in a Catholic hospital. Surprisingly, this is the only hospital in our area with nurse-midwives who work autonomously. Although they operate under the supervision of an obstetrician, they can manage prenatal care and deliver without the presence of physicians in routine deliveries. The fact that one of the two nurse-midwives is also a lesbian (we located her through our lesbian network) is ironic given the persistence and vehemence with which the Catholic Church has opposed same-sex marriage and civil union legislation in Connecticut and elsewhere. Regardless, the hospital is close to our home, is smaller, offers more flexibility than the public hospital in our city, and has accessible parking.

We are the only lesbian couple in our racially diverse childbirth class. My presence as the only woman coach in the class serves as a direct challenge to the gender essentialism associated with pregnancy, childbirth, and parenting. In contrast, as a pregnant woman, my partner finds herself easily drawn into conversations with the heterosexual women about the biological and emotional experiences of pregnancy and childbirth, highlighting how little of this world she shared before the pregnancy. Stein (1997) noted that a lesbian who becomes a biological mother can enjoy a new societal acceptance that renders lesbian identity less salient. In contrast, the comother must assert and explain her relationship to the child in every interaction, outing herself and her family form in multiple settings throughout each day.

The process of adopting her own children further reinscribes the nonbiological comother's otherness in a variety of frustrating ways. The adoption procedure includes a thorough assessment of personal background, including a criminal background check, and a home study by the Department of Children and Family Services to assess how suitable the home is for "the proper rearing of children." Some courts require the appointment of a guardian *ad litem* to represent the child in the court proceedings and may require an announcement in the newspaper to notify any potential interested parties about the adoption. In adoptions by step-fathers or step-mothers who are married to the biological parent, the process is streamlined, another privilege that accrues through marriage. According to Dalton (2001), second-parent adoptions can take up to 10 months, leaving lesbian and gay coparents at risk of losing their children if something happens to the birth mother before the adoption process is complete. In the case of assisted reproduction, the names of nonbiological fathers who are married to the biological mothers can be placed on the birth certificate automatically. As a result of the court ruling permitting same-sex marriage in Massachusetts, a lesbian coparent who was married to her partner could put her name on her child's birth certificate (Ross 2004). This marks a new chapter in state regulation of lesbian and gay sexuality and an official decoupling of reproduction and heterosexual privilege (Polikoff 2002).

However, when couples who live in other states decide to marry in Massachusetts, it is unclear whether their marriages will be recognized by home states. Several cases are now pending that will test the portability of marriage rights for same-sex couples.

Another alternative is for couples to enter into civil unions, which became legal in Vermont on 1 July 2000.[6] Maureen Murphy, a civil rights and family law attorney who founded the Connecticut Gay and Lesbian Law Association, cautions lesbians and gay men in Connecticut who wish to apply for coparent adoption against obtaining a civil union in Vermont. She explained that "entering into a civil union before completing adoption matters could complicate the adoption process—or even make you ineligible to adopt (especially if you are considering international adoptions)" (True Colors 2004).

The salience of the heteronormative family form is evident everywhere we turn. As a child-free lesbian couple, my partner and I could pass seemingly unnoticed in our everyday lives. Exceptions occur when we ask a hotel clerk for a queen size bed rather than two double beds and are met with a look of horror, as happened on one trip to Norway. Having children as a lesbian couple foregrounds our relationship in ways that we could not have anticipated, even though our fields of study are gender and sexuality. With few exceptions, my partner and I must define our relationship with the children-to-be to doctors, nurses, baby store employees, and in some new ways, to family and friends (Sullivan 2001).

We are changing the field of vision for those we interact with as we come out about our decision and "have children" together (Naples 2001). Our own field of vision and understanding of how heteronormativity shapes our worldview is also being altered as we become publicly visible as pregnant lesbian and partner. On one recent occasion, as we were waiting to order food at a roadside stand, a woman and her two children joined us in line. She turned to my partner who, at the time, was about six months pregnant, and asked, "Do you know what you're having?" My partner replied, "Fish and chips." After an awkward pause, she realized that she answered the wrong question. Similarly, too much time has been spent answering the wrong question: "Is the call for same-sex marriage an assimilationist or transformative strategy?" Rather, I believe the question we need to ask and answer is, "How can we harness the political energy that has been unleashed by the debates over same-sex marriage and queer parenting to destabilize the taken-for-granted notions of what counts as a family and what can be in the best interests of children in a resilient and inclusive society?" As Bernstein (2001, 440) argues, "Legal change may reduce the costs of coming out and transform public consciousness in the long run, but it is unlikely that by itself legal change will create acceptance or transform dominant cultural values." Queering family and parenting, and destabilizing the powerful hegemony of heteronormativity, involves daily negotiations, strategic choices, and a commitment to challenging heterosexual privilege in everyday life. At the same time, efforts to control and limit marriage have raised awareness among the members of the lesbian, gay, bisexual, and transgendered people about the costs as well as the benefits of campaigns for same-sex marriage.

NOTES

1. On 22 July, the U.S. House of Representatives approved The Marriage Protection Act, which bars all federal courts, including the U.S. Supreme Court, from hearing cases concerning the constitutionality of the Defense of Marriage Act. It also prohibits states, U.S. territories, and American Indian tribes from recognizing same-sex marriage licenses issued in other jurisdictions. Only state courts could hear cases concerning same-sex marriage. However, the vote (233 to 194) indicates that there are insufficient votes needed to pass the Federal Marriage Amendment in the House.

2. The Defense of Marriage Act permits each state to recognize or deny any marriage-like relationship between persons of the same sex that has been recognized in another state. It also explicitly defines marriage as "a legal union of one man and one woman as husband and wife" and states that a spouse "refers only to a person of the opposite sex who is a husband or a wife." To date, 38 states have enacted laws denying the recognition of same-sex unions, which is the same number of states needed to amend the United States Constitution.

3. Many conservatives who argue against same-sex marriage draw on social science literature to make their case (Stacey and Biblarz 2001). For an insightful analysis of the challenges of participating as a public intellectual in the debates around same-sex marriage and gay and lesbian parenting, see Stacey (2004).

4. Adam (2003) noted that almost 40 states have either passed legislation or are trying to pass legislation that would prohibit same-sex marriage. In stark contrast, laws recognizing same sex relationships have been passed in many industrial countries including South Africa, Germany, France, and New Zealand (Adam 2003, 259).

5. In addition to Connecticut, seven states plus Washington, D.C., recognize second-parent adoption. Judges have ruled in favor of second-parent adoptions in at least 20 other states.

6. In 2003, a lesbian couple who reside in Vermont and who took advantage of Vermont's civil union law won the right to have their names on their adoptive child's birth certificate after a Mississippi judge ruled in their favor (their adoptive child was born in that state) (Lambda Legal Defense and Education Fund 2003).

REFERENCES

Adam, Barry D. 2003. The Defense of Marriage Act and American exceptionalism: The "gay marriage" panic in the United States. *Journal of the History of Sexuality* 12 (2): 259–76.

Battle, Juan, Cathy J. Cohen, Dorian Warren, Gerard Fergerson, and Suzette Audam. 2002. *Say it loud: I'm Black and I'm proud.* New York: Policy Institute of the National Gay and Lesbian Task Force.

Bernstein, Mary. 2001. Gender transgressions and queer family law: Gender, queer family policies, and the limits of law. In *Queer families, queer politics: Challenging culture and the state.* New York: Columbia University Press.

Chambers, David. 2001. "What if?" The legal consequences of marriage and the legal needs of lesbian and gay male couples. In *Queer families, queer politics: Challenging culture and the state.* New York: Columbia University Press.

Dalton, Susan E. 2001. Protecting our parent-child relationships: Understanding the strengths and weaknesses of second-parent adoption. In *Queer families, queer politics: Challenging culture and the state,* edited by Mary Bernstein and Renate Reimann. New York: Columbia University Press.

Fineman, Martha. 1995. *The neutered mother, the sexual family and other twentieth century tragedies.* New York: Routledge.

Hulse, Carl. 2004. Gay-marriage ban faces loss in early vote. *New York Times,* 14 July.

Lambda Legal Defense and Education Fund. 2003. Mississippi judge orders state to list lesbian mothers on child's birth certificate. News release, 19 March.

Murphy, Julien S. 2001. Should lesbians count as infertile couples? Antilesbian discrimination in assisted reproduction. In *Queer families, queer politics: Challenging culture and the state,* edited by Mary Bernstein and Renate Reimann. New York: Columbia University Press.

Naples, Nancy A. 2001. A member of the funeral: An introspective ethnography. In *Queer families, queer politics: Challenging culture and the state,* edited by Mary Bernstein and Renate Reimann. New York: Columbia University Press.

Newman, Leslea, and Diana Souza. 1989. *Heather has two mommies.* New York: Alyson.

O'Brien, Jodi. 2004. Seeking normal? Considering same-sex marriage. *Seattle Journal of Social Justice* 2. Retrieved from http://www.law.seattleu.edu/sjsj/current.htm.

Osborn, Torie. 1996. *Coming home to America.* New York: St. Martin's.

Polikoff, Nancy D. 2002. Raising children: Lesbian and gay parents face the public and the courts. In *Creating change: Sexuality, public policy and civil rights,* edited by J. D'Emilio, W. B. Turner, and U. Vaid. New York: St. Martin's.

Ross, Casey. 2004. Moms the word—Lesbian couple first on birth certificate. *Boston Herald,* 16 July.

Stacey, Judith. 2004. Marital suitors court social science spinsters: The unwittingly conservative effects of public sociology. *Social Problems* 51 (1): 131–45.

Stacey, Judith, and Timothy Biblarz. 2001. (How) does the sexual orientation of parents matter? *American Sociological Review* 66 (2): 159–83.

Stein, Arlene. 1997. *Sex and sensibility: Stories of a lesbian generation.* Berkeley: University of California Press.

Sullivan, Maureen. 2001. Alma mater: Family "outings" and the making of the modern other mother (MOM). In *Queer families, queer politics: Challenging culture and the state,* edited by Mary Bernstein and Renate Reimann. New York: Columbia University Press.

True Colors, Inc. Sexual Minority Youth and Family Services of Connecticut. 2004. *Co-parent adoption tips and tidbits.* Retrieved from http://www.ourtruecolors.org/kinnections/co_parent.htm.

Walters, Suzanna. 2004. Gay marriage in America. *Political Sociology: States, Power, and Societies* 10 (2): 1, 4.

Sexualities

The processes of socialization encourage women and men to develop different views of and approaches to sexuality and intimate relationships. Women learn strong interpersonal and emotional skills in preparation for roles as wives and mothers and for employment in professions associated with care work, such as teaching and nursing. At the same time, women's and men's different positions in social institutions mean that we enter our intimate and sexual relationships with different amounts and kinds of resources, power, networks, and expectations. In addition, we are surrounded by a culture that portrays women and men as having intrinsically different sexual needs, desires, and obligations. As we have already seen, such differences between women and men are shaped as well by class, race, ethnicity, sexuality, nation, ability, and age. The readings in this section discuss how even such a seemingly personal matter as sexuality is *socially constructed* in various ways in different contexts.

We begin with Deborah Tolman's "Doing Desire: Adolescent Girls' Struggles for/with Sexuality," an examination of how adolescent girls understand their sexuality. Adolescents have been the subject of considerable recent public debate over sexuality, with many politicians suggesting that teenage sexual activity should be discouraged. Yet adolescence is the life stage during which we begin to develop our sexual selves and form a sense of our intimate connections to others. Tolman examines how diverse adolescent girls construct desire, tracing the complex mix of pleasure and desire with danger and fear, highlighting differences of sexual identity. As a result of the cultural repression of women's sexuality, Tolman argues,

adolescent girls are "denied full access to the power of their own desire." How do the girls Tolman discusses come to understand their sexual selves in this context? What are the "possibilities of empowerment"?

The next article, "After the Sexual Revolution: Gender Politics in Teen Dating," explores recent reports of a decline in sexual activity among black and white (but not Latina/o) American teenagers. Barbara Risman and Pepper Schwartz question that finding, suggesting instead that sex among teenagers is becoming more responsible (thus more likely to prevent pregnancy and disease), largely because it more often occurs within relationships. By looking at the gender and racial/ethnic dimensions of levels of sexual activity, Risman and Schwartz argue that the sexual revolution is a *fait accompli* even if the gender revolution is not. What racial and ethnic differences do they identify in terms of sexual behavior? Do you think Risman and Schwartz are right in their hypothesis that boys are beginning to behave more like girls in terms of sexual activity? In what ways do the authors see remnants of the double standard of sexual morality? Based on this article as well as Tolman's, what do you think needs to be taught in sex education classes, and at what ages?

From a very different perspective, Patricia Hill Collins takes up the relationship among race, gender, and sexuality in an excerpt from her new book, *Black Sexual Politics: African Americans, Gender, and the New Racism*. Making connections between historical and contemporary cultural phenomena, Collins analyzes the role of sexuality in what she calls "the new racism" of the twenty-first century. The dominant culture has long portrayed black bodies as hypersexualized, with different consequences for women and men. How does hypersexualization affect black women and men? How does sexuality enter into the new racism Collins discusses?

The concept of the social construction of sexuality—so central to Collins's analysis—has been most extensively developed in considering the history of same-sex sexuality. In "Toward a Global History of Same-Sex Sexuality," Leila Rupp explores the diverse experiences of individuals who have desired, loved, or engaged in sexual activity with someone with a genitally alike body at different times and in different places. She argues that such relationships have often been less about similar bodies than about different ages or genders and that we also have to ask the question, what counts as "sex"? Why do you think that contemporary American society holds such rigid notions of sexual identity, insisting that people fit into a category of heterosexuality, bisexuality, or homosexuality? What is required for an individual to move from one category to another? Is it about desire, or love, or sexual activity?

In the final article in this section, "Becoming 100% Straight," Michael Messner raises similar questions about adolescent male sexuality. Using his own experience as a student athlete, he rethinks his conviction that he had always been entirely heterosexual by analyzing a crush he developed on another boy and his subsequent hostile reaction to him. Contrasting his own story to that of Tom Waddell, a closeted gay male athlete, he raises questions about the connections among heterosexuality, masculinity, and sport. He argues that men perform masculinity and heterosexuality through sport, and he asks why and what kind of consequences follow from that performance. How do you read Messner's story of his turn against Timmy? How important do you think sport is for young men today? Do you think sport has similar or different consequences for women as they perform femininity and heterosexuality? How do Messner's stories compare to Tolman's analysis of adolescent girls' sexual desires?

Like family life, sexuality and intimate relationships are both a source of support and strength for women and a location of oppression. What do these readings suggest about how diverse women find sexuality to be a means of fulfillment and an expression of self-definition? In contrast, how do the readings show sexuality to be a means of social control? How is sexuality shaped differently for people in different social groups?

Doing Desire: Adolescent Girls' Struggles for/with Sexuality

In order to perpetuate itself, every oppression must corrupt or distort those various sources of power within the culture of the oppressed that can provide energy for change. For women, this has meant suppression of the erotic as a considered source of power and information within our lives.

(Lorde 1984, 53)

Recent research suggests that adolescence is the crucial moment in the development of psychological disempowerment for many women (e.g., Brown and Gilligan 1992; Gilligan 1990). As they enter adolescence, many girls may lose an ability to speak about what they know, see, feel, and experience evident in childhood as they come under cultural pressure to be "nice girls" and ultimately "good women" in adolescence. When their bodies take on women's contours, girls begin to be seen as sexual, and sexuality becomes an aspect of adolescent girls' lives; yet "nice" girls and "good" women are not supposed to be sexual outside of heterosexual, monogamous marriage (Tolman 1991). Many girls experience a "crisis of connection," a relational dilemma of how to be oneself and stay in relationships with others who may not want to know the truth of girls' experiences (Gilligan 1989). In studies of adolescent girls' development, many girls have demonstrated the ironic tendency to silence their own thoughts and feelings for the sake of relationships, when what they think and feel threatens to be disruptive (Brown and Gilligan 1992). At adolescence, the energy needed for resistance to crushing conventions of femininity often begins to get siphoned off for the purpose of maintaining cultural standards that stand between women and their empowerment. Focusing explicitly on embodied desire,

Tolman and Debold (1993) observed similar patterns in the process of girls learning to look at, rather than experience, themselves, to know themselves from the perspective of men, thereby losing touch with their own bodily feelings and desires. It is at this moment in their development that many women will start to experience and develop ways of responding to their own sexual feelings. Given these realities, what are adolescent girls' experiences of sexual desire? How do girls enter their sexual lives and learn to negotiate or respond to their sexuality?

Despite the real gains that feminism and the sexual revolution achieved in securing women's reproductive rights and increasing women's sexual liberation (Rubin 1990), the tactics of silencing and denigrating women's sexual desire are deeply entrenched in this patriarchal society (Brown 1991). The Madonna/whore dichotomy is alternately virulent and subtle in the cultures of adolescents (Lees 1986; Tolman 1992). Sex education curricula name male adolescent sexual desire; girls are taught to recognize and to keep a lid on the sexual desire of boys but not taught to acknowledge or even to recognize their own sexual feelings (Fine 1988; Tolman 1991). The few feminist empirical studies of girls' sexuality suggest that sexual desire is a complicated, important experience for adolescent girls about which little is known. In an ethnographic study, Fine noticed that adolescent girls' sexuality was acknowledged by adults in school, but in terms that denied the sexual subjectivity of girls; this "missing discourse of desire" was, however, not always absent from the ways girls themselves spoke about their sexual experiences (Fine 1988). Rather than being "educated," girls' bodies are suppressed under surveillance and silenced in the schools (see also Lesko 1988). Although Fine ably conveys the existence of girls' discourse of desire, she does not articulate that discourse. Thompson collected 400 girls' narratives about sexuality, romance, contraception, and pregnancy (Thompson 1984, 1990) in which girls' desire seems frequently absent or not relevant to the terms of their sexual relationships. The minority of girls who spoke of sexual pleasure voiced more sexual agency than girls whose experiences were devoid of pleasure. Within the context of girls' psychological development, Fine's and Thompson's work underscores the need to understand what girls' experiences of their sexual desire are like.

A psychological analysis of this experience for girls can contribute an understanding of both the possibilities and limits for sexual freedom for women in the current social climate. By identifying how the culture has become anchored in the interior of women's lives—an interior that is birthed through living in the exterior of material conditions and relationships—this approach can keep distinct women's psychological responses to sexual oppression and also the sources of that oppression. This distinction is necessary for avoiding the trap of blaming women for the ways our minds and bodies have become constrained.

METHODOLOGICAL DISCUSSION

Sample and Data Collection

To examine this subject, I interviewed thirty girls who were juniors in an urban and a suburban public high school ($n = 28$) or members of a gay and lesbian youth group ($n = 2$). They were 16.5 years old on average and randomly selected. The girls in the larger study are a heterogeneous group, representing different races and ethnic backgrounds (Black, including Haitian and African American; Latina, including Puerto Rican and Colombian; Euro-American, including Eastern and Western European), religions (Catholic, Jewish, and Protestant), and sexual experiences. With the exception of one Puerto Rican girl, all of the girls from the suburban school were Euro-American; the racial/ethnic diversity in the sample is represented by the urban school. Interviews with school personnel confirmed that the student population of the urban school was almost exclusively poor or working class and the students in the suburban school were middle and upper-middle class. This information is important in that my focus is on how girls' social environments shape their understanding of their sexuality. The fact that girls

who live in the urban area experience the visibility of and discourse about violence, danger and the consequences of unprotected sex, and that the suburban girls live in a community that offers a veneer of safety and stability, informs their experiences of sexuality. Awareness of these features of the social contexts in which these girls are developing is essential for listening to and understanding their narratives about sexual experiences.

The data were collected in one-on-one, semistructured clinical interviews (Brown and Gilligan 1992). This method of interviewing consists of following a structured interview protocol that does not direct specific probes but elicits narratives. The interviewer listens carefully to a girl, taking in her voice, and responding with questions that will enable the girl to clarify her story and know she is being heard. In these interviews, I asked girls direct questions about desire to elicit descriptions and narratives. Most of the young women wove their concerns about danger into the narratives they told.

Analytic Strategy

To analyze these narratives, I used the Listening Guide—an interpretive methodology that joins hermeneutics and feminist standpoint epistemology (Brown et al. 1991). It is a voice-centered, relational method by which a researcher becomes a listener, taking in the voice of a girl, developing an interpretation of her experience. Through multiple readings of the same text, this method makes audible the "polyphonic and complex" nature of voice and experience (Brown and Gilligan 1992, 15). Both speaker and listener are recognized as individuals who bring thoughts and feelings to the text, acknowledging the necessary subjectivity of both participants. Self-consciously embedded in a standpoint acknowledging that patriarchal culture silences and obscures women's experiences, the method is explicitly psychological and feminist in providing the listener with an organized way to respond to the coded or indirect language of girls and women, especially regarding topics such as sexuality that girls and women are not supposed to speak of. This method leaves a trail of evidence for the listener's interpretation, and thus leaves room for other interpretations by other listeners consistent with the epistemological stance that there is multiple meaning in such stories. I present *a* way to understand the stories these young women chose to tell me, our story as I have heard and understood it. Therefore, in the interpretations that follow I include my responses, those of an adult woman, to these girls' words, providing information about girls' experiences of sexual desire much like countertransference informs psychotherapy.

Adolescent Girls' Experiences of Sexual Desire

The first layer of the complexity of girls' experiences of their sexual desire was revealed initially in determining whether or not they felt sexual feelings. A majority of these girls (two-thirds) said unequivocally that they experienced sexual desire; in them I heard a clear and powerful way of speaking about the experience of feeling desire that was explicitly relational and also embodied. Only three of the girls said they did not experience sexual feelings, describing silent bodies and an absence of or intense confusion about romantic or sexual relationships. The remaining girls evidenced confusion or spoke in confusing ways about their own sexual feelings. Such confusion can be understood as a psychic solution to sexual feelings that arise in a culture that denigrates, suppresses, and heightens the dangers of girls' sexuality and in which contradictory messages about women's sexuality abound.

For the girls who said they experienced sexual desire, I turned my attention to how they said they responded to their sexual feelings. What characterized their responses was a sense of struggle; the question of "doing desire"—that is, what to do when they felt sexual desire—was not straightforward for any of them. While speaking of the power of their embodied feelings, the girls in this sample described the difficulties that their sexual feelings posed, being aware of both the potential for pleasure and the threat of danger that their desire holds for them. The struggle took different shapes for different girls, with some notable patterns emerging. Among the urban girls, the focus was on how to stay safe from bodily harm, in and out of the context of relational or social consequences, whereas among the suburban girls the most pronounced issue was how to maintain a sense of themselves as "good" and "normal" girls (Tolman 1992). In this article, I will offer portraits of three girls. By focusing on three girls in depth, I can balance an approach to "variance" with the kind of case study presentation that enables me to illustrate both similarities and differences in how girls in the larger sample spoke about their sexual

feelings. These three girls represent different sexual preferences—one heterosexual, one bisexual, and one lesbian.[1] I have chosen to forefront the difference of sexual preference because it has been for some women a source of empowerment and a route to community; it has also been a source of divisiveness among feminists. Through this approach, I can illustrate *both* the similarities and differences in their experiences of sexual desire, which are nested in their individual experiences as well as their social contexts. Although there are many other demarcations that differentiate these girls—social class, race, religion, sexual experience—and this is not the most pervasive difference in this sample,[2] sexual preference calls attention to the kinds of relationships in which girls are experiencing or exploring their sexual desire and which take meaning from gender arrangements and from both the presence and absence of institutionalization (Fine 1988; Friend 1993). Because any woman whose sexuality is not directly circumscribed by heterosexual, monogamous marriage is rendered deviant in our society, all adolescent girls bear suspicion regarding their sexuality, which sexual preference highlights. In addition, questions of identity are heightened at adolescence.

Rochelle Doing Desire　Rochelle is a tall, larger, African-American girl who is heterosexual. Her small, sweet voice and shy smile are a startling contrast to her large body, clothed in white spandex the day of our interview. She lives in an urban area where violence is embedded in the fabric of everyday life. She speaks about her sexual experience with a detailed knowledge of how her sexuality is shaped, silenced, denigrated, and possible in relationships with young men. As a sophomore, she thought she "had to get a boyfriend" and became "eager" for a sexual relationship. As she describes her first experience of sexual intercourse, she describes a traditional framing of male–female relationships:

> I felt as though I had to conform to everything he said that, you know, things that a girl and a guy were supposed to do, so like, when the sex came, like, I did it without thinking, like, I wish I would have waited . . . we started kissing and all that stuff and it just happened. And when I got, went home, I was like, I was shocked, I was like, why did I do that? I wish I wouldn't a did it.
> *Did you want to do it?*
> Not really. Not really. I just did it because, maybe because he wanted it, and I was always like tryin' to

please him and like, he was real mean, mean to me, now that I think about it. I was like kind of stupid, cause like I did everything for him and he just treated me like I was nothing and I just thought I had just to stay with him because I needed a boyfriend so bad to make my life complete but like now it's different.

Rochelle's own sexual desire is absent in her story of defloration—in fact, she seems to be missing altogether. In a virtual caricature of dominant cultural conventions of femininity, Rochelle connects her disappearance at the moment of sex—"it just happened"—to her attempts to fulfill the cultural guidelines for how to "make [her] life complete." She has sex because "he wanted it," a response that holds no place for whether or not she feels desire. In reflecting on this arrangement, Rochelle now feels she was "stupid . . . to do everything for him" and in her current relationship, things are "different." As she explains: "I don't take as much as I did with the first guy, cause like, if he's doin' stuff that I don't like, I tell him, I'll go, I don't like this and I think you shouldn't do it and we compromise, you know. I don't think I can just let him treat me bad and stuff."

During the interview, I begin to notice that desire is not a main plot line in Rochelle's stories about her sexual experiences, especially in her intimate relationships. When I ask her about her experiences of sexual pleasure and sexual desire, she voices contradictions. On one hand, as the interview unfolds, she is more and more clear that she does not enjoy sex: "I don't like sex" quickly becomes "I hate sex . . . I don't really have pleasure." On the other hand, she explains that

there are certain times when I really really really enjoy it, but then, that's like, not a majority of the times, it's only sometimes, once in a while . . . if I was to have sex once a month, then I would enjoy it . . . if I like go a long period of time without havin' it then, it's really good to me, cause it's like, I haven't had something for a long time and I miss it. It's like, say I don't eat cake a lot, but say, like every two months, I had some cake, then it would be real good to me, so that's like the same thing.

Rochelle conveys a careful knowledge of her body's hunger, her need for tension as an aspect of her sexual pleasure, but her voiced dislike of sex suggests that she does not feel she has much say over when and how she engages in sexual activity.

In describing her experiences with sexuality, I am overwhelmed at how frequently Rochelle says that she

"was scared." She is keenly aware of the many consequences that feeling and responding to her sexual desire could have. She is scared of being talked about and getting an undeserved reputation: "I was always scared that if I did that (had sexual intercourse) I would be portrayed as, you know, something bad." Even having sex within the confines of a relationship, which has been described by some girls as a safe haven for their sexuality (Rubin 1990; Tolman 1992), makes her vulnerable; she "could've had a bad reputation, but luckily he wasn't like that"; he did not choose to tell other boys (who then tell girls) about their sexual activity. Thinking she had a sexually transmitted disease was scary. Because she had been faithful to her boyfriend, having such a disease would mean having to know that her boyfriend cheated on her and would also make her vulnerable to false accusations of promiscuity from him. Her concern about the kind of woman she may be taken for is embedded in her fear of using contraception: "When you get birth control pills, people automatically think you're having sex every night and that's not true." Being thought of as sexually insatiable or out of control is a fear that many girls voice (Tolman 1992); this may be intensified for African-American girls, who are creating a sexual identity in a dominant cultural context that stereotypes Black women as alternately asexual and hypersexual (Spillers 1984).

Rochelle's history provides other sources of fear. After her boyfriend "flattened [her] face," when she realized she no longer wanted to be with him and broke off the relationship, she learned that her own desire may lead to male violence. Rochelle confided to me that she has had an abortion, suffering such intense sadness, guilt, and anxiety in the wake of it that, were she to become pregnant again, she would have the baby. For Rochelle, the risk of getting pregnant puts her education at risk, because she will have to sacrifice going to college. This goal is tied to security for her; she wants to "have something of my own before I get a husband, you know, so if he ever tries leavin' me, I have my own money." Given this wall of fears, I am not surprised when Rochelle describes a time when simply feeling desire made her "so scared that I started to cry." Feeling her constant and pervasive fear, I began to find it hard to imagine how she can feel any other feelings, including sexual ones.

I was thus caught off guard when I asked Rochelle directly if she has felt desire and she told me that she does experience sexual desire; however, she explained "most of the time, I'm by myself when I do." She launched, in breathless tones, into a story about an experience of her own sexual desire just the previous night:

> Last night, I had this crank call. . . . At first I thought it was my boyfriend, cause he likes to play around, you know. But I was sitting there talking, you know, and thinking of him and then I found out it's not him, it was so crazy weird, so I hang the phone up and he called back, he called back and called back. And then I couldn't sleep, I just had this feeling that, I wanted to have sex so so bad. It was like three o'clock in the morning. And I didn't sleep the rest of the night. And like, I called my boyfriend and I was tellin' him, and he was like, what do you want me to do, Rochelle, I'm sleeping! [Laughs.] I was like, okay, okay, well I'll talk to you later, bye. And then, like, I don't know, I just wanted to, and like, I kept tossin' and turnin'. And I'm trying to think who it was, who was callin' me, cause like, it's always the same guy who always crank calls me, he says he knows me. It's kinda scary. . . . I can't sleep, I'm like, I just think about it, like, oh I wanna have sex so bad, you know, it's like a fever, drugs, something like that. Like last night, I don't know, I think if I woulda had the car and stuff, I probably woulda left the house. And went over to his house, you know. But I couldn't, cause I was baby-sitting.

When I told her that it sounds a little frightening but it sounds like there's something exciting about it, she smiled and leaned forward, exclaiming, "Yeah! It's like sorta arousing." I was struck by the intensity of her sexual feelings and also by the fact that she is alone and essentially assured of remaining alone due to the late hour and her responsibilities. By being alone, not subject to observation or physical, social, emotional, or material vulnerability, Rochelle experienced the turbulent feelings that are awakened by this call in her body. Rochelle's desire has not been obliterated by her fear; desire and fear both reverberate through her psyche. But she is not completely alone in this experience of desire, for her feelings occur in response to another person, whom she at first suspects is her boyfriend speaking from a safe distance, conveying the relational contours of her sexual desire. Her wish to bring her desire into her relationship, voiced in her response of calling her boyfriend, is in conflict with her fear of what might happen if she did pursue her wish— getting pregnant and having a baby, a consequence that Rochelle is desperate to avoid.

I am struck by her awareness of both the pleasure and danger in this experience and how she works the contradiction without dissociating from her own strong feelings. There is a brilliance and also a sadness in the logic her body and psyche have played out in the face of her experiences with sexuality and relationships. The psychological solution to the dilemma that desire means for her, of feeling sexual desire only when she cannot respond as she says she would like to, arises from her focus on these conflicts as personal experiences, which she suffers and solves privately. By identifying and solving the dilemma in this way, Rochelle is diminished, as is the possibility of her developing a critique of these conflicts as not just personal problems but as social inequities that emerge in her personal relationships and on her body. Without this perspective, Rochelle is less likely to become empowered through her own desire to identify that the ways in which she must curtail herself and be curtailed by others are socially constructed, suspect, and in need of change.

Megan Doing Desire   Megan, a small, freckled, perky Euro-American, is dressed in baggy sweats, comfortable, unassuming, and counterpointed by her lively engagement in our interview.[3] She identifies herself as "being bisexual" and belongs to a gay youth group; she lives in a city in which wealth and housing projects coexist. Megan speaks of knowing she is feeling sexual desire for boys because she has "kind of just this feeling, you know? Just this feeling inside my body." She explains: "My vagina starts to kinda like act up and it kinda like quivers and stuff, and like I'll get like tingles and and, you can just feel your hormones (laughing) doing something weird, and you just, you get happy and you just get, you know, restimulated kind of and it's just, and Oh! Oh!" and "Your nerves feel good." Megan speaks about her sexual desire in two distinct ways, one for boys and one for girls. In our interview, she speaks most frequently about her sexual feelings in relation to boys. The power of her own desire and her doubt about her ability to control herself frighten her: "It scares me when I'm involved in a sexual situation and I just wanna go further and further and cause it just, and it scares me that, well, I have control, but if I even just let myself not have control, you know? . . . I'd have sex and I can't do that." Megan knows that girls who lose control over their desire like that can be called "sluts" and ostracized.

When asked to speak about an experience of sexual desire, Megan chooses to describe the safety of a heterosexual, monogamous relationship. She tells me how she feels when a boyfriend was "feeling me up"; not only is she aware of and articulate about his bodily reactions and her own, she narrates the relational synergy between her own desire and his:

> I just wanted to go on, you know? Like I could feel his penis, you know, 'cause we'd kinda lied down you know, and, you just really get so into it and intense and, you just wanna, well you just kinda keep wanting to go on or something, but it just feels good. . . . His penis being on my leg made, you know, it hit a nerve or something, it did something because it just made me start to get more horny or whatever, you know, it just made me want to do more things and stuff. I don't know how, I can't, it's hard for me to describe exactly how I felt, you know like, (intake of breath) . . . when he gets more excited then he starts to do more things and you can kind of feel his pleasure and then you start to get more excited.

With this young man, Megan knows her feelings of sexual desire to be "intense," to have a momentum of their own, and to be pleasurable. Using the concrete information of his erection, she describes the relational contours of her own embodied sexual desire, a desire that she is clear is her own and located in her body but that also arises in response to his excitement.

Although able to speak clearly in describing a specific experience she has had with her desire, I hear confusion seep into her voice when she notices that her feelings contradict or challenge societal messages about girls and sexuality:

> It's so confusing, 'cause you have to like say no, you have to be the one to say no, but why should you be the one to, cause I mean maybe you're enjoying it and you shouldn't have to say no or anything. But if you don't, maybe the guy'll just keep going and going, and you can't do that, because then you would be a slut. There's so [much] like, you know, stuff that you have to deal with and I don't know, just I keep losing my thought.

Although she knows the logic offered by society—that she must "say no" to keep him from "going and going," which will make her "a slut"—Megan identifies what is missing from that logic, that "maybe you're"—she, the girl—"the one who is enjoying it." The fact that she may be experiencing sexual desire makes the scripted response—to silence his body—dizzying. Because she does feel her own desire and can identify the potential

of her own pleasure, Megan asks the next logical question, the question that can lead to outrage, critique, and empowerment: "Why should you have to be the one to [say no]?" But Megan also gives voice to why sustaining the question is difficult; she knows that if she does not conform, if she does not "say no"—both to him and to herself—then she may be called a slut, which could lead to denigration and isolation. Megan is caught in the contradiction between the reality of her sexual feelings in her body and the absence of her sexual feelings in the cultural script for adolescent girls' sexuality. Her confusion is an understandable response to this untenable and unfair choice: a connection with herself, her body, and sexual pleasure or a connection with the social world.

Megan is an avid reader of the dominant culture. Not only has she observed the ways that messages about girls' sexuality leave out or condemn her embodied feelings for boys, she is also keenly aware of the pervasiveness of cultural norms and images that demand heterosexuality:

> Every teen magazine you look at is like, guy this, how to get a date, guys, guys, guys, guys, guys. So you're constantly faced with I have to have a boyfriend, I have to have a boyfriend, you know, even if you don't have a boyfriend, just [have] a fling, you know, you just want to kiss a guy or something. I've had that mentality for so long.

In this description of compulsory heterosexuality (Rich 1983), Megan captures the pressure she feels to have a boyfriend and how she experiences the insistence of this demand, which is ironically in conflict with the mandate to say no when with a boy. She is aware of how her psyche has been shaped into a "mentality" requiring any sexual or relational interests to be heterosexual, which does not corroborate how she feels. Compulsory heterosexuality comes between Megan and her feelings, making her vulnerable to a dissociation of her "feelings" under this pressure.

Although she calls herself bisexual, Megan does not describe her sexual feelings for girls very much in this interview. In fact, she becomes so confused that at one point she says she is not sure if her feelings for girls are sexual:

> I mean, I'll see a girl I really really like, you know, because I think she's so beautiful, and I might, I don't know. I'm so confused. . . . But there's, you know, that same mentality as me liking a guy if he's really cute,

I'm like, oh my God, you know, he's so cute. If I see a woman that I like, a girl, it's just like wow, she's so pretty, you know. See I can picture like hugging a girl; I just can't picture the sex, or anything, so, there's something being blocked.

Megan links her confusion with her awareness of the absence of images of lesbian sexuality in the spoken or imagistic lexicon of the culture, counterpointing the pervasiveness of heterosexual imagery all around her. Megan suggests that another reason that she might feel "confused" about her feelings for girls is a lack of sexual experience. Megan knows she is feeling sexual desire when she can identify feelings in her own body— when her "vagina acts up"—and these feelings occur for her in the context of a sexual relationship, when she can feel the other person's desire. Because she has never been in a situation with a girl that would allow this embodied sexual response, she posits a connection between her lack of sexual experience with girls and her confusion.

Yet she has been in a situation where she was "close to" a girl and narrates how she does not let her body speak:

There was this one girl that I had kinda liked from school, and it was like really weird 'cause she's really popular and everything. And we were sitting next to each other during the movie and, kind of her leg was on my leg and I was like, wow, you know, and that was, I think that's like the first time that I've ever felt like sexual pleasure for a girl. But it's so impossible, I think I just like block it out, I mean, it could never happen.... I just can't know what I'm feeling.... I probably first mentally just say no, don't feel it, you know, maybe. But I never start to feel, I don't know. It's so confusing. 'Cause finally it's all right for me to like a girl, you know? Before it was like, you know, the two times that I really, that it was just really obvious that I liked them a lot, I had to keep saying no no no no, you know, I just would not let myself. I just hated myself for it, and this year now that I'm talking about it, now I can start to think about it.

Megan both narrates and interprets her dissociation from her embodied sexual feelings and describes the disciplinary stance of her mind over her body in how she "mentally" silences her body by saying "no," preempting her embodied response. Without her body's feelings, her embodied knowledge, Megan feels confused. If she runs interference with her own sexual feelings by silencing her body, making it impossible for her to feel her desire for girls, then she can avoid the problems she knows will inevitably arise if she feels sexual feelings she "can't know"—compulsory heterosexuality and homophobia combine to render this knowledge problematic for her. Fearing rejection, Megan keeps herself from feelings that could lead to disappointment, embarrassment, or frustration, leaving her safe in some ways, yet also psychologically vulnerable.

Echoing dominant cultural constructions of sexual desire, Megan links her desire for girls with feelings of fear: "I've had crushes on some girls . . . you can picture yourself kissing a guy but then if you like a girl a lot and then you picture yourself kissing her, it's just like, I can't, you know, oh my God, no (laughs), you know it's like scary . . . it's society . . . you never would think of, you know, it's natural to kiss a girl." Megan's fear about her desire for girls is different from the fears associated with her desire for boys; whereas being too sexual with boys brings the stigma of being called a "slut," Megan fears "society" and being thought of as "unnatural" when it comes to her feelings for girls. Given what she knows about the heterosexual culture in which she is immersed—the pressure she feels to be interested in "guys" and also given what she knows about homophobia—there is an inherent logic in Megan's confused response to her feelings for girls.

Melissa Doing Desire   Melissa, dressed in a flowing gypsy skirt, white skin pale against the lively colors she wears, is clear about her sexual desire for girls, referring to herself as "lesbian"; she is also a member of a gay/lesbian youth group. In speaking of her desire, Melissa names not only powerful feelings of "being excited" and "wanting," but also more contained feelings; she has "like little crushes on like millions of people and I mean, it's enough for me." Living in a world defined as heterosexual, Melissa finds that "little crushes" have to suffice, given a lack of opportunity for sexual exploration or relationship: "I don't know very many people my age that are even bisexual or lesbians . . . so I pretty much stick to that, like, being hugely infatuated with straight people. Which can get a little touchy at times . . . realistically, I can't like get too ambitious, because that would just not be realistic."

At the forefront of how Melissa describes her desire is her awareness that her sexual feelings make her vulnerable to harm. Whereas the heterosexual girls in this study link their vulnerability to the outcomes of responding to their desire—pregnancy, disease, or getting a bad reputation—Melissa is aware that even the existence of her sexual desire for girls can lead to anger or violence if others know of it: "Well I'm really lucky that like nothing bad has happened or no one's gotten mad at me so far, that, by telling people about them, hasn't gotten me into more trouble than it has, I mean, little things but not like, anything really awful. I think about that and I think it, sometimes, I mean, it could be more dangerous." In response to this threat of violence, Melissa attempts to restrain her own desire: "Whenever I start, I feel like I can't help looking at someone for more than a few seconds, and I keep, and I feel like I have to make myself not stare at them or something." Another strategy is to express her desire covertly by being physically affectionate with other girls, a behavior that is common and acceptable; by keeping her sexuality secret, she can "hang all over [girls] and stuff and they wouldn't even think that I meant anything by it." I am not surprised that Melissa associates feeling sexual desire with frustration; she explains that she "find(s) it safer to just think about the person than what I wanna do, because if I think about that too much and I can't do it, then that'll just frustrate me," leading her to try to intervene in her feelings by "just think[ing] about the person" rather than about the more sexual things she "want(s) to do." In this way, Melissa may jeopardize her ability to know her sexual desire and, in focusing on containing what society has named improper feelings, minimize or exorcise her empowerment to expose that construction as problematic and unjust.

My questions about girls' sexual desire connect deeply with Melissa's own questions about herself; she is in her first intimate relationship, and this interview proves an opportunity to explore and clarify painful twinges of doubt that she had begun to have about it. This relationship began on the initiative of the other girl, with whom she had been very close, rather than out of any sexual feelings on Melissa's part. In fact, Melissa was surprised when her friend had expressed a sexual interest, because she had not "been thinking that" about this close friend. After a history of having to hold back her sexual desire, of feeling "frustrated" and being "hugely infatuated with straight people," rather than having the chance to explore her sexuality, Melissa's response to this potential relationship was that she "should take advantage of this situation." As the interview progresses, Melissa begins to question

whether she is sexually attracted to this girl or "it's just sort of like I just wanted something like this for so long that I'm just taking advantage of the situation."

When I ask Melissa questions about the role of her body in her experience of sexual desire, her confusion at first intensifies:

Is that [your body] part of what feels like it might be missing?

(eight-second pause) It's not, well, sometimes, I mean I don't know how, what I feel all the time. It's hard like, because I mean I'm so confused about this. And it's hard like when it's actually happening to be like, OK, now how do I feel right now? How do I feel right now? How am I gonna feel about this? . . . I don't know, 'cause I don't know what to expect, and I haven't been with anyone else so I don't know what's supposed to happen. So, I mean I'm pretty confused.

The way she speaks about monitoring her body suggests that she is searching for bodily feelings, making me wonder what, if anything, she felt. I discern what she does not say directly; that her body was silent in these sexual experiences. Her hunger for a relationship is palpable: "I really wanted someone really badly, I think, I was getting really sick of being by myself. . . . I would be like God, I really need someone." The desperation in her voice, and the sexual frustration she describes, suggest that her "want" and "need" are distinctly sexual as well as relational.

One reason that Melissa seems to be confused is that she felt a strong desire to be "mothered," her own mother having died last year. In trying to distinguish her different desires in this interview, Melissa began to distinguish erotic feelings from another kind of wanting she also experienced: she said that "it's more of like but I kind of feel like it's really more of like a maternal thing, that I really want her to take care of me and I just wanna touch someone and I just really like the feeling of just how I mean I like, when I'm with her and touching her and stuff. A lot, but it's not necessarily a sexual thing at this point." In contrast to her feelings for her girlfriend, Melissa describes feeling sexually attracted to another girl. In so doing, Melissa clarifies what is missing in these first sexual adventures, enabling her to know what had bothered her about her relationship with her girlfriend:

I don't really think I'm getting that much pleasure, from her, it's just, I mean it's almost like I'm getting experience, and I'm sort of having fun, it's not even that exciting, and that's why I think I don't really like her . . . because my friend asked me this the other day, well, I mean does it get, I mean when you're with her does it get really, I don't remember the word she used, but just really, like what was the word she used? But I guess she meant just like, exciting [laughing]. But it doesn't, to me. It's weird, because I can't really say that, I mean I can't think of like a time when I was really excited and it was like really, sexual pleasure, for me, because I don't think it's really like that. I mean not that I think that this isn't good because, I don't know, I mean, I like it, but I mean I think I have to, sort of realize that I'm not that much attracted to her, personally.

Wanting both a relationship and sexual pleasure, a chance to explore closeness and her sexual curiosity, and discovering that this relationship leaves out her sexual desire, Melissa laments her silent body: "I sort of expect or hope or whatever that there would be some kind of more excited feeling just from feeling sexually stimulated or whatever. I would hope that there would be more of a feeling than I've gotten so far." Knowing consciously what she "knows" about the absence of her sexual feelings in this relationship has left her with a relational conflict of large proportions for her: "I'm not that attracted to her and I don't know if I should tell her that. Or if I should just kind of pretend I am and try to . . . anyway." I ask her how she would go about doing that—pretending that she is. She replies, "I don't think I could pretend it for too long." Not being able to "pretend" to have feelings that she knows she wants as part of an intimate relationship, Melissa faces a dilemma of desire that may leave her feeling isolated and lonely or even fraudulent.

ADOLESCENT GIRLS' SEXUAL DESIRE AND THE POSSIBILITIES OF EMPOWERMENT

All of the girls in this study who said they felt sexual desire expressed conflict when describing their responses to their sexual feelings—conflict between their embodied sexual feelings and their perceptions of how those feelings are, in one way or another, anathema or problematic within the social and relational contexts of their lives. Their experiences of sexual desire are strong and pleasurable, yet they speak very often not of the power of desire but of how their desire may get them into trouble. These girls are beginning to voice the internalized oppression of their women's bodies; they knew and spoke about, in explicit or more indirect ways, the pressure they felt to silence their desire, to dissociate from those bodies in which they inescapably live. Larger societal forces of social control in the form of compulsory heterosexuality (Rich 1983), the policing of girls' bodies through school codes (Lesko 1988), and media images play a clear part in forcing this silence and dissociation. Specific relational dynamics, such as concern about a reputation that can easily be besmirched by other girls and by boys, fear of male violence in intimate relationships, and fear of violent repercussion of violating norms of heterosexuality are also audible in these girls' voices.

To be able to know their sexual feelings, to listen when their bodies speak about themselves and about their relationships, might enable these and other girls to identify and know more clearly the sources of oppression that press on their full personhood and their capacity for knowledge, joy, and connection. Living in the margins of a heterosexual society, the bisexual and lesbian girls voice an awareness of these forces as formative of the experiences of their bodies and relationships; the heterosexual girls are less clear and less critical about the ways that dominant constructions of their sexuality impinge on their embodied and relational worlds. Even when they are aware that societal ambivalence and fears are being played out on their minds and bodies, they do not speak of a need for collective action, or even the possibility of engaging in such activities. More often, they speak of the danger of speaking about desire at all. By dousing desire with fear and confusion, or simple, "uncomplicated" denial, silence, and dissociation, the girls in this study make individual psychological moves whereby they distance or disconnect themselves from discomfort and danger. Although disciplining their bodies and curbing their desire are a very logical and understandable way to stay physically, socially, and emotionally safe, they also heighten the chance that girls and women may lose track of the fact that an inequitable social system, and not a necessary situation, renders women's sexual desire a source of danger rather than one of pleasure and power in their lives. In "not knowing" desire, girls and women are at risk for not knowing that there is nothing wrong with having sexual feelings and responding to them in ways that bring joy and agency.

Virtually every girl in the larger study told me that no woman had ever talked to her about sexual desire and pleasure "like this"—in depth, listening to her speak about her own experiences, responding when she asked questions about how to masturbate, how to have cunnilingus, what sex is like after marriage. In the words of Rubin: "The ethos of privacy and silence about our personal sexual experience makes it easy to rationalize the refusal to speak [to adolescents]" (1990, 83; Segal 1993). Thompson (1990) found that daughters of women who had talked with them about pleasure and desire told narratives about first intercourse that were informed by pleasure and agency. The recurrent strategy the girls in my study describe of keeping their desire under wraps as a way to protect themselves also keeps girls out of authentic relationships with other girls and women. It is within these relationships that the empowerment of women can develop and be nurtured through shared experiences of both oppression and power, in which collectively articulated critiques are carved out and voiced. Such knowledge of how a patriarchal society systematically keeps girls and women from their own desire can instigate demand and agency for social change. By not talking about sexual desire with each other or with women, a source for empowerment is lost. There is a symbiotic interplay between desire and empowerment: to be empowered to desire one needs a critical perspective, and that critical perspective will be extended and sustained through knowing and experiencing the possibilities of desire and healthy embodied living. Each of these girls illustrates the phenomenon observed in the larger study—the difficulty for girls in having or sustaining a critical perspective on the culture's silencing of their sexual desire. They are denied full access to the power of their own desire and to structural supports for that access.

Common threads of fear and joy, pleasure and danger, weave through the narratives about sexual desire in this study, exemplified by the three portraits. Girls have the right to be informed that gaining pleasure and a strong sense of self and power through their bodies does not make them bad or unworthy. The experiences of these and other adolescent girls illustrate why girls deserve to be educated about their sexual desire. Thompson concludes that "to take possession of sexuality in the wake of the anti-erotic sexist socialization that remains the majority experience, most teenage girls need an erotic education" (1990, 406). Girls need to be educated about the duality of their sexuality, to have safe contexts in which they can explore both

danger and desire (Fine 1988), and to consider why their desire is so dangerous and how they can become active participants in their own redemption. Girls can be empowered to know and act on their own desire, a different educational direction than the simplistic strategies for avoiding boys' desire that they are offered. The "just say no" curriculum obscures the larger social inequities being played out on girls' bodies in heterosexual relationships and is not relevant for girls who feel sexual feelings for girls. Even adults who are willing or able to acknowledge that girls experience sexual feelings worry that knowing about their own sexual desire will place girls in danger (Segal 1993). But keeping girls in the dark about their power to choose based on their own feelings fails to keep them any safer from these dangers. Girls who trust their minds and bodies may experience a stronger sense of self, entitlement, and empowerment that could enhance their ability to make safe decisions. One approach to educating girls is for women to speak to them about the vicissitudes of sexual desire—which means that women must let themselves speak and know their own sexual feelings, as well as the pleasures and dangers associated with women's sexuality and the solutions that we have wrought to the dilemma of desire: how to balance the realities of pleasure and danger in women's sexuality.

Asking these girls to speak about sexual desire, and listening and responding to their answers and also to their questions, proved to be an effective way to interrupt the standard "dire consequences" discourse adults usually employ when speaking at all to girls about their sexuality. Knowing and speaking about the ways in which their sexuality continues to be unfairly constrained may interrupt the appearance of social equity that many adolescent girls (especially white, middle-class young women) naively and trustingly believe, thus leading them to reject feminism as unnecessary and mean-spirited and not relevant to their lives. As we know from the consciousness-raising activities that characterized the initial years of second-wave feminism, listening to the words of other girls and women can make it possible for girls to know and voice their experiences, their justified confusion and fears, their curiosities. Through such relationships, we help ourselves and each other to live in our different female bodies with an awareness of danger, but also with a desire to feel the power of the erotic, to fine-tune our bodies and our psyches to what Audre Lorde has called the "yes within ourselves" (Lorde 1984, 54).

NOTES

1. The bisexual girl and the lesbian girl were members of a gay/lesbian youth group and identify themselves using these categories. As is typical for members of privileged groups for whom membership is a given, the girls who feel sexual desire for boys and not for girls (about which they were asked explicitly) do not use the term "heterosexual" to describe themselves. Although I am aware of the debate surrounding the use of these categories and labels to delimit women's (and men's) experience, because my interpretive practice is informed by the ways society makes meaning of girls' sexuality, the categories that float in the culture as ways of describing the girls are relevant to my analysis. In addition, the bisexual and lesbian girls in this study are deeply aware of compulsory heterosexuality and its impact on their lives.

2. Of the thirty girls in this sample, twenty-seven speak of a desire for boys and not for girls. This pattern was ascertained by who appeared in their desire narratives and also by their response to direct questions about sexual feelings for girls, designed explicitly to interrupt the hegemony of heterosexuality. Two of the thirty girls described sexual desire for both boys and girls and one girl described sexual desire for girls and not for boys.

3. Parts of this analysis appear in Tolman (1994).

REFERENCES

Brown, L. 1991. Telling a girl's life: Self authorization as a form of resistance. In *Women, Girls and Psychotherapy: Reframing Resistance,* ed. C. Gilligan, A. Rogers, and D. Tolman. New York: Haworth.

Brown, L., E. Debold, M. Tappan, and C. Gilligan. 1991. Reading narratives of conflict for self and moral voice: A relational method. In *Handbook of Moral Behavior and Development: Theory, Research, and Application,* ed. W. Kurtines and J. Gewirtz. Hillsdale, NJ: Lawrence Erlbaum.

Brown, L., and C. Gilligan. 1992. *Meeting at the Crossroads: Women's Psychology and Girls' Development.* Cambridge, MA: Harvard University Press.

Fine, Michelle. 1988. Sexuality, schooling and adolescent females: The missing discourse of desire. *Harvard Educational Review* 58:29–53.

Friend, Richard. 1993. Choices, not closets. In *Beyond Silenced Voices,* ed. M. Fine and L. Weis. New York: State University of New York Press.

Gilligan, Carol. 1989. Teaching Shakespeare's sister. In *Making Connections: The Relational World of Adolescent Girls at Emma Willard School,* ed. C. Gilligan, N. Lyons, and T. Hamner. Cambridge, MA: Harvard University Press.

———. 1990. Joining the resistance: Psychology, politics, girls and women. *Michigan Quarterly Review* 29:501–36.

Lees, Susan. 1986. *Losing Out: Sexuality and Adolescent Girls.* London: Hutchinson.

Lesko, Nancy. 1988. The curriculum of the body: Lessons from a Catholic high school. In *Becoming Feminine: The Politics of Popular Culture,* ed. L. Roman. Philadelphia: Falmer.

Lorde, Audre. 1984. The uses of the erotic as power. In *Sister Outsider: Essays and Speeches.* Freedom, CA: Crossing Press.

Rich, Adrienne. 1983. Compulsory heterosexuality and lesbian existence. In *Powers of Desire: The Politics of Sexuality,* ed. A. Snitow, C. Stansell, and S. Thompson. New York: Monthly Review Press.

Rubin, Lillian. 1990. *Erotic Wars: What Happened to the Sexual Revolution?* New York: HarperCollins.

Segal, Lynne. 1993. Introduction. In *Sex Exposed: Sexuality and the Pornography Debate,* ed. L. Segal and M. McIntosh. New Brunswick, NJ: Rutgers University Press.

Spillers, Hortense. 1984. Interstices: A small drama of words. In *Pleasure and Danger: Exploring Female Sexuality,* ed. C. Vance. Boston: Routledge and Kegan Paul.

Thompson, Sharon. 1984. Search for tomorrow: On feminism and the reconstruction of teen romance. In *Pleasure and Danger: Exploring Female Sexuality,* ed. C. Vance. Boston: Routledge and Kegan Paul.

———. 1990. Putting a big thing in a little hole: Teenage girls' accounts of sexual initiation. *Journal of Sex Research* 27:341–61.

Tolman, Deborah L. 1991. Adolescent girls, women and sexuality: Discerning dilemmas of desire. *Women, Girls, and Psychotherapy: Reframing Resistance,* ed. C. Gilligan, A. Rogers, and D. Tolman. New York: Haworth.

———. 1992. Voicing the body: A psychological study of adolescent girls' sexual desire. Unpublished dissertation, Harvard University.

———. 1994. Daring to desire: Culture and the bodies of adolescent girls. In *Sexual Cultures: Adolescents, Communities and the Construction of Identity,* ed. J. Irvine. Philadelphia: Temple University Press.

Tolman, Deborah, and Elizabeth Debold. 1993. Conflicts of body and image: Female adolescents, desire, and the no-body. In *Feminist Treatment and Therapy of Eating Disorders,* ed. M. Katzman, P. Failon, and S. Wooley. New York: Guilford.

Barbara Risman
Pepper Schwartz

After the Sexual Revolution: Gender Politics in Teen Dating

News of apparent decreasing sexual activity among teens, as well as possible success in abstinence programs and church- and government-based "just say no" campaigns, is widely greeted as a positive development. Americans generally regard teen sexuality as a social problem—regardless of whether it results in abortion, single teen motherhood or sexually transmitted disease.

Signs of a new teenage conservatism are, however, at least exaggerated and, more probably, misinterpreted. Hints of increased conservatism apply only to boys, and a great deal of evidence shows that teens continue to be active sexually. Why, then, are social commentators so insistent on making the case for a teenage sexual retreat?

THE CASE FOR A TEENAGE SEXUAL COUNTERREVOLUTION

Much research suggests that teens became more sexually conservative during the last decade of the 20th century. Several studies show that a smaller proportion of youth had coitus between the ages of 15 and 17. For example, the Youth Risk Behavior Survey, designed by the Center for Disease Control (CDC) to find out which behaviors most affect student health, was conducted several times throughout the 1990s, and every replication found a lower percentage of sexually active teens under age 18. In this nationally representative study of over 10,000 students, the percentage of high school students, ages 15 to 17, who reported they had engaged in sexual intercourse dropped from 54.1 percent in 1991 to 48.4 percent by 1997, a dramatic decrease of some 5.7 percent in a short time. Similar trends were reported in three other nationally representative surveys. While black students continue to be more sexually active than whites, the trends found in this study are similar for blacks and whites. The trend is much less pronounced for Hispanic youth (Figure 1).

Accompanying these statistics is additional good news about the problems that often accompany teenage sexual activities. Not only did the percentage of teens engaging in coital sex fall, but also the serious problems that can result from irresponsible teenage sexuality declined. The teen pregnancy rate showed an impressive 14 percent reduction, lower than any time since 1975 (from a Peak of 117 per 1,000 young women in 1991 to 103 in 1995). Fewer teen pregnancies mean fewer teenage mothers and fewer abortions. Reports from the Alan Guttmacher Institute show that the abortion rate decreased 31 percent from 1986 to 1996. The birth rate among teens rose until 1991 and fell steadily since, with a 25 percent decline between 1986 and 1996. When teens did have sex, they waited until somewhat older ages. The percentage of students in grades 9 and 10 who reported ever having had sexual intercourse was 43.7 percent in 1991, but by 1997 the percentage decreased to 40.3 percent. Even among juniors and seniors in high school, the rates of coitus fell nearly 10 percent in that time. Most research finds that the

FIGURE I   PERCENTAGE OF SEXUALLY ACTIVE HIGH SCHOOL STUDENTS BY RACE

Source: Authors' tabulations from 1991 and 1997 Youth Risk Behavior Surveys.

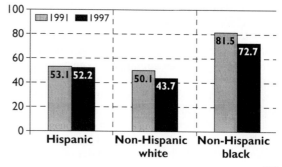

rate of sexually transmitted diseases also declined throughout the 1990s.

WHY THE APPARENT DECLINES?

These findings have many explanations, and most contradict one another. The various speculations for the decline in both sexual activity and the problems associated with it include the following: the success of abstinence education, the positive effect of comprehensive sex education, the cultural backlash against the sexual revolution, or the fear of disease (or some combination of these factors). Douglas Kirby's comprehensive analysis of the research on sex education indicates that while good studies show that comprehensive sex education delays the age of first intercourse, none indicate that abstinence—only education is similarly effective. A recent, highly publicized study suggests that abstinence pledges themselves (without actual education) deter teens from sexual activity. While this study was widely reported in the mass media, the story is much more complicated. We believe the claim is inaccurate and explain later in this article why solid scientific research can be distorted when it enters public discourse.

Some commentators have extolled newly conservative values among high school students as the explanation for less teen sex. According to this view, girls especially grew tired of the excesses of the previous decades and wanted to find safety and dignity in less sexualized relationships. Youths looked at the carnage of their parents' generation—divorce, disease, and a loss of status for women's choice to say no—and decided to reestablish their power through less, not more, sexuality. The explanation sounds possible, but little research exists to test this assertion. Fear of disease does seem to be one part of the puzzle. Considerable evidence indicates that some people have changed their sexual habits because of the perceived risk of contracting a permanent or fatal sexually transmitted disease.

Weighing these various explanations is complicated. Reports that the rates of birth, abortion, and sexually transmitted diseases fell much faster than rates of coitus convince us that young people are acting more responsibly when they are sexually active. Responsible sex, rather than postponed sex, seems to explain these improvements. For example, the Alan Guttmacher Institute calculates that less than 25 percent of the decline in pregnancy rates can be attributed to increased abstinence; they attribute the remainder of the decline to the more efficient use of birth control by sexually experienced women. Teens are primarily becoming sexually more responsible and only secondarily less sexually active. Whether such responsibility is attributable to comprehensive sex education or simply to the fear of disease, heightened by mass media reports on AIDS and other sexually transmitted diseases, remains unclear.

While credible competing explanations vie for credit when it comes to explaining the reduction of adolescent pregnancy, we still doubt the underlying premise that sexual activity is on the decline.

A CLOSER LOOK AT THE DATA

When we separate the data by gender, the story changes dramatically. Several rigorous studies indicate that the number of high school boys—but not girls—under 18 who remain virgins dramatically increased.

The drama of this decrease in sexual activity among high school boys was hidden in the earlier data that combined the sexes because girls' behavior did not change significantly (Figure 2). And yet the story is even more complicated. Sexual trends follow the same direction for white, black and Hispanic boys, but the picture is more complex for girls (Figures 3 and 4).

The rate of sexual activity among white and Hispanic girls has remained generally stable. Black girls, however, reduced their rates of sexual activity, moving toward levels comparable to that of white and Hispanic girls.

FIGURE 2   PERCENTAGE OF SEXUALLY ACTIVE HIGH SCHOOL STUDENTS BY GENDER

Source: Authors' tabulations from 1991 and 1997 Youth Risk Behavior Surveys.

FIGURE 3   PERCENTAGE OF SEXUALLY ACTIVE HIGH SCHOOL FEMALES BY RACE

Source: Authors' tabulations from 1991 and 1997 Youth Risk Behavior Surveys.

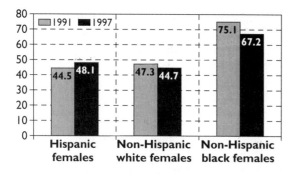

FIGURE 4   PERCENTAGE OF SEXUALLY ACTIVE HIGH SCHOOL MALES BY RACE

Source: Authors' tabulations from 1991 and 1997 Youth Risk Behavior Surveys.

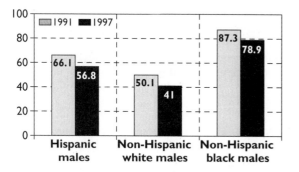

So what is going on? Boys' sexual behavior is becoming more like girls' behavior. Among whites, boys are less likely than girls to be sexually active by age 17. Black and Hispanic boys are still more likely than girls to report sexual intercourse, but the gaps are closing here, too.

We can only speculate about the explanations for the complexity of these changes. We draw on several intensive interview and observational research studies to help understand the reasons for the decrease in teenage boys' sexual experience while in high school. Our best sociologically informed guess is that the cultural norms for girls' sexuality have dramatically changed. Girls are now presumed sexually active inside, but not outside, romantic relationships. Boys are therefore now much more likely to begin their sexual lives with a girlfriend.

The decline in problematic outcomes such as pregnancies is the result, we believe, of girls' increased influence in intimate relationships. In the past, boys were often introduced to sex in a furtive encounter with a girl outside their social circle, one stigmatized by her own sexual appetite or with a desperate need for any kind of approval or inclusion. These girls were often ostracized and stigmatized by both sexes and cruelly smeared as sluts. In previous decades when boys were more sexually active than girls at younger ages, a small pool of "bad" girls probably serviced many boys (otherwise, how could so many fewer girls be sexually experienced than boys?). Nowadays, with boys and girls reporting more similar rates of sexual activity (although only equal rates at the moment for whites), more boys apparently have their first sexual experiences inside a "relationship" of some sort. Adult observers may, however, have to stretch their imagination a bit to define the word *relationship* as casually as teens do, since it may mean accepting the idea of a two-week acquaintance as a relationship. Nonetheless, there seems to be good reason to suspect that the decrease in boys' activity must have something to do with girls' increasing control over the conditions of sexual intercourse.

We also speculate that girls are more likely to insist on safer sex. Dana Lear's interview study with college students at UC Berkeley found that even in that educationally elite context, it was women who responded to the threat of disease as well as pregnancy and insisted on the use of condoms, at least until the relationship generated enough trust to move toward other means of birth control. Girls' increasing ability to define sex as part of a relationship is one of the reasons for more responsible teen behavior. To the extent that boys have sexual relations with girlfriends, we would expect more condom use and less problematic outcomes of coitus.

Does this mean that the gender revolution is over, that girls are now their boyfriends' equals as sexual partners? We think not. White girls are as likely as white boys to be sexually active. But beyond that, a remnant of the sexual double standard is alive and well. In studies from London to several American college campuses to urban and rural high schools, young women still report being worried about being labeled a slut. A new definition of the word *slut*, however, has surfaced—one that demonstrates that the sexual revolution is over, even while the gender revolution has hardly been won. Girls today may be able to have sex without stigma, but only with a steady boyfriend. For girls, love justifies desire. A young woman still cannot be respected if she admits an appetite-driven sexuality. If a young woman has sexual liaisons outside of publicly acknowledged "coupledom," she is at risk of being defamed. If a girl changes boyfriends too often and too quickly, she risks being labeled a slut. This puts her one down as a power player in her relationship, because her boyfriend does not have to worry about moving on too quickly and being stigmatized for his sexual choices.

While dating relationships may continue to be somewhat inequitable, the research clearly shows that today's teenagers are sophisticated sexual actors. No evidence indicates that sex in most high schools has once again been stigmatized. In fact, survey data suggest that a variety of sexual expressions are a part of "relationships." Most boys who report coitus also report having had oral sex performed on them and having performed it themselves. Even among virgins, over one-third of the students have masturbated a member of the opposite sex to orgasm. No one really knows if oral sex is more common now or simply more openly discussed, but teens clearly often do not consider oral sex as "real" sex, nor do they understand that disease can be transmitted this way. In one study, one-third of sex educators did not even consider oral sex as real sex.

Another finding is clear. While the incidence of coitus among teenage boys under age 18 has decreased, by the end of the teen years nearly all American youth are sexually active. Nine out of ten Americans are sexually active by the time they are 20. Nearly one-half of teens who are not sexually active by age 17 have become so by their senior year or perhaps immediately after graduation. It is now the statistically atypical woman (one out of four) or man (one out of five) who is still a virgin at the end of the teen years.

Still, some changes have turned in the direction of conservatism. For example, approval of casual sex is down. It was a rare boy or girl in the 1990s who openly approved of casual sex or claimed to engage in it. But the definition of being in a relationship is a social one, and a relationship of only two weeks may count. Therefore the participants may not consider the sex that happens within it as casual sex, although it might be so defined by researchers, parents and policymakers. Young American women no longer hold any attitudes that can be interpreted as a double standard. The majority of American women college students believe that sex with affection is acceptable for women and men, and nearly none of them support the right to casual sex for

themselves or others, men or women. And yet, boys do not report being worried about being labeled as promiscuous for having too many partners or for changing partners too often. And while teenage males no longer hold any double standard for the rights of women and men to have sexual relationships with affection, they do hold a double standard in that they approve of casual sex more often for men than for women.

Teenagers are now sexual actors, if not at age 16, then by the time they are old enough to drink legally. The severing of the necessary connection between sexual activity and marriage is irrevocable. What has changed is that teens are not getting into as much trouble as they once did because of their sexual activity.

WHAT DOES IT ALL MEAN?

The sexual revolution is a fait accompli; no counterrevolution has taken place. Instead, the revolution was such an overwhelming success that it has revised the entire framework of how American society thinks about sex. Premarital, unmarried, and post-divorce sex are now seen as individual choices for both women and men. The revolutionary principle that divorced the right to sexual pleasure from marriage (at least for adults) is no longer controversial; it goes unchallenged by nearly everyone but the most conservative of religious fundamentalists. It is the gender revolution that is unfinished and still progressing. And it is this revolution still in the making that shows up as we see the evidence that girls are beginning to successfully assert their own right to sexuality and to negotiate more control in their heterosexual relationships.

Why are teens protecting themselves more from the unintended negative consequences of sexual activity? Our best guess is that it is related to the increasing power of girls in their sexual encounters. If we are correct in asserting that the decrease in boys' sexual activity at younger ages reflects girls' increasing negotiation power to restrict sex to relationships (however loosely defined), it is a consequence of more relational and less casual sex that aids more responsible sexual activity.

Despite decreases in abortions, teen pregnancy rates, and sexually transmitted diseases, scientists still write about teenage sexuality as if it is inherently a social problem. On even the most liberal sex education sites on the Internet (Planned Parenthood, the Sex Information and Education Council of the United States [SIECUS] and the Alan Guttmacher institute), discussion of teenage sexuality is couched in the somber and concerned tones of what might go wrong and what has gone wrong. Yet because of the underlying presumption of nearly all the scientific literature that teen sex is necessarily bad, it is easy to underestimate how much has already been accepted about sexuality and youth in our society. The sexual revolution has changed the very way we think about this "social problem."

Note that most public concern is focused on teens in high school, not young adults or college students. Polls show that premarital sexuality is acceptable to most Americans, at least for adults. What would have been shocking during the heyday of the sexual revolution now goes unnoticed. Not long ago, Victoria's Secret ads would have been considered soft pornography, and jokes about oral sex would not have been allowed on prime-time TV. While concern with teenage sexuality continues, the public does not seem willing to desexualize the greater culture that shapes teen experiences. Rather, there seems to be some strange cultural desire, fueled by the mass media, to distort both the scientific research and the reality of teens' lives.

Every American knows that our culture is highly sexualized. We use sex to sell products to teens as well as to adults. Yet our culture is remarkably ambivalent about teens desiring sexual pleasure. Jocelyn Elders lost her position as surgeon general of the United States because she publicly advocated that masturbation be discussed, and even promoted as "safe" sex, as a part of sex education. She suggested that such self-gratification might delay entry into too early or more risky sexual activities simply to satisfy sexual appetites. The reactions to her comments were outrage, loathing, and anger far above the general distaste for sex education itself. The prompt and widely publicized dismissal of Elders indicates that at least publicly, our society denies the legitimation of safe sexual expression to teens and may have difficulty accepting sexual feelings outside of a spiritual, relational or reproductive context. The Elders incident reflects the American ambivalence toward and queasiness about the sexuality of youth. Teenage sexuality challenges both the public and the research community because teen sex is obviously not about reproduction or long-term mating behavior in kin groups—or even about love. Teen sex makes adults admit that sex may be purely about play and pleasure. Furthermore, even though today's parents lived through the sexual revolution, many are not comfortable allowing their own children the freedom they enjoyed (although they clearly cannot hinder sexual activity very effectively).

Perhaps this is why scientific studies on teen sex are often misrepresented in the media. Recently, a study of abstinence pledges was highly publicized, often with headlines such as "Abstinence Pledges Work." Yet, the headlines were hardly accurate. Indeed, Peter Bearman and Hannah Bruckner's rigorous study suggests that abstinence pledges succeed in delaying coitus only when neither too many nor too few peers pledge, so that abstinence becomes the membership badge of a social clique. When the majority of students pledge virginity or too few teens pledge to make a reasonable peer group, the pledges are ineffective. Abstinence pledges are headlined as "working" when in fact they may postpone intercourse only for 14- and 15-year-olds within an identifiable clique, and then for a total of 18 months. And when such pledges do work, they come with an unwelcome side effect: the pledgers are less likely to use condoms when their sexual activity does begin. Many in our culture are so desperate to justify the money put into abstinence programs that there is little desire to look at the downside of such programs.

The dialogue on teenage sexuality could be more useful if writers and researchers openly addressed their value presumptions about whether adolescent sexuality is developmentally appropriate or inherently pathological. Presently, the usually unstated assumption is that teenage sex is inherently a social problem. We do not believe the data support such a conclusion. Sexual exploration may in fact be part of the developmental journey of adolescence.

Whichever values one holds—that teen sex is either pathological or natural—American society cannot afford to continue to define teen sexuality as necessarily problematic. Both younger and older people no longer tie sexuality to long-term personal or institutional commitments. Teens and adults have sex before, during, and after marriage with a variety of partners over their life course. A policy that denies this reality cannot provide adequate medical and social education that promotes responsibility and safety. For most people, a sexual life begins during adolescence and is likely to include all kinds of sexual behaviors, including coitus, before people reach the legal age for drinking alcohol.

The sexual revolution has changed us. It redefined sexual activity as a right of individuals and not merely as a means for reproduction or even marital intimacy. This new view of sex is no longer a revolutionary ideal or even a liberal notion but has become a mainstream American value. Teenagers are simply living in the same culture as the rest of us. The sexual revolution is social history, the gender revolution continues, and teenagers struggle to create new norms that work for them in the 21st century.

RECOMMENDED RESOURCES

Alan Guttmacher Institute. Occasional Report. "Why Is Teenage Pregnancy Declining? The Roles of Abstinence, Sexual Activity, and Contraceptive Use." 1996. Online. www.agi.org.

Bearman, Peter S., and Hannah Bruckner. "Promising the Future: Virginity Pledges and First Intercourse." *American Journal of Sociology* 106, 4 (2001): 859–912.

Christopher, F. Scott, and Susan Sprecher. "Sexuality in Marriage, Dating, and Other Relationships: A Decade Review." *Journal of Marriage and the Family* 62 (2000): 999–1017.

Gates, G. J., and F. L. Sonenstein. "Heterosexual Genital Sexual Activity among Adolescent Males: 1988 and 1995." *Family Planning Perspectives* 32, 6 (2000): 295–97, 304.

Kaiser Family Foundation. Fact Sheet. "Sexually Transmitted Diseases in the United States." February 2000. Online. www.kff.org/content/archive/1447/std_fs.html.

Kaiser Family Foundation. Press Release. "New KFF/YM Magazine National Survey of Teens on Dating, Intimacy, and Sexual Experiences." May 1998. Online. www.kff.org/content/archive/1373/datingrel.html.

Kirby, Douglas. "No Easy Answers: Research Findings on Programs to Reduce Teen Pregnancy." March 1997. Washington, D.C.: National Campaign to Prevent Teen Pregnancy. Online. www.teenpregnancy.org/fmnoeasy.html.

Lear, Dana. *Sex and Sexuality: Risk and Relationships in the Age of AIDS*. Thousand Oaks, Calif.: Sage Publications, 1997.

Martin, Karin A. *Puberty, Sexuality, and the Self: Girls and Boys at Adolescence*. New York: Routledge, 1996.

Santelli, John, Laura Duberstein Lindberg, Joyce Abma, Clea Sucoff McNeely, and Michael Resnick. "Adolescent Sexual Behavior: Estimates and Trends from Four Nationally Representative Surveys." *Family Planning Perspectives* 32, 4 (2000): 156–65.

Thompson, Sharon. *Going All the Way: Teenage Girls' Tales of Sex, Romance, and Pregnancy*. New York: Hill and Wang, 1995.

Tolman, Deborah. "Doing Desire: Adolescent Girls' Struggles for/with Sexuality." *Gender & Society* 8, 3 (1994): 324–42.

READING *30*   **Patricia Hill Collins**

Black Sexual Politics

2001: The career of Jennifer Lopez skyrockets. A Puerto Rican woman, Lopez's rise to fame came after her feature film appearance as Selena, the first Chicana superstar. News of J-Lo is everywhere; especially her much discussed love relationship and subsequent break-up with hip-hop artist Puff Daddy (aka P Diddy). One special feature of Lopez's routinely makes the news—her seemingly large bottom. From late night American talk shows to South African radio programs to Internet websites, J-Lo's butt is all the rage. Recognizing its value, it is rumored that Lopez insures her buttocks for 1 billion dollars, as one website mischievously described it, 500 million dollars per cheek.

2000: The photo insert for *Survivor*, Destiny's Child third CD, shows the three African American women standing legs akimbo, holding hands, and dressed in animal skin bikinis. Selling over 15 million albums and singles worldwide, *Survivor's* success reflects a savvy marketing strategy that promoted the song "Independent Woman" as part of the soundtrack for the hit movie *Charlie's Angels* and foreshadowed the success of group member Beyoncé Knowles. *Survivor's* message of female power also fuels its popularity. Counseling women to be resilient and financially independent, Destiny's Child proclaim, "I'm a survivor, I'm gonna make it." *Survivor* suggests sexual independence as well. In their highly popular song "Bootylicious," written by Beyoncé, they refer to their butts as "jelly" and ask, "Can you handle it?" The term *bootylicious* proves to be so popular that, along with *hottie* and *roadrage*, it is added to the 2002 edition of *Merriam-Webster's Collegiate Dictionary*.

1925: Born in a poor community in East St. Louis, Missouri, African American entertainer Josephine Baker moves to Paris. She becomes a sensation in the American production of *La Revue Nègre*. Performing bare-breasted in a jungle setting and clad only in a short skirt of banana leaves, Ms. Baker's rump-shaking banana dance becomes an instant hit with Parisian audiences. When asked whether she will return to the United States, Ms. Baker replies, "they would make me sing mammy songs and I cannot feel mammy songs, so I cannot sing them." Instead, in 1937 Ms. Baker becomes a French citizen and garners lifelong accolades as the "Black Venus" of France. Upon her death in 1975, she receives a twenty-one-gun salute, the only such honor given by France to an American-born woman.[1]

1816: After several years of being exhibited in Paris and London as the "Hottentot Venus," Sarah Baartman, a Khoi woman from what is now South Africa, dies. In the London exhibit, she is displayed caged, rocking back and forth to emphasize her supposedly wild and dangerous nature. She wears a tight-fitting dress whose brown color matches her skin tones. When ordered to do so, she leaves her cage and parades before the audience who seems fascinated with what they see as her most intriguing feature—her buttocks. Some in the audience are not content to merely look. One eyewitness recounts with horror how Baartman endures poking and prodding, as people try to ascertain for themselves whether her buttocks are real. In the context of popular London shows that display as forms of entertainment talking pigs, animal monsters and human oddities such as the Fattest Man on Earth, midgets, giants, and similar "freaks of nature," these reactions to Baartman's exhibition are not unusual. Upon Sarah Baartman's death, George Cuvier, one of the fathers of modern biology, claims her body in the interests of science. Her subsequent dissection becomes one of at least seven others completed on the bodies of women of color from 1814 to 1870. Their goal—to advance the field of classical comparative anatomy.[2]

Contemporary sexual politics in the United States present African American women and men with a complicated problem. From the display of Sarah Baartman as a sexual "freak" of nature in the early nineteenth century to Josephine Baker dancing bare-breasted for Parisian society to the animal-skin bikinis worn by "bootylicious" Destiny's Child to the fascination with Jennifer Lopez's buttocks, women of African

descent have been associated with an animalistic, "wild" sexuality. Expressed via an ever-changing yet distinctive constellation of sexual stereotypes in which Sarah Baartman's past frames J-Lo's present, this association of sexuality with Black women helps create ideas about racial difference. Black men have their own variety of racial difference, also constructed from ideas about violence and dangerous sexuality. African American heavyweight boxer Jack Johnson certainly sparked controversy when, in 1910, he fought the formerly unbeaten White champion Jim Jeffries. During the fight itself, over 30,000 men stood outside the *New York Times'* offices, waiting to hear the outcome. Johnson's bloody victory sparked race riots in every Southern state. Johnson's predilection for White women only fueled the fires of White reaction. When authorities discovered that Johnson was having an affair with an eighteen-year-old blonde from Minnesota, they charged him under the Mann Act with engaging in white slavery. Johnson's ability to wield violence and his seeming attractiveness to White women made him threatening to White middle-class men.[3] For both women and men, Western social thought associates Blackness with an imagined uncivilized, wild sexuality and uses this association as one lynchpin of racial difference. Whether depicted as "freaks" of nature or as being the essence of nature itself, savage, untamed sexuality characterizes Western representations of women and men of African descent.[4]

For their respective audiences, the distinctive sexualized spectacles performed by Baartman, Baker, Destiny's Child, and Lopez invoke sexual meanings that give shape to racism, sexism, class exploitation, and heterosexism. Each spectacle marks the contradictions of Western perceptions of African bodies and of Black women's agency concerning the use of their bodies. Together they frame an invented discourse of *Black sexuality*.[5] For French and British audiences, Sarah Baartman served as a sign of racial difference used to justify the growing belief in the superiority of White civilization and the inferiority of so-called primitive peoples necessary for colonialism. Her treatment helped create modern Black sexual stereotypes of the jezebel, the mammy, and the welfare queen that, in the United States, helped uphold slavery, Jim Crow segregation, and racial ghettoization.[6] Illustrating through stark historical example how common sense understandings of race and gender flow smoothly into those of biology, medicine, and Western science itself, her body marked the intersection of entertainment, science, and commerce. Sarah Baartman could be enjoyed while alive and, upon her death, studied under the microscope for the burgeoning field of comparative anatomy. As South African writer Yvette Abrahams and filmmaker Zola Maseko's video recording on the life of Baartman point out, we know little about Baartman's agency in this arrangement.[7] What Baartman lost by being displayed as a "freak" is far clearer to us through our modern sensibilities than what she might have gained for herself and her family.

Baartman may not have been aware of the power of the sexual stereotypes that were created in her image, but women of African descent who followed most certainly were.[8] Black women struggled to exercise agency and self-definition concerning these images and the social practices that they defended. Evidently aware of the sexual stereotypes applied to women of African descent, Josephine Baker played the part of the "primitive," but for her own reasons.[9] Baker entertained the French with her openness about her body, an important example of how an imagined, uncivilized, wild sexuality remained associated with Blackness within Western social thought and continued as a sign of racial difference. But was Baker really sexually liberated, or was her performance a carefully planned illusion that, in the African American trickster tradition, was designed to titillate and manipulate the tastes of her European audiences? Baker's biography suggests a level of sophistication that enabled her to move far beyond her initial depiction as a bare-breasted "primitive." Baker may have initially done banana dances, but from her point of view, she escaped performing the ubiquitous "mammy songs" assigned to Hattie McDaniel, Ethel Waters, and other talented African American women then performing in the United States. In France, Baker ensured that she was well compensated for her performances.

The work of contemporary artists such as Destiny's Child also invokes the contradictions of sexualized spectacle and Black women's agency or self-determination. Transported from the immediacy of live stage performances, Destiny's Child perform in the intimate yet anonymous terrain of CDs, music videos, movies, Internet websites, and other forms of contemporary mass media. Here each consumer of "Independent Woman" or "Bootylicious" can imagine a one-on-one relationship with one, two, or all three members of Destiny's Child, whose images and artistry are purchased, rented, or downloaded under the control of the consumer. Under conditions of racial segregation, mass media provides a way that racial difference can safely enter racially segregated private spaces of living rooms and bedrooms. Destiny's Child may not be like the girls next door, but they can be seen on home theater and heard via headphones within the privacy of individual consciousness. In this new mass media context, Black sexual stereotypes are rendered virtually invisible by their ubiquity; yet, they persist through a disconnected mélange of animal skins, sexually explicit lyrics, breast worship, and focus on the booty. Destiny's Child may entertain and titillate; yet, their self-definitions as "survivors" and "independent women" express female power and celebration of the body and booty. The women in Destiny's Child are also wealthy. Just who is being "controlled" in these new arenas? For what purpose? Their message contains a defiance denied to Bartmann and Baker—"It's my body, it's my booty, and I'll do what I want with it—can you handle it?"

What are we to make of Jennifer Lopez? As a Latina,[10] where does she fit in this story of Western constructions of "wild" Black sexuality, the social construction of racial difference, and Black people's reactions to them? Like Josephine Baker before her, Jennifer Lopez is celebrated and makes a considerable amount of money. Elevating Jennifer Lopez's buttocks to icon status invokes historical meanings of Black female sexuality and takes the politics of race and sexuality to an entirely new plane. In this case, a Latina brushed with the hint of Blackness and not clearly of African descent carries the visible sign of Black sexuality. In order to be marketed, Black sexuality need not be associated solely with bodies that have been racially classified as "Negro," "mulatto," or "Black." Western imaginations have long filled in the color, moving women from Black to White and back again depending on the needs of the situation. In antebellum Charleston, South Carolina, and New Orleans, Louisiana, White men desired quadroons and octoroons as prostitutes because such women looked like White women, but they were actually Black women, with all that that implied about women's sexuality.[11] J-Lo's fluid ethnicity in her films, from the Chicana in *Selena* to the racial/ethnic ambiguity in subsequent roles, illustrates the shifting contours of racial/ethnic classification. When it comes to "hot-blooded" Latinas, one might ask which part of their "blood" carries the spice of sexual looseness?[12] This all seems to be a far cry from the commodification of Sarah Baartman's—buttocks—or is it?

The fact that these examples involve women of actual or imputed African descent is no accident because the racial difference assigned to Black people has often come in gender specific forms. In the nineteenth century, women stood as symbols of race and women from different races became associated with differentially valued expressions of sexuality. During this period marked by the rise of European nationalism, England, France, Spain, Portugal, Germany, the Netherlands, and Italy all jockeyed with varying degrees of success to define themselves as nation-states. Each followed its own distinctive path in constructing its own national identity and that of its colonies. Yet they shared one overriding feature—the treatment of women within each respective nation-state as well as within the colonies were important to national identity.[13] Ideas of pure White womanhood that were created to defend women of the homeland required a corresponding set of ideas about hot-blooded Latinas, exotic Suzy Wongs, wanton jezebels, and stoic native squaws. Civilized nation-states required uncivilized and backward colonies for their national identity to have meaning, and the status of women in both places was central to this entire endeavor. In this context, Black women became icons of hypersexuality.[14]

Men of African descent were also seen as hypersexual beings that have generated similar icons.[15] During the era of live entertainment, and until the onset of the technologies that made mass media possible, men were objectified differently from women. The West African slave trade and Southern auction blocks treated both Black women's and men's bodies as objects for sale, yet women participated in sexual spectacles to a greater degree than did men, because Western ideas about women and femininity itself have long been more tightly wedded to ideas about women's physical beauty and sexual attractiveness. Even today, men are far more likely to stare at and comment upon women's breasts, buttocks, legs, face, and other body parts than are women to subject men's bodies to this type of scrutiny. Like all women, Black women were objects to be seen, enjoyed, purchased, and used, primarily by White men with money. African women's sexuality may have piqued the prurient interest of Western audiences, but African men's sexuality was seen as dangerous and in need of control. Live expressions of Black male sexuality needed to be hidden from White spectators, especially audiences that might contain White women. Until recently, the very tenets of female respectability made it impossible for a female audience to cheer on a live male sex show, especially a White female audience viewing Black men as sexual beings. Assumptions of

heterosexuality also inhibit males viewing other males as sexual objects. A situation in which White men view Black male bodies as sexual objects potentially creates a homoerotic space that is incompatible with ideas of straight White masculinity.

Mass media technologies profoundly altered this reliance on face-to-face spectatorship and live entertainment. Television, video, DVD, and the Internet enabled images of Black women and men to enter living rooms, bedrooms, family rooms, and other private domestic spaces. Black male images could now enter private White spaces, one step safely removed because these were no longer live performances and Black men no longer appeared in the flesh. These technological advances enabled the reworking of Black male sexuality that became much more visible, yet was safely contained. Take, for example, the stylized music video performances of hip-hop artists. Camera angles routinely are shot from a lower position than the rapper in question, giving the impression that he is looming over the viewer. In real life, being this close to young African American men who were singing about sex and violence and whose body language included fists, angry gestures, and occasional crotch-grabbing might be anxiety provoking for the typical rap and hip-hop consumer (most are suburban White adolescents). Yet viewing these behaviors safely packaged within a music video protects consumers from any possible contact with Black men who are actually in the videos. Just who are these videos for? What are the imagined race, gender, and sexual orientations of the viewers? Black men have long given performances that placed sexuality center stage—Elvis Presley, Mick Jagger, and rapper Eminem all recognized and profited from this reality—but the sexual implications of viewing Black men in the flesh rarely made it out of African American settings where such performances had a different meaning. It is one thing to visit a Black nightclub to hear singer Millie Jackson's live performance of raunchy blues or gather in a neighbor's living room to listen to Redd Foxx records. It is entirely another to sit in an interracial audience and listen to comedian Eddie Murphy's uncensored boasting concerning Black male sexual prowess; or to count the times within a music video that the camera hones in on rapper Ja Rule's crotch.

Western perceptions of the sexuality of men of African descent also became central to the national identities of European nation-states engaged in colonial projects. England, France, and other colonial powers constructed their national identities by manipulating ideas about men in the home country and in their colonies. The United States followed a similar path, with ideas about race and masculinity intertwined with ideas about American citizenship.[16] Like their female counterparts, men of African descent were also perceived to have excess sexual appetite, yet with a disturbing additional feature, a predilection for violence. In this context, the "White heroes" of Western Europe and the United States became constructed in relation to the "Black beasts" of Africa.[17] Moreover, both were used to signal the hierarchical relationship between colonizers and colonies. Overall, colonialism, slavery, and racial segregation relied upon this discourse of Black sexuality to create tightly bundled ideas about Black femininity and Black masculinity that in turn influenced racial ideologies and racial practices.

As these systems of racial rule recede in the post–civil rights era, what if anything is taking their place? Over one hundred years ago, African American intellectual William E. B. DuBois predicted that the problem of the twentieth century would be the presence of the color line. By that, DuBois meant that the policies of colonialism and racial segregation were designed to create, separate, and rank the various "races" of man. Until legally outlawed in the 1950s and 1960s, the color line policies of Jim Crow racial segregation kept the vast majority of African Americans from quality educations, good jobs, adequate health care, and the best neighborhoods. In contrast, the problem of the twenty-first century seems to be the seeming *absence* of a color line. Formal legal discrimination has been outlawed, yet contemporary social practices produce virtually identical racial hierarchies as those observed by DuBois. By whatever measures used in the United States or on a global scale, people of African descent remain disproportionately clustered at the bottom of the social hierarchy. The effects of these historical exclusions persist today under a new racism.[18]

It is important to note that the new racism of the early twenty-first century has not replaced prior forms of racial rule, but instead incorporates elements of past racial formations. As a result, ideas about race, gender, sexuality, and Black people as well as the social practices that these ideas shape and reflect remain intricately part of the new racism, but in changed ways. The new racism thus reflects a situation of permanence and change. Just as people of African descent were disadvantaged within prior forms of economic organization, a similar outcome exists today. On a global

scale, wealth and poverty continue to be racialized. This is permanence. At the same time, racial hierarchy is produced in a context of massive economic, political, and social change that organizes racial hierarchy differently. The processes used to maintain the same outcome are also different. In a similar fashion, ideas about sexuality and gender that were very much a part of prior forms of racial rule remain as important today. They too are differently organized to produce remarkably similar results.

First, new forms of global capitalism frame the new racism. Globalization itself is certainly not new—it was a core characteristic of former patterns of racism. The African slave trade had a global reach and its legacy created the contemporary African Diaspora. The colonial wealth of Europe was based on a global system of racial subordination of people of color. Yet the increasing concentration of capital in the hands of fewer and fewer corporations distinguishes the contemporary global capitalism from its nineteenth-century counterpart. Today, relatively few transnational corporations are driving the world economy and their decisions affect the global distribution of wealth and poverty. These new forms of global organization have polarized world populations. On one end are elites who are wealthy beyond the imagination, and who have the freedom to come and go as they please, wherever and whenever they want. The locals, the people who are stuck in one place, without jobs, and for whom time seems to creep by, populate the other end.[19]

People of African descent are routinely disadvantaged in this global economy in which corporations make the decisions and in which "the company is free to move; but the consequences of the move are bound to stay."[20] Within a global context, Black people and other people of color are those more likely to lose jobs in local labor markets. They are the ones who lack control over oil, mineral wealth, or other natural resources on their land; who lose their land to global agribusiness; and who are denied basic services of electricity and clean water, let alone the luxury goods of the new information age. The benefits of telecommunications and other new technologies have had a far greater impact on Whites than on people of African descent and other people of color. For example, though Europe and North America constitute 20 percent of the world's population, two-thirds of all televisions and radios are owned and controlled in these two regions.[21]

The new racism is also characterized by a changing political structure that disenfranchises people, even if they appear to be included. In the United States, for example, people may vote, but corporations and other propertied entities wield tremendous influence in deciding the outcome of elections because they fund campaigns. All levels of government have been affected by a growing concentration of economic power that has fostered corporate influence over public policy. This same process operates in a transnational context. Global corporations increasingly dominate national, regional, and local governance. This concentrated economic power erodes the authority of national governments and has created unprecedented migrations of people and jobs both within and between nation-states. The ineffectiveness of transnational governance and domestic policies of racial desegregation in reducing Black poverty suggests an important link joining the experiences of people of African descent with postcolonial governance and the experiences of African Americans in the United States with racial desegregation. The outcome is reconfigured social hierarchies of race, class, gender, and sexuality, with people of African descent clumped at the bottom. Patterns of desegregation and subsequent resegregation of African Americans in the United States resemble the decolonization and recolonization that characterizes the global context.[22]

The new racism also relies more heavily on mass media to reproduce and disseminate the ideologies needed to justify racism. There are two themes here—the substance of racial ideologies under the new racism and the forms in which ideologies are created, circulated, and resisted. Ideas about Black sexuality certainly appear in contemporary racial ideologies. But the growing significance of Black popular culture and mass media as sites for creating and resisting racial ideologies is also striking. The films, music, magazines, music videos, and television shows of global entertainment, advertising, and news industries that produce superstars like Jennifer Lopez help manufacture the consent that makes the new racism appear to be natural, normal, and inevitable.[23]

The challenges of the new racism have been especially pronounced for African American women and men, the subjects of this book. The issues associated with the politics of the new racism and with the manipulation of ideologies within them, in the case of African Americans, the discourse on Black sexuality, affect everyone. But the specific form that race and gender politics take for African Americans can serve as an important site for examining these larger issues. Moreover, the African American community contains a crucial subpopulation in these debates. A generation of young African American men and women who were born after the struggles for civil rights, Black power, and African nation-state independence has come of age under this new racism. Referred to as the hip-hop generation, this group has encountered, reproduced, and resisted new forms of racism that continue to rely on ideas about Black sexuality. Expecting a democratic, fair society with equal economic opportunities, instead, this group faced disappearing jobs, crumbling schools, drugs, crime, and the weakening of African American community institutions. The contradictions of the post–civil rights era affect all African Americans, yet they have been especially pronounced for Black youth.[24]

AMERICA—A SEXUALLY REPRESSIVE SOCIETY?

Sexualized Black bodies seem to be everywhere in contemporary mass media, yet within African American communities, a comprehensive understanding of sexual politics remains elusive. In a social context that routinely depicts men and women of African descent as the embodiment of deviant sexuality, African American politics has remained curiously silent on issues of gender and sexuality. As a result, African Americans lack a vibrant, public discussion of the complex issues that the prevailing discourse on Black sexuality has raised for African American men and women. In more candid moments, however, some African American thinkers stress how damaging the absence of a self-defined Black sexual politics can be. As African American cultural critic Cheryl Clarke pointed out over twenty years ago:

> Like all Americans, black Americans live in a sexually repressive culture. And we have made all manner of compromise regarding our sexuality in order to live here. We have expended much energy trying to debunk the racist mythology which says our sexuality is depraved. Unfortunately, many of us have overcompensated and assimilated the Puritan value that sex is for procreation, occurs only between men and women, and is only valid within the confines of heterosexual marriage. . . . Like everyone else in America who is ambivalent in these respects, black folk have to live with the contradictions of this limited sexual system by repressing or closeting any other sexual/erotic urges, feelings, or desires.[25]

Given the saturation of American mass media with sexual themes, and the visibility of sexualized spectacles that include men and women of African descent within movies, music videos, and popular music in particular, Clarke's comments may seem to be odd. How can American culture be "sexually repressive" when sexuality seems to be everywhere? White actresses routinely play roles that include graphic sex scenes. Moreover, Black women are not downtrodden rape victims, but instead, also seem to be in control of their own sexuality. Director Spike Lee's African American leading lady Nola Darling seemed to be calling the shots in *She's Gotta Have It,* Lee's groundbreaking film about Black female sexuality. Destiny's Child and J-Lo certainly do not seem "repressed." How can African Americans be sexually "closeted" when Black sexuality itself serves as an icon for sexual freedom?

For African Americans, these questions are crucial, especially in the context of the post-civil rights era in which Black popular culture and mass media are increasingly important for racial rule. Sexual regulation occurs through repression, both by eliminating sexual alternatives and by shaping the public debates that do exist. In order to prosper, systems of oppression must regulate sexuality, and they often do so by manufacturing ideologies that render some ideas commonsensical while obscuring others. The expanding scope of mass media makes this process more visible and, more important, in the United States, does seem to have produced a "sexually repressive culture."

The treatment of human sexuality in American society reflects a curious combination of censorship and excessive visibility (e.g., hypervisibility), of embarrassed silences and talk-show babble. On the one hand, since colonial times, selected groups within U.S. society have striven to suppress a wide range of sexual ideas and practices.[26] American colonists paid close attention to the sexual behavior of individuals, not to eliminate sexual expression but to channel it into what they thought was its proper setting and purpose, namely, as a "duty and a joy within marriage, and for purposes of procreation."[27] More recently, the election of conservative Republican Ronald Reagan in 1980 emboldened the Christian Right to advance a fundamentalist family values discourse. Resembling the colonial discourse from the 1600s, the contemporary family values position argues (1) all sexual practices should occur only within the confines of heterosexual marriage; (2) the fundamental purpose of sexuality is procreation; and (3) children should be protected from

all sexual information with the exception of abstinence as the preferred form of birth control before marriage.

This historical and contemporary agenda that has suppressed and often censored a range of ideas concerning human sexuality has made it difficult to have open, candid, and fact-based public debates. This censorship not only affects public dialogues but it also influences research on human sexuality.[28] Heterosexism, with its ideas about what constitutes normal and deviant sexuality holds sway to the point where significant gaps exist in the social science literature on human sexuality. Despite the conservative thrust since 1980, the suppression of a range of ideas about human sexuality is not new. Research done in the 1950s by Alfred Kinsey and his colleagues at Indiana University provides a textbook case of sexual censorship. Kinsey's work treated all sexual practices, including homosexuality and bisexuality, as inherently "normal" and defined the array of sexual practices reported by study participants as benign indicators of human difference. But Kinsey's work virtually ground to a halt when funding for this line of scientific research dried up.

It has taken the field some time to recover from this censorship. In essence, heterosexism and its accompanying assumptions of heterosexuality operate as a hegemonic or taken-for-granted ideology that has influenced research on human sexuality. Societal norms that install heterosexuality as the only way to be normal still hold sway.[29] For example, the term *sexuality* itself is used so synonymously with *hetero*sexuality that schools, churches, and other social institutions treat heterosexuality as natural, normal, and inevitable. Studying sexual practices that stray too far from prevailing norms, for example, sex outside of marriage, adolescent sexuality, homosexuality, and formerly taboo sexual practices such as anal and oral sex, become situated within a social problems framework. This approach not only stigmatizes individuals and groups who engage in alternative sexual practices but it also reinforces views of human sexuality itself as being a problem that should not be discussed in public. Alternately, research on human sexuality is often annexed to bona fide social problems, for example, adolescent pregnancy and people living with HIV/AIDS. Sexuality seems to be everywhere, but research that investigates variations in human sexuality outside of a social problems framework has only recently come to the forefront.

The treatment of sex education in American public schools illustrates how a sexually repressive culture strives to render human sexuality invisible. Sex education remains a hot topic, with students receiving spotty information at best. Topics that are important to adolescents have been difficult to include within sex education programs. Despite high student interest and a growing recognition that comprehensive sex education might save lives, programs tend to shy away from discussing sexuality before marriage, the use of contraception, homosexuality, and other controversial topics. Ironically, the checkered pattern of research on human sexuality offers a good case for how heterosexism operates as a system of power that negatively affects straight and lesbian, gay, bisexual, and transgendered (LGBT) students alike. Because adolescents of all sexual orientations are in the process of forming sexual identities, they are especially affected by heterosexism. For example, despite a high adolescent pregnancy rate, worrisome increases in the rate of HIV infection among American adolescents, and emerging research demonstrating that high school students grappling with LGBT identities are more prone to depression and suicide, the reluctance to talk openly about human sexuality within U.S. schools places students at risk. Similarly, a special report on adolescent sexuality points to the difficulties of collecting data on adolescent conceptions of abstinence.[30] Anecdotal reports suggest that many adolescents who engage in oral sex think that they are practicing abstinence because they are refraining from genital sexual intercourse. These practices may protect them from pregnancy, but they also expose adolescents to risks of sexually transmitted diseases, including HIV.[31]

Despite these repressive practices, on the other hand, sexual ideas and images within contemporary U.S. society enjoy a visibility that would have been unheard of in Kinsey's 1950s America. Recognizing that sex sells, corporations increasingly use it to sell cars, toothpaste, beer, and other consumer goods. This media saturation has made sexual spectacles highly visible within American popular culture. Soap operas, prime time television, billboards, music videos, movies, and the Internet all contain explicit sexual material. Making sex highly visible in marketplace commodity relations becomes important to maintaining profitability within the U.S. capitalist political economy. The goal is neither to stimulate debate nor to educate, but to sell products.

In the absence of other forums, talk shows on network television provide one important public medium for gaining sexual information. Unfortunately, such shows foster the commodification of sexuality. Stressing sexually explicit conversations that titillate rather than instruct, talk shows illustrate how marketplace relations profit from sexual spectacles. By the early 2000s, this market had segmented into a variety of shows, each carving out its specific identity, often based on distinctive norms regarding race, class, gender, and sexuality.[32] For example, The *Montel Williams Show* routinely trumpets the benefits of the heterosexual family, primarily by extolling the role of fathers in their children's lives. By itself, this message is fairly innocuous. However, the show's format creates sexual spectacles that function as modern-day morality plays about race, gender, and sexuality. Mr. Williams, an African American, routinely conducts paternity tests for women who are not "sure" who fathered their babies. The potential fathers are invited to hear the results of the paternity test on the air, with a stern talk by Mr. Williams concerning their "responsibility" to those branded as fathers by DNA evidence. This family drama is played out repeatedly, with Mr. Williams readying himself to deliver the message to wayward young men—if you take it out of your pants, you need to take care of your babies. Moreover, as an African American man married to a White woman, on his show Mr. Williams repeatedly brings on working-class, interracial couples in which young White mothers try to get their sexually irresponsible Black boyfriends to claim paternity. If this weren't enough, Mr. Williams also devotes shows to the pain experienced by biracial children in search of their wayward parents.

The *Maury Povich Show* also trades in this racial family drama, but with more emphasis on race and sexuality. Not only does Mr. Povich, a White American, present shows in which White women seek paternity tests for their Black male partners, Mr. Povich presents Black women and Black men in an especially stark light. One show, for example, featured a Black woman who brought on nine Black men as candidates for her six-month-old daughter's "baby daddy."[33] All nine failed the paternity test. After the revelation, with cameras rolling in search of the all-important "money shot,"[34] Mr. Povich followed the distraught young mother backstage, and volunteered to keep working with her until she had tracked down the Black deadbeat dad. Like Mr. Williams, Mr. Povich delivers a message about responsibility to the DNA-branded fathers. Via the choice of topic, and showing the African American woman whose sexuality was so out of control that she had no idea who had fathered her child, Mr. Povich panders to longstanding societal beliefs about Black sexuality.

The crying and raw emotion solicited on Mr. Williams's and Mr. Povich's shows pales in comparison to the staged sexual spectacles of *The Jerry Springer Show*. Reminiscent of the London freak shows of Sarah Bartmann's time, Mr. Springer's shows routinely combine sexuality and violence, two sure-fire audience builders. Here participants are invited to come on the air and reveal "secrets" to seemingly unsuspecting spouses, lovers, and friends. The "secrets" routinely involve cheating, lying, and false paternity. By his choice of guests, Mr. Springer's show also takes sexual spectacles to an entirely new level. Morbidly obese women parade across the stage in bikinis, verbally taunting the audience to comment on their appearance. In a context in which women's bodies are routinely sexualized, displaying seemingly hideous female bodies is designed to shock and solicit ridicule. These confessional talk shows also routinely conduct paternity tests, show pictures of babies who lack legal fathers, discuss sexual infidelity, and display audience members in sexually explicit clothing (or lack thereof). For many Americans, these shows substitute for public discussions of sexuality because few other outlets are available.

African Americans are well represented in the public spectacles provided by Mr. Williams's, Mr. Povich's, and Mr. Springer's talk shows. Guests on all three programs are clearly working-class, with many of them Black and Latino. These shows are not just about sexuality; they also signal clear messages about race and class. They depict the challenges of explaining a new, interracial class structure that can no longer rely on biological notions of race to differentiate poor people (assumed to be Black) from middle-class people (assumed to be White). In the new multicultural America, Blacks can be middle class (the hugely popular *Cosby Show* broke that barrier in the 1980s) and, in fact, a certain degree of Black middle-class visibility is needed to buttress arguments of equal opportunity (Oprah Winfrey and Montel Williams both exemplify this need for visible, accomplished Blacks). But how does one explain the persistence of poverty among *White* Americans if poverty has long been attributed to Black biological inferiority? They are not biologically Black, but their poverty and downward mobility can be explained if they are seen as being culturally or socially Black. Whites who embrace Black culture become positioned closer to Blacks and become stigmatized. In the context of the new racism, cultural explanations for economic success and poverty substitute for biological arguments concerning intelligence or genetic dispositions for immorality or violence.

Viewing stories about historically taboo interracial sexuality between White women and Black men becomes the new sexual spectacle, where working-class White women become "darkened" by their sexual relationships with irresponsible working-class Black men.[35] When accused of paternity by these "trashy" White women, Black men are depicted as proud of their irresponsible sexual behavior. Certainly White men are given paternity tests on these shows, but typically these are working-class or poor White men who are hauled in by working-class White mothers of their alleged children. In contrast to the White women who point the finger of paternity at both Black and White men, Black women rarely identify White men as the potential fathers of their babies. Given the history of interracial, institutionalized rape of Black women by White men, White fathers of Black children would hardly be newsworthy. Instead, Black women are presented as being so reckless that they do not know who fathered their children or, sharing a common fate with their White sisters, they point the finger at irresponsible Black men. Despite similarities that link all three shows, they do offer different scripts for solving the problems of these sexual spectacles. Part of the appeal of *The Montel Williams Show* lies in his role in this family drama—Williams plays the part of the caring yet stern Black patriarch who provides the fatherly discipline that so many of his guests seemingly lack. In contrast, Mr. Povich presents himself as a kindly White father, showing concern for his emotional albeit abnormal guests. Mr. Springer is merely a ringmaster—he doesn't get near his guests, preferring instead to watch the cursing and chair throwing from a safe distance. Discipline them, listen to them, or dismiss them—all three solutions apply to working-class and poor guests. Apparently, middle-class Americans (even Black ones) have little difficulty identifying which sexual partner conceived their children. Affluent, thirty-something White women awaiting the results of paternity tests for their biracial babies just do not appear on any of these shows.

Much more is at stake here than the accuracy of the depictions of African American women and men within talk shows and other forms of mass media. African Americans and Black culture are highly visible within the American movies, music, sports, dance, and fashion that help shape contemporary ideologies of race, gender, sexuality, and class in a global context. Sexual spectacles travel, and they matter. Historical context disappears, leaving seemingly free-floating images in its wake that become the new vocabulary that joins quite disparate entities. Terms such as "primitive," "backward," "jungle," "wild," and "freak" uncritically cycle through contemporary global culture, leaving undisturbed the pejorative historical meanings associated with this vocabulary. But history hides in the shadows of these terms, because these concepts are incomprehensible without a social context to give them meaning. For example, the pervasive use of animal imagery persists within some expressions of contemporary Black popular culture, as suggested by the decision to clothe Destiny's Child in animal-skin bikinis on their album cover. These depictions eerily resemble past practices of associating Africans with animals, particularly apes, monkeys, and chimpanzees. The choice of animal may change—no longer apes, Black men have taken on new identities as "dogs" energetically engaged in chasing the (kitty) "cat"—but associating Black men and women with lusty, animal sexual practices apparently has not. Although different meanings may be associated with animal imagery, Snoop Doggy Dog, Little Bow Wow, and the classic phrase "you my main dog" all invoke this same universe of animal imagery. Moreover, representations of Black men as "dogs" who have replaced the cool "cats" of prior eras of African American jazzmen, as well as the video "hos" who populate rap music videos suggest the emergence of an increasingly sophisticated gender-specific expression of ideas about Blackness sold in the global marketplace. Josephine Baker's banana dance and Destiny's Child's "bootylicious" would be meaningless without this history, even if those enjoying the images do not consciously see the connections.

African American theorist Cornel West identifies the paradox of a sexually repressive culture that, on the one hand, seems saturated with sexuality, but that, on the other hand, suppresses education and open dialogue concerning human sexuality. To West, race matters: "the paradox of the sexual politics of race in America is that, behind closed doors, the dirty, disgusting, and funky sex associated with Black people is often perceived to be more intriguing and interesting, while in public spaces talk about Black sexuality is virtually taboo."[36] Black sexuality is routinely invoked within American society, namely, the alleged sexual prowess of the Black men accused of fathering babies with White women, but analyzing it is discouraged. The result is a society fraught with contradictions. For example, well-off White teenagers can drive expensive cars to racially segregated high schools and college campuses that admit only a few handpicked African Americans, all the while booming the latest sexually explicit lyrics of their favorite Black hip-hop artist. American viewers can sit in their living rooms viewing talk shows that censure the African American man accused of fathering three out-of-wedlock children with two different White women, yet still be intrigued by his sexual prowess. Legions of young American men can wonder what it would be like to get Beyoncé Knowles from Destiny's Child or Jennifer Lopez in bed.

Like other Americans, African Americans must make sense of this curious sexual climate that accompanies the new racism. This task is made even more difficult by the fact that African Americans are included in these debates, often serving as examples of what *not* to be or, alternately, as icons of sexual freedom served up as the antidote to American sexual repression. As part of the color-blind racism that has accompanied the erasure of the color line, the ubiquitous *inclusion* of images of Black sexuality that permeate contemporary movies, television shows, and music videos can replicate the power relations of racism today just as effectively as the *exclusion* of Black images did prior to the 1960s. Thus, Cheryl Clarke's observation that African Americans live in a sexually repressive culture speaks less to the prominence of representations of Black sexuality within an increasingly powerful mass media than to the *function* of these images in helping to construct a "limited sexual system."

NOTES

1. Asante 1993.
2. The details of this version come from (Fausto-Sterling 1995). Depending on the intent of the author, Sarah Baartman's story takes on different meanings. For example, Anne Fausto-Sterling's account focuses on the nineteenth-century scientists who relentlessly probed her body and used Baartman as a vehicle for redefining Western concepts of race, gender, and sexuality. Fausto-Sterling's version points out how we learn much more about European scientists themselves via their treatment of Sarah Baartman than we gain any accurate information about her. In contrast, in his groundbreaking essay "The Hottentot and the Prostitute: Toward an Iconography of Female Sexuality," Sander Gilman's account traces how ideas about the Hottentot Venus as an icon of Black sexuality were crucial to nineteenth-century European perceptions of women's sexuality (Gilman 1985, 76–108). Advancing a materialist analysis, Zine Magubane takes issue with Gilman's claim

that, by the eighteenth century, the sexuality of African men and women became the icon for deviant sexuality in general. Rather, Magubane contends that the Baartman exhibition encapsulated the debates that were occurring concerning colonial labor needs (Magubane 2001). Grounded in a cultural studies framework, Susie Prestney explores how the image of the Hottentot Venus was central to conceptions of difference, especially those of freak shows and similar spectacles (Prestney 1997). Taking a different approach, Yvette Abrahams challenges the flawed historiography on the Khoi people and indigenous people in general that places Baartman outside history (Abrahams 1998). Finally, my own rendering of this narrative in *Black Feminist Thought* (Collins 2000a, 136–137, 141–145), and in this volume aim to place Sarah Baartman in an intersectional analysis of how race, class, gender, and sexuality affect women of African descent.

3. Bederman 1995, 1–5.

4. I use the terms *representations, stereotypes,* and *controlling images* to refer to the depiction of people of African descent within Western scholarship and popular culture. Each term has a different history. Representations need not be stereotypical and stereotypes need not function as controlling images. Of the three, controlling images are most closely tied to power relations of race, class, gender, and sexuality. For a discussion of controlling images, see Collins 2000a, 69–96.

5. As used here, the term *invented* resembles Benedict Anderson's notion of an *imagined* community (Anderson 1983). In his important study of nationalism, Anderson contends that members of nations can never know one another. They "imagine" or "invent" a community. Racial categories such as White, Black, and native are all, in this sense, invented. Also, the term *discourse* has a particular meaning of a set of ideas and practices that, when taken together, organize both the way a society defines certain truths about itself and how it deploys social power. An invented discourse is in some sense an oxymoron in that all discourses are social constructions that simultaneously shape and reflect actual social relations. For a good use of the term *invented* as the frame of an argument, see Oyèrónké Oyěwùmí's book *The Invention of Women: Making an African Sense of Western Gender Discourses* (Oyěwùmí 1997). All invented discourses typically contain contradictions and are often hotly contested, certainly the case with invented discourses on Black sexuality. For historical treatments of the invention of discourses of Black sexuality, see Jordan 1968, 136–178, especially 150–151; and D'Emilio and Freedman 1997, 34–37.

6. Collins 2000a, 69–96.

7. Abrahams 1998; Maseko 1998.

8. Morton 1991; Jewell 1993; Davis 1994; Asante 1994; Turner 1994.

9. The theme of primitivism of non-Western peoples was used to justify colonialism and slavery. For an analysis of how this idea was constructed and used, see Young 1995; Torgovnick 1990; McClintock 1995.

10. The term *Latina* addresses some of the multifaceted debates within contemporary racial theory that demonstrate the fluidity of racial classification. Research on how the different histories of people of African descent within Latin American countries coupled with a philosophy of "racial democracy" shows how Latin American populations approach race and ethnicity differently (Winant 2001, 219–248). In this context, Lopez's history as a Puerto Rican is significant, especially regarding the changing meaning of race in the United States as evidenced in the 2000 census (Rodriguez 2000). The category *Latina* refers to a wide range of national histories and migration streams into a new American ethnicity of *Hispanic.* Historically, Puerto Ricans have been viewed as reflecting a mulatto mixture resulting from European and African backgrounds as compared to a mestizo mixture of European and Indian of Chicana or Mexican-American populations. But the very categories of mulatto and mestizo may mask more than they reveal about the fluidity of racial and ethnic classification throughout the Americas. Both Puerto Rico and Mexico have varying combinations of racial mixtures, a situation that generates different approaches to skin color, hair texture, and the racial order itself. These ideas become layered upon North American ideas concerning race.

11. D'Emilio and Freedman 1997, 102–103.

12. Ironically, the theme of racial mixture of African, Indians, and Whites falters when Spain and Portugal are in the mix. Latinas have Spanish blood, but the Whiteness of this lineage can be questioned. Moors brought dark skin and Islam to Spain and intermingled with its peoples. Ferdinand and Isabella were celebrated for unifying Spain, "civilizing" it, and insisting on Catholicism as the way to prove membership and belonging in the emerging Spanish nation. Thus, Moors with their heathen Muslim beliefs and their dark skin became coded as savages.

13. The relationship among colonialism, European nationalism, and women has been explored by a variety of authors. For a representative work, see Yuval-Davis 1997.

14. People of African descent were not the only ones whose sexuality was pathologized in this process. Whereas the black/white binary is the anchor that frames all others, different race/gender groups found their sexuality differentially stereotyped and pathologized in this process. Enslaving people of African descent not only required enforcing the master/slave relationship, it also required erasing the presence of indigenous peoples (who faced genocidal policies) as well as claiming land that had been historically governed by Mexico (Takaki 1993). Racial ideologies constructed the sexualities of multiple groups in relation to one another (D'Emilio and Freedman 1997). Justifying slavery also required establishing a social class hierarchy among Whites while hiding the effects of this hierarchy under the assumed privileges attached to Whiteness.

15. For an early discussion of Black male sexuality, see Jordan 1968, 151–152. For more recent works that build on historical work, see Ferber 1998; Riggs 1999; Jones 1993.

16. For an analysis of how this process operated in the late nineteenth and early twentieth centuries, see Somerville 2000; Bederman 1995.

17. For a classic work on this process, see Hoch 1979.

18. The changes generated by postcoloniality, global capitalism, and new technologies have sparked a lively debate about the contours and meaning of the new racism in the United States. Some scrutinize the transformation of contemporary U.S. society as a racialized social system composed of structural and ideological dimensions (Bonilla-Silva 1996). When it comes to African Americans, structurally, American society has not made the gains in desegregating its housing, schools, and employment promised by the civil rights movement (Massey and Denton 1993). One study of Atlanta, Georgia, revealed that neighborhood-level racial resegregation is emerging as a new spatial pattern within major American cities, even those with a politically enfranchised and highly visible Black middle class (Orfield and Ashkinaze 1991). Other research points to the growth of a prison-industrial complex as an important new site for institutionalized racism confronting working-class and poor African Americans and Latinos (Miller 1996). Ideologically, a belief in upholding "color blindness" masks the continued inequalities of contemporary racism. By proclaiming that equal treatment of *individuals* under the law is sufficient for addressing racism, this ideology redefines *group*-based, antiracist remedies such as affirmative action as being "racist" (Crenshaw 1997). For a critique of color blindness and an analysis of how this racial ideology merits rethinking in the United States, see Guinier and Torres 2002.

19. For a thorough analysis of how globalization shapes contemporary racial formations, see Winant's analysis of the United States, South Africa, Brazil, and Europe in the post–World War II era (Winant 2001). Feminist analysis has also produced a broad literature on globalization and women's economic status, some of it focused on racism, sexism, and issues of globalization. For representative theoretical work in this tradition, see Alexander 1997; Mohanty 1997. African American scholars have also focused more attention on the global political economy. For representative works in this tradition, see Wilson 1996; Brewer 1994; Squires 1994.

20. Bauman 1998, 9.

21. Lusane 1997, 114.

22. M. Jacqui Alexander's discussion of the tourist industry in the Bahamas provides an especially insightful analysis of the effects of globalization on nation-state autonomy and on social problems within the Bahamas (Alexander 1997).

23. Cultural studies and studies of mass media underwent massive growth after 1980. For general work on the media, see Gitlin 2001. For race and media, see Entman 2000. The field of Black cultural studies has generated a range of literature. For representative works, consult Bobo 1995; Kelley 1994; Kelley 1997; Rose 1994; Wallace 1990; Gilroy 2000; Ransby and Matthews 1993; Gates 1992; Neal 2002; Watkins 1998; Cashmore 1997; Caponi 1999; Dent 1992b; Hall 1992; and Dyson 1996.

24. Kitwana 2002.

25. Clarke 1983, 199.

26. D'Emilio and Freedman suggest that the suppression of a range of sexual practices was part of colonization. Comparing the sexual practices of Native Americans, which varied widely, with European colonialist perceptions of such practices, in every region where Europeans and indigenous peoples came into contact, Europeans judged the sexual life of natives as "savage" and their own practices as "civilized." For example, most indigenous peoples did not associate either nudity or sexuality with sin. They accepted premarital intercourse, polygamy, or institutionalized homosexuality, all practices that were condemned by European church and state (D'Emilio and Freedman 1997, 6–7). They point out, "perhaps the most striking contrast between English and Indian sexual systems was the relative absence of sexual conflict among native Americans, due in part to their different cultural attitudes toward both property and sexuality. . . . In cultures in which one could not 'own' another person's sexuality, prostitution—the sale of sex—did not exist prior to the arrival to European settlers. Rape—the theft of sex—only rarely occurred, and it was one of the few sexual acts forbidden by Indian cultures" (D'Emilio and Freedman 1997, 8).

27. D'Emilio and Freedman 1997, 16.

28. A 1995 report published by the Social Science Research Council charts the political difficulties that have plagued scientific studies of sexuality within American social science (di Mauro 1995).

29. Hegemony is also a mode of social organization wherein the dissent of oppressed groups is absorbed and thereby rendered politically useless. Moreover, in hegemonic situations, power is diffused throughout a social system such that multiple groups police one another and suppress each other's dissent. For example, if African Americans come to believe the dominant ideology and accept ideas about Black masculinities and Black femininities constructed within the dominant framework, then Black political dissent about gender and about all things tied to gender becomes weakened. Because they are used to justify existing social hierarchies, hegemonic ideologies may seem invincible. But ideologies of all sorts are never static. Instead, they are always internally inconsistent and are always subject to contestation (Magubane 2001).

30. Remez 2000.

31. This history of suppression of sex education and the limits on discussions that do exist have an especially negative impact on African American adolescents. HIV/AIDS has had a significant impact on African American youth. For statistics, see http://www.cdc.gov/hiv/pubs/Facts/afam.pdf.

32. For an analysis of talk shows, especially the production of "trashy" talk shows, see Grindstaff 2002. Grindstaff does not emphasize race, but her study of how talk shows replicate and reproduce ideas about social class and gender provides insight into the general process of ideology construction and contestation. She notes that talk shows are typically geared to women, feature working-class guests, and aim to display ordinary people engaged in extraordinary behavior.

33. Mark Anthony Neal and Hortense Spillers offer two different interpretations of the emergence of the term "baby daddy" to describe unmarried fatherhood among African American men. Neal's chapter "Baby Mama (Drama) and Baby Daddy (Trauma): Post-Soul Gender Politics" uses Black popular culture (Neal 2002, 57–97). In contrast, Spillers's essay "Mama's Baby, Papa's Maybe: An American Grammar Book," also examines unmarried fatherhood in the context of American race relations and the exploitation of Black bodies under slavery (Spillers 2000).

34. Grindstaff borrows the phrase the "money shot" from pornography to describe the efforts of producers to get ordinary people to deliver strong emotions such as joy, sorrow, rage, or remorse that can be seen in visible, bodily terms. Crying, shaking, running, and other evidence of emotion besides just talk are solicited. As Grindstaff points out, "Like pornography, daytime talk is a narrative of explicit revelation in which people 'get down and dirty' and 'bare it all' for the pleasure, fascination, or repulsion of viewers. Like the orgasmic cum shot of pornographic films, the money shot of talk shows makes visible the precise moment of letting go, of losing control, of surrendering to the body and its 'animal' emotions" (Grindstaff 2002, 19). This is why Mr. Povich followed the woman backstage—he was in search of an authentic money shot.

35. Sociologist Abby Ferber describes how White supremacist literature remains obsessed with this theme of interracial sexuality generally and of protecting the body of the White woman (and thus the White race) from Black penetration. White women who willingly partner with Black men become redefined as "darkened," trashy women (Ferber 1998).

36. West 1993, 83.

BIBLIOGRAPHY

Abrahams, Yvette. 1998. "Images of Sara Bartman: Sexuality, Race, and Gender in Early-Nineteenth-Century Britain." *Nation, Empire, Colony: Historicizing Gender and Race.* Ed. Ruth Roach Pierson and Nupur Chadhuri, 220–236. Bloomington: Indiana University Press.

Alexander, M. Jacqui. 1997. "Erotic Autonomy as a Politics of Decolonization: An Anatomy of Feminist and State Practice in the Bahamas Tourist Industry." *Feminist Genealogies, Colonial Legacies, Democratic Futures.* Ed. M. Jacqui Alexander and Chandra Talpade Mohanty, 63–100. New York: Routledge.

Anderson, Benedict. 1983. *Imagined Communities: Reflections on the Origin and Spread of Nationalism.* London: Verso.

Asante, Kariamu Welsh. 1993. "Josephine Baker." *Black Women in America: An Historical Encyclopedia.* Ed. Darlene Clark Hine, 75–78. Vol. 1. New York: Carlson Publishing.

———. 1994. "Images of Women in African Dance: Sexuality and Sensuality as Dual Unity." *Sage* 8, no. 2 (fall): 16–19.

Bauman, Zygmunt. 1998. *Globalization: The Human Consequences.* New York: Columbia University Press.

Bederman, Gail. 1995. *Manliness and Civilization: A Cultural History of Gender and Race in the United States, 1890–1917.* Chicago: University of Chicago Press.

Bobo, Jacqueline. 1995. *Black Women as Cultural Readers.* New York: Columbia University Press.

Bonilla-Silva, Eduardo. 1996. "Rethinking Racism: Toward a Structural Interpretation." *American Sociological Review* 62 (June): 465–480.

Brewer, Rose. 1994. "Race, Class, Gender and U.S. State Welfare Policy: The Nexus of Inequality for African American Families." *Color, Class and Country: Experiences of Gender.* Ed. Gay Young and Bette J. Dickerson, 115–127. London: Zed.

Caponi, Gena Dagel, ed. 1999. *Signifyin(g), Sanctifyin', & Slam Dunking: A Reader in African American Expressive Culture.* Amherst: University of Massachusetts Press.

Cashmore, Ellis. 1997. *The Black Culture Industry.* New York: Routledge.

Clarke, Cheryl. 1983. "The Failure to Transform: Homophobia in the Black Community." *Home Girls: A Black Feminist Anthology.* Ed. Barbara Smith, 197–208. New York: Kitchen Table Press.

Collins, Patricia Hill. 2000a. *Black Feminist Thought: Knowledge, Consciousness, and the Politics of Empowerment.* New York: Routledge.

Crenshaw, Kimberlé Williams. 1997. "Color Blindness, History, and the Law." *The House That Race Built.* Ed. Wahneema Lubiano, 280–288. New York: Pantheon.

D'Emilio, John, and Estelle B. Freedman. 1997. *Intimate Matters: A History of Sexuality in America.* Chicago: University of Chicago Press.

Dent, Gina, ed. 1992b. *Black Popular Culture.* Seattle: Bay Press.

di Mauro, Diane. 1995. *Sexuality Research in the United States: An Assessment of the Social and Behavioral Sciences.* New York: Social Science Research Council, Sexuality Research Assessment Project.

Dyson, Michael Eric. 1996. *Between God and Gangsta Rap: Bearing Witness to Black Culture.* New York: Oxford University Press.

Entman, Robert M., and Rojecki Andrew. 2000. *The Black Image in the White Mind: Media and Race in America.* Chicago: University of Chicago Press.

Fausto-Sterling, Anne. 1995. "Gender, Race, and Nation: The Comparative Anatomy of 'Hottentot' Women in Europe, 1815–1817." *Deviant Bodies: Critical Perspectives on Difference in Science and Popular Culture.* Ed. Jennifer Terry and Jacqueline Urla, 19–48. Bloomington: Indiana University Press.

Ferber, Abby L. 1998. *White Man Falling: Race, Gender, and White Supremacy.* Lanham, Md.: Rowman & Littlefield.

Gates, Henry Louis. 1992. *Loose Canons: Notes on the Culture Wars.* New York: Oxford University Press.

Gilman, Sander L. 1985. *Difference and Pathology: Stereotypes of Sexuality, Race, and Madness.* Ithaca, N.Y.: Cornell University Press.

Gilroy, Paul. 2000. *Against Race: Imagining Political Culture Beyond the Color Line.* Cambridge, Mass.: Belknap Press of Harvard University Press.

Gitlin, Todd. 2001. *Media Unlimited: How the Torrent of Images and Sounds Overwhelms Our Lives.* New York: Henry Holt.

Grindstaff, Laura. 2002. *The Money Shot: Trash, Class, and the Making of TV Talk Shows.* Chicago: University of Chicago Press.

Guinier, Lani, and Gerald Torres. 2002. *The Miner's Canary: Enlisting Race, Resisting Power, Transforming Democracy.* Cambridge, Mass.: Harvard University Press.

Hall, Stuart. 1992. "What Is This 'Black' in Black Popular Culture?" *Black Popular Culture.* Ed. Gina Dent, 21–33. Seattle: Bay Press.

Hoch, Paul. 1979. *White Hero, Black Beast: Racism, Sexism, and the Mask of Masculinity.* London: Pluto Press.

Jewell, K. Sue. 1993. *From Mammy to Miss America and Beyond: Cultural Images and the Shaping of U.S. Social Policy.* New York: Routledge.

Jones, Jacquie. 1993. "The Construction of Black Sexuality: Towards Normalizing the Black Cinematic Experience." *Black American Cinema.* Ed. Manthia Diawara, 247–256. New York: Routledge.

Jordan, Winthrop D. 1968. *White Over Black: American Attitudes toward the Negro, 1550–1812.* New York: W. W. Norton.

Kelley, Robin D. G. 1994. *Race Rebels: Culture, Politics, and the Black Working Class.* New York: Free Press.

———. 1997. *Yo' Mama's DisFUNKtional!: Fighting the Culture Wars in Urban America.* Boston: Beacon Press.

Kitwana, Bakari. 2002. *The Hip Hop Generation: Young Blacks and the Crisis in African-American Culture.* New York: Basic Books.

Lusane, Clarence. 1997. *Race in the Global Era: African Americans at the Millennium.* Boston: South End Press.

Magubane, Zine. 2001. "Which Bodies Matter? Feminism, Poststructuralism, Race, and the Curious Theoretical Odyssey of the 'Hottentot Venus.'" *Gender and Society* 15, no. 6: 816–834.

Maseko, Zola. 1998. *The Life and Times of Sara Baartman: "The Hottentot Venus."* New York: First Run/Icarus Films.

Massey, Douglas S., and Nancy A. Denton. 1993. *American Apartheid: Segregation and the Making of the Underclass.* Cambridge, Mass.: Harvard University Press.

McClintock, Anne. 1995. *Imperial Leather: Race, Gender, and Sexuality in the Colonial Contest.* New York: Routledge.

Miller, Jerome G. 1996. *Search and Destroy: African-American Males in the Criminal Justice System.* New York: Cambridge University Press.

Mohanty, Chandra Talpade. 1997. "Women Workers and Capitalist Scripts: Ideologies of Domination, Common Interests, and the Politics of Solidarity." *Feminist Genealogies, Colonial Legacies, Democratic Futures.* Ed. M. Jacqui Mohanty Chandra and Talpade Alexander, 3–29. New York: Routledge.

Morton, Patricia. 1991. *Disfigured Images: The Historical Assault on Afro-American Women.* New York: Greenwood Press.

Neal, Mark Anthony. 2002. *Soul Babies: Black Popular Culture and the Post-Soul Aesthetic.* New York: Routledge.

Orfield, Gary, and Carole Ashkinaze. 1991. *The Closing Door: Conservative Policy and Black Opportunity.* Chicago: University of Chicago Press.

Oyěwùmí, Oyèrónké. 1997. *The Invention of Women: Making an African Sense of Western Gender Discourses.* Minneapolis: University of Minnesota Press.

Prestney, Susie. 1997. "Inscribing the Hottentot Venus: Generating Data for Difference." *At the Edge of International Relations: Postcolonialism, Gender & Dependency.* Ed. Phillip Darby, 86–105. New York: Pinter.

Ransby, Barbara, and Tracye Matthews. 1993. "Black Popular Culture and the Transcendence of Patriarchal Illusions." *Race and Class* 35, no. 1: 57–68.

Remez, Lisa. 2000. "Oral Sex among Adolescents: Is It Sex or Abstinence?" *Family Planning Perspectives* 32, no. 6: 298–304.

Riggs, Marlon T. 1999. "Black Macho Revisited: Reflections of a SNAP! Queen." *Black Men on Race, Gender, and Sexuality.* Ed. Devon W. Carbado, 306–311. New York: New York University Press.

Rodriguez, Clara E. 2000. *Changing Race: Latinos, the Census, and the History of Ethnicity in the United States.* New York: New York University Press.

Rose, Tricia. 1994. *Black Noise: Rap Music and Black Culture in Contemporary American.* Hanover, N.H.: Wesleyan University Press.

Somerville, Siobhan B. 2000. *Queering the Color Line: Race and the Invention of Homosexuality in American Culture.* Durham, N.C.: Duke University Press.

Spillers, Hortense J. 2000. "Mama's Baby, Papa's Maybe: An American Grammar Book." *The Black Feminist Reader.* Ed. Joy James and T. Denean Sharpley-Whiting, 57–87. Malden Mass.: Blackwell.

Squires, Gregory D. 1994. *Capital and Communities in Black and White: The Intersections of Race, Class, and Uneven Development.* Albany: State University of New York Press.

Takaki, Ronald T. 1993. *A Different Mirror: A History of Multicultural America.* Boston: Little, Brown.

Torgovnick, Marianna. 1990. *Gone Primitive: Savage Intellects, Modern Lives.* Chicago: University of Chicago Press.

Turner, Patricia A. 1994. *Ceramic Uncles and Celluloid Mammies: Black Images and Their Influence on Culture.* New York: Anchor.

Wallace, Michele. 1990. *Invisibility Blues: From Pop to Theory.* New York: Verso.

Watkins, S. Craig. 1998. *Representing: Hip Hop Culture and the Production of Black Cinema.* Chicago: University of Chicago Press.

Wilson, William Julius. 1996. *When Work Disappears: The World of the New Urban Poor.* New York: Knopf.

Winant, Howard. 2001. *The World Is a Ghetto: Race and Democracy since World War II.* New York: Basic Books.

Young, Robert J. C. 1995. *Colonial Desire: Hybridity in Theory, Culture and Race.* New York: Routledge.

Yuval-Davis, Nira. 1997. *Gender and Nation.* Thousand Oaks, Calif.: Sage.

R E A D I N G *31*   **Leila J. Rupp**

Toward a Global History of Same-Sex Sexuality

This is the presumptuous title of a paper I delivered for what I believe was the first-ever session on "Gay and Lesbian History/L'histoire de l'homo-sexualité" at the International Congress of Historical Sciences, held in August 2000 in Oslo. As I did there, let me hasten to say here that I do not claim knowledge of same-sex sexuality in every time and every place. But the blossoming of research on a wide range of manifestations of same-sex sexuality calls for an attempt at global thinking. Although my own work is rooted in U.S. and European history, I would like to make use of the work of scholars focusing on different parts of the world to reflect on what patterns might emerge. I take up this task from the perspective of one firmly committed to a social constructionist perspective on sexuality. Thus, I recognize that making transhistorical comparisons can be a risky business. Nevertheless, I think we can learn something by thinking about same-sex sexuality from a global viewpoint.

I favor the term "same-sex sexuality" as one that gets beyond the use of terms such as "queer," "gay," "lesbian," or "homosexual." Yet I would like to proceed by looking at manifestations of what we call "same-sex sexuality" in different times and places both to explore global patterns and to consider how those patterns make the two parts of the term "same-sex sexuality" problematic. That is, sometimes such manifestations cannot really be considered "same-sex," and sometimes they should not really be labeled "sexuality." These complications suggest that even the attempt to avoid assumptions about the meanings of desires, acts, and relationships by using a term such as "same-sex sexuality" may inadvertently lump together phenomena that are quite different. This is the difficulty of thinking about a global history of same-sex sexuality.

There are various ways that sexual acts involving two genitally alike bodies may in fact not be best conceptualized as "same-sex." In some cases, what is more important than genital similarity is the fact of some kind of difference: age difference, class difference, gender difference. As numerous scholars have pointed out, across time and space those differences have in more cases than not structured what we call same-sex acts in ways that are far more important to the people involved and to the societies in which they lived than the mere fact of the touching of similar bodies.[1] (My favorite way to explain this to my students is through the story of my colleague's five-year-old son, who was one day playing with the family dog and a girl from his school. The girl said, "I love Lily [the dog] so much I wish I could marry her. But I can't because she's a girl." My colleague's son, viewing the relevant categories in a different way, responded, "That's not the reason you can't marry Lily. You can't marry Lily because she's a dog!") Looking at the whole question of sameness and difference from an entirely different angle, Jens Rydström's work on homosexuality and bestiality in rural Sweden reminds us that these two categories of deviant acts were not conceptually distinct in the past.[2] Thus, the lines between same-sex and different-species acts were not clearly drawn.

To start, probably the most familiar example is from ancient Athenian society where age difference between older and younger men determined the ways they engaged in sex acts, and such relationships had educative functions that were as much the point as the sex. Furthermore (although this is a bit controversial), the lack of an age or other differential was considered deviant, while same-sex and different-age (or different-status) relationships were not. Adult male citizens of Athens could penetrate social inferiors, including women, boys, foreigners, and slaves.[3] The privilege of elite men to penetrate anyone other than their equals lingered on into early modern Europe. "Missing my whore, I bugger my page," wrote the Earl of Rochester in Restoration England.[4] Were such men "bisexual," or was the whole notion of sexual object choice irrelevant? Was this "same-sex sex"? Or are such relations or acts best described as "different-status sex"?

We find examples of age differences structuring sexual acts in other parts of the world as well. In seventeenth-century Japan, men expected to desire sexual relations with both women and boys.[5] Two different words described love of women and love of boys. Styles of dress and distinct haircuts differentiated youths from men, thus creating visible categories of difference based on age. When a youth became a man, ceremonially donning the proper garment and having his forelocks shaved, he would cease his role as the anally penetrated partner and take on the adult male penetrator role in a new relationship.

Yet age itself could become a socially constructed category. That is, although it was a violation of the norms, men might keep the boy role well past youth. In *The Great Mirror of Male Love,* a collection of short stories published in Japan in 1687, "Two Old Cherry Trees Still in Bloom" tells of two samurai lovers in their sixties who had first met when one was sixteen and the other nineteen. "Han'emon still thought of Mondo as a boy of sixteen. Though his hair was thinning and had turned completely white, Mondo sprinkled it with 'Blossom Dew' hair oil and bound it up in a double-folded topknot anyway. . . . There was no sign that he had ever shaved his temples; he still had the rounded hairline he was born with."[6] John Boswell, who vehemently denied that age difference structured male same-sex relations in ancient Athens and the Roman

Empire, suggests that the term "boy" might simply mean "beautiful man" or one who was beloved.[7] Boswell took this to signify that age difference was irrelevant, but it is also possible that this means, as in Japan, that age difference was crucial but that the concept of age might be only loosely tied, or not tied at all, to the number of years a person had lived.

In some societies, transgenerational same-sex relations are thoroughly institutionalized. We know the most about a number of cultures in New Guinea in which boys cannot grow into men without incorporating the semen of older men into their bodies, either through oral sex, anal sex, or simply smearing it on the skin.[8] Such "boy-inseminating rituals" transmit life-giving semen, which produces masculinity and a warrior personality. What is critical here is that all boys take part in the ritual, and once they become men (sometimes through marriage, sometimes through fathering a child), they take on the adult role. Different cultures prescribe different lengths of time for such same-sex relations, different rules for which men should penetrate which boys (sometimes a mother's brother, sometimes a sister's husband), and different ways to transmit the semen.

Note that almost all of the information we have about age-differentiated relationships is about men. True, the construction of Sappho as the mistress of a girls' school falling in love with her students hints at age difference, but this seems a bit far-fetched.[9] Martha Vicinus and Karin Lützen have both told tales about passion between students and teachers in English and Danish schools in the nineteenth century, but this is still a far cry from the evidence about men.[10] Perhaps more comparable is a ritual among the Baruya in Melanesia in which lactating mothers nourish young girls who are not their own daughters by offering a breast, believing that breast milk is produced from men's semen and thus essential to womanhood.[11] A young girl at the breast, however, is reminiscent of motherhood, while a boy enclosing a penis has nothing to do with traditional men's roles. A more convincing, if still very sketchy, example can be found in Big Nambas society in the New Hebrides, where higher-ranking women took younger girls as sexual partners.[12]

The point here, of course, is that our construction of these interactions as same-sex may be totally foreign to the people involved. That is even more true for transgenderal relations, which can be found in a variety of cultures throughout history and around the globe. For a number of reasons—spiritual, political, economic, social, cultural—individuals take on (or are forced to take on) the social role, dress, and other markers of the (here our language fails us) "other" sex. Sexual relations may then occur between biological males of female gender and biological males of male gender, or biological females of male gender and biological females of female gender. (Here again, our language describes just two genders where other cultures may see three or more.) Such "gender-transformed relationships" can be found in many parts of the world.

We know the most about transgenderal relations among North American native peoples. The term "berdache," a derogatory French word bestowed by the horrified European invaders, emphasized the sexual aspects of the role, but in fact the spiritual characteristics of what some scholars now call the "two-spirit person" were sometimes more important.[13] The male transgendered role could be found in over a hundred American Indian tribes, the female in about thirty.[14] Among the Mohave Indians in the western United States, both male (*alyha*) and female (*hwame*) two-spirit roles existed. A two-spirit male would take a female name, engage in female occupations, and even enact menstruation and childbirth. "Manly-hearted women" would take on male characteristics and have children with their wives through adoption. Men-women sought orgasm through anal sex, while women-men engaged in tribadism or genital rubbing, with the two-spirit on top.[15]

Third-gender roles also existed in a number of Polynesian societies. From the late eighteenth century, European explorers and missionaries commented on men dressed as women who were sexually involved with men in Tahiti. *Mahus,* as they are known, according to an English missionary, "chose this vile way of life when young; putting on the dress of a woman they follow the same employments, are under the same prohibitions with respect to food, etc., and seek the courtship of men as women do, nay are more jealous of the men who cohabit with them, and always refuse to sleep with women."[16] More recently, *mahus* tend to be effeminate and interested in women's household tasks but do not dress entirely as women. They seek oral sex with men, who may ridicule them in public but also seek them out for fellatio.

Other examples of transgenderal relations involve transformation of the body in some way. The *hijras* of India are defined by their sexual impotence with women.[17] Some are born hermaphrodites, but others simply lack desire for women and as a result undergo the surgical removal of their male genitals. They wear women's clothes and hairstyles, imitate women's walk and talk, and prefer male sexual partners. But they also exaggerate femininity and exhibit an aggressive sexuality that is unlike that of Indian women. They also have religious and ceremonial functions, performing at marriages and the birth of male children and serving as servants of Matar, the Mother goddess, at her temples. This is not to say that this is a high-status role in Indian society, for the *hijras* are much despised.

Not all cases of transgenderal relations have spiritual or religious origins or implications. The *travestis* of Brazil are transgendered prostitutes who, beginning at a young age, take female names and wear women's clothes as a result of their desire to attract men.[18] Although they do not, like the *hijras,* remove their genitals, they do take female hormones and inject silicone in order to enlarge their buttocks, thighs, and breasts. They work as prostitutes, attracting men who define themselves as resolutely heterosexual.

In the case of women who passed as men in early modern Europe, the motivation may have been a desire for occupational or literal mobility, although this is undoubtedly something we will never know for sure.[19] Women who dressed in men's clothing in order to join the army or take a man's job had to impersonate men in all ways, including in their relations with women. When discovered, punishment could be swift and severe for the usurpation of male privilege, particularly if it involved the use of what were called "material instruments" to "counterfeit the office of a husband," as a 1566 case put it.[20] In Germany in the early eighteenth century, a woman named Catharine Margaretha Linck dressed as a man, served in the army, and, after discharge, worked as a cotton dyer. She married a woman who, following a quarrel, confessed to her mother that her husband was not what he seemed. When the outraged mother took Linck to court and produced what another trial transcript in a similar case described as "the illicit inventions she used to supplement the shortcomings of her sex," Linck was sentenced to death for her crimes.[21] Were women who risked death looking only for better job prospects, or were these gender-crossers what we would today consider transgendered?

The connection between women's cross-dressing and same-sex desire becomes tighter over time. Lisa Duggan, in her analysis of the case of Alice Mitchell, a nineteen-year-old Memphis woman who murdered the girl she loved when their plans to elope came to naught, ties together the threads of romantic friendship, gender transgression, and the emerging definitions of lesbianism.[22] Jennifer Robertson's pathbreaking work on cross-dressing women in the Japanese Takarazuka Revue, founded in 1913, does much the same thing in a very different context. Exploring a rash of lesbian double suicides in Japan in the 1930s, Robertson details the erotics of fandom inspired by the Revue.[23] Like Duggan and Robertson, Lucy Chesser, in her dissertation on cross-dressing in Australia, shows the development over time of the idea that cross-dressing had something to do with same-sex desire.[24]

The point of all these examples is, once again, that sexual relations between two genitally alike (or originally alike) bodies are in many cases better defined as different-gender than same-sex relations. This seems clear in the case of two-spirit people or the *hijras* or *travestis,* but as the spectrum of transgendered relations moves from those who alter their bodies to those who simply take on some characteristics traditionally associated with the other/another gender, the lines get blurry. What about the "mollies" of eighteenth-century London? Like men in subcultures in other large European cities, including Paris and Amsterdam, "mollies" were effeminate men who frequented taverns, parks, and public latrines; sought out male sexual partners; and shared a style of feminine dress and behavior.[25] An agent of the English Societies for the Reformation of Manners entered a London club in 1714 and found men "calling one another my dear, hugging and kissing, tickling and feeling each other, as if they were a mixture of wanton males and females; and assuming effeminate voices, female airs."[26] What about the "roaring girls" of London or the "randy women" of Amsterdam, cross-dressed but not entirely? Mary Frith, known by her pseudonym, Moll Cutpurse, the model for a number of early-seventeenth-century English accounts, struck one observer as "both man and woman."[27] Examples of gender-differentiated pairings—the *bichas* (faggots) and *bofes* (real men) of Brazil, the *jotas* (homosexuals) and *mayates* (men who have sex with *jotas*) of Mexico City, the butches and fems of 1950s American bar culture, the "mine wives" and "husbands" of South Africa—can be found in many parts of the world, and how much they are perceived within their own cultures as different-gender and how much as same-sex is a tricky question.[28]

In the narrowest sense, then, "same-sex sexuality" may best refer to modern Western notions of relations between individuals undifferentiated by gender, age, class, or any other factors: in other words, those (or some of those) who adopt a "gay" or "lesbian" identity. That is an irony of a term designed to do just the opposite.

The second part of my critique of the term "same-sex sexuality" is already implicit here. That is, how do we determine what is "sexuality" and what is something else in these different interactions? Scholars have argued that "sexuality" itself is a relatively modern concept, that, for example, acts of fellatio or anal penetration in ancient Athens were expressions of power, acts of domination and submission, not "sexuality."[29] In the case of the Sambia boys in New Guinea who ingest semen through acts of fellatio on older men, we can ask, "Is that a sexual act? Or akin to taking vitamins?" Is it significant that the boys swallow the semen directly from a penis rather than from a bowl with a spoon?[30]

How can we know for sure what is a sexual act? There are really two questions here. How do we think about acts—such as fellatio, cunnilingus, anal penetration—that seem clearly sexual yet may have other meanings? What do we make of acts—such as kissing, hugging, cuddling—that may or may not be considered "sex"? These questions in turn raise a third: Are certain acts associated with specific forms of relationships?

We have already considered the possibility that fellatio and a girl's mouth on the breast of a woman not her mother may be about a kind of spiritual nutrition rather than sexuality; and even that a whole range of acts might be the assertion of elite male privilege, a sign of power. Some scholars argue that particular acts—especially anal penetration—carry meanings that are far more about power than sex and did so even before the advent of the concept "sexuality." Richard Trexler, for example, interprets the cross-gender male role in the Americas at the time of conquest as just another form of a long-lasting practice of men dominating other men by raping them, either literally or symbolically.[31] Eva Keuls, in her study of sexual politics in ancient Athens, argues that anal intercourse was an "initiatory rite of submission to the desires of the established class," an assertion of superiority rather than a source of pleasure. Agreeing with Trexler, Keuls asserts that "anal sex is charged with aggression and domination: the submitting partner is in a helpless position, penetration can be painful, and opportunity for the gratification of the passive participant is limited."[32] If these are accurate conclusions (and I know that a chorus of voices will be raised to shout that they are not!), can we think of such interactions as "same-sex sexuality" at all, or are they, rather, "same-sex domination"?

What about societies that make room for loving relations that seem sexual to outsiders but not to the participants? In Basotho society in contemporary Lesotho, girls and women exchange long kisses, putting their tongues in each others' mouths; they fondle each other and endeavor to lengthen the labia minora; they rub their bodies together and engage in cunnilingus without defining any of this as sexual. They fall in love and form marriage-like unions. In this context sex requires a penis and marriage means sex with a man, so there is no such concept as lesbian sex or lesbian relationships.[33] Are these sexual acts?

Looking at the question of what constitutes a sexual act from a different angle, we are faced, most prominently, with the case of romantic friendship in the eighteenth- and nineteenth-century Western world. One of the central debates in the history of sexuality focuses on whether or not these passionate, intense, loving, physically affectionate relationships between women (and, to a lesser extent, men) included sex. This raises in a direct way the question of whether some involvement of the genitals of at least one person is a necessary, even if not sufficient, condition for the existence of a sexual act. Because romantic friendships could warrant public approval, even appreciation, we have traditionally assumed that they involved nothing that either the participants or observers defined as sex, largely because of the societal assumption of women's lack of passion.[34] Thus, when twenty-nine-year-old married mother Sarah Butler Wister instructed Jeannie Field Musgrove, the friend she had met in school fifteen years earlier, to "fill a quarter page with caresses & expressions of endearment" and Jeannie responded with "a thousand kisses"; or poet Emily Dickinson felt "hot and feverish, and my heart beats so fast" at the prospect of seeing and kissing her friend Sue Gilbert, we call this "affection."[35]

Part of the problem of evaluating what counts as sex between women is that we have so little evidence of what women did with each other, in contrast to how they felt about each other. Some of this can be accounted for because religious and civil authorities— that is, male religious and civil authorities—could not really understand sex without a penis, so they were themselves never really sure what was taking place.

Consider the evidence we do have. Marie-Jo Bonnet has collected a range of images in European art from ancient times to the present, images of what she calls the "female couple," many of them engaged in what look to be quite explicitly sexual encounters.[36] The question remains, however, what such representations mean. At the very least, they make female same-sex acts visible.

Potentially sexual activities between women fall into several different categories across time. In written as well as visual sources, one kind of act that we find is the caressing of breasts. A twelfth-century nun in the monastery of Tegernsee in Bavaria wrote to another nun, "When I recall the kisses you gave me, / And how with tender words you caressed my little breasts, / I want to die / Because I cannot see you."[37] Centuries later across the Atlantic, Addie Brown, a domestic servant, and Rebecca Primus, a schoolteacher, both African American women who met in Hartford, Connecticut, in the 1860s, also engaged in what Karen Hansen calls "bosom sex." Addie worked at a girls' school and wrote Rebecca that the "girls are very friendly towards me. One of them wants to sleep with me. Perhaps I will give my consent some of these nights." In response to Rebecca's lost reply, Addie explained, "If you think that is my bosom that captivated the girl that made her want to sleep with me, she got sadly disappointed injoying it, for I had my back towards [her] all night and my night dress was butten up so she could not get to my bosom. I shall try to keep your favored one always for you. Should in my excitement forget [sic], you will pardon me I know." Like other romantic friends, and like the twelfth-century nuns, Rebecca and Addie also enjoyed kissing. "No kisses is like youres," Addie told Rebecca in another letter.[38]

Then we also have some evidence of genital contact, either tribadism or manual stimulation of the clitoris and/or vagina. Judith Brown recounts the story of Benedetta Carlini, the seventeenth-century Italian "lesbian nun." In the course of an investigation into Carlini's mystical claims of being the bride of Christ, Bartolomea Crivelli, a younger and less powerful sister in the convent where Carlini was abbess, testified that Carlini had forced her into "the most immodest acts." "Benedetta would grab her by the arm and throw her by force on the bed. Embracing her, she would put her under herself and kissing her as if she were a man, she would speak words of love to her. And she would stir on top of her so much that both of them corrupted themselves."[39]

There is also the tale of the early-nineteenth-century Scottish schoolteachers made famous by Lillian Hellman's *The Children's Hour.* As reconstructed by Lillian Faderman in *Scotch Verdict,* Marianne Woods and Jane Pirie were accused by a student of coming to each other's beds, lying on top of one another, kissing, and shaking the bed. The student, Jane Cumming, born of a liaison between an Indian woman and an aristocratic Scottish man serving the empire in the East, reported that Jane said one night, "You are in the wrong place," and Marianne replied, "I know," and asserted that she was doing it "for fun." Another night, she said, Jane whispered, "Oh, do it, darling." And then Jane Cumming described, through her tears, the noise that she heard as similar to "putting one's finger into the neck of a wet bottle."[40]

Perhaps the most extensive account we have of such sexual acts comes from the diary of Anne Lister, a nineteenth-century, upper-class, independent, mannish English woman. Anne recorded numerous sexual affairs with women, some of them married. In 1819, she detailed an encounter with the love of her life, Marianne, who married for economic and social status but continued her affair with Lister, passing on a venereal disease contracted from her husband through his own extramarital exploits. *Kiss* in Lister's diary is a code word for "orgasm." "From the kiss she gave me it seemed as if she loved me as fondly as ever. By & by, we seemed to drop asleep but, by & by, I perceived she would like another kiss & she whispered, 'Come again a bit, Freddy.' But soon, I got up a second time, again took off, went to her a second time &, in spite of all, she really gave me pleasure, & I told her no one had ever given me kisses like hers." Fed up with waiting for Marianne's all-too-healthy husband to die, Lister went to Paris in 1824, where she began to court a widow staying in the same pension. One night the widow came to her room and climbed into bed with her: "I was contented that my naked left thigh should rest upon her naked left thigh and thus she let me grubble her over her petticoats. All the while I was pressing her between my thighs. Now and then I held my hand still and felt her pulsation, let her rise towards my hand two or three times and gradually open her thighs, and felt that she was excited."[41]

Which of these descriptions qualify as "sex"? What is required? This question has been, historically, particularly difficult in the case of women, but even for men we are sometimes in the dark. At the same time that romantic friendship flourished among women, men in the United States might also kiss, hug, and share a bed with no sense that they were violating sexual norms. Jonathan Katz, in his forthcoming book, argues that the separation between love and lust—the notion not only that love between men had no connotations of sexuality, but also that sodomy was perceived as only sexual, with no connection to love—confused men who might

have felt both.[42] Although men might write, as did college students Albert Dodd and Anthony Halsey in the 1830s, of "how sweet" it was "to sleep with him, to hold his beloved form in my embrace, to have his arms about my neck, to imprint upon his face sweet kisses," they had no words to describe what they felt.[43] By the end of the nineteenth century, New Yorker Frederick S. Ryman expressed unease about the possible sexual meanings of his fondness for "the Oriental custom of men embracing & kissing each other." He described sleeping with his friend Rob's arms around him but insisted, perhaps too vigorously, that "I am certain there was no sexual sentiment on the part of either of us. We both have our mistresses . . . & I am certain that the thought of the least demonstration of unmanly & abnormal passion would have been as revolting to him as it is & ever has been to me."[44]

The association of romantic friendship in both its female and male forms with acts that are particularly hard to classify as either sex or not-sex suggests that there may be patterns in the kinds of acts that take place between individuals of the same sex in different varieties of relationships. Certainly it is clear that the particular part a man plays in a sexual act has always—or almost always?—been associated with gender and/or age or class, or, at least in some places, race or ethnicity. (Even here, though, I insert the "almost always" because evidence suggests that the "norm" of even societally deviant sex acts is not a firm description of reality. Both Don Kulick's work on the *travestis* of Brazil and Annick Prieur's study of the *jotas* of Mexico City point out that the "real men" who have sex with men dressed as women eventually, or sometimes, or often, want to reverse roles, even if they will never admit it. The drag queens that Verta Taylor and I are studying insist that, in private, what "straight" or bisexual men want is not what they say they want.)[45] Nevertheless, the act of putting one's penis in the mouth, vagina, or anus of another is privileged, but the act of enclosing a penis with one's mouth, vagina, or anus is not.

Putting aside such complications, are there other patterns? Does the intercrural sex—rubbing the penis between the thighs of another man—practiced between older and younger men in ancient Athens and in South African mine marriages (and among adolescents in the societies from which the miners came) have more loving and nurturing connotations than other acts? Is it true that anal sex has connotations of dominance, as Eva Keuls insists? Did romantic fiends only caress each others' breasts and engage in tribadism, and only women dressed as men penetrate their partners?

What about the fact that oral contact seems relatively infrequent on the global stage? Kissing, as we know, is not a universal erotic act, although it has a very long history in the Western world. In ancient Rome and in eighteenth-century Europe, fellatio was considered especially depraved. A Parisian hustler in 1783, according to a police agent who entrapped him, "says that he did it in all ways, *even that* if I wanted, I could consummate the act in his mouth." Another man offered as proof of his strong love for another man that he had "many times . . . kissed his genitals and even his anus."[46] Sex between men was so closely associated with anal intercourse that in 1914, when the police in Long Beach, California, arrested a group of men for deviant sexual behavior, they hardly knew what to make of what a reporter called "nothing more nor less than 'cocksucking.'" This was not, however, the same as "homosexualism," although it resembled it because "men find their sexual pleasure and gratification with men and boys rather than women and women on the other hand are attracted sexually toward girls and women instead of the opposite sex."[47] The men who engaged in this practice called it "the twentieth-century way." Liz Kennedy and Madeline Davis document the dawning acceptability of oral sex among Buffalo bar lesbians in the 1950s, suggesting that this might have been the "mid-twentieth-century way" for U.S. women.[48] Surely oral sex is not new—we can find references to "paired eating" between women in the Han dynasty in China—but perhaps it experienced a revival in modern times.[49] Is there then something "modern" about fellatio and cunnilingus?

Although I am bold enough to dare to address a global history of same-sex sexuality, I am not foolish enough to pretend to have answers to all of these questions. As the Euramerican nature of most of the evidence I use to consider the nature of sexual acts makes plain, we (or, certainly, I) do not know enough about such questions in other parts of the world to say anything even suggestive. But I do think these are good questions for future research.

I have spent all this time undermining the term "same-sex sexuality," but, in fact, I think that it is the best one we have. I have focused on the problems that arise from the term not because I think it is flawed, but because it in fact allows us to raise these very important questions about global patterns of love and desire between genitally alike bodies. I think we can see a limited number of patterns of same-sex interactions: differentiated by age or gender or class, or not differentiated in any of these ways; with spiritual or practical implications or based on desire and/or love; totally determining or determined by social roles, or not; clearly associated with specific acts, or not.[50] As we pursue our specific research projects, we would do well to remember that we need to consider carefully the ways that love, desire, and relationships are structured by differences or similarities, and the meaning of sex acts in their historical contexts. There are rich stories of same-sex sexuality out there that will tell us a great deal about gender, class, ethnicity, nationality, bodies, emotions, social relations, religion, law, identity, community, activism, culture, and just about every other thing that is part of what we think of as history.

NOTES

1. Stephen O. Murray, "Homosexual Categorization in Cross-Cultural Perspective," in *Latin American Male Homosexualities,* ed. Stephen O. Murray (Albuquerque: University of New Mexico Press, 1995), 3–32, cites a number of schemes for the social structuring of homosexuality and adopts that of Barry Adam, "Age, Structure, and Sexuality," *Journal of Homosexuality* 11 (1986): 19–33. This includes age-structured, gender-defined, profession-defined, and egalitarian. In Murray's most recent book, *Homosexualities* (Chicago: University of Chicago Press, 2000), he includes "profession-defined" under "gender-defined." John Howard, in his comment on the paper I delivered at Oslo, added race and ethnicity to this list, citing Nayan Shah's work on Indian and Chinese men arrested in British Columbia for their sexual relations with Anglo-Canadian men, and his own work on African American and white

same-sex interactions in the U.S. South. See Nayan Shah, "The Race of Sodomy: Asian Men, White Boys, and the Policing of Sex in North America" (paper presented at the Organization of American Historians conference, St. Louis, April 2000); John Howard, *Men Like That: A Southern Queer History* (Chicago: University of Chicago Press, 1999).

2. Jens Rydström, "Beasts and Beauties: Bestiality and Male Homosexuality in Rural Sweden, 1880–1950" (paper presented at the 19th International Congress of Historical Sciences, Oslo, Norway, August 2000).

3. The classic work is K. J. Dover, *Greek Homosexuality* (New York: Vintage, 1978). More recent studies include Eva C. Keuls, *The Reign of the Phallus: Sexual Politics in Ancient Athens* (New York: Harper and Row, 1985); David Halperin, *One Hundred Years of Homosexuality and Other Essays on Greek Love* (New York: Routledge, 1990); Eva Cantarella, *Bisexuality in*

the *Ancient World* (New Haven, CT: Yale University Press, 1992); and Wayne R. Dynes and Stephen Donaldson, eds., *Homosexuality in the Ancient World* (New York: Garland, 1992). See also Craig A. Williams, *Roman Homosexuality: Ideologies of Masculinity in Classical Antiquity* (New York: Oxford University Press, 1999). John Boswell, "Revolutions, Universals, and Sexual Categories," in *Hidden From History: Reclaiming the Gay and Lesbian Past,* ed. Martin Bauml Duberman, Martha Vicinus, and George Chauncey, Jr. (New York: New American Library, 1989), 17–36, disputes the notion that an age or status difference was essential to same-sex relations in Athenian society, and, more recently, Murray, in *Homosexualities,* has argued that undifferentiated (what he calls "egalitarian") relationships between men existed in ancient Greece and Rome (as well as in other premodern places) and that age difference did not always determine sexual role.

4. Quoted in James M. Saslow, "Homosexuality in the Renaissance: Behavior, Identity, and Artistic Expression," in *Hidden From History,* 90–105, quotation on 92. See Alan Bray, *Homosexuality in Renaissance England* (New York: Columbia University Press, 1982); Michael Rocke, *Forbidden Friendships: Homosexuality and Male Culture in Renaissance Florence* (New York: Oxford University Press, 1996); Louise Fradenburg and Carla Freccero, eds., *Premodern Sexualities* (New York: Routledge, 1996); Carolyn Dinshaw, *Getting Medieval: Sexualities and Communities, Pre- and Postmodern* (Durham, NC: Duke University Press, 1999); James M. Saslow, *Pictures and Passions: A History of Homosexuality in the Visual Arts* (New York: Viking, 1999); Glenn Burger and Steven F. Kruger, eds., *Queering the Middle Ages* (Minneapolis: University of Minnesota Press, 2001).

5. Paul Gordon Schalow, ed., *The Great Mirror of Male Love* (Stanford, CA: Stanford University Press, 1990); Stephen O. Murray, "Male Homosexuality in Japan before the Meiji Restoration," in *Oceanic Homosexualities,* ed. Stephen O. Murray (New York: Garland, 1992), 363–70; Gary P. Leupp, *Male Colors: The Construction of Homosexuality in Tokugawa Japan* (Berkeley: University of California Press, 1995).

6. Quoted in Paul Gordon Schalow, "Male Love in Early Modern Japan: A Literary Depiction of the 'Youth,'" in *Hidden from History,* 118–28, quotation of 126.

7. John Boswell, *Christianity, Social Tolerance, and Homosexuality* (Chicago: University of Chicago Press, 1980), 28–30.

8. David F. Greenberg, *The Construction of Homosexuality* (Chicago: University of Chicago Press, 1988), 26–40; Gilbert Herdt, *Same Sex, Different Cultures* (Boulder, CO: Westview Press, 1997), 64–88; Murray, *Oceanic Homosexualities.*

9. See Judith P. Hallett, "Sappho and Her Social Context: Sense and Sensuality," *Signs: Journal of Women in Culture and Society* 4: 447–64 (1979).

10. Martha Vicinus, "Distance and Desire: English Boarding School Friendships," *Signs: Journal of Women in Culture and Society* 9: 600–622 (1984); Karin Lützen, *Was das Herz begehrt: Liebe und Freundschaft zwischen Frauen* (Hamburg, Germany: Ernst Kabel Verlag, 1990).

11. Greenberg, *Construction of Homosexuality,* 29.

12. Herdt, *Same-Sex, Different Cultures,* 86.

13. Herdt, *Same-Sex, Different Cultures,* 90–102; Walter L. Williams, *The Spirit and the Flesh: Sexual Diversity in American Indian Culture* (Boston: Beacon Press, 1986); Sue-Ellen Jacobs, Wesley Thomas, and Sabine Lang, eds., *Two-Spirit People: Native American Gender Identity, Sexuality, and Spirituality* (Urbana: University of Illinois Press, 1997). There is disagreement about the status of transgendered individuals in the Americas. For a contrary view to those cited above, see Richard C. Trexler, *Sex and Conquest: Gendered Violence, Political Order, and the European Conquest of the Americas* (Ithaca, NY: Cornell University Press, 1995).

14. Herdt, *Same Sex, Different Cultures,* 91.

15. Herdt, *Same Sex, Different Cultures,* 92–94.

16. Quoted in Greenberg, *Construction of Homosexuality,* 58. See also Raleigh Watts, "The Polynesian Mahu," in Murray, *Oceanic Homosexualities,* 171–84.

17. Serena Nanda, "Hijras: An Alternative Sex and Gender Role in India," in *Third Sex, Third Gender: Beyond Sexual Dimorphism in Culture and History,* ed. Gilbert Herdt (New York: Zone Books, 1996), 373–417.

18. Don Kulick, *Travesti: Sex, Gender and Culture among Brazilian Transgendered Prostitutes* (Chicago: University of Chicago Press, 1998).

19. See Rudolf M. Dekker and Lotte C. van de Pol, *The Tradition of Female Transvestism in Early Modern Europe* (London: Macmillan Press, 1989).

20. Quoted in Lillian Faderman, *Surpassing the Love of Men* (New York: William Morrow, 1981), 51.

21. Faderman, *Surpassing the Love of Men,* 51–52.

22. Lisa Duggan, *Sapphic Slashers: Sex, Violence, and American Modernity* (Durham, NC: Duke University Press, 2001).

23. Jennifer Robertson, *Takarazuka: Sexual Politics and Popular Culture in Modern Japan* (Berkeley: University of California Press, 1998); Jennifer Robertson, "Dying to Tell: Sexuality and Suicide in Imperial Japan," *Signs: Journal of Women in Culture and Society* 25: 1–36 (1999).

24. Lucy Sarah Chesser, "'Parting with My Sex for a Season': Cross-Dressing, Inversion and Sexuality in Australian Cultural Life, 1850–1920," (Ph.D. diss., La Trobe University, 2001). See also Lucy Chesser, "'A Woman Who Married Three Wives': Management of Disruptive Knowledge in the 1879 Australian Case of Edward De Lacy Evans," *Journal of Women's History* 9: 53–77 (winter 1998).

25. Rictor Norton, *Mother Clap's Molly House: The Gay Subculture in England 1700–1830* (London: GMP Publishers, 1992); Michael Rey, "Parisian Homosexuals Create a Lifestyle, 1700–1750: The Police Archives," *Eighteenth-Century Life* 9, new series 3: 179–91 (1985); Jeffrey Merrick, "Sodomitical Scandals and Subcultures in the 1720s," *Men and Masculinities* 1: 365–84 (April 1999); Arend H. Huussen, Jr., "Sodomy in the Dutch Republic during the Eighteenth Century," *Unauthorized Sexual Behavior during the Enlightenment,*

ed. Robert P. Maccubbin (Williamsburg, VA: College of William and Mary Press, 1985), 169–78.

26. Randolph Trumbach, "The Birth of the Queen: Sodomy and the Emergence of Gender Equality in Modern Culture, 1660–1750," in *Hidden from History,* 129–40, quotation on 137. See also Randolph Trumbach, *Sex and the Gender Revolution: Heterosexuality and the Third Gender in Enlightenment London* (Chicago: University of Chicago Press, 1998).

27. Quoted in Faderman, *Surpassing the Love of Men,* 57. "Randy women" is a rough translation of *lollepotten,* a term analyzed by Myriam Everard in "Ziel en zinnen: Over liefde en lust tussen vrouwen in de tweede helft van de achttiende eeuw" (Ph.D. diss., Rijksuniversiteit Leiden, 1994).

28. See James N. Green, *Beyond Carnival: Male Homosexuality in Twentieth-Century Brazil* (Chicago: University of Chicago Press, 1999); Annick Prieur, *Mema's House, Mexico City: On Transvestites, Queens, and Machos* (Chicago: University of Chicago Press, 1998); Elizabeth Lapovsky Kennedy and Madeline D. Davis, *Boots of Leather, Slippers of Gold: The History of a Lesbian Community* (New York: Routledge, 1993); Stephen O. Murray and Will Roscoe, eds., *Boy-Wives and Female Husbands: Studies of African Homosexualities* (New York: St. Martin's, 1998).

29. David M. Halperin, "Sex before Sexuality: Pederasty, Politics, and Power in Classical Athens," in *Hidden from History,* 37–53.

30. This is a point made by Carole S. Vance, "Social Construction Theory: Problems in the History of Sexuality," in *Which Homosexuality?,* ed. Dennis Altman et al. (Amsterdam: Dekker/Schorer, 1989), 13–34. Vance credits a student with the incisive question about the bowl and spoon. On a Sambia man who sought out fellatio with initiates, see Gilbert H. Herdt, "Semen Depletion and the Sense of Maleness," in Murray, *Oceanic Homosexualities,* 33–68.

31. Trexler, *Sex and Conquest.*

32. Keuls, *The Reign of the Phallus,* 276.

33. Kendall, "'When a Woman Loves a Woman' in Lesotho: Love, Sex, and the (Western) Construction of Homophobia," in Murray and Roscoe, *Boy-Wires and Female Husbands,* 223–41.

34. There is a great deal of disagreement about the acceptability of romantic friendships. See Liz Stanley, "Romantic Friendship? Some Issues in Researching Lesbian History and Biography," *Women's History Review* 1: 193–216 (1992); Lisa Moore, "'Something More Tender Still Than Friendship': Romantic Friendship in Early-Nineteenth-Century England," *Feminist Studies* 18: 499–520 (1992); Martha Vicinus, "'They Wonder to Which Sex I Belong': The Historical Roots of the Modern Lesbian Identity," *Feminist Studies* 18: 467–97 (1992); Emma Donoghue, *Passions between Women: British Lesbian Culture 1668–1801* (New York: HarperCollins, 1993); Sylvia Martin, "'These Walls of Flesh': The Problem of the Body in the Romantic Friendship/Lesbianism Debate," *Historical Reflections/Réflexions Historiques* 20: 243–66 (1994); Marylynne Diggs, "Romantic Friends or a 'Different Race

of Creatures?' The Representation of Lesbian Pathology in Nineteenth-Century America," *Feminist Studies* 21: 317–40 (1995); Molly McGarry, Kanchana Natarajan, Dása Franèiková, Tania Navarro Swain, and Karin Lützen, "Carroll Smith-Rosenberg's 'The Female World of Love and Ritual' after Twenty-five Years," *Journal of Women's History* 12: 8–38 (2000). My argument, presented in "Romantic Friendship," in *Modern American Queer History,* ed. Allida Black and John Howard (Philadelphia, PA: Temple University Press, forthcoming), is that women could engage in quite passionate relationships without censure as long as they remained respectable by neither appearing masculine, rejecting men, nor seeming to have a relationship that would be defined as sexual.

35. Quoted in Carroll Smith-Rosenberg, "The Female World of Love and Ritual: Relations between Women in Nineteenth-Century America," *Signs: Journal of Women in Culture and Society* 1 (1): 1–29 (1975), quotation on 4–5; quoted in John D'Emilio and Estelle Freedman, *Intimate Matters: A History of Sexuality in America* (New York: Harper and Row, 1988), 126.

36. Marie-Jo Bonnet, *Les deux amies: Essai sur le couple de femmes dans l'art* (Paris: Éditions Blanche, 2000). See also Marie-Jo Bonnet, *Les relations amoureuses entre les femmes du XVIème au XXè siècle* (Paris: Odile Jacob, 1995).

37. Quoted in Boswell, *Christianity, Social Tolerance, and Homosexuality,* 220.

38. Quoted in Karen V. Hansen, "No Kisses Is Like Youres': An Erotic Friendship between Two African-American Women during the Mid-nineteenth Century," *Gender and History* 7: 153–82 (1995). See also Farah Jasmine Griffin, ed., *Beloved Sisters and Loving Friends: Letters from Rebecca Primus of Royal Oak, Maryland, and Addie Brown of Hartford, Connecticut, 1854–1868* (New York: Knopf, 1999).

39. Quoted in Judith Brown, *Immodest Acts: The Life of a Lesbian Nun in Renaissance Italy* (New York: Oxford University Press, 1986), 117–18.

40. Quoted in Lillian Faderman, *Scotch Verdict* (New York: Quill, 1983), 147.

41. Anne Lister, *I Know My Own Heart: The Diaries of Anne Lister (1791–1840),* ed. Helena Whitbread (New York: Virago, 1988), 104; Anne Lister, *No Priest but Love: The Journals of Anne Lister from 1824–1826,* ed. Helena Whitbread (New York: New York University Press, 1992), 65. On Lister, see Jill Liddington, "Anne Lister of Shibden Hall, Halifax (1791–1840): Her Diaries and the Historians," *History Workshop* 35: 45–77 (1993); and Anna Clark, "Anne Lister's Construcrion of Lesbian Identity," *Journal of the History of Sexuality* 7: 23–50 (1996).

42. Jonathan Ned Katz, *Love Stories: Sex between Men before Homosexuality* (Chicago: University of Chicago Press, forthcoming).

43. E. Anthony Rotundo, "Romantic Friendship: Male Intimacy and Middle-Class Youth in the Northern United States, 1800–1900," *Journal of Social History* 23: 1–25 (1989), quotation on 7.

44. Quoted in Martin Duberman, *About Time: Exploring the Gay Past,* rev. ed. (New York: Meridian Books, 1991), 63.

45. Leila J. Rupp and Verta Taylor, "What Makes a Man a Man: Drag Queens at the 801 Cabaret" (Chicago: University of Chicago Press, forthcoming). Murray makes the same point in *Homosexualities,* referring to "boy tops" in a number of different cultural settings.

46. Quoted in Rey, "Parisian Homosexuals," 184.

47. Sharon R. Ullman, "'The Twentieth Century Way': Female Impersonation and Sexual Practice in Turn-of-the-Century America," *Journal of the History of Sexuality* 5 (4): 573–600 (1995), quotation on 595.

48. Kennedy and Davis, *Boots of Leather.*

49. Bret Hinsch, *Passions of the Cut Sleeve: The Male Homosexual Tradition in China* (Berkeley: University of California Press, 1990).

50. In his comments at the Oslo conference, John Howard suggested that if we combine the myriad hierarchies of sexuality with the categories of age, gender, class, race, ethnicity, and so on, "we see a system of distinction-making that is virtually limitless in its permutations, in its capacity for normalizing and marginalizing." I think this is an important point, but I am still struck, as is Stephen Murray, by the fact that there "are not hundreds or even dozens of different social organizations of homosexual relations in human societies." See his "Homosexual Categorization in Cross-Cultural Perspective," in *Latin American Male Homosexualities,* ed. Stephen O. Murray (Albuquerque: University of New Mexico Press, 1995), 3–32, quotation on 4, and the introduction to *Homosexualities.*

READING *32* *Michael A. Messner*

Becoming 100% Straight

In 1995, as part of my job as the President of the North American Society for the Sociology of Sport, I needed to prepare a one-hour long Presidential Address for the annual meeting of some 200 people. This presented a challenge to me: how might I say something to my colleagues that was challenging, at least somewhat original, and above all, not boring. Students may think that their professors are especially boring in the classroom, but believe me, we are usually much worse at professional meetings. For some reason, many of us who are able to speak to our students in the classroom in a relaxed manner, and using relatively jargon-free language, seem at these meetings to become robots, dryly reading our papers—packed with impressively unclear jargon—to our yawning colleagues.

Since I desperately wanted to avoid putting 200 sport studies scholars to sleep, I decided to deliver a talk which I entitled "studying up on sex." The title, which certainly did get my colleagues' attention, was intended as a play on words—a double entendre. "Studying up" has one, generally recognizable colloquial meaning, but in sociology, it has another. It refers to studying "up" in the power structure. Sociologists have perhaps most often studied "down"—studied the

poor, the blue or pink-collar workers, the "nuts, sluts and perverts," the incarcerated. The idea of "studying up" rarely occurs to sociologists unless and until we are living in a time when those who are "down" have organized movements that challenge the institutional privileges of elites. So, for instance, in the wake of labor movements, some sociologists like C. Wright Mills studied up on corporate elites. And recently, in the wake of racial/ethnic civil rights movements, some scholars like Ruth Frankenberg have begun to study the social meanings of "whiteness." Much of my research, inspired by feminism, has involved a studying up on the social construction of masculinity in sport. Studying up, in these cases, has raised some fascinating new and important questions about the workings of power in society.

However, I realized, when it comes to understanding the social and interpersonal dynamics of sexual orientation in sport, we have barely begun to scratch the surface of a very complex issue. Although sport studies has benefited from the work of scholars like Helen Lenskyj, Brian Pronger, and others who have delineated the experiences of lesbians and gay men in sports, there has been very little extension of these scholars' insights into a consideration of the social construction of heterosexuality in sport. In sport, just as in the larger society, we seem obsessed with asking "how do people become gay?" Imbedded in this question is the assumption that people who identify as heterosexual, or "straight," require no explanation, since they are simply acting out the "natural" or "normal" sexual orientation. It's the "sexual deviants" who require explanation, we seem to be saying, while the experience of heterosexuals, because we are considered normal, seems to require no critical examination or explanation. But I knew that a closer look at the development of sexual orientation or sexual identity reveals an extremely complex process. I decided to challenge myself and my colleagues by arguing that although we have begun to "study up" on corporate elites in sport, on whiteness, on masculinity, it is now time to extend that by studying up on heterosexuality.

But in the absence of systematic research on this topic, where could I start? How could I explore, raise questions about, and begin to illuminate the social construction of heterosexuality for my colleagues? Fortunately, I had for the previous two years been working with a group of five men (three of whom identified as heterosexual, two as gay) who were mutually exploring our own biographies in terms of our earlier bodily experiences that helped to shape our gender and sexual identities. We modeled our project after that of a German group of feminist women, led by Frigga Haug, who created a research method which they call "memory work." In short, the women would mutually choose a body part, such as "hair," and each of them would then write a short story, based on a particularly salient childhood memory that related to their hair (for example, being forced by parents to cut your hair, deciding to straighten one's curly hair, in order to look more like other girls, etc.). Then, the group would read all of the stories, discuss them one-by-one, with the hope of gaining some more general understanding of, and raising new questions about, the social construction of "femininity." What resulted from this project was a fascinating book called *Female Sexualization,* which my men's group used as an inspiration for our project.

As a research method, memory work is anything but conventional. Many sociologists would argue that this is not really a "research method" at all, because the information that emerges from the project can't be used very confidently as a generalizable "truth," and especially because in this sort of project, the researcher is simultaneously part of what is being studied. How,

my more scientifically oriented colleagues might ask, is the researcher to maintain his or her objectivity in this project? My answer is that in this kind of research, objectivity is not the point. In fact, the strength of this sort of research is the depth of understanding that might be gained through a systematic group analysis of one's experience, one's *subjective* orientation to social processes. A clear understanding of the subjective aspect of social life—one's bodily feelings, emotions, and reactions to others—is an invaluable window that allows us to see and ask new sociological questions about group interaction and social structure. In short, group memory work can provide an important, productive, and fascinating insight into aspects of social reality, though not a complete (or completely reliable) picture.

So, as I pondered the lack of existing research on the social construction of heterosexuality in sport, I decided to draw on one of my own stories from my memory work men's group. Some of my most salient memories of embodiment are sports memories. I grew up the son of a high school coach, and I eventually played point guard on my dad's team. In what follows, I juxtapose one of my stories with that of a gay former Olympic athlete, Tom Waddell, whom I had interviewed several years earlier for a book that I wrote on the lives of male athletes.

TWO SEXUAL STORIES

Many years ago I read some psychological studies that argued that even for self-identified heterosexuals, it is a natural part of their development to have gone through "bisexual" or even "homosexual" stages of life. When I read this, it seemed theoretically reasonable, but it did not ring true in my experience. I have always been, I told myself, 100% heterosexual! The group process of analyzing my own autobiographical stories challenged this conception I had developed of myself, and also shed light on the way that the institutional context of sport provided a context for the development of my definition of myself as "100% straight." Here is one of the stories.

> When I was in the 9th grade, I played on a "D" basketball team, set up especially for the smallest of high school boys. Indeed, though I was pudgy with baby fat, I was a short 5'2", still pre-pubescent with no facial hair and a high voice that I artificially tried to lower. The first day of practice, I was immediately attracted to a boy I'll call Timmy, because he looked like the boy who

played in the Lassie TV show. Timmy was short, with a high voice, like me. And like me, he had no facial hair yet. Unlike me, he was very skinny. I liked Timmy right away, and soon we were together a lot. I *noticed* things about him that I didn't notice about other boys: he said some words a certain way, and it gave me pleasure to try to talk like him. I remember liking the way the light hit his boyish, nearly hairless body. I thought about him when we weren't together. He was in the school band, and at the football games, I'd squint to see where he was in the mass of uniforms. In short, though I wasn't conscious of it at the time, I was infatuated with Timmy—I had a crush on him. Later that basketball season, I decided—for no reason that I could really articulate then—that I hated Timmy. I aggressively rejected him, began to make fun of him around other boys. He was, we all agreed, a geek. He was a faggot.

Three years later, Timmy and I were both on the varsity basketball team, but had hardly spoken a word to each other since we were freshmen. Both of us now had lower voices, had grown to around 6 feet tall, and we both shaved, at least a bit. But Timmy was a skinny, somewhat stigmatized reserve on the team, while I was the team captain and starting point guard. But I wasn't so happy or secure about this. I'd always dreamed of dominating games, of being the hero. Halfway through my senior season, however, it became clear that I was not a star, and I figured I knew why. I was not aggressive enough.

I had always liked the beauty of the fast break, the perfectly executed pick and roll play between two players, and especially the long twenty-foot shot that touched nothing but the bottom of the net. But I hated and feared the sometimes brutal contact under the basket. In fact, I stayed away from the rough fights for rebounds and was mostly a perimeter player, relying on my long shots or my passes to more aggressive teammates under the basket. But now it became apparent to me that time was running out in my quest for greatness: I needed to change my game, and fast. I decided one day before practice that I was gonna get aggressive. While practicing one of our standard plays, I passed the ball to a teammate, and then ran to the spot at which I was to set a pick on a defender. I knew that one could sometimes get away with setting a face-up screen on a player, and then as he makes contact with you, roll your back to him and plant your elbow hard in his stomach. The beauty of this move is that your own body "roll" makes the elbow look like an accident. So I decided to try this move. I approached the defensive player, Timmy, rolled, and planted my elbow deeply into his solar plexus. Air

exploded audibly from Timmy's mouth, and he crumbled to the floor momentarily.

Play went on as though nothing had happened, but I felt bad about it. Rather than making me feel better, it made me feel guilty and weak. I had to admit to myself why I'd chosen Timmy as the target against whom to test out my new aggression. He was the skinniest and weakest player on the team.

At the time, I hardly thought about these incidents, other than to try to brush them off as incidents that made me feel extremely uncomfortable. Years later, I can now interrogate this as a *sexual* story, and as a *gender* story unfolding within the context of the heterosexualized and masculinized institution of sport. Examining my story in light of research conducted by Alfred Kinsey a half-century ago, I can recognize in myself what Kinsey saw as a very common **fluidity and changeability of sexual desire over the lifecourse.** Put simply, Kinsey found that large numbers of adult, "heterosexual" men had previously, as adolescents and young adults, experienced sexual desire for males. A surprisingly large number of these men had experienced sexual contact to the point of orgasm with other males during adolescence or early adulthood. Similarly, my story invited me to consider what is commonly called the **"Freudian theory of bisexuality."** Sigmund Freud shocked the post-Victorian world by suggesting that all people go through a stage, early in life, when they are attracted to people of the same sex. Adult experiences, Freud argued, eventually led most people to shift their sexual desire to what Freud called an appropriate "love object"—a person of the opposite sex. I also considered my experience in light of what lesbian feminist author Adrienne Rich called **institution of compulsory heterosexuality.** Perhaps the extremely high levels of homophobia that are often endemic in boys' and men's organized sports led me to deny and repress my own homoerotic desire through a direct and overt rejection of Timmy, through homophobic banter with male peers, and through the resultant stigmatization of the feminized Timmy. And eventually, I considered my experience in light of what the radical theorist Herbert Marcuse called the **sublimation of homoerotic desire** into an aggressive, violent act as serving to construct a clear line of demarcation between self-and-other. Sublimation, according to Marcuse, involves the driving underground, into the unconscious, of sexual desires that might appear dangerous due to their socially stigmatized status. But sublimation involves more than simple repression into the unconscious—it involves a transformation of sexual desire into something else—often into aggressive and violent acting out toward others, acts that clarify boundaries between one's self and others and therefore lessen any anxieties that might be attached to the repressed homoerotic desire.

Importantly, in our analysis of my story, my memory group went beyond simply discussing the events in psychological terms. My story did suggest some deep psychological processes at work, perhaps, but it also revealed the importance of social context—in this case, the context of the athletic team. In short, my rejection of Timmy and the joining with teammates to stigmatize him in ninth grade stands as an example of what sociologist R. W. Connell calls a **moment of engagement with hegemonic masculinity,** where I actively took up the male group's task of constructing heterosexual/masculine identities in the context of sport. The elbow in Timmy's gut three years later can be seen as a punctuation mark that occurred precisely because of my fears that I might be failing at this goal.

It is helpful, I think, to compare my story with gay and lesbian "coming out" stories in sport. Though we have a few lesbian and bisexual coming out stories among women athletes, there are very few gay male coming out stories. Tom Waddell, who as a closeted gay man finished sixth in the decathlon in the 1968 Olympics, later came out and started the Gay Games, an athletic and cultural festival that draws tens of thousands of people every four years. When I interviewed Tom Waddell over a decade ago about his sexual identity and athletic career, he made it quite clear that for many years sports *was* his closet. Tom told me,

> When I was a kid, I was tall for my age, and was very thin and very strong. And I was usually faster than most other people. But I discovered rather early that I liked gymnastics and I liked dance. I was very interested in being a ballet dancer . . . [but] something became obvious to me right away—that male ballet dancers were effeminate, that they were what most people would call faggots. And I thought I just couldn't handle that . . . I was totally closeted and very concerned about being male. This was the fifties, a terrible time to live, and everything was stacked against me. Anyway, I realized that I had to do something to protect my image of myself as a male—because at that time homosexuals were thought of primarily as men who wanted to be women. And so I threw myself into atheletics—I played football, gymnastics, track and field . . . I was a

jock—that's how I was viewed, and I was comfortable with that.

Tom Waddell was fully conscious of entering sports and constructing a masculine/heterosexual athletic identity precisely because he feared being revealed as gay. It was clear to him, in the context of the 1950s, that being revealed as gay would undercut his claims to the status of manhood. Thus, though he described the athletic closet as "hot and stifling," he remained in the closet until several years after his athletic retirement. He even knowingly played along with locker room discussions about sex and women, knowing that this was part of his "cover":

> I wanted to be viewed as male, otherwise I would be a dancer today. I wanted the male, macho image of an athlete. So I was protected by a very hard shell. I was clearly aware of what I was doing . . . I often felt compelled to go along with a lot of locker room garbage because I wanted that image—and I know a lot of others who did too.

Like my story, Waddell's story points to the importance of the athletic institution as a context in which peers mutually construct and re-construct narrow definitions of masculinity—and heterosexuality is considered to be a rock-solid foundation of this conception of masculinity. But unlike my story, Waddell's story may invoke what sociologist Erving Goffman called a "dramaturgical analysis": Waddell seemed to be consciously "acting" to control and regulate others' perceptions of him by constructing a public "front stage" persona that differed radically from what he believed to be his "true" inner self. My story, in contrast, suggests a deeper, less consciously strategic repression of my homoerotic attraction. Most likely, I was aware on some level of the dangers of such feelings, and was escaping the dangers, disgrace, and rejection that would likely result from being different. For Waddell, the decision to construct his identity largely within sport was a decision to step into a fiercely heterosexual/masculine closet that would hide what he saw to be his "true" identity. In contrast, I was not so much stepping into a "closet" that would hide my identify—rather, I was stepping out into an entire world of heterosexual privilege. My story also suggests how a *threat* to the promised privileges of hegemonic masculinity—my failure as an athlete—might trigger a momentary sexual panic that could lay bare the constructedness, indeed, the *instability* of the heterosexual/masculine identity.

In either case—Waddell's or mine—we can see how, as young male athletes, heterosexuality and masculinity were not something we "were," but something we were *doing*. It is very significant, I think, that as each of us was "doing heterosexuality," neither of us was actually "having sex" with women (though one of us desperately wanted to!). This underscores a point made by some recent theorists, that heterosexuality should not be thought of simply as sexual acts between women and men; rather, **heterosexuality is a constructed identity, a performance, and an institution** that is not necessarily linked to sexual acts. Though for one of us it was more conscious than for the other, we were both "doing heterosexuality" as an ongoing practice through which we sought (a) to avoid stigma, embarrassment, ostracism, or perhaps worse if we were even suspected of being gay; and (b) to link ourselves into systems of power, status, and privilege that appear to be the birthright of "real men" (i.e., males who are able to successfully compete with other males in sport, work, and sexual relations with women). In other words, each of us actively scripted our own sexual/gender performances, but these scripts were constructed within the constraints of a socially organized (institutionalized) system of power and pleasure.

QUESTIONS FOR FUTURE RESEARCH

As I prepared to tell my above sexual story publicly to my colleagues at the sport studies conference, I felt extremely nervous. Part of the nervousness was due to the fact that I knew some of my colleagues would object to my claim that telling personal stories can be a source of sociological insights. But a larger part of the reason for my nervousness was due to the fact that I was revealing something very personal about my sexuality in such a public way. Most of us aren't used to doing this, especially in the context of a professional conference. But I had learned long ago, especially from feminist women scholars, and from gay and lesbian scholars, that biography is linked to history, and that part of "normal" academic discourse has been to hide "the personal" (including the fact that the researcher is himself or herself a person, with values, feelings, and, yes, biases) behind a carefully constructed facade of "objectivity." Rather than trying to hide—or be ashamed of—one's subjective experience of the world, I was challenging myself to draw on my experience of the world as a resource. Not that I should trust my experience as the final word on "reality"—white, heterosexual males like myself have made the mistake for centuries of calling their own experience "objectivity," and then punishing anyone who does not share their world view as "deviant." Instead, I hope to use my experience as an example of how those of us who are in dominant sexual/racial/gender/class categories can get a new perspective on the "constructedness" of our identities by juxtaposing our subjective experiences against the recently emerging world views of gay men and lesbians, women, and people of color.

Finally, I want to stress that, juxtaposed, my and Tom Waddell's stories do not shed much light on the question of why some individuals "become gay" while others "become" heterosexual or bisexual. Instead, I'd like to suggest that this is a dead-end question, and that there are far more important and interesting questions to be asked:

- How has heterosexuality, as an institution and as an enforced group practice, constrained and limited all of us—gay, straight, and bi?
- How has the institution of sport been an especially salient institution for the social construction of heterosexual masculinity?
- Why is it that when men play sports they are almost always automatically granted masculine status, and thus assumed to be heterosexual, while when women play sports, questions are raised about their "femininity" and their sexual orientation?

These kinds of questions aim us toward an analysis of the workings of power within institutions—including the ways that these workings of power shape and constrain our identities and relationships—and point us toward imagining alternative social arrangements that are less constraining for everyone.

REFERENCES

Haug, Frigga. 1987. *Female Sexualization: A Collective Work of Memory*. London: Verso.

Katz, Jonathan Ned. 1995. *The Invention of Heterosexuality*. New York: Dutton.

Messner, Michael A. 1992. *Power at Play: Sports and the Problem of Masculinity*. Boston: Beacon Press.

———. 1994. "Gay Athletes and the Gay Games: An Interview with Tom Waddell," in M. A. Messner & D. F. Sabo (Eds.), *Sex, Violence and Power in Sports: Rethinking Masculinity* (pp. 113–119). Freedom, CA: The Crossing Press.

Pronger, Brian. 1990. *The Arena of Masculinity: Sports, Homosexuality, and the Meaning of Sex*. New York: St. Martin's Press.

MY WORDS TO VICTOR FRANKENSTEIN ABOVE
THE VILLAGE OF CHAMOUNIX

Susan Stryker

The transsexual body is an unnatural body. It is the product of medical science. It is a technological construction. It is flesh torn apart and sewn together again in a shape other than that in which it was born. In these circumstances, I find a deep affinity between myself as a transsexual woman and the monster in Mary Shelley's *Frankenstein*. Like the monster, I am too often perceived as less than fully human due to the means of my embodiment; like the monster's as well, my exclusion from human community fuels a deep and abiding rage in me that I, like the monster, direct against the conditions in which I must struggle to exist. . . .

I want to lay claim to the dark power of my monstrous identity without using it as a weapon against others or being wounded by it myself. I will say this as bluntly as I know how: I am a transsexual, and therefore I am a monster. Just as the words "dyke," "fag," "queer," "slut," and "whore" have been reclaimed, respectively, by lesbians and gay men, by anti-assimilationist sexual minorities, by women who pursue erotic pleasure, and by sex industry workers, words like "creature," "monster," and "unnatural" need to be reclaimed by the transgendered. By embracing and accepting them, even piling one on top of another, we may dispel their ability to harm us. A creature, after all, in the dominant tradition of Western European culture, is nothing other than a created being, a made thing. The affront you humans take at being called a "creature" results from the threat the term poses to your status as "lords of creation," beings elevated above mere material existence. As in the case of being called "it," being called a "creature" suggests the lack or loss of a superior personhood. I find no shame, however, in acknowledging my egalitarian relationship with non-human material Being; everything emerges from the same matrix of possibilities. "Monster" is derived from the Latin noun *monstrum*, "divine portent," itself formed on the root of the verb *monere*, "to warn." It came to refer to living things of anom-

alous shape or structure, or to fabulous creatures like the sphinx who were composed of strikingly incongruous parts, because the ancients considered the appearance of such beings to be a sign of some impending supernatural event. Monsters, like angels, functioned as messengers and heralds of the extraordinary. They served to announce impending revelation, saying, in effect, "Pay attention; something of profound importance is happening."

Hearken unto me, fellow creatures. I who have dwelt in a form unmatched with my desire, I whose flesh has become an assemblage of incongruous anatomical parts, I who achieve the similitude of a natural body only through an unnatural process, I offer you this warning: the Nature you bedevil me with is a lie. Do not trust it to protect you from what I represent, for it is a fabrication that cloaks the groundlessness of the privilege you seek to maintain for yourself at my expense. You are as constructed as me; the same anarchic Womb has birthed us both. I call upon you to investigate your nature as I have been compelled to confront mine. I challenge you to risk abjection and flourish as well as have I. Heed my words, and you may well discover the seams and sutures in yourself. . . .

Journal (February 18, 1993)

Kim sat between my spread legs, her back to me, her tailbone on the edge of the table. Her left hand gripped my thigh so hard the bruises are still there a week later. Sweating and bellowing, she pushed one last time and the baby finally came. Through my lover's back, against the skin of my own belly, I felt a child move out of another woman's body and into the world. Strangers' hands snatched it away to suction the sticky green meconium from its airways. "It's a girl," somebody said. Paul, I think. Why, just then, did a jumble of dark, unsolicited feelings emerge wordlessly from some quiet back corner of my mind? This moment of miracles was not the time to deal with them. I pushed them back, knowing they were too strong to avoid for long.

After three days we were all exhausted, slightly disappointed that complications had forced us to go to Kaiser instead of having the birth at home. I wonder what the hospital staff thought of our little tribe swarming all over the delivery room: Stephanie, the midwife; Paul, the baby's father; Kim's sister Gwen; my son Wilson and me; and the two other women who make up our family, Anne and Heather. And of course Kim and the baby. She named her Denali, after the mountain in Alaska. I don't think the medical folks had a clue as to how we all considered ourselves to be related to each other. When the labor first began we all took turns shifting between various supporting roles, but as the ordeal progressed we settled into a more stable pattern. I found myself acting as birth coach. Hour after hour, through dozens of sets of contractions, I focused everything on Kim, helping her stay in control of her emotions as she gave herself over to this inexorable process, holding on to her eyes with mine to keep the pain from throwing her out of her body, breathing every breath with her, being a companion. I participated, step by increasingly intimate step, in the ritual transformation of consciousness surrounding her daughter's birth. Birth rituals work to prepare the self for a profound opening, an opening as psychic as it is corporeal. Kim's body brought this ritual process to a dramatic resolution for her, culminating in a visceral, cathartic experience. But my body left me hanging. I had gone on a journey to the point at which my companion had to go on alone, and I needed to finish my trip for myself. To conclude the birth ritual I had participated in, I needed to move something in me as profound as a whole human life.

I floated home from the hospital, filled with a vital energy that wouldn't discharge. I puttered about until I was alone: my ex had come over for Wilson; Kim and Denali were still at the hospital with Paul; Stephanie had gone, and everyone else was out for a much-needed walk. Finally, in the solitude of my home, I burst apart like a wet paper bag and spilled the emotional contents of my life through the hands I cupped like a sieve over my face. For days, as I had accompanied my partner on her journey, I had been progressively opening myself and preparing to let go of whatever was deepest within. Now everything in me flowed out, moving up from inside and out through my throat, my mouth because these things could never pass between the lips of my cunt. I knew the darkness I had glimpsed earlier would reemerge, but I had vast oceans of feeling to experience before that came up again.

Simple joy in the presence of new life came bubbling out first, wave after wave of it. I was so incredibly happy. I was so in love with Kim, had so much admiration for her strength and courage. I felt pride and excitement about the queer family we were building with Wilson, Anne, Heather, Denali, and whatever babies would follow. We've all tasted an exhilarating possibility in communal living and these nurturing, bonded kinships for which we have no adequate names. We joke about pioneering on a reverse frontier: venturing into the heart of civilization itself to reclaim biological reproduction from heterosexism and free it for our own uses. We're fierce; in a world of "traditional family values," we need to be.

Sometimes, though, I still mourn the passing of old, more familiar ways. It wasn't too long ago that my ex and I were married, woman and man. That love had been genuine, and the grief over its loss real. I had always wanted intimacy with women more than intimacy with men, and that wanting had always felt queer to me. She needed it to appear straight. The shape of my flesh was a barrier that estranged me from my desire. Like a body without a mouth, I was starving in the midst of plenty. I would not let myself starve, even if what it took to open myself for a deep connectedness cut off the deepest connections I actually had. So I abandoned one life and built this new one. The fact that she and I have begun getting along again, after so much strife between us, makes the bitterness of our separation somewhat sweet. On the day of the birth, this past loss was present even in its partial recovery; held up beside the newfound fullness in my life, it evoked a poignant, hopeful sadness that inundated me.

Frustration and anger soon welled up in abundance. In spite of all I'd accomplished, my identity still felt so tenuous. Every circumstance of life seemed to conspire against me in one vast, composite act of invalidation and erasure. In the body

(continued)

I was born with, I had been invisible as the person I considered myself to be; I had been invisible as a queer while the form of my body made my desires look straight. Now, as a dyke I am invisible among women; as a transsexual, I am invisible among dykes. As the partner of a new mother, I am often invisible as a transsexual, a woman, and a lesbian. I've lost track of the friends and acquaintances these past nine months who've asked me if I was the father. It shows so dramatically how much they simply don't get what I'm doing with my body. The high price of whatever visible, intelligible, self-representation I have achieved makes the continuing experience of invisibility maddeningly difficult to bear.

The collective assumptions of the naturalized order soon overwhelmed me. Nature exerts such a hegemonic oppression. Suddenly I felt lost and scared, lonely and confused. How did that little Mormon boy from Oklahoma I used to be grow up to be a transsexual leatherdyke in San Francisco with a Berkeley Ph.D.? Keeping my bearings on such a long and strange trip seemed a ludicrous proposition. Home was so far gone behind me it was gone forever, and there was no place to rest. Battered by heavy emotions, a little dazed, I felt the inner walls that protect me dissolve to leave me vulnerable to all that could harm me. I cried, and abandoned myself to abject despair over what gender had done to me. . . .

By speaking as a monster in my personal voice, by using the dark, watery images of Romanticism and lapsing occasionally into its brooding cadences and grandiose postures, I employ the same literary techniques Mary Shelley used to elicit sympathy for her scientist's creation. Like that creature, I assert my worth as a monster in spite of the conditions my monstrosity requires me to face, and redefine a life worth living. I have asked the Miltonic questions Shelley poses in the epigraph of her novel: "Did I request thee, Maker, from my clay to mould me man? Did I solicit thee from darkness to promote me?" With one voice, her monster and I answer "no" without debasing ourselves, for we have done the hard work of constituting ourselves on our own terms, against the natural order. Though we forgo the privilege of naturalness, we are not deterred, for we ally ourselves instead with the chaos and blackness from which Nature itself spills forth.[1]

If this is your path, as it is mine, let me offer whatever solace you may find in this monstrous benediction: May you discover the enlivening power of darkness within yourself. May it nourish your rage. May your rage inform your actions, and your actions transform you as you struggle to transform your world.

NOTE

1. Although I mean "chaos" here in its general sense, it is interesting to speculate about the potential application of scientific chaos theory to model the emergence of stable structures of gendered identities out of the unstable matrix of material attributes, and on the production of proliferating gender identities from a relatively simple set of gendering procedures.

WORK CITED

Shelley, Mary. *Frankenstein, or The Modern Prometheus.* Orig. pub. 1817. New York: Signet/NAL, 1965.

SECTION 8

Bodies

It might seem that women's physical bodies and health are biological rather than social matters. In fact, however, factors such as access to health care, working conditions, and nutrition are all socially determined and have a big impact on our physical selves. In addition, cultural ideologies about women's bodies affect how we perceive our own bodies, as well as how social institutions regulate women's bodies and health. As with the other aspects of women's lives that we have explored so far, class, race, ethnicity, sexuality, and ability intersect with gender in shaping the social and cultural forces that affect women's health and physical well-being.

Women's bodies are contested terrain, the subject of struggle over political rights, reproductive rights, health care, and medical research. The ability to control reproduction, to live and work in conditions not injurious to health, and to receive safe, effective, and affordable medical care are central to all women's welfare. Feminists have devoted considerable energy to changing public health policy on women's behalf and to increasing research funding for women's health issues during the last two decades.

In the 1970s, a women's health movement developed in the United States as an outgrowth of the feminist and consumer health movements. Women's health advocates criticized and challenged the medical establishment's tendency to view women as abnormal and inherently diseased simply because the female reproductive cycle deviates from the male. Women today across the world are asserting the right to control their own bodies by exposing and resisting the medical abuse of women in forms ranging from forced sterilization and sex selection favoring male children to pharmaceutical experimentation. Women are also increasing their control over their own health care by enhancing access to information and specialized training that allows them more accurately to assess their health care needs and make informed decisions about medical treatment. These movements focused on improving women's health care have recently worked alongside other movements, such as those organizing against AIDS or working for improved nutrition and preventative health care for the poor in the United States as well as in third world countries.

This section explores different aspects of the social construction of women's bodies and the experiences of diverse women with body issues. Suzanne Kessler's article in Section Two ("The Medical Construction of Gender") showed that the medical system actively constructs sex categories. In "Hormonal Hurricanes: Menstruation, Menopause, and Female Behavior," Anne Fausto-Sterling discusses additional ways that medicine shapes our understandings of gender. She examines traditional research on menstruation and menopause and finds that it reflects a deep bias against women by advancing the view that women are "slaves of their reproductive physiologies." Reviewing feminist studies of premenstrual syndrome and menopause, Fausto-Sterling suggests other approaches to women's health issues. Her work shows us that social contexts deeply affect medical interpretations of the female reproductive cycle. Can you think of additional examples of how beliefs about gender are reflected in medical approaches to women's or men's reproductive health?

349

Social contexts also shape and create health problems. Becky Wangsgaard Thompson examines the social roots of women's eating problems in "'A Way Outa No Way': Eating Problems among African-American, Latina, and White Women." Thompson argues that compulsive eating, compulsive dieting, anorexia, and bulimia are coping strategies that women employ in response to sexual abuse, poverty, heterosexism, racism, and "class injuries." Eating problems thus are not just about conforming to a norm of physical appearance but are also a "serious response to injustices." Thompson's article illustrates how examining women's multiple oppressions—race, class, and sexuality, as well as gender—can alter feminist analyses. What differences does she see between the different groups she examines? What kinds of social change would be necessary to eliminate eating problems?

In "Loose Lips Sink Ships," Simone Weil Davis looks at a different kind of bodily "problem" beginning to gain attention in the United States: droopy labia. She compares women's dissatisfaction with their genitals, leading them to embrace cosmetic surgery, to the motivations behind genital cutting in some African societies. At the same time that she argues against genital surgery of any kind, she challenges us to forgo the assumption that U.S. women "choose" such surgeries while African women are helpless victims forced to undergo them. What are the forces that lead women in different contexts to alter their bodies? How does Davis's analysis compare to Gimlin's article in Section Three about other forms of cosmetic surgery? What do you think about the practice of labiaplasty? About other kinds of genital surgery?

Andrea Smith, in "Beyond Pro-Choice versus Pro-Life," questions the approaches of both sides of the abortion debate from the perspective of women of color, poor women, and women with disabilities. Beginning with the complicated responses of Native American women to the question of whether they were "pro-choice" or "pro-life," Smith challenges the reliance of both groups on imprisonment as a solution to issues of reproductive rights. Arguing that neither side attends to the issues of marginalized women, she advocates a more complex response to the barriers to reproductive justice for women both in the United States and abroad. What kinds of approaches might make a difference? How might feminists go about fighting for what Smith calls "reproductive justice"?

The last article in this section takes an irreverent approach to the "cult of the survivor" of cancer, specifically breast cancer. Barbara Ehrenreich tells the story of her experience of cancer and chemotherapy, taking off from it to analyze the politics and culture of cancer. Critical of the pink-ribbon culture and insistence that having cancer somehow ennobles one, Ehrenreich questions the role of environmental factors in causing cancer and drug companies in promoting the culture of cancer survivorship. How gendered is her experience of cancer? Do you agree with her criticism of the focus on the positive side of surviving cancer? How would you compare the treatment of women with breast cancer to that of women with other illnesses, such as cerebral palsy (see the boxed insert by Eli Clare)?

Together, these articles show the diverse ways in which bodies are socially constructed. What might a feminist agenda for the body include?

Hormonal Hurricanes: Menstruation, Menopause, and Female Behavior

Woman is a pair of ovaries with a human being attached, whereas man is a human being furnished with a pair of testes.

—Rudolf Virchow, MD (1821–1902)

Estrogen is responsible for that strange mystical phenomenon, the feminine state of mind.

—David Reuben, MD, 1969

In 1900, the president of the American Gynecological Association eloquently accounted for the female life cycle:

Many a young life is battered and forever crippled in the breakers of puberty; if it crosses these unharmed and is not dashed to pieces on the rock of childbirth, it may still ground on the ever-recurring shadows of menstruation and lastly upon the final bar of the menopause ere protection is found in the unruffled waters of the harbor beyond the reach of the sexual storms.[1]

Since then we have amassed an encyclopedia's worth of information about the existence of hormones, the function of menstruation, the regulation of ovulation, and the physiology of menopause. Yet many people, scientists and nonscientists alike, still believe that women function at the beck and call of their hormonal physiology. In 1970, for example, Dr. Edgar Berman, the personal physician of former Vice President Hubert Humphrey, responded to a female member of Congress:

Even a Congresswoman must defer to scientific truths . . . there just are physical and psychological inhibitants that limit a female's potential. . . . I would still rather have a male John F. Kennedy make the Cuban missile crisis decisions than a female of the same age

who could possibly be subject to the curious mental aberrations of that age group.[2]

In a more grandiose mode, Professor Steven Goldberg, a university sociologist, writes that "men and women differ in their hormonal systems . . . every society demonstrates patriarchy, male dominance, and male attainment. The thesis put forth here is that the hormonal renders the social inevitable."[3]

At the broadest political level, writers such as Berman and Goldberg raise questions about the competency of *any and all* females to work successfully in positions of leadership, while for women working in other types of jobs, the question is, Should they receive less pay or more restricted job opportunities simply because they menstruate or experience menopause? And further, do women in the throes of premenstrual frenzy frequently try to commit suicide? Do they really suffer from a "diminished responsibility" that should exempt them from legal sanctions when they beat their children or murder their boyfriends?[4] Is the health of large numbers of women threatened by inappropriate and even ignorant medical attention—medical diagnoses that miss real health problems, while resulting instead in the prescription of dangerous medication destined to create future disease?

The idea that women's reproductive systems direct their lives is ancient. But whether it was Plato, writing about the disruption caused by barren uteri wandering about the body,[5] Pliny, writing that a look from a menstruating woman will "dim the brightness of mirrors, blunt the edge of steel, and take away the polish from ivory,"[6] or modern scientists writing about the changing levels of estrogen and progesterone, certain messages emerge quite clearly. Women, by nature emotionally erratic, cannot be trusted in positions of responsibility. Their dangerous, unpredictable furies warrant control by the medical profession,[a] while ironically, the same "dangerous" females also need protection because their reproductive systems, so necessary for the procreation of the race, are vulnerable to stress and hard work.

"The breakers of puberty," in fact, played a key role in a debate about higher education for women, a controversy that began in the last quarter of the nineteenth century and still echoes today in the halls of academe. Scientists of the late 1800s argued on physiological grounds that women and men should receive different types of education. Women, they believed, could not survive intact the rigors of higher education. Their reasons were threefold: first, the education of young women might cause serious damage to their reproductive systems. Energy devoted to scholastic work would deprive the reproductive organs of the necessary "flow of power," presenting particular problems for pubescent women, for whom the establishment of regular menstruation was of paramount importance. Physicians cited cases of women unable to bear children because they pursued a course of education designed for the more resilient young man.[7] In an interesting parallel to modern nature–nurture debates, proponents of higher education for women countered biological arguments with environmental ones. One anonymous author argued that, denied the privilege afforded their brothers of romping actively through the woods, women became fragile and nervous.[8]

Opponents of higher education for women also claimed that females were less intelligent than males, an assertion based partly on brain size itself but also on the overall size differences between men and women. They held that women cannot "consume so much food as men . . . [because] their average size remains so much smaller; so that the sum total of food converted into thought by women can never equal the sum total of food converted to thought by men. It follows, therefore, that *men will always think more than women.*"[9] One respondent to this bit of scientific reasoning asked the thinking reader to examine the data: Aristotle and Napoleon were short, Newton, Spinoza, Shakespeare, and Comte delicate and of medium height, Descartes and Bacon sickly, "while unfortunately for a theory based upon superior digestion, Goethe and Carlyle were confirmed dyspeptics."[10] Finally, as if pubertal vulnerability and lower intelligence were not enough, it seemed to nineteenth-century scientists that menstruation rendered women "more or less sick and unfit for hard work"

"for one quarter of each month during the best years of life."[11]

Although dated in some of the particulars, the turn-of-the-century scientific belief that women's reproductive functions make them unsuitable for higher education remains with us today. Some industries bar fertile women from certain positions because of workplace hazards that might cause birth defects, while simultaneously deeming equally vulnerable men fit for the job.[b] Some modern psychologists and biologists suggest that women perform more poorly than do men on mathematics tests because hormonal sex differences alter male and female brain structures; many people believe women to be unfit for certain professions because they menstruate. Others argue that premenstrual changes cause schoolgirls to do poorly in their studies, to become slovenly and disobedient, and even to develop a "nymphomaniac urge [that] may be responsible for young girls running away from home . . . only to be found wandering in the park or following boys."[12]

If menstruation really casts such a dark shadow on women's lives, we ought certainly to know more about it—how it works, whether it can be controlled, and whether it indeed warrants the high level of concern expressed by some. Do women undergo emotional changes as they progress through the monthly ovulatory cycle? And if so, do hormonal fluctuations bring on these ups and downs? If not—if a model of biological causation is appropriate—how else might we conceptualize what happens?

THE SHADOWS OF MENSTRUATION: A READER'S LITERATURE GUIDE

The Premenstrual Syndrome

> *Science update: premenstrual strain linked to crime*
>
> —*Providence Journal*

> *Erratic female behavior tied to premenstrual syndrome*
>
> —*Providence Journal*

> *Violence by women is linked to menstruation*
>
> —*National Enquirer*

Menstruation makes news, and the headlines summarize the message. According to Dr. Katharina Dalton, premenstrual syndrome (PMS) is a medical problem of enormous dimensions. Under the influence of the tidal hormonal flow, women batter their children and husbands, miss work, commit crimes, attempt suicide, and suffer from up to 150 different symptoms, including headaches, epilepsy, dizziness, asthma, hoarseness, nausea, constipation, bloating, increased appetite, low blood sugar, joint and muscle pains, heart palpitations, skin disorders, breast tenderness, glaucoma, and conjunctivitis.[13] Although the great concern expressed in the newspaper headlines just quoted may come from a single public relations source,[14] members of the medical profession seem eager to accept at face value the idea that "70 to 90 percent of the female population will admit to recurrent premenstrual symptoms and that 20 to 40 percent report some degree of mental or physical incapacitation."[15]

If all this is true, then we have on our hands nothing less than an overwhelming public health problem, one that deserves a considerable investment of national resources in order to develop understanding and treatment. If, on the other hand, the claims about premenstrual tension are cut from whole cloth, then the consequences are equally serious. Are there women in need of proper medical treatment who do not receive it? Do some receive dangerous medication to treat nonexistent physiological problems? How often are women refused work, given lower salaries, taken less seriously because of beliefs about hormonally induced erratic behavior? In the game of PMS the stakes are high.

The key issues surrounding PMS are so complex and interrelated that it is hard to know where to begin. There is, as always, the question of evidence. To begin with we can look, in vain, for credible research that defines and analyzes PMS. Despite the publication of thousands of pages of allegedly scientific analyses, the most recent literature reviews simultaneously lament the lack of properly done studies and call for a consistent and acceptable research definition and methodology.[16] Intimately related to the question of evidence is that of conceptualization. Currently held theoretical views about the reproductive cycle are inadequate to the task of understanding the emotional ups and downs of people functioning in a complex world. Finally, lurking beneath all of the difficulties of research design, poor methods, and muddy thinking is the medical world's view of the naturally abnormal woman. Let's look at this last point first.

If you're a woman you can't win. Historically, females who complained to physicians about menstrual difficulties, pain during the menstrual flow, or physical or emotional changes associated with the premenstruum heard that they were neurotic. They imagined the pain and made up the tension because they recognized menstruation as a failure to become pregnant, to fulfill their true role as a woman.[17] With the advent of the women's health movement, however, women began to speak for themselves.[18] The pain is real, they said; our bodies change each month. The medical profession responded by finding biological/hormonal causes, proposing the need for doctor-supervised cures. A third voice, however, entered in: that of feminists worried about repercussions from the idea that women's natural functions represent a medical problem capable of preventing women from competing in the world outside the home. Although this multisided discussion continues, I currently operate on the premise that some women probably do require medical attention for incapacitating physical changes that occur in synchrony with their menstrual cycle. Yet in the absence of any reliable medical research into the problem it is impossible to diagnose true disease or to develop rational treatment. To start with, we must decide what is normal.

The tip-off to the medical viewpoint lies in its choice of language. What does it mean to say "70 to 90 percent of the female population will admit to recurrent premenstrual symptoms"?[19] The word *symptom* carries two rather different meanings. The first suggests a disease or an abnormality, a condition to be cured or rendered normal. Applying this connotation to a statistic suggesting 70 to 90 percent symptom formation leads one to conclude that the large majority of women are by their very nature diseased. The second meaning of *symptom* is that of a sign or signal. If the figure of 70 to 90 percent means nothing more than that most women recognize signs in their own bodies of an oncoming menstrual flow, the statistics are unremarkable. Consider then the following, written in 1974 by three scientists:

> It is estimated that from 25 percent to 100 percent of women experience some form of premenstrual or menstrual emotional disturbance. Eichner makes the discerning point that the few women who do not admit to premenstrual tension are basically unaware of it but one only has to talk to their husbands or co-workers to confirm its existence.[20]

Is it possible that up to 100 percent of all menstruating women regularly experience emotional disturbance? Compared to whom? Are males the unstated standard of emotional stability? If there is but a single definition of what is normal and men fit that definition, then women with "female complaints" must by definition be either crazy or in need of medical attention. A double bind indeed.

Some scientists explicitly articulate the idea of the naturally abnormal female. Professor Frank Beach, a pioneer in the field of animal psychology and its relationship to sexuality, suggests the following evolutionary account of menstruation. In primitive hunter–gatherer societies adult women were either pregnant or lactating, and since life spans were so short they died well before menopause; low-fat diets made it likely that they did not ovulate every month; they thus experienced no more than ten menstrual cycles. Given current life expectancies as well as the widespread use of birth control, modern women may experience a total of 400 menstrual cycles. He concludes from this reasoning that "civilization has given women *a physiologically abnormal status* which may have important implications for the interpretation of psychological responses to periodic fluctuations in the secretion of ovarian hormones"—that is, to menstruation (emphasis added).[21] Thus the first problem we face in evaluating the literature on the premenstrual syndrome is figuring out how to deal with the underlying assumption that women have "a physiologically abnormal status."

Researchers who believe in PMS hold a wide variety of viewpoints (none of them supported by scientific data) about the basis of the problem. For example, Dr. Katharina Dalton, the most militant promoter of PMS, says that it results from a relative end-of-the-cycle deficiency in the hormone progesterone. Others cite deficiencies in vitamin B$_6$, fluid retention, and low blood sugar as possible causes. Suggested treatments range from hormone injection to the use of lithium, diuretics, megadoses of vitamins, and control of sugar in the diet[22] (see Table 1 for a complete list). Although some of these treatments are harmless, others are not. Progesterone injection causes cancer in animals. What will it do to humans? And a recent issue of the *New England Journal of Medicine* contains a report that large doses of vitamin B$_6$ damage the nerves, causing a loss of feeling in one's fingers and toes.[23] The wide variety of PMS "causes" and "cures" offered by the experts is confusing, to put it mildly. Just what *is* this syndrome that causes such controversy? How can a woman know if she has it?

TABLE I   ALLEGED CAUSES AND PROPOSED TREATMENTS OF PMS

Hypothesized Causes of Premenstrual Syndrome	Various PMS Treatments (used but not validated)
Estrogen excess	Oral contraceptives (combination estrogen and progesterone pills)
Progesterone deficiency	
Vitamin B deficiency	Estrogen alone
Vitamin A deficiency	Natural progesterone
Hypoglycemia	Synthetic progestins
Endogenous hormone allergy	Valium or other tranquilizers
Psychosomatic	Nutritional supplements
Fluid retention	Minerals
Dysfunction of the neurointermediate lobe of the pituitary	Lithium
	Diuretics
Prolactin metabolism	A prolactin inhibitor/ dopamine agonist
	Exercise
	Psychotherapy, relaxation, education, reassurance

Sources: Robert L. Reid and S. S. Yen, "Premenstrual Syndrome," *American Journal of Obstetrics and Gynecology* 139 (1981): 85–104; and Judith Abplanalp, "Premenstrual Syndrome: A Selective Review." *Women and Health* 8 (1983): 107–24.

With a case of the measles it's really quite simple. A fever and then spots serve as diagnostic signs. A woman said to have PMS, however, may or may not have any of a very large number of symptoms. Furthermore, PMS indicators such as headaches, depression, dizziness, and loss or gain of appetite show up in everyone from time to time. Their mere presence cannot (as would measle spots) help one to diagnose the syndrome. In addition, whether any of these signals connote disease depends upon their severity. A slight headache may reflect nothing more than a lack of sleep, but repeated, severe headaches could indicate high blood pressure. As one researcher, Dr. Judith Abplanalp, succinctly put it: "There is no one set of symptoms which is considered to be the hallmark of or standard criterion for defining the premenstrual syndrome."[24] Dr. Katharina Dalton agrees but feels one can diagnose PMS quite simply by applying the term to "any symptoms or complaints which regularly come just before or during early menstruation but are absent at other times of the cycle."[25] Dalton contrasts this with men suffering from potential PMS "symptoms," because, she says, they experience them randomly during the month while women with the same physical indications acknowledge them only during the premenstruum.

PMS research usually bases itself on an ideal, regular, twenty-eight-day menstrual cycle. Researchers eliminate as subjects for study women with infrequent, shorter, or longer cycles. As a result, published investigations look at a skewed segment of the overall population. Even for those women with a regular cycle, however, a methodological problem remains because few researchers define the premenstrual period in the same way. Some studies look only at the day or two preceding the menstrual flow, others look at the week preceding, while workers such as Dalton cite cases that begin two weeks before menstruation and continue for one week after. Since so few investigations use exactly the same definition, research publications on PMS are difficult to compare with one another.[26] On this score if no other, the literature offers little useful insight, extensive as it is.

Although rarely stated, the assumption is that there is but *one* PMS. Dalton defines the problem so broadly that she and others may well lump together several phenomena of very different origins, a possibility heightened by the fact that investigators rarely assess the severity of the symptoms. Two women, one suffering from a few low days and the other from suicidal depression, may both be diagnosed as having PMS. Yet their difficulties could easily have different origins and ought certainly to receive different treatments. When investigators try carefully to define PMS, the number of people qualifying for study decreases dramatically. In one case a group used ten criteria (listed in Table 2) to define PMS only to find that no more than 20 percent of those who had volunteered for their research project met them.[27] In the absence of any clearly agreed-upon definition(s) of PMS, examinations of the topic should at least state clearly the methodology used; this would enable comparison between publications and allow us to begin to accumulate some knowledge about the issues at hand (Table 2 lists suggested baseline information). At the moment the literature is filled with individual studies that permit neither replication nor comparison with one another—an appropriate state,

TABLE 2 TOWARD A DEFINITION OF PREMENSTRUAL SYNDROME

Experimental criteria (rarely met in PMS studies):

Premenstrual symptoms for at least six preceding cycles

Moderate to severe physical and psychological symptoms

Symptoms *only* during the premenstrual period, with marked relief at onset of menses

Age between 18 and 45 years

Not pregnant

Regular menses for six previous cycles

No psychiatric disorder; normal physical examination and laboratory test profile

No drugs for preceding four weeks

Will not receive anxiolytics, diuretics, hormones, or neuroleptic drugs during the study

Minimal descriptive information to be offered in published studies of PMS (rarely offered in the current literature):

Specification of the ways in which subjects were recruited

Age limitations

Contraception and medication information

Marital status

Parity

Race

Menstrual history data

Assessment instruments

Operational definition of PMS

Psychiatric history data

Assessment of current psychological state

Criteria for assessment of severity of symptoms

Criteria for defining ovulatory status of cycle

Cutoff criteria for "unacceptable" subjects

Source: Judith Abplanalp, "Premenstrual Syndrome: A Selective Review," *Women and Health* 8 (1983): 107–24.

perhaps, for an art gallery but not for a field with pretensions to the scientific.

Despite the problems of method and definition, the conviction remains that PMS constitutes a widespread disorder, a conviction that fortifies and is fortified by the idea that women's reproductive function, so different from that of "normal" men, places them in a naturally diseased state. For those who believe that 90 percent of all women suffer from a disease called PMS, it becomes a reasonable research strategy to look at the normally functioning menstrual cycle for clues about the cause and possible treatment. There are, in fact, many theories but no credible evidence about the origins of PMS. In Table 1 I've listed the most frequently cited hypotheses, most of which involve in some manner the hormonal system that regulates menstruation. Some of the theories are ingenious and require a sophisticated knowledge of human physiology to comprehend. Nevertheless, the authors of one recent review quietly offer the following summary: "To date no one hypothesis has adequately explained the constellation of symptoms composing PMS."[28] In short, PMS is a disease in search of a definition and cause.

PMS also remains on the lookout for a treatment. That many have been tried is attested to in Table 1. The problem is that only rarely has the efficacy of these treatments been tested with the commonly accepted standard of a large-scale, double-blind study that includes placebos. In the few properly done studies "there is usually (1) a high placebo response and (2) the active agent is usually no better than a placebo."[29] In other words, women under treatment for PMS respond just as well to sugar pills as to medication containing hormones or other drugs. Since it is probable that some women experience severe distress caused by malfunctions of their menstrual system, the genuinely concerned physician faces a dilemma. Should he or she offer treatment until the patient says she feels better even though the drug used may have dangerous side effects; or should a doctor refuse help for as long as we know of no scientifically validated treatment for the patient's symptoms? I have no satisfactory answer. But the crying need for some scientifically acceptable research on the subject stands out above all. If we continue to assume that menstruation is itself pathological, we cannot establish a baseline of health against which to define disease. If, instead, we accept in theory that a range of menstrual normality exists, we can then set about designing studies that define the healthy female reproductive cycle. Only when we have some feeling for *that* can we begin to help women who suffer from diseases of menstruation.

Many of those who reject the alarmist nature of the publicity surrounding PMS believe nevertheless that women undergo mood changes during their menstrual cycle. Indeed, most western women would agree. But do studies of large segments of our population support this generality? And if so, what causes these ups and downs? In trying to answer these questions we confront another piece of the medical model of human behavior, the belief that biology is primary, that hormonal changes cause behavioral ones, but not vice versa. Most researchers use such a linear, unicausal model without thinking about it. Their framework is so much a part of their belief system that they forget to question it. Nevertheless it is the model from which they work, and failure to recognize and work skeptically with it often results in poorly conceived research combined with implausible interpretations of data. Although the paradigm of biological causation has until very recently dominated menstrual-cycle research, it now faces serious and intellectually stimulating challenge from feminist experts in the field. . . .

MENOPAUSE: THE STORM BEFORE THE CALM

An unlikely specter haunts the world. It is the ghost of former womanhood . . . "unfortunate women abounding in the streets walking stiffly in twos and threes, seeing little and observing less. . . . The world appears [to them] as through a grey veil, and they live as docile, harmless creatures missing most of life's values." According to Dr. Robert Wilson and Thelma Wilson, though, one should not be fooled by their "vapid cowlike negative state" because "there is ample evidence that the course of history has been changed not only by the presence of estrogen, but by its absence. The untold misery of alcoholism, drug addiction, divorce, and broken homes caused by these unstable estrogen-starved women cannot be presented in statistical form."[30]

Rather than releasing women from their monthly emotional slavery to the sex hormones, menopause involves them in new horrors. At the individual level one encounters the specter of sexual degeneration, described so vividly by Dr. David Reuben: "The vagina begins to shrivel, the breasts atrophy, sexual desire disappears. . . . Increased facial hair, deepening voice, obesity . . . coarsened features, enlargement of the clitoris, and gradual baldness complete the tragic picture. Not really a man but no longer a functional woman, these individuals live in the world of intersex."[31] At the demographic level, writers express foreboding about women of the baby-boom generation, whose life span has increased from an average forty-eight years at the turn of the century to a projected eighty years in the year 2000.[32] Modern medicine, it seems, has played a cruel trick on women. One hundred years ago they didn't live long enough to face the hardships of menopause but today their increased longevity means they will live for twenty-five to thirty years beyond the time when they lose all possibility of reproducing. To quote Dr. Wilson again: "The unpalatable truth must be faced that all postmenopausal women are castrates."[33]

But what medicine has wrought, it can also rend asunder. Few publications have had so great an effect on the lives of so many women as have those of Dr. Robert A. Wilson, who pronounced menopause to be a disease of estrogen deficiency. At the same time in an influential popular form, in his book *Feminine Forever*, he offered a treatment: estrogen replacement therapy (ERT).[34] During the first seven months following publication in 1966, Wilson's book sold one hundred thousand copies and was excerpted in *Vogue* and *Look* magazines. It influenced thousands of physicians to prescribe estrogen to millions of women, many of whom had no clinical "symptoms" other than cessation of the menses. As one of his credentials Wilson lists himself as head of the Wilson Research Foundation, an outfit funded by Ayerst Labs, Searle, and Upjohn, all pharmaceutical giants interested in the large potential market for estrogen. (After all, no woman who lives long enough can avoid menopause.) As late as 1976 Ayerst also supported the Information Center on the Mature Woman, a public relations firm that promoted estrogen replacement therapy. By 1975 some six million women had started long-term treatment with Premarin (the Ayerst Labs brand name for estrogen), making it the fourth or fifth most popular drug in the United States. Even today, two million of the forty million postmenopausal women in the United States contribute to the $70 million grossed each year from the sale of Premarin-brand estrogen.[35] The "disease of menopause" is not only a social problem: it's big business.[36]

The high sales of Premarin continue despite the publication in 1975 of an article linking estrogen treatment to uterine cancer.[37] Although in the wake of that publication many women stopped taking estrogen and many physicians became more cautious about prescribing it, the idea of hormone replacement therapy remains with us. At least three recent publications in

medical journals seriously consider whether the benefits of estrogen might not outweigh the dangers.[38] The continuing flap over treatment for this so-called deficiency disease of the aging female forces one to ask just what *is* this terrible state called menopause? Are its effects so unbearable that one might prefer to increase, even ever so slightly, the risk of cancer rather than suffer the daily discomforts encountered during "the change of life"?

Ours is a culture that fears the elderly. Rather than venerate their years and listen to their wisdom, we segregate them in housing built for "their special needs," separated from the younger generations from which we draw hope for the future. At the same time we allow millions of old people to live on inadequate incomes, in fear that serious illness will leave them destitute. The happy, productive elderly remain invisible in our midst. (One must look to feminist publications such as *Our Bodies, Ourselves* to find women who express pleasure in their postmenopausal state.) Television ads portray only the arthritic, the toothless, the wrinkled, and the constipated. If estrogen really is the hormone of youth and its decline suggests the coming of old age, then its loss is a part of biology that our culture ill equips us to handle.

There is, of course, a history to our cultural attitudes toward the elderly woman and our views about menopause. In the nineteenth century physicians believed that at menopause a woman entered a period of depression and increased susceptibility to disease. The postmenopausal body might be racked with "dyspepsia, diarrhea . . . rheumatic pains, paralysis, apoplexy . . . hemorrhaging . . . tuberculosis . . . and diabetes," while emotionally the aging female risked becoming irritable, depressed, hysterical, melancholic, or even insane. The more a woman violated social laws (such as using birth control or promoting female suffrage), the more likely she would be to suffer a disease-ridden menopause.[39] In the twentieth century, psychologist Helene Deutsch wrote that at menopause "woman has ended her existence as a bearer of future life and has reached her natural end—her partial death—as a servant of the species."[40] Deutsch believed that during the postmenopausal years a woman's main psychological task was to accept the progressive biological withering she experienced. Other well-known psychologists have also accepted the idea that a woman's life purpose is mainly reproductive and that her postreproductive years are ones of inevitable decline. Even in recent times postmenopausal women have been "treated" with tranquilizers, hormones, electro-shock, and lithium.[41]

But should women accept what many see as an inevitable emotional and biological decline? Should they believe, as Wilson does, that "from a practical point of view a man remains a man until the end," but that after menopause "we no longer have the 'whole woman'—only the 'part woman'"?[42] What is the real story of menopause?

The Change: Its Definition and Physiology

In 1976, under the auspices of the American Geriatric Society and the medical faculty of the University of Montpellier, the First International Congress on the Menopause convened in the south of France. In the volume that emerged from that conference, scientists and clinicians from around the world agreed on a standard definition of the words *menopause* and *climacteric*. "Menopause," they wrote, "indicates the final menstrual period and occurs during the climacteric. The climacteric is that phase in the aging process of women marking the transition from the reproductive stage of life to the nonreproductive stage."[43] By consensus, then, the word *menopause* has come to mean a specific event, the last menstruation, while *climacteric* implies a process occurring over a period of years.[c]

During the menstrual cycle, the blood levels of a number of hormones rise and fall on a regular basis. At the end of one monthly cycle, the low levels of estrogen and progesterone trigger the pituitary gland to make follicle-stimulating hormone (FSH) and luteinizing hormone (LH). The FSH influences the cells of the ovary to make large amounts of estrogen, and induces the growth and maturation of an oocyte. The LH, at just the right moment, induces ovulation and stimulates certain ovarian cells to form a progesterone-secreting structure called a corpus luteum. When no pregnancy occurs the life of the corpus luteum is limited and, as it degenerates, the lowered level of steroid hormones calls forth a new round of follicle-stimulating and luteinizing hormone synthesis, beginning the cycle once again. Although the ovary produces the lion's share of these steroid hormones, the cells of the adrenal gland also contribute, and this contribution increases in significance after menopause.

What happens to the intricately balanced hormone cycle during the several years preceding menopause is little understood, although it seems likely that gradual changes occur in the balance between pituitary activity (FSH and LH production) and estrogen synthesis.[44] One thing, however, is clear: menopause does not mean the *absence* of estrogen, but rather a gradual lowering in the availability of *ovarian* estrogen. Table 3 summarizes some salient information about changes in steroid hormone levels during the menstrual cycle and after menopause. In looking at the high point of cycle synthesis and then comparing it to women who no longer menstruate, the most dramatic change is seen in the estrogenic hormone estradiol.[d] The other estrogenic hormones, as well as progesterone and testosterone, drop off to some extent but continue to be synthesized at a level comparable to that observed during the early phases of the menstrual cycle. Instead of concentrating on the notion of estrogen deficiency, however, it is more important to point out that (1) postmenopausally the body makes different kinds of estrogen; (2) the

TABLE 3   HORMONE LEVELS AS A PERCENTAGE OF MID-MENSTRUAL-CYCLE HIGH POINT

Stage of Menstrual Cycle	TYPE OF ESTROGEN			Progesterone	Testosterone	Androstenedione
	Estrone	Estradiol	Estriol			
Premenopausal stage						
Early (menses)	20%	13%	67%	100%	55%	87%
Mid (ovulation)	100	100	—	—	100	100
Late (premenstrual)	49	50	100	—	82	—
Postmenopausal stage	17	3	50	50	23	39

Source: Wulf H. Utian, *Menopause in Modern Perspectives* (New York: Appleton-Century-Crofts, 1980), 32.

ovaries synthesize less and the adrenals more of these hormones; and (3) the monthly ups and downs of these hormones even out following menopause.

While estrogen levels begin to decline, the levels of FSH and LH start to increase. Changes in these hormones appear as early as eight years before menopause.[45] At the time of menopause and for several years afterward, these two hormones are found in very high concentrations compared to menstrual levels (FSH as many as fourteen times more concentrated than premenopausally, and LH more than three times more). Over a period of years such high levels are reduced to about half their peak value, leaving the postmenopausal woman with one-and-one-half times more LH and seven times more FSH circulating in her blood than when she menstruated regularly.

It is to all of these changes in hormone levels that the words *climacteric* and *menopause* refer. From these alterations Wilson and others have chosen to blame estrogen for the emotional deterioration they believe appears in postmenopausal women. Why they have focused on only one hormone from a complex system of hormonal changes is anybody's guess. I suspect, however, that the reasons are (at least) twofold. First, the normative biomedical disease model of female physiology looks for simple cause and effect. Most researchers, then, have simply assumed estrogen to be a "cause" and set out to measure its "effect." The model or framework out of which such investigators work precludes an interrelated analysis of all the different (and closely connected) hormonal changes going on during the climacteric. But why single out estrogen? Possibly because this hormone plays an important role in the menstrual cycle as well as in the development of "feminine" characteristics such as breasts and overall body contours. It is seen as the quintessential female hormone. So where could one better direct one's attention if, to begin with, one views menopause as the loss of true womanhood?

Physical changes do occur following menopause. Which, if any, of these are caused by changing hormone levels is another question. Menopause research comes equipped with its own unique experimental traps.[46] The most obvious is that a postmenopausal population is also an aging population. Do physical and emotional differences found in groups of postmenopausal women have to do with hormonal changes or with other aspects of aging? It is a difficult matter to sort out. Furthermore, many of the studies on menopause have been done on preselected populations, using women who volunteer because they experience classic menopausal "symptoms" such as the hot flash. Such investigations tell us nothing about average changes within the population as a whole. In the language of the social scientist, we have no baseline data, nothing to which we can compare menopausal women, no way to tell whether the complaint of a particular woman is typical, a cause for medical concern, or simply idiosyncratic.

Since the late 1970s feminist researchers have begun to provide us with much-needed information. Although their results confirm some beliefs long held by physicians, these newer investigators present them in a more sophisticated context. Dr. Madeleine Goodman and her colleagues designed a study in which they drew information from a large population of women ranging in age from thirty-five to sixty. All had undergone routine multiphasic screening at a health maintenance clinic, but none had come for problems concerning menopause. From the complete clinic records they selected a population of women who had not menstruated for at least one year and compared their health records with those of women who still menstruated, looking at thirty-five different variables, such as cramps, blood glucose levels, blood calcium, and hot flashes, to see if any of these symptoms correlated with those seen in postmenopausal women. The results are startling. They found that only 28 percent of Caucasian women and 24 percent of Japanese women identified as postmenopausal "reported traditional menopausal symptoms such as hot flashes, sweats, etc., while in nonmenopausal controls, 16 percent in Caucasians and 10 percent in Japanese also reported these same symptoms."[47] In other words, 75 percent of menopausal women in their sample reported no remarkable menopausal symptoms, a result in sharp contrast to earlier studies using women who identified themselves as menopausal.

In a similar exploration, researcher Karen Frey found evidence to support Goodman's results. She wrote that menopausal women "did not report significantly greater frequency of physical symptoms or concern about these symptoms than did pre- or post-menopausal women."[48] The studies of Goodman, Frey, and others[49] draw into serious question the notion that menopause is generally or necessarily associated with a set of disease symptoms. Yet at least three physical changes—hot flashes, vaginal dryness and irritation, and osteoporosis—and one emotional one—depression—remain associated in the minds of many with the decreased estrogen levels of the climacteric. Goodman's work indicates that such changes may be far less widespread than previously believed, but if they are troublesome to 26 percent of all menopausal women they remain an appropriate subject for analysis.

We know only the immediate cause of hot flashes: a sudden expansion of the blood flow to the skin. The technical term to describe them, *vasomotor instability*, means only that nerve cells signal the widening of blood vessels, allowing more blood into the body's periphery. A consensus has emerged on two things: (1) the high concentration of FSH and LH in blood probably causes hot flashes, although exactly how this happens remains unknown; and (2) estrogen treatment is the only currently available way to suppress the hot flashes. One hypothesis is that by means of a feedback mechanism, artificially raised blood levels of estrogen signal the brain to tell the pituitary to call off the FSH and LH. Although estrogen does stop the hot flashes, its effects are only temporary; remove the estrogen and the flashes return. Left alone, the body eventually adjusts to the changing levels of FSH and LH. Thus a premenopausal woman has two choices in dealing with hot flashes: she can either take estrogen as a permanent medication, a course Wilson refers to as embarking "on the great adventure of preserving or regaining your full femininity,"[50] or suffer some discomfort while nature takes its course. Since the longer one takes estrogen, the greater the danger of estrogen-linked cancer, many health care workers recommend the latter.[51]

Some women experience postmenopausal vaginal dryness and irritation that can make sexual intercourse painful. Since the cells of the vaginal wall contain estrogen receptors, it is not surprising that estrogen applied locally or taken in pill form helps with this difficulty. Even locally applied, however, the estrogen enters into the bloodstream, presenting the same dangers as when taken in pill form. There are alternative treatments, though, for vaginal dryness. The Boston Women's Health Collective, for example, recommends the use of nonestrogen vaginal creams or jellies, which seem to be effective and are certainly safer. Continued sexual activity also helps—yet another example of the interaction between behavior and physiology.

Hot flashes and vaginal dryness are the *only* climacteric-associated changes for which estrogen unambiguously offers relief. Since significant numbers of women do not experience these changes and since for many of those that do the effects are relatively mild, the wisdom of ERT must be examined carefully and on an individual basis. Both men and women undergo certain changes as they age, but Wilson's catastrophic vision of postmenopausal women—those ghosts gliding by "unnoticed and, in turn, notic[ing] little"[52]—is such a far cry from reality that it is a source of amazement that serious medical writers continue to quote his work.

In contrast to hot flashes and vaginal dryness, osteoporosis, a brittleness of the bone which can in severe cases cripple, has a complex origin. Since this potentially life-threatening condition appears more frequently in older women than in older men, the hypothesis of a relationship with estrogen levels seemed plausible to many. But as one medical worker has said, a unified theory of the disease "is still nonexistent, although sedentary lifestyles, genetic predisposition, hormonal imbalance, vitamin deficiencies, high-protein diets, and cigarette smoking all have been implicated."[53] Estrogen treatment seems to arrest the disease for a while, but may lose effectiveness after a few years.[54]

Even more than in connection with any physical changes, women have hit up against a medical double bind whenever they have complained of emotional problems during the years of climacteric. On the one hand physicians dismissed these complaints as the imagined ills of a hormone-deficient brain, while on the other they generalized the problem, arguing that middle-aged women are emotionally unreliable, unfit for positions of leadership and responsibility. Women had two choices: to complain and experience ridicule and/or improper medical treatment, or to suffer in silence. Hormonal changes during menopause were presumed to be the cause of psychiatric symptoms ranging from fatigue, dizziness, irritability, apprehension, and insomnia to severe headaches and psychotic depression. In recent years, however, these earlier accounts have been supplanted by a rather different consensus now emerging among responsible medical researchers.

To begin with, there are no data to support the idea that menopause has any relationship to serious depression in women. Postmenopausal women who experience psychosis have almost always had similar episodes premenopausally.[55] The notion of the hormonally depressed woman is a shibboleth that must be laid permanently to rest. Some studies have related irritability and insomnia to loss of sleep from nighttime hot flashes. Thus, for women who experience hot flashes, these emotional difficulties might, indirectly, relate to menopause. But the social, life history, and family contexts in which middle-aged women find themselves are more important links to emotional changes occurring during the years of the climacteric. And these, of course, have nothing whatsoever to do with hormones. Quite a number of studies suggest that the majority of women do not consider menopause a time of crisis. Nor do most women suffer from the so-called "empty nest syndrome" supposedly experienced when children leave home. On the contrary, investigation suggests that women without small children are less depressed and have higher incomes and an increased sense of well-being.[56] Such positive reactions depend upon work histories, individual upbringing, cultural background, and general state of health, among other things.

In a survey conducted for *Our Bodies, Ourselves*, one which in no sense represents a balanced cross section of U.S. women, the Boston Women's Health Collective recorded the reactions of more than two hundred menopausal or postmenopausal women, most of whom were suburban, married, and employed, to a series of questions about menopause. About two-thirds of them felt either positively or neutrally about a variety of changes they had undergone, while a whopping 90 percent felt okay or happy about the loss of childbearing ability![57] This result probably comes as no surprise to most women, but it flies in the face of the long-standing belief that women's lives and emotions are driven in greater part by their reproductive systems.

No good account of adult female development in the middle years exists. Levinson,[58] who studied adult men, presents a linear model of male development designed primarily around work experiences. In his analysis, the male climacteric plays only a secondary role. Feminist scholars Rosalind Barnett and Grace Baruch have described the difficulty of fitting women into Levinson's scheme: "It is hard to know how to think of women within this theory—a woman may not enter the world of work until her late thirties, she seldom has a mentor, and even women with lifelong career commitments rarely are in a position to reassess their commitment pattern by age forty," as do the men in Levinson's study.[59]

Baruch and Barnett call for the development of a theory of women in their middle years, pointing out that an adequate one can emerge only when researchers set aside preconceived ideas about the central role of biology in adult female development and listen to what women themselves say. Paradoxically, in some

sense we will remain unable to understand more about the role of biology in women's middle years until we have a more realistic *social* analysis of women's post-adolescent psychological development. Such an analysis must, of course, take into account ethnic, racial, regional, and class differences among women, since once biology is jettisoned as a universal cause of female behavior, it no longer makes sense to lump all women into a single category.

Much remains to be understood about menopause. Which biological changes, for instance, result from ovarian degeneration and which from other aspects of aging? How does the aging process compare in men and women? What causes hot flashes and can we find safe ways to alleviate the discomfort they cause? Do other aspects of a woman's life affect the number and severity of menopausally related physical symptoms? What can we learn from studying the experience of menopause in other, especially nonwestern, cultures? A number of researchers have proposed effective ways of finding answers to these questions.[60] We need only time, research dollars, and an open mind to move forward.

CONCLUSION

The premise that women are by nature abnormal and inherently diseased dominates past research on menstruation and menopause. While appointing the male reproductive system as normal, this viewpoint calls abnormal any aspect of the female reproductive life cycle that deviates from the male's. At the same time, such an analytical framework places the essence of a woman's existence in her reproductive system. Caught in her hormonal windstorm, she strives to attain normality but can do so only by rejecting her biological uniqueness, for that too is essentially deformed: a double bind indeed. Within such an intellectual structure no medical research of any worth to women's health can be done, for it is the blueprint itself that leads investigators to ask the wrong questions, look in the wrong places for answers, and then distort the interpretation of their results.

Reading through the morass of poorly done studies on menstruation and menopause, many of which express deep hatred and fear of women, can be a discouraging experience. One begins to wonder how it can be that within so vast a quantity of material so little quality exists. But at this very moment the field of menstrual-cycle research (including menopause) offers a powerful antidote to that disheartenment in the form of feminist researchers (both male and female) with excellent training and skills, working within a new analytical framework. Rejecting a strict medical model of female development, they understand that men and women have different reproductive cycles, *both* of which are normal. Not binary opposites, male and female physiologies have differences *and* similarities. These research pioneers know too that the human body functions in a social milieu and that it changes in response to that context. Biology is not a one-way determinant but a dynamic component of our existence. And, equally important, these new investigators have learned not only to *listen* to what women say about themselves but to *hear* as well. By and large, these researchers are not in the mainstream of medical and psychological research, but we can look forward to a time when the impact of their work will affect the field of menstrual-cycle research for the better and for many years to come.

NOTES

a. In the nineteenth century, control took the form of sexual surgery such as ovarietomies and hysterectomies, while twentieth-century medicine prefers the use of hormone pills. The science of the 1980s has a more sophisticated approach to human physiology, but its political motives of control and management have changed little. For an account of medicine's attitudes toward women, see Barbara Ehrenreich and Deidre English, *For Her Own Good: 150 Years of Experts' Advice to Women* (New York: Doubleday, 1979); and G. J. Barker-Benfield, *The Horrors of the Half-Known Life* (New York: Harper & Row, 1977).

b. The prohibited work usually carries a higher wage.

c. There is also a male climacteric, which entails a gradual reduction in production of the hormone testosterone over the years as part of the male aging process. What part it plays in that process is poorly understood and seems frequently to be ignored by researchers, who prefer to contrast continuing male reproductive potency with the loss of childbearing ability in women.[61]

d. Estrogens are really a family of structurally similar molecules. Their possibly different biological roles are not clearly delineated.

REFERENCES

1. Carroll Smith-Rosenberg and Charles Rosenberg, "The Female Animal: Medical and Biological Views of Woman and Her Role in 19th Century America," *Journal of American History* 60 (1973): 336.

2. Edgar Berman, Letter to the Editor, *New York Times*, 26 July 1970.

3. Steven Goldberg, *The Inevitability of Patriarchy* (New York: William Morrow, 1973), 93.

4. Herbert Wray, "Premenstrual Changes," *Science News* 122 (1982): 380–81.

5. Ilza Veith, *Hysteria: The History of a Disease* (Chicago: University of Chicago Press, 1965).

6. Pliny the Elder, quoted in M. E. Ashley and Montagu, "Physiology and Origins of the Menstrual Prohibitions," *Quarterly Review of Biology* 15 (1940): 211.

7. Smith-Rosenberg and Rosenberg, "The Female Animal"; Henry Maudsley, "Sex in Mind and in Education," *Popular Science Monthly* 5 (1874): 200; and Joan Burstyn, "Education and Sex: The Medical Case against Higher Education for Women in England 1870–1900," *Proceedings of the American Philosophical Society* 177 (1973): 7989.

8. Carroll Smith-Rosenberg, "The Hysterical Woman: Sex Roles and Role Conflict in 19th Century America," *Social Research* 39 (1972): 652–78.

9. M. A. Hardaker, "Science and the Woman Question," *Popular Science Monthly* 20 (1881): 583.

10. Nina Morais, "A Reply to Ms. Hardaker on: The Woman Question," *Popular Science Monthly* 21 (1882): 74–75.

11. Maudsley, "Sex in Mind and in Education," 211.

12. Katharina Dalton, *Once a Month* (Claremont, Calif.: Hunter House, 1983), 78.

13. Ibid.; Katharina Dalton, *The Premenstrual Syndrome* (London: William Heinemann Medical Books, 1972).

14. Andrea Eagan, "The Selling of Premenstrual Syndrome," *Ms.* Oct. 1983, 26–31.

15. Robert L. Reid and S. S. Yen, "Premenstrual Syndrome," *American Journal of Obstetrics and Gynecology* 139 (1981): 86.

16. J. Abplanalp, R. F. Haskett, and R. M. Rose, "The Premenstrual Syndrome," *Advances in Psychoneuroendocrinology* 3 (1980): 327–47.

17. Dalton, *Once a Month.*

18. Boston Women's Health Collective, *Our Bodies, Ourselves* (New York: Simon and Schuster, 1979).

19. Reid and Yen, "Premenstrual Syndrome," 86.

20. John O'Connor, M. Shelley Edward, and Lenore O. Stern, "Behavioral Rhythms Related to the Menstrual Cycle," in *Biorhythms and Human Reproduction*, ed. M. Fern et al. (New York: Wiley, 1974), 312.

21. Frank A. Beach, Preface to chapter 10, in *Human Sexuality in Four Perspectives* (Baltimore: Johns Hopkins University Press, 1977), 271.

22. M. B. Rosenthal, "Insights into the Premenstrual Syndrome," *Physician and Patient* (April 1983): 46–53.

23. Herbert Schaumberg et al., "Sensory Neuropathy from Pyridoxine Abuse," *New England Journal of Medicine* 309 (1983): 446–48.

24. Judith Abplanalp, "Premenstrual Syndrome: A Selective Review," *Women and Health* 8 (1983): 110.

25. Dalton, *Once a Month*, 12.

26. Abplanalp, Haskett, and Rose, "The Premenstrual Syndrome"; and Abplanalp, "Premenstrual Syndrome: A Selective Review."

27. Abplanalp, "Premenstrual Syndrome: A Selective Review."

28. Reid and Yen, "Premenstrual Syndrome," 97.

29. G. A. Sampson, "An Appraisal of the Role of Progesterone in the Therapy of Premenstrual Syndrome," in *The Premenstrual Syndrome*, ed. P. A. vanKeep and W. H. Utian (Lancaster, England: MTP Press Ltd. International Medical Publishers, 1981), 51–69; and Sampson, "Premenstrual Syndrome: A Double-Bind Controlled Trial of Progesterone and Placebo," *British Journal of Psychiatry* 135 (1979): 209–15.

30. Robert A. Wilson and Thelma A. Wilson, "The Fate of the Nontreated Postmenopausal Woman: A Plea for the Maintenance of Adequate Estrogen from Puberty to the Grave," *Journal of the American Geriatric Society* 11 (1963): 352–56.

31. David Reuben, *Everything You Always Wanted to Know about Sex but Were Afraid to Ask* (New York: McKay, 1969), 292.

32. Wulf H. Utian, *Menopause in Modern Perspectives* (New York: Appleton-Century-Crofts, 1980).

33. Wilson and Wilson, "The Fate of the Nontreated Postmenopausal Woman," 347.

34. Robert A. Wilson, *Feminine Forever* (New York: M. Evans, 1966).

35. Marilyn Grossman and Pauline Bart, "The Politics of Menopause," in *The Menstrual Cycle*, vol. 1, ed. Dan, Graham, and Beecher.

36. Kathleen MacPherson, "Menopause as Disease: The Social Construction of a Metaphor," *Advances in Nursing Science* 3 (1981): 95–113; A. Johnson, "The Risks of Sex Hormones as Drugs," *Women and Health* 2 (1977): 8–11.

37. D. Smith et al., "Association of Exogenous Estrogen and Endometrial Carcinoma," *New England Journal of Medicine* 293 (1975): 1164–67.

38. H. Judd et al., "Estrogen Replacement Therapy," *Obstetrics and Gynecology* 58 (1981): 267–75; M. Quigley, "Postmenopausal Hormone Replacement Therapy: Back to Estrogen Forever?" *Geriatric Medicine Today* 1 (1982): 78–85; and Thomas Skillman, "Estrogen Replacement: Its Risks and Benefits," *Consultant* (1982): 115–27.

39. C. Smith-Rosenberg, "Puberty to Menopause: The Cycle of Femininity in 19th Century America," *Feminist Studies* 1 (1973): 65.

40. Helene Deutsch, *The Psychology of Women* (New York: Grune and Stratton, 1945), 458.

41. J. H. Osofsky and R. Seidenberg, "Is Female Menopausal Depression Inevitable?" *Obstetrics and Gynecology* 36 (1970): 611.

42. Wilson and Wilson, "The Fate of the Nontreated Postmenopausal Woman," 348.

43. P. A. vanKeep, R. B. Greenblatt, and M. Albeaux-Fernet, eds., *Consensus on Menopause Research* (Baltimore: University Park Press, 1976), 134.

44. Utian, *Menopause in Modern Perspectives.*

45. Ibid.

46. Madeleine Goodman, "Toward a Biology of Menopause," *Signs* 5 (1980): 739–53.

47. Madeleine Goodman, C. J. Stewart, and F. Gilbert, "Patterns of Menopause: A Study of Certain Medical and Physiological Variables among Caucasian and Japanese Women Living in Hawaii," *Journal of Gerontology* 32 (1977): 297.

48. Karen Frey, "Middle-Aged Women's Experience and Perceptions of Menopause," *Women and Health* 6 (1981): 31.

49. Eve Kahana, A. Kiyak, and J. Liang, "Menopause in the Context of Other Life Events," in *The Menstrual Cycle*, vol. 1, ed. Dan, Graham, and Beecher, 167–78.

50. Wilson, *Feminine Forever*, 134.

51. A. Voda and M. Eliasson, "Menopause: The Closure of Menstrual Life," *Women and Health* 8 (1983): 137–56.

52. Wilson and Wilson, "The Fate of the Nontreated Postmenopausal Woman," 356.

53. Louis Avioli, "Postmenopausal Osteoporosis: Prevention vs. Cure," *Federation Proceedings* 40 (1981): 2418.

54. Voda and Eliasson, "Menopause: The Closure of Menstrual Life."

55. G. Winokur and R. Cadoret, "The Irrelevance of the Menopause to Depressive Disease," in *Topics in Psychoendocrinology*, ed. E. J. Sachar (New York: Grune and Stratton, 1975).

56. Rosalind Barnett and Grace Baruch, "Women in the Middle Years: A Critique of Research and Theory," *Psychology of Women Quarterly* 3 (1978): 187–97.

57. Boston Women's Health Collective, *Our Bodies, Ourselves.*

58. D. Levinson et al., "Periods in the Adult Development of Men: Ages 18–45," *The Counseling Psychologist* 6 (1976): 21–25.

59. Barnett and Baruch, "Women in the Middle Years," 189.

60. Ibid.; Goodman, "Toward a Biology of Menopause"; and Voda, Dinnerstein, and O'Donnell, eds., *Changing Perspectives on Menopause.*

61. Marcha Flint, "Male and Female Menopause: A Cultural Put-on," in *Changing Perspectives on Menopause*, ed. A. M. Voda, M. Dinnerstein, and S. O'Donnell (Austin: University of Texas Press, 1982).

"A Way Outa No Way": Eating Problems among African-American, Latina, and White Women

Bulimia, anorexia, binging, and extensive dieting are among the many health issues women have been confronting in the last twenty years. Until recently, however, there has been almost no research about eating problems among African-American, Latina, Asian-American, or Native American women, working-class women, or lesbians.[1] In fact, according to the normative epidemiological portrait, eating problems are largely a white, middle-, and upper-class heterosexual phenomenon. Further, while feminist research has documented how eating problems are fueled by sexism, there has been almost no attention to how other systems of oppression may also be implicated in the development of eating problems.

In this article, I reevaluate the portrayal of eating problems as issues of appearance based in the "culture of thinness." I propose that eating problems begin as ways women cope with various traumas, including sexual abuse, racism, classism, sexism, heterosexism, and poverty. Showing the interface between these traumas and the onset of eating problems explains why women may use eating to numb pain and cope with violations to their bodies. This theoretical shift also permits an understanding of the economic, political, social, educational, and cultural resources that women need to change in correcting their relationship to food and their bodies.

EXISTING RESEARCH ON EATING PROBLEMS

There are three theoretical models used to explain the epidemiology, etiology, and treatment of eating problems. The biomedical model offers important scientific research about possible physiological causes of eating problems and the physiological dangers of purging and starvation (Copeland 1985; Spack 1985). However, this model adopts medical treatment strategies that may disempower and traumatize women (Garner 1985; Orbach 1985). In addition, this model ignores many social, historical, and cultural factors that influence women's eating patterns. The psychological model identifies eating problems as "multidimensional disorders" that are influenced by biological, psychological, and cultural factors (Garfinkel and Garner 1982). While useful in its exploration of effective therapeutic treatments, this model, like the biomedical one, tends to neglect women of color, lesbians, and working-class women.

The third model, offered by feminists, asserts that eating problems are gendered. This model explains why the vast majority of people with eating problems are women, how gender socialization and sexism may relate to eating problems, and how masculine models of psychological development have shaped theoretical interpretations. Feminists offer the culture-of-thinness model as a key reason why eating problems predominate among women. According to this model, thinness is a culturally, socially, and economically enforced requirement for female beauty. This imperative makes women vulnerable to cycles of dieting, weight loss, and subsequent weight gain, which may lead to anorexia and bulimia (Chernin 1981; Orbach 1978, 1985; Smead 1984).

Feminists have rescued eating problems from the realm of individual psychopathology by showing how the difficulties are rooted in systematic and pervasive attempts to control women's body sizes and appetites. However, researchers have yet to give significant attention to how race, class, and sexuality influence women's understanding of their bodies and appetites. The handful of epidemiological studies that include African-American women and Latinas casts doubt on the accuracy of the normative epidemiological portrait. The studies suggest that this portrait reflects which particular populations of women have been studied rather than actual prevalence (Andersen and Hay 1985; Gray, Ford, and Kelly 1987; Hsu 1987; Nevo 1985; Silber 1986).

More important, this research shows that bias in research has consequences for women of color. Tomas Silber (1986) asserts that many well-trained professionals have either misdiagnosed or delayed their diagnoses of eating problems among African-American and Latina women due to stereotypical thinking that these problems are restricted to white women. As a consequence, when African-American women or Latinas are diagnosed, their eating problems tend to be more severe due to extended processes of starvation prior to intervention. In her autobiographical account of her eating problems, Retha Powers (1989), an African-American woman, describes being told not to worry about her eating problems since "fat is more acceptable in the Black community" (p. 78). Stereotypical perceptions held by her peers and teachers of the "maternal Black woman" and the "persistent mammy-brickhouse Black woman image" (p. 134) made it difficult for Powers to find people who took her problems with food seriously.

Recent work by African-American women reveals that eating problems often relate to women's struggles against a "simultaneity of oppression" (Clarke 1982; Naylor 1985; White 1991). Byllye Avery (1990), the founder of the National Black Women's Health Project, links the origins of eating problems among African-American women to the daily stress of being undervalued and overburdened at home and at work. In Evelyn C. White's (1990) anthology, *The Black Woman's Health Book: Speaking for Ourselves*, Georgiana Arnold (1990) links her eating problems partly to racism and racial isolation during childhood.

Recent feminist research also identifies factors that are related to eating problems among lesbians (Brown 1987; Dworkin 1989; Iazzetto 1989; Schoenfielder and Wieser 1983). In her clinical work, Brown (1987) found that lesbians who have internalized a high degree of homophobia are more likely to accept negative attitudes about fat than are lesbians who have examined their internalized homophobia. Autobiographical accounts by lesbians have also indicated that secrecy about eating problems among lesbians partly reflects their fear of being associated with a stigmatized illness ("What's Important" 1988).

Attention to African-American women, Latinas, and lesbians paves the way for further research that explores the possible interface between facing multiple oppressions and the development of eating problems. In this way, this study is part of a larger feminist and sociological research agenda that seeks to understand how race, class, gender, nationality, and sexuality inform women's experiences and influence theory production.

METHODOLOGY

I conducted eighteen life history interviews and administered lengthy questionnaires to explore eating problems among African-American, Latina, and white women. I employed a snowball sample, a method in which potential respondents often first learn about the study from people who have already participated. This method was well suited for the study since it enabled women to get information about me and the interview process from people they already knew. Typically, I had much contact with the respondents prior to the interview. This was particularly important given the secrecy associated with this topic (Russell 1986; Silberstein, Striegel-Moore, and Rodin 1987), the necessity of women of color and lesbians to be discriminating about how their lives are studied, and the fact that I was conducting across-race research.

To create analytical notes and conceptual categories from the data, I adopted Glaser and Strauss's (1967) technique of theoretical sampling, which directs the researcher to collect, analyze, and test hypotheses during the sampling process (rather than imposing theoretical categories onto the data). After completing each interview transcription, I gave a copy to each woman who wanted one. After reading their interviews, some of the women clarified or made additions to the interview text.

Demographics of the Women in the Study

The eighteen women I interviewed included five African-American women, five Latinas, and eight white women. Of these women, twelve are lesbian and six are heterosexual. Five women are Jewish, eight are Catholic, and five are Protestant. Three women grew up outside of the United States. The women represented a range of class backgrounds (both in terms of origin and current class status) and ranged in age from nineteen to forty-six years old (with a median age of 33.5 years).

The majority of the women reported having had a combination of eating problems (at least two of the following: bulimia, compulsive eating, anorexia, and/or extensive dieting). In addition, the particular types of eating problems often changed during a woman's life span. (For example, a woman might have been bulimic during adolescence and anorexic as an adult.) Among the women, 28 percent had been bulimic, 17 percent had been bulimic and anorexic, and 5 percent had been anorexic. All of the women who had been anorexic or bulimic also had a history of compulsive eating and extensive dieting. Of the women, 50 percent were compulsive eaters and dieters (39 percent) or compulsive eaters (11 percent) but had not been bulimic or anorexic.

Two-thirds of the women have had eating problems for more than half of their lives, a finding that contradicts the stereotype of eating problems as transitory. The weight fluctuation among the women varied from 16 to 160 pounds, with an average fluctuation of 74 pounds. This drastic weight change illustrates the degree to which the women adjusted to major changes in body size at least once during their lives as they lost, gained, and lost weight again. The average age of onset was eleven years old, meaning that most of the women developed eating problems prior to puberty. Almost all of the women (88 percent) consider themselves as still having a problem with eating, although the majority believe they are well on the way to recovery.

THE INTERFACE OF TRAUMA AND EATING PROBLEMS

One of the most striking findings in this study was the range of traumas the women associated with the origins of their eating problems, including racism, sexual abuse, poverty, sexism, emotional or physical abuse, heterosexism, class injuries, and acculturation.[2] The particular constellation of eating problems among the women did not vary with race, class, sexuality, or nationality. Women from various race and class backgrounds attributed the origins of their eating problems to sexual abuse, sexism, and emotional and/or physical abuse. Among some of the African-American and Latina women, eating problems were also associated with poverty, racism, and class injuries. Heterosexism was a key factor in the onset of bulimia, compulsive eating, and extensive dieting among some of the lesbians.

These oppressions are not the same nor are the injuries caused by them. And certainly, there are a variety of potentially harmful ways that women respond to oppression (such as using drugs, becoming a workaholic, or committing suicide). However, for all these women, eating was a way of coping with trauma.

Sexual Abuse

Sexual abuse was the most common trauma that the women related to the origins of their eating problems. Until recently, there has been virtually no research exploring the possible relationship between these two phenomena. Since the mid-1980s, however, researchers have begun identifying connections between the two, a task that is part of a larger feminist critique of traditional psychoanalytic symptomatology (DeSalvo 1989; Herman 1981; Masson 1984). Results of a number of incidence studies indicate that between one-third and two-thirds of women who have eating problems have been abused (Oppenheimer et al. 1985; Root and Fallon 1988). In addition, a growing number of therapists and researchers have offered interpretations of the meaning and impact of eating problems for survivors of sexual abuse (Bass and Davis 1988; Goldfarb 1987; Iazzetto 1989; Swink and Leveille 1986). Kearney-Cooke (1988) identifies dieting and binging as common ways in which women cope with frequent psychological consequences of sexual abuse (such as body image disturbances, distrust of people and one's own experiences, and confusion about one's feelings). Root and Fallon (1989) specify ways that victimized women cope with assaults by binging and purging: bulimia serves many functions, including anesthetizing the negative feelings associated with victimization. Iazzetto's innovative study (1989), based on in-depth interviews and art therapy sessions, examines how a woman's relationship to her body changes as a consequence of sexual abuse. Iazzetto discovered that the process of leaving the body (through progressive phases of numbing, dissociating, and denying) that often occurs during sexual abuse parallels the process of leaving the body made possible through binging.

Among the women I interviewed, 61 percent were survivors of sexual abuse (eleven of the eighteen women), most of whom made connections between sexual abuse and the beginning of their eating problems. Binging was the most common method of coping identified by the survivors. Binging helped women "numb out" or anesthetize their feelings.

Eating sedated, alleviated anxiety, and combated loneliness. Food was something that they could trust and was accessible whenever they needed it. Antonia (a pseudonym) is an Italian-American woman who was first sexually abused by a male relative when she was four years old. Retrospectively, she knows that binging was a way she coped with the abuse. When the abuse began, and for many years subsequently, Antonia often woke up during the middle of the night with anxiety attacks or nightmares and would go straight to the kitchen cupboards to get food. Binging helped her block painful feelings because it put her back to sleep.

Like other women in the study who began binging when they were very young, Antonia was not always fully conscious as she binged. She described eating during the night as "sleep walking. It was mostly desperate—like I had to have it." Describing why she ate after waking up with nightmares, Antonia said, "What else do you do? If you don't have any coping mechanisms, you eat." She said that binging made her "disappear," which made her feel protected. Like Antonia, most of the women were sexually abused before puberty; four of them before they were five years old. Given their youth, food was the most accessible and socially acceptable drug available to them. Because all of the women endured the psychological consequences alone, it is logical that they coped with tactics they could do alone as well.

One reason Antonia binged (rather than dieted) to cope with sexual abuse is that she saw little reason to try to be the small size girls were supposed to be. Growing up as one of the Italian Americans in what she described as a "very WASP town," Antonia felt that everything from her weight and size to having dark hair on her upper lip were physical characteristics she was supposed to hide. From a young age she knew she "never embodied the essence of the good girl. I don't like her. I have never acted like her. I can't be her. I sort of gave up." For Antonia, her body was the physical entity that signified her outsider status. When the sexual abuse occurred, Antonia felt she had lost her body. In her mind, the body she lived in after the abuse was not really hers. By the time Antonia was eleven, her mother put her on diet pills. Antonia began to eat behind closed doors as she continued to cope with the psychological consequences of sexual abuse and feeling like a cultural outsider.

Extensive dieting and bulimia were also ways in which women responded to sexual abuse. Some women thought that the men had abused them because

of their weight. They believed that if they were smaller, they might not have been abused. For example when Elsa, an Argentine woman, was sexually abused at the age of eleven, she thought her chubby size was the reason the man was abusing her. Elsa said, "I had this notion that these old perverts liked these plump girls. You heard adults say this too. Sex and flesh being associated." Looking back on her childhood, Elsa believes she made fat the enemy partly due to the shame and guilt she felt about the incest. Her belief that fat was the source of her problems was also supported by her socialization. Raised by strict German governesses in an upper-class family, Elsa was taught that a woman's weight was a primary criterion for judging her worth. Her mother "was socially conscious of walking into places with a fat daughter and maybe people staring at her." Her father often referred to Elsa's body as "shot to hell." When asked to describe how she felt about her body when growing up, Elsa described being completely alienated from her body. She explained,

> Remember in school when they talk about the difference between body and soul? I always felt like my soul was skinny. My soul was free. My soul sort of flew. I was tied down by this big bag of rocks that was my body. I had to drag it around. It did pretty much what it wanted and I had a lot of trouble controlling it. It kept me from doing all the things that I dreamed of.

As is true for many women who have been abused, the split that Elsa described between her body and soul was an attempt to protect herself from the pain she believed her body caused her. In her mind, her fat body was what had "bashed in her dreams." Dieting became her solution, but, as is true for many women in the study, this strategy soon led to cycles of binging and weight fluctuation.

Ruthie, a Puerto Rican woman who was sexually abused from twelve until sixteen years of age, described bulimia as a way she responded to sexual abuse. As a child, Ruthie liked her body. Like many Puerto Rican women of her mother's generation, Ruthie's mother did not want skinny children, interpreting that as a sign that they were sick or being fed improperly. Despite her mother's attempts to make her gain weight, Ruthie remained thin through puberty. When a male relative began sexually abusing her, Ruthie's sense of her body changed dramatically. Although she weighed only 100 pounds, she began to feel fat and thought her size was causing the abuse. She had seen a movie on television about Romans who made themselves throw up and so she began doing it, in hopes that she could look like the "little kid" she was before the abuse began. Her symbolic attempt to protect herself by purging stands in stark contrast to the psychoanalytic explanation of eating problems as an "abnormal" repudiation of sexuality. In fact, her actions and those of many other survivors indicate a girl's logical attempt to protect herself (including her sexuality) by being a size and shape that does not seem as vulnerable to sexual assault.

These women's experiences suggest many reasons why women develop eating problems as a consequence of sexual abuse. Most of the survivors "forgot" the sexual abuse after its onset and were unable to retrieve the abuse memories until many years later. With these gaps in memory, frequently they did not know why they felt ashamed, fearful, or depressed. When sexual abuse memories resurfaced in dreams, they often woke feeling upset but could not remember what they had dreamed. These free-floating, unexplained feelings left the women feeling out of control and confused. Binging or focusing on maintaining a new diet were ways women distracted or appeased themselves, in turn, helping them regain a sense of control. As they grew older, they became more conscious of the consequences of these actions. Becoming angry at themselves for binging or promising themselves they would not purge again was a way to direct feelings of shame and self-hate that often accompanied the trauma.

Integral to this occurrence was a transference process in which the women displaced onto their bodies painful feelings and memories that actually derived from or were directed toward the persons who caused the abuse. Dieting became a method of trying to change the parts of their bodies they hated, a strategy that at least initially brought success as they lost weight. Purging was a way women tried to reject the body size they thought was responsible for the abuse. Throwing up in order to lose the weight they thought was making them vulnerable to the abuse was a way to try to find the body they had lost when the abuse began.

Poverty

Like sexual abuse, poverty is another injury that may make women vulnerable to eating problems. One woman I interviewed attributed her eating problems directly to the stress caused by poverty. Yolanda is a Black Cape Verdean mother who began eating compulsively when she was twenty-seven years old.

After leaving an abusive husband in her early twenties, Yolanda was forced to go on welfare. As a single mother with small children and few financial resources, she tried to support herself and her children on $539 a month. Yolanda began binging in the evenings after putting her children to bed. Eating was something she could do alone. It would calm her, help her deal with loneliness, and make her feel safe. Food was an accessible commodity that was cheap. She ate three boxes of macaroni and cheese when nothing else was available. As a single mother with little money, Yolanda felt as if her body was the only thing she had left. As she described it,

> I am here, [in my body] 'cause there is no where else for me to go. Where am I going to go? This is all I got . . . that probably contributes to putting on so much weight cause staying in your body, in your home, in yourself, you don't go out. You aren't around other people . . . You hide and as long as you hide you don't have to face . . . nobody can see you eat. You are safe.

When she was eating, Yolanda felt a momentary reprieve from her worries. Binging not only became a logical solution because it was cheap and easy but also because she had grown up amid positive messages about eating. In her family, eating was a celebrated and joyful act. However, in adulthood, eating became a double-edged sword. While comforting her, binging also led to weight gain. During the three years Yolanda was on welfare, she gained seventy pounds.

Yolanda's story captures how poverty can be a precipitating factor in eating problems and highlights the value of understanding how class inequalities may shape women's eating problems. As a single mother, her financial constraints mirrored those of most female heads of households. The dual hazards of a race- and sex-stratified labor market further limited her options (Higginbotham 1986). In an article about Black women's health, Byllye Avery (1990) quotes a Black woman's explanation about why she eats compulsively. The woman told Avery,

> I work for General Electric making batteries, and, I know it's killing me. My old man is an alcoholic. My kid's got babies. Things are not well with me. And one thing I know I can do when I come home is cook me a pot of food and sit down in front of the TV and eat it. And you can't take that away from me until you're ready to give me something in its place. (p. 7)

Like Yolanda, this woman identifies eating compulsively as a quick, accessible, and immediately satisfying way of coping with the daily stress caused by conditions she could not control. Connections between poverty and eating problems also show the limits of portraying eating problems as maladies of upper-class adolescent women.

The fact that many women use food to anesthetize themselves, rather than other drugs (even when they gained access to alcohol, marijuana, and other illegal drugs), is partly a function of gender socialization and the competing demands that women face. One of the physiological consequences of binge eating is a numbed state similar to that experienced by drinking. Troubles and tensions are covered over as a consequence of the body's defensive response to massive food intake. When food is eaten in that way, it effectively works like a drug with immediate and predictable effects. Yolanda said she binged late at night rather than getting drunk because she could still get up in the morning, get her children ready for school, and be clearheaded for the college classes she attended. By binging, she avoided the hangover or sickness that results from alcohol or illegal drugs. In this way, food was her drug of choice since it was possible for her to eat while she continued to care for her children, drive, cook, and study. Binging is also less expensive than drinking, a factor that is especially significant for poor women. Another woman I interviewed said that when her compulsive eating was at its height, she ate breakfast after rising in the morning, stopped for a snack on her way to work, ate lunch at three different cafeterias, and snacked at her desk throughout the afternoon. Yet even when her eating had become constant, she was still able to remain employed. While her patterns of eating no doubt slowed her productivity, being drunk may have slowed her to a dead stop.

Heterosexism

The life history interviews also uncovered new connections between heterosexism and eating problems. One of the most important recent feminist contributions has been identifying compulsory heterosexuality as an institution which truncates opportunities for heterosexual and lesbian women (Rich 1986). All of the women interviewed for this study, both lesbian and heterosexual, were taught that heterosexuality was compulsory, although the versions of this enforcement were shaped by race and class. Expectations about heterosexuality were partly taught through messages that girls learned about eating and their bodies. In some homes, boys were given more food than girls, especially as teenagers, based on the rationale that girls need to be thin to attract boys. As the girls approached puberty, many were told to stop being athletic, begin wearing dresses, and watch their weight. For the women who weighed more than was considered acceptable, threats about their need to diet were laced with admonitions that being fat would ensure becoming an "old maid."

While compulsory heterosexuality influenced all of the women's emerging sense of their bodies and eating patterns, the women who linked heterosexism directly to the beginning of their eating problems were those who knew they were lesbians when very young and actively resisted heterosexual norms. One working-class Jewish woman, Martha, began compulsively eating when she was eleven years old, the same year she started getting clues of her lesbian identity. In junior high school, as many of her female peers began dating boys, Martha began fantasizing about girls, which made her feel utterly alone. Confused and ashamed about her fantasies, Martha came home every day from school and binged. Binging was a way she drugged herself so that being alone was tolerable. Describing binging, she said, "It was the only thing I knew. I was looking for a comfort." Like many women, Martha binged because it softened painful feelings. Binging sedated her, lessened her anxiety, and induced sleep.

Martha's story also reveals ways that trauma can influence women's experience of their bodies. Like many other women, Martha had no sense of herself as connected to her body. When I asked Martha whether she saw herself as fat when she was growing up she said, "I didn't see myself as fat. I didn't see myself. I wasn't there. I get so sad about that because I missed so much." In the literature on eating problems, *body image* is the term that is typically used to describe a woman's experience of her body. This term connotes the act of imagining one's physical appearance. Typically, women with eating problems are assumed to have difficulties with their body image. However, the term *body image* does not adequately capture the complexity and range of bodily responses to trauma experienced by the women. Exposure to trauma did much more than distort the women's visual image of themselves. These traumas often jeopardized their capacity to consider themselves as having bodies at all.

Given the limited connotations of the term *body image*, I use the term *body consciousness* as a more useful way to understand the range of bodily responses to trauma.[3] By body consciousness I mean the ability to reside comfortably in one's body (to see oneself as embodied) and to consider one's body as connected to oneself. The disruptions to their body consciousness that the women described included leaving their bodies, making a split between their body and mind, experiencing being "in" their bodies as painful, feeling unable to control what went in and out of their bodies, hiding in one part of their bodies, or simply not seeing themselves as having bodies. Binging, dieting, or purging were common ways women responded to disruptions to their body consciousness.

Racism and Class Injuries

For some of the Latinas and African-American women, racism coupled with the stress resulting from class mobility related to the onset of their eating problems. Joselyn, an African-American woman, remembered her white grandmother telling her she would never be as pretty as her cousins because they were lighter skinned. Her grandmother often humiliated Joselyn in front of others, as she made fun of Joselyn's body while she was naked and told her she was fat. As a young child, Joselyn began to think that although she could not change her skin color, she could at least try to be thin. When Joselyn was young, her grandmother was the only family member who objected to Joselyn's weight. However, her father also began encouraging his wife and daughter to be thin as the family's class standing began to change. When the family was working class, serving big meals, having chubby children, and keeping plenty of food in the house was a sign the family was doing well. But, as the family became mobile, Joselyn's father began insisting that Joselyn be thin. She remembered, "When my father's business began to bloom and my father was interacting more with white businessmen and seeing how they did business, suddenly thin became important. If you were a truly well-to-do family, then your family was slim and elegant."

As Joselyn's grandmother used Joselyn's body as territory for enforcing her own racism and prejudice about size, Joselyn's father used her body as the territory through which he channeled the demands he faced in the white-dominated business world. However, as Joselyn was pressured to diet, her father still served her large portions and bought treats for her and the neighborhood children. These contradictory

messages made her feel confused about her body. As was true for many women in this study, Joselyn was told she was fat beginning when she was very young even though she was not overweight. And, like most of the women, Joselyn was put on diet pills and diets before even reaching puberty, beginning the cycles of dieting, compulsive eating, and bulimia.

The confusion about body size expectations that Joselyn associated with changes in class paralleled one Puerto Rican woman's association between her eating problems and the stress of assimilation as her family's class standing moved from poverty to working class. When Vera was very young, she was so thin that her mother took her to a doctor who prescribed appetite stimulants. However, by the time Vera was eight years old, her mother began trying to shame Vera into dieting. Looking back on it, Vera attributed her mother's change of heart to competition among extended family members that centered on "being white, being successful, being middle class, . . . and it was always, 'Ay Bendito. She is so fat. What happened?'"

The fact that some of the African-American and Latina women associated the ambivalent messages about food and eating to their family's class mobility and/or the demands of assimilation while none of the eight white women expressed this (including those whose class was stable and changing) suggests that the added dimension of racism was connected to the imperative to be thin. In fact, the class expectations that their parents experienced exacerbated standards about weight that they inflicted on their daughters.

EATING PROBLEMS AS SURVIVAL STRATEGIES

Feminist Theoretical Shifts

My research permits a reevaluation of many assumptions about eating problems. First, this work challenges the theoretical reliance on the culture-of-thinness model. Although all of the women I interviewed were manipulated and hurt by this imperative at some point in their lives, it is not the primary source of their problems. Even in the instances in which a culture of thinness was a precipitating factor in anorexia, bulimia, or binging, this influence occurred in concert with other oppressions.

Attributing the etiology of eating problems primarily to a woman's striving to attain a certain beauty ideal is also problematic because it labels a common way that women cope with pain as essentially appearance-based disorders. One blatant example of sexism is the notion that women's foremost worry is about their appearance. By focusing on the emphasis on slenderness, the eating-problems literature falls into the same trap of assuming that the problems reflect women's "obsession" with appearance. Some women were raised in families and communities in which thinness was not considered a criterion for beauty. Yet, they still developed eating problems. Other women were taught that women should be thin, but their eating problems were not primarily in reaction to this imperative. Their eating strategies began as logical solutions to problems rather than problems themselves as they tried to cope with a variety of traumas.

Establishing links between eating problems and a range of oppressions invites a rethinking of both the groups of women who have been excluded from research and those whose lives have been the basis of theory formation. The construction of bulimia and anorexia as appearance-based disorders is rooted in a notion of femininity in which white middle- and upper-class women are portrayed as frivolous, obsessed with their bodies, and overly accepting of narrow gender roles. This portrayal fuels women's tremendous shame and guilt about eating problems—as signs of self-centered vanity. This construction of white middle- and upper-class women is intimately linked to the portrayal of working-class white women and women of color as their opposite: as somehow exempt from accepting the dominant standards of beauty or as one step away from being hungry and therefore not susceptible to eating problems. Identifying that women may binge to cope with poverty contrasts the notion that eating problems are class bound. Attending to the intricacies of race, class, sexuality, and gender pushes us to rethink the demeaning construction of middle-class femininity and establishes bulimia and anorexia as serious responses to injustices.

Understanding the link between eating problems and trauma also suggests much about treatment and prevention. Ultimately, their prevention depends not simply on individual healing but also on changing the social conditions that underlie their etiology. As Bernice Johnson Reagon sings in Sweet Honey in the Rock's song "Oughta Be a Woman," "A way outa no way is too much to ask/too much of a task for any one woman" (Reagon 1980).[4] Making it possible for women to have healthy relationships with their bodies and eating is a comprehensive task. Beginning steps in this direction include insuring that (1) girls can grow up without being sexually abused, (2) parents have adequate resources to raise their children, (3) children of color grow up free of racism, and (4) young lesbians have the chance to see their reflection in their teachers and community leaders. Ultimately, the prevention of eating problems depends on women's access to economic, cultural, racial, political, social, and sexual justice.

NOTES

1. I use the term *eating problems* as an umbrella term for one or more of the following: anorexia, bulimia, extensive dieting, or binging. I avoid using the term *eating disorder* because it categorizes the problems as individual pathologies, which deflects attention away from the social inequalities underlying them (Brown 1985). However, by using the term *problem* I do not wish to imply blame. In fact, throughout, I argue that the eating strategies that women develop begin as logical solutions to problems, not problems themselves.

2. By trauma I mean a violating experience that has long-term emotional, physical, and/or spiritual consequences that may have immediate or delayed effects. One reason the term *trauma* is useful conceptually is its association with the diagnostic label *post-traumatic stress disorder (PTSD)* (American Psychological Association 1987). PTSD is one of the few clinical diagnostic categories that recognize social problems (such as war or the Holocaust) as responsible for the symptoms identified (Trimble 1985). This concept adapts well to the feminist assertion that a woman's symptoms cannot be understood as solely individual, considered outside of her social context, or prevented without significant changes in social conditions.

3. One reason the term *consciousness* is applicable is its intellectual history as an entity that is shaped by social context and social structures (Delphy 1984; Marx 1964). This link aptly applies to how the women described their bodies because their perceptions of themselves as embodied (or not embodied) directly relate to their material conditions (living situations, financial resources, and access to social and political power).

4. Copyright © 1980. Used by permission of Songtalk Publishing.

REFERENCES

American Psychological Association. 1987. *Diagnostic and Statistical Manual of Mental Disorders.* 3rd ed. rev. Washington, DC: American Psychological Association.

Andersen, Arnold, and Andy Hay. 1985. Racial and socioeconomic influences in anorexia nervosa and bulimia. *International Journal of Eating Disorders* 4:479–87.

Arnold, Georgiana. 1990. Coming home: One Black woman's journey to health and fitness. In *The Black Women's Health Book: Speaking for Ourselves,* Evelyn C. White. Seattle, WA: Seal Press.

Avery, Byllye Y. 1990. Breathing life into ourselves: The evolution of the National Black Women's Health Project. In *The Black Women's Health Book: Speaking for Ourselves,* Evelyn C. White. Seattle, WA: Seal Press.

Bass, Ellen, and Laura Davis. 1988. *The Courage to Heal: A Guide for Women Survivors of Child Sexual Abuse.* New York: Harper & Row.

Brown, Laura S. 1985. Women, weight and power: Feminist theoretical and therapeutic issues. *Women and Therapy* 4: 61–71.

———. 1987. Lesbians, weight and eating: New analyses and perspectives. In *Lesbian Psychologies,* the Boston Lesbian Psychologies Collective. Champaign: University of Illinois Press.

Chernin, Kim. 1981. *The Obsession: Reflections of the Tyranny of Slenderness.* New York: Harper & Row.

Clarke, Cheryl. 1982. *Narratives.* New Brunswick, NJ: Sister Books.

Copeland, Paul M. 1985. Neuroendocrine aspects of eating disorders. In *Theory and Treatment of Anorexia Nervosa and Bulimia: Biomedical, Sociocultural, and Psychological Perspectives,* Steven Wiley Emmett. New York: Brunner/Mazel.

Delphy, Christine. 1984. *Close to Home: A Materialist Analysis of Women's Oppression.* Amherst: University of Massachusetts Press.

DeSalvo, Louise. 1989. *Virginia Woolf: The Impact of Childhood Sexual Abuse on Her Life and Work.* Boston, MA: Beacon.

Dworkin, Sari H. 1989. Not in man's image: Lesbians and the cultural oppression of body image. In *Loving Boldly: Issues Facing Lesbians,* Ester D. Rothblum and Ellen Cole. New York: Harrington Park Press.

Garfinkel, Paul E., and David M. Garner. 1982. *Anorexia Nervosa: A Multidimensional Perspective.* New York: Brunner/Mazel.

Garner, David. 1985. Iatrogenesis in anorexia nervosa and bulimia nervosa. *International Journal of Eating Disorders* 4: 701–26.

Glaser, Barney G., and Anselm L. Strauss. 1967. *The Discovery of Grounded Theory: Strategies for Qualitative Research.* New York: Aldine DeGruyter.

Goldfarb, Lori. 1987. Sexual abuse antecedent to anorexia nervosa, bulimia and compulsive overeating: Three case reports. *International Journal of Eating Disorders* 6:675–80.

Gray, James, Kathryn Ford, and Lily M. Kelly. 1987. The prevalence of bulimia in a Black college population. *International Journal of Eating Disorders* 6:733–40.

Herman, Judith. 1981. *Father-Daughter Incest.* Cambridge, MA: Harvard University Press.

Higginbotham, Elizabeth. 1986. We were never on a pedestal: Women of color continue to struggle with poverty, racism and sexism. In *For Crying Out Loud,* Rochelle Lefkowitz and Ann Withorn. Boston, MA: Pilgrim Press.

Hsu, George. 1987. Are eating disorders becoming more common in Blacks? *International Journal of Eating Disorders* 6: 113–24.

Iazzetto, Demetria. 1989. When the body is not an easy place to be: Women's sexual abuse and eating problems. Ph.D. diss., Union for Experimenting Colleges and Universities, Cincinnati, Ohio.

Kearney-Cooke, Ann. 1988. Group treatment of sexual abuse among women with eating disorders. *Women and Therapy* 7:5–21.

Marx, Karl. 1964. *The Economic and Philosophic Manuscripts of 1844.* New York: International.

Masson, Jeffrey. 1984. *The Assault on the Truth: Freud's Suppression of the Seduction Theory.* New York: Farrar, Strauss & Giroux.

Naylor, Gloria. 1985. *Linden Hills.* New York: Ticknor & Fields.

Nevo, Shoshana. 1985. Bulimic symptoms: Prevalence and the ethnic differences among college women. *International Journal of Eating Disorders* 4:151–68.

Oppenheimer, R., K. Howells, R. L. Palmer, and D. A. Chaloner. 1985. Adverse sexual experience in childhood and clinical eating disorders: A preliminary description. *Journal of Psychiatric Research* 19:357–61.

Orbach, Susie. 1978. *Fat Is a Feminist Issue.* New York: Paddington.

———. 1985. Accepting the symptom: A feminist psychoanalytic treatment of anorexia nervosa. In *Handbook of Psychotherapy for Anorexia Nervosa and Bulimia,* David M. Garner and Paul E. Garfinkel. New York: Guilford.

Powers, Retha. 1989. Fat is a Black women's issue. *Essence,* Oct., 75, 78, 134, 136.

Reagon, Bernice Johnson. 1980. "Oughta be a woman." On Sweet Honey in the Rock's album *Good News.* Music by Bernice Johnson Reagon; lyrics by June Jordan. Washington, DC: Songtalk.

Rich, Adrienne. 1986. Compulsory heterosexuality and lesbian existence. In *Blood, Bread and Poetry.* New York: Norton.

Root, Maria P. P., and Patricia Fallon. 1988. The incidence of victimization experiences in a bulimic sample. *Journal of Interpersonal Violence* 3:161–73.

———. 1989. Treating the victimized bulimic: The functions of binge–purge behavior. *Journal of Interpersonal Violence* 4:90–100.

Russell, Diana E. 1986. *The Secret Trauma: Incest in the Lives of Girls and Women.* New York: Basic Books.

Schoenfielder, Lisa, and Barbara Wieser, eds. 1983. *Shadow on a Tightrope: Writings by Women about Fat Liberation.* Iowa City, IA: Aunt Lute Book Co.

Silber, Tomas. 1986. Anorexia nervosa in Blacks and Hispanics. *International Journal of Eating Disorders* 5:121–28.

Silberstein, Lisa, Ruth Striegel-Moore, and Judith Rodin. 1987. Feeling fat: A woman's shame. In *The Role of Shame in Symptom Formation*, Helen Block Lewis. Hillsdale, NJ: Lawrence Erlbaum.

Smead, Valerie. 1984. Eating behaviors which may lead to and perpetuate anorexia nervosa, bulimarexia, and bulimia. *Women and Therapy* 3:37–49.

Spack, Norman. 1985. Medical complications of anorexia nervosa and bulimia. In *Theory and Treatment of Anorexia*

Nervosa and Bulimia: Biomedical, Sociocultural, and Psychological Perspectives, Steven Wiley Emmett. New York: Brunner/Mazel.

Swink, Kathy, and Antoinette E. Leveille. 1986. From victim to survivor: A new look at the issues and recovery process for adult incest survivors. *Women and Therapy* 5:119–43.

Trimble, Michael. 1985. Post-traumatic stress disorder: History of a concept. In *Trauma and Its Wake: The Study and Treatment of Post-traumatic Stress Disorder*, C. R. Figley. New York: Brunner/Mazel.

What's important is what you look like. 1988. *Gay Community News*, July, 24–30.

White, Evelyn C., ed. 1990. *The Black Women's Health Book: Speaking for Ourselves.* Seattle, WA: Seal Press.

———. 1991. Unhealthy appetites. *Essence*, Sept., 28, 30.

READING *35*   **Simone Weil Davis**

Loose Lips Sink Ships

[They are] two excresences of muscular flesh which hang, and in some women, fall outside the neck of the womb; lengthen and shorten as does the comb of a turkey, principally when they desire coitus. . . .

—Ambroise Paré (1579), quoted in Lisa Jean Moore and Adele E. Clarke, "Clitoral Conventions and Transgressions: Graphic Representations in Anatomy Texts, c1900–1991," Feminist Studies 21 (summer 1995)

DESIGNER VAGINAS

Perhaps you noticed some of the articles in women's magazines that came out in 1998; *Cosmopolitan, Marie Claire,* and *Harper's Bazaar* each carried one, as did *Salon* on-line, articles with titles like "Labia Envy," "Designer Vaginas," and "The New Sex Surgeries." More recently, *Jane* magazine covered the topic, and Dan Savage's nationally syndicated advice column, "Savage Love," stumbled explosively upon it as well.

These pieces all discussed labiaplasty, a relatively recent plastic surgery procedure that involves trimming away labial tissue and sometimes injecting fat from another part of the body into labia that have been deemed excessively droopy. In contrast to the tightening operation known as "vaginal rejuvenation," labiaplasty is sheerly cosmetic in purpose and purports to have no impact on sensation (unless something were to go terribly awry).[1] Throughout coverage here and in Canada, the aptly named Doctors Alter, Stubbs, and Matlock shared much of the glory and the public relations. In the name of consumer choice, these articles provoke consumer anxiety. The *Los Angeles Times* quotes Dr. Matlock: "The woman is the designer . . . the doctor is just the instrument. . . . Honestly, if you look at *Playboy,* those women, on the outer vagina area, the vulva is very aesthetically appealing, the vulva is rounded. It's full, not flat. . . . Women are coming in saying, I want something different, I want to change things. They look at *Playboy,* the ideal woman per se, for the body and the shape and so on. You don't see women in there with excessively long labia minora."[2]

All the popular articles about the "new sex surgeries" that I've reviewed also include remarks from skeptical colleagues and from polled readers who feel okay about their labia. (In an unfortunate turn of phrase, one plastic surgeon describes Dr. Matlock as a bit too "cutting edge.") Despite this apparently balanced coverage, a brand-new worry is being planted, with the declaration in *Salon* that "many women had been troubled for years about the appearance of their labia minora," and with the use of words like "normal" and "abnormal" to describe nonpathological variations among genitalia. The November 1998 article in *Cosmopolitan* has an eye-catching blurb: "My labia were so long, they'd show through my clothes!" Having taken *that* in, the reader suddenly looks up at the accompanying photo with new eyes: the photograph is of a slim woman in fairly modest underwear; because of the picture's cropping, she is headless, but the posture is distinctive, awkward. She's somewhat hunched forward, her hands are both crotch-bound, and one finger slips beneath the edge of her panties. Having read the caption, you think, "My God, she's tucking in her labia!"[3]

Ellen Frankfort's 1972 book, the women's liberationist *Vaginal Politics,* begins with the following scene.[4] Carol from the Los Angeles Self-Help Clinic "slips out of her dungarees and underpants," hops onto a long table in an old church basement and inserts a speculum into her vagina. The 50 other women present file up and look with a flashlight, and learn, too, how to self-examine with a speculum and a dimestore mirror. This self-exploration of what has often been referred to as "the dark continent" or just "down there" seemed the perfect symbol for the early claim of women's liberation that "the personal is political." How could a woman call for sexual autonomy without self-awareness? To reverse the phrasing of one of Second Wave feminism's most famous byproducts, how could we know "our selves" without knowing "our bodies" first?[5] This image of women using a well-placed mirror to demystify and reclaim their own bodies is rooted dimly in my teen-years memory. I found it eerily resurrected when the *Salon* piece by Louisa Kamps came up on my computer screen. Kamps starts off like this: "'Ladies, get out your hand mirrors,' begins a curious press release I find at my desk one Monday morning. 'Yes, it is true . . . the newest trend in surgically enhanced body beautification: Female Genital Cosmetic Surgery.'" The hand mirror this time is used to alert the would-be vagina shopper to any deficiencies "down below" that she may have been blithely ignoring. From 1970s' consciousness-raising groups and Judy Chicago's dinner plates, through Annie Sprinkle's speculum parties of the 1980s, and on to Eve Ensler's collaborative *Vagina Monologues,*[6] we came at the end of the 1990s to Dr. Alter and Dr. Stubbs. What's the trajectory from Second Wave feminist "self-discovery and celebration" to the current almost-craze for labiaplasty? And does the fact of this trajectory provide us with a warning?

THE CLEAN SLIT

The vagina. According to Freud, its first sighting is the first scandal. It is *the* secret, invariably broken, that, once seen, changes you forever, especially if "you" are a little boy in turn-of-the-century Vienna, stumbling in upon your mother *en déshabillé*. You discover, all at once, in a rude shock, that she lacks a penis. You tremble at the threat that her missing phallus implies to *your* little member: if it happened to her, it could happen to you (especially because you've got the gall to compete with your father for your mother's affections). For Freud, his followers, and even many of his feminist revisionists, the "scandal" of a woman's genitals is supposed to be due to what *isn't* there, not what *is*. This article is not about lack, however. It is about excess. And it is not (exactly) about what Jacques Lacan and Hélène Cixous celebrated as *jouissance*. It's about labia.

So the vagina betokens the horror of castration, we're told. Many have remarked that perhaps this scandal is more accurately defined as one of interiority. In a society that revolves around the visual, an orgasm that doesn't include ejaculation can seem maddeningly uncontrollable: you can't prove it (outside of a laboratory), and thus it can be faked.[7] Discussing hard-core cinematic pornography, Linda Williams claims that "[t]he woman's ability to fake the orgasm that the man can never fake . . . seems to be at the root of all the genre's attempts to solicit what it can never be sure of: the out-of-control confession of pleasure, a hard-core 'frenzy of the visible.'"[8]

In the Amero-European world of the late-eighteenth and the early-nineteenth centuries, an earlier notion of women's natural lustiness was transformed into the myth of feminine modesty.[9] This purported lady-like decorum has always been depicted as simultaneously innate for the female *and* a massively big job. For the same social world that generated the mythos of the delicate, proper lady has also continually spawned and recycled dirty jokes about "vagina dentata," fatal odors, and other horror-story imagery about female genitalia.[10] The off-color disgust has always been tied in a complex way to a vast, off-color desire, and these both have been concomitant with the prescription to stay dainty—no matter what—for at least three hundred years. The paradoxical welding of abhorrence and adoration is often "resolved" socially through a stereotyped decoupling of the two, although mythologies of the lurid and the pure female are in fact too interdependent ever to be truly unbraided. Women have been branded good or bad, refined or fallen, on the basis of their race, their profession, their station in life, and so forth, with the judgments conveniently supporting the political, economic, and racial status quo (about which, more later). That being said, the paradox is also one that women negotiate individually, and this has been so for a remarkably long time. . . .

Although "feminine modesty" used to be the answer to this subtextual concern about vaginas, now the shameful zone needs to be brought into line for display, rather than hidden. The vulva is becoming a pioneer territory for cosmetic enhancement—surgical practitioners need above all to capitalize both on that preexisting shame and on the ever-greater need to provide a cyborgian spectacle of porno-gloss. The relative mainstreaming of the sex industry (think of Demi Moore in *Striptease,* for example) and the blurring of the lines between hard-core and advertising imagery (think Calvin Klein) have led to a perpetually increasing sense of pressure among many women, the pressure to develop and present a seamlessly sexualized, "airbrushed" body.[11] Drs. Alter, Stubbs, and Matlock want that sought-after body to include a specific labial look, one desirable enough to be worth "buying."

Before people will spend money on something as expensive and uncomfortable as cosmetic surgery, they need to be motivated not only by desire but by concern or self-doubt. Bringing the authoritative language of medical science to the aestheticization of the vagina is one key way to trigger such anxiety. Advertisers have frequently invoked and generated medicalized norms to sell products. Roland Marchand describes perhaps the classic example of this phenomenon: after the liquid known as Listerine proved a lackluster general antiseptic, it was decided to dramatize its function as a mouthwash. Foul tasting as it was, consumer incentive would be needed. The term "halitosis" was "exhumed

from an old medical dictionary" by an advertising firm and became the driving force behind a subsequent, energetic scare campaign about the medical, social, and romantic risks of bad breath.[12] Advertisers have always been both matter-of-fact and explicit about delineating and then steadily working to create a sense of deficiency where once there was indifference or even, God forbid, enjoyment, working to incite new arenas of insecurity, new personal anxieties, so that more things can be marketed and sold.

Cosmetic surgery has worked with the same principles throughout its more than 100-year history, as detailed in histories of the profession by Kathy Davis, Elizabeth Haiken, and Sander Gilman.[13] For instance, in a particularly unnerving chapter on "micromastia" (the "disease" of flat-chestedness) and the surgeries developed to "correct" it, Haiken quotes a 1958 article by plastic surgeon Milton T. Edgerton and psychiatrist A.R. McClary, on "the psychiatry of breast augmentation": "Literally thousands of women in this country alone, are seriously disturbed by feelings of inadequacy in regard to concepts of the body image. Partly as a result of exposure to advertising propaganda and questionable publicity, many physically normal women develop an almost paralyzing self-consciousness focused on the feeling that they do not have the correct size bosom."[14] The rationale laid out here, which explains *but also helps create* "inferiority complexes," can be applied across the full topography of the human form, as borne out by the increasing prevalence of liposuction, face-lifts, buttock and tummy tucks. The latest realm to be scoured for "abnormalities" is the vagina, formerly spared from the scrutiny of the market because it was considered both too reviled and too quakingly desired to be addressed commercially.

These days, in part because of the video dissemination and the main-streaming of pornography, women, regardless of gender preference, can see the vaginas of a lot of different other women. They may desire those vaginas, they may simultaneously identify with them, but if they are rich enough or have great credit, they can definitely have them built.[15] A 1997 article in the Canadian magazine *See* interviews a patient of Dr. Stubbs in Toronto. Deborah "has had her eyes done and had breast implants and some liposuction. She says that she started thinking about her labia when her first husband brought home porn magazines and she started comparing herself. 'I saw some other ones that were cuter than mine' and I thought, 'Hey, I want that one,' she laughs."[16] Of course, the images we relish or bemoan in pornography are almost always tweaked technically. As Deborah did her "catalog shopping," the women she was admiring were perhaps themselves surgically "enhanced," but additionally, they were posed, muted with makeup and lighting, and the resultant photographic images were then edited with an airbrush or the digital modifications of Photoshop.

This is especially true of pornography that presents itself as "upscale," whether soft or hard core. As Laura Kipnis helps us realize, there's a crucial link between *Hustler*'s targeting of a working-class market and its being the first of the big three glossy "wank mags" to show what it called "the pink."[17] *Hustler*'s aggressive celebration of vulgarity informed its initial rejection of soft-core decorum about genitals; thus, its representations of vaginas were matter-of-fact, and often enough contextualized with very explicit, poorly lit Polaroid shots sent in by readers. When the vagina finally came to the pages of *Penthouse*, by contrast, it was as flaw-free and glossy as the rest of the models' figures. In "The Pussy Shot: An Interview with Andrew Blake," sex writer Susie Bright discusses the classed aesthetics of this pornographer, whose trademarks are his lavish sets (straight out of *Architectural Digest*, Bright remarks) and high-end production values: in this posh setting, it comes as no surprise that the star's labia are small and her "pussy is perfectly composed, with every hair in place."[18]

The evolution of a new strict standard of "beauty," rigid enough to induce surgery, does not occur in a vacuum. Among other factors, economics are in play—not just in the eagerness of a few cosmetic surgeons to up their patient load but in a far more intricate web of drives and desires intersecting with technological shifts and cultural and financial power plays. I will only nod here to the complexity of this phenomenon. A first example: in *Venus Envy: A History of Cosmetic Surgery*, Haiken points out that research catalyzed by World War I and II led to technological innovations that furthered the cosmetic surgery industry. Wars, which maim and disfigure people, increase the demand for and respectability of plastic surgery, allowing surgeons the grim opportunity to improve their skills and their public relations. Additionally, war means the invention and/or increased availability of new materials, like silicone and polyurethane, both of which were used for breast augmentation in the wake of World War II.[19] Could this new material on hand have *led* (in part) to the 1950s' notorious obsession with large breasts?

Here is a more recent example of the subtle interplay of cultural and economic forces that can help shape changes in beauty standards: Perhaps Rudolph Giuliani's New York City should be thought of as undergoing an urban labiaplasty. In this zoned, regulated era, newly comfortable for tourists if not for New Yorkers, the sex industry has been radically curtailed. This change has meant, tellingly enough, that almost all the sex clubs "connected" enough to remain open after 1998 favor "clone" women—Caucasian bodies, tidy tan lines, big blonde hair, collagen lips, surgically removed ribs, liposucked bottoms, and implanted breasts. With time, their labia may also be ubiquitously trimmed. Many women with bodies that diverge from the approved stereotype—biker chicks, Latina and Black dancers, plump or small-breasted women, the pierced girl with the monster tattoo—women who used to be able to dance erotically for an income, have been "sheered away," forced into unemployment, prostitution, or departure. These days in New York, only the clones can dance, and it is clone bodies alone that New York City strip club patrons now ogle.[20] The ripple effects such a change works, no doubt, multiply, and the Bloomberg era will see them continue.

In part because of the prevalence of just such a mainstreamed *Penthouse* and *Playboy* aesthetic, labias in pornography are often literally tucked away (in the most low-tech variant of body modification).[21] If you review enough porn, however, especially lesbian porn or that which is unsqueamishly "déclassé" as in *Hustler*, you will see a wide variety in the female genitalia on display—wide enough to evoke the "snowflake uniqueness" analogy that is bandied around in popular coverage of the new cosmetic enhancement surgeries. And indeed the before-and-after shots available at some of the surgeons' web sites that I've found so far do reveal, unsurprisingly, that the single favored look for these "designer vaginas" is . . . the clean slit. Louisa Kamps of *Salon* magazine agrees: "What strikes me in the 'after' shots is the eerie similarity between the women . . . their genitalia are carbon copies of each other."

In a subtle but nontrivial way, this particular aesthetic and the surgery that manifests it cut back on women's experience of self-on-self contact, of tactility: Luce Irigaray celebrates the nonvisual, sensory experience women perpetually enjoy as their vaginal lips press and move against one another. She suggests that this physiological status makes women psychologically less invested in the myth of the monadic, self-reliant individual than are men. Irigaray's "two lips which are not one" would not touch each other much in a world of women "Altered."[22] What do the aesthetics of a streamlined vulva signify? The smooth groin of our favorite plastic android prototype, Barbie? A desire to approximate prepubescence? A fastidious minimization of marginal zones?[23]

Mary Russo writes of "the female grotesque" in terms that are relevant here: "The images of the grotesque body are precisely those which are abjected from the bodily canons of classical aesthetics. The classical body is transcendent and monumental, closed, static, self-contained, symmetrical, and sleek.... The grotesque body is open, protruding, secreting, multiple and changing...."[24] Russo's contrasting of the grotesque with the classical is particularly resonant in this context, as plastic surgeons often invoke classical aesthetics and the metaphor of surgeon-as-sculptor; Stubbs even illustrates his site with photographs of classical statuary and presents his "before-and-after" shots in a "Surgical Art Gallery" captioned by Hippocrates: "'Ars longa, vita brevis'—Art is long and life is short."[25] Elizabeth Haiken discusses "the classical context in which [early plastic surgeons] wished to place themselves; the term *plastic surgery* derives from the Greek *plastikos,* to shape or mold."[26] The asymmetries, protrusions, and changeability of Russo's grotesque are what the labiaplasty is meant to "shape or mold" and *cut* away.

Bodies do change with the passage of time, of course. If the living body is to approximate sculpture, change itself must be managed, *fixed*. Reading the following quote from Dr. Alter's web site, one is reminded of the Renaissance theory of the wandering womb, whereby female hysteria and misbehavior were deemed the results of a uterus that had dislodged and begun to storm about internally, wreaking havoc. A woman's "womb was like a hungry animal; when not amply fed by sexual intercourse or reproduction, it was likely to wander about her body, overpowering her speech and senses."[27] In Dr. Alter's prose, the older woman, "in dialogue with gravity,"[28] may find her previously pleasing vagina dangerously "on the move": "The aging female may dislike the descent of her pubic hair and labia and desire re-elevation to its previous location," Dr. Alter warns. So, it is woman's work to make sure her genitalia are snug, not wayward.

We are talking about vaginal aesthetics, and aesthetic judgments almost always evidence socially relevant metaphors at work on the material and visual planes. Ideas about feminine beauty are ever-changing: the classic example is a comparison of Rubens's fleshy beauties and the wraithlike super-model Kate Moss (who succeeded Twiggy). But, in a world where many women have never thought about judging the looks of

their genitals, even if they care about their appearance more generally, we should ask what criteria make for a good-looking vagina, and who is assigned as arbiter. These (mutating) criteria should tell us something about the value system that generates them. To tease out some answers to these questions, this article goes on to put the labiaplasty phenomenon in a contextual frame with other vaginal modifications.

MODIFYING/CLASSIFYING

What representations of vulvas circulate in our society? And who, beyond Dr. Tight, is modifying the female genitalia, how and why? For one, among alternative youth (and the not-so-alternative, not-so-youthful, too) piercings are being sought to modify and decorate the labia, sometimes to extend them, and, ideally, to add to clitoral stimulation. What sensibilities mark these changes? Among body modifiers on the Web, conversation about body image, self-mutilation, and, contrarily, healing, is common, with an accepted understanding that many turn to piercing as a means of overcoming perceived past abuse. "'Most folks use BodMod to get back in touch with the parts of themselves that were hurt or misused by others.' 'BodMod has helped me undemonize pain.... I was able to handle [childbirth] better, knowing that I'd survived...two ten-gauge labial piercings....'" Changing one's relationship to one's genitalia by becoming their "modifier" leads here to an aesthetic reassessment: "'You know, I never liked to look at my puss until I got my rings. I have well-developed inner labia that always show, and I was always envious of those women who seemed to have nice neat little pussies with everything tucked inside. My puss looked like an old whore's cunt to me! So one reason I *know* I wasn't mutilating myself when I got my privates pierced was how much I liked to look at myself after the work was done. You might actually say I'm *glad* my labia are the way they are now.'"[29]

"Glad" is what the cosmetic surgeons do *not* want you to be about prominent labia minora. If you look at the opening paragraph of Ensler's *Vagina Monologues*, you begin to wonder if the unruliness now coming under the governance of the cosmetic surgeon isn't at least as symbolic as it is aesthetic. This is Ensler, introducing her project (interviews with real women, transcribed, performed onstage, and then collected in a book):

I was worried about vaginas. I was worried about what we think about vaginas, and even more worried that we don't think about them. . . . So I decided to talk to women about their vaginas, to do vagina interviews, which became vagina monologues. I talked with over two hundred women. I talked to old women, young women, married women, single women, lesbians, college professors, actors, corporate professionals, sex workers, African American women, Hispanic women, Asian American women, Native American women, Caucasian women, Jewish women. At first women were reluctant to talk. They were a little shy. But once they got going, you couldn't stop them.[30]

Just as Ensler's own catalog of interviewees seems to burgeon and proliferate, so too the women with whom she spoke were "unstoppable." With a similar metaphoric expansion, in the cosmetic surgeons' promotional material, not only are women's *labia* depicted as in danger of distention, but one woman customer also described her *"hang-up"* about her preoperative labia as "just growing and growing," until the doctor cut it short, that is. Loose lips sink ships.

I received a "free consultation" from one doctor who performs labiaplasties, and this doctor explained to me that the ideal look for labia minora was not only minimal and unextended but also symmetrical, "homogeneously pink," and "not wavy."[31] To the dangers and allures of what's hidden about the vagina, now is added the "too muchness" of labial tissue. In their heterogeneous dappling and their moist curves, labia mark the lack of tidy differentiation between inside and outside and that's just *too much*. One effect of this procedure is to reduce this sense of a "marginal" site between exterior and interior corporeality. Labia can be seen as "gateway" tissue, in other words, tissue that is somewhat indeterminate in texture and hue, yielding slowly from outer to inner and blurring the boundary between the fetishized gloss of the outer dermis and the wet, mushy darkness of the inside. This indeterminacy, actually a function of the labia's protective role, may be part of their association with excess.[32] In *Public Privates: Performing Gynecology from Both Ends of the Speculum*, Terry Kapsalis "reads" the images in a widely used medical text, *Danforth's Obstetrics and Gynecology*. She is struck by the lack of representations of healthy vaginas in *Danforth's* and argues that ultimately the work's visual logic pathologizes female genitalia per se. Using language parallel to that which I have used here, she writes: "Perhaps it is not a lack that is threatening, but an excess. The fact is that even if no pathology exists, there *is* something there—namely, a

vulva with labia, a clitoris, and so on, a marginal site occupying both the inside and the outside, an abject space (according to Julia Kristeva) that threatens to devour the penis (vagina dentata)."[33]

In the medical realm, much effort is expended to overcome the mysterious liminality of the vagina. Since the eras of the ancient anatomists Galen and Hippocrates and especially since the rise of gynecology in the nineteenth century, vaginas have been diagrammed and cataloged in medical textbooks. Running parallel, a variant of pornography has always picked up and parodied the objectifying eroticism of scientific conquest.[34] In this realm, large labia have often been associated with deviance—at least since the sixteenth century they have indicated to doctors the alleged presence of hypersexuality, onanism, and possible "tribadism" or lesbian tendencies. Jennifer Terry discusses a 1930s' study conducted in New York City, "under the auspices of the Committee for the Study of Sex Variants," in order "to identify, treat, and prevent homosexuality." A moderate-sized group of self-proclaimed lesbians were examined by a battery of experts, so that their "traits" could be characterized and profiled. These experts included gynecologists. The overseer of the project, one Dr. Dickinson, ultimately "identified ten characteristics which he argued set the sex variant [lesbian] apart from 'normal' women: (1) larger than average vulvas; (2) longer labia minora; (3) 'labia minora protrude between the labia majora and are wrinkled, thickened, or *brawny*'; (4) 'the prepuce is large or wrinkled or in folds'; (5) the clitoris is 'notably erectile'. . .; (6) 'eroticism is clearly in evidence on examination, as shown by dusky flush of the parts, with free flow of clear, glairy mucus, and with definite clitoris erection. . . .'" The study concludes that all "these findings can be the result of strong sex urge [presumably an innate or congenital condition], plus: (a) Vulvar and vulvovaginal self-friction; or (b) Homosexual digital or oral play; or (c) Heterosexual manual or coital techniques, singly or in any combination."[35] Terry rightly emphasizes the researchers' apparent fascination with the concept that homo/hypersexual desire (often conflated) could be strong enough that it could make the vulva a site of transformation. The prurience behind this possibility that perverted sex play could "rebuild" a vagina seems great enough that it is allowed to overshadow the theory of a congenital distinction between heterosexual and homosexual anatomy.

Many American and British clitoridectomies and female castrations (the removal of healthy ovaries) were performed in the nineteenth century and as recently as the 1970s, as a response to just such indicators.[36] Isaac Baker Brown began to perform clitoridectomies in Britain in 1858, in order to reduce "hysteria" and other nervous ailments, but particularly to combat "excessive" masturbation. He was, by the 1860s, soundly critiqued in his own country and indeed expelled from Britain's Obstetrical Society in 1867; but his procedure (and its milder variant, circumcision of the clitoral hood) became popular in the United States by the late 1860s and was performed in this country for decades. Although experimentation in the development phases of sexual surgeries generally was exacted on the bodies of poor and disenfranchised women (mostly African American), the lady of leisure became the expressed target for these operations. Upper-middle-class and upper-class women had disposable incomes and time on their hands (to masturbate . . . or to recover from genital surgery). Robert Battey developed the practice of removing healthy ovaries to address a whole slew of complaints, from kleptomania to epilepsy, and this procedure was surprisingly widespread, particularly between 1880 and 1910. One 1893 proponent of female castration claimed that "the moral sense of the patient is elevated. . . . She becomes tractable, orderly, industrious and cleanly." Although depleted misrule seems an unsurprising "benefit" of such operations, one would not expect *aesthetics* to spring up as a concern in this context, but Ben Barker-Benfield cites some clitoridectomy and castration patients who thought of the trend as a "fashionable fad" and found their scars "as pretty as the dimple on the cheek of sweet sixteen."[37]

In the 1970s and 1980s, James Burt, an Ohio gynecologist, gained notoriety—and eventually lost his license—performing what he called "the surgery of love" on more than 4,500 patients, apparently often without even garnering the pretense of informed consent, while they were anesthetized and "on the table" for another procedure. This procedure included a clitoral circumcision and a vaginal reconstruction that changed the angle of the vagina; he insisted before and after the malpractice suits that he had enhanced the sexual pleasure of 99 percent of the women upon whom he'd operated and that he was "correcting" the female anatomy, which he saw as God's mistake, by repositioning the genitalia. Women were left with loss of erotic sensation, enormous pain during intercourse, chronic bowel and urination problems requiring

regular catheter use, and ongoing serious infections; the same set of medical sequelae have been reported among infibulated women.[38] In 1997, the Ohio Supreme Court ultimately awarded forty women compensation amounting to a total of $20 million. This award came after spectacular struggles in the courts over an eleven-year-period. The organization Patients-in-Arms, led by Carla Miller (who describes herself as "a victim of FGM" [female genital mutilation]), is devoted to helping women speak out about abuse and disfigurement at the hands of gynecologists. A review of the cases toward which Ms. Miller can direct one makes it excruciatingly clear both that this phenomenon is quite widespread and that it is made possible by the common and interlinked phenomenon of the "white wall of silence" that reduces the doctors' risk of being brought to task.[39]

In a related phenomenon that persists to this day, the erotic tissue of "intersexed" or ambiguously gendered babies and children is routinely, in fact just about ubiquitously, modified through surgery without the minor's consent, in what the medical profession calls a "psychosocial emergency." These modifications have been shown to leave behind serious psychological scarring; often enough, the surgeries profoundly compromise the sexual sensation of the people forced to undergo them. In a piece called "The Tyranny of the Aesthetic: Surgery's Most Intimate Violation," Martha Coventry explains that "girlhood is [almost always] the gender approximated through surgery in such circumstances." "It's easier to poke a hole than build a pole," as one surgeon remarks. Coventry quotes Suzanne Kessler, whose work represents an important contribution to the study of intersexed experience: "Genital ambiguity is corrected not because it is threatening to the infant's life, but because it is threatening to the infant's culture."[40]

The genitalia are cultural terrain that must conform to identificatory norms; this has been driven home by the historians of gynecological science. When mid-nineteenth-century physician Marion Sims developed the duck-billed speculum and an examination protocol that gave him a good view, he used the language of an imperial conquistador, beholding still uncharted territory: "I saw everything, as no man had seen before."[41] Much has been written, particularly by Irigaray, about the mythologization of female genitalia as "the dark continent," the "nothing to see," an Unknown supposedly waiting to be penetrated by pioneering masculine experts; Mary Ann Doane and Anne McClintock are among those who have etched out the linkage that such a metaphor immediately suggests between gender politics and racial imperialism.[42]

What if the "nothing," the furor about female absence, is in part a stand-in scandal for the *something* that is the vaginal bloom—just as the "vast wildernesses" of the Americas and Africa were an invader's myth that suppressed the inconvenient fact of inhabitation? It is exactly in the realms where gender and race intersect that we can see this being played out. Sander Gilman and Michele Wallace are among those who have discussed Saartjie (or Sara) Baartman, dubbed the Hottentot Venus. She and other African women were taken from their homes and put on show in the early nineteenth century; in this display, their labial "aprons" were rumored about and peeked at with as much eroticized condemnation as were their "steoptygic" buttocks, although the latter were more plainly in view.[43] When George Cuvier, Geoffrey St. Hilaire, and Henri de Blainville, eminent naturalists all, attempted to force a scientific examination of Baartman, de Blainville reported that "she hid her apron carefully between her thighs—her movements were brusque and capricious like those of apes. . . . It was only with great sorrow that she let drop her handkerchief for a moment."[44] The outrage of invasion so evident here is aggravated by the dehumanization of Baartman that drove the tragic endeavor. In the same commentary, Cuvier describes elements of her appearance as being "like an orangutan," "like an animal," and "like a dog."[45] Eager to inspect her labia, particularly as they were seeking a classificatory wedge that would distinguish the Hottentot from the European on the level of species, the scientists spent three days trying to convince Baartman to submit to the physical, even offering her money, which she refused. Alas, her early death afforded them ready access to her private parts, however, and Cuvier made a plaster cast of her body and had her brain and genitals preserved in jars. Although the skeleton remains at Paris's Musée de l'Homme, her body is due to be returned to South Africa for burial . . . and her brain and genitals have disappeared.[46]

It is no coincidence that the aforementioned Marion Sims, early American gynecologist, developed his surgery techniques only by repeated, public operations on the bodies of African American slaves and poor, white "washerwomen."[47] Doing symbolic work, nonwhite women in the Euro-American context have endured the exposure of their bodies only to have them decried and desired, first as heathenish, then as "abnormal." Meanwhile, the nonprostitute white woman's vagina was hidden, protected—shamed, too, but out of the limelight.

OUR VULVAS, OUR SELVES

Perhaps this context needs to be kept in mind when we consider another role played contemporarily by images of female genitals: among activists opposed to the circumcision of African females, even among those who are extremely sensitive to the liabilities of cultural bias, the documenting photo has a special, and somewhat problematic, status. In "Desiring the 'Mutilated' African Woman," Wacuka Mungai points out that there is a heated and eerily prurient interest expressed over the Web in accessing documentary photos of girls and women who have undergone cliterodectomies, excisions, and infibulation.[48] Although photographs of excised and infibulated vaginas are available at "kinky" web sites alongside other images deemed freakish or gory, I agree with Mungai that, even beyond the overtly pornographic, their status as emblems of an "Othered" barbarity is also tinged with unacknowledged eroticism. As Mungai explains, these photos are typically taken with something like consent, but under circumstances when a girl would be hard pressed to withhold permission—in exchange for treatment, a foreign, light-skinned doctor who doesn't speak your language asks that you let her photograph you. You are not likely to refuse her, even though there may be trauma in the taking, and even though the photos then circulate the globe, representing only the wounded status of the African female. Like the gynecological diagram, like Baartman's genitals so long on formaldehyde display in Paris, like the "monster shot" in porn flicks, these images are partial, headless . . . vaginas emphatically dissevered from whole people, made creatures of their own—treated perhaps as the essence of the woman, the cut vagina the truest thing about her, a dangerous metonymy. Mungai points out that, by the same token, in media coverage of the debates over female circumcision among immigrants, the portraits of "cut" women's faces that accompany articles decrying the practice often serve to bring about the same delimiting reduction.

One North American woman with whom I spoke who had elected to have a labiaplasty laughed uproariously with me at the nerve of a European television news program that had approached her to ask if she'd like to do a segment on their show about her operation. The very *thought* of her face being linked to her imagined, modified vagina was preposterous to her, and she would certainly never have consented to being part of the show. Our laughter should continue to ring until it has turned livid, as we think about the many African girls and women who experience just this representational conflation. . . .

CONFOUNDING THE BOUNDARIES

The U.S. Congress passed a measure criminalizing the circumcision of a minor female in 1996, and nine or ten states have passed anti-FGO acts since 1996 as well. In Illinois, Minnesota, Rhode Island, and Tennessee, this legislation felonizes operations performed on adults as well as on minors. But *which* operations? Anti-FGO laws that now exist in a number of U.S. states describe procedures that would definitely include those practiced by Drs. Alter and Matlock, but they use only language that addresses the "ritual" or custom and belief-based cutting of African immigrant bodies. Meanwhile, this legal language either elides or okays both the "corrective" cutting of the intersexed child and the surgery sought by the unsettled consumer who has been told by plastic surgeons that her labia are unappealing and aberrant. Thus American law marks out relations between the state and its citizen bodies that differ depending on birthplace, cultural context, and skin color.

In fact, however, it is a (prevalent) mistake to imagine a quantum distinction between Euro-American and African reshapings of women's bodies: far too often, they are measured with entirely different yardsticks, rather than on a continuum. Nahid Toubia, executive director of the advocacy group Rainbo, remarks that "[t]he thinking of an African woman who believes that 'FGM is the fashionable thing to do to become a real woman' is not so different from that of an American woman who has breast implants to appear more feminine."[49] In keeping with Toubia's remark, I propose here that a subtler and less culturally binaristic analysis of such phenomena will lead, not to political paralysis in the name of cultural relativism, but to deeper understanding of core issues like the nature of consent, of bodily aesthetics and social control, and of cross-cultural activist collaboration.[50]

Soraya Miré, Somali maker of the film *Fire Eyes*, remarks in Inga Muscio's (wo)manifesto, *Cunt: A*

Declaration of Independence: "[Western women] come into conversations waving the American flag, forever projecting the idea that they are more intelligent than I am. I've learned that American women look at women like me to hide from their own pain. . . . In America, women pay *the money that is theirs and no one else's* to go to a doctor who cuts them up so they can create or sustain an image men want. Men are the mirror. Western women cut themselves up voluntarily."[51] Significantly, in Miré's construction, consent to genital surgery does *not* okay it so much as it marks the degrading depths of women's oppression. Although consent is at the heart of the issue of genital operations on children, a topic both urgent and not to be downplayed, we must also look at the social and cultural means whereby consent is manufactured, regardless of age, in the West as well as in African and other countries engaging in FGOs. In the North American popular imagination, the public address of advertising is not understood as infringing upon our power of consent. Indeed, the freedom to "pay the money that is [one's] own" is too often inscribed as the quintessential exemplar of life in a democracy. Perhaps due to that presumption, beauty rituals hatched on Madison Avenue or in Beverly Hills do not bear the onus of "barbarism" here, despite the social compulsions, psychological drives, and magical thinking that impel them.

By the same token, American oversimplifications suppress the fact that African women's relations to female genital operations are complex and variable, as are the operations themselves, of course. The operations can be roughly grouped into four sorts: circumcision, the removal of the clitoral hood or "female prepuce"; clitoridectomy, "the partial or total removal of the clitoris"; excision, "the removal of the clitoris and all or part of the labia minora"; and infibulation, "the removal of all external genitalia followed by the stitching together of most of the vaginal opening."[52] As will be discussed, motivations for any of these practices are highly variable across time and between individuals as well as between cultures. Vicki Kirby points out the distortions that come with Western monolithizing: "What is 'other' for the West must thereby forfeit its own internal contradictions and diversities in this singular and homogenizing determination of alterity."[53]

Additionally, African vaginal aesthetics are not limited to such sheerings away of vulvular tissue. Although now it is predominantly the members of the royal family who still practice this technique (which is thus a sign of status), the Buganda people in Uganda have a tradition of stretching and massaging the labia and clitoris from childhood to extend them (for feminine beautification). As Londa Schiebinger describes, some say that the "Hottentot aprons," so fetishized by Europeans, were also the result of cosmetic manipulations, on the part of African women seeking beauty.[54]

If one considers all female circumcision practices in Africa to be analogous, as is too commonly the case in popular American analysis of the phenomenon, not only does one miss the dramatic differences between the different forms of FGO, but one also fails to understand the relevant differences between people who practice it as a part of their cultural life and those who experience it as a part of their religious life. Crucial issues of consent are blurred with such elisions. Western critics of African genital surgeries can also miss completely the role that it often plays in the symbolism of resistance and political struggle, both colonial and tribal.[55] In *Facing Mt. Kenya: The Tribal Life of the Kikuyu* (1953), Jomo Kenyatta remarks that "the overwhelming majority of [the local people] believe that it is the secret aim of those who attack this country's old customs to disintegrate their social order and thereby hasten their Europeanization."[56] An additional point: although female circumcision is not explicitly directed by any religious text, it is practiced as an expression of Muslim, Christian, and Jewish religious observance among various African populations. Overall, it should not be imagined as concomitant with Islam (which it regularly is, often in an anti-Arab conflation), or even as a primarily religious practice.

In most regions, female circumcision practices are determined more by cultural factors, and by ethnic, national, tribal, and postcolonial politics, than by religion. They are by no means solely or exotically "ritualistic" in a way that entirely distinguishes them from nonimmigrant American operations on vaginas. Female genital operations are understood, variously, as hygiene, as beautification, as a curb to female sexuality, as a clarification of the difference between the sexes, as an enhancement of male sexual pleasure, as conducive to fertility and/or monogamy, as disease prevention, and as a means of conforming with social norms and ensuring that one's daughter will be marriageable, that she will be able to take her place among her age set, and that the solidarity and social strength of older women's organizations will be able to flourish.[57]

SURGERY, SISTERLINESS, AND THE "RIGHT TO CHOOSE"

Among the key motivating factors raised by African women who favor female genital surgeries are beautification, transcendence of shame, and the desire to conform; these clearly matter to American women seeking cosmetic surgery on their labia, as well. Thus, the motivations that impel African-rooted FGOs and American labiaplasties should not be envisioned as radically distinct. Not only does such oversimplification lead to a dangerous reanimation of the un/civilized binary, but it also leaves the feminist with dull tools for analysis of either phenomenon. There are aesthetic parallels between the Western and the African procedures. The enthusiasm for the clean slit voiced so vigorously by the American plastic surgeon I consulted is echoed among a group of Egyptian mothers discussing female genital operations for their daughters in the 1990 documentary, *Hidden Faces*. Although several of the women laughingly nudge each other and say they wouldn't want the excisers to interfere much with "the front" (showing a clear zest for clitoral pleasure), one woman voices an aesthetic principle about which she feels strongly. Energetically, she decries the ugliness of dangling labia, and explains to the filmmaker, with appropriate hand gestures, "Do you want her to be like a boy, with this floppy thing hanging down? Now, it should be straight. Shhh. Smooth as silk." This aesthetic judgment is in keeping not only with the views of labiaplasters in the United States but also with the vocabulary of Mauritanian midwives: one such woman, who has argued to her colleagues for a milder version of circumcision in place of vigorous excision, "use[s] two words to refer to female circumcision, 'tizian,' which means to make more beautiful, and 'gaaad,' which means to cut off and make even."[58]

The group of women chatting on a rooftop in *Hidden Faces* invokes another continuum between African and American women's approaches to feminine beauty rituals and vaginal modifications. Simplistic depictions of a global patriarchy, wherein men curb, cow, cut, and dominate "their" women, may drive home the ubiquity of female subjugation, but they leave out an important factor at the same time: although both labiaplasties and African female circumcision should be (and are here) investigated through a feminist lens, that feminism should be informed by an awareness of women's agency. A knee-jerk celebration of that agency misleads, but its disavowal in the name of victimhood leads to dangerous blind spots. Across many different cultural contexts, female genital operations are contemplated and undergone by girls and women in a social and psychological framework shaped *in part* by other women.

The plastic surgeon whose office I visited provided me with two referrals, patients who had had the procedure done by him. As part of what seemed a well-worn sales pitch, he referred often to "self-help groups," a network of supportive, independent women helping each other find the professional care they wanted and deserved, in the face of an unfeeling, disbelieving medical profession. I was interested by what seemed an invocation of rather feminist sensibilities and wondered about this swelling, grassroots support group he seemed to be conjuring up for me. And, indeed, the image of the surgery consumer as a liberated woman and an independent self-fashioner did provide a crucial spin for the doctor, throughout his consultation. The consumer-feminist in support of other women he condoned; by contrast, he expressed an avowed disapproval of the women who came to him solely to please a domineering partner. He brought up this posited bad, weak, man-centric woman three times as we spoke, and each time his face clouded, he frowned, and his brow furrowed: he said that it was only this type of woman who complained of pain after the procedure, for instance, just to get the attention of her partner, whereas for most women, he insisted, the pain was minimal. He seemed to use these diverging models of female behavior to answer in advance any reservations the prospective client might have about a cosmetic operation on the genitalia (such as, "Should I really do something so drastic to my body just to please men?"). By insisting on his antipathy toward women who kowtowed to the male perspective, and celebrating the fearless vision of the pioneer consumer of "cutting edge" surgery, the doctor tried, I suspect, to ward off potential surges of feminist resistance to the procedure.

In the same spirit, one web site advertising the surgery fuels itself on a long-standing feminist call for a more responsive medical establishment by contrasting the surgeon being advertised with other doctors less sensitive to the needs of women. "Very few physicians are concerned with the appearance of the female external genitalia. A relative complacency exists that frustrates many women."[59] Rachel Bowlby has addressed the theoretical conflations between feminist freedom and the "freedom" to choose as a consumer.[60] The surgeon to whose sales pitch I listened and the creators of

the web site noted here certainly understood that the feminist discourse of choice can be appropriated, funneled toward the managed choosing-under-duress of the consumer, becoming saturated along the way with commodity culture's directives.

One goal of this article is to raise the question of this ready appropriation. In *States of Injury: Power and Freedom in Late Modernity*, Wendy Brown examines some of the liabilities of the Left's reliance on the rhetoric of identity, injury, and redress, suggesting that it can result in a politics of state domination.[61] From Bakke on, we have certainly seen the language of affirmative action hauled into the arena of "reverse racism." Perhaps by the same token, the language of choice, as central to the feminist project in this country as we could imagine, sprang up in a culture where the glories of consumer "choice" had already been mythologized. Revisiting and perhaps refiguring the conceptual framework behind "choice" in the face of manufactured consent, then, is to enable, not critique feminism. The hand mirror that allowed feminists of the 1960s and 1970s to get familiar with "our bodies, our selves" is positioned again so that we can see our vaginas. Only, it comes now with the injunction to look critically at what we see and to exert our selfhood through expenditure and remodeling of a body that is not "ourself" any longer but which is "ours," commodified and estranged, to rebuild.

Although the approach of the doctor I visited seemed agenda-driven and rather theatricalized, when I talked with the women to whom he referred me, I was struck by how very friendly and supportive they *did* seem. I had found the doctor likable but showy, like a much rehearsed salesman, but these women were engaged, candid, and genuinely warm. They were generous with their time (and with their permission to be cited anonymously in the present article), and they made it clear that they really did want to help other women with their "experience, strength, and hope." Perhaps these women were "incentivized" to speak well of the doctor (about whose care they raved): maybe they received discounted work in exchange for talking with prospective clients. Even with this possibility in mind they seemed sincerely ready to assume a common perspective, in fact an intimacy, between women discussing their bodies and body image. To overlook their candor, generosity, and *sisterliness* in order to critique the misogynist judgments that may have driven them to surgery would be to mischaracterize the phenomenon of gender display. We typically learn about and develop a gendered bodily performance, not in isolation, but as members of both real and imagined female "communities."[62] And in 2002, one senses the cultural shading that twentieth-century feminism has, ironically, brought to this community building: the rhetoric of choice making and of solidarity developed during the Second Wave ghosts through our conversations. It's a stereotypical joke that women *really* dress for each other—a deeper look at how this female-to-female hodgepodge of peer pressure and peer support really manifests itself is useful. And again, a look at the web of relations among women is helpful in understanding African female genital operations as well.

One on-line World Health Organization report discusses the impact of female circumcisions on girls' psychological health. Importantly, it mentions not only "experiences of suffering, devaluation and impotence" but also the "desirability of the ceremony for the child, with its social advantage of peer acceptance, personal pride and material gifts." Claire Robertson points out that among the functions of the circumcision ceremony in Central Kenya is the role female initiation plays in maintaining the social strength of organizations of older women.[63] The flip side of approving support, of course, is peer pressure. "When girls of my age were looking after the lambs, they would talk among themselves about their circumcision experiences and look at each other's genitals to see who had the smallest opening. If there was a girl in the group who was still uninfibulated, she would always feel ashamed since she had nothing to show the others."[64]

A reminiscent bodily shame lurks behind the support for labial modifications that my American patient contacts expressed. One (heterosexual) woman explained to me that although none of her boyfriends had ever remarked on her labia, "ever since I was fourteen, I felt like I had this abnormalcy; I felt uncomfortable changing in front of girl-friends." She went on to say that she felt she had to hide her vagina around other women and could never enjoy skinny-dipping because of her concerns about other women judging her appearance. Another labiaplasty patient reported a "120% shift" in her "mental attitude," and a "night-and-day" improvement in the looks of her genitalia, thanks to the surgery. "As sad as it is, it makes you feel inferior," she commented.[65] Her use of the second person (or the ethical dative, as it's known), so intimate in its extension of subjectivity, meant that her language included me. . . . I too felt sad, I too felt inferior. And for a fee, the kind doctor was there to correct me.

NEW RITES

It is probably obvious from this piece that, even in the age where both informational and medical technology have led to bodies being reshaped, extended, reconfigured, and reconceptualized like never before, I believe that erotic tissue is far better enjoyed than removed.[66] In approaching the politics of female genital operations, however, I would argue that it is imperative that both consent issues and vaginal modifications themselves be considered *on a continuum* that is not determined along hemispheric, national, or racial lines. Instead, we peer at female genital operations with a prurient, bifurcating tunnel vision and pretend a clean break between the "primitive barbarism" of "ritual" cutting of African women, who are far too often represented as undifferentiated victims, and the aesthetic or medical "fixings" of those Amero-European women who are presented as either mildly deformed people in the wise hands of experts or consumer-designers of a cyborgian gender display.

In "Arrogant Perception, World-Traveling, and Multicultural Feminism: The Case of Female Genital Surgeries," Isabelle R. Gunning attempts to define and model a responsible approach to thinking about genital operations across cultures. She urges activists "to look at one's own culture anew and identify [. . .] practices that might prove 'culturally challenging' or negative to some other," and "to look in careful detail at the organic social environment of the 'other' which has produced the culturally challenging practice being explored."[67] I have tried, in this article, to meet her first criterion, and I hope that rendering American cosmetic surgery strange through a heedful look at this latest, not-yet-naturalized procedure can aid us in contextualizing and understanding genital surgeries born in other contexts as well.

Gunning examines some of the ramifications of legal "remedies" for African genital operations and concludes that criminalization of FGOs, whether on the grounds of violating human rights, women's rights, or children's rights, can seem to characterize African women and men as morally blighted, criminally bad parents, and blinded by a cultural tradition that would best be replaced with Western values. Stan Meuwese and Annemieke Wolthuis of Defense for Children International remark that a "legal approach to the phenomenon . . . especially the use of criminal law, shows very clearly the limitations of the juridical system to combat historically and socially deeply-rooted behavior." One Somali woman points out that "if Somali women change, it will be a change done by us, among us. When they order us to stop, tell us what we must do, it is offensive to the black person or Muslim person who believes in circumcision. To advise is good, but not to order."[68]

Gunning, Robertson, and writers at Rainbo's web site are among those who advise that the socioeconomic dependency of women upon men is perhaps the key context for understanding and ultimately abandoning female genital surgeries.[69] They call for a two-pronged strategy: (1) work to improve women's socioeconomic autonomy, both globally and locally and (2) facilitate autonomous, community-generated cultural evolution rather than imposing punitive restrictions. These do seem fruitful emphases, as applicable in the American as in the African context. That they are realizable can be seen with the following story.

In 1997, Malik Stan Reaves reported in the *African News Service* about an alternative ritual that was replacing female circumcision in some rural sections of Kenya. I quote from his article:

> A growing number of rural Kenyan families are turning to an alternative to the rite of female circumcision for their daughters. "Circumcision Through Words" grows out of collaborations between rural families and the Kenyan national women's group, Maendeleo ya Wanawake Organization (MYWO), which is committed to ending FGM in Kenya, . . . with the close cooperation of the Program for Appropriate Technology in Health (PATH), a nonprofit, nongovernmental, international organization which seeks to improve the health of women and children. . . .
>
> "People think of the traditions as themselves," said Leah Muuya of MYWO. "They see themselves in their traditions. They see they are being themselves because they have been able to fulfill some of the initiations." . . . Circumcision Through Words brings the young candidates together for a week of seclusion during which they learn traditional teachings about their coming roles as women, parents, and adults in the community, as well as more modern messages about personal health, reproductive issues, hygiene, communications skills, self-esteem, and dealing with peer pressure. The week is capped by a community celebration of song, dancing, and feasting which affirms the girls and their new place in the community.[70]

Willow Gerber, of PATH, confirms that as of December 2001, the Circumcision Through Words program is still ongoing and has been, over the last several years,

expanded to other districts by a consortium of donors.[71] Considering this impressive endeavor, which has seen more than 1,900 girls grow to womanhood uncut, one is reminded of the words of Claire Robertson: "Central Kenyan women have been making increasingly successful efforts to stop FGM . . . [they show] strengths that U.S. women might well emulate in seeking to better their own status.[72]

How *might* we emulate "Circumcision Through Words"? Newly formed rituals in this country, at least those formally recognized as such, usually emerge in either New Age or evangelical settings and can grate the sensibilities of people beyond those spheres. Initiation of our girls into womanhood is often enough left to the devices of Madison Avenue and magazines like *YM, Teen People,* and *CosmoGirl.* And yet, for all the unconsciousness with which so many of us muddle through our life transitions in this country, nonetheless we too "feel that we have been ourselves" when we fulfill what we see as society's expectations for people at our stage of life. This is not an emotion to be belittled. (One Arabic term for the genital scar is *nafsi,* "my own self.")[73] Without the "years of research and discussion" that helped MYWO develop Circumcision Through Words, we would be hard pressed to generate new ways of bringing "our bodies, ourselves" into a symbolic relation with the social world that would prove both intelligible and affirmative. Just as analogies between genital cuttings are both important and exceedingly difficult to draw, so too is the conscious development of new, performative practices both worth emulating and only circuitously "applicable." Even in rural Kenya, the approach to "circumcision through words" varies dramatically from district to district."[74]

So I will not conclude this article with a glib, faux ritual for American women trained to hate the specificities of their bodies in the interest of capital accumulation. I will see, however, if I can leave you in a performative mode, offering a coda that I hope can "act" upon and through the reader as a textual "rite of antidote," speaking back to the cited language of abnormality, pathology, and sexual distrust with which this article began.

CODA

Dan Savage, syndicated sex advice columnist, responded to one reader concerned about the aesthetic effect of her long labia minora, by suggesting the work of Dr. Stubbs. He received many letters of protest, providing paeans to the appeal of prominent labia and/or suggesting that he advise self-admiration, not surgery. The enthusiastic adjectives these letter writers employed ("lavish," "luscious," "extravagant"), coupled with their emphasis on erotic pleasure, can remind us that perhaps "beauty" results from a harmony between form and function, and one key genital function is *pleasure*. I offer excerpts from some of these letters here.[75]

- . . . You might have told Jagger Lips to toss her unappreciative lovers out of bed and find a boyfriend who sees the beauty of her as she exists. . . .
- . . . I have long inner labia and most of the women I've seen naked have inner labia that extend past the outer labia. . . . If someone wants to see what vulvas really look like, they should put down *Penthouse* and start sleeping with lots of women.
- . . . many men, myself included, don't find a thing wrong with longer labia minora. My girlfriend has one [*sic*] and I find it quite the enjoyable thing to suck on. . . .

- Does female sexual pleasure mean anything to you? Not only do the labia minora engorge during sexual stimulation and have lots of nerve endings, they also increase friction. . . .
- I am writing to Jagger Lips to discourage her from chopping off her labia minora. I prefer long labia. I find that they lend themselves more readily to being tugged, stretched, nibbled, etc. . . .
- . . . I remember a gorgeous actor, Savannah, who sadly committed suicide in the mid-1990s, who had a beautiful snatch with extravagant labia spilling (an inch and a half, easy) from her soft and salty cornucopia of love. She was rad, I hope she's resting in peace, and I'd recommend your reader try and rustle up a video. . . .
- Our society tends not to be so pussy-positive, and most commercial pussy pictures are airbrushed on Planet Barbie, and shouldn't be considered reality. Labia (inner and outer) have lots of nerves and feel really good when they get stroked.
- . . . Please tell the woman with the lavish labia not to have them removed. . . . You were much too hasty to recommend clipping her butterfly wings! . . .

NOTES

Thanks to former students Jenn Sanders and Wacuka Mungai for their help in developing this article.

1. Things certainly can happen. See Louisa Kamps, "Labia Envy," 16 Mar. 1998, <http://www.salon.com/mwt/feature/1998/03/16feature.html> (9 Dec. 2001).
2. *Los Angeles Times*, 5 Mar. 1998. See, too, the following Internet resources on labiaplasty: Dr. Alter: "Female Cosmetic and Reconstructive Genital Surgery," <http://www.altermd.com/female/index.html> (9 Dec. 2001); Julia Scheeres, "Vaginal Cosmetic Surgery," 16 Apr. 2001, <http://thriveonline.oxygen.com/sex/sexpressions/vaginal-cosmetic-surgery.html> (9 Dec. 2001); Dr. Stubbs, <http://psurg.com>; Laser Rejuvenation Center of LA, <http://www.drmatlock.com>; Dan Savage, "Long in the Labia," 16 Dec. 1999, <http://www.the stranger.com/1999-12-16/savage.html> (13 Dec. 2001); iVillage.com Archive Message Board, "Cosmetic Surgery," 7 Jan. 2000, <http://boards.allhealth.com/messages/get/bhcosmeticsx2.html> (13 Dec. 2001); Patients' chatboard, <http://boards.allhealth.com/messages/get/bhcosmeticsx2.html>.
3. See Kamps. Also, see Carrie Havranek, "The New Sex Surgeries," *Cosmopolitan*, November 1998, 146.
4. Ellen Frankfort, *Vaginal Politics* (New York: Quadrangle, 1972). See, too, Julia Scheeres, "Vulva Goldmine: How Cosmetic Surgeons Snatch Your Money," *Bitch* 11 (January 2000): 70–84.

5. Boston Women's Health Collective, *Our Bodies, Ourselves* (New York: Simon & Schuster, 1973). Updated editions have continued to be released. See Boston Women's Health Collective, *Our Bodies, Ourselves for the New Century: A Book by and for Women* (New York: Simon & Schuster, 1998).
6. See Amelia Jones, ed., *Sexual Politics: Judy Chicago's Dinner Party in Feminist Art History* (Berkeley: University of California Press, 1996); Shannon Bell, "Prostitute Performances: Sacred Carnival Theorists of the Female Body," from her *Reading, Writing, and Rewriting the Prostitute Body* (Bloomington: Indiana University Press, 1994), 137–84; and Eve Ensler, *The Vagina Monologues* (New York: Villard Press, 1998).
7. Although some women enjoy orgasmic ejaculation, it remains an exception to the rule.
8. Linda Williams's book is about pornographic films, especially those of the 1970s: *Hard Core: Power, Pleasure, and the "Frenzy of the Visible"* (Berkeley: University of California Press, 1989), 50.
9. See Michel Foucault, *The History of Sexuality*, vol. 1, *An Introduction* (New York: Random House, 1978).
10. See Gershon Legman, *Rationale of the Dirty Joke: An Analysis of Sexual Humor* (New York: Breaking Point Press, 1975), 547.
11. In a mode that both ridicules and familiarizes the body modifications of plastic surgery, tabloids regularly feature articles about the "work" being done on celebrities, with a special emphasis on implant disasters. See, for instance,

"Hollywood's Plastic Surgery Nightmares: When Breast Implants Go Bad," *National Enquirer*, 4 May 1999, 28–33. Kathy Davis discusses popular coverage of celebrity surgeries in *Reshaping the Female Body: The Dilemma of Cosmetic Surgery* (New York: Routledge, 1995), 18.

12. See the work of the late historian Roland Marchand, *Advertising the American Dream: Making Way for Modernity, 1920–1940* (Berkeley: University of California Press, 1985), 18–20.

13. Davis; Elizabeth Haiken, *Venus Envy: A History of Cosmetic Surgery* (Baltimore: Johns Hopkins University Press, 1997); Sander Gilman, *Making the Body Beautiful: A Cultural History of Aesthetic Surgery* (Princeton: Princeton University Press, 1999). Also, see Claudia Springer, *Electronic Eros: Bodies and Desire in the Postindustrial Age* (Austin: University of Texas Press, 1996).

14. Milton T. Edgerton and H.R. McClary, quoted in Haiken, 244.

15. On the thin line between identification and desire, between wanting to be like someone and wanting to bed down with them (so exploited in consumer culture), see Diana Fuss, "Fashion and the Homospectatorial Look," in *On Fashion*, ed. Shari Benstock and Suzanne Ferriss (New Brunswick, N.J.: Rutgers University Press, 1994), 211–32; and Judith Butler, *Gender Trouble: Feminism and the Subversion of Identity* (New York: Routledge, 1990), esp. 57–72.

16. Josey Vogels, "My Messy Bedroom," *See*, 10 July 1997, <http://www.greatwest.ca/SEE/Issues/1997/970710/josey.html> (13 Dec. 2001).

17. Laura Kipnis, *Bound and Gagged: Pornography and the Politics of Fantasy in America* (New York: Grove, 1996).

18. Susie Bright, "The Pussy Shot: An Interview with Andrew Blake," *Sexwise* (New York: Cleis Press, 1995), 82.

19. Haiken, 29–34, 136–45, 237, 246.

20. See Richard Goldstein, "Porn Free," *Village Voice*, 1 Sept. 1998, 28–34. My own research for a work-in-progress, "Choosing the Moves: Choreography in the Strip Club," also bears this out.

21. See Nedahl Stelio, "Do You Know What a Vagina Looks Like?" *Cosmopolitan*, August 2001, 126–28, on sex magazines' doctoring of vaginas and the increased prevalence of labiaplasty.

22. Luce Irigaray, *This Sex Which Is Not One*, trans. Catherine Porter (Ithaca: Cornell University Press, 1985), 209. Also see her *Speculum of the Other Woman* (Ithaca: Cornell University Press, 1986).

23. See Mary Douglas on a cross-cultural tendency to approach marginal zones, marginal people, and marginal periods with great apprehension, in *Purity and Danger: An Analysis of the Concepts of Pollution and Taboo* (1966; reprint, New York: Routledge, 1992).

24. Mary Russo, *The Female Grotesque: Risk, Excess, and Modernity* (New York: Routledge, 1994), 8.

25. See <http://www.psurg.com/gallery.html> (13 Dec. 2001).

26. Haiken, 5.

27. Natalie Zemon Davis, "Women on Top," in her *Society and Culture in Early Modern France* (Stanford: Stanford University Press, 1975), 124. See 124–31.

28. Denise Stoklos, remark made in Solo Performance Composition, her course offered by the Performance Studies Department, New York University, Spring 2000. "Our primary dialogue is with gravity," Stoklos says.

29. See Ambient, Inc., "Body Modification: Is It Self-Mutilation—Even if Someone Else Does It for You?" 2 Feb. 1998, <http://www.ambient.on.ca/bodmod/mutilate.htm> (13 Dec. 2001). Another web site dealing with body modification is <www.perforations.com> (13 Dec. 2001).

30. Ensler, 3–5.

31. This and all subsequent quotations from this plastic surgeon are from an office visit in a major American city—location to remain unspecified to ensure anonymity—in April 1999.

32. Elizabeth Grosz: "[W]omen's corporeality is inscribed as a mode of seepage." See her *Volatile Bodies: Toward a Corporeal Feminism* (Bloomington: Indiana University Press, 1994), 203.

33. Terri Kapsalis, *Public Privates: Performing Gynecology from Both Ends of the Speculum* (Durham: Duke University Press, 1997), 89. She references Julia Kristeva, *Powers of Horror: An Essay on Abjection* (New York: Columbia University Press, 1982). On the cultural and political implications of representations of genitalia in anatomical textbooks, see Lisa Jean Moore and Adele E. Clarke, "Clitoral Conventions and Transgressions: Graphic Representations in Anatomy Texts, c1900–1991," *Feminist Studies* 21 (summer 1995): 255–301; and Susan C. Lawrence and Kae Bendixen, "His and Hers: Male and Female Anatomy in Anatomical Texts for U.S. Medical Students, 1890–1989," *Social Science and Medicine* 35 (October 1992): 925–34. Also, see Katharine Young, "Perceptual Modalities: Gynecology," in her *Presence in the Flesh* (Cambridge: Harvard University Press, 1997), 46–79.

34. Thomas Laqueur, *Making Sex: Body and Gender from the Greeks to Freud* (Cambridge: Harvard University Press, 1990). And see Lynn Hunt, *The Invention of Pornography* (New York: Zone, 1993).

35. Jennifer Terry, "Lesbians under the Medical Gaze: Scientists Search for Remarkable Differences," *Journal of Sex Research* 27 (August 1990): 317–39, 332 (emphasis added), 333.

36. See Ben Barker-Benfield, "Sexual Surgery in Late-Nineteenth-Century America," *International Journal of Health Services* 5, no. 2 (1975): 279–98; Andrew Scull and Diane Favreau, "The Clitoridectomy Craze," *Social Research* 53 (summer 1986): 243; Barbara Ehrenreich and Deirdre English, *Complaints and Disorders: The Sexual Politics of Sickness* (New York: City University of New York Press, 1973); and Rachel P. Maines, *The Technology of Orgasm: "Hysteria," the Vibrator, and Women's Sexual*

Satisfaction (Baltimore: Johns Hopkins University Press, 1999).

37. Barker-Benfield, 287, 298.

38. See Daniel Gordon, "Female Circumcision and Genital Operations in Egypt and the Sudan: A Dilemma for Medical Anthropology," *Medical Anthropology Quarterly* 5 (March 1991): 7.

39. For more on this and similar cases, see Carla Miller's statement at <www.InMemoryoftheSufferingChild.com>. For coverage of the Burt case, see, for instance, Sandy Theis, "His Peers Waved Red Flags: Monitors' Concern Went beyond Love Surgery," *Dayton Daily News*, 4 Aug. 1991, 1A; Rob Modic, "Painful Testimony: Woman Testifies of Trust for Gynecologist Burt," *Dayton Daily News*, 1 June 1991, 1A; Judith Adler Hennessee, "The Love Surgeon," *Mademoiselle*, August 1989, 206; Gerry Harness and Judy Kelman, "A Mother's True Story: 'My Gynecologist Butchered Me!'" *Redbook*, July 1989, 22. Also see <http://www.nocirc.org> (13 Dec. 2001); <http://www.SexuallyMutilatedChild.org/index.html> (13 Dec. 2001).

40. See Suzanne Kessler, *Gender: An Ethnomethodological Approach* (1978; reprint, Chicago: University of Chicago Press, 1985), quoted by Martha Coventry in "The Tyranny of the Aesthetic: Surgery's Most Intimate Violation," <http://www.fgm.org/coventryarticle.html> (20 Dec. 2001).

41. Deborah Kuhn McGregor, *From Midwives to Medicine: The Birth of American Gynecology* (New Brunswick, N.J.: Rutgers University Press, 1998), 49. She is quoting Sims's autobiography. See also Kapsalis, chap. 2.

42. Mary Ann Doane, "Dark Continents: Epistemologies of Racial and Sexual Difference in Psychoanalysis and the Cinema," in her *Femmes Fatales: Feminism, Film Theory, Psychoanalysis* (New York: Routledge, 1991), 209–48; and Anne McClintock, *Imperial Leather: Race Gender, and Sexuality in the Colonial Contest* (New York: Routledge, 1995), esp. 1–4, and 21–31.

43. See Zola Maseko, director, *The Life and Times of Sara Baartman, "The Hottentot Venus,"* videorecording, London: Dominant 7, Mail and Guardian Television, France 3, and SABC 2, 1998.

44. Henri de Blainville, quoted in Maseko.

45. See Londa Schiebinger, *Nature's Body: Gender in the Making of Modern Science* (Boston: Beacon, 1995), chap. 5.

46. Maseko.

47. McGregor, 46–51.

48. Wacuka Mungai, "Desiring the 'Mutilated' African Woman," paper, 1999. Mungai is a doctoral student at New York University and assistant program director at Rainbo, an organization devoted in large part to advocating for African women around the issue of female circumcision.

49. Nahid Toubia, *Female Genital Mutilation: A Call for Global Action*, 3d ed. (New York: Women, Ink, 1995), 35.

50. See Janice Boddy, "Body Politics: Continuing the Anticircumcision Crusade"; and Faye Ginsburg, "What Do Women Want? Feminist Anthropology Confronts Clitoridectomy," both in *Medical Anthropology Quarterly* 5 (March 1991): 15–19.

51. Inga Muscio, *Cunt: A Declaration of Independence* (Toronto: Seal Press, 1998), 134–35.

52. "Female Genital Mutilation: A Human Rights Information Pack" (London: Amnesty International, 1997).

53. Vicki Kirby, "On the Cutting Edge: Feminism and Clitoridectomy," *Australian Feminist Studies* 5 (summer 1987): 35–56.

54. In New York City, March 1999, Wacuka Mungai shared one anecdote with me about a Buganda woman who took one trip to a gynecologist in North America: the doctor was flabbergasted and wanted to rush in a crowd of residents to stare at her. Of course, this reaction was not welcomed by the patient and she shied away from the entire profession afterward, rather than risk a reoccurrence of the circus atmosphere the doctor had created. See also, Lauran Neergard, "Doctors See More Female Circumcision," 17 Sept. 1999, posted at <http://www.worldafricannet.com/news/news7861.html>. And see this web site, that catalogs body modifications across cultures: <http://www.cadewalk.com/mods/modify.htm>. Also, see Schiebinger.

55. See Claire Robertson, "Grassroots in Kenya: Women, Genital Mutilation, and Collective Action, 1920–1990," *Signs* 21 (spring 1996): 615–42, on some of the history of circumcision's changing meaning in Kenya over the course of the twentieth century. Mungai suggested that the *tribal* politics, in addition to the politics of colonial resistance, were perhaps more complex than Robertson's article describes. See also, Isabelle R. Gunning, "Arrogant Perception, World Traveling, and Multicultural Feminism: The Case of Female Genital Surgeries," *Columbia Human Rights Law Review* 23 (Summer 1992): 189–248.

56. Jomo Kenyatta, quoted in Gunning, 228.

57. See, for instance, Nadia Kamal Khalifa, "Reasons Behind Practicing Re-circumcision among Educated Sudanese Women," *Ahfad Journal* 11, no. 2 (1994): 16–32; Anke van der Kwaake, "Female Circumcision and Gender Identity: A Questionable Alliance?" *Social Science and Medicine* 35, no. 6 (1992): 777–87.

58. Claire Hunt and Kim Longinotto, with Safaa Fathay, *Hidden Faces,* videorecording (New York: Twentieth Century Vixen Production/Women Make Movies, 1990). And see Elizabeth Oram, introduction to Zainaba's "Lecture on Clitoridectomy to the Midwives of Touil, Mauritania" (1987), in *Opening the Gates: A Century of Arab Feminist Writing*, ed. Margot Badran and Miriam Cooke (Bloomington: Indiana University Press, 1990), 63–71.

59. See <http://www.altermd.com/female/index.html> (13 Dec. 2001).

60. See Rachel Bowlby, in *Shopping with Freud: Items on Consumerism, Feminism, and Psychoanalysis* (New York: Routledge,

1993), on theoretical conflations between feminist freedom and the "freedom" to choose as a consumer.

61. Wendy Brown, *States of Injury: Power and Freedom in Late Modernity* (Princeton: Princeton University Press, 1995).

62. Anonymous telephone interviews with two West Coast labiaplasty patients, August 1999. For an on-line example of this, see the fascinating archived chat between women about cosmetic surgery at iVillage, "Cosmetic Surgery Archive Board," 7 Jan. 2001, <http://boards.allhealth.com/messages/get/bhcosmeticsx2.html> (13 Dec. 2001).

63. See Robertson.

64. Anab's story, from "Social and Cultural Implications of Infibulation in Somalia," by Amina Wasame, in *Female Circumcision: Strategies to Bring about Change* (Somali Women's Democratic Organization), quoted in Toubia, 41.

65. Anonymous telephone interview with author, August 1999.

66. An important caveat: As the transgendered community has made clear, for some individuals, erotic enjoyment is enhanced via the genital modification that comes along with reassigning gender, even if that surgery has resulted in a reduction in nerve endings or sensation.

67. Gunning, 213.

68. See Frances A. Althaus, "Female Circumcision: Rite of Passage or Violation of Rites?" *International Family Planning Perspectives* 23 (September 1997), <http://www.agi-usa.org/pubs/journals/2313097.html#21> (20 Dec. 2001).

69. Alan Worsley, "Infibulation and Female Circumcision," *Journal of Obstetrics and Gynecology of the British Empire* 45, no. 4 (1938): 687.

70. For more information, see the web site for the Gender Learning Network, a partnership between twenty-three women-run NGOs, including MYWO, "working to promote women's rights and status in Kenya," <http://arcc.or.ke/gln/glnl3sec.html> (13 Dec. 2001). And here are two relevant links to PATH's web site: (1) Anonymous, "Alternative rituals raise hope for eradication of Female Genital Mutilation," 20 Oct. 1997, <http://www.path.org/resources/press/19971020-FGM.html> (13 Dec. 2001), and (2) Anonymous, "Modern Rites of Passage," <http://www.path.org/resources/closerlooks/f_modern_rites_of_passage.htm> (13 Dec. 2001).

71. PATH's Michelle Folsom heads a ten-year office in Kenya, and oversees the organization's collaboration on this and other projects with MYWO, and their work receives the support of the Kenyan government. See "Program for Appropriate Technology in Health," *Promoting a Healthy Alternative to FGM: A Tool for Program Implementers* (Washington, D.C.: PATH, 2001). See also, Davan Maharaj, "Kenya to Ban Female Genital Excision," *Los Angeles Times*, 15 Dec. 2001.

72. Robertson, 615. See also, Carolyn Sargent, "Confronting Patriarchy: The Potential for Advocacy in Medical Anthropology," *Medical Anthropology Quarterly* 5 (March 1991): 24–25.

73. Alan Worsley, 687.

74. See "Modern Rites of Passage," <http://www.path.org/closerlooks/f_modern_rites_of_passage.html> (13 Dec. 2001).

75. All letters quoted in Dan Savage, "Savage Love," *Village Voice*, 18 Jan. 2000, 126.

READING *36* *Andrea Smith*

Beyond Pro-Choice versus Pro-Life: Women of Color and Reproductive Justice

Once, while taking an informal survey of Native women in Chicago about their position on abortion—were they "pro-life" or "pro-choice"—I quickly found that their responses did not neatly match up with these media-mandated categories.

Example 1:

ME: Are you pro-choice or pro-life?
RESPONDENT 1: Oh I am definitely pro-life.
ME: So you think abortion should be illegal?

RESPONDENT 1: No, definitely not. People should be able to have an abortion if they want.

ME: Do you think then that there should not be federal funding for abortion services?

RESPONDENT 1: No, there should be funding available so that anyone can afford to have one.

Example 2:

ME: Would you say you are pro-choice or pro-life?

RESPONDENT 2: Well, I would say that I am pro-choice, but the most important thing to me is promoting life in Native communities.

These responses make it difficult to categorize the Native women queried neatly into "pro-life" or "pro-choice" camps. Is Respondent #1 pro-life because she says she is pro-life? Or is she pro-choice because she supports the decriminalization of and public funding for abortion? I would argue that, rather than attempt to situate these respondents in pro-life or pro-choice camps, it is more useful to recognize the limitations of the pro-life/pro-choice dichotomy for understanding the politics around reproductive justice. Unlike pro-life versus pro-choice advocates who make their overall political goal either the criminalization or decriminalization of abortion, the reproductive frameworks these Native women are implicitly articulating are based on fighting for life and self-determination of their communities. The criminalization of abortion may or may not be a strategy for pursuing that goal.

In previous works, I have focused more specifically on Native women and reproductive justice (Smith 2001). Here, I am using these Native women's responses to questions about abortion to argue that the pro-life versus pro-choice paradigm is a model that marginalizes women of color, poor women, and women with disabilities. The pro-life versus pro-choice paradigm reifies and masks the structures of white supremacy and capitalism that undergird the reproductive choices that women make, and it also narrows the focus of our political goals to the question of criminalization of abortion. Ironically, I will contend, while the pro-choice and pro-life camps on the abortion debate are often articulated as polar opposites, both depend on similar operating assumptions that do nothing to support either life or real choice for women of color. In developing this analysis, I seek to build on previous scholarship that centers women of color as well as

reflect on my fifteen years as an activist in the reproductive justice movement through such organizations as Illinois National Abortion and Reproductive Rights Action League (NARAL), the Chicago Abortion Fund, Women of All Red Nations, Incite! Women of Color Against Violence, and Committee on Women, Population and the Environment. I begin by examining the limitations of the pro-life position. I then explore the problems with the pro-choice position. The paper concludes with suggestions for moving beyond this binary stalemate between "pro-life" and "pro-choice."

PRO-LIFE POLITICS, CRIMINALIZATION OF ABORTION, AND THE PRISON INDUSTRIAL COMPLEX

The fetus is a life—but sometimes that life must be ended.

—Jeanette Bushnell, Seattle-based
Native health activist (2004)

The pro-life position maintains that the fetus is a life; hence abortion should be criminalized. Consequently, the pro-life camp situates its position around moral claims regarding the sanctity of life. In a published debate on pro-life versus pro-choice positions on the issue of abortion, Gray Crum (former vice-president of South Carolina Citizens for Life) argues that the pro-life position is "ethically pure" (Crum and McCormack 1992, 54). Because of the moral weight he grants to the protection of the life of the fetus, Crum contends that abortion must be criminalized. Any immoral actions that impact others should be a "serious crime under the law" (1992, 28). The pro-choice position counters this argument by asserting that the fetus is not a life, and hence policy must be directed toward protecting a woman's ability to control her own body. To quote sociologist Thelma McCormack's response to Crum: "Life truly begins in the . . . hospital room, not in the womb" (Crum and McCormack 1992, 121). Gloria Feldt, president of Planned Parenthood, similarly asserts that if the fetus is established as a life, the principles of *Roe v. Wade* must necessarily be discarded (Feldt 2004, 90).

Jeanette Bushnell's statement that *"The fetus is a life—but sometimes that life must be ended"* suggests, however, a critical intervention in the pro-life argument. That is, the major flaw in the pro-life position is NOT the claim that the fetus is a life, but the conclusion it draws from this assertion: that because the fetus is a life, abortion should be criminalized. In this regard, reproductive rights activists and scholars could benefit from the analysis of the anti-prison movement which questions criminalization as an appropriate response to social issues. As I shall demonstrate, assuming a criminal justice regime fails to address social problems or to adjudicate reproductive issues and results in further marginalization of poor women and women of color. To make this connection, I must first provide a critical history of the failures of the prison system to deal effectively with social problems.

The anti-prison industrial complex movement has highlighted the complete failure of the prison system to address social concerns. In fact, not only do prisons not solve social problems, such as "crime," they are more likely to increase rather than decrease crime rates (Currie 1998; Donziger 1996; Walker 1998). Most people in prison are there for drug or poverty-related crimes. Prisons do not provide treatment for drug addiction, and it is often easier to access drugs in prison than on the outside. For people who are in prison because of poverty-related crimes, a prison record ensures that it will be much more difficult for them to secure employment once they are released. Consistently, study after study indicates that prisons do not have an impact on decreasing crime rates. For instance, the Rand Corporation found that California's three strikes legislation, which requires life sentences for three-time convicted felons, did not reduce the rate of "murders, rapes, and robberies that many people believe to be the law's principal targets" (Walker 1998, 139). In fact, changes in crime rates often have more to do with fluctuations in employment rates than with increased police surveillance or increased incarceration rates (Box and Hale 1982; Jankovic 1977). In addition, as documented by prison activist groups such as the Prison Activist Resource Center, government monies are siphoned away from education and social services into prisons, thus destabilizing communities of color and increasing their vulnerability to incarceration (Prison Activist Resource Center 2004).

The failure of prisons is well known to policymakers. In fact, John Dilulio, prominent right-wing analyst who was one of the major advocates for the build-up of the prison industrial complex, later renounced his position and came out in support of a prison moratorium (Dilulio 1999). Given that this failure is well known, it then becomes apparent that the purpose of prisons has never been to stop crime. Rather, as a variety of scholars and activists have argued, the purpose has

been in large part to control the population of communities of color. As Michael Mancini (1991) and Angela Davis (2003) point out, the racial background of the prison population prior to the Civil War was white. After the Civil War, the Thirteenth Amendment was passed, which prohibits slavery—except for prisoners. The slavery system was then essentially replaced by the convict leasing system, which was often even more brutal than the former. Under slavery, slave-owners at least had a financial incentive to keep slaves alive. In the convict leasing system, no such incentive existed—if a prisoner died, she or he could simply be replaced by another prisoner (Davis 2003; Mancini 1991). The regime of the prison was originally designed to "reform" the prisoner by creating conditions for penitence (hence the term "penitentiary") (Ignatieff 1978). After the Civil War, however, the prison adopted similar regimes of punishment found in the slavery system that coincided with the re-enslavement of black communities into the convict leasing system (Davis 2003). As Davis argues, "racisms . . . congeal and combine in prisons"; they exist to maintain the capitalist and white supremacist underpinnings of U.S. society (Davis 2003, 26). The continuing racism of the prison system is evidenced by who is in prison. In 1994, for instance, one out of every three African American men between the ages of 20 and 29 was under some form of criminal justice supervision (Mauer 1999). Two-thirds of men of color in California between the ages of 18 and 30 have been arrested (Donziger 1996, 102–4). Six of every ten juveniles in federal custody are American Indian and two-thirds of women in prison are women of color (Prison Activist Resource Center 2004).

In a statement that also applies to the criminalization of abortion, Davis further argues that it is critical to disarticulate the equation between crime and punishment because the primary purpose is not to solve the problem of crime.

> "Punishment" does not follow from "crime" in the neat and logical sequence offered by discourses that insist on the justice of imprisonment, but rather punishment—primarily through imprisonment (and sometimes death)—is linked to the agendas of politicians, the profit drive of corporations, and media representations of crime. Imprisonment is associated with the racialization of those most likely to be punished. . . . If we . . . strive to disarticulate crime and punishment . . . then our focus must not rest only on the prison system as an isolated institution but must

also be directed at all the social relations that support the permanence of the prison. (2003, 112)

Prisons simply are not only ineffective institutions for addressing social concerns, they drain resources from institutions that could be more effective. They also mark certain peoples, particularly people of color, as inherently "criminal," undeserving of civil and political rights—thus increasing their vulnerability to poverty and further criminalization.

Davis's principle of disarticulation is critical in reassessing the pro-life position. That is, whether or not one perceives abortion to be a crime, it does not therefore follow that punishment in the form of imprisonment is a necessary response. Criminalization individualizes solutions to problems that are the result of larger economic, social, and political conditions. Consequently, it is inherently incapable of solving social problems or addressing crime. Alternative social formations and institutions that can speak to these large scale political and economic conditions are the appropriate place to address social issues, such as reproductive justice. As Davis argues: "Prison needs to be abolished as the dominant mode of addressing social problems that are better solved by other institutions and other means. The call for prison abolition urges us to imagine and strive for a very different social landscape" (Rodriguez 2000, 215). Thus, even if we hold that a top social priority is to reduce the number of abortions, there is no evidence to suggest that involving the criminal justice system will accomplish that goal, given that it has not been effective in reducing crime rates or addressing social problems. In addition, increased criminalization disproportionately affects people of color—and in the case of abortion, women of color and poor women. An interrogation of the assumptions behind the pro-life movement suggests that what distinguishes the pro-life position is not so much a commitment to life (since criminalization promotes death rather than life, particularly in communities of color and poor communities), but rather a commitment to criminal justice interventions in reproductive justice issues.

An assessment of recent debates within the anti-domestic/sexual assault movements further illustrates this argument. As I, and others, have argued, the anti-violence movement, as it became increasingly funded by the state, began to rely on criminal justice interventions (Smith 2005/in press). Domestic violence and sexual assault agencies formed their strategy around the slogan that sexual and domestic violence

is a crime. The response then of activists was to push for increased criminalization of sexual and domestic violence through mandatory arrest policies, no-drop prosecution policies, and longer sentencing. Sadly, the result of this approach was that not only did it not reduce violence rates, it often contributed further to women's victimization. For instance, under mandatory arrests laws, the police often arrest the women who are being battered. In fact, *The New York Times* recently reported that the impact of strengthened anti-domestic violence legislation is that battered women kill their abusive partners less frequently; however, batterers do *not* kill their partners less frequently, and this is more true in black than white communities (Butterfield 2000). Thus, ironically, laws passed to protect battered women are actually protecting their batterers! While prisons currently are not filled with batterers and rapists, this approach contributed to the growth of the prison industrial complex by implicitly buying into a criminal justice regime on which the prison system depends. Legislators attach violence against women provisions (such as the Violence Against Women Act) to repressive anti-crime bills, and by so doing legislators can then rely on anti-violence activists to support the legislation as a whole.

Similarly, the pro-life position implicitly supports the prison industrial complex by unquestioningly supporting a criminal justice approach that legitimizes rather than challenges the prison system. As Davis (2003) argues, it is not sufficient to challenge the criminal justice system; we must build alternatives to it. Just as the women of color anti-violence movement is currently developing strategies for ending violence (Smith 2005/in press), a consistent pro-life position would require activists to develop responses to abortion that do not rely on the prison industrial complex. Otherwise, these pro-life activists will continue to support policies that are brutally oppressive, particularly to communities of color and poor communities.

Interestingly, this critique of the prison system is prevalent even within conservative evangelical circles. For example, Charles Colson, a prominent Christian Right activist, founder of Prison Fellowship, and former attorney with the Nixon administration, served time in prison for his role in the Watergate break-in. Following his imprisonment, Colson began to work on prison reform, organizing the Prison Fellowship and its associated lobbying arm, Justice Fellowship. Many platforms implicitly or explicitly supported by Prison and Justice Fellowship could be used to question the wisdom of the criminalization of abortion: decarceration for drug offenders (Colson 1977, 17; Colson 1980, 52); minimum wage compensation for prison labor (Lawton 1988, 38); decarceration of all nonviolent offenders ("The first thing we have to do with prisons today is to get the nonviolent people out") (Forbes 1982, 33: Smarto 1993, 46); prison construction moratoriums (Colson 1985, 29; Mill 1999; Van Ness 1985); eradication of mandatory sentencing (Forbes 1982, 33); suffrage for convicted felons (Colson 1985, 34); and expansion of community sentencing programs (Colson 1985, 29; Pulliam 1987; Van Ness 1985). In fact, Colson argues that 50 percent of people in prison today should be released immediately (Fager 1982, 23). To quote Colson:

> The whole system of punishment today is geared toward taking away people's dignity, putting them in an institution, and locking them up in a cage. Prisons are overcrowded, understaffed, dirty places. Eighty percent of American prisons are barbaric—not just brutal, but barbaric. . . . Prison as a punishment is a failure. Mandatory sentences and longer sentences are counterproductive . . . the tougher the laws, I'm convinced, the more lawless and violent we will become. As for public safety, it can hardly be said that prisons contribute to public safety. . . . Prisons obviously are not deterring criminal conduct. The evidence is overwhelming that the more people we put in prison, the more crime we have. All prisons do is warehouse human beings and at exorbitant cost. (Colson 1983, 15; Fager 1982, 23; Forbes 1982, 34)[1]

Yet, despite his sustained critique of the failure of the prison system, Colson never critiques the wisdom of criminalization as the appropriate response to abortion. In the name of promoting life, the pro-life movement supports one of the biggest institutions of violence and death in this society. But given that this critique of criminalization is not inaccessible to large sectors of the pro-life movement, there should be opportunities to make anti-criminalization interventions into pro-life discourse. Thus, the major flaw in the pro-life position is not so much its claim that the fetus is a life, but its assumption that because the fetus is a life, abortion should be criminalized. A commitment to criminalization of social issues necessarily contributes to the growth of the prison system because it reinforces the notion that prisons are appropriate institutions for addressing social problems rather than causes of the problems. Given the disproportionate impact of criminalization on communities of color, support for criminalization as public policy also implicitly supports racism.

In addition, I am suggesting that those committed to pro-choice positions will be more effective and politically consistent if they contest the pro-life position from an anti-prison perspective. For instance, increasingly, poor women and women of color are finding their pregnancies criminalized. As Dorothy Roberts (1997) and others have noted, women of color are more likely to be arrested and imprisoned for drug use because, as a result of greater rates of poverty in communities of color, they are more likely to be in contact with government agencies where their drug use can be detected. While white pregnant women are slightly *more* likely to engage in substance abuse than black women, public health facilities and private doctors are more likely to report black women than white women to criminal justice authorities (Maher 1990; Roberts 1997, 175). Meanwhile, pregnant women who would like treatment for their addiction can seldom get it because treatment centers do not meet the needs of pregnant women. One study found that two-thirds of drug treatment centers would not treat pregnant women (Roberts 1997, 189). Furthermore, the criminalization approach is more likely to drive pregnant women who are substance abusers from seeking prenatal or other forms of health care for fear of being reported to the authorities (Roberts 1997, 190). Roberts critiques communities of color for often supporting the criminalization of women of color who have addictions and for failing to understand this criminalization as another strategy of white supremacy that blames women for the effects of poverty and racism. Lisa Maher (1990) and Rickie Solinger (2001, 148) note that a simple choice perspective is not effective for addressing this problem because certain women become marked as women who make "bad choices" and hence deserve imprisonment.

Similarly, Elizabeth Cook-Lynn (1998) argues in "The Big Pipe Case" that at the same time Native peoples were rallying around Leonard Peltier, no one stood beside Marie Big Pipe when she was incarcerated on a felony charge of "assault with intent to commit serious bodily harm" because she breast-fed her child while under the influence of alcohol. She was denied services to treat her substance abuse problem and access to abortion services when she became pregnant. But not only did her community not support her, it supported her incarceration. Cook-Lynn argues that in doing so, the community supported the encroachment of U.S. federal jurisdiction on tribal lands for an issue that would normally be under tribal jurisdiction (1998, 110–25). Cook-Lynn recounts how this demonization of Native women was assisted by the publication of Michael Dorris's (1989) *The Broken Cord,* which narrates his adoption of a Native child who suffered from fetal alcohol syndrome. While this book has been crucial in sensitizing many communities to the realities of fetal alcohol syndrome, it also portrays the mother of the child unsympathetically and advocates repressive legislative solutions targeted against women substance abusers. Thus, within Native communities, the growing demonization of Native women substance abusers has prompted tribes to collude with the federal government in whittling away their own sovereignty.

In the larger society, Barbara Harris started an organization called CRACK (Children Requiring a Caring Kommunity) in Anaheim, California, which gives women $200 to have sterilizations. Their mission is to "'save our welfare system' and the world from the exorbitant cost to the taxpayer for each 'drug addicted birth' by offering 'effective preventive measures to reduce the tragedy of numerous drug-affected pregnancies'" (Kigvamasud'Vashi 2001). Some of CRACK's initial billboards read, "Don't let a pregnancy ruin your drug habit" (Kigvamasud'Vashi 2001). The organization has since opened chapters in several cities around the country, and has changed its name to Positive Prevention to present a less inflammatory image. Nonetheless, its basic message is the same—that poor women who are substance abusers are the cause of social ills and that the conditions that give rise to poor women becoming substance abusers do not need to be addressed.

Unfortunately, as both Roberts (1997) and Cook-Lynn (1998) point out, even communities of color, including those who identify as both pro-life and pro-choice, have supported the criminalization of women of color who have addiction issues. The reason they support this strategy is because they focus on what they perceive to be the moral culpability of women of color for not protecting the life of their children. If we adopt an anti-prison perspective, however, it becomes clear that even on the terms of moral culpability (which I am not defending) it does not follow that the criminal justice approach is the appropriate way to address this social concern.[2] In fact, criminal justice responses to unwanted pregnancies and/or pregnant women who have addiction issues demonstrate an inherent contradiction in the pro-life position. Many pro-life organizations have been ardent opponents of population control programs and policies—advocating against the promotion of dangerous contraceptives or the promotion of sterilization in third-world countries. Yet, their position depends on the prison industrial complex that is an institution of population control for communities of color in the United States.

Meanwhile, many pro-choice organizations, such as Planned Parenthood, have supported financial incentives for poor and criminalized women to be sterilized or to take long-acting hormonal contraceptives (Saletan 2003).[3] As I will discuss later, part of this political inconsistency is inherent in the articulation of the pro-choice position. But another reason is that many in the pro-choice camp have also not questioned criminalization as the appropriate response for addressing reproductive health concerns. The pro-choice camp may differ from pro-life groups regarding which acts should be criminalized, but it does not necessarily question the criminalization regime itself.

THE PRO-CHOICE POSITION AND CAPITALISM

The pro-choice camp claims a position that offers more choices for women making decisions about their reproductive lives. A variety of scholars and activists have critiqued the choice paradigm because it rests on essentially individualist, consumerist notions of "free" choice that do not take into consideration all the social, economic, and political conditions that frame the so-called choices that women are forced to make (Patchesky 1990; Smith 1999; Solinger 2001). Solinger further contends that in the 1960s and 1970s, abortion rights advocates initially used the term "rights" rather than choice; rights are understood as those benefits owed to all those who are human regardless of access to special resources. By contrast, argues Solinger, the concept of choice is connected to possession of resources, thus creating a hierarchy among women based on who is capable of making legitimate choices (2001, 6). Consequently, since under a capitalist system, those with resources are granted more choices, it is not inconsistent to withdraw reproductive rights choices from poor women through legislation such as the Hyde Amendment (which restricts federal funding for abortion) or family caps for TANF (Temporary Assistance for Needy Families) recipients.[4] Solinger's argument can be demonstrated in the writings of Planned Parenthood. In 1960, Planned Parenthood commissioned a study which concluded that poor and working-class families lacked the rationality to do family planning, and that this lack of "rationality and early family planning as middle-class couples" was "embodied in the particular personalities, world views, and ways of life" of the poor themselves (Rainwater 1960, 5, 167). As Solinger states:

> "Choice" also became a symbol of middle-class women's arrival as independent consumers. Middle-class women could afford to choose. They had earned the right to choose motherhood, if they liked. According to many Americans, however, when choice was associated with poor women, it became a symbol of illegitimacy. Poor women had not earned the right to choose. (2001, 199–200)

What Solinger's analysis suggests is that, ironically, while the pro-choice camp contends that the pro-life position diminishes the rights of women in favor of "fetal" rights; the pro-choice position actually does not ascribe inherent rights to women either. Rather, women are viewed as having reproductive choices if they can afford them or if they are deemed legitimate choice-makers.

William Saletan's (1998) history of the evolution of the pro-choice paradigm illustrates the extent to which this paradigm is a conservative one. Saletan contends that pro-choice strategists, generally affiliated with National Abortion and Reproductive Rights Action League (NARAL), intentionally rejected a rights-based framework in favor of one that focused on privacy from *big government*. That is, government should not intervene in the woman's right to decide if she wants to have children. This approach appealed to those with libertarian sensibilities who otherwise might have had no sympathy with feminist causes. The impact of this strategy was that it enabled the pro-choice side to keep *Roe v. Wade* intact—but only in the most narrow sense. This strategy undermined any attempt to achieve a broader pro-choice agenda because the strategy could be used against a broader agenda. For instance, the argument that government should not be involved in reproductive rights decisions could also be used by pro-life advocates against federal funding for abortions (Saletan 2003). Consequently, Saletan argues, "Liberals have not won the struggle for abortion rights. Conservatives have" (1998, 114).

Furthermore, this narrow approach has contributed to some pro-choice organizations, such as Planned Parenthood and NARAL, often developing strategies that marginalize women of color. Both supported the

Freedom of Choice Act in the early 1990s that retained the Hyde Amendment (Saletan 2003). The Hyde Amendment, besides discriminating against poor women by denying federal funding for abortion services, discriminates against American Indian women who largely obtain healthcare through Indian Health Services, a federal agency. One of NARAL's petitions stated: "The Freedom of Choice Act (FOCA) will secure the original vision of *Roe v. Wade*, giving *all* women reproductive freedom and securing that right for future generations [emphasis mine]."[5] Apparently, poor women and indigenous women do not qualify as "women."[6]

Building on this analysis, I would argue that while there is certainly a sustained critique of the choice paradigm, particularly among women of color reproductive rights groups, the choice paradigm continues to govern much of the policies of mainstream groups in a manner that sustains the marginalization of women of color, poor women, and women with disabilities. One example is the extent to which pro-choice advocates narrow their advocacy around legislation that affects the one choice of whether or not to have an abortion without addressing all the conditions that gave rise to a woman having to make this decision in the first place. Consequently, politicians, such as former President Bill Clinton, will be heralded as "pro-choice" as long as they do not support legislative restrictions on abortion regardless of their stance on other issues that may equally impact the reproductive choices women make. Clinton's approval of federal welfare reform that places poor women in the position of possibly being forced to have an abortion because of cuts in social services, while often critiqued, is not viewed as an "anti-choice" position. On Planned Parenthood's and NARAL's websites (www.plannedparenthood.org; www.naral.org) there is generally no mention of welfare policies in these organizations' pro-choice legislation alerts.

A consequence of the choice paradigm is that its advocates frequently take positions that are oppressive to women from marginalized communities. For instance, this paradigm often makes it difficult to develop nuanced positions on the use of abortion when the fetus is determined to have abnormalities. Focusing solely on the woman's choice to have or not have the child does not address the larger context of a society that sees children with disabilities as having worthless lives and that provides inadequate resources to women who may otherwise want to have them. As Martha Saxton notes: "Our society profoundly limits the 'choice' to love and care for a baby with a disability" (1998, 375). If our response to disability is to simply facilitate the process by which women can abort fetuses that may have disabilities, we never actually focus on changing economic policies that make raising children with disabilities difficult. Rashmi Luthra (1993) notes, by contrast, that reproductive advocates from other countries such as India, who do not operate from this same choice paradigm, are often able to develop more complicated political positions on issues such as this one.

Another example is the difficulty pro-choice groups have in maintaining a critical perspective on dangerous or potentially dangerous contraceptives, arguing that women should have the "choice" of contraceptives. Many scholars and activists have documented the dubious safety record of Norplant and Depo-Provera, two long-acting hormonal contraceptives (Krust and Assetoyer 1993; Masterson and Guthrie 1986; Roberts 1997; Smith 2001). In fact, lawsuits against Norplant have forced an end to its distribution (although Norplant that remains on the shelves can be sold to women). In 1978, the FDA denied approval for Depo-Provera on the grounds that: (1) dog studies confirmed an elevated rate of breast cancer; (2) there appeared to be an increased risk of birth defects in human fetuses exposed to the drug; and (3) there was no pressing need shown for use of the drug as a contraceptive (Masterson and Guthrie). In 1987, the FDA changed its regulations and began to require cancer testing in rats and mice instead of dogs and monkeys; Depo-Provera did not cause cancer in these animals, but major concerns regarding its safety persist (Feminist Women's Health Centers 1997). Also problematic is the manner in which these contraceptives are frequently promoted in communities of color and often without informed consent (Krust and Assetoyer 1993; Masterson and Guthrie 1986; Smith 2001).[7] Yet none of the mainstream pro-choice organizations have ever seriously taken a position on the issue of informed consent as part of their agenda.[8] Indeed, Gloria Feldt, president of Planned Parenthood, equates opposition to Norplant and Depo-Provera as opposition to "choice" in her book The War on Choice (Feldt 2004, 34, 37). Planned Parenthood and NARAL opposed restrictions against sterilization abuse, despite the thousands of women of color who were being sterilized without their consent, because they saw such policies as interfering with a woman's "right to choose" (Nelson 2003, 144; Patchesky 1990, 8).

Particularly disturbing has been some of the support given by these organizations to the Center for Research on Population and Security, headed by Stephen Mumford and Elton Kessel, which distributes globally a form of sterilization, Quinacrine. Quinacrine is a drug that is used to treat malaria. It is inserted into the uterus where it dissolves, causing the fallopian tubes to scar, rendering the woman irreversibly sterile. Family Health International conducted four in vitro studies and found Quinacrine to be mutagenic in three of them (Controversy Over Sterilization Pellet 1994; Norsigian 1996). It, as well as the World Health Organization, recommended against further trials for female sterilization, and no regulatory body supports Quinacrine. However, the North Carolina–based Center for Research on Population and Security has circumvented these bodies through private funding from such organizations as the Turner Foundation and Leland Fykes organization (which incidentally funds pro-choice and anti-immigrant groups). The Center for Research on Population and Security has been distributing Quinacrine for free to researchers and government health agencies. There are field trials in eleven countries, with more than 70,000 women sterilized. In Vietnam, a hundred female rubber plant workers were given routine pelvic exams during which the doctor inserted the Quinacrine without their consent. Thus far, the side effects linked to Quinacrine include ectopic pregnancy, puncturing of the uterus during insertion, pelvic inflammatory disease, and severe abdominal pains. Other possible concerns include heart and liver damage and exacerbation of pre-existing viral conditions. In one of the trials in Vietnam, a large number of cases that had serious side effects were excluded from the data (Controversy Over Sterilization Pellet 1994; Norsigian 1996).

Despite the threat to reproductive justice that this group represents, Feminist Majority Foundation featured the Center for Research on Population and Security at its 1996 Feminist Expo because, I was informed by the organizers, they promoted choice for women. Then in 1999, Planned Parenthood almost agreed to sponsor a Quinacrine trial in the United States until outside pressure forced it to change its position (Committee on Women, Population and the Environment 1999). A prevalent ideology within the mainstream pro-choice movement is that women should have the choice to use whatever contraception they want. This position does not consider: (1) that a choice among dangerous contraceptives is not much of a choice;

(2) the millions of dollars pharmaceutical companies and the medical industry have to promote certain contraceptives, compared to the few resources women's advocacy groups have to provide alternative information on these same contraceptives; and (3) the social, political, and economic conditions in which women may find themselves are such that using dangerous contraceptives may be the best of even worse options.

One reason that such groups have not taken a position on informed consent in the case of potentially dangerous contraceptives is due to their investment in population control. As Betsy Hartmann (1995) has argued, while contraceptives are often articulated as an issue of choice for white women in the first world, they are articulated as an instrument of population control for women of color and women in the third world (Hartmann 1995). The historical origins of Planned Parenthood are inextricably tied to the eugenics movement. Its founder, Margaret Sanger, increasingly collaborated with eugenics organizations during her career and framed the need for birth control in terms of the need to reduce the number of those in the "lower classes" (Roberts 1997, 73). In a study commissioned in 1960, Planned Parenthood concluded that poor people "have too many children" (Rainwater 1960, 2); yet something must be done to stop this trend in order to "disarm the population bomb" (Rainwater 1960, 178). Today, Planned Parenthood is particularly implicated in this movement as can be seen clearly by the groups it lists as allies on its website (www.plannedparenthood.org): Population Action International, the Population Institute, Zero Population Growth, and the Population Council. A central campaign of Planned Parenthood is to restore U.S. funding to the United Nations Population Fund. In addition it asserts its commitment to addressing *rapid population growth* on this same website. I will not repeat the problematic analysis, critiqued elsewhere, of this population paradigm that essentially blames third-world women for poverty, war, environmental damage, and social unrest, without looking at the root causes of all these phenomena (including population growth)—colonialism, corporate policies, militarism, and economic disparities between poor and rich countries (Bandarage 1997; Hartmann 1995; Silliman and King 1999).

As Hartmann (1995) documents, the United Nations Population Fund has long been involved in coercive contraceptive policies throughout the world. The Population Council produced Norplant and assisted in Norplant trials in Bangladesh and other countries without the informed consent of the trial participants

(Hartmann 1995). In fact, trial administrators often refused to remove Norplant when requested (Cadbury 1995). All of these population organizations intersect to promote generally long-acting hormonal contraceptives of dubious safety around the world (Hartmann 1995). Of course, Planned Parenthood provides valuable family planning resources to women around the world as well, but it does so through a population framework that inevitably shifts the focus from family planning as a right in and of itself to family planning as an instrument of population control. While population control advocates, such as Planned Parenthood, are increasingly more sophisticated in their rhetoric and often talk about ensuring social, political, and economic opportunity, the *population* focus of this model still results in its advocates working to reduce population rather than to provide social, political, and economic opportunity.

Another unfortunate consequence of uncritically adopting the choice paradigm is the tendency of reproductive rights advocates to make simplistic analyses of who our political friends and enemies are in the area of reproductive rights. That is, all those who call themselves pro-choice are our political allies while all those who call themselves pro-life are our political enemies. An example of this rhetoric is Gloria Feldt's description of anyone who is pro-life as a "right-wing extremist" (Feldt 2004, 5). As I have argued elsewhere, this simplistic analysis of who is politically progressive versus conservative does not actually do justice to the complex political positions people inhabit (Smith 2002). As a result, we often engage uncritically in coalitions with groups that, as anti-violence activist Beth Richie states, "do not pay us back" (2000, 31). Meanwhile, we often lose opportunities to work with people with whom we may have sharp disagreements, but who may, with different political framings and organizing strategies, shift their positions.

To illustrate: Planned Parenthood is often championed as an organization that supports women's rights to choose with whom women of color should ally. Yet, as discussed previously, its roots are in the eugenics movement and today it is heavily invested in the population establishment. It continues to support population control policies in the third world, it almost supported the development of Quinacrine in the United States, and it opposed strengthening sterilization regulations that would protect women of color. Meanwhile, the North Baton Rouge Women's Help Center in Louisiana is a crisis pregnancy center that articulates its pro-life position from an anti-racist perspective. It argues that Planned Parenthood has advocated population control, particularly in communities of color. It critiques the Black Church Initiative for the Religious Coalition for Reproductive Choice for contending that charges of racism against Sanger are *scare tactics* (Blunt 2003, 22). It also attempts to provide its services from a holistic perspective—it provides educational and vocational training, GED classes, literacy programs, primary health care and pregnancy services, and child placement services. Its position: "We cannot encourage women to have babies and then continue their dependency on the system. We can't leave them without the resources to care for their children and then say, 'Praise the Lord, we saved a baby'" (Blunt 2003, 23).

It would seem that while the two organizations support some positions that are beneficial to women of color, they both equally support positions that are detrimental to them. If we are truly committed to reproductive justice, why should we presume that we should necessarily work with Planned Parenthood and reject the Women's Help Center? Why would we not instead position ourselves independently from both of these approaches and work to shift their positions to a stance that is truly liberatory for all women?

BEYOND PRO-LIFE VERSUS PRO-CHOICE

To develop an independent position, it is necessary to reject the pro-life versus pro-choice model for understanding reproductive justice. Many reproductive advocates have attempted to expand the definitions of either pro-life or pro-choice depending on which side of this divide they may rest. Unfortunately, they are trying to expand concepts that are inherently designed to exclude the experiences of most women, especially poor women, women of color, indigenous women, and women with disabilities.

If we critically assess the assumptions behind both positions, it is clear that these camps are more similar than they are different. As I have argued, they both assume a criminal justice regime for adjudicating reproductive issues (although they may differ as to which women should be subjected to this regime). Neither position endows women with inherent rights to their body—the pro-life position pits fetal rights against women's rights whereas the pro-choice position argues that women should have freedom to make choices rather than possess inherent rights to their bodies regardless of their class standing. They both support positions that reinforce racial and gender hierarchies that marginalize women

of color. The pro-life position supports a criminalization approach that depends on a racist political system that will necessarily impact poor women and women of color who are less likely to have alternative strategies for addressing unwanted pregnancies. Meanwhile, the pro-choice position often supports population control policies and the development of dangerous contraceptives that are generally targeted toward communities of color. And both positions do not question the capitalist system—they focus solely on the decision of whether or not a woman should have an abortion without addressing the economic, political, and social conditions that put women in this position in the first place.

Consequently, it is critical that reproductive advocates develop a framework that does not rest on the pro-choice versus pro-life framework. Such a strategy would enable us to fight for reproductive justice as a part of a larger social justice strategy. It would also free us to think more creatively about who we could work in coalition with while simultaneously allowing us to hold those who claim to be our allies more accountable for the positions they take. To be successful in this venture, however, it is not sufficient to simply articulate a women of color reproductive justice agenda—we must focus on developing a nationally coordinated women of color movement. While there are many women of color reproductive organizations, relatively few actually focus on bringing new women of color into the movement and training them to organize on their own behalf. And to the extent that these groups do exist, they are not generally coordinated as national mobilization efforts. Rather, national work is generally done on an advocacy level with heads of women of color organizations advocating for policy changes, but often working without a solid base to back their demands (Silliman et al. 2005/in press).

Consequently, women of color organizations are not always in a strong position to negotiate with power brokers and mainstream pro-choice organizations or to hold them accountable. As an example, many women of color groups mobilized to attend the 2004 March for Women's Lives in Washington, D.C., in order to expand the focus of the march from a narrow pro-choice abortion rights agenda to a broad-based reproductive rights agenda. While this broader agenda was reflected in the march, it became co-opted by the pro-choice paradigm in the media coverage of the event. My survey of the major newspaper coverage of the march indicates that virtually no newspaper described it as anything other than a pro-choice or abortion rights march.[9] To quote New Orleans health activist Barbara Major,

"When you go to power without a base, your demand becomes a request" (2003). Base-building work, on which many women of color organizations are beginning to focus, is very slow work that may not show results for a long time. After all, the base-building of the Christian Right did not become publicly visible for 50 years (Diamond 1989). Perhaps one day, we will have a march for women's lives in which the main issues addressed and reported will include: (1) repealing the Hyde Amendment; (2) stopping the promotion of dangerous contraceptives; (3) decriminalizing women who are pregnant and who have addictions; and (4) ending welfare policies that punish women, in addition to other issues that speak to the intersections of gender, race, and class in reproductive rights policies.

At a meeting of the United Council of Tribes in Chicago, representatives from the Chicago

Pro-Choice Alliance informed us that we should join the struggle to keep abortion legal or else we would lose our reproductive rights. A woman in the audience responded, "Who cares about reproductive rights; we don't have any rights, period." What her response suggests is that a reproductive justice agenda must make the dismantling of capitalism, white supremacy, and colonialism *central* to its agenda, and not just as principles added to organizations' promotional material designed to appeal to women of color, with no budget to support making these principles a reality. We must reject single-issue, pro-choice politics of the mainstream reproductive rights movement as an agenda that not only does not serve women of color, but actually promotes the structures of oppression which keep women of color from having real choices or healthy lives.

NOTES

1. This block quote is a compilation of Colson quotes from three different sources (Colson 1983, 15; Fager 1982, 23; Forbes 1982, 34).
2. As Roberts (1997) and Maher (1990) note, addiction is itself a result of social and political conditions, such as racism and poverty, which the U.S. government does not take steps to alleviate, and then blames women who are victimized by these conditions. Furthermore, the government provides no resources for pregnant women to end their addictions; it simply penalizes them for continuing a pregnancy. Thus assigning moral culpability primarily to pregnant women with addiction problems is a dubious prospect.
3. Additionally, several reproductive rights advocates at the historic *SisterSong* Conference on Women of Color and Reproductive Justice held in Atlanta, November 13–16, 2003, noted that some local Planned Parenthood agencies were currently offering financial incentives for women who are addicted to accept long-acting contraceptives or were distributing literature from CRACK. This policy was not uniform among Planned Parenthood chapters, however, and many Planned Parenthood chapters condemn this practice.
4. For further analysis of how welfare reform marks poor women and women of color as women who make "bad choices" and hence should have these choices restricted through marriage promotion, family caps (or cuts in payments if recipients have additional children), and incentives to use long-acting hormonal contraceptives, see Mink 1999.
5. The petition can be found on the Web at http://www.wanaral.org/s01takeaction/200307101.shtml
6. During this period, I served on the board of Illinois National Abortion and Reproductive Rights Action League (NARAL), which was constituted primarily of women

of color. Illinois NARAL broke with National NARAL in opposing the Freedom of Choice Act (FOCA). Despite many heated discussions with NARAL president Kate Michelman, she refused to consider the perspective of women of color on this issue.
7. I was a co-organizer of a reproductive rights conference in Chicago in 1992. There, hotline workers from Chicago Planned Parenthood reported that they were told to tell women seeking contraception that Norplant had no side effects. In 2000, women from a class I was teaching at University of California, Santa Cruz, informed the class that when they asked Planned Parenthood workers what were the side effects of Depo-Provera, the workers said that they were not allowed to tell them the side effects because they were supposed to promote Depo-Provera. Similar problems in other Planned Parenthood offices were reported at the previously mentioned *SisterSong* conference. These problems around informed consent are not necessarily a national Planned Parenthood policy or uniform across all Planned Parenthood agencies.
8. In 1994 when NARAL changed its name from the National Association for the Repeal of Abortion Laws to the National Abortion and Reproductive Rights Action League, it held a strategy session for its state chapters which I attended. Michelman and her associates claimed that this name change was reflective of NARAL's interest in expanding its agenda to new communities, and informed consent around contraceptives would be included in this expanded agenda. I asked how much of NARAL's budget was going to be allocated to this new agenda. Their reply: none. They were going to release a report on these new issues, but they were going to work only on the issues NARAL had addressed traditionally.

9. Newspapers surveyed which focused solely on abortion rights include *The New York Times* (Toner 2004); *Connecticut Post* ("Abortion-Rights Marchers Crowd D.C." 2004); *New York Newsday* (Phelps 2004); *Syracuse Post Standard* (Gadoua 2004); *The Record* (Varoqua 2004); *The Baltimore Sun* (Gibson 2004); *The Commercial Appeal* (Wolfe 2004); *Richmond Times Dispatch* (Smith 2004); *Marin Independent Journal* ("Marchers Say Bush Policies Harm Women" 2004); *Salt Lake Tribune* (Stephenson 2004); *The Capital Times* (Segars 2004); *Dayton Daily News* (Dart 2004); *Milwaukee Journal Sentinel* (Madigan 2004); *Cleveland Plains Dealer* (Diemer 2004); *Minneapolis Star Tribune* (O'Rourke 2004); *Chicago Daily Herald* (Ryan 2004); *Chicago Sun-Times* (Sweeney 2004); *The Columbus Dispatch* (Riskind 2004); *San Francisco Chronicle* (Marinucci 2004); and *Dayton Daily News* (Wynn 2004). The coverage of "other" issues in a few papers was limited to "The concerns they voiced extended beyond the issues of abortion to health care access, AIDS prevention, birth control and civil rights" in *San Francisco Chronicle* (Marinucci 2004); "Another group flashed signs calling for the government to recognize same-sex marriage" in the *Houston Chronicle* (Black 2004); "Various trends and vendors on the Mall also promoted other political causes, including welfare, the Falun Gong movement in China, homosexual 'marriage,' the socialist movement, environmentalism, and striking Utah coal miners" in the *Atlanta Journal-Constitution* (Dart and Pickel 2004); "'This morning I was saying that I was mainly here for abortion,' said Gresh, reflecting on the march. 'But now, going through this, I realize that there are so many issues. Equal pay is a big issue. And globalization, and women's rights around the world'" in the *Pittsburgh Post-Gazette* (Belser 2004).

REFERENCES

"Abortion-Rights Marchers Crowd D.C." 2004. *Connecticut Post,* April 26.

Bandarage, Asoka. 1997. *Women, Population and Global Crisis.* London: Zed.

Belser, Ann. 2004. "Local Marchers Have Many Issues." *Pittsburgh Post-Gazette,* April 26, A4.

Black, Joe. 2004. "Marchers Rally for Abortion Rights." *Houston Chronicle,* April 26, A1.

Blunt, Sheryl. 2003. "Saving Black Babies." *Christianity Today* 47 (February):21–3.

Box, Steve, and Chris Hale. 1982. "Economic Crisis and the Rising Prisoner Population in England and Wales." *Crime and Social Justice* 17:20–35.

Bushnell, Jeanette. 2004. Interview with author, 21 May.

Butterfield, Fox. 2000. "Study Shows a Racial Divide in Domestic Violence Cases." *The New York Times,* May 18, A16.

Cadbury, Deborah. 1995. *Human Laboratory.* Video, BBC.

Colson, Charles. 1985. "God Behind Bars." *Christian Life* 47 (September):28–32.

———. 1983. "Why Charles Colson's Heart Is Still in Prison." *Christianity Today* 27 (September 16):12–4.

———. 1980. "Prison Reform: Your Obligation as a Believer." *Christian Life* 41 (April):23–4; 50–6.

———. 1977. "Who Will Help Penitents and Penitentiaries?" *Eternity* 28 (May): 12–7, 34.

Committee on Women, Population and the Environment. 1999. Internal Correspondence.

Controversy over Sterilization Pellet. 1994. *Political Environments* 1 (Spring):9.

Cook-Lynn, Elizabeth. 1998. *Why I Can't Read Wallace Stegner and Other Essays.* Madison: University of Wisconsin Press.

Crum, Gary, and Thelma McCormack. 1992. *Abortion: Pro-Choice or Pro-Life?* Washington, DC: American University Press.

Currie, Elliott. 1998. *Crime and Punishment in America.* New York: Metropolitan Books.

Dart, Bob. 2004. "Abortion-Rights Backers March." *Dayton Daily News,* April 26, A1.

Dart, Bob, and Mary Lou Pickel. 2004. "Abortion Rights Supporters March." *Atlanta Journal-Constitution,* April 26, 1A.

Davis, Angela. 2003. *Are Prisons Obsolete?* New York: Seven Stories Press.

Diamond, Sara. 1989. *Spiritual Warfare.* Boston: South End Press.

Diemer, Tom. 2004. "Thousands Rally for Choice 500,000 to 800,000 March in D.C. in Support of Abortion Rights." *Cleveland Plains Dealer,* April 26, A1.

Dilulio, John. 1999. Keynote Address, Justice Fellowship Conference. Washington, D.C., February.

Donziger, Steven. 1996. *The Real War on Crime.* New York: Harper Collins.

Dorris, Michael. 1989. *The Broken Cord.* New York: Harper & Row.

Fager, Charles. 1982. "No Holds Barred." *Eternity* 33 (April 1982):20–4.

Feldt, Gloria. 2004. *The War on Choice.* New York: Bantam Books.

Feminist Women's Health Centers. 1997. "Depo-Provera (The Shot)," http://www.fwhc.org/bcdepo.html.

Forbes, Cheryl. 1982. "What Hope for America's Prisons." *Christian Herald* 105 (April): 32–40.

Gadoua, Renee. 2004. "A Woman Should Decide." *Post-Standard,* April 26, B1.

Gibson, Gail. 2004. "Thousands Rally for Abortion Rights." *Baltimore Sun,* April 26, 1A.

Hartmann, Betsy. 1995. *Reproductive Rights and Wrongs: The Global Politics of Population Control.* Boston: South End Press.

Ignatieff, Michael. 1978. *A Just Measure of Pain*. New York: Pantheon Books.

Jankovic, Ivan. 1977. "Labour Market and Imprisonment." *Crime and Social Justice* 8:17–31.

Kigvamasud'Vashi, Theryn. 2001. "Fact Sheet on Positive Prevention/CRACK (Children Requiring a Caring Community)." Seattle: Communities Against Rape and Abuse.

Krust, Lin, and Charon Assetoyer. 1993. "A Study of the Use of Depo-Provera and Norplant by the Indian Health Services." Lake Andes: South Dakota: Native American Women's Health Education Resource Center.

Lawton, Kim. 1988. "So What Should We Do with Prisoners." *Christianity Today* 32 (November 4):38–9.

Luthra, Rashmi. 1993. "Toward a Reconceptualization of 'Choice': Challenges at the Margins." *Feminist Issues* 13 (Spring):41–54.

Madigan, Erin. 2004. "Hundreds of Thousands March for Abortion Rights." *Milwaukee Journal Sentinel*, April 26, 3A.

Maher, Lisa. 1990. "Criminalizing Pregnancy—The Downside of a Kinder, Gentler Nation?" *Social Justice* 17 (Fall): 111–35.

Major, Barbara. 2003. Keynote Address, National Women's Studies Association National Conference. New Orleans, June.

Mancini, Michael. 1991. *One Dies, One Gets Another*. Columbia: University of South Carolina Press.

"Marchers Say Bush Policies Harm Women." 2004. *Marin Independent Journal*, April 26, Nation/World.

Marinucci, Carla. 2004. "Hundreds of Thousands in D.C. Pledge to Take Fight to Polls." *San Francisco Chronicle*, April 26, A1.

Masterson, Mike, and Patricia Guthrie. 1986. "Taking the Shot." *Arizona Republic*, n.p.

Mauer, Marc. 1999. *Race to Incarcerate*. New York: New Press/WW Norton.

Mill, Manny. 1999. "No Prisons in Heaven." *New Man* 8 (January/February):74.

Mink, Gendolyn, ed. 1999. *Whose Welfare?* Ithaca: Cornell University Press.

Nelson, Jennifer. 2003. *Women of Color and the Reproductive Rights Movement*. New York: New York University Press.

Norsigian, Judy. 1996. "Quinacrine Update." *Political Environments* 3 (Spring):26–7.

O'Rourke, Lawrence. 2004. "Thousands Rally for Abortion Rights." *Star Tribune*, April 26, 1A.

Patchesky, Rosalind. 1990. *Abortion and Woman's Choice*. Boston: Northeastern University Press.

Phelps, Timothy. 2004. "Demonstration in D.C." *New York Newsday*, April 26, A05.

Prison Activist Resource Center. 2004. http://www.prisonactivist.org.

Pulliam, Russ. 1987. "A Better Idea than Prison." *Christian Herald* 110 (November):28–31.

Rainwater, Lee. 1960. *And the Poor Get Children*. Chicago: Quadrangle Books.

Richie, Beth. 2000. "Plenary Presentation." In *The Color of Violence: Violence Against Women of Color*, ed. Incite! Women of Color Against Violence, 124. University of California, Santa Cruz: Incite! Women of Color Against Violence.

Riskind, Jonathan. 2004. "Supporters of Abortion Rights Seek Forefront." *The Columbus Dispatch*, April 25, 1A.

Roberts, Dorothy. 1997. *Killing the Black Body*. New York: Pantheon Books.

Rodriguez, Dylan. 2000. "The Challenge of Prison Abolition." *Social Justice* 27 (Fall):212–8.

Ryan, Joseph. 2004. "Abortion Rights Supporters Jump in to Rejuvenate Cause." *Chicago Daily Herald*, April 26, 15.

Saletan, William. 2003. *Bearing Right*. Berkeley: University of California Press.

———. 1998. "Electoral Politics and Abortion." In *The Abortion Wars*, ed. Rickie Solinger, 111–23. Berkeley: University of California Press.

Saxton, Martha. 1998. "Disability Rights." In *The Abortion Wars*, ed. Rickie Solinger, 374–93. Berkeley: University of California Press.

Segars, Melissa. 2004. "Rally For Women's Rights." *The Capital Times*, April 26, 1A.

Silliman, Jael, Loretta Ross, Marlene Gerber Fried, and Elena Gutierrez. 2005/in press. *Undivided Rights*. Boston: South End Press.

Silliman, Jael, and Ynestra King, eds. 1999. *Dangerous Intersections: Feminist Perspectives on Population, Environment and Development*. Boston: South End Press.

Smarto, Don, ed. 1993. *Setting the Captives Free*. Grand Rapids: Baker Book House.

Smith, Andrea. 2005/in press. "Domestic Violence, the State, and Social Change." In *Domestic Violence at the Margins: A Reader at the Intersections of Race, Class, and Gender*, ed. Natalie Sokoloff. New Brunswick: Rutgers University Press.

———. 2002. "Bible, Gender and Nationalism in American Indian and Christian Right Activism." Santa Cruz: University of California.

———. 2001. "'Better Dead Than Pregnant' The Colonization of Native Women's Health." In *Policing the National Body*, ed. Anannya Bhattacharjee and Jael Silliman. 123–46. Boston: South End Press.

Smith, Justine. 1999. "Native Sovereignty and Social Justice: Moving Toward an Inclusive Social Justice Framework." In *Dangerous Intersections: Feminist Perspectives on Population, Environment and Development*, ed. Jael Silliman and Ynestra King, 202–13. Boston: South End Press.

Smith, Tammie. 2004. "Marchers Call for 'A Choice' About Reproductive Rights." *Richmond Times Dispatch*, April 26, A1.

Solinger, Rickie. 2001. *Beggers and Choosers*. New York: Hill and Wang.

Stephenson, Kathy. 2004. "Utahns Take Part in D.C. and at Home." *Salt Lake Tribune*, April 26, A6.

Sweeney, Annie. 2004. "Chicagoans Head to D.C. for Pro-Choice March." *Chicago Sun-Times*, April 26, 18.

Toner, Robin. 2004. "Abortion Rights Marches Vow to Fight Another Bush Term." *The New York Times*, April 26, A1.

Van Ness, Daniel. 1985. "The Crisis of Crowded Prisons." *Eternity* 36 (April): 33–7

Varoqua, Eman. 2004. "N.J. Supporters Form Large Column for Rights." *The Record*, April 26, A01.

Walker, Samuel. 1998. *Sense and Nonsense about Crime.* Belmont: Wadsworth Publishing Company.

Wolfe, Elizabeth. 2004. "Rights March Packs Mall." *The Commercial Appeal*, April 26, A4.

Wynn, Kelli. 2004. "Hundreds Go to D.C. for March Today." *Dayton Daily News*, April 25, B1.

R E A D I N G *37*　**Barbara Ehrenreich**

Welcome to Cancerland

A mammogram leads to a cult of pink kitsch

I was thinking of it as one of those drive-by mammograms, one stop in a series of mundane missions including post office, supermarket, and gym, but I began to lose my nerve in the changing room, and not only because of the kinky necessity of baring my breasts and affixing tiny X-ray opaque stars to the tip of each nipple. I had been in this place only four months earlier, but that visit was just part of the routine cancer surveillance all good citizens of HMOs or health plans are expected to submit to once they reach the age of fifty, and I hadn't really been paying attention then. The results of that earlier session had aroused some "concern" on the part of the radiologist and her confederate, the gynecologist, so I am back now in the role of a suspect, eager to clear my name, alert to medical missteps and unfair allegations. But the changing room, really just a closet off the stark windowless space that houses the mammogram machine, contains something far worse, I notice for the first time now—an assumption about who I am, where I am going, and what I will need when I get there. Almost all of the eye-level space has been filled with photocopied bits of cuteness and sentimentality: pink ribbons, a cartoon about a woman with iatrogenically flattened breasts, an "Ode to a Mammogram," a list of the "Top Ten Things Only Women Understand" ("Fat Clothes" and "Eyelash Curlers" among them), and, inescapably, right next to the door, the poem "I Said a Prayer for You Today," illustrated with pink roses.

It goes on and on, this mother of all mammograms, cutting into gym time, dinnertime, and lifetime generally. Sometimes the machine doesn't work, and I get squished into position to no purpose at all. More often, the X ray is successful but apparently alarming to the invisible radiologist, off in some remote office, who calls the shots and never has the courtesy to show her face with an apology or an explanation. I try pleading with the technician: I have no known risk factors, no breast cancer in the family, had my babies relatively young and nursed them both. I eat right, drink sparingly, work out, and doesn't that count for something? But she just gets this tight little professional smile on her face, either out of guilt for the torture she's inflicting or because she already knows something that I am going to be sorry to find out for myself. For an hour and a half the procedure is repeated: the squishing, the snapshot, the technician bustling off to consult the radiologist and returning with a demand for new angles and more definitive images. In the intervals while she's off with the doctor I read the *New York Times* right down to the personally irrelevant sections like theater and real estate, eschewing the stack of women's magazines provided for me, much as I ordinarily enjoy a quick read about sweat-proof eyeliners and "fabulous sex tonight," because I have picked up this warning vibe in the changing room, which, in my increasingly anxious state, translates into: femininity is death. Finally there is nothing left to read but one of the free local weekly newspapers, where I find, buried deep in the classifieds, something even more unsettling than the growing prospect of major disease—a classified ad for a "breast cancer teddy bear" with a pink ribbon stitched to its chest.

Yes, atheists pray in their foxholes—in this case, with a yearning new to me and sharp as lust, for a clean and honorable death by shark bite, lightning strike, sniper fire, car crash. Let me be hacked to death by a madman, is my silent supplication—anything but suffocation by the pink sticky sentiment embodied in that bear and oozing from the walls of the changing room.

My official induction into breast cancer comes about ten days later with the biopsy, which, for reasons I cannot ferret out of the surgeon, has to be a surgical one, performed on an outpatient basis but under general anesthesia, from which I awake to find him standing perpendicular to me, at the far end of the gurney, down near my feet, stating gravely, "Unfortunately, there is a cancer." It takes me all the rest of that drug-addled day to decide that the most heinous thing about that sentence is not the presence of cancer but the absence of me—for I, Barbara, do not enter into it even as a location, a geographical reference point. Where I once was—not a commanding presence perhaps but nonetheless a standard assemblage of flesh and words and gesture—"there is a cancer." I have been replaced by it, is the surgeon's implication. This is what I am now, medically speaking.

In my last act of dignified self-assertion, I request to see the pathology slides myself. This is not difficult to arrange in our small-town hospital, where the pathologist turns out to be a friend of a friend, and my rusty Ph.D. in cell biology (Rockefeller University, 1968) probably helps. He's a jolly fellow, the pathologist, who calls me "hon" and sits me down at one end of the dual-head microscope while he mans the other and moves a pointer through the field. These are the cancer cells, he says, showing up blue because of their overactive DNA. Most of them are arranged in staid semicircular arrays, like suburban houses squeezed into a cul-de-sac, but I also see what I know enough to know I do not want to see: the characteristic "Indian files" of cells on the march. The "enemy," I am supposed to think—an image to save up for future exercises in "visualization" of their violent deaths at the hands of the body's killer cells, the lymphocytes and macrophages. But I am impressed, against all rational self-interest, by the energy of these cellular conga lines, their determination to move on out from

the backwater of the breast to colonize lymph nodes, bone marrow, lungs, and brain. These are, after all, the fanatics of Barbaraness, the rebel cells that have realized that the genome they carry, the genetic essence of me, has no further chance of normal reproduction in the postmenopausal body we share, so why not just start multiplying like bunnies and hope for a chance to break out?

It has happened, after all; some genomes have achieved immortality through cancer. When I was a graduate student, I once asked about the strain of tissue-culture cells labeled "HeLa" in the heavy-doored room maintained at body temperature. "HeLa," it turns out, refers to one Henrietta Lacks, whose tumor was the progenitor of all HeLa cells. She died; they live, and will go on living until someone gets tired of them or forgets to change their tissue-culture medium and leaves them to starve. Maybe this is what my rebel cells have in mind, and I try beaming them a solemn warning: The chances of your surviving me in tissue culture are nil. Keep up this selfish rampage and you go down, every last one of you, along with the entire Barbara enterprise. But what kind of a role model am I, or are multicellular human organisms generally, for putting the common good above mad anarchistic individual ambition? There is a reason, it occurs to me, why cancer is our metaphor for so many runaway social processes, like corruption and "moral decay": we are no less out of control ourselves.

After the visit to the pathologist, my biological curiosity drops to a lifetime nadir. I know women who followed up their diagnoses with weeks or months of self-study, mastering their options, interviewing doctor after doctor, assessing the damage to be expected from the available treatments. But I can tell from a few hours of investigation that the career of a breast-cancer patient has been pretty well mapped out in advance for me: You may get to negotiate the choice between lumpectomy and mastectomy, but lumpectomy is commonly followed by weeks of radiation, and in either case if the lymph nodes turn out, upon dissection, to be invaded—or "involved," as it's less threateningly put—you're doomed to chemotherapy, meaning baldness, nausea, mouth sores, immunosuppression, and possible anemia. These interventions do not constitute a "cure" or anything close, which is why the death rate from breast cancer has changed very little since the 1930s, when mastectomy was the only treatment available. Chemotherapy, which became a routine part of breast-cancer treatment in the eighties, does not confer anywhere near as decisive an advantage as patients are often led to believe, especially in post-menopausal women like myself—a two or three percentage point difference in ten-year survival rates,[1] according to America's best known breast-cancer surgeon, Dr. Susan Love.

I know these bleak facts, or sort of know them, but in the fog of anesthesia that hangs over those first few weeks, I seem to lose my capacity for self-defense. The pressure is on, from doctors and loved ones, to do something right away—kill it, get it out now. The endless exams, the bone scan to check for metastases, the high-tech heart test to see if I'm strong enough to withstand chemotherapy—all these blur the line between selfhood and thing-hood anyway, organic and inorganic, me and it. As my cancer career unfolds, I will, the helpful pamphlets explain, become a composite of the living and the dead—an implant to replace the breast, a wig to replace the hair. And then what will I mean when I use the word "I"? I fall into a state of unreasoning passive aggressivity: They diagnosed this, so it's their baby. They found it, let them fix it.

I could take my chances with "alternative" treatments, of course, like punk novelist Kathy Acker, who succumbed to breast cancer in 1997 after a course of alternative therapies in Mexico, or actress and Thigh-Master promoter Suzanne Somers, who made tabloid headlines last spring by injecting herself with mistletoe brew. Or I could choose to do nothing at all beyond mentally exhorting my immune system to exterminate the traitorous cellular faction. But I have never admired the "natural" or believed in the "wisdom of the body." Death is as "natural" as anything gets, and the body has always seemed to me like a retarded Siamese twin dragging along behind me, an hysteric really, dangerously overreacting, in my case, to everyday allergens and minute ingestions of sugar. I will put my faith in science, even if this means that the dumb old body is about to be transmogrified into an evil clown—puking, trembling, swelling, surrendering significant parts, and oozing post-surgical fluids. The surgeon—a more genial and forthcoming one this time—can fit me in; the oncologist will see me. Welcome to Cancerland.

Fortunately, no one has to go through this alone. Thirty years ago, before Betty Ford, Rose Kushner, Betty Rollin, and other pioneer patients spoke out, breast cancer was a dread secret, endured in silence and euphemized in obituaries as a "long illness." Something about the conjuncture of "breast," signifying sexuality and nurturance, and that other word, suggesting

the claws of a devouring crustacean, spooked almost everyone. Today however, it's the biggest disease on the cultural map, bigger than AIDS, cystic fibrosis, or spinal injury, bigger even than those more prolific killers of women—heart disease, lung cancer, and stroke. There are roughly hundreds of websites devoted to it, not to mention newsletters, support groups, a whole genre of first-person breast-cancer books; even a glossy, upper-middle-brow, monthly magazine, *Mamm*. There are four major national breast-cancer organizations, of which the mightiest, in financial terms, is The Susan Komen Foundation, headed by breast-cancer veteran and Bush's nominee for ambassador to Hungary Nancy Brinker. G. Komen organizes the annual Race for the Cure, which attracts about a million people—mostly survivors, friends, and family members. Its website provides a microcosm of the new breast-cancer culture, offering news of the races, message boards for accounts of individuals' struggles with the disease, and a "marketplace" of breast-cancer-related products to buy.

More so than in the case of any other disease, breast-cancer organizations and events feed on a generous flow of corporate support. Nancy Brinker relates how her early attempts to attract corporate interest in promoting breast cancer "awareness" were met with rebuff. A bra manufacturer, importuned to affix a mammogram-reminder tag to his product, more or less wrinkled his nose. Now breast cancer has blossomed from wallflower to the most popular girl at the corporate charity prom. While AIDS goes begging and low-rent diseases like tuberculosis have no friends at all, breast cancer has been able to count on Revlon, Avon, Ford, Tiffany, Pier 1, Estee Lauder, Ralph Lauren, Lee Jeans, Saks Fifth Avenue, JC Penney, Boston Market, Wilson athletic gear—and I apologize to those I've omitted. You can "shop for the cure" during the week when Saks donates 2 percent of sales to a breast-cancer fund; "wear denim for the cure" during Lee National Denim Day, when for a $5 donation you get to wear blue jeans to work. You can even "invest for the cure," in the Kinetics Assets Management's new no-load Medical Fund, which specializes entirely in businesses involved in cancer research.

If you can't run, bike, or climb a mountain for the cure—all of which endeavors are routine beneficiaries of corporate sponsorship—you can always purchase one of the many products with a breast-cancer theme. There are 2.2 million American women in various stages of their breast-cancer careers, who, along with anxious relatives, make up a significant market for all things breast-cancer-related. Bears, for example: I have identified four distinct lines, or species, of these creatures, including "Carol," the Remembrance Bear; "Hope," the Breast Cancer Research Bear, which wears a pink turban as if to conceal chemotherapy-induced baldness; the "Susan Bear," named for Nancy Brinker's deceased sister, Susan; and the new Nick & Nora Wish Upon a Star Bear, available, along with the Susan Bear, at the Komen Foundation website's "marketplace."

And bears are only the tip, so to speak, of the cornucopia of pink-ribbon-themed breast-cancer products. You can dress in pink-beribboned sweatshirts, denim shirts, pajamas, lingerie, aprons, loungewear, shoelaces, and socks; accessorize with pink rhinestone brooches, angel pins, scarves, caps, earrings, and bracelets; brighten up your home with breast-cancer candles, stained-glass pink-ribbon candleholders, coffee mugs, pendants, wind chimes, and night-lights; pay your bills with special BreastChecks or a separate line of Checks for the Cure. "Awareness" beats secrecy and stigma of course, but I can't help noticing that the existential space in which a friend has earnestly advised me to "confront [my] mortality" bears a striking resemblance to the mall.

This is not, I should point out, a case of cynical merchants exploiting the sick. Some of the breast-cancer tchotchkes and accessories are made by breast-cancer survivors themselves, such as "Janice," creator of the "Daisy Awareness Necklace," among other things, and in most cases a portion of the sales goes to breast-cancer research. Virginia Davis of Aurora, Colorado, was inspired to create the "Remembrance Bear" by a friend's double mastectomy and sees her work as more of a "crusade" than a business. This year she expects to ship 10,000 of these teddies, which are manufactured in China, and send part of the money to the Race for the Cure. If the bears are infantilizing—as I try ever so tactfully to suggest is how they may, in rare cases, be perceived—so far no one has complained. "I just get love letters," she tells me, "from people who say, 'God bless you for thinking of us.'"

The ultrafeminine theme of the breast-cancer "marketplace"—the prominence, for example, of cosmetics and jewelry—could be understood as a response to the treatments' disastrous effects on one's looks. But the infantilizing trope is a little harder to account for, and teddy bears are not its only manifestation. A tote bag distributed to breast cancer patients by the Libby Ross Foundation (through places such as the Columbia Presbyterian Medical Center) contains, among other items, a tube of Estee Lauder Perfumed Body Creme, a hot-pink satin pillowcase, an audiotape "Meditation to Help You with Chemotherapy," a small tin of peppermint pastilles, a set of three small inexpensive rhinestone bracelets, a pink-striped "journal and sketch book," and—somewhat jarringly—a small box of crayons. Maria Willner, one of the founders of the Libby Ross Foundation, told me that the crayons "go with the journal for people to express different moods, different thoughts . . ." though she admitted she has never tried to write with crayons herself. Possibly the idea is that regression to a state of childlike dependency puts one in the best frame of mind with which to endure the prolonged and toxic treatments. Or it may be that, in some versions of the prevailing gender ideology, femininity is by its nature incompatible with full adulthood—a state of arrested development. Certainly men diagnosed with prostate cancer do not receive gifts of Matchbox cars.

But I, no less than the bear huggers, need whatever help I can get, and start wading out into the Web in search of practical tips on hair loss, lumpectomy versus mastectomy, how to select a chemotherapy regimen, what to wear after surgery and eat when the scent of food sucks. There is, I soon find, far more than I can usefully absorb, for thousands of the afflicted have posted their stories, beginning with the lump or bad mammogram, proceeding through the agony of the treatments; pausing to mention the sustaining forces of family, humor, and religion; and ending, in almost all cases, with warm words of encouragement for the neophyte. Some of these are no more than a paragraph long—brief waves from sister sufferers; others offer almost hour-by-hour logs of breast-deprived, chemotherapized lives:

Tuesday, August 15, 2000: Well, I survived my 4th chemo. Very, very dizzy today. Very nauseated, but no barfing! It's a first. . . . I break out in a cold sweat and my heart pounds if I stay up longer than 5 minutes.

Friday, August 18, 2000: . . . By dinner time, I was full out nauseated. I took some meds and ate a rice and vegetable bowl from Trader Joe's. It smelled and tasted awful to me, but I ate it anyway. . . . Rick brought home some Kern's nectars and I'm drinking that. Seems to have settled my stomach a little bit.

I can't seem to get enough of these tales, reading on with panicky fascination about everything that can go wrong—septicemia, ruptured implants, startling recurrences a few years after the completion of treatments, "mets" (metastases) to vital organs, and—what scares me most in the short term—"chemo-brain," or the cognitive deterioration that sometimes accompanies chemotherapy. I compare myself with everyone, selfishly impatient with those whose conditions are less menacing, shivering over those who have reached Stage IV ("There is no Stage V," as the main character in Wit, who has ovarian cancer, explains), constantly assessing my chances.

Feminism helped make the spreading breast-cancer sisterhood possible, and this realization gives me a faint feeling of belonging. Thirty years ago, when the disease went hidden behind euphemism and prostheses, medicine was a solid patriarchy, women's bodies its passive objects of labor. The Women's Health Movement, in which I was an activist in the seventies and eighties, legitimized self-help and mutual support and encouraged women to network directly, sharing their stories, questioning the doctors, banding together. It is hard now to recall how revolutionary these activities once seemed, and probably few participants in breast-cancer chat rooms and message boards realize that when post-mastectomy patients first proposed meeting in support groups in the mid-1970s, the American Cancer Society responded with a firm and fatherly "no." Now no one leaves the hospital without a brochure directing her to local support groups and, at least in my case, a follow-up call from a social worker to see whether I am safely ensconced in one. This cheers me briefly, until I realize that if support groups have won the stamp of medical approval this may be because they are no longer perceived as seditious.

In fact, aside from the dilute sisterhood of the cyber (and actual) support groups, there is nothing very feminist—in an ideological or activist sense—about the mainstream of breast-cancer culture today. Let me pause to qualify: You can, if you look hard enough, find plenty of genuine, self-identified feminists within the vast pink sea of the breast-cancer crusade, women who are militantly determined to "beat the epidemic" and insistent on more user-friendly approaches to treatment. It was feminist health activists who led the campaign, in the seventies and eighties, against the most savage form of breast-cancer surgery—the Halsted radical mastectomy, which removed chest muscle and lymph nodes as well as breast tissue and left women permanently disabled. It was the Women's Health Movement that put a halt to the surgical practice, common in the seventies, of proceeding directly from biopsy to mastectomy without ever rousing the patient from anesthesia. More recently, feminist advocacy groups such as the San Francisco–based Breast Cancer Action and the Cambridge-based Women's Community Cancer Project helped blow the whistle on "high-dose chemotherapy," in which the bone marrow was removed prior to otherwise lethal doses of chemotherapy and later replaced—to no good effect, as it turned out.

Like everyone else in the breast-cancer world, the feminists want a cure, but they even more ardently demand to know the cause or causes of the disease without which we will never have any means of prevention. "Bad" genes of the inherited variety are thought to account for fewer than 10 percent of breast cancers, and only 30 percent of women diagnosed with breast cancer have any known risk factor (such as delaying childbearing or the late onset of menopause) at all. Bad lifestyle choices like a fatty diet have, after brief popularity with the medical profession, been largely ruled out. Hence suspicion should focus on environmental carcinogens, the feminists argue, such as plastics, pesticides (DDT and PCBs, for example, though banned in this country, are still used in many Third World sources of the produce we eat), and the industrial runoff in our ground water. No carcinogen has been linked definitely to human breast cancer yet, but many have been found to cause the disease in mice, and the inexorable increase of the disease in industrialized nations—about one percent a year between the 1950s and the 1990s—further hints at environmental factors, as does the fact that women migrants to industrialized countries quickly develop the same breast-cancer rates as those who are native born. Their emphasis on possible ecological factors, which is not shared by groups such as Komen and the American Cancer Society, puts the feminist breast-cancer activists in league with other, frequently rambunctious, social movements—environmental and anticorporate.

But today theirs are discordant voices in a general chorus of sentimentality and good cheer; after all, breast cancer would hardly be the darling of corporate America if its complexion changed from pink to green. It is the very blandness of breast cancer, at least in mainstream perceptions, that makes it an attractive object of corporate charity and a way for companies to brand themselves friends of the middle-aged female market. With breast cancer, "there was no concern that you might actually turn off your audience because of the life style or sexual connotations that AIDS has,"

Amy Langer, director of the National Alliance of Breast Cancer Organizations, told the *New York Times* in 1996. "That gives corporations a certain freedom and a certain relief in supporting the cause." Or as Cindy Pearson, director of the National Women's Health Network, the organizational progeny of the Women's Health Movement, puts it more caustically: "Breast cancer provides a way of doing something for women, without being feminist."

In the mainstream of breast-cancer culture, one finds very little anger, no mention of possible environmental causes, few complaints about the fact that, in all but the more advanced, metastasized cases, it is the "treatments," not the disease, that cause illness and pain. The stance toward existing treatments is occasionally critical—in Mamm, for example—but more commonly grateful; the overall tone, almost universally upbeat. The Breast Friends website, for example, features a series of inspirational quotes: "Don't Cry Over Anything that Can't Cry Over You," "I Can't Stop the Birds of Sorrow from Circling my Head, But I Can Stop Them from Building a Nest in My Hair," "When Life Hands Out Lemons, Squeeze Out a Smile," "Don't wait for your ship to come in ... Swim out to meet it," and much more of that ilk. Even in the relatively sophisticated Mamm, a columnist bemoans not cancer or chemotherapy but the end of chemotherapy, and humorously proposes to deal with her separation anxiety by pitching a tent outside her oncologist's office. So pervasive is the perkiness of the breast-cancer world that unhappiness requires a kind of apology, as when "Lucy," whose "long term prognosis is not good," starts her personal narrative on breastcancertalk.org by telling us that her story "is not the usual one, full of sweetness and hope, but true nevertheless."

There is, I discover, no single noun to describe a woman with breast cancer. As in the AIDS movement, upon which breast-cancer activism is partly modeled, the words "patient" and "victim," with their aura of self-pity and passivity, have been ruled un-P.C. Instead, we get verbs: Those who are in the midst of their treatments are described as "battling" or "fighting," sometimes intensified with "bravely" or "fiercely"—language suggestive of Katharine Hepburn with her face to the wind. Once the treatments are over, one achieves the status of "survivor," which is how the women in my local support group identify themselves, A.A.-style, as we convene to share war stories and rejoice in our "survivorhood": "Hi, I'm Kathy and I'm a three-year survivor." For those who

cease to be survivors and join the more than 40,000 American women who succumb to breast cancer each year—again, no noun applies. They are said to have "lost their battle" and may be memorialized by photographs carried at races for the cure—our lost, brave sisters, our fallen soldiers. But in the overwhelmingly Darwinian culture that has grown up around breast cancer, martyrs count for little; it is the "survivors" who merit constant honor and acclaim. They, after all, offer living proof that expensive and painful treatments may in some cases actually work.

Scared and medically weakened women can hardly be expected to transform their support groups into bands of activists and rush out into the streets, but the equanimity of breast-cancer culture goes beyond mere absence of anger to what looks, all too often, like a positive embrace of the disease. As "Mary" reports, on the Bosom Buds message board:

> I really believe I am a much more sensitive and thoughtful person now. It might sound funny but I was a real worrier before. Now I don't want to waste my energy on worrying. I enjoy life so much more now and in a lot of aspects I am much happier now.

Or this from "Andee":

> This was the hardest year of my life but also in many ways the most rewarding. I got rid of the baggage, made peace with my family, met many amazing people, learned to take very good care of my body so it will take care of me, and reprioritized my life.

Cindy Cherry, quoted in the *Washington Post*, goes further:

> If I had to do it over, would I want breast cancer? Absolutely. I'm not the same person I was, and I'm glad I'm not. Money doesn't matter anymore. I've met the most phenomenal people in my life through this. Your friends and family are what matter now.

The First Year of the Rest of Your Life, a collection of brief narratives with a foreword by Nancy Brinker and a share of the royalties going to the Komen Foundation, is filled with such testimonies to the redemptive powers of the disease: "I can honestly say I am happier now than I have ever been in my life—even before the breast cancer." "For me, breast cancer has provided a good kick in the rear to get me started rethinking my life. . . ." "I have come out stronger, with a new sense of priorities . . ." Never a complaint about lost time, shattered sexual confidence, or the long-term weakening of the arms caused by lymph-node dissection and radiation. What does not destroy you, to paraphrase Nietzsche, makes you a spunkier, more evolved, sort of person.

The effect of this relentless brightsiding is to transform breast cancer into a rite of passage—not an injustice or a tragedy to rail against, but a normal marker in the life cycle, like menopause or graying hair. Everything in mainstream breast-cancer culture serves, no doubt inadvertently, to tame and normalize the disease: the diagnosis may be disastrous, but there are those cunning pink rhinestone angel pins to buy and races to train for. Even the heavy traffic in personal narratives and practical tips, which I found so useful, bears an implicit acceptance of the disease and the current barbarous approaches to its treatment: you can get so busy comparing attractive head scarves that you forget to question a form of treatment that temporarily renders you both bald and immunoincompetent. Understood as a rite of passage, breast cancer resembles the initiation rites so exhaustively studied by Mircea Eliade: First there is the selection of the initiates—by age in the tribal situation, by mammogram or palpation here. Then come the requisite ordeals—scarification or circumcision within traditional cultures, surgery and chemotherapy for the cancer patient. Finally, the initiate emerges into a new and higher status—an adult and a warrior—or in the case of breast cancer, a "survivor."

And in our implacably optimistic breast-cancer culture, the disease offers more than the intangible benefits of spiritual upward mobility. You can defy the inevitable disfigurements and come out, on the survivor side, actually prettier, sexier, more femme. In the lore of the disease—shared with me by oncology nurses as well as by survivors—chemotherapy smoothes and tightens the skin, helps you lose weight; and, when your hair comes back, it will be fuller, softer, easier to control, and perhaps a surprising new color. These may be myths, but for those willing to get with the prevailing program, opportunities for self-improvement abound. The American Cancer Society offers the "Look Good . . . Feel Better" program, "dedicated to teaching women cancer patients beauty techniques to help restore their appearance and self-image during cancer treatment." Thirty thousand women participate a year, each copping a free makeover and bag of makeup

donated by the Cosmetic, Toiletry, and Fragrance Association, the trade association of the cosmetics industry. As for that lost breast: after reconstruction, why not bring the other one up to speed? Of the more than 50,000 mastectomy patients who opt for reconstruction each year, 17 percent go on, often at the urging of their plastic surgeons, to get additional surgery so that the remaining breast will "match" the more erect and perhaps larger new structure on the other side.

Not everyone goes for cosmetic deceptions, and the question of wigs versus baldness, reconstruction versus undisguised scar, defines one of the few real disagreements in breast-cancer culture. On the more avantgarde, upper-middle-class side, *Mamm* magazine—which features literary critic Eve Kosofsky Sedgwick as a columnist—tends to favor the "natural" look.

Here, mastectomy scars can be "sexy" and baldness something to celebrate. The January 2001 cover story features women who "looked upon their baldness not just as a loss, but also as an opportunity: to indulge their playful sides . . . to come in contact, in new ways, with their truest selves." One decorates her scalp with temporary tattoos of peace signs, panthers, and frogs; another expresses herself with a shocking purple wig; a third reports that unadorned baldness makes her feel "sensual, powerful, able to recreate myself with every new day." But no hard feelings toward those who choose to hide their condition under wigs or scarves; it's just a matter, *Mamm* tells us, of "different aesthetics." Some go for pink ribbons; others will prefer the Ralph Lauren Pink Pony breast-cancer motif. But everyone agrees that breast cancer is a chance for creative self-transformation—a makeover opportunity, in fact.

Now, cheerfulness, up to and including delusion and false hope, has a recognized place in medicine. There is plenty of evidence that depressed and socially isolated people are more prone to succumb to diseases, cancer included, and a diagnosis of cancer is probably capable of precipitating serious depression all by itself. To be told by authoritative figures that you have a deadly disease, for which no real cure exists, is to enter a liminal state fraught with perils that go well beyond the disease itself. Consider the phenomenon of "voodoo death"—described by ethnographers among, for example, Australian aborigines—in which a person who has been condemned by a suitably potent curse obligingly shuts down and dies within a day or two. Cancer diagnoses could, and in some cases probably do, have the same kind of fatally dispiriting effect. So, it could be argued, the collectively pumped-up optimism of breast-cancer culture may be just what the doctor ordered. Shop for the Cure, dress in pink-ribbon regalia, organize a run or hike—whatever gets you through the night.

But in the seamless world of breast-cancer culture, where one website links to another—from personal narratives and grassroots endeavors to the glitzy level of corporate sponsors and celebrity spokespeople— cheerfulness is more or less mandatory, dissent a kind of treason. Within this tightly knit world, attitudes are subtly adjusted, doubters gently brought back to the fold. In *The First Year of the Rest of your Life*, for example, each personal narrative is followed by a study question or tip designed to counter the slightest hint of negativity—and they are very slight hints indeed, since the collection includes no harridans, whiners, or feminist militants:

> Have you given yourself permission to acknowledge you have some anxiety or "blues" and to ask for help for your emotional well-being?
>
> Is there an area in your life of unresolved internal conflict? Is there an area where you think you might want to do some "healthy mourning"?
>
> Try keeping a list of the things you find "good about today."

As an experiment, I post a statement on the Komen.org message board, under the subject line "angry," briefly listing my own heartfelt complaints about debilitating treatments, recalcitrant insurance companies, environmental carcinogens, and, most daringly, "sappy pink ribbons." I receive a few words of encouragement in my fight with the insurance company, which has taken the position that my biopsy was a kind of optional indulgence, but mostly a chorus of rebukes. "Suzy" writes to say, "I really dislike saying you have a bad attitude towards all of this, but you do, and it's not going to help you in the least." "Mary" is a bit more tolerant, writing, "Barb, at this time in your life, it's so important to put all your energies toward a peaceful, if not happy, existence. Cancer is a rotten thing to have happen and there are no answers for any of us as to why. But to live your life, whether you have one more year or 51, in anger and bitterness is such a waste . . . I hope you can find some peace. You deserve it. We all do. God bless you and keep you in His loving care. Your sister, Mary."

"Kitty," however, thinks I've gone around the bend: "You need to run, not walk, to some counseling. . . .

Please, get yourself some help and I ask everyone on this site to pray for you so you can enjoy life to the fullest."

I do get some reinforcement from "Gerri," who has been through all the treatments and now finds herself in terminal condition: "I am also angry. All the money that is raised, all the smiling faces of survivors who make it sound like it is o.k. to have breast cancer. IT IS NOT OK!" But Gerri's message, like the others on the message board, is posted under the mocking heading "What does it mean to be a breast-cancer survivor?"

"Culture" is too weak a word to describe all this. What has grown up around breast cancer in just the last fifteen years more nearly resembles a cult—or, given that it numbers more than two million women, their families, and friends—perhaps we should say a full-fledged religion. The products—teddy bears, pink-ribbon brooches, and so forth—serve as amulets and talismans, comforting the sufferer and providing visible evidence of faith. The personal narratives serve as testimonials and follow the same general arc as the confessional autobiographies required of seventeenth-century Puritans: first there is a crisis, often involving a sudden apprehension of mortality (the diagnosis or, in the old Puritan case, a stern word from on high); then comes a prolonged ordeal (the treatment or, in the religious case, internal struggle with the Devil); and finally, the blessed certainty of salvation, or its breast-cancer equivalent, survivorhood. And like most recognized religions, breast cancer has its great epideictic events, its pilgrimages and mass gatherings where the faithful convene and draw strength from their numbers. These are the annual races for a cure, attracting a total of about a million people at more than eighty sites—70,000 of them at the largest event, in Washington, D.C., which in recent years has been attended by Dan and Marilyn Quayle and Al and Tipper Gore. Everything comes together at the races: celebrities and corporate sponsors are showcased; products are hawked; talents, like those of the "Swinging, Singing Survivors" from Syracuse, New York, are displayed. It is at the races, too, that the elect confirm their special status. As one participant wrote in the *Washington Post*:

> I have taken my "battle scarred" breasts to the Mall, donned the pink shirt, visor, pink shoelaces, etc. and walked proudly among my fellow veterans of the breast cancer war. In 1995, at the age of 44, I was diagnosed and treated for Stage II breast cancer. The experience continues to redefine my life.

Feminist breast-cancer activists, who in the early nineties were organizing their own mass outdoor events—demonstrations, not races—to demand increased federal funding for research, tend to keep their distance from these huge, corporate-sponsored, pink gatherings. Ellen Leopold, for example—a member of the Women's Community Cancer Project in Cambridge and author of *A Darker Ribbon: Breast Cancer, Women, and Their Doctors in the Twentieth century*—has criticized the races as an inefficient way of raising money. She points out that the Avon Breast Cancer Crusade, which sponsors three-day, sixty-mile walks, spends more than a third of the money raised on overhead and advertising, and Komen may similarly fritter away up to 25 percent of its gross. At least one corporate-charity insider agrees. "It would be much easier and more productive," says Rob Wilson, an organizer of charitable races for corporate clients, "if people, instead of running or riding, would write out a check to the charity."

To true believers, such criticisms miss the point, which is always, ultimately, "awareness." Whatever you do to publicize the disease—wear a pink ribbon, buy a teddy, attend a race—reminds other women to come forward for their mammograms. Hence, too, they would argue, the cult of the "survivor": If women neglect their annual screenings, it must be because they are afraid that a diagnosis amounts to a death sentence. Beaming survivors, proudly displaying their athletic prowess, are the best possible advertisement for routine screening mammograms, early detection, and the ensuing round of treatments. Yes, miscellaneous businesses—from tiny distributors of breast-cancer wind chimes and note cards to major corporations seeking a woman-friendly image—benefit in the process, not to mention the breast-cancer industry itself, the estimated $12–16 billion-a-year business in surgery, "breast health centers," chemotherapy "infusion suites," radiation treatment centers, mammograms, and drugs ranging from anti-emetics (to help you survive the nausea of chemotherapy) to tamoxifen (the hormonal treatment for women with estrogen-sensitive tumors). But what's to complain about? Seen through pink-tinted lenses, the entire breast-cancer enterprise—from grassroots support groups and websites to the corporate providers of therapies and sponsors of races—looks like a beautiful example of synergy at work: cult activities, paraphernalia, and testimonies encourage women to undergo the diagnostic

procedures, and since a fraction of these diagnoses will be positive, this means more members for the cult as well as more customers for the corporations, both those that provide medical products and services and those that offer charitable sponsorships.

But this view of a life-giving synergy is only as sound as the science of current detection and treatment modalities, and, tragically, that science is fraught with doubt, dissension, and what sometimes looks very much like denial. Routine screening mammograms, for example, are the major goal of "awareness," as when Rosie O'Donnell exhorts us to go out and "get squished." But not all breast-cancer experts are as enthusiastic. At best the evidence for the salutary effects of routine mammograms—as opposed to breast self-examination—is equivocal, with many respectable large-scale studies showing a vanishingly small impact on overall breast-cancer mortality. For one thing, there are an estimated two to four false positives for every cancer detected, leading thousands of healthy women to go through unnecessary biopsies and anxiety. And even if mammograms were 100 percent accurate, the admirable goal of "early" detection is more elusive than the current breast-cancer dogma admits. A small tumor, detectable only by mammogram, is not necessarily young and innocuous; if it has not spread to the lymph nodes, which is the only form of spreading detected in the common surgical procedure of lymph-node dissection, it may have already moved on to colonize other organs via the bloodstream. David Plotkin, director of the Memorial Cancer Research Foundation of Southern California, concludes that the benefits of routine mammography "are not well established; if they do exist, they are not as great as many women hope." Alan Spievack, a surgeon recently retired from the Harvard Medical School, goes further, concluding from his analysis of dozens of studies that routine screening mammography is, in the words of famous British surgeon Dr. Michael Baum, "one of the greatest deceptions perpetrated on the women of the Western world."

Even if foolproof methods for early detection existed,[2] they would, at the present time, serve only as portals to treatments offering dubious protection and considerable collateral damage. Some women diagnosed with breast cancer will live long enough to die of something else, and some of these lucky ones will indeed owe their longevity to a combination of surgery, chemotherapy, radiation, and/or anti-estrogen drugs such as tamoxifen. Others, though, would have lived untreated or with surgical excision alone, either because their cancers were slow-growing or because their bodies' own defenses were successful. Still others will die of the disease no matter what heroic, cell-destroying therapies are applied. The trouble is, we do not have the means to distinguish between these three groups. So for many of the thousands of women who are diagnosed each year, Plotkin notes, "the sole effect of early detection has been to stretch out the time in which the woman bears the knowledge of her condition." These women do not live longer than they might have without any medical intervention, but more of the time they do live is overshadowed with the threat of death and wasted in debilitating treatments.

To the extent that current methods of detection and treatment fail or fall short, America's breast-cancer cult can be judged as an outbreak of mass delusion, celebrating survivorhood by downplaying mortality and promoting obedience to medical protocols known to have limited efficacy. And although we may imagine ourselves to be well past the era of patriarchal medicine, obedience is the message behind the infantilizing theme in breast-cancer culture, as represented by the teddy bears, the crayons, and the prevailing pinkness. You are encouraged to regress to a little-girl state, to suspend critical judgment, and to accept whatever measures the doctors, as parent surrogates, choose to impose.

Worse, by ignoring or underemphasizing the vexing issue of environmental causes, the breast-cancer cult turns women into dupes of what could be called the Cancer Industrial Complex: the multinational corporate enterprise that with the one hand doles out carcinogens and disease and, with the other, offers expensive, semi-toxic pharmaceutical treatments. Breast Cancer Awareness Month, for example, is sponsored by AstraZeneca (the manufacturer of tamoxifen), which, until a corporate reorganization in 2000, was a leading producer of pesticides, including acetochlor, classified by the EPA as a "probable human carcinogen." This particularly nasty conjuncture of interests led the environmentally oriented Cancer Prevention Coalition (CPC) to condemn Breast Cancer Awareness Month as "a public relations invention by a major polluter which puts women in the position of being unwitting allies of the very people who make them sick." Although AstraZeneca no longer manufactures

pesticides, CPC has continued to criticize the breast-cancer crusade—and the American Cancer Society for its unquestioning faith in screening mammograms and careful avoidance of environmental issues. In a June 12, 2001, press release, CPC chairman Samuel S. Epstein, M.D., and the well-known physician activist Quentin Young castigated the American Cancer Society for its "longstanding track record of indifference and even hostility to cancer prevention. . . . Recent examples include issuing a joint statement with the Chlorine Institute justifying the continued global use of persistent organochlorine pesticides, and also supporting the industry in trivializing dietary pesticide residues as avoidable risks of childhood cancer. ACS policies are further exemplified by allocating under 0.1 percent of its $700 million annual budget to environmental and occupational causes of cancer."

In the harshest judgment, the breast-cancer cult serves as an accomplice in global poisoning—normalizing cancer, prettying it up, even presenting it, perversely, as a positive and enviable experience.

When, my three months of chemotherapy completed, the oncology nurse calls to congratulate me on my "excellent blood work results," I modestly demur. I didn't do anything, I tell her, anything but endure—marking the days off on the calendar, living on Protein Revolution canned vanilla health shakes, escaping into novels and work. Courtesy restrains me from mentioning the fact that the tumor markers she's tested for have little prognostic value, that there's no way to know how many rebel cells survived chemotherapy and may be carving out new colonies right now. She insists I should be proud; I'm a survivor now and entitled to recognition at the Relay for Life being held that very evening in town.

So I show up at the middle-school track where the relay's going on just in time for the Survivors' March: about 100 people, including a few men, since the funds raised will go to cancer research in general, are marching around the track eight to twelve abreast while a loudspeaker announces their names and survival times and a thin line of observers, mostly people staffing the raffle and food booths, applauds. It could be almost any kind of festivity, except for the distinctive stacks of cellophane-wrapped pink Hope Bears for sale in some of the booths. I cannot help but like the funky small-town Gemutlichkeit of the event, especially when the audio system strikes up that universal anthem of solidarity, "We Are Family," and a few people of various ages start twisting to the music on the gerry-rigged stage. But the money raised is going far away, to the American Cancer Society, which will not be asking us for our advice on how to spend it.

I approach a woman I know from other settings, one of our local intellectuals, as it happens, decked out here in a pink-and-yellow survivor T-shirt and with an American Cancer Society "survivor medal" suspended on a purple ribbon around her neck. "When do you date your survivorship from?" I ask her, since the announced time, five and a half years, seems longer than I recall. "From diagnosis or the completion of your treatments?" The question seems to annoy or confuse her, so I do not press on to what I really want to ask: At what point, in a downwardly sloping breast-cancer career, does one put aside one's survivor regalia and admit to being in fact a die-er? For the dead are with us even here, though in much diminished form. A series of paper bags, each about the right size for a junior burger and fries, lines the track. On them are the names of the dead, and inside each is a candle that will be lit later, after dark, when the actual relay race begins.

My friend introduces me to a knot of other women in survivor gear, breast-cancer victims all, I learn, though of course I would not use the V-word here. "Does anyone else have trouble with the term 'survivor'?" I ask, and, surprisingly, two or three speak up. It could be "unlucky," one tells me; it "tempts fate,"

says another, shuddering slightly. After all, the cancer can recur at any time, either in the breast or in some more strategic site. No one brings up my own objection to the term, though: that the mindless triumphalism of "survivorhood" denigrates the dead and the dying. Did we who live "fight" harder than those who've died? Can we claim to be "braver," better, people than the dead? And why is there no room in this cult for some gracious acceptance of death, when the time comes, which it surely will, through cancer or some other misfortune?

No, this is not my sisterhood. For me at least, breast cancer will never be a source of identity or pride. As my dying correspondent Gerri wrote: "IT IS NOT O.K.!" What it is, along with cancer generally or any slow and painful way of dying, is an abomination, and, to the extent that it's manmade, also a crime. This is the one great truth that I bring out of the breast-cancer experience, which did not, I can now report, make me prettier or stronger, more feminine or spiritual—only more deeply angry. What sustained me through the "treatments" is a purifying rage, a resolve, framed in the sleepless nights of chemotherapy, to see the last polluter, along with, say, the last smug health-insurance operative, strangled with the last pink ribbon. Cancer or no cancer, I will not live that long of course. But I know this much right now for sure: I will not go into that last good night with a teddy bear tucked under my arm.

NOTES

1. In the United States, one in eight women will be diagnosed with breast cancer at some point. The chances of her surviving for five years are 86.8 percent. For a black woman this falls to 72 percent; and for a woman of any race whose cancer has spread to the lymph nodes, to 77.7 percent.

2. Some improved prognostic tools, involving measuring a tumor's growth rate and the extent to which it is supplied with blood vessels, are being developed but are not yet in use.

STOLEN BODIES, RECLAIMED BODIES: DISABILITY AND QUEERNESS

Eli Clare

I want to write about the body, not as a metaphor, symbol, or representation, but simply as the body. To write about my body, our bodies, in all their messy, complicated realities. I want words shaped by my slurring tongue, shaky hands, almost steady breath; words shaped by the fact that I am a walkie—someone for whom a flight of stairs without an accompanying elevator poses no problem—and by the reality that many of the people I encounter in my daily life assume I am "mentally retarded." Words shaped by how my body—and I certainly mean to include the mind as part of the body—moves through the world.

Sometimes we who are activists and thinkers forget about our bodies, ignore our bodies, or reframe our bodies to fit our theories and political strategies. For several decades now, activists in a variety of social change movements, ranging from black civil rights to women's liberation, from disability rights to queer liberation, have said repeatedly that the problems faced by any marginalized group of people lie, not in their bodies, but in the oppression they face. But in defining the external, collective, material nature of social injustice as separate from the body, we have sometimes ended up sidelining the profound relationships that connect our bodies with who we are and how we experience oppression.

. . .

Disentangling the body from the problems of social injustice has served the disability rights movement well. The dominant paradigms of disability—the medical, charity, supercrip, and moral models—all turn disability into problems faced by individual people, locate those problems in out bodies, and define those bodies as wrong. The medical model insists on disability as a disease or condition that is curable and/or treatable. The charity model declares disability to be a tragedy, a misfortune, that must be tempered or erased by generous giving. The supercrip model frames disability as a challenge to overcome and disabled people as superheroes just for living our daily lives. The moral model transforms disability into a sign of moral weakness. . . .

In resistance to this, the disability rights movement has created a new model of disability, one that places emphasis on how the world treats disabled people: Disability, not defined by our bodies, but rather by the material and social conditions of ableism; not by the need to use a wheelchair, but rather by the stairs that have no accompanying ramp or elevator. Disability activists fiercely declare that it's not our bodies that need curing. Rather, it is ableism—disability oppression, as reflected in high unemployment rates, lack of access, gawking, substandard education, being forced to live in nursing homes and back rooms, being seen as childlike and asexual—that needs changing. . . .

. . .

Irrevocable difference could be a cause for celebration, but in this world it isn't. The price we pay for variation from the norm that's defined and upheld by white supremacy, patriarchy, and capitalism is incredibly high. And in my life, that price has been body centered. I came to believe that my body was utterly wrong. Sometimes I wanted to cut off my right arm so it wouldn't shake. My shame was that plain, that bleak. Of course, this is one of the profound ways in which oppression works—to mire us in body hatred. Homophobia is all about defining queer bodies as wrong, perverse, immoral. Transphobia, about defining trans bodies as unnatural, monstrous, or the product of delusion. Ableism, about defining disabled bodies as broken and tragic. Class warfare, about defining the bodies of workers as expendable. Racism, about defining the bodies of people of color as primitive, exotic, or worthless. Sexism, about defining female bodies as pliable objects. These messages sink beneath our skin.

There are so many ways oppression and social injustice can mark a body, steal a body, feed lies and poison to a body. I think of the kid tracked into "special education" because of his speech

(continued)

impediment, which is actually a common sign of sexual abuse. I think of the autoimmune diseases, the cancers, the various kinds of chemical sensitivities that flag what it means to live in a world full of toxins. I think of the folks who live with work-related disabilities because of exploitative, dangerous work conditions. I think of the people who live downwind of nuclear fallout, the people who die for lack of access to health care, the rape survivors who struggle with post-traumatic stress disorder. The list goes on and on.

The stolen bodies, the bodies taken for good, rise up around me. Rebecca Wight, a lesbian, shot and killed as she hiked the Appalachian Trail with her lover. James Byrd Jr., an African American, dragged to death behind a pickup driven by white men. Tyra Hunter, a transgendered person living as a woman, left to bleed to death on the streets of D.C. because the EMT crew discovered she had a penis and stopped their work. Tracy Latimer, a twelve-year-old girl with severe cerebral palsy, killed by her father, who said he did it only to end her unbearable suffering. Bodies stolen for good. Other bodies live on—numb, abandoned, full of self-hate, trauma, grief, aftershock. The pernicious stereotypes, lies, and false images can haunt a body, stealing it away as surely as bullets do.

But just as the body can be stolen, it can also be reclaimed. The bodies irrevocably taken from us, we can memorialize in quilts, granite walls, and candlelight vigils. We can remember and mourn them, use their deaths to strengthen our will. And as for the lies and false images: we need to name them, transform them, create something entirely new in their place. Something that comes close and finally true to the bone, entering our bodies as liberation, as joy, as fury, as a will to refigure the world. ...

. . .

In the end, I am asking that we pay attention to our bodies—our stolen bodies and our reclaimed bodies. To the wisdom that tells us the causes of the injustice we face lie outside our bodies, and also to the profound relationships our bodies have to that injustice, to the ways our identities are inextricably linked to our bodies. We need to do this because there are disability activists so busy defining disability as an external social condition that they neglect the daily realities of our bodies: the reality of living with chronic pain; the reality of needing personal attendants to help us pee and shit (and of being at once grateful for those PAs and deeply regretting our lack of privacy); the reality of disliking the very adaptive equipment that makes our day-to-day lives possible. We need to do this because there are disability thinkers who can talk all day about the body as metaphor and symbol but never mention flesh, and blood, bone and tendon—never even acknowledge their own bodies. We need to do this because without our bodies, without the lived bodily experience of identity and oppression, we won't truly be able to refigure the world. . . .

SECTION 9

Violence against Women

Violence against women manifests itself in many forms. Verbal harassment, sexual imposition, sexual assault, rape, domestic battering, lesbian bashing, and child abuse all contribute to a social climate that encourages women to comply with men's desires or to restrict their activities in order to avoid assault. The threat of violence against women is pervasive across cultures. In addition to violence against women and girls, other forms of violence—against gay men (or those presumed to be gay), boys, people of color, and transgendered people—serve to reinforce the subordination of those groups and, often, reinforce the notion that transgressing acceptable boundaries of gender is risky and dangerous. Feminist analyses of violence against women focus on the extent to which violence serves as a means for the institutionalized control of women, children, and sexual minorities by men. The articles in this section analyze various forms of violence against women and contrast beliefs and actualities about various kinds of male violence. Often, sexist ideologies encourage us to accept violence against women as either harmless or deserved. Feminist analyses take the position that this violence constitutes a system through which men frighten and therefore control and dominate women.

Patricia Yancey Martin and Robert A. Hummer also explore the implications of heterosexual male bonding in "Fraternities and Rape on Campus." Fraternity members' negative attitudes toward women, rigid ideas about masculinity, and pressures to demonstrate simultaneously their heterosexuality and their utter loyalty to the "brotherhood" create fraternity cultures in which men use women to prove their masculinity and

worth. What are some other social contexts in which similar pressures for men to be hypermasculine exist?

Hate crimes are crimes motivated by prejudice against particular groups. Because violence against women is so widespread, we sometimes fail to recognize it as a crime of hate. Gloria Steinem argues that mass killings in schools such as Columbine, Colorado, and Jonesboro, Arkansas; serial killings by criminals such as Edmond Kemper and Son of Sam; and other multiple sadistic killings of strangers are linked to male domination. In "Supremacy Crimes," Steinem argues that we should regard most such crimes not as individual and apolitical assaults by deranged men. Rather, they are crimes against women as a group, committed for the most part by white heterosexual males and motivated by men's desire for power and superiority. Think about the coverage of the mass killings in schools that occurred at the end of the 1990s. Did the media acknowledge the gender of the killers and most of the victims and the role gender might have played in what happened?

Violence against women is shaped by the intersections between race, class, and gender. In "Mapping the Margins: Intersectionality, Identity Politics, and Violence against Women of Color," Kimberlé Crenshaw examines the relationship between gender and race in domestic violence. Domestic violence, she shows, is shaped by race in several ways. First, there are proscriptions within communities of color against publicizing or politicizing domestic violence, out of the fear of reinforcing stereotypes of black men as violent. Controversy over feminism (often seen as a white movement) and reluctance to report violence to an often-racist police force further contribute to the problem. At the same time, efforts to address domestic violence by feminists and policy makers often either ignore women of color or include them in a tokenistic way. Services to help women who are battered, such as shelters, are often inaccessible to women of color because of language barriers or the lack of incorporation of women of color into leadership positions in shelters. What does Crenshaw suggest would be necessary to address domestic violence more effectively in all communities? To what extent do the other readings in this section use an intersectional approach to violence, taking into account how it is shaped by race as well as gender?

Violence against women, as all these articles point out, is not simply the act of individual men against individual women. Instead, it is created and perpetuated by social institutions. In the final article in this section, "Sex and War: Fighting Men, Comfort Women, and the Military-Sexual Complex," Joane Nagel discusses the many ways that violence against women is related to military organizations and ethnic conflict. These include Korean prostitution—around military bases in South Korea and within the United States—and similar sexual dynamics around other military bases. Reinforcing both the masculinity of U.S. soldiers and the exoticized sexual image of the women, prostitution serves many interests, Nagel argues. During wartime, Nagel argues that rape is one weapon in ethnic conflicts, and serves not only to attack the women who are raped but also to "terrorize and humiliate" the enemy as a whole. According to UN reports, Serbian soldiers systematically raped and tortured Bosnian women as a tool of war, and the hearings surrounding these horrific events have begun to raise international awareness about sexual assault as a violation of human rights.

Despite the overt nature of sex crimes during war, Nagel contends that sex is militarized during peacetime as well, through the network of military bases, which she argues have institutionalized prostitution on a large scale around the world. In general, Nagel points out, these sexual relationships occur between military members and local residents who are seen as different, other, because of their race, ethnicity, and nationality. These "ethnosexual" industries also exist outside the military. Building from the prostitution and "entertainment" networks created during the Vietnam War, a large sex tourism industry has arisen in Thailand which now serves men from Japan, Europe, Australia, and the United States. For Nagel, the dynamics and industries she describes are not simply a manifestation of male dominance over women, but are a sexualization of ethnic dominance, a "sexual means to an ethnic end."

Can you identify other instances of the sexualization of ethnic difference and conflict? What is the role and existence of prostitution in your own community, and in what ways is it shaped by ethnic inequalities? Locate news accounts of recent developments in the UN-sponsored International Criminal Tribunals dealing with Rwanda or the former Yugoslavia. How are sexual assaults discussed in these hearings, and what are the attitudes exhibited toward these assaults? What evidence is there of the use of sexual violence in the Iraq War? What effects would you expect the Iraq War to have on what Nagel calls the "military-sexual complex"? How is rape in wartime similar to and different from rape in the contexts described in the other articles in this section?

READING *38* **Patricia Yancey Martin**
Robert A. Hummer

Fraternities and Rape on Campus

Rapes are perpetrated on dates, at parties, in chance encounters, and in specially planned circumstances. That group structure and processes, rather than individual values or characteristics, are the impetus for many rape episodes was documented by Blanchard (1959) thirty years ago (also see Geis 1971), yet sociologists have failed to pursue this theme (for an exception, see Chancer 1987). A recent review of research (Muehlenhard and Linton 1987) on sexual violence, or rape, devotes only a few pages to the situational contexts of rape events, and these are conceptualized as potential risk factors for individuals rather than qualities of rape-prone social contexts.

Many rapes, far more than come to the public's attention, occur in fraternity houses on college and university campuses, yet little research has analyzed fraternities at American colleges and universities as rape-prone contexts (cf. Ehrhart and Sandler 1985). Most of the research on fraternities reports on samples of individual fraternity men. One group of studies compares the values, attitudes, perceptions, family socioeconomic status, psychological traits (aggressiveness, dependence), and so on, of fraternity and nonfraternity men (Bohrnstedt 1969; Fox, Hodge, and Ward 1987; Kanin 1967; Lemire 1979; Miller 1973). A second group attempts to identify the effects of fraternity membership over time on the values, attitudes, beliefs, or moral precepts of members (Hughes and Winston 1987; Marlowe and Auvenshine 1982; Miller 1973; Wilder, Hoyt, Doren, Hauck, and Zettle 1978; Wilder, Hoyt, Surbeck, Wilder, and Carney 1986). With minor exceptions, little research addresses the group and organizational context of fraternities or the social construction of fraternity life (for exceptions, see Letchworth 1969; Longino and Kart 1973; Smith 1964).

Gary Tash, writing as an alumnus and trial attorney in his fraternity's magazine, claims that over 90 percent of all gang rapes on college campuses involve fraternity men (1988, p. 2). Tash provides no evidence to substantiate this claim, but students of violence against women have been concerned with fraternity men's frequently reported involvement in rape episodes (Adams and Abarbanel 1988). Ehrhart and Sandler (1985) identify over fifty cases of gang rapes on campus perpetrated by fraternity men, and their analysis points to many of the conditions that we discuss here. Their analysis is unique in focusing on conditions in fraternities that make gang rapes of women by fraternity men both feasible and probable. They identify excessive alcohol use, isolation from external monitoring, treatment of women as prey, use of pornography, approval of violence, and excessive concern with competition as precipitating conditions to gang rape (also see Merton 1985; Roark 1987).

The study reported here confirmed and complemented these findings by focusing on both conditions and processes. We examined dynamics associated with the social construction of fraternity life, with a focus on processes that foster the use of coercion, including rape, in fraternity men's relations with women. Our examination of men's social fraternities on college and university campuses as groups and organizations led us to conclude that fraternities are a physical and sociocultural context that encourages the sexual coercion of women. We make no claims that all fraternities are "bad" or that all fraternity men are rapists. Our observations indicated, however, that rape is especially probable in fraternities because of the kinds of organizations they are, the kinds of members they have, the practices their members engage in, and a virtual absence of university or community oversight. Analyses that lay blame for rapes by fraternity men on "peer pressure" are, we feel, overly simplistic (cf. Burkhart 1989; Walsh 1989). We suggest, rather, that fraternities create a sociocultural context in which the use of coercion in sexual relations with women is normative and in which the mechanisms to keep this pattern of behavior in check are minimal at best and absent at worst. We conclude that unless fraternities change in fundamental ways, little improvement can be expected.

417

METHODOLOGY

Our goal was to analyze the group and organizational practices and conditions that create in fraternities an abusive social context for women. We developed a conceptual framework from an initial case study of an alleged gang rape at Florida State University that involved four fraternity men and an eighteen-year-old coed. The group rape took place on the third floor of a fraternity house and ended with the "dumping" of the woman in the hallway of a neighboring fraternity house. According to newspaper accounts, the victim's blood-alcohol concentration, when she was discovered, was .349 percent, more than three times the legal limit for automobile driving and an almost lethal amount. One law enforcement officer reported that sexual intercourse occurred during the time the victim was unconscious: "She was in a life-threatening situation" (*Tallahassee Democrat* 1988b). When the victim was found, she was comatose and had suffered multiple scratches and abrasions. Crude words and a fraternity symbol had been written on her thighs (*Tampa Tribune* 1988). When law enforcement officials tried to investigate the case, fraternity members refused to cooperate. This led, eventually, to a five-year ban of the fraternity from campus by the university and by the fraternity's national organization.

In trying to understand how such an event could have occurred, and how a group of over 150 members (exact figures are unknown because the fraternity refused to provide a membership roster) could hold rank, deny knowledge of the event, and allegedly lie to a grand jury, we analyzed newspaper articles about the case and conducted open-ended interviews with a variety of respondents about the case and about fraternities, rapes, alcohol use, gender relations, and sexual activities on campus. Our data included over 100 newspaper articles on the initial gang rape case; open-ended interviews with Greek (social fraternity and sorority) and non-Greek (independent) students ($n = 20$); university administrators ($n = 8$, five men, three women); and alumni advisers to Greek organizations ($n = 6$). Open-ended interviews were held also with judges, public and private defense attorneys, victim advocates, and state prosecutors regarding the processing of sexual assault cases. Data were analyzed using the grounded theory method (Glaser 1978; Martin and Turner 1986). In the following analysis, concepts generated from the data analysis are integrated with the literature on men's social fraternities, sexual coercion, and related issues.

FRATERNITIES AND THE SOCIAL CONSTRUCTION OF MEN AND MASCULINITY

Our research indicated that fraternities are vitally concerned—more than with anything else—with masculinity (cf. Kanin 1967). They work hard to create a macho image and context and try to avoid any suggestion of "wimpishness," effeminacy, and homosexuality. Valued members display, or are willing to go along with, a narrow conception of masculinity that stresses competition, athleticism, dominance, winning, conflict, wealth, material possessions, willingness to drink alcohol, and sexual prowess vis-à-vis women.

Valued Qualities of Members

When fraternity members talked about the kind of pledges they prefer, a litany of stereotypical and narrowly masculine attributes and behaviors was recited and feminine or woman-associated qualities and behaviors were expressly denounced (cf. Merton 1985). Fraternities seek men who are "athletic," "big guys," good in intramural competition, "who can talk college sports." Males "who are willing to drink alcohol," "who drink socially," or "who can hold their liquor" are sought. Alcohol and activities associated with the recreational use of alcohol are cornerstones of fraternity social life. Nondrinkers are viewed with skepticism and rarely selected for membership.[1]

Fraternities try to avoid "geeks," nerds, and men said to give the fraternity a "wimpy" or "gay" reputation. Art, music, and humanities majors, majors in traditional women's fields (nursing, home economics, social work, education), men with long hair, and those whose appearance or dress violate current norms are rejected. Clean-cut, handsome men who dress well (are clean, neat, conforming, fashionable) are preferred. One sorority woman commented that "the top-ranking fraternities have the best looking guys."

One fraternity man, a senior, said his fraternity recruited "some big guys, very athletic" over a two-year period to help overcome its image of wimpiness. His fraternity had won the interfraternity competition for highest grade-point average several years running but was looked down on as "wimpy, dancy, even gay." With their bigger, more athletic recruits, "our reputation improved; we're a much more recognized fraternity now." Thus a fraternity's reputation and status depend on members' possession of stereotypically masculine qualities. Good grades, campus leadership, and community service are "nice" but masculinity dominance—for example, in athletic events, physical size of members, athleticism of members—counts most.

Certain social skills are valued. Men are sought who "have good personalities," are friendly, and "have the ability to relate to girls" (cf. Longino and Kart 1973). One fraternity man, a junior, said: "We watch a guy [a potential pledge] talk to women . . . we want guys who can relate to girls." Assessing a pledge's ability to talk to women is, in part, a preoccupation with homosexuality and a conscious avoidance of men who seem to have effeminate manners or qualities. If a member is suspected of being gay, he is ostracized and informally drummed out of the fraternity. A fraternity with a reputation as wimpy or tolerant of gays is ridiculed and shunned by other fraternities. Militant heterosexuality is frequently used by men as a strategy to keep each other in line (Kimmel 1987).

Financial affluence or wealth, a male-associated value in American culture, is highly valued by fraternities. In accounting for why the fraternity involved in the gang rape that precipitated our research project had been recognized recently as "the best fraternity chapter in the United States," a university official said: "They were good-looking, a big fraternity, had lots of BMWs [expensive, German-made automobiles]." After the rape, newspaper stories described the fraternity members' affluence, noting the high number of members who owned expensive cars (*St. Petersburg Times* 1988).

The Status and Norms of Pledgeship

A pledge (sometimes called an associate member) is a new recruit who occupies a trial membership status for a specific period of time. The pledge period (typically ranging from ten to fifteen weeks) gives fraternity brothers an opportunity to assess and socialize new recruits. Pledges evaluate the fraternity also and decide if they want to become brothers. The socialization experience is structured partly through assignment of a Big Brother to each pledge. Big Brothers are expected to teach pledges how to become a brother and to support them as they progress through the trial membership period. Some pledges are repelled by the pledging experience, which can entail physical abuse; harsh discipline; and demands to be subordinate, follow orders, and engage in demeaning routines and activities, similar to those used by the military to "make men out of boys" during boot camp.

Characteristics of the pledge experience are rationalized by fraternity members as necessary to help

pledges unite into a group, rely on each other, and join together against outsiders. The process is highly masculinist in execution as well as conception. A willingness to submit to authority, follow orders, and do as one is told is viewed as a sign of loyalty, togetherness, and unity. Fraternity pledges who find the pledge process offensive often drop out. Some do this by openly quitting, which can subject them to ridicule by brothers and other pledges, or they may deliberately fail to make the grades necessary for initiation or transfer schools and decline to reaffiliate with the fraternity on the new campus. One fraternity pledge who quit the fraternity he had pledged described an experience during pledgeship as follows:

> This one guy was always picking on me. No matter what I did, I was wrong. One night after dinner, he and two other guys called me and two other pledges into the chapter room. He said, "Here, X, hold this 25-pound bag of ice at arms' length 'til I tell you to stop." I did it even though my arms and hands were killing me. When I asked if I could stop, he grabbed me around the throat and lifted me off the floor. I thought he would choke me to death. He cussed me and called me all kinds of names. He took one of my fingers and twisted it until it nearly broke. . . . I stayed in the fraternity for a few more days, but then I decided to quit. I hated it. Those guys are sick. They like seeing you suffer.

Fraternities' emphasis on toughness, withstanding pain and humiliation, obedience to superiors, and using physical force to obtain compliance contributes to an interpersonal style that de-emphasizes caring and sensitivity but fosters intragroup trust and loyalty. If the least macho or most critical pledges drop out, those who remain may be more receptive to, and influenced by, masculinist values and practices that encourage the use of force in sexual relations with women and the covering up of such behavior (cf. Kanin 1967).

Norms and Dynamics of Brotherhood

Brother is the status occupied by fraternity men to indicate their relations to each other and their membership in a particular fraternity organization or group. Brother is a male-specific status; only males can become brothers, although women can become "Little Sisters," a form of pseudomembership. "Becoming a brother" is a rite of passage that follows the consistent and often lengthy display by pledges of appropriately masculine qualities and behaviors. Brothers have a quasifamilial relationship with each other, are normatively said to share bonds of closeness and support, and are sharply set off from nonmembers. Brotherhood is a loosely defined term used to represent the bonds that develop among fraternity members and the obligations and expectations incumbent upon them (cf. Marlowe and Auvenshine [1982] on fraternities' failure to encourage "moral development" in freshman pledges).

Some of our respondents talked about brotherhood in almost reverential terms, viewing it as the most valuable benefit of fraternity membership. One senior, a business-school major who had been affiliated with a fairly high-status fraternity throughout four years on campus, said:

> Brotherhood spurs friendship for life, which I consider its best aspect, although I didn't see it that way when I joined. Brotherhood bonds and unites. It instills values of caring about one another, caring about community, caring about ourselves. The values and bonds [of brotherhood] continually develop over the four years [in college] while normal friendships come and go.

Despite this idealization, most aspects of fraternity practice and conception are more mundane. Brotherhood often plays itself out as an overriding concern with masculinity and, by extension, femininity. As a consequence, fraternities comprise collectivities of highly masculinized men with attitudinal qualities and behavioral norms that predispose them to sexual coercion of women (cf. Kanin 1967; Merton 1985; Rapaport and Burkhart 1984). The norms of masculinity are complemented by conceptions of women and femininity that are equally distorted and stereotyped and that may enhance the probability of women's exploitation (cf. Ehrhart and Sandler 1985; Sanday 1981, 1986).

Practices of Brotherhood

Practices associated with fraternity brotherhood that contribute to the sexual coercion of women include a preoccupation with loyalty, group protection and secrecy, use of alcohol as a weapon, involvement in violence and physical force, and an emphasis on competition and superiority.

Loyalty, Group Protection, and Secrecy　　Loyalty is a fraternity preoccupation. Members are reminded constantly to be loyal to the fraternity and to their brothers. Among other ways, loyalty is played out in the practices of group protection and secrecy. The fraternity must be shielded from criticism. Members are admonished to avoid getting the fraternity in trouble and to bring all problems "to the chapter" (local branch of a national social fraternity) rather than to outsiders. Fraternities try to protect themselves from close scrutiny and criticism by the Interfraternity Council (a quasigoverning body composed of representatives from all social fraternities on campus), their fraternity's national office, university officials, law enforcement, the media, and the public. Protection of the fraternity often takes precedence over what is procedurally, ethically, or legally correct. Numerous examples were related to us of fraternity brothers' lying to outsiders to "protect the fraternity."

Group protection was observed in the alleged gang rape case with which we began our study. Except for one brother, a rapist who turned state's evidence, the entire remaining fraternity membership was accused by university and criminal justice officials of lying to protect the fraternity. Members consistently failed to cooperate even though the alleged crimes were felonies, involved only four men (two of whom were not even members of the local chapter), and the victim of the crime nearly died. According to a grand jury's findings, fraternity officers repeatedly broke appointments with law enforcement officials, refused to provide police with a list of members, and refused to cooperate with police and prosecutors investigating the case (*Florida Flambeau* 1988).

Secrecy is a priority value and practice in fraternities, partly because full-fledged membership is premised on it (for confirmation, see Ehrhart and Sandler 1985; Longino and Kart 1973; Roark 1987). Secrecy is also a boundary-maintaining mechanism, demarcating in-group from out-group, us from them. Secret rituals, handshakes, and mottoes are revealed to pledge brothers as they are initiated into full brotherhood. Since only brothers are supposed to know a fraternity's secrets, such knowledge affirms membership in the fraternity and separates a brother from others. Extending secrecy tactics from protection of private knowledge to protection of the fraternity from criticism is a predictable development. Our interviews indicated that individual members knew the difference between right and wrong, but fraternity norms that emphasize loyalty, group protection, and secrecy often overrode standards of ethical correctness.

Alcohol as Weapon　　Alcohol use by fraternity men is normative. They use it on weekdays to relax after class and on weekends to "get drunk," "get crazy," and "get laid." The use of alcohol to obtain sex from women is pervasive—in other words, it is used as a weapon against sexual reluctance. According to several fraternity men whom we interviewed, alcohol is the major tool used to gain sexual mastery over women (cf. Adams and Abarbanel 1988; Ehrhart and Sandler 1985). One fraternity man, a twenty-one-year-old senior, described alcohol use to gain sex as follows: "There are girls that you know will fuck, then some you have to put some effort into it. . . . You have to buy them drinks or find out if she's drunk enough."

A similar strategy is used collectively. A fraternity man said that at parties with Little Sisters: "We provide them with 'hunch punch' and things get wild. We get them drunk and most of the guys end up with one." "'Hunch punch,'" he said, "is a girls' drink made up of overproof alcohol and powdered Kool-Aid, no water or anything, just ice. It's very strong. Two cups will do a number on a female." He had plans in the next academic term to surreptitiously give hunch punch to women in a "prim and proper" sorority because "having sex with prim and proper sorority girls is definitely a goal." These women are a challenge because they "won't openly consume alcohol and won't get openly drunk as hell." Their sororities have "standards committees" that forbid heavy drinking and easy sex.

In the gang rape case, our sources said that many fraternity men on campus believed the victim had a drinking problem and was thus an "easy make." According to newspaper accounts, she had been drinking alcohol on the evening she was raped; the lead assailant is alleged to have given her a bottle of wine after she arrived at his fraternity house. Portions of the rape occurred in a shower, and the victim was reportedly so drunk that her assailants had difficulty holding her in a standing position (*Tallahassee Democrat* 1988a). While raping her, her assailants repeatedly told her they were members of another fraternity under the apparent belief that she was too drunk to know the difference. Of course, if she was too drunk to know who they were, she was too drunk to consent to sex (cf. Allgeier 1986; Tash 1988).

One respondent told us that gang rapes are wrong and can get one expelled, but he seemed to see nothing wrong in sexual coercion one-on-one. He seemed unaware that the use of alcohol to obtain sex from a woman is grounds for a claim that a rape occurred (cf. Tash 1988). Few women on campus (who also may not know these grounds) report date rapes, however; so the odds of detection and punishment are slim for fraternity men who use alcohol for "seduction" purposes (cf. Byington and Keeter 1988; Merton 1985).

Violence and Physical Force   Fraternity men have a history of violence (Ehrhart and Sandler 1985; Roark 1987).

Their record of hazing, fighting, property destruction, and rape has caused them problems with insurance companies (Bradford 1986; Pressley 1987). Two university officials told us that fraternities "are the third riskiest property to insure behind toxic waste dumps and amusement parks." Fraternities are increasingly defendants in legal actions brought by pledges subjected to hazing (Meyer 1986; Pressley 1987) and by women who were raped by one or more members. In a recent alleged gang rape incident at another Florida university, prosecutors failed to file charges but the victim filed a civil suit against the fraternity nevertheless (*Tallahassee Democrat* 1989).

Competition and Superiority   Interfraternity rivalry fosters in-group identification and out-group hostility. Fraternities stress pride of membership and superiority over other fraternities as major goals. Interfraternity rivalries take many forms, including competition for desirable pledges, size of pledge class, size of membership, size and appearance of fraternity house, superiority in intramural sports, highest grade-point averages, giving the best parties, gaining the best or most campus leadership roles, and, of great importance, attracting and displaying "good-looking women." Rivalry is particularly intense over members, intramural sports, and women (cf. Messner 1989).

FRATERNITIES' COMMODIFICATION OF WOMEN

In claiming that women are treated by fraternities as commodities, we mean that fraternities knowingly, and intentionally, *use* women for their benefit. Fraternities use women as bait for new members, as servers of brothers' needs, and as sexual prey.

Women as Bait

Fashionably attractive women help a fraternity attract new members. As one fraternity man, a junior, said, "They are good bait." Beautiful, sociable women are believed to impress the right kind of pledges and give the impression that the fraternity can deliver this type of woman to its members. Photographs of shapely, attractive coeds are printed in fraternity brochures and videotapes that are distributed and shown to potential pledges. The women pictured are often dressed in bikinis, at the beach, and are pictured hugging the brothers of the fraternity. One university official says such recruitment materials give the message: "Hey, they're here for you, you can have whatever you want," and, "we have the best-looking women. Join us and you can have them too." Another commented: "Something's wrong when males join an all-male organization as the best place to meet women. It's so illogical."

Fraternities compete in promising access to beautiful women. One fraternity man, a senior, commented that "the attraction of girls [i.e., a fraternity's success in attracting women] is a big status symbol for fraternities." One university official commented that the use of women as a recruiting tool is so well entrenched that fraternities that might be willing to forgo it say they cannot afford to unless other fraternities do so as well. One fraternity man said, "Look, if we don't have Little Sisters, the fraternities that do will get all the good pledges." Another said, "We won't have as good a rush [the period during which new members are assessed and selected] if we don't have these women around."

In displaying good-looking, attractive, skimpily dressed, nubile women to potential members, fraternities implicitly, and sometimes explicitly, promise sexual access to women. One fraternity man commented that "part of what being in a fraternity is all about is the sex" and explained how his fraternity uses Little Sisters to recruit new members:

> We'll tell the sweetheart [the fraternity's term for Little Sister], "You're gorgeous; you can get him." We'll tell her to fake a scam and she'll go hang all over him during a rush party, kiss him, and he thinks he's done wonderful and wants to join. The girls think it's great too. It's flattering for them.

Women as Servers

The use of women as servers is exemplified in the Little Sister program. Little Sisters are undergraduate women who are rushed and selected in a manner parallel to the recruitment of fraternity men. They are affiliated with the fraternity in a formal but unofficial way and are able, indeed required, to wear the fraternity's Greek letters. Little Sisters are not full-fledged fraternity members, however; and fraternity national offices and most universities do not register or regulate them. Each fraternity has an officer called Little Sister Chairman who oversees their organization and activities. The Little Sisters elect officers among themselves, pay monthly dues to the fraternity, and have well-defined roles. Their dues are used to pay for the fraternity's social events, and Little Sisters

are expected to attend and hostess fraternity parties and hang around the house to make it a "nice place to be." One fraternity man, a senior, described Little Sisters this way: "They are very social girls, willing to join in, be affiliated with the group, devoted to the fraternity." Another member, a sophomore, said: "Their sole purpose is social—attend parties, attract new members, and 'take care' of the guys."

Our observations and interviews suggested that women selected by fraternities as Little Sisters are physically attractive, possess good social skills, and are willing to devote time and energy to the fraternity and its members. One undergraduate woman gave the following job description for Little Sisters to a campus newspaper:

> It's not just making appearances at all the parties but entails many more responsibilities. You're going to be expected to go to all the intramural games to cheer the brothers on, support and encourage the pledges, and just be around to bring some extra life to the house. [As a Little Sister] you have to agree to take on a new responsibility other than studying to maintain your grades and managing to keep your checkbook from bouncing. You have to make time to be a part of the fraternity and support the brothers in all they do. (*The Tomahawk* 1988)

The title of Little Sister reflects women's subordinate status; fraternity men in a parallel role are called Big Brothers. Big Brothers assist a sorority primarily with the physical work of sorority rushes, which, compared to fraternity rushes, are more formal, structured, and intensive. Sorority rushes take place in the daytime and fraternity rushes at night so fraternity men are free to help. According to one fraternity member, Little Sister status is a benefit to women because it gives them a social outlet and "the protection of the brothers." The gender-stereotypic conceptions and obligations of these Little Sister and Big Brother statuses indicate that fraternities and sororities promote a gender hierarchy on campus that fosters subordination and dependence in women, thus encouraging sexual exploitation and the belief that it is acceptable.

Women as Sexual Prey

Little Sisters are a sexual utility. Many Little Sisters do not belong to sororities and lack peer support for refraining from unwanted sexual relations. One fraternity man (whose fraternity has sixty-five members and eighty-five Little Sisters) told us they had recruited "wholesale" in the prior year to "get lots of new women." The structural access to women that the Little Sister program provides and the absence of normative supports for refusing fraternity members' sexual advances may make women in this program particularly susceptible to coerced sexual encounters with fraternity men.

Access to women for sexual gratification is a presumed benefit of fraternity membership, promised in recruitment materials and strategies and through brothers' conversations with new recruits. One fraternity man said: "We always tell the guys that you get sex all the time, there's always new girls. . . . After I became a Greek, I found out I could be with females at will." A university official told us that, based on his observations, "no one [i.e., fraternity men] on this campus wants to have 'relationships.' They just want to have fun [i.e., sex]." Fraternity men plan and execute strategies aimed at obtaining sexual gratification, and this occurs at both individual and collective levels.

Individual strategies include getting a woman drunk and spending a great deal of money on her. As for collective strategies, most of our undergraduate interviewees agreed that fraternity parties often culminate in sex and that this outcome is planned. One fraternity man said fraternity parties often involve sex and nudity and can "turn into orgies." Orgies may be planned in advance, such as the Bowery Ball party held by one fraternity. A former fraternity member said of this party:

> The entire idea behind this is sex. Both men and women come to the party wearing little or nothing. There are pornographic pinups on the walls and usually porno movies playing on the TV. The music carries sexual overtones. . . . They just get schnockered [drunk] and, in most cases, they also get laid.

When asked about the women who come to such a party, he said: "Some Little Sisters just won't go. . . . The girls who do are looking for a good time, girls who don't know what it is, things like that."

Other respondents denied that fraternity parties are orgies but said that sex is always talked about among the brothers and they all know "who each other is doing it with." One member said that most of the time, guys have sex with their girlfriends "but with socials, girlfriends aren't allowed to come and it's their [members'] big chance [to have sex with other women]." The use of alcohol to help them get women into bed is a routine strategy at fraternity parties.

CONCLUSIONS

In general, our research indicated that the organization and membership of fraternities contribute heavily to coercive and often violent sex. Fraternity houses are occupied by same-sex (all men) and same-age (late teens, early twenties) peers whose maturity and judgment is often less than ideal. Yet fraternity houses are private dwellings that are mostly off-limits to, and away from scrutiny of, university and community representatives, with the result that fraternity house events seldom come to the attention of outsiders. Practices associated with the social construction of fraternity brotherhood emphasize a macho conception of men and masculinity, a narrow, stereotyped conception of women and femininity, and the treatment of women as commodities. Other practices contributing to coercive sexual relations and the cover-up of rapes include excessive alcohol use, competitiveness, and normative support for deviance and secrecy (cf. Bogal-Allbritten and Allbritten 1985; Kanin 1967).

Some fraternity practices exacerbate others. Brotherhood norms require "sticking together" regardless of right or wrong; thus rape episodes are unlikely to be stopped or reported to outsiders, even when witnesses disapprove. The ability to use alcohol without scrutiny by authorities and alcohol's frequent association with violence, including sexual coercion, facilitates rape in fraternity houses. Fraternity norms that emphasize the value of maleness and masculinity over femaleness and femininity and that elevate the status of men and lower the status of women in members' eyes undermine perceptions and treatment of women as persons who deserve consideration and care (cf. Ehrhart and Sandler 1985; Merton 1985).

Androgynous men and men with a broad range of interests and attributes are lost to fraternities through their recruitment practices. Masculinity of a narrow and stereotypical type helps create attitudes, norms, and practices that predispose fraternity men to coerce women sexually, both individually and collectively (Allgeier 1986; Hood 1989; Sanday 1981, 1986). Male athletes on campus may be similarly disposed for the same reasons (Kirshenbaum 1989; Telander and Sullivan 1989).

Research into the social contexts in which rape crimes occur and the social constructions associated with these contexts illumine rape dynamics on campus. Blanchard (1959) found that group rapes almost always have a leader who pushes others into the crime. He also found that the leader's latent homosexuality, desire to show off to his peers, or fear of failing to prove himself a man are frequently an impetus. Fraternity norms and practices contribute to the approval and use of sexual coercion as an accepted tactic in relations with women. Alcohol-induced compliance is normative, whereas, presumably, use of a knife, gun, or threat of bodily harm would not be because the woman who "drinks too much" is viewed as "causing her own rape" (cf. Ehrhart and Sandler 1985).

Our research led us to conclude that fraternity norms and practices influence members to view the sexual coercion of women, which is a felony crime, as sport, a contest, or a game (cf. Sato 1988). This sport is played not between men and women but between men and men. Women are the pawns or prey in the interfraternity rivalry game; they prove that a fraternity is successful or prestigious. The use of women in this way encourages fraternity men to see women as objects and sexual coercion as sport. Today's societal norms support young women's right to engage in sex at their discretion, and coercion is unnecessary in a mutually desired encounter. However, nubile young women say they prefer to be "in a relationship" to have sex while young men say they prefer to "get laid" without a commitment (Muehlenhard and Linton 1987). These differences may reflect, in part, American puritanism and men's fears of sexual intimacy or perhaps intimacy of any kind. In a fraternity context, getting sex without

giving emotionally demonstrates "cool" masculinity. More important, it poses no threat to the bonding and loyalty of the fraternity brotherhood (cf. Farr 1988). Drinking large quantities of alcohol before having sex suggests that "scoring" rather than intrinsic sexual pleasure is a primary concern of fraternity men.

Unless fraternities' composition, goals, structures, and practices change in fundamental ways, women on campus will continue to be sexual prey for fraternity men. As all-male enclaves dedicated to opposing faculty and administration and to cementing in-group ties, fraternity members eschew any hint of homosexuality. Their version of masculinity transforms women, and men with womanly characteristics, into the out-group. "Womanly men" are ostracized; feminine women are used to demonstrate members' masculinity. Encouraging renewed emphasis on their founding values (Longino and Kart 1973), service orientation and activities (Lemire 1979), or members' moral development (Marlowe and Auvenshine 1982) will have little effect on fraternities' treatment of women. A case for or against fraternities cannot be made by studying individual members. The fraternity qua group and organization is at issue. Located on campus along with many vulnerable women, embedded in a sexist society, and caught up in masculinist goals, practices, and values, fraternities' violation of women—including forcible rape—should come as no surprise.

ACKNOWLEDGMENTS

We gratefully thank Meena Harris and Diane Mennella for assisting with data collection. The senior author thanks the graduate students in her fall 1988 graduate research methods seminar for help with developing the initial conceptual framework. Judith Lorber and two anonymous *Gender & Society* referees made numerous suggestions for improving our article and we thank them also.

NOTE

1. Recent bans by some universities on open-keg parties at fraternity houses have resulted in heavy drinking before coming to a party and an increase in drunkenness among those who attend. This may aggravate, rather than improve, the treatment of women by fraternity men at parties.

REFERENCES

Adams, Aileen, and Gail Abarbanel. 1988. *Sexual Assault on Campus: What Colleges Can Do.* Santa Monica, CA: Rape Treatment Center.

Allgeier, Elizabeth. 1986. "Coercive Versus Consensual Sexual Interactions." G. Stanley Hall Lecture to American Psychological Association Annual Meeting, Washington, DC, August.

Blanchard, W. H. 1959. "The Group Process in Gang Rape." *Journal of Social Psychology* 49: 259–66.

Bogal-Allbritten, Rosemarie B., and William L. Allbritten. 1985. "The Hidden Victims: Courtship Violence among College Students." *Journal of College Student Personnel* 43: 201–4.

Bohrnstedt, George W. 1969. "Conservatism, Authoritarianism and Religiosity of Fraternity Pledges." *Journal of College Student Personnel* 27: 36–43.

Bradford, Michael. 1986. "Tight Market Dries Up Nightlife at University." *Business Insurance* (March 2): 2, 6.

Burkhart, Barry. 1989. Comments in Seminar on Acquaintance/ Date Rape Prevention: A National Video Teleconference, February 2.

Burkhart, Barry R., and Annette L. Stanton. 1985. "Sexual Aggression in Acquaintance Relationships." pp. 43–65 in *Violence in Intimate Relationships*, ed. G. Russell. Englewood Cliffs, NJ: Spectrum.

Byington, Diane B., and Karen W. Keeter. 1988. "Assessing Needs of Sexual Assault Victims on a University Campus." pp. 23–31 in *Student Services: Responding to Issues and Challenges*. Chapel Hill: University of North Carolina Press.

Chancer, Lynn S. 1987. "New Bedford, Massachusetts, March 6, 1983–March 22, 1984: The 'Before and After' of a Group Rape." *Gender & Society* 1: 239–60.

Ehrhart, Julie K., and Bernice R. Sandler. 1985. *Campus Gang Rape: Party Games?* Washington, DC: Association of American Colleges.

Farr, K. A. 1988. "Dominance Bonding through the Good Old Boys Sociability Network." *Sex Roles* 18: 259–77.

Florida Flambeau. 1988. "Pike Members Indicted in Rape." (May 19): 1, 5.

Fox, Elaine, Charles Hodge, and Walter Ward. 1987. "A Comparison of Attitudes Held by Black and White Fraternity Members." *Journal of Negro Education* 56: 521–34.

Geis, Gilbert. 1971. "Group Sexual Assaults." *Medical Aspects of Human Sexuality* 5: 101–13.

Glaser, Barney G. 1978. *Theoretical Sensitivity: Advances in the Methodology of Grounded Theory*. Mill Valley, CA: Sociology Press.

Hood, Jane. 1989. "Why Our Society Is Rape-Prone." *New York Times*, May 16.

Hughes, Michael J., and Roger B. Winston, Jr. 1987. "Effects of Fraternity Membership on Interpersonal Values." *Journal of College Student Personnel* 45: 405–11.

Kanin, Eugene J. 1967. "Reference Groups and Sex Conduct Norm Violations." *The Sociological Quarterly* 8: 495–504.

Kimmel, Michael, ed. 1987. *Changing Men: New Directions in Research on Men and Masculinity*. Newbury Park, CA: Sage.

Kirshenbaum, Jerry. 1989. "Special Report, An American Disgrace: A Violent and Unprecedented Lawlessness Has Arisen among College Athletes in all Parts of the Country." *Sports Illustrated* (February 27): 16–19.

Lemire, David. 1979. "One Investigation of the Stereotypes Associated with Fraternities and Sororities." *Journal of College Student Personnel* 37: 54–57.

Letchworth, G. E. 1969. "Fraternities Now and in the Future." *Journal of College Student Personnel* 10: 118–22.

Longino, Charles F., Jr., and Cary S. Kart. 1973. "The College Fraternity: An Assessment of Theory and Research." *Journal of College Student Personnel* 31: 118–25.

Marlowe, Anne F., and Dwight C. Auvenshine. 1982. "Greek Membership: Its Impact on the Moral Development of College Freshmen." *Journal of College Student Personnel* 40: 53–57.

Martin, Patricia Yancey, and Barry A. Turner. 1986. "Grounded Theory and Organizational Research." *Journal of Applied Behavioral Science* 22: 141–57.

Merton, Andrew. 1985. "On Competition and Class: Return to Brotherhood." *Ms.* (September): 60–65, 121–22.

Messner, Michael. 1989. "Masculinities and Athletic Careers." *Gender & Society* 3: 71–88.

Meyer, T. J. 1986. "Fight Against Hazing Rituals Rages on Campuses." *Chronicle of Higher Education* (March 12): 34–36.

Miller, Leonard D. 1973. "Distinctive Characteristics of Fraternity Members." *Journal of College Student Personnel* 31: 126–28.

Muehlenhard, Charlene L., and Melaney A. Linton. 1987. "Date Rape and Sexual Aggression in Dating Situations: Incidence and Risk Factors." *Journal of Counseling Psychology* 34: 186–96.

Pressley, Sue Anne. 1987. "Fraternity Hell Night Still Endures." *Washington Post* (August 11): B1.

Rapaport, Karen, and Barry R. Burkhart. 1984. "Personality and Attitudinal Characteristics of Sexually Coercive College Males." *Journal of Abnormal Psychology* 93: 216–21.

Roark, Mary L. 1987. "Preventing Violence on College Campuses." *Journal of Counseling and Development* 65: 367–70.

Sanday, Peggy Reeves. 1981. "The Socio-Cultural Context of Rape: A Cross-Cultural Study." *Journal of Social Issues* 37: 5–27.

———. 1986. "Rape and the Silencing of the Feminine." pp. 84–101 in *Rape*, ed. S. Tomaselli and R. Porter. Oxford: Basil Blackwell.

St. Petersburg Times. 1988. "A Greek Tragedy." (May 29): 1F, 6F.

Sato, Ikuya. 1988. "Play Theory of Delinquency: Toward a General Theory of 'Action.'" *Symbolic Interaction* 11: 191–212.

Smith, T. 1964. "Emergence and Maintenance of Fraternal Solidarity." *Pacific Sociological Review* 7: 29–37.

Tallahassee Democrat. 1988a. "FSU Fraternity Brothers Charged" (April 27): 1A, 12A.

———. 1988b. "FSU Interviewing Students about Alleged Rape" (April 24): 1D.

———. 1989. "Woman Sues Stetson in Alleged Rape" (March 19): 3B.

Tampa Tribune. 1988. "Fraternity Brothers Charged in Sexual Assault of FSU Coed" (April 27): 6B.

Tash, Gary B. 1988. "Date Rape." *The Emerald of Sigma Pi Fraternity* 75(4): 1–2.

Telander, Rick, and Robert Sullivan. 1989. "Special Report, You Reap What You Sow." *Sports Illustrated* (February 27): 20–34.

The Tomahawk. 1988. "A Look Back at Rush, A Mixture of Hard Work and Fun" (April/May): 3D.

Walsh, Claire. 1989. Comments in Seminar on Acquaintance/ Date Rape Prevention: A National Video Teleconference, February 2.

Wilder, David H., Arlyne E. Hoyt, Dennis M. Doren, William E. Hauck, and Robert D. Zettle. 1978. "The Impact of Fraternity and Sorority Membership on Values and Attitudes." *Journal of College Student Personnel* 36: 445–49.

Wilder, David H., Arlyne E. Hoyt, Beth Shuster Surbeck, Janet C. Wilder, and Patricia Imperatrice Carney. 1986. "Greek Affiliation and Attitude Change in College Students." *Journal of College Student Personnel* 44: 510–19.

MEN CHANGING MEN

Robert L. Allen and Paul Kivel

Batterers need to be penalized for their actions, but the future safety of women and children depends on stopping the violence before it starts. With prevention in mind, Robert Allen and Paul Kivel discuss the work they do with boys and men in the Oakland Men's Project (OMP). Formed in 1979, this California-based group is a nonprofit, multiracial organization of men and women, devoted to community education and eradicating male violence, racism, and homophobia. The group has worked with thousands of boys and men. Its workshops are designed to encourage participants to examine gender roles, violence and discrimination, and alternatives to violence.

Why do men batter women? We have to discard the easy answers. Portraying batterers as ogres only serves to separate "them" from "us." But men who batter and men who don't are not all that different. Male violence is normal in our society and vast numbers of men participate. Men batter because we have been trained to; because there are few social sanctions against it; because we live in a society where the exploitation of people with less social and personal power is acceptable. In a patriarchal society boys are taught to accept violence as a manly response to real or imagined threats, but they get little training in negotiating intimate relationships. And all too many men believe that they have the right to control or expect certain behavior from "their" women and children; many view difficulties in family relationships as threats to their manhood, and they respond with violence.

Young people's definitions of femininity and masculinity often reflect rigid expectations of what they must live up to in order to be a "real" woman or a "real" man. Time and again we hear boys say that they are supposed to be tough, aggressive, in control, that they are not to express any feelings except anger, not to cry, and never to ask for help. And many boys expect girls to acquiesce to men and be dependent on them.

How do boys get these ideas about male identity and manhood? Often from parents, but our whole society contributes to the process. As many as one of every six boys is sexually assaulted, and many, many more are hit, yelled at, teased, and goaded into fighting to prove they're tough. At the project, we believe that many boys become convinced that they will be violated until they learn to use force to protect themselves. Then they move to take their pain and anger out on others the way older males have done to them.

In our work we often use role play as a way of getting at some of these issues. One particularly effective exercise involves a ten-year-old and his father: the father arrives home from work and demands that the boy turn off the TV, then berates him for the messiness of his room. The boy tries to explain; the father tells him to shut up, to stop making excuses. Fueling the father's anger is the fact that he's disappointed by the boy's school report card. The father shoves the report card in his son's face and demands to know why he has gotten a "D" in math. The boy says he did his best. The father tells him that he is stupid. The boy protests and begins to stand up. The father shoves him down, saying, "Don't you dare get up in my face!" The boy is visibly upset, and begins to cry. The father explodes: "Now what? You little mama's boy! You sissy! You make me sick. When are you going to grow up and start acting like a man?"

When we do this exercise in schools, it gets the boys' undivided attention because most have experienced being humiliated by an older male. Indeed, the power of this exercise is that it is so familiar. When asked what they learned from such encounters, the boys often say things like: A man is tough. A man is in control. A man doesn't cry. A man doesn't take crap.

We write the boy's comments on a blackboard, draw a box around them, and label it the "Act Like a Man" box. We talk about how males in this culture are socialized to stay in the box. Eventually we ask: What happens if you step out of it, if you stop acting tough enough or man enough? Invariably we hear that you get called names like "fag," "queer," "mama's boy," "punk," "girl." Asked why, the boys say it's a challenge, that they're expected to fight to prove themselves. Homophobia, and fear of being identified with women, are powerful messages boys get from an early age, and they are expected to fight to prove that they're tough and not gay—that they're in the box.

Using exercises, like the father/son interchange, helps us examine how the male sex role often sets men up to be dominating, controlling, and abusive. We ask: How safe is it to stay in the "Act Like a Man" box? Usually, most admit that it isn't safe, because boys and men continually challenge each other to prove that they're in the box. When a boy or man is challenged, he can prove he's a man either by fighting the challenger or by finding someone "weaker"—a female or a more vulnerable male—to dominate. Hurting girls relieves any anxiety that we may not be tough enough and establishes our heterosexual credentials. It's both a sign of our interest (we're paying attention to them) and a symbol of our difference (we're in control).

Because we are taught that women are primarily sexual objects, this behaviour seems perfectly natural. And many men come to believe that a woman is just another material possession. We initiate dates, pay for our time together, protect them on the streets, and often marry them. We are trained to think that in return, girls should show their appreciation by taking care of us emotionally, putting their own concerns and interest aside, and putting out sexually.

This unspoken contract is one that many heterosexual men operate by, and it often leads to the assumption that women are our dumping ground. If we've had a hard day at work, were embarrassed or humiliated by a boss—challenged in the box—the contract leads us to believe that we can take those feelings out on "our" women, and thus regain our power. If we end up hitting her, then we have to blame her in order to deny our aggression and keep our self-esteem intact. So we say things like: She asked for it. She pushed my buttons. She deserved it.

Invariably it comes as a surprise to us that women don't meekly accept our violence. So we respond by minimizing and justifying our actions: I didn't mean it, You're too sensitive. That's the way guys are. It was just the heat of the moment.

In order to get men to take responsibility for their own actions, we have to get them to talk about what they did, and what they said, and what they felt. Making the connection between how they have been trained and hurt and how they have learned to pass that pain on by hurting women or young people is essential.

To get men to reflect on their experiences and behaviors, we use exercises we call "stand ups." We ask everyone to be silent, and then slowly pose a series of questions or statements, and ask men to stand every time one applies to them. For example, we may ask, Have you ever:

- worried you were not tough enough?
- been called a wimp, queer, or fag?
- been told to "act like a man"?
- been hit by an older man?
- been forced to fight?
- been physically injured and hid the pain?
- been sexually abused, or touched in a way you didn't like?
- used alcohol or drugs to hide your pain?
- felt like blowing yourself away?

Later in the workshop we ask, Have you ever:

- interrupted a woman by talking louder?
- made a comment in public about a woman's body?
- discussed a woman's body with another man?
- been told by a woman that she wanted more affection and less sex from you?
- used your voice or body to intimidate a woman?
- hit, slapped, shoved, or pushed a woman?
- had sex with a woman when you knew she didn't want to?

Each participant is asked to look around and see other men standing, which helps break down their sense of isolation and feeling of shame. Since we are not a therapy group, no one is questioned or confronted about his own experiences. All of our work involves challenging the notion that males are naturally abusive and that females are natural targets of male abuse. We give boys and men a way of analyzing social roles by drawing insights from their own experiences, and help them to recognize that social interactions involve making choices, that we can break free of old roles by supporting each other in choosing alternatives to violence.

An important part of our work is getting men and boys to look at how power, inequality, and the ability to do violence to others are structured into social relationships in this country. We discuss how

(continued)

these inequalities are maintained and how violence against one targeted group encourages violence against others. This is not to excuse men's behavior; it is done in the belief that in order to make better choices, men must understand the framework of power and violence that constantly pressures us to be in control and on top.

There are growing numbers of men who are critical of sexism. All too often they are isolated and fearful of raising their concerns with other men because they worry about being targeted for violence. We try to help them break through the fear and reach out to other men. But we also work to get men to understand how they are damaged by sexism and how male violence against women keeps us from the collective action needed to confront racial, gender-based, and economic injustice.

For us personally this is powerful, life-changing work. We were each drawn to it because of troubling issues in our own lives: issues around our relationships with our fathers (one emotionally abusive, the other emotionally distant); relationships with women partners where we found ourselves repeating controlling, sexist behaviors that make us feel guilty, ashamed, defensive; and the fear that we might do to our children what had been done to us as children. Through the work we have discovered that many men share these concerns, but they are hesitant to talk about this with other men. Sadly, we have all learned that "real" men don't admit vulnerability. But despite their initial hesitation, many men are eager to talk about their lives, and to change the controlling and abusive behavior they've been trained to pass on. Doing this work is healing for us and for those we work with.

Men are responsible for battery and for stopping male violence. If we are to counter the myth that men's abuse of women is natural, men must challenge each other to stop the violence. We must defy notions of manhood that lead us to injure or kill those we say we love. We must confront male friends when we see them heading down the destructive path of domestic violence and urge them to get help. While it is critical that domestic violence cases be taken more seriously by the police and criminal justice system, it is equally important to examine and to change underlying social attitudes and practices that promote and excuse domestic violence. This is truly men's work.

READING *39*   **Gloria Steinem**

Supremacy Crimes

From domestic violence to sexual harassment, naming a crime has been the first step toward solving it. But another crime is hiding in plain sight. You've seen the ocean of television coverage, you've read the headlines: "How to Spot a Troubled Kid," "Twisted Teens," "When Teens Fall Apart."

After the slaughter in Colorado that inspired those phrases, dozens of copycat threats were reported in the same generalized way: "Junior high students charged with conspiracy to kill students and teachers" (in Texas); "Five honor students overheard planning a June graduation bombing" (in New York); "More than 100 minor threats reported statewide" (in Pennsylvania). In response, the White House held an emergency strategy session titled "Children, Violence, and Responsibility." Nonetheless, another attack was soon reported: "Youth With 2 Guns Shoots 6 at Georgia School."

I don't know about you, but I've been talking back to the television set, waiting for someone to tell us the obvious: it's not "youth," "our children," or "our teens." It's our sons—and "our" can usually be read as "white," "middle class," and "heterosexual." We know that hate crimes, violent and otherwise, are overwhelmingly committed by white men who are apparently straight. The same is true for an even higher percentage of impersonal, resentment-driven, mass killings like those in Colorado; the sort committed for no economic or rational gain except the need to say, "I'm superior because I can kill." Think of Charles Starkweather, who reported feeling powerful and serene after murdering ten women and men in the 1950s; or the shooter who climbed the University of Texas Tower in 1966, raining down death to gain celebrity. Think of the engineering student at the University of Montreal who resented females' ability to study that subject, and so shot to death fourteen women students in 1989, while saying, "I'm against feminism." Think of nearly all those who have killed impersonally in the workplace, the post office, McDonald's.

White males—usually intelligent, middle class, and heterosexual, or trying desperately to appear so—also account for virtually all the serial, sexually motivated, sadistic killings, those characterized by stalking, imprisoning, torturing, and "owning" victims in death. Think of Edmund Kemper, who began by killing animals, then murdered his grandparents, yet was released to sexually torture and dismember college students and other young women until he himself decided he "didn't want to kill *all* the coeds in the world." Or David Berkowitz, the Son of Sam, who murdered some women in order to feel in control of all women. Or consider Ted Bundy, the charming, snobbish young would-be lawyer who tortured and murdered as many as forty women, usually beautiful students who were symbols of the economic class he longed to join. As for John Wayne Gacy, he was obsessed with maintaining the public mask of masculinity, and so hid his homosexuality by killing and burying men and boys with whom he had had sex.

These "senseless" killings begin to seem less mysterious when you consider that they were committed disproportionately by white, nonpoor males, the group most likely to become hooked on the drug of superiority. It's a drug pushed by a male-dominant culture that presents dominance as a natural right; a racist hierarchy that falsely elevates whiteness; a materialist society that equates superiority with possessions, and a homophobic one that empowers only one form of sexuality.

As Elliott Leyton reports in *Hunting Humans: The Rise of the Modern Multiple Murderer*, these killers see

their behavior as "an appropriate—even 'manly'— response to the frustrations and disappointments that are a normal part of life." In other words, it's not their life experiences that are the problem, it's the impossible expectation of dominance to which they've become addicted.

This is not about blame. This is about causation. If anything, ending the massive cultural cover-up of supremacy crimes should make heroes out of boys and men who reject violence, especially those who reject the notion of superiority altogether. Even if one believes in a biogenetic component of male aggression, the very existence of gentle men proves that socialization can override it.

Nor is this about attributing such crimes to a single cause. Addiction to the drug of supremacy is not their only root, just the deepest and most ignored one. Additional reasons why this country has such a high rate of violence include the plentiful guns that make killing seem as unreal as a video game; male violence in the media that desensitizes viewers in much the same way that combat killers are desensitized in training; affluence that allows maximum access to violence-as-entertainment; a national history of genocide and slavery; the romanticizing of frontier violence and organized crime; not to mention extremes of wealth and poverty and the illusion that both are deserved.

But it is truly remarkable, given the relative reasons for anger at injustice in this country, that white, nonpoor men have a near-monopoly on multiple killings of strangers, whether serial and sadistic or mass and random. How can we ignore this obvious fact? Others may kill to improve their own condition—in self-defense, or for money or drugs; to eliminate enemies; to declare turf in drive-by shootings; even for a jacket or a pair of sneakers—but white males addicted to supremacy kill even when it worsens their condition or ends in suicide.

Men of color and females are capable of serial and mass killing, and commit just enough to prove it. Think of Colin Ferguson, the crazed black man on the Long Island Railroad, or Wayne Williams, the young black man in Atlanta who kidnapped and killed black boys, apparently to conceal his homosexuality. Think of Aileen Carol Wuornos, the white prostitute in Florida who killed abusive johns "in self-defense," or Waneta Hoyt, the upstate New York woman who strangled her five infant children between 1965 and 1971, disguising their cause of death as sudden infant death syndrome. Such crimes are rare enough to leave a haunting refrain of disbelief, as evoked in Pat Parker's poem "jonestown": "Black folks do not/ Black folks do not/Black folks do not commit suicide." And yet they did.

Nonetheless, the proportion of serial killings that are not committed by white males is about the same as the proportion of anorexics who are not female. Yet we discuss the gender, race, and class components of anorexia, but not the role of the same factors in producing epidemics among the powerful.

The reasons are buried deep in the culture, so invisible that only by reversing our assumptions can we reveal them.

Suppose, for instance, that young black males—or any other men of color—had carried out the slaughter in Colorado. Would the media reports be so willing to describe the murderers as "our children"? Would there be so little discussion about the boys' race? Would experts be calling the motive a mystery, or condemning the high school cliques for making those young men feel like "outsiders"? Would there be the same empathy for parents who gave the murderers luxurious homes, expensive cars, even rescued them from brushes with the law? Would there be as much attention to generalized causes, such as the dangers of violent video games and recipes for bombs on the Internet?

As for the victims, if racial identities had been reversed, would racism remain so little discussed? In fact, the killers themselves said they were targeting blacks and athletes. They used a racial epithet, shot a black male student in the head, and then laughed over the fact that they could see his brain. What if *that* had been reversed?

What if these two young murderers, who were called "fags" by some of the jocks at Columbine High School, actually had been gay? Would they have got the same sympathy for being gay-baited? What if they had been lovers? Would we hear as little about their sexuality as we now do, even though only their own homophobia could have given the word "fag" such power to humiliate them?

Take one more leap of the imagination: suppose these killings had been planned and executed by young women—of any race, sexuality, or class. Would the media still be so uninterested in the role played by gender-conditioning? Would journalists assume that female murderers had suffered from being shut out of access to power in high school, so much so that they were pushed beyond their limits? What if dozens, even hundreds of young women around the country had made imitative threats—as young men have done— expressing admiration for a well-planned massacre and promising to do the same? Would we be discussing their youth more than their gender, as is the case so far with these male killers?

I think we begin to see that our national self-examination is ignoring something fundamental, precisely because it's like the air we breathe: the white male factor, the middle-class and heterosexual one, and the promise of superiority it carries. Yet this denial is self-defeating—to say the least. We will never reduce the number of violent Americans, from bullies to killers, without challenging the assumptions on which masculinity is based: that males are superior to females, that they must find a place in a male hierarchy, and that the ability to dominate *someone* is so important that even a mere insult can justify lethal revenge. There are plenty of studies to support this view. As Dr. James Gilligan concluded in *Violence: Reflections on a National Epidemic*, "If humanity is to evolve beyond the propensity toward violence . . . then it can only do so by recognizing the extent to which the patriarchal code of honor and shame generates and obligates male violence."

I think the way out can only be found through a deeper reversal: just as we as a society have begun to raise our daughters more like our sons—more like whole people—we must begin to raise our sons more like our daughters—that is, to value empathy as well as hierarchy; to measure success by other people's welfare as well as their own.

But first, we have to admit and name the truth about supremacy crimes.

Mapping the Margins: Intersectionality, Identity Politics, and Violence against Women of Color

. . . My objective [is to explore] the race and gender dimensions of violence against women of color. . . . I consider how the experiences of women of color are frequently the product of intersecting patterns of racism and sexism. . . .

[Based on] a brief field study of battered women's shelters located in minority communities in Los Angeles,[1] [I found that in most cases], the physical assault that leads women to these shelters is merely the most immediate manifestation of the subordination they experience. Many women who seek protection are unemployed or under-employed, and a good number of them are poor. Shelters serving these women cannot afford to address only the violence inflicted by the batterer; they must also confront the other multi-layered and routinized forms of domination that often converge in these women's lives, hindering their ability to create alternatives to the abusive relationships that brought them to shelters in the first place. Many women of color, for example, are burdened by poverty, child care responsibilities, and the lack of job skills.[2] These burdens, largely the consequence of gender and class oppression, are then compounded by the racially discriminatory employment and housing practices women of color often face, as well as by the disproportionately high unemployment among people of color that makes battered women of color less able to depend on the support of friends and relatives for temporary shelter.[3]

Where systems of race, gender, and class domination converge, as they do in the experiences of battered women of color, intervention strategies based solely on the experiences of women who do not share the same class or race backgrounds will be of limited help to women who because of race and class face different obstacles.[4] Such was the case in 1990 when Congress amended the marriage fraud provisions of the Immigration and Nationality Act to protect immigrant women who were battered or exposed to extreme cruelty by the United States citizens or permanent residents these women immigrated to the United States to marry. Under the marriage fraud provisions of the Act, a person who immigrated to the United States to marry a United States citizen or permanent resident had to remain "properly" married for two years before even applying for permanent resident status,[5] at which time applications for the immigrant's permanent status were required of both spouses. Predictably, under these circumstances, many immigrant women were reluctant to leave even the most abusive of partners for fear of being deported.[6] When faced with the choice between protection from their batterers and protection against deportation, many immigrant women chose the latter. Reports of the tragic consequences of this double subordination put pressure on Congress to include in the Immigration Act of 1990 a provision amending the marriage fraud rules to allow for an explicit waiver for hardship caused by domestic violence.[7] Yet many immigrant women, particularly immigrant women of color, have remained vulnerable to battering because they are unable to meet the conditions established for a waiver. The evidence required to support a waiver "can include but is not limited to, reports and affidavits from police, medical personnel, psychologists, school officials, and social service agencies.[8] For many immigrant women, limited access to these resources can make it difficult for them to obtain the evidence needed for a waiver. And cultural barriers often further discourage immigrant women from reporting or escaping battering situations. Tina Shum, a family counselor at a social service agency, points out that "[t]his law sounds so easy to apply, but there are cultural complications in the Asian community that make even these requirements difficult. . . . Just to find the opportunity and courage to call us is an accomplishment for many."[9] The typical immigrant spouse, she suggests, may live "[i]n an extended family where several generations live together, there may be no privacy on the telephone, no opportunity to leave the house and no understanding of public phones.[10] As a consequence, many immigrant women are wholly dependent on their husbands as their link to the world outside their homes.

Immigrant women are also vulnerable to spousal violence because so many of them depend on their husbands for information regarding their legal status.[11] Many women who are now permanent residents continue to suffer abuse under threats of deportation by their husbands. Even if the threats are unfounded, women who have no independent access to information will still be intimidated by such threats. And even though the domestic violence waiver focuses on immigrant women whose husbands are United States citizens or permanent residents, there are countless women married to undocumented workers (or who are themselves undocumented) who suffer in silence for fear that the security of their entire families will be jeopardized should they seek help or otherwise call attention to themselves.

Language barriers present another structural problem that often limits opportunities of non-English-speaking women to take advantage of existing support services. Such barriers not only limit access to information about shelters, but also limit access to the security shelters provide. Some shelters turn non-English-speaking women away for lack of bilingual personnel and resources.[12]

These examples illustrate how patterns of subordination intersect in women's experience of domestic violence. . . .

A. THE POLITICIZATION OF DOMESTIC VIOLENCE

[T]he political interests of women of color are obscured and sometimes jeopardized by political strategies that ignore or suppress intersectional issues, [This] is illustrated by my [research]. I attempted to review Los Angeles Police Department statistics reflecting the rate of domestic violence interventions by precinct because such statistics can provide a rough picture of arrests by racial group, given the degree of racial segregation in Los Angeles.[13] L.A.P.D., however, would not release the statistics. A representative explained that

one reason the statistics were not released was that domestic violence activists both within and outside the Department feared that statistics reflecting the extent of domestic violence in minority communities might be selectively interpreted and publicized so as to undermine long-term efforts to force the Department to address domestic violence as a serious problem. I was told that activists were worried that the statistics might permit opponents to dismiss domestic violence as a minority problem and, therefore, not deserving of aggressive action.

The informant also claimed that representatives from various minority communities opposed the release of the statistics. They were concerned, apparently, that the data would unfairly represent Black and Brown communities as unusually violent, potentially reinforcing stereotypes that might be used in attempts to justify oppressive police tactics and other discriminatory practices. These misgivings are based on the familiar and not unfounded premise that certain minority groups—especially Black men—have already been stereotyped as uncontrollably violent. Some worry that attempts to make domestic violence an object of political action may only serve to confirm such stereotypes and undermine efforts to combat negative beliefs about the Black community.

This account sharply illustrates how women of color can be erased by the strategic silences of antiracism and feminism. The political priorities of both were defined in ways that suppressed information that could have facilitated attempts to confront the problem of domestic violence in communities of color.

I. Domestic Violence and Antiracist Politics

Within communities of color, efforts to stem the politicization of domestic violence are often grounded in attempts to maintain the integrity of the community. The articulation of this perspective takes different forms. Some critics allege that feminism has no place within communities of color, that the issues are internally divisive, and that they represent the migration of white women's concerns into a context in which they are not only irrelevant but also harmful. At its most extreme, this rhetoric denies that gender violence is a problem in the community and characterizes any effort to politicize gender subordination as itself a community problem. This is the position taken by Shahrazad Ali in her controversial book, *The Blackman's Guide to Understanding the Blackwoman*.[14] In this stridently antifeminist tract, Ali draws a positive correlation between domestic violence and the liberation of African Americans. Ali blames the deteriorating conditions within the Black community on the insubordination of Black women and on the failure of Black men to control them.[15] Ali goes so far as to advise Black men to physically chastise Black women when they are "disrespectful."[16] While she cautions that Black men must use moderation in disciplining "their" women, she argues that Black men must sometimes resort to physical force to reestablish the authority over Black women that racism has disrupted.[17]

Ali's premise is that patriarchy is beneficial for the Black community, and that it must be strengthened through coercive means if necessary. Yet the violence that accompanies this will to control is devastating, not only for the Black women who are victimized, but also for the entire Black community. The recourse to violence to resolve conflicts establishes a dangerous pattern for children raised in such environments and contributes to many other pressing problems. It has been estimated that nearly forty percent of all homeless women and children have fled violence in the home,[18] and an estimated sixty-three percent of young men between the ages of eleven and twenty who are imprisoned for homicide have killed their mothers' batterers.[19] And yet, while gang violence, homicide, and other forms of Black-on-Black crime have increasingly been discussed within African-American politics, patriarchal ideas about gender and power preclude the recognition of domestic violence as yet another compelling incidence of Black-on-Black crime.

Efforts such as Ali's to justify violence against women in the name of Black liberation are indeed extreme. The more common problem is that the political or cultural interests of the community are interpreted in a way that precludes full public recognition of the problem of domestic violence. While it would be misleading to suggest that white Americans have come to terms with the degree of violence in their own homes, it is nonetheless the case that race adds yet another dimension to why the problem of domestic violence is suppressed within nonwhite communities. People of color often must weigh their interests in avoiding issues that might reinforce distorted public perceptions against the need to acknowledge and address intracommunity problems. Yet the cost of suppression is seldom recognized in part because the failure to discuss the issue shapes perceptions of how serious the problem is in the first place.

The controversy over Alice Walker's novel *The Color Purple* can be understood as an intracommunity debate about the political costs of exposing gender violence within the Black community.[20] Some critics chastised Walker for portraying Black men as violent brutes.[21] One critic lambasted Walker's portrayal of Celie, the emotionally and physically abused protagonist who finally triumphs in the end. Walker, the critic contended, had created in Celie a Black woman whom she couldn't imagine existing in any Black community she knew or could conceive of.[22]

The claim that Celie was somehow an unauthentic character might be read as a consequence of silencing discussion of intracommunity violence. Celie may be unlike any Black woman we know because the real terror experienced daily by minority women is routinely concealed in a misguided (though perhaps understandable) attempt to forestall racial stereotyping. Of course, it is true that representations of Black violence—whether statistical or fictional—are often written into a larger script that consistently portrays Black and other minority communities as pathologically violent. The problem, however, is not so much the portrayal of violence itself as it is the absence of other narratives and images portraying a fuller range of Black experience. Suppression of some of these issues in the name of antiracism imposes real costs. Where information about violence in minority communities is not available, domestic violence is unlikely to be addressed as a serious issue.

The political imperatives of a narrowly focused antiracist strategy support other practices that isolate women of color. For example, activists who have attempted to provide support services to Asian- and African-American women report intense resistance from those communities.[23] At other times, cultural and social factors contribute to suppression. Nilda Rimonte, director of Everywoman's Shelter in Los Angeles, points out that in the Asian community, saving the honor of the family from shame is a priority.[24] Unfortunately, this priority tends to be interpreted as obliging women not to scream rather than obliging men not to hit.

Race and culture contribute to the suppression of domestic violence in other ways as well. Women of color are often reluctant to call the police, a hesitancy likely due to a general unwillingness among people of color to subject their private lives to the scrutiny and control of a police force that is frequently hostile. There is also a more generalized community ethic against public intervention, the product of a desire to create a private world free from the diverse assaults on the public lives of racially subordinated people. The home is not simply a man's castle in the patriarchal sense, but may also function as a safe haven from the indignities of life in a racist society. However, but for this "safe haven" in many cases, women of color victimized by violence might otherwise seek help.

There is also a general tendency within antiracist discourse to regard the problem of violence against women of color as just another manifestation of racism. In this sense, the relevance of gender domination within the community is reconfigured as a consequence of discrimination against men. Of course, it is probably true that racism contributes to the cycle of violence, given the stress that men of color experience in dominant society. It is therefore more than reasonable to explore the links between racism and domestic violence. But the chain of violence is more complex and extends beyond this single link. Racism is linked to patriarchy to the extent that racism denies men of color the power and privilege that dominant men enjoy. When violence is understood as an acting-out of being denied male power in other spheres, it seems counterproductive to embrace constructs that implicitly link the solution to domestic violence to the acquisition of greater male power. The more promising political imperative is to challenge the legitimacy of such power expectations by exposing their dysfunctional and debilitating effect on families and communities of color. Moreover, while understanding links between racism and domestic violence is an important component of any effective intervention strategy, it is also clear that women of color need not await the ultimate triumph over racism before they can expect to live violence-free lives.

2. Race and the Domestic Violence Lobby

Not only do race-based priorities function to obscure the problem of violence suffered by women of color; feminist concerns often suppress minority experiences as well. Strategies for increasing awareness of domestic violence within the white community tend to begin by citing the commonly shared assumption that battering is a minority problem. The strategy then focuses on demolishing this strawman, stressing that spousal abuse also occurs in the white community. Countless first-person stories begin with a statement like, "I was not supposed to be a battered wife." That battering occurs in families of all races and all classes seems to be an ever-present theme of anti-abuse campaigns.

First-person anecdotes and studies, for example, consistently assert that battering cuts across racial, ethnic, economic, educational, and religious lines.[25] Such disclaimers seem relevant only in the presence of an initial, widely held belief that domestic violence occurs primarily in minority or poor families. Indeed some authorities explicitly renounce the "stereotypical myths" about battered women.[26] A few commentators have even transformed the message that battering is not exclusively a problem of the poor or minority communities into a claim that it equally affects all races and classes.[27] Yet these comments seem less concerned with exploring domestic abuse within "stereotyped" communities than with removing the stereotype as an obstacle to exposing battering within white middle- and upper-class communities.

Efforts to politicize the issue of violence against women challenge beliefs that violence occurs only in homes of "others." While it is unlikely that advocates and others who adopt this rhetorical strategy intend to exclude or ignore the needs of poor and colored women, the underlying premise of this seemingly universalistic appeal is to keep the sensibilities of dominant social groups focused on the experiences of those groups. Indeed, as subtly suggested by the opening comments of Senator David Boren (D-Okla.) in support of the Violence Against Women Act of 1991, the displacement of the "other" as the presumed victim of domestic violence works primarily as a political appeal to rally white elites. Boren said:

> Violent crimes against women are not limited to the streets of the inner cities, but also occur in homes in the urban and rural areas across the country.
>
> Violence against women affects not only those who are actually beaten and brutalized, but indirectly affects all women. Today, our wives, mothers, daughters, sisters, and colleagues are held captive by fear generated from these violent crimes—held captive not for what they do or who they are, but solely because of gender.[28]

Rather than focusing on and illuminating how violence is disregarded when the home is "othered," the strategy implicit in Senator Boren's remarks functions instead to politicize the problem only in the dominant community. This strategy permits white women victims to come into focus, but does little to disrupt the patterns of neglect that permitted the problem to continue as long as it was imagined to be a minority problem. The experience of violence of minority women is ignored, except to the extent it gains white support for domestic violence programs in the white community.

Senator Boren and his colleagues no doubt believe that they have provided legislation and resources that will address the problems of all women victimized by domestic violence. Yet despite their universalizing rhetoric of "all" women, they were able to empathize with female victims of domestic violence only by looking past the plight of "other" women and by recognizing the familiar faces of their own. The strength of the appeal to "protect our women" must be its race and class specificity. After all, it has always been someone's wife, mother, sister, or daughter that has been abused, even when the violence was stereotypically Black or Brown, and poor. The point here is not that the Violence Against Women Act is particularistic on its own terms, but that unless the Senators and other policymakers ask why violence remained insignificant as long as it was understood as a minority problem, it is unlikely that women of color will share equally in the distribution of resources and concern. It is even more unlikely, however, that those in power will be forced to confront this issue. As long as attempts to politicize domestic violence focus on convincing whites that this is not a "minority" problem but their problem, any authentic and sensitive attention to the experiences of Black and other minority women probably will continue to be regarded as jeopardizing the movement.

While Senator Boren's statement reflects a self-consciously political presentation of domestic violence, an episode of the CBS news program *48 Hours*[29] shows how similar patterns of "othering" nonwhite women are apparent in journalistic accounts of domestic violence as well. The program presented seven women who were victims of abuse. Six were interviewed at some length along with their family members, friends, supporters, and even detractors. The viewer got to know something about each of these women. These victims were humanized. Yet the seventh woman, the only nonwhite one, never came into focus. She was literally unrecognizable throughout the segment, first introduced by photographs showing her face badly beaten and later shown with her face electronically altered in the videotape of a hearing at which she was forced to testify. Other images associated with this woman included shots of a bloodstained room and blood-soaked pillows. Her boyfriend was pictured handcuffed while the camera zoomed in for a close-up of his bloodied sneakers. Of all the presentations in the episode, hers was the most graphic and impersonal. The overall point

of the segment "featuring" this woman was that battering might not escalate into homicide if battered women would only cooperate with prosecutors. In focusing on its own agenda and failing to explore why this woman refused to cooperate, the program diminished this woman, communicating, however subtly, that she was responsible for her own victimization.

Unlike the other women, all of whom, again, were white, this Black woman had no name, no family, no context. The viewer sees her only as victimized and uncooperative. She cries when shown pictures. She pleads not to be forced to view the bloodstained room and her disfigured face. The program does not help the viewer to understand her predicament. The possible reasons she did not want to testify—fear, love, or possibly both—are never suggested. Most unfortunately, she, unlike the other six, is given no epilogue. While the fates of the other women are revealed at the end of the episode, we discover nothing about the Black woman. She, like the "others" she represents, is simply left to herself and soon forgotten.

I offer this description to suggest that "other" women are silenced as much by being relegated to the margin of experience as by total exclusion. Tokenistic, objectifying, voyeuristic inclusion is at least as disempowering as complete exclusion. The effort to politicize violence against women will do little to address Black and other minority women if their images are retained simply to magnify the problem rather than to humanize their experiences. Similarly, the antiracist agenda will not be advanced significantly by forcibly suppressing the reality of battering in minority communities. As the *48 Hours* episode makes clear, the images and stereotypes we fear are readily available and are frequently deployed in ways that do not generate sensitive understanding of the nature of domestic violence in minority communities.

3. Race and Domestic Violence Support Services

Women working in the field of domestic violence have sometimes reproduced the subordination and marginalization of women of color by adopting policies, priorities, or strategies of empowerment that either elide or wholly disregard the particular intersectional needs of women of color. While gender, race, and class intersect to create the particular context in which women of color experience violence, certain choices made by "allies" can reproduce intersectional subordination within the very resistance strategies designed to respond to the problem.

This problem is starkly illustrated by the inaccessibility of domestic violence support services to many non-English-speaking women. In a letter written to the deputy commissioner of the New York State Department of Social Services, Diana Campos, Director of Human Services for Programas de Ocupaciones y Desarrollo Economico Real, Inc. (PODER), detailed the case of a Latina in crisis who was repeatedly denied accommodation at a shelter because she could not prove that she was English-proficient. The woman had fled her home with her teenaged son, believing her husband's threats to kill them both. She called the domestic violence hotline administered by PODER seeking shelter for herself and her son. Because most shelters would not accommodate the woman with her son, they were forced to live on the streets for two days. The hotline counselor was finally able to find an agency that would take both the mother and the son, but when the counselor told the intake coordinator at the shelter that the woman spoke limited English, the coordinator told her that they could not take anyone who was not English-proficient. When the women in crisis called back and was told of the shelter's "rule," she replied that she could understand English if spoken to her slowly. As Campos explains, Mildred, the hotline counselor, told Wendy, the intake coordinator

> that the woman said that she could communicate a little in English. Wendy told Mildred that they could not provide services to this woman because they have house rules that the woman must agree to follow. Mildred asked her, "What if the woman agrees to follow your rules? Will you still not take her?" Wendy responded that all of the women at the shelter are required to attend [a] support group and they would not be able to have her in the group if she could not communicate. Mildred mentioned the severity of this woman's case. She told Wendy that the woman had been wandering the streets at night while her husband is home, and she had been mugged twice. She also reiterated the fact that this woman was in danger of being killed by either her husband or a mugger. Mildred expressed that the woman's safety was a priority at this point, and that once in a safe place, receiving counseling in a support group could be dealt with.[30]

The intake coordinator restated the shelter's policy of taking only English-speaking women, and stated further that the woman would have to call the shelter herself for screening. If the woman could communicate with them in English, she might be accepted. When the woman called the PODER hotline later that day, she was in such a state of fear that the hotline counselor who had been working with her had difficulty understanding her in Spanish.[31] Campos directly intervened at this point, calling the executive director of the shelter. A counselor called back from the shelter. As Campos reports,

> Marie [the counselor] told me that they did not want to take the woman in the shelter because they felt that the woman would feel isolated. I explained that the son agreed to translate for his mother during the intake process. Furthermore, that we would assist them in locating a Spanish-speaking battered women's advocate to assist in counseling her. Marie stated that utilizing the son was not an acceptable means in communication for them, since it further victimized the victim. In addition, she stated that they had similar experiences with women who were non-English-speaking, and that the women eventually just left because they were not able to communicate with anyone. I expressed my extreme concern for her safety and reiterated that we would assist them in providing her with the necessary services until we could get her placed someplace where they had bilingual staff.[32]

After several more calls, the shelter finally agreed to take the woman. The woman called once more during the negotiation; however, after a plan was in place, the woman never called back. Said Campos, "After so many calls, we are now left to wonder if she is alive and well, and if she will ever have enough faith in our ability to help her to call us again the next time she is in crisis.[33]

Despite this woman's desperate need, she was unable to receive the protection afforded English-speaking women, due to the shelter's rigid commitment to exclusionary policies. Perhaps even more troubling than the shelter's lack of bilingual resources was its refusal to allow a friend or relative to translate for the woman. This story illustrates the absurdity of a feminist approach that would make the ability to attend a support group without a translator a more significant consideration in the distribution of resources than the risk of physical harm on the street. The point is not that the shelter's image of empowerment is empty, but rather that it was imposed without regard to the disempowering consequences for women who didn't match the kind of client the shelter's administrators imagined. And thus they failed to accomplish the basic priority of the shelter movement—to get the woman out of danger.

Here the woman in crisis was made to bear the burden of the shelter's refusal to anticipate and provide for the needs of non-English-speaking women. Said Campos "It is unfair to impose more stress on victims by placing them in the position of having to demonstrate their proficiency in English in order to receive services that are readily available to other battered women."[34] The problem is not easily dismissed as one of well-intentioned ignorance. The specific issue of monolingualism and the monistic view of women's experience that set the stage for this tragedy were not new issues in New York. Indeed, several women of color reported that they had repeatedly struggled with the New York State Coalition Against Domestic Violence over language exclusion and other practices that marginalized the interests of women of color.[35] Yet despite repeated lobbying, the Coalition did not act to incorporate the specific needs of non-white women into its central organizing vision.

Some critics have linked the Coalition's failure to address these issues to the narrow vision of coalition that animated its interaction with women of color in the first place. The very location of the Coalition's headquarters in Woodstock, New York—an area where few people of color live—seemed to guarantee that women of color would play a limited role in formulating policy. Moreover, efforts to include women of color came, it seems, as something of an afterthought. Many were invited to participate only after the Coalition was awarded a grant by the state to recruit women of color. However, as one "recruit" said, "they were not really prepared to deal with us or our issues. They thought that they could simply incorporate us into their organization without rethinking any of their beliefs or priorities and that we would be happy."[36] Even the most formal gestures of inclusion were not to be taken for granted. On one occasion when several women of color attended a meeting to discuss a special task force on women of color, the group debated all day over including the issue on the agenda.[37]

The relationship between the white women and the women of color on the Board was a rocky one from beginning to end. Other conflicts developed over differing definitions of feminism. For example, the Board decided to hire a Latina staffperson to manage outreach programs to the Latino community, but the white members of the hiring committee rejected candidates favored by Latina committee members who did not have recognized feminist credentials. As Campos pointed out, by measuring Latinas against their own biographies, the white members of the Board failed to recognize the different circumstances under which feminist consciousness develops and manifests itself within minority communities. Many of the women who interviewed for the position were established activists and leaders within their own community, a fact in itself suggesting that these women were probably familiar with the specific gender dynamics in their communities and were accordingly better qualified to handle outreach than other candidates with more conventional feminist credentials.[38]

The Coalition ended a few months later when the women of color walked out.[39] Many of these women returned to community-based organizations, preferring to struggle over women's issues within their communities rather than struggle over race and class issues with white middle-class women. Yet as illustrated by the case of the Latina who could find no shelter, the dominance of a particular perspective and set of priorities within the shelter community continues to marginalize the needs of women of color.

The struggle over which differences matter and which do not is neither an abstract nor an insignificant debate among women. Indeed, these conflicts are about more than difference as such; they raise critical issues of power. The problem is not simply that women who dominate the antiviolence movement are different from women of color but that they frequently have power to determine, either through material or rhetorical resources, whether the intersectional differences of women of color will be incorporated at all into the basic formulation of policy. Thus, the struggle over incorporating these differences is not a petty or superficial conflict about who gets to sit at the head of the table. In the context of violence, it is sometimes a deadly serious matter of who will survive—and who will not. . . .

NOTES

1. During my research in Los Angeles, California, I visited Jenessee Battered Women's Shelter, the only shelter in the Western states primarily serving Black women, and Everywoman's Shelter, which primarily serves Asian women. I also visited Estelle Chueng at the Asian Pacific Law Foundation, and I spoke with a representative of La Casa, a shelter in the predominantly Latino community of East L.A.

2. One researcher has noted, in reference to a survey taken of battered women's shelters, that "many Caucasian women were probably excluded from the sample, since they are

more likely to have available resources that enable them to avoid going to a shelter. Many shelters admit only women with few or no resources or alternatives." Mildred Daley Pagelow, *Woman-Battering: Victims and Their Experiences*, 97 (1981). On the other hand, many middle- and upper-class women are financially dependent upon their husbands and thus experience a diminution in their standard of living when they leave their husbands.

3. More specifically, African Americans suffer from high unemployment rates, low incomes, and high poverty rates. According to Dr. David Swinton, Dean of the School of Business at Jackson State University in Mississippi, African Americans "receive three-fifths as much income per person as whites and are three times as likely to have annual incomes below the federally defined poverty level of $12,675 for a family of four." Urban League Urges Action, *N.Y. Times*, Jan 9, 1991, at A14. In fact, recent statistics indicate that racial economic inequality is "higher as we begin the 1990s than at any other time in the last 20 years." David Swinton, The Economic Status of African Americans: "Permanent" Poverty and Inequality, in *The State of Black America 1991*, 25 (1991).

The economic situation of minority women is, expectedly, worse than that of their male counterparts. Black women, who earn a median of $7,875 a year, make considerably less than Black men, who earn a median income of $12,609 a year, and white women, who earn a median income of $9,812 a year. *Id.* at 32 (Table 3). Additionally, the percentage of Black female-headed families living in poverty (46.5%) is almost twice that of white female-headed families (25.4%). *Id.* at 43 (Table 8). Latino households also earn considerably less than white households. In 1988, the median income of Latino households was $20,359 and for white households, $28,840—a difference of almost $8,000. *Hispanic Americans: A Statistical Sourcebook* 149 (1991), Analyzing by origin, in 1988, Puerto Rican households were the worst off, with 34.1% earning below $10,000 a year and a median income for all Puerto Rican households of $15,447 per year. *Id.* at 155. 1989 statistics for Latino men and women show that women earned an average of $7,000 less than men. *Id.* at 169.

4. . . . Racial differences marked an interesting contrast between Jenessee's policies and those of other shelters situated outside the Black community. Unlike some other shelters in Los Angeles, Jenessee welcomed the assistance of men. According to the Director, the shelter's policy was premised on a belief that given African Americans' need to maintain healthy relations to pursue a common struggle against racism, anti-violence programs within the African American community cannot afford to be antagonistic to men. For a discussion of the different needs of Black women who are battered, see Beth Richie, Battered Black Women: A Challenge for the Black Community, *Black Scholar* 40 (Mar./Apr. 1985).

5. §U.S.C. §1186a (1988), . . .

6. Immigration activists have pointed out that "[t]he 1986 Immigration Reform Act and the Immigration Marriage Fraud Amendment have combined to give the spouse applying for permanent residence a powerful tool to control his partner. "Jorge Banales, Abuse Among Immigrants; As Their Numbers Grow So Does the Need for Services, *Washington Post*, Oct. 16, 1990, at E5. . . . In one egregious instance described by Beckie Masaki, executive director of the Asian Women's Shelter in San Francisco, the closer the Chinese bride came to getting her permanent residency in the United States, the more harshly her Asian-American husband beat her. Her husband, kicking her in the neck and face, warned her that she needed him, and if she did not do as he told her, he would call immigration officials. Deanna Hodgin, "Mail-Order" Brides Marry Pain to Get Green Cards, *Washington Times*, Apr. 16, 1991, at El.

7. Immigration Act of 1990, Pub. L. No. 101–649, 104 Stat. 4978. . . .

8. H.R.Rep. No. 723(1). 101st Cong., 2d Sess. 79 (1990), *reprinted in* 1990 U.S.C.C.A.N. 6710, 6759.

9. Hodgin, *supra* note 6.

10. *Id.*

11. A citizen or permanent resident spouse can exercise power over an alien spouse by threatening not to file a petition for permanent residency. If he fails to file a petition for permanent residency, the alien spouse continues to be undocumented and is considered to be in the country illegally. These constraints often restrict an alien spouse from leaving. Dean Ito Taylor tells the story of "one client who has been hospitalized—she's had him arrested for beating her—but she keeps coming back to him because he promises he will file for her. . . . He holds that green card over her head." Hodgin, *supra* note 6. . . .

12. . . . To combat this lack of appropriate services for women of color at many shelters, special programs have been created specifically for women from particular communities. A few examples of such programs include the Victim Intervention Project in East Harlem for Latina women, Jenessee Shelter for African American women in Los Angeles, Apna Gar in Chicago for South Asian women, and, for Asian women generally, the Asian Women's Shelter in San Francisco, the New York Asian Women's Center, and the Center for the Pacific Asian Family in Los Angeles. Programs with hotlines include Sakhi for South Asian Women in New York, and Manavi in Jersey City, also for South Asian women, as well as programs for Korean women in Philadelphia and Chicago.

13. Most crime statistics are classified by sex or race but none are classified by sex and race. Because we know that most rape victims are women, the racial breakdown reveals, at best, rape rates for Black women. Yet, even given this head start, rates for other non-white women are difficult to collect. While there are some statistics for Latinas, statistics for Asian and Native American women are virtually nonexistent. Cf. G. Chezia Carraway, Violence Against Women of Color, *Stan. L. Rev.* 43 (1993); 1301.

14. Shahrazad Ali, *The Blackman's Guide to Understanding the Blackwoman* (1989). Ali's book sold quite well for an independently published title, an accomplishment no doubt due in part to her appearances on the Phil Donahue, Oprah Winfrey, and Sally Jesse Raphael television talk shows. For public and press reaction, see Dorothy Gilliam, Sick, Distorted Thinking, *Washington Post*, Oct. 11, 1990, at D3; Lena Williams, Black Woman's Book Starts a Predictable Storm, *New York Times*, Oct 2, 1990, at C11; see also Pearl Cleague, *Mad at Miles: A Black Women's Guide to Truth* (1990). The title clearly styled after Ali's, *Mad at Miles* responds not only to issues raised by Ali's book, but also to Miles Davis's admission in his autobiography, *Miles: The Autobiography* (1989), that he had physically abused, among other women, his former wife, actress Cicely Tyson.

15. Shahrazad Ali suggests that the "[Blackwoman] certainly does not believe that her disrespect for the Blackman is destructive, nor that her opposition to him has deteriorated the Black nation." S. Ali, *supra* note 14, at viii. Blaming the problems of the community on the failure of the Black woman to accept her "real definition," Ali explains that "[n]o nation can rise when the natural order of the behavior of the male and the female have been altered against their wishes by force. No species can survive if the female of the genus disturbs the balance of her nature by acting other than herself." *Id.* at 76.

16. Ali advises the Blackman to hit the Blackwoman in the mouth, "[b]ecause it is from that hole, in the lower part of her face, that all her rebellion culminates into words. Her unbridled tongue is a main reason she cannot get along with the Blackman. She often needs a reminder." *Id.* at 169. Ali warns that "if [the Blackwoman] ignores the authority and superiority of the Blackman, there is a penalty. When she crosses this line and becomes viciously insulting, it is time for the Blackman to soundly slap her in the mouth." *Id.*

17. Ali explains that, "[r]egretfully some Blackwomen want to be physically controlled by the Blackman." *Id.* at 174. "The Blackwoman, deep inside her heart" Ali reveals, "wants to surrender but she wants to be coerced." *Id.* at 72. "[The Blackwoman] wants [the Blackman] to stand up and defend himself even if it means he has to knock her out of the way to do so. This is necessary whenever the Blackwoman steps out of the protection of womanly behavior and enters the dangerous domain of masculine challenge." *Id.* at 174.

18. [Women and Violence: Hearings Before the Senate Comm. on the Judiciary on Legislation to Reduce the Growing Problem of Violent Crime Against Women, 101st Cong., 2d Sess., pt. 2, at 142] (statement of Susan Kelly-Dreiss) (discussing several studies in Pennsylvania linking homelessness to domestic violence).

19. *Id.* at 143 (statement of Susan Kelly-Dreiss).

20. Alice Walker, *The Color Purple* (1982). The most severe criticism of Walker developed after the book was filmed as a movie. Donald Bogle, a film historian, argued that part of the criticism of the movie stemmed from the one-dimensional portrayal of Mister, the abusive man. See Jacqueline Trescott, Passions Over Purple; Anger and Unease Over Film's Depiction of Black Men, *Washington Post*, Feb. 5, 1986, at C1. Bogle argues that in the novel, Walker linked Mister's abusive conduct to his oppression in the white world—since Mister "can't be himself, he has to assert himself with the black woman." The movie failed to make any connection between Mister's abusive treatment of Black women and racism, and thereby presented Mister only as an "insensitive, callous man." *Id.*

21. See, e.g., Gerald Early, Her Picture in the Papers: Remembering Some Black Women, *Antaeus*, Spring 1988, at 9; Daryl Pickney, Black Victims, Black Villains, *New York Review of Books*, Jan. 29, 1987, at 17; Trescott, *supra* note 20.

22. Trudler Harris, On the Color Purple, Stereotypes, and Silence, *Black Am. Lit. F.* 18 (1984), 155.

23. The source of the resistance reveals an interesting difference between the Asian-American and African-American communities. In the African-American community, the resistance is usually grounded in efforts to avoid confirming negative stereotypes of African-Americans as violent; the concern of members in some Asian-American communities as to avoid tarnishing the model minority myth. Interview with Nilda Rimonte, Director of the Everywoman Shelter, in Los Angeles, California (April 19, 1991).

24. Nilda Rimonte, A Question of Culture: Cultural Approval of Violence Against Women in the Pacific-Asian Community and the Cultural Defense, *Stan. L. Rev.* 43 (1991), 1311; see also Nilda Rimonte, Domestic Violence Against Pacific Asians, in Asian Women United of California ed., *Making Waves: An Anthology of Writings By and About Asian American Women*; 327, 328 (1989). . . .

When—or, more importantly, how—to take culture into account when addressing the needs of women of color is a complicated issue. Testimony as to the particularities of Asian "culture" has increasingly been used in trials to determine the culpability of both Asian immigrant women and men who are charged with crimes of interpersonal violence. A position on the use of the "cultural defense" in these instances depends on how "culture" is being defined as well as on whether and to what extent the "cultural defense" has been used differently for Asian men and Asian women. See Leti Volpp, (Mis) Identifying Culture: Asian Women and the "Cultural Defense," (unpublished manuscript).

25. See, e.g., Lenore F. Walker, *Terrifying Love: Why Battered Women Kill and How Society Responds*, 101–102 (1989). ("Battered women come from all types of economic, cultural, religious, and racial backgrounds. . . . They are women like you. Like me. Like those whom you know and love."); Murray A. Straus, Richard J. Gelles & Suzanne K. Steinmetz, *Behind Closed Doors: Violence in the American Family*, 31 (1980) ("Wife-beating is found in every class, at every income level."). . . .

26. For example, Susan Kelly-Dreiss states: "The public holds many myths about battered women—they are poor, they

are women of color, they are uneducated, they are on welfare, they deserve to be beaten and they even like it. However, contrary to common misperceptions, domestic violence is not confined to any one socioeconomic, ethnic, religious, racial or age group." Hearings on Violent Crime Against Women, *supra* note 18, pt. 2, at 139 (testimony of Susan Kelly-Dreiss, Executive Director, Pennsylvania Coalition Against Domestic Violence). Kathleen Waits offers a possible explanation for this misperception: "It is true that battered women who are also poor are more likely to come to the attention of governmental officials than are their middle- and upper-class counterparts. However, this phenomenon is caused more by the lack of alternative resources and the intrusiveness of the welfare state than by any significantly higher incidence of violence among lower-class families." Kathleen Waits, The Criminal Justice System's Response to Battering: Understanding the Problem, Forging the Solutions, *Washington U.L. Rev.* 60 (1985), 267, 276–277.

27. However, no reliable statistics support such a claim. In fact, some statistics suggest that there is a greater frequency of violence among the working classes and the poor. See M. Straus, R. Gelles & S. Steinmetz, *supra* note 25, at 31. Yet these statistics are also unreliable because, to follow Waits's observation, violence in middle- and upper-class homes remains hidden from the view of statisticians and governmental officials alike. I would suggest that assertions that the problem is the same across race and class are driven less by actual knowledge about the prevalence of domestic violence in different communities than by advocates' recognition that the image of domestic violence as an issue involving primarily the poor and minorities complicates efforts to mobilize against it.

28. 137 Cong. Rec. S611 (daily ed. Jan. 14, 1991) (statement of Sen. Boren). Senator William Cohen (D-Me.) followed with a similar statement. . . . *Id.* (statement of Sen. Cohen).

29. *48 Hours: Till Death Do Us Part* (CBS television broadcast, Feb. 6, 1991).

30. Letter of Diana M. Campos, Director of Human Services, PODER, to Joseph Semidei, Deputy Commissioner, New York State Department of Social Services (Mar. 26, 1992).

31. The woman had been slipping back into her home during the day when her husband was at work. She remained in a heightened state of anxiety because he was returning shortly and she would be forced to go back out into the streets for yet another night.

32. PODER Letter, *supra* note 30.

33. *Id.*

34. *Id.*

35. Roundtable Discussion on Racism and the Domestic Violence Movement (April 2, 1992). The participants in the discussion—Diana Campos, Director, Bilingual Outreach Project of the New York State Coalition Against Domestic Violence: Elsa A. Rios, Project Director, Victim Intervention Project (a community-based project in East Harlem, New York, serving battered women); and Haydee Rosario, a social worker with the East Harlem Council for Human Services and a Victim Intervention Project volunteer—recounted conflicts relating to race and culture during their association with the New York State Coalition Against Domestic Violence, a state oversight group that distributed resources to battered women's shelters throughout the state and generally set policy priorities for the shelters that were part of the Coalition.

36. *Id.*

37. *Id.*

38. *Id.*

39. Ironically, the specific dispute that led to the walk-out concerned the housing of the Spanish-language domestic violence hotline. The hotline was initially housed at the Coalition's headquarters, but languished after a succession of coordinators left the organization. Latinas on the Coalition board argued that the hotline should be housed at one of the community service agencies, while the board insisted on maintaining control of it. The hotline is now housed at PODER. *Id.*

Sex and War: Fighting Men, Comfort Women, and the Military-Sexual Complex

Several years ago a student came to see me during office hours to discuss a research project he was planning for that semester. He said he wanted to write a paper on Korean prostitution in Junction City, Kansas. I looked at him blankly, thinking there was some kind of miscommunication between us. He was an international student, and perhaps we were having a language problem. Either I did not understand his description of the project or he did not understand the assignment. What would Koreans (especially Korean prostitutes) be doing in a small town 150 miles west of Kansas City? As we discussed his project further, I began to understand what this Korean student already knew—that both South Korea and Kansas are ethnosexual destinations where the global meets the local in the pursuit of racialized sex and romance.

. . . This [reading] will focus on the geopolitics of ethnicity and sexuality mainly in the twentieth century, and will examine the ethnosexual dimensions of international conflicts, civil wars, the Cold War, and the post-Soviet "new world order." We will survey the ways that sexuality is deployed in military missions and the uses of sexual technologies in making war and keeping the peace.

SEX AND THE MILITARY MAN

Since the Korean War of 1950–1953 hundreds of thousands of U.S. armed services personnel have been stationed on dozens of military bases and installations in South Korea. For instance, in 2001 U.S. Forces in Korea officials reported that there were ninety-five military bases and installations of various sorts in South Korea, forty-one of which were "major sized bases/installations" staffed by approximately thirty-seven thousand troops and service personnel.[1] Some of these troops are based stateside in Junction City, Kansas, home of

the U.S. Army's First Infantry Division—"The Big Red One." While they are stationed in South Korea many American servicemen frequent hundreds of bars and brothels surrounding military bases, some of which were set up and are inspected by U.S. and Korean authorities. These Americans sate their sexual desire and spread their sexual seed among thousands of Korean and other mainly Asian prostitutes servicing these servicemen. For instance, Katharine Moon estimates that

[s]ince the war, over one million Korean women have served as sex providers for the U.S. military. And millions of Koreans and Americans have shared a sense of special bonding, for they have together shed blood in battle and mixed blood through sex and Amerasian offspring.[2]

GIs in Korea do not simply have sex with local women, some marry Korean women who return with them to the United States when the men complete their tours of duty. Moon reports that "from the early 1950s to the early 1990s, over 100,000 Korean women have immigrated to the United States as wives of servicemen."[3] Some of these marriages are, no doubt, affairs of convenience arranged for profit or immigration purposes, and some are matches made for love or romance. Some marriages last, some do not.

In the United States, Korean women from dissolved unions often find themselves strangers in a new land, attempting to establish an independent life, possessing only a limited knowledge of English and few job skills, competing for employment in local labor markets primarily oriented to providing services to the military base. These women have easy access linguistically and culturally to already established Korean businesses catering to soldiers, and many find work as waitresses, bargirls, dancers, masseuses, and prostitutes. This

combination of military, marriage, and migration accounted for what initially seemed to me to be the unlikely presence of Korean prostitutes in Junction City,
Kansas.

The number of Korean prostitutes in Junction City
is no doubt small and represents a tiny proportion of
the number of American prostitutes working near U.S.
military bases across the United States. Korean prostitutes in Junction City are, of course, only a tiny fraction
of the number of Korean and other Asian prostitutes
working near U.S. military bases in Korea, and still a
smaller fraction of German and other European prostitutes working near U.S. military bases in Germany, or
the number of Japanese, Okinawan, and other Asian
prostitutes working near U.S. military bases in Japan,[4]
or Filipino prostitutes who worked near U.S. military
bases in the Philippines until those bases were closed in
1992,[5] or Panamanian and Latin American prostitutes
who worked near bases in the former U.S. Canal Zone
before the canal was turned over to Panama in 1999.
These are to name but a few of the ethnosexual work
zones surrounding U.S. and other countries' military
bases around the world. These militarized ethnosexual
frontiers are collateral creations of the global defense
and warfare system.

An important aspect of Korean prostitution in Korea
and Kansas involves the place of Asian women in
Western erotic meaning systems. Lynn Thiesmeyer argues that the imaginary construction of Asian women's
sexuality is accomplished by "discourses of seduction"
in which the Asian female body is characterized by
servile sexual availability. She argues that this long-
standing, performative Western sexual stereotype of
Asian women works to silence dissident discourses and
mask inconvenient realities of Asian women's physical abuse, forced servitude, and sexual exploitation by
both Western and non-Western men.

> The western image of the Asian female, the Asian
> body, and Asian sexuality has been reproduced, yet
> scarcely updated for centuries. As a late twentieth-
> century representative body of cultural feudalism and
> exoticism, the Asian/Asian-American woman has no
> parallel in the fantasies of the West. Wendy Chapkis
> points out that "advertisements using Asian women,
> for example, are evocative not only of the sexual mys-
> tery but also the docility and subservience supposedly
> 'natural to the oriental female.' . . . These women thus
> become metaphors for adventure, cultural difference,
> and sexual sub-servience."[6]

Thus, for American servicemen the sexual recreation
areas that surround U.S. military bases, especially in
Asia, are ethnosexual sites where Western fantasies of
Asian female sexuality meet material manifestations
of Asian women, and where the marriage of geopolitics
and racial cosmologies is consummated nightly.

Although the presence of U.S. bases provides the
customer base for the local and immigrant prostitutes,
the bars and brothels that ring military installations are
owned and regulated by a variety of economic players.
Aida Santos argues that there are many local groups
and actors directly or indirectly involved in the sex
industry: local club owners, organized crime rings,
politicians and party officials, law enforcement; she
also cites local patriarchal cultural patterns, especially
"male political privilege that underlies the institutionalized use of women's bodies."[7] Saundra Sturdevant
and Brenda Stoltzfus's discussion of the bar system in
Olongapo that was situated near the Subic Bay U.S.
military base in the Philippines described a similar
local/foreign partnership:

> The bar owners are Filipinos, Chinese, and American
> ex-Navy men who either have married a Filipina or
> have a front in order to own a bar. They are community
> members active in the Lion's and Rotary Clubs. The
> mayor also owns several clubs. The club owners have
> an association, which enables them to control what
> happens in the bar system.[8]

There are many interests served by the sexual service industry. There is money to be made, troops to be
entertained, tensions to be released, strategic interests
to be protected, and masculinity to be militarized.
Cynthia Enloe argues that militaries and military operations depend on

> particular presumptions about masculinity in order to
> sustain soldiers' morale and discipline. Without a sexual-
> ized "rest and recreation" (R&R) period, would the U.S.
> military command be able to send young men off on long,
> often tedious sea voyages and ground maneuvers? With-
> out myths of Asian women's compliant sexuality would
> many American men be able to sustain their own iden-
> tities of themselves as manly enough to act as soldiers.
> Women who . . . work as prostitutes around American
> bases in Asia tell us how a militarized masculinity is con-
> structed and reconstructed in smoky bars and in sparsely
> furnished boardinghouses. If we only look at boot camps
> and the battlefield—the focus of most investigations into

the formation of militarized masculinity—we will not be able adequately to explain just how masculinity is created and sustained in the peculiar ways necessary to sustain a military organization.[9]

Enloe is joined by a number of critics of the U.S. global military presence who argue that the military mobilization of masculinity to serve national interests—economic and geopolitical, foreign and domestic—is not without its costs—to the men themselves and to the country as a whole. The presence of the U.S. military is deeply resented in many countries, not the least because of the local presence of American culture and consumers, especially sexual consumers. Chalmers Johnson argues that

[f]ew Americans who have never served in the armed forces overseas have any conception of the nature or impact of an American base complex, with its massive military facilities, post exchanges, dependents' housing estates, swimming pools, and golf courses, and the associated bars, strip clubs, whore-houses, and venereal disease clinics that they attract. . . . They can extend for miles, dominating localities and in some cases whole nations.[10]

In such cases, the American presence can be experienced by locals as an occupation by foreign men, women, equipment, vehicles, buildings, war machinery and materiel, as an invasion of Western culture, ideas, and desires, and as a source of pollution and corruption. Johnson links anti-American sentiment and actions, such as attacks on U.S. military and civilian targets, to the "blowback" from America's international presence and foreign policy that, he argues, are hidden from average Americans or conveniently denied by informed Americans and their government.[11]

FIGHTING MEN AND COMFORT WOMEN

As Enloe notes, sexuality has always been an important, though often disregarded aspect of all militaries and military operations. Throughout history women have been among "camp followers" providing services such as laundry, nursing, companionship, and sex to soldiers on military missions during peace and war.[12] Sometimes these women have been wives, relatives, or girlfriends, but always among their ranks have been prostitutes as well. Women who have had sex with servicemen around the world, however, have not always

been volunteers. Throughout history local women have been involuntarily "drafted" in the sexual service of militaries as rape victims and sexual slaves.[13]

Rape in war is at its core an ethnosexual phenomenon. Whether a war is fought across national borders or inside state boundaries, the military front is typically an ethnosexual frontier. Differences in nationality, race, or ethnicity separate the combatants and identify the targets of aggression in military operations. Whether violence in war is from combat or sexual attack, and whether it is guns or bodies that are used as weapons, those who are physically or sexually assaulted almost always are different in some ethnic way. Men at war do not, as a rule, rape their "own" women unless, of course, those women are suspected of disloyalty, especially sexual disloyalty or "collaboration."

Sexual exploitation and abuse are important weapons of war, and rape is perhaps the most common component of war's sexual arsenal. Susan Brownmiller documents the routine practice of rape, especially gang rape, in war.[14] Moving or occupying armies use the rape of "enemy" women and girls as both a carrot and a stick: raping local women is a spoil of war for the troops to enjoy, and rape is also a technique of terror and warfare designed to dominate and humiliate enemy men by sexually conquering their women. Rape in war, as in many other ethnosexual settings, is best understood as a transaction between men, where women are the currency used in the exchange. Sexually taking an enemy's women amounts to gaining territory and psychological advantage. In countries around the world, rape often is defined as a polluting action, a way to soil the victim, her kin, and her nation physically and symbolically. Sexual warfare can extend beyond the moment of violation in situations where victims are reputationally smeared, physically mutilated, or when pregnancies or births result from sexual assaults. For instance, the widespread rape of mainly Muslim and some Croatian women by Serbian men in Bosnia in the early 1990s was partly intended to impregnate the women so that they would bear Serbian babies, "little Chetniks."[15] In order to guarantee that these rape victims could not obtain abortions, the Serbs set up concentration camps where pregnant women were imprisoned until they gave birth.[16]

Probably the best-known instance of rape in war is the so-called Rape of Nanking that occurred during the Japanese invasion of China in the winter and spring of 1938–1939, when Japanese soldiers raped an estimated eighty thousand Chinese women and girls.[17] A less well-known instance of Japanese wartime sexual exploits was the sexual enslavement of thousands of mainly Asian women by the Japanese Imperial Army during World War II. Sexual slavery in war is a variation on the theme of wartime rape. Slavery extends the tactic of rape as a short-term strategy of a military mission into a permanent feature of military operations. The Japanese military established camps of so-called military comfort women (*Jugun Ianfu*) in Japan and other countries where Japanese troops were stationed. While there were some mainly lower-class Japanese women forced into sexual slavery, most of the estimated 200,000 women enslaved by the Japanese army were ethnic or national Others brought from Korea, China, Taiwan, Indonesia, Malaysia, and the Philippines to sexually service the troops.[18] Kazuko Watanabe reports that in such settings a woman's worth as a sexual commodity was based on her class and her ethnicity.[19] . . .

Soldiers' rankings of and preferences for women of particular races and nationalities enslaved in rape camps were not unique to the Japanese military.[20] Japan was not the only country that established large-scale organized operations of forced sexual servitude during World War II. The Nazis used concentration camps in Germany and other occupied countries for more than industrial and war-related labor, their program of genocide against the Jews, and the mass deportation and killing of Roma (gypsies) and other "non-Aryan" peoples. Sexual labor was also demanded of women internees, and both men and women prisoners were used for sexual experimentation by Nazi scientists and physicians. German concentration camps were sites of forced prostitution and sexual assault, and as was the case with Japan, not all women in the German camps were treated as "equal" when it came to sexual abuse. A woman's age, youth, and physical appearance made her more or less likely to be the target of Nazi sexual aggression.[21] And, as in so many areas of social life, even (especially) in wartime concentration camps, ethnicity mattered. There were official prohibitions against German soldiers having sex with Jewish women, though these rules often were not enforced. Many Jewish women survivors reported extensive sadistic sexual torture, as well as rape, and these assaults often were accompanied by a barrage of racial and anti-Semitic verbal abuse.[22]

The Allies also were involved in sexual violence and exploitation during World War II. Some was in the form of mass rapes, such as those committed against German women by the Soviet army.[23] In other cases, sexual abuse and exploitation resulted when military personnel capitalized on the vulnerability of women who faced economic hardship, malnourishment, or starvation because of the war's disruption of local economies and food production. Many women in occupied or liberated countries found sexual liaisons or prostitution preferable to the grim alternatives available for themselves and their dependent families. U.S. troops also committed rapes during the war and the occupation that followed. In her examination of U.S. Army records, Brown-miller found 947 rape *convictions,* not simply charges or trials of American soldiers in Army general courts-martial during the period from January 1942 to July 1947.[24]

Wartime rape did not stop at the end of World War II, nor did its ethnosexual character change after 1945. The practice of rape in war extended into major and minor conflicts during the second half of the twentieth century—in civil wars, wars of independence, and military invasions, interventions, and operations in countries and regions around the world including Bangladesh, Vietnam, Iraq, Kuwait, Bosnia, Croatia, Serbia, Rwanda, Liberia, Kashmir, and Sierra Leone.[25] The logic of rape in war is always the same: rapes are committed across ethnosexual boundaries, and rape is used by both sides for the familiar time-honored reasons—to reward the troops, to terrorize and humiliate the enemy, and as a means of creating solidarity and protection through mutual guilt among small groups of soldiers. Ethnic loyalty and ethnic loathing join hands in rape in war.

In the post-Soviet era East European nationalist conflicts the use of rape as a weapon of war has begun to move from the shadows more fully into view. For instance, during the 1990s warfare occurred along a number of ethnic and national borders in the former Yugoslavia—between Croats and Serbs, Christians and Muslims, and against Roma, among others. The most notorious of these ethnic conflicts was in Bosnia; the conflict's notoriety stemmed in part from its sexual character, especially the mass rape of Bosnian Muslim women by Orthodox Christian Serbian men. Many of these men and women were former neighbors. Muslims and Christians had lived side by side in the city of Sarajevo and elsewhere in Bosnia for decades and many had intermarried. That peace was shattered in 1992 when "ethnic cleansing" began.

Ethnic cleansing, or the removal of one ethnic group from a territory claimed by another, followed a common pattern across the region. Groups of armed Serbian men (sometimes uniformed troops and sometimes "irregulars" who were not officially in the military and not in uniform) roamed Bosnian towns and villages in groups, opportunistically looting and pillaging houses and businesses, raping and killing mainly unarmed Muslims they encountered along the way. Survivors reported that the Serbs came through the same towns several times in waves. During the first wave, typically, some of the Muslim men were killed and the rest were rounded up to be killed later or to be interned in concentration camps. Muslim women, children, and the elderly were left behind. It was during the next waves of Serbs passing through the towns that they raped local non-Serbian girls and women.

Munevra was a forty-eight-year-old widow with three sons ranging in age from fourteen to twenty-four, ages that made them targets for the Serbs to kill or deport to concentration camps. She kept the young men hidden in the cellar as small groups of armed Serbian men repeatedly came through the town. In the spring of 1992, two men came to her house and sexually assaulted her. Please note, Munevra's account of her abuse and the testimony of other rape victims below may be very disturbing to some readers.

I was afraid my sons would hear me. I was dying of fear 'cause of my sons. They're decent people. . . . Then this man touched my breasts. He pulled up my blouse and took out my breasts. . . . He said, "For a woman your age your breasts aren't bad." Then they brought me to the other room. . . . I begged him and cried, and I crossed my legs. Then he took out his thing, you know, and he did it and sprayed it on me. When he was done the other one came and did the same thing. . . . When they left, my sons came out and . . . they asked me what happened: "What'd they do to you?" I said, "Nothing." I couldn't tell them about it. . . . I'd rather die than have them find out about it.[26]

Women's and families' shame about such incidents were part of the process of victimization and violation.[27] Munevra's experience occurred relatively early in the nationalist conflict; far worse sexual violations were in store for women as the war escalated.

The scene in Serbian so-called rape camps was a longer, more brutal nightmare for Muslim and other non-Serbian women and girls. Twenty-six-year-old Ifeta was arrested by Serbian soldiers, most of whom she knew, and taken to a women's camp in Doboj:

Three drunken [Serbian army] soldiers . . . dragged her into a classroom . . . here she was raped by all three men "at the same time," says Ifeta, pointing to her mouth and backside. "And while they were doing it they said I was going to have a baby by them". . . . After that the rapes were a part of Ifeta's daily life. . . . It was always a gang rape, they always cursed and humiliated her during it, and the rapists very frequently forced her to have oral sex with them.[28]

Another camp internee, Kadira, described the weeks she spent at Doboj:

"They pushed bottle necks into our sex, they even stuck shattered, broken bottles into some women. . . . Guns too. And then you don't know if he's going to fire, you're scared to death". . . . Once she was forced to urinate on the Koran. Another time she and a group of women had to dance naked for the Serbian guards and sing Serbian songs. . . . She has forgotten how many times she was raped.[29]

The same pattern of sexual terror, torture, and rape used by the Serbs in their campaigns of ethnic cleansing and warfare in Bosnia was repeated in Kosovo, Yugoslavia, in 1998–1999. Once again groups of Serbian men—police, soldiers, irregulars—swept through villages invading homes and raping Kosovar Albanian (mainly Muslim) female occupants, sexually attacking Kosovar Albanian women refugees fleeing combat zones, and sexually assaulting Kosovar Albanian women who were being held hostage or detained. The Kosovo conflict ended when NATO troops entered Kosovo in June 1999.[30]

In spring 2000, the UN convened the *International Criminal Tribunal for the Former Yugoslavia* in The Hague, Netherlands, to investigate and prosecute those ordering mass killing and mass rape in the various ethnic conflicts in the former Yugoslavia.[31] This investigation raised the issue of whether rape and sexual slavery are "crimes against humanity." Enloe argues that this question reflects a new awareness and public airing of what has been a long hidden history of sexual assault, torture, and exploitation of women during war:

[T]he rapes in Bosnia have been documented by women's organizations . . . [that] have helped create an international political network of feminists who are making news of the Bosnian women's victimization not to institutionalize women as victims, not to incite men to more carnage, but to explain anew how war makers rely on peculiar ideas about masculinity . . . [F]eminist reporters are using news of wartime sexual assaults by male soldiers to rethink the very meanings of both sovereignty and national identity. . . . If they succeed, the construction of the entire international political arena will be significantly less vulnerable to patriarchy.[32]

As the reports of human rights hearings and organizations document every year, it is not only enemy women who are the targets of sexual abuse and torture in war. I have not seen reported the establishment of rape camps with men as sexual slaves, however, men often are assaulted sexually as part of intimidation, torture, and combat in international conflicts and wars, as well as in military or paramilitary operations against internal political or ethnic insurgents. For instance, in Bosnia, there were numerous reports of cases in which Muslim and Croatian men were castrated or forced to castrate one another:

> In villages, towns, cities, the countryside, and concentration camps, male and female adults and children are raped as part of more extensive torture. Many of the atrocities committed are centered on the genitalia . . . [T]estimonies of castrations enforced on Bosnian-Herzegovinian and Croatian prisoners, and in particular of orders under threat of death that they castrate each other with various instruments and at times with their teeth, are widely available, as the [United Nations] Bassiouni Report makes clear.[33]

Men also can be vulnerable to sexualized warfare in more indirect ways. In her critique of Japan's patriarchal Confucianist view of all women and racist treatment of non-Japanese men and women, Kazuko Watanabe also identifies a danger for men. She argues that in many countries men are trapped in masculinist roles, and forced to act out patriarchal and sexual scripts that commodify and endanger them as well as the women they victimize. . . .[34]

Watanabe's analysis suggests that although they are perpetrators of the rape and sexual abuse of both women and other men in times of war, men pay a psychological, social, and physical price for their complicity in patriarchal masculinist systems of sexual and ethnosexual violence. For instance, many soldiers display varying degrees of post-traumatic stress or "shell shock" following combat. Michael Kimmel reports that during World War I officers and doctors tended to view such disorders as "failures to conform to gender demands":

> Most psychiatric treatments for shell shock involved treating the disease as the result of insufficient manliness. T. J. Calhoun, assistant surgeon with the Army of the Potomac, argued that if the soldier could not be "laughed out of it by his comrades" or by "appeals to his manhood," then a good dose of battle was the best "curative."[35]

Although modern-day soldiers suffering from post-traumatic stress are viewed with more sympathy than their historical counterparts, many, including those working in the health care industry, still view soldiers exhibiting symptoms arising from combat and military operations with some suspicion, as malingerers, frauds, or weaklings.[36]

SEX AND PEACE

A state of war is not a necessary condition for the militarization of sex. Even in peacetime or as part of a "defense" strategy, the presence of military troops, operations, or bases creates a convenient and lucrative market for the sex industry, and occupying or peacekeeping troops find ample opportunity for sexual associations with and sexual attacks against local women and girls. It is the scale of military operations, not the occurrence of actual combat, that determines the amount and intensity of sexual action—commercial, congenial, and coercive—on the ethnosexual frontiers surrounding military installations and troops. For instance, the Cold War changed the character of military-related prostitution, which was already operating on a large scale at the end of World War II. After the war, the Allied powers established permanent military bases in former hostile states (e.g., Germany, Japan, Italy) and in many friendly countries as part of the North Atlantic Treaty Organization (NATO) and various mutual defense agreements and treaties (e.g., with the Philippines, Panama, Guam).

During the Cold War, the creation of a global network of military bases and pacts by the U.S. and its allies and by the Soviet Union and its allies greatly expanded the number of armed forces and military installations around the world. These new military consumers generated unprecedented demand for many products and services for military operations and personnel, including sexual services. Military bases became permanent features of the geopolitical landscape in the second half of the twentieth century, and expanded in size and personnel during various Cold War proxy combat engagements such as those in Korea, Vietnam, Central America, and Southern Africa. Prostitution became a large-scale, stable industry around military bases in many parts of the world. Not just U.S. bases were involved. Soldiers are a diverse set of global ethnosexual adventurers. For instance, Enloe reported during the 1980s there were

> British bases in West Germany, Cyprus, the Falklands and Belize . . . [and] Northern Ireland. . . . The Indian

government stationed 45,000 of its soldiers on counter-insurgency duty in Sri Lanka. There have been 50,000 Cuban soldiers stationed in Angola. The Soviet Union maintains bases in Vietnam and Eastern Europe. Vietnamese troops only now are withdrawing from Kampuchea. The French military bases 8,000 of its soldiers in Chad, the Central African Republic, Gabon, Senegal, the Ivory Coast and Djibouti, as well as others in its remaining Pacific and Caribbean colonies. Canada sends troops to its bases in West Germany. Finnish, Fijian, Irish and other men serve overseas as part of United Nations peace-keeping forces.[37]

The sex workers who provided services to these troops typically were ethnically distinct from their clients since soldiers often are stationed in regions of a country with ethnically different populations or in countries where local or immigrant sex workers are of different nationalities from occupying forces. It is important to note in this thus far almost exclusively heterosexual discussion that the sex workers visited by military men are not always women. For instance, U.S. servicemen stationed abroad also seek exotic sexual encounters with Other men. During his tour in the U.S. Marine Corps in the 1980s, former Chief Scout/Sniper David Anthony Tyeeme Clark reported much gossip and bragging by Marines about their sexual exploits with "benny boys"—male sex workers who provided presumably straight Marines with something new and different during their shore "liberty."

> My enlistment was for six years beginning in 1982 . . . [those] years corresponded with the Reagan/ Gipper/John Wayne administration . . . when men were men and benny boys provided the best shore leave memories. . . . In my memory of those conversations, guys would insist that benny boys were even better than women (the logic was something like benny boys had insider [sexual] knowledge, something women had to depend on men for learning).[38]

Clark argues that by othering these often gay, ethnically different male sex workers, Marines managed to create the distance they needed to maintain a hypermasculine, hyperheterosexual image of themselves and the Marine Corps. The exotic strangeness they attributed to the benny boys seemed to allow the Marines to camouflage the fact that they were having sex with other men.[39]

The last five decades of postwar global militarization has institutionalized female and male prostitution on an unparalleled scale in the many countries around the world that served NATO and Eastern bloc military operations. The disintegration of the Soviet Union in the early 1990s and the subsequent end of the Cold War changed the logic of many of these military base and personnel placements from superpower competition to international peacekeeping. UN and NATO peacekeeping operations have expanded as has the U.S. military's involvement in peacekeeping. As a result, the international circulation of soldiers remains an important feature of the global system. These new peacekeeping troops are no more celibate than their Cold War predecessors, and the new military missions have generated continuing demand for sexual services. For instance, Judith Stiehm reports that during the United Nations' peacekeeping mission in Namibia in 1989–1990

> some male peacekeepers moved local women into their quarters, UN vehicles were parked in front of brothels, and even high-ranking officials were believed to exploit local women hired by the UN. . . . [In Cambodia in the early 1990s] the abuse of local women and children by UN troops and civilian police was brought to public attention. . . . Apparently the fear of AIDS made "virgins" highly desirable, and younger and younger girls were being recruited for prostitution.[40]

In contrast to the historically casual, even approved links between national armies and sexual service suppliers, Stiehm found that international peacekeeping troops and officials' sexual excursions into local towns and countrysides became controversial as the 1990s progressed. For the first time serious questions were being raised about the taken-for-granted, "boys will be boys" attitude of UN senior officials. Stiehm attributes this change of heart and mind to the presence of women UN workers and peacekeepers and to the involvement of religious NGOs (nongovernmental organizations, such as charitable or relief organizations), both of whom challenged longstanding military men's sexual perquisites.[41] Exposure and criticism of UN troops' ethnosexual appetites and indulgences pressured United Nations officials to design new policies to restrict such behavior. Established ethnosexual practices die hard, however, especially where there is money to be made. . . .

An important aspect of military-related prostitution, even in peacekeeping settings, is that it illustrates very clearly the links among geopolitics, ethnicity, and sexuality. Even away from war fronts with their direct ethnic and national confrontations, sexual encounters involving foreign military personnel and local people are almost without exception ethnosexual encounters. The women and men providing sexual services to peace-time military and police personnel are invariably racial, ethnic, and national Others. Such sexual encounters often are the only real interactions that occur between locals and foreign soldiers. As a result of this limited, distorted relationship, the commercial sexualized image each has of the other magnifies the stereotypes and prejudices that so often are associated with racial, ethnic, or national differences. The hypersexualization of local women, the commercialization of sexual culture, and the presence of an entrenched sex industry, all of which stem from the militarization of sexuality, often persist long after the wars are over. . . .

THE MILITARY-SEXUAL COMPLEX

Despite the end of the Korean War, Vietnam War, and Cold War, the sex industries they helped to generate and expand have remained permanent niches in many national economies. Besides continuing to service ongoing military operations around the world, a central legacy of the militarized global sex trade is sex tourism.[42] Sex tourism is part of a large sex-for-profit industry which includes, for example, prostitution, pornography, sexual media, materials, and equipment, and nude and exotic dancing. Sex tourism destinations are concentrated commercial sex spaces that provide a wide array of establishments and services to which consumers travel for sex. Sex tourist destinations can draw customers from local populations or from more distant national and international venues. Sex tours often are advertised and arranged by agencies and organizations specializing in sex tourism. Both sex tourism and the broader sex industry of which it is a part are organized commercial operations with legal and illegal components and with some well-paid and some exploited workers.

Sex tourism represents another chapter in the history of sex and war. Sex tourism developed as the international industry it is today with the help of the U.S. military. The strategy of delivering large groups of consumers to commercial sex service destinations began, in part, as a strategy for entertaining the troops during the Vietnam War. Ryan Bishop and Lillian Robinson argue that there is a historical connection between sex-for-sale operations catering to soldiers and sex for sale to tourists: "sex tourism builds on an infrastructure established

for military R&R and extended through corporate recreational contracts. . . .[43] They detail a fascinating link between the U.S. military and the World Bank in the development of the notorious Thai sex industry:

> In 1967, Thailand contracted with the U.S. government to provide "Rest and Recreation" . . . services to the troops during the Vietnam War. Today's customers at the go-go bars spawned by those contracts are not only white Americans but also European and Australian—all *farangs* to the Thais. . . . It was in 1971, while the war in Southeast Asia still raged, that World Bank President Robert McNamara, who had been U.S. Secretary of Defense when the R&R contracts with Thailand were signed, went to Bangkok to arrange for the bank's experts to produce a study of Thailand's postwar tourism prospects.[44]

Because of the presence and profitability of the wartime sex industry, the World Bank's advice, which Thailand followed, to specialize in tourism resulted in a large-scale sexualization of the tourist trade. The U.S. military and the World Bank thus became partners in developing what is perhaps the most famous, or infamous depending on one's point of view, sex industry in the world. Phil Williams concurs with Bishop and Robinson's summary of this connection:

> The importance of Thailand in the global sex industry, for example, is generally traced back to the late 1960s and the use of Thailand as a place for "rest and recreation" for American G.I.s in Vietnam. The recommendation by the World Bank in [the 1970s] that Thailand develop "mass tourism" as a means to pay off its debts, encouraged what became, in effect, the peace-time institutionalization of the sex industry in Thailand.[45]

Some scholars argue that historical and cultural aspects of Thai society made it especially suitable for the development of a large-scale sex sector. For instance, although David Leheny agrees with other researchers about the link between Thailand's agreement to provide R&R for U.S. soldiers during the Vietnam war and the burgeoning of its sex industry, he also cites earlier agreements and legislation that set the stage for the present, in particular

> the Bowring Treaty of 1855 which opened Thailand to foreign laborers. Most immigrants were young men from rural South China, planning to earn money for

their families by mining tin in Phuket. A large number of Chinese prostitutes accompanied the men, establishing the largest sex centers Thailand had experienced at that time. . . . A 1909 law to prevent the spread of venereal disease effectively legalized prostitution.[46]

Ryan Bishop also supports analyses that identify historical antecedents to contemporary patterns of ethnosexual commerce. He is suspicious of other claims, however, especially those made by sex tourists, that Thai Buddhism and traditions of concubinage provide religious and cultural support for the commercial sex industry:

> It is a bit too neat that "going native" just happens to mesh with one's deepest, darkest desires. . . . [Thailand's] Theravada Buddhism is just as proscriptive about premarital sex, if not more so, than any monotheistic system. In fact, virginity is such an important part of a woman's status as a desirable bride that procurers for the sex trade regularly rape young women, rendering them "damaged goods" and unavailable for marriage.[47]

Kazuko Watanabe sees reflections more of history than of any specific religious or cultural traditions in the present-day sex trade throughout Asia. She argues, for instance, that there are many social, political, and economic parallels between Japan's wartime policy of forcing mainly foreign women into prostitution and its current role as a consumer market for the sex industry, in particular sex tourism, which also involves mainly foreign women as sexual service provider. . . .[48]

CONCLUSION

Ethnicity and sexuality are unlikely but constant companions on war fronts around the world. Ethnosexual exploitation is a common weapon of war and a routine price of peace. In conflicts across and within national borders, differences in language, religion, culture, and color often become justifications for sexual assault; alien ethnic homelands are sighted for sexual strikes and sexual warfare is waged against ethnically defined enemies. Casualties of ethnosexual assaults are not collateral damage associated with military campaigns; they are designated targets of sexual attack; they are victims who are guilty of ethnic Otherness; they are in the wrong skin in the wrong place at the wrong time; they are the sexual means to an ethnic end, a sexual stopover on the path toward a final solution.

The drama of sex and war is not restricted to combat theatres. The post–World War II period with its economic competition and superpower geopolitical rivalry produced a massive military-sexual complex to feed its large-scale manpower's equally large-scale sexual appetites. The militarization of sexuality has outlived the Cold War in the form of an international sex industry that serves military personnel around the world in conflicts and peacekeeping operations and satisfies the growing civilian market for ethnosex.

NOTES

1. Major William H. MacDonald, EUSA/USFK Public Affairs Office, personal communication, July 11, 2001; for a critical view of the U.S. military presence in South Korea, see http://www.apcjp.org/women's_network/skorea.htm.
2. Katharine H. S. Moon, *Sex among Allies: Military Prostitution in U.S.-Korea Relations* (New York: Columbia University Press, 1997), 1.
3. Ibid., 175, fn. 42.
4. U.S. military bases were established in Japan during the Allied occupation of the country following the end of World War II; 75 percent of U.S. military bases in Japan are on Okinawa Island; Kazuko Watanabe reports that controversies and demands that the U.S. close its military bases in Japan are the result not only of public opposition to the large sex industry on the island, but also because of the history of sexual assaults against Okinawan women by U.S. soldiers; see Kazuko Watanabe, "Trafficking in Women's Bodies, Then and Now: The Issue of Military Comfort Women," *Peace & Change* 20 (1995): 501–14. For a discussion of sexual collaboration between U.S. and Japanese authorities during the allied occupation of Japan, see Yuki Tanaka. *Japan's Comfort Women: Sexual Slavery and Prostitution during World War II and the U.S. Occupation* (New York: Routledge, 2002): my thanks to Ayako Mizumura for bringing this book to my attention.
5. Jean Enriquez reports that in recent years since the closing of U.S. bases in the Philippines and the beginning of the Asian economic crisis, "Filipino women have been migrating in flocks to neighboring countries"; many of these women go to South Korea which now "ranks 7th in terms of destination of deployed overseas Filipino workers"; some of these women are willingly recruited and others are unwillingly required to work in the Korean sex industry; see Jean Enriquez, "Filipinas in Prostitution around U.S. Military Bases in Korea: A Recurring Nightmare," *Coalition against Trafficking in Women-Asia-Pacific*, July 11,

2001, http://www.uri.edu/artsci/wms/hughes/catw/filkorea.htm.

6. Lynn Thiesmeyer, "The West's 'Comfort Women' and the Discourses of Seduction," in *Transnational Asia Pacific: Gender, Culture, and the Public Sphere*, ed. Shirley G. Lim, Larry E. Smith, and Wimal Dissanayake (Urbana: University of Illinois Press, 1999), 81; see also, Wendy Chapkis, *Beauty Secrets: Women and the Politics of Appearance* (Boston: South End Press, 1986), 53–54; Lisa Lowe argues that there is not a unified Euro-American historical imagining of Asian women, rather there are similarities between regional and historical different "orientalisms"; Lowe, *Immigrant Acts*, 178, n. 7.

7. Aida F. Santos, "Gathering the Dust: The Base Issue in the Philippines," in *Let the Good Times Roll: Prostitution and the U.S. Military in Asia*, ed. Saundra Pollock Sturdevant and Brenda Stoltzfus (New York: The New Press, 1992), 39; Cynthia Enloe provides an even more extensive list of men she argues "contribute to the construction and maintenance of prostitution around any government's military base: husbands and lovers, bar owners, local and foreign, local public-health officials, local government zoning-board members, local police officials, local mayors, national treasury or finance-ministry officials, national-defense officials, male soldiers in the national forces, local male prostitution customers, foreign male soldier-customers, foreign male soldiers' buddies, foreign base commanders, foreign military medical officers, foreign national-defense planners, foreign national legislators" (Cynthia Enloe, "It Takes Two," in *Let the Good Times Roll*, 24–25); see also Cynthia Enloe, *The Morning After: Sexual Politics and the End of the Cold War* (Berkeley: University of California Press, 1993).

8. Saundra Pollock Sturdevant and Brenda Stoltzfus, "Olongapo: The Bar System," in *Let the Good Times Roll*, 46–47.

9. Enloe, "It Takes Two," 23–24.

10. Chalmers Johnson, *Blowback: The Costs and Consequences of American Empire* (New York: Metropolitan Books, 2000), 35; see also Cynthia Enloe, *Maneuvers: The International Politics of Militarizing Women's Lives* (Berkeley: University of California Press, 2000).

11. Ibid., as its 2000 publication date indicates, Johnson's book was written before the September 11, 2001, attacks on New York and Washington, but he does link the 1996 bombing of the Khobar Towers apartments in Saudi Arabia, an attack that has been attributed to the same suspected perpetrators of the 2001 attacks, to the presence of U.S. military in Saudi Arabia, a presence that was invited by the Saudi government in the early 1990s following Iraq's invasion of Kuwait, but which is resented by "devoutly Muslim citizens of that kingdom [who] see [U.S.] presence as a humiliation to the country and an affront to their religion" (92); my thanks to Norm Yetman, American Studies, University of Kansas, for bringing this book to my attention.

12. See for instance, Butler, *Daughters of Joy, Sisters of Misery*.

13. For a recent overview see Barstow, *War's Dirty Secret*.

14. Brownmiller, *Against Our Will*.

15. Allen, *Rape Warfare*, 96.

16. Ibid., 96.

17. See Iris Chang, *The Rape of Nanking: The Forgotten Holocaust of World War II* (New York: Basic Books, 1997); James Yin and Shi Young, *The Rape of Nanking: An Undeniable History in Photographs* (Chicago: Innovative Publishing Group, 1997).

18. Japan has yet to make satisfactory restitution to Korean and Filipina "comfort women" who were sexually enslaved during World War II, and some former victims have come forward to demand a public apology and accounting for their treatment; see Seth Mydans, "Inside a Wartime Brothel: The Avenger's Story," *New York Times*, November 12, 1996:A3; Maria Rosa Henson, *Comfort Woman: A Filipina's Story of Prostitution and Slavery under the Japanese Military* (Lanham, MD: Rowman and Littlefield Publishers, 1999); Sangmie Choi Schellstede, *Comfort Women Speak: Testimony by Sex Slaves of the Japanese Military* (New York: Holmes and Meier, 2000); for discussions of Japan's system of brothels, see George L. Hicks, *The Comfort Women: Japan's Brutal Regime of Enforced Prostitution in the Second World War* (New York: W.W. Norton, 1995); Keith Howard, *True Stories of the Korean Comfort Women* (London: Cassell, 1995); Sayoko Yoneda, "Sexual and Racial Discrimination: A Historical Inquiry into the Japanese Military's 'Comfort' Women System of Enforced Prostitution," in *Nation, Empire, Colony: Historicizing Gender and Race*, ed. Ruth Roach Pierson and Nupur Chaudhuri (Bloomington: Indiana University Press, 1989), 237–50; for a discussion of restitution in general and specifically as it relates to the women enslaved by Japan during World War II, see Elazar Barkan, *The Guilt of Nations: Restitution and Negotiating Historical Injustices* (New York: W.W. Norton, 2000), especially chapter 3.

19. Watanabe, "Trafficking in Women's Bodies," 503–504.

20. Both sexual and nonsexual labor were also demanded of women enslaved by the Japanese (ibid., 503); the Japanese also used rape as an instrument of terror and domination, most infamous is the "rape of Nanking" in which thousands of women were raped and killed; see Brownmiller, *Against Our Will*, 53–60.

21. Brownmiller, *Against Our Will*, 61–62.

22. For firsthand accounts of women's treatment in the camps, see Sarah Nomberg-Przytyk, *Tales from a Grotesque Land* (Chapel Hill: University of North Carolina Press, 1985), 14–20; Livia E. Bitton Jackson, *Elli: Coming of Age in the Holocaust* (New York: Times Books, 1980) 59–61; Cecile Klein, *Sentenced to Live* (New York: Holocaust Library, 1988), 73–77; Lore Shelley, *Auschwitz: The Nazi Civilization* (Lanham, MD: University Press of America, 1992).

23. See Cornelius Ryan, *The Last Battle* (New York: Simon and Schuster, 1966); Barstow, *War's Dirty Secret*.

24. Brownmiller, *Against Our Will*, 76–77; these 947 convictions are only part of a much greater universe of sexual

assault by U.S. troops for several reasons: most rape is not reported and when it is, convictions are relatively rare even today, much less back in the 1940s during a state of war and/or military occupation; further, these were *convictions* where the soldier was found guilty, and did not include what could only have been a much larger number of charges filed and trials conducted; further still, these records were only for convictions of Army and Air Force personnel, and did not include data on the U.S. Navy or Marine Corps; finally, these records did not include information on charges, trials, or convictions for lesser sexual crimes than rape, such as sodomy or assault with the intent to commit rape or sodomy.

25. See Americas Watch and the Women's Rights Project, *Untold Terror: Violence against Women in Peru's Armed Conflict* (New York: Americas Watch, 1992); Asia Watch and Physicians for Human Rights, *Rape in Kashmir: A Crime of War* (New York: Asia Watch, 1993); Ximena Bunster, "Surviving beyond Fear: Women and Torture in Latin America," in *Women and Change in Latin America,* ed. June Nash and Helen Safa (South Hadley, MA: Bergin & Garvey, 1986), 297–325; Samir al-Khalil, *Republic of Fear: The Politics of Modern Iraq* (Berkeley: University of California Press, 1989).

26. Stiglmayer, "The Rapes in Bosnia-Herzegovina," 101.

27. See Elizabeth Bumiller, "Deny Rape or Be Hated: Kosovo Victims' Choice," *New York Times,* June 22, 1999:1; Peter Finn, "Signs of Rape Sear Kosovo; Families' Shame Could Hinder Investigation," *Washington Post,* June 27, 1999:1.

28. Stiglmayer, "The Rapes in Bosnia-Herzegovina," 117–18.

29. Ibid., 118–19.

30. Human Rights Watch reports that although both sides committed sexual assault during the conflict, rates of rape by Serbian men far outnumbered instances of sexual abuse by Kosovar Albanian men during the conflict; see Human Rights Watch Report, "Kosovo: Rape as a Weapon of 'Ethnic Cleansing'" (March 21, 2000); my thanks to Hsui-hua Shen, Department of Sociology, University of Kansas, for bringing this report to my attention.

31. For early reports on the hearings and judgments of that tribunal, see Marlise Simons, "Bosnian Serb Trial Opens: First on Wartime Sex Crimes," *New York Times,* March 21, 2000:3; John-Thor Dahlburg, "Bosnian Witness Says She Endured Series of Rapes; Courts: Victim No. 50 Testifies in The Hague," *Los Angeles Times,* March 30, 2000:1; Chris Bird, "UN Tribunal Told of Bosnian Rape Camp Horrors," *Guardian,* April 21, 2000:1; Roger Thurow, "A Bosnian Rape Victim Suffers from Scars that Do Not Fade," *Wall Street Journal,* July 17, 2000:18.

32. Cynthia Enloe, "Afterword: Have the Bosnian Rapes Opened a New Era of Feminist Consciousness?" in *Mass Rape,* 219–30; progress continues to be made, slowly, in the shift toward defining rape as a human rights violation and in the prosecution of those responsible for the sexual assaults in the former Yugoslavia: on June 29, 2001,

the Serbian government turned over former Yugoslavian president Slobodan Milosevic to the United Nations war crimes tribunal in The Hague, Netherlands; Marlise Simons with Carlotta Gall, "Milosevic Is Given to U.N. for Trial in War-Crime Case," *New York Times,* June 29, 2001:1; it is important to note that at about the same time the rapes and killings were happening in Yugoslavia and Bosnia, millions of men, women, and children were being raped, mutilated, and murdered in Rwanda; while Western governments dithered and delayed responding to both the Yugoslavian and Rwandan massacres and atrocities, and while an international tribunal was established in 1994 to prosecute Rwandans for their war crimes, the issue of rape as a war crime came to the fore in Yugoslavia, but not in the much larger-scale Rwandan case; perhaps it required reports of the mass rapes and sexual enslavement of white women, albeit Muslim white women, for the "civilized" world to take notice of ethnosexual violence in war.

33. Allen, *Rape Warfare,* 78; the "Bassiouni Report" is the result of an October 1992 decision by the Secretary-General of the United Nations to appoint a commission of experts "to examine and analyze information gathered with a view to providing the Secretary-General with its conclusions on the evidence of grave breaches of the Geneva Conventions and other violations of international humanitarian law committed in the territory of the former Yugoslavia" (ibid., 43).

34. Watanabe, "Trafficking in Women's Bodies," 506–507.

35. Kimmel, *Manhood in America,* 133–34.

36. See, for instance, Tracy X. Karner, *Masculinity, Trauma, and Identity: Life Narratives of Vietnam Veterans with Post Traumatic Stress Disorder* (Ph.D. diss., University of Kansas, 1994).

37. Enloe, *Bananas, Beaches, and Bases,* 66.

38. Personal communication, July 22, 2001; Clark was a Corporal in the First Battalion, Seventh Marines, Strategic and Target Acquisition (STA) Platoon.

39. Ibid.; Clark goes on to say:

> It is funny that during a period in U.S. military history when a "good" president restored military "honor," guys were in the Philippines and Thailand receiving oral sex (and who knows what else) from guys—and then talking about it later, giving no indication at all that they might just have participated in sex acts that challenged their masculinity. At the same time, new recruits were being instructed in the "manly" arts of beating up "fags," Naval Intelligence was hunting down "evidence" that guys with HIV and AIDS actually were gay, and Marines having sex with Marines (men) and caught in the "act" were being "punished" with hysterical physical violence in response. (ibid.)

See also Steven Zeeland, *The Masculine Marine: Homoeroticism in the U.S. Marine Corps* (New York: Harrington Park Press, 1996); Tim Bergling, "A Few Good Men," *Genre*

(November/December 1997) (http://www.davidclemens
.com/gaymilitary/fgm.htm) and Anonymous, "Standby
Warning" (http://www.subicbaymarines.com/Standby.htm).

40. Judith Hicks Stiehm, "United Nations Peacekeeping:
Men's and Women's Work," in *Gender Politics in Global Gov-
ernance,* ed. Mary K. Meyer and Elisabeth Prugl (Lanham,
MD: Rowman and Littlefield, 1999), 50–54.

41. Stiehm attributes the "boys will be boys" comment to Yasushi
Akashi of Japan, the head of the UN peacekeeping mission in
Cambodia; the comment was in response to "a letter signed
by more than 180 women [that] was sent to Akashi charging
sexual harassment of staff by UNTAC personnel and harassment of women on the street and asserting that there was no
channel for redressing this behavior" (ibid., 54).

42. Sex tourism is distinct from the general sex industry in
that it is the sector of the sex trade that actually provides
organized travel and tours to bring sex consumers to concentrated sex service destinations.

43. Ryan Bishop and Lillian S. Robinson, *Night Market: Sexual
Cultures and the Thai Economic Miracle* (New York: Routledge, 1998), 248.

44. Ibid., 8–9.

45. Phil Williams, "Trafficking in Women and Children: A
Market Perspective," in *Illegal Immigration and Commercial
Sex: The New Slave Trade,* ed. Phil Williams (London: Frank
Cass, 1999), 154; see also Lisa Law, "A Matter of 'Choice':
Discourses on Prostitution in the Philippines," in *Sites of
Desire, Economies of Pleasure: Sexualities in Asia and the Pa-
cific,* ed. Lenore Manderson and Margaret Jolly (Chicago:
University of Chicago Press, 1997), 233–61.

46. David Leheny, "A Political Economy of Asian Sex Tourism," *Annals of Tourism Research* 22 (1995): 367–84, 373; Annette Hamilton also finds images of a sexualized Thailand
in 1950s fiction, images that lead her to argue that Thailand
was already a "privileged site" in the "Western masculinist imagination" before the Vietnam War era; she does not
conclude, however, that the large-scale commercialization of sex that occurred as a result of the war was irrelevant to contemporary images of a sexualized Thailand;
see Annette Hamilton, "Primal Dream: Masculinism, Sin,
and Salvation in Thailand's Sex Trade," in *Sites of Desire,
Economies of Pleasure,* 157.

47. Ryan Bishop, personal communication, March 16, 2001; see
also Bishop and Robinson, *Night Market,* 160–61; see also
Thanh-Dam Truong, *Sex, Money, and Morality: Prostitution
and Tourism in South-East Asia* (London: Zed Books, 1990);
Lenore Manderson, "Public Sex Performances in Patpong
and Explorations of the Edges of Imagination," *The Journal
of Sex Research* 29 (1992): 451–75.

48. Watanabe, "Trafficking in Women's Bodies," 506. Sex tourism has become a controversial business in many destination and consumer countries. In Thailand, a number
of organizations, including "Empower" and "Friends of
Women," work directly with women in the sex tourism industry to teach them about AIDS prevention, and "Daughters Education Programme" provides education for village
girls to increase their employability outside of sex tourism
and to enhance their local status; Enloe, *Bananas, Beaches
and Bases,* 38; June Kane, *Sold for Sex* (Brookfield, VT:
Arena, 1998), 122–23. Other international anti–sex trade/
sex tourism organizations include the Asian Women's
Human Rights Council, ECPAT (End Child Prostitution
in Asian Tourism), the Global Alliance Against Traffic in
Women, and the Coalition Against Trafficking in Women;
see Skrobanek et al., *The Traffic in Women,* 81, 110–16; Kane,
Sold for Sex, 4; the website for the Coalition Against Trafficking in Women is http://www.uri.edu/artsci/wms/
hughes/catw/catw.htm; Julia Davidson reports several
demonstrative methods of protesting sex tourism:

> There have been instances of direct action against clients—
> for example, that organized by Japanese feminist groups
> at airports, which involved ridiculing and insulting men
> arriving home from sex tours, and that proposed by the
> Filipino guerrilla group that adopted the slogan, "Kill a
> sex tourist a day." Public humiliation has also been used as
> an instrument to control Taiwanese businessmen caught
> using prostitutes while in mainland China. (Davidson,
> *Prostitution, Power, and Freedom,* 198)

Davidson quotes Ren's description of Chinese humiliation
techniques:

> Chinese authorities not only sent them to a poultry farm
> in the outskirts of Bejing for a short period of labor reform,
> but also sent letters to their employers in Taiwan to inform
> them of the "repulsive deeds" committed by their employ-
> ees in China. Hoping that public exposure will deter such
> behavior, Chinese authorities have also stamped the words
> "patron of prostitution" on the travel documents of those
> men who have been found guilty of committing "repulsive
> deeds." (Ren, "China," in *Prostitution: An International
> Handbook on Trends, Problems, and Policies,* ed. Nanette Davis
> [Westport, CT: Greenwood Press, 1993], 102–103)

PART FOUR

SOCIAL CHANGE

Thus far we have emphasized the stability of gender inequality. We have examined how socialization, social definitions of gender, and the structure and content of all the major institutional arenas of social life converge to produce a world in which males and females are understood as essentially different and are differentially valued and rewarded. The forces that perpetuate gender inequality are so intricately interwoven into the social fabric and so deeply embedded in the identities of individuals that changing them is beyond the power of any one individual, no matter how well intentioned that individual might be.

Yet societies can and do change. Anyone who has lived through the past three decades in the United States cannot help but notice that there has been substantial change in the position, behaviors, and consciousness of women and men. In earlier readings, we discussed some of the dynamic forces that have unintentionally recast gender consciousness and inequality, including new cultural meanings, technological innovations, demographic processes, and economic factors. To understand fully how systems of gender inequality change, we must also examine the ways that women have sought collectively and intentionally to reduce their disadvantage. Certainly every society or group contains individuals who are nonconformists, but significant and lasting social change is ultimately the result of collective rather than individual action.

In Part Four, we turn our attention to struggles to transform culture and social institutions in two arenas. Section Ten focuses on the politicization of gender in the state and global politics. Section Eleven documents the rich history and diversity of women's movements and examines continuity and change in the history of American feminism. To understand the part that women themselves have played in improving their status, we focus, on the one hand, on women's actions "within the system" by conventional and orderly means and, on the other, on women's collective actions "outside the system" by unconventional and disorderly means.

Politics is generally thought to refer to the institutionalized or authoritative system by which a society makes decisions, allocates power, and distributes resources. According to the traditional view, voting, campaigning, lobbying, conducting organizational activities, holding office, and working in political parties are classified as politics because they take place in the context of formal governmental structure.

Feminist scholars have pointed out that the standard definition of politics is too narrow, however, for understanding women's political participation. It not only assumes a particular type of state and political system but ignores the fact that in most industrialized societies women have been denied access to the formal political process until fairly recently.

In the United States, women were not allowed to vote, hold office, or sit on juries until the twentieth century. Even after women received the vote with the passage of the Nineteenth Amendment to the U.S. Constitution in 1920, their participation in electoral politics, involvement in major political parties, and election to public offices lagged significantly behind men's. African-American women, moreover, like African-American men remained effectively disenfranchised in southern states by racist voter registration rules until the late 1960s.

It was not until a half century after women got the vote that the gap between men's and women's party involvement and office holding began to shrink, and even today women fare better in local and state politics than in the national arena. Voting turnout differences between women and men finally disappeared in 1976. But it took until 1980 for women to use the electoral process to express *their collective dissatisfaction by voting in line with their interests in women's equality, creating for the first time what has come to be known as the "gender gap."*

Elections, participation in party politics, running for office, and lobbying are not the only ways to express grievances, influence public policy, and achieve social change. Politics also include social movements, protests, and other group actions intended to change cultural beliefs and influence the distribution of power and resources in a state or community. This definition is broad enough to encompass women's long history of participation in collective action on their own behalf through the feminist movement, as well as in pursuit of other human rights causes through female reform societies, women's church groups, alternative religious societies, women's clubs, and other social movements.

Social movements are collective attempts to bring about change. They originate outside of the established political system, forge links between individuals and groups who share common concerns, and mobilize the people and resources necessary to pursue the goal of social change. In democratic societies, social movements and the tactics they employ—marches, boycotts, strikes, demonstrations, and protests—are a regular part of the democratic process. Movements act as pressure groups on behalf of people excluded from routine decision-making processes and the dominant power structure; they are a major source of new social patterns and cultural understandings.

Because participants in social movements typically challenge conventional ideas and behaviors, they are often stereotyped by the larger society as deviant and irrational and are accused of exaggerating their claims. If we take a historical perspective on social movements, we will often find that today's social institution is likely to have been yesterday's social movement. In other words, social movement participants are not qualitatively different from other kinds of social actors, and their actions are governed by the same norms that underlie other groups.

Although popular opinion often presents the women's movement as a relatively recent phenomenon, its roots are well-grounded historically. Indeed, the similarities between the views of contemporary feminists and earlier feminists are remarkable. More than 200 years ago, for example, Abigail Adams gave this warning to her husband, John,

when he was fashioning the Constitution of the United States:

> *In the new code of laws which I suppose will be necessary for you to make, I desire you would remember the ladies and be more generous and favorable to them than your ancestors. Do not put such unlimited power in the hands of husbands. Remember, all men would be tyrants if they could. If particular care and attention is not paid to the ladies, we are determined to foment a rebellion, and will not hold ourselves bound by any laws in which we have no voice or representation.*

Unfortunately, John Adams failed to take his wife's warning seriously. He urged her to be patient and said that there were more important issues than the rights of "ladies."

As this example illustrates, in the United States, as in much of the industrialized world, the history of feminist activism is long and rich. Until the past three decades, however, knowledge of the women's movement remained mostly buried. Initially most scholars studying the women's movement held that feminism in the United States has come in waves. The first wave began in the nineteenth century as a broad attack on male domination, continued for almost a century, and then died precipitously in 1920 with the passage of the suffrage amendment granting women the right to vote, which by then had become the movement's major goal. Supposedly, a 40-year lull followed before the second wave, or new feminist movement, erupted in the mid-1960s.

As a result of new research, a different interpretation of the history of the U.S. women's movement has emerged that emphasizes the continuity and persistence of women's resistance. The newer work recognizes the great waves of mass feminist activism, but also points to the survival of feminism in less highly mobilized periods. It focuses not only on the continuity of the movement but on changes in feminist ideology, goals, constituency, tactics, and organizational style. In addition to self-proclaimed feminists, working-class women and women of color also have a long history of struggle on their own behalf, in labor unions, socialist and communist groups, women's clubs, and within churches and communities. Any analysis of contemporary feminism and the backlash against it must consider the multiple forms of the enduring struggle against gender inequality.

The readings thus far suggest the depth, pervasiveness, and persistence of gender inequality and the intersection of gender with inequalities of race, class, and sexuality. It is not surprising, then, that contemporary feminism encompasses a wide range of struggles, from local efforts to improve women's daily lives to broad visions of fundamentally restructuring all institutions that perpetuate and sustain male dominance. The media have repeatedly proclaimed the present period the "postfeminist era," and many women disavow the feminist label—yet, as we shall see, women's movements remain very much alive. Feminist groups can be found within every major institution: in the professions, academia, labor, religion, politics, the arts, music, and literature. Feminist groups have mobilized around practically every issue imaginable, including employment and equal pay issues, reproductive rights, health, depression, substance abuse, pornography, prostitution, disability rights, spirituality, child care, nuclear weaponry, lesbianism, incest, battering, racism, and older women's rights. Feminists organize around sexual, racial and ethnic, and class identities.

The flourishing of women's organizing in these multiple forms has been considered a "third wave" of feminism that builds on the successes and lessons of earlier activism. Third-wave feminism is characterized by the view that gender is multiple and variable because it is also shaped by race, class, sexuality, nationality, and other factors. But the differences and conflicts between second- and third-wave feminism have also been exaggerated. What is important is that because feminism addresses every facet of social life, it has had a major and lasting impact not only on economic, political, and cultural institutions but also on the consciousness and lives of individual women and men.

In Part Four, we examine the diversity of women's participation in contemporary women's movements, emphasizing the continuity and global nature of feminist challenges as well as changes and differences in feminist goals, constituencies, and tactics. The readings document the multiple forms that feminist resistance can take. They recognize that protest can be directed at the structural, cultural, or individual level and that resistance varies across cultural and national contexts. We begin with an overview of the U.S. women's movement and a look to the future. As you think about these readings, consider the ways in which the efforts of women to transform gender have succeeded.

Global Politics and the State

National governments, international relations, and transnational economies and cultures exert wide-ranging influence on gender systems. Government-controlled economies shape differences in women's and men's wages and the prices of goods that women and men produce and consume. National and international policies on education, welfare, health, and various forms of violence against women affect women's daily lives in profound ways.

Because governmental policies frequently reflect dominant antiwoman ideologies, they often serve to reinforce the disadvantaged position of women in most countries. The state, in fact, plays a central part in maintaining a social structure of inequalities between women and men and between people of different social groups. That is, the state plays a crucial role in perpetuating inequalities of class (through regulation of the labor market or of minimum wages, for example) and of race and ethnicity and nationality (for example, through legislative policies regarding affirmative action or immigration).

Feminist scholars focus on the ways that state actions and policies create and perpetuate gender categories, ideologies of women's inferiority, and differential access of women and men to valued resources and power. The state's role in upholding gender stratification, of course, is inextricably linked to its role in reinforcing race and class stratification, as the articles in this section point out.

The increasing forces of globalization mean that women's lives are shaped not only by the governmental policies of their own countries but also by transnational politics and economics as well. A complex web of interrelationships among transnational corporations, states, transnational social movements, technology, and ideologies of gender, race, ethnicity, and religion shape relations among women, states, and global politics. In this section, contributors examine the relationships among constructions of gender, the forces of globalization, women's lives and activism, and the state, both in the United States and transnationally.

We begin with Cynthia Enloe's discussion of the transnational economics and politics of women's labor in "The Globe Trotting Sneaker." Enloe makes clear that women workers' interests have been left behind as outsourcing and globalization has increased. Taking sneaker manufacturing as an example, she shows how multinational corporations profit from the labor of underpaid and exploited women workers on the global assembly line. Documenting the activism of women workers in South Korea, Enloe shows why Nike moved its manufacturing from South Korea to such countries as China and Indonesia, where women were less organized. Yet, she suggests, increasing transnational organizing by women workers holds the potential for social change, particularly if women in the United States and other countries of the global North join them. Where are your running shoes and clothing produced? How does your standard of living depend on the work of the women workers Enloe discusses? What would be the consequences if workers earned a living wage all around the globe? What might you and other Americans do to improve the living situation of women workers abroad?

Grace Chang, in "From the Third World to the 'Third World Within,'" like Enloe, attends to the ways that women workers are fighting the forces of globalization. In the context of the globalization of poverty and its consequences, including the migration of millions of women from the Third World to the First, Chang focuses on the activism of Filipina migrant workers in the United States and Canada. Chang links the impact on women of structural adjustment programs forced on countries of the global South—from the slashing of social services to economic changes that leave no option for survival other than migration—to welfare reform in the United States. Her stories of Filipina workers echo those of the Latin American nannies recounted by Hondagneu-Sotelo in Section Five. How do various governments benefit from the migration of women from the Third to the First World? What strategies are women employing to resist the consequences of globalization?

Sharon Ann Navarro is also concerned with the impact of globalization on women workers and with women's resistance. In "*Las Mujeres Invisibles*/The Invisible Women," she documents the struggles of women in El Paso. El Paso sits on the Texas-Mexico border across from Juárez, where women workers are being murdered (see the boxed insert). Through a nongovernmental organization (NGO) called *La Mujer Obrera* (The Woman Worker), Mexican-American women draw on Mexican history and culture to mobilize constituents and work for change. How has globalization affected Mexican-American women in El Paso? How are the efforts of *La Mujer Obrera* similar to those of the Filipinas Chang discusses?

Chang and Navarro both show women of color committed to fighting oppression. When the United States went to war in Afghanistan after the attacks of September 11, 2001, one of the rationales was the need to liberate Afghan women. Lila Abu-Lughod addresses the question, "Do Muslim Women Really Need Saving?" reminding us that Afghan women, like Filipinas in North America and Mexican-American women in El Paso, have their own history of activism. Critiquing the "missionary" notion of saving other women, Abu-Lughod calls for a serious appreciation of differences among women around the globe. Why do you think there is so much focus in the United States on the "oppression" of Muslim women? How does Abu-Lughod suggest we deal with differences?

The final article in this section returns to the United States, where the welfare reform of 1996 parallels the cutting of social services in countries undergoing structural adjustment. Gwendolyn Mink, a feminist scholar and activist, argues that income support for caregivers is essential for women's equality—meaning that welfare should be an inalienable right of poor single mothers. Do you agree? Why was the women's movement so uninvolved in the fight against welfare reform?

As the forces of globalization increase, the economic, political, and cultural power of the global North affects women everywhere. Yet we need to be respectful of difference, as Lila Abu-Lughod argues. Once again, this section returns to the question of the commonalities and differences among women. Given the disparities of wealth and power among women around the world, especially between the global North and South, do you think diverse women have anything in common by virtue of their gender?

READING *42* **Cynthia Enloe**

The Globe Trotting Sneaker

Four years after the fall of the Berlin Wall marked the end of the Cold War, Reebok, one of the fastest-growing companies in United States history, decided that the time had come to make its mark in Russia. Thus it was with considerable fanfare that Reebok's executives opened their first store in downtown Moscow in July 1993. A week after the grand opening, store managers described sales as well above expectations.

Reebok's opening in Moscow was the perfect post–Cold War scenario: commercial rivalry replacing military posturing; consumerist tastes homogenizing heretofore hostile peoples; capital and managerial expertise flowing freely across newly porous state borders. Russians suddenly had the "freedom" to spend money on US cultural icons like athletic footwear, items priced above and beyond daily subsistence: at the end of 1993, the average Russian earned the equivalent of $40 a month. Shoes on display were in the $100 range. Almost 60 percent of single parents, most of whom were women, were living in poverty. Yet in Moscow and Kiev, shoe promoters had begun targeting children, persuading them to pressure their mothers to spend money on stylish, western sneakers. And as far as strategy goes, athletic shoe giants have, you might say, a good track record. In the United States many inner-city boys who see basketball as a "ticket out of the ghetto" have become convinced that certain brand-name shoes will give them an edge.

But no matter where sneakers are bought or sold, the potency of their advertising imagery has made it easy to ignore this mundane fact: Shaquille O'Neal's Reeboks are stitched by someone; Michael Jordan's Nikes are stitched by someone; so are your roommate's, so are your grandmother's. Those someones are women, mostly Asian women who are supposed to believe that their "opportunity" to make sneakers for US companies is a sign of their country's progress—just as a Russian woman's chance to spend two months' salary on a pair of shoes for her child allegedly symbolizes the new Russia.

As the global economy expands, sneaker executives are looking to pay women workers less and less, even though the shoes that they produce are capturing an ever-growing share of the footwear market. By the end of 1993, sales in the United States alone had reached $11.6 billion. Nike, the largest supplier of athletic footwear in the world, posted a record $298 million profit for 1993—earnings that had nearly tripled in five years. And sneaker companies continue to refine their strategies for "global competitiveness"—hiring supposedly docile women to make their shoes, changing designs as quickly as we fickle customers change our tastes, and shifting factories from country to country as trade barriers rise and fall.

The logic of it all is really quite simple; yet trade agreements such as the North American Free Trade Agreement (NAFTA) and the General Agreement of Tariffs and Trade (GATT) are, of course, talked about in a jargon that alienates us, as if they were technical matters fit only for economists and diplomats. The bottom line is that all companies operating overseas depend on trade agreements made between their own governments and the regimes ruling the countries in which they want to make or sell their products. Korean, Indonesian, and other women workers around the world know this better than anyone. They are tackling trade politics because they have learned from hard experience that the trade deals their governments sign do little to improve the lives of workers. Guarantees of fair, healthy labor practices, of the rights to speak freely and to organize independently, will usually be left out of trade pacts—and women will suffer. The recent passage of both NAFTA and GATT ensures that a growing number of private companies will now be competing across borders without restriction. The result? Big business will step up efforts to pit working women in industrialized countries against much lower-paid working women in "developing" countries, perpetuating the misleading notion that they are inevitable rivals in the global job market. (See Figure 1.)

All the "New World Order" really means to corporate giants like athletic shoemakers is that they now

FIGURE 1   HOURLY WAGES IN ATHLETIC FOOTWEAR FACTORIES

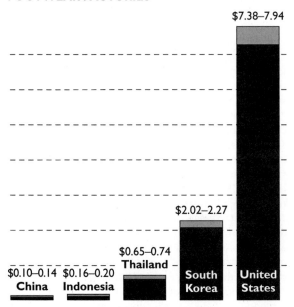

$7.38–7.94

$2.02–2.27

$0.65–0.74
Thailand

$0.10–0.14 $0.16–0.20
China **Indonesia** | **South Korea** | **United States**

have the green light to accelerate long-standing industry practices. In the early 1980s, the field marshals commanding Reebok and Nike, which are both US-based, decided to manufacture most of their sneakers in South Korea and Taiwan, hiring local women. L.A. Gear, Adidas, Fila, and Asics quickly followed their lead. In short time, the coastal city of Pusan, South Korea, became the "sneaker capital of the world." Between 1982 and 1989 the United States lost 58,500 footwear jobs to cities like Pusan, which attracted sneaker executives because its location facilitated international transport. More to the point, South Korea's military government had an interest in suppressing labor organizing, and it had a comfortable military alliance with the United States. Korean women also seemed accepting of Confucian philosophy, which measured a woman's morality by her willingness to work hard for her family's well-being and to acquiesce to her father's and husband's dictates. With their sense of patriotic duty, Korean women seemed the ideal labor force for export-oriented factories.

US and European sneaker company executives were also attracted by the ready supply of eager Korean male entrepreneurs with whom they could make profitable arrangements. This fact was central to Nike's strategy in particular. When they moved their production sites to Asia to lower labor costs, the executives of the

Oregon-based company decided to reduce their corporate responsibilities further. Instead of owning factories outright, a more efficient strategy would be to subcontract the manufacturing to wholly foreign-owned—in this case, South Korean—companies. Let them be responsible for workers' health and safety. Let them negotiate with newly emergent unions. Nike would retain control over those parts of sneaker production that gave its officials the greatest professional satisfaction and the ultimate word on the product: design and marketing. Although Nike was following in the footsteps of garment and textile manufacturers, it set the trend for the rest of the athletic footwear industry.

But at the same time, women workers were developing their own strategies. As the South Korean prodemocracy movement grew throughout the 1980s, increasing numbers of women rejected traditional notions of feminine duty. Women began organizing in response to the dangerous working conditions, daily humiliations, and low pay built into their work. Such resistance was profoundly threatening to the government, given the fact that South Korea's emergence as an industrialized "tiger" had depended on women accepting their "role" in growing industries like sneaker manufacture. If women reimagined their lives as daughters, as wives, as workers, as citizens, it wouldn't just rattle their employers; it would shake the very foundations of the whole political system.

At the first sign of trouble, factory managers called in government riot police to break up employees' meetings. Troops sexually assaulted women workers, stripping, fondling, and raping them "as a control mechanism for suppressing women's engagement in the labor movement," reported Jeong-Lim Nam of Hyosung Women's University in Taegu. It didn't work. It didn't work because the feminist activists in groups like the Korean Women Workers Association (KWWA) helped women understand and deal with the assaults. The KWWA held consciousness-raising sessions in which notions of feminine duty and respectability were tackled along with wages and benefits. They organized independently of the male-led labor unions to ensure that their issues would be taken seriously, in labor negotiations and in the prodemocracy movement as a whole.

The result was that women were at meetings with management, making sure that in addition to issues like long hours and low pay, sexual assault at the hands of managers and health care were on the table. Their activism paid off: in addition to winning the right to organize women's unions, their earnings grew. In 1980,

South Korean women in manufacturing jobs earned 45 percent of the wages of their male counterparts; by 1990, they were earning more than 50 percent. Modest though it was, the pay increase was concrete progress, given that the gap between women's and men's manufacturing wages in Japan, Singapore, and Sri Lanka actually *widened* during the 1980s. Last but certainly not least, women's organizing was credited with playing a major role in toppling the country's military regime and forcing open elections in 1987.

Without that special kind of workplace control that only an authoritarian government could offer, sneaker executives knew that it was time to move. In Nike's case, its famous advertising slogan—"Just Do It"—proved truer to its corporate philosophy than its women's "empowerment" ad campaign, designed to rally women's athletic (and consumer) spirit. In response to South Korean women workers' newfound activist self-confidence, the sneaker company and its subcontractors began shutting down a number of their South Korean factories in the late 1980s and early 1990s. After bargaining with government officials in nearby China and Indonesia, many Nike subcontractors set up shop in those countries, while some went to Thailand. China's government remains nominally Communist; Indonesia's ruling generals are staunchly anti-Communist. But both are governed by authoritarian regimes who share the belief that if women can be kept hard at work, low paid, and unorganized, they can serve as a magnet for foreign investors.

Where does all this leave South Korean women—or any woman who is threatened with a factory closure if she demands decent working conditions and a fair wage? They face the dilemma confronted by thousands of women from dozens of countries. The risk of job loss is especially acute in relatively mobile industries; it's easier for a sneaker, garment, or electronics manufacturer to pick up and move than it is for an automaker or a steel producer. In the case of South Korea, poor women had moved from rural villages into the cities searching for jobs to support not only themselves but parents and siblings. The exodus of manufacturing jobs has forced more women into the growing "entertainment" industry. The kinds of bars and massage parlors offering sexual services that had mushroomed around US military bases during the Cold War have been opening up across the country.

But the reality is that women throughout Asia are organizing, knowing full well the risks involved. Theirs is a long-term view; they are taking direct aim at companies' nomadic advantage, by building links among workers in countries targeted for "development" by multinational corporations. Through sustained grassroots efforts, women are developing the skills and confidence that will make it increasingly difficult to keep their labor cheap. Many are looking to the United Nations conference on women in Beijing, China, [1996], as a rare opportunity to expand their cross-border strategizing.

The Beijing conference will also provide an important opportunity to call world attention to the hypocrisy of the governments and corporations doing business in China. Numerous athletic shoe companies followed Nike in setting up manufacturing sites throughout the country. This included Reebok—a company claiming its share of responsibility for ridding the world of "injustice, poverty, and other ills that gnaw away at the social fabric," according to a statement of corporate principles.

Since 1988, Reebok has been giving out annual human rights awards to dissidents from around the world. But it wasn't until 1992 that the company adopted its own "human rights production standards"—after labor advocates made it known that the quality of life in factories run by its subcontractors was just as dismal as that at most other athletic shoe suppliers in Asia. Reebok's code of conduct, for example, includes a pledge to "seek" those subcontractors who respect workers' rights to organize. The only problem is that independent trade unions are banned in China. Reebok has chosen to ignore that fact, even though Chinese dissidents have been the recipients of the company's own human rights award. As for working conditions, Reebok now says it sends its own inspectors to production sites a couple of times a year. But they have easily "missed" what subcontractors are trying to hide—like 400 young women workers locked at night into an overcrowded dormitory near a Reebok-contracted factory in the town of Zhuhai, as reported last August in the *Asian Wall Street Journal Weekly*.

Nike's cofounder and CEO, Philip Knight, has said that he would like the world to think of Nike as "a company with a soul that recognizes the value of human beings." Nike, like Reebok, says it sends in inspectors from time to time to check up on work conditions at its factories; in Indonesia, those factories are run largely by South Korean subcontractors. But according to Donald Katz in a recent book on the company, Nike spokesman Dave Taylor told an in-house newsletter that the factories are "[the subcontractors'] business to run." For the most part, the company relies on regular reports from subcontractors regarding its "Memorandum of Understanding," which managers must sign, promising to impose "local government standards" for wages, working conditions, treatment of workers, and benefits.

In April, the minimum wage in the Indonesian capital of Jakarta will be $1.89 *a day*—among the highest in a country where the minimum wage varies by region. And managers are required to pay only 75 percent of the wage directly; the remainder can be withheld for "benefits." By now, Nike has a well-honed response to growing criticisms of its low-cost labor strategy. Such wages should not be seen as exploitative, says Nike, but rather as the first rung on the ladder of economic opportunity that Nike has extended to workers with few options. Otherwise, they'd be out "harvesting coconut meat in the tropical sun," wrote Nike spokesman Dusty Kidd, in a letter to the *Utne Reader*. The all-is-relative response craftily shifts attention away from reality: Nike didn't move to Indonesia to help Indonesians; it moved to ensure that its profit margin continues to grow. And that is pretty much guaranteed in a country where "local standards" for wages rarely take a worker over the poverty line. A 1991 survey by the International Labor Organization (ILO) found that 88 percent of women working at the Jakarta minimum wage at the time—slightly less than a dollar a day—were malnourished.

A woman named Riyanti might have been among the workers surveyed by the ILO. Interviewed by the *Boston Globe* in 1991, she told the reporter who had asked about her long hours and low pay: "I'm happy working here. . . . I can make money and I can make friends." But in fact, the reporter discovered that Riyanti had already joined her co-workers in two strikes, the first to force one of Nike's Korean subcontractors to accept a new women's union and the second to compel managers to pay at least the minimum wage. That Riyanti appeared less than forthcoming about her activities isn't surprising. Many Indonesian factories have military men posted in their front offices who find no fault with managers who tape women's mouths shut to keep them from talking among

themselves. They and their superiors have a political reach that extends far beyond the barracks. Indonesia has all the makings for a political explosion, especially since the gap between rich and poor is widening into a chasm. It is in this setting that the government has tried to crack down on any independent labor organizing—a policy that Nike has helped to implement. Referring to a recent strike in a Nike-contracted factory, Tony Nava, Nike representative in Indonesia, told the *Chicago Tribune* in November 1994 that the "troublemakers" had been fired. When asked about Nike policy on the issue, spokesman Keith Peters struck a conciliatory note: "If the government were to allow and encourage independent labor organizing, we would be happy to support it."

Indonesian workers' efforts to create unions independent of governmental control were a surprise to shoe companies. Although their moves from South Korea have been immensely profitable [see Figure 2], they do not have the sort of immunity from activism that they had expected. In May 1993, the murder of a female labor activist outside Surabaya set off a storm of local and international protest. Even the US State Department was forced to take note in its 1993 worldwide human rights report, describing a system similar to that which generated South Korea's boom twenty years earlier: severely restricted union organizing, security forces used to break up strikes, low wage for men, lower wages for women—complete with government rhetoric celebrating women's contribution to national development.

Yet when President Clinton visited Indonesia last November, he made only a token effort to address the country's human rights problem. Instead, he touted the benefits of free trade, sounding indeed more enlightened, more in tune with the spirit of the post–Cold War era than do those defenders of protectionist trading policies who coat their rhetoric with "America

FIGURE 2   A $70 PAIR OF NIKE PEGASUS: WHERE THE MONEY GOES

Labor $1.66
(Total allocation for the 45 to 50 employees who work on the one pair of shoes)

Subcontractor's profit $1.19

Nike markup $22.95
(After paying subcontractor $14.85, Nike adds on $22.95 for costs and profits, selling shoes to retailer for $37.80)

Retail markup $32.20
(Retailer adds on $32.20 for costs and profits, selling shoes for $70)

Administration and overhead $2.82

Materials $9.18

first" chauvinism. But "free trade" as actually being practiced today is hardly *free* for any workers—in the United States or abroad—who have to accept the Indonesian, Chinese, or Korean workplace model as the price of keeping their jobs.

The not-so-new plot of the international trade story has been "divide and rule." If women workers and their government in one country can see that a sneaker company will pick up and leave if their labor demands prove more costly than those in a neighbor country, then women workers will tend to see their neighbors not as regional sisters, but as competitors who can steal their precarious livelihoods. Playing women off against each other is, of course, old hat. Yet it is as essential to international trade politics as is the fine print in GATT.

But women workers allied through networks like the Hong Kong-based Committee for Asian Women are developing their own post–Cold War foreign policy, which means addressing women's needs: how

to convince fathers and husbands that a woman going out to organizing meetings at night is not sexually promiscuous; how to develop workplace agendas that respond to family needs; how to work with male unionists who push women's demands to the bottom of their lists; how to build a global movement.

These women refuse to stand in awe of the corporate power of the Nike or Reebok or Adidas executive. Growing numbers of Asian women today have concluded that trade politics have to be understood by women on their own terms. They will be coming to Beijing this September [1996] ready to engage with women from other regions to link the politics of consumerism with the politics of manufacturing. If women in Russia and Eastern Europe can challenge Americanized consumerism, if Asian activists can solidify their alliances, and if US women can join with them by taking on trade politics—the post–Cold War sneaker may be a less comfortable fit in the 1990s.

ACKNOWLEDGMENTS

This article draws from the work of South Korean scholars Hyun Sook Kim, Seung-kyung Kim, Katherine Moon, Seungsook Moon, and Jeong-Lim Nam.

READING *43*   *Grace Chang*

From the Third World to the "Third World Within": Asian Women Workers Fighting Globalization

The present form of globalization has not produced enough jobs for all those who seek them or in the places where they are most needed. This is probably its biggest failure.

Juan Somavia
Director-General, International Labor Organization[1]

I want to begin to dispel the myths. It's not about mail-order brides. Hello, this is a global world. . . . We are a global population.

Mike Krosky
Owner, Cherry Blossoms[2]

INTRODUCTION

These observations on globalization probably could not have come from more distant corners. Juan Somavia's comment, addressed to representatives from 175 International Labor Organization member countries was intended to be sobering. He warned that the failure of globalization to create new jobs in developing countries has fueled and will continue to fuel massive migration worldwide. He estimated that about 500 million jobs will have to be created over the next decade just to accommodate the young people and women now entering the labor market.

In contrast, Mike Krosky's comment from an interview about his Cherry Blossoms business is positively celebratory. Krosky's business lists over 6000 women available for order through print catalogs and a web site, half of whom are Filipina. The next largest group is Indonesian, and the group showing the greatest increase comes from Eastern European countries. Krosky celebrates globalization not only because of huge business profits, but also for his personal satisfaction as the happy husband of a Filipina more than 18 years his junior, whom he met through his own service.

Both these comments speak directly or otherwise to an important but often neglected aspect of globalization: migrations of Third World people from their homes as a result of the destruction wrought by globalization on their abilities to survive at home.

I want to address this dimension of globalization, particularly Third World women's migrations, and, like Mike Krosky, I want to begin to dispel the myths. I also want to address the reality that in today's globalized context, virtually all migration can be seen as coerced through economic means, through the institutionalized underdevelopment and impoverishment of Third World nations and people.

A few years ago I had the privilege of speaking on an International Women's Day radio program with Ethel Long Scott of the Women's Economic Agenda Project. Scott remarked that we must talk about globalization in its proper terms, as the *globalization of poverty*—that is, the creation, perpetuation, and exacerbation of poverty worldwide. Scott also cautioned listeners not to think that the ravages of globalization are confined "over there" in the Third World but to examine its impacts in our own communities of color.[3] Scott raised an important point missing from many debates surrounding globalization—that those in the Third World and those in the "Third World within" First World countries share these conditions and thus are central to the struggles against this globalization of poverty.[4]

I will examine how women of color and migrant women in First World host nations experience the impact of globalization on their lives and livelihoods daily and forge resistance to these impact daily. Specifically, I look at the struggles of Filipina migrant workers in the U.S. and Canada—women who suffer these impacts on both ends of the global "trade route." I interviewed members of two migrant domestic worker organizations, one in Vancouver, Canada, and the other in Bronx, New York, who provide important models for critical gender analyses of globalization and organized resistance against it.

Many of us who attended the 1995 Non-Governmental Organizations (NGO) Forum on Women as members of the U.S. women of color delegation were humbled by our Third World sisters who danced circles around us in their analyses and first-hand knowledge of global economic restructuring and its impact. Poor women of color throughout the world suffer first and worst under globalization. They experience so-called "development" and "free trade" as losses in status, freedom, safety, education, access to basic needs of food, water, housing, and health care—indeed, as assaults on their very survival. As the first victims of globalization, poor women of color are also the primary leaders in fighting back, in resisting the so-called "New World Order" that they know is not new at all but a continuation of neo-imperialist activities into the 21st century.

GLOBAL ECONOMIC RESTRUCTURING

At the Fourth World NGO Forum on Women held in China in 1995, women from Africa, Latin America, the Middle East, and Asia echoed the same truth in their testimonies: Global economic restructuring embodied in Structural Adjustment Programs (SAPs) strikes poor women of color around the world the hardest, rendering them most vulnerable to exploitation both at home and in the global labor market. Since the 1980s, the World Bank, International Monetary Fund (IMF), and other international financial institutions based in the First World have routinely prescribed structural adjustment policies to the governments of indebted countries as preconditions for loans. These prescriptions included cutting government expenditures on social programs, slashing wages, liberalizing imports, opening markets to foreign investment, expanding exports, devaluing local currency, and privatizing state enterprises.

Women have consistently reported increasing poverty and rapidly deteriorating nutrition, health, and work conditions as a direct result of SAPs. When wages and food subsidies are cut, wives and mothers adjust household budgets often at the expense of their own and their children's nutrition. As public health care and education vanish, women suffer from lack of prenatal care and become nurses to ill family members at home; girls are the first family members to leave school to help at home or go to work. When export-oriented agriculture is encouraged—indeed, coerced—peasant families are evicted from their lands to make room for corporate farms, and women become seasonal workers in the fields or in processing areas instead of land-owning farmers.

Lands once used to raise staples like rice are used instead for raising shrimp, oranges, and orchids—all for export, not for local consumption—or for golf courses and luxury hotels for tourists. Essentially, SAPs lead to destruction of both subsistence and social service systems in Third World nations so that women have no viable options to sustain their families and leave them behind to migrate in search of work. Usually women go from villages to cities within their home countries first and then migrate to the First World to pursue service work, sex work, and manufacturing jobs.[5]

Since the 1995 NGO Forum, women of color around the world have spoken in no uncertain terms to these continuing trends that globalization imposes on their lives.[6] They report the persistence of the most devastating impact of globalization on their abilities to support their children and families in the form of increased assaults on their reproductive rights. In short, globalization threatens the very survival of people of color by hindering the ability of their women to reproduce and maintain their families and communities.

In 1999, before the Seattle protests against the World Trade Organization (WTO), the Northwest Labor and Employment Law Office (LELO), a multiracial community and labor organization, recognized the need for education to build awareness of these issues and the linkages between workers' struggles in the U.S. and abroad. LELO brought together several grassroots groups, including the Seattle Young People's Project, Committee Against Repression in Mexico, Community Coalition for Environmental Justice, and the Washington Alliance for Immigrant and Refugee Justice to form the Workers' Voices Coalition. The coalition sponsored the participation of eight women labor-rights organizers from Third World countries in the WTO protest activities and a post-WTO conference.

Cenen Bagon, a participant, responded to comments by Michael Moore, then WTO director-general, when he addressed the International Confederation of Free Trade Unions. Moore said, "There is also a darker side to the backlash against globalization. For some, the attacks on economic openness are part of a broader assault on internationalism, on foreigners, immigration, a more pluralistic and integrated world. . . . " Bagon, who works with Filipina and other immigrant women workers in Canada through the Vancouver Committee for Domestic Workers and Caregivers Rights, countered sharply:

> Moore and others like him, in his ideological dogma, forget to add, and I'm sure it's quite intentional, that what we are against are the realities brought about by trade

authored by the backers of capitalist globalization. . . . And if these so-called leaders are really looking for indicators of whether their programs are truly creating economic improvements, they should look beyond the country's balance of payment and budget deficits and analyze how women are affected by these programs. . . . Supporters of structural adjustment programs should visit the night life in Japan, Hong Kong, and certain places in Canada and listen to the stories of Filipino and other women who unknowingly left their countries as entertainers and ended up being prostituted by their recruiters. They should also listen to the stories of domestic workers who left not only their countries . . . but their families and their own children, as well, to care for other women's children and households. . . . [7]

Bagon calls for world leaders to view the migration of women forced to leave their homelands and families because of the ravages of SAPs as true indicators of the impacts of global economic restructuring. Extending on this, the experiences of immigrant women workers can serve not only as measures of the effects, but as true indicators of the *intentions* of SAPs and other neo-liberal economic policies. The sheer magnitude of women's migration urges us to examine this phenomenon and view it as both an effect of globalization and as a calculated feature of global economic restructuring.

In other words, it is important to understand the economic interventions in Third World nations embodied in SAPs and free-trade policies as deliberate. They facilitate the extraction of resources, especially labor and people, from the Third World and their importation into the First World. In effect, they support trade in and traffic of migrant women workers and their exploitation at both ends of the so-called trade route. This trade or forced migration is orchestrated through economic interventions compelling migration from the Third World coupled with welfare, labor, and immigration policies in the First World that channel these women into service work at poverty wages in host or receiving countries.

I have argued elsewhere that structural adjustment in the Third World and welfare reform in the First World are inextricably linked; indeed, they are two sides of the same coin. For example, in the U.S., domestic forms of structural adjustment, including privatization and cutbacks in health care and the continued lack of subsidized child care, contribute to expanded demand among dual-career middle-class households for child care, elder care, home health care, and housekeeping workers. The slashing of benefits and social services under "welfare reform" helps guarantee that this demand is met by a pool of migrant women readily available to serve as cheap labor. The dismantling of public support in the U.S. in general and the denial of benefits and services to immigrants in particular act in tandem with structural adjustment in the Third World to force migrant women into low-wage service work in the U.S.[8]

Migrant women workers from indebted nations are kept pliable by both the dependence of their families on remittances sent home and by the severe restrictions on immigrant access to almost all forms of assistance in the U.S. Their vulnerability is further reinforced by First World immigration policies explicitly designed to recruit migrant women as contract or temporary workers yet deny them the protections and rights afforded citizens. This phenomenon is readily apparent in the cases of both U.S. and Canadian immigration policies structured to ensure a ready supply of women workers available for nursing aide, home care, domestic care, child care, and elder care work at low wages and under conditions most citizens would not accept.

"FILIPINOS FOR THE WORLD"

The massive migration of women from the Philippines to all corners of the First World illustrates clearly how structural adjustments imposed on the Philippines and welfare and immigration policies in First World receiving countries combine to make the global traffic in Filipinas an explicit government practice and highly profitable industry on both ends of the trade route. Every day, an average of 2700 people are estimated to leave the Philippines in search of work. Currently, more than 8 million Filipino migrant workers live in over 186 countries, and an estimated 65% are women.[9] Although the Philippine government denies that it has an official export policy now, an agency called the Philippine Overseas Employment Administration (POEA) was established in the 1970s to promote migrant labor with the stated goals of (1) earning foreign currency and (2) easing the Philippines' unemployment rate.[10]

Confining the analysis for the moment only to the benefits of this trade to the Philippine government and capital, the numbers are staggering. One woman migrating to Canada reported paying 1900 pesos at the embassy in the Philippines, 1500 pesos for a medical examination, and 5000 pesos to the POEA according to the research by the Philippine Women's Centre.[11] If we multiply this total 8400 pesos ($181 US) for typical bureaucratic expenses paid by one individual migrating from the Philippines by the average daily exodus of 2700 people leaving the country, the Philippine government receives

the equivalent of almost half a million U.S. dollars in revenue daily for processing exports of people. Moreover, the remittances sent home to families by Filipino workers overseas infuse into the economy what amounts to the Philippines' largest source of foreign currency—far more than income from sugar and mineral exports.

Although the absolute numbers are remarkable, taken in context they are particularly telling. For example, in the year 2000, remittances from overseas workers were estimated at $6.23 billion officially, reported as channeled through the Central Bank of the Philippines. This does not include funds received through informal channels. The $6.23 billion represented 5.2% of the gross domestic product and exceeded the entire interest payment on the country's foreign debt that hovers around $5 billion a year.[12]

Philippine President Gloria Macapagal-Arroyo launched a program known as "Filipinos for the World" to celebrate and further institutionalize this exportation of workers for profit. Arroyo (unaffectionately referred to as GMA) persists in glorifying these migrant workers, following a long line of Philippines officials who once called women in particular the country's "modern heroes." In even more crass economic terms, GMA now calls them "overseas Philippines investors" and "internationally shared resources."[13] She is promoting her new labor export plan announced in June of 2002 as a push to have 100 million overseas Filipinos serving others across the globe. Arroyo's program will certainly serve her interests well. As one observer remarked, "Arroyo seeks not only the remittances from the migrant workers, but their absentee ballots to keep her in office and bolster her unstable position. She wants not only the dollars but the 8 million Filipinos abroad in her pocket at election time."[14]

It is particularly useful to examine the experiences of Filipinas trained as nurses who migrate to work in the U.S. and Canada. They provide cheap and highly skilled labor and also serve to further the neo-liberal agenda of privatizing health care. In both countries, immigration policy is structured to keep these trained workers underemployed and deskilled in exploitative situations closely resembling indentured servitude and debt bondage. Nursing schools graduating hundreds of thousands of registered nurses abound in the Philippines, but few graduates reside in their own country.

The Philippine Women Centre (PWC) of British Columbia, a group of Filipino–Canadian women working to educate, organize, and mobilize Filipina migrant workers in Canada, identifies this phenomenon as the "commodification of the nursing profession in the

Philippines." The group observes that nursing training is promoted as "a quick route to work abroad," rather than as a means to serve the needs of Filipinos. As a result Filipina nurses are seen as exportable commodities.[15] A survey of members of the group revealed that 77% of participants studied nursing with the specific intention of going abroad, and 62% took entrance exams allowing foreigners to practice nursing in the U.S.[16]

Clearly, exclusion from both welfare benefits and workers' rights through immigration policy makes immigrant women workers available for—indeed, unable to refuse—low-wage service work in the U.S. In Canada, the connection between labor control and immigration policy is even more explicit because of the use of both immigration and nursing accreditation issues to prevent foreign-trained nurses from being able to practice nursing for several years after arrival in Canada. In tandem, the policies serve to exclude immigrant nurses from their professions and channel them into low-paid care work as nannies, domestics, and home support workers.

The Live-in Caregiver Program (LCP) is the immigration policy through which the vast majority of Filipina migrants enter Canada and become trapped in low-wage care work. Established in 1992 to facilitate the importation of primarily Filipino women, the program provides that a Canadian employer (individual or employment agency) may apply through the Canadian Employment Office for a prospective employee after showing that an attempt was made to find a Canadian to do the job. A job applicant must have 2 years of post-secondary education, 6 months of formal training or 12 months of experience in caregiving work, and be in good health. Once matched with an employer, she must notify the Ministry of Citizenship and Immigration if she wishes to change employers. After 2 years of live-in work, a nanny can apply for landed-immigrant status, but during those 2 years she is considered a temporary migrant. Three years after applying for landed-immigrant status, she can become a Canadian citizen.[17]

The PWC undertook a community-based participatory action research project, interviewing 30 Filipina nurses who entered Canada via the LCP and performed domestic work. According to Cecilia Diocson, founding chairperson of the PWC, the interviews revealed that women with up to 15 years of nursing experience in operating rooms, cancer units, and other facilities were becoming deskilled while working as nannies and home support workers.[18] Others were indeed using their skills, working around the clock and performing nursing tasks, but they were not recognized or compensated

as such. Many of their tasks included heavy lifting; transferring; personal care duties; administering medications; and tube feeding for elderly, ill, and disabled clients. One nurse, Mary Jane reported:

> Because of the LCP requirements, we become responsible for our employers 24 hours a day, but we are only paid for 8 hours, with no overtime pay. For some of us, we accompany our employers to the hospital and even sleep at our employer's bedside at the hospital.[19]

Many of those interviewed did not realize when they migrated that they would not be doing nursing work after they entered Canada through the LCP. Many believed that they would perform nursing in private homes or care for disabled children. Moreover, many did not know that working as a nanny would mean so much labor demanded of them beyond caring for children. For example, Pamela, a registered nurse in the Philippines who left three children behind to seek work in Vancouver, said:

> I thought being a nanny, as the dictionary says, is child's nurse. In the Philippines, a yaya [Tagalog for nanny] works for the kids only, right? They don't do other jobs in the house. They just change the kids, feed them and put them to bed. . . . When I came here, I was shocked. I said, why is it a package? Three children in a big house, 5 bedrooms, 1½ baths, and 3 living rooms. . . . I feel like I'm going to die. My female employer didn't work. She stays at home. Then, she said that I'm not clean enough. I told her that I have to prioritize the work and I asked her, what's more important, the kids or cleaning? . . . It was so hard I quit.[20]

After Pamela quit, her former employer refused to give her a reference, nanny agencies would not accept her, and she decided to advertise for a job caring for the elderly. Several prospective employers who answered her ad sought caregivers willing to provide sexual services. After several such experiences and trying to work as a nanny for one more family, she found a job caring for a single woman.

Pamela supports her husband, who is a student, and her three children in the Philippines by sending a quarter of her wages home each month. She spoke of the hardships of separation from her family and her doubts and fears about reuniting:

> I'm confused whether I should get my family or not. The separation is really hard for me, but I also think

if my family is here, my husband and I have to chip in. I fear that communication will be through messages on the refrigerator. We don't see each other any more. That's why sometimes I feel that maybe it's better for them to stay in the Philippines because they write to me and there's an attachment still. Here, it seems that you're not really intact.[21]

Mary Jane, another Filipina nurse working as a nanny, reflected on the pain of separation from her children and the great financial hardship of maintaining contact:

My children are now 5 and 8. I spent so much money on the long distance because sometimes when I call, my child will say, "Mommy I still want to sing." You know, you didn't see your child for 4 years and she will tell you she wants to sing, you cannot say no. . . . I said I will call everyday so that [her youngest child] will not forget my voice. I only stopped calling because my phone bill is over $500.

For these women, the agony of separation from their own children is surely not diminished by caring for their employers' children. For many of the women interviewed, the hope of eventually being able to bring their families to join them in Canada influenced them to stay in unhappy and often abusive working situations in order to fulfill the 2-year live-in work requirement of the LCP as quickly as possible. The policy prohibits them from earning any extra income to supplement their low wages as caregivers and explicitly stipulates that working for anyone other than the employer named on the employment authorization is illegal, and unauthorized employment will not count toward satisfying the 2-year employment requirement to apply for permanent residence.[22] Thus, women are effectively kept bonded to the employers named on their original LCP employment authorizations at whatever wages and conditions the employer chooses to provide. As Pamela reports:

Filipinos are abused because they are pressured to stay with the 24-month requirement. . . . You stay because it's not that easy to find an employer. And you get exploited and we are highly educated. . . . That's really racism.

In addition to these barriers that essentially lock trained nurses into nanny and home support work for at least 2 years, migrant Filipinas face more hurdles in trying to gain accreditation to practice nursing even after

serving the 2-year live-in requirement. Applicants must take English tests that are irrelevant and extremely costly, about US $410. According to Leah Diana, a registered nurse and volunteer with the Filipino Nurses Support Group (FNSG) in Vancouver, Filipino nurses are usually educated in English, used English while employed in the Philippines and elsewhere, and passed mandatory English interviews before arrival in Canada. Diana says, "The English tests required are only based on the racist assumption that people of color can't speak English." These barriers are particularly outrageous when viewed in the context of Canada's recognized nursing shortage. A Canadian Nurses' Association study showed an expected shortage of 59,000 to 113,000 registered nurses in Canada by the year 2011.[23]

Cecilia Diocson reports that the mainstream, predominantly white nursing unions in Canada have not been good allies. They have not supported allowing Filipina nurses to practice despite shortages. Diocson expressed outrage that the president of a nursing union tried to pass this off as concern that "the Philippines needs them." She said:

We responded, "Don't give us that kind of rationalization. The nurses are already here, and in crisis, and we are seeking solidarity. Is the real issue that we are nonwhite, from the Third World, and foreign-trained? Are you threatened by our presence?" It's so clear that this is just racism. Otherwise, they would support and struggle with us.

Beyond the presence of women of color born and trained in the Third World, the existence of a surplus of low-wage workers and ostensible competitors is perhaps most threatening. Migrant women workers are well aware that the Canadian government can and does use their presence in the country and their exclusion through the LCP from the nursing profession to render them available to do other low-wage care and service work while keeping Canadian citizen nurses wary of competition. As Gemma Gambito, a member of FNSG who graduated from nursing school in the Philippines in 1993 and went to Canada in 1997 under the LCP, says:

Our presence in Canada is used to drive down the wages of Canadian nurses and health care workers. Once completing our temporary work contract and becoming landed immigrants, many become home support workers, nursing aides, or continue to do domestic work for low wages. A pool of highly skilled yet low paid health workers has been created by the Canadian government's LCP.[24]

The LCP and its attendant racism facilitate the privatization of health care and help ensure the lack of movement or alliance building for subsidized child care, health care, and other staples of feminist and worker agendas. Dr. Lynn Farrales, a co-chair of the PWC, observes that the LCP functions simply to bring in women who are educated and trained nurses to do domestic work and provide live-in child care and private home care for the disabled and elderly for less than minimum wage. Farrales says:

> Canada, a country without a national day care program and a health care system moving towards increased privatization, has established in the LCP a means of importing highly educated and skilled workers to fulfill the need for flexible and cheap labor in the spheres of child care and health care. The economic and social consequences of the LCP have been devastating for Filipino women. They are highly exploited, oppressed, and de-skilled. Despite being highly educated, many are trapped in minimum wage jobs after completion of the LCP, and are effectively legislated into poverty.[25]

Moreover, Farrales notes that these negative consequences extend to the next generation of Filipino youth as well, including the effects of years of separation of mothers and children and the systemic racism in Canadian institutions that Filipino–Canadian youths encounter. Because Filipino youths drop out of high school at high rates, they join their mothers working for low wages in the service sector. Thus, the Canadian government achieves what Farrales calls the "commodification of the migration of the entire family as a package deal of cheap labor."[26] Meanwhile, ironically, with rapidly privatizing health care and the continuing nursing shortage in the public sector, health care becomes inaccessible for working-class Canadians, including Filipina nurses and their families. Thus, the Canadian government provides middle- and upper-class Canadian citizens with quality, low-cost, in-home child care and health care, literally at the expense of Filipina women workers and their families, who cannot afford these services for themselves.

Filipina migrant workers understand all too well how the Philippine government benefits and profits from this trade in women and thus plays a calculated role in ensuring its smooth functioning. The following statement of the PWC reflects this analysis of the past and current complicity of the Philippine government in this trade:

> The migration and commodification of Filipinos is sanctioned by official Philippine government policy. Known as the Labour Export Policy (LEP), this scheme of systematically exporting labour is part of the Structural Adjustment Programs (SAPs) imposed by the IMF and World Bank as conditionalities for borrowing. Ultimately, the LEP and SAPs are part of the neoliberal policies of the globalization agenda. The LEP seeks to alleviate the continuing problems of massive unemployment, trade deficits, foreign debt and social unrest. . . . The government relies upon the remittances of these migrants to prop up the economy and pay off the massive foreign debt owed to the IMF and the World Bank. Instead of selling coconuts and sugar, the Philippine government is now engaged in the sophisticated practice of selling its own people to industrialized countries.[27]

This statement reflects these women's clear recognition that the official Philippine government labor export policy is part and parcel of structural adjustment programs that wreak havoc on their lives and force them to migrate in the first place. The LEP institutionalizes the exportation of Filipina women to other countries for cheap labor and effectively guarantees that remittances from these migrant women workers are used to pay off foreign debt.

TURNING THE "NEW WORLD ORDER" UPSIDE DOWN

Carol de Leon is now program director for the Women Workers Project at CAAAV (formerly Committee Against Anti-Asian Violence): Organizing Asian Communities in the Bronx, New York. She grew up in the Philippines, where she was a youth activist until she left in 1987 to work abroad as a nanny. She recalls that when she was in Hong Kong she applied to go to Canada, but it did not materialize, and this was probably fortunate. In the mid-1980s, the Canadian government was "very lenient, inviting people to come into the country, so at the time it was so easy to find an employer and go to Canada." In the 1990s, the Canadian government instituted requirements such as educational background checks for 2 to 3 years of college education. She comments:

> It seems very appealing to go to Canada when you are in other countries . . . for a Third World woman to go there—but in reality that structure is not

well-implemented. When you go there, you'll end up working for a family for 2 or 3 years, and if you are being exploited, you can't leave while applying for a change in status. So the employer has all of the control, because the worker will end up staying anyway.[28]

de Leon knows that she is lucky not to be speaking from the experience of being trapped as a live-in caregiver in Canada. Although some aspects of her initial experiences in the U.S. were very similar, she not only was able to escape these exploitative situations, but is now organizing women like her to mobilize against the common abuses they face.

de Leon says that although the U.S. has no program like the Canadian LCP, it has a formal legal structure for au pairs who are usually young students from Europe. She says employers can hire them through agencies and arrange for them to have connections to church and school here. She also emphasizes that these "young students are treated very well and respected for what they do, compared to immigrant women who work as professional nannies." Third World women working for corporate executives do not get working permits. de Leon says, "You just get a visa that is tied to an employer." She had a contract to work as a live-in nanny for a family; her working papers described her as a "personal servant to American family." She added, "I really hated that because it sounded like back in the days when women and men are being brought here from Africa against their will and became enslaved. To me, *servant* means *slave*, and I'm certainly not one." She started working a few months after arrival in the New York City suburb of Ardsley. The people and weather appeared strange. Her job conditions were "a nightmare—I did everything from waking up the children, giving them breakfast, walking the dog, shoveling the snow, and cleaning the house." She worked from 6:30 a.m. to 9 p.m. 6 days a week. After a year, she asked for another day off after noting that others had 2 days off. Her employer, who worked for Philip Morris Corporation, said that he had seen that the common practice in Hong Kong was only one day off and refused her request on that basis.

She took the initiative to call the labor department to find out about the minimum wage and overtime pay and asked her employer to adjust her salary. Again, her employer said that the contract they signed was based on earnings in Hong Kong. de Leon pointed out that she could not support herself on those wages. When she asked for overtime, saying she understood the law

limited the workday to 8 hours, her employers demanded to know where she got the information. After telling them that her source was the labor department, they still refused, then gave her a $25 raise. de Leon calculated that her earnings after the raise amounted to $2 an hour when the minimum wage was $4. After that, she decided that she wanted to leave, but met the typical tactics of exploitative household employers:

> When I told them that I'd rather leave, they said I couldn't break the contract. I said that in a contract, either party can break the contract if you are not happy, so I'm giving you 2 weeks' notice. They insisted that I couldn't do it, and tried to manipulate me, asking where I was going, if I was going back to my country. To me, that's an implication that I was going to starve! I told her that it's none of her business.

Ultimately de Leon decided to stay because she signed a contract to work for 2 years—"the reality is that I felt I was legally trafficked." She remarks that women who are brought here by executives or diplomats have no way to network with others and no assistance from employers to find a community. Instead, she observes, workers are discouraged from meeting others and deliberately isolated in the suburbs, where they had no contact with other nannies, not even in the park. She adds that, "Without other people giving me support, I decided to stay and finish my contract and just survive," recalling that this also happened to her in Hong Kong. She was finally able to leave and find a live-out job from 11 a.m. to 7 p.m. that allowed her to start going to the park:

> That's when I realized that in this industry the majority of workers are women from the Third World. I met other domestic workers from all over the Third World. I realized that these conditions were widespread, whether you were from Indonesia, Malaysia, Philippines, Barbados, Guyana, Trinidad, most domestic workers face long hours, low wages, and isolation, and lack of control of our living and working conditions. Labor laws are not enforced in this industry. And labor laws simply do not protect our basic human rights to decent housing, food, shelter, and livable wages. And many laws, like those protecting workers against discrimination in the workplace, including sexual harassment and racism, specifically exclude domestic workers.

de Leon recalls many accounts of women who were subject to abuse and exploitation, worked long hours even when they were sick, and were forced to terminate pregnancies. After 7 years, she met people from CAAAV when they were handing out fliers in the park. de Leon approached them, "they took my number, and the next week I met with them and ended up going to weekly meetings."

Now, de Leon leads the Women Workers Project, which holds monthly meetings to improve working and living conditions among women in the domestic work industry. The project members began drafting standard guidelines and a pay scale to make recommendations for how much should be paid per child, for housekeeping tasks, etc.:

> We started looking at the industry, and realized that we had to be strategic about it, doing outreach with women from other ethnicities, and women really embraced it. We did a survey in 2000 in parks, indoor playgrounds, train stations, to see the conditions of women—who gets minimum wage, overtime pay, sick days, holidays. One woman who was being sponsored was forced to work 6 days a week, over 65 hours. She wanted to have one day to go to church. She started asking and showing papers from the labor department, and her employers were furious. Employers will try all their ways to not follow the regulations.

de Leon remarks on the lack of regulation of the industry: "We're not even protected from sexual harassment or any other abuses." Moreover, she notes that employers try many different tactics, including using race to divide household workers. For example, they make comparisons and say women from the Philippines are "better than from other countries, to create tensions between workers." They also "discriminate against us because of race, language, and immigration status."

Domestic Workers United, a project sponsored by CAAAV and Andolan, a South Asian workers' group, is pushing now for legislation that de Leon's group drafted. Led by a steering committee composed mostly of women from the Caribbean, the group used their research to design a standard contract and approached the New York City Council to pass a new law regulating the industry. Essentially, the law will regulate the Department of Consumer Affairs, the agency that licenses employment agencies recruiting and placing domestic workers. Seventy-five percent of domestic workers get their jobs through such agencies. The agencies should serve to protect these workers' rights, yet, de Leon says, when a worker has an abusive employer and calls her agency, "they advise

you to stay for at least 3 or 4 months because they want to receive their fees from the employers." Otherwise, the agency will have to give the money back to the employer or provide another employee without a fee. de Leon explains, "What we are asking for is a code of conduct, so that the agency provides a contract with your work conditions, including minimum wage, 2 weeks' paid vacation, etc. and the agency should enforce it."[29]

The group introduced the bill in March 2002 and provided supporting testimony at a hearing in May with the chair of the committee on labor. Supporters like Councilwoman Gail Brewer said the bill should have been easy to pass because it involved no cost to the city. The group staged a city-wide action on October 5, 2002, starting with a rally at Washington Square Park, followed by a march to City Hall. Participants wore yellow rubber gloves and aprons, just as they did when they introduced the bill. Media coverage surpassed their expectations: although the turnout for the action was strong at 500, the press coverage put the numbers above 1000.[30]

de Leon reflects on the Women Workers' Project and the demands of the bill. She also describes the nature of her organization's work and, more broadly, the movement she is helping build. The measure is in some ways modest and yet revolutionary:

> The bill is very basic—how we should be treated, working conditions, minimum wage, overtime pay, legal holidays and sick days—but really, we want to turn the industry upside down and change the notions that immigrant workers are lazy and uneducated. Because it relates to history, because this country inherited this industry through American slavery and ideas that this is women's work, etc. We're calling for respect and recognition for women in this industry.

de Leon says the group continues to wait patiently for a meeting on the bill with the Department of Consumer Affairs but will stage another action if necessary. In the meantime, her project offers an immigrant rights law clinic through New York University students working with CAAAV to provide advice on negotiating with employers and maneuvering the health care system. The project also provides courses for nannies on child care, psychology, and cardiopulmonary resuscitation training leading to Red Cross certification.[31]

Similarly, while the PWC in Vancouver pursues its long-term campaign to dismantle the LCP, its members work to build the movement for immigrant workers' rights in Canada every day in myriad ways. For example, the PWC has rented a house for use as a drop-in center for members who yearn for camaraderie and some comforting elements of Philippine culture. Cecilia Diocson, founding chairperson and director, describes how the center serves as a place for women to congregate, eat, and talk with women in similar situations:

The women started to educate each other, bringing their stories to discuss at the center. We have had a lot of successes in making these women more assertive in their employers' homes after gathering these stories over food. They report having to pay for their own room and board, sleeping in the garage without heat, and being "shared" by two employers. They say, "It's like being in prison from Monday through Friday." The majority work 14 to 16 hours and are underpaid. We found out that they are getting underfed too. They want rice at least twice a day, but lots of white employers don't eat rice, just pasta and potatoes. The regulars on Friday afternoon would be rushing to the kitchen, saying "I'm so hungry. I haven't had rice all week." They could hardly work because they were so hungry.

Clearly, the drop-in center provides more than a refuge for hungry workers. It serves as a space for these women to build a community base from which to organize. The effectiveness of the other work of the PWC is closely tied to this base, as much of it evolves from participatory research and is advanced through popular education including cultural events and political theater. The center has been able to conduct longitudinal studies, following women through 8- to 10-year time spans, to document the segregation and lack of mobility Filipinas face in the labor market in Canada.

The most recent research relates to the way the increasing number of Filipinas who enter Canada via the LCP led to growth over the past 20 years of the mail-order bride industry—"another category of slave," as Diocson says. The PWC also plans to launch a women's studies program with guest lecturers at the center for women who cannot afford to attend universities.[32]

At a recent international women's conference, Diocson presented an analysis of global migration and particularly the cases of Filipina women forced to migrate to Canada in the context of global capitalism. Her cogent analysis, both as a trained nurse who migrated from the Philippines and as a radical political organizer, is one of the most well-articulated analyses I have encountered in a variety of contexts. She commented about the LCP:

Instead of instituting a universal day care system to address the needs of women who are leaving the home to join the workplace, the Canadian state's response to this economic restructuring is to import cheap but highly educated and relatively skilled foreign domestic workers. This confers several advantages both to the Canadian state and Canadians who can afford a foreign domestic worker.... [T]he Canadian state earns revenue through the processing of migration documents and taxation of these foreign domestic workers.... [F]oreign domestic workers help provide a stable base of cheap "reserve army of labor" that keeps wages down and ensures continuous accumulation of capital.... Thus, the foreign domestic worker is functional to the maintenance of the existing capitalist system in Canada. On the other side of the ledger, the sending country also benefits much from its export of foreign domestic workers.[33]

In my experience, Third World women migrant workers have always been many steps ahead of us in formulating and articulating these analyses of globalization, perhaps because of its direct and dire impacts on the conditions of these women's lives. They have much at stake to develop strategies to resist these conditions effectively, and it is only fitting that those who have suffered first and worst under globalization will lead the way out from under its oppressive forces. The women of the Workers' Voices Coalition, the PWC, Domestic Workers United, and many other grassroots organizations are doing revolutionary work in the face of what they all know is surely not new under globalization. They remind us through their fierce struggles and sharp analyses that they will revolutionize not only their work force and their adopted societies, but the antiglobalization movement itself.

ACKNOWLEDGMENTS

Portions of this [reading] are reprinted from Chang, G., "The Global Trade in Filipina Workers," in *Dragon Ladies: Asian American Feminists Breathe Fire*, South End Press, Boston, 1997, p. 132; Chang, G., *Disposable Domestics: Immigrant Women Workers in the Global Economy*, South End Press, Boston, 2000, p. 123.

NOTES

1. "Globalization's Inability to Create Jobs Fuels Mass Migration: ILO Chief," *Tehran Times*, June 13, 2002.

2. Nishioka, J., "Marriage by Mail: The Internet Makes It Easier for Potential Mates to Connect across Seas," *Asian-Week*, July 29, 1999. [Cherry Blossoms is identified by all but Krosky as an international mail-order bride business.]

3. KPFA Radio, Morning Show with host Andrea Lewis, International Women's Day Program, 2001, guests: Grace Chang and Ethel Long Scott.

4. See "Third World Within" cited in *CAAAV Voice*, Special Issue on Women, Race and Work, Vol. 10, Fall 2000, p. 17. Cindy Domingo, founder of the Workers' Voices Coalition, in her call for seizing the moment after the Battle at Seattle, 1999, said: "We saw the profound deterioration in the conditions of immigrant and women workers worldwide as a direct result of free trade policies, globalization and privatization. In the United States, immigrant workers have become scapegoats for the failures of the global economy because U.S. workers don't see their interests as one and the same with workers in Latin America, Asia or Africa. The WTO coming to our city gave us a once-in-a-lifetime opportunity to draw links between conditions faced by working people in developing countries and those faced by immigrants and people of color in the United States," cited by Joy, K. in "Gender, Immigration and the WTO," *Network News*, Winter 2000, p. 12.

5. Testimony of representative of the International Organization of Prostitutes, Gabriela Workshop, September 3, 1995.

6. See Sandrasagra, M.J., "Globalisation Heightening Gender Inequalities:," IPS, October 10, 2000; Tauli-Corpuz, V., "Asia-Pacific Women Grapple with Financial Crisis and Globalisation," Roundtable Discussion on the Economic, Social, and Political Impacts of the Southeast Asian Financial Crisis, Manila, April 12–14, 1998, and Rural and Indigenous Women Speak Out on the Impact of Globalisation, Chiangmai, Thailand, May 22–25, 1998.

7. Testimony of Cenen Bagon, "Voices of Working Women," Proceedings of "Beyond the WTO: Conference on Women and Immigration the Global Economy" organized by North-west Labor and Employment Law Office (LELO) and Workers' Voice Coalition. Seattle, Washington, December 4, 1999, p. 16.

8. See Chang, G., "The Global Trade in Filipina Workers," in *Dragon Ladies: Asian American Feminists Breathe Fire*, South End Press, Boston, 1997, p. 132; Chang, G., *Disposable Domestics: Immigrant Women Workers in the Global Economy*, South End Press, Boston, 2000, p. 123.

9. Filipino Nurses Support Group, "Contextualizing the Presence of Filipino Nurses in BC," in *Advancing the Rights and Welfare of Non-Practicing Filipino and Other Foreign-Trained Nurses,"* proceedings of national consultation for Filipino and other foreign-trained nurses, December 7–9, 2001. The Philippines Department of Labor and Employment estimates that about 2748 Filipinos leave the country daily.

10. This number does not include women who are trafficked, illegally recruited, or migrate for marriage or students and tourists who eventually become undocumented workers. Data compiled by Kanlungan Center Foundation from Philippine Overseas Employment Administration and Department of Labor and Employment statistics, 1995; Vincent, I., "Canada Beckons Cream of Nannies: Much-Sought Filipinas Prefer Work Conditions," *Globe and Mail*, January 20, 1996, p. A1. Other authors more extensively address trafficking in women for the sex, entertainment, and mail-order bride industries. See Rosca, N., "The Philippines' Shameful Export," *Nation*, April 17, 1995, p. 523; Kim, E., "Sex Tourism in Asia: A Reflection of Political and Economic Equality," *Critical Perspectives of Third World America*, 2, Fall 1984, p. 215; Blitt, C., Producer, "Sisters and Daughters Betrayed: The Trafficking of Women and Girls and the Fight to End It," Video, Global Fund for Women.

11. Testimony of Pamela, "Filipino Nurses Doing Domestic Work in Canada: A Stalled Development," Philippine Women Centre of British Columbia, March 2000, p. 20.

12. Philippine Overseas Employment Administration, 2000, bulatlat.com.

13. Presentation by Ethel Farrales, Filipino–Canadian Youth Alliance, Vancouver, "Link Arms, Raise Fists: U.S. Out of the Philippines Now!" North American Conference, July 6–7, 2002.

14. Comments of youth member of Overseas Filipino Workers' Organization, Vancouver, "Link Arms, Raise Fists: U.S. Out of the Philippines Now!" North American Conference, San Francisco, July 6–7, 2002.

15. Philippine Women Centre of British Columbia, "Filipino Nurses Doing Domestic Work in Canada: A Stalled Development," Vancouver, March 2000, p. 10.

16. Ibid., p. 16.

17. Ibid., p. 11.

18. Diocson, C., Philippine Women Centre of British Columbia, Vancouver, Phone Interview, August 2002.

19. Statement of Sheila Farrales, "The Use of Filipino Nurses in the Scheme to Privatize Health Care," Conference Proceedings: Advancing the Rights and Welfare of Non-Practicing Filipino and Other Foreign-Trained Nurses, Filipino Nurses' Support Group, Burnaby, British Columbia, December 7–9, 2001, p. 51.

20. Testimony of Pamela, "Filipino Nurses Doing Domestic Work in Canada: A Stalled Development," Philippine Women Centre of British Columbia, March 2000, p. 19.

21. Ibid., p. 20.

22. Ibid., p. 29.

23. Statement of Sheila Farrales, ibid.

24. Statement of Gemma Gambito, ibid., p. 61.

25. Statement of Lynn Farrales, ibid., p. 42.

26. Ibid.

27. Philippine Women Centre of B.C., "Filipino Nurses Doing Domestic Work in Canada: A Stalled Development," March 2000, p. 7.

28. de Leon, C., Women Workers Project, CAAAV, Bronx, NY, Phone interview, September 2002.

29. de Leon, C., Women Workers Project, CAAAV, Bronx, NY, Phone Interviews, September 2002 and February 2003.

30. Alapo, L., "Bill to Protect Domestic Workers," *Newsday*, March 25, 2002; Greenhouse, S., "Wage Bill Would Protect Housekeepers and Nannies," *New York Times*, March 25, 2002; Richardson, L., "A Union Maid? Actually a Nanny, Organizing," *New York Times*, April 4, 2002; Ginsberg, A.,

"Nannies March for Fair Pay, OT," *Daily News*, October 6, 2002; Ramirez, M., "Domestic Workers Seek Wage, Personal Protection," *Newsday*, October 6, 2002; Geron, T., "All in a Day's Work," *AsianWeek*, July 11, 2002; Lee, C., "Revolt of the Nannies," *Village Voice*, March 9, 2002.

31. de Leon, C., Women Workers Project, CAAAV, Bronx, NY, Phone Interview, September 2002.

32. Diocson, C., Philippine Women Centre of British Columbia, Phone Interview, August 2002.

33. Diocson, C., "Forced Migration: Perpetuation of Underdevelopment," paper presented at Ninth International Forum, Association for Women's Rights in Development, Guadalajara, Mexico, October 3–6, 2002.

READING *44* **Sharon Ann Navarro**

Las Mujeres Invisibles/*The Invisible Women*

NAFTA is a story of violence against women. It is a treaty that created violence against women and their families. There are tremendous implications, the economic implications and the whole impact it has had on women's health, their lives, their future, and their families. It is as violent as any beating, if not more destructive.

—*La Mujer Obrera*

El Paso, Texas, is a microcosm of the inherent contradictions created by the North American Free Trade Agreement (NAFTA) along the border. On the one hand, NAFTA profoundly shifted the focus of national and international commerce, moving it from an "East-West" emphasis to a "North-South" paradigm. In doing so, El Paso became the gateway to the tremendous economic opportunities available to Mexico and Latin America (Ortega 2000). At the same time, north of the U.S.-Mexican border, NAFTA acted as a catalyst, another force, or another trend, that is steadily squeezing Mexican-American women workers (in the garment industry) to the margins of the economic sector in El Paso. These Mexican-American garment workers are typically low-skilled and low-income women. As the garment industries close down their businesses and move across the border, the Mexican-American women

that once worked in these businesses are being left out of the economic restructuring taking place under NAFTA. These women are being marginalized. The type of work that they have done—in some cases for more than twenty years—is now becoming obsolete and replaced by advanced technology.

Before this study is presented to you, it is important to note that NAFTA is not characterized as *the main factor* for the displacement (or permanent layoffs) of female garment workers in El Paso. NAFTA is instead used by one grassroots non-governmental women's organization, La Mujer Obrera (LMO), as a symbol of what they face as female workers in a border city, as a tool for political activism and mobilization. The women's organization examined in this study has succeeded in contextualizing NAFTA as a tangible culprit, the *primary cause* of their current struggle for a better quality of life for the displaced workers and their families.

LMO's direct response to globalization, as manifested in NAFTA, should not be interpreted to mean that one organization is simply bashing NAFTA only. Instead, because of the attention given to NAFTA by politicians, various interest groups, and scholars alike, NAFTA has simply become the topic of selection that organizations like LMO use as the source of their struggle. Similar agreements, such as the General

Agreement on Tariffs and Trade, the Free Trade Area of the Americas, or the Multilateral Agreement on Investment, could just have easily been targeted.

For the Mexican-American garment workers in El Paso, an entire way of life and standard of living are fast disappearing. These Spanish-speaking women have worked all of their lives to provide for up to four generations of their families. Now they have lost their livelihood, their health-care insurance, their homes, and their futures. When NAFTA was first introduced in the late 1980s, various organizations with labor interests believed that NAFTA was going to be their opportunity to set labor standards for workers in the three participating countries. However, that was not at all what the crafters of NAFTA intended. Instead, labor interests were left out of NAFTA.

And so NAFTA became an incitement to discourse, an invitation to review the voices whose identities, as Spanish-speaking, female garment workers, are vehicles for political expression. This woman's nongovernmental organization mobilized to express their anxieties about the way NAFTA has affected their economic subsistence, their way of life. The struggle for this grassroots organization is not over the politics of influence, but to transform the terms and nature of the debate; it is a struggle to integrate previously excluded groups, voices, and issues into local and national politics.

Drawing on literature from political science, as well as from a wealth of new data obtained through fieldwork,[1] this study examines LMO's use of central icons, traditions, history, and customs from Mexican culture to mobilize constituents in appeals to U.S. local, state, and federal government institutions. More important, this study explores how one women's organization used the U.S.-Mexico border to highlight its struggle in the post-NAFTA era.

This [reading] is divided into three sections. The first focuses on the uniqueness of a border city in the post-NAFTA era. The second offers a gendered look at globalization as manifested in NAFTA. The last section looks at culture as a mobilizing tool for LMO, paying particular attention to the way in which LMO embraces Mexican culture to highlight the displaced workers' struggle.

EL PASO: A BORDER BETWEEN TWO WORLDS

The physical designation of a boundary may serve as an observable reminder that the politics, economics, and culture of countries and subnationalities differ (Agnew, Mercer, and Sopher 1984). The uniqueness of El Paso–Ciudad Juarez stems from the fact that a city from the First World shares a border with a developing city from the Third World. Boundaries create cultures and identities that impose order on cities, communities, and individuals by shaping them in a way that embodies the values and beliefs of a society or geographic location. The physical and cultural closeness of the United States and Mexico, as well as the political, social, and economic ties that connect them, creates an intriguing bicultural arrangement that provide a laboratory for studying identity formation and mobilization across borders.

In theory, a border is a line that separates one nation from another or, in the case of internal entities, one province or locality from another. The essential functions of a border are to keep people in their own space and to prevent, control, or regulate interactions among them. For the purposes of this study, the terms *border, borderland,* and *frontera* are used interchangeably. The terms are used to denote an area that is physically distant from the core of the nation; it is a zone of transition, a place where people and institutions are shaped by natural and human forces that are not felt in the core or heartland of the United States or Mexico.

For example, the U.S.-Mexico boundary is the busiest land border in the world, the longest and most dramatic meeting point between a rich and a poor country, and the site of the most intensive interaction between law enforcement and law evasion. Nowhere has the state more aggressively loosened and tightened its territorial border grip at the same time. Nowhere else do the contrasting state practices of market liberalization and criminalization more visibly overlap. The result has been the construction of both a borderless economy (via NAFTA) and a barricaded border. More concretely, the politics of opening the border to legal economic flows is closely connected to the politics of making it appear more closed to illegal flows: illegal drugs and migrant labor.

Oscar Martinez, one of the leading scholars on the U.S.-Mexico border, acknowledges the political, economic, and social cultural significance of the frontera. He proposes that the dynamics of the border create four models of borderland interaction: alienated borderlands, coexistent borderlands, interdependent borderlands, and integrated borderlands. Each model illustrates a different degree of cross-border interaction (Grimes 1998). For example, today interdependence is overwhelmingly dominant in the U.S.-Mexico borderlands, and therefore the most appropriate designation for that binational zone is the interdependent frontera. That is not to say, however, that elements of alienation, coexistence, and even integration are not part of the zone at a given time. Martinez's findings are nothing new for this border city and its border people. The influence of Ciudad Juarez on El Paso is a natural daily occurrence.

The uniqueness of the US.-Mexico border, specifically the border city in question, plays a critical role in the sociopolitical construction of identities. Kimberly Grimes, in her study of migration to the United States from Putla de Guerro, Oaxaca, Mexico, suggests that identities are rooted in geography. Grimes's claim holds the key to understanding the seemingly contradictory strategy of LMO, which on the one hand embraces the Mexican culture—which is suggestive of a "borderless cultural region"—to mobilize its members, but at the same time reemphasizes the U.S.-Mexico border to highlight the struggles of displaced workers. According to Grimes, borders play an important role in distinguishing "us" from "them." Moreover, people's sense of self includes identification with particular geographical spaces. People negotiate constructed political, economic, and social (cultural) borders of self-identification. Identities are gounded in space and time, and they transform as time passes, as people move across spaces, and as national policies and global conditions transform. People react to these changes and constructions by accommodating or challenging and/or resisting them.

MEXICAN-AMERICAN WOMEN WORKERS IN EL PASO: A GENDERED LOOK AT GLOBALIZATION

For the close to 20,000 displaced workers, NAFTA and ongoing deep economic restructuring have not ushered in the new dawn of prosperity hailed by political leaders. The explosive growth of lower-paid export manufacturing jobs in the maquiladora sector in Mexico has been offset by the immense loss of jobs in the domestic manufacturing sector in the United States and Canada.

The globalization of capital necessary for economic restructuring is being deliberately hastened by most national governments, by international institutions like the International Monetary Fund and the World Bank, and by global corporations themselves. While international trade is nothing new, our system of nation-based economies is rapidly changing toward a "new world economy" (Takaki 1993). At the center of this change lies a sharp increase in capital mobility. Computer, communication, and transportation technologies continue to shorten geographical distances, making possible the coordination of production and commerce on a global scale. Lower tariffs have reduced national frontiers as

barriers to commerce, thus encouraging transnational production and distribution. Corporations are becoming global not only to reduce production costs, but also to expand markets, elude taxes, acquire resources, and protect themselves against currency fluctuations and other risks, including the growth of organizations like LMO that would mobilize workers and demand that their interests and voices be heard in the new world economy (see also Brecher and Costello 1994).

Three hundred companies now own an estimated one-quarter of the productive assets of the world (Barnet and Cavanagh 1994, 15). Of the top 100 economies in the world, 47 are corporations—each with more wealth than 130 countries (Harison 1994). International trade and financial institutions like the International Monetary Fund, the World Bank, the European Union (EU), and the new World Trade Organization have cultivated powers formerly reserved for nation-states. Conversely, national governments have become less and less able to control their own economies. This new system, which is controlled by the so-called Corporate Agenda, is not based on the consent of the governed (Brecher, Childs, and Cutler 1993), and it has no institutional mechanism to hold it accountable to those whom its decisions affect.

In general, the effects of capital mobility, which is designed to increase economic efficiency, have been malignant for workers. An unregulated global economy forces workers, communities, and countries to compete with each other in an effort to attract corporate investment. Each tries to reduce labor, social, and environmental costs below the others.[2]

In the debates surrounding NAFTA, globalization and regionalization are often interpreted as homogenizing vehicles, without regard to the fact that women, and in particular women of color, are paying a disproportionate share of the costs of the processes of neoliberalism. Globalization hits especially hard racial/ethnic minorities in the United States and female factory workers in the U.S. (Larudee 1999, 123–63). It has profoundly changed the lives of women in El Paso, Texas, creating inequalities that interact with pre-existing class, ethnic, gender, and regional cleavages (Gabriel and Macdonald 1994, 535–62).

Job losses have been especially substantial in the apparel sector in El Paso and in some small communities that are heavily dependent on factories, which shut down and moved to Mexico. Since NAFTA took effect in 1994, El Paso has lost between 15,000 and 20,000 jobs.[3] Table 1 shows the number of job losses from 1994 to 2000. Table 2 shows how Texas ranks in comparison

TABLE I   NAFTA JOB LOSSES IN EL PASO, JANUARY 1994–NOVEMBER 2000

Year	Number of Displaced Workers
1994	1,045
1995	2,193
1996	2,573
1997	3,435
1998	3,641
1999	2,125
2000	1,940
TOTAL	18,975

Source: Texas Workforce Commission.

TABLE 2   NAFTA-TAA CERTIFIED WORKERS, BY STATE AS OF MID-JULY 1997

State	Number	State	Number
Texas	*	Massachusetts	1,315
North Carolina	*	West Virginia	1,288
Pennsylvania	*	Kansas	1,184
New York	*	Kentucky	1,016
California	7,476	Alaska	780
Georgia	6,186	Louisiana	778
Indiana	5,811	Arizona	684
Tennessee	5,640	Connecticut	631
Arkansas	5,397	Montana	613
New Jersey	4,471	Maine	432
Ohio	4,413	Wyoming	392
Wisconsin	4,405	Vermont	361
Michigan	3,783	Minnesota	336
Washington	3,445	North Dakota	300
Missouri	3,329	Utah	292
Illinois	2,902	New Mexico	242
Florida	2,804	Oklahoma	230
Iowa	2,785	Nebraska	220
Oregon	2,550	New Hampshire	139
South Carolina	2,305	Maryland	86
Virginia	2,166	Idaho	83
Colorado	1,990	Nevada	76
Alabama	1,383	South Dakota	65

*The Department of Labor does not have the total number of displaced workers for the states of Texas, North Carolina, Pennsylvania, and New York, but claim they are the states with the highest numbers.

Source: Department of Labor, NAFTA Trade Adjustment Assistance Office.

Note: Certifications are for January 1, 1994, to July 18, 1997.

to other states with respect to displaced workers. Free trade and the reduction of tariffs made it easier for companies to close plants and move to Mexico only to continue as maquiladoras (Myerson 1998, 1C, 22C).

In December 1998, El Paso's average unemployment rate was almost three times (11 percent) the state unemployment rate of 4.4 percent and the U.S. rate of 4 percent (Kolence 1999c, B10). The community of El Paso was for a very long time advertised as a low-wage, low-skill manufacturing paradise. A 1993–94 study conducted by the Greater El Paso Chamber of Commerce Foundation Inc. reported, "[I]f you want to be the low wage paying capital of the world, don't do anything, you're already there" (El Paso Greater Chamber of Commerce 1997, 10). Cheap Mexican labor, in particular, has always been El Paso's strongest selling point (also see Garcia 1981). Roberto Franco, director of the City's Economic Development Agency, articulated this point best when he said, "El Paso was perceived as the jeans and slacks capital of the United States" (Kolence 1999a, 4).

Approximately 80 percent of the garment workers in El Paso's garment and other manufacturing industries were Mexican-American women. Their subordinate social status limits their employment opportunities and makes them vulnerable to exploitation. As a result of NAFTA, however, thousands of Mexican-American workers, many of whom had migrated from Mexico to El Paso in search of a better life, lost their jobs. A total of 97 percent of the displaced Mexican-American workers in El Paso are Hispanic, and 80 percent are women (Gilot 1999, 10B). One-third of these women head single households. Half are between the ages of 30 and 45, while the majority of

the other half are older than 45. In addition, most of the affected workers are sustaining up to four generations of their families—themselves, their parents, their children and their grandchildren (La Mujer Obrera 1999a, 1). Using an average figure of four persons per household, the population affected by NAFTA in El Paso can be estimated at 40,000. When taking only into account the number of so-called certified NAFTA displaced workers,[4] the at-risk population is at least 80,000—13 percent of El Paso's population—and the potentially affected population is as large as 200,000. The women's job skills cannot easily be transferred from low-tech to the mid- to high-tech manufacturing jobs entering El Paso in record numbers (El Puente CDC/La Mujer Obrera 1999, 6). The testimonies of displaced Mexican-American women workers reveal their immense financial struggles. Typically over 45 years of age, with less than a fourth-grade education in Mexico, they have lost health insurance and other benefits because the businesses they worked for shut down production, and they are typically two to three months past due on rent and utilities.[5] The lead organizer of the Asociacion de Trabajadores Fronterizos (Association of Borderland Workers), Guillermo Glenn (1999), describes the burden globalization has foisted on female Mexican-American displaced woman workers:

> In El Paso, women suffer what is called a *"doble jornada"* (double day's work) because they have two jobs, one at home and one at the factory (or school since there are very few factories open). They suffer all the discrimination. Language discrimination, discrimination because they are Mexican, and discrimination because they are women. . . . There is still a lot of discrimination in terms of their role, in terms of their decision-making, in terms of how they are treated.

LMO has been working for nearly five years to make the conditions of Spanish-speaking NAFTA-displaced women workers visible locally, regionally, and nationally. The seeds of LMO were planted in 1972, when a campaign to unionize workers in the Farah plant (the biggest jean maker at the time) in El Paso intensified (see Coyle, Hershatter, and Honig 1980, 117–43). LMO was formed because women felt that the Amalgamated Clothing and Textile Workers of America, or for that matter, any union (such as the AFL-CIO), did nothing to address their needs, ignored their rights as *women* workers, and did not respect their membership as *women* members in the union (Flores 1998). This devaluation of women's work is deeply rooted in the history of U.S. labor unions. According to Glenn (1999), the old labor movement of the 1970s—including the one that organized Farah workers—"characterized itself as . . . [a]very macho kind of an organization. We (LMO) feel that the labor unions have not gotten away from that." For example, during the strike against Farah, male organizers in both the Amalgamated Clothing Workers

of America and the AFL-CIO ignored women worker's concerns, such as sexual harassment, health care, child care, domestic violence, political education, and verbal abuse by their employers (Flores 1998). Moreover, employers often view the income of the female workers as "extra" or "supplemental" to their husband's income.

In 1981, following the Farah campaign, LMO was legally established as a non-profit community-based organization of women workers in El Paso. LMO has defined itself, first and foremost, as a *woman's* organization (La Mujer Obrera 1993, 3). It combines community organizing, popular education, leadership development and advocacy into a comprehensive struggle for a better quality of life for the women and their families. Like other organizations operating in a resource-poor environment, the organization relies on outside funding (La Mujer Obrera 1999, 1 and 2). The organization turns to national churches, private foundations, the federal government, and local entities for financial support (Arnold 1999a). LMO initially had a yearly budget of $150,000, and in 1998–1999 its budget was between $500,000 and $750,000 (Arnold 1999b). The organization employs a total of six women as full-time organizers. The board of directors is made up of two men and five women, all of whom have been displaced by NAFTA. The support staff consists of a paid secretary and a grant writer as well as various interns and volunteers.

The organization struggles to achieve *siete necesidades basicas* (seven basic goals): decent, stable employment, housing, education, nutrition, health care, peace, and political liberty. One of LMO's principal objectives is to educate workers so that they are able to defend their rights and to take leadership positions in their own communities. Educational programs form the basis for organizing work and raise workers' awareness of their roles as *women* and as economic producers. Like other women's movements, LMO has struggled to integrate previously excluded issues into politics by pushing women's concerns (e.g., child care and health care) (Peterson 1992, 183–206). LMO also serves at a safe place where friendships develop, experiences are shared, and where women become educated not only about their rights as workers, but, perhaps most important, their rights as women, mothers, and spouses. To this end, LMO has established a child care center where displaced workers may leave their children while they attend school, look for work, or go to their jobs.[6]

To achieve institutional changes that will lead to the creation of genuine economic alternatives for workers in the midst of globalization, La Mujer Obrera has also recently reorganized and broadened its structure (La Mujer Obrera 1998, 4). The most critical developments have been the emergence of two new quasi-independent organizations under LMO's corporate umbrella. One is the Asociacion de Trabajadores Fronterizos, which has taken on the worker and community organizing, direct action, and mass mobilization components of LMO's work (5). The association includes Spanish-speaking men and women workers who were employed and laid off from the manufacturing plants in El Paso. Launched during the summer of 1996 with the support of LMO, the association extends beyond LMO's traditional base of women garment workers and incorporates displaced men, workers from electronics, plastics, medical supply manufacturing, and other labor intensive industries. Growing from an initial membership of 20 workers to a current roster of more than 700 active members, the association has built a countywide network with representatives of LMO in seven factories and school committees throughout El Paso (6–7).

Through these networks, the association has the participation of more than 2,000 workers, the majority of whom are women, and a governing board of 14 displaced workers, two elected from and by each of the seven factory and school committees (26). At the same time, LMO began constructing its capacity to develop and operate community economic development programs on behalf of, and with, displaced workers. In December of 1997, LMO established El Puente Community Development Corporation as a vehicle for developing training and education, jobs, self-employment, housing, the development of microenterprises, access to credit and neighborhood revitalization strategies as a means to create jobs, income, and economic self-sufficiency for the workers and the organization. Moving into this arena has required that LMO negotiate and work with local, state, and federal agencies and officials for financial support (26–27).

By creating a space in the political and economic arena, LMO has already produced tangible results for the displaced workers. The organization succeeded in getting a $45 million grant—the largest grant ever given by the U.S. Department of Labor—to retrain displaced workers. To get this grant, LMO made its concerns known locally and nationally with one act that proved to be a turning point for LMO. On June 1997, several Mexican-American women (all from LMO) blocked the Zaragoza International Port of Entry, which is one of El Paso's busiest commercial bridges with Ciudad Juarez, Mexico, for one hour by stretching a rope across the port. The goal of the protest was to bring the plight of NAFTA-displaced workers to the attention of Secretary Robert Rubin of the Department of the Treasury, which is responsible for a variety of NAFTA programs. But instead of meeting with him, his representative, or other state or local authorities, protesters were arrested and charged with obstructing highway commerce.

The $45 million grant allows LMO to institute alternatives to existing federal and state retraining programs. These programs entitle displaced workers to benefits while attending English classes, courses for their general equivalency diploma (GED), and retraining within an 18-month period. Many of these programs, however, are plagued with a variety of problems, especially inadequate buildings and equipment, outdated curricula, incompetent or poorly trained teachers, and administrators who make racial/ethnic slurs and personal insults (Klapmeyer 1998).

In the summer of 1999, Margarita Calderon, a researcher at Johns Hopkins University, tested 60 displaced workers at 12 different schools to see what they had learned. The results were shocking. Only two of the 60 students, some of whom had spent up to five years in various federally subsided training programs, had learned enough to handle an interview in English. Calderon, an expert in bilingual education, found that retraining schools set up for displaced workers had been using rigid teaching techniques long abandoned by better language schools, such as lectures and translation exercises (quoted in Templin 2000, B1 and B4). In addition, there is a perception among case managers, state and local agencies, school administrators, and teachers that "the displaced workers are just there to get paid and don't want to learn" (Klapmeyer 1998). Frustrated with many of the inept retraining schools, LMO opened up its own school for displaced workers on February 1, 1999. It hired a full-time teacher to teach English, the general equivalency examination and microenterprise training. LMO has also established a business incubator that will support the self-employment initiatives of displaced workers. Further, LMO is currently in the process of developing a bilingual adult education curriculum specifically designed for displaced workers in El Paso. This curriculum will be the standard curriculum for every school in El Paso if they are to accept displaced workers in their schools. LMO has also played an instrumental role in helping El Paso win the Empowerment Zone designation that provides federal funds for economic development. As a result, the poorest area of the city—South Central—will receive much needed federal money for revitalization, which would create jobs. LMO plays a role in deciding how that money will be spent.

THE USES OF MEXICAN CULTURE FOR MOBILIZATION

For LMO, culture has become a unique dimension in women's activism. In her study of two Chicano struggles in the Southwest, Laura Pulido (1998, 31–60) points out that culture plays a key role in mobilization efforts both by "providing familiar and meaningful guideposts and by facilitating collective identity." The use of symbols, customs, traditions reminds people of who they are, of their shared traditions past and present, and of what they can achieve by uniting and acting collectively.

In the 1960s and 1970s Latinos/Chicanos became aware of how their culture not only differed from, but was also maligned by, mainstream Anglo America. Once-shameful cultural icons were reappropriated and turned into symbols of resistance. In the course of building a movement, farmworkers and activists publicly displayed statues and posters of La Virgen de Guadalupe not only as a source of solace and inspiration, but also (and far more consciously at times) as an expression of pride in the Mexican culture and a tool of mobilization. By openly engaging in ritual prayer, they asserted their identity to the larger society (see Herrera-Sobek 1990; Rodriguez 1994). LMO similarly uses La Virgen de Guadalupe as an expression of inspiration and as a vehicle of mobilization and consciousness raising. For the women of LMO, La Virgen de Guadalupe thus not only represents strength, hope, and respect, but "she is also viewed as a woman and a mother who has suffered with the death of her son and, like her, we (displaced workers) are suffering for our families and our children (Orquiz 1999).[7]

In a study of Mexican-American women in East Los Angeles, Mary Pardo examines how they transform "traditional" networks and resources based on family and culture into political assets to defend the quality of urban life. Here, the women's activism arises out of seemingly "traditional" roles, addresses wider social and political issues, and capitalizes on formal associations sanctioned by the community. Religion, commonly viewed as a conservative force, becomes intertwined with politics. Often, women speak of their communities and their activism as extensions of their family and household responsibility. Women's grassroots struggles center around quality of life and challenge conventional assumptions about the powerlessness of women as well as static definitions of culture and tradition (Pardo 1998).

LMO also identifies with the Mexican culture and its members through its landscape. Outside its building, LMO has corn (maize) stalks growing in place of an assortment of bushes or flowers. As Refugio Arrieta explains, "The maize is symbolic of our Mexican culture. It is a symbol of the resistance too. . . . It is more like the resistance that leads to maintaining the culture here and helping it live and grow here in the U.S. and not simply being forced to abandon the Mexican culture" (Arrieta 1998).

Moreover, LMO also tries to maintain and reinterpret its history and heritage with Mexico in symbolic remembrance of Emiliano Zapata and the Zapatista rebels. Hanging from some of the walls of LMO are portraits and pictures of Emilio Zapata and Zapatista *women* rebels. For LMO, Zapata and the Zapatista rebels represent the struggle of resistance against neoliberalism, specifically NAFTA. They represent in Mexico the voice of people who have been eliminated in Mexico by NAFTA. As one member stated, "We are kindred spirits because of what the U.S. economy is doing to and Mexican-American factory workers what the Mexican economy is doing to the indigenous people of Mexico" (Anonymous 1998). To some extent, LMO believes, like the Zapatistas in southern Mexico, that NAFTA will eliminate them from an economy that was built on their backs.

LMO further uses the Mexican *corrido* as a mobilizing mechanism that reflects their political situation.[8] For example, during Guillermo Glenn's trial on March 17, 1999, after he was arrested for his participation in the blocking of the Zaragoza Bridge, LMO members gathered outside the courthouse in protest. With the news stations there, LMO members began to sing the "Corrido de los Desplazados" (The ballad of the displaced), which they had written themselves:

Ano de 94	In the year of '94
Comenzo la pesadilla	The nightmare started
Se robaron los trabajos,	They stole the jobs,
Nos dejaron en la orilla	They left us at the edge
Los obreros en El Paso,	The workers in El Paso,
Recuerdan bien ese dia.	Remember well that day.

The "Corrido de los Desplazados" embraces all displaced workers, raises their level of consciousness, unites them, and inspires them to mobilize. This type of cultural practice also represents the organization's strategy of activism and mobilization. It adds to more conventional forms of political participation, such as voting, in an effort to stress demands for respect, dignity, and justice of the Mexican-American workers and their traditions. Cindy Arnold (1999b), coordinator of El Puente at LMO, summed up the organization's philosophy of political participation as follows: "For us, political involvement is not based on an electoral or party process, but [is seen] in terms of on-going dialogue with political leaders at all the different levels." As a political actor, LMO emphasizes that it has no political affiliation and does not endorse any particular political party or politician. Its legal charter as a community-based organization does not permit it to become involved in electoral politics. Now that half of its members are citizens and thus eligible to vote (a change that became evident in the last city election), it will also encourage its members to vote.

Yet the March 1999 protest in support of Guillermo Glenn also illustrated one of the obstacles to LMO organizing efforts, which stems from the roles typically ascribed to women in Mexican culture. These roles make Mexican women feel uneasy about their political activism—despite the fact that they do not see it as political. As local news cameras panned the crowd of LMO protesters, which included both men and women, some women hid their faces behind the protest signs because their husbands would be angry with them for appearing on television. One woman said, "My husband would be humiliated by his friend if they saw me on television" (Anonymous, 1999; my translation of the original Spanish).

In other instances, LMO activists have been accused by their spouses of neglecting their family obligations when they became involved with the organization (Olvera 1990, A12). Women in leadership roles often reveal that they have strained relationships with their husbands because they refused to adhere to the role of a traditional Mexican wife (I. Montoya 1999). Other women reported that it was okay for them to participate in LMO as long as they also did what was expected of them as mothers, housekeepers, and wives (Reyes 1999; see also Fernandez-Kelly 1990; Garcia 1981). Some women describe the difficulty of getting away from housework and their husbands. Maria Acosta describes the problem she has with her jealous husband: "Every time I get ready to come to the meetings, my husband gives me a hard time. He says that I come to [La] Mujer Obrera because I am either looking for a boyfriend or I come to meet my boyfriend."[9] According to Acosta's husband, there could be no other reason for her to come to LMO, despite the fact that it is helping her to get into a retraining program.

CONCLUSION

LMO's activism in response to global economic restructuring, as manifested in NAFTA, relies on contradictory yet successful mobilization strategy. On the one hand,

LMO became visible when its members literally reemphasized the U.S.-Mexico border to highlight NAFTA's disastrous effects on Mexican-American women garment workers. On the other hand, LMO de-emphasized the U.S.-Mexico border culturally by embracing the Mexican culture. This is what makes the border city of El Paso unique. Displaced by NAFTA, the lives of the LMO women have been disrupted and forever changed by the corporate agenda driving NAFTA. Spanish-speaking women, who once migrated to El Paso in search of a better life, have received a rude awakening after dedicating their entire lives to building the city's economy. After having been subject to exploitation and limited employment in El Paso, these women are now being marginalized and slowly eliminated from an increasingly internationalized economy.

To mobilize these women, LMO has focused on Mexican culture as a vehicle that links individual members to the organization. The use of Mexican religious symbols, traditions, histories, and customs has served to reinforce a bond between the organization and its members, as well as to contextualize the plight of the NAFTA-displaced workers. At the same time, its creation of a transnationally shared space of Mexican culture has enabled LMO to become a legitimate economic actor in the city's economic restructuring. Symbols such as the *Virgen de Guadalupe*, the cultivation of corn stalks, pictures of the Zapatistas, and the use of the Mexican *corrido* have served as icons of political resistance against a transnational agreement that has affected their lives. The success of this strategy has manifested itself in the fact that no other organization in the U.S.-Mexico border region has achieved as much as has LMO. It has helped obtain El Paso's designation as an Empowerment Zone, won a $45 million grant for displaced workers, created two umbrella organizations—the Asociacion de Trabajadores and El Puente—opened its own school for displaced workers, is currently developing the first bilingual adult curriculum for displaced workers, and has established a child-care center. All of its achievements serve as a testament to the power of a transnational culture in women's political activism. But, be that as it may, a much larger question looms: Although this essay is about one grassroots globalization movement at the U.S.-Mexico border, are there lessons to be learned from its experiences?

Certainly the first lesson points to the fact that any one specific identity—in this case the Mexican identity—may not necessarily be enough to forge a cross-border alliance. Other principal factors may come into play, such as shared gender, shared experiences, values, beliefs, ideology. For example, a much more useful and broader theme that workers could mobilize around could be the pursuit for social justice among all workers, specifically the push for "living wages." By mobilizing around the theme of social justice, LMO would broaden its support base by being inclusive of other grassroots organizations and perhaps catapult them into the international area where their voices would be much more difficult to stifle. The most recent example of this was seen in the Summit of the Americas meeting on April 20–22, 2001, in Quebec City, where numerous grassroots movements gathered to protest the expansion of economic integration (free trade) at the expense of social justice.

In addition, what becomes evident in this essay is the importance of contextualizing the workers situation under NAFTA. What this case study suggests is that mobilization depends upon the way in which an organization chooses to construct, define, identify, or contextualize itself given a certain set of circumstances. The way in which an organization chooses to identify itself and whether or not that particular identity resonates with its members has bearing on the organization's behavior and the perception external agencies, individuals, and institutions have of that organization. The perception of others outside of the organization may have significant political repercussions. For example, the identity of an organization can affect its access to resources made available only by governmental agencies.

Moreover, this essay also points to the growing participation of women in grassroots mobilization, specifically as leaders, against NAFTA, the Free Trade for the Americas Initiative scheduled for completion in 2005, as it is for the Multilateral Agreement on Investment and other similar agreements. Lisa Montoya and her colleagues correctly point out that political scientists have tended to neglect or discount Latina leadership and participation in electoral and community politics (Montoya, Hardy-Fanta, Garcia 2000, 555–61). A key issue within the debate about gender differences is whether there is an essential divide between the public and private dimensions of politics. For Latina women, much more than men, the boundary between these supposedly distinct spheres of life is blurred, indistinct. With their emphasis on grassroots politics, survival politics, and the politics of everyday life and through their emphasis on the development of political consciousness, Latina women see connections between the problems they face personally and community issues stemming from government policies.

NOTES

1. This study is based on 56 face-to-face interviews I conducted from August of 1998 through August 1999 in El Paso, Texas, with active women who have lost their jobs because of NAFTA—that is, businesses moving from El Paso to Mexico. I have defined as "active" those women who dedicate 20 hours to LMO by either attending weekly meetings, belonging to committees within the organization, volunteering their time, or attending and helping in organizing fiestas (parties), rallies, and protests. The interviews were conducted in Spanish (and on occasion in English) at LMO, protest and rally sites, and, when it was convenient for the person interviewed, over the phone. I have also included interviews with the lead organizers of LMO, a former bilingual teacher, who was employed to teach these women English at one of the many schools that offer English classes, a public relations spokesperson from one of the last mammoth garment industries (Levi Strauss) in El Paso, politicians, and various governmental/political officials. Depending on the individual, these interviews lasted between 15 and 75 minutes. In LMO, the women speak only Spanish, range in age from 35 to 72, and more than half have no more than a fourth-grade education in Mexico. At the time of my interviews with the women of LMO, almost all of them were either in school learning English, studying for their high school equivalancy diploma, or in some retraining program.

2. According to Brecher and Costello (1994), "race to the bottom" is the reduction in labor, social, and environmental conditions that results from global competition for jobs and investment.

3. This is the only credible number that I have seen reported.

4. In speaking with John Ownby of the Dislocated Worker Service Unit at the Texas Workforce Commission, I was told that being classified as "certified NAFTA displaced worker" might not reflect the true number of displaced workers. Businesses that close up shop because of NAFTA are supposed to certify their workers with the Texas Workforce Commission, which simply means that the workers were laid off because the business closed down due solely to NAFTA. Certification by the Texas Workforce Commission ensures that the displaced worker will be eligible for retraining programs. However, the Texas Workforce Commission does not have the manpower to see that businesses due in fact register their workers as certified NAFTA displaced workers. Thus, the number of certified displaced workers may not be a true account of displaced workers. Ownby believes the number to be much higher (Ownby 1999).

5. This information is based on face-to-face interviews and informal discussions with women.

6. The power of culture as a mobilizing force is not a new phenomenon. It has been instrumental in the civil rights movement, the Chicano movement, and the farmworkers movement as well as many others.

7. In both my formal and informal conversations with LMO and staff members, this was the response given by all.

8. A *corrido* is a simple narrative ballad that relates an event of interest only to a small region; it may be a love song or a comment on a political situation.

9. This name has been altered to protect the identity of the woman. The information was revealed in a private informal conversation.

BIBLIOGRAPHY

Agnew, John A., John Mercer, and David Sopher, eds. 1984. *The City in Cultural Context.* Boston: Allen & Unwin.

Anonymous. 1998. Personal interview, November 4.

Anonymous. 1999. Personal interview, March 17.

Arnold, Cindy. 1999a. Personal interview, January 9.

———. 1999b. Personal interview, June 21.

Arrieta, Refugio. 1998. Personal interview, November 5.

Barnet, Richard, La Barricada, and John Cavanagh. 1994. *Global Dreams.* New York: Simon & Schuster.

Brecher, Jeremy, John Brown Childs, and Jill Cutler, eds. 1993. *Global Visions.* Boston: South End Press.

Brecher, Jeremy, and Tim Costello. 1994. *Global Village or Global Pillage: Economic Reconstruction from the Bottom Up.* Boston: South End.

Coyle, Laurie, Gail Hershatter, and Emily Honig, "Women at Farah: An Unfinished Story." Pp. 117–43 in *Mexican Women in the United States,* ed. Magdalena Mora and Adelaida del Castillo. (Los Angeles: Chicano Studies Research Center, University of California, 1980).

El Paso Greater Chamber of Commerce. 1997. "The El Paso Labor Market: A Training Gap Analysis, Final Report," December.

El Puente CDC/La Mujer Obrera. 1999. *Building Employment and Economic Development Bridges in South Central El Paso for Displaced Workers, Strategic Plan.* El Paso, TX: La Mujer Obrera.

Fernandez-Kelly, Maria Patricia, 1990. "Power Surrendered, Power Restored: The Politics of Work and Family among Hispanic Garment Workers in California and Florida." Pp. 130–49 in *Women, Politics and Change,* ed. Louise Tilly and Patricia Gurin. New York: Russell Sage.

Flores, Maria Antonia. 1998. Personal interview, October 13.

Gabriel, Christina, and Laura Macdonald. 1994. "NAFTA, Women, and Organizing in Canada and Mexico: Forging a Feminist Internationality." *Millennium: Journal of International Studies* 23(3):535–62.

Garcia, Mario T. 1981. *Desert Immigrants.* New Haven, CT: Yale University Press.

Gilot, Louie. 1999. "Displaced Workers Want City to Help Find Jobs Quickly." *El Paso Times,* August 31.

Glenn, Guillermo. 1999. Personal interview, January 27.

Grimes, Kimberly M. 1998. *Crossing Borders: Changing Social Identities in Southern Mexico.* Tucson: University of Arizona Press.

Harison, Bennett. 1994. *Lean and Mean: The Changing Landscape of Corporate Power in the Age of Flexibility.* New York: Basic Books.

Herrera-Sobek, Maria. 1990. *The Mexican Corrido.* Bloomington: Indiana University Press.

Klapmeyer, Keith. 1998. Personal interview, November 19.

Kolence, Vic. 1999a. "Apparel Industry Was Precursor to Maquiladoras." *El Paso Times,* February 21.

La Mujer Obrera. 1993. *Orientation Center La Mujer Obrera* El Paso, TX: La Mujer Obrera.

———. 1998. *Progress Report.* El Paso, TX: La Mujer Obrera.

———. 1999a. *Stop NAFTA? Violence against Women Workers.* El Paso, TX: La Mujer Obrera.

———. 1999b. *Women Working Together: Goals and Activities.* El Paso, TX: La Mujer Obrera.

Larudee, Mehrene. 1999. "NAFTA's Impact on U.S. Labor Markets, 1994–1997." Pp. 123–63 in *Pulling Apart: The Deterioration of Employment and Income in North America under Free Trade,* ed. Bruce Campbell, Maria Teresa Gutierrez Haces, Andrew Jackson, and Mehrene Larudee. Ottawa, Ontario: Canadian Center for Policy Alternatives.

Montoya, Irma. 1999. Personal interview, February 24.

Montoya, Lisa, Carol Hardy-Fanta, and Sonia Garcia. 2000. "Latina Politics: Gender, Participation, and Leadership." *Political Science and Politics* 33(3).

Myerson, Alan. 1998. "Borderline Working Class: Texas Labor Is Feeling Trade Pact's Pinch." *New York Times,* May 8.

Olvera, Joe. 1990. "Hunger Strikers Face New Battle on Home Front." *El Paso Times,* September 2, p. A12.

Orquiz, Paz. 1999. Personal interview, January 20.

Ortega, Roy. 2000. "Trade Soars Both Ways after NAFTA." *El Paso Times,* July 9, pp. El–2.

Ownby, John. 1999. Personal interview, September 1.

Pardo, Mary. 1998. *Mexican American Women Activists.* Philadelphia: Temple University Press.

Peterson, V. Spike. 1992. "Transgressing Boundaries: Theories of Knowledge, Gender, and International Relations." *Millennium: Journal of International Studies* 21(2).

Pulido, Laura. 1998. *Environmental and Economic Justice.* Tucson: University of Arizona Press.

Reyes, Lorenza. 1999. Personal interview, January 13.

Rodriquez, Jeanette. 1994. *Our Lady of Guadalupe: Faith among Mexican-American Women.* Austin: University of Texas Press.

Takaki, Ronald. 1993. *A Different Mirror: A History of Multicultural America.* Boston: Little, Brown.

Templin, Neal. 2000. "Anatomy of a Jobs Program That Went Awry." *Wall Street Journal,* February 11.

FEMICIDE IN JUÁREZ

Pheona Donohoe

Pink and black crosses mark the street poles in downtown Ciudad Juárez. They are a constant reminder of how easy it is for a woman to disappear. Symbolizing the victims of femicide, each pole is hand-painted by a family member of the murdered and missing women from Juárez. Earlier this year Amnesty International estimated that 373 women had been murdered in Juárez since 1993. Many were killed as the result of domestic violence, gang or drug related, or from the horrifying kidnap, rape and torture by alleged serial killers. Despite the Juárez femicide becoming a mass-media commodity, these crimes have not ceased with two more murders in the past several months. This gross abuse of human rights is happening within kilometres of El Paso, Texas. On one side of the border is poverty and corruption. On the other is democracy, justice and freedom. America's international dominance has come at cost however, and is partially to blame for the moral chaos in Juárez.

Logos for American corporations are plastered on the exterior walls of 80% of the factories in Juárez. Some of these factories assemble parts for General Motors, Sony, Ford, Phillips and RCA. Since the North American Free Trade Agreement (NAFTA) took effect, Juárez became the largest industrial zone in Mexico, housing almost 300 maquiladora's (foreign-owned sweatshops). A majority of the factory workers are female and many have relocated to Juárez from remote villages and towns from the south of Mexico. Over the past 10 years, many of the women employed at maquiladora's have disappeared. Some bodies have been found in the Chihuahua desert, some remain missing.

The last victim in the Juárez femicide is Alma Brisa Molina Baca, a maquiladora worker who never made it home on Saturday July 24. Her body was found on waste ground several days later. Autopsies revealed she had been raped and strangled. This follows the death of Guadalupe Santos Gomez, a 24-year-old bar waitress originally from southern Mexico. Her strangled body was found in an empty lot in a south Juárez suburb on Monday May 28. Santos shared physical traits consistent with two

thirds of the victims; dark skinned, tall and thin, with long, dark hair, aged between 11 and 25. Over one third of the victims have never been identified.

To date, the handling of the Juárez murders by local authorities has been a farce. State authorities have lost, contaminated and even washed evidence, wrongly identified bodies, announced victims' names to the media before their families, forced suspects into confessing after torturing them with electric prods, threatened and harassed family members of the victims, and allegedly have a direct involvement in the murders. In early July the Mexican government bowed to pressure and released its first report on the murders in Juárez. Compiled by Maria Lopez Urbina, the federal prosecutor in charge of investigating the femicide, this was the first real analysis of the situation despite its eleven-year history. This report was not why or how the women were killed, but rather how the investigation of their murders was handled by officials. Not surprisingly, 81 Chihuahua officials were harshly criticised for their incompetent handing of the cases; 24 police officers, 17 forensic experts, 30 state investigators and three investigative supervisors. Most alarmingly, the report only contained information on 50 of the murders.

In addition to victims' families receiving little to no help from authorities to solve the murders, they are currently being exploited by media outlets capitalising on their loss and turning the femicide into pop-culture. Dozens of movies, TV shows, songs, theatre performances, artwork and books are in production with storylines inspired by the femicide in Juárez, many sensationalising and glorifying the murders. Most recently, Mexico's second largest television network, TV Azteca, began airing a five-part, soap-opera style drama called *Tan Infinito Como El Desierto* (*As Infinite as the Desert*). Shot on location in Juárez, the series dramatises a different type of murder each episode suggesting women fell victim to snuff movies, satanic rituals and copycat murders inspired by serial killers. The executive producer Genoveva Martinez claims that the episodes are based on police investigations. Family members in Juárez are infuriated by the series and many have threatened legal action against the broadcast company for unauthorised use of their daughters' names and images.

In addition to the Mexican television show there is a film by Kevin James Dobson *The Virgin of Juárez* currently in production, a book by Diana Washington Valdez *Harvest of Women* due to be released later this year, a text/illustration book compiled by actress Mia Kirshner is due in 2006, a song Mujeres de Juárez on the new los Tigres del Norte album, and other documentaries in the making. Chihuahua state has responded quickly and on April 21 the president of the state assembly, Victor Valencia, banned the los Tigres del Norte song claiming it was immoral for the band to be making money from singing about the murders. A respectful insight into the Juárez murders is the 2001 documentary *Senorita Extraviada (Young Missing Women)* by Mexican-American filmmaker Lourdes Portillo. Containing interviews with victims'

families and a survivor of police brutality, the documentary helped to raise international awareness including a recent screening in Melbourne, Australia. The Melbourne documentary screening drew a sell-out crowd to the Australian Centre for the Moving Image and launched a fundraising campaign which also included a concert and series of t-shirts. AUD$5,500 was raised and forwarded to Amigos de las Mujeres de Juárez in New Mexico.

Despite the international attention, Mexican federal government reports and constant media coverage, the pink and black crosses continue to fill the streets of Juárez where men kill with impunity. Twenty-four years ago The Pop Group released an album *How Much Longer Do We Tolerate Mass Murder?* We've learned little in the quarter century since that album's release and in Juárez the authorities don't just tolerate it, they cover it up.

READING *45*   **Lila Abu-Lughod**

Do Muslim Women Really Need Saving? Anthropological Reflections on Cultural Relativism and Its Others

What are the ethics of the current "War on Terrorism," a war that justifies itself by purporting to liberate, or save, Afghan women? Does anthropology have anything to offer in our search for a viable position to take regarding this rationale for war?

I was led to pose the question of my title in part because of the way I personally experienced the response to the U.S. war in Afghanistan. Like many colleagues whose work has focused on women and gender in the Middle East, I was deluged with invitations to speak—not just on news programs but also to various departments at colleges and universities, especially women's studies programs. Why did this not please me, a scholar who has devoted more than

20 years of her life to this subject and who has some complicated personal connection to this identity? Here was an opportunity to spread the word, disseminate my knowledge, and correct misunderstandings. The urgent search for knowledge about our sister "women of cover" (as President George Bush so marvelously called them) is laudable and when it comes from women's studies programs where "transnational feminism" is now being taken seriously, it has a certain integrity (see Safire 2001).

My discomfort led me to reflect on why, as feminists in or from the West, or simply as people who have concerns about women's lives, we need to be wary of this response to the events and aftermath of September 11, 2001. I want to point out the minefields—a metaphor that is sadly too apt for a country like Afghanistan, with the world's highest number of mines per capita—of this obsession with the plight of Muslim women. I hope to show some way through them using insights from anthropology, the discipline whose charge has been to understand and manage cultural difference. At the same time, I want to remain critical of anthropology's complicity in the reification of cultural difference.

CULTURAL EXPLANATIONS AND THE MOBILIZATION OF WOMEN

It is easier to see why one should be skeptical about the focus on the "Muslim woman" if one begins with the U.S. public response. I will analyze two manifestations of this response: some conversations I had with a reporter from the PBS *NewsHour with Jim Lehrer* and First Lady Laura Bush's radio address to the nation on November 17, 2001. The presenter from the *NewsHour* show first contacted me in October to see if I was willing to give some background for a segment on Women and Islam. I mischievously asked whether she had done segments on the women of Guatemala, Ireland, Palestine, or Bosnia when the show covered wars in those regions; but I finally agreed to look at the questions she was going to pose to panelists. The questions were hopelessly general. Do Muslim women believe "x"? Are Muslim women "y"? Does Islam allow "z" for women? I asked her: If you were to substitute Christian or Jewish wherever you have Muslim, would these questions make sense? I did not imagine she would call me back. But she did, twice, once with an idea for a segment on the meaning of Ramadan and another time on Muslim women in politics. One was in response to the bombing and the other to the speeches by Laura Bush and Cherie Blair, wife of the British Prime Minister.

What is striking about these three ideas for news programs is that there was a consistent resort to the cultural, as if knowing something about women and Islam or the meaning of a religious ritual would help one understand the tragic attack on New York's World Trade Center and the U.S. Pentagon, or how Afghanistan had come to be ruled by the Taliban, or what interests might have fueled U.S. and other interventions in the region over the past 25 years, or what the history of American support for conservative

groups funded to undermine the Soviets might have been, or why the caves and bunkers out of which Bin Laden was to be smoked "dead or alive," as President Bush announced on television, were paid for and built by the CIA.

In other words, the question is why knowing about the "culture" of the region, and particularly its religious beliefs and treatment of women, was more urgent than exploring the history of the development of repressive regimes in the region and the U.S. role in this history. Such cultural framing, it seemed to me, prevented the serious exploration of the roots and nature of human suffering in this part of the world. Instead of political and historical explanations, experts were being asked to give religio-cultural ones. Instead of questions that might lead to the exploration of global interconnections, we were offered ones that worked to artificially divide the world into separate spheres—recreating an imaginative geography of West versus East, us versus Muslims, cultures in which First Ladies give speeches versus others where women shuffle around silently in burqas.

Most pressing for me was why the Muslim woman in general, and the Afghan woman in particular, were so crucial to this cultural mode of explanation, which ignored the complex entanglements in which we are all implicated, in sometimes surprising alignments. Why were these female symbols being mobilized in this "War against Terrorism" in a way they were not in other conflicts? Laura Bush's radio address on November 17 reveals the political work such mobilization accomplishes. On the one hand, her address collapsed important distinctions that should have been maintained. There was a constant slippage between the Taliban and the terrorists, so that they became almost one word—a kind of hyphenated monster identity: the Taliban-and-the-terrorists. Then there was the blurring of the very separate causes in Afghanistan of women's continuing malnutrition, poverty, and ill health, and their more recent exclusion under the Taliban from employment, schooling, and the joys of wearing nail polish. On the other hand, her speech reinforced chasmic divides, primarily between the "civilized people throughout the world" whose hearts break for the women and children of Afghanistan and the Taliban-and-the-terrorists, the cultural monsters who want to, as she put it, "impose their world on the rest of us."

Most revealingly, the speech enlisted women to justify American bombing and intervention in Afghanistan and to make a case for the "War on Terrorism" of which it was allegedly a part. As Laura Bush said, "Because of our recent military gains in much of Afghanistan, women are no longer imprisoned in their homes. They can listen to music and teach their daughters without fear of punishment.... The fight against terrorism is also a fight for the rights and dignity of women" (U.S. Government 2002).

These words have haunting resonances for anyone who has studied colonial history. Many who have worked on British colonialism in South Asia have noted the use of the woman question in colonial policies where intervention into sati (the practice of widows immolating themselves on their husbands' funeral pyres), child marriage, and other practices was used to justify rule. As Gayatri Chakravorty Spivak (1988) has cynically put it: white men saving brown women from brown men. The historical record is full of similar cases, including in the Middle East. In Turn of the Century Egypt, what Leila Ahmed (1992) has called "colonial feminism" was hard at work. This was a selective concern about the plight of Egyptian women that focused on the veil as a sign of oppression but gave no support to women's education and was professed loudly by the same Englishman, Lord Cromer, who opposed women's suffrage back home.

Sociologist Marnia Lazreg (1994) has offered some vivid examples of how French colonialism enlisted women to its cause in Algeria. She writes:

Perhaps the most spectacular example of the colonial appropriation of women's voices, and the silencing of those among them who had begun to take women revolutionaries ... as role models by not donning the veil, was the event of May 16, 1958 [just four years before Algeria finally gained its independence from France after a long bloody struggle and 130 years of French control—L.A.]. On that day a demonstration was organized by rebellious French generals in Algiers to show their determination to keep Algeria French. To give the government of France evidence that Algerians were in agreement with them, the generals had a few thousand native men bused in from nearby villages, along with a few women who were solemnly unveiled by French women.... Rounding up Algerians and bringing them to demonstrations of loyalty to France was not in itself an unusual act

during the colonial era. But to unveil women at a well-choreographed ceremony added to the event a symbolic dimension that dramatized the one constant feature of the Algerian occupation by France: its obsession with women. [Lazreg 1994:135]

Lazreg (1994) also gives memorable examples of the way in which the French had earlier sought to transform Arab women and girls. She describes skits at awards ceremonies at the Muslim Girls' School in Algiers in 1851 and 1852. In the first skit, written by "a French lady from Algiers," two Algerian Arab girls reminisced about their trip to France with words including the following:

Oh! Protective France: Oh! Hospitable France! ...
Noble land, where I felt free
Under Christian skies to pray to our God: ....
God bless you for the happiness you bring us!
And you, adoptive mother, who taught us
That we have a share of this world,
We will cherish you forever! [Lazreg 1994:68–69]

These girls are made to invoke the gift of a share of this world, a world where freedom reigns under Christian skies. This is not the world the Taliban-and-the-terrorists would "like to impose on the rest of us."

Just as I argued above that we need to be suspicious when neat cultural icons are plastered over messier historical and political narratives, so we need to be wary when Lord Cromer in British-ruled Egypt, French ladies in Algeria, and Laura Bush, all with military troops behind them, claim to be saving or liberating Muslim women.

POLITICS OF THE VEIL

I want now to look more closely at those Afghan women Laura Bush claimed were "rejoicing" at their liberation by the Americans. This necessitates a discussion of the veil, or the burqa, because it is so central to contemporary concerns about Muslim women. This will set the stage for a discussion of how anthropologists, feminist anthropologists in particular, contend with the problem of difference in a global world. In the conclusion, I will return to the rhetoric of saving Muslim women and offer an alternative.

It is common popular knowledge that the ultimate sign of the oppression of Afghan women under the Taliban-and-the-terrorists is that they were forced to wear the burqa. Liberals sometimes confess their surprise that even though Afghanistan has been liberated from the Taliban, women do not seem to be throwing off their burqas. Someone who has worked in Muslim regions must ask why this is so surprising. Did we expect that once "free" from the Taliban they would go "back" to belly shirts and blue jeans, or dust off their Chanel suits? We need to be more sensible about the clothing of "women of cover," and so there is perhaps a need to make some basic points about veiling.

First, it should be recalled that the Taliban did not invent the burqa. It was the local form of covering that Pashtun women in one region wore when they went out. The Pashtun are one of several ethnic groups in Afghanistan and the burqa was one of many forms of covering in the subcontinent and Southwest Asia that has developed as a convention for symbolizing women's modesty or respectability. The burqa, like some other forms of "cover" has, in many settings, marked the symbolic separation of men's and women's spheres, as part of the general association of women with family and home, not with public space where strangers mingled.

Twenty years ago the anthropologist Hanna Papanek (1982), who worked in Pakistan, described the burqa as "portable seclusion." She noted that many saw it as a liberating invention because it enabled women to move out of segregated living spaces while still observing the basic moral requirements of separating and protecting women from unrelated men. Ever since I came across her phrase "portable seclusion," I have thought of these enveloping robes as "mobile homes." Everywhere, such veiling signifies belonging to a particular community and participating in a moral way of life in which families are paramount in the organization of communities and the home is associated with the sanctity of women.

The obvious question that follows is this: If this were the case, why would women suddenly become immodest? Why would they suddenly throw off the markers of their respectability, markers, whether burqas or other forms of cover, which were supposed to assure their protection in the public sphere from the harassment of strange men by symbolically signaling to all that they were still in the inviolable space of their homes, even though moving in the public realm? Especially when these are forms of dress that had become so conventional that most women gave little thought to their meaning.

To draw some analogies, none of them perfect, why are we surprised that Afghan women do not throw off their burqas when we know perfectly well that it would not be appropriate to wear shorts to the opera? At the time these discussions of Afghan women's burqas were raging, a friend of mine was chided by her husband for suggesting she wanted to wear a pantsuit to a fancy wedding: "You know you don't wear pants to a WASP wedding," he reminded her. New Yorkers know that the beautifully coiffed Hasidic women, who look so fashionable next to their dour husbands in black coats and hats, are wearing wigs. This is because religious belief and community standards of propriety require the covering of the hair. They also alter boutique fashions to include high necks and long sleeves. As anthropologists know perfectly well, people wear the appropriate form of dress for their social communities and are guided by socially shared standards, religious beliefs, and moral ideals, unless they deliberately transgress to make a point or are unable to afford proper cover. If we think that U.S. women live in a world of choice regarding clothing, all we need to do is remind ourselves of the expression, "the tyranny of fashion."

What had happened in Afghanistan under the Taliban is that one regional style of covering or veiling, associated with a certain respectable but not elite class, was imposed on everyone as "religiously" appropriate, even though previously there had been many different styles, popular or traditional with different groups and classes—different ways to mark women's propriety, or, in more recent times, religious piety. Although I am not an expert on Afghanistan, I imagine that the majority of women left in Afghanistan by the time the Taliban took control were the rural or less educated, from nonelite families, since they were the only ones who could not emigrate to escape the hardship and violence that has marked Afghanistan's recent history. If liberated from the enforced wearing of burqas, most of these women would choose some other form of modest headcovering, like all those living nearby who were not under the Taliban—their rural Hindu counterparts in the North of India (who cover their heads and veil their faces from affines) or their Muslim sisters in Pakistan.

Even *The New York Times* carried an article about Afghan women refugees in Pakistan that attempted to educate readers about this local variety (Fremson 2001). The article describes and pictures everything from the now-iconic burqa with the embroidered eye-holes, which a Pashtun woman explains is the proper dress for her community, to large scarves they call chadors, to the new Islamic modest dress that wear-ers refer to as *hijab*. Those in the new Islamic dress are characteristically students heading for profes-sional careers, especially in medicine, just like their counterparts from Egypt to Malaysia. One wearing the large scarf was a school principal; the other was a poor street vendor. The telling quote from the young street vendor is, "If I did [wear the burqa] the refu-gees would tease me because the burqa is for 'good women' who stay inside the home" (Fremson 2001:14). Here you can see the local status associated with the burqa—it is for good respectable women from strong families who are not forced to make a living selling on the street.

The British newspaper *The Guardian* published an interview in January 2002 with Dr. Suheila Siddiqi, a respected surgeon in Afghanistan who holds the rank of lieutenant general in the Afghan medical corps (Goldenberg 2002). A woman in her sixties, she comes from an elite family and, like her sisters, was educated. Unlike most women of her class, she chose not to go into exile. She is presented in the ar-ticle as "the woman who stood up to the Taliban" be-cause she refused to wear the burqa. She had made it a condition of returning to her post as head of a major hospital when the Taliban came begging in 1996, just eight months after firing her along with other women. Siddiqi is described as thin, glamor-ous, and confident. But further into the article it is noted that her graying bouffant hair is covered in a gauzy veil. This is a reminder that though she re-fused the burqa, she had no question about wearing the chador or scarf.

Finally, I need to make a crucial point about veil-ing. Not only are there many forms of covering, which themselves have different meanings in the commu-nities in which they are used, but also veiling itself must not be confused with, or made to stand for, lack of agency. As I have argued in my ethnography of a Bedouin community in Egypt in the late 1970s and 1980s (1986), pulling the black head cloth over the face in front of older respected men is considered a volun-tary act by women who are deeply committed to being moral and have a sense of honor tied to family. One of the ways they show their standing is by covering their faces in certain contexts. They decide for whom they feel it is appropriate to veil.

To take a very different case, the modern Islamic modest dress that many educated women across the Muslim world have taken on since the mid-1970s now both publicly marks piety and can be read as a sign of educated urban sophistication, a sort of modernity (e.g., Abu-Lughod 1995, 1998; Brenner 1996; El Guindi 1999; MacLeod 1991; Ong 1990). As Saba Mahmood (2001) has so brilliantly shown in her ethnography of women in the mosque movement in Egypt, this new form of dress is also perceived by many of the women who adopt it as part of a bodily means to cultivate vir-tue, the outcome of their professed desire to be close to God.

Two points emerge from this fairly basic discussion of the meanings of veiling in the contemporary Mus-lim world. First, we need to work against the reductive interpretation of veiling as the quintessential sign of women's unfreedom, even if we object to state impo-sition of this form, as in Iran or with the Taliban. (It must be recalled that the modernizing states of Turkey and Iran had earlier in the century banned veiling and required men, except religious clerics, to adopt West-ern dress.) What does freedom mean if we accept the fundamental premise that humans are social beings, always raised in certain social and historical contexts and belonging to particular communities that shape their desires and understandings of the world? Is it not a gross violation of women's own understandings of what they are doing to simply denounce the burqa as a medieval imposition? Second, we must take care not to reduce the diverse situations and attitudes of millions of Muslim women to a single item of clothing. Perhaps it is time to give up the Western obsession with the veil and focus on some serious issues with which feminists and others should indeed be concerned.

Ultimately, the significant political-ethical problem the burqa raises is how to deal with cultural "others." How are we to deal with difference without accept-ing the passivity implied by the cultural relativism for which anthropologists are justly famous—a relativism that says it's their culture and it's not my business to judge or interfere, only to try to understand. Cultural relativism is certainly an improvement on ethnocen-trism and the racism, cultural imperialism, and impe-riousness that underlie it; the problem is that it is too late not to interfere. The forms of lives we find around the world are already products of long histories of interactions.

I want to explore the issues of women, cultural relativism, and the problems of "difference" from three angles. First, I want to consider what feminist anthropologists (those stuck in that awkward relationship, as Strathern [1987] has claimed) are to do with strange political bedfellows. I used to feel torn when I received the e-mail petitions circulating for the last few years in defense of Afghan women under the Taliban. I was not sympathetic to the dogmatism of the Taliban; I do not support the oppression of women. But the provenance of the campaign worried me. I do not usually find myself in political company with the likes of Hollywood celebrities (see Hirschkind and Mahmood 2002). I had never received a petition from such women defending the right of Palestinian women to safety from Israeli bombing or daily harassment at check-points, asking the United States to reconsider its support for a government that had dispossessed them, closed them out from work and citizenship rights, refused them the most basic freedoms. Maybe some of these same people might be signing petitions to save African women from genital cutting, or Indian women from dowry deaths. However, I do not think that it would be as easy to mobilize so many of these American and European women if it were not a case of Muslim men oppressing Muslim women—women of cover for whom they can feel sorry and in relation to whom they can feel smugly superior. Would television diva Oprah Winfrey host the Women in Black, the women's peace group from Israel, as she did RAWA, the Revolutionary Association of Women of Afghanistan, who were also granted the *Glamour Magazine* Women of the Year Award? What are we to make of post-Taliban "Reality Tours" such as the one advertised on the internet by Global Exchange for March 2002 under the title "Courage and Tenacity: A Women's Delegation to Afghanistan"? The rationale for the $1,400 tour is that "with the removal of the Taliban government, Afghan women, for the first time in the past decade, have the opportunity to reclaim their basic human rights and establish their role as equal citizens by participating in the rebuilding of their nation." The tour's objective, to celebrate International Women's Week, is "to develop awareness of the concerns and issues the Afghan women are facing as well as to witness the changing political, economic, and social conditions which have created new opportunities for the women of Afghanistan" (Global Exchange 2002).

To be critical of this celebration of women's rights in Afghanistan is not to pass judgment on any local

women's organizations, such as RAWA, whose members have courageously worked since 1977 for a democratic secular Afghanistan in which women's human rights are respected, against Soviet-backed regimes or U.S.-, Saudi-, and Pakistani-supported conservatives. Their documentation of abuse and their work through clinics and schools have been enormously important.

It is also not to fault the campaigns that exposed the dreadful conditions under which the Taliban placed women. The Feminist Majority campaign helped put a stop to a secret oil pipeline deal between the Taliban and the U.S. multinational Unocal that was going forward with U.S. administration support. Western feminist campaigns must not be confused with the hypocrisies of the new colonial feminism of a Republican president who was not elected for his progressive stance on feminist issues or of administrations that played down the terrible record of violations of women by the United States' allies in the Northern Alliance, as documented by Human Rights Watch and Amnesty International, among others. Rapes and assaults were widespread in the period of infighting that devastated Afghanistan before the Taliban came in to restore order.

It is, however, to suggest that we need to look closely at what we are supporting (and what we are not) and to think carefully about why. How should we manage the complicated politics and ethics of finding ourselves in agreement with those with whom we normally disagree? I do not know how many feminists who felt good about saving Afghan women from the Taliban are also asking for a global redistribution of wealth or contemplating sacrificing their own consumption radically so that African or Afghan women could have some chance of having what I do believe should be a universal human right—the right to freedom from the structural violence of global inequality and from the ravages of war, the everyday rights of having enough to eat, having homes for their families in which to live and thrive, having ways to make decent livings so their children can grow, and having the strength and security to work out, within their communities and with whatever alliances they want, how to live a good life, which might very well include changing the ways those communities are organized.

Suspicion about bedfellows is only a first step; it will not give us a way to think more positively about what to do or where to stand. For that, we need to confront two more big issues. First is the acceptance of the possibility of difference. Can we only free Afghan women to be like us or might we have to recognize that even after "liberation" from the Taliban, they might want different things than we would want for them? What do we do about that? Second, we need to be vigilant about the rhetoric of saving people because of what it implies about our attitudes.

Again, when I talk about accepting difference, I am not implying that we should resign ourselves to being cultural relativists who respect whatever goes on elsewhere as "just their culture." I have already discussed the dangers of "cultural" explanations; "their" cultures are just as much part of history and an interconnected world as ours are. What I am advocating is the hard work involved in recognizing and respecting differences—precisely as products of different histories, as expressions of different circumstances, and as manifestations of differently structured desires. We may want justice for women, but can we accept that there might be different ideas about justice and that different women might want, or choose, different futures from what we envision as best (see Ong 1988)? We must consider that they might be called to personhood, so to speak, in a different language.

Reports from the Bonn peace conference held in late November to discuss the rebuilding of Afghanistan revealed significant differences among the few Afghan women feminists and activists present. RAWA's position was to reject any conciliatory approach to Islamic governance. According to one report I read, most women activists, especially those based in Afghanistan who are aware of the realities on the ground, agreed that Islam had to be the starting point for reform. Fatima Gailani, a U.S.-based advisor to one of the delegations, is quoted as saying, "If I go to Afghanistan today and ask women for votes on the promise to bring them secularism, they are going to tell me to go to hell." Instead, according to one report, most of these women looked for inspiration on how to fight for equality to a place that might seem surprising. They looked to Iran as a country in which they saw women making significant gains within an Islamic framework—in part through an Islamically oriented feminist movement that is challenging injustices and reinterpreting the religious tradition.

The situation in Iran is itself the subject of heated debate within feminist circles, especially among Iranian feminists in the West (e.g., Mir-Hosseini 1999; Moghissi 1999; Najmabadi 1998, 2000). It is not clear whether and in what ways women have made gains and whether the great increases in literacy, decreases in birthrates, presence of women in the professions and government, and a feminist flourishing in cultural fields like writing and film-making are because of or despite the establishment of a so-called Islamic Republic. The concept of an Islamic feminism itself is also controversial. Is it an oxymoron or does it refer to a viable movement forged by brave women who want a third way?

One of the things we have to be most careful about in thinking about Third World feminisms, and feminism in different parts of the Muslim world, is how not to fall into polarizations that place feminism on the side of the West. I have written about the dilemmas faced by Arab feminists when Western feminists initiate campaigns that make them vulnerable to local denunciations by conservatives of various sorts, whether Islamist or nationalist, of being traitors (Abu-Lughod 2001). As some like Afsaneh Najmabadi are now arguing, not only is it wrong to see history simplistically in terms of a putative opposition between Islam and the West (as is happening in the United States now and has happened in parallel in the Muslim world), but it is also strategically dangerous to accept this cultural opposition between Islam and the West, between fundamentalism and feminism, because those many people within Muslim countries who are trying to find alternatives to present injustices, those who might want to refuse the divide and take from different histories and cultures, who do not accept that being feminist means being Western, will be under pressure to choose, just as we are: Are you with us or against us?

My point is to remind us to be aware of differences, respectful of other paths toward social change that might give women better lives. Can there be a liberation that is Islamic? And, beyond this, is liberation even a goal for which all women or people strive? Are emancipation, equality, and rights part of a universal language we must use? To quote Saba Mahmood, writing about the women in Egypt who are seeking to become pious Muslims, "The desire for freedom and liberation is a historically situated desire whose motivational force cannot be assumed a priori, but needs to be reconsidered in light of other desires aspirations, and capacities that inhere in a culturally and historically located subject" (2001:223). In other words, might other desires be more meaningful for different groups of people? Living in close families? Living in a godly way? Living without war? I have done fieldwork in Egypt over more than 20 years and I cannot think of a single woman I know, from the poorest rural to the most educated cosmopolitan, who has ever expressed envy of U.S. women, women they tend to perceive as bereft of community, vulnerable to sexual violence and social anomie, driven by individual success rather than morality, or strangely disrespectful of God.

Mahmood (2001) has pointed out a disturbing thing that happens when one argues for a respect for other traditions. She notes that there seems to be a difference in the political demands made on those who work on or are trying to understand Muslims and Islamists and those who work on secular-humanist projects. She, who studies the piety movement in Egypt, is consistently pressed to denounce all the harm done by Islamic movements around the world—otherwise she is accused of being an apologist. But there never seems to be a parallel demand for those who study secular humanism and its projects, despite the terrible violences that have been associated with it over the last couple of centuries, from world wars to colonialism, from genocides to slavery. We need to have as little dogmatic faith in secular humanism as in Islamism, and as open a mind to the complex possibilities of human projects undertaken in one tradition as the other.

BEYOND THE RHETORIC OF SALVATION

Let us return, finally, to my title, "Do Muslim Women Really Need Saving?" The discussion of culture, veiling, and how one can navigate the shoals of cultural difference should put Laura Bush's self-congratulation about the rejoicing of Afghan women liberated by American troops in a different light. It is deeply problematic to construct the Afghan woman as someone in need of saving. When you save someone, you imply that you are saving her from something. You are also saving her *to* something. What violences are entailed in this transformation, and what presumptions are being made about the superiority of that to which you are saving her? Projects of saving other women depend on and reinforce a sense

of superiority by Westerners, a form of arrogance that deserves to be challenged. All one needs to do to appreciate the patronizing quality of the rhetoric of saving women is to imagine using it today in the United States about disadvantaged groups such as African American women or working-class women. We now understand them as suffering from structural violence. We have become politicized about race and class, but not culture.

As anthropologists, feminists, or concerned citizens, we should be wary of taking on the mantles of those 19th-century Christian missionary women who devoted their lives to saving their Muslim sisters. One of my favorite documents from that period is a collection called *Our Moslem Sisters*, the proceedings of a conference of women missionaries held in Cairo in 1906 (Van Sommer and Zwemmer 1907). The subtitle of the book is *A Cry of Need from the Lands of Darkness Interpreted by Those Who Heard It*. Speaking of the ignorance, seclusion, polygamy, and veiling that blighted women's lives across the Muslim world, the missionary women spoke of their responsibility to make these women's voices heard. As the introduction states, "They will never cry for themselves, for they are down under the yoke of centuries of oppression" (Van Sommer and Zwemer 1907:15). "This book," it begins, "with its sad, reiterated story of wrong and oppression is an indictment and an appeal. . . . It is an appeal to Christian womanhood to right these wrongs and enlighten this darkness by sacrifice and service" (Van Sommer and Zwemer 1907:5).

One can hear uncanny echoes of their virtuous goals today, even though the language is secular, the appeals not to Jesus but to human rights or the liberal West. The continuing currency of such imagery and sentiments can be seen in their deployment for perfectly good humanitarian causes. In February 2002, I received an invitation to a reception honoring an international medical humanitarian network called Médecins du Monde/Doctors of the World (MdM). Under the sponsorship of the French Ambassador to the United States, the Head of the delegation of the European Commission to the United Nations, and a member of the European Parliament, the cocktail reception was to feature an exhibition of photographs under the clichéd title "Afghan Women: Behind the Veil."

The invitation was remarkable not just for the colorful photograph of women in flowing burqas walking across the barren mountains of Afghanistan but also for the text, a portion of which I quote:

> For 20 years MdM has been ceaselessly struggling to help those who are most vulnerable. But increasingly, thick veils cover the victims of the war. When the Taliban came to power in 1996, Afghan Women became faceless. To unveil one's face while receiving medical care was to achieve a sort of intimacy, find a brief space for secret freedom and recover a little of one's dignity. In a country where women had no access to basic medical care because they did not have the right to appear in public, where women had no right to practice medicine, MdM's program stood as a stubborn reminder of human rights. . . . Please join us in helping to lift the veil.

Although I cannot take up here the fantasies of intimacy associated with unveiling, fantasies reminiscent of the French colonial obsessions so brilliantly unmasked by Alloula in *The Colonial Harem* (1986), I can ask why humanitarian projects and human rights discourse in the 21st century need rely on such constructions of Muslim women.

Could we not leave veils and vocations of saving others behind and instead train our sights on ways to make the world a more just place? The reason respect for difference should not be confused with cultural relativism is that it does not preclude asking how we, living in this privileged and powerful part of the world, might examine our own responsibilities for the situations in which others in distant places have found themselves. We do not stand outside the world, looking out over this sea of poor benighted people, living under the shadow—or veil—of oppressive cultures; we are part of that world. Islamic movements themselves have arisen in a world shaped by the intense engagements of Western powers in Middle Eastern lives.

A more productive approach, it seems to me, is to ask how we might contribute to making the world a more just place. A world not organized around strategic military and economic demands; a place where certain kinds of forces and values that we may still consider important could have an appeal and where there is the peace necessary for discussions, debates, and transformations to occur within communities. We need to ask ourselves what kinds of world conditions we could contribute to making such that popular desires will not be overdetermined by an overwhelming sense of helplessness in the face of forms of global injustice. Where we seek to be active in the affairs of distant places, can we do so in the spirit of support for those within those communities whose goals are to make women's (and men's) lives better (as Walley has argued in relation to practices of genital cutting in Africa [1997])? Can we use a more egalitarian language of alliances, coalitions, and solidarity, instead of salvation?

Even RAWA, the now celebrated Revolutionary Association of the Women of Afghanistan, which was so instrumental in bringing to U.S. women's attention the excesses of the Taliban, has opposed the U.S. bombing from the beginning. They do not see in it Afghan women's salvation but increased hardship and loss. They have long called for disarmament and for peacekeeping forces. Spokespersons point out the dangers of confusing governments with people, the Taliban with innocent Afghans who will be most harmed. They consistently remind audiences to take a close look at the ways policies are being organized around oil interests, the arms industry, and the international drug trade. They are not obsessed with the veil, even though they are the most radical feminists working for a secular democratic Afghanistan. Unfortunately, only their messages about the excesses of the Taliban have been heard, even though their criticisms of those in power in Afghanistan have included previous regimes. A first step in hearing their wider message is to break with the language of alien cultures, whether to understand or eliminate them. Missionary work and colonial feminism belong in the past. Our task is to critically explore what we might do to help create a world in which those poor Afghan women, for whom "the hearts of those in the civilized world break," can have safety and decent lives.

ACKNOWLEDGMENTS

I want to thank Page Jackson, Fran Mascia-Lees, Tim Mitchell, Rosalind Morris, Anupama Rao, and members of the audience at the symposium "Responding to War," sponsored by Columbia University's Institute for Research on Women and Gender (where I presented an earlier version), for helpful comments, references, clippings, and encouragement.

REFERENCES CITED

Abu-Lughod, Lila. 1986. *Veiled Sentiments: Honor and Poetry in a Bedouin Society.* Berkeley: University of California Press.

———. 1995. Movie Stars and Islamic Moralism in Egypt. *Social Text* 42:53–67.

———. 1998. *Remaking Women: Feminism and Modernity in the Middle East.* Princeton: Princeton University Press.

———. 2001. Orientalism and Middle East Feminist Studies. *Feminist Studies* 27(1):101–113.

Ahmed, Leila. 1992. *Women and Gender in Islam.* New Haven, CT: Yale University Press.

Alloula, Malek. 1986. *The Colonial Harem.* Minneapolis: University of Minnesota Press.

Brenner, Suzanne. 1996. Reconstructing Self and Society: Javanese Muslim Women and "the Veil." *American Ethnologist* 23(4):673–697.

El Guindi, Fadwa. 1999. *Veil: Modesty, Privacy and Resistance.* Oxford: Berg.

Fremson, Ruth. 2001. Allure Must Be Covered. Individuality Peeks Through. *New York Times*, November 4: 14.

Global Exchange. 2002. Courage and Tenacity: A Women's Delegation to Afghanistan. Electronic document, http://www.globalexchange.org/tours/auto/2002-03-05_CourageandTenacityAWomensDele.html. Accessed February 11.

Goldenberg, Suzanne. 2002. The Woman Who Stood Up to the Taliban. *The Guardian,* January 24. Electronic document, http://222.guardian.co.ur/afghanistan/story/0,1284,63840.

Hirschkind, Charles, and Saba Mahmood. 2002. Feminism, the Taliban, and the Politics of Counter-Insurgency. *Anthropological Quarterly* 75(2):107–122.

Lazreg, Marnia. 1994. *The Eloquence of Silence: Algerian Women in Question.* New York: Routledge.

MacLeod, Arlene. 1991. *Accommodating Protest.* New York: Columbia University Press.

Mahmood, Saba. 2001. Feminist Theory, Embodiment, and the Docile Agent: Some Reflections on the Egyptian Islamic Revival. *Cultural Anthropology* 16(2):202–235.

Mir-Hosseini, Ziba. 1999. *Islam and Gender: The Religious Debate in Contemporary Iran.* Princeton: Princeton University Press.

Moghissi, Haideh. 1999. *Feminism and Islamic Fundamentalism.* London: Zed Books.

Najmabadi, Afsaneh. 1998. Feminism in an Islamic Republic. In *Islam, Gender and Social Change.* Yvonne Haddad and John Esposito, eds. Pp. 59–84. New York: Oxford University Press.

———. 2000. (Un)Veiling Feminism. *Social Text* 64:29–45.

Ong, Aihwa. 1988. Colonialism and Modernity: Feminist Re-Presentations of Women in Non-Western Societies. *Inscriptions* 3–4:79–93.

———. 1990. State Versus Islam: Malay Families, Women's Bodies, and the Body Politic in Malaysia. *American Ethnologist* 17(2):258–276.

Papanek, Hanna. 1982. Purdah in Pakistan: Seclusion and Modern Occupations for Women. In *Separate Worlds.* Hanna Papanek and Gail Minault, eds. Pp. 190–216. Columbus, MO: South Asia Books.

Safire, William. 2001. "On Language." *New York Times Magazine*, October 28: 22.

Spivak, Gayatri Chakravorty. 1988. Can the Subaltern Speak? In *Marxism and the Interpretation of Culture.* Cary Nelson and Lawrence Grossberg, eds. Pp. 271–313. Urbana: University of Illinois Press.

Strathern, Marilyn. 1987. An Awkward Relationship: The Case of Feminism and Anthropology. *Signs* 12:276–292.

U.S. Government. 1907. *Our Moslem Sisters: A Cry of Need from Lands of Darkness Interpreted by Those Who Heard It.* New York: Fleming H. Revell Co.

———. 2002. Electronic document, http://www.whitehouse.gov/news/releases/2001/11/20011117. Accessed January 10.

Walley, Christine. 1997. Searching for "Voices": Feminism, Anthropology, and the Global Debate over Female Genital Operations. *Cultural Anthropology* 12(3):405–438.

GLOBALIZATION OF BEAUTY MAKES SLIMNESS TRENDY

Norimitsu Onishi

Lagos, Nigeria—With no success, Nigeria had been sending contestants to the Miss World pageant for years. Winners of the Most Beautiful Girl in Nigeria went year after year to the Miss World competition, and year after year the beauty queens performed remarkably poorly.

Guy Murray-Bruce, the executive director of Silverbird Productions, which runs the Most Beautiful Girl contest, said he had almost resigned himself to the fact that black African women had little chance of winning an international competition in a world dominated by Western beauty ideals.

Then in 2000 he carried out a drastic change of strategy in picking the Most Beautiful Girl and Nigeria's next international representative.

"The judges had always looked for a local queen, someone they considered a beautiful African woman," Mr. Murray-Bruce, 38, said. "So I told the judges not to look for a local queen, but someone to represent us internationally."

The new strategy's success was immediate. The Most Beautiful Girl of 2001, Agbani Darego, went on to clinch the Miss World title in Sun City, South Africa, last October. She became the first African winner in the contest's 51-year history.

Her victory stunned Nigerians, whose country had earned a worldwide reputation for corruption and fraud. Now, all of a sudden, Nigeria was No. 1 in beautiful women. Ms. Darego, who was 18 at the time, instantly became a national heroine.

But soon pride gave way to puzzlement. In a culture where Coca-Cola-bottle voluptuousness is celebrated and ample backsides and bosoms are considered ideals of female beauty, the new Miss World shared none of those attributes. She was 6 feet tall, stately and so, so skinny. She was, some said uncharitably, a white girl in black skin.

The perverse reality was that most Nigerians, especially those over 40, did not find the new Miss World particularly beautiful.

The story does not end there, though. In the year since her victory, a social transformation has begun to take hold across this nation, Africa's most populous.

The change is an example of the power of Western culture on a continent caught between tradition and modernity. Older Nigerians' views of beauty have not changed. But among young, fashionable Nigerians, voluptuousness is out and this is in.

"After Agbani won, girls look up to me and ask me how to get slim," said Linda Ikeji, 22, an English major at the University of Lagos.

"Before, fat girls were the rave of the moment," said Ms. Ikeji, who is 5 feet 8, weighs 130 pounds and now finds work as a part-time model. "Some fat girls thought they had an advantage over me. But Agbani changed everything."

Here in Lagos, the commercial capital, the thin "It" girls are now called lepa, using a Yoruba word that means thin but that was not applied to people before. The lepa girl has had a popular song written about her, called simply "Lepa." Nigeria's booming film industry has capitalized on the trend by producing a movie, "Lepa Shandi"; the title means a girl as slim as a 20-naira bill.

To anyone who has traveled across the continent, especially in West and Central Africa, the cultural shift is striking. In the United States slimness may be an ideal, but many ethnic groups in this region hold festivals celebrating big women. In Niger many women take livestock feed or vitamins to bulk up.

Among the Calabari people in southeastern Nigeria, fat has traditionally held a cherished place. Before their weddings, brides are sent to fattening farms, where their caretakers feed them huge amounts of food and massage them into rounder shapes. After weeks inside the fattening farms, the big brides are finally let out and paraded in the village square.

Ms. Darego, the same Miss World who has helped change young Nigerians' perception of beauty, belongs to the Calabari ethnic group—and thus may seem particularly unattractive to her own people.

"If she was in a crowd of other African women, I wouldn't regard her as a beautiful woman," said Ken Calebs-Olumese, who does not belong to that ethnic group but, as the owner of the exclusive Coliseum nightclub here, knows beautiful women.

"The average African woman is robust, has big hips, a lot of bust," he said. "That's what she offers in terms of beauty. It's in our culture." Mr. Calebs-Olumese, who is 56, drew a blank at the mention of lepa. Still, he acknowledged that he was "Speaking from my generation's perspective."

While the transformation in youthful tastes was linked to the Miss World victory, it started, some said, with an earlier event.

"In 1998, M-Net, the South African network seen across Africa on satellite television, opened a search for the "Face of Africa." The winner was promised a three-year, $150,000 modeling contract with the Elite agency in New York.

Not surprisingly, M-net, which shows mostly American movies and TV shows, chose a skinny, 6-foot-2 teenager from Lagos, Oluchi Onweagba, who was not considered particularly pretty here but became a hit on the runways.

"That was the start," said Frank Osodi, 36, a fashion designer whose studio in the Surulere district in Lagos was a hive for models and beauty queens one recent morning. "Before, if you were thin, people thought you were sick, like an AIDS patient. Now if you have a skinny member in your family, you don't have to be ashamed."

Indeed, parents are now urging their daughters to take part in beauty pageants. In the past, the Most Beautiful Girl competition drew just enough contestants to hold a pageant, Mr. Murray-Bruce said. For the 2001 contest there were only 40; this year there were 400.

No one is predicting whether the youthful preference for thinness represents a fad or a lasting cultural change. But Maureen and Mary-Jane Mekowulu, slim 18-year-old twins who are students at the University of Nsukka in southeastern Nigeria and were visiting their parents here, said they would continue to exercise every morning and abstain from eating after 6 P.M.

"Because of Agbani, people have realized that slim is beautiful," Maureen said of the Miss World.

And the Most Beautiful Girl of 2002 would reinforce that impression, said the contest's producer, Mr. Murray-Bruce. "She's even skinnier than Agbani," he said.

READING *46*   ***Gwendolyn Mink***

The Lady and the Tramp (II): Feminist Welfare Politics, Poor Single Mothers, and the Challenge of Welfare Justice

I have worked in various political venues on welfare issues for ten years—for about as long as I have been researching and writing about women and U.S. social policy.[1] Most recently, I worked as a Steering Committee member and cochair of the Women's Committee of 100, a feminist mobilization against punitive welfare reform. I signed up with the Women's Committee of 100 in March or April of 1995—roughly a year after completing a book on welfare policy history and around the same time as the book's publication.[2]

I have always done both politics and scholarship, so directing my activism toward my field of professional expertise at first did not seem especially odd or problematic. However, I had just published a book critical of experts like me—a book which, among other things, faulted solipsistic women welfare innovators of the early twentieth century for building a welfare state harmful to women and to gender equality. The book was barely between covers, and I had already embarked on a path of policy advocacy that veered disturbingly close to the reformers I had criticized. There I was, consorting with a group of super-educated, do-good feminists, most of whom would never need a welfare check. And there we were, using our social and professional positions to gain entry into congressional offices, where we spoke against reforms that would affect not us but poor women. It seemed to me that maybe I hadn't really internalized the lessons I had drawn from early-twentieth-century welfare history.

I struggled a bit with my own contradictions—between what I felt compelled to do as a feminist activist confronted by the political crisis of welfare reform and what I had cautioned against as a student of elite women reformers. But I didn't have to struggle long. It quickly became apparent that any historical analogies I feared were the product of academic overinterpretation. An awesome collection of women makes up the Committee of 100—none of whom, to my knowledge, has any interest in mothering the poor as our forebears did earlier in the century and all of whom reject the morally and culturally prescriptive politics of early-twentieth-century welfare innovation and of late-twentieth-century welfare reform.

We mobilized not to speak for poor mothers but with them—to speak for ourselves as feminists frustrated by the absence of women's voices and by the lack of gender equality concerns in the welfare debate. Although members of Congress paid scant attention, in our lobbying, letter writing, and media efforts, we repeatedly explained how welfare reform risks many of the rights and protections upon which women's security and equality depends. Often speaking of "welfare as a women's issue," we argued that "a war against poor women is a war against all women."

This was a strategically clever rallying cry, but it failed to rally many women—even feminists. In fact, the war against poor women was just that: a war against poor women. And it was a war in which many middle-class women participated on the anti-welfare side. All but one woman in the U.S. Senate supported the Personal Responsibility Act when it

first was taken up in the summer of 1995.[3] In 1996, twenty-six of thirty-one Democratic women in the House of Representatives voted for their party's substitute bill, which, like the Personal Responsibility Act, stripped poor single mothers of their entitlement to welfare.[4] Meanwhile, across the country, a National Organization for Women Legal Defense and Education Fund appeal for contributions to support an economic justice litigator aroused so much hate mail that NOW LDEF stopped doing direct mail on the welfare issue.[5]

Although the feminist Women's Committee of 100 campaigned ardently against the welfare bill, Republicans won their war against poor single mothers with the complicity of millions of other feminists. Feminist members of Congress did not write the Personal Responsibility Act, of course. Nor did NOW members or contributors to Emily's List comprise the driving force behind the most brutal provisions of the new welfare law. My point is not that feminists were uniquely responsible for how Congress reformed welfare. It is that they were uniquely positioned to make a difference. We have made a difference in many arenas across the years, even during inauspicious Republican presidencies—reforming rape laws, winning recognition of sexual harassment as a form of sex discrimination, and securing passage of a federal law against domestic violence. Feminists certainly could have made a difference when a friendly Democratic president began casting about for ways to reform welfare in 1993; and although we could not have changed Republican intentions in the 104th Congress, we surely could have pressured the Democrat we helped elect to the White House to veto the Republican bill.

In the absence of widespread feminist opposition to the welfare reform principles of the Personal Responsibility Act, the legislative record is devoid of a counternarrative that might temper administrative and judicial enforcement of the new law. Moreover, it is devoid of any discursive precedent for women-friendly, equality-enhancing amendments to the new law. Because most feminists did not contest or disturb the Republican welfare paradigm, about all they can do now to fix the new welfare mess is urge that more money be spent on job training and childcare and that broader exceptions for battered women be adopted. These are important goals, but they do not repair the damage wrought by the new welfare law on the lives and rights of poor single mothers.

Why were so many feminists unconcerned that welfare reform not only repealed poor single mothers' entitlement to cash assistance but encroached on their basic civil rights as well? Given the degree of harm inflicted on poor single mothers by the new welfare law, why were there no candlelight vigils like there were against O. J. Simpson? Why were there no marches like there have been to defend *Roe v. Wade?* Why were no boycotts waged like there were against the film *The People vs. Larry Flynt?*

These questions are the fruit of my frustration as a welfare activist. They have renewed my scholarly attention to the relationship between welfare and equality, on the one hand, and between welfare and feminism, on the other. Out of these concerns has emerged a new scholarly project . . . a new book.[6] The book is a broadside against the Personal Responsibility Act, culminating in defense of welfare. It is also a call to middle-class feminists to practice true "sisterhood": by upholding poor mothers' rights as we do our own.

Although the Personal Responsibility Act deserves boundless criticism for its seismic practical consequences—for driving a million more children into poverty, for example—my book is concerned less with the economic than with the political impact of welfare reform. The new welfare law distinguishes poor single mothers as a separate caste, subject to a separate system of law. Poor single mothers are the only people in America forced by law to work outside the home. They are the only people in America whose decisions to bear children are punished by government. They are the only people in America of whom government may demand the details of intimate relationships. And they are the only mothers in America compelled by law to make room for biological fathers in their families.

Based on lessons drawn from eighteen months of struggle against the Personal Responsibility Act, one of my goals in the book is to defend welfare as an affirmative right of poor single mothers, a right backed up by the reproductive, associational, family, and vocational rights assured to all persons under the Constitution. Toward this end, I argue that welfare (by which I mean income support for caregivers) is a condition of women's equality (by which I mean full and independent citizenship).

Without welfare, mothers who work inside the home are deprived of equal citizenship, for they alone are not paid for their labor. Moreover, lacking earnings for their economic and social contributions, women who work full- or part-time as caregivers for their children are ideologically unequal in a political culture that prizes income-producing work as the currency of virtue. Further, unwaged mothers do not have marital freedom: lacking the financial means to exit marriages, they lack the freedom to choose to stay in them. When they do dare to exit or avoid marriage, mothers do not enjoy vocational liberty: unpaid for their work in the home, they are forced either by law or by economic circumstance to choose wages over children.

We should not think of welfare as a subsidy for dependence but as insurance for the rights that comprise independence. Nor should we think of welfare as an income substitute for the wage earned by breadwinners—fathers—in the labor market. Rather, we should reconceive welfare as the income owed to persons who work inside the home caring for, nurturing, and protecting children—mothering.

The idea that welfare should support mothers in their caregiving roles should not be terribly controversial. This was a core premise of mothers' pension programs early in the century and a justification for including Aid to Dependent Children in the New Deal's Social Security Act.[7] The problem is that the caregiving work performed by poor mothers has lost its luster over the past thirty years; who welfare mothers are explains why.

In the popular imagination, welfare participants are reckless breeders who bear children to avoid work. Such vintage stereotypes have bipartisan roots and were popularized beginning in the 1960s by Republican Richard Nixon, southern Democrat Russell Long, and sometime Democrat George Wallace. Even Lyndon Johnson, often credited for expanding welfare as part of his War on Poverty, shared these views: he called for limits on payments to nonmarital children and complained that their mothers "sit around and breed instead of going out to work."[8] Into the 1990s, the racial mythology of welfare cast the welfare mother as Black, pinned the need for reform on her character, and at least implicitly defined Black women as other people's workers rather than their own families' mothers.[9] Racially charged images of lazy, promiscuous, and matriarchal women have dominated welfare discourse for quite some time, inflaming demands that mothers who need welfare—although perhaps not their children—must pay for their improvident behavior through work, marriage, or destitution.[10]

If racism has permitted policymakers to negate poor single mothers as mothers, middle-class feminism has provided them an excuse. New attitudes about wage earning by mothers amplified by successful feminist challenges to employment discrimination have turned work outside the home into a rhetorical resource for critics of welfare. Middle-class feminists' emphasis on women's right to work outside the home also has inflected welfare politics among women, diminishing the scale of coalitions for welfare justice—especially by comparison to coalitions for abortion rights or against rape or domestic violence. This created something of a vacuum in the defense of poor mothers' political and economic rights.

Part of the problem, I think, is that white and middle-class feminists—who are the mainstream of the women's movement—view mothers who need welfare as mothers who need feminism. They see welfare mothers as victims—of patriarchy, may be of racism, possibly of false consciousness. They don't see welfare mothers as feminist agents of their own lives—as women who are entitled to and capable of making independent and honorable choices about what kind of work they will do and how many children they will have and whether they will marry. As a result, when many white, middle-class feminists weighed into the welfare debate, it was to prescribe reforms to assimilate welfare mothers to white feminists' own goals—principally, independence through paid employment.

Most of the policy claims made by Second-Wave feminists have emphasized women's right to participate in men's world and have made work outside the home a defining element for women's full and equal citizenship. Middle-class feminists responded to their particular historical experiences, experiences drawn by an ethos of domesticity which confined middle-class women to the home. From this perspective, the home is the site of oppression for women, while the labor market is potentially liberating. But when middle-class women moved into the labor market, they did not trade in their caregiving obligations. Now doubly taxed by the dual responsibilities of earning and caring, many feminists have demanded labor market policies to address the family needs that fall disproportionately on women—parental leave and childcare, for example.[11] However, they have been less interested in winning social policies to support women where we meet our family responsibilities: in the home. In the absence of widespread feminist attention to the social value of the childraising and home management work mothers do,

poor mothers' right to do motherwork has been only faintly defended.

The popular feminist claim that women earn independence, autonomy, and equality through wages historically has divided feminists along class and race lines, as women of color and poor white women have not usually earned equality from sweated labor. To the contrary. Especially for women of color, wage work has been a mark of inequality: expected by the white society for whom they work; necessary because their male kin cannot find jobs or cannot earn family-supporting wages; and exploitative because their earnings keep them poor. Thus, the right to care for their own children—to work inside the home—has been a touchstone goal of their struggles for equality. The fact that women are positioned divergently in the nexus among caregiving, wage earning, and inequality separated feminists one from another on the welfare issue and separated employed middle-class feminists from mothers who need welfare.

Out of the middle-class feminist emphasis on winning rights in the workplace has emerged, sotto voce, an expectation that women ought to work outside the home and an assumption that any job outside the home—including caring for other people's children—is more socially productive than caring for one's own. Feminists in Congress betrayed this bias, voting unfazed to require poor single mothers to work outside the home both as a condition of welfare and as a consequence of time limits.

Although feminism is fundamentally about winning women choices, our labor market bias has put much of feminism not on the side of vocational choice—the choice to work inside or outside the home—but on the side of wage earning for all women. Thus, most congressional feminists, along with many feminists across the country, have conflated their right to work outside the home with poor single mothers' obligation to do so. This is an obligation of no small significance for poor single mothers, who are conscripted into wagework under the new welfare law.

Most single mothers work outside the home, and most single mothers who receive welfare want to. The question is whether social policy should dictate that they must. Poor single mothers already shoulder a double burden in parenting: should social policy require them to perform yet another job?

Except for a few young men in my classes who insist that mothering is love, not work, I think most people understand that the caregiving mostly provided by mothers is work. Disagreements arise over whether that work is worth anything if it is performed for one's own family. Or, more accurately, disagreements arise over when that work is worth something and in what kinds of families.

When Republicans and Democrats have wanted to, they have acknowledged mothers' caregiving work in public policy: they've even remunerated it. The very week it negated the motherwork of poor single women by giving final approval to the Personal Responsibility Act, Congress affirmed the mother-work of middle-class homemakers by granting them rights to their own IRAs.[12] Representative Nancy Johnson hailed the measure as forwarding equality for homemakers. Others hailed it for honoring them. Viewed alongside welfare reform, IRAs for homemakers deepened existing differentiations in law between married and unmarried mothers, between white women and women of color, and between rich women and poor. It also created a distinction between poor single mothers' activities in the home and married, middle-class mothers' work there. IRAs, after all, are an untaxed portion of earned income.

Clearly, legislators do understand that what (some) domestic mothers do is not pass the time but work. The challenge, then, is to lead policymakers to give poor mothers' caregiving work the dignity it is due by providing it an income. Payments for mothers' caregiving work ought not to be too difficult to calculate, for much of the work done by caregiving mothers already has a market price if performed for someone else's family. We pay teachers, for example, as well as psychologists, nurses, accountants, chauffeurs, launderers, housecleaners, cooks, waitresses, even personal shoppers.[13]

To some extent we can derive a right to a caregiver's income through constitutional reasoning: a socially provided income guarantee ought to be a condition of reproductive, marital, family, and vocational freedoms—as well as a matter of equal protection. Although the Constitution does not oblige us to provide for one another's economic security, it does permit us to imagine different ways to enforce its meaning legislatively: the Fourteenth Amendment gives Congress the responsibility to enact laws that enforce its provisions, including its clause promising "equal protection of the law." Moreover, the Constitution permits us to defend rights with remedies, including remedial social supports—legal assistance for poor criminal defendants, for example—without which the rights of some citizens would disappear.

Welfare remedies poor single mothers' inequality, specifically the inequality of economic disfranchisement. Mothers' economic disfranchisement comes from our failure to impute economic value to the work that they do. In marriages, mothers who work inside the home surrender their economic personhood to husbands and occupy the legal status of dependent. Such married mothers' lack of their own economic resources—earnings—skew power relations in the family; some mothers may feel tethered to husbands because they could not survive the economic consequences of leaving them. Single mothers, meanwhile, must accept destitution as a condition of caring for their children. Unpaid and disdained, they are expected to forswear childraising for full-time wage earning. Full-time caregiving mothers, then, are disproportionately dependent on men if married and disproportionately poor, if not. These private inequalities have public effects, foreclosing mother-workers' independent citizenship.

We would begin to redress these inequalities by providing caregivers who are parenting alone an income in recognition of their family work. A socially provided income for solo parents who bear the dual responsibilities of providing care for their children and financing it, welfare is a condition of equality in the family, in the labor market, and in the state. As such, welfare should be a right, not an entitlement—a claim backed by law and courts that should be irresistible, or at least impossible for a rogue Congress to deny. Unless we can establish a right to welfare, we cannot cure inequality where it is most gendered—in sexual, reproductive, and family relations.

A right to income support in return for poor single mothers' caregiving work tackles the neglected side of the gender divide, the side that has defined women as the legal and economic dependents of men. But although a caregiver's income would address the gender divide, it need not reproduce that divide. Rights that accommodate mothers' caregiving work need not ascribe mother-work to all women, nor only to women: men can mother, too. Nor need rights that accommodate mothers' caregiving work disparage women's choices and equality claims in the labor market. Such rights should widen options for solo caregivers of either gender by backing up the choice to work outside the home with the means not to. Ending welfare by redefining it in this way will enable equality—in the safety net, between the genders, among women, and under the Constitution.

NOTES

1. "Lady and the tramp" refers to my essay, "The Lady and the Tramp: Gender, Race, and the Origins of the American Welfare State," in *Women, the State, and Welfare,* ed. Linda Gordon (Madison: University of Wisconsin Press, 1990), 92–122.

2. Gwendolyn Mink, *The Wages of Motherhood: Inequality in the Welfare State, 1917–1942* (Ithaca: Cornell University Press, 1995).

3. The Republican initiative (H.R. 4) was first introduced in January 1995. Passed by the House in March and by the Senate in the late summer, the bill died with the 1995 budget impasse. In 1996, the Congress passed and the president signed a new bill, H.R. 3734, or P.L. 104–193. The new law repealed the Aid to Families with Dependent Children program.

4. This was the Castle-Tanner substitute amendment to H.R. 3734. See *Congressional Record,* 18 July 1996, H7907–7974.

5. Felicia Kornbluh, "Feminists and the Welfare Debate: Too Little? Too Late?" *Dollars and Sense,* November/December 1996, 25.

6. Mink, *Welfare's End* (Ithaca: Cornell University Press, 1998). Some material in this article is taken from this book with the permission of the publisher.

7. Mink, *Wages of Motherhood,* chap. 6.

8. President Lyndon Johnson to his budget director, LBJ White House telephone tapes, CNN Morning News, 18 Oct. 1996.

9. Dorothy Roberts, "The Value of Black Mothers' Work," *Connecticut Law Review* 26 (spring 1994): 871–73; Lucy A. Williams, "Race, Rat Bites, and Unfit Mothers: How Media Discourse Informs Welfare Legislation Debate," *Fordham Urban Law Journal* 22 (summer 1995): 1159–96.

10. See, e.g., Charles Murray, *Losing Ground: American Social Policy, 1950–1980* (New York: Basic Books, 1984).

11. See, for example, Barbara Bergman and Heidi Hartmann, "A Welfare Reform Based on Help for Working Parents," *Feminist Economics* 1 (summer 1995): 85–91.

12. The IRAs for homemakers provision was part of the Small Business Job Protection and Minimum Wage Increase Act, H.R. 3448 (104th Congress, 2d session).

13. In 1972, Chase Manhattan Bank economists concluded that the weekly value of a family caregiver's work was at least $257.53, or $13,391.56 a year (1972 dollars). See Ann Crittenden Scott, "The Value of Housework: For Love or Money?" *Ms.,* July 1972, 56–59.

Social Protest and the Feminist Movement

Throughout *Feminist Frontiers* we have begun to understand the breadth and magnitude of the social forces working to differentiate women and men and to disadvantage women. Socialization, the organization of social institutions, and social and economic policies all come together to hinder women's full political participation, self-determination, economic security, and even health and safety.

Despite the ubiquitous forms of inequality embedded in our social institutions, women resist. As we have seen, women often struggle against oppression in individual ways. Women also come together to take collective action to pursue social change. This section explores contemporary forms of social protest, noting how feminist movements attract different constituencies, develop different ideas, articulate different goals, and utilize different tactics and strategies issues across time and place.

In the first article, Verta Taylor, Nancy Whittier, and Cynthia Fabrizio Pelak present an overview of the multiple ideologies and forms of the feminist movement in the United States from its emergence in the 1960s to the present. "The Women's Movement: Persistence through Transformation" considers the larger social and economic conditions responsible for the rise of women's movements in the Western world and describes the transnational context of feminism. Taylor, Whittier, and Pelak focus on the way feminist movements have changed over time as a result of activists' own ideas and goals and the larger social and political

context, including antifeminist countermovements that have arisen to oppose the aims of the women's movement. Based on their analysis, what do you think might be the future of feminism?

Feminism, as this article demonstrates, has a long and vibrant history and strong prospects for the future. A great deal of attention has been devoted to the generational divisions in feminism. Some see a "third wave" of feminism (see the boxed insert); others see the death of feminism in the "postfeminist" generation. Pamela Aronson, in "Feminists or 'Postfeminists'?" explores attitudes toward feminism through interviews with a diverse sample of young women. She shows that the majority of her sample is aware that the women's movement increased opportunity and that inequality remains, but that young women embrace a range of positions on the question of whether they identify as feminists. What difference do class, race, and life experience make in shaping young women's perspectives? Where would you fit on a spectrum of attitudes toward feminism?

In "Punks, Bulldaggers, and Welfare Queens," Cathy Cohen calls for a new form of progressive and transformative coalition building. She embraces queer activists' in-your-face strategies intended to challenge the invisibility of gay, lesbian, bisexual, and transgendered people and to embrace sexual difference. But she criticizes the narrowness of queer politics for its overemphasis on deconstructing the historically and culturally recognized categories of homosexual and heterosexual.

Such a strategy, she argues, exaggerates the similarities among individuals categorized under the label of "heterosexual" and ignores the way other systems of oppression regulate the lives of women and men of all races, classes, and sexualities. A truly queer politics, she suggests, would bring together those, like punks, bulldaggers, and welfare queens, who live outside not heterosexuality, but heteronormativity. What might the kinds of coalitions Cohen envisages look like?

Susan Muaddi Darraj, an Arab Christian young feminist, explains why Arab feminism is not an oxymoron. Discussing her sense of alienation from white Western feminism, Darraj exposes the double standard by which Arabic culture is criticized and exoticized as patriarchal, while American culture is viewed as more advanced despite its own patriarchal nature. She recounts the development of her own sense of feminism through the work of Black feminist writers and Arab feminist

networks. How is her Arab feminism different from white Western feminism? How does it compare to the varieties of feminism presented in the other readings?

Finally, looking at women's activism transnationally, we end with the declaration from the Fourth World Conference on Women in Beijing in 1995 and a press release on the 2005 reaffirmation of support (originally contested by the United States) of the Platform for Action adopted at Beijing. What do these pieces tell us about the challenges of building women's movements across differences?

Women's movements in the twenty-first century are becoming more diverse than ever and hold great promise for transforming for the better the lives of both women and men. As you finish reading *Feminist Frontiers,* think about what changes you would like to see in your world. How do you propose to work for these changes?

READING 47 *Verta Taylor*
Nancy Whittier
Cynthia Fabrizio Pelak

The Women's Movement:
Persistence through Transformation

INTRODUCTION

Popular authors and scholars alike described the 1980s and 1990s as a "postfeminist" era of political apathy during which former feminists traded their political ideals for career mobility and cell phones and younger women single-mindedly pursued career goals and viewed feminism as an anachronism. Yet this was not the first time that commentators proclaimed the death of feminism. In the 1920s, after women won the right to vote, images of young women abandoning the struggle for rights in favor of jobs and good times filled the media. Then as now, feminism changed form, but neither the movement nor the injustices that produced it have vanished. Of all the manifestations of social activism in the 1960s, feminism is one of the few that persist. We explore here continuity and change in the American women's movement from the 1960s to the present. First we consider the structural preconditions of women's movements in the Western world and the international context for activism. Then we focus on the changing ideologies, structures, political contexts, and strategies of the women's movement in the United States. We conclude our discussion by considering historically specific antifeminist countermovements that have emerged in response to challenges of the women's movement.

STRUCTURAL PRECONDITIONS OF WESTERN FEMINIST MOVEMENTS

From a social movement perspective, women have always had sufficient grievances to create the context for feminist activity. Indeed, instances of collective action on the part of women abound in history, especially if one includes female reform societies, women's church groups, alternative religious societies, and women's clubs. However, collective activity on the part of women directed specifically toward improving their own status has flourished primarily in periods of generalized social upheaval, when sensitivity to moral injustice, discrimination, and social inequality has been widespread in the society as a whole (Chafe 1977; Staggenborg 1998a). The first wave of feminism in the United States grew out of the abolitionist struggle of the 1830s and peaked during an era of social reform in the 1890s, and the contemporary movement emerged out of the general social discontent of the 1960s. Although the women's movement did not die between these periods of heightened activism, it declined sharply in the 1930s, 1940s, and 1950s after the passage of the Nineteenth Amendment to the Constitution guaranteeing women the right to vote as a response to the changing social, political, and economic context (Rupp and Taylor 1987). During this period, women who had played important roles in obtaining women's suffrage managed to keep the flames of feminism alive by launching a campaign to pass an Equal Rights Amendment (ERA) to the Constitution.

Despite national differences in feminist movements, scholars identify certain basic structural conditions that have contributed to the emergence of feminist protest in most parts of the western world (Oppenheimer 1973; Huber and Spitze 1983; Chafetz and Dworkin 1986). Broad societal changes in the patterns of women's participation in the paid labor force, increases in women's formal educational attainment, and shifts in women's fertility rates and reproductive roles disrupt traditional social arrangements and set the stage for women's movements. As industrialization and urbanization bring greater education for women, expanding public roles create role and status conflicts for middle-class women, who then develop the discontent and gender consciousness necessary for political action (Chafetz and Dworkin 1986). Specifically, when women, especially married middle-class women, enter the paid labor force, their gender consciousness increases because they are more likely to use men as a reference group when assessing their access to societal rewards. Similarly, women often experience strains and discrepancies in their lives as their gender consciousness is raised through formal education (Klein 1984).

Other important structural factors that serve as preconditions for feminist mobilization include changes in family relationships, marriage, fertility, and sexual mores (Ferree and Hess 1994). Declines in women's childbearing and increases in their age at first marriage can improve women's educational attainment and participation in the paid labor force—which, in turn, raise their gender consciousness (Klein 1984). Moreover, changes in the traditional relationships between women and men in marriage and in sexual mores, such as the shift from authoritarian marriages to romantic or companionate marriages at the turn of the last century in the United States and the "sexual revolution" of the 1960s, can politicize gender relations and create the motivations for feminist mobilization.

Certainly, the specific configuration of structural preconditions underlying the genesis of feminist collective mobilizations varies with historical and geographic context. Not only the political context but also the demographic, economic, and cultural processes that have given rise to feminist movements in the United States are different from those in Third World countries. Such political and cultural variations are reflected in national and regional variations in the way women define their collective interests, in the distinct ideologies, organizational forms, and strategies adopted by feminist movements in different times and places, and ultimately in the possibilities for feminist mobilization. Nonetheless, scholars recognize some important commonalties among women's movements around the world.

FEMINIST MOVEMENTS IN AN INTERNATIONAL CONTEXT

We focus here on the women's movement in the United States. It is nonetheless important to acknowledge the multiple forms of feminist resistance around the world and to underscore the importance of the historical and geographic specificity of feminist activism. Throughout modern history, women in all regions of the world have organized collectively against the injustice and

oppression in their lives and communities (Basu 1995). Such mobilizations in diverse political, cultural, and historical contexts have varied widely in their organizations, strategies, ideologies, and structures. Gender oppression for some Third World feminists cannot be divorced from issues and histories of colonization, immigration, racism, or imperialism, and thus feminist activism in some Third World contexts may be organized around a constellation of oppressions rather than specifically around gender oppression (Jayawardena 1986; Mohanty, Russo, and Torres 1991).

In some instances, ideological, organizational, and strategic differences in women's movements lie in fundamental differences in the political culture of a region (Ray 1999). In Calcutta, India, for example, which is dominated by the Communist Party and a strong and traditional left culture, the women's movement functions more as a political party and uses the party structure to address issues such as employment, poverty, and literacy that do not directly threaten the gender status quo. The women's movement in Bombay, on the other hand, which exists in a more open, contested political field and culture, is more explicitly feminist and uses more autonomous forms of organizing to spotlight issues that are more threatening to men, such as violence against women, religious fundamentalism, and women's restricted roles in the family. Although national and regional differences exist, there are important commonalties that link women's movements over time and place (Chafetz and Dworkin 1986; Katzenstein and Mueller 1987; Giele 1995; Miles 1996).

Women's movements, particularly those in industrialized countries, generally have emerged in two waves of heightened activism. In their cross-cultural, historical analysis of forty-eight countries, Chafetz and Dworkin (1986) found that the mass-scale, independent women's movements of the first wave, such as those in European societies and the United States, occurred in the closing decades of the nineteenth century and the first decades of the twentieth century, while the second-wave women's movements have emerged since the 1960s. Major goals of the first wave of activism included women's suffrage, educational opportunities for women, basic legal reforms, inheritance and property rights, and employment opportunities for women. Women's demands during this first wave often were framed around middle-class women's roles as wives and mothers and reinforced gender difference by valorizing women's special virtues and moral superiority over men. Smaller-scale movements during the first wave were more likely to challenge basic role differentiation between women and men and to resist doctrines and images of femininity in the culture.

To the extent that the large-scale changes brought on by urbanization and industrialization in Western countries created dramatic changes in the workplace, the family, and the lives of women and men, it is not surprising there was considerable ideological debate and diversity among first-wave feminists. In the United States, for example, some factions of the nineteenth-century women's movement were grounded in essentialist views of sex differences and were more interested in nonfeminist social reforms, for which the vote was only a prerequisite (Buechler 1990; Giele 1995). Other branches of the nineteenth-century women's movement rejected essentialist notions of gender and, by pursuing more radical changes such as sexual freedom and the expansion of women's roles in the workplace and politics, sought to transform the gender order in more fundamental ways (Cott 1987).

Women's movements of the second wave in western countries, blossoming since the 1960s, have mobilized around an even broader range of issues, such as reproductive rights, sexual and economic exploitation, and violence against women (Chafetz and Dworkin 1986; Ferree and Hess 1994). Modern feminist movements often have developed around women's commonalities, but differences of race, class, ethnicity, and nationality are also expressed in the collective identities deployed by feminists (Moraga and Anzaldúa 1981; Mohanty, Russo, and Torres 1991). African-American women have organized around interlocking structures of oppression that affect women differently depending on their ethnicity, class, or sexual identities (Collins 1990). For example, African-American and Latina women from low-income urban neighborhoods have struggled for quality education, affordable and safe housing, and expanded child care services for their families and communities (Naples 1992).

Since the 1970s, there has been a phenomenal growth in regional, interregional, and international networking among feminist groups (Miles 1996), although the origins of international women's organizations date back to the closing decades of the nineteenth century (Rupp 1997). The United Nations' International Women's Year (1975) and Decade for Women (1975–1985) helped foster global feminist dialogues and stimulated independent, locally based feminist activities in all parts of the world. Since the beginning of the UN Decade for Women, there have been four official UN world conferences of government representatives devoted to women's issues, with four unofficial forums of women's groups running alongside each of these conferences. Since the first forum in Mexico City in 1975, participation by women in the unofficial forums has increased sharply, challenging the notion that feminism has died in recent years.

Although these conferences and forums have been sites of considerable debate and conflict over the meaning of "women's issues" and the definition of feminism, the events have sparked multiple forms and foci of feminist resistance and a global awareness of women's oppression that reaches beyond women's groups. Feminists are forging global relations around a diverse set of issues including "health, housing, education, law reform, population, human rights, reproductive and genetic engineering, female sexual slavery and trafficking in women, violence against women, spirituality, peace and militarism, external debt, fundamentalism, environment, development, media, alternative technology, film, art and literature, publishing, and women's studies" (Miles 1996:142). The trajectory of the US women's movement can be fully understood only in this global context.

THE CONTEMPORARY FEMINIST MOVEMENT: CONTINUITY AND CHANGE

Most scholarly analyses of the women's movement of the late 1960s—what scholars call the "second-wave feminist movement"—divide it into two wings, with origins in the grievances and preexisting organizations of two groups of women: older professional women, who formed bureaucratic organizations with a liberal ideology and adopted legal reform strategies, and younger women from the civil rights and New Left movements, who formed small collective organizations with radical ideology and employed "personal as political" strategies such as consciousness-raising groups (Freeman 1975; Cassell 1977; Ferree and Hess 1994; Buechler 1990). During a period of resurgence dating to the founding of the National Organization for Women (NOW) in 1966, the movement established itself, forming organizations and ideologies and moving into the public eye (Buechler 1990; Ryan 1992). By 1971, major segments of feminism had crystallized: liberal feminism, embodied in the formation of groups such as NOW, the Women's Equity Action League (WEAL) in 1967, and the National Women's Political Caucus (NWPC) in 1971; radical feminism and socialist feminism, emerging from consciousness-raising groups, theory groups, and small action groups such as Redstockings and the Feminists in 1969; and lesbian feminism, organized in such groups as Radicalesbians in 1970 and the Furies (initially called "Those Women") in 1971 (Echols 1989).

The year 1972 was pivotal both for the movement's success and for its opposition. The Equal Rights Amendment (ERA) passed the Congress, and Phyllis Schlafly launched her first antifeminist attacks. This can be considered the movement's heyday because the feminist revolution seemed to be on the move. The campaign to ratify the ERA in the states brought mass mobilization, fostering female solidarity and enlisting women into feminism; women's studies programs proliferated on college campuses; the number and variety of feminist organizations increased phenomenally; and the movement entered the political arena and encountered active opposition (Matthews and DeHart 1990; Ryan 1992). Not only did feminism flourish in the ERA ratification campaign but it spread into the political mainstream, while radical and lesbian feminist organizing heightened outside it.

Following the ERA's defeat in 1982, the women's movement entered a period of the doldrums, in which it developed new structural forms to survive a declining membership and an increasingly nonreceptive environment. The 1980s saw a turning away from the values of equality, human rights, and social justice and even a deliberate backlash against the feminist momentum of the 1970s. Rights won by feminists in the 1960s and 1970s— from affirmative action to legal abortion—were under siege throughout the 1980s and 1990s. Yet the so-called postfeminist era of the 1980s and 1990s no more marks the death of the women's movement than did the earlier premature announcements of feminism's demise. In fact, although the women's movement of the turn of the twenty-first century takes a different form than it did twenty years earlier, it remains vital and influential.

Feminist Ideology

While ideas do not necessarily cause social movements, ideology is a central component in the life of any social movement (Morris and Mueller 1992). The modern feminist movement, like most social movements, is not ideologically monolithic. Feminist ideology encompasses numerous ideological strands that differ in the scope of change sought, the extent to which gender inequality is linked to other systems of domination— especially class, race, ethnicity, and sexuality—and the significance attributed to gender differences. We focus here on the evolution of the dominant ideologies that have motivated participants in the two major branches of the feminist movement from its inception, liberal feminism and radical feminism.

The first wave of the women's movement in the nineteenth century was, by and large, a liberal feminist reform movement. It sought equality within the existing social structure and, indeed, in many ways functioned like other reform movements to reaffirm existing values within the society (Ferree and Hess 1994). Nineteenth-century feminists believed that if they obtained the right to an education, the right to own property, the right to vote, employment rights—in other words, equal civil rights under the law—they would attain equality with men. Scholars have labeled this thinking "individualist" or "equity" feminism, linking the goal of equal rights to gender assumptions about women's basic sameness with men (Offen 1988; Black 1989).

The basic ideas identified with contemporary liberal or "mainstream" feminism have changed little since their formulation in the nineteenth century, when they seemed progressive, even radical (Eisenstein 1981). Contemporary liberal feminist ideology holds that women lack power simply because we are not, as women, allowed equal opportunity to compete and succeed in the male-dominated economic and political arenas but, instead, are relegated to the subordinate world of home, domestic labor, motherhood, and family. The major strategy for change is to gain legal and economic equalities and to obtain access to elite positions in the workplace and in politics. Thus, liberal feminists tend to place as much emphasis on changing individual women as they do on changing society. For instance, teaching women managerial skills or instructing rape victims in "survival" strategies strikes a blow at social definitions that channel women into traditionally feminine occupations or passive behaviors that make them easy targets of aggression from men.

Liberal feminists ironically provided ideological support through the 1970s and 1980s for the massive transformation in work and family life that was occurring as the United States underwent the transition to a postindustrial order (Mitchell 1986; Stacey 1987). Some writers even contend that by urging women to enter the workplace and adopt a male orientation, the equal opportunity approach to feminism unwittingly contributed to a host of problems that further disadvantaged women (especially working-class women and women of color), including the rise in divorce rates, the "feminization" of working-class occupations, and the devaluation of motherhood and traditionally female characteristics (Gordon 1991).

Radical feminist ideology dates to Simone de Beauvoir's early 1950s theory of "sex class," which was developed further in the late 1960s among small groups of radical women who fought the subordination of women's liberation within the New Left (Beauvoir 1952; Firestone 1970; Millett 1971; Atkinson 1974; Rubin 1975; Rich 1976, 1980; Griffin 1978; Daly 1978; Eisenstein 1981; Hartmann 1981; Frye 1983; Hartsock 1983; MacKinnon 1983). The radical approach recognizes women's identity and subordination as a "sex class," emphasizes women's fundamental difference from men, views gender as the primary contradiction and foundation for the unequal distribution of a society's rewards and privileges, and recasts relations between women and men in political terms (Echols 1989). Defining women as a "sex class" means no longer treating patriarchy in individual terms but acknowledging the social and structural nature of women's subordination. Radical feminists hold that in all societies, institutions and social patterns are structured to maintain and perpetuate gender inequality and female disadvantage permeates virtually all aspects of sociocultural and personal life. Further, through the gender division of labor, social institutions are linked so that male superiority depends upon female subordination (Hartmann 1981). In the United States, as in most industrialized societies, power, prestige, and wealth accrue to those who control the distribution of resources outside the home, in the economic and political spheres. The sexual division of labor that assigns child care and domestic responsibilities to women not only ensures gender inequality in the family system but perpetuates male advantage in political and economic institutions as well.

To unravel the complex structure on which gender inequality rests requires, from a radical feminist perspective, a fundamental transformation of all institutions in society. To meet this challenge, radical feminists formulated influential critiques of the family, marriage, love, motherhood, heterosexuality, sexual violence, capitalism, reproductive policies, the media, science, language and culture, the beauty industry, sports, politics, the law, technology, and more. Radical feminism's ultimate vision is revolutionary in scope: a fundamentally new social order that eliminates the sex-class system and replaces it with new ways—based on women's difference—of defining and structuring experience. Central to the development of radical feminist ideology was the strategy of forming small groups for the purpose of "consciousness-raising." Pioneered initially among New Left women, consciousness-raising

can be understood as a kind of conversion in which women come to view experiences previously thought of as personal and individual, such as sexual exploitation or employment discrimination, as social problems that are the result of gender inequality.

By the late 1970s, the distinction between liberal and radical feminism was becoming less clear (Carden 1978; Whittier 1995). Ideological shifts took place at both the individual and organizational levels. Participation in liberal feminist reform and service organizations working on such issues as rape, battering, abortion, legal and employment discrimination, and women's health problems raised women's consciousness, increased their feminist activism, and contributed to their radicalization as they came to see connections between these issues and the larger system of gender inequality (Schlesinger and Bart 1983; Whittier 1995). Women were also radicalized by working through their own personal experiences of sexual harassment, divorce, rape, abortion, and incest (Huber 1973; Klein 1984).

Radicalization has occurred at the group level as well. By the end of the 1970s, liberal feminist organizations such as NOW, the Women's Legal Defense Fund, and the National Abortion Rights Action League (NARAL) which had been pursuing equality within the law, began to adopt strategies and goals consistent with a more radical stance. NOW included in its 1979 objectives not only such legal strategies as the ERA and reproductive choice, but broader issues such as the threat of nuclear energy to the survival of the species, lesbian and gay rights, homemakers' rights, the exploitation of women in the home, and sex segregation in the workplace (Eisenstein 1981). Even the ERA, which sought equality for women within the existing legal and economic structure, was based on the fact that women are discriminated against as a "sex class" (Mansbridge 1986).

Beginning in the mid-1980s, with the defeat of the unifying issue of the ERA and the growing diversification of the movement, feminist ideology de-emphasized the question of women's similarity to or difference from men in favor of "deconstructing" the term *woman*. Women of color, Jewish women, lesbians, and working-class women challenged radical feminists' idea of a "sex class" that implied a distinctive and essential female condition. Since women are distributed throughout all social classes, racial and ethnic groupings, sexual communities, cultures, and religions, disadvantage for women varies and is multidimensional (Spelman 1988). The recognition that the circumstances of women's oppression differ has given way to a new feminist paradigm that views race, class, gender, ethnicity, and sexuality as interlocking systems of oppression, forming what Patricia Hill Collins (1990) refers to as a "matrix of domination."

Some scholars have charged that focusing on women's differences from one another has resulted in a retreat to "identity politics" and the demise of the women's movement. Alice Echols (1989) links disputes over difference and a focus on identity to a concentration on building an alternative women's culture rather than confronting and changing social institutions. In a similar vein, Barbara Ryan (1989) argues that internal debates over the correctness of competing feminist theories and the political implications of personal choices—what she terms "ideological purity"—tore the women's movement apart. But other scholars see the sometimes vehement arguments over women's differences from one another as a sign of life (Taylor and Rupp 1993). Feminists organizing around diverse identities sometimes seek out new arenas of challenge that differ from traditional definitions of political activism and thus extend the reach of feminism. Self-help movements focused on the self and the body, for example—drug and alcohol abuse, incest, postpartum depression, battering, breast cancer—offer a complex challenge to traditional notions of femininity, motherhood, and sexuality and carry the potential to mobilize new constituencies (Taylor and Van Willigen 1996; Gagné 1998).

In any case, ideas alone are an incomplete explanation of either the direction or the consequences of a social movement (Marx and Wood 1975; McCarthy and Zald 1977). Much depends on a movement's structures and strategies, as well as on the larger political context.

Feminist Organizational Structures

Social movements do not generally have a single central organization or unified direction. Rather, the structure of any general, broad-based social movement is more diffuse—composed of a number of relatively independent organizations that differ in ideology, structure, goals, and tactics. A social movement is characterized by decentralized leadership; it is loosely connected by multiple and overlapping memberships and by friendship networks that work toward common goals (Gerlach and Hine 1970). The organizational structure of the modern feminist movement has conformed to this model from its beginnings (Freeman 1975; Cassell 1977; Ferree and

Martin 1995). While the movement as a whole is characterized by a decentralized structure, the various organizations that comprise it vary widely in structure. The diversity of feminist organizational forms reflects both ideological differences and the movement's diverse membership base (Freeman 1979).

There have been two main types of organizational structure in the modern feminist movement since its resurgence, reflecting the two sources of feminist organizing in the late 1960s: bureaucratically structured movement organizations with hierarchical leadership and democratic decision-making procedures, such as the National Organization for Women; and smaller collectively structured groups that formed a more diffuse social movement community held together by a feminist political culture. Collectively organized groups, at least in theory, strove to exemplify a better way of structuring society by constructing a distinctive women's culture that valorized egalitarianism, the expression of emotion, and the sharing of personal experience. It is important to recognize, however, that while the two strands of the women's movement emerged separately, they have not remained distinct and opposed to each other. Most women's movement organizations are mixed in form from the outset. The two structures have increasingly converged as bureaucratic organizations adopted some of the innovations of collectivism and feminist collectives became more formally structured (Staggenborg 1988, 1989; Martin 1990; Ryan 1992; Ferree and Martin 1995; Whittier 1995). In addition, many individual activists are involved in a variety of organizations with differing structures.

The bureaucratically structured and professionalized movement organizations initially adopted by liberal groups such as NOW were well suited to work within the similarly structured political arena and to members' previous experience in professional organizations. The structures that radical feminist groups initially adopted, on the other hand, built on their prior involvement in the New Left (Evans 1979). Collectivist organizations grew from radical feminists' attempts to structure relations among members, processes of decision making, and group leadership in a way that reflected or prefigured the values and goals of the movement (Rothschild-Whitt 1979; Breines 1982). Feminist collectivist organizations made decisions by consensus, rotated leadership and other tasks among members, and shared skills to avoid hierarchy and specialization. Such groups often failed to meet their ideals and did, in fact, spawn unacknowledged hierarchies

(Freeman 1972/3). Nevertheless, the conscious effort to build a feminist collective structure has had a lasting impact on the women's movement and has led to the growth of a social movement community (Buechler 1990). That is, the movement consists of not only formal organizations but also more informally organized communities, made up of networks of people who share the movement's political goals and outlook and work toward common aims. The collectivist branch of the women's movement initially sparked the growth of a feminist social movement community in which alternative structures guided by a distinctively feminist women's culture flourished—including bookstores, theater groups, music collectives, poetry groups, art collectives, publishing and recording companies, spirituality groups, vacation resorts, self-help groups, and a variety of feminist-run businesses. This "women's culture," though it includes feminists of diverse political persuasions, has been largely maintained by lesbian feminists. It nurtures a feminist collective identity that is important to the survival of the women's movement as a whole (Taylor and Whittier 1992; Taylor and Rupp 1993).

Both bureaucratic organizations working within mainstream politics and the alternative feminist culture have expanded and converged since the movement's emergence in the 1960s. Organizations such as NOW and NARAL incorporated some of the innovations of collectivism, including consciousness-raising groups, modified consensus decision making, and the use of direct-action tactics and civil disobedience. A host of structural variations emerged, including formally structured groups that use consensus decision making, organizations with deliberately democratic structures, and groups that officially operate by majority-rule democracy but in practice make most decisions by consensus (Staggenborg 1988, 1989; Martin 1990; Ryan 1992; Taylor 1996). At the same time, feminist collectives shifted their focus from consciousness-raising and radical feminist critique to the development of feminist self-help and service organizations such as rape crisis centers, shelters for battered women, job training programs for displaced homemakers, and lesbian peer counseling groups. Moreover, many feminist collectives revised their structure to depend less on consensus decision making and to permit specialization of skills. The widespread acceptance of the feminist analysis of rape as an act of violence and power rather than a strictly sexual act further attested to the impact of the feminist antirape movement. Feminist antirape groups received financial support from government agencies and private foundations to provide rape-prevention and treatment services in public schools and universities (Matthews 1994). The distinction between "working outside the system" and "working within the system," so important in the late 1960s, no longer had the same significance.

In conjunction with the ideological shift from a universal to a differentiated category of "woman," the structures of the women's movement diversified as well. Although individual women of color and working-class women had participated in the founding of NOW and in the early protests against sexism in the civil rights movement, the women's movement attracted primarily white middle-class women. Not that women of color and working-class or poor women experienced no oppression as women or opposed feminist goals. A 1989 *New York Times*/CBS News poll revealed that, while only 64 percent of white women saw a need for a women's movement, 85 percent of African-American women and 76 percent of Hispanic women thought the women's movement was needed (Sapiro 1991). Yet the feminist movement remained predominantly white both because it continued to define its goals based on the concerns of white middle-class women and because many Black women and other women of color placed a priority on working in their own racial communities to advance their collective interests, despite the recognition of sexism within such organizations (Barnett 1993; Robnett 1996).

Independent organizing by women of color did grow during the 1970s, and when African-American activists in the women's movement formed the National Black Feminist Organization in 1973 it grew to a membership of 1,000 within its first year (Deckard 1983). In the 1980s and 1990s, independent feminist organizations and networks of women of color such as the National Black Women's Health Project and the National Coalition of 100 Black Women emerged. Women of color also formed active caucuses within predominantly white feminist organizations, such as the National Women's Studies Association, to work against racism within the women's movement (Leidner 1993). Likewise, Jewish women, who had historically played important roles within the women's movement, organized their own groups in the 1980s and spoke out against antisemitism within the movement (Beck 1980; Bulkin, Pratt, and Smith 1984). Some scholars have argued that the Black feminist movement generally does not mobilize through institutionalized formal organizations but operates through informal networks in local communities. Such informal networks include self-help groups, book clubs, "girlfriend" (women-only) parties and gatherings, and explicitly political groups. For example, in the 1990s, after the much publicized appeal of convicted rapist and professional boxer Mike Tyson one such informal network served as a springboard to launch an antirape education program geared to the Black community (White 1999).

Union women played a significant role in the formation of NOW in 1966 by providing office space and clerical services until NOW's endorsement of the ERA in 1967 forced the women of the United Auto Workers, an organization that at the time opposed the ERA, to withdraw such support. Women committed to both feminism and the union movement, like women of color, formed their own organization, the Coalition of Labor Union Women (CLUW) in 1974 (Balser 1987). CLUW claimed 16,000 members by 1982 and had made progress in its fight to win AFL-CIO support for feminist issues. Union women also participated in deeply gendered ways in labor movement activity such as the 1985 Wheeling-Pittsburgh Steel strike, both affirming and challenging gender (Fonow 1998). The basic class and race composition of the movement may have changed little throughout the 1970s and 1980s, but by the beginning of the twenty-first century "a movement that began as unconsciously class-bound and race-bound has now become consciously class-bound and race-bound" (Buechler 1990:158).

Collective action by the women's movement has created new institutions and moved into almost every major institution of our society. However, in direct proportion to the successes of the women's movement, a countermovement successfully reversed some feminist gains, stalled progress on others, and changed the face of the women's movement.

The Antifeminist Political Context

The early 1980s saw a rapid decrease in the number of feminist organizations and a transformation in the form and activities of the women's movement. In part, this was a response to the successes of the New Right: so powerful were antifeminist sentiments and forces that members of the Republican party were elected in 1980 on a platform developed explicitly to "put women back in their place." After forty years of faithful support of the ERA, the Republican party dropped it from its platform, called for a constitutional amendment to ban abortion, and aligned itself with the economic and social policies of the New Right. After the election of the conservative Reagan administration in 1980, federal funds and grants were rarely available to feminist service organizations, and because other social service organizations were also hard hit by budget cuts, competition increased for relatively scarce money from private foundations. As a result, many feminist programs such as rape crisis centers, shelters for battered women, abortion clinics, and job training programs were forced to close or limit their services.

The failure of the ERA in 1982 seemed to reflect the changed political climate and set the stage for other setbacks throughout the 1980s. Abortion rights, won in 1973 with the Supreme Court's decision in *Roe v. Wade,* were curtailed in 1989 by the Supreme Court's decision in *Webster v. Reproductive Services* permitting states to enact restrictions on abortion (Staggenborg 1991: 137–38). Following the *Webster* decision, state governments set increasingly tight restrictions on abortion, ranging from "informed consent" laws that required a waiting period before women could obtain abortion surgery, to parental consent laws for underage women, to outright bans on abortion unless the woman's life was in danger. In 1991, the Supreme Court further limited abortion rights by ruling that federally funded family planning clinics could be barred from providing information on abortion. The antiabortion movement also escalated and hardened its tactics in the late 1980s and 1990s: it bombed abortion clinics, picketed doctors who performed abortions, and attempted to dissuade women entering clinics from having abortions (Staggenborg 1991; Simonds 1996).

Further, women's studies programs in colleges and universities, which had been established in the 1970s in response to feminist agitation, came under attack by conservatives in the late 1980s and early 1990s. A backlash against "multiculturalism" and "political correctness" in academia sought to restore the traditional academic focus on the "great thinkers" of Western European history and thus to maintain the primacy of white male perspectives and experiences. Joining the attack, feminists such as Camille Paglia, Katie Roiphe, and Elizabeth Fox-Genovese drew media attention by holding radical and lesbian feminists responsible for alienating mainstream women and men from the women's movement.

The women's movement suffered not only from such attacks but also from its apparent success. Overt opposition to the feminist movement had been muted in the mid- to late 1970s. Elites in politics, education, and industry gave the appearance of supporting feminist aims through affirmative action programs and the appointment of a few token women to high positions in their respective areas. Meanwhile, the popular image of feminism advanced by the mass media suggested that the women's movement had won its goals. Despite the real-life difficulties women encountered trying to balance paid employment and a "second shift" of housework and child care (Hochschild 1989), the image of the working woman became the feminine ideal. The public discourse implied that since women had already achieved equality with men, they no longer needed a protest movement. Women who continued to press for gender equality were described increasingly in negative terms, as lesbians, man-haters, and, in the words of right-wing talk show host Rush Limbaugh, "feminazis."

But the women's movement did not die. Rather, it went into abeyance in order to survive in a hostile political climate. Movements in abeyance are in a holding pattern, during which activists from an earlier period maintain the ideology and structural base of the movement but few new recruits join (Taylor 1989). A movement in abeyance is primarily oriented toward maintaining itself rather than confronting the established order directly. Focusing on building an alternative culture, for example, is a means of surviving when external resources are not available and the political structure is not amenable to challenge. The structure and strategies of the women's movement have changed, then, as mass mobilization has declined and opposition to feminism has swelled. Nevertheless, feminist resistance continues—just in different forms.

Multiple Strategies and the Challenge to Gender

Gender resistance, challenge, and change can occur at three levels: the individual level of consciousness and interactions, the social structural level, and the cultural level (Collins 1990). This conceptualization of feminist activism allows us to recognize that movements adopt many strategies and to acknowledge the important role of women's movements in the reconstruction of gender.

Resisting Gender Practices   At the level of consciousness and social interactions, individual women can and do resist norms and expectations of the dominant gender system (Thorne 1994, 1995). It is, however, social movements or collectives, rather than isolated individuals, who perform the critical role of refashioning the gender code and calling institutions to account for

gender inequality (Huber 1976; Chafetz 1990; Connell 1987). One of the primary goals of the modern feminist movement has been to change the unequal power relations between women and men. A general strategy used by feminists to achieve this goal has been to resist and challenge sexist practices within a diverse set of social contexts, ranging from heterosexual marriage to the gender division of labor in rearing and nurturing children to the gendered workplace and male-dominated medical establishment.

The formation of consciousness-raising groups facilitated the process of resisting and challenging gender practices and politicizing everyday life. Because consciousness-raising enables women to view the "personal as political," for most women it is an identity-altering experience. Becoming a feminist can transform a woman's entire self-concept and way of life: her biography, appearance, beliefs, behavior, and relationships (Cassell 1977; Esterberg 1997). As women's consciousness changes through personalized political strategies, women individually and collectively defy traditionally feminine role expectations for women and, in so doing, reconstruct the meanings of women, femininity, and interpersonal relationships between women and men. For example, some breast cancer activists have chosen to resist societal conceptions of femininity that link women's sexuality to breast beauty by refusing to wear prostheses or displaying mastectomy scars following breast surgery.

Women active in the feminist movement of the 1960s and 1970s continued to shape their lives in the 1980s and 1990s around their feminist beliefs, even when they were not involved in organized feminist activity. They continued to choose leisure activities, significant relationships, dress, and presentation of self consistent with feminist ideology (Whittier 1995). Many held jobs in government, social service organizations, or women's studies departments and other academic programs that allowed them to incorporate their political goals into their work. Even the consciousness and lives of women who did not identify as feminist have been altered by the women's movement. In a study of gender and family life in the Silicon Valley of California, Judith Stacey (1987) found that in the 1980s some women incorporated portions of feminism into traditional family and work structures by combining a feminist emphasis on developing satisfying careers, sharing household work with husbands, and increasing men's emotional expressiveness with fundamentalist Christianity and its focus on the importance of the family. Such women critiqued men's absence from families and lack of emotional expression, reflecting both feminism and traditional religion. The effects of the women's movement stretch far beyond policies and practices that are explicitly labeled feminist.

Another example of women resisting gender practices at the interactional level is found among young African-American women involved in little sister fraternity programs on college campuses in the 1990s. Such women embrace a collective identity built on notions of sisterhood and womanly strength to challenge the sexist practices of fraternities (Stombler and Padavic 1997). Further, these women use the fraternity little sister program to satisfy their own agendas of community service and self-enhancement. Even within the most traditional male-dominated organizations, then, gender relations are not immutable and women are employing diverse strategies to resist gender inequality.

Challenging the Structure of Gender Inequality   The challenge to gender inequality and the dominant gender order is also waged at the social structural level. As we have seen, the liberal bureaucratic strand of the modern feminist movement has employed legal reform strategies and engaged in street protests to counter sex discrimination in the economic, education, political, and domestic spheres. The legislative campaigns for equal pay for work of comparable worth and for maternity leave policies in the workplace challenge institutions that essentialize differences between women and men and rank "masculine" values and attributes above those identified as "feminine" (Vogel 1993). The women's movement has created a feminist policy network of elected officials, lobbying organizations, social movement organizations, and individuals who have mobilized to address issues ranging from abortion rights, domestic violence, and pregnancy discrimination to day care, sexual harassment, and welfare rights (Ferree and Hess 1994; Staggenborg 1996; Gagné 1998).

As part of its legislative or legal strategies, the modern feminist movement has engaged in street protests such as picketing, mass demonstrations, and civil disobedience. Even within the conservative political climate of the 1980s, the feminist movement sparked some of the largest feminist demonstrations and actions in years. In April 1989, The National Organization for Women and abortion rights groups organized a national demonstration in Washington, DC, that drew between 300,000 and 600,000 women and men to protest restrictions on abortion. Additional national and local demonstrations followed. Prochoice activists organized

electoral lobbying, defended abortion clinics, held conferences, and attempted to form coalitions across racial and ethnic lines and among women of different ages (Staggenborg 1991; Ryan 1992). The National Abortion Rights Action League experienced a growth in membership from 200,000 in 1989 to 400,000 in 1990 (Staggenborg 1991:138). NOW also continued to grow in the late 1980s and 1990s. After a decline in the early 1980s, it reached a membership of 250,000 in 1989 and maintained that membership level throughout the 1990s.

A wide variety of feminist organizations continued to pursue social change at state and local levels in the late 1990s (Ferree and Martin 1995). The Lesbian Avengers, a direct-action group founded in the 1990s with affiliates in several large cities, uses dramatic street theater to focus on issues of sexism and homophobia. For example, outside a police station in Delaware, Lesbian Avengers protested the police department's lack of action to catch a serial rapist by drawing chalk outlines of bodies on the sidewalk to represent women who had been raped during the past year. Veteran feminist organizations, such as NOW, continued to hold public protests in the late 1990s. For instance, in 1999, NOW chapters across the country staged pickets outside Wal-Mart retail stores to protest the corporation's refusal to sell the emergency contraception kit PREVEN to those who wish to prevent unintended pregnancies.

Beyond street politics, feminist activism in the 1980s and 1990s moved into diverse institutional settings. As an indication of the success and influence of feminist mobilization in earlier years, women found niches from which to challenge and transform institutional policies and structures, from pay equity to sexual harassment to occupational sex segregation (Blum 1991). Women in the military, for example, have formed pressure groups such as Women Military Aviators, who fought for the opening up of combat aviation positions for women. In the Catholic Church, radical religious orders have become protected spaces for women who challenge hierarchy within the institutional church (Katzenstein 1998). In major corporations, feminists have joined with gay activists to campaign successfully for domestic partnership benefits for lesbian and gay employees. Such unobtrusive mobilization within institutional boundaries refutes the notion of the death of feminism (Katzenstein 1997). Although the form and location of feminist protest have changed, this does not mean the women's movement has been deradicalized. The transformative potential of feminist activism within institutional settings may in some contexts be greater than that of pressure from outside.

Reconstructing the Culture of Gender At the cultural level, the feminist social movement community has challenged cultural values, beliefs, and norms around gender and the gender order through building alternative social and cultural institutions for women outside mainstream institutions. The strategy of creating autonomous institutions is rooted in radical feminist ideology, which emphasizes that women need to have places and events away from patriarchal society where they can develop strength and pride as women. Since the early years of the women's movement, an extensive network of institutions has emerged within which a feminist culture flourishes (Taylor and Whittier 1992). Feminist communities contribute to the reconstruction of the culture of gender by challenging the devaluation of the feminine and undermining androcentric values and beliefs at the same time that they rearticulate alternative femininities and woman-centered values and beliefs (Taylor and Rupp 1993).

Into the new century, the feminist cultural community has continued to thrive with events such as an "annual multicultural multiracial conference on aging" for lesbians (*Off Our Backs* 1991:12), feminist cruises, annual women's music festivals, and women's comedy festivals in different parts of the country (Staggenborg 1998b). Gatherings and conferences include groups such as Jewish lesbian daughters of holocaust survivors, women motorcyclists, fat dykes, pagans, Asian lesbians, practitioners of herbal medicine, and survivors of incest. Newsletters and publications exist for a multitude of groups, among them women recovering from addictions, women's music professionals and fans, lesbian separatists, disabled lesbians, lesbian mothers, feminists interested in sadomasochism, and feminists opposed to pornography.

The growth of the feminist community underscores the flowering of lesbian feminism in the late 1980s and 1990s (Esterberg 1997; Stein 1997). A wide variety of lesbian and lesbian feminist books and anthologies have been published on topics ranging from lesbian feminist ethics to separatism to sexuality to lesbian parenthood to commitment ceremonies for lesbian couples (see, for example, Hoagland 1988; Hoagland and Penelope 1988; Loulan 1990; Butler 1991), reflecting diverse perspectives that have been hotly debated in the pages of lesbian publications and at conferences and festivals. For example, a series of letters to the editor in a national lesbian newsletter during 1991 argued about the correct lesbian feminist response to lesbians serving in the armed forces in the Persian Gulf War: some readers held

that the war was a manifestation of patriarchy and that lesbians in the military should be criticized; others argued that lesbian soldiers should be supported because they are lesbians in a homophobic institution, regardless of one's support of or opposition to the war; still others argued that the Gulf War was justified and that lesbian servicewomen should be celebrated for their patriotic service (*Lesbian Connection* 1991). Clearly, the task of building a community based on the identity "lesbian" has proven complex, if not impossible. Nevertheless, the institutional structure of the social movement community has continued to expand, and within the community feminists construct and reinforce a collective identity based on opposition to dominant conceptions of women and lesbians (Taylor and Whittier 1992).

Another example of resistance on the cultural level is the emergence of women's self-help groups, which sprang directly out of the early women's health movement and continue to model support groups on feminist consciousness-raising (Rapping 1996; Simonds 1996). Some feminist writers contend that women's self-help diverts the feminist agenda away from social and political change and directs women, instead, to change themselves (Kaminer 1992). Others argue that explicitly feminist self-help movements, such as strands of the postpartum depression and breast cancer movements, are contributing to the reconstruction of gender through the collective redefinition of womanhood and the cultural articulation of alternative femininities (Taylor 1996; Taylor and Van Willigen 1996; Klawiter 1999). These self-help movements are not depoliticized and purely individually focused; they perform a critical role of challenging institutional gender biases and refashioning the dominant gender code (Taylor 1996; Taylor 1999).

All of these diverse strategies, operating at different levels, challenge traditional societal definitions of femininity and masculinity and the dominant gender order. From the individual to the social structural to the cultural plane, we can see the continuous impact of the women's movement.

Movement Continuity and Change into the Twenty-first Century

Social movement scholars understand that social movements affect one another. The abolitionist movement in the mid-nineteenth century influenced the first wave of the women's movement in the United States, and the civil rights and New Left movements of the 1960s shaped the course of the second wave (Buechler 1990).

In turn, the women's movement has had a substantial impact on other social movements. Meyer and Whittier (1994) argue that "the ideas, tactics, style, participants, and organizations of one movement often *spill over* its boundaries to affect other social movements" (277, emphasis in the original). The gay and lesbian movement, transgender, AIDS, recovery from addictions, New Age, and animal-rights movements have been profoundly influenced by feminist values and ideology, including the emphasis on collective structure and consensus, the notion of the personal as political, and the critique of patriarchy extended to the mistreatment of animals and ecological resources (Jasper and Poulsen 1995; Einwohner 1999).

The women's movement also trained a large number of feminist activists in the 1970s (particularly lesbians), who have participated in new social movements and integrated feminism into them (Cavin 1990; Whittier 1995). The gay and lesbian movement, for example, has expanded its health concerns to include breast cancer as well as AIDS and has used strategies of the feminist antirape movement to confront violence against gays and lesbians. In addition, feminists have renewed coalitions with the peace, environmental, socialist, anti-US intervention in Latin America, and antiapartheid movements, transforming these movements both by creating separate feminist organizations that address these issues and by moving into mixed-sex organizations (Whittier 1995). In a sense the women's movement has come full circle, rejoining the 1990s versions of the movements that composed the New Left in the 1960s, when many feminists split off to form a separate autonomous women's movement.

Although the women's movement has changed form and location, the level of mass mobilization and confrontation of the social structural system has clearly declined since the 1980s. Because feminism came to focus more on consciousness and culture and established roots in other social movements of the period, feminist protest is less visible than it was during the heyday of the women's movement. According to some studies (Schneider 1988; Dill unpublished), despite support for feminist goals, many young women do not identify themselves as feminists, apparently because the term is stigmatized. A feminist is seen as someone who deviates from gender norms by being unattractive, aggressive, hostile to men, unfeminine, opposed to marriage and motherhood, and lesbian. Despite the gain made by women in some areas, gender norms are still so rigid and deeply internalized that they successfully deter many women who support the feminist agenda from participating in the movement.

Yet some younger women have joined the women's movement despite the risks entailed in identifying with a stigmatized and unpopular cause. A new generation of women has been recruited to feminism primarily through women's studies courses and through the transmission of feminism from mothers to daughters. The institutionalized gains of the heyday of feminist activism in the 1970s are enabling the women's movement to survive and to disseminate its ideas to new recruits. What direction the self-proclaimed "third-wave" feminists (Kamen 1991; Walker 1992, 1995) will take is not at all clear, but the history of the women's movement suggests that a new constituency will revise feminist ideology, renovate existing structures, respond to a changing political climate, and further develop feminist strategies.

ANTIFEMINIST COUNTERMOVEMENTS

The emergence of organized opposition is one indication of the successes of feminist movements. In general, it is when social movements pose a serious threat to the status quo that countermovements appear (Chafetz and Dworkin 1987). Antifeminist resistance movements mobilized in response to first- and second-wave feminist movements in the United States when feminists began to gain political legitimacy and influence. For example, as the first wave of the women's movement was building support for suffrage in the late nineteenth century, an organized antisuffrage movement began to coalesce (Marshall 1997). Likewise, when the feminist movement of the 1970s was gaining political ground on the ratification of the Equal Rights Amendment, an anti-ERA movement blossomed (Marshall 1984).

Antifeminist countermovements, like feminist movements, are not monolithic. They vary over time and place by ideology, strategy, and organization (Marshall 1985; Buechler 1990; Blee 1991). Chafetz and Dworkin (1987) contend that antifeminist countermovements are composed of two constituencies: vested-interest groups, which are typically male-dominated and oppose feminist change movements on the basis of class interests; and voluntary grassroots associations made up of women who are reacting to the threat to their status as privileged traditional women.

Compared to the scholarship on movements, countermovements have been understudied and undertheorized (Meyer and Staggenborg 1996). Research on organized opposition to feminism by women is also limited (Klatch 1990; Marshall 1997). Women's participation in antifeminist countermovements challenges the radical feminist notion that women are a "sex class" with clearly defined gender interests (Luker 1984; Blee 1991). Scholars often characterize antifeminist women as victims of false consciousness or as women who are passively expressing their husbands' interests. Marshall (1997) argues that these are overly simplistic interpretations and that an appreciation for the ways in which antisuffragist leaders used their wealth, social networks, and political power to build an oppositional identity in the antisuffrage movement suggests "a conceptual shift of the locus of conflict over suffrage from culture to politics" (p. 13). In this light, antifeminist women should be viewed as political actors who take up gendered class interests independently of their husbands (Marshall 1997).

The interaction between opposing movements is a prominent feature of contemporary US society. Any social movement analysis is incomplete without a consideration of the interdependence of movements and countermovements. For example, we cannot fully understand the tactics, strategies, organizational forms, and feminist identities characteristic of the feminist movement during the 1980s and 1990s without considering the effects of the antiabortion mobilization and the rise of the New Right.

The modern women's movement in the United States has been opposed by a variety of conservative antifeminist groups. In the early 1970s, the Stop ERA campaign initiated by Phyllis Schlafly fought to block passage of the ERA by state legislatures. Through the 1970s, the New Right grew larger and more influential, linking conservative issues like opposition to busing, abortion, gay rights, the ERA, and governmental regulation of business through affirmative action and health and safety programs (Klatch 1990). With the election of Ronald Reagan to the presidency in 1980, the New Right gained state support for its agenda.

The antifeminist movement in the late 1980s and 1990s spent considerable energy opposing abortion, and its successes in that area have been impressive in terms of judicial and legislative gains and disruptive demonstrations at abortion clinics (Staggenborg 1991; Simonds 1996). Over the years a number of aggressive splinter groups, such as Operation Rescue, developed out of the mainstream National Right to Life Committee, which originated within the Catholic Church. The murders of Drs. David Gunn in Pensacola, Florida, and Barnett Slepian in Buffalo, New York, are potent examples of the radical tactics advocated by some anti-abortion rights groups.

The prevalence of antifeminist resistance throughout history highlights the significance of the family, sexuality, and reproduction for the maintenance of the dominant social order. The growth of antifeminism, however, does not imply that the women's movement has failed or run its course. On the contrary, it attests to feminism's successful challenge to the status quo.

CONCLUSION

The history of the women's movement and its present survival, despite the challenges it has confronted from within its own ranks and from a conservative political climate, suggest that because feminism is a response to the fundamental social cleavage of gender it will continue to exist (Taylor and Rupp 1993). As one generation of feminists fades from the scene with its ultimate goals unrealized, another takes up the challenge (Rossi 1982).

But each new generation of feminists does not simply carry on where the previous generation left off. Rather, it speaks for itself and defines its own objectives and strategies, often to the dismay and disapproval of feminists from earlier generations. A new generation of feminists may organize a "warm line" for women suffering postpartum depression (Taylor 1996), or construct a public clothesline of T-shirts representing the victims of domestic violence to raise awareness of violence against women, or march together in a Take Back the Night event to empower survivors of sexual violence and reclaim the streets for women. They may put on "drag king" performances to challenge the restrictions placed on expressions of women's sexuality, or distribute condoms and dental dams to women for AIDS prevention, or organize "kiss-ins" with Queer Nation. While earlier generations of activists may not view such endeavors as feminist, as Myra Ferree and Beth Hess (1985:182) point out, "feminism is not simply a form of received wisdom" but something that evolves with each new cycle of feminist activism. Just as the women's movement of the twentieth century has endured and persisted through transformation, feminism of the twenty-first century will be characterized by continuity and change.

REFERENCES

Atkinson, T. G. (1974). *Amazon Odyssey.* New York: Links.

Balser, Diane. (1987). *Sisterhood and Solidarity: Feminism and Labor in Modern Times.* Boston: South End Press.

Barnett, Bernice McNair. (1993). Invisible southern black women leaders in the civil rights movement: The triple constraints of gender, race, and class. *Gender & Society, 7,* 162–182.

Basu, Amrita, ed. (1995). *The Challenge of Local Feminisms: Women's Movements in Global Perspective.* Boulder, CO: Westview Press.

Beauvoir, S. de. (1952). *The Second Sex.* New York: Bantam.

Beck, E. T. (1980). *Nice Jewish girls: A Lesbian Anthology.* Watertown, MA: Persephone.

Black, Naomi. (1989). *Social Feminism.* Ithaca, NY: Cornell University Press.

Blee, Kathleen M. (1991). *Women of the Klan: Racism and Gender in the 1920s.* Berkeley, CA: University of California Press.

Blum, Linda M. (1991). *Between Feminism and Labor: The Significance of the Comparable Worth Movement.* Berkeley, CA: University of California Press.

Breines, W. (1982). *Community and Organization in the New Left, 1962–68.* New York: Praeger.

Buechler, Steven M. (1990). *Women's Movements in the United States.* New Brunswick, NJ: Rutgers.

Bulkin, Elly, Minnie Bruce Pratt, & Barbara Smith. (1984). *Yours in Struggle: Three Feminist Perspectives on Anti-Semitism and Racism.* New York: Long Haul Press.

Butler, Becky. (1991). *Ceremonies of the Heart: Celebrating Lesbian Unions.* Seattle, WA: The Seal Press.

Carden, Maren. (1978). The proliferation of a social movement. In Louis Kriesberg, ed., *Research in Social Movements, Conflict, and Change,* vol. 1 (pp. 179–196). Greenwich, CT: JAI Press.

Cassell, J. (1977). *A Group Called Women: Sisterhood and Symbolism in the Feminist Movement.* New York: David McKay.

Cavin, Susan. (1990). The invisible army of women: Lesbian social protests, 1969–88. In Guida West & Rhoda Blumberg, eds. *Women and Social Protest* (pp. 321–332). New York: Oxford University Press.

Chafe, W. H. (1977). *Women and Equality: Changing Patterns in American Culture.* New York: Oxford University Press.

Chafetz, Janet. (1990). *Gender Equity: An Integrated Theory of Stability and Change.* Newbury Park, CA: Sage.

Chafetz, Janet, & Gary Dworkin. (1986). *Female Revolt.* Totowa, NJ: Rowman and Allenheld.

———. (1987). In the face of threat: Organized antifeminism in comparative perspective. *Gender & Society, 1,* 33–60.

Collins, Patricia Hill. (1990). *Black Feminist Thought.* New York: Routledge.

Cornell, R. W. (1987). *Gender and Power.* Stanford, CA: Stanford University Press.

Cott, Nancy. (1987). *The Grounding of Modern Feminism.* New Haven, CT: Yale University Press.

Daly, Mary. (1978). *Gyn/ecology.* Boston: Beacon.

Deckard, Barbara Sinclair. (1983). *The Women's Movement.* New York: Harper and Row.

Dill, Kim. Unpublished. "Feminism in the nineties: The influence of collective identity and community on young feminist activists." Master's thesis, The Ohio State University, 1991.

Echols, Alice. (1989). *Daring to Be Bad: Radical Feminism in America 1967–1975.* Minneapolis: University of Minnesota Press.

Einwohner, Rachel L. (1999). Gender, class, and social movement outcomes: Identity and effectiveness in two animal rights campaigns. *Gender & Society, 13,* 56–76.

Eisenstein, Z. (1981). *The Radical Future of Liberal Feminism.* New York: Longman.

Esterberg, Kristin G. (1997). *Lesbian and Bisexual Identities: Constructing Communities, Constructing Selves.* Philadelphia: Temple University Press.

Evans, Sarah. (1979). *Personal Politics.* New York: Knopf.

Ferree, Myra Marx, & Beth B. Hess. [1985] (1994). *Controversy and Coalition: The New Feminist Movement.* Boston: Twayne.

Ferree, Myra Marx, & Patricia Yancey Martin. (1995). *Feminist Organizations: Harvest of the New Women's Movement.* Philadelphia: Temple University Press.

Firestone, S. (1970). *The Dialectic of Sex.* New York: William Morrow.

Fonow, Mary Margaret. (1998). Protest engendered: The participation of women steelworkers in the Wheeling-Pittsburgh steel strike of 1985. *Gender & Society, 12,* 710–728.

Freeman, Jo. (1972/3). The tyranny of structurelessness. *Berkeley Journal of Sociology, 17,* 151–164.

———. (1975). *The Politics of Women's Liberation.* New York: David McKay.

———. (1979). Resource mobilization and strategy: A model for analyzing social movement organization actions. In M. N. Zald & J. D. McCarthy, eds. *The Dynamics of Social Movements* (pp. 167–89). Cambridge, MA: Winthrop.

Frye, Marilyn. (1983). *The Politics of Reality: Essays in Feminist Theory.* Trumansburg, NY: Crossing Press.

Gagné, Patricia. (1998). *Battered Women's Justice: The Movement for Democracy and the Politics of Self-defense.* New York: Twayne Publishers.

Gerlach, L. P., & V. H. Hine. (1970). *People, Power, Change: Movements of Social Transformation.* Indianapolis: Bobbs-Merrill.

Giele, Janet Zollinger. (1995). *Two Paths to Women's Equality: Temperance, Suffrage, and the Origins of Modern Feminism.* New York: Twayne Publishers.

Gordon, Suzanne. (1991). *Prisoners of Men's Dreams.* New York: Little, Brown.

Griffin, S. (1978). *Women and Nature.* New York: Harper & Row.

Hartmann, Heidi. (1981). The family as the locus of gender, class, and political struggle: The example of housework. *Signs, 6,* 366–394.

Hartsock, Nancy. (1983). *Money, Sex, and Power: Toward a Feminist Historical Materialism.* New York: Longman.

Hoagland, Sarah Lucia. (1988). *Lesbian Ethics: Toward New Value.* Palo Alto, CA: Institute of Lesbian Studies.

Hoagland, Sarah Lucia, & Julia Penelope, eds. (1988). *For Lesbians Only.* London: Onlywomen Press.

Hochschild, Arlie. (1989). *The Second Shift.* New York: Avon.

Huber, Joan. (1973). From sugar and spice to professor. In A. S. Rossi & A. Calderwood, *Academic Women on the Move.* New York: Russell Sage Foundation.

———. (1976). Toward a sociotechnological theory of the women's movement. *Social Problems,* 23, 371–388.

Huber, Joan, & Glenna Spike. (1983). *Sex Stratification: Children, Housework, and Jobs.* New York: Academic.

Jasper, James M., & Jane D. Poulsen. (1995). Recruiting strangers and friends: Moral shocks and social networks in animal rights and anti-nuclear protests. *Social Problems,* 42, 493–512.

Jayawardena, Kumari. (1986). *Feminism and Nationalism in the Third World.* London: Zed Books.

Kamen, Paula. (1991). *Feminist Fatale: Voices from the "Twenty-something" Generation Explore the Future of the Women's Movement.* New York: Donald I. Fine.

Kaminer, Wendy. (1992). *I'm Dysfunctional, You're Dysfunctional: The Recovery Movement and Other Self-help Fashions.* Reading, MA: Addison-Wesley.

Katzenstein, Mary Fainsod. (1997). Stepsisters: Feminist movement activism in different institutional spaces. In David Meyer & Sidney Tarrow, eds. *A Movement Society? Contentious Politics for a New Century.* Boulder, CO. Rowland and Littlefield.

———. (1998). *Faithful and Fearless: Moving Feminist Protest inside the Church and Military.* Princeton, NJ: Princeton University Press.

Katzenstein, Mary Fainsod, & Carol McClurg Mueller. (1987). *The Women's Movements of the United States and Western Europe.* Philadelphia: Temple University Press.

Klatch, Rebecca. (1990). The two worlds of women of the new right. In Louise A. Tilly & Patricia Gurin, eds. *Women, Politics and Change.* New York: Russell Sage Foundation.

Klawiter, Maren. (1999). Racing for the Cure, walking women, and toxic touring: Mapping cultures of action within the Bay Area terrain of breast cancer. *Social Problems,* 46, 104–126.

Klein, Ethel. (1984). *Gender Politics.* Cambridge, MA: Harvard University Press.

Leidner, Robin. (1993). Constituency, accountability, and deliberation: Reshaping democracy in the National Women's Studies Association. *NWSA Journal,* 5, 4–27.

Lesbian Connection. (1991). Vols. 13 & 14. Lansing, MI: Ambitious Amazons.

Loulan, JoAnn. (1990). *The Lesbian Erotic Dance.* San Francisco: Spinsters Book Company.

Luker, Kristin. (1984). *Abortion and the Politics of Motherhood.* Berkeley: University of California Press.

MacKinnon, C. A. (1983). Feminism, Marxism, method, and the state: Toward feminist jurisprudence. *Signs,* 8, 635–668.

Mansbridge, Jane. (1986). *Why We Lost the ERA.* Chicago: University of Chicago Press.

Marshall, Susan E. (1984). Keep us on the pedestal: Women against feminism in twentieth-century America. In Jo Freeman, ed., *Women: A Feminist Perspective* (pp. 568–581). Palo Alto: Mayfield.

———. (1985). Ladies against women: Mobilization dilemmas of antifeminist movements. *Social Problems,* 32, 348–362.

———. (1997). *Splintered Sisterhood: Gender and Class in the Campaign against Woman Suffrage.* Madison, WI: The University of Wisconsin Press.

Martin, Patricia Yancey. (1990). Rethinking feminist organizations. *Gender & Society,* 4, 182–206.

Marx, G. T., & J. L. Wood. (1975). Strands of theory and research in collective behavior. *Annual Review of Sociology,* 1, 363–428.

Matthews, Nancy. (1994). *Confronting Rape: The Feminist Anti-rape Movement and the State.* London: Routledge.

Matthews, Donald G., & Jane Sheffon DeHart. (1990). *Sex, Gender and the Politics of ERA: A State and the Nation.* New York: Oxford.

McCarthy, J. D., & M. N. Zald. (1977). Resource mobilization and social movements: A partial theory. *American Journal of Sociology,* 82, 1212–1239.

Meyer, David S., & Nancy Whittier. (1994). Social movement spillover. *Social Problems,* 41, 277–298.

Meyer, David S., & Suzanne Staggenborg. (1996). Movements, countermovements, and the structure of political opportunity. *American Journal of Sociology,* 101, 1628–1660.

Miles, Angela. (1996). *Integrative Feminisms: Building Global Visions, 1960s–1990s.* New York: Routledge.

Millett, K. (1971). *Sexual Politics.* New York: Avon.

Mitchell, Juliet. (1986). Reflections on twenty years of feminism. In Juliet Mitchell & Ann Oakley, eds. *What Is Feminism?* (pp. 34–48). Oxford: Basil Blackwell.

Mohanty, Chandra Talpade, Ann Russo, & Lordes Torres, eds. (1991). *Third World Women and the Politics of Feminism.* Bloomington, IN: Indiana University Press.

Moraga, Cherríe & Gloria Anzaldúa. (1981). *This Bridge Called My Back: Writings by Radical Women of Color.* Watertown, MA: Persephone.

Morris, Aldon D., & Carol McClurg Mueller, eds. (1992). *Frontiers in Social Movement Theory.* New Haven, CT: Yale University Press.

Naples, Nancy A. (1992). Activist mothering: Cross-generational continuity in the community work of women from low-income neighborhoods. *Gender & Society,* 6, 441–463.

Off Our Backs (1991). Passages 7—Beyond the barriers. Vol. 21 (6), 12.

Offen, Karen. (1988). Defining feminism: A comparative historical approach. *Signs,* 14, 119–157.

Oppenheimer, Valerie Kincade. (1973). Demographic influence on female employment and the status of women. In Joan Huber, ed. *Changing Women in a Changing Society* (pp. 184–199). Chicago: University of Chicago Press.

Rapping Elayne. (1996). *The Culture of Recovery: Making Sense of the Recovery Movement in Women's Lives.* Boston: Beacon Press.

Ray, Raka. (1999). *Fields of Protest: Women's Movements in India.* Minneapolis: University of Minnesota Press.

Rich, Adrienne. (1976). *Of Woman Born.* New York: Norton.

———. (1980). Compulsory heterosexuality and lesbian existence. *Signs,* 5, 631–660.

Robnett, Belinda. (1996). African-American women in the civil rights movement, 1954–1965: Gender, leadership, and micro-mobilization. *American Journal of Sociology,* 101, 1661–1693.

Rossi, Alice S. (1982). *Feminist in Politics: A Panel Analysis of the First National Women's Conference.* New York: Academic Press.

Rothschild-Whitt, Joyce. (1979). The collectivist organization: An alternative to rational-bureaucratic models. *American Sociological Review,* 44, 509–527.

Rubin, G. (1975). "Traffic in women: Notes on the 'political economy' of sex." In *Toward an Anthropology of Women,* Rayne Reiter, ed. New York: Monthly Review Press.

Rupp, Leila J. (1997). *Worlds of Women: The Making of an International Women's Movement.* Princeton, NJ: Princeton University Press.

Rupp, Leila J., & Verta Taylor. (1987). *Survival in the Doldrums: The American Women's Rights Movement, 1945 to 1960s.* New York: Oxford University Press.

Ryan, Barbara. (1989). Ideological purity and feminism: The U.S. women's movement from 1966 to 1975. *Gender & Society,* 3, 239–257.

———. (1992). *Feminism and the Women's Movement.* New York: Routledge.

Sapiro, V. (1991). In Janet Boles, ed. *The Annals of the American Academy of Political and Social Science,* May, 515.

Schlesinger, M. B., & P. Bart. (1983). Collective work and self-identity: The effect of working in a feminist illegal abortion collective. In L. Richardson & V. Taylor, eds. *Feminist Frontiers.* Reading, MA: Addison-Wesley.

Schneider, Beth. (1988). Political generations in the contemporary women's movement. *Sociological Inquiry,* 58, 4–21.

Simonds, Wendy. (1996). *Abortion at Work: Ideology and Practice in a Feminist Clinic.* New Brunswick, NJ: Rutgers University Press.

Spelman, Elizabeth. (1988). *Inessential Woman: Problems of Exclusion in Feminist Thought.* Boston: Beacon Press.

Stacey, Judith. (1987). Sexism by a subtler name? Postindustrial conditions and postfeminist consciousness. *Socialist Review,* 17, 7–28.

Staggenborg, Suzanne. (1988). The consequences of professionalization and formalization in the pro-choice movement. *American Sociological Review,* 53, 585–606.

———. (1989). Stability and innovation in the women's movement: A comparison of two movement organizations. *Social Problems,* 36, 75–92.

———. (1991). *The Pro-choice Movement.* New York: Oxford University Press.

———. (1996). The survival of the women's movement: Turnover and continuity in Bloomington, Indiana. *Mobilization,* 1, 143–158.

———. (1998a). *Gender, Family, and Social Movements.* Thousand Oaks, CA: Pine Forge Press.

———. (1998b). Social movement communities and cycles of protest: The emergence and maintenance of a local women's movement. *Social Problems,* 45, 180–204.

Stein, Arlene. (1997). *Sex and Sensibility: Stories of a Lesbian Generation.* Berkeley, CA: University of California Press.

Stombler, Mindy, & Irene Padavic. (1997). Sister acts: Resisting men's domination in black and white fraternity little sister programs. *Social Problems,* 44, 257–275.

Taylor, Verta. (1989). Social movement continuity: The women's movement in abeyance. *American Sociological Review,* 54, 761–775.

———. (1996). *Rock-a-by Baby: Feminism, Self-help, and Postpartum Depression.* New York: Routledge.

———. (1999). Gender and social movements: Gender processes and women's self-help movements. *Gender & Society,* 13, 8–33.

Taylor, Verta, & Leila Rupp. (1993). Women's culture and lesbian feminist activism: A reconsideration of cultural feminism. *Signs,* 19, 32–61.

Taylor, Verta, & Marieke Van Willigen. (1996). Women's self-help and the reconstruction of gender: The postpartum support and breast cancer movements. *Mobilization: An International Journal,* 2, 123–142.

Taylor, Verta, & Nancy Whittier. (1992). Collective identity in social movement communities: Lesbian feminist mobilization. In Aldon Morris & Carol Mueller, eds. *Frontiers of Social Movement Theory.* New Haven, CT: Yale University Press.

Thorne, Barrie. (1994). *Gender Play: Girls and Boys in School.* New Brunswick, NJ: Rutgers University Press.

———. (1995). Symposium on West and Fenstermaker's "Doing Difference." *Gender & Society,* 9, 498–499.

Vogel, Lise. (1993). *Mothers on the Job: Maternity Policy in the U.S. Workplace.* New Brunswick, NJ: Rutgers University Press.

Walker, Rebecca. (1992). Becoming the third wave. *Ms.,* 2 (January/February), 39–41.

———. (1995). *To Be Real: Telling the Truth and Changing the Face of Feminism.* New York: Anchor.

White, Aaronette M. (1999). Talking feminist, talking back: Micromobilization processes in a collective protest against rape. *Gender & Society,* 13, 77–100.

Whittier, Nancy E. (1995). *Feminist Generations: The Persistence of the Radical Women's Movement.* Philadelphia: Temple University Press.

Feminists or "Postfeminists"? Young Women's Attitudes toward Feminism and Gender Relations

A late 1990s cover of *Time* magazine with the caption "Is feminism dead?" featured photos of prominent feminist activists, including one of the flighty television lawyer character, Ally McBeal (Bellafante 1998). Such media pronouncements of the "death" of feminism rest on widespread presumptions that young women do not appreciate gains made by the women's movement, are not concerned about discrimination, and do not support feminism. These suppositions have rarely been tested.

How do young women view their own opportunities and obstacles, particularly when compared to those faced by women of their mothers' generation? How do they perceive and experience gender discrimination? How do they identify themselves with respect to feminism, and how can we make sense of their seemingly contradictory perspectives? Finally, what are the impacts of racial and class background and life experience on attitudes toward feminism? Although prior studies have considered aspects of these questions, my research examines them through interviews with a diverse sample. This diversity reveals the importance not only of race and class, but also life experience, in the development of attitudes toward feminism. Furthermore,

Author's note: This research was supported by a National Research Service Award from the National Institute of Mental Health (Training Program in Identity, Self, Role, and Mental Health—PHST 32 MH 14588), the National Institute of Mental Health (MH 42843, Jeylan T. Mortimer, principal investigator), the Personal Narratives Award from the Center for Advanced Feminist Studies, University of Minnesota, and a Graduate School Block Grant Stipend Award from the Department of Sociology, University of Minnesota. The author would like to thank a number of people who provided comments and suggestions on earlier versions of this article: Ronald Aronson, Christine Bose, Donna Eder, Debbie Engelen-Eigles, Amy Kaler, Barbara Laslett, Jane McLeod, Jeylan T. Mortimer, Irene Padavic, Katie See, Beth Schneider, and Kim Simmons, as well as the social psychology seminar members at Indiana University and several anonymous reviewers.

by not imposing a set definition of feminism but letting it emerge from the interviewees themselves, my study reveals great ambiguity in the meanings of feminism today and suggests that we need to rethink some of the assumptions about young women's identities.

LITERATURE REVIEW: GROWING UP IN THE SHADOW OF THE WOMEN'S MOVEMENT[1]

Since the mid-1980s, 30 to 40 percent of women have called themselves feminists, and by 1990, nearly 80 percent favored efforts to "strengthen and change women's status in society" (Marx Ferree and Hess 1995, 88). Although the media often question why so few women call themselves feminists, Marx Ferree and Hess (1995) pointed out that the number of women who do so represents the same percentage of people who label themselves as Republicans or Democrats. Addressing the same concerns, Gurin (1985, 1987) distinguished between four components of gender consciousness: identification (recognizing women's shared interests), discontent (recognizing women's lack of power), assessment of legitimacy (seeing gender disparities as illegitimate), and collective orientation (believing in collective action). Although women historically have become more critical of men's claims to power, women's gender consciousness has been weaker than the group consciousness of African Americans, the working class, and the elderly. At the same time, women, especially employed women, are often conscious of women's structural disadvantage in the labor market (Gurin 1985). However, an average woman may have somewhat vague understandings of political labels such as "feminism," as activists and political elites are generally more consistent and coherent in their positions (Converse 1964; Unger 1989).

In the early 1980s, the media began to label women in their teens and twenties as the "postfeminist" generation[2] (Bellafante 1998; Bolotin 1982; Whittier 1995). Twenty years later, the term continues to be applied to young women, who are thought to benefit from the women's movement through expanded access to employment and education and new family arrangements but at the same time do not push for further political change. Postfeminism has been the subject of considerable debate, since its usage connotes the "death" of feminism and because the equality it assumes is largely a myth (Coppock, Haydon, and Richter 1995; Overholser 1986; Rosenfelt and Stacey 1987; Whittier 1995). The term has been used by researchers to reflect the current cycle and stage of the women's movement (Taylor 1989; Taylor and Rupp 1993; Whittier 1995). Indeed, Rossi (1982) has written of a cyclical generational pattern in the women's movement, with each feminist wave separated by roughly fifty years, or two generations. "Quiet periods" (Rossi 1982, 9) see diminished political action, but continued progress in private arenas, such as education and employment. Because movement stages greatly influence how women identify with the movement (Taylor 1989; Taylor and Rupp 1993; Whittier 1995), women's individual attitudes toward feminism are likely to vary.

The second-wave women's movement has simultaneously experienced great successes and backlash. Successes include the maintenance of movement organizations (Marx Ferree and Yancey Martin 1995; Whittier 1995), as well as a "broadly institutionalized and effective interest group," with an institutional base in academia, particularly women's studies programs (Brenner 1996, 24). Backlash is evident in a decline in grassroots mobilization and negative public discourse by antifeminist organizations and media figures (Faludi 1991; Marx Ferree and Hess 1995; Schneider 1988).

Scholars have found that young women tend to be depoliticized and individualistic and that few identify as feminists (Rupp 1988; Stacey 1987)—they typically focus on individual solutions (Budgeon and Currie 1995) and express feminist ideas without labeling them as such (Henderson-King and Stewart 1994; Morgan 1995; Percy and Kremer 1995; Renzetti 1987; Rupp 1988; Stacey 1987; Weis 1990). Many of these apolitical women assume that discrimination will not happen to them (Sigel 1996). The lack of grassroots mobilization results in no framework for understanding individual experiences in politicized terms (Aronson 2000; Taylor 1996) and limits "postfeminists" to viewing gender disparities as illegitimate, rather than in collective terms or in terms of women's shared interests (Gurin 1985, 1987). Their attitudes are also influenced by the media, which have supported the antifeminist backlash (Faludi 1991; Marx Ferree and Hess 1995) and have implied that "no further feminist action is needed" (Schneider 1988, 11).

This generally negative picture of contemporary feminist consciousness is occasionally countered by researchers who have been discovering a "third wave." They point to more than one micro cohort within the postfeminist generation, noting that women who came of age in the 1990s more frequently support feminist goals and are more politically active to achieve these goals (e.g., abortion rights activism) than women who came of age in the 1980s (Whittier 1995). From activists who seek to represent a diversity of young women's experiences (Walker 1995), to the Riot Grrrl movement in music (Rosenberg and Garofalo 1998; Wald 1998), third-wave feminism is said to explicitly embrace hybridity, contradiction, and multiple identities (particularly "connections between racial, sexual and gender identities," Heywood and Drake 1997, 7, 8, 15). However, this new emphasis is questioned by scholars arguing that African American and Chicana feminists have focused historically, and continue to focus, on organizing not only in terms of gender but also along racial lines (Hurtado 1998; Springer 2002). In addition, the third wave is sometimes perceived as nonactivist in nature (Heywood and Drake 1997).

Although not explicitly defining themselves as feminists, other women are said to have the "potential for feminist critique" (Weis 1990, 179). Stacey (1991, 262) argued that young women have "semiconsciously incorporated feminist principles into their gender and kinship expectations and practices." This approach includes "taking for granted" many recent gains: women's work opportunities, combining work with family, sexual autonomy and freedom, and male participation in domestic work and child rearing (Stacey 1991, 1987). This "simultaneous incorporation, revision and depoliticization" (Stacey 1987, 8) of feminism indicates that worldviews include more feminist principles while being less explicitly feminist.

The negative as well as the positive prognosis of these studies should be taken with a grain of salt. They tend to operate with uniform definitions of feminism, ignore generational differences, and/or study groups that are too homogeneous to provide conclusions about the full diversity of today's young women. My study seeks to correct each of these limitations and hopes to provide insights that are more nuanced, complex, and attentive to diversity.

Some research has assumed that when women are asked their views of feminism, they react to a common, uncontested definition. For example, Renzetti (1987) asked college women to respond to an attitudinal inventory survey and found that about a quarter agreed with the statement "I consider myself to be a feminist." Similarly, Boxer's (1997) survey found that three-quarters of women of all ages agreed that the status of women has improved in the past twenty-five years, although only about a third considered themselves to be feminists. By requiring women to define themselves as either for or against feminism, these studies are not likely to tap into the highly complex and contested meanings of feminism today and the ways these diverse meanings influence people's reactions to the term itself. In contrast, my study did not impose a uniform definition of feminism when probing or interpreting interviewees' attitudes but instead left this term for the women themselves to define. In so doing, I did not assume that feminism's meaning is commonly understood or agreed upon.

Research that has recognized feminism's multiple meanings has either focused on a broad age span of women or has centered on homogenous groups of young women. Focusing on more than one cohort, Taylor's (1996) study (with women aged 18 to 43 who were active in the postpartum depression movement) found that feminist identification can be classified on a continuum: Some women call themselves feminists, others reject the label "feminist" but support its principles, while some reject feminism altogether. In her study of women of all ages,[3] Sigel (1996, 113) observed that feminism was often characterized by ambivalence: Women felt that the movement had been positive but that it may have "gone too far" and negatively affected relations with men. The women in Sigel's study called themselves feminists, endorsed feminist goals but rejected the label, or were uncertain about their positions. Neither of these studies explored the potential generational differences in these attitudes. However, a generation has common experiences that structure its worldview (Mannheim 1952). A political generation—persons coming of age in a particular historical period—shares a similar consciousness (Schneider 1988, 6). Despite such a "a common interpretative framework"(Whittier 1995, 16), an individual's place within the social structure and the extent to which she

or he is aware and involved in politics can influence her or his belief systems (Converse 1964).

Studies based on homogenous samples may obscure important differences in feminist orientations. For example, Renzetti (1987) surveyed college students at a predominately white, Catholic university—a very privileged sample. Similarly, Stacey's (1987) insights about "postfeminist consciousness" are based on her interviews with two "kinship networks." Kamen (1991), a journalist, reports a similar continuum of identification as Taylor (1996) described, yet she did not examine the perspectives of women with diverse backgrounds and life experiences.

In fact, no prior studies examine differences in the attitudes of young women with diverse life experiences. We might expect, however, that varying life experiences or class backgrounds will lead to divergent ideas about feminism. Women of some backgrounds have greater supports for the development of feminist identities than others, especially those who have taken women's studies courses in college and have thus been exposed to the institutional legitimization of feminist ideas. Other women are limited to conceptions of feminism advanced by their family and friends and institutions such as the media. These life paths can be tied to class differences. Many middle-class feminist issues, such as the "glass ceiling" and alienation from the housewife role, are far from the daily struggle to make ends meet that is faced by working-class women. Even feminist activists develop different feminist identities as a result of their social class backgrounds (Reger 2002).

In addition, women of different racial and ethnic backgrounds may develop varying views of feminism and gender relations. Women of color have argued that the women's movement has put white, middle-class concerns at its center and ignored the ideas of women of color (Hill Collins 1991). Historically, women of color have not been "full participants in white feminist organizations," despite these organizations' claims that their concerns are universal to all women (Hill Collins 1991, 7). For women of color, racial identities might also be more salient and politicized than gender identities, constituting barriers to the development of feminist identification (Hunter and Sellers 1998). At the same time, prior studies suggest that African Americans are more likely than whites are to support feminist positions, to have egalitarian gender role attitudes, and to engage in collective action (Hunter and Sellers 1998).

This article explores young women's attitudes toward feminism in relation to differences in background and life experience. In contrast to prior research, I recognize the ambivalent and sometimes contradictory orientations of the women who have grown up in the shadow of the women's movement. While prior research has given some attention to the contexts within which feminist attitudes develop (Sigel 1996; Stacey 1987; Taylor 1996; Whittier 1995), many studies have not directly considered women's perceptions of some key goals of feminist organizing, such as advancing women's opportunities, and the obstacles and discrimination that feminism addresses. To discern the context of young women's attitudes toward gender relations, I begin my analysis with an examination of perceptions of women's opportunities, obstacles, and discrimination. I continue the analysis by considering young women's attitudes toward feminism and the impact of race, class, and life experience on these attitudes. Taken together, this article reveals support for feminist goals and complexity in attitudes toward the term *feminism*.

METHOD

This study is based on in-depth interviews with members of a panel study of young people, the Youth Development Study, an ongoing longitudinal study of adolescent development and the transition to adulthood (Jeylan Mortimer is the principal investigator). The larger survey sample ($N = 1,000$) was randomly chosen from a list of enrolled ninth-grade students in St. Paul, Minnesota. Respondents completed surveys annually, with the first year (ninth grade) in 1988. Of the original 1,000 panel members who took part in the first year of data collection, the Youth Development Study retained 77.5 percent through 1995, the last year of the survey before my interview study.

For my in-depth interviews, I followed Glaser and Strauss's (1967) suggestions for theoretical sampling and interviewed women with varying trajectories of life experience and background, as reported in surveys during the four years following high school (1991 to 1995). I focused on differences in education, parenthood, and careers and interviewed nearly equal proportions of women in each group. Obviously, these categories of experience are not mutually exclusive. However, the groups were defined as nonoverlapping categories for this reason. A "school" group had attended a four-year college or university for at least eight months annually in three of the four years following high school. A "parent" group had become mothers by the eighth year of the study and could also be

engaged in school and/or work. A "labor force" group did not have an extensive school trajectory, nor had they become mothers. Instead, they typically worked full-time or moved between postsecondary school and work after high school.

By mail, the Youth Development Study invited 138 women to be interviewed; 42 consented by returning a postcard indicating their interest. Interviews took place in 1996 and 1997. Of the 448 Youth Development Study women who responded in the eighth year of the larger study (1995), I interviewed 9.4 percent. The women were aged twenty-three or twenty-four at the time of my interviews. Among them, 33 percent were women of color (11.9 percent African American, 9.5 percent Asian American, 9.5 percent biracial and multiracial, and 2.4 percent Latina). Their socioeconomic backgrounds included 31 percent from working-class families, 48 percent from the middle class, and 21 percent from upper-middle-class backgrounds.[4] At the time of the interviews, two-thirds of the women were working full-time (28), 3 were working part-time, 7 were in school full-time (and not working), and 4 were out of the labor force for other reasons (2 were caring for their young children, 1 was not working as a result of a severe disability, and 1 was in prison). Slightly more than one-third had completed a bachelor's degree.

Half of the interviewees were involved in committed relationships: 10 were married, 3 were engaged, 8 were in exclusive relationships, and 1 was divorced and involved in a new relationship. Although none of the women directly labeled themselves as lesbians, 2 suggested this possibility. One woman was questioning her sexuality, although she had never had an intimate relationship. The other (who had been in prison since she was a teenager) suggested that her intimate relationships had been with women, although she was looking forward to having a relationship with a man. Although it would be interesting to examine whether young lesbian and bisexual women would report different perceptions of feminism than heterosexual young women, this issue cannot be adequately addressed with my sample.

One-third (14) of the interviewees had become mothers by the time of the interviews. Ten of these women were single parents, while 4 of them were married. However, nearly all had previously been single parents; only 1 woman was married prior to becoming a parent.

Interviews were conducted face to face, in a place chosen by each participant, and were tape-recorded and transcribed. They ranged from 45 minutes to

3 hours long, although most lasted 1½ hours. The interviews were "structured conversations" (Taylor and Rupp 1991, 126) and allowed space for participants to bring up issues they found to be important. After each interview, I wrote field notes, including the main themes, my reflections, and emerging research questions. A qualitative data analysis program (QSR NUD*IST 1996) facilitated the identification and organization of emergent themes.

The interview guide covered a range of themes related to education, work, family, and feminism (Aronson 1998, 1999). The study relied on grounded theory (Glaser and Strauss 1967). This inductive approach served my purpose well as I left open the possibility of multiple meanings of feminism. In the analysis that follows, using pseudonyms for my respondents, I examine several key issues that emerged during the interviews. First, to provide a context for attitudes toward feminism, I consider two themes about women's treatment by society: perceptions of opportunities and obstacles, and experiences with gender discrimination. I then explicate the five approaches to feminist identification that came out of my analysis of the interviews.

PERCEPTIONS OF OPPORTUNITIES AND OBSTACLES

My interviews revealed a general optimism about women's expanded opportunities, coupled with a realization that older women have struggled to create these new opportunities. At the same time, most (35 out of 42) of the interviewees were quite aware that gender-based obstacles still remained. These perspectives were shared by women of all racial and class backgrounds and life experiences.

A majority (36) of the interviewees discussed women's current opportunities in terms of expanded educational and career choices, which have in turn led to women's independence from men and new family arrangements. For example, Hoa, a middle-class Vietnamese American woman who was in law school at the time of the interview, said that women used to think "'I will *marry* a doctor. I will *marry* a lawyer.' It was never: 'I will *become* one.'" Nora, a working-class Hispanic woman, saw this issue in generational terms:

When my mom was growing up, *men* pretty much *ruled* it. . . . [Men] decided what would happen *when* and where you were going to go and where you're going to live. Nowadays men have an opinion, but

that's all it is. . . . Women have their opinions and can go with what they want to do. . . . They can make their own decisions without men.

There was widespread awareness that changes resulted from the struggles of older women, who helped to create new opportunities. Although most of the interviewees attributed these changes to an aggregate of individuals who became "fed up" or "got sick and tired" of gender inequalities, a number credited the women's movement directly.

At the same time, 35 of the interviewees also observed that women continue to face many obstacles, including sexism, difficulty balancing conflicting work and family demands, greater responsibility than men for child rearing and domestic work, and violence against women. For example, Esther, a working-class white woman, said, "Although it's changing, I think that there's a lot of things that are still real male dominated." Nine of the interviewees mentioned that new opportunities have produced new strains, particularly balancing work and family. As Linda, a middle-class white woman working in a traditionally male field, put it, "Companies aren't supportive yet of working mothers."

This recognition of the need for further social change diverges from prior research on the postfeminist generation in two ways. While the micro cohort of women I interviewed here may be more aware of obstacles than prior postfeminist micro cohorts (Whittier 1995), my respondents were more diverse in background than prior studies and thus may have been more apt to perceive obstacles. At the same time that this recognition of inequalities and their illegitimacy suggests significant gender consciousness, my interviewees stopped short of a collective orientation focused on women's movement activism (Gurin 1985, 1987).

EXPERIENCES WITH GENDER DISCRIMINATION

Have these young women experienced discrimination? Although only 6 (14 percent) of the 42 interviewees felt they had experienced blatant instances of gender discrimination, nearly all had experienced what they considered to be minor instances of discrimination or were aware of its possibility in the future. Specifically, a third (14) were concerned about workplace inequality and discrimination. Nearly a quarter (10) approached discrimination somewhat paradoxically: They did not expect that gender discrimination would have an impact on their lives, despite the subtle instances of discrimination that they had experienced. The final quarter (12 out of 42) of interviewees focused on individual solutions to discrimination, such as confronting their perpetrator. In all, these findings reveal a substantial awareness of gender discrimination.

Of the six women who recounted instances of blatant gender discrimination, the main problem was workplace discrimination and sexual harassment. For example, Shonda, a working-class African American woman, experienced both gender and racial discrimination on the job. Although she was aware that she could have filed a lawsuit, her more immediate concern of financially supporting her two children took precedence.

One-third of the women were concerned about future discrimination, including pay equity, hitting a "glass ceiling," and career advancement. Reflecting the career trajectories that these women anticipated, most of those with this approach were middle-class white women with college educations. For example, Linda, a middle-class white woman who worked in the field of accounting, said, "I can see being a woman coming in the way. I work for a company that does still have a little bit of the old boy's club at the upper management."

Nearly a quarter of the interviewees did not originally label their own experiences "discrimination" but realized through telling their stories that gender inequalities were, in fact, part of their life experience. For example, when I asked Sherri, an upper-middle-class white woman who worked in a hospital, whether she had experienced discrimination, she said, "I never thought about it. Probably because in my field it's mostly women." She went on to say the following:

> The highest paid people around here are *men*. I *do* think that's a big obstacle for women—that it's a male, white, male-dominated world, and they're the ones who make the rules. . . . It's not something that I worry about, but I think that's a big obstacle for women.

Similarly, Hillary, a working-class Korean American woman, never felt less "capable" as a result of being a woman, yet she described women's second shift with regard to household responsibilities and her anger at feeling afraid to walk alone at night. Illustrating both an awareness, and the minimizing, of gender discrimination, she said, "Other than the constraints that I felt being a woman, I really don't think that I've . . . missed out on opportunities . . . because I'm a woman, luckily." This paradoxical approach indicates that some women are reluctant to label their experiences with inequality as "discrimination" because they define discrimination narrowly in terms of blatant workplace harassment.

The remaining quarter of the women in this study focused on individual solutions to the problem of discrimination, such as confronting the perpetrator. For example, Felicia, a middle-class white woman, said she wouldn't "tolerate" discrimination: "I feel . . . like I can take care of myself. Some man might want to put me back in my place, but I think I'm a tough little bitch . . . ! Take some karate classes!" Here, individual resistance to discrimination resulted in feelings of personal strength, yet it is important to note that this approach is based on an assumption that individuals must be strong enough to defend themselves against discriminatory actions. Other women focused on the impact of their own choices, particularly choosing female-dominated careers. For example, Kelly, a middle-class white woman who worked in female-dominated retail, said that discrimination "*definitely* hasn't affected me. . . . I haven't been in a situation where it's been more of a man's field. . . . I've never, *ever* felt discriminated [against]."[5]

In sum, although only a small proportion of the interviewees felt that they had experienced blatant gender discrimination, most of the women had known it in minor ways and expressed some concern about it in the future. These findings run contrary to past studies, which imply that young women are unrealistic about the forces that have the potential to hold them back (Coppock, Haydon, and Richter 1995; Sigel 1996; Stacey 1987).[6] At the same time, the term *discrimination* was itself often defined in a narrow way, to include only blatant instances of workplace inequality. This low level of awareness may result from the successes of the women's movement, which have made discrimination less pronounced than in the past. It may also reflect arguments made by other scholars: Women partially accept discrimination as a given because they try to protect themselves from its negative effects (Sigel 1996), or they may feel helpless when thinking of themselves as victims (Gurin 1987). The extent of gender consciousness observed here does not include a collective orientation (Gurin 1985, 1987) since the emphasis was on individual responsibility rather than a broader framework of inequality. It may be that such a political vision, based on social movement involvement, is not available to these women.

ATTITUDES TOWARD FEMINISM

When asked about their attitudes toward feminism, nearly half of these women's responses could be categorized on the continuums developed in previous studies (e.g., Kamen 1991; Taylor 1996) including those who identified as feminists, those who called themselves feminists but qualified their support, and those who said they were not feminists but supported a range of feminist issues. However, suggesting ambiguity in the term *feminism* and its negative connotations, more than half of these women did not want to explicitly define themselves in relation to feminism at all. Most of these interviewees were, in the words of one woman, "fence-sitters": They embraced a number of feminist principles yet rejected others and failed to classify themselves as either feminists or nonfeminists. In addition, nearly a quarter had never thought about feminism as a concept and were unable to articulate an opinion altogether. Despite this ambiguity, nearly all of the interviewees were supportive of feminist issues.

Racial and Class Background and Life Experience

Attitudes toward feminism were differentiated by racial and class background and life experience (see Table 1). In the interviews, nearly a quarter of the women (10 out of 42) identified themselves as feminists. Among this group, 6 defined themselves as feminists without qualifying what they meant by the term *feminist,* while 4 qualified their support by outlining the specific aspects of feminism with which they agreed and disagreed. Those who did not qualify their support were nearly all white or middle class; all were college educated and came to feminism as a result of their experiences with women's studies courses. The women who qualified their feminist identities were women of color or white working-class women who had nearly all attended college but had no experience with women's studies courses.

As young women are most commonly characterized in other research, eight of the interviewees (19 percent) defined themselves as not being feminists but agreed with many of the principles of feminist ideology. Nearly all of these interviewees were from quite privileged backgrounds—close to 90 percent were white and middle to upper-middle class. However, unlike the nearly all-white and middle-class group who called themselves feminists, only two of these women

had attended college and neither had taken women's studies courses.

One-third of the interview sample (13 out of 42 interviewees) were what one woman called "fence-sitters" since they would not position themselves in relation to feminism as an identity. These women were evenly divided in their life experiences and proportionally divided along racial lines, although a greater proportion were from working-class backgrounds.

One-quarter of the interviewees (11 out of 42) were uncertain about their attitudes toward feminism yet endorsed an ideology of equality. Among these women who never thought about feminism, the majority (7 out of 11) were young parents—typically single parents—while the others were focused on the full-time labor force; none had completed a four-year college degree. In addition, a disproportionate number of these interviewees were women of color. A number of these women experienced great stress in daily living, leaving little time for reflection about such issues. This suggests that not only racial and class background but also life paths and life experience in early adulthood may be linked to attitudes toward feminism. I will now consider each of these approaches in turn.

"I'm a Feminist"

Among those who identified as feminists without qualifying their support, feminism was viewed primarily as an ideology of equality. The women in this group were supportive of equal opportunity, abortion rights, equality in childhood socialization, and "social justice" and were concerned about issues such as sexual assault. These interviewees largely came to see themselves as feminists as a result of taking women's studies courses. Tina, a working-class white woman, said that a woman's studies course "started the whole movement for *me.* . . . If I hadn't taken that class . . . I could be married with 60 children right now!" Involvement in women's studies courses reveals that young feminists are not only highly educated but also exposed to feminist ideologies through an institutional location that supports and legitimates feminist perspectives.

"I'm a Feminist, But . . ."

Those who defined themselves as feminists but qualified their support came to their views not through women's studies courses but through assumptions of equality inherent in the attitudes of their families when

TABLE I ATTITUDES TOWARD FEMINISM BY BACKGROUND AND LIFE EXPERIENCE

Attitudes toward Feminism	Interviewees in Group		BACKGROUND								LIFE EXPERIENCE					
			Working-Class White Women		Working-Class Women of Color		Middle-Class and Higher White Women		Middle-Class and Higher Women of Color		"School" Group		"Parent" Group		"Labor Force" Group	
	%	n	%	n	%	n	%	n	%	n	%	n	%	n	%	n
I'm a feminist	14.3	6	16.7	1	0	0	66.7	4	16.7	1	83.3	5	0	0	16.7	1
I'm a feminist, but …	9.5	4	25	1	25	1	0	0	50	2	75	3	0	0	25	1
I'm *not* a feminist, but …	19	8	0	0	0	0	87.5	7	12.5	1	25	2	25	2	50	4
I'm a fence-sitter	31	13	30.8	4	23.1	3	38.5	5	7.7	1	38.5	5	38.5	5	23	3
I never thought about feminism	26.2	11	9.1	1	18.2	2	45.5	5	27.3	3	0	0	63.6	7	36.4	4
Total	100	42	16.7	7	14.3	6	50	21	19.1	8	35.7	15	33.3	14	31	13

they were growing up. Although they called themselves feminists, they also distanced themselves from certain negative associations of feminism. For example, Esther, a working-class white woman, said, "Feminism has gotten a bad rap . . . that it's sort of this *angry, radical* [view-point]. . . . I consider myself a feminist, definitely. I consider myself a *strong* feminist, but I'm not someone who is always needing to assert it." Although she endorsed an ideology of equality and supported diversity in men's and women's work and family arrangements, Esther distanced herself from two negative associations with feminism: those who "always assert" their viewpoints and those who "want to alienate men."

These women grew up with an assumption of equality in their families, yet this may itself explain why they qualify their feminist identities. As Esther put it,

> Feminism isn't something that I've had to *discover* on my own. . . . People who *just* discover . . . *activism* or *feminism* . . . are . . . more vocal about it and . . . *champion* it because it's new and different. And I feel like it's just a *given* that everyone should be treated equally. It's just a *given* that . . . because I'm a woman, that doesn't stop me from doing whatever I want to do.

"I'm Not a Feminist, But . . ."

Nineteen percent of the interviewees distanced themselves from feminism while endorsing many of the principles of feminist ideology. One example of this perspective comes from Betsy, a middle-class white woman, who said, "I'm *not* a feminist, I would say. Probably a lot of feminists wouldn't like me. But, well, I mean I guess it depends on what feminism. . . . I think everybody should be treated equally at the base." These women gave several reasons for distancing themselves from the identity of "feminist." A number of interviewees felt that feminism goes "too far." Whitney, a middle-class Korean American woman, said that "a lot of feminism goes overboard," yet she suspected that she had this view because she herself had never faced discrimination: "Maybe people who are a little bit older or have been discriminated against [call themselves feminists] and I haven't really experienced that. So, I mean if I had, maybe I would become a feminist, but I either don't *see* it [or] haven't *been*" discriminated against. Here, feminism is seen as a place where grievances against discrimination can be voiced, rather than a perspective that sees power inequalities influencing every domain of gender relations.

Other interviewees distanced themselves from activism and political engagement. Dawn, an upper-middle-class white woman, appreciated the benefits of the women's movement, particularly educational and occupational opportunities, and was supportive of equality more generally. At the same time, she said, "I *don't* believe that *I* would consider *myself* a feminist." Implying that it was activism from which she distanced herself, she said, "I don't go out every day and say 'women's rights and more opportunities for women.' . . . I don't think about it on a day-to-day basis." Similarly, Linda, a middle-class white woman, said of feminism: "Folks should just live their lives and not get so caught up in everything." Clearly, these women's gender consciousness does not include a collective orientation (Gurin 1985, 1987).

These women also distanced themselves from feminism as a result of negative perceptions of feminists, particularly lesbianism and separatism from men. For example, although Alice, a middle-class white woman, said, "I just think that everybody is *equal*," she did not want to distance herself from men: "I don't go around bashing men. . . . I *like* men." Linda thought that being a feminist meant that she could not live the type of life she wanted to lead:

> I have a couple of feminist friends that have *very* different views than I do. . . . My boyfriend's sister is a feminist, and she will *never* have children. She will probably *never* get married. And that's fine, but that's not what I want to do. That's not the life that I want to lead. I want to raise a family.

This perspective reflects the antifeminist movement and the media's construction of feminists as lesbians and militants (Faludi 1991; Marx Ferree and Hess 1995). As was also the case in previous eras (e.g., Marshall 1997), the media have perpetuated "the social climate of antifeminism and thwart[ed] the possibility of mobilizing discontented women" (Rupp and Taylor 1987).

"I'm a Fence-Sitter"

The fence-sitting approach (taken by one-third of the women) reveals a paradox: support for feminist issues, as well as the ambiguous connotations of "feminism" today. Rather than identifying themselves in relation to feminist identity, these women focused on evaluating the ideologies and stereotypes associated with feminism. This group is distinct from the others because they would not classify themselves as either feminists or nonfeminists. In embracing ambiguity, they truly remained "on the fence." In some respects, they evaded the interview questions and chose instead to support and critique aspects of the term *feminism*.

One woman who took this approach was Ann, who is working class and white. When I asked her thoughts about feminism, she said, "I'd be supportive," yet she stopped short of calling herself a feminist. She went on to call herself a fence-sitter and said, "I would still be reserved about some things." When asked to elaborate, she discussed only her support of feminist issues: eradicating the "perpetuation" of stereotypes about women, violence against women, governmental cuts in welfare, and sexual harassment and favoring comparable worth and gay rights. Likewise, Susan, a middle-class white woman, said that "a lot of feminism is lesbianism" and she did not want to "go hate men." She also recognized this stereotype as a "big generalization" about feminists. In fact, she had enjoyed taking women's studies courses in college: "As far as identifying similar experiences and . . . feeling like you're not alone, that's what I *like* about feminism."

Other studies have also found that some women reject feminism because they are worried about creating "male antagonism" (Sigel 1996, 114). These views may reflect a general reluctance to express anger over discrimination because some women accept unfairness, see discrimination as realistic, or want to protect themselves from recognizing inequality (Sigel 1996). Stereotypes against feminists have been powerfully advanced by the antifeminist movement and the media, which may have influenced these women's views.

"I Never Thought about Feminism"

The remaining quarter (11 out of 42) of the interviewees expressed a great deal of uncertainty about their attitudes toward feminism, had no opinion on the topic, or had substantial difficulty defining the term itself. Of these women, most felt that they were unable to comment because they did not know enough about feminism or had never thought about it in enough depth to express an opinion. One interviewee who was unable to articulate an opinion was Kelly, a middle-class white woman. Although she felt that "women should have the same rights as a man does," she said that she had "never been a real *strong*

activist." Kelly went on to explain her view as follows: "I don't really have a lot of feelings on that because I kind of take it as it is. . . . I don't really think about that kind of stuff." Kim, a middle-class white woman, said, "I don't even really know what [feminism] *is*."

Why were these women unable or unwilling to articulate an opinion of feminism? Some of the interviewees were simply confused over the definition of feminism. For others, feminism was implicitly defined as an activist approach that addressed discrimination and thus did not have personal relevance. For example, when I asked Caroline, an upper-middle-class white woman, about her view of feminism, she said that "nothing has *happened* to me that I would have to be that way." Here, being "that way" connotes that feminist perspectives go along with discrimination: without it, there was no need to think about feminism. Other women also saw feminism as irrelevant to their everyday lives. Jill, a middle-class, white, single parent of two children, was explicit that she had more pressing daily issues to worry about than feminism:

> I don't care. No big thing. I've never been treated unfairly by a man. I don't think I have. . . . I blow off things, because I'm an easy come, easy go [person]. I'm already stressed out with kids and a job. . . . I don't need to be stressed out about things like that. So [in terms of] *feminism*, I don't *care*. Who *cares?*

To Jill, feminism is irrelevant, perhaps even frivolous, when compared with the struggles of combining work and single motherhood. Feminism is primarily a way to redress workplace discrimination, in contrast to confronting issues that are central to basic survival as a woman. Ironically, both Caroline and Jill (in another part of the interview) also recounted their own experiences with domestic violence, suggesting that some of the women who would benefit the most from a feminist political perspective or agenda see it as the least relevant to their own lives.

At the same time, these women were supportive of equality between men and women. For example, Yolanda, a working-class biracial (African American and white) single parent said,

> I can change a tire. I can change oil . . . and I don't have a problem with it. And I can move my *own* furniture, *pregnant* or *not*, you know?! . . . When a guy tells me I

can't do something, I'll tell him to *prove* it. . . . I'll tell a guy off real quick if he tells *me* that [I can't do something] because of my gender.

As I explore elsewhere (Aronson 1999, 2001), the young women in this study (even the engaged and married women) emphasized the importance of their own independence from men in many areas of their lives—career, finances, childbearing and child rearing, and self-development. In fact, marital status does not seem to make any difference in attitudes toward feminism, as women with different relationships to men were evenly dispersed among the groups examined here.

CONCLUSIONS

My findings about the widespread awareness of the extent of gender inequality run contrary to prior studies of the postfeminist generation (Renzetti 1987; Rupp 1988; Sigel 1996; Stacey 1987, 1991). And while many of the interviewees fit on a continuum of feminist identification previously defined by other researchers (Kamen 1991; Sigel 1996; Taylor 1989), more than half of the young women in this study approached feminism even more ambiguously than previously reported, especially the fence-sitters who embrace some aspects of feminism while rejecting others and avoid defining themselves in relation to the identity of feminist.

My findings also extend prior research by illustrating that attitudes toward feminism are shaped by racial and class background, and also by life experience. No prior studies have examined the role of diverse types of life experience in developing particular attitudes toward feminism. I have shown that the feminist identification without qualification and the "I'm not a feminist, but . . ." approach are associated with more privileged racial and class backgrounds. The feminists were more likely to be college educated, and most had taken women's studies courses. Those who qualified their feminist identities and those who had never thought about feminism were disproportionately from less privileged racial and class backgrounds, but their life experience differentiates them from the other groups as well. The "qualified" feminists were college-educated, working-class women and/or women of color who came to feminism as a result of assumptions of equality when growing up. Among the women who had never thought about feminism, two-thirds had

become parents early in life, and none had pursued a college degree.

My findings also indicate that young women's development of a feminist perspective and identity is tied closely with institutions that support and nurture such a perspective—particularly women's studies programs. This institutionalization of feminism has occurred at the same time as antifeminist organizations and media figures have advanced negative stereotypes that have become incorporated in some young women's conceptions of feminism. In addition, although the women of color that I interviewed were supportive of equality, most distanced themselves from the identity of feminist, suggesting that the institutional supports for feminism may be more appealing or available to white women.

This study also suggests that having the space to think about political issues such as feminism may be a luxury that some young women, especially single mothers, cannot afford. For these women, feminism was seen as lacking personal relevance and viewed primarily as a place to redress workplace discrimination. Many of these women had never thought about their positions on feminism or saw it as frivolous when compared with the struggles of supporting and raising their children. Obviously, this is a broader problem than simply creating better public relations within feminist organizations, as it involves developing new initiatives and expanding institutional power. A new wave of political organizing might in turn lead to new personal understandings of feminism at later points in the life course (Aronson 2000).

Most important, whether or not young women call themselves feminists, they support feminist goals. In fact, the young women I interviewed were more supportive of feminism than had been found in past research, and none expressed antifeminist sentiments. The fence-sitting stance, while not as politicized as in previous generations, is not entirely individualized and apolitical either. Although most researchers and the media have painted a pessimistic view of young women's ambivalence, I believe that my results offer some promise for feminism. Many of these young women may be passive supporters rather than agents of change, but they are supporters nonetheless. Their endorsement may represent the seeds of change, which, under the right historical conditions, and in interaction with the growth of grassroots feminist organizing, could blossom into the next wave of the women's movement.

NOTES

1. I would like to thank Karen Lutfey for the origination of this phrase.
2. This term had also been used after the first-wave women's movement (Taylor 1996).
3. The exact age range is not specified in her book.
4. Social class background was based on parents' income and education as reported in the parent surveys in the first year of the study (1988). "Working class" includes those whose parents had less than a bachelor's degree and earned less than $30,000 per year in 1988. "Middle class" includes four subgroups: parents who had high educational attainment (at least a bachelor's degree) and low income (less than $30,000 per year in 1988), low educational attainment (less than a bachelor's degree) but high income (at least $50,000 per year in 1988), high education (at least a bachelor's degree) and middle income

(between $30,000 and $50,000 per year in 1988), and low education (less than a bachelor's degree) and middle income. "Upper-middle class" includes those parents who had high educational attainment (at least a bachelor's degree) and earned a middle to high income (more than $50,000 per year in 1988).

5. This lack of salience of gender discrimination within female-dominated occupations is supported by Slevin and Wingrove's (1998) findings that African American women do not find race to be extremely salient when working in African American organizations.
6. It is possible that the differences between my study and prior findings result from historical shifts—that this micro cohort of young women is more aware of inequalities than prior micro cohorts of the postfeminist generation (Whittier 1995).

REFERENCES

Aronson, Pamela. 1998. Coming of age in the 1990s: Women's identities, life paths, and attitudes towards feminism. Ph.D. diss., University of Minnesota, Minneapolis.

———. 1999. The balancing act: Young women's expectations and experiences of work and family. In *Research in the sociology of work*, vol. 7, edited by Toby Parcel. Stamford, CT: JAI.

———. 2000. The development and transformation of feminist identities under changing historical conditions. In *Advances in life course research: Identity across the life course in cross-cultural perspective*, vol. 5, edited by Timothy J. Owens. Stamford, CT: JAI.

———. 2001. The markers and meanings of growing up: Contemporary young women's transition to adulthood. Paper presented at the annual meeting of the American Sociological Association, Anaheim, CA.

Bellafante, Ginia. 1998. Is feminism dead? *Time Magazine,* 29 June, 25.

Bolotin, Susan. 1982. Views from the post-feminist generation. *New York Times Magazine*, 17 October, 29–31, 103–16.

Boxer, Sarah. 1997. One casualty of the women's movement: Feminism. *New York Times*, 14 December, 3.

Brenner, Johanna. 1996. The best of times, the worst of times: Feminism in the United States. In *Mapping the women's movement: Feminist politics and social transformation in the North*, edited by Monica Threlfall. London: Verso.

Budgeon, Shelley, and Dawn Currie. 1995. From feminism to postfeminism: Women's liberation in fashion magazines. *Women's Studies International Forum* 18 (2): 173–86.

Converse, Philip E. 1964. The nature of belief systems in mass publics. In *Ideology and discontent*, edited by David E. Apter. London: Free Press of Glencoe.

Coppock, Vicki, Deena Haydon, and Ingrid Richter. 1995. *The illusions of "post-feminism": New women, old myths*. London: Taylor and Francis.

Faludi, Susan. 1991. *Backlash: The undeclared war against American women*. New York: Crown.

Glaser, Barney, and Anselm Strauss. 1967. *The discovery of grounded theory*. Chicago: Aldine.

Gurin, Patricia. 1985. Women's gender consciousness. *Public Opinion Quarterly* 49 (2): 143–63.

———. 1987. The political implications of women's statuses. In *Spouse, parent, worker: On gender and multiple roles*, edited by Faye J. Crosby. New Haven, CT: Yale University Press.

Henderson-King, Donna, and Abigail Stewart. 1994. Women or feminists? Assessing women's group consciousness. *Sex Roles* 31 (9–10): 505–16.

Heywood, Leslie, and Jennifer Drake. 1997. Introduction. *Third wave agenda: Being feminist, doing feminism*, edited by Leslie Heywood and Jennifer Drake. Minneapolis: University of Minnesota Press.

Hill Collins, Patricia. 1991. *Black feminist thought: Knowledge, consciousness and the politics of empowerment*. New York: Routledge.

Hunter, Andrea, and Sherrill Sellers. 1998. Feminist attitudes among African American women and men. *Gender & Society* 12 (1): 81–99.

Hurtado, Aida. 1998. Sitios y lenguas: Chicanas theorize feminisms. *Hypatia* 13 (2): 134–61.

Kamen, Paula. 1991. *Feminist fatale: Voices from the "twenty-something" generation explore the future of the "women's movement."* New York: Donald I. Fine.

Mannheim, Karl. 1952. *Essays on the sociology of knowledge*. London: Routledge Kegan Paul.

Marshall, Susan. 1997. *Splintered sisterhood: Gender and class in the campaign against woman suffrage.* Madison: University of Wisconsin Press.

Marx Ferree, Myra, and Beth B. Hess. 1995. *Controversy and coalition: The new feminist movement across four decades of change.* 3d ed. New York: Routledge.

Marx Ferree, Myra, and Patricia Yancey Martin. 1995. *Feminist organizations: Harvest of the new women's movement.* Philadelphia: Temple University Press.

Morgan, Debi. 1995. Invisible women: Young women and feminism. In *Feminist activism in the 1990s.* edited by Gabriele Griffin. London: Taylor and Francis.

Overholser, Geneva. 1986. What "post-feminism" really means. *New York Times,* 19 September, 30.

Percy, Carol, and John Kremer. 1995. Feminist identifications in a troubled society. *Feminism and Psychology* 5 (2): 201–22.

QSR NUD*IST. 1996. Thousand Oaks, CA: Qualitative Solutions and Research Pty. Ltd.

Reger, Jo. 2002. Organizational dynamics and construction of multiple feminist identities in the National Organization for Women. *Gender & Society* 16 (5): 710–27.

Renzetti, Claire. 1987. New wave or second stage? Attitudes of college women toward feminism. *Sex Roles* 16 (5/6): 265–77.

Rosenberg, Jessica, and Gitana Garofalo. 1998. Riot grrrl: Revolutions from within. *Signs: Journal of Women in Culture and Society* 23 (3): 809–41.

Rosenfelt, Deborah, and Judith Stacey. 1987. Second thoughts on the second wave. *Feminist Studies* 13 (2): 341–61.

Rossi, Alice. 1982. *Feminists in politics.* New York: Academic.

Rupp, Lelia, and Verta Taylor. 1987. *Survival in the doldrums: The American women's rights movement, 1945 to the 1960s.* New York: Oxford University Press.

Rupp, Rayna. 1988. Is the legacy of second-wave feminism postfeminism? *Socialist Review* (January–March):52–57.

Schneider, Beth. 1988. Political generations and the contemporary women's movement. *Sociological Inquiry* 58:4–21.

Sigel, Roberta. 1996. *Ambition and accommodation: How women view gender relations.* Chicago: University of Chicago Press.

Slevin, Kathleen F., and C. Ray Wingrove. 1998. *From stumbling blocks to stepping stones: The life experiences of fifty professional African American women.* New York: New York University Press.

Springer, Kimberly. 2002. Third wave Black feminism? *Signs: Journal of Women in Culture and Society* 27 (4): 1059–82.

Stacey, Judith. 1987. Sexism by a subtler name? Postindustrial conditions and postfeminist consciousness in the Silicon Valley. *Socialist Review* 17 (6): 7–28.

———. 1991. *Brave new families: Stories of domestic upheaval in late twentieth century America.* New York Basic Books.

Taylor, Verta. 1996. *Rock-a-by baby: Feminism, self-help, and postpartum depression.* New York: Routledge.

———. 1989. Social movement continuity: The women's movement in abeyance. *American Sociological Review* 54:761–75.

Taylor, Verta, and Lelia Rupp. 1991. Researching the women's movement: We make our own history, but not just as we please. In *Beyond methodology: Feminist scholarship as lived research,* edited by Mary Margaret Fonow and Judith A. Cook. Bloomington: Indiana University Press.

———. 1993.Women's culture and lesbian feminist activism: A reconsideration of cultural feminism. *Signs: Journal of Women in Culture and Society* 19 (1): 32–61.

Unger, Rhoda. 1989. Explorations in feminist ideology: Surprising consistencies and unexamined conflicts. In *Representations: Social constructions of gender,* edited by Rhoda Unger. Amityville, NY: Baywood.

Wald, Gayle. 1998. Just a girl? Rock music, feminism, and the cultural construction of female youth. *Signs: Journal of Women in Culture and Society* 23 (3): 585–610.

Walker, Rebecca. 1995. *To be real: Telling the truth and changing the face of feminism.* New York: Anchor.

Weis, Lois. 1990. *Working class without work: High school students in a de-industrializing economy.* New York: Routledge.

Whittier, Nancy. 1995. *Feminist generations: The persistence of the radical women's movement.* Philadelphia: Temple University Press.

THE END OF FEMINISM'S THIRD WAVE

Lisa Jervis

"Are you in the third wave?"

"When did the third wave start?"

"What's the most important issue to third wavers?"

I get asked this a lot—at campus lectures, during radio interviews, at publishing conferences. I hate these questions. There are so many ways to answer, none of them entirely satisfactory.

I always want to pepper my interlocutor with questions instead:

Do you want to know how *I* identify, or how others would label me? Are you asking when the term was coined? When the first feminists who are considered part of the third wave became politicized? When the first riot grrl zine was published? What makes you think it's possible to elevate one issue over all others? Which definition of the third wave are we talking about here, the chronological or the ideological?

This reluctance isn't just me being cranky and not wanting to answer any hard questions. Here is the reality: We've reached the end of the wave terminology usefulness. What was at first a handy-dandy way to refer to feminism's history and its present and future potential with a single metaphor has become shorthand that invites intellectual laziness, an escape hatch from the hard world of distinguishing between core beliefs and a cultural moment.

Using the simplest and most straightforward definition, I am, indisputably, a member of the third wave: I was born in 1972, right smack in the demographics that people think about when they think about the third wave. But discussions of the waves are only nominally about demographics. The metaphor wraps up differences in age, ideology, tactics and style, and pretends that distinguishing among these factors is unimportant.

Even the more nuanced discussions of third-wavers tend to cast them (or, given my birthday, should I say "us"?) as sex-obsessed young thangs with a penchant for lip gloss and a disregard for recent history, or sophisticated identity politicians who have moved past the dated concerns of their predecessors.

It's no mystery why the discourse that has developed around the waves is divisive and oppositional. Writers and theorists love oppositional categories—they make things so much easier to talk about. Similarities are much more difficult. So, naturally, much has been said and written about the disagreements, conflicts, differences and antagonisms between feminists of the second and third waves, while hardly *anything* is ever said about our similarities and continuities.

The rap goes something like this: Older women drained their movement of sexuality; younger women are uncritically sexualized. Older women won't recognize the importance of pop culture; younger women are obsessed with media representation. Older women have too narrow a definition of what makes a feminist issue; younger women are scattered and don't know what's important.

Stodgy versus frivolous. Won't share power versus spoiled and ignorant.

Nothing on this list is actually true—but, because this supposedly great generational divide has been constructed out of very flimsy but readily available materials, the ideas persist in the face of overwhelming evidence to the contrary.

It's just so much easier to hit on the playful cultural elements of the third wave and contrast them with the brass-tacks agenda—and impressive gains—of the second wave: It's become the master narrative of feminism's progression (or regression, as some see it).

But when has it ever been a good idea to trust a master narrative? After all, the oft-repeated notion among self-described third-wavers that those labeled as hopelessly second-wave reject humor, fashion, sex or anything else that might be fun is just a slightly—and only slightly—more nuanced and polite version of the stone-faced, hairy-legged manhater whom we all know to be a myth that originated in the sexist culture at large and was cultivated and amplified by conservative, anti-feminist and/or just plain clueless journalists and pundits.

The image of the frivolous young pseudofeminist has the same provenance. Take *Time*'s infamous June 29, 1998, cover story "Is Feminism Dead?" for instance. In lambasting young women for being more interested in celebrity than the wage gap and seeing vibrators as more important than protests, writer Ginia Bellafante had to carefully ignore the vibrant anti-sweatshop movement spawning on college campuses at the time, or organizations like the Third Wave Foundation, feminist.com, SOUL, Home Alive or many of the other activist projects founded and run by women born in the '70s and after.

When feminists engage in this kind of nuance-deprived conflation of age and ideology, we're doing little more than reinscribing the thoroughly debunked notion that we need to agree with each other all the time.

As we all know, feminism has always held within it multitudes of ideologies, tactics and priorities. The movement's two current generations have come to be painted as internally monolithic, but they are each as diverse philosophically as feminism itself—they have to be; they *are* feminism itself.

There are elements of both that are playful and take pop culture as both their medium and their subject matter: The 1968 Miss America protests defined the very start of the second wave, and their lineage extends to guerrilla theater groups like Ladies Against Women in the '80s and the Radical Cheerleaders today.

There are elements of both that are relentlessly—and appropriately—serious. Combating rape and domestic violence was a key issue 35 years ago; its importance has not changed. Affordable, accessible child care is no less a concern now than it was in the '70s.

Chronologically third-wave publications such as *Feminista!* share their ideologies about pornography and sex work with Catharine MacKinnon and Andrea Dworkin. The riot grrls groups that sprang up in the early '90s have clear connections to consciousness-raising groups. Last April's hugely successful and inspiring March for Women's Lives was intergenerational in both planning and attendance.

There's certainly no shortage of disagreements both large and small within feminism. There are those who see transgender folks as interlopers in feminist spaces, and those who see genderqueers as the frontline soldiers against sexist systems of power.

There are those who would like to see "feminine" values replace "masculine" values as the defining characteristics of our society, and those who reject the very notion that these values have any gender apart from what's been assigned by a sexist culture.

There are those who see gender as the overarching factor that shapes women's oppression, and those who think that raising the minimum wage would achieve more feminist goals in one fell swoop than any other single act.

The issues motivating both sides of the '80s sex wars are very much still with us. Even if some views are more common among one generation than another at their roots these are ideological disagreements—but they can't be discussed productively while in disguise as generational issues. That disguise keeps us distracted from the real work before the movement today.

Here's what we all need to recognize so that we can move on: Those in their 20s and 30s who don't see their concerns reflected in the feminism of their elders are ignorant of history; those in their 50s and beyond who think that young women aren't politically active—or active enough, or active around the right issues—don't know where to look.

We all want the same thing: To borrow bell hooks' phrase, we want gender justice.

We may not all agree on exactly what it looks like or how to get it. We should never expect to agree. Feminism has always thrived on and grown from internal discussions and disagreements. Our many different and often opposing perspectives are what push us forward, honing our theories, refining our tactics, driving us toward a more thorough dismantling of the white-supremacist, capitalist patriarchy (to borrow another phrase from hooks).

I want to see these internal disagreements continue. I want to see as much wrangling over them as ever. But I want them articulated accurately. And that means recognizing the generational divide for what it is—an illusion.

49   *Cathy J. Cohen*

Punks, Bulldaggers, and Welfare Queens: The Radical Potential of Queer Politics?

On the eve of finishing this essay my attention is focused not on how to rework the conclusion (as it should be) but instead on news stories of alleged racism at Gay Men's Health Crisis (GMHC). It seems that three black board members of this largest and oldest AIDS organization in the world have resigned over their perceived subservient position on the GMHC board. Billy E. Jones, former head of the New York City Health and Hospitals Corporation and one of the board members to quit, was quoted in the *New York Times* as saying, "Much work needs to be done at GMHC to make it truly inclusive and welcoming of diversity. . . . It is also clear that such work will be a great struggle. I am resigning because I do not choose to engage in such struggle at GMHC, but rather prefer to fight for the needs of those ravaged by HIV" (Dunlap).

This incident raises mixed emotions for me, for it points to the continuing practice of racism many of us experience on a daily basis in lesbian and gay communities. But just as disturbingly it also highlights the limits of a lesbian and gay political agenda based on a civil rights strategy, where assimilation into, and replication of, dominant institutions are the goals. Many of us continue to search for a new political direction and agenda, one that does not focus on integration into dominant structures but instead seeks to transform the basic fabric and hierarchies that allow systems of oppression to persist and operate efficiently. For some of us, such a challenge to traditional gay and lesbian politics was offered by the idea of queer politics. Here we had a potential movement of young antiassimilationist activists committed to challenging the very way people understand and respond to sexuality. These activists promised to engage in struggles that would disrupt dominant norms of sexuality, radically transforming politics in lesbian, gay, bisexual, and transgendered communities.

Despite the possibility invested in the idea of queerness and the practice of queer politics, I argue that a truly radical or transformative politics has not resulted from queer activism. In many instances, instead of destabilizing the assumed categories and binaries of sexual identity, queer politics has served to reinforce simple dichotomies between heterosexual and everything "queer." An understanding of the ways in which power informs and constitutes privileged and marginalized subjects on both sides of this dichotomy has been left unexamined.

I query in this essay whether there are lessons to be learned from queer activism that can help us construct a new politics. I envision a politics where one's relation to power, and not some homogenized identity, is privileged in determining one's political comrades. I'm talking about a politics where the *nonnormative* and *marginal* position of punks, bulldaggers, and welfare queens, for example, is the basis for progressive transformative coalition work. Thus, if there is any truly radical potential to be found in the idea of queerness and the practice of queer politics, it would seem to be located in its ability to create a space in opposition to dominant norms, a space where transformational political work can begin.

EMERGENCE OF QUEER POLITICS AND A NEW POLITICS OF TRANSFORMATION

Theorists and activists alike generally agree that it was in the early 1990s that we began to see, with any regularity, the use of the term "queer."[1] This term would come to denote not only an emerging politics, but also a new cohort of academics working in programs primarily in the humanities centered around social and cultural criticism (Morton 121). Individuals such as Judith Butler, Eve Sedgwick, Teresa de Lauretis, Diana Fuss, and Michael Warner produced what are now thought of as the first canonical works of "queer theory." Working from a variety of postmodernist and poststructuralist theoretical perspectives, these scholars focused on identifying and contesting the discursive and cultural markers found within both dominant and marginal identities and institutions which prescribe and reify "heterogendered" understandings and behavior.[2] These theorists presented a different conceptualization of sexuality, one which sought to replace socially named and presumably stable categories of sexual expression with a new fluid movement among and between forms of sexual behavior (Stein and Plummer 182).

Through its conception of a wide continuum of sexual possibilities, queer theory stands in direct contrast to the normalizing tendencies of hegemonic sexuality rooted in ideas of static, stable sexual identities and behaviors. In queer theorizing the sexual subject is understood to be constructed and contained by multiple practices of categorization and regulation that systematically marginalize and oppress those subjects thereby defined as deviant and "other." And, at its best, queer theory focuses on and makes central not only the socially constructed nature of sexuality and sexual categories, but also the varying degrees and multiple sites of power distributed within all categories of sexuality, including the normative category of heterosexuality.

It was in the early 1990s, however, that the postmodern theory being produced in the academy (later to be recategorized as queer theory) found its most direct interaction with the real-life politics of lesbian, gay, bisexual, and transgendered activists. Frustrated with what was perceived to be the scientific "degaying" and assimilationist tendencies of AIDS activism, with their invisibility in the more traditional civil rights politics of lesbian and gay organizations, and with increasing legal and physical attacks against lesbian and gay community members, a new generation of activists began the process of building a more confrontational political formation—labeling it queer politics (Bérubé and Escoffier 12). Queer politics, represented most notoriously in the actions of Queer Nation, is understood as an "in your face" politics of a younger generation. Through action and analysis these individuals seek to make "queer" function as more than just an abbreviation for lesbian, gay, bisexual, and transgendered. Similar to queer theory, the queer politics articulated and pursued by these activists first and foremost recognizes and encourages the fluidity and movement of people's sexual lives. In queer politics sexual expression is something that always entails the possibility of change, movement, redefinition, and subversive performance—from year to year, from partner to partner, from day to day, even from act to act. In addition

to highlighting the instability of sexual categories and sexual subjects, queer activists also directly challenge the multiple practices and vehicles of power which render them invisible and at risk. However, what seems to make queer activists unique, at this particular moment, is their willingness to confront normalizing power by emphasizing and exaggerating their own antinormative characteristics and nonstable behavior. Joshua Gamson, in "Must Identity Movements Self-Destruct? A Queer Dilemma," writes that

> queer activism and theory pose the challenge of a form of organizing in which, far from inhibiting accomplishments, the *destabilization* of collective identity is itself a goal and accomplishment of collective action.
>
> The assumption that stable collective identities are necessary for collective action is turned on its head by queerness, and the question becomes: *When and how are stable collective identities necessary for social action and social change?* Secure boundaries and stabilized identities are necessary not in general, but in the specific, a point social movement theory seems currently to miss. (403, original emphasis)

Thus queer politics, much like queer theory, is often perceived as standing in opposition, or in contrast, to the category-based identity politics of traditional lesbian and gay activism. And for those of us who find ourselves on the margins, operating through multiple identities and thus not fully served or recognized through traditional single-identity-based politics, *theoretical conceptualizations* of queerness hold great political promise. For many of us, the label "queer" symbolizes an acknowledgment that through our existence and everyday survival we embody sustained and multisited resistance to systems (based on dominant constructions of race and gender) that seek to normalize our sexuality, exploit our labor, and constrain our visibility. At the intersection of oppression and resistance lies the radical potential of queerness to challenge and bring together all those deemed marginal and all those committed to liberatory politics.

The problem, however, with such a conceptualization and expectation of queer identity and politics is that in its present form queer politics has not emerged as an encompassing challenge to systems of domination and oppression, especially those normalizing processes embedded in heteronormativity. By "heteronormativity" I mean both those localized practices and those centralized institutions which legitimize and privilege heterosexuality and heterosexual relationships as fundamental and "natural" within society. I raise the subject of heteronormativity because it is this normalizing practice/power that has most often been the focus of queer politics (Blasius 19–20; Warner xxi–xxv).

The inability of queer politics to effectively challenge heteronormativity rests, in part, on the fact that despite a surrounding discourse which highlights the destabilization and even deconstruction of sexual categories, queer politics has often been built around a simple dichotomy between those deemed queer and those deemed heterosexual. Whether in the infamous "I Hate Straights" publication or queer kiss-ins at malls and straight dance clubs, very near the surface in queer political action is an uncomplicated understanding of power as it is encoded in sexual categories: all heterosexuals are represented as dominant and controlling and all queers are understood as marginalized and invisible. Thus, even in the name of destabilization, some queer activists have begun to prioritize sexuality as the primary frame through which they pursue their politics.[3] Undoubtedly, within different contexts various characteristics of our total being—for example, race, gender, class, sexuality—are highlighted or called upon to make sense of a particular situation. However, my concern is centered on those individuals who consistently activate only one characteristic of their identity, or a single perspective of consciousness, to organize their politics, rejecting any recognition of the multiple and intersecting systems of power that largely dictate our life chances.

It is the disjuncture, evident in queer politics, between an articulated commitment to promoting an understanding of sexuality that rejects the idea of static, monolithic, bounded categories, on the one hand, and political practices structured around binary conceptions of sexuality and power, on the other hand, that is the focus of this article. Specifically, I am concerned with those manifestations of queer politics in which the capital and advantage invested in a range of sexual categories are disregarded and, as a result, narrow and homogenized political identities are reproduced that inhibit the radical potential of queer politics. It is my contention that queer activists who evoke a single-oppression framework misrepresent the distribution of power within and outside of gay, lesbian, bisexual, and transgendered communities, and therefore limit the comprehensive and transformational character of queer politics.

Recognizing the limits of current conceptions of queer identities and queer politics, I am interested in examining the concept of "queer" in order to think about how we might construct a new political identity that is truly liberating, transformative, and inclusive of all those who stand on the outside of the dominant constructed norm of state-sanctioned white middle- and upper-class heterosexuality.[4] Such a broadened understanding of queerness must be based on an intersectional analysis that recognizes how numerous systems of oppression interact to regulate and police the lives of most people. Black lesbian, bisexual, and heterosexual feminist authors such as Kimberle Crenshaw, Barbara Ransby, Angela Davis, Cheryl Clarke, and Audre Lorde have repeatedly emphasized in their writing the intersectional workings of oppression. And it is just such an understanding of the interlocking systems of domination that is noted in the opening paragraph of the now famous black feminist statement by the Combahee River Collective:

> The most general statement of our politics at the present time would be that we are actively committed to struggling against racial, sexual, heterosexual, and class oppression and see as our particular task the development of *integrated* analysis and practice based upon the fact that the major systems of oppression are interlocking. The synthesis of these oppressions creates the conditions of our lives. As Black women we see Black feminism as the logical political movement to combat the manifold and simultaneous oppressions that all women of color face. (272)

This analysis of one's place in the world which focuses on the intersection of systems of oppression is informed by a consciousness that undoubtedly grows from the lived experience of existing within and resisting multiple and connected practices of domination and normalization. Just such a lived experience and analysis have determined much of the progressive and expansive nature of the politics emanating from people of color, people who are both inside and outside of lesbian and gay communities.

However, beyond a mere recognition of the intersection of oppressions, there must also be an understanding of the ways our multiple identities work to limit the entitlement and status some receive from obeying a heterosexual imperative. For instance, how would queer activists understand politically the lives of women—in particular women of color—on welfare, who may fit into the category of heterosexual, but whose sexual choices are not perceived as normal, moral, or worthy of state support? Further, how do queer activists understand and relate politically to those whose same-sex sexual identities position them within the category of queer, but who hold other identities based on class, race and/or gender categories which provide them with membership in and the resources of dominant institutions and groups?

Thus, inherent in our new politics must be a commitment to left analysis and left politics. Black feminists as well as other marginalized and progressive scholars and activists have long argued that any political response to the multilayered oppression that most of us experience must be rooted in a left understanding of our political, economic, social, and cultural institutions. Fundamentally, a left framework makes central the interdependency among multiple systems of domination. Such a perspective also ensures that while activists should rightly be concerned with forms of discursive and cultural coercion, we also recognize and confront the more direct and concrete forms of exploitation and violence rooted in state-regulated institutions and economic systems. The Statement of Purpose from the first Dialogue on the Lesbian and Gay Left comments specifically on the role of interlocking systems of oppression in the lives of gays and lesbians. "By leftist we mean people who understand the struggle for lesbian and gay liberation to be integrally tied to struggles against class oppression, racism, and sexism. While we might use different political labels, we share a commitment to a fundamental transformation of the economic, political and social structures of society."

A left framework of politics, unlike civil rights or liberal frameworks, brings into focus the systematic relationship among forms of domination, where the creation and maintenance of exploited, subservient, marginalized classes is a necessary part of, at the very least, the economic configuration. Urvashi Vaid, in *Virtual Equality,* for example, writes of the limits of civil rights strategies in confronting systemic homophobia:

> Civil rights do not change the social order in dramatic ways; they change only the privileges of the group asserting those rights. Civil rights strategies do not challenge the moral and antisexual underpinnings of homophobia, because homophobia does not originate in our lack of full civil equality. Rather, homophobia arises from the nature and construction of the political, legal, economic, sexual, racial and family systems within which we live. (183)

Proceeding from the starting point of a system-based left analysis, strategies built upon the possibility of incorporation and assimilation are exposed as simply expanding and making accessible the status quo for more privileged members of marginal groups, while the most vulnerable in our communities continue to be stigmatized and oppressed.

It is important to note, however, that while left theorists tend to provide a more structural analysis of oppression and exploitation, many of these theorists and activists have also been homophobic and heterosexist in their approach to or avoidance of the topics of sexuality and heteronormativity. For example, Robin Podolsky, in "Sacrificing Queers and other 'Proletarian' Artifacts," writes that quite often on the left lesbian and gay sexuality and desire have been characterized as "more to do with personal happiness and sexual pleasure than with the 'material basis' of procreation—we were considered self-indulgent distractions from struggle . . . [an example of] 'bourgeois decadence'" (54).

This contradiction between a stated left analysis and an adherence to heteronormativity has probably been most dramatically identified in the writing of some feminist authors. I need only refer to Adrienne Rich's well-known article, "Compulsory Heterosexuality and Lesbian Existence," as a poignant critique of the white, middle-class heterosexual standard running through significant parts of feminist analysis and actions. The same adherence to a heterosexual norm can be found in the writing of self-identified black left intellectuals such as Cornel West and Michael Eric Dyson. Thus, while these writers have learned to make reference to lesbian, gay, bisexual, and transgendered segments of black communities—sparingly—they continue to foreground black heterosexuality and masculinity as the central unit of analysis in their writing—and most recently in their politics, witness their participation in the Million Man March.

This history of left organizing and the left's visible absence from any serious and sustained response to the AIDS epidemic have provoked many lesbian, gay, bisexual and transgendered people to question the relevance of this political configuration to the needs of our communities. Recognizing that reservations of this type are real and should be noted, I still hold that a left-rooted analysis which emphasizes economic exploitation and class structure, culture, and the systemic nature of power provides a framework of politics that is especially effective in representing and challenging the numerous sites and systems of oppression. Further, the left-centered approach that I embrace is one that designates sexuality and struggles against sexual normalization as central to the politics of all marginal communities.

THE ROOT OF QUEER POLITICS: CHALLENGING HETERONORMATIVITY?

In the introduction to the edited volume *Fear of a Queer Planet: Queer Politics and Social Theory*, Michael Warner asks the question: "What do queers want?" (vii). He suggests that the goals of queers and their politics extend beyond the sexual arena. Warner contends that what queers want is acknowledgment of their lives, struggles, and complete existence; queers want to be represented and included fully in left political analysis and American culture. Thus what queers want is to be a part of the social, economic, and political restructuring of this society; as Warner writes, queers want to have queer experience and politics "taken as starting points rather than as footnotes" in the social theories and political agendas of the left (vii). He contends that it has been the absence or invisibility of lived queer experience that has marked or constrained much of left social and political theories and "has posited and naturalized a heterosexual society" in such theories (vii).

The concerns and emerging politics of queer activists, as formulated by Warner and others interested in understanding the implications of the idea of queerness, are focused on highlighting queer presence and destroying heteronormativity not only in the larger dominant society but also in extant spaces, theories, and sites of resistance, presumably on the left. He suggests that those embracing the label of "queer" understand the need to challenge the assumption of heteronormativity in every aspect of their existence:

Every person who comes to a queer self-understanding knows in one way or another that her stigmatization is connected with gender, the family, notions of individual freedom, the state, public speech, consumption and desire, nature and culture, maturation, reproductive politics, racial and national fantasy, class identity, truth and trust, censorship, intimate life and social display, terror and violence, health care, and deep cultural norms about the bearing of the body. Being queer means fighting about these issues all the time, locally and piecemeal but always with consequences. (xiii)

Now, independent of the fact that few of us could find ourselves in such a grandiose description of queer consciousness, I believe that Warner's description points to the fact that in the roots of a lived "queer" existence are experiences with domination and in particular heteronormativity that form the basis for genuine transformational politics. By transformational, again, I mean a politics that does not search for opportunities to integrate into dominant institutions and normative social relationships, but instead pursues a political agenda that seeks to change values, definitions, and laws which make these institutions and relationships oppressive.

Queer activists experiencing displacement both within and outside of lesbian and gay communities rebuff what they deem the assimilationist practices and policies of more established lesbian and gay organizations. These organizers and activists reject cultural norms of acceptable sexual behavior and identification and instead embrace political strategies which promote self-definition and full expression. Members of the Chicago-based group Queers United Against Straight-acting Homosexuals (QUASH) state just such a position in the article "Assimilation Is Killing Us: Fight for a Queer United Front" published in their newsletter, WHY I HATED THE MARCH ON WASHINGTON:

Assimilation is killing us. We are falling into a trap. Some of us adopt an apologetic stance, stating "that's just the way I am" (read: "I'd be straight if I could."). Others pattern their behavior in such a way as to mimic heterosexual society so as to minimize the glaring differences between us and them. No matter how much [money] you make, fucking your lover is still illegal in nearly half of the states. Getting a corporate job, a fierce car and a condo does not protect you from dying of AIDS or getting your head bashed in by neo-Nazis. The myth of assimilation must be shattered.

. . . Fuck the heterosexual, nuclear family. Let's make families which promote sexual choices and liberation rather than sexual oppression. We must learn from the legacy of resistance that is ours: a legacy which shows that empowerment comes through grassroots activism, not mainstream politics, a legacy which shows that real change occurs when we are inclusive, not exclusive. (4)

At the very heart of queer politics, at least as it is formulated by QUASH, is a fundamental challenge to the heteronormativity—the privilege, power, and normative status invested in heterosexuality—of the dominant society.

It is in their fundamental challenge to a systemic process of domination and exclusion, with a specific focus on heteronormativity, that queer activists and queer theorists are tied to and rooted in a tradition of political struggle most often identified with people of color and other marginal groups. For example, activists of color have, through many historical periods, questioned their formal and informal inclusion and power in prevailing social categories. Through just such a process of challenging their centrality to lesbian and gay politics in particular, and lesbian and gay communities more generally, lesbian, gay, bisexual, and transgendered people of color advanced debates over who and what would be represented as "truly gay." As Steven Seidman reminds us in "Identity and Politics in a 'Postmodern' Gay Culture: Some Historical and Conceptual Notes," beyond the general framing provided by postmodern queer theory, gay and lesbian—and now queer—politics owes much of its impetus to the politics of people of color and other marginalized members of lesbian and gay communities.

> Specifically, I make the case that postmodern strains in gay thinking and politics have their immediate social origin in recent developments in the gay culture. In the reaction by people of color, third-world-identified gays, poor and working-class gays, and sex rebels to the ethnic/essentialist model of identity and community that achieved dominance in the lesbian and gay cultures of the 1970s, I locate the social basis for a rethinking of identity and politics. (106)

Through the demands of lesbian, gay, bisexual, and transgendered people of color as well as others who did not see themselves or their numerous communities in the more narrowly constructed politics of white gays and lesbians, the contestation took shape over who and what type of issues would be represented in lesbian and gay politics and in larger community discourse.

While similarities and connections between the politics of lesbians, gay men, bisexuals, and transgendered people of color during the 1970s and 1980s and queer activists of today clearly exist, the present-day rendition of this politics has deviated significantly from its legacy. Specifically, while both political efforts include as a focus of their work the radicalization and/or expansion of traditional lesbian and gay politics, the politics of lesbian, gay, bisexual, and transgendered people of color have been and continue to be much broader in its understanding of transformational politics.

The politics of lesbian, gay, bisexual, and transgendered people of color has often been guided by the type of radical intersectional left analysis I detailed earlier. Thus, while the politics of lesbian, gay, bisexual, and transgendered activists of color might recognize heteronormativity as a primary system of power structuring our lives, it understands that heteronormativity interacts with institutional racism, patriarchy, and class exploitation to define us in numerous ways as marginal and oppressed subjects.[5] And it is this constructed subservient position that allows our sisters and brothers to be used either as surplus labor in an advanced capitalist structure and/or seen as expendable, denied resources, and thus locked into correctional institutions across the country. While heterosexual privilege negatively impacts and constrains the lived experience of "queers" of color, so too do racism, classism, and sexism.

In contrast to the left intersectional analysis that has structured much of the politics of "queers" of color, the basis of the politics of some white queer activists and organizations has come dangerously close to a single-oppression model. Experiencing "deviant" sexuality as the prominent characteristic of their marginalization, these activists begin to envision the world in terms of a "hetero/queer" divide. Using the framework of queer theory in which heteronormativity is identified as a system of regulation and normalization, some queer activists map the power and entitlement of normative heterosexuality onto the bodies of all heterosexuals. Further, these activists naively characterize all those who exist under the category of "queer" as powerless. Thus, in the process of conceptualizing a decentered identity of queerness, meant to embrace all those who stand on the outside of heteronormativity, a monolithic understanding of heterosexuality and queerness has come to dominate the political imagination and actions of many queer activists.

This reconstruction of a binary divide between heterosexuals and queers, while discernible in many of the actions of Queer Nation, is probably most evident in the manifesto "I Hate Straights." Distributed at gay pride parades in New York and Chicago in 1990, the declaration written by an anonymous group of queers begins,

> I have friends. Some of them are straight.
>
> Year after year, I see my straight friends. I want to see how they are doing, to add newness to our long and complicated histories, to experience some continuity.
>
> Year after year I continue to realize that the facts of my life are irrelevant to them and that I am only half

listened to, that I am an appendage to the doings of a greater world, a world of power and privilege, of the laws of installation, a world of exclusion. 'That's not true,' argue my straight friends. There is the one certainty in the politics of power; those left out of it beg for inclusion, while the insiders claim that they already are. Men do it to women, whites do it to blacks, *and everyone does it to queers.*

. . . The main dividing line, both conscious and unconscious, is procreation . . . and that magic word—Family. (emphasis added)

Screaming out from this manifesto is an analysis which places not heteronormativity, but heterosexuality, as the central "dividing line " between those who would be dominant and those who are oppressed. Nowhere in this essay is there recognition that "nonnormative" procreation patterns and family structures of people who are labeled heterosexual have also been used to regulate and exclude *them*. Instead, the authors declare. "Go tell them [straights] to go away until they have spent a month walking hand in hand in public with someone of the same sex. After they survive that, then you'll hear what they have to say about queer anger. Otherwise, tell them to shut up and listen." For these activists, the power of heterosexuality is the focus, and queer anger the means of queer politics. Missing from this equation is any attention to, or acknowledgment of, the ways in which identities of race, class, and/or gender either enhance or mute the marginalization of queers, on the one hand, and the power of heterosexuals, on the other.

The fact that this essay is written about and out of queer anger is undoubtedly part of the rationale for its defense (Berlant and Freeman 200). But I question the degree to which we should read this piece as just an aberrational diatribe against straights motivated by intense queer anger. While anger is clearly a motivating factor for such writing, we should also understand this action to represent an analysis and politics structured around the simple dichotomy of straight and queer. We know, for instance, that similar positions have been put forth in other anonymously published, publicly distributed manifestos. For example, in the document *Queers Read This*, the authors write, "Don't be fooled, straight people own the world and the only reason you have been spared is you're smart, lucky or a fighter. Straight people have a privilege that allows them to do whatever they please and fuck without fear." They continue by stating: "Straight people are your enemy."

Even within this document, which seems to exemplify the narrowness of queer conceptions, there is a surprising glimpse at a more enlightened left intersectional understanding of what queerness might mean. For instance, the authors continue, "being queer is not about a right to privacy; it is about the freedom to be public, to just be who we are. It means everyday fighting oppression; homophobia, racism, misogyny, the bigotry of religious hypocrites and our own self-hatred." Evident in this one document are the inherent tensions and dilemmas many queer activists currently encounter: how does one implement in real political struggle a decentered political identity that is not constituted by a process of seemingly reductive "othering"?

The process of ignoring or at least downplaying queers' varying relationships to power is evident not only in the writing of queer activists, but also in the political actions pursued by queer organizations. I question the ability of political actions such as mall invasions (pursued by groups such as the Queer Shopping Network in New York and the Suburban Homosexual Outreach Program [SHOP] in San Francisco), to address the fact that queers exist in different social locations. Lauren Berlant and Elizabeth Freeman describe mall invasion projects as

[an attempt to take] the relatively bounded spectacle of the urban pride parade to the ambient pleasures of the shopping mall. "Mall visibility actions" thus conjoin the spectacular lure of the parade with Hare Krishna-style conversion and proselytizing techniques. Stepping into malls in hair-gelled splendor, holding hands and handing out fliers, the queer auxiliaries produce an "invasion" that conveys a different message. "We're here, we're queer, *you're* going shopping." (210)

The activity of entering or "invading" the shopping mall on the part of queer nationals is clearly one of attempted subversion. Intended by their visible presence in this clearly coded heterosexual family economic mecca is a disruption of the agreed-upon segregation between the allowable spaces for queer "deviant" culture and the rest of the "naturalized" world. Left unchallenged in such an action, however, are the myriad ways, besides the enforcement of normative sexuality, in which some queers feel alienated and excluded from the space of the mall. Where does the mall as an institution of consumer culture and relative economic privilege play into this analysis? How does this action account for the varying economic relationships queers have to consumer culture? If you are a poor or working-class queer the exclusion and alienation you experience when entering the mall may not be limited to the normative sexual codes associated with the mall, but may also be centered on the assumed economic status of those shopping in suburban malls. If you are a queer of color your exclusion from the mall may, in part, be rooted in racial norms and stereotypes which construct you as a threatening subject every time you enter this economic institution. Queer activists must confront a question that haunts most political organizing: How do we put into politics a broad and inclusive left analysis that can actually engage and mobilize individuals with intersecting identities?

Clearly, there will be those critics who will claim that I am asking too much from any political organization. Demands that every aspect of oppression and regulation be addressed in each political act seem, and are indeed, unreasonable. However, I make the critique of queer mall invasions neither to stop such events nor to suggest that every oppression be dealt with by this one political action. Instead, I raise these concerns to emphasize the ways in which varying relation to power exist not only among heterosexuals, but also among those who label themselves queer.

In its current rendition, queer politics is coded with class, gender, and race privilege, and may have lost its potential to be a politically expedient organizing tool for addressing the needs—and mobilizing the bodies—of people of color. As some queer theorists and activists call for the destruction of stable sexual categories, for example, moving instead toward a more fluid understanding of sexual behavior, left unspoken is the class privilege which allows for such fluidity. Class or material privilege is a cornerstone of much of queer politics and theory as they exist today. Queer theorizing which calls for the elimination of fixed categories of sexual identity seems to ignore the ways in which some traditional social identities and communal ties can, in fact, be important to one's survival. Further, a queer politics which demonizes all heterosexuals discounts the relationships—especially those based on shared experiences of marginalization—that exist between gays and straights, particularly in communities of color.

Queers who operate out of a political culture of individualism assume a material independence that allows them to disregard historically or culturally recognized categories and communities or at the very least to move fluidly among them without ever establishing permanent relationships or identities within them.

However, I and many other lesbian and gay people of color, as well as poor and working-class lesbians and gay men, do not have such material independence. Because of my multiple identities, which locate me and other "queer" people of color at the margins in this country, my material advancement, my physical protection and my emotional well-being are constantly threatened. In those stable categories and named communities whose histories have been structured by shared resistance to oppression, I find relative degrees of safety and security.

Let me emphasize again that the safety I feel is relative to other threats and is clearly not static or constant. For in those named communities I also find versions of domination and normalization being replicated and employed as more privileged/assimilated marshal group members use their associations with dominant institutions and resources to regulate and police the activities of other marginal group members. Any lesbian, gay, bisexual, or transgendered person of color who has experienced exclusion from indigenous institutions, such as the exclusion many out black gay men have encountered from some black churches responding to AIDS, recognizes that even within marginal groups there are normative rules determining community membership and power (Cohen). However, in spite of the unequal power relationships located in marginal communities, I am still not interested in disassociating politically from those communities, for queerness, as it is currently constructed, offers no viable political alternative, since it invites us to put forth a political agenda that makes invisible the prominence of race, class, and to varying degrees gender in determining the life chances of those on both sides of the hetero/queer divide.

So despite the roots of queer politics in the struggles of "queer" people of color, despite the calls for highlighting categories which have sought to regulate and control black bodies like my own, and despite the attempts at decentralized grassroots activism in some queer political organizations, there still exist—for some, like myself—great misgivings about current constructions of the term "queer." Personally speaking, I do not consider myself a "queer" activist or, for that matter, a "queer" anything. This is not because I do not consider myself an activist; in fact I hold my political work to be one of my most important contributions to all of my communities. But like other lesbian, gay, bisexual, and transgendered activists of color, I find the label "queer" fraught with unspoken assumptions which inhibit the radical political potential of this category.

The alienation, or at least discomfort, many activists and theorists of color have with current conceptions of queerness is evidenced, in part, by the minimal numbers of theorists of color who engage in the process of theorizing about the concept. Further, the sparse numbers of people of color who participate in "queer" political organizations might also be read as a sign of discomfort with the term. Most important, my confidence in making such a claim of distance and uneasiness with the term "queer" on the part of many people of color comes from my interactions with other lesbian, gay, bisexual, and transgendered people of color who repeatedly express their interpretation of "queer" as a term rooted in class, race, and gender privilege. For us, "queer" is a politics based on narrow sexual dichotomies which make no room either for the analysis of oppression of those we might categorize as heterosexual, or for the privilege of those who operate as "queer." As black lesbian activist and writer Barbara Smith argues in "Queer Politics: Where's the Revolution?":

> Unlike the early lesbian and gay movement, which had both ideological and practical links to the left, black activism and feminism, today's "queer" politicos seem to operate in a historical and ideological vacuum. "Queer" activists focus on "queer" issues, and racism, sexual oppression and economic exploitation do not qualify, despite the fact that the majority of "queers" are people of color, female or working class. . . . Building unified, ongoing coalitions that challenge the system and ultimately prepare a way for revolutionary change simply isn't what "queer" activists have in mind. (13–14)

It is this narrow understanding of the idea of queer that negates its use in fundamentally reorienting the politics and privilege of lesbian and gay politics as well as more generally moving or transforming the politics of the left. Despite its liberatory claim to stand in opposition to static categories of oppression, queer politics and much of queer theory seem in fact to be static in the understanding of race, class, and gender and their roles in how heteronormativity regulates sexual behavior and identities. Distinctions between the status and the acceptance of different individuals categorized under the label of "heterosexual" go unexplored.

I emphasize the marginalized position of some who embrace heterosexual identities not because I want to lead any great crusade to understand more fully the plight of "the heterosexual." Rather, I recognize the potential for shared resistance with such individuals.

This potential not only for coalitional work but for a shared analysis is especially relevant, from my vantage point, to "queer" people of color. Again, in my call for coalition work across sexual categories, I do not want to suggest that same-sex political struggles have not, independently, played an essential and distinct role in the liberatory politics and social movements of marginal people. My concern, instead, is with any political analysis or theory which collapses our understanding of power into a single continuum of evaluation.

Through a brief review of some of the ways in which nonnormative heterosexuality has been controlled and regulated through the state and systems of marginalization we may be reminded that differentials in power exist within all socially named categories. And through such recognition we may begin to envision a new political formation in which one's relation to dominant power serves as the basis of unity for radical coalition work in the twenty-first century.

HETEROSEXUALS ON THE (OUT)SIDE OF HETERONORMATIVITY

In this section I want to return to the question of a monolithic understanding of heterosexuality. I believe that through this issue we can begin to think critically about the components of a radical politics built not exclusively on identities, but on identities as they are invested with varying degrees of normative power. Thus, fundamental to my concern about the current structure and future agenda of queer politics is the unchallenged assumption of a uniform heteronormativity from which all heterosexuals benefit. I want again to be clear that there are, in fact, some who identify themselves as queer activists who do acknowledge relative degrees of power, and heterosexual access to that power, even evoking the term "straight queers." "Queer means to fuck with gender. There are straight queers, bi queers, tranny queers, lez queers, fag queers, SM queers, fisting queers in every single street in this apathetic country of ours" (anonymous, qtd. McIntosh 31).

Despite such sporadic insight, much of the politics of queer activists has been structured around the dichotomy of straight versus everything else, assuming a monolithic experience of heterosexual privilege for all those identified publicly with heterosexuality. A similar reductive dichotomy between men and women has consistently reemerged in the writing and actions of some feminists. And only through the demands, the actions, and the writing of many "feminists" and/or lesbians of color have those women who stand outside the norm of white, middle-class, legalized heterosexuality begun to see their lives, needs, and bodies represented in feminist theory (Carby; Collins; hooks). In a similar manner lesbian, gay, bisexual, and transgendered people of color have increasingly taken on the responsibility for at the very least complicating and most often challenging reductive notions of heteronormativity articulated by queer activists and scholars (Alexander; Farajaje-Jones; Lorde; Moraga and Anzaldúa; B. Smith).

If we follow such examples, complicating our understanding of both heteronormativity and queerness, we move one step closer to building the progressive coalition politics many of us desire. Specifically, if we pay attention to both historical and current examples of heterosexual relationships which have been prohibited, stigmatized, and generally repressed, we may begin to identify those spaces of shared or similar oppression and resistance that provide a basis for radical coalition work. Further, we may begin to answer certain questions: In narrowly positing a dichotomy of heterosexual privilege and queer oppression under which we all exist, are we negating a basis of political unity that could serve to strengthen many communities and movements seeking justice and societal transformation? How do we use the relative degrees of ostracization all sexual/cultural "deviants" experience to build a basis of unity for broader coalition and movement work?

A little history (as a political scientist a little history is all I can offer) might be helpful in trying to sort out the various ways heterosexuality, especially as it has intersected with race, has been defined and experienced by different groups of people. It should also help to underscore the fact that many of the roots of heteronormativity are in white supremacist ideologies which sought (and continue) to use the state and its regulation of sexuality, in particular through the institution of heterosexual marriage, to designate which individuals were truly "fit" for full rights and privileges of citizenship. For example, the prohibition of marriages between black women and men imprisoned in the slave system was a component of many slave codes enacted during the seventeenth and eighteenth centuries. M.G. Smith, in his article on the structure of slave economic systems, succinctly states, "As property slaves were prohibited from forming legal relationships or marriages which would interfere with and restrict their owner's property

rights" (71–72). Herbert G. Gutman, in *The Black Family in Slavery and Freedom, 1750–1925*, elaborates on the ideology of slave societies which denied the legal sanctioning of marriages between slaves and further reasoned that Blacks had no conception of family.

> The *Nation* identified sexual restraint, civil marriage, and family "stability" with "civilization" itself.
>
> Such mid-nineteenth-century class and sexual beliefs reinforced racial beliefs about Afro-Americans. As slaves, after all, their marriages had not been sanctioned by the civil laws and therefore "the sexual passion" went unrestrained. . . . Many white abolitionists denied the slaves a family life or even, often, a family consciousness because for them [whites] the family had its origins in and had to be upheld by the civil law. (295)

Thus it was not the promotion of marriage or heterosexuality per se that served as the standard or motivation of most slave societies. Instead, marriage and heterosexuality, as viewed through the lenses of profit and domination, and the ideology of white supremacy, were reconfigured to justify the exploitation and regulation of black bodies, even those presumably engaged in heterosexual behavior. It was this system of state-sanctioned, white male, upper-class, heterosexual domination that forced these presumably black *heterosexual* men and women to endure a history of rape, lynching, and other forms of physical and mental terrorism. In this way, marginal group members, lacking power and privilege although engaged in heterosexual behavior, have often found themselves defined as outside the norms and values of dominant society. This position has most often resulted in the suppression or negation of their legal, social, and physical relationships and rights.

In addition to the prohibition of marriage between slaves, A. Leon Higginbotham, Jr., in *The Matter of Color—Race and the American Legal Process: The Colonial Period*, writes of the legal restrictions barring interracial marriages. He reminds us that the essential core of the American legal tradition was the preservation of the white race. The "mixing" of the races was to be strictly prohibited in early colonial laws. The regulation of interracial heterosexual relationships, however, should not be understood as exclusively relegated to the seventeenth, eighteenth and nineteenth centuries. In fact, Higginbotham informs us that the final law prohibiting miscegenation (the "interbreeding" or marrying of individuals from different "races"—actually meant to inhibit the "tainting" of the white race) was not repealed until 1967:

> Colonial anxiety about interracial sexual activity cannot be attributed solely to seventeenth-century values, for it was not until 1967 that the United States Supreme Court finally declared unconstitutional those statutes prohibiting interracial marriages. The Supreme Court waited thirteen years after its *Brown* decision dealing with desegregation of schools before, in *Loving v. Virginia*, it agreed to consider the issue of interracial marriages. (41)

It is this pattern of regulating the behavior and denigrating the identities of those heterosexuals on the outside of heteronormative privilege, in particular those perceived as threatening systems of white supremacy, male domination, and capitalist advancement, that I want to highlight. An understanding of the ways in which heteronormativity works to support and reinforce institutional racism, patriarchy, and class exploitation must therefore be a part of how we problematize current constructions of heterosexuality. As I stated previously, I am not suggesting that those involved in publicly identifiable heterosexual behavior do not receive political, economic, and social advantage, especially in comparison to the experiences of some lesbian, transgendered, gay, and bisexual individuals. But the equation linking identity and behavior to power is not as linear and clear as some queer theorists and activists would have us believe.

A more recent example of regulated nonnormative heterosexuality is located in current debates and rhetoric regarding the "underclass" and the destruction of the welfare system. The stigmatization and demonization of single mothers, teen mothers, and, primarily, poor women of color dependent on state assistance has had a long and suspicious presence in American "intellectual" and political history. It was in 1965 that Daniel Patrick Moynihan released his "study" entitled *The Negro Family: The Case for National Action*. In this report, which would eventually come to be known as the Moynihan Report, the author points to the "pathologies" increasingly evident in so-called Negro families. In this document were allegations of the destructive nature of Negro family formations. The document's introduction argues that

> the fundamental problem, in which this is most clearly the case, is that of family structure. The evidence—not

final, but powerfully persuasive—is that the Negro family in urban ghettos is crumbling. A middle-class group has managed to save itself, but for vast numbers of the unskilled, poorly educated city working class the fabric of conventional social relationships has all but disintegrated.

Moynihan, later in the document, goes on to describe the crisis and pathologies facing Negro family structure as being generated by the increasing number of single-female-headed households, the increasing number of "illegitimate" births and, of course, increasing welfare dependency:

> In essence, the Negro community has been forced into a matriarchal structure which, because it is so out of line with the rest of the American society, seriously retards the progress of the group as a whole, and imposes a crushing burden on the Negro male and, in consequence, on a great many Negro women as well. . . . In a word, most Negro youth are in danger of being caught up in the tangle of pathology that affects their world, and probably a majority are so entrapped. . . . Obviously, not every instance of social pathology afflicting the Negro community can be traced to the weakness of family structure. . . . Nonetheless, at the center of the tangle of pathology is the weakness of the family structure. (29–30)

It is not the nonheterosexist behavior of these black men and women that is under fire, but rather the perceived nonnormative sexual behavior and family structures of these individuals, whom many queer activists—without regard to the impact of race, class, or gender—would designate as part of the heterosexist establishment or those mighty "straights they hate."

Over the last thirty years the demonization of poor women, engaged in nonnormative heterosexual relationships, has continued under the auspices of scholarship on the "underclass." Adolph L. Reed, in "The 'Underclass' as Myth and Symbol: The Poverty of Discourse about Poverty," discusses the gendered and racist nature of much of this literature, in which poor, often black and Latina women are portrayed as unable to control their sexual impulses and eventual reproductive decisions, unable to raise their children with the right moral fiber, unable to find "gainful" employment to support themselves and their "illegitimate children," and of course unable to manage "effectively" the minimal assistance provided by the state. Reed writes:

> The underclass notion may receive the greatest ideological boost from its gendered imagery and relation to gender politics. As I noted in a critique of Wilson's *The Truly Disadvantaged*, "family" is an intrinsically ideological category. The rhetoric of "disorganization," "disintegration," "deterioration" reifies one type of living arrangement—the ideal type of the bourgeois nuclear family—as outside history, nearly as though it were decreed by natural law. But—as I asked earlier—why exactly is out-of-wedlock birth pathological? Why is the female-headed household an indicator of disorganization and pathology? Does that stigma attach to *all* such households—even, say, a divorced executive who is a custodial mother? If not, what are the criteria for assigning it? The short answer is race and class bias inflected through a distinctively gendered view of the world. (33–34)

In this same discourse of the "underclass," young black men engaged in "reckless" heterosexual behavior are represented as irresponsible baby factories, unable to control or restrain their "sexual passion" (to borrow a term from the seventeenth century). And unfortunately, often it has been the work of professed liberals like William Julius Wilson, in his book *The Truly Disadvantaged*, that, while not using the word "pathologies," has substantiated in its own tentative way the conservative dichotomy between the deserving working poor and the lazy, Cadillac-driving, steak-eating welfare queens of Ronald Reagan's imagination. Again, I raise this point to remind us of the numerous ways that sexuality and sexual deviance from a prescribed norm have been used to demonize and to oppress various segments of the population, even some classified under the label "heterosexual."

The policies of politicians and the actions of law enforcement officials have reinforced, in much more devastating ways, the distinctions between acceptable forms of heterosexual expression and those to be regulated—increasingly through incarceration. This move toward the disallowance of some forms of heterosexual expression and reproductive choice can be seen in the practice of prosecuting pregnant women suspected of using drugs—nearly 80 percent of all women prosecuted are women of color; through the forced sterilization of Puerto Rican and Native American women; and through the state-dictated use of Norplant by women answering to the criminal justice system and by women receiving state assistance.[6] Further, it is the "nonnormative" children of many of these nonnormative women that Newt Gingrich would place in orphanages. This is the same Newt Gingrich who, despite his clear disdain for gay and lesbian "lifestyles," has invited lesbians and gay men into the Republican party. I need not remind you that he made no such offer to the women on welfare discussed above. Who, we might ask, is truly on the outside of heteronormative power—maybe *most* of us?

CONCLUSION: DESTABILIZATION AND RADICAL COALITION WORK

While all this may, in fact, seem interesting or troubling or both, you may be wondering: What does it have to do with the question of the future of queer politics? It is my argument, as I stated earlier, that one of the great failings of queer theory and especially queer politics has been their inability to incorporate into analysis of the world and strategies for political mobilization the roles that race, class, and gender play in defining people's differing relations to dominant and normalizing power. I present this essay as the beginning of a much longer and protracted struggle to acknowledge and delineate the distribution of power within and outside of queer communities. This is a discussion of how to build a politics organized not merely by reductive categories of straight and queer, but organized instead around a more intersectional analysis of who and what the enemy is and where our potential allies can be found. This analysis seeks to make clear the privilege and power embedded in the categorizations of, on the one hand, an upstanding, "morally correct," white, state-authorized, middle-class, male *heterosexual*, and on the other, a culturally deficient, materially bankrupt, state-dependent, *heterosexual* woman of color, the latter found most often in our urban centers (those that haven't been gentrified), on magazine covers, and on the evening news.

I contend, therefore, that the radical potential of queer politics, or any liberatory movement, rests on its ability to advance strategically oriented political identities arising from a more nuanced understanding of power. One of the most difficult tasks in such an endeavor (and there are many) is not to forsake the complexities of both how power is structured and how we might think about the coalitions we create. Far too often movements revert to a position in which membership and joint political work are based upon a necessarily similar history of oppression—but this is too much like identity politics (Phelan). Instead, I am suggesting that the process of movement building be rooted not in our shared history or identity, but in our shared marginal relationship to dominant power which normalizes, legitimizes, and privileges.

We must, therefore, start our political work from the recognition that multiple systems of oppression are in operation and that these systems use institutionalized categories and identities to regulate and socialize. We must also understand that power and access to dominant resources are distributed across the boundaries of "het" and "queer" that we construct. A model of queer politics that simply pits the grand "heterosexuals" against all those oppressed "queers" is ineffectual as the basis for action in a political environment dominated by Newt Gingrich, the Christian Right, and the recurring ideology of white supremacy. As we stand on the verge of watching those in power dismantle the welfare system through a process of demonizing poor and young, primarily poor and young women of color—many of whom have existed for their entire lives outside the white, middle-class, heterosexual norm—we have to ask if these women do not fit into society's categories of marginal, deviant, and "queer." As we watch the explosion of prison construction and the disproportionate incarceration rates of young men and women of color, often as part of the economic development of poor white rural communities, we have to ask if these individuals do not fit society's definition of "queer" and expendable.

I am not proposing a political strategy that homogenizes and glorifies the experience of poor heterosexual people of color. In fact, in calling for a more expansive left political identity and formation I do not seek to erase the specific historical relation between the stigma of "queer" and the sexual activity of gay men, lesbians, bisexual, and transgendered individuals. And in no way do I mean to, or want to, equate the experiences of marginal heterosexual women and men to the lived experiences of queers. There is no doubt that heterosexuality, even for those heterosexuals who stand outside the norms of heteronormativity, results in some form of privilege and feelings of supremacy. I need only recount the times when other women of color, more economically vulnerable than myself, expressed superiority and some feelings of disgust when they realized that the nice young professor (me) was "that way."

However, in recognizing the distinct history of oppression lesbian, gay, bisexual, and transgendered people have confronted and challenged, I am not willing to embrace every queer as my marginalized political ally. In the same way, I do not assume that shared racial, gender, and/or class position or identity guarantees or produces similar political commitments. Thus, identities and communities, while important to this strategy, must be complicated and destabilized through a recognition of the multiple social positions and relations to dominant power found *within* any one category or identity. Kimberle Crenshaw, in "Mapping the Margins: Intersectionality, Identity Politics, and Violence against Women of Color," suggests that such a project use the idea of intersectionality to reconceptualize or problematize the identities and communities that are "home" to us. She demands that we challenge those identities that seem like home by acknowledging the other parts of our identities that are excluded:

> With identity thus reconceptualized [through a recognition of intersectionality], it may be easier to understand the need to summon up the courage to challenge groups that are after all, in one sense, "home" to us, in the name of the parts of us that are not made at home. . . . The most one could expect is that we will dare to speak against internal exclusions and marginalizations, that we might call attention to how the identity of "the group" has been centered on the intersectional identities of a few. . . . Through an awareness of intersectionality, we can better acknowledge and ground the differences among us and negotiate the means by which these differences will find expression in constructing group politics. (1299)

In the same ways that we account for the varying privilege to be gained by a heterosexual identity, we must also pay attention to the privilege some queers receive from being white, male, and upper class. Only through recognizing the many manifestations of power, across and within categories, can we truly begin to build a movement based on one's politics and not exclusively on one's identity.

I want to be clear that what I and others are calling for is the destabilization, and not the destruction or abandonment, of identity categories.[7] We must reject a queer politics which seems to ignore, in its analysis of the usefulness of traditionally named categories, the roles of identity and community as paths to survival, using shared experiences of oppression and resistance to build indigenous resources, shape consciousness, and act collectively. Instead, I would suggest that it is the multiplicity and interconnectedness of our identities which provide the most promising avenue for the *destabilization and radical politicalization* of these same categories.

This is not an easy path to pursue because most often this will mean building a political analysis and political strategies around the most marginal in our society, some of whom look like us, many of whom do not. Most often, this will mean rooting our struggle in, and addressing the needs of, communities of color. Most often this will mean highlighting the intersectionality of one's race, class, gender, and sexuality and the relative power and privilege that one receives from being a man and/ or being white and/or being middle class and/or being heterosexual. This, in particular, is a daunting challenge because so much of our political consciousness has been built around simple dichotomies such as powerful/ powerless; oppressor/victim; enemy/comrade. It is difficult to feel safe and secure in those spaces where both your relative privilege and your experiences with marginalization are understood to shape your commitment to radical politics. However, as Bernice Johnson Reagon so aptly put it in her essay, "Coalition Politics: Turning the Century," "if you feel the strain, you may be doing some good work" (362).

And while this is a daunting challenge and uncomfortable position, those who have taken it up have not only survived, but succeeded in their efforts. For example, both the needle exchange and prison projects pursued through the auspices of ACT UP New York point to the possibilities and difficulties involved in principled transformative coalition work. In each project individuals from numerous identities—heterosexual, gay, poor, wealthy, white, black, Latino—came together to challenge dominant constructions of who should be allowed and who deserved care. No particular identity exclusively determined the shared political commitments of these activists; instead their similar positions, as marginalized subjects relative to the state—made clear through the government's lack of response to AIDS—formed the basis of this political unity.

In the prison project, it was the contention of activists that the government which denied even wealthy gay men access to drugs to combat this disease must be regarded as the same source of power that denied incarcerated men and women access to basic health care, including those drugs and conditions needed to combat HIV and AIDS. The coalition work this group engaged in involved a range of people, from formerly incarcerated individuals, to heterosexual men and women of color, to those we might deem privileged white lesbians and gay men. And this same group of people who came together to protest the conditions of incarcerated people with AIDS also showed up to public events challenging the homophobia that guided the government's and biomedical industries' response to this epidemic. The political work of this group of individuals was undoubtedly informed by the public identities they embraced, but these were identities that they further acknowledged as complicated by intersectionality and placed within a political framework where their shared experience as marginal, nonnormative subjects could be foregrounded. Douglas Crimp, in his article "Right On, Girlfriend!" suggests that through political work our identities become remade and must therefore be understood as *relational*. Describing such a transformation in the identities of queer activists engaged in, and prosecuted for, needle exchange work, Crimp writes:

> But once engaged in the struggle to end the crisis, these queers' identities were no longer the same. It's not that "queer" doesn't any longer encompass their sexual practices; it does, but it also entails a *relation* between those practices and other circumstances that make very different people vulnerable both to HIV infection and to the stigma, discrimination, and neglect that have characterized the societal and governmental response to the constituencies most affected by the AIDS epidemic. (317–18)

The radical potential of those of us on the outside of heteronormativity rests in our understanding that we need not base our politics in the dissolution of all categories and communities, but we need instead to work toward the destabilization and remaking of our identities. Difference, in and of itself—even that difference designated through named categories—is not the problem. Instead it is the power invested in certain identity categories and the idea that bounded categories are not to be transgressed that serve as the basis of domination and control. The reconceptualization not only of the content of identity categories, but the intersectional nature of identities themselves, must become part of our political practice.

We must thus begin to link our intersectional analysis of power with concrete coalitional work. In real terms this means identifying political struggles such as the needle exchange and prison projects of ACT UP that transgress the boundaries of identity to highlight, in this case, both the repressive power of the state and the normalizing power evident within both dominant and marginal communities. This type of principled coalition work is also being pursued in a more modest fashion by the Policy Institute of the National Gay and Lesbian Task Force. Recently, the staff at the Task Force distributed position papers not only on the topics of gay marriages and gays in the military, but also on right-wing attacks against welfare and affirmative action. Here we have political work based in the knowledge that the rhetoric and accusations of nonnormativity that Newt Gingrich and other right-wingers launch against women on welfare closely resemble the attacks of nonnormativity mounted against gays, lesbians, bisexuals, and transgendered individuals. Again it is the marginalized relation to power, experienced by both of these groups—and I do not mean to suggest that the groups are mutually exclusive—that frames the possibility for transformative coalition work. This prospect diminishes when we do not recognize and deal with the reality that the intersecting identities that gay people embody—in terms of race, class, and gender privilege—put some of us on Gingrich's side of the welfare struggle (e.g., Log Cabin Republicans). And in a similar manner a woman's dependence on state financial assistance in

no way secures her position as one supportive of gay rights and/or liberation. While a marginal identity undoubtedly increases the prospects of shared consciousness, only an articulation and commitment to mutual support can truly be the test of unity when pursuing transformational politics.

Finally, I realize that I have been short on specifics when trying to describe how we move concretely toward a transformational coalition politics among marginalized subjects. The best I can do is offer this discussion as a starting point for reassessing the shape of queer/lesbian/gay/bisexual/transgendered politics as we approach the twenty-first century. A reconceptualization of the politics of marginal groups allows us not only to privilege the specific lived experience of distinct communities, but also to search for those interconnected sites of resistance from which we can wage broader political struggles. Only by recognizing the link *between* the ideological, social, political, and economic marginalization of punks, bulldaggers, and welfare queens can we begin to develop political analyses and political strategies effective in confronting the linked yet varied sites of power in this country. Such a project is important because it provides a framework from which the difficult work of coalition politics can begin. And it is in these complicated and contradictory spaces that the liberatory and left politics that so many of us work for is located.

ACKNOWLEDGMENTS

The author would like to thank Mark Blasius, Nan Boyd, Ed Cohen, Carolyn Dinshaw, Jeff Edwards, Licia Fiol-Matta, Joshua Gamson, Lynne Huffer, Tamara Jones, Carla Kaplan, Ntanya Lee, Ira Livingston, and Barbara Ransby for their comments on various versions of this paper. All shortcomings are of course the fault of the author.

NOTES

1. The very general chronology of queer theory and queer politics referred to throughout this article is not meant to write the definitive historical development of each phenomenon. Instead, the dates are used to provide the reader with a general frame of reference. See Epstein for a similar genealogy of queer theory and queer politics.
2. See Ingraham for a discussion of the heterogendered imaginary.
3. I want to be clear that in this essay I am including the destruction of sexual categories as part of the agenda of queer politics. While a substantial segment of queer activists and theorists call for the *destabilization* of sexual categories, there are also those self-avowed queers who embrace a politics

built around the *deconstruction* and/or elimination of sexual categories. For example, a number of my self-identified queer students engage in sexual behavior that most people would interpret as *transgressive* of sexual identities and categories. However, these students have repeatedly articulated a different interpretation of their sexual behavior. They put forth an understanding that does not highlight their transgression of categories, but one which instead represents them as individuals who operate outside of categories and sexual identities altogether. They are sexual beings, given purely to desire, truly living sexual fluidity, and not constrained by any form of sexual categorization or identification. This interpretation seems at least one step removed from that held by people who embrace the fluidity of sexuality while still recognizing the political usefulness of categories or labels for certain sexual behavior and communities. One example of such people might be those women who identify as lesbians and who also acknowledge that sometimes they choose to sleep with men. These individuals exemplify the process of destabilization that I try to articulate within this essay. Even further removed from the queers who would do away with all sexual categories are those who also transgress what many consider to be categories of sexual behaviors while they publicly embrace one stable sexual identity (for example, those self-identified heterosexual men who sleep with other men sporadically and secretly).

4. I want to thank Mark Blasius for raising the argument that standing on the outside of heteronormativity is a bit of a misnomer, since as a dominant normalizing process it is a practice of regulation in which we are all implicated. However, despite this insight I will on occasion continue to use this phrasing, understanding the limits of its meaning.

5. See Hennessy for a discussion of left analysis and the limits of queer theory.

6. For an insightful discussion of the numerous methods used to regulate and control the sexual and reproductive choices of women, see Shende.

7. See Jones for an articulation of differences between the destabilization and the destruction of identity categories.

REFERENCES

Alexander, Jacqui. "Redrafting Morality: The Postcolonial State and the Sexual Offences Bill of Trinidad and Tobago." *Third World Women and the Politics of Feminism*, ed. C. T. Mohanty, A. Russo, and L. Torres. Bloomington: Indiana UP, 1991. 133–52.

Berlant, Lauren, and Elizabeth Freeman. "Queer Nationality." Warner 193–229.

Bérubé, Allan, and Jeffrey Escoffier. "Queer/Nation." *Out/Look: National Lesbian and Gay Quarterly* II (Winter 1991): 12–14.

Blasius, Mark. *Gay and Lesbian Politics: Sexuality and the Emergence of a New Ethic*. Philadelphia: Temple UP, 1994.

Butler, Judith. *Gender Trouble*. New York Routledge, 1990.

Carby, Hazel. *Reconstructing Womanhood: The Emergence of the Afro-American Woman Novelist*. New York: Oxford UP, 1987.

Clarke, Cheryl. "The Failure to Transform: Homophobia in the Black Community." Smith, *Home Girls* 197–208.

Cohen, Cathy J. "Contested Membership: Black Gay Identities and the Politics of AIDS." *Queer Theory/Sociology*, ed. S. Seidman, Oxford: Blackwell, 1996. 362–94.

Collins, Patricia Hill. *Black Feminist Thought: Knowledge, Consciousness, and the Politics of Sociology Empowerment*. New York: Harper, 1990.

Combahee River Collective. "The Combahee River Collective Statement." Smith, *Home Girls* 272–82.

Crenshaw, Kimberle. "Mapping the Margins: Intersectionality, Identity Politics, and Violence against Women of Color." *Stanford Law Review* 43 (1991): 1241–99.

Crimp, Douglas. "Right On, Girlfriend!" Warner 300–20.

Davis, Angela Y. *Women, Race and Class*. New York Vintage, 1983.

De Lauretis, Teresa. "Queer Theory: Lesbian and Gay Sexualities." *Differences* 3.2 (Summer 1991): iii–xviii.

Dunlap, David W. "Three Black Members Quit AIDS Organization Board." *New York Times* 11 Jan. 1996: B2.

Dyson, Michael Eric. *Between God and Gangsta Rap*. New York: Oxford UP, 1996.

Epstein, Steven. "A Queer Encounter: Sociology and the Study of Sexuality." *Sociological Theory* 12 (1994): 188–202.

Farajaje-Jones, Elias. "Ain't I a Queer." Creating Change Conference, National Gay and Lesbian Task Force, Detroit, Michigan, 8–12 Nov. 1995.

Fuss, Diana, ed. *Inside/Outside*. New York: Routledge, 1991.

Gamson, Joshua. "Must Identity Movements Self-destruct? A Queer Dilemma." *Social Problems* 42 (1995): 390–407.

Gutman, Herbert G. *The Black Family in Slavery and Freedom, 1750–1925*. New York: Vintage, 1976.

Hennessy, Rosemary. "Queer Theory, Left Politics," *Rethinking MARXISM* 7.3 (1994): 85–111.

Higginbotham, A. Leon, Jr. *In the Matter of Color—Race and the American Legal Process: The Colonial Period*. New York: Oxford UP, 1978.

hooks, bell. *Feminist Theory: From Margin to Center*. Boston: South End, 1984.

Ingraham, Chrys. "The Heterosexual Imaginary: Feminist Sociology and Theories of Gender." *Sociological Theory* 12 (1994): 203–19.

Jones, Tamara. "Inside the Kaleidoscope: How the Construction of Black Gay and Lesbian Identities Inform Political Strategies." Unpublished. Yale University, 1995.

Lorde, Audre. *Sister Outsider: Essays and Speeches by Audre Lorde*. New York: The Crossing P. 1984.

McIntosh, Mary. "Queer Theory and the War of the Sexes." *Activating Theory: Lesbian, Gay, Bisexual Politics*, ed. J. Bristow and A. R. Wilson. London: Lawrence and Wishart, 1993. 33–52.

Moraga, Cherríe, and Gloria Anzaldúa, eds. *This Bridge Called My Back: Writings by Radical Women of Color*. New York: Kitchen Table/Women of Color, 1981.

Morton, Donald. "The Politics of Queer Theory in the (Post) Modern Moment," *Genders* 17 (Fall 1993): 121–15.

Moynihan, Daniel Patrick. *The Negro Family: The Case for National Action*. Washington D.C.: Office of Policy Planning and Research. U.S. Department of Labor, 1965.

Phelan, Shane. *Identity Politics: Lesbian Feminism and the Limits of Community*. Philadelphia: Temple UP, 1989.

Podolsky, Robin. "Sacrificing Queer and other 'Proletarian' Artifacts." *Radical America* 25.1 (January 1991): 53–60.

Queer Nation. "I Hate Straights" manifesto. New York, 1990.

Queers United Against Straight-acting Homosexuals. "Assimilation Is Killing Us: Fight for a Queer United Front." WHY I HATED THE MARCH ON WASHINGTON (1993): 4.

Ransby, Barbara, and Tracye Matthews. "Black Popular Culture and the Transcendence of Patriarchical Illusions." *Race & Class* 35.1 (July–September 1993): 57–70.

Reagon, Bernice Johnson. "Coalition Politics: Turning the Century." Smith, *Home Girls* 356–68.

Reed, Adolph L., Jr. "The 'Underclass' as Myth and Symbol: The Poverty of Discourse about Poverty." *Radical America* 24.1 (January 1990): 21–40.

Rich, Adrienne. "Compulsory Heterosexuality and Lesbian Existence." *Powers of Desire: The Politics of Sexuality*, ed. A. Snitow, C. Stansell and S. Thompson. New York: Monthly Review, 1983. 177–206.

Sedgwick, Eve. *The Epistemology of the Closet*. Berkeley: U of California P, 1990.

Seidman, Steven. "Identity and Politics in a 'Postmodern' Gay Culture." Warner 105–42.

Shende, Suzanne. "Fighting the Violence against Our Sisters: Prosecution of Pregnant Women and the Coercive Use

of Norplant." *Women Transforming Politics: An Alternative Reader,* ed. C. Cohen, K. Jones, and J. Tronto, New York: New York UP, 1997.

Smith, Barbara. "Queer Politics: Where's the Revolution?" *The Nation* 257.1 (July 5, 1993): 12–16.

——, ed. *Home Girls: A Black Feminist Anthology.* New York: Kitchen Table/Women of Color, 1983.

Smith, M. G. "Social Structure in the British Caribbean about 1820." *Social and Economic Studies* 1.4 (August 1953): 55–79.

"Statement of Purpose." Dialogue on the Lesbian and Gay Left. Duncan Conference Center in Del Ray Beach, Florida. 1–4 April 1993.

Stein, Arlene, and Ken Plummer. "'I Can't Even Think Straight': 'Queer' Theory and the Missing Sexual Revolution in Sociology." *Sociological Theory* 12 (1994): 178–87.

Vaid, Urvashi. *Virtual Equality: The Mainstreaming of Gay & Lesbian Liberation.* New York: Anchor, 1995.

Warner, Michael, ed. *Fear of a Queer Planet: Queer Politics and Social Theory.* Minneapolis: U of Minnesota P, 1993.

West, Cornel. *Race Matters.* Boston: Beacon, 1993.

Wilson, William Julius. *The Truly Disadvantaged: The Inner City, the Underclass, and Public Policy.* Chicago: U of Chicago P, 1987.

R E A D I N G *50*   **Susan Muaddi Darraj**

It's Not an Oxymoron: The Search for an Arab Feminism

I see no reason to say that the Arab woman is less intelligent and energetic and sincere than the [W]estern woman.

—*Ghada Samman, 1961*

My father is a feminist, although he would probably never admit it. It is difficult to even write the two words "father" and "feminist" next to each other in the same sentence (despite the nice alliterative sound). I can imagine him hearing it and shrinking away from the word, shaking his head vehemently and saying, in his thick Middle Eastern accent that all my girlfriends find so charming, "No, no, no, not me, thank you." And yet, despite his denial, my father has helped me form my own unique feminist identity more than that other F-word—Friedan.

I remember sitting in a feminist theory class in graduate school, feeling strangely unmoved by the words of Betty Friedan and the second-wave feminist writers. I understood their struggles and respected their courage—there was not a doubt in my mind that it took a lot of courage to resist Western patriarchal demands on women's lives. But these were not representative feminists. In *The Feminine Mystique*, Friedan expounds on the woes of being a mere housewife, but it seemed there was a certain level of class privilege that accompanied her position. The role of a "housewife" usually developed when there was a man to support the family, when he could do it all on his own salary. Although my mother swept the floor and cooked most of our meals, I realized that housework was not her only "work." She also worked full-time in the business that she and my father ran together.

Sitting in that class, with other women who expounded on the oppression of housework, I dared once to ask, "Who will do the housework then?" Seventeen pairs of eyes turned to me, and I continued: "If men don't do it and women don't do it, who will? It has to be done. Do you propose that we hire *other women* to come and do it? Other women who clean people's homes because they have the opportunity to do nothing else?"

Silence greeted my question, as I had expected. I realized then that most of the women in the class were upper-middle- and middle-class white women—and I felt like a complete outsider. Perhaps they could understand Friedan because her brand of feminism spoke directly to their experience. But it didn't speak to mine. I didn't view housework as a mark of oppression. There was a certain sense of pride placed on a clean, welcoming home, and both my parents had always placed value on it. That was why my father spent his weekends trimming the lawn and sweeping the walkways and why my mother mopped the kitchen floor and wiped the windows until they sparkled. It was why my brothers and I were marched off to various rooms every Saturday morning, armed with furniture polish and dust rags. We all did housework. No, this version of feminism did not appeal to me. But then again, what version did? For a long time I thought that this was the only brand of feminism that existed. If that was true, I certainly wasn't a card-carrying member.

Furthermore, I didn't like the way that this feminism viewed people like my mother and grandmothers and aunts—and me, for that matter. I was tired of turning on the evening news, eager to learn news of the Middle East, and seeing women clad in heavy, black robes, their eyes lowered but barely visible behind the slits in their face veils as they scurried past the television cameras. I have been to the Middle East. I am an Arab Christian, and I know many Arab Christian and Muslim women. Some—but definitely not all—of my Muslim friends veil themselves, as do a few of the older, conservative Christian women, especially before entering a church. Why did Americans equate Muslim women with veils so completely, and why did the cameras seem to pick out only these women?

The answer was an uncomplicated one: because this was the quaint vision of the Middle East with which America felt comfortable. This vision included heavily robed and mustachioed sheiks, belly dancers, tents, camels and—of course—veiled women. This vision was, to use an orientalist cliché, a desert mirage, concocted by the same Hollywood producers who created Rudolph Valentino (*The Sheik*).

American feminists, like the rest of the nation and the Western world, had accepted the flawed image of the Middle East and Middle Eastern women without question. "Of course, they [meek and silent Arab women] are oppressed; *we* [liberated, assertive Western women with voices] must help *them*." I have heard similar statements (with the notions in the brackets implied) from white American feminists who wanted to save their Arab sisters but not to understand them. They wanted to save them from the burden of their families and religion but not from the war, hunger, unemployment, political persecution and oppression that marked their daily lives and that left them with only their families and religion as sole sources of comfort. The tone of white Western feminism—with its books about "lifting the veil on Arab women" and Arab women "lifting the veil of silence"—was that Arab feminism was nothing greater than an amusing oxymoron.

The apparent hypocrisy and condescension that white Western feminists held for Arab women confused me. I felt betrayed by a movement that claimed to create a global sisterhood of women; it seemed that the Arab woman was the poor and downtrodden stepsister in this family.

Where was my feminism?

It was my father who first taught me "feminism," who told me that I could do anything I wanted—achieve any goal, reach any height—and that he would support me in that climb. I don't remember ever feeling that my culture—and in my mind my father embodied that culture almost completely—stood in my way, although others thought my culture was a jungle of patriarchal pitfalls.

One day my father told me a story that rocked my world. It was that of Jamila Bouhereid, the Algerian woman who had played an instrumental role in the Algerian resistance against the colonial French forces. It was one of those stories that he and his generation had heard about while growing up in Palestine, nations away from Algeria, though the story stirred them nonetheless. Bouhereid had been captured by the French and tortured in unspeakable ways, but she refused to divulge essential information about the resistance. The torture continued until it finally killed her. He told me the story during one of our many marathon conversations that usually lasted through the night, while we sat at the kitchen table, sipping coffee and eating oranges. I became obsessed with Bouhereid's story and tried to find out everything I could about her. Unfortunately, there was very little information about her—or Arab women in general—available in English.

My futile search was not a complete failure, however, only the opening of a new door. I came across the names of other Arab women whose names I had heard: Huda Sha'rawi, the founder of the Egyptian Feminist Union, who had called for the ban of the veil at the beginning of the twentieth century; Mai Ziyyadah, a feminist writer and a contemporary of Sha'rawi, who called for men to free women in order to free themselves; even Khadijah, the first wife of the Prophet Muhammad, who had financed his travels, owned a lucrative business and been the first convert to Islam. I searched the Internet for information on more modern Arab women: Hanan Ashrawi, a chief spokesperson for the Palestinians; Leila Ahmed, a feminist and scholar who wrote about Arab women with accuracy, honesty and pages of solid research; and Fatima Mernissi, who sought to rediscover Islam's valuation of women.

I also searched for something that neither the Internet nor the library's shelves could offer me: a real, hard, searing look at the lives of modern, everyday Arab women. I saved my pennies and, armed with my notebooks and pens, traveled to Egypt, Jordan and Palestine over the course of a few years. I met women in my family and made some new friends. One summer, I spent three months in the West Bank, in the city of Ramallah, and studied at Birzeit University. Ramallah and Birzeit were a mere half-hour taxicab ride away from Taybeh, the small village where my parents grew up and where my grandmother and several aunts, cousins and uncles lived. Although I was thrilled to spend time with my relatives, I also wanted to meet and interact with Palestinian college women, and I met quite a few and listened to their stories. At many points and on many occasions I felt like I was looking into a mirror, at what I would have been like had my father and mother never left the political oppression and insecurities of Palestine.

One woman, a twenty-four-year-old student, told me how it was a struggle to get to the university every day, not because her father wouldn't permit it (for he actually encouraged her), but because she had to take a multipassenger taxi in which she had been groped many times by the male passengers. Another woman, also in her mid-twenties, described how her parents were proud that she had been accepted at the university, but she often skipped semesters because money usually ran low. It often was a choice of buying textbooks or

letting her younger siblings go without meat for several months. She estimated that at that rate it would take another six years to finish her bachelor's degree. Another woman, who veiled herself, explained to me how as a religious person she felt compelled to educate herself for her own betterment and for that of her family.

It struck me that many of the women whom I met could be considered feminists, perhaps not by the standards of the white Western feminism that I had encountered in my feminist theory class, but by the standards of a different feminism—one that allowed women to retain their culture, to have pride in their traditions and to still vocalize the gender issues of their community. These were women whom I considered feminists because they believed in the dignity and potential for upward mobility of every woman; they wanted to erase class lines between women; they worked so that they could have choices in their lives and not be channeled into one way of life.

I realized upon my return to the United States that fall that, more than ever, I longed for a feminism that would express who I was and what my experiences were as an Arab-American woman. That feminism was within my grasp, but I discerned several obstacles that blocked my path. The chief one was the seeming universality of white Western feminism, which appears to leave no room for other visions. This caused various conflicts within me. Another obstacle to voicing my own feminism to white Western feminists was that the various traditions in my Arabic culture were indeed the markings of a patriarchal culture. Many feminist texts and discourses on the Middle East highlighted such traditions, although most modern-day societies, including that of the United States, can be accurately described as patriarchal.

One such tradition is that Arab parents are usually referred to by the name of their eldest son. Thus, a couple whose eldest son is named Abdallah would be referred to socially as Im Abdallah (mother of Abdallah) and Abu Abdallah (father of Abdallah). I am the eldest child in my family, but my parents are called by the name of my brother, who is a year younger. There is generally an emphasis on having at least one male child in Arab families, and the boys are often named after their grandfathers; my brother Abdallah was given the name of my grandfather Abdallah. As a woman, this certainly bothers me, and it strikes a sour note with many Arab women. After all, why the big deal about boys? What is so disappointing about girls? It seems to me that American feminists overly criticize this tradition, however, while forgetting that it is no different than American boys being named David, Jr. or Jonathan So-and-so, III. As far as I can remember, American girls aren't dubbed Michelle, Jr. and Jennifer IV, unless they are European monarchs, but this point does not occupy chapters in Arab feminist texts on the West.

Another unfairly beleaguered custom is that of the traditional Arabic marriage, which has wrinkled many a conversation with my American feminist friends. In the Middle East and among Middle Easterners living in other parts of the world, when a couple decides to get married, it is expected that a *toulbeh* takes place. During the toulbeh the potential bridegroom arrives at the home of the potential bride, escorted by several members of his family. The bride's family waits, and members of her extended family wait with them. The eldest male of the groom's family requests the bride's hand from the eldest male in her family. When the expected "yes" is announced (because the question is a formality, after all), the two families celebrate their upcoming union. Of course, this is a patriarchal tradition, one in which a woman is viewed as a person who should not answer for herself. Again, is it different than in American culture, where it is considered a sweet gesture and a romantic leftover from traditional times for a man to ask for the bride's hand from her father? And don't fathers still walk their daughters down the aisle and "give them away"? The endless explanations of Arab wedding customs that I had to offer my American feminist friends, however, would have led one to think that it was utterly barbaric.

In the aftermath of the events of September 11 and with the recent conflict in Afghanistan, the same stilted media coverage would make anyone think that *every* Middle Eastern woman saw the world from between the peepholes of her burqa's face netting. These traditions are usually used as examples that create a picture of the Arab world as a *1,001 Nights*–like land of wicked and despotic sultans and silenced and imprisoned harem girls—women who need the West to enlighten, educate and save them (But Scheherazade, a Muslim Arab woman and the heroine of *1,001 Nights*, saved herself and her countrywomen, so it doesn't make sense to me *why* Arab culture is attacked as anti-woman, as if no other culture has gender-oppressive traditions of which to be ashamed).

These naming and wedding traditions, and others like them, made me second-guess my professed need to find a feminism that suited me. After all, on one level I liked these traditions—they were deeply embedded in my culture and in myself as a person. When I got married, my husband's eldest uncle asked for my hand from my eldest uncle. Did that mean that I wasn't a feminist? Some of my friends, upon hearing this, wrinkled their noses in disgust and shook their heads sadly at me as if to say, "Poor thing! She's just condemned herself to a lifetime of constant pregnancies, Little League games and soap operas." My God, I thought, was I being kicked out of the club before I had even officially joined?

This experience—feeling emotionally torn between my culture and what white Western feminism told me I had to be—relates almost inversely to another conflict that obstructed the recognition of my feminist identity: America's exoticism of Arab women. Although we were considered veiled and meek, we were simultaneously and ironically considered sultry, sexual and "different." People, especially white feminists, were often intrigued by my "exoticness" and asked me silly questions, like whether Arab women knew how to belly-dance or whether I knew of any women who lived in harems. I was also frequently mistaken as a Muslim, because many people couldn't conceive of an Arab Christian (although Arab Christians and Muslims have long allied themselves against the pervasive stereotypes that threaten to categorize us both). They wanted to know if I had ever ridden a camel and if I would have an arranged marriage and would my husband be taking other wives as well? If this was how little people in general, and feminists in particular, knew of my culture, what was the hope that I would be seriously received as a feminist?

Some Muslim women see no contradiction between feminism and Islam. In her book *Palestinian Women: Patriarchy and Resistance in the West Bank*, Cheryl Rubenberg studies Palestinian women who live in the camps and villages of the West Bank and highlights the phenomenon of the Muslim Sisters *(Ikhwat al-musilmat)*. Sometimes called "Islamist feminists," the Muslim Sisters believe that Islam gives women full rights but that the religion has been corrupted by men to suit their patriarchal agenda. One Muslim Sister whom Rubenberg interviewed said that their mission is to bring people back to the true Islam, which historically allowed women the right to be educated, to work, to participate in public life and to own property. According to the Sisters, however, Islam has been perverted by men's patriarchal ambitions in the centuries since the Prophet Muhammad's death.

Because of anti-Muslim sentiments (which are inextricably linked to anti-Arab sentiments) and the general misconceptions of Islam in the West (that all Muslim men are terrorists with long beards and all Muslim women are battered and wear veils), it would be difficult for a Western, non-Muslim person to understand the desire of Arab Muslim women to retain both their religion and their sense of feminism.

Another conflict that threatened my development of a feminist voice was my split vision—my ability to thrive in American culture but to also appreciate Arab culture. Further, it was my frustration with white Western feminists who took up issues like keeping one's name after marriage but who sniffed at Arab women, who had always kept their names[1] and whose biggest problem was how to afford bread for dinner? I was living in America, land of the free and home of the brave, while cousins in the West Bank were throwing stones at Israeli tanks and working extra jobs to help my aunts and uncles pay the bills. While I was hopping in my car to work every day, perhaps stopping at a Starbucks for my morning coffee, they were walking to the taxi stop to see if a car was available and willing to drive them around the road-blocks that the Israelis had set up—all just to get to class on time for a final exam. Even worse, it was U.S. money and foreign aid to Israel that kept Palestinians locked in a seemingly hopeless situation that robbed them of their futures.

I think that I had a guilt complex as a result of this split vision: I loathed having to write papers on the "Angel of the House" theory and the imagery of women trapped behind wallpaper, while Arab women were dealing with issues of physical survival.[2] Although I admired the work of white feminists and respected the ways in which they surpassed their own obstacles, those were not my obstacles. I could not focus on the complexities of white Western feminist theory when I knew that Arab women faced very different issues.

And I returned once again to my initial question: Where did I fit in all this?

A few years ago, through a strange set of coincidences, I found an answer. I had started reading the work of Black feminists, such as bell hooks, who took on Betty Friedan full force. She challenged the relevance of Friedan's ideas about housewives to Black women, who have always had to work. Her work led me to Gloria Anzaldúa, who led me to Barbara Smith, and the list grew. I was heartened by the fact that Black women and other women of color had the courage to carve a feminism of their own out of the monolithic block that was generally accepted as "feminism."

About this time I caught up with a friend of mine, an assertive and lively Arab woman from San Francisco, who was visiting when I lived in Philadelphia. I was twenty-four. It was a gloriously sunny day in the city, and we decided to go out. We sat in a coffee shop on Philadelphia's hip South Street section and talked about the way that we both felt locked out of feminism and the lack of relevance that feminism seemed to have for our lives. We also talked about the way that analyses of Arab women's issues seemed to be largely conducted by white Western women.

"But it's white Western feminism that doesn't relate to my life," I interjected.

"True," she agreed. "There *is* actually a group of Arab women who deal with gender issues—their association is called AWSA, the Arab Women's Solidarity Association."

"Arab feminists?" I asked, unbelieving.

"Yeah. I think that you can call them feminists." She gave me the Web site information, and I checked it out immediately upon my return home. I found out that AWSA is a network for Arab women, meant to provide support and to serve as the basis for the Arab women's movement. It was founded by Nawal el-Saadawi, an Egyptian doctor and leading feminist. That sunny Philadelphia afternoon initiated my awareness of AWSA members, who were scholars, artists, writers and everyday women who felt that gender issues in the Arab world and among Arabs in other countries should be discussed and diagnosed by a circle that included Arab women themselves.

Another life-changing event occurred around this time: I met the man I eventually married. As an Arab woman, romance had never been easy because of the strong cultural taboo on dating. I often watched movies and television shows in which girlfriends chatted with each other (usually while doing each other's hair at slumber parties) about the good looks of a new boyfriend, the disappointment of a blind date, the elation over a romantic dinner or the pain of a breakup. I could never chat so easily about romance because it was a distant, remote experience, one that I knew only vicariously through television, films and books. Furthermore, it was difficult to meet American men who were not entranced by my "exoticness" (probably the most ridiculous comment I've ever heard) and the aspects of my culture that they didn't understand (such as not showing someone the bottom of my shoes or genuinely enjoying time with my family, etc.). I also met some Arab men who, ironically, thought I was too "Americanized": my unaccented, perfect English littered with slang; my tendency to wear boots and blue jeans; and my refusal to spend more than three minutes on my hair and makeup testified to that, I suppose, not to mention my vocalized interest in pursuing my career and my (equally vocalized) lack of desire to have children for a long time.

But meeting my future husband was an eye-opening experience. I felt that I finally had met someone who could understand and even relate to my split vision. Not only was he kind and caring, but he respected my intellect, my career goals and my opinions. In other words, he allowed me to be myself—and comfortably so. When, over dinner, I mentioned to him the topic of feminism—a word I had uttered to few men, save my father—he said that I didn't strike him as a feminist. I asked why not, and he offered me an interesting response: "Well, I guess I'm thinking of 'feminists' as what I see here in the States. And they seem largely self-involved. But you care about all kinds of issues, not just the ones that affect you. And I think that you consider the concept of family to be above that of the individual."

I pointed out that women have traditionally been reared to ignore and neglect themselves for the sakes of others (children, husbands, in-laws, etc.). This included Arab women. Women in general had also never had the opportunity to focus on their own development and their own goals. But I also realized that he was thinking of traditional, American, white feminism when he said that, and I explained that I felt that there might be another kind of feminism out there, one that appealed more to women like me, who wanted to be feminists and spouses and mothers.

I could see that he was intrigued by what I was saying, and he admitted that this conversation had redefined feminism for him. "Besides," he asked casually, "Why does there have to be a choice between feminism and family? I think a woman can have both."

He was right.

I knew at that point that with the recent riveting conglomeration of coincidental events in my life—my interest in Black feminism, AWSA and the discovery of a possible Arab feminism, and meeting my future husband—that something exciting was happening. My feminist self—my own version of feminism—was emerging.

It required no great sacrifice of my Arab heritage, no shame at my close ties to my family and no compromise of my own needs. It involved two of the most important men in my life—my father and my husband—unlike the ways in which I saw American feminism making a conscious split from male influence (I should also mention here that although my father and husband are the two best men that I personally know, they are not rare examples of Arab men—their mentalities are not unusual in the Arab world, despite what CNN says). There was no need to define independence as living in isolation from my family and making decisions without their support and advice. There was no imperative to shake my head at the thought of having my own family and being a mother. I could be a feminist in a way that suited *my* life, not in a feminism that would mold me to its ideal shape. After all, wasn't feminism supposed to be about making my own choices?

So here I am—an Arab-American feminist. I am happily married. I work. I write. I plan to have children in a few years. I read the newspaper every day. I call my congressperson about U.S. foreign policy issues that negatively affect Arab women. I follow the news in Palestine and Israel religiously, on both American and Arab news channels (thanks to satellite technology). I cringe first and take action second whenever I come across hackneyed "exotic" portrayals of Arab women. I eagerly read the ever-growing body of work being produced about Arab women. This lifestyle is what feminism means to me now, although I once thought that I would never use this word to describe myself.

Most important, once I realized my own version of feminism, I found myself better able to understand white Western feminism and the many outer storms and internal divisions it has had to weather. Now that I have my own foundation, I see the need for a cross-cultural feminist dialogue, especially after the September 11 attacks on the United States, which have led to an overthrow of the Taliban and an intensified interest on the part of Americans to understand Islam in general. As that interest expands to include the issues of Muslim women and Arab women, it should be clarified that any resulting dialogues must be inclusive of Arab voices in order to be successful. I applaud American feminism for attempting to bridge an intimidatingly wide gap, but that bridge must be rooted in firm ground at *both* ends of the divide. It should no longer be possible to write about Arab women with any aura of expertise or authority without *first* knowing what Arab women need and want.

NOTES

1. In Arabic culture women traditionally keep their family names when they marry. Their children assume the names of their fathers, but women are considered to be members of their original families always. This is unlike the Western tradition of marriage, in which a woman is symbolically "given away" by her father to her husband's family.

2. The "Angel in the House" is a theory put forth by Virginia Woolf in her essay *A Room of One's Own.* She says that the Angel in the House is the epitome of Victorian womanhood, whose image haunts Woolf as a writer and attempts to stop her creativity. The Angel represents an era in which "feminine" women were uneducated and uncritical of their own oppression. The "wallpaper" allusion refers to Charlotte Perkins Gilman's story *The Yellow Wallpaper,* in which a woman goes mad when her husband restricts her ability to write.

The title is from Cheryl Rubenberg's poem, "It's Not An Oxymoron: The Search for an Arab Feminism" from *Palestinian Women: Gender and Patriarchy in the West Bank,* by Cheryl A. Rubenberg. Copyright © 2001 by Lynne Rienner Publishers, Inc. Reprinted with permission of the publisher.

UN COMMISSION APPROVES DECLARATION REAFFIRMING GOALS OF 1995 WOMEN'S CONFERENCE AFTER U.S. DROPS ANTIABORTION AMENDMENT

08 Mar 2005

The 45-member . . . U.N. Commission on the Status of Women on Friday unanimously approved a one-page declaration supporting the Platform for Action adopted at the 1995 Fourth World Conference on Women in Beijing after the United States dropped an amendment that would have clarified that the platform does not include a right to abortion or create any new international human rights, the *AP/San Francisco Chronicle* reports (Lederer, *AP/San Francisco Chronicle,* 3/5). The U.N. commission at the end of last month—ahead of a two-week review of the conference, which began last week—proposed a declaration asking the participating countries to reaffirm progress toward the Beijing platform, which stated that abortion should be safe in places where it is legal and that criminal charges should not be filed against any woman who undergoes an illegal abortion. The platform also stated that women have the right to "decide freely and responsibly on matters related to their sexuality . . . free of coercion, discrimination and violence." Bush administration representatives at first said the United States would not sign the declaration because of concerns that the platform classified legal abortion as a human right and proposed an amendment that would reaffirm U.S. commitment to the platform and declaration "while reaffirming that they do not create any new international human rights and that they do not include the right to abortion."

However, most member nations rejected even a "watered down" version of the U.S. amendment, with delegates from the European Union, African Union and Mercosur trading bloc in South America all insisting that the declaration remain in its original form (*Kaiser Daily Reproductive Health Report,* 3/4).

U.S. Drops Amendment, Declares Victory

U.S. Ambassador to the United Nations Ellen Sauerbrey on Friday said the U.S. delegation would drop its amendment after "receiving assurances" that the platform approved at the 1995 conference does not create "a new global right to abortion," the *AP/Chronicle* reports (*AP/San Francisco Chronicle,* 3/5). "We have heard from countries that our interpretation is their interpretation," Sauerbrey said at a news conference, adding, "So the amendment, we recognize, is really redundant, but it has accomplished its goals" (Lynch, *Washington Post,* 3/5). Charlotte Bunch, executive director of the Center for Women's Global Leadership, said the amendment was "an effort to inject U.S. politics into a broad international consensus," adding, "The reality is that [the United States] heard loud and clear the voices of 6,000 women here [at the conference] saying 'No,' echoing millions of other women worldwide" (*AP/San Francisco Chronicle,* 3/5).

FOURTH WORLD CONFERENCE ON WOMEN BEIJING DECLARATION

Declaration

1. We, the Governments participating in the Fourth World Conference on Women,
2. Gathered here in Beijing in September 1995, the year of the fiftieth anniversary of the founding of the United Nations,
3. Determined to advance the goals of equality, development and peace for all women everywhere in the interest of all humanity,
4. Acknowledging the voices of all women everywhere and taking note of the diversity of women and their roles and circumstances, honoring the women who paved the way and inspired by the hope present in the world's youth,
5. Recognize that the status of women has advanced in some important respects in the past decade but that progress has been uneven, inequalities between women and men have persisted and major obstacles remain, with serious consequences for the well-being of all people,
6. Also recognize that this situation is exacerbated by the increasing poverty that is affecting the lives of the majority of the world's people, in particular women and children, with origins in both the national and international domains,
7. Dedicate ourselves unreservedly to addressing these constraints and obstacles and thus enhancing further the advancement and empowerment of women all over the world, and agree that this requires urgent action in the spirit of determination, hope, cooperation and solidarity, now and to carry us forward into the next century.

We Reaffirm Our Commitment to:

8. The equal rights and inherent human dignity of women and men and other purposes and principles enshrined in the Charter of the United Nations, to the Universal Declaration of Human Rights and other international human rights instruments, in particular the Convention on the Elimination of All Forms of Discrimination against Women and the Convention on the Rights of the Child, as well as the Declaration on the Elimination of Violence against Women and the Declaration on the Right to Development;
9. Ensure the full implementation of the human rights of women and of the girl child as an inalienable, integral and indivisible part of all human rights and fundamental freedoms;
10. Build on consensus and progress made at previous United Nations conferences and summits—on women in Nairobi in 1985, on children in New York in 1990, on environment and development in Rio de Janeiro in 1992, on human rights in Vienna in 1993, on population and development in Cairo in 1994 and on social development in Copenhagen in 1995 with the objective of achieving equality, development and peace;
11. Achieve the full and effective implementation of the Nairobi Forward-Looking Strategies for the Advancement of Women;
12. The empowerment and advancement of women, including the right to freedom of thought, conscience, religion and belief, thus contributing to the moral, ethical, spiritual and intellectual needs of women and men, individually or in community with others and thereby guaranteeing them the possibility of realizing their full potential in society and shaping their lives in accordance with their own aspirations.

We Are Convinced That:

13. Women's empowerment and their full participation on the basis of equality in all spheres of society, including participation in the decision-making process and access to power, are fundamental for the achievement of equality, development and peace;
14. Women's rights are human rights;
15. Equal rights, opportunities and access to resources, equal sharing of responsibilities for the family by men and women, and a harmonious partnership between them are critical to their

well-being and that of their families as well as to the consolidation of democracy;

16. Eradication of poverty based on sustained economic growth, social development, environmental protection and social justice requires the involvement of women in economic and social development, equal opportunities and the full and equal participation of women and men as agents and beneficiaries of people-centered sustainable development;

17. The explicit recognition and reaffirmation of the right of all women to control all aspects of their health, in particular their own fertility, is basic to their empowerment;

18. Local, national, regional and global peace is attainable and is inextricably linked with the advancement of women, who are a fundamental force for leadership, conflict resolution and the promotion of lasting peace at all levels;

19. It is essential to design, implement and monitor, with the full participation of women, effective, efficient and mutually reinforcing gender-sensitive policies and programmes, including development policies and programmes, at all levels that will foster the empowerment and advancement of women;

20. The participation and contribution of all actors of civil society, particularly women's groups and networks and other non-governmental organizations and community-based organizations, with full respect for their autonomy, in cooperation with Governments, are important to the effective implementation and follow-up of the Platform for Action;

21. The implementation of the Platform for Action requires commitment from Governments and the international community. By making national and international commitments for action, including those made at the Conference, Governments and the international community recognize the need to take priority action for the empowerment and advancement of women.

We Are Determined to:

22. Intensify efforts and actions to achieve the goals of the Nairobi Forward-Looking Strategies for the Advancement of Women by the end of this century;

23. Ensure the full enjoyment by women and the girl child of all human rights and fundamental freedoms and take effective action against violations of these rights and freedoms;

24. Take all necessary measures to eliminate all forms of discrimination against women and the girl child and remove all obstacles to gender equality and the advancement and empowerment of women;

25. Encourage men to participate fully in all actions towards equality;

26. Promote women's economic independence, including employment, and eradicate the persistent and increasing burden of poverty on women by addressing the structural causes of poverty through changes uneconomic, ensuring equal access for all women, including those in rural areas, as vital development agents, to productive resources, opportunities and public services;

27. Promote people-centered sustainable development, including sustained economic growth, through the provision of basic education, life-long education, literacy and training, and primary health care for girls and women;

28. Take positive steps to ensure peace for the advancement of women and, recognizing the leading role that women have played in the peace movement, work actively towards general and complete disarmament under strict and effective international control, and support negotiations on the conclusion, without delay, of a universal and multilaterally and effectively verifiable comprehensive nuclear-test-ban treaty which contributes to nuclear disarmament and the prevention of the proliferation of nuclear weapons in all its aspects;

29. Prevent and eliminate all forms of violence against women and girls;

30. Ensure equal access to and equal treatment of women and men in education and health care and enhance women's sexual and reproductive health as well as education;

31. Promote and protect all human rights of women and girls;

32. Intensify efforts to ensure equal enjoyment of all human rights and fundamental freedoms for all women and girls who face multiple barriers to

their empowerment and advancement because of such factors as their race, age, language, ethnicity, culture, religion, or disability, or because they are indigenous people;

33. Ensure respect for international law, including humanitarian law, in order to protect women and girls in particular;

34. Develop the fullest potential of girls and women of all ages, ensure their full and equal participation in building a better world for all and enhance their role in the development process.

We Are Determined to:

35. Ensure women's equal access to economic resources, including land, credit, science and technology, vocational training, information, communication and markets, as a means to further the advancement and empowerment of women and girls, including through the enhancement of their capacities to enjoy the benefits of equal access to these resources, inter alia, by means of international cooperation;

36. Ensure the success of the Platform for Action, which will require a strong commitment on the part of Governments, international organizations and institutions at all levels. We are deeply convinced that economic development, social development and environmental protection are interdependent and mutually reinforcing components of sustainable development, which is the framework for our efforts to achieve a higher quality of life for all people. Equitable social development that recognizes empowering the poor, particularly women living in poverty, to utilize environmental resources sustainably is a necessary foundation for sustainable development. We also recognize that broad-based and sustained economic growth in the context of sustainable development is necessary to sustain social development and social justice. The success of the Platform for Action will also require adequate mobilization of resources at the national and international levels as well as new and additional resources to the developing countries from all available funding mechanisms, including multilateral, bilateral and private sources for the advancement of women; financial resources to strengthen the capacity of national, subregional, regional and international institutions; a commitment to equal rights, equal responsibilities and equal opportunities and to the equal participation of women and men in all national, regional and international bodies and policy-making processes; and the establishment or strengthening of mechanisms at all levels for accountability to the world's women;

37. Ensure also the success of the Platform for Action in countries with economies in transition, which will require continued international cooperation and assistance;

38. We hereby adopt and commit ourselves as Governments to implement the following Platform for Action, ensuring that a gender perspectives reflected in all our policies and programmes. We urge the United Nations system, regional and international financial institutions, other relevant regional and international institutions and all women and men, as well as non-governmental organizations, with full respect for their autonomy, and all sectors of civil society, in cooperation with Governments, to fully commit themselves and contribute to the implementation of this Platform for Action.

ACKNOWLEDGMENTS

Lila Abu-Lughod, "Do Muslim Women Really Need Saving?" from *American Anthropologist* 104, no. 3 (2002). Copyright © 2002 by the American Anthropological Association. Reprinted with permission.

Paula Gunn Allen, "Where I Come From Is Like This" from *The Sacred Hoop: Recovering the Feminine Side in American Indian Traditions*. Copyright © 1986 by Paula Gunn Allen. Reprinted with the permission of Beacon Press.

Robert L. Allen and Paul Kivel, "Men Changing Men" from *Ms.* (September/October 1994). Copyright © 1994. Reprinted with the permission of *Ms.* Magazine.

American Association of University Women, from *Hostile Hallways: The AAUW Survey on Sexual Harassment in America's Schools*. Copyright © 1993 by the American Association of University Women. Reprinted with permission.

Pamela Aronson, "Feminists or Postfeminists?" from *Gender & Society* 17, no. 6 (December 2003). Copyright © 2003 by Sociologists for Women in Society. Reprinted with the permission of Sage Publications, Inc.

Ingrid Banks, "Hair Still Matters." Reprinted with the permission of the author.

Eileen Boris, "The Living Wage as a Women's Issue" from *Living Wage Now! The Newsletter of the Coalition for a Living Wage* (February 2001). Reprinted with the permission of the Coalition for a Living Wage.

Eileen Boris, from "'You Wouldn't Want One of 'Em Dancing with Your Wife': Racialized Bodies on the Job in World War II" from *American Quarterly* 50.1 (1998). Copyright © 1998 by The American Studies Association. Reprinted with the permission of The Johns Hopkins University Press.

Christine E. Bose and Rachel Bridges Whaley, "Sex Segregation in the U.S. Labor Force" from *Gender Mosaics: Social Perspectives*, edited by Dana Vannoy. Copyright © 2001 by Roxbury Publishing Company. Reprinted with the permission of the publisher.

Grace Chang, "From the Third World to the 'Third World Within'" from *Labor Versus Empire: Race, Gender, and Migration*, edited by Gilbert G. Gonzalez, Raul Fernandez, Vivian Price, David Smith, and Linda Trinh Vo. Copyright © 2001 by Taylor & Francis Books, Inc. Reprinted with the permission

of Routledge/Taylor & Francis Group, LLC. This selection contains material from: (1) "Beyond the WTO: Conference on Women and Immigration the Global Economy" (Northwest Labor and Employment Law Office and Workers' Voice Coalition, Seattle, Washington, December 4, 1999). Reprinted from LELO's Tyree Scott International Worker-to-Worker Project; (2) "The Use of Filipino Nurses in the Scheme to Privatize Health Care," Conference Proceedings: Advancing the Rights and Welfare of Non-Practicing Filipino and Other Foreign-Trained Nurses (Filipino Nurses' Support Group, Burnaby, British Columbia, December 2001); and (3) From "Filipino Nurses Doing Domestic Work in Canada: A Stalled Development," Philippine Women Centre of British Columbia (March 2000).

Cecilia Diocson, from "Forced Migration: Perpetuation of Underdevelopment" (paper presented at Ninth International Forum, Association for Women's Rights in Development, Guadalajara, Mexico, October 2002).

Eli Clare, "Stolen Bodies" from "Stolen Bodies, Reclaimed Bodies: Disability and Queerness" from *Public Culture* 13(3): 359–365. Copyright © 2001 by Duke University Press. All rights reserved. Used by permission of the publisher.

Cathy Cohen, "Punks, Bulldaggers, and Welfare Queens: The Radical Potential of Queer Politics?" from *GLQ: A Journal of Lesbian and Gay Studies* 3, no. 4 (1997): 437–65. Copyright © 1997 by Duke University Press. All rights reserved. Reprinted with the permission of the publisher.

Patricia Hill Collins, from *Black Sexual Politics: African Americans, Gender, and the New Racism*. Copyright © 2004 by Patricia Hill Collins. Reprinted with the permission of Routledge.

R. W. Connell, "Masculinities and Globalization" from *Men and Masculinities* 1 (1999). Copyright © 1999 by Sage Publications, Inc. Reprinted with the permission of Sage Publications, Inc.

Kimberlé Crenshaw, "Mapping the Margins: Intersectionality, Identity Politics, and Violence against Women of Color" from *Stanford Law Review* 1241 (1991). Reprinted with the permission of the author and the *Stanford Law Review*, Stanford University School of Law.

Susan Muaddi Darraj, "It's Not an Oxymoron" from *Colonize This!: Young Women of Color on Today's Feminism*, edited by Daisy

Hernandez and Bushra Rehman. Copyright © 2002 by Susan Muaddi Darraj. Reprinted with the permission of Seal Press.

Simone Weil Davis, "Loose Lips Sink Ships" from *Feminist Studies* 28, No. 1 (Spring 2002). Reprinted with the permission of the publisher, Feminist Studies, Inc.

Pheona Donohoe, "Femicide in Juárez." Reprinted by permission of the author.

Barbara Ehrenreich, "Welcome to Cancerland" from *Harper's* (November 2001). Copyright © 2001 by Barbara Ehrenreich. Reprinted with the permission of International Creative Management, Inc.

Cynthia Enloe, "The Globe Trotting Sneaker" from *Ms.* (March/April 1995). Copyright © 1995. Reprinted with the permission of *Ms.* Magazine.

Yen Le Espiritu, "We Don't Sleep Around Like White Girls Do" from *Signs: Journal of Women in Culture and Society* 26, no. 2 (Winter 2001). Copyright © 2001 by The University of Chicago. Reprinted with permission.

Shane Faber, Queen Latifah, Mark James, Anthony Peaks, and Simone A. Johnson, "Ladies First." Copyright © 1989 by Warner-Tamerlane Publishing Corp. (BMI), Now and Then Music (BMI), WB Music Corp. (ASCAP), Queen Latifah Music Inc. (ASCAP), and Simone Johnson Publishing Designee. All rights on behalf of itself and Now and Then Music administered by Warner-Tamerlane Publishing Corp. All rights on behalf of itself, Queen Latifa Music Inc., Forty Five King Music, Forked Tongue Music and Simon Johnson Publishing Designee administered by Alfred Publishing Co., Inc. All rights reserved. Used by permission.

Anne Fausto-Sterling, "Hormonal Hurricanes: Menstruation, Menopause, and Female Behavior" adapted from *Myths of Gender: Biological Theories about Women and Men*. Copyright © 1986 by Basic Books, Inc. Reprinted with the permission of Basic Books, a member of Perseus Books LLC.

Marilyn Frye, "Oppression" from The *Politics of Reality: Essays in Feminist Theory*. Copyright © 1983 by Marilyn Frye. Reprinted with the permission of The Crossing Press, Freedom, California.

Roberta Galler, "The Myth of the Perfect Body" from *Pleasure and Danger: Exploring Female Sexuality*, edited by Carole S. Vance. Copyright © 1984 by Roberta Galler. Reprinted with the permission of the author.

Kathleen Gerson, "Moral Dilemmas, Moral Strategies, and the Transformation of Gender" from *Gender & Society* 16, No. 1 (February 2002): 8–28. Copyright © 2002 by Sociologists for Women in Society. Reprinted with the permission of the author and Sage Publications, Inc.

Debra Gimlin, "Cosmetic Surgery: Paying for Your Beauty" from *Body Work: Beauty and Self-Image in American Culture.*

Copyright © 2002 by the Regents of the University of California. Reprinted with the permission of the University of California Press.

Lois Gould, "X: A Fabulous Child's Story." Copyright © 1978 by Lois Gould. Reprinted with the permission of the Charlotte Sheedy Literary Agency.

Pierrette Hondagneu-Sotelo, "Maid in L.A." from *Doméstica: Immigrant Workers Cleaning and Caring in the Shadows of Affluence*. Copyright © 2001 by the Regents of the University of California. Reprinted with the permission of the University of California Press.

Hung Cam Thai, "For Better or Worse: Gender Allures in the Vietnamese Global Marriage Market." Revised by Verta Taylor and Nancy Whittier from Hung Cam Thai, "Clashing Dreams: Highly-Educated Vietnamese Brides and Their Low-Wage Overseas Husbands" in *Global Women*, edited by Arlie Russell Hochschild and Barbara Ehrenreich (New York: Metropolitan Books, 2003). Reprinted with the permission of the author. Lisa Jervis, "The End of Feminism's Third Wave" from *Ms.* (Winter 2004). Reprinted with permission.

Sarah Jones, "Your Revolution." Copyright © by Sarah Jones. Reprinted with the permission of the author.

Miliann Kang, "The Managed Hand: The Commercialization of Bodies and Emotions in Korean Immigrant-Owned Nail Salons" from *Gender & Society* 17, no. 6 (December 2003): 820–839. Copyright © 2003 by Sociologists for Women in Society. Reprinted with the permission of the author and Sage Publications, Inc.

Suzanne J. Kessler, "The Medical Construction of Gender" from *Lessons from the Intersexed*. Copyright © 1990 by The University of Chicago. Copyright © 1998 by Suzanne J. Kessler. Reprinted with the permission of the author and The University of Chicago Press.

Cheryl Keyes, "Empowering Self, Making Choices, Creating Spaces: Black Female Identity via Rap Music Performance" from *Journal of American Folklore* 113: 255–269. Reprinted with permission.

Michael Kimmel, "What Are Little Boys Made Of?" from *Ms.* (October/November 1999). Copyright © 1999. Reprinted with the permission of the author.

William J. Kole and Aida Cerkez-Robinson, excerpts from "U.N. Police Accused of Involvement in Bosnia," Associated Press (July 6, 2001). Copyright © 2001 Associated Press. All rights reserved. Distributed by Valeo IP.

Laura M. Lopez and Frances S. Hasso, "Frontlines and Borders: Identity Thresholds for Latinas and Arab-American Women" from *Everyday Inequalities: Critical Inquiries*, edited by Jodi O'Brien and Judith A. Howard. Copyright © 1998 by Blackwell Publishers, Ltd. Reprinted with the permission of the publisher.

Judith Lorber, "'Night to His Day': The Social Construction of Gender" from *Paradoxes of Gender*. Copyright © 1993 by Yale University. Reprinted with the permission of Yale University Press.

Audre Lorde, "The Master's Tools Will Never Dismantle the Master's House" from *Sister Outsider: Essays and Speeches*. Copyright © 1984 by Audre Lorde. Reprinted with the permission of The Crossing Press, Freedom, California.

Audre Lorde, "Thanks to Jesse Jackson" from *The Marvelous Arithmetics of Distance: Poems 1987–1992*. Copyright © 1993 by Audre Lorde. Reprinted with the permission of W. W. & Norton, Inc.

Patricia Yancy Martin and Robert A. Hummer, "Fraternities and Rape on Campus" from *Gender & Society* 3, no. 4 (December 1989). Copyright © 1989 by Sociologists for Women in Society. Reprinted with the permission of the authors and Sage Publications, Inc.

Peggy McIntosh, "White Privilege: Unpacking the Invisible Knapsack." Copyright © 1988 by Peggy McIntosh. Permission to reprint must be obtained from the author, Wellesley College Center for Research on Women, Wellesley, MA 02481, (781) 283-2520.

Michael A. Messner, "Becoming 100% Straight" from *Inside Sports*, edited by Jay Coakley and Peter Donnelly. Copyright © 1999. Reprinted with the permission of Routledge.

Gwendolyn Mink, "The Lady and the Tramp (II)" from *Feminist Studies* 24, no. 1 (Spring 1998): 55–64. Reprinted with the permission of the publisher, Feminist Studies, Inc.

Wendy Mink and Anna Marie Smith, "Gay or Straight, Marriage May Not Be Bliss" from Women's eNews, www.womensenews.org. Reprinted with the permission of Women's eNews.

Chandra Talpade Mohanty, from *Feminism without Borders: Decolonizing Theory, Practicing Solidarity*. Copyright © 2002 by Duke University Press. All rights reserved. Reprinted with the permission of the publisher.

Melissa Morrison, "Bridal Wave" from *Bitch: Feminist Response to Pop Culture* (Summer 2004).

Joane Nagel, "Sex and War" from *Race, Ethnicity, and Sexuality: Intimate Intersections, Forbidden Frontiers*. Copyright © 2003 by Oxford University Press, Inc. Reprinted with the permission of Oxford University Press, Inc.

Nancy Naples, "Queer Parenting in the New Millennium" from *Gender & Society* 18, No. 6 (December 2004): 679–684. Copyright © 2004 by Sociologists for Women in Society. Reprinted with the permission of Sage Publications, Inc.

Sharon Ann Navarro, "*Las Mujeres Invisibles*/The Invisible Women" from *Women's Activism and Globalization: Linking Local Struggle and Transnational Politics*, edited by Nancy A. Naples and Manisha Desai. Copyright © 2002 by Routledge. Reprinted with the permission of Routledge/Taylor & Francis, Inc.

Mary Oliver, from "When Death Comes" from *New and Selected Poems*. Copyright © 1992 by Mary Oliver. Reprinted with the permission of Beacon Press, Boston.

Norimitsu Onishi, "Globalization of Beauty Makes Slimness Trendy" from *The New York Times* (October 3, 2002). Copyright © 2002 by The New York Times Company. Reprinted with permission.

Dana Owens, "The Evil That Men Do." Copyright © 1989 by WB Music Corp (ASCAP) and Queen Latifah Music Inc. (ASCAP). All rights administered by Alfred Publishing Co., Inc. All rights reserved. Used by permission.

Barbara Reskin, excerpt from "The Realities of Affirmative Action in Employment" from *The Realities of Affirmative Action in Employment*. Copyright © 1998 by the American Sociological Association. Reprinted with the permission of the author and the American Sociological Association.

Barbara Reskin and Irene Padavic, "Moving Up and Taking Charge" (editors' title, originally titled "Sex Differences in Moving Up and Taking Charge") from *Women and Men at Work*, 2nd ed. (Thousand Oaks, Calif.: Pine Forge, 2002). Copyright © 2002 by Sage Publications, Inc. Reprinted with the permission of the authors.

From Barbara Reskin and Irene Padavic, *Women and Men at Work*, 2nd ed. (Thousand Oaks, Calif.: Pine Forge, 2002). Copyright © 2002 by Sage Publications, Inc. Reprinted with the permission of the authors.

Laurel Richardson, "Gender Stereotyping in the English Language" adapted from *The Dynamics of Sex and Gender: A Sociological Perspective*, 3rd ed. (New York: Harper & Row, 1987). Copyright © 1981 by Houghton Mifflin Company. Copyright © 1987 by Harper & Row, Publishers, Inc. Reprinted with the permission of the author.

Barbara Risman and Pepper Schwartz, "After the Sexual Revolution: Gender Politics in Teen Dating" from *Contexts* 1, no. 1 (Spring 2002). Copyright © 2002 by the American Sociological Association. Reprinted with the permission of the University of California Press.

Judy Rohrer, "Haole Girl: Identity and White Privilege in Hawai'i" in *Social Process in Hawai'i* (Honolulu: University of Hawai'i Press, 1997). Copyright © 1997 by the University of Hawai'i. Reprinted with the permission of Dr. Kiyoshi Ikeda, Department of Sociology, University of Hawai'i.

Leila J. Rupp, "Toward a Global History of Same-Sex Sexuality" from *Journal of the History of Sexuality* 10, No. 2 (April 2001). Copyright © 2001 by the University of Texas Press. Reprinted with permission.

Lauren Sandler, "The *Ms.* of Baghdad" from *Ms.* (Spring 2004): 28. Copyright © 2004. Reprinted with permission.

Denise A. Segura, "Working at Motherhood: Chicana and Mexican Immigrant Mothers and Employment" from *Mothering: Ideology, Experience, and Agency*, edited by Evelyn Nakano Glenn, Grace Chang, and Linda Rennie Forcey. Copyright © 1994 by Routledge. Reprinted with the permission of the author and Routledge/Taylor & Francis Books, Inc.

Somini Sengupta, "Live Clothed Girls May Be Stripped of Their Dance Jobs" from *The New York Times* (May 2, 2005). Copyright © 2005 by The New York Times Company. Reprinted with permission.

A. Sivanandan, excerpt from "All That Melts into Air Is Solid: The Hokum of the New Times" from *Communities of Resistance: Writings on Black Struggles for Socialism*. Originally published in *Race and Class* 31, no. 3 (1990): 18–19. Reprinted with the permission of Verso.

Andrea Smith, "Beyond Pro-Choice versus Pro-Life" from *NWSA Journal* 17.1 (2005): 119–140. Copyright © 2005. Reprinted with the permission of Indiana University Press.

Gloria Steinem, "Supremacy Crimes" from *Ms.* (August-September 1999). Copyright © 1999 by Gloria Steinem. Reprinted with the permission of the author.

Alexandra Stiglmayer, from "The Rapes in Bosnia-Herzegovina" from *Mass Rape: The War Against Women in Bosnia-Herzegovina*, edited by Alexandra Stiglmayer, translations by Marion Faber. Copyright © 1993 by Kore Verlag GmbH. Copyright © 1994 by the University of Nebraska Press. Reprinted with the permission of University of Nebraska Press.

Susan Stryker, excerpts from "My Words to Victor Frankenstein above the Village of Chamounix: Performing Transgender Rage" from *GLQ: A Journal of Lesbian and Gay Studies* 1(3): 227–254. Copyright © 1994 by Duke University Press. All rights reserved. Reprinted with the permission of the publisher.

Verta Taylor, Nancy Whittier, and Cynthia Fabrizio Pelak, "The New Feminist Movement: Persistence through Transformation." Reprinted with the permission of the authors.

Becky Wangsgaard Thompson, "'A Way Outa No Way': Eating Problems among African American, Latina, and White Women" from *Gender & Society* 6, no. 4 (December 1992). Copyright © 1994 by Sociologists for Women in Society. Reprinted with the permission of the author.

Barrie Thorne, "Girls and Boys Together . . . But Mostly Apart: Gender Arrangements in Elementary Schools" from *Relationships and Development*, edited by Willard W. Hartup and Zick Rubin (Hillsdale, New Jersey: Lawrence Erlbaum Associates, 1986). Volume sponsored by the Social Science Research Council. Copyright © 1986 by Lawrence Erlbaum Associates. Reprinted with the permission of the author and publisher.

Deborah L. Tolman, "Doing Desire: Adolescent Girls' Struggles for/with Sexuality" from *Gender & Society* 8, no. 3 (September 1994). Copyright © 1994 by Sociologists for Women in Society. Reprinted with the permission of Sage Publications, Inc.

France Winddance Twine, "Brown-Skinned White Girls" from *Displacing Whiteness: Essays in Social and Cultural Criticism*, edited by Ruth Frankenberg. Copyright © 1997 by Duke University Press. All rights reserved. Used by permission of the publisher.

"UN Commission Approves Declaration Reaffirming Goals of 1995 Women's Conference" from Kaiser Daily Reproductive Health Report, 3/4/05.

Mary-Jane Wagle, "Abstinence-only: Breeding Ignorance" from *Daily Hampshire Gazette* (December 13, 2004). Reprinted with the permission of the author.

Alice Walker, "Womanist" from *In Search of Our Mothers' Gardens: Womanist Prose*. Copyright © 1983 by Alice Walker. Reprinted with the permission of Harcourt, Inc.

Kazuko Watanabe, excerpts from "Trafficking in Women's Bodies, Then and Now: The Issue of Military Comfort Women" from *Peace and Change* 20 (1995): 501–514. Copyright © 1995 by Sage Publications, Inc. Reprinted with the permission of the publishers.

Riki Ann Wilchins, "17 Things You Don't Say to a Transsexual" from *Read My Lips: Sexual Subversion and the End of Gender*. Reprinted with the permission of Firebrand Books.

Maxine Baca Zinn and Bonnie Thornton Dill, "Theorizing Difference from Multiracial Feminism" from *Feminist Studies* 22, no. 2 (Summer 1996). Reprinted with the permission of Feminist Studies, Inc.